THE PAPERS

of

JOHN C. CALHOUN

THOMAS GREEN CLEMSON

*This portrait of Calhoun's only son-in-law was painted
by Joseph B. Ord about 1830 while Clemson was a student
in Paris. The portrait is now at Fort Hill.*

THE PAPERS

of

JOHN C. CALHOUN

Volume XIX, 1844

Edited by

CLYDE N. WILSON

Shirley Bright Cook, *Associate Editor*

Alexander Moore, *Assistant Editor*

UNIVERSITY OF SOUTH CAROLINA PRESS, 1990

CONTENTS

▥

PREFACE

◫

This volume covers the middle portion of Calhoun's service as Secretary of State. The volume is highly selective, including not much more than a third of the extant Calhoun documents for its period. The Preface and Introduction of the immediately preceding volume (Volume XVIII) explain amply the policies of selectivity and other editorial considerations that have governed our treatment of Calhoun's State Department period.

At this time Calhoun was an administrator, in charge of the foreign relations and some of the internal administration of the Union, under the President. Yet, perhaps surprisingly, the papers for this period are as densely relevant to all of the major issues and developments of the day as are those created when he was a Senator. The future users of this book will find not only Calhoun's career and the State Department but most of the larger aspects of the history of the United States in the mid-nineteenth century illuminated with depth and relevance.

Our continuing editorial effort is made possible by the Program for Editions of the National Endowment for the Humanities, the University of South Carolina, and the National Historical Publications and Records Commission.

CLYDE N. WILSON

Columbia, S.C., August, 1988

INTRODUCTION

〇

John C. Calhoun was not of that common American type of the nineteenth century (and the twentieth) who believed that being "practical" is the beginning and end of all wisdom and virtue. His attitude toward life, and government, resembled more the classically-derived "prudence" of the eighteenth century than it did the utilitarianism of later times. A certain philosophical bent he often displayed led his critics, especially among politicians of the sort who grew uneasy when principles and long-range consequences were mentioned, to regard him as troublesomely "metaphysical." Politicians, for the most part, feel more at home managing interests than ideas.

Calhoun in the State Department

Despite all this, the 62-year-old South Carolinian who took over the State Department in 1844 was one of the most experienced and disciplined administrators in the American government, even though he had spent the preceding eleven years as a parliamentarian. It was not in his character to be a token department head. As an administrator he was thorough, "practical," and decisive, without being authoritarian. His demeanor was that of a leader seeking to inspire his subordinates by his own professionalism and courtesy. Calhoun "is decidedly one of the most indefatigable members of the Cabinet," reported a New York newspaper correspondent. "His popularity with all the clerks as well as all who have business with that Department is very great."[1]

The volume in hand is devoted to the middle portion of Calhoun's service as Secretary of State. The greater part of the Secretary's attention at this time had to be given to the greater matters—though not to the complete neglect of many lesser matters. These greater matters were Texas and Oregon.

This volume documents the next-to-the-last phase of the Texas

[1] The New York, N.Y., *Herald,* quoted in the Charleston, S.C., *Mercury,* September 26, 1844, p. 2.

question in American politics and diplomacy. The treaty of annexation which Calhoun had negotiated was rejected by the Senate on June 8. This did not end the issue. Even the major opponents of the treaty—Martin Van Buren, Henry Clay, and Thomas H. Benton—claimed they were opposed only to immediate annexation, not to annexation per se. In the months following rejection of the treaty the issue was projected into the politics of Presidential and Congressional electioneering.

It was well understood by the Tyler administration and Congressional supporters that the game was not over. There was some consideration of calling Congress back into session early, after public opinion had had a chance to develop, since the treaty itself provided for six months' consideration (that is, until October 12) before it expired as a proposal. This was not done, but it was also well understood that the treaty, which required a two-thirds vote of the Senate, might be set aside and the same objective be accomplished by a joint resolution admitting Texas to Statehood, which would require only a simple majority in each house. This was under discussion by early May if not before.[2] This was what was eventually done, although not until after the elections and the reconvening of Congress.

The Secretary of State's papers during this interim waiting period provide much information about the relationship between the United States and the independent Republic of Texas (they shared a long and partly undefined border); about the history of Texas itself in the last period of independence; and about American public opinion in regard to Texas.

One of Calhoun's chief concerns, which many others shared, was that, in the meantime, Texas, through discouragement, necessity, or the machinations of some of its leaders, might be seduced away to an alliance with a foreign power. Much effort and eloquence was devoted to dealing with this contingency and maintaining cordial relations.[3]

The existing situation also presented a problem of relations with Mexico, which had not recognized the independence of its former State, though such independence had been de facto and de jure for

---

[2] Entry for May 6 in the diary of Charles J. Ingersoll of Pa., annexation leader in the House of Representatives. William M. Meigs, *The Life of Charles Jared Ingersoll* (Philadelphia: J.B. Lippincott, 1900), p. 265.

[3] See Calhoun's instructions herein to the U.S. Chargé d'Affaires to Texas, Tilghman A. Howard, June 18, 1844; also to Howard's successor, Andrew J. Donelson, August 23, 1844. See also Donelson's letter of July 29 to Calhoun, enclosing a copy of a letter of Andrew Jackson to Sam Houston.

eight years. There was always the possibility that whatever forces prevailed in the constant changes of Mexican government might launch new hostilities against Texas. This might range from minor forays to a full scale effort at reconquest. Such a possibility presented grave political, Constitutional, and military questions for the Tyler administration. What was the moral obligation of the United States in regard to the defence of Texas while annexation was pending? What was the Constitutional authority of the executive to meet this obligation while Congress was not in session? The lines of power between executive and legislature in military matters have been a perennial source of tension in the American system. The Secretary of State had necessarily to deal with this situation.[4]

Whether hostilities were renewed or not, Mexican relations had to be managed. This was troublesome even in the best of times. The Secretary's papers yield a great amount of information about internal events and conditions in Mexico, as seen by many different Americans. A good deal of the Secretary's attention had to be devoted to dealing with American citizens who had claims against the Mexican government. These arose mostly out of confiscations and oppressions that had been inflicted on foreign traders and investors in the conditions of anarchy and civil war that had obtained frequently since independence. Some of the claimants had demands that had already been settled by convention and were awaiting instalment payments which might or might not appear. Others had claims as yet unsettled.

There was also a necessity to justify the annexation of Texas in an international context. The Republic of Texas was recognized by and had relations with foreign powers. In the case of Great Britain this had gone as far as offers of mediation with Mexico, accompanied by conditions and guarantees. This broader necessity of the Texas question Calhoun embraced gladly, since it coincided with his international offensive against abolitionism.[5]

The other great question of the day was Oregon. This matter, too, was in an interim stage. The middle period of Calhoun's State

[4] See especially in this connection Calhoun's instructions to the U.S. Minister to Mexico, Wilson Shannon, June 20, September 10, and September 11, 1844, herein. During September and later there is considerable correspondence reflecting an effort to deal with the problems created by the refitting of two Mexican warships at New York City and with suspected Mexican manipulation of the more warlike Indian tribes against Texas.

[5] Calhoun's most important paper in this respect is his letter to the U.S. Minister to France, William R. King, August 12, 1844, herein.

Department service is the time of his most intense negotiations of this issue with the British Minister, Richard Pakenham, who had been sent to America chiefly to settle this question. It was not yet possible to decide conclusively the future of the vast territory in the northwest of North America, to which both Britain and the United States had claims, but Calhoun devoted a great deal of time and talent to it.[6] The succeeding Polk administration, after much unproductive bluster and maneuvering, essentially settled on the basis that Calhoun had developed. Calhoun's admirers always considered that his role in the peaceful settlement of this vast matter had been decisive. Richard K. Crallé, at the time of the negotiations Calhoun's Chief Clerk, later put it: ". . . in the adjustment of the Oregon controversy, some years afterwards, the boundary line between the two countries was finally adopted, as designated by Mr. Calhoun."[7]

Texas, Mexico, and Oregon by no means exhaust the subjects reflected in Calhoun's papers in this volume. The papers also tell a good deal about American involvement, through both the public and private sectors, in the Caribbean, South America, the Pacific, Asia, and Europe, especially northern Europe, where German-American trade agreements were on the table. The Senate had adjourned without definite action on a commercial treaty with the German Zollverein, and it required all of Calhoun's discretion to keep the matter alive until Congress reconvened in December.[8] And while Oregon was being discussed, the British-American settlement of the northeastern boundary line, in the Treaty of Washington of 1842 (the Webster-Ashburton Treaty), was being implemented with occasional difficulties.

Robert M.T. Hunter, a Calhoun intimate, visited Washington on his way to and from the Democratic National Convention at Baltimore. He found Calhoun working after hours in the State Department. According to Hunter, Calhoun "had taken rather a fancy to the work in his Department. He said that small work and the claims of individuals had been too much neglected by his predecessors in office. That generally absorbed in some one great question they neglected what they deemed small matters."[9]

[6] See especially Calhoun's letters to the British Minister, Richard Pakenham, September 3 and September 20, 1844, herein.

[7] Richard K. Crallé, ed., *The Works of John C. Calhoun* (6 vols. Columbia, S.C.: printed by A.S. Johnston, 1851, and New York: D. Appleton & Co., 1853–1857), 5:415.

[8] See especially Calhoun's two letters to Henry Wheaton, U.S. Minister to Prussia, on June 28, 1844, herein.

[9] Hunter's ms. memoir of Calhoun, Virginia State Library, pp. 286–288.

Calhoun's correspondence reflects the considerable attention he devoted to understanding and evaluating many individual claims against foreign governments, determining whether they were worthy, and if so what steps to take in regard to them. His letters of instructions to various American representatives in South America are interesting documents, both for their grasp of detail and for their moderate and insightful approach to American relations with those countries. These and other able Calhoun state papers not related to Texas and Oregon have not been much noticed.[10]

Confronting the Abolitionist International

The claims to which Calhoun turned his attention were of many types, but there was a certain category that attracted particular notice. Hunter later summarized Calhoun's remarks to him on this subject:

> It had been very unfortunate that when questions arose involving the rights of slaveholders they [his predecessor Secretaries of State] neglected them for some reason or other[;] perhaps they were afraid of them. The Amistad he said was not the only case of that sort. It was a great misfortune to the South he said that all such cases had not been taken up promptly in a manner to show that the whole government in all its departments felt bound to protect the rights of the Slaveholder from Foreign wrongs.[11]

Calhoun was determined to employ every legal and diplomatic means to defend the rights of American citizen-slaveholders when such rights came into conflict with the actions of other nations. He saw this as a function, natural and logical, of a just, moral, and lawful system of domestic slavery. To do any less would be to give countenance to the presumption that the system that existed was immoral or unlawful and would thus damage the South at its most sensitive point, its honor.

As a prescient defender of Southern society, Calhoun was aware that abolitionism was an international movement, centered in the

---

[10] For instance, see instructions to newly-appointed American representatives in Latin America, published in this volume or the immediately preceding volume: to Henry A. Wise, Brazil, May 25 and July 18, 1844; William Crump, Chile, May 28, 1844; William Brent, Jr., Argentina, July 15, 1844. Also interesting in this connection herein: to Robert Wickliffe, Jr., Sardinia, June 17, 1844, on the proper general conduct of U.S. representatives; to Washington Irving, August 23, 1844, on Spanish policies toward American Consuls; and to William W. Irwin, September 13, 1844, on the perennial question of the Danish Sound Dues.

[11] Hunter's ms. memoir of Calhoun, p. 286.

heart of the British Empire, London. Thus, for him, the defense of slavery was not only Constitutional, it was a part of the defense of American republican liberty and independence from a traditional enemy. Abolitionism was a new manifestation of interference with American independence, with which some Americans were willing to collaborate.

The British government had, in the post-Napoleonic period, undertaken to suppress the African slave trade and then to liberate the black slaves of its own New World colonies. Americans had a certain sympathy with the first goal and a limited interest in the second. But, so it seemed to Calhoun and many others, antislavery had lately taken a new turn that carried it beyond philanthropy and into imperialism. In response to American questions about Texas, the British Secretary of State for Foreign Affairs had insisted that Great Britain did not wish to "interfere unduly" in the internal affairs of Texas or any other country. But at the same time it continued to "feel it to be our duty to promote such a consummation" as worldwide black emancipation.[12]

For Calhoun and many other Americans, this apparently benevolent mission to abolish one particular form of servitude among many, wherever it was found, was crafty hypocrisy to cover those motives of domination and profit which they believed always controlled British dealings with other societies. It was merely one face of that imperial process which was bringing a quarter of the world under one or another form of British dominance. The staples of the United States and other slave societies in the New World were vital commodities in advantageous competition with British colonial produce. The one certain effect of emancipation would be to diminish competition and enhance British wealth.

Given the constant thrust of British power, both armed and subtle, all over the world at this time, this was an extremely plausible line of reasoning for many Americans.[13] It was convenient to the defense of slavery, but also quite sincere, especially for those Americans with

[12] Lord Aberdeen's statement, enclosed with a letter from Richard Pakenham to Abel P. Upshur, February 26, 1844, in *The Papers of John C. Calhoun,* 18:53–54.

[13] See the musings of John R. Mathewes, a nonpolitical friend of Calhoun, in letters dated at the end of April, 1844, and May 12, 1844, in *The Papers of John C. Calhoun,* 18:373–380 and 494–496. Or see the letter from William P. Duval, July 4, 1844, herein, or Duval's letter of May 20, 1844, *The Papers of John C. Calhoun,* 18:561–563. This was almost a commonplace of Southern opinion.

firsthand memories of British scalp-buying on the frontier and of the narrow repulse at New Orleans in 1815 of a British fleet with a complete colonial government for the Mississippi valley on board.

One place to join the fight was to take a firm line against British interference in the New World on abolition grounds, such as making emancipation a condition for support for Texas. Calhoun devoted a good deal of effort to unmasking British presumption and hypocrisy in this regard, and did it in an official way which could not be ignored. His forthright letter to the U.S. Minister to France, William R. King, on August 12, 1844, was intended for wider circulation. Calhoun knew this stand would appeal to many Americans and also to foreign powers naturally suspicious of the British.

Another place the issue could be joined officially was in the cases of the "Foreign wrongs" which Calhoun had mentioned to Hunter. The British government maintained that the jurisdiction of British law automatically dictated emancipation for a bondsman. There had been a number of cases in which British colonial authorities in the Bahamas and elsewhere had freed slaves found on board American coasting vessels that had come into their power through act of nature or man.

Calhoun had been raising inquiries about such cases in the Senate for some years, and such cases had a considerable history of State Department negotiation behind them already in which American demands for compensation had generally been sustained. Calhoun's emphasis there had been on international law—to refute the contention that American vessels lost the protection of American law when in foreign ports accidentally.

The Treaty of Washington of 1842 devoted one of its articles to a system of extradition of criminals between British and American authorities. This presented a new aspect to the question of fugitive slaves which Calhoun now took up vigorously.[14] What was to occur when the fugitive slaves were under indictment for theft or murder, as was often the case? Calhoun was determined to establish that neither international law nor the treaty permitted the British to refuse to deliver fugitives on grounds that their own law did not recognize slavery.

There was another class of cases, less pressing and clear-cut, but numerous, which involved hardships and indignities inflicted upon American merchant vessels by the British navy in the course of its

[14] See Calhoun's instructions to Edward Everett, U.S. Minister to Great Britain, August 7, August 12, and September 25, 1844, herein.

efforts to suppress the African slave trade. This was a touchy matter for Americans. Most of them, including Calhoun and most Southerners, were sympathetic to the goal, which had been American law since 1808, and were willing to cooperate with it. But actions against the African slave trade by the British fleet also touched Americans at a traditionally very sensitive point—the arrogant pretensions of British naval power in regard to neutral shipping on the seas. The Webster-Ashburton treaty had included an article providing for a degree of British-American cooperation in interdicting the African slave trade, and this had been used as an argument against the treaty by some, notably Thomas H. Benton.

Calhoun and the Tyler administration were willing to fulfill legal and treaty obligations for the suppression of the slave trade, and to do so conscientiously. But they also vigorously contended on two related issues against the British. These were compensation for American vessels unjustly suspected and damaged, and the restriction of British actions to very carefully codified and pre-announced rules. Calhoun's papers reflect both of these interests.

The suppression of the slave trade primarily involved the interception of ships plying between Africa and Brazil and, to a lesser extent, Cuba. Besides the Spanish and Portuguese, the chief participants in this trade were Americans. An American representative in Brazil, a Middle Westerner, remarked:

> . . . eight out of ten of all the vessels employed in this nefarious traffic are from Beverly, Salem and other eastern [that is, New England] ports of the United States, where the people profess to be opposed to anything approaching involuntary servitude and are constantly interfering in the domestic institutions of the Southern States of the Union.[15]

It is noteworthy that Calhoun and other Southern defenders of slavery were conscientious in their enforcement of legal and treaty obligations against the slave trade. Calhoun's papers as Secretary of State contain materials about the apprehension and prosecution of guilty Americans. Such U.S. representatives in Brazil as Henry A. Wise, future Governor of Virginia and Confederate general, were evidently sincere in their repugnance at the trade and efforts to curtail it. Calhoun and other Southerners felt no contradiction between the defense of slavery and the opposition to the trade. The two stands supported each other in both interest and sentiment.

[15] George H. Proffit to Abel P. Upshur, February 27, 1844, *The Papers of John C. Calhoun,* 18:57.

Calhoun could reasonably hope that his unmasking of British pseudo-philanthropy would be welcomed by other nations. The French had every reason to be resentful of British influence in the New World and elsewhere. The Spanish had an interest in the protection of their slave-holding colony, Cuba; and there was a coincidence of interest in this respect between the slave-holding part of the United States and the other great American slave-holding power, Brazil.

Calhoun's papers reflect a considerable American interest in Cuba.[16] It was a strategic location and there was a general American desire to prevent it from falling under British control. For many Americans, there was considerable sympathy for the native planter class. Like Americans in the past they were threatened by an arbitrary colonial power which would not hesitate to use the slave population against their rights and safety. At the same time Calhoun, as was to be expected from so conscientious a patriot, was zealous in seeking protection of American citizens oppressed in Cuba, even those who were suspected, usually wrongly, of complicity in slave revolts.[17]

And in keeping with the same views, anti-abolition Americans were greatly interested in what they considered to be the failures and disasters of emancipation in Haiti and in such British colonies as Jamaica. The veteran U.S. Consul in Kingston, Jamaica, Robert Monroe Harrison, a Virginian, was indefatigable in bringing to the attention of the Secretary of State the post-emancipation condition of that island. And Calhoun could not avoid being interested in events in Hispaniola because of the ceaseless complaints by American traders, nearly all New Englanders, about conditions there.

Tyler, Polk, and Rhett

Not a lot emerges from Calhoun's papers about the nature of his relationship with the President, John Tyler, his junior in years and

[16] Among many other examples see Calhoun's letter to Robert B. Campbell, U.S. Consul in Havana, June 26, 1844, herein. See also the letters of Alexander H. Everett of Mass. to Calhoun, June 17, 1844, herein, and April 13, 1844, *The Papers of John C. Calhoun*, 18:224–229.

[17] See Calhoun to Thomas M. Rodney, U.S. Consul at Matanzas, July 24 and August 31, 1844, herein; Calhoun to Robert B. Campbell, U.S. Consul at Havana, August 31, 1844, herein; Calhoun to Franklin Gage, U.S. Consul at Cardenas, April 25, 1844, *The Papers of John C. Calhoun*, 18:328.

fame. Charles J. Ingersoll, a Representative from Pennsylvania who was on close terms with both men, recorded a conversation in which Calhoun told him "that he had differed with Jackson because he required flattery as Tyler does, and that he, Calhoun, had never flattered anyone."[18] This statement may well record the thrust of Calhoun's remarks, though it is probably an interpretive paraphrase since the language is less subtle and restrained than Calhoun usually employed in personal remarks. Calhoun and Tyler were both courteous and tactful men, and they agreed on the larger issues. There would have been no profit for either in disagreement or lack of cooperation. Possibly they treated each other with reserved respect.

One point on which Calhoun did clearly disagree with the President and keep a quiet distance was that of appointments. The author of the famous Report on the Extent of the Executive Patronage of 1835 did not wish to be seen as a part of the systematic removals and replacements of officeholders which Tyler carried on in a vain hope of building Presidential support for himself. If Calhoun's correspondents are to be believed when they wrote him about numerous local situations, Tyler's maneuvers in this regard were often mistaken and counterproductive, more than a few times resulting in the removal of the loyal or inoffensive for the benefit of false and shallow friends.[19]

Calhoun told an intimate "in strict confidence" that Tyler "makes most of his appointments on his own responsibility without consulting the appropriate Department."[20] This simplified the situation for Calhoun, as did his policy of declining to take any aggressive interest in appointments outside his own department. As Calhoun told his daughter in declining to actively support one of her in-laws, he had found it "necessary to establish it as a rule, not to interfere with the appointments in the other departments, in order to prevent them interfering with mine . . . ." He was opposed to turning out officeholders. However, if a "fair opportunity" offered to serve a worthy friend, he would take it.[21]

In his own sphere, when Presidential removals were inevitable,

---

[18] Meigs, *Ingersoll*, p. 267 (May 18).

[19] Among others, see the letters to Calhoun from Simeon Hubbard, April 4, 1844, from Joseph R. Flanders, May 6, 1844, and from Moses Stuart, May 20, 1844, in *The Papers of John C. Calhoun*, 18:149–152, 443–445, and 571–572.

[20] To Robert M.T. Hunter, July 30, 1844, herein.

[21] To Anna Maria Calhoun Clemson, May 10, 1844, *The Papers of John C. Calhoun*, 18:469–470.

or where there were legitimate opportunities, he sought to influence appointments. To a Virginia follower, James A. Seddon, he "advised measures [that] should be taken to secure the favourable consideration of the President" for a deserving candidate.[22] Calhoun thought of the appointing power in terms of rewarding qualified and meritorious citizens, including his own supporters and friends, but he did so somewhat passively and obviously without any systematic plan of organization-building in mind. He told Charles J. Ingersoll at this time that "abuse of the appointing power is ruining this country, and will infallibly do it, if continued as practiced by Van Buren, unless checked by some great chief magistrate . . . ."[23]

Calhoun was a national political figure to whom many looked for guidance. As soon as the Democratic National Convention had nominated James K. Polk and George M. Dallas on a pro-Texas platform, Calhoun gave the ticket his firm allegiance. "My friends every where will give the ticket hearty support; and I have strong hope it will succeed," Calhoun told a young Northern admirer.[24] This support was sincere and in a closely contested election perhaps significant. The support was also optimistic. To an Alabama friend he expressed the opinion that Polk's election was "in a great measure certain." If he realized the expectations of those who thought as Calhoun did, "his administration will mark a great & salutary era in our political history . . . ."[25] What Calhoun thought of James K. Polk personally he did not say. This is merely speculation, based on a knowledge of Calhoun's general attitude rather than evidence, but he must have regarded Polk as, in abilities, a rather pedestrian party politician. He perhaps hoped that Polk's situation and his worthy character would lead him in the right direction.

While visiting Washington immediately after the Convention, Robert M.T. Hunter asked Calhoun what he would have his friends do in the election. Calhoun responded, as paraphrased later by Hunter:

> Pull off your coats and go to work. You have all sacrificed too much already to retain your hold on the party for the sake of the South to sacrifice it now by want of exertion. If Polk is willing

[22] James A. Seddon to Robert M.T. Hunter, August 9, 1844, in Charles H. Ambler, ed., *Correspondence of Robert M.T. Hunter, 1826–1876* (Washington: U.S. Government Printing Office, 1918), p. 66.

[23] Meigs, *Ingersoll*, p. 267 (May 18).

[24] To Francis Wharton, July 14, 1844, herein.

[25] To David Hubbard, September 22, 1844, herein.

to risk anything and if his heart is in the cause he might perhaps save the South even now by wisdom and firmness. Try him. I see no other chance.[26]

Hunter was willing to follow Calhoun's advice, but was less hopeful that such a course would lead to the benefits expected. Such reservations were felt even more strongly by others who had in the past followed Calhoun's lead. It was during the election campaign of 1844 that these followers, led by the most talented and intransigent of the South Carolina radicals, Robert Barnwell Rhett, launched what was known to contemporary reporters and later historians as "the Bluffton movement."

Calhoun's strategy in 1844 was similar to that of 1828. To await the results of the Presidential election, after which the tariff and abolition would be dealt with on a broad base of Southern cooperation. This policy had not worked in 1828, and South Carolina had resorted to Nullification. Calhoun sincerely and with some foundation believed that the prospects were better in 1844. Public opinion on the tariff and abolition, within the Democratic party, had moved in South Carolina's direction, and there was no longer a bullheaded Andrew Jackson to deflect the proper course of policy.

The South Carolinians who followed Rhett were not willing to wait. The unsatisfactory tariff of 1842 and the waffling of Northern and cautious Southern politicians on abolition and Texas whetted their appetite for more drastic action and pressure—nullification and perhaps secession. They were sure that only drastic action, as in 1832, would bring redress and, perhaps, were not averse to agitation for its own sake. This episode has fascinated historians, perhaps because they feel it represents one of the few open rebellions in South Carolina against the leadership of the great Calhoun and because it was a portent of post-Calhoun developments. The rise, brief flourishing, and containment of the "Bluffton movement" can be traced in Calhoun's papers of July through September.[27]

Calhoun was aware that such action, rather than mobilizing Southern opinion, would merely revive the old suspicions of South Carolina disunionism and lower the influence of the State. And he valued the doctrine of nullification so highly that he wished to see it preserved for later occasions when the need and the possibilities of

[26] Hunter's ms. memoir of Calhoun, p. 288.

[27] For the reaction of Calhoun friends in another State, see the Hunter-Seddon correspondence in Ambler, ed., *Correspondence of Robert M.T. Hunter*, pp. 66–72.

success might be greater.[28]   The movement was contained, with
relative ease, by Calhoun's friends in the State.

While a small rebellion in South Carolina was interesting, other
more pervasive political conditions and more dangerous political
events perhaps concerned him more.   Too many Southerners suffered from short-sighted enthusiasms for parties and candidates.   In
late September, as Calhoun was on his way home for a vacation,
a straw Presidential poll was taken among the passengers of the
steamboat on which he was traveling.   A newspaper reported: ". . .
the vote stood: For Clay sixty-one; for Polk ten; for Cass two. Mr.
Calhoun did not vote."[29]   The unthinking inertial allegiance of
masses of fellow Southerners to Henry Clay presented a greater
problem to Calhoun than did Rhett's mini-rebellion.

The furor of a closely contested campaign between the Whigs
and Democrats turned up a new development much more portentous
for the future and less noticed than the "Bluffton movement." Towards the end of the summer of 1844 Calhoun began to receive reports from friends in the Old Northwest that he had become a focus
for attack by Whig stump orators seeking to damage the Democracy
in the minds of the voters.   The core of these attacks was the charge
that Calhoun, in defending the slave system of the South, had por-
trayed slavery as the natural condition for labor.   The implication
was that there was a Southern hostility to the freedom of the white
working men of the North.

"So far from ever having entertained such an abominable sentiment," Calhoun wrote, "my whole life has been devoted to endeavoring to uphold our free and popular system of government . . . ."   In
his view, the great danger to liberty came not from the traditional
ways of the South, but from the economic program of the Whigs,
"which I firmly believe is calculated to subvert the liberty of the
people, and reduce the laboring class in this country to the wretched
condition to which they have been reduced by the same policy in
England."[30]

The charge against Calhoun was demagoguery, "a calumny, utterly destitute of foundation."[31]   It would be difficult to imagine
anything more damaging to the harmony of the Union if any signifi-

[28] To Armistead Burt, August 7, 1844, herein.

[29] Washington, D.C., *Daily National Intelligencer*, October 2, 1844, p. 3.

[30] To Robert I. Alexander and others, St. Clairsville, Ohio, September 12,
1844, herein.

[31] *Ibid.*

cant number of Northern citizens were persuaded to give it credit. But that such a charge had been put forth at all indicated a belief on the part of some politicians that there was fertile ground for it. And that indicated a dangerous dysfunction in communication between the sections. Those "practical" politicians who did not like to have to cope with the Calhoun element in national affairs said he had brought it upon himself by insisting on making an issue of slavery with the British.

THE PAPERS

of

JOHN C. CALHOUN

▯

Volume XIX

JUNE 9–17, 1844

〇

The sixty-two-year-old South Carolinian, John C. Calhoun, was a week into his third month at the head of the State Department when, on June 8, the Senate of the United States voted down the treaty he had concluded in April with the Texas Republic. The next largest piece of business pending before the Senate from the State Department was a trade treaty with the German Zollverein, which many looked to as a step toward free trade and which certainly could be regarded as a boon to unprotected American agriculture. On June 15, after a negative report by the Foreign Relations Committee, the Senate tabled this treaty without approving or rejecting it.

Calhoun was an experienced and conscientious administrator and doubtless worked hard at the business of his department. The last weeks of the first session of the 28th Congress, which ended on June 17, were demanding in terms of appointments, appropriations, and calls for information. But, in addition to this legislative business and much minor continuing work, Calhoun had to meet numerous demands from foreign representatives. Those of Spain, Portugal, and the Netherlands had complaints in regard to the interpretation of the Tariff of 1842, as it affected their imports into the United States. The Belgian representative wanted to smooth the way for immigrants. The Consul General of the Pontifical States was concerned about anti-Catholic rioting in Philadelphia. The chief Prussian representative hoped to take the developing friendship of the two countries a step further by calling on American good offices to assist the fledgling Prussian whaling industry in the Pacific.

Various aspects of the implementation of the Treaty of Washington of 1842 had to be overseen, especially the continuing survey of the northeastern boundary. And, though the Texas treaty had been rejected, the issue which it represented was very much alive. It was necessary to continue to manage relations with the republics of Texas and Mexico, the most important points in the foreign relations of the Union at the moment. The Senators had refused to confirm the American representative in Texas, William S. Murphy, after his nomination had been before them many months. It was necessary to appoint a new one—Tilghman A. Howard, recently a member of

3

Congress from Indiana, who had been born in Calhoun's neighborhood.

Texas was not only a diplomatic issue—it was even more alive as a political issue. There was a Presidential campaign going on amidst widespread public excitement. John C. Calhoun, political leader, received advice from many quarters.

〔〕

From ROBERT B. CAMPBELL

Consulate of the United States of America
Havana, June 9th 1844

Sir, Since my last communication there has been no occurrence of sufficient importance to be made the subject of a letter, except the reduction of duties on some articles of the first necessity, and the growth of the United States. This intelligence will be found in the diario [newspaper] of yesterday accompanying this communication.

The Government are still engaged in finding & arresting the suspected parties to the intended insurrection, in this part of the Island there has not been any additional arrests of American Citizens, so far as I have been able to ascertain. Among the arrests made, are a great many Englishmen and rumor says a British fleet will shortly visit the Island to demand redress.

I forward to the Dept. a partial file of Buenos airean papers, perhaps of later dates than have been received. A battle of a sanguinary character has been recently fought near Monte Video. I have the honor to be with great respect your Mo[st] Ob[edien]t Serv[an]t, Robert B. Campbell.

ALS in DNA, RG 59 (State Department), Consular Despatches, Havana, vol. 19 (T-20:19), received 6/22.

From W[ILLIAM] S. MURPHY

Legation of the United States
Galveston, 9th June 1844

Sir, Having a moment only between the arrival and departure of the, Union, I can only say, that the rebellion, of which I had the Honor to advise you in my despatch of the 29th May (No. 29) is reported to be gaining strength: That [Mariano] Ariste is certainly at its head.

Gen[era]l [Samuel] Houston is at Washington [Texas], attending the trial of Commodore [Edwin W.] Moore Etal. All is peace and quiet on the Texan border, except an occasional incursion of Indians, in small thieving bands. The British party in Galveston are elated at the prospect of the failure of the Treaty of annexation in the Senate of the United States: and not a little delighted also, at the prospect of the rejection of my nomination, by that body. The American portion of the Citizens, ent[ert]ain strong hopes of final success ["in" *interlined*] one way, or another; and this hope, I also fondly entertain. I transmit a copy of instructions given to the Consulate here, by this Legation, in which I hope the Department of State, will concur. I have the Honor to be Your ob[edien]t Serv[an]t, W.S. Murphy.

ALS (No. 30) with En in DNA, RG 59 (State Department), Diplomatic Despatches, Texas, vol. 2 (T-728:2, frames 349–355), received 6/24; FC in DNA, RG 84 (Foreign Posts), Records of the Texas Legation. NOTE: The enclosed letter of 6/4/1844 from Murphy to A[rchibald] M. Green, headed "Instructions From the Legation of the U.S., to the Consulate at Galveston Texas," cautions Green against taking any action that would impair relations between Texas and the U.S. and emphasizes that Green has no authority to issue any orders to U.S. military forces. Murphy feels that the *Scioto Belle* case should be left to the decision of the Texas admiralty court before which it is pending.

From W[ILLIAM] S. MURPHY

Legation of the U. States
Galveston, 9th June 1844

Sir, I enclose for the information of the Department of State, the "National Vindicator," The Government paper here, containing the correspondence between the Charge d'Affaires of her Majesty's Govt. here [Charles Elliot], & the Dept. of State, of this Rep[u]b[lic] in relation to the Treaty of Annexation. I have the Honor to be Your ob[edien]t Serv[an]t, W.S. Murphy.

ALS (No. 31) with En in DNA, RG 59 (State Department), Diplomatic Despatches, Texas, vol. 2 (T-728:2, frames 355–360), received 6/24. NOTE: The enclosed newspaper, the Washington, Tex., *National Vindicator* of 6/1/1844, contains letters of 3/22/1844 and 4/3/1844 from Elliot to Anson Jones and a letter of 3/25/1844 from Jones to Elliot. In his letter of 3/22 Elliot states that the British government has been working with Mexico to encourage recognition of Texan independence by that country and has induced France to join her in these efforts. The continuance of these negotiations is possible only if Texas discourages efforts at annexation to the U.S. Elliot knows of [Samuel Houston's] and Jones's disinclination towards annexation and assumes that the present talks are meant to avoid giving offense to the U.S. Jones replied on 3/25 to Elliot that Mexico has shown that she is "indisposed to any amicable settlement, upon reasonable and admissible terms" of her difficulties with Texas. Should the U.S. government "yield its assent to the assurances which the representatives of this are required to ask of it, the Government of Texas will view the policy of annexation as the most proper one left it under all existing circumstances at the present time to pursue." Elliot states in his letter of 4/3 that he views the situation differently and hopes that Texas "will not make the incalculably heavy sacrifice of their separate national existence, under the impression that the prospect of amicable settlement with Mexico has passed away." "The undersigned cannot refrain from observing that there is no want of evidence in the press of the United States, that very eminent and practised statesmen in that country, are firmly opposed to the annexation of Texas to that Union, either at all, or at least under any other condition than the consent of Mexico, peacefully obtained: neither does it seem to be doubtful, judging from the same sources, that these opinions are shared by a large part of the people of that confederacy." Elliot closes with the expression of his belief that "the preservation of their independence is the best security of the people of Texas, for their ultimate prosperity, both political and commercial."

From W[ILLIA]M RUFUS PAGE

Hallowell Maine, June 9th 1844

Dear Sir, The object of the present communication is to say that in 1842 my Father Mr. Rufus K. Page of this town sent to the Levant a Steamer which for the last 18 months has under my direction done a good business despite all the discourag[e]ments & obstacles she has had to contend with. I was obliged to place her under the Turkish Flag before she could be admitted to the priveleges which are accorded to Austrian, Russian, French & English Steamers in the same waters. It is a humiliating circumstance to an American to meet with such invidious distinctions abroad, particularly when they operate as uneaqual and consequently as unjust commercial restrictions.

I am now building a costly steamer of about 400 tons—expressly for the trade of the Levant, and shall be ready to leave this country for Constantinople about the middle of August. Apart from the benefit it may be to me in a pecuniary manner[,] as an American I feel an earnest desire that our steam ship may be permitted to carry her own flag. It is the interest which I feel in this matter which has emboldened me to invite your attention to the subject with the hope that some suggestion of yours may be offered for my service & guidance in the matter; that through your councils & aid and (should you think the matter sufficiently important) your instructions to our minister at the Sublime Porte on the subject, we may enjoy at least the rights & priveleges which are accorded to Steam vessels of other nations in the same seas.

I think no person can better than yourself appreciate the advantage to our commerce[,] our citizens & our national fame[?] of having a beautiful American merchant Steamship plying prosperously in the Levant carrying proudly in those distant seas its own protection in its own flag.

With the hope Sir, that you will pardon the liberty with which I have addressed you and will appreciate the motives by which I am influenced. I have the honor to be Sir Your most ob[edien]t Serv[an]t, Wm. Rufus Page.

ALS in DNA, RG 59 (State Department), Miscellaneous Letters (M-179:104, frames 518–519); CC in DNA, RG 84 (Foreign Posts), Turkey, Instructions, 3:61–63.

From W[illia]m Fort

Lost Cedar[,] Randolph County Mo.
June 10th 1844

Sir, Though an entire stranger to you, it is hoped that it will not be considered an unnessesary [*sic*] intrusion on you, to address you on the momentious subject of the rean[n]exation of Texas to the U.S. This subject is at this moment agitating this vast republic from center, to its extremities; and it is feared that the Senate of ["the" *interlined*] Union without stop[p]ing to consult their confiding constituency have er[e] this rejected the Treaty an[n]exing to the United States the Republic of Texas. Should this be the case, have not the misrepresented constituency, of the recresant [*sic*; recreant?] Senators, no alternative, no remedy, is the glorious, the noble prize lost forever? *Will not Gallant Texas wait but a short space of time?*, and she shall hear the thundering voice of an insulted, and misrepresented people, proclaiming to there [*sic*] Senators, and the world, that Texas is, and shall be ours, now, and forever.

It is understood in this section of the union that should Texas be rejected at this time she will not consent to a union with the U.S. at a future time, if this is not the case the error should be immediately corrected otherwise the ardor of the friends of rean[n]exation will be paralized, and our enemies may obtain an advantage in our approaching elections.

On the subject of an[n]exation I speak with confidence when I say to you that ⅔ of the people are in favor of immediate an[n]exation in this section of Missouri, and I think I may safely say of the State, at least we have a sufficient majority to controle the vote of Missouri after next Nov., at which time we elect two Senators, to the U.S. Senate; and should the Texas question continue an open one the State of Missouri after that time will come to the rescue. *Of this Texas and its friends every where may be assured.*

One word as to my self and I have done. Permit me to refer you to the Hon. Cave Johnson of Tennessee or any one or all our delegation from Missouri in Congress for my character and standing in society or you may refer to the Journals of the House of Representatives of Missouri for the last fifteen or twenty years with the exception of the last session at which time my name may be found recorded a State Senator.

I have been for 30 years an ardent Democrattic States right Republican, and you Sir, I prefer, to any man in our beloved country for the office of President of the U.S. My motto is, and shall ever be, every thing for the cause, nothing for men.

Be pleased to favour me with your views on the subjects conta[i]ned in this hasty and imperfect letter, either for the public, or private eye as you may elect. I am D[ea]r Sir Yours truly, Wm. Fort.

[P.S.] Direct to Huntsville Missouri.

ALS in ScCleA. NOTE: One of Fort's Senators, Thomas H. Benton, had voted against the annexation treaty.

From W[illiam] S. Fulton, [Senator from Ark.], 6/10. He encloses a letter from Josiah Gregg asking that a passport for a Mr. Alvarez, who is now on his way to Santa Fe, be transmitted to Independence, Missouri. ALS in DNA, RG 59 (State Department), Passport Applications, vol. 31, no. 2220 (M-1372:14).

From LOUIS MARK

Washington, 10 June 1844

Sir, You receive herewith an original Letter of Mr. B[ernard] Graham one of the partners of the house of P[eter] Harmony & Nephews & Co. of New York [City] in which he states his conviction that no wrong was intended by me either to his house or the Government. Owing to the absence of another Partner of this house from New York it has been impossible as yet to obtain all the Documents I wish relative to my Bond but ample proof will be forwarded to you to prove that no wrong was intended or can be attributed to me in that transaction.

Some malicious Person has published an *anonymous* Letter in the Newspapers stating that I had written a Letter to Mr. Fred[eri]ck Diergardt of Viersin, requesting money to be sent to bribe this Government to ratify the German Treaty—ridiculous as such an accusation is, still I think proper to state that the only Letter I wrote to Mr. Diergardt was to furnish me with Samples as proofs that Germany could furnish Silk Goods as cheap as England or France as the Times English Newspaper stated that by this German Treaty we would get worse Articles at a higher Price. I only rec[eive]d here his reply to that Letter which I inclose as also the Letter of one of his N. York Correspondents confirming this Statement and am ready to furnish any farther proofs that may be required.

My humble part in this German Convention causes many of its opponents to calumniate me. I therefore take the liberty to state that I was educated in New York—that I married a Sister of General [Alexander] Macomb who with my Children are now in Bavaria[;] that I was nominated to Consulships in Europe by Mr. [James] Monroe, Gen[era]l [Andrew] Jackson and Mr. [John] Tyler and allways confirmed by the Senate during their Administrations—that in the Archives of your Department you will find Statements from Mr. [Hugh S.] Legare and Mr. [Henry] Wheaton praising my Patriotism, and that they received more information from me as to the Commerce and political Economy of Germany, than from *any* and all *other sources put together* and as I continue to enjoy the confidence and friendship of Mr. Wheaton I hope you will also favor me with your protection. With the greatest Respect I remain Your Ob[edient] Ser[van]t, Louis Mark.

ALS with Ens in DNA, RG 59 (State Department), Consular Despatches, Munich, vol. 1 (T-261:1).

From Ro[bert] Tyler, "Private"

No. 34 7th Street
[Philadelphia?, *ca.* June 10?] 1844

My dear Sir, I have this morning been made acquainted with a nasty intrigue in progress here to defeat Judge [Edward] King's Confirmation as supreme [court] Judge by the Senate. The object is to have George M. Read, a *particular friend* of [James] Buchanan, or in a *certain Contingency* Buchanan himself, nominated to the place. That pragmatical two-horse circus rider politician, [Attorney General] John Nelson, is the Washington agent in this traffic. The object of this letter is to put you on your guard against such influences. Judge King is clearly our man. He will certainly be opposed by [Thomas H.] Benton & Co. He is known here as a liberal politician. He commenced political life in [18]24 your warm friend—was one of the conductors or special writers for the Franklin Gazette—went down with you here when those very men (some of them) deserted you. In [18]28 he was a presidential elector & voted for you as vice President. He has been with us for the last four years.

These are the facts. I am never mistaken in my men, for I never believe what others ["or themselves" *interlined*] say. I trace their history step by step. We southern men have no idea of the political profligacy of these lying & oft disgrac[e]d[?] impostors at the north. Experience teaches a man something, & I have had a *little* lesson taught me now & then. Judge King is possessed of unquestioned abilities, & is backed by a larger popular influence than these men altogether have. With assurances of my perfect respect, y[ou]r fr[ie]nd & ob[edien]t S[ervan]t, Ro: Tyler.

ALS in ScCleA. NOTE: On 6/5 John Tyler sent King's nomination as Associate Justice of the Supreme Court to the Senate. It was not voted on before the Congressional session ended on 6/17. At the next session of Congress the nomination was again made, but eventually withdrawn. This letter is undated except for "1844" which is so written as to suggest it may have been added at a time after the writing of the rest of the ms. Robert Tyler was a son of the President. A June date is conjectural. The date of the letter might possibly be December, 1844, when the nomination of King was resubmitted.

From W[illiam] S. Archer, "Private"

Senate, June 11/44

Dear Sir, I deem it incumbent on me to communicate my opinion to you, that no Outfit [for a diplomatic mission] will pass the Senate unless the nomination shall have first met the confirmation of the Senate.

The nomination [of Tilghman A. Howard] to Texas, will be confirmed. Why is an outfit asked for Constantinople? Is it for a new Mission, or is the Outfit of the last year[']s Minister in arrear?

I have to request information as to the time and grounds, of the Institution of the Mission to Buenos Ayres. The Outfit asked is I presume for the Charge [Harvey M. Watterson] who has just been rejected. Respectf[ull]y y[our]s, W.S. Archer.

ALS in ScCleA. NOTE: Archer, a Va. Whig, was chairman of the Senate Committee on Foreign Relations.

To W[illiam] S. Archer, Chairman, Senate Committee on Foreign Relations, 6/11. "I have the honor to enclose a copy of a letter, addressed to the Chairman of the [Senate] Committee on Finance [George Evans], in relation to appropriations for civil and diplomatic expenses; and to invite the attention of the Committee on Foreign Relations to that part of it respecting appropriations for diplomatic purposes." FC in DNA, RG 59 (State Department), Accounting Records: Miscellaneous Letters Sent, 1832–1916, vol. for 2/1–9/30/-1844, p. 227.

To GEORGE EVANS, Chairman of the Senate Committee on Finance

Department of State
Washington, 11 June 1844

Sir, I have the honor to inform the Committee of Finance, that sundry appropriations for which estimates have been submitted by this Department, are omitted in the Bill (H.R. No. 32,) making appropriations for the civil and diplomatic expenses of Government for the fiscal year ending on the 30th of June 1845, and for other purposes. The following are the items referred to, and to which I invite the attention of the Committee.

First. Previous to the present year the appropriation for the Contingent expenses of this Department was $25,000, including the cost of publishing and distributing the laws. The estimate for the present and ensuing year was $20,000, each—and this amount for the year ending the 30th of June, 1845, has been reduced in the Bill to $18,600, by taking from it, on account of extra clerk hire, the sum of $1,400.

This item of expenditure was estimated at $3,400, instead of $2,000, as in the appropriation bill of the last session; (for experience had shewn that the estimate was too small,) but the aggregate amount was not increased, the sum added to this item having been taken from other heads of Contingent expenditure.

Second. Under the head of "Intercourse with Foreign Nations," the sums estimated for salaries of a Minister to China, ($9,000,) and of a Secretary of Legation, ($2,000,) have been omitted in the Bill now before the Senate; as, also, the estimates for outfits of Ministers to China, Mexico, and Austria, ($27,000). These appropriations are required for the public service, for the Representative of ["our Government, to" *interlined*] China [Caleb Cushing], is by this time at his post: and our Minister to Mexico [Wilson Shannon] awaits the necessary appropriation in order to [make] his departure. It is also understood that Mr. [Daniel] Jenifer, our Minister at Vienna will return to the United States during the summer, and it will be important to fill the vacancy immediately thereafter.

Third. The appropriation for outfits of our Chargés des Affaires in Sardinia, Chile, and Belgium, ($13,500,) is also omitted—as also the sum of $3000, for the salary of our Commissioner at the Sandwich Islands, and the sum of $500 for our Consul at Beyrout; for both of whom provision was made in the appropriation bill of the year ending the 30th of June, 1844.

In regard to [Henry W. Hilliard] our Chargé d'Affaires to Belgium, I have to state that letters have been received from him, requesting that he may be allowed to resign his situation during the summer, in consequence, as he states, of the death of his brother in law, and the private obligations which that event has devolved on him—and that the President has acceded to his request. In the present state of our relations with that power, it is highly important that the vacancy should be filled without delay. The Chargé to Chile [William Crump] awaits the necessary appropriation to enable him to proceed to that country—and the Chargé at Sardinia [Robert Wickliffe, Jr.] has been for some time in the discharge of his duties; but as yet no provision has been made for his outfit.

Fourth. The estimate submitted for defraying the expenses of an overland mail from Chagres to Panama, and the conveyance of despatches at and between these places, including the compensation of an Agent at each, amounting to $3000, has also been omitted. The arrangement is important to the safe and speedy transmission of intelligence to and from our Diplomatic and Consular Agents in the countries bordering on, and the Islands lyeing in the Pacific. The sum of $1000 was appropriated to this object for the present year, and Agents have been accordingly appointed.

Fifth. The estimate for the relief and protection of American Seamen in foreign countries amounted to $75,000. The amount appropriated by the Bill is only $30,000. As to the inadequacy of this sum, I beg leave to refer you to a communication, addressed by this Department to [James I. McKay] the Chairman of the [House of Representatives] Committee of Ways and Means, of date the 7th instant.

The appropriation for the Contingent expenses of all the Missions abroad has also been reduced by the Bill, from $20,000 to $15,000—an amount deemed inadequate to the demands of the ensuing year. On this point I ask leave to refer you to a communication which I had the honor to address to the Chairman of the Committee of Ways and Means, dated the 20th [*sic*; 28th] Ultimo—with the additional remark that the contingent expenses of, at least, twenty three missions have to be paid out of this sum.

I have further to state that, in consequence of the non-concurrence of the Senate in the appointment of [William S. Murphy] the present Chargé d'Affaires to Texas, an appropriation of $4,500, will be necessary for the outfit of a successor to be appointed in his place. I have the honor to be, Sir, Your obedient Servant, J.C. Calhoun.

LS in DNA, RG 233 (U.S. House of Representatives), 28A-D30.6; FC in DNA, RG 59 (State Department), Accounting Records: Miscellaneous Letters Sent, 1832–1916, vol. for 2/1–9/30/1844, pp. 223–226; CC (dated 6/10) in ScCleA.

To Francis J. Grund, 6/11. Grund is informed that he has been appointed and confirmed as U.S. Consul for Antwerp. Information related to taking up the duties of the office is enclosed. FC in DNA, RG 59 (State Department), Consular Instructions, 10:249–250.

To Samuel Haight, Antwerp, 6/11. "I have to inform you that Francis J. Grund, Esq. has been appointed to succeed you in the Consulate of the United States at Antwerp, and to request that you will deliver to him the Archives and other property appertaining to the office." FC in DNA, RG 59 (State Department), Consular Instructions, 10:250.

From JOHN HOGAN, "Private"

Utica New York, June 11th 1844

My dear Sir, I have now reached home where I ["am" *interlined*] under my own "vine & fig tree," and where I can look over the late field of contest deliberately an[d] calculate its consequences &c. So total a defeat never did man receive than my *friend* from N[ew] York [Martin Van Buren] and in truth all of that class of men and what is more they feel the sting. I am told that Gov. [William L.] Ma[r]cy, Gov. [William] Bouck[,] [Edwin] Croswell[,] Vanderpool [*sic*; Aaron Vanderpoel, Samuel] Beardsley and that class of men who were on the side of the Abolitionists & in fact had formed a Coalition with them are all without exception in hot water. The calculation of those fellows was to get V[an] Buren nominated then ["fo" *altered to* "to"] force Gov. Bouck again on the ticket untie [*sic*; unite] with the Abolitionists & carry this State under the guise of Democracy & then go into a regular crusade for the Spoils. They are *foiled* in all their projects. They now dare not go over in full to the Abolitionists but they will get a *stride the fence*. They are all without exception bitterly hostile to the Annexation of Texas and I am told that ["that" *altered to* "they"] now boast that they will get Mr. [John] Tyler to run & have an Electoral Ticket in each State and in that way defeat the matter. The Post Master [John L.] Graham of the City of New York I am fearful is in that plot. You are better see Gov. [Charles A.] Wickliff[e] the Post Master Gen. & put him on his guard against those men. [William] Jones the Post Master of Washington City is I am told one. They together with John Cramer of this State and a Mr. [Chesselden] Ellis a Member of Congress from Cramer's District are engaged in that matter. They for the purpose of holding office go to Mr. Tyler & urge him to run for the Presidency. They wish to get up an Electoral Ticket in each State as the friend[s] of Mr. Tyler but really their object is to divide so as to let Mr. Clay come in. Mr. Clay with Mr. Webster & the New England People will of course prevent the annexation of Texas to the Union. The Old Hunkers of this State are in that Boat. You know Beardsley's course. That is an index that Class of Men are Abolitionists. They are able & shrewd set of men. Now you are in possession of the whole ground. Mr. Polk will be defeated by those men if possible. You are better see Mr. [Dixon H.] Lewis, Mr. [Robert J.] Walker, Mr. [Willie P.] Mangum & that Class of men who will look into the matter. Recollect one thing that those Gent[lemen] in this

State look toward yourself & friends with more than a jealous eye as they ["say" *interlined*] it was yourself & friends that defeated them. Mr. [Edmund S.] Derry of New York will be in Washington in a few days. He will do all in his power to aid you. *Could* I afford it I would without delay go to Washington & there remain ["thus" *canceled*] for three months and direct the Artillery in this State. We are struggling hard in this State. *We will succeed.* There is an application for one of your friends to be appointed Post Master of this City (Utica) in the place of the present incumbent A[ugustine] G. Danby whose term expires in July. Danby is one of the Van Buren Bure [*sic*] men. Will you call & have Mr. Wickliffe the Post Master Gen. & have him interpose with [the] President to get your friend appointed in place of (Danby). Now I believe I have put all these matters fairly before you. Now I call [*ms. torn*] a matter of much more interest to me personally[,] that is in a pecuniary point of view. I see by the papers that the Senate have rejected Mr. Waterson [Harvey M. Watterson] as Minister to Buenosayres. Who will get that appointment[?]

I will now go into my own matters fully & fairly. The reason that I have not been in the Congress of the U.S. was my pecuniary matters. I should have long since been there contending by your side for those principles of Gov[ernment] but I was deter[r]ed by having been left with a large family of my Father[']s to sustain & therefore had to look to my profession for a livelihood. *It is so yet.* Therefore I am compelled to defer for a time. My object in asking the appoint[ment] I seek is to enable me to return & go to Congress there to maintain & sustain the noble principles that you have advanced. If I could get a full Mission that would give me a Spur that I would at once take the field. I feel that I am asking of my friend to[o] much[,] a place that is sought after by men higher in place [and] consequently more claim. Still I throw my self wholly on you and look to your friendship for support. *This* State N[ew] York has no foreign minister & has but one charge d affa[i]res Mr. [George W.] Lay who is at the Court of Denmark. The time might come when I could in a slight measure repay your friendship. I will write [no] more for some days least you would become tired of my letters. I hope Mrs. Calhoun & family are well. I [am] Sir with the greatest respect your ob[edien]t Serv[an]t, John Hogan.

ALS in ScCleA.

From STEWART NEWELL, [Galveston]

Consulate of the U. States
Sabine [Texas], June 11th 1844

Sir, I beg leave to enclose a Letter [of 6/8/1844] of C[arter] Beaman relative to Steamer "Scioto Belle" and to request the same to be filed with other Documents relative to said vessel.

Also Copy of Letter [of 4/13/1844] from Gen[era]l [William S.] Murphy to me as refer[r]ed to in Letter of C. Beaman. I have the honor to be most Respectfully your Ob[edien]t Serv[an]t, Stewart Newell.

ALS (No. 18) with Ens in DNA, RG 59 (State Department), Consular Despatches, Texas, vol. 1 (T-153:1), received 6/21. NOTE: Beaman's letter to Newell discusses the sale of the *Scioto Belle* as directed by Newell according to William S. Murphy's instructions and the subsequent claims against her by three former seamen and her former captain, James J. Wright. Beaman feels that Murphy has tended to assist those filing this suit even though he knows of their bad character and reputation. He feels that he has been victimized in this affair. The copy of Murphy's letter enclosed expresses the hope that Newell can without further delay "find some way of restoring to the Owner [Carter Beaman], the Steamer Scioto Belle." A Clerk's EU on the despatch reads "I should like to have all the papers in this case briefed, so as to present the points involved to the Secretary, with the evidence[?] stated briefly."

From [CHARLES SERRUYS, Belgian Chargé d'Affaires]

Washington, June 11th 1844

There exists in the Provinces of the Rhine a great disposition to emigrate to the United States. The Belgian Government for[e]sees the moment when the same disposition will extend itself in Belgium.

Before giving its Sanction or encouragement to emigration, the Belgian Government wishes to know the moral & material situation of emigrants in the United States. This mission has been given to Baron van der Straten-Ponthoz, Secretary of the Belgian Legation at Washington.

To further the views of his Government, B[ar]on van der Straten intends to visit the States of New York, Ohio, Indiana, Illinois, Michigan, & Missouri; the Territories of Wisconsin & Iowa. He thinks that it would be useful to have a passport to establish his character with the local authorities, in the different places he is to visit.

He also wishes to receive letters of introduction to the Governors & Agents of the Public land in the States & Territories mentioned above.

B[ar]on van der Straten would be pleased to correspond with the Agent of the Public Land at Washington, & officers of the Treasury Department, who could give him information upon the subject of emigration in the United States, the laws of navigation concerning the transportation of emigrants, & the privileges bestowed to them at the Custom House.

ADU in DNA, RG 59 (State Department), Notes from Foreign Legations, Belgium, vol. 1 (M-194:1).

From McC[lintock] Young, Secretary of the Treasury ad interim, 6/11. "I have the honor to acknowledge the receipt of the letters of Mr. Jno. Bachman [*not found*] & Mr. W[illia]m C. Sully transmitted by you, soliciting an appointment in the Revenue Marine, and would state, that the corps is full and the number of applicants unusually large." LS in DNA, RG 59 (State Department), Miscellaneous Letters (M-179:104, frame 522).

From W[ILLIAM] S. ARCHER

Senate, June 12/44

Sir, I have to request on behalf of the Committee of Foreign Relations of the Senate, to be furnished with the correspondence between your Department and the Chargé of the Netherlands [Jean Corneille Gevers] on the subject of the exaction by our Government of a differential duty on British as distinguished from Coffee from Brazil[,] Cuba &c &c.

A note apprizing me of the grounds taken by the Department in the discussion will probably be equivalent to the correspondence and save the trouble of preparing it. I am, Very Resp[ectfull]y, Y[ou]rs, W.S. Archer.

ALS in ScCleA.

Rich[ar]d K. Crallé to W[ILLIAM] S. ARCHER

Department of State
Washington, June 12th 1844

In reply to your note of this morning asking for the correspondence between this Department, & the Chargé d'Affaires of the Netherlands [Jean Corneille Gevers], or a Statement in brief, of the grounds assumed by it in the discussion, I have the honor (in obedience to the instructions of the Secretary of State) to transmit to you the enclosed copy of a letter from the Secretary of the Treasury *ad interim* [McClintock Young], to the Collector of Customs at Philadelphia [Calvin Blythe] in relation to the Subject in question. Also a copy from the communication from the same to this Department on the same Subject. This Department concurs in the views contained in these communications, so far as the existing treaties and laws are concerned. As to the course which congress may think it expedient to adopt under the circumstances, this Department has expressed no opinion. Richd. K. Crallé, Ch[ie]f Cl[er]k.

FC in DNA, RG 59 (State Department), Domestic Letters, 34:344–345 (M-40:32).

R[ichard] K. Crallé to W[ILLIAM] S. ARCHER

Department of State
Washington, June 12th 1844

Sir, The Mission of the United States which it is proposed to renew a[t] Buenos Ayres, is considered to be of great importance[,] especially at this juncture.

The direct trade between this Country and the Argentine Confederation is of considerable and growing value, as the Treasury Statements Show. According to those Statements, our Exports to that Country for the fiscal year of 1841 amounted to ($661,946) Six hundred and Sixty one thousand nine hundred and forty six dollars, and our imports thence to ($1,612,513) One million Six hundred and twelve thousand, five hundred and thirteen dollars. For the first fiscal year of 1842, our exports were ($411,261) four hundred and eleven thousand, two hundred and Sixty one dollars, and our imports ($1,835,623) One million eight hundred & thirty five thousand, Six hundred and twenty three dollars.

Taking into view the unsettled state of that Country, it is desirable that this trade Should be regulated by a Treaty, an advantage which it does not now enjoy, whereas a Treaty between Great Britain and Buenos Ayres has for a number of years been in operation, from which the trade of the former Country has, as is understood, direct and Superior benefits. The Tonnage duties on vessels of the United States entering ports of the Argentine Confederation are double those exacted from British Vessels.

There are also claims of Citizens of the United States pending against that Government to a Serious amount. Our Citizens living in and resorting to the country are constantly Subjected to greviences [*sic*], from which they would most probably be exempt if this Government had a chargé d'Affaires on the spot; or the claims would be much more certain to obtain prompt redress through the representations of such an agent, than through those of a Consul, merely.

There is no prospect of an immediate termination of the existing war between Buenos Ayres and Monte Video. In its progress hitherto, citizens of the United States have in Several instances, Suffered aggressions upon their neutral rights of one or the other party, in a way which would not have happened, if we had had a formal diplomatic Agent at Buenos Ayres to Assist and Counsel them.

An officer of that character would also be Useful for the purpose of opening the way to Commercial & diplomatic relations, between the United States and the Republic of Paraguay, whose Territories border on those of the Argentine Republic.

These general considerations may be Strengthened by an inspection of the instructions of Mr. [Abel P.] Upshur to Mr. [Harvey M.] Watterson, the original draft of which, is herewith transmitted, and which I will thank you to return. I have the honor to be &c &c, R.K. Crallé, Ch[ie]f Cl[er]k.

FC in DNA, RG 59 (State Department), Domestic Letters, 34:345–347 (M-40:32).

From Robert B. Campbell, Havana, 6/12. Campbell encloses a copy of a note, dated 6/11, from Captain General Leopoldo O'Donnell, concerning the punishment of Manuel Martinez for the murder of U.S. seaman Michael Murphy. According to the note, Martinez was convicted and sentenced to four months imprisonment, but O'Donnell, believing the sentence too lenient, revoked it and sentenced Martinez to two years. ALS with En (and translation) in DNA, RG 59 (State Department), Consular Despatches, Havana, vol. 19 (T-20:19), received 6/24.

From ROBERT B. CAMPBELL

Consulate of the United States of America

Havana, June 12th 1844

Sir, I have the honor herewith to enclose to you a copy of a letter just received from the Capt. Gen[era]l, in reply to a letter addressed to him by me (a copy of which has been forwarded to you) in relation to the arrest and imprisonment of [William] Bisby and Mofford [*sic*; Samuel Moffat] at Cardenas, referred to in your communication of the 26th of April last. Not having been on the spot nor having the evidence of witnesses who might substantiate the facts, I cannot say whether the Capt. Gen[era]l has been deceived or not by the representations made to him of the treatment of Bisby & Mofford. I have the honor to be with considerations of very great respect y[ou]r mo[st] ob[edien]t Ser[van]t, Robert B. Campbell.

ALS (marked "Copy") with En in DNA, RG 59 (State Department), Consular Despatches, Havana, vol. 19 (T-20:19), received 6/25. NOTE: Campbell enclosed a copy of Captain General Leopoldo O'Donnell's note of 6/11. According to a translation filed with this correspondence, O'Donnell stated that Bisby and Moffat had been held briefly in leg irons before being transferred to the Cardenas prison, which was described as healthy and decent.

From JOHN COMMERFORD

New York [City,] June 12th 1844

Dear Sir, I understand that through the wishes of your friends, that you advise the President [John Tyler] in the selection of the appointments in our City. For my own part I know nothing of what is going on with regard to these matters and if what I have stated is ["not" *interlined*] true you must not be offended at me[.] The fact is that I have no disposition to mingle with any small body of men for to accomplish certain purposes[.] As a prominent member of the Administration of Mr. Tyler I think that whatever appertains to his credit or discredit in the selections he may make reflects on all of his Cabinet. It is therefore ["this idea" *interlined*] that prompts me to address you at this time. I am told that the President is about to appoint Mr. Henry C. Atwood as U.S. Marshall or Surveyor of this Port. If this is the case the President will make a most unfortunate Selection, because the man is well known throughout our City, as the Keeper of a disreputable Grog[g]ery. He is remarkable for nothing

but as a Rum House Brawler. It is true that by the Rum House influence he obtained his nomination as Sheriff of this County, but it
is also true that ["he" *interlined*] was defeated by over 3,000 majority
whilst the other democratic candidates were elected[.] I am told
that Mr. ["Ely" *interlined*] Moore is ["spoken of as" *interlined*] a
Candidate for the Surveyorship and although he had a preference for
another Candidate for the Presidency yet I am satisfied that he entertains good feelings towards yourself[.] And I am also satisfied
that the Selection of Mr. Moore would give far more Satisfaction to
the entire Democracy of our City than any other man that can be
selected[.] Mr. Moore and myself have talked over our preferences
for the Presidency and he always maintained that as to the qualifications of intellect and availibility he would go for him who enjoyed
this favor of the people. Very respectfully Your fellow citizen, John
Commerford.

ALS in ScCleA.

From L U C I U S Q. C. E L M E R, [Representative from N.J.]

House of Representatives, June 12th 1844
Sir, Dr. Franklin Lippencott [*sic*; Lippincott] of the State of New
Jersey, is desirous of obtaining the appointment of Consul at Leghorn,
Italy, which office is now held as I understand by a foreigner [Joseph
Binda] and not by an American. This gentleman belongs to that
part of New Jersey in which I reside myself, and knowing him to be
peculiarly deserving, I am ["the" *canceled*] anxious that he should
succeed. My colleagues join with me in the hope that you may be
willing to recommend his appointment. We feel that we may the
more pressingly urge his claim, because but one appointment to an
office abroad has been made from our State, so far as we are aware,
for many years.

Dr. Lippencott was graduated as a Dr. of Medicine in the University of Penns[ylvani]a in the year 1840 and has a strong recommendation from Dr. [Nathaniel] Chapman a distinguished professor
of that institution. His great motive for wishing a situation in Italy
is that his health is delicate, altho he is perfectly able to attend to
business. He is recommended, by the Governor of New Jersey, by
all the democratic members of the Legislature, and most of the whigs,

by Gen[era]l [Garret D.] Wall late Senator, by Gov. [Peter D.] Vroom, and by James S. Green Esq. of Princeton, as well as by the members of Congress from New Jersey, thus combining a support from our State which but few persons could command.

My attention is so much engrossed at this moment by the business pressing upon us at the close of the session, that I cannot wait on you in person, and have therefore taken the liberty of making this communication and of asking that it may receive your favorable consideration at as early a period as may be practicable. Very respectf[ull]y Your ob[edien]t Servant, Lucius Q.C. Elmer.

ALS in DNA, RG 59 (State Department), Applications and Recommendations, 1837–1845, Lippincott (M-687:19, frames 492–494).

From R[amon] L. Irarrazaval, [Chilean Minister of Foreign Affairs], Santiago, 6/12. Irarrazaval uses the occasion of John S. Pendleton's return to the U.S. to state the Chilean position on American claims against Chile stemming from the Sitana affair in 1821, which claims have been the subject of correspondence between Pendleton and himself. Chile asserts the principle of "prescription, with regard to antiquated claims, on which the parties have omitted to take, in proper time, the measures necessary for the recognition of the rights alleged on their part." Although the Chilean government places its refusal on this ground it possesses sufficient proof of the legality of its actions in 1821 to defeat the claim. He also animadverts upon the tone used by Pendleton in his correspondence on the subject. ALS (in Spanish) and State Dept. translation in DNA, RG 59 (State Department), Notes from Foreign Legations, Chile, vol. 1 (M-73:1).

To [ANSON JONES], Secretary of State of Texas

Department of State
Washington, 12th June, 1844

Sir: Mr. William S. Murphy, who has for some time been accredited to the Government of the Republic of Texas as Chargé d'Affaires of the United States, being about to return to his country, I have directed him to take leave of Your Excellency and to embrace the opportunity which will thereby be afforded him, to convey to Your Excellency the expression of the friendly sentiments entertained by

The President [John Tyler] towards the Republic of Texas, and his intention, at an early period, to renew the representation of the United States in that country.

I avail myself of this occasion to offer Your Excellency the assurance of my very distinguished consideration. J.C. Calhoun.

LS in Tx, Records of the Texas Republic Department of State, U.S. Diplomatic Correspondence; FC in Tx, Records of the Texas Republic Department of State, Copybooks of Letters Received from Texan and Foreign Representatives, vol. 2–1/98, p. 512; FC (dated 6/4) in DNA, RG 59 (State Department), Credences, 3:82.

To W[illia]m B. Lewis, [Washington], 6/12. "Mr. Calhoun presents his compliments to Major Lewis, and will cheerfully comply with Suggestion contained in the letter of the Prussian Consul at New York [City, Johann W. Schmidt], of the 10th inst., upon the receipt of an application addressed directly to the Department of State, by that functionary." FC in DNA, RG 59 (State Department), Domestic Letters, 34:344 (M-40:32).

To W[ILLIAM] S. MURPHY

Department of State
Washington, 12th June, 1844
Sir: I have to inform you that on the 23d of last month, the Senate resolved not to advise and consent to your appointment as Chargé d'Affaires of the United States to the Republic of Texas. A letter to the Secretary of State of that Republic [Anson Jones] announcing the termination of your mission, is accordingly herewith transmitted. You will avail yourself of the occasion of delivering it and, also, of that of taking leave of the Chief Magistrate of Texas [Samuel Houston], to offer renewed assurances of the friendly disposition of the President [John Tyler] towards that Republic, of his hope that it will be reciprocated, and that nothing may take place which will have a tendency to weaken that disposition on either part.

Before you set out from that country, you will commit the books and papers of the Legation to the custody of the Consul of the United States at Galvezton, provided your successor should not have arrived. I am, Sir, your obedient servant, J.C. Calhoun.

LS (No. 20) in DNA, RG 84 (Foreign Posts), Records of the Texas Legation, received 7/3; FC in DNA, RG 59 (State Department), Diplomatic Instructions, Texas, 1:95 (M-77:161).

From B. W. SHARP and Others

Boonville ["Mo." *interlined*] June 12th 1844
Dear Sir, The undersigned were appointed a committee of arrangements in behalf of the "Boonville Democratic Association" to make preparitory preperations for a State central convention of ratification, to be held at this place on the 17th day of July next; We therefore in the name of the aforesaid Association and of the Democracy of the State of ["Missouri" *interlined*] beg leave to present you this manifestation of our particular regard for your close adherence to the principles of true republicanism, and your untiring efforts in opposition to the host of oppressive measures, which whiggery has endeavoured to foist upon the American people during their ["unfortunate" *interlined*] reign of power, and to respectfully invite you to attend the said convention. We have the honor to remain with ev[e]ry assurance of our highest consideration and respect your obedient Servants, B.W. Sharp, Dr. F.W.G. Thomas, H.E. McDearmon, Eli Collier, H. Martin, Charles Chilten, E[dward] B. McPherson, H[enry] W. Crowther, John Asetlyne, F.A. Williams, William Harley, W[illia]m Gray, Isaac Lionberger, J.M. Crane, H.E. Moore, James Tankesley, J.D. Blair, J.S. Watson, Benj[amin] E. Ferry, Addison Bronough, Hamilton Tinney, W.T. Moore, John Wells, R.P. Bowman, Dr. E.E. Buckner.

LS in ScCleA.

To [JOHN TYLER]

Department of State
Washington, 12th June, 1844

To the President of the United States.

The Secretary of State, to whom was referred the Resolution of the Senate of the 4th instant, requesting the President "if not incompatible with the public interest to communicate to the Senate the correspondence between the late Minister of the United States in Mexico [Waddy Thompson, Jr.] and the Minister of Foreign Affairs of that Republic [José M. de Bocanegra] upon the subject of an order issued by the Mexican government expelling all natives of the United States from Upper California and other Departments of the Mexican

Republic, and also the correspondence between the said American Minister and the Mexican Minister of Foreign Affairs upon the order prohibiting foreigners the privilege of the retail trade in Mexico, and which has taken place subsequently to that heretofore communicated to Congress on the same subject"—has the honor to lay before the President the papers of which a list is subjoined, and which are believed to be all those on the files of this Department called for by the Resolution. Respectfully submitted. J.C. Calhoun.

LS in DNA, RG 46 (U.S. Senate), 28A-E3; FC in DNA, RG 59 (State Department), Reports of the Secretary of State to the President and Congress, 6:110–111; PC with Ens in Senate Document No. 390, 28th Cong., 1st Sess., pp. 1–19; PC with Ens in the Washington, D.C., *Daily National Intelligencer*, July 13, 1844, p. 2; PC with Ens in *Niles' National Register*, vol. LXVI, no. 21 (July 20, 1844), pp. 332–335. NOTE: Tyler transmitted this letter and its Ens to the Senate on 6/12. Enclosed were copies of 19 communications exchanged by Thompson and de Bocanegra between 12/23/1843 and 2/8/1844. The resolution to which the above is a reply is found in DNA, RG 59 (State Department), Miscellaneous Letters (M-179:104, frame 486), and *Senate Journal*, 28th Cong., 1st Sess., p. 682.

From HENRY WHEATON

Berlin, 12 June, 1844

Sir, Your Despatch, No. 56, has been duly received.

I have the honor to enclose Copies of my Correspondence with the Envoy of the Grand Duchy of Baden at this Court, relating to the conclusion of a convention with that State, for the mutual abolition of the *Droit d'Aubaine*, taxes on emigration, &c, between the United States, & the Government of Baden. It will be perceived, from Mr. de Frankenberg's Letter to me, that his Government declines, for the present, entering into a Treaty for this purpose, upon the ground that certain of its subjects have vested rights in the taxes on emigration, which require to be regulated by municipal legislation; before such an arrangement can be made with any foreign Power. I have the honor to be, with the highest Consid[eratio]n, Sir, Y[ou]r ob[e]d[ien]t Serv[an]t, Henry Wheaton.

LS (No. 252) with Ens (in French) in DNA, RG 59 (State Department), Diplomatic Despatches, Germany, vol. 3 (M-44:4), received 7/10; FC with Ens in DNA, RG 84 (Foreign Posts), Germany, Despatches, 4:134–137.

From H[ENRY] WHEATON, "Private"

Berlin, 12 June, 1844

My dear Sir, I had the pleasure to write you on the 10 & 17 April.

In the first of these Letters, I took the liberty of referring you to my official correspondence with the Department upon the subject of the Danish Sound Duties, & our existing treaties of navigation with Denmark, the Hanse-towns, &c.

As the Session of Congress is now terminated, I trust you will find time to examine these important questions. Should you come to the same conclusion which I have arrived at respecting the Navigation treaties, a negotiation will be necessary for their *revision*, & I have already mentioned in several of my Despatches that the Hanseatic minister at this Court has frequently expressed to me the desire of his constituents, if the ["treat" *canceled*] existing treaty is to be put an end to, that the negotiations for its renewal, with such modifications as may be agreed on, should be carried on *here*. Should the President [John Tyler] think fit to entrust this negotiation to me, & should he adopt the basis I have suggested of confining Hanseatic vessels to the direct trade between the United States & Germany, including the mouths of the Rhine, Meuse, & Scheldt, as being the natural outlets of German trade, it will only be necessary to notify to them the cessation of the existing Treaty in 12 months, & give me the necessary instructions & full power to treat for its revision. I do not wish to be considered as asking for this employment, which naturally falls within that division of Germany assigned to the Legation at Berlin, but merely make the suggestion to you, as a friend, to be acted on as you may think fit.

In respect to the Danish Sound duties, my impression is that we ought to confine ourselves to endeavouring to reduce them to the original standard of one per centum, instead of seeking to suppress them altogether, in which attempt we should not be supported by Prussia & other Powers, who have a political interest in sustaining Denmark, though certainly the right is very questionable. If we were to make it a *casus belli*, we could not well refuse the mediation & arbitration of a third Power, who would certainly decide against us upon the question of the general right, though it might recommend an equitable compromise. This subject is connected with our existing treaty of commerce & navigation with Denmark, as we are placed by the 5th article of that treaty on the footing of the most favored nation in respect to the payment of Sound Duties, which the Danes insist is an implied acknowledgment of their preexisting right. The whole of this matter is fully explained in my Despatch, No. 173, & the Memoir accompanying it, from which Mr. [Daniel] Webster's Report of the 24 May, 1841, so far as respects this subject, was drawn up. The Prussian Government has been, for some time past, negotiating at Copenhagen, with the view of reducing the duties to the original standard, & to ["hav"(?) *canceled*] make them payable at Stettin & the other Prussian ports in the Baltic, in order to avoid the vexatious delay at Elsinore. Mr. [Frederick] Schillow, our Consul at Stettin, informs me that in a recent Report to the Department he had made some suggestions respecting the matter, the precise nature of which you will learn by inspecting his Despatch. I am, my dear Sir, ever truly your faithful friend, H. Wheaton.

ALS in ScCleA.

From W[ILLIAM] S. ARCHER

Senate, June 13/44

Sir, A nomination has been made to the Senate, of Jasper Hall Livingston, as Secretary of Legation to Spain. I have to request to be furnished with the evidence on which this nomination has been commended to the Senate, not haveing been able to get this information from other sources.

It will be desirable to have the information today.

I have also to request the immediate communication, of the correspondence of our late Minister to Mexico [Waddy Thompson Jr.], called for by a recent Resolution of the Senate. I am Resp[ectfull]y & &, W.S. Archer.

ALS in ScCleA.

From C[ALEB] CUSHING

Macao, 13 June 1844

Sir: I have the honor to ["transmit to" *interlined*] you Copies in English of correspondence between the Imperial Commissioner Keying and myself.

The tenor of these letters is of the best possible augury for the success of the Mission.

In explanation of one particular of the correspondence I have to state that in the address of the two letters of the 29th of April and 31st of May as originally presented to me, the name of the Chinese Government stood higher in column by one character than that of the United States. As the Chinese have the custom of indicating in this way the relative dignity of parties to a correspondence and I did not choose to submit to any form of writing or expression which derogated in the slightest degree from the dignity of the United States, I accordingly returned these letters to Keying, under the circumstances set forth in the correspondence even at the hazard of at once cutting off all negociation.

The result seems to have justified this step on my part; as Keying immediately transmitted to me corrected originals of the two letters, accompanied with a note wholly unexceptionable in its spirit.

Chinese copies of all these letters, exhibiting the points of difference, will be sent to the Department by the earliest suitable opportunity.

Keying is to come here, attended by three persons of high distinction to aid him with their Counsel, and a numerous suite, and has had suitable apartments prepared for his own residence and that of his advisers and followers.

I hope, in a very short time therefore, to be able to transmit to you a satisfactory Treaty between the United States and China. I am With great respect Your obed[ien]t ser[van]t, C. Cushing.

LS (No. 66) with Ens in DNA, RG 59 (State Department), Diplomatic Despatches, China, vol. 2 (M-92:3), received 10/22; PC with Ens in Senate Document No. 67, 28th Cong., 2nd Sess., pp. 34–38. NOTE: This despatch was addressed to A[bel] P. Upshur.

From A[UGUSTINE] G. DANBY, "Private"

P[ost] O[ffice,] Utica, June 13, [18]44
Dear Sir, The importance of the subject upon which I write is my only apology for addressing one with whom I have a slight personal acquaintance, but for whom I have for years, cherished the most profound sentiments of respect; and who I am convinced occupies, at this time, a position, that enables him to save the Democratic party from a most calamitous defeat. You have more than once came to its rescue in the time of its greatest need; but never has it required the Exertion of your great talents and patriotic services, more than at this

period, to save it from destruction. The nominations of Messrs. [James K.] Polk and [George M.] Dallas, have every where been received with decided marks of approbation; and it is confidently believed that their Election will put an end to a political dynasty, which has become odious and intolerable to a vast majority of Republicans in almost all the States of the Union.

I appreciate fully the delicacy of your position. You are a member of Mr. [John] Tyler's administration, and no doubt will honorably perform all the duties which grow out of your personal & political relations with him; but none of these I trust & believe, will be found incompatible with your higher obligations to your country and your party. I profess to be a true friend of the President and believe that the Democratic party owe him a great debt of gratitude—a debt of honor, which must and will be paid, and while I condemn those selfish politicians who have so unwisely and ungratefully persecuted him who has done so much for the rescusitation of the Democracy from its overwhelming defeat in 1840, I cannot be insensible to the dangers which menace it from having two Republican Presidential candidates in the field to divide and paralize its strength[.]

Should Mr. Tyler run on an independent ticket I fear the result would be the Success of the [Henry] Clay Electoral ticket in several States, where the Democratic party, single handed, would be victorious. This course the friends of Mr. Clay are exceedingly anxious should be pursued, and there are some who at this time, are *clamorous* Tyler men, (in *profession* merely) who assert that they had rather die in such a cause, than triumph under any other leader. We have a few such individuals here, but they are *known* to be not the sincere friends of the President, but the decided friends of Mr. Clay, whose election they hope to secure by keeping the Republican party divided. I wish to prevent this result by combining the whole strength of the party upon one individual; and this it seems to me can be done in a manner highly creditable to Mr. Tyler; and certainly no friend would ask him to make a sacrifice incompatible with his interests, his honor or his fame. Under existing circumstances, however, it appears to me, he cannot hope to be elected; and conceding that he cannot be, what can he or his friends gain by his remaining a candidate. By withdrawing at this time, he may not lessen the malignity of his persecutors; but he will unite the Republican party; ensure its triumph; and win the gratitude and favor of every member of it not callous to every magnanimous and generous emotion; and he will occupy a position which must, in the event of the election of Mr. Polk, secure for him and his friends all that they may, with propriety, desire to obtain. I will not enlarge on this subject; but submit it to your consideration, with a perfect confidence that whether my opinions are or are not in unison with your own, that they will be regarded by you as the honest convictions of one who has no other object in view than the interest of the party to which he has for the last twenty years devoted his best energies of mind and body.

Altho' at the late Baltimore Convention the *united vote* of this State was given to Mr. [Martin] Van Buren, there are many Democrats who would have been gratified with your nomination for the Presidency; and they are looking forward to 1848 to see their wishes, on this subject, realized; and in the mean time they are anxious that you should occupy such a position in the coming contest as will enable them to act with as little embarrassment and as much efficiency as possible in your favor. There may be relations and circumstances, which I do not understand, but from the imperfect view I have taken of our public affairs, it seems to me that your interests, at this time, are identified with those of Mr. Polk, and that his success cannot fail, provided he acts with fairness, to strengthen your position.

I think you may calculate with considerable certainty—I may say with entire certainty should Mr. T[yler] decline his nomination, that the Electoral vote of this State will be given for Polk and Dallas. With great regard Your ob[edien]t serv[an]t, A.G. Danby.

ALS in ScCleA; PC in Boucher and Brooks, eds., *Correspondence*, pp. 238–240. NOTE: An AEU by Calhoun reads: "Mr. Danby[,] relates to the Presidential election."

From [J.C.] de Figanieře e Morão, [Portuguese Minister to the U.S.], 6/13. He asks that Calhoun do everything possible to encourage the House of Representatives to take up bill No. 118 to "carry into effect the Treaty between Portugal & the United States" before the end of the day. ALS in DNA, RG 59 (State Department), Notes from Foreign Legations, Portugal, vol. 3 (M-57:3, frame 519).

From HENRY W. HILLIARD

Legation of the United States
Brussels, 13th June 1844
Sir: It has been for some years the wish of the Belgian Government to revise its whole commercial system, and construct one suited to the present condition of the country. There were very strong po-

litical reasons for the revolution [in 1839] which separated Belgium from Holland but this event impaired the prosperity of some great interests in this country and made it necessary to cultivate new commercial relations. This led to the appointment of a committee instructed to institute an "enquête commerciale" and to report a system suited to the new position which Belgium had acquired. This report I had the honor to forward some weeks since, and I now enclose several documents, which exhibit the new System of "Droits differentiels" which it is proposed to establish. You will, of course, be prepared upon examining these papers to see to what extent our trade will be affected by the adoption of this system. The subject has engaged the attention of the Chamber of Representatives and has undergone an animated discussion. The Ministry have insisted that the system will operate beneficially for our country, while the opposition deny that this will be its effect. I have endeavored to examine it carefully and my impression is, that if a good understanding shall be preserved between our Government and that of Belgium, it will be found favorable to us, for it is the intention of this Government to use the power confided to it, and assimilate the flag of the United States to that of Belgium, as far as it can be done. I regarded the system, at first, with some distrust for I apprehended it was the purpose of this Government to discriminate to a great and injurious extent between its own flag and that of other nations. I thought it best, therefore, to state to Count [Albert Joseph] Goblet, Minister of Foreign Affairs, that it would disturb the commercial relations between the United States and Belgium and I addressed him a letter to that effect. I have the honor to forward a copy of my correspondence with him on this subject, and you will perceive that he hastens to assure me of the purpose of the Government to exercise its full authority in abolishing all discrimination between the flags of the two nations in the ports of this country. This will apply, however, to the direct trade only, leaving the new system to take effect on the importation of articles not the productions of the soil and the industry of our country. I have endeavored, as will be seen in my correspondence, to have this difference abolished likewise, believing that the interest of our trade with this country, requires reciprocity. I am aware that different opinions are entertained upon the subject of extending the reciprocity principle to other nations, but so far as Belgium is concerned, I am persuaded that we may not only conduct our trade with advantage upon the basis of perfect reciprocity, but that our interests strongly demand it. The shipping of this country is inconsiderable and competition with us is out of the question;

under a liberal arrangement we shall do almost the entire carrying trade. We find here a growing market for our productions, and the completion of the rail-road between Antwerp and the Rhine opens to that port an interesting part of Germany from which a large amount of produce destined for the United States must come. If the shipping interest of Belgium were large, the question would wear a different aspect, but it is really so very inconsiderable that it need not give rise to the slightest apprehension of even feeble rivalry. I trust that these views, which I have felt it my duty to present, will meet your approbation.

It will appear from the accompanying correspondence, that the arrangement to permit productions not those of our own soil and industry, to enter Belgium when imported under the flag of the United States, upon the same footing, as when imported under the Belgian flag, can be effected only by some positive international arrangement. This is very much desired by the present Government, and the Minister of Foreign Affairs has submitted a formal request that I would make known to the Government of the United States the wish of the Government of Belgium to enter upon the negotiation of a treaty of commerce and navigation. He desires me, too, to apply for powers to conduct the negotiation here. He supposes, of course, that our past experience in negotiations with this Government will induce us to insist upon this course, and to claim an approval of the treaty on the part of the treaty-making power of this country before it is submitted to our own Government for ratification. Two former negotiations, which were approved by the Government of the United States were permitted to fall through here. An ample apology has been tendered for this, but it certainly entitles us to claim, some sufficient guarantee that a new negotiation will not meet the same fate before entering upon it. The completion of the commercial inquiry so long prosecuted, enables the Government to make its new offer with entire confidence and to comprehend the extent of its power. It was the opinion of Mr. [Abel P.] Upshur, that the negotiation, when renewed, should be conducted at Washington, but I have thought it best in the new state of things here to submit the whole subject to your decision. There exists on the part of the present Government a friendly disposition towards the United States and a full appreciation of the importance of cultivating commercial relations with us. This is exhibited in debate and in conversation; Mr. [Jean Baptiste] Nothomb, Minister of the Interior, and much the ablest man in the Cabinet, took especial care to explain while defending the proposed tariff in the Chamber of Representatives that its provisions which threatened to disturb commercial relations with the United States would be arranged by treaty. I dined with their Majesties at the Chateau of Laeken near this place, on Saturday last, where I met Count Goblet, and he was very eager to know if the explanations given by him in his letter of that day were satisfactory. In my interviews with him, he has shown the greatest anxiety to preserve a good understanding with us. On Monday I dined with Mr. [Adolphe] Dechamps, Minister of Public Works and a very influential member of the Cabinet, he arranged that I should be seated next him at the table and made our affairs the subject of conversation, observing among other things that we must have a treaty. I may assure you with entire confidence that there exists a very strong disposition on the part of the present Government to arrange relations with our country upon the most favorable footing. This disposition does not extend to some other countries; there is by no means a good understanding with Holland, indeed, the Dutch Minister has addressed a strong note to the Belgian Government threatening reprisals if the proposed tariff of differential duties should be adopted. The British Government, too, is hostile to the new measure, and it is understood has addressed a vigorous note to this Government on the subject. The Representative of that power at this Court [Sir George Hamilton Seymour] called on me, some days since, and desired to know how I thought it would affect us, stating, that it would in his opinion injure the trade both of the United States and of Great Britain. This is not now my opinion so far as we are concerned. My apprehension was, that the distinction made between the flag of the United States and that of Belgium in favor of the latter, as to the importation of the productions of other countries, when taken from the warehouses of the United States might lead to retaliatory measures on the part of our Government and that we might lose the benefits of the reciprocity principle even in its application to the direct trade. Upon this subject, however, I think the letters of Count Goblet are satisfactory and I hope we shall derive benefits from the system.

There exists a disposition, on the part of some members of the Chambers to modify the scheme of the Minister of Finance upon the subject of tobacco, in every essential feature, that is, to abolish the clauses of the "Projet" which propose to tax the growth, sale and consumption of tobacco and to lay a heavy duty upon its importation. This would affect us very unfavorably and I had an interview with Count Goblet on the subject, in which I urged him to resist this change. He pledged himself to me to do so and assured me the

Ministry would press my views. I was much gratified, therefore, when the Minister of Finance, yesterday, in addressing the Chamber of Representatives expressed the determination of the Government to maintain this ground. I took occasion in my interview with Count Goblet to impress upon him the importance of avoiding any increase of the duties of importation upon *cotton, tobacco,* and other unmanufactured productions of the United States. This policy the Government will advocate and favor, and I hope, sustain. You will perceive that *cotton* is to be admitted upon terms as favorable as could be desired.

These questions are yet to undergo discussion and may not be disposed of before another session, but, I am very confident that the present Government will adhere to a most liberal system so far as the United States are concerned.

I have endeavored most faithfully to do my duty here, in advocating the general interests of our country and in protecting the rights of citizens of the United States. My intercourse too with the Government and with other members of the Diplomatic Corps has been of the most agreeable character, and now that my duties here are drawing towards a close, I shall continue to discharge them in such a manner that I may bear with me the consciousness of having performed every obligation which my position imposed with perfect fidelity.

I forward my accounts with the accompanying vouchers for the last quarter. I have the honor to be, Sir, Very Respectfully, Your obedient servant, Henry W. Hilliard.

LS (No. 19) with Ens in DNA, RG 59 (State Department), Diplomatic Despatches, Belgium, vol. 2 (M-193:3), received 7/5. NOTE: Hilliard was a distant kinsman of Calhoun by his sister having married William W. Waddel of Ga., son of the Rev. Moses Waddel.

From G. W. JOHNSTON and Others

Maracaybo [Venezuela,] June 13th 1844
Sir, We the undersigned Merchants and residents in Maracaybo beg to call your attention to the vacancy in the Consulate at this Port. We are aware of the appointment of Mr. Cochrane and subsequently of Mr. [Charles A.] Leas, but do not think that any gentleman will come out for the perquisites of an office not exceeding Three Hundred

Dollars. Therefore we ask the appointment of Mr. Roland Dubs a brother of our former Consul and now a resident merchant here. We presume that the fact that this petition is signed by every American now residing in Maracaybo, together with many others of high respectability Your Honour will see the propriety of the appointment. G.W. Johnston, W. Cook, A.M. Peñac, M.D., Geo[rge] Alonzo Taylor, Wm. Hutton, F. Bousquet, Fran[cis?] Alexandre Boyer, Victer Belloit[?], P. Casaun[?], Eldad[?] Whiting, J[u]n[io]r, S.A. Wait, master of Brig Emma, William Angus, Silas C. Bateman, William Piggott, Anthony Belany, Ira C. Price, John O. McPash[?], J.A. Spalding, M.D., Oliver Taylor, Henry B. Taylor, George Farish.

LS in DNA, RG 59 (State Department), Applications and Recommendations, 1845–1853, Dubs (M-873:24, frame 458). NOTE: This memorial was enclosed with a letter of Fernando Wood to Calhoun on 8/8/1844.

From JOHN A. MCCLERNAND,
[Representative from Ill.]

House of Representatives
Congress U.S.   June 13, 1844
Sir, If I mistake not, the "Illinois Republican" a paper lately published at Shawneetown, was appointed by ["the" *canceled*] Mr. [Daniel] Webster to print the laws of Congress. I think the paper was unworthy of the appointment in the first place, though Mr. W[ebster] may not have been aware of it. Since the paper has been discontinued.

My object now is to obtain the appointment of the [Shawneetown] "Illinois State Gazette" for the same purpose. You will therefore confer a favor on a friend if you will make the appointment. Your ob[e]d[ien]t Serv[an]t, John A. McClernand, Shawneetown, Ill[inoi]s.

ALS in DNA, RG 59 (State Department), Miscellaneous Letters Received Regarding Publishers of the Laws. NOTE: A Clerk's EU reads "Inform him there is no authority to publish out of the District."

From J[ohn] Y. Mason, [Secretary of the Navy], 6/13. In reply to a letter referred by Calhoun, Mason states that there is "no vacancy in the grade of Pursers. When one shall occur, the application of

Mr. [Francis S.?] Claxton will be respectfully considered." LS in DNA, RG 59 (State Department), Miscellaneous Letters (M-179: 104, frame 532); FC in DNA, RG 45 (Naval Records), Miscellaneous Letters Sent by the Secretary of the Navy, 33:471 (M-209:12).

To W[ILLIAM] S. ARCHER, Chairman of the Senate Committee on Foreign Relations

Department of State
Washington, 14th June, 1844
Sir: Upon the repeated solicitations of the Chargé d'Affaires of the United States at Brussels [Henry W. Hilliard], to be permitted to return home, the President [John Tyler] consented to accept his resignation, being entirely satisfied with the reasons and considerations which prompted the request. That this indulgence was granted with reluctance, owing to the very important interests at stake between the two countries, will abundantly appear from a perusal of the late instructions [of 6/7?] to Mr. Hilliard, a copy of which I have the honor to enclose. Under the circumstances of the case, I feel confident that this explanation will be sufficient to warrant and induce Congress to make provision for the outfit of a successor. I am, Sir, with great consideration, Your obedient Servant, J.C. Calhoun.

LS in DNA, RG 46 (U.S. Senate), 28A-D5; FC in DNA, RG 59 (State Department), Domestic Letters, 34:348 (M-40:32).

From W[ILLIA]M M. BLACKFORD

Legation of U.S.
Bogotá, June 14/44
Sir, I had the honor to receive, by the last mail, Despatch No. 17—announcing your appointment as Secretary of State—an event upon which I beg leave to offer my congratulations.

The news of the deplorable catastrophe of the 28th February last, produced no ordinary sensation in this city. The President [Pedro Alcantara Herran], Secretary of State [Joaquin Acosta], and the members of the Diplomatic corps honored me with official visits of sympathy and condolence; and from many private citizens, I received assurances of the profound regret which they felt for a calamity, which deprived the nation of so much private worth and official rank. I need not say I was much gratified at these evidences of respect for our country, manifested by the authorities of New Granada & by my colleagues of the Diplomatic Corps.

In my last Despatch, I dwelt, at some length, upon the condition, at that date, of the negotiation in the case of the Brig "Morris," and detailed the circumstances, which would induce me still to abide by the offer I had made in January last. The perusal of that Despatch and of the accompanying correspondence between myself and the Secretary of Foreign Affairs in April last, probably left no doubt upon your mind that the claim was, ere this, adjusted. I had every reason to expect such an issue, but you will observe a paragraph, in which a different result is contemplated as possible. Referring to my several Despatches and the copies, therewith transmitted, of the various notes, which passed between myself and the Granadian Government, I beg leave briefly to recapitulate the most material points of the negotiation.

It was not until the establishment of a separate Department for Foreign Affairs, in October last, that I was enabled to have the case taken up. On the 30th of that month, the new Secretary, himself, opened the correspondence upon the subject. After a reference to the act of June 1842, he proceeds to say, that the alleged outrage occurred in Venezuela—and that, altho' acting in the name of the Republic of Colombia, the courts, which took cognizance of the case, were, in fact, Venezuelan—that, it would be an act of which Venezuela might with reason complain, if New Granada should take the initiative in the settlement of a case, which Venezuela, from a more perfect knowledge of the details, could better understand—and this, notwithstanding he admits, that Republic had maintained that the decision of one of the component states of the late Republic should not affect the rest.

In my answer I combatted the positions he had taken, and showed that the United States had always held the three Republics jointly and severally bound, and that Venezuela might, with more propriety, insist upon New Granada, as the larger and metropolitan State, taking the initiative—and that this fastidious delicacy as to precedence, if acted upon by both States, would effectually & forever prevent an adjustment, as Venezuela had declined, most positively, all joint action. I protested, therefore, against the action of Venezuela being considered as a condition precedent of the action of New Granada in the premises, and insisted upon a conference and the mutual production and collation of evidence, as the easiest mode of arriving at a settlement. His reply and my rejoinder were marked by some asperity, but need not be noticed here. On the 16th November, I sent in a long note, recapitulating all the facts of the seizure and eventual condemnation of the "Morris," with an application of the Law of Nations to the case—and concluding by a demand for Indemnity, as follows—

1st   for value of the Brig,
2d   for value of the Cargo,
3d   for freight to Gibraltar,
4th   for the money taken from on board
5th   for adequate demur[r]age
6th   for Interest on each of these items.

On the 11th December, the Secretary answered this note, by one of great length, and—I must say—of considerable ability. Many of my statements were contradicted—new facts alleged, and issue joined upon various points of Law. He concluded by offering to make indemnity,

1st   for the nett proceeds of the sale of the Brig,
2d   for the nett proceeds of the sale of the Cargo, acquitted in the first trial—&
3d   for Interest from 27 Oct. 1827.

I promptly refused to accept these terms. I endeavored to prove that the Treaty of Bogotá was in force at the date of the Capture—though it took place before the Exchange of Ratifications—and again pressed for a Conference. He rejoined at length and combatted the assertion that a Treaty had efficacy before the date of the Exchange of Ratifications—and finally appointed the 5th of January, for a conference.

After a full and free conversation and examination of papers, at this and subsequent conferences, I stated that I would abandon the claim for that part of the cargo which was, confessedly, Spanish, and abide by the 1st sentence—considering it as not conditional—of the Admiralty Court of Puerto Cabello and, finally, having been convinced that the Treaty could not be considered in force at the date of the capture, and my opinion of the case having been somewhat modified, by the examination of testimony on the other side, I submitted, in writing, as my ultimatum, a demand for Indemnity, as follows:

1st.	for value of Brig as insured	6,000
2	for value of owner's part of cargo, as p[e]r invoice	6,982.07
3d	for value of Backers' part of cargo, as p[e]r invoice	7,530.88
4th	for Demur[r]age 1 year	5,000.00
		$25,512.95

With interest from 12 Jan[uar]y 1826 at 6 p[e]r cent per ann[um] till paid.

In our next conference, he said that the sum demanded was considered extravagant, and that his Government wished to procure information from St. Jago de Cuba as to the authentic[it]y of the document, presented to the court at Puerto Cabello, and accepted by it as satisfactory, to prove the neutral character of the "Morris"—that he had written, some weeks ago, for this information and might expect an answer in four or five weeks. He desired, therefore, that I would not press for a definitive answer then—that I would lose nothing by the delay, as a convention could be made before Congress was prepared, in the routine of business, to take it up for consideration.

I answered, that I inferred, from his remarks, the demand I had made was considered unreasonable and inadmissible—and that, if this were the case, I could not consent to any delay, but must close the negotiation at once, however I might regret its unsatisfactory issue—as I could not lessen the sum in the slightest degree. He replied that I was under a misapprehension—that he had not intended to create the impression the Government would not accede to my proposition—that the object in procuring the information from St. Jago de Cuba was to enable him to present himself, in a stronger position, before the Chambers, and thus to secure the ratification of any Convention we might conclude. Under these circumstances, I agreed to await, for a few weeks, the arrival of the expected document.

In all the subsequent informal conversations held upon the subject, I was led to believe that he considered the claim as settled. He spoke of the description of money and instalments, in which payment was to be made—pointed out particular members of Congress, whose support of the Convention it would be advisable to secure—and regretted that an unfortunate prejudice, which existed against himself, personally, might lead to a rejection of any arrangement he should make.

Having heard, about the 1st of April, of the offer made by Venezuela to pay $18,000 cash, in full of her portion of liability in the case, I showed him that the sum I was willing to take, was far less than the proportionate share of New Granada, assuming the offer of Venezuela as the basis—reminded him that, Venezuela having already settled the claim, he could not, according to the positions assumed in his note of 30th October, longer refuse to act—and pressed him to sign a Convention at once. He admitted the terms I offered were very favorable—did not object to the amount, and seemed to consider the sum as agreed upon. His objection to concluding a convention had reference to the *time* only. He dwelt upon the relation which he held to the Chambers—the strong prejudice, entertained by a majority in both houses, against himself, which had been carried so far as to induce them to refuse the appropriation for his salary—that the Convention, if submitted to the present Congress, would certainly be rejected, on grounds apart from its merits—that I would lose no time by deferring the signing until after the adjournment &c.

I told him I might expect instructions to demand a sum proportionate to that granted by Venezuela, and that I must have an assurance of my offer being accepted, or that I should not consider myself longer bound by its terms. He tried to show that I could not absolve myself from the obligation to abide by my offer.

I addressed to him, therefore, my note of 12th April, which he answered on the 16th. Copies of these communications were transmitted with my No. 24 and I request your particular attention to the latter part of his answer, which I could, under the circumstances, understand as nothing else than a pledge to sign a convention, so soon as the Congress adjourned—and in a subsequent conference he almost admitted it to be such. I told him, as against instructions, I no longer held myself bound by my offer—but that, should none arrive in the meantime, I would, the week after the adjournment, renew it.

Congress adjourned on the 29th of May, and, after some difficulty, I succeeded in inducing him to appoint a day for a Conference, at which, I told him, the case must be definitively settled. He named the 6th Inst.

From what I have related you may judge of my surprize, when he announced that his Government would not accede to my terms, and saw no reason to enlarge the offer, which it had already made, and which I had rejected as preposterously inadequate.

I expressed my surprize & regret in strong terms—recapitulated the various circumstances which had justified me in expecting a different result—insinuated that insincerity and bad faith had been practised by his Government in the negotiation, and that, whether intentionally or not on his part, I had been grossly deceived. He attempted no justification, but held out a hope that the affair might yet be settled, and hinted at a reference of the question—which was merely one of amount—to the arbitration of a third party.

I told him I was done with the case—that self respect would prevent my taking, voluntarily, another step in the negotiation—that it must now rest with my Government to take such measures, as might, in its judgment, be deemed necessary—and that I forbore to anticipate the character of those measures.

I have thus, at the risk of being tedious, related these particulars, that you might, without reference to previous despatches, have a general idea of the case. I proceed now, in accordance with the intimation, contained in my last despatch, to give my views of the course the Government should adopt. I will do so, under the fullest sense of the responsibility I incur, but, at the same time, with the most thorough conviction of the policy & necessity of the measures I recommend.

I beg leave then, most respectfully, to suggest, that instructions be sent to me to demand of this Government an amount of Indemnity, proportionate to the $18,000, granted by Venezuela; that these Instructions be brought to Santa Martha, by an officer in command of a small Squadron of four or five sloops of war or smaller vessels; that he be ordered to remain on the coast, until he hear the result of my demand; and that, in the event of its rejection, he be authorised to blockade the ports of Santa Martha and Carthagena—for which purpose the force I have indicated will be amply sufficient, though a larger one would be advisable.

The West India Squadron is in the habit of spending the months of August, September and October in port. The vessels would be as safe and the crews as healthy, in the ports of this country as in Pensacola—hurricanes being unknown on the coast, and the climate very healthy. The proposed demonstration then would involve no additional expense. It would be but the concentration of a Naval force on the coast of this country, which, otherwise, for the same space of time, would remain inactive in our harbors at home. I have not the remotest idea, that there would be necessity for resorting to a blockade. The exhibition of a respectable squadron, before the ports specified, with the explicit assurance that a blockade would be enforced, in case of non compliance with the demand, would be sufficient. There is great disaffection among the people of the provinces of the Coast, & the Government here knows very well that such a measure would be the signal for those provinces to assert their Independence. There is nothing, therefore, that is so much dreaded as a Blockade, not only from political, but from financial, considerations—the far greater portion of the revenue of the country being derived from duties on imports. There is no reason to apprehend, therefore, that a blockade will be necessary—the threat & the presence of the means to enforce it, will promptly bring this Government to terms.

The Squadron, after remaining a fortnight at Santa Martha, if thought advisable, might proceed on a cruise, or bear up for Curacoa, and return at the expiration of a month—by which time, my despatches, conveying the result of the demand, would await the arrival of the commanding officer. It would be proper that the squadron make its first appearance about the 1st of October, and that the Commander be ordered to put himself in communication with myself.

The measure recommended may appear too strong, if it be supposed to have reference merely to the claim of the Morris—but this is far from being the case. The archives of this Legation abound in claims of American citizens, for acts of piratical outrage committed by Colombian Privateers, upon our commerce. There is not the remotest hope of effecting a settlement of these long standing claims by an appeal to the sense of justice of New Granada. Our long forbearance has been, not only unappreciated but, construed into a consciousness, on our part, of the injustice of the claims, or of inability to enforce them. This Government now considers itself as the injured party, when redress is demanded for these antiquated injuries. Further delay will only aggravate the difficulty, and render a settlement more hopeless.

The claim of the "Morris" is the one, the justice of which is the most unquestionable—so unquestionable, indeed, that the Court before which the case was first brought, could but decide in favor of the vessel. It has been pending for near twenty years, and, until lately, this Government has never been induced to take it into consideration. It has now been elaborately discussed, and its justice clearly established—and if, in this case, New Granada still refuses to make indemnification, what reason have we to hope for success in other claims, which, however well founded, have not been sanctioned by decisions of their own courts?

I have no hesitation in saying, that further negotiation touching these claims, whilst it would be altogether futile, does not comport with the dignity of our Government. The time has arrived when, a more energetic line of conduct is required, if we desire to procure justice, or even to maintain the respect of this people. I have indicated the policy, which I think it advisable to pursue. I believe it would be entirely efficacious, not only in the case immediately under consideration, but in bringing to a speedy settlement all the other claims. Its moral influence upon this Government, as well as upon that of every other South American State, would be most salutary and important.

I have discharged what I conceive my duty in making these suggestions, which I submit to the better judgment of yourself and the President. I have only further to remark, that the threat of a Blockade in the absence of a naval force, would have no effect whatever, and, indeed, be worse than useless—and that the efficacy of any minatory, or coercive, measure, which may be adopted, will be doubled by its prompt execution.

Despatch No. 16, enclosing the commission of Mr. [J.A.] Townsend, as Consul for the Port of Panama was received—the Exequatur obtained—and, together with the commission, forwarded to that gentleman at his post.

I have the honor to enclose to you the receipts of Mr. Gooding, for the 8th, 9th & 10th Instalments of the "By-Chance" money.

In the statement of the claim of Mr. Alexander Ruden, Jr., transmitted with my despatch No. 22, I have discovered a small error. I enclose a corrected statement, & have requested a friend to pay into the Department the sum of Three Dollars & forty four cents ($3.44)— the remittance, made by me, being less than it should have been, by that sum.

The Congress appropriated the money, stipulated to be paid, as indemnity to Capt. John Hugg, by the Convention of the 22d of April last, in the case of the Henrietta. The first instalment is payable on the 1st of October next.

I have New York papers to the 5th April—but my latest dates from my family are no later than the 23d February. I must again, and earnestly, request, that all letters, received for me at the Department, may be forwarded to my own Agents, Messrs. Murray & Lanman, 63 Water Street N.Y., and not to the Despatch Agent, from whose ignorance, or negligence, I have already suffered sufficiently.

I shall await with anxiety the answer to this Despatch, & I beg to be favored with the views of the Department upon the suggestion I have made, at the earliest moment.

I beg leave, respectfully, to commend to your favorable consideration the application for a leave of absence, contained in my last despatch. I have the honor to be, with high respect, Your Ob[edien]t S[ervan]t, Wm. M. Blackford.

ALS (No. 25) with Ens in DNA, RG 59 (State Department), Diplomatic Despatches, Colombia, vol. 10 (T-33:10, frames 220–234), received 7/21; CC in DNA, RG 84 (Foreign Posts), Colombia, Despatches, vol. B4.

To F[idericio] Bourman, [Spanish Chargé d'Affaires], 6/14. Bourman's note of 1/20 [to Abel P. Upshur] concerning U.S. import duties on wines from the Grand Canary Island has been referred to the House Committee on Foreign Affairs. FC in DNA, RG 59 (State Department), Notes to Foreign Legations, Spain, 6:111 (M-99:85).

To D[ANIEL] C. CROXALL,
U.S. C[onsul], Marseilles

Department of State
Washington, June 14, 1844

Sir, In reply to your letter of the 27th of April last, in relation to the refusal of colored Seamen, thrown on your hands to proceed in Vessels bound to the Ports of New Orleans and Charleston, I have to state that upon their refusal to take passage, according to the provisions of the Act of the 28th of February 1803, in the first American Vessel bound to the United States, they lose their right to support from the Government, and you will in all such cases withhold that support from them. I am Sir &c, J.C. Calhoun.

FC in DNA, RG 59 (State Department), Consular Instructions, 12:84.

From DANIEL J. DESMOND

Consulate General of the Pontifical States in the United States
Philad[elphi]a, June 14, 1844

Sir, The recent riots in this City have given strong reason to entertain apprehension that the Consulate General might not be safe in the event of their recurrence. During their existence every Institution which belonged to the Catholic Church was threatened with destruction. In order to create this dangerous fanaticism invectives have been constantly directed by a few papers against the Pope; and rediculous, false and malicious assertions made regarding his temporal power in this Country. The efforts of a new party appear to be directed against existence of Religious Liberty. The excesses recently committed in the burning of Catholic churches, Parsonage Houses, Libraries and Seminary have withdrawn the feeling of Security and shewn the Catholic Citizen that he has no efficient protection when popular excitement and violence are created by designing and bad Men. With this Knowledge of these facts I deem it a duty I owe the Government that has so honourably distinguished me to provide for any contingency and I therefore beg leave to ask to what Officer or Authority of the United States in this City I may if necessary apply for the protection of the Consulate General[,] my family & my person. I make this application that neither I, or the officer may be under any misapprehension as to *my right* to protection or *his duty* to afford it efficiently and promptly. I have been told that as I am a Native American Citizen I am perfectly safe but I would not discharge my duty to the Government which has confided to me the Highest Office it has in this Country if I depended on any other protection than that guarranteed me by my recognition by the President of the United States as the Consul General of His Holiness The Pope. I have the Honor to remain with distinguished Consideration Your most obedient Serv[an]t, Daniel J. Desmond.

ALS in DNA, RG 59 (State Department), Miscellaneous Letters (M-179:104, frames 535–536).

From EDWARD EVERETT

London, 14 June 1844

Sir, A few days ago Mr. H. Ewbank, a partner in one of the houses principally interested in the importation into this country of Rough Rice from the United States, called upon me, and shewed me a memorial addressed by a large number of manufacturing houses in Manchester and the vicinity, inviting the attention of this government to the convention recently negotiated by Mr. [Henry] Wheaton with the German Zollverein. Aware that it would be regarded by you as a paper of some interest, I desired Mr. Ewbank to furnish me with a copy to be transmitted to my government; a request with which he readily complied. The copy which he handed me will accompany this despatch.

I thought it proper in order to avoid the misconception which might arise from my silence on that point, to say to Mr. Ewbank, that I conceived that there was no foundation for the rumor alluded to by the memorialists to the effect that "the refusal or delay on the part of Her Majesty's Government to afford redress for what the President in his late message to Congress, calls a contravention of the commercial convention between the two nations, touching the duties levied on Rough Rice and exportation of Woollens, may be made the ground by America for the proposed treaty with Germany."

Although the conduct of this government, in continuing to levy and refusing to repay the duties in question, might justify measures of retaliation, yet, not supposing in point of fact, that it had had any influence in reference to the negociation of the convention with the German league, I thought it would be injudicious to permit that convention to be represented as such a measure. This would be to admit, that it contravenes the commercial convention between Great Britain and the United States of July 1815.

In the measure now before parliament for a modification of the duties on foreign sugar, of which an important feature is a descriminating duty in favor of sugar not the growth of Slave labor, there is a provision that sugar the growth of countries, with which England has treaties of reciprocity, may be admitted on the same terms, although such sugar should be the produce of slave labor. It is understood that this provision is intended to meet the case of the United States. In a conversation with Lord Aberdeen a short time since, he informed me that since intelligence had been received of the negociation of a treaty for the annexation of Texas to the United States, the question had suggested itself, whether, in case that annexation should take place, sugar the growth of Texas would be entitled to the same privilege, in virtue of the convention between the United States and Great Britain; that the question had been referred to the law officers of the crown; but that their opinion had not yet been given.

In reference to the demand, which I have been so long pressing on this Government for the restitution of the duties improperly levied on "Rough Rice," my note to Lord Aberdeen of the 18th of October last remains unanswered. Shortly after it was sent to the Foreign Office, Lord Aberdeen observed to me casually, in the course of an interview on a different subject, that he understood I had made him another communication on the subject of Rough Rice; that he had not read it; but that he was told I had stated the case very strongly. I felt somewhat encouraged by this remark, to hope for ultimate success; a hope however which soon became less confident. An unfavorable answer to my note was, I have reason to think, nearly or quite prepared, when the news of Mr. Wheaton's convention arrived. In a conversation with Lord Aberdeen on that subject, I understood him to say, that the further consideration of the Rice question would be suspended for the present; that he considered our convention with the Zollverein to be precisely such a violation of the treaty between the two countries as we erroneously charged to them in reference to the duties on Rough Rice, unless we were prepared unconditionally to admit British manufactures on the same duties as those on which we had agreed, in the new convention, to admit the manufactures of the States of the Zoll-Verein: if we did this he owned he did not see how they could refuse the re-imbursement of the descriminating duties that had been levied on our Rough Rice.

Lord Aberdeen did not appear to feel in making this remark, that he indirectly admitted, what he had a moment before denied, for if, as he said, we *erroneously* charged them with violating the convention, in levying descriminating duties on our Rough Rice, why should they be obliged to re-imburse those duties, because we admit them (as they say we are bound to do) to the privileges of the treaty with the Zollverein, without receiving the equivalents on their part? I am, sir, with great respect, your obedient servant, Edward Everett.

Document transmitted with Despatch Nro. 142.

Memorial of the manufacturers of Manchester & the vicinity on the subject of the convention with the Zoll-Verein.

LS (No. 142) with En in DNA, RG 59 (State Department), Diplomatic Despatches, Great Britain, vol. 52 (M-30:48), received 7/5; FC in DNA, RG 84 (Foreign Posts), Great Britain, Despatches, 8:284–289; FC in MHi, Edward Everett Papers, 49:221–226 (published microfilm, reel 23, frames 111–114).

From [Jean Corneille, Chevalier] Gevers, Chargé d'Affaires of His Majesty the King of the Netherlands, Washington, 6/14. Gevers suspects that the U.S. Congress will not alter during the present session the tariff of 1842 to remove duties upon Java coffee imported into the U.S. from Holland. Therefore he inquires whether the Executive can take any temporary action to admit Java coffee "free of duty into the United States on the same footing as Brasil coffee is allowed to be imported." He encloses a copy of the House of Representatives Committee on Foreign Affairs report [dated 6/1/1844] on the discriminating duty on Dutch-imported coffee. LS with En in DNA, RG 59 (State Department), Notes from Foreign Legations, Netherlands, vol. 2 (M-56:2, frames 169–175).

To "the GOVERNORS of the States of New York, Ohio, Indiana, Illinois, Michigan & Missouri and of the Territories of Wisconsin and Iowa"

> Department of State
> Washington, 14th June 1844

A disposition to emigrate to the United States similar to that which exists in the provinces of the Rhine, has manifested itself in Belgium, and the Government of that Country anxious to obtain in advance all the information that can be collected respecting the real condition of emigrants in this country, has authorised and instructed Baron Vander Straten Ponthoy to visit several of the States and Territories for the purpose of inquiring into the subject with a view to communicate authentic information in regard to it.

I annex to this letter a copy of a memorandum [of 6/11] upon the subject, which was handed to this Department by the Belgian Minister [Charles Serruys], as explanations of the object of the Baron[']s Mission, and I have much pleasure in soliciting for him all the facility and aid towards its accomplishment which it may be in your power to render him. I am, with much consideration, your Obedient Servant, John C. Calhoun.

FC in DNA, RG 59 (State Department), Domestic Letters, 34:238 (M-40:32).

From Major J[AMES] D. GRAHAM

> Washington, June 14th 1844

Sir, In answer to the enquiries made of me by the State Department a few days ago, I have the honour to state that after I ["was" *interlined*] appointed, in March 1843, head of the Scientific Corps on the part of the United States, to aid in the demarcation of the Boundary between the U.S. and the British Provinces under the treaty of Washington, the following officers from the Corps of Topographical Engineers were detailed, under the law, for that Service vizt.

Brevet Captain J[oseph] E. Johnston
1st Lieut: Tho[ma]s J. Lee
2d Lieut: George Thom
2d Lieut: George G. Meade

In addition to the above, three assistant Civil Engineers were appointed and attached to the Scientific Corps on the part of the

United States, and a detail was made from the 1st Regiment of artillery, of one Lieutenant, one Sergeant, one corporal, and 15 privates, to act in a Similar Capacity with the detail on the part of Great Britain from the Royal Corps of Sappers & Miners. The members of this Corps are well versed in the practical duties of Surveying embracing in some cases the highest practical operations in geodesy. We have no Similar Corps in our Service, and although the detachment from the Artillery performed the duties assigned it, embracing the measurement of experimental lines, the care of instruments in moving from one point to another, the use of the compass in some cases, &c. and promised to be still farther useful by the aid of more practical experience, yet we must look to the grade of junior Lieutenants, or to civil Engineers in our Country, to obtain persons Capable of performing the duties which are performed upon this Survey by the non-commissioned officers of the Corps of Sappers & Miners, in the British Service.

The Scientific Corps on the part of the British Government, consisted last season of

2 Captains of Engineers
1 Lieut: of Engineers
8 Non commissioned officers of the Corps of Sappers & Miners attached to the Corps of Royal Engineers
2 Assistant Civil Engineers
1 other d[itt]o as draftsman.

Since that time, as I have been apprised by a letter from Lieut: Colonel [James B.] Estcourt, the Commissioner on the part of Great Britain, dated in May, an addition has been made to his corps of 14 from the corps of Sappers & Miners all of whom are supposed to be non-commissioned officers.

During the last winter Lieut: Meade was, at his own request, relieved from duty upon the boundary Service, and within a few days past Brevet Captain Johnston, & 1st Lieut: Lee have also been relieved from it, and assigned to the coast Survey. In lieu of the three officers above named, 1st Lieut: [William H.] Emory of the Top[ographical] Engineers has been detailed for the Boundary Service, and 2d Lieut: [Amiel W.] Whipple, Corps of Top[ographical] Engineers & Brevet 2d Lieut: [William F.] Raynolds, Corps Top[ographica]l Engineers, have been designated for that duty, and orders have, within a few days past, been issued from the head quarters of the Army augmenting the detail from the rank & file of the Artillery (1st & 2d Regiments) So as to make the whole, as it now stands, consist of 1 Lieutenant, 1 Sergeant, 2 Corporals, & 26 privates. The object of the two governments, from the beginning, was to have the Scientific Corps on both sides, as nearly alike, and as nearly of equal strength as possible. This would seem to justify the employment of the three assistant civil Engineers on the part of the U.S. to correspond with an equal number of the same Class on the part of Great Britain. But as regards the Military Engineers, the large number of efficient non-commissioned officers from the Sappers & Miners who are generally excellent practical Surveyors, places the preponderance as to strength undoubtedly upon the side of Great Britain. To restore the equality in this respect, I would respectfully suggest the propriety of attaching to the Corps on the part of the U.S. two graduates of the Military Academy, from the Class of this year, to be selected with an especial regard to their proficiency in science, and attached as 2d Lieutenants by brevet to the Topographical Engineers. This would enable us to have as many heads of parties as there will be on the British side, and the rank & file from the Artillery will, by practice, soon become very efficient & very useful in the capacities for which they are intended, and will moreover save the expence of employing persons at a much higher compensation. I would also respectfully suggest, as an arrangement essential to the successful performance of this important duty, that the detail from the corps of Topographical Engineers, and also that from the Artillery be made permanent, and not liable to change by transfers for other service until the field and office duties in connection with the survey & demarcation of the boundary shall have been completed. It is not only necessary that the officers for this service should possess the requisite acquirements in science, but that they should also be ready and efficient astronomical observers. The whole operation is based upon astronomical determinations, and these are required to be very accurate, otherwise valuable territory may wrongfully be assigned to the one or the other government. Practice & experience can alone produce efficiency in this important branch of the duties, & when acquired it should be made available for this object until it is completed. The officers of Engineers who act as astronomers on the part of Great Britain possess the advantage of the requisite science aided by a course of practice under the Astronomer Royal at the Greenwich observatory. Our own officers possess in an eminent degree the necessary science, but it requires much time & practice to make efficient observers, a qualification necessary to place us upon an equality with our British colleagues. The Artillery detachment was, last season, transported & subsisted at the expence of the Quartermaster's & Subsistence Departments of the Army, and the estimates of the U.S. Commissioner, were based upon a continuation of the same system in future. I have the honour to be very respectfully, Your ob[edien]t Serv[an]t, J.D. Graham, Major Top[ographical] Engineers, Head of Scient[ifi]c Corps on the part of the U.S.

LS in DNA, RG 92 (Quartermaster General), Consolidated Correspondence, Boundary, Northeast Survey.

From J[AMES] HAMILTON, [JR.]

Oswichee Bend [near Fort Mitchell, Ala.,] June 14[t]h 1844
My Dear Sir, Since my last to you the Baltimore Convention has meet [*sic*] & done its *nothingness*—for I really consider the nomination of [James K.] Polk as nothing. I do not pretend to decide on the policy of your friends dropping you, but there is something certainly peculiarly unfortunate in the ["fortunes" *canceled and* "fate or condition" *interlined*] of a party which compels it to pass over the *first* of its men & to rally on those scarcely above mediocrity. Mr. [John] Tyler[']s nomination, would in reference to the Question of Annexation have been far more just & congruous than that of Polk. It must have been made by the [Martin] Van Buren men expressly to be defeated—or to illustrate the amiable fable of the Dog in the manger.

We passed on the 8[t]h of June Resolutions ["in this County" *interlined*] providing for the call of a So[uthern] Convention—with a view to a Convention of all the States—To take into consideration the Slave Question. An address is ordered which I am to prepare to appear after the adjournment of Congress—that we may avail ourselves of the result of its final proceedings on Annexation. I will endeavour to combine both moderation & prudence in the paper with *a proper spirit.* We are however without advices from our members of Congress who have kept us entirely in the dark as to questions of remedy & redress.

I wish to see whether the South has any pluck left[;] if not the sooner we settle down into quiet submission & capitulate with the enemy the better. We have talked & Bullied enough.

I have written to [Franklin H.] Elmore to request [Dixon H.] Lewis to stop at Columbus [Ga.] to meet me. If any thing is to be done I think we may put Alabama in the lead[;] if nothing[,] why I will quietly return to my cotton fields & wait with what fortitude I ["am"(?) *canceled*] can the bursting of the Storm that cannot be a

53

long way off. Come what may you have done yourself honor. I remain My Dear Sir with sincere esteem Yours faithfully, J. Hamilton.

P.S. I wish [Thomas H.] Benton had been present at Crawford [Ala.] last Saturday. To the mirth of the people I handled him without gloves.

ALS in ScCleA; PC in Jameson, ed., *Correspondence*, pp. 962–963.

From W[illia]m Hogan

Boston, June 14th 1844

I do myself the honor, Sir, of addressing you, not with a view of annoying or perplexing you, nor to ask any favors from ["yourself" *changed to* "you"] but to prevent you, if possible, from unconsciously falling into a trap which is laid for you here by one of the most consum[m]ate political knaves in New England; one, who has no power nor influence of his own, who has neither the confidence nor respect of a single individual, possessing influence, fortune or talents in this community; who for fifteen years, has been struggling by trickery, knavery & political juggling to obtain Executive favour but who untill he succeeded in imposing upon that honest & guileless man President [John] Tyler never obtained any from Whig or Democrat; I allude to Robert Rantoul of this place, who—if rumor be true—is to be appointed Secr[etar]y of the Treasury as soon as Congress adjourns.

In a case of this kind I will take the liberty of speaking freely to you even at the expence of incurring your displeasure. There is no man in the United States, who stands higher—as to intentions and purity of motive—than you do with the mercantile community of this City; whatever your peculiar opinions may be, on national questions, you have ever been & are now, looked upon by them as a man of untainted honour & motives pure as ["their own" *changed to* "the"] icicles which hang from their own mountains, and permit me to say, that if you ever stoop to encourage—as it is thought you are now doing—the advancement of this Rantoul to the head of the Treasury department or degrade yourself by sitting with him in the same Cabinet, you forfeit the respect & confidence of one of the most honourable mercantile communities in the world. This, Sir, is strong language, but such is my respect for you personally & such my veneration for genius & talents, wherever I see them that I risk now, as I have ever done, my own popularity & even your good opinion, to protect them from contamination by such reptiles as that Abolitionist, ["as that reptile" *canceled*] Robert Rantoul. Apart from all this, Sir, what avail your letters against Abolition, if in the face of this country, you stoop to be a member of the same Cabinet with an avowed Abolitionist, such as Rantoul confesses himself to be. Enclosed [*not found*] you will find his letter upon the subject. I am told he is now base enough to tell you & the President that he has changed his opinion upon slavery. Will he do so through the public press? Will he do so while here? Neither and yet President Tyler, and the Secr[etar]y of State, are seen & believed to be fondling this miserable man, this little district politician, this little demagogue of one or two speeches ["of" *canceled*] as their associate in the supreme Council of our nation. Do not, Sir, require of your friends to witness the humiliating spectacle of seeing *John C. Calhoun*—a man whose name belongs to the world & to whose ashes alone Americans have any peculiar claim, sitting in the same Cabinet with Robert "Rantoul Jun[io]r." If he has done any service let him have some little office of fifteen hundred or two thousand a year but in the name of all that is respectable, never lend your aid to place him on a level with you as Cabinet Counsellor. It can only reflect discredit upon your name & bring the Administration of President Tyler to a most ignominious & inglorious termination, & to this end it has been approaching ever since the President[']s first connection with R. Rantoul & a few more petty scheeming politicians of Boston, who are using him, pretty much after the fashion that a few wags in Philadelphia formerly used Col. Pluck. I have long since taken the liberty of apprising the President of this, but his Sons differed with me, & I have concluded to adopt—so far as his Excellency & his Sons are concerned—the old Roman maxim *"qui vult decipi decipiatul"* [*sic*; decipiatur; Let him that wishes to be deceived be deceived]. I have the honor to remain Sir Respectfully, Wm. Hogan.

ALS in ScCleA.

From Ch[ristopher] Hughes, "Private"

The Hague; 14 June; 1844
My dear Sir, There is nothing—of any interest to us—to write about. All is quiet, peacefulness & tranquillity here! The Newspapers tell every thing.

We had a very short visit—of 24 hours—of [Nicholas I] the Emperor of Russia—on his return from England; He hastened homewards—in consequence of very alarming accounts—brought to Him from Petersburg—of the health of his Daughter—the Grand Duchess Alexandrine of Hesse! She was married only Six Months ago; it is feared, that she is in a galloping Consumption. The Emperor meant to pass a few days here—& some weeks at one of the Spas of Germany; but all these plans were changed & he set out, immediately—for St. Petersburg. He declined receiving the Corps Diplomatique—from the shortness of his stay.

The King [of Holland, William II] gave a military Parade and the Emperor passed the Review of several Regiments of all arms; & expressed great satisfaction at the order & condition of the Dutch Troops. The Emperor conferred a great number of orders & decorations amongst the dutch officers; and he made the most magnificent presents—indeed of quite enormous sums of money—& of valuable Rings & Gold Watches—to all the Royal Household, & to all persons—both here and at Rotterdam—who had been in any—the slightest way—employed in the arrangements and services for the journey of His Imperial Majesty. The splendour of his presents surpasses all example—and is almost fabulous; both here & in England, He lavished his Gold & Diamonds upon all who had charge of the slightest duty about his person.

One of the medical men of his Court came from Petersburg to the Hague—as Courier—with the distressing news of his Daughter's alarming state! His grief was extreme; & when not before the public—he passed his time in his Rooms—weeping with uncontrollable agony! In the world there is not a more affectionate and devoted Father, than the Emperor Nicholas.

I forward—with this letter—despatches to [William Wilkins] the Secretary of War (to whom, I beg to be particularly recalled—& in terms of the most friendly recollection; with assurances of my heartfelt joy—at his marvellous preservation—on board the Princeton)— from Colonel [Sylvanus] Thayer; who arrived here—last Evening & goes on—to Amsterdam & the North—tomorrow morning. I need not say—that I have felt great pleasure in seeing Col. Thayer & in rendering him every service & facility—in the furtherance of the objects of his visit to Holland. His health appears to be very feeble; &, I fear, he travels too fast—and fatigues himself too much, in the discharge of the duties of his military observation & inspection. I have enjoined on him, to be more careful of his health & represented *this* as his first & chief duty to his Country; & I implored him, to rest

& pass a few days quietly here, with me! but in vain! He goes on & I rather fear for the Consequences of his zeal & *conscience*.

Col. Thayer has with him—a very amiable & promising youth— Mr. Parker; son of General [Daniel?] Parker of Washington; an old Friend of mine—who will be pleased to hear—that his Son is in excellent health; & employing his time & opportunities, wisely & profitably. I am now about to call for my two Countrymen, & conduct them to see some of the *Curiosities* of the Hague! & this will explain the haste with which I write.

I have written you a gossipping Letter; but there is no public topic to write on; & you will indulge me in using the freedom allowable in a *"Private"* epistle. I am, my dear Sir, respectfully & Sincerely y[ou]r obed[ien]t Serv[an]t, Ch. Hughes.

P.S. I recommend the enclosed family letter to your kindness [for forwarding]: & I pray you to present my respects to the President. C.H.

ALS in ScCleA.

To C[harles] J. Ingersoll, Chairman, House Committee on Foreign Affairs, 6/14. He encloses a copy of a note of 1/20 from [Fidericio] Bourman [Spanish Chargé d'Affaires] with an enclosure concerning the duties levied in U.S. ports on wines of the Grand Canary Island under the Tariff of 1842. FC in DNA, RG 59 (State Department), Domestic Letters, 34:240 (M-40:32).

To John Y. Mason, Secretary of the Navy

Department of State
Washington, 14th June, 1844
Sir: For the information of your Department, I have the honor to enclose an extract from a communication [of 9/28/1843] which accompanied a recent note to this Department, from the Spanish Minister near this Government, being a representation from the Ayuntamiento, or Board of Administration of the Island of the Grand Canary; the passage quoted going to show the advantages which that Island, as a place of resort and rendezvous, offers to our ships of war. I am, Sir, respectfully, Your obedient Servant, J.C. Calhoun.

LS with En in DNA, RG 45 (Naval Records), Letters from Federal Executive Agents, 1837–1886, 6:166 (M-517:2, frames 365–367); FC in DNA, RG 59 (State Department), Domestic Letters, 34:238–239 (M-40:32).

From John H. Miller, 6/14. Describing himself as "one of your oldest & fastest friends," Miller recommends Philip O. Hughes for appointment as U.S. Marshal for Southern Miss. Miller describes Hughes as being "honest and capable" and names others from whom Calhoun can obtain testimony as to Hughes's qualifications. ALS in DNA, RG 59 (State Department), Applications and Recommendations, 1837–1845, Hughes (M-687:16, frames 534–535).

From C[harles] Morris, [Commodore, U.S. Navy]

Washington, June 14, 1844
Sir, I have the honour to submit the enclosed account for your decision.

It was necessary for me to leave the "Delaware" and visit Buenos Ayres, ["three times" *canceled and* "twice" *interlined*], & for several weeks at each time, to give proper attention to the Instructions from the Department of State.

The expense incurred during these absences from the "Delaware" constitute the amount stated in the account. With much Respect Y[ou]r O[bedien]t Servant, C. Morris.

LS in DNA, RG 59 (State Department), Accounting Records: Miscellaneous Letters Received. NOTE: A Clerk's EU reads "a/c paid 21 [June]."

From H[aym] M. Salomon

Galleburn[']s Hotel [Washington] June 14, [18]44
Dear Sir, About *four years* since there was a Gentleman occupying at Washington the first office under the Commissioner that of examiner of Patents—*Doctor T.W.* Donnavan a graduate of medicine, a man of great Study in Natural History and Medical Science—he came to New York and applied for the hand of my eldest daughter, conceiving that such a place was like one in the Army or Navy, not removeable, I consented though he was a most ultra writer as a radical democrat.

When Mr. [Daniel] Webster became the Governing Power of that department as Secretary of State one Doctor [Charles G.] Page a relative or particular friend of his had long desired *the place*. Doctor Donnavan *was* removed to give this snug berth to a favourite successor and to heal the wound of Dr. D[onnavan] he was *promised* something else—a *promise* never *redeemed*.

I have understood that an appropriation was made yesterday of 4000 Doll[ars] towards certain expenses in the patent buildings for managing the National institute department. For the direction of which under the order of the Commissioner the Doctor is eminently capable.

A Physician in a city where there are already more than 700 Doctors finds it utterly impracticable without waiting for years to get into a living practice among the paying portion, and the poor are provided for by the dispensaries. The Doctor and his lady are now living at our house in New York [City]. He is without a single disqualification of the character of a Gentleman unless a warmth ["of" *canceled*] in political writing against Mr. [Henry] Clay might be so termed but unaccompanied by any vulgarity of expression.

I have a letter yesterday from him expressing a willingness to take a place in the establishment if it were only 1000 Dollars. I have thought it not impracticable from the conversation yesterday with Mr. [Henry L.] El[l]sworth that we might thro your goodness obviate some of the difficulties that have taken place through the political or partial Supercedin[g]s of your honourable predecessor. Very respectfully your Oblig[e]d Ser[van]t, H.M. Salomon.

ALS in DNA, RG 59 (State Department), Applications and Recommendations, 1837–1845, Donnavan (M-687:9, frames 406–408).

To [JOHN TYLER]

Department of State
Washington, June 14th, 1844

To the President of the United States:

The Secretary of State to whom was referred the Resolution of the Senate of June 12th. 1844 (in Executive Session,) requesting the President "to cause the Senate to be informed whether Mr. Duff Green has been paid any money out of the Treasury of the United States, or out of the Contingent fund for foreign intercourse, for services rendered since the 4th day of March in the year 1841; and if so, how much? and also, whether the said Mr. Duff Green has further known claims or demands for such services?"; has the honor to report to the President that the amount of expenditures paid out of the fund for the contingent expenses of Foreign intercourse, from the 1st of December, 1840, to the 1st of December, 1843, together with the names of the individuals to whom the payments were made, as well as the objects of such payments, may be seen by reference to the letter of the Secretary of State to the Speaker of the House of Representatives, dated December 9, 1841, (Doc. No. 4, State Dept.), and a Report made by the undersigned to the Chairman of the Committee on the expenditures of the Department of State, (in answer to a Resolution of the House of Representatives) dated April 8, 1844, (Rep[ort] No. 484, Ho[use] of Rep[resentative]s). From these Documents it appears that, on the 3rd. day of November 1841, there was paid to Mr. Duff Green, out of the fund for the Contingent expenses of foreign intercourse, the sum of $500.00 as bearer of despatches to London and Paris. And again on the 9th. day of December 1842, there was paid to the same individual, out of the same fund, the sum of $500. for expenses and compensation as bearer of despatches to Paris. These items include all the payments which appear from the files of this Department to have been made to Mr. Duff Green from the 1st day of December 1840 to the 1st. day of December 1843; and since this last date, it does not appear that any amount has been paid by this Department to the said Green; nor any evidence on its files that he has or holds further claims or demands for services against it. Respectfully submitted, J.C. Calhoun.

LS in DNA, RG 46 (U.S. Senate), 28B-B12; FC in DNA, RG 59 (State Department), Reports of the Secretary of State to the President and Congress, 6:113–114; PC in Jameson, ed., *Correspondence*, p. 597. NOTE: Tyler transmitted this letter to the Senate on 6/17 with a letter of his own in which he defended the President's right to employ the contingency fund of the State Department "without any requisition upon him for a disclosure of the names of persons employed . . . ." In this instance, however, "I feel no desire to with[h]old the fact" that Green was employed in Europe "to collect such information from private or other sources as was deem'd important to assist the Executive in undertaking a negociation then contemplated, but afterwards abandon'd . . . ." Tyler added that $1,000 paid Green in full for his services and that an additional claim which was submitted was disallowed. Tyler to the President of the Senate, 6/17/1844, LS in DNA, RG 46 (U.S. Senate), 28B-B12. The Senate resolution of 6/12 which elicited the above responses can be found in DNA, RG 59 (State Department), Miscellaneous Letters (M-179:104, frames 528–529) and *Senate Executive Journal*, 6:319.

To [JOHN TYLER]

Department of State
Washington, 14th June 1844

To the President of the United States.

The Secretary of State to whom has been referred the Resolution of the House of Representatives of the 4th inst., requesting the President, if not incompatible with the public interests to communicate to that body "All the correspondence between this Government and the Government of Great Britain, alluded to in his annual message to Congress, with respect to the duties exacted by the Government of Great Britain on rough Rice exported from this Country to Great Britain contrary to the Treaty of 1815"—has the honor to report to the President the accompanying copies and extracts from Documents on file in this Department which embrace all the correspondence referred to in the above cited Resolution, with the exception of that portion which has been previously transmitted to Congress. Respectfully submitted, John C. Calhoun.

FC in DNA, RG 59 (State Department), Reports of the Secretary of State to the President and Congress, 6:114–115; PC with Ens in House Document No. 278, 28th Cong., 1st Sess. NOTE: Tyler transmitted this letter to the House on 6/15. Appended to the FC is a list of accompanying documents that indicates that seventeen letters and extracts of letters between Everett and the Secretary of State from December 1841 through April [1844] were enclosed. The resolution to which the above letter is a reply can be found in DNA, RG 59 (State Department), Miscellaneous Letters (M-179:104, frames 484–485) and in *House Journal*, 28th Cong., 1st Sess., p. 1002.

From **Sam T. Bicknell**, Maryville, Blount County, E[ast] Tennessee, 6/15. Bicknell informs Calhoun that, as one who "has contributed so largely to the dignity of our American Union," he has been elected unanimously as an honorary member of the Beth Hackma Ve-Berith Society of Maryville College. ALS in ScCleA.

To DABNEY S. CARR, [Constantinople]

Department of State
Washington, 15th June, 1844

Sir: I transmit a copy of a letter addressed to this Department on the 9th Instant, by W[illia]m Rufus Page, of Hallowell, in the State of Maine, who states that he is building a Steamer for the Levant trade, and that he is desirous to secure for her, by the intervention of his Government, the rights and privileges, which, it is alleged, have been accorded by the Turkish Government to the Steamers of other nations, running in the same waters.

You will inquire what these alleged rights and privileges are, and the grounds upon which they have been granted to others; and if the result of the inquiry will warrant it, you will make a proper application to the Turkish Government upon the subject, with a view to secure their enjoyment, if practicable, to the citizens of the United States. The Steamer referred to, in Mr. Page's letter, as having been sent out in 1842, by his father, to the Levant, is presumed to be the Bangor, of Boston; respecting which, the correspondence you will find on file in your Legation, will furnish light.

Mr. Page will receive a copy of these instructions, and be directed to communicate with you on his arrival at Constantinople, when you will acquaint him with his rights, as well as with any favors, which you may have been able to procure for American citizens proposing to navigate the Turkish waters in Steamers.

Your despatches Nos. 2, 3, 4, 5 and 6, and Mr. [John P.] Brown's letter of the 1st September, have been received at the Department. I am, Sir, respectfully, Your obedient Servant, J.C. Calhoun.

LS (No. 8) with En in DNA, RG 84 (Foreign Posts), Turkey, 3:57–64; FC in DNA, RG 59 (State Department), Diplomatic Instructions, Turkey, 1:307–308 (M-77:162).

From a COMMITTEE at Charlotte, N.C.

Charlotte, 15th June 1844

Sir, The Democracy of Mecklenburg County have resolved to give a public Barbacue in this place, on the 23d of next month, (July) in token of their approbation of the nominations recently made by our Party at Baltimore for President & V[ice-]Pres[iden]t. Relying upon you, as we do, as the chief & ever vigilant defender of our principles & rights, we most cordially invite you, in the name of the Democracy of this County & State, to meet with us on the day above named, on the birth-spot of American Independence, and unite our efforts for the restoration of the Republican Party to power. With sentiments of the highest regard we are Your friends, W[illiam] J. Alexander, B. Morrow, C[harles] G. Alexander, J[oseph] W. Hampton,

C[harles] J. Fox, P.C. Caldwell, C.T. Alexander, T.L. Hutchison, John Walker, J[ennings] B. Kerr, Com[mittee] of Invitation.

LS in ScCleA. NOTE: An AEU by Calhoun reads: "Invitation to a Barbecue in N. Carolina."

From EDWARD EVERETT

London, 15 June 1844

Sir, I transmit with this despatch a copy of a note addressed by me to Lord Aberdeen on the subject of the seizure of the "Jones," in the roads of St. Helena in September 1840. The case of this vessel was discussed at great length in my note to Lord Aberdeen of the 18th May 1843, to which I beg leave respectfully to refer for a history of the transaction. Shortly after that note was written, I had an interview with Lord Aberdeen, in which he spoke of my argument, in a manner which led me to think that it had carried conviction to his mind.

In despatch Nro. 46 the views of the department in reference to this case were communicated to me by the late Mr. [Hugh S.] Legaré, confirming those which I had myself taken. I had felt with him that its weak point was that no appeal was taken at Sierra Leone from the judgment of the court there. It is true it does not appear that, at the time the decree of the court was given throwing the costs upon the owners, there was any one at Sierra Leone to represent them. But no reason is given why the Captain did not follow her from St. Helena.

There is also some obscurity hanging over the preliminary transactions at St. Helena, as I have observed in my despatch Nro. 44; but upon the whole, the narrative of the Captain is so circumstantial, the defence of Mr. Littlehales so contradictory and improbable, and the entire complexion of the case so suspicious against him, that I have felt convinced in my own mind, that the representations made to the government by the owners may be substantially relied upon.

What effect the technical plea that no appeal was taken, may have upon the ultimate decision of this government, it is impossible to foresee. I have argued the case, in my note of the 18th May 1843, as much as possible on grounds calculated to meet that objection, without however giving it too much prominence.

I felt last year a good deal of confidence that compensation would be granted, and nothing has occurred to make me think, that Lord Aberdeen's first impressions after reading my note have been changed. Unfortunately the allowance of claims, which create a heavy draft on the Treasury, habitually meets with a resistance from the officers immediately in charge of that Department all but insuperable. I am, sir, very respectfully, your obedient servant, Edward Everett.

Transmitted with despatch No. 143.
Mr. Everett to the Earl of Aberdeen, 14 June 1844.

LS (No. 143) with En in DNA, RG 59 (State Department), Diplomatic Despatches, Great Britain, vol. 52 (M-30:48), received 7/5; FC in DNA, RG 84 (Foreign Posts), Great Britain, Despatches, 8:290–292; FC in MHi, Edward Everett Papers, 49:226–229 (published microfilm, reel 23, frames 114–115). NOTE: The *Jones* had been seized for "being in the waters of a British possession without a national character, & being equipped for the Slave trade." She was taken from St. Helena by Lt. Littlehales to Sierra Leone for trial. The court there found no evidence to support the charges against the *Jones* but levied the cost of the legal proceedings against the vessel and owners. Everett had protested the entire proceeding in this case. (Everett to Lord Aberdeen, May 18, 1843; FC in MHi, Edward Everett Papers, 46:194–227 [published microfilm, reel 22, frames 590–606]).

From [BEN E. GREEN]

Legation of the U.S. of A.
Mexico [City], June 15th 1844

Sir, I had the honor a few days since to send a copy of my note of the 31st ult[im]o, in answer to Mr. [José M. de] Bocanegra's very harsh note of the 30th. I now send you a copy of his reply of the 6th inst., to which I deemed it proper to reply in the terms of mine of the 10th inst., a copy of which I send you (no. 2). I have just received an answer, dated June 12th, of which no. 3 is a copy. To this I shall not reply, before hearing further from you, notwithstanding the singular position it assumes, that the U.S., by their treaty of limits with Mexico, were bound to guaranty the integrity of the territory of Mexico, and the possession of Texas.

I hope that the ground taken in my 2d note, and the tone of the last, which I now send, will be approved by the President.

In the Diario [official newspaper] of the 13th, you will find a sanguinary order, addressed to Gen[era]l [Adrian] Woll, of the Army of the North, which directs that any individual, who may be found beyond a league's distance from the left bank of the River Bravo, shall be punished as a traitor, after a summary military trial. I called to see Mr. Bocanegra upon the subject (of this order), and told him that I hoped it would not be put in force against any citizen of the U.S.; that an example had been set in the revolution of Mexico herself; that Commodore [David] Porter, and many other citizens of the U.S. had taken part with Mexico, but none had ever, when taken prisoners, been treated by Spain, as traitors. He replied, that the order applied only to Mexican citizens. I answered that I was glad to hear him say so; but regretted that the order had been so vaguely and generally worded, and hoped that no mistakes would be made as far as citizens of the U.S. were concerned.

I send you also the Diario of the 11th June, in which you will find a message from the minister of war to the Congress; & recommend particularly to your attention the 3d paragraph, which I have marked. In the Diario of the 13th, you will also find some remarks addressed to the Chambers by the Minister of justice. Both the message of the minister of war, and the speech of the minister of Justice support the opinion advanced in my last despatch, namely that the vital importance of Texas to the security of the U.S. is well understood here; that they know that sooner or later the annexation must take place, unless Mexico avails herself of the delay to reconquer that country, and that their hopes of its defeat for the present are based upon the supposed opposition of the Senate of the U.S. to Mr. Tyler personally.

As yet the Congress has not been able to settle down on any plan for raising the four millions of dollars, called for by Santa Anna to begin the campaign against Texas. Various plans are proposed, but all liable to great opposition.

When the Congress first met, Santa Anna intrigued for "extraordinary powers," which the Congress were found unwilling to grant. Then he called on them to raise $4,000,000, and 30,000 men. They were afraid to take the responsibility of raising the taxes, already insufferable; and proffered the extraordinary powers. It was now his time to refuse, as he wished to throw on them the responsibility of raising money.

It is believed by many that he wants this sum of money, not to make war upon Texas, but for his own ambitious purposes at home; and that the present question of Texas is merely an excuse for carrying into effect his favorite measure, the increase of the army. Meanwhile, however, troops have been secretly despatched for the northern frontier; a troop of cavalry is to follow in a day or two; and this morning proposals for supplies of provisions, clothing &c &c, to be deposited at Mier & Matamoros, are posted at the corners of the

65

streets. This looks something like reality, and it is probable that Gen[era]l [Valentin] Canalizo, with a considerable force, will be sent to make another attempt to reconquer Texas.

Our Govt. is much mistaken, if it supposes that the present ruling powers in this country would be influenced, by fear of English interference, to consent to our occupation of Texas. On the contrary, Santa Anna would much rather see England, than the U.S., in possession of that country; and England will be the friend of Mexico or of Texas, just as she thinks most is to be gained.

[State Department translation of enclosure:]
J.M. de Bocanegra to Benjamin E. Green

National Palace
Mexico [City,] June 6th 1844

The Undersigned, Minister of Foreign Relations and Government, had the honor to receive the note, addressed to him under date of the 31st of May, by the Chargé d'Affaires ad interim of the United States of America, in reply to that from the Undersigned, written in answer to one of the 23d of the same month, respecting the grave and important matter of the treaty, signed by the Executive of the United States, for the annexation of the Department of Texas to that Union.

The Undersigned would certainly have fulfilled, all that is required by Diplomatic propriety and Etiquette, should he confine himself ["to" *interlined*] simply acknowledging the receipt of the above mentioned note; as it however contains various points of the highest interest to all concerned, in the question at issue, he finds himself under the necessity of answering Mr. Green, in the order observed in the said note, from the American Legation.

The term extraordinary applied by Mr. Green to the Undersigned's answer of the 30th of May, might certainly be more naturally and properly assigned, to the note, to which the present is a reply; since it may be asserted, with the utmost confidence, that all that is extraordinary, consists in the fact, that the American Legation, having by order of its Government opened the discussion of a matter, brought forward by the same Legation, in its note of the 23d of May, the Mexican Government had no other course left, and could follow none other, than to reply, in the terms, and upon the bases used in its note of the 30, to which Mr. Green replies.

The communication from the Chargé d'Affaires ad interim, is however extraordinary, considering that as he had given to the Mexican communication a certain direction by transmitting it to his

Government, with the expression of a desire that it should give the answer, nothing was more natural, nothing more obvious, than to await that answer, requested by the Legation itself, in the manner and terms stated by the Chargé d'Affaires ad interim, in his said note. It was in truth most natural, most just, and undoubtedly most consonant with the ordinary mode, to reply to what is placed in discussion and asked.

The Chargé d'Affaires ad interim declared in his note of the 23d of May, the principal motive, which induced his Government to sign the treaty for the annexation of Texas; stating that for the convenience, and security of the United States of America, and in order to free themselves from the policy of Great Britain, they had determined to occupy Texas; without leaving to Mexico any farther liberty or right, than that of settling the boundaries. And was no answer to be made to this? Was Mexico to leave in silence and condemn to oblivion, the justice with which she claims and demands what is due to her, and what is required by the right, which all nations possess, when they can appeal, as in the present case, to the international right established by treaties? Is the Mexican nation to remain silent, whilst it is deeply wounded in its dignity, and seriously compromised by the difficult position in which it is placed by the failure of compliance with international stipulations and compacts?

How can it be considered extraordinary, that Mexico should have replied to and protested, against the usurpation of what belongs to her, and has belonged legally to ["her" *canceled*] her, by a thousand titles, ever since the period of her independence and emancipation? What can Mr. Green find extraordinary in this conduct? what can he see new in a nation's claiming back, that which is usurped from it, on the ground of convenience and security, as declared (by another nation) solely on its own authority? Is it extraordinary that Mexico should repeat what she has advanced so frequently, with proofs and reasons, relying not only upon her own words, but on just, precise and indefeasible titles? Should she have limited herself to a simple acknowledgement of receipt? Would that have been consistent, with the principles adopted and given to the world with publicity? Was it not Mr. Green, who opened and provoked the discussion? and is it not he who has continued it? Who therefore acts extraordinarily? The answer is simple and very easy; and the Undersigned doubts not, that it will be given by all who yield to the voice of impartial justice. There cannot certainly be found a single man, who after reading and comparing the notes, will not see and confess, that

Mexico, while acting with energy and firmness restrains herself within the limits of moderation, in her expressions, and views, as the importance and nature of the subject under consideration requires.

The Chargé d'Affaires ad interim, in his note which the Undersigned is answering, employs exactly these words—"he considers the note of the 30 of May indecorous, and the importance of the affair little worthy of his official character as the representative of a powerful nation whose generosity Mexico has often experienced."

Thus Mr. Green considers it indecorous that an other nation as worthy of consideration as the rest, especially when it is claiming its own lawful real and existing property, should address him in the language of international law, which gives power rigour and justice, protesting against the infraction of treaties. Though this be in his opinion indecorous, Mexico regards it as legal and compatible with the principles of national Law and even of common law, as the Undersigned has already had the honor, upon an other occasion to say, by order of his Government to the American Legation; while addressing to it those protests, which the Chargé d'Affaires on his own authority, pronounces unfounded, declaring them so, without any other proof than his own assertion. To no one can it appear indecorous, that Mexico should express and maintain her rights in resistance to the usurpation, with all the force derived from the justice of her cause; and on the other hand, the Mexican Republic would be unworthy to be reckoned among nations, who know how to value their sovereignty and independence, if it were to remain silent and passive, with degradation and contempt, in a matter of vital importance, affecting so deeply the rights, which all the nations of the earth maintain & have maintained, from duty, from use, and even from custom. Mexico is then to be silent and to receive as orders, the infraction of treaties, committed without precedent, and without reason. Mr. Green should remember that he who uses his right offends no one; and if Mexico has asserted the rights which she has, over the Department of Texas, she has done so, with resolution, without transgressing the limits of what is due to reason and courtesy. This is not indecorous, nor has it ever been so considered. The Chargé d'Affaires alludes to the generosity with which Mexico has been more than once treated; the Undersigned wishes that those acts of generosity had been specified, in order that they may thus be made known, and acknowledged as such.

Mr. Green says he regrets to be obliged to mention, some points in the note of the 30th of May from the Undersigned, as offensive.

The Chargé d'Affaires, will however allow the Undersigned to tell him, that this reproach deserves to be considered in no other light, than as gratuitous; and to assure him that it will be completely done away, by a simple comparison of the notes, exchanged between the Legation and the Mexican Ministry; and it would be sufficient to transcribe literally, the proposition as made by the Chargé d'Affaires, and that stated by Mexico, to answer an assertion, in which it is forgotten, that while refuting it, the proof in favor of Mexico was established in these words "and not wanting in the respect due to Mexico his Government [*illegible word*] that the U.S. have been obliged for their own security to adopt this measure[?]."

This is not altering but shewing truely how far the respect due to Mexico can be reconciled with the adoption of the treaty, founded on the security and interests of the United States.

The Government of the United States, says Mr. Green, in addressing this communication to Mexico, neither directly nor indirectly, admits that she is the legitimate possessor of Texas: the independence of which has been acknowledged, not only by the United States, but also by the other principal powers; The Chargé d'Affaires however took care to be silent, as to the essential and notable circumstance, that, Mexico has protested against this acknowledgement, of the independence of Texas, from the moment when it was first made; that she has repeatedly claimed her rights, and maintained and defended them, on the just titles, which have been and are in her favour; declaring constantly, that certain extraordinary acts could not lessen the rights of Mexico, nor can nor could accrue to her injury; unless an act can be considered as compatible with the principles of national law, which is directly at variance with, and repugnant to, natural right, the highest of all rights, guarantying alike the property of nations and individuals. Will it, on the contrary be said, that a violent occupation and detention, is superior to the legal power which a proprietor holds over what is his own?

The question turns not on possession, but on the right of property, which is certainly not lost, because force interposes to usurp it. The common law, repeats the Undersigned, and the law of nations, considers and applies to individuals, without excepting nations, and their Governments, comprehending and embracing them, under the immutable rules of reason and justice.

The Government of the United States continues Mr. Green has thought proper to communicate with Mexico in a friendly manner, while exposing the motives of its conduct, not as having a right to Texas, but as being situated contiguous to that Department and to the United States, and moreover as being a member of the family of American Republics. The Undersigned however does not know how it happened that the Ch[a]rgé d'Affaires did not notice the contradiction which results from communicating with Mexico in a friendly manner in exposing the motives of their conduct, and at the same time excluding her from the right which constitutes her title to that consideration; for it is as much as to say that the belief that Mexico is worthy of consideration and of having communicated to her, the causes which actuate cabinet of Washington, was an erroneous belief; or at least that Mr. Green who set it forth, has withdrawn from the opinion presented by him in explanation. If it were so, it is positively an offense ["given" *interlined*] and an injury ["given" *canceled*] committed without any other motive than the resistance legally offered to a declared usurpation, and a direct infraction of treaties.

No less offensive to Mexico, is the pretext, which the Undersigned will take the liberty of repelling, as he does, that the vicinity of Texas and of the United States, is the motive of the latter, in giving to Mexico, the intimation of the present affair.

That pretext is strange and absolutely new, in questions of this nature, and importance; Mr. Green will allow the Undersigned not only to term it extraordinary, but to refuse to admit it, in any way as he has express orders to do.

The Chargé d'Affaires announces his surprise, that Mexico should repeat the protests, which he has been pleased to term as unfounded; and assumes as established, that this Republic in sustaining ["its" *interlined*] authority over Texas, sustains new and extraordinary principles; making at the same time, allusions really strange, which Mr. Green will allow the Undersigned to term inadmissible in matters of social convention: If Mexico has protested and does protest, she has done so, and does so, in virtue of just titles, well recognised and establishing her dominion over Texas, from the period of her emancipation; titles which have been acknowledged and approved in the most serious public acts, by nations with which she fortunately, maintains the best relations of friendship; and most particularly by the United States, where treaties of amity and limits, present the most irrefragable evidence of the right of Mexico, to complain and to protest against the infraction of the compacts which bind nations together.

Circumstances inevitable and more or less complicated, occurring, some in the bosom of this Republic, and others out of it, have retarded the accomplishment of the recovery of Texas; but is it not true and well known to the United States, that Mexico has maintained and does maintain an army, which has on several occasions, and in several victorious expeditions, marched over that territory, until the very recent act of the suspension of its military movements, in consequence of an armistice, for the purpose of dislodging the usurpers from the Mexican territory? What is the act, which can be considered as the renunciation of rights, with respect to that integrant part of the Republic? Is not that really a seizure and usurpation, which it has been thought proper to call a possession? A possession cannot exist where good faith is not to be found.

The Government of the Undersigned, has been surprised to see, the Chargé d'Affaires of the United States assert, that Mexico has despised amicable propositions to settle the questions which gave rise to the present events; and His Excellency the President of the Republic, orders the Undersigned to say to you expressly, as he now has the honor to do, that no other proposition has been made to him, except the indirect and confused one, relative to limits, and which is contained in vague language, in the first communication from Mr. Green; and even should such have been made, the Undersigned has been expressly authorised to inform the American legation, that Mexico, being most jealous of her rights, her dignity, and her independence, and most attentive to what is due to her sovereignty and integrity, is resolved to maintain by every means, and in every respect, those favorable titles, preferring glory and honor always to degradation and ignominy.

The appeal made by Mr. Green, to the world, has been made by Mexico long since, and recently; the Government and nation on whose part, the Undersigned has the honor to speak, indulging the expectation, that in order to obtain a just decision, it will be necessary merely to compare the notes exchanged, and their contents, so as to shew that neither the dispute, nor the war, are provoked by Mexico; but by the party which takes possession of an other's property, under the pretext of such a course being required, for its security and interest in contempt of international law, as well as of the rights of nations.

The whole world will know, how to place this controversy, in its true point of view; and civilised and just nations, will examine the precedents, and will analize and determine the conduct of both Republics.

If, unfortunately, the evils of war should hereafter be felt, they will fall on the head of the party, which has made itself responsible, and liable to the impartial and severe judgement, which condemns those worthy of reprobation and censure.

The Undersigned repeats &c, J.M. de Bocanegra.

[Enclosure]
Ben E. Green to J.M. de Bocanegra

Legation of the U.S. of A.
Mexico, June 10th 1844

The undersigned, Chargé d'affaires of the U.S. of A. (ad interim) has the honor to acknowledge the receipt of the note of H.E. J.M. de Bocanegra, of the 6th inst., in relation to the "grave and important" subject of the Treaty, lately concluded at Washington, for the annexation of the Republic of Texas to the U.S. of A.

The undersigned is gratified to see, that, although his last note upon this subject has been incorrectly translated in many respects, H.E. Mr. Bocanegra, has felt the full force of the reference, therein made, to the harsh language and unjust insinuations, directed in H.E.'s note of the 30th ult[im]o, against the Govt. and people, whom the undersigned is proud to represent. He is still more gratified to see, that H.E., by so laboured and lengthy an effort to defend himself from the imputation of a want of courtesy, fully admits the impropriety of using discourteous, or heated language in treating of so delicate a subject. H.E. should, and doubtless does, know full well, that harsh words prove nothing in favor of the justice of the cause they espouse, that on the contrary, they are an argument of weakness, being generally the last resort of those, to whom arguments are wanting. Such invectives are inadmissible even in the quarrels of individuals. Much less are they allowable in national differences. The consequences of the latter are of such magnitude, and the evils, to which they sometimes lead, so great and so extensive, as to call for great moderation & calmness in those, to whose hands are entrusted the destinies of a great people. Reproaches and denunciations are the language of passion; they neither convince the mind, nor remove difficulties; but, on the contrary, add fuel to excited spirits, and end in bloodshed and evil. Well convinced of this, the undersigned will continue to avoid everything calculated to irritate or estrange. He knows, that, if by invective and rejoinder ["(as it only can be)" *interlined*], this question is pushed to the extreme of an appeal to arms, the blood of many victims will cry curses from the earth upon those, who, by inconsiderate warmth, shall have brought about so powerful a consummation.

The undersigned must be permitted to add, that he considers the note of H.E. Mr. Bocanegra, of the 30th ult[im]o, as also that of the 6th inst., discourteous and highly objectionable. The charges of usurpation, atrocity, bad faith and violation of treaties, so often repeated; and the rash & ungracious insinuation contained in that passage of H.E.'s note of the 30th *March* ["May" *interlined*] beginning in these words: "La espenencia ha venide a declarar &c &c", are as objectionable, as they are gratuitous and unfounded; and the undersigned hopes that they will not be repeated. He has also the express orders of his Govt., (given on a former, but applicable to the present occasion) to say to that of Mexico, that he can hold no intercourse with it, except on such terms of courtesy and respect as are due to the honor and dignity of the U.S.

H.E. Mr. Bocanegra, promises to answer the note of the undersigned in the same order observed therein. But singularly enough, H.E. immediately grapples with an argument, certainly never advanced by the undersigned. After narrating that notice had been given to the Mexican Govt. of the conclusion of a Treaty for the annexation of the Republic of Texas to the U.S., H.E. exclaims: "And was not this to be answered? Was the justice, with which Mexico sustains & demands that, which is her due and which she exacts by the right, which all nations have when they interpose, as in the present case, international right by the medium of treaties, to be left in silence and condemned to forgetfulness? Is it wished that the Mexican nation should remain silent, seeing itself highly offended in its dignity and seriously compromised by the difficult position, in which the failure to comply with international stipulations & compacts places it."

The undersigned must be excused for noticing in the above extract two material departures from the rules of sound logic. It contains both the "*petitio principii*" and the *assumptio falsi* of the logicians. It assumes that the U.S. have violated their treaties, which the undersigned by no means admits. It also assumes that an indignity has been offered to Mexico; that the undersigned wished her to bear it in silence; and did not wish H.E. to answer the note of the 23d ult[im]o. In all this H.E. is mistaken. Neither the acts, nor the notes of the undersigned bear such a construction. He has never expressed, nor entertained such a sentiment. On the contrary, he wish[e]d and expected an answer. But he expected that that answer would be couched in those terms of courtesy and respect, which every Govt. owes to itself and to others. He expected that it would contain nothing to embitter and enflame passion; and he regrets, that, in this respect, he was mistaken.

The undersigned can not admit that either he or his Govt., has offered any indignity to Mexico. Certainly none has been intentionally offered. Neither would he desire that Mexico should bear a supposed indignity in silence. If Mexico thinks that she has rights over Texas, or that those rights have been violated, the U.S. are ever ready to lend a patient hearing to her claims, and to do her justice. They are equally ready to defend their own rights against any opponent, or at any cost. The language of remonstrance will never pass unheeded by the American people, nor by their Govt., but threat and abuse are alike inadequate to turn them from their course, where their right is clear, as in the present case, to treat with Texas as an independent power.

H.E. goes on to say, that the undersigned, on his own responsibility and without other authority than his own word, calls the protests of Mexico unfounded. The undersigned must be permitted again to correct H.E., and to remind him, that in thus characterizing those protests, he has spoken, not on his own authority alone, but on that of his own govt., of France, G[reat] Britain, & many other powerful nations.

The undersigned must also be permitted to express his surprise, that H.E. Mr. Bocanegra, should in one place charge him with having unwarrantably spoken of those protests; and that, immediately afterwards, he should say that the undersigned was very careful not to mention them. In this there is a strange inconsistency, for which the undersigned is at a loss to account. He can not charge it to the inaccuracy of H.E.'s translator, nor indeed to anything else than an inadvertence of H.E. himself.

The undersigned by no means sought silence on this point. On the contrary his note expressly alluded to it, and it was his chief object, by calm and courteous argument, to prove, that the U.S., in treating with the Republic of Texas as an independent nation, had never infringed any of the rights of Mexico; and that those protests were therefore unfounded. Upon those arguments it appears that H.E. has sought to keep silence, passing them over with the simple remark, that they were "inadmissible on a matter of social agreement." The undersigned begs leave to say that H.E. would have come nearer the mark, if, instead of declaring them to be inadmissible, he had acknowledged them to be facts, & facts unanswerable.

H.E. also says that he does not know how the undersigned overlooked the contradiction, which results from communicating to Mexico, in a friendly manner, the motives of the conduct of the U.S., and at the same time denying to her the right, which constitutes her title to that consideration. H.E. is either again mistaken, or misrepresents. The undersigned has not denied to Mexico the right which constitutes her title to that consideration. On the contrary he expressly admitted that the communication was due to Mexico, and as expressly stated the grounds, on which she was entitled to that consideration.

The undersigned is also free to admit that the claims urged by Mexico, although, in the opinion of the undersigned & of his Govt., untenable, may have had some influence in determining the Govt. of the U.S. to make its views known to Mexico in the language of conciliation & kindness. And in this the Govt. of the U.S. has shown a commendable & generous regard for whatever rights Mexico could allege, whilst it has not forgotten its own rights, and is determined to sustain them.

The undersigned deems it out of place, in answering a communication like the present, to enumerate the instances of generosity & kind feeling, which Mexico has experienced at the hands of the people & Govt. of the U.S. But he must be permitted to express his surprise, that a gentleman so intelligent and well informed ["in the history of Mexican independence" *interlined*] as H.E. Mr. Bocanegra, should plead ignorance, or need to be informed of them.

The undersigned regrets extremely the warmth and character of this discussion, for which he considers himself in no way responsible. His first note on this subject was in the language of peace and kindness, and he deeply regretted to see himself forced to notice the disparaging language of H.E.'s reply. If the undersigned had suffered that language to pass without rebuke, he would have merited the reprobation of his countrymen, and the reproof of his Govt. Neither could he suffer to pass unnoticed the pretended admission of the rights of Mexico, which H.E., with more ability than candor, sought to deduce from the conciliatory tone of the note of the undersigned. He hopes that in the future discussion of this subject the language of recrimination will be dropt, as unworthy of the greatness of either nation; and whenever the discussion is confined to the real question at issue, to wit, whether the U.S. are authorized to treat with Texas as an independent Govt., and whether by so doing they infringe upon any of the rights of Mexico?, the undersigned, or his Govt. will be always ready to answer Mexico in courteous and convincing argument; or otherwise, to act, as their honor & interests require.

The undersigned avails himself of this occasion &c &c &c, (Signed) Ben E. Green.

[State Department translation of enclosure:]
Jose Maria de Bocanegra to B[enjamin] E. Green

Palace of the National Government

Mexico [City,] June 12th 1844

The Undersigned, Minister of Foreign Relations and Government, would wish not to find himself under the absolute necessity, of answering the note addressed to him on the 10th inst., by the Chargé d'Affaires ad interim of the United States, reiterating the reply which he had made to the answers given by the Undersigned, in consequence of their having been provoked, by the Chargé d'Affaires, in beginning the discussion, and sustaining it, in the undeniable language, exhibited in the correspondence itself.

This correspondence, shews beyond doubt, that the American Legation has been proceeding, to place the Mexican ministry in the inevitable position, of continuing a discussion, which has been gradually becoming more and more complicated, so far as to make Mr. Green willing to enter into the signification of words, the accuracy of translations, and even logical propriety; moreover bringing into opposition, in the course which he has adopted in this grave and serious affair, other incoherent and strange matters, which become prominent and striking, on reading the said note of the 10th instant, requiring severe criticism, in order to form an impartial judgement on them.

The want of courtesy, of which Mr. Green speaks, the heat and irritation, which, I may be permitted to say, he supposes to exist, and the numerous charges which he has thought proper to bring again[s]t the Undersigned, and his communications—on all these points, he would find ample satisfaction, and answer, if he would again read over the notes, exchanged between the Legation and the Ministry; for those written by him alone will show where are the irritating and uncourteous expressions, the offensive allusions, and the references to points entirely foreign, to the discussion—take for example the fourth paragraph of the note of the 31st May, in which Mr. Green, besides asserting that the protests of Mexico are vain and existing merely on paper proceeds to assert that "Mexico might as well by protests declare the whole world to be her possession and all the nations inhabiting it her subjects and expect to have her rights admitted." The sense of these expressions, and of others to which that gentleman ["likewise" *interlined*] gave utterance, in that communication, and ["in" *interlined*] the one to which the undersigned is now replying is offensive and certainly at variance with the acknowledged proprieties of diplomacy. This may be said in virtue of the duty of the Undersigned, and the orders which he has received from his Government, to sustain the dignity of a nation, which like Mexico has the great advantage of resting on justice, and of being engaged in the defence of that, which is its own. The Undersigned repeats, that good sense, and the reading of the notes, will be sufficient to shew, that by comparing those notes, with impartiality and without, either prejudice or sympathy, it will be found, that the notes on the part of Mexico, display energy and firmness, in defence of those rights, but nothing of that discourteous character, which it has pleased Mr. Green to attribute to them—unless that name be gratuitously applied to words proper and adequate, and really and truly signifying, what is said, and serving to explain, the subject of the discussion, agreeably to its very nature.

As a discussion on the propriety or impropriety of translations, would be but to multiply useless observations, and might perhaps afford grounds for saying, that the translations of Mr. Green are incorrect, and it would be entering upon a question of words, which setting aside the essential and principal part of the business, would leave that part in confusion and oblivion, it would have been much better to waive the examination of phrases or points of syntax, well or ill applied, and to have brought proofs, that Mexico did not and does not possess the rights, which she did and does claim on just titles, over a territory which has been usurped by adventurers and speculators, proclaiming an independence, which would not have existed; as it wants every thing that right requires in such cases.

The Undersigned has always been, and now is, by express order of His Excellency the Constitutional President—ready for proper defence on this vital question, affecting not only the Republic, but also the nations, which may be now, or hereafter, under circumstances such as those in which Mexico has been placed.

The Ministry, in defending its cause, has not had recourse to improper means, nor to caustic expressions; and has always kept itself within the bounds of the civility due even to persons; relying upon the principles established by natural law, the law of nations, and international Law, which latter, as Mr. Green well knows, arises from reciprocal stipulations, and treaties between nations. The Undersigned will hereafter have the honor to prove, in the clearest manner, the flagrant violation by the Executive of the United States, of the Treaty concluded between Mexico and those States, on the 1st of December 1832, by entering into a treaty of annexation with Texas, which cannot be admissible, under any legal view of the matter.

The Undersigned in answering Mr. Green's note of the 23d of

May, conceives that the Mexican ministry, was performing its principal and most sacred duty, in declaring clearly and decisively, that its Government would always assert the rights and dignity of the Mexican Republic, which could not be disavowed, either by usurpation, committed by the first colonists, or by the situation in which the protectors and abettors of those colonists endeavoured to place them; or by the unavoidable obstacles, which have constantly retarded the vindication of those rights. The principles of right as regards acquisition and dominion, and the manner of losing dominion, favors nations as well as individuals, when they are in positions, such as that in which Mexico is placed.

The Chargé d'Affaires, will permit the Undersigned to remind him, that the right of property, the full knowledge, not peculiar to Mexico, but common to all civilized nations, that every occupation without a legal title, is an usurpation, have sustained Mexico, in asserting, as she has asserted, that this right has been wounded, in the deepest manner, by the very act, of the signature on the part of the Executive of the United States of America, of a treaty, wherein is settled and determined, what should at the least be regarded as in dispute, in virtue of public and repeated protests. History and nations will do justice to Mexico, and will pronounce upon the act in question, according to what ["is required by" *interlined*] the nature of the outrage committed, by a free just and civilized nation, labouring with constancy and determination, in the most direct spoliation, which has been seen for ages; a spoliation the more remarkable, for the manner in which it is proposed to be effected.

When the Undersigned said, in his note of the 30th May, that experience had confirmed the suspicions of Mexico, and that what had been conjectured, has now been realized, that could in no wise have been regarded as offensive; and least of all, when it was not a capricious or intrusive assertion, nor one of those which generally involve and confound matters, but was based on public and notorious circumstances, on certain and completed acts, which present that assertion, with all ["the" *interlined*] evidence and force of conviction. Had this been otherwise, it would have been necessary to have recourse to the subterfuge, of denying the existence of what is seen and felt. For this reason it was, that the Undersigned, in the note in question, made an illusion though very slight, to the circumstances which led Mexico to conjecture, that the States contiguous to Texas, which supplied arms, troops, and munitions of war, did not act solely with the view of assisting the insurgents, in supporting and preserving their independence; but principally with the clear intention of extending and maintaining the degradation of the human race; or what is the same thing—Slavery, thwarting, according to their principles, the efforts of those, who desire to abolish it, whether their fellow citizens or foreigners; and for this cause, the territory of Texas has been sustained and succoured, as well as its annexation, as the most certain means of carrying the project into effect. And is this not exactly, what Mr. Green has revealed to us, and said clearly and unequivocally in third paragraph of his note of the 23d of May last? The Undersigned would have desired to have been able to do, what cannot be done, namely to say things in the language of truth in which he should speak, without presenting them as they are, but as he could wish them to be. Mexico thus has without violence, and gradually, succeeded in establishing the proposition, that she could not lose the dominion of a ["Country" *canceled*] territory, which she acquired in the most glorious legitimate and determined manner.

The Chargé d'Affaires of the United States, has thought proper to enumerate, among the observations which he terms harsh and offensive, the assertion, that the treaties between the two Republicks have been violated, and in truth, as the only answer to and proof of this, the Undersigned will not transcribe literally, but he will mention, the first Article of the Treaty of Amity, commerce and navigation, between Mexico and the United States of December 1, 1832, and the part relative to boundaries, also concluded between the two Republics. These portions compared with the notes, give the victory to the Mexican Ministry, which has done no more, than rely upon Conventions and agreements.

By the tenor of these articles, it will be immediately seen, that the frank, sincere, and durable friendship promised in these stipulations, was not merely abstract phrases, or general terms; nor is it to be supposed, ["that" *interlined*] they were intended to bind only the Governments of the two Republics and without reference to their respective subjects; but on the contrary, it was meant that there should be reciprocal friendship, between the ["two" *canceled*] Governments and their citizens. It is therefore clear, that comparing the obligation contracted, and produced by the treaties, with the conduct hitherto observed and practised by the United States, in the unfortunate affair of Texas, it results that, the stipulations have not been fulfilled on their part? a conclusion at which, the Undersigned doubts not, that every one will arrive, who judges actions and occurrences with impartiality and rectitude.

As to the treaty of Amity, the United States of America have acknowledged in the most formal and solemn manner, that the boundaries between ["them" *changed to* "themselves"] and the Mexican Republic, are the same which were designated as the dividing line, on settling that matter, between the United States and Spain, in the treaty concluded to that effect, between the two last mentioned nations. The Undersigned considers this to be sufficient for his purpose, of answering Mr. Green's note, in which he has been engaged; inasmuch as the force and the notoriety of the right on which he relies, and the desire of avoiding disagreeable repetitions, lead him to the examination of another point.

The Chargé d'Affaires in his last note of the 10th of June, has touched on the point of the recognition of the independence of Texas; but as he dwells on that essential and serious matter, not as he formerly did in an indirect and transitory way, but presenting it as an argument and proof of the right, acquired in favor of the Republic of Washington, and as a loss of right on the part of ["the" *interlined*] Mexican Republic, he will have the kindness to listen to the reflections, which the Undersigned addresses to him on this subject. Mr. Green says that, the recognition of the independence of Texas, by the United States, and by other powers, destroys the rights of Mexico, and nullifies the protests, which this Republic has made opportunely, and repeatedly, for the preservation of a territory, which belongs to it; The Chargé d'Affaires declaring at the same time, that he advances this argument, not as from himself, but as speaking from authority of his ["own" *interlined*] Government, of that of Great Britain, and that of France, which have all given the acknowledgement.

If it be remembered, that the United States acknowledged the independence of Texas, it should also be remembered, that Mexico protested against that act, as she also did with regard to the other two powers, mentioned. But it is to be observed that the annexation to the Union of the United States, in virtue of the treaty signed by that nation does not rest on this acknowledgement but on the circumstance, as stated by Mr. Green in his above mentioned note of the 23d of May, "that this step had been forced upon the Government of the United States in self defence in consequence of the policy, adopted by Great Britain, in reference to the abolition of Slavery in Texas. It was impossible for the United States to witness with indifference, the efforts of Great Britain to abolish slavery in that territory. They could not but see, that she had the means in her power, in the actual condition of Texas, to accomplish the objects of her policy, unless prevented by the most efficient measures; and that if accomplished, it would lead to a state of things, dangerous in the extreme to the adjacent States, and to the Union itself." The Undersigned must here refer, as he does, to what he has already said, upon the subject of this recognition by the United States, and upon the manner in which the act of annexation is viewed, in virtue of a treaty concluded by the Executive, without having paid any respect to a Republic, with which it is bound, by the most sacred bonds, acknowledged among civilized nations. Respect to Mexico was abandoned, when the act of annexation was consummated, by the Executive; and it was restored, only by the Law and the wisdom of the Senate. Mr. Green will also admit, what the Undersigned had the honor to state to him, on this point in his previous notes; And as the Chargé d'Affaires had founded arguments and reasoning, on the acknowledgement of the Independence of Texas, by Great Britain and France, the Undersigned may be allowed to say to him, that ["if" *interlined*] these two Great nations did lend themselves to this acknowledgement of Independence ["they" *interlined*] did so as in those acts, by acknowledging a fact, and nothing more. Neither of those two nations, denied to Mexico her rights at that time; nor has either of them since, treated the protests of the Mexican Republic, as unfounded, and existing only on paper, as Mr. Green has been pleased to do. On the contrary France and England have on various occasions, interposed their high respect and worthy influence, to procure a cessation of the war; never however have they termed it unjust, but only injurious and pernicious, from its very nature.

Nor could such great powers have acted in any other way in acknowledging that in a country independent in fact, but depending in right upon a mother country, the fact alone, and not the right can be acknowledged; much less could they give to the country, the right to be acknowledged as a sovereign nation, for that act is peculiar to the mother country, and to her and to her alone, belongs the acknowledgement which produces emancipation. All this is legal: these are not new ideas; they are principally universally admitted; they have been uttered by these same great powers above named, in treating of the independence of countries, which had been their colonies; and what is here said, has just been heard in the United States, from the mouth of one of their most distinguished citizens. And certainly the question of annexation by the treaty made in the United States, is entirely different, and cannot possibly be terminated, by reference to the recognition made by other nations, and regarding merely a fact, without also taking into consideration rights, which from their very essential nature, have been reserved in those cases, by the powers who performed those acts.

The importance and seriousness of the present matter, the propriety of not involving in it ideas and circumstances, which unless useful for conviction, often degenerate into offensiveness, and other considerations most essential in this question, induce the Undersigned to proceed to collect and reply to the last observations addressed to him by Mr. Green, in the note which he is now answering; and for this reason, he will allow the Undersigned to say that when he stated that the Chargé d'Affaires of the United States of America, spoke on his own authority, he formed that opinion from reading the fourth paragraph of the note of the 31st of May last, where these words occur "The Undersigned takes the liberty," where he emits[?] the opinion above mentioned; and if in truth Mr. Green in no way desires the point to which the present notes relate to remain under silence, the Undersigned has succeeded in treating it without deviating from or parrying the question. And though in Mr. Green's opinion, the Government of the United States has not been wanting in respect for the rights of Mexico, including a treaty with the so called Republic of Texas, the Undersigned has answered and has presented, what he had to say in reply; entering directly into the matter of the difficulty freeing it as far as he could, from all that could complicate and confuse it, as appeared to be required by the seriousness and importance of the case. For this reason, the Undersigned, in his note of the 6th instant, whilst noticing the allusions made by Mr. Green, at the conclusion of his fourth paragraph above mentioned, merely indicated that they were strange, and inadmissible, in matters of convention. This is clear, and it will be sufficient to read it.

The Chargé d'Affaires of the United States, asserts that it would be out of place to enumerate the instances of generosity and kind feeling, on the part of the United States towards Mexico; and he refers the Undersigned for a knowledge of them, to the history of the independence of Mexico. The Chargé d'Affaires will not however take it ill, if the Undersigned should assure him, that he is unacquainted with the facts to which Mr. Green refers, and he knows only those alleged on the other side. It does not seem in place now to speak of the history of Mexico; and the Undersigned repeats by order of his Government, that whensoever those acts of kind feeling and generosity, supposing them to exist, be set forth and particularised, it will acknowledge and esteem them, according to their real value and consideration; and will then proceed to set forth and particularise, the acts of good feeling and generosity, which will doubtless be found also in her history.

As the Chargé d'Affaires has chosen to raise a question of courtesy, the Undersigned should in duty assure him, as he has the honor to do, that the notes of the Mexican Ministry cannot consistently with impartiality be styled uncourteous; inasmuch as the expressions therein used are such as are suggested by the rights of Mexico, and are demanded by the very nature of the affair in question. The ideas and propositions advanced, are those of invariable and eternal justice; they are the same which are invoked in the United States themselves, and are published by the press, against the annexation of Texas, resting on the respectable names of [John Quincy] Adams, [Henry] Clay ["and" *canceled*; Martin] Van Buren and other notable persons, who know what is advantageous to their own Country, yet wish to do no ill to Mexico, being convinced that it is material for a Republic which has professed the political faith of walking always in the path, traced by reason, not to change the principles they adopted, by offending a friendly Republic, which has offered abundant and irrefragable proofs, of its honour, good faith and benevolent feelings. The Undersigned may be allowed to attribute the observation of Mr. Green, to the circumstance, that probably her moderation may have given ground for such imputations; things may have come to that extremity, that courtesy is to be regarded as meaning humiliation, and quietly receiving orders, in place of Diplomatic notes.

The Chargé d'Affaires states, that he has orders from his Government, though given in reference to an other matter, to say to the Government of Mexico, that he can hold no intercourse with it, except upon such terms of courtesy and respect, as are due to the United States. And it is precisely the notes of Mr. Green, which have caused an order to the same effect, to be given to the Undersigned, by His Excellency the Constitutional President of the Republic, declaring in the same manner, that so long as the discussion relates substantially to the serious matter under consideration, and it is conducted with proper courtesy and respect, it should be also properly prosecuted, and maintained by Mexico. And as the conclusion and termination of this serious affair, depends upon the wisdom, prudence, and circumspection of the Senate of the United States of America, upon whose decision will rest exclusively and entirely, either the responsibility or the glory of the result of a question, in which Mexico is so clearly and palpably in the right, the Undersigned repeats in the name of his Government, what he has already advanced, in behalf of the rights of the Republic; hoping that the voice of his Country may be heard by nations, and the world to which it has already appealed; and flattering himself with the belief that as Mexico has relied on virtue and truth, the world will approve the manner in which she has acted, in the present affair, which has ["been" *interlined*] fortunately exposed, and submitted to the light, in every way, so as to establish its justice most evidently. The Undersigned has the honor to repeat to the Chargé d'Affaires of the United States of America the assurances of his distinguished consideration. Jose Maria de Bocanegra.

ALU (No. 7) with Ens and State Department translations in DNA, RG 59 (State Department), Diplomatic Despatches, Mexico, vol. 12 (M-97:13), received 7/15; FC in DNA, RG 84 (Foreign Posts), Mexico, Despatches, pp. 500–502; draft in NcU, Duff Green Papers (published microfilm, roll 5, frames 581–584); PEx with Ens in Senate Document No. 1, 28th Cong., 2nd Sess., pp. 60–74; PEx with Ens in House Document No. 2, 28th Cong., 2nd Sess., pp. 59–74.

Richard K. Crallé to TILGHMAN A. HOWARD

Department of State
Washington, 15th June, 1844

Sir: I am directed by the Secretary of State to inform you, that the President of the United States [John Tyler], by and with the advice and consent of the Senate, has appointed you Chargé d'Affaires of this Government to the Republic of Texas. Should you accept this appointment, you will be so good as to give the earliest information of the fact to this Department, and say when it will be in your power to leave the United States to enter upon the discharge of the duties of the station. Your commission and instructions will be forwarded to you immediately on the receipt of your reply. I have the honor to be, Sir, your obedient servant, Richard K. Crallé, Chief Clerk.

FC in DNA, RG 59 (State Department), Diplomatic Instructions, Texas, 1:95–96 (M-77:161). NOTE: Howard was a native of S.C. who had been a resident of Ind. since 1830. He had served in the U.S. House of Representatives from Ind. and had been the unsuccessful Democratic candidate for Governor in 1840.

From GEORGE W. LAY

Legation of the United States
Stockholm, June 15, 1844

Sir, I have observed in the newspapers an account of a Report made by Mr. [Charles J.] Ingersoll [Representative] of Pennsylvania on the subject of our Foreign intercourse. With a view to economy he proposes to consolidate several of our Foreign Missions. This is not a new idea. It has already been adopted by the King of Holland, and the Emperor of Brazil. The experience and observation which I have had abroad, enables me to speak on this subject more understandingly than many of ["our" *interlined*] Countrymen who have seen nothing of Foreign Courts. As I have made it my practice through life to speak fearles[s]ly & sincerely on all matters appertaining either to the interest or honour of my Country, I shall give you a brief view of my ideas on this subject, hoping that if they meet with your views, the question may be brought before Congress at its next meeting, and some modification made in the laws relating to our foreign intercourse. It is certain to all who know any thing in relation to the expenses of our Foreign intercourse, that our expenses are much greater ["than" *interlined*] that of most other nations, without attaining the principal object of keeping up our Foreign missions.

This arises principally from the constant change made in our Diplomatic Agents abroad. The custom of making nearly an entire change in our Foreign Ministers abroad, with every change of Administration has been too long sanctioned by the usage and practice of every successive Administration, to expect that any change in this respect will ever be adopted. Could this be effected then I should most assuredly advise as the best course to raise the national character abroad, and elevate us in the eyes of the world to that high position to which we are entitled amongst the nations of the earth, that we should place in every respect our foreign representatives, upon an equal footing at all of the Courts abroad, with those of the great Powers of Europe. A Position inferior in rank to that of other great powers renders the situation of a representative embarrassing, and it is impossible for him whatever may be his acquirements or talents to create that feeling of respect in the eyes of a foreign Court and a foreign people, that rank alone can give. This arises from the education and habits of the people of all the European nations. They judge of a whole nation by its immediate Representative, and no dignity of character or power of intellect can accomplish in their eyes half as much as rank & external appearances. National reputation, says the author of Common Sense "is of as much importance as independence itself." ["]It possesses a charm which wins[?] upon the world & makes even enemies civil."

Now let me inquire what is the object of keeping up our Diplomatic Relations on the Continent of Europe? Not most assuredly for the fear of any national rupture with those nations in these piping[?] times of peace—nor is it on account of our commercial relations, as we have subsisting treaties with all the nations with whom we have commercial dealings & in case of any change, we can with the greatest ease send out a Special Agent to negotiate a new treaty, and when the treaty is negotiated, there would be an end to his Diplomatic career[?] & the expenses of the mission.

The only answer to the question is, that we consider it for our nation's reputation to keep up our Diplomatic relations with other nations, & endeavour to foster & cherish a kind feeling on their part toward us and our Country. Now in this we most signally fail. The low grade of our ministers abroad generally, & the continued changes going on, subject us to the severest animadversions ["of" *altered to* "at"] every Court in Europe.

This I hear continually & not without pain I assure you, for a person abroad merges all private & party feeling, & is only sensitive to the reputation and honour of his Country. No American can be abroad either in a diplomatic, or private capacity without seeing & feeling this. Whatever opinions may be entertained in the United States in regard to the rank of our ministers abroad, here in Europe it is of the greatest moment. It is of so much consequence at all the Courts of Europe, that admitting it is not thought advisable to change the salary, I should advise by all means to raise the Chargé d'Affaires to the rank of Envoys Extraordinary & Ministers Plenipotentiary, or abolish it at once altogether. Having reflected much upon the subject & knowing the difficulties, attending an in[n]ovation where the expenses are to be considerably increased, it is my decided opinion that it is for the interest as well as reputation of the Government of the United States, to abolish at once all our foreign missions (excepting that of England, France & Russia) and substitute in their place Commercial Agents with suitable salaries & fees, and make the Office of a certain & fixed duration, so that without cause, no one could be removed, within the period limited by law. These Commercial Agents could attend to every thing relating to the commerce of the country, with much more efficiency than a minister, and could easily possess himself of all the information, necessary or useful to the Government. I speak with great sincerity when I say, that I cannot see of what earthly benefit to our Government, are the several Chargé d'Affaires at the various Courts in Europe. What services have they or can they render to their Government? A late Chargé d'Affaires [Henry Wheaton?] at the Court of Denmark, who had represented the United States at that Court for Eight years, wrote home to the Department, but two Dispatches during the whole of his residence at Copenhagen, and from the tenor of those, & style, I could well imagine, that it must have been a relief to the Department, not to have heard oftener from him. I have made it a point to write to the Department every month, but must admit, that without alluding frequently to matters which could not be particularly interesting or useful, I have sometimes been much perplexed what I should write that might not be considered irrelevant or useless. This I am satisfied is also the case with our ministers at most of the Courts of Europe & if consulted would give the same opinion.

My argument in brief is that our Diplomatic Corps as at present organized does not & cannot succeed in accomplishing the sole object for which it is kept up in times of peace & when no chance of any rupture can be anticipated.

That it is attended with a useless & unnecessary expense, and that all the objects sought or expected to be attained can be equally well, if not better accomplished by Commercial Agents.

Should this meet with your views I hope you will second my wishes & cause the same to be laid before the next Congress, should Mr. Ingersoll's bill not succeed. As there will then be a new Administration to come in, it would be a good beginning to commence with a new system, which has greater economy to reccommend it than the plan of Mr. Ingersoll & in my opinion much more efficient. Yours Respectfully, George W. Lay, Chargé.

ALS (No. 23) in DNA, RG 84 (Foreign Posts), Sweden, Despatches, 6:76–82.

From John F. McGregor, [U.S. Consul at Campeche], 6/15. McGregor reports that all is quiet in Yucatan. Trade has fallen off as a result of the noncompliance of the Mexican government with treaties made with Yucatan by which Yucatan's products are to be admitted free into Mexican ports. "None of your communications have been as yet received." (This despatch was addressed to Abel P. Upshur.) ALS (No. 6) in DNA, RG 59 (State Department), Consular Despatches, Campeche, vol. 2 (M-286:1), received 9/25.

To Commodore Cha[rle]s Morris, U.S. Navy

Department of State
Washington, 15 June 1844

Sir, I have received your note of the 14th instant, enclosing for my decision, an account for expenses incurred by you, whilst absent from the U.S. Ship "Delaware," in the River La Plata, attending to duties prescribed by this Department, in its instructions dated 30th September, 1841, and 22d March, 1842.

In order that the Department may be enabled to decide upon your claim, you are requested ["to" *interlined*] transmit to it a detailed account of those expenses, properly certified and supported by vouchers: or, if that is not practicable, an account, regularly certified, stating the number of days that you were on shore, engaged in the performance of the duties assigned by this Department. I am, Sir, Your obedient servant, J.C. Calhoun.

FC in DNA, RG 59 (State Department), Accounting Records: Miscellaneous Letters Sent, 1832–1916, vol. for 2/1–9/30/1844, p. 240.

MEMORANDUM [on Commodore Charles Morris's Accounts]

[State Department, *ca.* June 15, 1844]

Memorandum. In consequence of the United States being without a diplomatic agent at Monte Video, on the 30th of September, 1841, Commodore [Charles] Morris was instructed by this Department to present to the government at that place a demand of satisfaction for injuries inflicted by military officers of the Republic of Uruguay upon George Johnson, a citizen of the United States. The Commodore entered into a correspondence with that government upon the subject which resulted in an agreement on its part to render the satisfaction required and it has since been received by the aggrieved party.

This government being also without a diplomatic representative at Buenos Ayres, on the 22nd of March, 1842, the Commodore was instructed at large by the Secretary of State upon the subject of a claim of Mr. T[homas] L. Halsey against the Buenos Ayrean government for upwards of a hundred thousand dollars, which claim he was directed to present to that government.

Pursuant to this instruction, the Commodore entered into a voluminous correspondence with the Buenos Ayrean Secretary of State which, however, did not bring about a payment of the claim.

It is presumed that the discharge of these duties required personal interviews also ["on shore," *interlined*] with the officers of those governments and especially with those of Buenos Ayres, the Delaware, the Commodore's flag ship not being able to approach the latter City within several miles.

There is also reason to believe that an object, if not the primary one, for sending the Commodore to Buenos Ayres, was to draw from that government an expression of its disposition to receive a diplomatic agent from the United States. In this the Commodore succeeded. His business at Buenos Ayres extended through most of the autumn of 1842.

ADU in ScCleA. NOTE: This undated memorandum is in an unknown hand. Found among Calhoun's papers at ScCleA is another undated memorandum which is probably related to the above. The second memorandum, a one-page document, describes the circumstances under which a claim by Capt. [Isaac] McKeever of the U.S. Navy was settled. McKeever spent 37 days on shore at Buenos Ayres in 1833 during a time of disturbances when no representative of the State Department was present. His expenses were allowed by Secretary of State [Louis] McLane even in the absence of vouchers.

From J[AMES] C. PICKETT

Legation of the U. States
Lima, June 15, 1844

Sir: I have not yet received an official notification of the death of Judge [Abel P.] Upshur, but letters and papers have come to hand within the last week, that confirm but too fully, the account which had reached us here, circuitously, of the awful catastrophe, by which he lost his life.

The civil war in Peru continues, and is waged with some activity and with much rancor, but nothing decisive seems yet to have taken place. There has been a little skirmishing, in which the partisans of Gen. [Manuel] Vivanco have had the advantage. He himself has retreated to Arequipa, about 700 miles from Lima, losing on the march, one third of his army, by desertions—there was no fighting. Gen. [Ramon] Castilla pursued him and is now not far from him, it is supposed—each with about three thousand troops, probably.

Vivanco left Lima, six months ago, saying that he would march at once against Castilla and annihilate him; but after much delay and apparent irresolution, he took the road to Arequipa instead of the one to Ayacucho, where his antagonist was waiting for him. Some say that this movement is a stroke of consummate generalship— others that it is a proof of consummate cowardice, and indifferent persons incline generally, to the latter opinion, I think.

It does not appear that Castilla has yet attempted to carry into execution, his decree of *guerra a muerte* (war without quarter) mentioned in my 93rd number. He and Vivanco are both bad enough, I dare say, but not so bad perhaps, as they are willing to be thought, and as they represent themselves to be, taking their public measures for true exponents of their principles. Castilla was minister of Finance in Peru, in 1839–40, and those who were hostile to him admitted that he was officially honest—that he neither plundered, himself, nor suffered others to plunder the public revenue, if he could prevent it; which was admitting a great deal in favor of a Peruvian military chief. He is very violent and arbitrary though.

Vivanco became somewhat popular, last year, through the extreme unpopularity of his rivals, Vidal and [Antonio] La Fuente. He is superior however, in some respects, to many of his military contemporaries here. He has some education and is considered to be personally decent, which they are not all. But he seems to be but ill qualified for a ruler, being vain, presumptuous and selfish, and as a military commander, below mediocrity. He has been called, notwithstanding, by his countrymen, the Washington of Peru and compared by them to Napoleon; and to this ridiculous stuff, he listens very complacently. There is some excuse for his vanity though, for scarcely any man in modern times, has been the object of more gross and nauseating adulation. His flatterers having exhausted the Castilian, copious as it is, have had recourse to the learned languages, and he is made to figure in a latin ode, as *praesul, clarissima cives, salus, spes patriae decusque Minervae,* &c. &c.—And the misfortune is, that being weak enough to believe all this flummery, it has completely turned his head.

The English at Tahiti (Otaheite) complain loudly and not without cause, perhaps, of the violent and arbitrary proceedings of the French in that island: But their conduct has not been more reprehensible, I imagine, than Lord [George] Paulet's was at Oahu, and of that no Englishman in the Pacific complained, probably.

It appears to me that it would have been more to the advantage of the United States, had the English taken possession of Tahiti, the French occupying the Marquesas, for the reason that as it cannot be presumed we shall ever be at war with both of them at the same time, there would then have been, in the event of a war with either, ports to which our whaling and other trading vessels could repair and find themselves in perfect safety. But now, should the U. States engage in hostilities with France, our commerce in those regions will be greatly exposed, unless the naval force in the Pacific should be considerably increased.

It is said in the English papers which have reached Lima, that the British government has definitively recognised the independence of the Sandwich Islands: Consequently, the extravagant doings of Lord Paulet have been disapproved in good earnest, and it may be supposed that they will not be repeated soon—at all events, I do not think they will be, whilst the present commander of the British naval force in the Pacific, (Admiral [Richard] Thomas) is on the Station. He is I believe, a just and honorable man, and no doubt other British officers commanding ships in these seas, are also just and honorable men: They are not all of the Paulet school. I have the honor to be, with great respect, Sir, Your Ob[edien]t Servant, J.C. Pickett.

ALS (No. 95) in DNA, RG 59 (State Department), Diplomatic Despatches, Peru, vol. 6 (T-52:6, frames 501–503), received 12/30.

From Joseph Ray, Washington, 6/15. Ray states that he has a claim on the Brazilian government that was, as early as 1830, to be presented to that government. Having heard no news of the claim, he asks that Calhoun ascertain its present status and inform him of any attempts by the U.S. to present the claim and to obtain payment of it. ALS in DNA, RG 59 (State Department), Miscellaneous Letters (M-179:104, frames 540–541).

From J[OHANN] W. SCHMIDT

Consulate of Prussia
New York [City,] 15th June 1844

Sir, A company has been formed at Stettin for the purpose of carrying on the Whaling bussiness in the South Seas. The Government has done much to promote an undertaking entirely new in Prussia and the King himself [Frederick William IV] takes a great and personal interest in the success of the enterprize.

The first Ship fitted out by the Company "The Borussia, Capt[ai]n Hartwig" has arrived at New Bedford, there to complete her equipment and to engage able and experienced Americans, as officers, harpooners & boatSteerers, and will shortly proceed on her voyage.

Prussia has no Agents whatsoever in those regions, where her flag is probably entirely unknown. The United States on the contrary are well represented, and as occurrences may take place, when the advice[,] assistance or protection of a public functionary would be most beneficial and essential for Capt[ai]n Hartwig and his Crew and considering more that the same is, in part composed of american Citizens, I venture to ask of you the favor to grant to the Borussia, a circular letter addressed to the Consuls of the U.S. residing in the regions generally visited by Whaling ships, by which they are requested to extend such assistance and protection to Capt[ai]n Hartwig and his crew as occassion may call for and as may be compatible with their station, and I beg you to be assured that such an act of courtesy and friendly feeling will not fail to meet with due appreciation from my Government. With the highest consideration I have the honour to be Sir your most obed[ien]t Serv[an]t, J.W. Schmidt, Consul of Prussia.

ALS in DNA, RG 59 (State Department), Notes from Foreign Consuls, vol. 2 (M-664:2, frames 391–393).

To CHARLES SERRUYS, [Belgian Chargé d'Affaires]

Department of State
Washington, 15th June, 1844

Sir: I have the honor to communicate to you, a letter [of 6/14] addressed to the Governors of several States introducing Baron Vander Stratten Ponthoz, & asking for him such facilities as they may be able to afford, in furtherance of the objects of his tour through the States.

I also communicate for the use of the Baron, a letter from [McClintock Young] the Secretary of the Treasury, *ad interim*, to the Collectors of the Customs, Receivers and Registers of Land Offices, and Surveyors General of the Public Lands.

These letters, written in accordance with the wishes of your Government, as presented in a late communication [of 6/11] from you, it is confidently hoped, will meet your views, and enable Baron Vander Stratten Ponthoz to fulfil the instructions of the Belgian Government. I am, Sir, with great Consideration, Your obedient Servant, J.C. Calhoun.

FC in DNA, RG 59 (State Department), Notes to Foreign Legations, Belgium, 6:36–37 (M-99:5).

From R[OBERT] WICKLIFFE, JR.

Legation of The United States
Turin, June 15, 1844

Sir, I have the honor to acknowledge by this days mail the receipt of your circular of the 1st of April (No. 3), in which you inform me that you had been appointed by the President Secretary of State and had on that day entered upon the discharge of the duties of that office.

The circumstances under which you have been called to the management of our Foreign Relations are alike honorable to him and yourself. The wisdom which he displayed in selecting the most suitable man in the country to conduct our Foreign Affairs at this most critical juncture, and the patriotic sacrifice which you have made in relinquishing the quiet enjoyments and peaceful pursuits of private life for no other end than the good of the country, entitle both to the lasting gratitude of the Republic. That your appointment should not only have commanded the approbation but drawn forth the applause of all parties and of all men though doubtless highly gratifying to yourself, has not been surprising to me. That such unanimity should prevail with regard to its peculiar propriety, when parties are so numerous, when the nation is agitated by the approaching election, and when two of the most momentous questions that have arisen since the last war, are unsettled and placed in your hands, is the proudest evidence which you could receive of the confidence which the people repose not merely in your ability, but in your personal character and political integrity.

In those feelings of joy so generally and so freely expressed from all quarters, permit me to say that I heartily join. It was my good fortune to enjoy the confidence and friendship of the late lamented Secretary of State [Abel P. Upshur] and it shall be my great ambition during my residence near this Royal Court, to endeavor, in some slight degree to merit your approbation.

I avail myself of this occasion to offer you the assurances of my most distinguished Consideration! R. Wickliffe, Jr.

ALS (No. 7) in DNA, RG 59 (State Department), Diplomatic Despatches, Sardinia, vol. 4 (M-90:5), received 7/19; slightly variant ALS (No. 8, marked "Copy") in the same file; FC (dated 6/12) in DNA, RG 84 (Foreign Posts), Italy, Sardinia, 2:[230–231]. NOTE: Robert Wickliffe, Jr., was of a prominent Ky. family and a nephew of Postmaster General Charles A. Wickliffe. He had been appointed Chargé d'Affaires to Sardinia by John Tyler in 1843.

From A[LEXANDER] D. BACHE

Office of W[eigh]ts & Measures &c.
[Treasury Department] June 17, 1844
Dear Sir, Allow me to introduce to you my friend Prof. R[ichard] S. McCulloh, & to request that you will have the kindness to give him facilities in obtaining authentic information in reference to subjects recently referred to this office by the Treasury Department, from sources within the Department of State. Prof. McCulloh will more fully explain the objects referred to. With great respect Yours very truly, A.D. Bache.

ALS in DNA, RG 59 (State Department), Miscellaneous Letters (M-179:104, frame 548). NOTE: An AES by R[obert] Greenhow, Librarian of the State Department, reads "Leave given verbally by the Secretary of State for Mr. McCulloh to have recourse to the Library and take out books in reference to subjects aforesaid."

From H[ENRY] W. CONNER, "Private"

Charleston, June 17, 1844
The annexed slip is from the [Charleston] Mercury of this morning & is copied you perceive from the South Carolinian of Columbia.

Judging from the experience of the past I think its object is to keep you out of the Senate of the U. States that another may occupy the place.

The public are extremely reluctant that you should retire from public life in view of the Great Crisis now evidently approaching & the desire is universally expressed that you should be prevailed upon to go back to the Senate whenever you may leave the State department.

Hence this paragraph of those two papers[;] you will receive this opinion for so much as it is worth. It is the settled conviction of my mind & I presume to communicate it only because I think you should be put upon your guard at least until you could give the matter due consideration. Understanding my motive you will I am sure pardon the manner in which I now approach you.

The people since the rejection of the Treaty are ready & anxious to act & are only waiting for a plan of proceeding to be furnished to make a powerful move at once & a meeting of the friends of union & Texas throughout the U.S. I understand is in contemplation. It is concentration & organization that the democratic ["party" *interlined*] alone[?] want—as I understand they are now united—now to succeed & no possible delay should be allowed to intervene. I advert to this course of policy because I have recently witnessed the evil effects of a contrary course.

I have confidential letters from North Carolina & Tennessee that say the annexation question is carrying both States for the Democrats. Very Truly yours &c, H.W. Conner.

P.S. I do not at all mean to allude to Mr. [Francis W.] Pickens.

ALS with En in ScCleA. NOTE: The enclosed newspaper clipping states that Pickens is a candidate for the State Senate. The clipping adds: "Let our ablest men go into the State Legislature, where they can be of infinitely more service to us at the present time, than in Congress. Would that we could see enough of them there, and Mr. Calhoun in the Gubernatorial chair!" Henry Workman Conner (1797–1861) was a native of N.C. who had come to Charleston as a young man. He was president of the Bank of Charleston, 1839–1840 and 1843–1850, and president of the South Carolina Railroad, 1850–1853.

From A[LEXANDER] H. EVERETT, "Private & Confidential"

Boston, June 17, 1844

Dear Sir, I transmitted to your department, during the course of the present and past year, at the request of the writer, extracts from several letters, which I had received from a most intelligent and respectable correspondent in the island of Cuba, concerning the present critical situation of that superb colony. The writer has since temporarily left the Havana, and is now at Paris. I received a letter from him, a short time since, dated from that place, of which he wishes me to make a similar disposition, and of which I now enclose a translation.

I am not at liberty to mention the name of the writer, which, if known, would stamp his communications with a character of the highest authority; but they carry with them, in their style and substance, internal evidence of the sagacity, liberality and patriotism, by which they are dictated.

The troubles, now existing in the island of Cuba, have verified the anticipations, expressed in these letters, and render its present situation a matter of the deepest concern to this country. They have also an important bearing upon the question of the re-annexation of

Texas. The policy avowed by the British Government in regard to that republic is the same, upon which they have acted for some years past in regard to Cuba. The troubles, now existing in Cuba, exhibit the practical operation of the system, and afford the means of judging with certainty how far it may, with safety to us, be carried into effect in a contiguous territory.

I have requested my correspondent to send me a copy of the memorial on the situation of the island, which he has laid before the Spanish Ambassador at Paris, and, if I obtain it, I will take the liberty of communicating it to you. I am, with high respect, dear Sir, very truly & faithfully yours, A.H. Everett.

[Enclosure]
Translation
Extract from a letter dated at Paris, March 20, 1844.

. . . . I have learned with great pleasure, since my arrival here, the reappointment of Don Angel Calderon de la Barca, as Minister Plenipotentiary to the United States, not only because I consider him, as eminently qualified for the place, but on account of his intimate relations with you and other persons in the Union. I trust that you & they will induce him to convey to his government at Madrid more correct notions in regard to the proper method of administering the affairs of the island of Cuba.

You have seen how completely all my predictions, in regard to impending troubles in the island, have unfortunately been verified. Insurrections among the blacks succeed each other with frightful rapidity, & have assumed so alarming a character that the most intelligent planters are constantly expecting some tremendous catastrophe. The danger is increased by the fatal blindness—to give it no other name—with which [Captain] General [Leopoldo] O'Donnell connives at the slave trade. At the very moment, when the conspiracies, which had been formed at the Sabanilla were made known at Matanzas and Havana, fresh importations of blacks were introduced into those ports, and ships were being fitted out for still farther supplies. This open violation of the treaties with England exasperates the British Government, while the Abolitionists scarcely attempt to conceal their hostile intentions upon Cuba. They publicly avowed in the Anti-Slavery Convention, held last year at London, that, instead of sending agents and books to the island, they should in future employ other means, which they did not specify. Their nature is sufficiently explained by the existing insurrections. The conspiracy, which was brought to light by Oviedo in the Sabanilla estate, was most artfully contrived; and it is shewn beyond a doubt by the confessions of the leaders, that there were whites engaged in it. The local authorities, acting under the direction of the Captain General, have inflicted sanguinary punishments upon the leaders. This is the amount of what has been done in the way of repression, and this only serves to produce additional irritation. In the mean time the plantations throughout the island, all of which are now so many hot beds of insurrection, remain without defence, for the troops never leave the capitol. To complete the picture, there are daily new importations of Africans. The remonstrances of the wealthiest and most respectable planters of Matanzas and the Havana have been very badly received by the Captain General. He has also imposed silence upon Mr. de Betancourt, a most enlightened and respectable citizen of Puerto Principe, who, as I mentioned to you, has been attempting to solve, theoretically and practically, the important problem of introducing white labor into Cuba.

I have had several interviews with the Spanish Ambassador at this Court, Don F. Martinez de la Rosa, and have addressed to him a written memorial on the critical state of the island. He has promised to transmit it to Madrid, and to recommend it strongly to the attention of the Ministry, but I have very little hope from that quarter on account of the revolutionary state of the peninsula, and the continual changes in the Ministry. Little or nothing can be done, excepting on the island itself, through influence, exercised upon the mind of the Captain General. He should be induced, if possible, to open his eyes and adopt a different line of conduct. Some influence of this kind may, I think, be exercised by our Minister in the United States.

You will make use of my letters in any way that you may think best fitted to promote the object, observing, of course, the necessary discretion; and I trust that you will employ your personal influence in favor of our unhappy island, which reckons you among her friends and benefactors. . . .

ALS with En in ScCleA; PC of letter and PEx of En in Boucher and Brooks, eds., *Correspondence*, pp. 240, 216–217.

From [J.C.] de Figaniere e Morão, 6/17. He regrets that House bill No. 118, which would have lowered the import duties on Portuguese wines, was not enacted into law by Congress and hopes that some executive action can be taken to place the duties charged on Portuguese wines on the basis of those charged on wines of the most favored nations. ALS in DNA, RG 59 (State Department), Notes from Foreign Legations, Portugal, vol. 3 (M-57:3, frames 517–518).

From JOHN D. GARDINER, "Confidential"

Sag Harbor [N.Y.,] June 17th 1844

My very Dear Friend and Class-mate, Since our seperation at Yale nearly forty years have passed away. Though, during this period, we have passed thro' many trying scenes, it is, be assured, at this time a source of much pleasure to me, to think, that our friendship formed at that early day, yet continues in undiminished strength. No change of circumstances, no lapse of years, no vicissitudes of life have soiled the links, or, in the least weakened the chain that bound us together.

In all the spheres of public action, in which you have been called to move by the voice of our country, I have always esteemed you the same man, the same firm and ste[a]dfast friend, as on the memorable day of our seperation.

Of your entire public course I have been no inattentive or indifferent observer. And I am [*one word altered to* "happy"], to say, that, to the present hour, your political principles and conduct have met with my entire approval; and shewn me that you have always been the same true and undeviating Republican, in principle and practice, that you were forty years ago. In the full belief of these same principles I have hitherto lived; and in the faith of ["their" *interlined*] correctness, I trust we shall both die; for, in my estimation, they lie at the foundation of all our Free institutions, and form the only immoveable basis of our Republican Government. Let these pillars be torn away, and the whole beautiful Fabric, that rests upon them, will fall and tumble into ruins. To undermine and pull them down, old Federalism has been long at work, in a great variety of ways: But, thank heaven, all its labours have hitherto been in vain. The temple of Liberty, erected upon the bones and cemented by the blood of our Patriot Fathers, still stands unshaken, as the rock amid the waves, bidding defiance to its foes. My prayer is that it may abide forever. As this is a letter of true friendship, you will permit me to speak of my family, in which you have ever taken the livel[i]est interest. I have five promising sons, the youngest of whom is your name ["sake" *interlined*] Calhoun; now in his eighteenth year, and all of them, like their Father, Republicans to the heart. This I am proud to say, My eldest son, Samuel, was educated at Yale, studied law in the City of New York, and is now married and Settled in this place. My second and third sons are engaged in the merchantile business; my fourth son is in the University of the City of New York, and educated by his Uncle, the Brother of my wife, and is said to be one [of] the best scholars and speakers in that Institution. He is nearly twenty years of age. Calhoun is at home. I have kept him at school from childhood until recently. He has made commendable progress in his mathematical and Classical studies; and as I have not been able to obtain a situation for him at West Point, it was my desire to send him to College; but, as my pecuniary circumstances will not permit me to do it, unless providence should open the way, by which I may be enabled to accomplish this fondest desire of my heart, he must stop in his progress, and enter upon some other course. This, to me, is matter of very deep regret; and what more especially causes this regret is, that he is gifted with one of the finest minds, capable of grasping almost any subject with great facility, and developing itself rapidly.

Never do I feel so strong a desire to seize upon the mines of Potosi, as when I think of the education of the youth of our land, endowed with such intellects, but who for the want of the means of mental improvement, must live and die in comparitive uselessness and obscurity. But so it is—Necessity has no laws. I have but one hope left, that Calhoun may yet obtain a liberal education, and that is the promise of my eldest son Samuel, who says, he should be able to assist his brother Calhoun with means sufficient to go on with his studies, and complete his education if President [John] Tyler would give him the Collectorship of this place. It is a small office worth some four hundred & fifty dollars a year; and paid by the government as a sallery [*sic*]; as no duties are collected here worth the name. Of his qualifications for the office he could furnish the strongest testimonials from his Republican Friends & neighbors in this Community, and in the City of New York, who wish his appointment. Of the present Incumbent [Henry T. Dering], it need only be stated that he has held the office some twelve or fourteen years; that his Father held it before him thirty years, that he is a strong Modern Whig, belongs to that Party, is a warm friend, and devoted advocate of Mr. [Henry] Clay and his antidemocratic principles, that he is associated with the old Federalists; the bitterest & most vindictive enemies to President Tyler and his Administration, in the whole State; men who constitute a large majority of the voters in this place. The journal printed here semi-weekly, Called the Corrector, is their Organ & mouth piece; and which pours forth from its Columns, the vilest abuse, the lowest scurrility and the grossest falsehoods, against him and all his measures, while, the Watchman, the Republican organ here, has pursued a course directly the opposite. The best and only friends of his administration here, are old Republicans; who wish to have those of like feelings and views put in office. Among other considerations, an ardent wish for the Education of your name sake, joined to a sincere desire, that he ["may" *interlined*] be qualified to do honor, in future life, to that distinguished name, have prompted me to trouble you with this letter. You will allow me further to state, that during the late war, when the Cannon of the enemy was daily thundering in my ears, and, for more than two years, was threatining us daily with destruction and death; and, when the Federal peace party here, were pouring forth loud excrecrations [*sic*] against President [James] Madison, and all who supported the war, I shouldered my musket, went into the fort in the defence of the place & the Country; entered into the Camp from week to week; and, as a Republican Minister of the gospel, addressed the Soldiers, and endeavored by pourtraying the character of the enemy and the justice of our cause, to fire their bosoms with the spirit of patriotic ardor. And in this, I only did my duty as an American Citizen; and while most of the Clergy here as well as in New England and elsewhere, were uttering from the pulpit their sanctimonious denunciations, against the Administration and the war, I dared to defend them publically, with all my feeble powers of speech & pen, without the least disposition to yield an inch of ground to foes without or within. These facts are well known on this [Long] Island, and in this part of the Country. Another fact you will permit me to mention. In 1824 many of my Parishioners seceded from the Republican party and joined the Federalists and Mr. [John Quincy] Adams, and became identified with him in his political views. Some of these finding me ste[a]dfast in the doctrines of the old ["school" *interlined*] of [17]98, and unwilling to take a stand with them, manifested a degree of coolness towards me, and at length by their monied influence, brought others of the Congregation into their views; and in a few years they became the majority of the place. Finding that I could not be induced to go with them, they began to make influence against me as their Minister in the Presbyterian Congregation. This produced such an unhappy state of things, as led to the dissolution of my connection with them. This of course cut off my public support; and compelled me to rely wholly upon my own private & limited resources, for the Education of my children, and the maintenance of a large & helpless Family. Unwilling to leave my friends & my native Island, and seek for another settlement, I have since 1835 lived in retirement, devoting my time chiefly to books & the instruction of my Children; ["in which" *canceled*] In which I found the greatest earthly enjoyment; for never had a man a better wife & more promising children.

My oldest Son, Samuel, whom I have mentioned, is now 27 and settled in[?] as an attorney & Counsellor at Law here, and is much esteemed & respected. He looks to his profession entirely for the support of his family, and at present has not the means to educate his younger brother Calhoun, or he would cheerfully do it. That this may be done, with my last hope and last effort I now come to you as your old & faithful friend with these facts, and respectfully, but earnestly solicit your aid & influence with the President, to obtain the appointment of my Son Samuel to the place I have named. Your willingness, at all times, to afford me your assistance, has induced me to presume to ["ask" *interlined*] us[?] this particular favor at your hands. It is not for myself that I do it, but for the assistance of your name sake in his education. May I say it never was, & never will be needed more. The time has come when I must decide, whether Calhoun is to go on in his education, or to abandon it forever, and enter upon some other pursuit. My decission [*sic*] of this question, will depend upon the success or failure of this application. If successful he will be able to proceed, other wise he cannot. At this trying crisis of his life, he comes to you, as his and Father's Friend, and throws himself wholly upon your goodness, as his last resort, and will wait, with patience the result. I can say & do no more.

Should you succeed in his behalf, I trust, at some future day, he will meet you, with eyes filled, with tears of overflowing gratitude & joy; and feel that whatever, of consideration, he may hereafter attain in life, he is entirely indebted for it to the kindness of the Hon[orab]l[e] John C. Calhoun, his Father[']s old & faithful friend. I now leave the thing with you, without a doubt, that you ["will" *interlined*] do every thing, which you can for its accomplishment; and, at the same time, beg the favor of hearing from you, on the subject, at the earliest convenient opportunity. My health is good and my family well. I received a letter, a few days since, from our Class mate the Rev. Abel M'Ewen of New London [Conn.], stating that all the surviving members of our Class were ["request" *altered to* "requested"] to meet, in august next, in New Haven; on the day preceding Commencement. I hope to attend the meeting, & to have the pleasure of seeing you there. Is it probable that you will attend? If so please to inform me; as there is none of my class mates, to whom I have so strong an attachment, & whom I should be so much gratified to see. Whether I shall ever have this pleasure I know not; I will however indulge the pleasing hope. But my feelings have impelled me to trespass upon your time & patience quite to[o] long. Of this I am fully sensible. You will therefore pardon, the almost irresistible promptings of a warm & friendly heart. Hoping to hear from you soon I will only add, that you have my best wishes, & fervent prayers, for the health, prosperity, & happiness of your self & family. With sentiments of the highest esteem & respect, I remain your friend & Class mate, John D. Gardiner.

ALS in ScCleA.

From BEN E. GREEN

Legation of the U.S. of A.
Mexico, June 17th 1844

Dear Sir, In my despatch no. 7 [dated 6/15], accompanying this letter, I have expressed the opinion that Gen[era]l Santa Anna would rather see Texas in the hands of G[reat] B[ritain] than of the U.S. The reasons for this opinion are plain and powerful. The English merchants here are all in favor of his Govt.; because under his administration, negocios, (which in English may be rendered transactions effected by bribery) are most frequent and most profitable. They are his best customers; they pay most liberally for exclusive licenses to import, &c, &c. They put money in their pockets; he amasses golden ounces. They serve each other, and the interest of G[reat] B[ritain] is on his side. That you may have some idea of the extent to which this is carried, I mention the fact, (of the truth of which I was assured by Gen[era]l [Waddy] Thompson) that a Minister of the Treasury made over $100,000 in three months by these "negocios."

Naturally enough then he leans to the side of English interest. At the same time, he hates our Govt. and our people. The disgrace and misfortunes of San Jacinto he can neither forget nor forgive; and he would gladly see G[reat] B[ritain] encircle us on every side, & strangle our growing commerce and power in her strong embrace. His panegyrists pronounce him brave and generous. But the order, which he gave for the massacre of Fanning's [*sic*; James W. Fannin's] men [in the Texas war for independence], & which even [Gen. José] Urrea refused to execute, and the recent order of the 11th June, prove him [to] be more revengeful than brave, & more bloodthirsty than generous. He is now making preparations to invade Texas with a large force. The question arises, what are his views? A few months ago, the Minister of War acknowledged to Gen[era]l Thompson that it was impossible for Mexico to reconquer Texas. That he spoke Santa Anna's sentiments I do not doubt, for they are the sentiments of most intelligent men, in and out of Mexico. What then is his purpose in preparing an expedition and sending troops secretly to the frontier? Is it the mere thirst of blood? Is it that he merely seeks to ravage the country, to surprise, kill and make prisoners, and then retire, after the manner of Gen[era]l [Adrian] Wol[l] from Bejar?

I informed you in my last despatch that a special messenger had been sent to England in the last Havana packet. Immediately afterwards, it was rumoured that he had been sent to offer to England the sale of Texas. This I could not for a moment believe; for besides, that Mexico, not being in possession of Texas, could not sell, England, having acknowledged the independence of Texas, could not buy of Mexico. I have since however been led to believe (chiefly from the change of feeling towards Texas in the B[ritish] legation here) that there may be some truth in what I supposed at first to be the most ridiculous of rumours.

["I informed you in my" *canceled*.] Mexico has rejected the opportunity of settling this Texas war, from which the Mexican Govt. itself has no hopes of a favourable conclusion. Supposing that the feelings of Mexico were friendly to the U.S., the Treaty of annexation, accompanied with the explanations offered to Mexico, afforded a favourable opportunity, and what, Gen[era]l Thompson was convinced, Santa Anna desired. The latter now proposes, at heavy expense and with an exhausted treasury, to renew what he knows to be a fruitless struggle. With an army of 30,000 men he may overrun the country; but he can not keep possession or subdue it. He has no hopes that the Texans will either submit to his Govt., or that he will be able to drive them permanently from the country. He knows that, though once defeated, they will rally, gathering strength from each defeat. Why then does he persist? Will a sanguinary and vindictive spirit account for it, fully & satisfactorily? It might perhaps, were it not that the feelings of the English Legation here have wonderfully changed of late, as regards Texas. From being her warm friends and the advocates of her independence, they now *damn* the Texans, and the British Minister says, that his Govt. committed a great mistake in ever recognizing their independence. Why? *Because as yet they had gained nothing by it.*

It may then be that Santa Anna expects, by a rapid movement

103

with a large army, to overrun Texas; & hold it some 60 or 90 days, & then by a hasty transfer, sell it to England, before the Texans shall be able to rally and drive him back.

That this is Santa Anna's expectation, I have little doubt. That England would accept such a proposition, with the certainty of a war with the U.S. as the consequence, is more questionable, and I, for one, can not believe that she would. Certain I am, however, that the desire of the British Legation here, *now* is, not for the independence of Texas, but for her subjugation; and I deem it proper to inform you of the ["present" *interlined*] feelings of that legation here, to put you on the "qui vive", and to leave you to draw your own inferences. When the sanguinary order of the 11th inst. appeared in the Diario, I applied to the British Minister to unite with me in protesting against it. His reply was that he presumed the Texans were to be treated by Mexico as rebels, and he declined to do more than to speak to Mr. [Jose M. de] Bocanegra, requesting verbally that the order should not be put in force against English subjects. Very Respectfully Your ob[edien]t Serv[an]t, Ben E. Green.

[Enclosure]
Waddy Thompson [Jr.] to Ben E. Green

Vera Cruz, Mar[ch] 27th 1844

My Dear Sir, If the Texas Commissioners [to Mexico] arrive, tell them that [Jose M.] Tornel told me, a few days before I left—"Texas is gone forever from Mexico. All we desire is to save the 'decoro nacional.' Let them only acknowledge our supremacy, and pay us some nominal sum, say $20,000, and they will then be practically independent."

I told Santa Anna in a conversation on the subject that the great difficulty would be the slavery question. He replied, that unfortunately they had a Treaty with England, which stipulated that slavery should not exist in any part of Mexico; that he was sorry for it, but that there was no remedy. He said that the most that could be done would be to say nothing about it in the negotiation. But that he had no expectation whatever of a favourable result.

But they are very anxious for a settlement. &c &c &c (Signed), Waddy Thompson.

(See over [for Memorandum by Green])

Memorandum—Here is an acknowledgement that Mexico is unable to enforce the right, which she asserts, to reconquer Texas. The person, who makes it, is one of the Cabinet, the Minister of War, who ought to be best informed on the subject of Mexico's military abilities.

At the time it was made, he was universally admitted to be the best informed and ablest of the Cabinet, of which he was a leading spirit, & whose sentiments he spoke.

How long then are other nations to wait upon the "decoro nacional" of Mexico? Certainly not longer than their own safety & interests permit.

ALS (Private) with En in DNA, RG 59 (State Department), Diplomatic Despatches, Mexico, vol. 12 (M-97:13), received 7/15; draft (dated 6/7) in NcU, Duff Green Papers (published microfilm, roll 5, frames 564–566).

From Rob[er]t Monroe Harrison

United States Consulate
Kingston, Jamaica, 17th June 1844
Sir, I do myself the honor to inform you that General [Jean Pierre] "Boyer" late President of Haiti returned to this island on the 15th inst. in the last Packet inconsequence of the climate of France being too cold (as it is here given out by some persons) for his constitution; whilst others are of an opinion that overtures have been made to him by either France or England, as both seem well disposed to take that pretended Republic under their protection.

If that should be the case I think the former will be before hand with the latter, as it is understood here that she is already in possession of "Samana" a place where there is a fine Harbour and Safe Bay, capable of containing the fleets of both nations and a very healthy place—Said to have been ceded to them by the Spanish inhabitants who have separated from the "Haitians." And as an instalment is now due the French Government from that Republic which is without a cent, the possession may be considered as permanently secured.

The Mulattos are favourably inclined to the English, but as they are not the one twentieth part as strong as the negroes, they will have to succumb to the wishes of the latter, who it is said have no good will to either the English or French. [Philippe] "Guerrier" (a negro) who is now President, is a drunken old fellow very illiterate and it is therefore supposed that he will not retain his situation for any length of time.

Captain [Thomas W.] "Freelon" of the United States Ship "Preble" who was induced to go to "Aux Cayes" at my request, has rendered very important Services not only to our own Citizens trading to that place but to foreigners and Haitians also, whose property would have been sacrificed but for his active and timely interference. With profound respect I have the honor to be Sir Your Ob[edien]t & most humble Servant, Robt. Monroe Harrison.

LS (No. 290) in DNA, RG 59 (State Department), Consular Despatches, Kingston, vol. 9 (T-31:9), received 7/19.

T[ILGHMAN] A. HOWARD
to Rich[ar]d [K.] Crallé

Washington City, 17 June 1844

Sir, In answer to your letter of the ["morning" *canceled and* "1st inst." *interlined*] informing me of my appointment by the president of the U. States by and with the advice & consent of the Senate as Chargé de'affaires to the republic of Texas, I have the honor to state that in in [*sic*] pursuance of assurances already given by me to the president & to the Secretary of State, I accept the appointment, and hold myself in readiness to leave the U. States to enter upon the duties of the station as soon as it shall please the Department to require my departure. I have the honor to be Sir Y[ou]r Ob[e]d[ien]t Servant, T.A. Howard.

ALS in DNA, RG 59 (State Department), Diplomatic Despatches, Texas, vol. 2 (T-728:2, frame 371), received 6/17.

To TILGHMAN A. HOWARD

Department of State
Washington, 17th June, 1844

Sir: It is expected that the books and papers of the Legation of the United States in Texas will be found in the custody of Mr. [William S.] Murphy, your predecessor, or in that of Mr. [Archibald M.] Green, our Consul at Galvezton, to whom Mr. Murphy was directed to deliver them in case he should leave that country before you arrived. All the books and documents with which it is customary to furnish the Legations abroad have, from time to time, been sent to that in Texas; and it is consequently presumed that you will find a complete sett of them there. If, however, any should be missing, the department, when informed of the deficiencies, will endeavor to supply them.

Herewith you will receive the following documents, which will be useful or necessary for the discharge of your official duties.

1. Your Commission [dated 6/11] as Chargé d'Affaires of the United States to the Republic of Texas.

2. A letter accrediting you in that character to the Secretary of State of that Republic [Anson Jones].

3. A special passport [dated 6/17].

4. Printed personal instructions, with which you will strictly comply.

According to a general rule, the salary of a diplomatic agent of the United States begins with the date of his Commission, provided he sets out for his post within thirty days from that date or assigns satisfactory reasons for further delay. Your salary will consequently begin on the 11th of this month. As it becomes due, you will draw on this department for it and, also, for the contingent expenses of the Legation, which last must not exceed five hundred dollars a year without special authority. I am, Sir, your obedient servant, J.C. Calhoun.

LS (No. 2) with Ens in DNA, RG 84 (Foreign Posts), Records of the Texas Legation; variant FC in DNA, RG 59 (State Department), Diplomatic Instructions, Texas, 1:101 (M-77:161). NOTE: Enclosed with the first version of this letter is the "printed personal instructions" mentioned by Calhoun. This is an undated pamphlet of eight pages (with a three-page supplement) entitled *Personal Instructions to the Diplomatic Agents of the United States in Foreign Countries.* It sets forth detailed information about duties, conduct, compensation, accounts, and other matters.

To [ANSON JONES], Secretary of State of Texas

Department of State
Washington, 17th June, 1844

Sir: The President of the United States [John Tyler] having thought proper to name Tilghman A. Howard their Chargé d'Affaires to the Republic of Texas, I have the honor of announcing the same to Your Excellency and of praying you to give credence to whatever he shall say to you on my part. He knows the concern our Republic takes in the interest and prosperity of Texas, our strong desire to cultivate its friendship, and to deserve it by all the good offices which may be in our power. He knows also my zeal to promote these by whatever may depend upon my Ministry. I have no doubt that Mr. Howard will so conduct himself as to meet your confidence, and I avail myself with pleasure of this occasion of tendering to you assurances of my high and distinguished consideration. J.C. Calhoun.

LS and CC in Tx, Records of the Texas Republic Department of State, U.S. Diplomatic Correspondence; FC in Tx, Records of the Texas Republic Department of State, Copybooks of Letters Received from Texan and Foreign Representatives, vol. 2–1/98, p. 512; FC in DNA, RG 59 (State Department), Credences, 3:83.

From Pleasant Jordan, Little Rock, 6/17. He asks for an appointment to be U.S. District Attorney for Ark. He has practiced law in Little Rock for two years and plans to live there permanently. He will submit testimonials of his character and qualifications if necessary but reminds Calhoun of their short personal acquaintance when he studied law at Pendleton and Anderson, S.C. ALS in DNA, RG 59 (State Department), Applications and Recommendations, 1837–1845, Jordan (M-687:17, frames 692–694).

To [John Y.] Mason, Secretary of the Navy, 6/17. Calhoun introduces Dr. Eli S. Davis. "The Doctor resided many years in South Carolina, but has been a resident at Memphis Tennessee for several years since. You will find him intelligent and well informed in relation to that portion of our country. He will explain the object he has in view." ALU (signature clipped) in DNA, RG 45 (Naval Records), Miscellaneous Letters Received by the Secretary of the Navy, 1844, June:139 (M-124:206).

From JOHN W. NESBITT and Others

Philadelphia, June 17, 1844

Sir, The undersigned Committee appointed by the Democratic Citizens of the first Congressional District of Pennsylvania, respectfully tender to you an invitation to unite with them in the Celebration of the 4th of July 1844. In thus addressing you we are actuated by an exalted opinion of your eminent talents and distinguished Public Services and also by a desire to extend an humble mark of respect to that Chivalrous State of the South, with whose honour and interests your name is so closely identified. Should your engagements permit your acceptance, we promise you on behalf of our Constituents a hearty welcome. We have the Honour to be very respectfully Your friends & fellow Citizens, John W. Nesbitt, Thomas McCully, B[enjamin] M. Evans, W[illia]m Harleson, John Thomson, Committee on Invitations.

LS in ScCleA. NOTE: An AEU by Calhoun reads: "Invitation to dine on the 4th July."

To R[ICHARD] PAKENHAM

Department of State
Washington, 17th June, 1844

Sir: I have the honor to acknowledge the receipt of your letter of the 10th instant, transmitting, with a view to the fulfilment of the 4th article of the treaty of Washington, authenticated copies of three grants of lands situated on the south side of the St. John's river, and within the territory of the United States, which documents had been forwarded to you for this purpose by His Excellency the Lieutenant Governor of New Brunswick [Thomas Carleton]; and at the same time acquainting me that an act had been passed by the Legislature of New Brunswick to enable the Government of the Province to carry into effect the provisions of the article referred to, in respect to lands situated on the north side of the river and within British Territory.

I will not fail to take an early occasion to communicate copies of these papers, together with a transcript of your letter, to their Excellencies the Governors of the States of Massachusetts and of Maine [George N. Briggs and Hugh J. Anderson], respectively, who have been for some time past, very desirous to be put in possession of certified copies of the grants in question. I have the honor to be, With high consideration, Sir, Your obedient servant, J.C. Calhoun.

FC in DNA, RG 59 (State Department), Notes to Foreign Legations, Great Britain, 7:19 (M-99:36); PC in House Document No. 110, 29th Cong., 1st Sess., pp. 35–36. NOTE: The disposition of land grants along the Maine–New Brunswick border, in accordance with the Treaty of Washington of 1842, was the subject of much subsequent correspondence of Calhoun with Pakenham and with the governors of Mass. and Maine, most of which correspondence is omitted from this publication.

To Alexander Powell, Philadelphia, 6/17. "Your nomination as Consul of the U.S. for Altona [in Germany] having been rejected by the Senate, it becomes my duty to inform you that the Commission given you in the recess of that body, expires this day." FC in DNA, RG 59 (State Department), Consular Instructions, 10:252.

To ROBERT WICKLIFFE, JR., Turin

Department of State
Washington, 17th June, 1844

Sir: The Senate having advised, and consented to, your appointment, as Chargé d'Affaires of the United States to Sardinia, I herewith transmit to you, your commission in that character.

Your despatches of the 17th, 21st and 30th of March—the last communicating the opinions of the American Consuls at London and Liverpool [Thomas Aspinwall and James Hagarty, respectively], on the subject of protests, to which the two former despatches related—have been received. A reference to the Treaty of Commerce, which subsists between the United States and Sardinia, will show, that there are no principles in it, which were intended to, or can overrule, or control, the established municipal law of that country, in regard to the admissibility of evidence in any of His Sardinian Majesty's Courts, or to the forms to be observed by Captains of American vessels arriving in the ports of Sardinia; unless such regulation should operate in favor of the national or any other flag, to the disadvantage of our own.

However onerous and peculiar the requirements of the Sardinian Government may be in these respects, it must be obvious that we have no just ground of complaint. It is certainly the duty of the American Representative to use every exertion to procure modifications in the laws and regulations of the country in which he resides, calculated to facilitate commerce and simplify the formal proceedings required upon the entry of American ships; but, at the same time, acting under higher and more general considerations, the greatest care should always be taken by him, never to vex and annoy the Government to which he may be accredited, by presenting to, or urging upon, it claims that may be regarded as either unreasonable or dubious.

By an examination of the list of books, and documents, given in your No. 2, of the 17th February, it is perceived that your Legation is supplied with all the volumes allowed by the Department.

Your despatches of the 19th March, No. 4, and of the 10th April, (not numbered), have also been received. That of the 17th March, however, was not numbered. I am, Sir, respectfully, Your obedient Servant, J.C. Calhoun.

FC (No. 5) in DNA, RG 59 (State Department), Diplomatic Instructions, Italy, 1:27–29 (M-77:101); FC in DNA, RG 84 (Foreign Posts), Italy, Sardinia, 2:236–[237]; PC in Jameson, ed., *Correspondence*, pp. 598–599.

To WILLIAM WILKINS, Secretary of War

Department of State
Washington, June 17th 1844
Sir: This Department has been informed by a letter of the 7th instant from the Colonel of Topographical Engineers [John J. Abert], in answer to inquiries upon the subject, that some changes have recently been made in the detail of officers from that Corps for duty in the joint demarkation of the boundary under the 1st article of the treaty of Washington.

The detail, it appears, consists at present of the following officers, vizt.

Major J[ames] D. Graham, head of the Scientific Corps, and principal Astronomer for the U.S.
1st Lieut[enant] W[illiam] H. Emory
2d Lieut[enant] George Thom
2d Lieut[enant] A[miel] W. Whipple
Br[eve]t 2d Lieut[enant] W[illiam] F. Raynolds.

This Department has to request that two more officers of the Corps of Topographical Engineers may be detailed for this service, and that the detail from that Corps as well as that which has been made from the artillery, of 1 Lieutenant, 1 Sergeant, 2 Corporals, and 26 privates may be ordered as a permanent detail, and not liable to change by transfers for other Service until the field and office duties in connexion with the Survey and demarcation of the boundary shall have been completed. It is essential that the Officers upon this duty should be ready and efficient astronomical observers and Computers, and the instruction and experience which are once required should be made available until the whole work is completed.

The Department has also to request that the necessary orders may be given to the Quartermaster's and Commissary's Departments for furnishing the necessary transportation, subsistence and Camp equipage for the artillery detachment, upon the requisition of the officer in command of the Scientific Corps.

In order to carry on a system of signals for the determination of differences of longitude along the line, it is requested that one hundred two pound rockets of good quality, with Socket Sticks, and 100 port fires each 16 or 18 inches long, may be immediately furnished on the requisition of the head of the Scientific Corps.

As early an answer as may be convenient is respectfully asked from the Hon[ora]ble the Secretary of War. I have the honor to be, Very respectfully, Your obedient Servant, J.C. Calhoun.

LS in DNA, RG 92 (Quartermaster General), Consolidated Correspondence File, Boundary, Northeast Survey; FC in DNA, RG 59 (State Department), Domestic Letters, 34:279–281 (M-40:32).

JUNE 18–30, 1844

◫

The adjournment of Congress on June 17 meant no cessation of work for the Secretary of State. He could, however, turn his attention to difficult and pressing matters. Prominent among his many correspondents were the numerous American citizens who had outstanding financial claims against Mexico. Their uneasiness was evident. Always problematic, the satisfaction of such claims was rendered even more so by the prospect of broken relations with Mexico over the annexation of Texas. These citizens included both those whose claims had not yet been settled and those who feared the interruption of instalment payments promised in earlier conventions.

Pending claims was only one of several delicate matters that Calhoun had to deal with in careful instructions on June 20 to Wilson Shannon, just resigned as Governor of Ohio in order to depart for Mexico as the American Minister there. Equally careful orders had to be drafted, two days before, for Tilghman A. Howard, about to depart for the capital of the Texas Republic. Texas was to be assured that "the loss of the Treaty does not necessarily involve the failure of the great object [of annexation] which it contemplated." In fact, Calhoun felt that annexation could be regarded as nearly certain, though there was to be an unfortunate delay while the domestic political situation resolved itself by means of the Presidential election in November and the meeting of Congress in December. There were two serious problems in the meantime. One of these was the delicate political, diplomatic, military, and Constitutional question of the defense of Texas while annexation was unconsummated.

The other problem was evident in Calhoun's concluding remarks to Howard. Annexation "has taken so deep and general a hold on the public mind that it must ultimately triumph, should it not be abandoned by the Government and People of Texas." The last few words expressed Calhoun's greatest anxiety—that Texas in need or despair would turn away to other alliances, which would be a disaster to the future of the American Union.

Relations with Europe also claimed attention. An equally delicate, if not so urgent and perilous a situation as Texas, had to be

113

handled in instructions on June 28 to Henry Wheaton, the able American Minister in Berlin. The Senate had neither ratified nor rejected the treaty with the German Customs Union which had been concluded in March by Wheaton after arduous labors. How to keep open the hope and possibility of future ratification, without giving promises beyond the power of the executive branch to keep, and still perpetuate the friendly relations that had been developing?

A more pleasant event in regard to European relations occurred on the last day of the Congressional session, as Calhoun wrote to his daughter, Anna Maria, the next day, June 18. Anna's husband, Thomas G. Clemson, already an experienced student, engineer, and traveller in Europe, was unanimously confirmed by the Senate as United States Chargé d'Affaires in Belgium. Given Calhoun's well-known distaste for political spoils, it doubtless added to his pleasure that this successful appointment had required no removal. Clemson was to replace an incumbent who had long been pleading for permission to resign and come home.

〚〛

CIRCULAR to U.S. Consuls and Commercial Agents "Residing on the Western Coast of South America, & the Islands of the Pacific"

Department of State
Washington, June 18th 1844

Gentlemen, The Consul of Prussia residing in New York, Mr. J[ohann] W. Schmidt, having informed this Department, that a company has been formed at Stettin, for the purpose of carrying on the Whaling business, in the South Seas, in the success of which the King of Prussia himself takes a great and personal interest, and his Government being without Agents of any kind in those Regions, where her flag is probably entirely unknown, having asked that the advice, assistance, and protection, compatible with their official station, of the Consuls and Commercial Agents of the U. States, may be extended to the Ship "Borussia" Capt. Hartwig and her Crew, which Ship fitted out by the said Company, has arrived as he states at New Bedford, for the purpose of completing her equipment, & to engage able & experienced Americans, as Officers, Harpooners & Boatsteerers and will shortly proceed on her voyage, I now in a ready compliance therewith address to you this Circular letter, and request, that you will should occasion call for it, render to the said Ship "Borussia," her Captain and Crew, such advice, aid, protection and assistance as may be in your power & as may be consistent with your public station & the laws of the Country in which you reside. I am, &c, J.C. Calhoun.

FC in DNA, RG 59 (State Department), Consular Instructions, 11:248–249.

To A[nna] M[aria Calhoun] Clemson, [Edgefield District, S.C.]

Washington, 18th June 1844
My dear Anna, I have delayed answering your letter [of 6/1] till I could reply with certainty to your several enquiries.

Mr. [Thomas G.] Clemson was yesterday nominated to Belgium, as Charge de Affairs, and unanimously confirmed. The appointment takes effect after the 1st of August, so that he ought to be here by that time or shortly after. The outfit is $4500 ["&" *canceled*] with an annual salary of the same amount.

I do not feel myself prepared to answer, as to the arrangement he ought to make ["as" *canceled and* "in reference" *interlined*] to his place and his affairs. It seems to me, however, indispensible, that he should get some one in the neighbourhood in whose judgement he can confide in, to visit the place frequently & to have the power of general superintendence, invested in him with the right, if he should think proper, of dissmising[?] and ["appoint" *canceled*] employing ["another" *canceled*] overseers. To secure the service of such an one, he ought not to hesitate to give an adequate compensation. It ought to be made his duty to visit & inspect the place at least once a week, and to give such orders as he may deem necessary. It might be made his duty to write to me from time to time & to give me all necessary information ["as to" *interlined*] how the affairs of the place are conducted, & to obey such instructions, in reference to it, as I might think proper to give. I make these ["remarks" *interlined*] as suggestions.

In reference to a nurse, if you cannot succeed in getting a suitable one in Charleston, I would advise you to postpone the employment of one till you get to New York, where, I have no doubt, you can succeed, through the aid of [James] Ed[ward] Boisseau, to get one that will suit you well.

Patrick [Calhoun] & John [C. Calhoun, Jr.] left here two weeks since. I had a letter from the latter dated at Louisville. He was delighted with the journey, & thinks his health is improved. He has great confidence in the good effect of the excursion. I do hope it may be realised, but I cannot but be very uneasy about him. I fear the disease has taken a deep hold.

I am much pressed for time & you must excuse a short letter. My health remains good. Kiss the children [John Calhoun Clemson and Floride Elizabeth Clemson] for their grand father. With love to Mr. Clemson, I am your affectionate father, [J.C. Calhoun.]

ALU (signature clipped) in ScCleA.

From Tho[ma]s G. Clemson

Cane Brake [Edgefield District, S.C.] June 18th 1844
My dear Sir, Herewith I enclose a letter to Mr. [J.B.] Crockett[,] my attorney in St. Louis[.] You would oblige me by putting your frank on the back of it & expediting it.

We are all well & the crop doing as well as could be anticipated. The corn crop looks like a cane Brake in reality. For the last week we have had abundant rains, too much for good[,] and the weather has been cold & chilly[,] so much so that I am now sitting by a fire. The wet weather is bringing out the grass & weeds most rapidly so that we are kept very busy.

I am very much pleased to hear that Dr. [James H.] Relfe speaks so confidently of John[']s [that is, John C. Calhoun, Jr.'s] recovery[.] I hope & trust that it may be so, for he is really a fine fellow.

I have written to Mr. Crockett the purport of the conversation you were kind enough to have with Dr. Relfe on the subject of the mine La Motte suit. I have requested him (Mr. Crockett) to receive any propositions the parties might make & forward them to me but I will leave the letter open so that if [*one word canceled*] you have leisure & inclination you can peruse it[;] if not please seal it [and] send it on.

I am of course very much obliged to you for your kind intercession with the President [John Tyler] in my behalf. I wrote you a letter of queries connected with the subject in order that I may act advisedly. From what I know of Belgium I think a residence of [a] year there can not otherwise than give great pleasure to Anna [Maria Calhoun Clemson]. If you can put your hand on any document relative to our transactions with that country (Belgium) you would oblige me by sending it to me, or if you know of any work particularly useful on Diplomatic correspondence I should be happy to have its name that I may procure it for perusal.

Anna joins me in sending much love. Your affectionate son, Thos. G. Clemson.

N.B. Anna requests me to say that she wrote & sent her letter to Edgefield & hopes you got it. I should like to hear from you as soon as possible as I shall remain in uncertainty until I hear & wishing to time my arrangements. T.G.C.

ALS in ScCleA.

To TILGHMAN A. HOWARD, [U.S. Chargé d'Affaires to Texas, Washington]

Department of State
Washington, June 18th 1844

Sir: Your letter of the 17th Instant notifying your acceptance of the appointment tendered you by the President [John Tyler] as Chargé d'Affaires of the United States near the Government of Texas, and expressing your readiness to proceed on your mission, has been received at this Department; and I have now the honor to enclose to you your Commission, together with a Credential Letter, addressed to the Secretary of State of that Republic, with an open copy of the same, for your inspection and use. In presenting this letter of credence you will take the occasion to express to the Secretary of State the warm interest felt by the President of the United States in the happiness and prosperity of the Government and People of Texas, and the earnest desire which animates him to preserve and strengthen the bonds of good feeling and kind relations which now happily subsist between the two Countries. The recent rejection of the Treaty of Annexation by the Senate, has placed these relations in a very delicate and hazardous state; and the great object of your mission is to prevent, by every exertion in your power, the dangerous consequences to which it may lead.

The first step towards the accomplishment of so desirable a result, will be to satisfy the Government of Texas that the loss of the Treaty does not necessarily involve the failure of the great object which it contemplated. It is now admitted that what was sought to be effected by the Treaty, submitted to the Senate, may be secured by a Joint Resolution of the two Houses of Congress, incorporating all its provisions. This mode of effecting it will have the advantage of requiring only a majority of the two Houses, instead of two-thirds of the Senate. A Joint Resolution for this purpose has accordingly been introduced, by Mr. [George] McDuffie, of South Carolina, in the Senate, and was laid on the table by a vote of 19 to 27, (many members being absent), on the ground that there was not sufficient time to act on it. Three of the absentees, and also three who voted to lay on the table, were known to be favourable to Annexation; which shows that, in a full Senate, and supposing the other absentees unfavourable, but two Senators are required to constitute a majority of the whole number.

In the other House the indications are still more favourable; as appears by the votes to which the President's recent Message, communicating the Treaty and accompanying Documents to that body, gave rise. On the motion to lay the Message and Documents on the Table, the vote stood 66 yeas to 118 nays: and on that to suspend the rules, with a view to the printing of 15,000 extra copies, it stood 108 yeas to 79 nays. All of which would seem to indicate that there is already a majority in the House in favor of Annexation. In addition to these facts, it may be safely stated, from the indications in the Country, that, amongst the people, a far larger proportion is in favour of Annexation, and that it is still on the increase. On this point, however, it is not deemed necessary to enlarge; as your residence here, during the past winter, with all the facilities of ascertaining the state and current of public opinion, will enable you to sustain its correctness from your own information. Indeed the force of the popular sentiment in favour of Annexation, is believed to be so strong, as to afford just grounds to hope that, on ["the return to" *canceled and* "consulting with" *interlined*] their constituents, it will ["compel" *canceled and* "induce" *interlined*] a sufficient number to make a majority, especially from the South and West, to ["change their opinions and" *canceled*] vote for the measure, and you may assure the Government of Texas that the President is resolved to call an extra session of Congress, whenever there is cause to believe that there is a sufficient change to secure the passage of a Joint Resolution by both Houses.

The importance of satisfying the Government of Texas that the non-approval of the Treaty does not involve the loss of Annexation, and that there is still reasonable grounds to hope for its success, is based on the belief that the Government and people of Texas are so deeply devoted to the measure, that they will not abandon it so long as there is any reasonable hope of its success. In this belief we cannot feel that we are mistaken. The evidences they have given of such a disposition, are so numerous and strong, that we cannot permit ourselves to doubt. Indeed, an opposite conclusion would imply, that they were not only insensible to the feelings and sympathies which belong to a common origin, but blind to their own future safety and prosperity. The danger is, that the revulsion of disappointed hopes highly excited, may be seized upon by an interested and wily diplomacy, and made the means of seducing them to seek and form other alliance with the Power, which, ["there is reason to fear," *interlined*] has been eagerly watching the favourable opportunity.

Of all the results which could follow, this, in the end, would be the most disastrous to Texas, to the United States, and to the whole American Continent. The Government of Texas would be blind, indeed, not to see that Great Britain, in seeking its alliance, seeks it for purposes purely selfish. She looks to her interests exclusively, not to the interests of Texas; and that whatever motive may be held out, the result, in the end, must be abject submission and degradation on the part of Texas. Such has ever been the fate of the smaller in alliances between them and larger communities; and in none would the connection be followed by more oppressive consequences, than between Texas and Great Britain. Their interests would be opposite in many and important particulars. Her vast East-Indian Possessions exercise a controlling influence over her in all commercial questions in which their interests come in conflict with the products of this Continent. To those she has already sacrificed her West-India Islands; and it would be the height of folly for Texas—as a dependent community—to expect a better fate. The enlightened Chief Magistrate of the Republic of Texas [Samuel Houston], has too much intelligence not to see that this would be the consequence of such an alliance; and too much patriotism to seek it while one hope remained of incorporating it into our glorious Union. He has already acquired too much fame to hazard it by a step which Texas would long deplore; and which, in after times could not fail to impair his just renown; while, on the other hand, by successfully carrying out the measure with which he is so intimately identified, he would fill the measure of his Country's glory, and his own.

In regard to the orders which have been, heretofore, given to the officers in command of the Military and Naval force of the United States, in the Gulf of Mexico, and on the frontiers of Texas, you may assure the Government of Texas that there will be no ["material" *interlined*] change, except that the communications made to it by the officer commanding the military as well as the naval force, will be made through the Chargé d'Affaires of the United States.

You will consider these, as constituting the general outline of your instructions. Much must be left to your judgment and discretion as to the means and matters most proper to be employed in securing the attachment of the Government and People of Texas, in removing existing, and preventing future causes of discontent and alienation, and of advancing the great object of Annexation so essential to the peace and safety of both Countries. In conclusion, you may give assurance that Annexation has been defeated at the present time mainly by the controlling influence of ["the Presidential election" *canceled and* "temporary causes" *interlined*]; but that ["let the election terminate as it may," *canceled*] the ["cause" *canceled and* "measure" *interlined*] has taken so deep and general a hold on the public mind that it must ultimately triumph, should it not be abandoned by the Government and People of Texas. I am, Sir, very respectfully, Your obedient Servant, J.C. Calhoun.

LS (No. 1) in DLC, Andrew Jackson Donelson Papers; FC in DNA, RG 59 (State Department), Diplomatic Instructions, Texas, 1:96–100 (M-77:161); CCEx in Tx, Records of the Texas Republic Department of State, Letters and Dispatches Sent by the Texas Legation in Washington, vol. 1.

John Tyler to Gen. [TILGHMAN A.] HOWARD

Washington, June 18 1844

D[ea]r Sir, I cannot permit you to take your departure from Washington without placing in your hands the copy of a communication made me two days ago, and which you will recognize as being signed by many of the leading members of the H[ouse] of R[epresentatives]. The paper pledges the associates of the signers to use their efforts to possess the people with the merits of the Texas question— and to elicit an expression of public sentiment in its favor. You will also perceive that it bears the signature of a member from every delegation but that of three States—and I do not doubt but that the

Democracy of those States, as well as the others will cause their voices plainly to be heard upon the question.

Wishing you a prosperous trip to Texas and a glorious success in accomplishing the high purposes of your mission I salute you most cordially and sincerely, John Tyler.

[Enclosure]

June 15th 1844

We the undersigned, Members of the House of Representatives, from the respective States attached to our names, desire to assure the President, that we have not and shall not surrender the cause of annexing Texas to this Union; but that we are resolved immediately after the adjournment of the present session of Congress to return to our respective States and to use the most active means to bring the question directly before the people to elicit an expression of their opinions in its favour—and we feel assured in this effort we shall be sustained by our democratic associates. Edw[ar]d Cross of Arkansas, Jno. Slidell of Louisiana, W[illiam] H. Hammett of Miss., Jno. Jamieson [sic; Jamison] of Mis[s]ouri, A[aron] V. Brown of Tennessee, Jno. W. Tibbetts of Kentucky, James E. Belsur [sic; Belser] of Alabama, Edw[ar]d J. Black of Georgia, R[obert] B. Rhett of South Carolina, R[omulus] M. Saunders of North Carolina, J.H. [sic; Thomas H.] Bayly of Virginia, Samuel Simons Con[n]ecticut, Richd. [sic; Shepard] Cary Maine, A[lexander] Duncan Ohio, C[harles] J. Ingersoll Pen[n]s[ylvani]a, S[tephen] A. Douglass [sic] Illinois, Edmund Burke, New Hampshire, Tho[ma]s [J.] Hendley [sic; Henley] Indiana.

ALS with En in DNA, RG 84 (Foreign Posts), Texas.

From STEWART NEWELL

Consulate of the United States
Port of Sabine
June 18th 1844

Sir, As expressed in my former letter, which I had the Honor, to address to the Department, I indulged the hope, that nothing should occur, to require further complaint from me, relative to the conduct, of our late Charge de'Affaires, and I assure the Hon. Secretary, a matter of trifling moment, would not have induced this, communication, but if the Department, are in possession, of the Despatches, forwarded from this Legation, to the Department, as announced in the Public Press, of New Orleans, on the 3d inst., there, will be developed, a scheme of ruin, to my private, and official character, that my firm conviction, induces the belief, will be stamped, with the character it deserves, for Malice, and misrepresentation towards me, and my Acts, that requires more, than an expression of feeling, in private, from me, and ["for" *interlined*] a refutation of which, for the first time, in *my* life, I have been dragged before the Public, to defend myself, from Slander, and serious charges, that no honorable Man, would tamely submit to, and against which, if no adequate punishment, exists within the Department, leaves *no* alternative, but for the parties, to defend themselves, in such manner, as may be best suited, to the case.

Gen[era]l [William S.] Murphy thought proper, to forward some despatches, as we, are Publickly informed, to New Orleans, and delivered them, as p[e]r previous arrangement, into the custody ["of" *interlined*] a certain J[ames] J. Wright, who is well known, throughout most of Texas, as a Man of notorious bad character, and whose bad reputation, was known to Gen[era]l Murphy, at the time. *He* upon his arrival, communicated certain portions of said Despatches, as will be found, in the Republican, and Jeffersonian, published in N[ew] Orleans, on the 3d inst. Certain facts, relative to the Steamer Scioto Belle, and this, Wright[']s, connection with her, as Master, have been, before laid, before the Department, and others, now enclosed, will I hope, prove sufficient, to establish his proper reputation, with the Department. This is the Man, selected to carry these Despatches, and whose Expences, amounting to about Fifty dollars, as stated by Gen[era]l Murphy, in Public, should be paid, by the Collector, at New Orleans, if not, should be by him (Murphy) of course ultimately by the Department.

The Hon. Secretary, will perceive by the Editorials, of said papers, "that by permission of J.J. Wright, bearer of Despatches," they the Editors, were allowed to publish them. The credit for this permission, given to Wright, whom the Department will judge, by whose sanction, and Agency, they were published, and the object intended, by their being published, a long time before, I, could have a knowledge of them, and refute those, having a refference to me, and my Acts, the whole of which statements, are false, and induced only by the desire express[e]d by (Murphy) to find some person or thing, that would affect me, with the Department, or my fellow Citizens. I have before express[e]d my desire, to have my Acts examined by the Department, and I do not object, to an impartial trial, by public opinion, but to be charged by such Men, and through such channels, as those referr[e]d to, and in secret, deprives me, of the advantage of a proper examination, before the only proper tribunal, the Department, and to be found guilty, or acquit[t]ed, as the case may be, but I am charged, witnesses of bad character, introduced, judgement pronounced, against me, at the instance of the Minister, of my Country, who instead, of aiding my exertions, to do my duty, is found, by such means, opposing me, and bringing the Govt., and her Laws into disrepute. The Case of the Sch[oone]r "Cabot" referr[e]d to, in publication, having been communicated to the Dep[art]m[en]t requires no further notice, this vessel, arrived four times, at Sabine from New Orleans, ["the Master" *interlined*] refused to, or neglected to, comply with the Law of 1803, twice, and paid fees of $4 to Consul, but once, being on her return from N[ew] Orleans, after being reported to Dep[art]m[en]t.

The James [W.] Wood, who signs the Affidavit, published, is the Master of the Steamer Col. Woods, referr[e]d to in my *No. 8*, and who, on or about the 28th day of March 1844, discharged his Crew, or such part, of them, as from whom testimony, could have been had, relative to the Death of a Seaman, on board said vessel, and with which Wood, stood charged. These Men, were discharged, without payment of Wages, or the three Months wages extra, and no notice given to the Consul, of the discharge, until the same had proceeded, to Sea. The said Master Wood, stated he had no Crew List. I enclose Certificate of the Facts. The limited time allowed me, has not permitted me, to obtain Certificate of Collector at Sabine, as to my conduct Private & Official, and services rendered to the Masters and vessels, at Sabine. The Documents herewith enclosed, may aid the Department, in a view of these Matters.

I beg leave to refer the Hon. Secretary, to my *No. 7* relative to the jurisdiction, claimed by the Collector at Sabine, and to my remonstrance against the authority claimed by him. Also to my *No. 8*, for reference to the Master of a Steam Boat, who a short time previous, had been making arrangements, to introduce Slaves, into Sabine, *the same,* * J.J. Wright, who has thus been introduced, to the Department, and who also commanded, an armed Boat from Galveston, some Two Years since, and captured the American Schooners, "Jane Eliza," at Anchor off the Mississippi River, carried her into Galveston, and for which vessel, the Owner, I am informed, has not yet received compensation.

I have the honor to acknowledge, the receipt of Letter, from the Department, in reply to my No. 11, and dated May 1st 1844. I have the honor to be, most Respectfully, Your Ob[edien]t Servant, Stewart Newell.

*And now in New Orleans for *same* purpose furnished with Money to purchase a vessel. James Wood has left Texas for Wheeling Va. to join his family where he can be found. Resp[ectfull]y &c, S. Newell.

ALS (No. 18) with Ens in DNA, RG 59 (State Department), Consular Despatches, Texas, vol. 1 (T-153:1), received 7/20.

From John Tyler, Jr., "Private Secretary, President's Office," 6/18. Tyler transmits to Calhoun a letter of 6/7 from Charles S. Robinson of Binghamton, N.Y., to President John Tyler, seeking aid to recover money currently held in trust in a bank in Amsterdam, Holland. "The President is desirous of obtaining your views as to the action necessary to be had in the case, if any be necessary at all." According to Robinson's letter, the funds belong to the Beauvais family of N.Y. and Mich. The family had received annual interest payments from the bank until 1814 when the payments ceased. Robinson writes in behalf of the family and of Hallam Eldredge, their attorney and agent, to learn what actions can be taken to recover the funds. LS with En in DNA, RG 59 (State Department), Miscellaneous Letters (M-179:105, frames 70–72).

From JOHN BALDWIN and Others

[Washington] June 19th 1844
Sir, The undersigned are among those citizens of the United States having claims upon the Government of Mexico, in whose favor awards were made by the Board of Commissioners appointed under the Convention between the two Governments. After the rights of the parties were adjusted and determined by that Board, the United States assented to another arrangement with Mexico by which a period of five years was allowed her for making payment. The amount due was now made payable in instalments at the expiration of each succeeding three months.

It has so happened that with the exception of one instalment which was brought to the United States by an agent specially deputed for that purpose, the money payable by Mexico has never reached the claimants until a long time after the period prescribed in addition to the time required to transport the money to the United States. The instalment payable in January was not as we are informed paid at the time appointed, and that payable in April was not paid at the date of the last advices from Mexico.

It must be apparent that this irregularity and uncertainty materially depreciate the value of the certificates which we hold, and as is well known they cannot be disposed of in the market even in the present abundance of money, for any thing approaching to the nominal value.

We therefore respectfully and earnestly implore the Government of the United States, which has taken this entire business into its own hands to take such measures as to it shall seem most appropriate and effective for causing the prompt payment of what is now due and regularity in future payments, and the transportation of the money when paid without unnecessary delay or expense to the United States. John Baldwin, Rich[ar]d S. Coxe, James H. Causten, Francis A. Dickins, Aaron Leggett.

LS in DNA, RG 59 (State Department), Miscellaneous Letters (M-179:104, frames 557–558); CC in DNA, RG 84 (Foreign Posts), Mexico, Instructions, vol. 5.I; CC in DLC, Causten-Pickett Papers. NOTE: An EU on the LS reads "To be copied, and the copy to be filld [*sic*] with the papers placed in the hands of Gov. [Wilson] Shannon."

From HENRY W. HILLIARD

Legation of the United States
Brussels, 19th June 1844
Sir; The project of the law upon tobacco, some time since submitted by the Minister of Finance, was, yesterday, brought to a vote in the Chamber of Representatives. It will be remembered that he proposed to tax the consumption of tobacco, and the question submitted yesterday was, Shall an excise be laid on tobacco? This was decided in the negative by a vote of 64 to 17—all the Ministers voting in the affirmative. This, of course, disposes of the retro-active principle which made a part of the Minister's scheme, and relieves those who are interested in the tobacco now in this country, from all apprehension of an increase of duties, unless another scheme, involving this principle, should be adopted by the Chambers. I do not, however, apprehend this, for the Ministers felt embarrassed by this feature in the late scheme and I resisted it in such strong terms, that

I do not think they will consent to revive it. It is very gratifying to find that I have not resisted this measure in vain, and to be able to assure you that our citizens, who hold a large amount of tobacco which has been sent to this country for sale, may be relieved from all apprehension of the infliction of the unjust measure which for some time threatened their interests. Even if the ministerial scheme had been adopted which proposed to tax the consumption of tobacco, I think that the retro-active principle would have been abandoned, and, in my opinion, the Ministers adhered to it after they became convinced that it was impolitic to apply it to prevent the sudden introduction into Belgium of large quantities of tobacco, which might have been imported to avoid the provisions of the new law, upon the eve of its adoption. After this vote, the Chamber passed to the discussion of several propositions relative to a new arrangement "des droits de douane," to be applied to tobacco. There are several propositions submitted, which will come up for discussion to-day, and will, perhaps, be brought to a decisive vote in time for me to inform you of the result by the "Great Western," which sails from Liverpool the 22nd of this month. I shall withhold this communication until the latest moment possible, before the closing of the mail this afternoon in the hope of being able to give you this information.

In my last despatch, I expressed the hope that we should derive great benefits from the new Tariff of differential duties which has just passed the Chamber of Representatives, and further reflection has confirmed me in this opinion. I hope, therefore that it will meet your approbation and that our Government will appreciate the disposition manifested by the Government of this country to cultivate liberal commercial relations with the United States.

4 o'clock. I have just received an un-official note from Count [Albert Joseph] Goblet, Minister of Foreign Affairs, who informs me that the general discussion upon the tobacco question has not yet closed, but that the vote will probably be taken to-day, too late, however, for the result to be given in the present despatch. I have the honor to be, Sir, Very respectfully, Your obedient servant, Henry W. Hilliard.

LS (No. 20) in DNA, RG 59 (State Department), Diplomatic Despatches, Belgium, vol. 2 (M-193:3), received 7/10.

From HENRY W. HILLIARD

Brussels, 19th June 1844

My Dear Sir, I take it for granted the President [John Tyler] will accept my resignation, and you will greatly oblige me by giving me the earliest information as to the appointment of my successor. If it is desired that I shall remain until his arrival, I ought to be informed immediately, as I shall be obliged to stay until *October,* unless I can get away by the 12th August, for the unfavorable season for going to sea then comes on, and I should be unwilling to sail in the month of September. If I had the power in my hands I am sure that I could conclude an advantageous Treaty with this Govt. and take it home with me. I could avail myself of my acquaintance with the views of Ministers and the policy of the Govt.

I shall make my arrangements with the expectation of leaving on the day named by me, and I hope you will be good enough to make the necessary orders to facilitate this.

Mr. [Samuel] Haight, the Consul at Antwerp[,] thinks that some movement has been made against him at home, and I am sure you will pardon the liberty I take in saying, that I believe he has discharged his duty faithfully. My friend Mr. [Virgil] Maxcy who preceded me, was very favorable to Mr. Haight's retaining his office, and appeared to have confidence in his capacity.

I could not say less than this and I am sure you will appreciate my frankness. I have the honor to be Sir, Very respectfully Your ob[edien]t Serv[an]t, Henry W. Hilliard.

ALS in ScCleA.

To W[illia]m Rufus Page, Hallowell, Maine, 6/19. "Your letter of the 9th Ins[tan]t has been received and I have directed a copy of the instructions sent to the American Minister at Constantinople, on the subject to which your communication relates, to be made out and transmitted with this letter." FC in DNA, RG 59 (State Department), Domestic Letters, 34:246 (M-40:32).

To J[ohann] W. Schmidt, "Consul of Prussia, New York [City]," 6/19. "In compliance with the request of your note of the 15th Instant, I have pleasure in transmitting a circular letter [of 6/18] addressed by me to the Consuls and Agents of the United States, enjoining upon them the duty of rendering protection and succor to the Ship Borussia, Captain Hartwig, from Stettin, about to proceed on a whaling voyage to the South Seas." FC in DNA, RG 59 (State Department), Notes to Foreign Legations, German States, 6:94 (M-99:27).

From Ro[bert] Tyler

White House, June 19th [1844]
My Dear Sir, I have a small favor to ask of you. Mr. [S.D.] Dakin a Gentleman of great worth & Intelligence, a personal friend of mine, and a man well known to the scientific world as the author of "Dakin's plan of Dry Dock" desires, in the prosecution of his work, to visit Europe. He wishes some little Government position to give value to his efforts in behalf of his work. If you could give him some Despatches to bear ["wh" *canceled*] sometime during the summer, especially if they should carry him into the north of Europe, you would serve an excellent & very intelligent gentleman & confer a *personal favor* on me. Any other diplomatic engagement would be equally acceptable. He merely wishes to visit Europe in a capacity to assist him in the promotion of his "plan of Dry Dock." With very sincere respect Y[ou]r Ob[edien]t S[ervan]t, Ro: Tyler.

ALS in DNA, RG 59 (State Department), Applications and Recommendations, 1837–1845, Dakin (M-687:8, frames 52–54).

From Rich[ar]d S. Coxe and Others

[Washington] June 20th 1844
Sir, You have been apprised of the fact that a number of individual citizens of the United States have large claims upon the government of Mexico, for outrages committed upon their persons & property; that these claims are of many years standing; that the government of the United States including both the Executive and Legislative Departments have investigated the circumstances upon which these claims rest, have represented as well to Mexico as to the individuals interested the obligations which it feels imposed upon it to require that these demands should be promptly and satisfactorily adjusted.

We beg leave to refer you, to our several communications addressed to the Hon. Daniel Webster and the Hon. A[bel] P. Upshur which will present you with the prominent facts in these cases—in a brief compass. We also request your particular attention to the Executive communications to Congress particularly that of June 13, 1842, Senate Doc. 27th Cong. 2d Sess. Doc. 320.

In this last document you will perceive the impediments which have been thrown by Mexico in the way of the claimants. That she stands charged by the American Commissioners with endeavouring to impose upon the Board false and forged testimony to rebut these claims; that when this charge was made her Commissioners against the remonstrances of their colleagues and the distinct objections of the State Department withdrew the papers which contained the evidence to substantiate the accusation and then assigned to Mr. Webster reasons for their conduct which were utterly false in fact.

You will perceive that ["eighteen months" *canceled and* "a year & a half" *interlined*] have elapsed since that Board of Commissioners adjourned leaving a large mass of business unsettled: that from that period the claimants have been urgent in their solicitations to your Department to press these matters to a conclusion. You will perceive that nearly a year since Mexico was called upon to accede to a convention embodying the principles upon which these claims should be adjudicated, and that this call upon her was made in terms which indicated that this government would insist upon a concurrence in them. By some means wholly inexplicable to us the convention was signed by the Representative of the two governments with alterations as to the place where the new board should hold its sittings, a change which the claimants regarded as tantamount to an entire abandonment of their cases. The Senate refused to ratify this Convention without modifying this extraordinary provision—and in the month of february the paper was again transmitted to Mexico with a full and distinct exhibition of the grounds upon which the Executive called for the proposed change.

We need scarcely suggest to you that although this proposition has now been before the Mexican government upwards of three months there has been no definite action upon it. The claimants after having the cup of hope raised to their lips by the energetic manner in which their rights have been asserted have again seen it dashed by the recent intelligence from Mexico that the business remains precisely where it stood fifteen months since.

When Sir you review the past history of this business you cannot but come to the conclusion that the claimants have experienced the most harsh and cruel treatment; that their means of support have been torn from them and the most flagrant outrages have been perpetrated upon them by Mexico: that they have every right to the energetic and effective interposition of their own government to obtain redress for the wrongs they have endured—and compensation for spoliations which they have suffered. This they have been assured they should obtain—this Mexico has been informed would be exacted.

We now respectfully ask whether we have not been delayed long enough—whether there is to be any limit to our endurance. We now learn that Mexico is unable to pay the comparatively small instalments as they fall due under the awards of the late Board, and we see but little prospect of her being enabled to meet the greatly enlarged demands which must be awarded to us if we obtain any thing approaching to justice.

We earnestly ask therefore that more energetic means may be adopted to enforce our long procrastinated rights; that Mexico may be required to do that justice she has so long withheld; and that the amount due to us may be fairly and promptly adjusted and when adjusted be liquidated and paid. Richd. S. Coxe, John Baldwin, W[illia]m S. Parrott, J. Prentiss, G[ilbert] L. Thompson.

LS in DNA, RG 59 (State Department), Miscellaneous Letters (M-179:104, frames 561–563); CC in DNA, RG 84 (Foreign Posts), Mexico, Instructions, vol. 5.I.

To DANIEL J. DESMOND, "Consul General of the Pontifical States, Philadelphia"

Department of State
Washington, 20th June, 1844

Sir: Your communication of the 14th Instant has been received.

This Government does not, in any manner, participate in the apprehensions expressed by you in that communication. No country has been more exempt than the United States from mobs, and wherever in this country popular outbreaks have, unhappily, occurred, fewer lives have been lost, and less blood shed, than in any country where similar scenes have been enacted. Nor is there a single instance known, where a diplomatic or consular Representative, or any public functionary residing here has been molested.

The Department, under the circumstances, feels compelled to remark, that your application is without a precedent, and that the granting of it, would, in its opinion, be highly offensive to the authorities of the City and State, in which you reside, and every way calculated to revive and increase the excitement, which you seem to think exists so alarmingly at the present moment. I am, Sir, with due consideration, Your most obedient Servant, J.C. Calhoun.

FC in DNA, RG 59 (State Department), Notes to Foreign Legations, Italian States, Greece, and Turkey, 6:69–70 (M-99:61).

From F[RANCIS] M. DIMOND

United States Consulate
Vera Cruz, June 20th 1844

Sir, I have the honour to acknowledge the receipt of your letter of the 18th ult[im]o in relation to the Schooner Vigilant; by the next opportunity I shall hav[e] the honour to furnish the Department with the particulars respecting her Capture and condemnation.

I have now the honour to transmit despatches from our Legation at Mexico [City] and this is the first opportunity I have had to forward them.

The U.S. Frigate Potomac Commodor[e David] Conner arrived at Sacrificios on the 16th and is hourly expecting the Vincennes and the Somers. The U.S. Cutter is also here waiting the instalment from Mexico due on the 30th April and not paid on the 16th inst.

I mentioned in my last respects that a vessel had been fitted out of New Orleans having on board Gen[era]l Samana [*sic*; Francisco Sentmanat], the former Governor of Tabasco with 70 officers and men armed[,] the Object of which was to land near Tabasco and join others and take possession of that State, the said Samana having been expelled [from] the State last year. The Government having been informed by their Consul at New Orleans sent two national vessel[s] to watch his movement. They discovered this Schooner under the American flag and ran her on shore 20 miles this side of Tabasco. Gen[era]l [Pedro de] Ampudia having command of the Government Troops at Tabasco immediately went in pursuit and after killing 14 took the others prisoners. General Samana was shot and his head cut off and fried in oil. Thus has ended this wild expedition. It is reported here that these troops were embarked in open day at New Orleans and that it was generally known the object they had in view. I have however contradicted the report for I could [not] believe that such things would have been allowed by the authorities of New

131

Orleans. I have the honour to be Sir most Respectfully Your Ob[edient] s[ervan]t, F.M. Dimond.

ALS (No. 225) in DNA, RG 59 (State Department), Consular Despatches, Vera Cruz, vol. 5 (M-183:5), received 7/12.

From F[RANKLIN] H. ELMORE

Charleston, June 20, 1844

My Dear Sir, I returned today from Columbia & on the Rail Road had as a Companion Professor [William H.] Ellet of our College, from whom I ascertained some highly interesting facts which may be of the greatest importance to us in South Carolina & indeed the whole gold region—if half of what he believes he has ascertained holds good. He informs me that he has analyzed about 30 Specimens of gold ores latterly—that in none of these has he failed to extract greatly more gold than has been ascertained by the working process. The ores tried were of various qualities—from [T.P.?] Black[']s mine in Spartanburg he tried several samples. The richest was a fair sample of what Black claims to have yielded him about $160 to the bushel—this Prof. Ellet pronounces good for $1000. Another specimen Black reported as yielding less than $2—Ellet says gives at the rate of $62. He says there is & can be no mistake—that as a proof, independent of the analysis, that the specimen which yielded at the rate of $62 to the bushel, did not exhibit a particle of gold to the eye or the microscope. He tells me also that the best of the No. Ca. [ores] are shipped to London & worked up there. He says he offered Black $400 for every bushel of his best ore (from a small vein in his mine) deliverable at Columbia—and he assures me that he is perfectly convinced that a most ruinous waste is made in our mines by the mode of working them.

I have given you the above hasty & imperfect sketch of what he tells me for several purposes—it may be vastly important if correct to yourself as well as to many others of us—and Professor Ellet thinks that it may be made available in the best form by introducing the Russian process for separating the gold—that process he says is one of smelting in furnaces somewhat like our iron furnaces. But he says that every effort he has made to ascertain the mode has failed. It struck me that you could procure it through our Minister in Russia or the Russian Ambassador & I suggested it to him. He gave me the heads of inquiry. He gave me also the idea which was most upon his mind as to the operation. He is under the impression that the furnaces are constructed upon principles analogous to the blast furnace, for smelting iron ores—that the ores of gold are mixed with some iron ore—the product is gold & iron. This, mixed in a mass, is put into vessels of vitriol where the iron is dissolved—the vitriol is increased in value by it for the market & the gold is left as the residuum. He feels satisfied that immense results may be reached by this process. What is necessary to be known is:

1. The description of the furnace—size—construction—form &c.

2. The mode of working it—applying blast—cold or heated—with one—two or more twiers [*sic*; tuyeres].

3. ["The" *canceled*] The degree of heat proper—whether it should [be] forced rapidly—slowly—or how.

4. The mode of charging the furnace—what ["fluses" *altered to* "flues"] are to be used—the proportions of each—in short the fullest directions for the processes both of preparation & working—fuel &c.

5. If iron ores are used, what kind are best—should they & the gold ores be pounded small—should they be put in the furnace as dug out of the mines or roasted before used?

You may remember that in 1839 one of the Messrs. Bissel [J. Humphrey Bissell?] was at Washington on his way to Europe to procure information of some newly discovered process for working gold mines. Prof. [Ellet] tells me he understands that Mr. Bissel has a furnace at work, but he has it walled around & will let no one see its operations & gives nobody any information about it.

I believe I have upon this matter discharged myself of all I learned from Prof. Ellet, except perhaps the suggestion that the information sought for may perhaps be got in France or Belgium.

The Professor also seemed solicitous on another matter. There are he says a set of weights & measures prepared under orders of [*sic*] by the late Mr. [Ferdinand R.] Hassler for this State which are in some of the Departments. He thinks they ought to be lodged in the College—and asks if they could not be sent on to Columbia, where the Legislature might be moved to order them deposited in the College. Can you give any aid in this? I am my Dear Sir Yours truly, F.H. Elmore.

ALS in ScCleA; CCEx in DNA, RG 84 (Foreign Posts), Russia, Letters Received, vol. 4337; CCEx in DNA, RG 84 (Foreign Posts), Russia, Instructions, 4406:27–28; CCEx in DNA, RG 59 (State Department), Miscellaneous Letters (M-179:104, frames 559–560). NOTE: AEU's by Calhoun on the ALS read: "Show to Mr. Clemson," and "Mr. Willingham[?]."

From E[DMUND] W. HUBARD, [Representative from Va.]

Washington, June 20th 1844

My Dear Sir, I have talked with Mr. [William H.] Haywood [Jr., Senator from N.C.] who made the motion about the proceedings on the Wheaton Treaty. He wrote on a card which I have enclosed to Mr. [Asbury] Dickens [Secretary of the Senate] that in his verbal motion he included the Treaty "et omnes." This card I have sent to the Clerk & asked him to inform you whether I could have a copy of the Treaty. If he answers in the affirmative, please send me a copy forthwith—direct to Curdsville, Buckingham [County], Va. Y[ou]r mo[st] ob[edien]t serv[an]t, E.W. Hubard.

ALS in ScCleA.

From THOMAS O. LARKIN

Consulate of the United States
of America, Monterey, June 20 1844

Sir, I have the honour to inform you that the French Gover[n]ment have their Transport Ship "Leon," Captain Bonnet, on this coast for the purpose of taking samples of Lumber, Spars, Dry or jerked Beef, and other produce, also Cows for supplying the Marquesas Islands.

Captain Bonnet now receives on board about 300 head of cattle. He informs me his Government wishes to send for some thousand head, and will open an extensive trade between the Marquesas and California, for the purpose of supplying the former with the produce of this country paying in drafts made out, signed and counter signed in France, for five hundred francs and upwards.

The "Leon" was allowed to take on board all she wanted without paying any port charges or tonnage duties, General [Manuel] Micheltorena reserving to himself the right of referring the subject to his Government.

I find by the debates in Congress of February and March last, in the Oregon debate, that Mr. [Rufus] Choate of the senate [from Mass.] and some other Members, are of opinion that the Hudson Bay Company on the Columbia River are merely employing Dr. [John] McLaughlin and some trappers, and that when the game are gone, the hunters will follow; that our American settlers will sweep them from the country. This appears the tenor of Mr. Choate's speech of the 22 of February last.

As you may wish for the latest information on this subject, I take the liberty of informing you that the H[udson] B[ay] Company besides trapping, are cultivating the soil and building mills, they are shipping flour and lumber to the Sandwich Islands and this country, and I believe to the Russians. They are purchasing cattle from California and stocking their farms largely. They have an Agent doing business in Oahu for them, and one stationed in San Francisco with his family and servants, where they have purchased land and the best house in the place, selling goods and purchasing hides to ship in their vessels, not being able to return loaded to England.

Dr. [John] McLaughlin has wrote this year to California requesting an extensive grant of land on the Sacrament river, about the Lat. 40 N. promising, that if Government will grant the land, to settle it immediately, and as an inducement says, that all the settlers will bring money, and that some of them are wealthy; we are daily looking for the arrival in this Port of a H[udson] B[ay] Company's ship, with a large cargo of English goods for their San Francisco establishment.

I have reason to think, that many of the emigrants already in the Oregon, are dissatisfied and will move to California; some have already arrived here, and are settling on the waters entering into the Bay of San Francisco; there can be no comparison between the two countries.

I do not know as this information is of consequence to your department. I however take the liberty of informing you of it. Sir I am with much respect, your most obedient servant, Thomas O. Larkin.

LS (No. 7) in DNA, RG 59 (State Department), Consular Despatches, Monterey (M-138:1), received 8/31; FC in CU, Bancroft Library, Larkin Collection; PC in Hammond, ed., *Larkin Papers*, 2:140–141.

To Jasper Hall Livingston, Madrid, 6/20. Calhoun transmits to Livingston his commission, passport, instructions, and letter of credit for the post of Secretary of Legation in Spain to which he has been appointed. FC in DNA, RG 59 (State Department), Diplomatic Instructions, Spain, 14:178 (M-77:142).

From William Nibb, Jr., [Washington, *ca.* 6/20]. He applies for employment as a copyist in the State Department and states that he has been recommended by President [John Tyler] for a post. ALS in DNA, RG 59 (State Department), Applications and Recommendations, 1837–1845, Nibb (M-687:24, frames 190–191).

From S[hadrach] Penn, Jr., St. Louis, 6/20. Penn advises that a pardon be granted to John and David McDaniel and James Brown, convicted of the murder of Mexican trader [Antonio José] Chavis. Their conviction was obtained largely on the testimony of [William] Mason, a member of their band and a man of bad character who Penn would not believe "under any circumstances." If a pardon cannot be obtained, he recommends a respite to allow time for further study of the case. ALS in DNA, RG 59 (State Department), Petitions for Pardon and Related Briefs, 1800–1849, no. 292A.

To WILSON SHANNON

Department of State
Washington, June 20th, 1844

Sir, I have the honor to acknowledge the receipt of your letter of the 17th of April last, announcing your acceptance of the appointment tendered you by the President of the United States [John Tyler] as Envoy Extraordinary and Minister Plenipotentiary to the Republic of Mexico; and notifying this Department of your readiness to enter on the discharge of the duties of your office. You have already received your Commission; and I herewith enclose to you a full power, a special passport, printed personal instructions, a sealed Letter, accrediting you to the President of the Mexican Republic [Santa Anna], and an open copy of the same for your own use. In presenting this Letter of Credence to the President, you will avail yourself of the occasion to express to the President of Mexico, the sincere desire of the President of the United States to maintain the most amicable relations with the Government of the Mexican Republic, and his purpose to promote this end by every proper means in his power.

By a Convention between the United States and the Mexican Republic signed on the 11th day of April 1839, a joint Commission was agreed upon for the purpose of adjusting the Claims of the citizens of the former on the Government of the latter. This Commission, agreeably to the provisions of the Convention, met in the City of Washington in August 1840: but ["much" *interlined*] of the time allowed for the transaction and close of its business was consumed by the Commissioners of the two Governments in discussing the organization of the Board and proper forms of procedure to be adopted before it. The consequence was that at the expiration of the period when, by the terms of the Convention, the Commission should expire, many of the claims submitted for its decision remained undecided by the Board; while others referred to the Umpire, were left in the same state, as he considered his functions terminating with those of the Commission.

The Convention also provided that the claims which should be allowed might be discharged by the payment of Mexican Treasury notes: but as these were much depreciated in value at the time when the Commission expired, it became a matter of importance to effect some arrangement by which specie should be substituted in their stead. To this end your predecessor was empowered and instructed to enter into a negotiation with the Government of Mexico, and a Convention was concluded on the 30th of January 1843, providing for the payment of the awards and the interest accruing thereon in specie, in five years from the 30th day of April 1843, in equal instalments every three months. These instalments have been paid punctually with the exception of that which fell due in the month of February last, a part only of which was paid on the day; and though the balance has since been discharged, it is important to the interests involved that the strictest punctuality should be observed. The last instalment due on the 30th of April 1844, had not been paid at the date of our last advices from Mr. [Ben E.] Green, the Chargé d'Affaires *ad interim* of the United States, though repeated applications had been made by him to the Minister of Foreign Relations [José M. de Bocanegra]. This neglect of solemn and express stipulations, cannot be otherwise regarded than as violations of national faith, injurious alike to the honor of Mexico and to the interests of the United States. It will therefore be your duty to remonstrate, in the strongest terms, against this apparent indifference to the obligations of Contracts; and to urge upon the Government of Mexico the necessity of complying with the stipulations of the Convention, agreeably to its terms.

By the 6th article of the Convention of January 30th 1843, certain stipulations were entered into with a view to the final adjustment of the claims of the citizens of the United States against Mexico which had not been decided by the Commission under the Convention of 1839, as well as of others held by the respective people and Governments on each other. On the 20th of November 1843, this Convention was concluded and signed by the accredited Agents of the two

137

Governments, and submitted by the President to the Senate at an early period of the late session, by which it was approved, except as to the articles relating to the adjustment of the claims of the two Governments on each other, and the designation of the City of Mexico, instead of Washington as the place where the Board should hold its sessions. It therefore became necessary to refer the Convention with these amendments or alterations back to the Government of Mexico for its approval; and although this was promptly done, no definitive action of that Government in the premises has yet been communicated to this Department.

The views which seem to have influenced the Senate in its decision on these two points are so fully and ably set forth in the instructions of ["the late" interlined; Secretary of State] Mr. [Abel P.] Upshur to Mr. [Waddy] Thompson, of the —— day of January last, that I need but refer you to them for a thorough understanding of the subject. And should the matter be still pending on your arrival at Mexico, it will be your duty to urge upon the Government the necessity of some speedy and definitive action on its part.

You will find on the files of the Legation a correspondence between your Predecessor[,] Mr. Thompson, and the Mexican Minister of Foreign Relations, in regard to an order addressed by the Mexican Secretary of War, dated the 14th July, 1843, to the Governors of the States of California, Sonora, Sinaloa and Chihuahua, directing the expulsion of the citizens of the United States from their territories respectively. The result of this correspondence seems to have been none other than an enlargement of the terms of the order, so as to embrace foreigners generally; or such of them as might be deemed vagrants or dangerous to the public peace.

It is not designed to enter into a grave argument to expose the character of such an order, or to show its opposition to the Treaty of the 5th of April 1831. The correspondence referred to will put you in possession of the points in issue, and the views of the Government in regard to them.

As a large number of our citizens for the purpose of trade, have settled themselves in the States referred to, whose property and liberty may be endangered by its enforcement, it will be necessary that you give to the subject your earliest attention. You will perceive by the reference to the correspondence on the files of the Legation, that the Governors of the States to whom the order is addressed, are empowered arbitrarily to fix the time when those deemed obnoxious shall leave the Country—while no opportunity seems to be vouchsafed to the suspected to vindicate their characters. In the execution of such an order it is more than probable that much individual wrong and suffering may be inflicted; and while you will protest, in strong terms, against the order itself as a flagrant violation of the Treaty of 1831, you will at the same time exert your utmost vigilance to protect the persons and property of those who may be made unjustly the subjects of its operations; enjoining on our citizens on the one hand, a proper obedience to the Laws of Mexico as a condition of your interference in their behalf; and on the other, giving the Mexican Government to understand ["that the United States" *interlined*] cannot allow their citizens, induced to take up their residence in its territories under the solemn sanctions of a Treaty, to be driven from their abodes or otherwise injured in their persons or property, on frivolous pretexts.

Another question of very grave importance, and which is still pending between the two Governments, grows out of the Mexican Decree of the 23rd September 1843, prohibiting foreigners resident in Mexico, from engaging in the Retail Trade. Your Predecessor, Mr. Thompson, was instructed to protest against the application of this Decree to the citizens of the United States, as a direct and palpable infringement of the 3rd article of the Treaty of 1831; and incompatible with other stipulations contained in it. The Mexican Minister for Foreign Affairs attemp[t]s to sustain the Decree, on the general ground, that, by the Treaty, the citizens of each Country resident in the other, are subject to their respective Laws and usages. This, as a general truth, may be admitted, but surely it cannot be pretended that rights guarrantied by Treaty between two independent powers may be abridged and modified by the municipal regulations of one of the Parties, without, and against the consent of the other. Such a position is so utterly untenable that it would be needless to dwell on it.

This subject will demand your prompt attention, for it is of the highest importance to prevent the injustice, injury and distress which must necessarily attend the execution of the Decree, rather than to resort to protracted negotiations in order to repair them.

You will, therefore, inform the Government of Mexico, in firm but conciliatory language, that while the United States concedes to Mexico the right to enact laws not inconsistent with her Treaty stipulations, they cannot tamely submit to the execution of this Decree; and that it is confidently expected it will be countermanded so far as their citizens are concerned.

Another Decree, dated in August last, was also issued by the Mexican Government, which appears to conflict, very clearly, with the stipulations of the Treaty of 1831. By the fourth article of this Decree, merchandize, lawfully imported into the territories of Mexico, is subjected to forfeiture after a limited time, unless it be sold or re-shipped in one year. This is so obviously in contravention of the 26th article of the Treaty existing between the two Countries, and so hostile in its spirit to those relations of friendship which it was intended to secure, that in the last interview between your predecessor, Mr. Thompson, and the President of Mexico, a promise was made by that Functionary so to modify the said Decree as to divest it of its obnoxious provisions in respect to the citizens of the United States. You will avail yourself of the first occasion, after your arrival, to bring the subject to the notice of the Mexican Government, and to urge the immediate fulfilment of the promise made to your predecessor.

You will embrace some convenient opportunity after you have complied with the foregoing instructions to address a note to the Mexican Government in which you will say, that you are instructed to inform it that the President perceives with regret it has entirely misconceived the object of the communication which the Secretary of the Legation of the U. States, in conformity with his instructions, made to it, in reference to the Treaty recently entered into with Texas. Its object, as it plainly imports to be, was to announce to the Government of Mexico, that the Treaty had been signed and submitted to the Senate for its approval; that the measure had been adopted with no unfriendly or hostile feelings to Mexico; and that the Government of the United States was ready to adjust, on liberal terms, the question of boundary, and any other that might grow out of the treaty. It constituted no part of its object to invite a discussion as to its right to make the Treaty. To suppose so would be to assume that it had made it, without duly examining and establishing, to its entire satisfaction, its right to do so; a supposition which would neither comport with the fact, nor what is due to its honor and dignity. Such being the case, it cannot, consistently with either, permit itself to be drawn into a controversy with the Government of Mexico as to its right to make the treaty; and you will inform it accordingly that you have been instructed to pass unnoticed the inconclusive arguments by which it has attempted to controvert our right to enter into it. We hold Texas to be independent *de jure* as well as *de facto*; and as competent, in every respect, to enter into a Treaty of Cession, or any other, as Mexico herself, or any other independent power; and that, in entering into the Treaty of annexation with her, we violated no prior engagement or stipulation with Mexico. We would, indeed, have been glad, in doing so, to have acted with the concurrence of Mexico, if circumstances had permitted; not because we believed ["that" *interlined*] she had any rightful claim of sovereignty over Texas, or that the latter was not competent, of itself, to transfer the full and lawful right and title to its territory; but because in our desire to preserve the most friendly relations with Mexico, we were disposed to treat her with respect, however unfounded we believed her claim to Texas to be. It was in conformity with this desire that the instructions were given to make the communication to the Government of Mexico, announcing the signature of the Treaty, and our readiness to adjust all questions which might grow out of it, between the two Countries, on the most liberal terms.

You will also state that you are instructed to pass over, unnoticed, the menaces and offensive language which the Government of Mexico has thought proper to use. It makes a great mistake in supposing that the United States can be deterred by menaces from adopting a measure which after mature deliberation, they have determined they have a right to do, and which they believe to be essential to their safety and prosperity. They are desirous of peace with Mexico and all other nations; but they always stand prepared to defend themselves, if need be, against any attack, to which they may be subjected, in pursuing a line of policy by themselves deemed just and expedient. Nor can they be provoked to retort the offensive language used. The Government of the United States is too mindful of what is due to its own self-respect and dignity, to be driven, by any provocation, however unwarranted, or great, from that decorum of language which ought ever to be observed in the official Correspondence of independent States. In their estimation a good cause needs no such support, and a bad one cannot be strengthened by it.

From the failure of the Senate to approve the Treaty of annexation with Texas, it is not deemed advisable to instruct you to make any overtures or propositions to the Government of Mexico in relation to that subject, but should any disposition be manifested on its part, to open negotiations or any propositions be made in reference to it, you will receive and immediately transmit them to this Department. I am, Sir, Your obedient Servant, J.C. Calhoun.

LS (No. 1) in DNA, RG 84 (Foreign Posts), Mexico, Instructions vol. 5.I; FC in DNA, RG 59 (State Department), Diplomatic Instructions, Mexico, 15:297–305 (M-77:111); PC in Senate Document No. 1, 28th Cong., 2nd Sess., pp. 21–24; PC in House Document No. 2, 28th Cong., 2nd Sess., pp. 21–24; PC in *Congressional Globe*, 28th Cong., 2nd Sess., Appendix, pp. 1–2; PC in the

Washington, D.C., *Globe*, December 6, 1844, p. 1; PC in the Washington, D.C., *Daily Madisonian*, December 7, 1844, p. 3; PC in the Washington, D.C., *Daily National Intelligencer*, December 7, 1844, p. 2; PC in *Niles' National Register*, vol. LXVII, no. 15 (December 14, 1844), pp. 230–231; PC in Crallé, ed., *Works*, 5:349–356.

To William C. Anderson, U.S. Marshal, St. Louis, 6/21. Calhoun encloses the President's [John Tyler's] respite of David McDaniel from execution for one year. FC in DNA, RG 59 (State Department), Domestic Letters, 34:253 (M-40:32).

To William C. Anderson, St. Louis, 6/21. Calhoun encloses the President's [John Tyler's] respite for one year "of such sentence as may be or has been pronounced against" Thomas Towson. FC in DNA, RG 59 (State Department), Domestic Letters, 34:252–253 (M-40:32).

From William Brent, Jr., "near Georgetown, D.C.," 6/21. "I received on yesterday a commission from the President of the United States [John Tyler], as Chargé d'Affaires of the United States of America to the Republic of Buenos Ayres. I accept this appointment & await the instructions of the department." LS with En in DNA, RG 59 (State Department), Diplomatic Despatches, Argentina, vol. 5 (M-69:6).

From H[enry] L. Ellsworth, [Commissioner of the] Patent Office, 6/21. He asks that he be given a leave of absence. He normally takes such leave during the recess of Congress, "employing the time in collecting agricultural statistics as required by an act of Congress." The Chief Clerk of the Patent Office is ready to assume the duties of Commissioner in Ellsworth's absence. ALS in DNA, RG 59 (State Department), Miscellaneous Letters (M-179:104, frames 565–566).

From BEN E. GREEN, [Secretary of Legation and Chargé d'Affaires ad interim]

Legation of the U.S. of A.
Mexico, June 21st 1844

Sir, In my last despatches & private letter, I informed you of the state of things here, and the probable views of Santa Anna. I also informed you that the Clergy are much opposed to a renewal of the war with Texas, foreseeing, with their usual sagacity, that the contest is a hopeless one, and that they will have to pay the expenses. Nor are the clergy the only persons, who see the matter in its true lights. There are many others, who are of the same opinion, and oppose, as far as they dare, the renewal of the war. The Congress also are suspicious of Santa Anna. The committee, to whom was referred his iniciative [*sic*] have brought in their report, which gives him great dissatisfaction. I send you a copy of this long & singular document, & have marked those parts worthy of attention. It is stamped with that singular dread of Santa Anna, under which everything & everybody in this country seems to be clouded, and while it attacks the "extraordinary Govt.," disclaims all intention of blaming him, and throws the whole burden on the shoulders of the Ministry. You will see that they refuse to give him more than $1,000,000; oppose, in toto, the great increase of the army, which he desires; and propose the alternative of calling out the militia if, as he says, the "national independence" is in danger. The abuse of this is also guarded against by providing that the militia shall not be sent out of their respective districts, without the consent of Congress. Santa Anna would not suffer the Report of the Committee to be published in the "Diario del Gobierno," the Govt. organ, and tried to prevent its appearance in the Siglo XIX.

Many rumors are afloat. Some say that Santa Anna will dissolve the Congress, and proclaim again the 7a Base of Tacubaya. Others, that it is his purpose to resign, accusing Congress of a disregard for the "national honor, independence &c;" & then cause himself to be proclaimed Dictator by the Army. His reliance is the Army, and his stock in trade consist[s] of charges of usurpation against the U.S. and the cry that the *national independence*" is in danger from their "*treacherous neighbours of the North.*"

Under these circumstances I have thought it adviseable to depart from my first determination (of not answering Mr. [José M. de] Bocanegra's note of the 12th inst., which I sent you a few days since); and to send him a note [dated 6/20] of which No. 1 [enclosed] is a copy. In this note I have endeavoured, coolly & dispassionately, to answer his invectives by the example of Mexico herself, and to show ["that the U.S." *interlined*] have but acted on the principles, which Mexico herself has always sustained. I have hopes that this may strengthen the party favourable to us, and force Santa Anna either to acknowledge the independence of Texas, or to suffer that country to fall into our hands, instead of those of G. Britain. One of these

143

three must happen. It is impossible for Mexico to reconquer ["&
hold" *interlined*] Texas, & Santa Anna knows it.

I have taken this step with great hesitation; but I feel that I
should be culpable, were I to shrink from any responsibility, when
by incurring that responsibility there is so favourable a prospect of
doing good. I have the honor to be Very Respectfully Your ob[e-
dien]t Serv[an]t, Ben E. Green.

ALS (No. 8) with En in DNA, RG 59 (State Department), Diplomatic Despatches, Mexico, vol. 12 (M-97:13), received 7/16; variant FC in DNA, RG 84
(Foreign Posts), Mexico, Despatches; draft (undated) in NcU, Duff Green
Papers (published microfilm, roll 5, frames 713–714); PEx with En in Senate
Document No. 1, 28th Cong., 2nd Sess., pp. 75–77; PEx with En in House Document No. 2, 28th Cong., 2nd Sess., pp. 74–76. NOTE: Both the FC and the
draft close the second paragraph with the following sentence: "The charges are
well made use of by the man, whose aim is the dictatorship or the throne."

From Wilson Lumpkin, [former Governor of Ga.], Athens [Ga.],
6/21. He recommends the appointment of Henderson Willingham
as U.S. Marshal. Willingham is now the principal acting Deputy
Marshal of Ga. and is a "man of honor & integrity of character." An
AEU by Calhoun reads: "Mr. Lumpkin Recommends Mr. Willingham for Marshall [*sic*]." ALS in DNA, RG 59 (State Department),
Applications and Recommendations, 1837–1845, Willingham (M-
687:34, frames 434–436).

Rich[ar]d K. Crallé, Chief Clerk, State Department, to J[ohn] Y.
Mason, Secretary of the Navy, 6/21. "The Secretary of State directs
me to inform you that he assents to your suggestions in regard to
Gov. [Wilson] Shannon, who has been informed of the proposed arrangement [for his transportation to Mexico], and will probably be
in this city on his way to Norfolk by the 2nd day of July next. It
would be desirable that the Falmouth should be got ready for sea
at as early a day after that date as possible." (An endorsement, possibly by Mason, reads, "let order be issued to have the Falmouth
ready as early as possible.") ALS in DNA, RG 45 (Naval Records),
Letters from Federal Executive Agents, 1837–1886, 6:180 (M-517:2,
frames 385–386).

From Geo[rge] Moore, U.S. Consul, Trieste, 6/21. So far in
1844, 14 ships have arrived at Trieste from U.S. ports, of which only
five were American ships—the rest Swedish, Prussian, English, and
Austrian. "The low rates of Freight accepted by these Foreign vessels is complained of as very injurious to the American Shipping In-

terest." LS (No. 58) in DNA, RG 59 (State Department), Consular Despatches, Trieste, vol. 3 (T-242:3), received 7/19.

To Joseph Ray, Washington, 6/21. Calhoun acknowledges Ray's letter of 6/15 "upon the subject of your claim against the Brazilian Government." Although the State Department does not usually "communicate to claimants upon foreign Governments the particulars respecting the prosecution of their claims when a negotiation for that purpose is pending," Calhoun wishes to correct some misapprehensions on Ray's part. First, the U.S. Ministers to Brazil have not been instructed to "demand" of the Brazilian Government reparation on Ray's behalf, nor have those representatives been told to present "officially" Ray's claims. They were simply instructed to employ their influence in presenting the claims "so far as they might think proper" to do so. FC in DNA, RG 59 (State Department), Domestic Letters, 34:251–252 (M-40:32).

From LEMUEL SAWYER

N[ew] York [City,] June [*ca.* 21] 1844
Dear Sir, I observe that on the 26th of April the president [John Tyler], in obedience to a resolution of the senate of the 22d sent a map of Texas to that body, produced under the direction of Col. [John J.] Abert of the topo[graphical] engineer corps. I should take it as a very great favour to get a rough copy of it from your office. It will be of great importance to our company, (the Rio Grande & Texas) & to the friends of annexation generally to see that map, & thro it to make a fair & practical southern boundary line, between Texas & Mexico. We observe with great dissatisfaction, the imaginary line suggested by Col. [Thomas H.] Benton, in his 2d Speech in the senate of the 20th Ult[im]o—which proposes to establish the boundary *to the East* of the Nueces, & west thro the desert Prairies &c. of that river. This would afford the friends of Texas the same ground of complaint, of one of the court of Richard the 2d that the party had "emasculated" this our Kingdom." It would cut off more than half the possessions of the RioGrande company, & *throw their Town* of Dolores (which they founded in 1833, at a cost of $40,000) entirely out of the garbled limits of this emasculated state. As to any southern boundary being adopted, this side of that natural & well established one of the Rio Del Norte, it is preposterous. Were

it not trespassing too much upon your business, I could write a full answer in refutation of Col. B[enton]'s arguments & reasons in support of his proposed line.

I shall be very glad to receive a copy of the map, a sketch can readily be drawn on thin, fine paper, & enclosed by mail. I remain very Resp[ectfull]y Your Ob[edient] ser[van]t, Lemuel Sawyer.

ALS in ScCleA. NOTE: An AEU by Calhoun reads: "Mr. Sawyer[,] desires a map of Texas." This letter was postmarked on 6/21.

From R.M. Aycock, Lafayette, Ga., 6/22. Aycock writes on behalf of Martha Maroney, widow of Philip Maroney, a Revolutionary soldier. She wishes to obtain a pension and thinks that Calhoun knew her husband when he lived in Pendleton and in Greenville, S.C. Aycock will appreciate any information that Calhoun can furnish in this matter. (An AEI by Calhoun refers this letter to [James L. Edwards] and reads: "It is not in my power to furnish any information on the points referred to within; and I enclose this to you, as I suppose it may be in your power to give some information on the subject." A Clerk's EU indicates that this letter was answered by Edwards on 7/24 and "sent under cover to Mr. Aycock (26th July) at La Fayette.") ALS in DNA, RG 59 (State Department), Miscellaneous Letters (M-179:104, frames 570–572).

To Messrs. Baring Brothers & Co., London, 6/22. Calhoun has received today a duplicate of the Barings' letter to the Treasury Department enclosing their account with the U.S. for the State Department for the quarter that ended on 3/31. He asks them to have such letters and accounts sent directly to the State Department rather than the Treasury—and that as promptly as practicable—in order that the State Department will be enabled to know when remittances should be made to the Barings. Calhoun calls their attention also to the fact that in this most recent quarterly account the objects or purposes for which three disbursements were made was not stated. FC in DNA, RG 59 (State Department), Accounting Records: Miscellaneous Letters Sent, 1832–1916, vol. for 2/1–9/30/1844, p. 254.

To W[illia]m Brent, Jr., 6/22. Calhoun answers Brent's note of yesterday. The appropriation "for your outfit" [as Chargé d'Affaires in Argentina] having been included in an act for the fiscal year that will begin on 7/1/1844, the Treasury will not issue a warrant for a payment to Brent "before that date." FC in DNA, RG 59 (State

Department), Accounting Records: Miscellaneous Letters Sent, 1832–1916, vol. for 2/1–9/30/1844, p. [253].

From JAMES H. CAUSTEN

Washington, June 22d 1844

Sir: I have the honor to inform you, that, under the provisions of the Convention with Mexico of the 11th of April 1839, and before the Commissioners appointed to carry it into effect, I represented as agent and attorney many claims to indemnity due to Citizens of the United States, as set forth in the following abstract:

Class 1. Claims definitively awarded = $185,466.59. On these ["awards" *interlined*] three quarterly instalments of five per cent each have been paid by Mexico. The fourth quarterly instalment of five per cent fell due on the 30th of April last, and has *not* been paid.

Class 2. Claims on which the American Commissioners made awards to the amount of $256,186.89; but not being concurred in by the Mexican Commissioners, were referred to the Umpire, who returned them to the Board without examination or decision—and they so remain at this day. The whole number of claims of that discription so returned by the Umpire is Seventy two, whereof forty six are represented by the undersigned. Nearly the entire of said forty six cases arise out of the capture of three Schooners, the Julius Caesar, Champion, & Louisiana.

The circumstances of the three Schooners named (they were regarded diplomatically as one case) constitute, in all stages of action had and to be had, a marked exception from all ["cases" *canceled and* "the other classes" *interlined*] of claims. They were captured by a Mexican National Ship of War, for an alleged breach of a pretended Blockade: and the captor was himself, for that act, forcibly subdued, and, while in the waters of Mexico, captured by a National vessel of War of the United States and carried by her as prize, in charge of a prize crew, into a port of the United States, avowedly to respond for the restoration of the three Schooners & to respond to the Government for the gross violation of its flag and dignity. This violent exercise of National force on each side, caused great excitement in both countries—Mexico seized the American vessels in her ports, and an open rupture was seriously threatened by each Government. Active diplomatic discussion resulted in an acknowledgment by Mexico of the illegality of the pretended Blockade, and was followed with an admission that the capture of the three Schooners was illegal. (See Senate documents 2d Session 25th Congress[,] Vol. 1[,] Doc. 1[,] page 154); and, on the other hand, the United States restored the Mexican capturing ship of war. The acknowledged illegality of capture of the three Schooners put entirely to rest all question of the right to indemnity due to the owners; and therefore the claim was with confidence submitted to the Board.

But the Mexican Commissioners, under the unfounded pretext that the United States had given notice to Mexico, that they excepted this case from the provisions of said Convention and from the action of said Board, in order to treat on it directly and diplomatically, delayed with evident intention all proceedings on it until so near the close of the Commission that its failure to receive definitive decision was within their own control, which they used with effect.

The American Commissioners had made awards on the three vessels at an early period, and in order to counteract the chicane and delay of the Mexican Commissioners before mentioned, took the unexampled course of addressing a formal official letter to the Umpire, setting forth the meritorious character of this claim and that it was entitled to priority of decision: it was, nevertheless, not acted on by him, but was returned without decision to the joint Board—and thereupon, the Mexican Commissioners stole from the files of the office and carried away (and have not since returned) all the Spanish papers and documents filed in the case and indispensable to its support (which had been procured by the claimants at great cost & labor, and was their exclusive property) against the earnest remonstrance of the American Commissioners, followed by the explicit injunction of the Secretary of State—who was moved thereto by the invocation of the undersigned, followed by his formal protests. (See said protests, detailed statement of claims &c. &c. among the printed documents accompanying the President[']s message, of June 13, 1842, in Senate Documents 2d Session 27th Congress Doc. No. 320—a copy whereof, for more convenient reference, I have the honor to present herewith).

The two classes of claims to which I have thus invited your attention, say 1st class or awards $185,466.59, and 2d class, returned by the Umpire, say, $256,186.89, making together an aggregate of $441,653.48, are held to be in the charge of the United States; and no doubt is entertained that our Government will manifest and make effectual proper efforts to secure promptly the rights and interests of the long suffering claimants, in a manner that shall best comport with its own dignity; and with that view, and to that end, the whole matter is now most respectfully submitted. I have the honor to be, With much respect, Your most ob[edient] Ser[van]t, James H. Causten.

ALS in DNA, RG 59 (State Department), Miscellaneous Letters (M-179:104, frames 591–592); draft (dated 6/21) in DLC, Causten-Pickett Papers.

To James H. Causten, Washington, 6/22. Calhoun acknowledges Causten's letter of today "relative to certain claims against the Mexican government for which you are agent." In reply, Calhoun assures Causten that no "proper efforts" will be spared in attempting to obtain any reparations that may be due. FC in DNA, RG 59 (State Department), Domestic Letters, 34:255 (M-40:32).

To R[ICHARD] S. COX[E], JOHN BALDWIN, and Others, Washington

Dept. of State, June 22nd 1844

Gentlemen, I have received the letters which you addressed to me under date the 19th and 20th Instant, upon the subjects of payment by the Mexican government under the convention of the 30th Jan[ular]y 1843, and of claims against the Mexican government in which you are interested. In reply, I have to assure you, that all proper means within the competency of the Executive shall be employed for the purpose of bringing about the object desired by you. I am, Gentlemen, your Obedient Serv[an]t, John C. Calhoun.

FC in DNA, RG 59 (State Department), Domestic Letters, 34:256 (M-40:32). NOTE: Other addressees were James H. Causten, Francis A. Dickins, Aaron Leggett, J. Prentiss, William S. Parrott, and G[ilbert] L. Thompson.

To W[arder] Cresson, Philadelphia, 6/22. "I am instructed by the President [John Tyler] to inform you, that, having reconsidered the proposal to establish a Consulate at Jerusalem, he is of opinion it is not called for by the public service and therefore declines to establish it at present." FC in DNA, RG 59 (State Department), Domestic Letters, 34:255–256 (M-40:32).

To Caleb Cushing, [Macao], 6/22. "The Senate having confirmed your appointment as Commissioner of the United States to

China, I have the honor to transmit to you, herewith, the commission consequent upon that confirmation." FC (No. 8) in DNA, RG 59 (State Department), Diplomatic Instructions, China, 1:23 (M-77: 38).

From S. D. DAKIN

Brown's Hotel, Washington, June 22d 1844
D[ea]r Sir, I hand you herewith a letter [of 6/19] from my friend, Mr. [Robert] Tyler, which partly explains my views in making this application to you. The adoption of my improved plan of dry dock by the Navy Department of my own country, encourages me to offer it to the maratime powers of Europe. If I could go abroad in some diplomatic capacity, consistent with this object, it would aid me essentially in my efforts to bring this important improvement to their attention. It has occurred to me that I might serve my country while serving myself, particularly in the north of Europe, in a way which I will proceed briefly to hint at, & will leave your own more sagacious & well informed mind to carry out the idea in detail.

I have thought, since the protective tariff policy has obtained such a strong hold upon the Country, that the most effectual method to combat its insidious errors & give a new direction to public sentiment, was to present countervailing commercial advantages to the consideration of the country, & open new resources of trade founded upon a necessary reduction of our present restrictions. Those who are opposed to the protective policy, would then be able to back up their arguments by an appeal to the immediate interests of the community, & to offer a positive equivalent for the relinquishment of the advantages claimed by the friends of that policy. If, for instance, this Government could open far more extensive markets than we now enjoy for our domestic productions, by forming treaties with the Zoll Verein,* [*Marginal interpolation:* *"The unfavorable reception of the treaty already made with the Zoll Verein, by the Senate, is perhaps rather discouraging, yet an extension of the system with results more favorable than were secured by that treaty which I think might be effected, will compel them to yeild."] Austria & other Germanic states, Holland, Denmark, Sweden, Russia &c, providing for the reduction of their duties on our cotton, rice, tobacco & other productions, in consideration of a corresponding reduction of ["our" *interlined*] duties on some articles the growth or manufacture of those countries, it would then be apparent to the satisfaction of every body, that an adherence to the ultra protective policy was inflicting a direct, positive & palpable injury on the country, by depriving it of the benefit of these certain, specific & definable advantages proposed by these treaties. The friends of free trade could then show to the country, that, by reducing our present high protective tariff upon certain articles of importation, we could procure a reduction of foreign duties & open a more extended foreign Market for certain articles of exportation; & that their doctrines are not only sound in theory, but also palpably beneficial in practice, in a case actually in hand.

An agent, appointed to bear despatches to our ministers resident at the several courts of these powers, & instructed to press upon their attention the views of this Government on this subject, would be able in the course of a few months probably to start negotiations in several quarters at nearly the same time, & in the course of a year or two, several treaties would no doubt be formed, whose combined advantages would not fail to make an offsett that could not be gainsayed to the pretended benefits of the protective tariff, & make a profound impression on the country, which would give that system a blow from which it would never recover.

I do not propose to specify in this communication the particular objects to which the attention of the ministers resident near the several governments should be called. They naturally suggest themselves to any reflecting mind on examining the state of our trade with the several nations. It would not become me to go into such details, however familiar I might be with them, & I content myself with a few general hints on the subject, leaving it to be more fully developed by yourself, if it should meet with your favorable consideration.

So far as these proposed efforts may affect the protective tariff policy, the result will be rather incidental than direct; & no one would have any right to regard them as undertaken with the express & exclusive design to attack that system. The independent advantages which would accrue from their success, would be sufficient to justify the undertaking & secure the approbation of the whole country.

Feeling confident that if you will turn this subject over in your mind, you will be favorably impressed with my hasty suggestions, (if you have not already anticipated them) I am, with profound respect, Your ob[edien]t serv[an]t, S.D. Dakin.

P.S. I will call on you personally in a few days. I think the President [John Tyler] is favorable to my ["views" *canceled and* "having such a position" *interlined*], & I should be pleased to have you speak to him—before he leaves town. I had a letter to you from Charles Gould Esq. of N.Y.

ALS in DNA, RG 59 (State Department), Applications and Recommendations, 1837–1845, Dakin (M-687:8, frames 48–52).

From F[rancis] M. Dimond

United States Consulate
Vera Cruz, June 22, 1844

Sir, I have the honour herewith to transmit dispatches recced [*sic*; received] by this morning[']s mail from our Charge at Mexico [City].

There appears to be considerable preparations making to rais[e] money and Troops to invade Texas. My opinion is that Santa Anna will make one great effort to conquer and if not successful give it up.

Presuming you have every information from our Legation at Mexico, I do not deem it proper to trouble you with reports and conjectures, on the subject.

Having received permission some time since from the Acting Secretary of State, to visit my Family in R[hode] Island[,] I shall avail myself of it, as soon as I learn the Fate of the Treaty with Texas in the Senate of the U. States. I have the honour to be Sir most respectfully Your ob[edient] Serv[an]t, F.M. Dimond.

[P.S.] The U.S. Frigate Potomac and Brig Somers are here—and Vincennes hourly expected.

ALS (No. 226) in DNA, RG 59 (State Department), Consular Despatches, Veracruz, vol. 5 (M-183:5), received 7/15.

To Dr. David Martin, Philadelphia, 6/22. Calhoun informs Martin that "owing to the name of the consulate for the Island of Trinidad having been mistaken for that of the Consulate at Trinidad de Cuba," Martin's nomination for the U.S. Consulship at the Island of Trinidad was mistakenly sent to and confirmed by the Senate as U.S. Consul at Trinidad, Cuba. Because of the recent appointment of the Consul there, [Samuel] McLean, the President [John Tyler] declines issuing a commission to Martin "conformably to the confirmation of your nomination." (An EU reads: "sent to care of Rob[er]t Tyler.") FC in DNA, RG 59 (State Department), Domestic Letters, 34:256–257 (M-40:32).

From P.A. Sage, "Publisher of the 'German National Gazette'," 6/22. "In the instructions communicated to the undersigned with his appointment as publisher of the Laws, treaties etc. of the U.S., some emphasis is laid upon the precept, to copy verbatim from the Madisonian of this city. As however in the publication in that paper of yesterday's date, of the recent convention with France, numerous gross violations of the French language occur, which to the undersigned seem ill to befit an official publication—probably through the ignorance of that idiom, of the copyist or compositor—leave is respectfully asked to correct the errors at this office." ALS in DNA, RG 59 (State Department), Miscellaneous Letters (M-179:104, frame 593).

From HENRY SAVAGE

Guat[emal]a, 22nd June 1844

I send herewith enclosed copy of a note [dated 5/22/1844] addressed to me by directions of the President of this State [José Mariano Rodriguez], purporting to forewarn me of the invasion of the territory of Guatemala by troops of the State of San Salvador, and the reply thereto [of 5/30], I have judged proper to make.

The invasion of the State of Guatemala by forces of San Salvador, arises from the fact, that in April last, certain persons in authority under the Government of Guatemala, furnished muskets to an exile of S[an] Salvador, for the purpose of subverting that Government, but the expedition proving fruitless and the authorities of that State succeeding in repelling the attempt, the insurgents returned to Guatemala, but were shortly after followed by 4000 armed men, headed by the President of San Salvador and who occupied a village called Jutiapa, situated on the frontiers of Guatemala.

Immediately on the receipt of this intelligence, martial law was proclaimed and preparations of a hostile character commenced, with its attendant requisitions of forced loans from the inhabitants, as is the custom in this country. I have however, to remark for the first time, that foreigners have been exempted from these vexations.

Up to this time, nothing of greater importance has occurred, than, that on the 19th advices were received, that the invaders had abandoned the territory of Guatemala; this movement I ascribe to the influence of the Confederation (composed of three States, Nicaragua, Honduras, & S[an] Salvador) which has assumed the position of aggressor, & at the same time inviting Guatemala to appoint Commissioners to negotiate a treaty to restore the friendly relations between Guatemala and S[an] Salvador.

This Government seems fully prepared for defence and has sent out troops to observe the movements of the invaders.

Enclosed you will also find a printed decree issued [on 3/7/1844] by the Legislative Assembly of the State of San Salvador in regard to foreigners, as likewise copy of a protest [dated 4/22] which I have sent to that Government, and which I trust will meet with your approval.

I have only to refer you to a Convention concluded between the Government of Guatemala and the Consul of France, for payment of certain french claims upon this Government; it is inserted in the "Gaceta Oficial" No. 145, Feb[ruar]y 8/[18]44 sent heretofore; and to the declaration of the Blockade of the port of San Juan de Nicaragua, by Sir Charles Adam, communicated to this Government by the British ["Government" *canceled and* "Consul" *interlined*], as will be seen in the No. 151 of same Gazette. I am with great respect Your Obed[ien]t Serv[an]t, Henry Savage [Acting Consul?].

ALS (No. 14) with Ens in DNA, RG 59 (State Department), Diplomatic Despatches, Guatemala, vol. 1 (M-219:4).

From W[ILLIA]M SMITH,
[former Representative from Va.]

Warrenton [Va.,] June 22nd 1844
Dear Sir, May I trouble you so far as to ask you that one of your messengers may collect for you a copy of [Absalom H.] Chappell[']s [Representative from Ga.] letter on the tariff; [Linn] Boyd[']s [Representative from Ky.] speech on the Bargain &C; and [Thomas H.] Benton[']s & [Robert J.] Walker[']s D[itt]o on Texas, all in pamphlet; & that you will forward them to me, as early as your leisure will permit. If you could send me a copy of Charles Francis Adams' recent pamphlet on Texas you would oblige me.

Is Benton to join the enemy? A distinguished Fed[eralist], here, this day pronounced him a patriot & a statesman; and the Richmond Whig has said that "Bullion ought to be a Whig." Certain it is, that his course on Texas is with the Democracy, the shirt of Nessus, to him. And what madness rules the hour with the [Washington] Globe? Are its Editors [Francis P. Blair and John C. Rives] so blind as not to see that their strength & power alone depends on their intimate connection with the whole democracy? The readiness with which Mr. [Martin] V[an] B[uren] has been given up proves a predisposition in the public mind, so to do—and the eagerness with which Colo[nel James K.] Polk has been adopted in his stead conclusively proves it. Mr. V[an] B[uren']s Texas letter [*two words changed to* "came most"] opportunely to this mood of the public mind and it eagerly seized upon it. Col. B[enton] & the Globe are in a somewhat like predicament; & time will show that both can be abandoned with great alacrity.

Excuse me however, I commenced by putting you to some trouble; and I have run off into rather dangerous metaphysics.

Please send me the last annual Army & ["Navy" *interlined*] Register & the annual treasury statement of the commerce &C of the U.S. Y[ou]rs most truly, Wm. Smith.

ALS in ScCleA.

From HENRY F. FISH

[Washington? *ca.* June 24, 1844]
Sir, I respectfully solicit from you the appointment of Consul at The Bermudas, or at some other foreign and southern port.

Among some of the motives prompting me to desire such an appointment, may I be permitted to remark that I have long been familiar with commercial affairs: that the incumbent at Bermuda is a British subject, more or less unqualified to a full discharge of a Consul's duties: that I am a native citizen, about to seek a residence abroad, without resources for occupation: And that a residence of two seasons at Bermuda has given me a good knowledge of the country and its principal citizens.

Respectfully referring you to the accompanying letters, and humbly protesting my sincere desire, if appointed, faithfully to discharge all the duties of my trust, I subscribe myself, Sir, With profound personal respect, Your Very Humble Servant, Henry F. Fish.

ALS in DNA, RG 59 (State Department), Applications and Recommendations, 1837–1845, Fish (M-687:11, frames 273–274).

From ALEX[ANDER] JONES

Baton Rouge La., June 24th 1844

Dear Sir, Since I had the honor of seeing you last in Washington I have made quite an extensive tour. I reached Wheeling on the Ohio [River] from Baltimore, and descended that River ["as far" *canceled*] to Cincinnati, from thence to Louisville, where I took a boat for New Orleans[,] which city I reached on the 21st Inst., where I spent a day, or two on business, then left and arrived in this place, on yesterday, 130 miles above[.]

Every where I have directed my inquiries, and observations towards the state of public opinion & feeling with regard to the pending questions of the day, and especially as respects the present canvass for the Presidency. I am happy to inform you that in reference to the questions of free trade, and the Annexation of Texas[,] which may be considered questions of the greatest importance, I found the opinions of the people much more favourable than I expected. I am glad to find, the cotton planters of Carolina do not now as formerly almost stand alone on the question of a protective Tarriff [*sic*]. For the first time in the history of the Government, the great farming interest of the west are coming to their senses on this subject. They are forced into the consideration of the subject, by the current course of events. They find every thing they consume advancing while all they produce has a downward tendency. Flour is selling in New Orleans at $3.00 per Barrell. Bacon at 3 to 3¼ c[ents] per pound— Whiskey at 17 to 18 c[ents] per Gallon[.] Western provisions have become to be [*sic*] a drug. I am disposed to think that the manufacturers are fast loosing the ear of the west, and once gone they will probably never recover it. Because, right, reason, & common sense are all against it.

The Texas question is a much stronger one than I apprehended even in Indiana & Illinois. In the latter State it is the most powerful question agitated[,] especially in southern Illinois. I saw many persons in & from this State, all of whom concur in saying that this State will give Polk & Dallas [a] 10,000 majority. The accounts from Indiana seem to leave not a shadow of doubt but the State will give a large Democratic majority. In Kentucky Col. [William O.] Butler is the candidate for Governor who is said to be the most popular man in the State. With his popularity is joined the influence of [Charles A.] Wickliff[e] and his family, with that of Tom Marshall. I was assured by some intelligent gentlemen, that this State would cast the largest Democratic vote this year, that it probably has ever done for a long period past. They seem to think it may not be impossible to carry the State. I saw a large ["number" *interlined*] of Tennesseans. They say all is safe in that State. Not a shadow of doubt rest[s] upon Mississippi or Arkansas.

In this State, the election takes place next ["place" *canceled*] next [*sic*] week. The contest will be a close one. It is also mixed up with the election of members to a State Convention, which brings into the canvass a strong local question. Yet all seem to agree that the Democraty [*sic*] will carry the State. Many of the sugar planters, still adhere most warmly to [Henry] Clay, ["an" *canceled*] on account of the sugar duty; but a ["lar" *canceled*] large defection has taken place among them and other whigs of the State on the Texas question, which is a powerful question in this State.

I saw a large sugar planter of Bayou Plaquemine, 9 miles below this place, who stated that in his election precinct of the Parish of Ibberville [*sic*; Iberville] there were 45 voters, all of whom in 1840 with some two or three exceptions voted for Gen[era]l [William Henry] Harrison. Now he says, every one with 2 or 3 exceptions have declared they will vote for [James K.] Polk. Many of the sugar planters themselves express the greatest indignation against Mr. [Alexander] Barrow [Senator from La.] and say his letter in opposition to the annexation of Texas, ["was an" *canceled and* "is an" *interlined; one word canceled*] insult to their understandings. He ["told" *canceled*] told them annexation would cause a depreciation in the value of their lands and negroes. They ["said" *interlined*] even admitting a temporary depression to follow annexation, what would it amount to, compared with the possibility of *total & permanent destruction*, without annexation? You may set down this State for Polk, though the result next week will be no criterion to judge by[.] Upon the whole, I think the prospect of success was never more encouraging[.] The day is coming when right principles will prevail, and that very soon.

Immense destruction has been sustained by the cotton crop on account of the Inundations of the Mississippi[,] Red & Arkansas Rivers. No one estimates the damage at less than 150,000 Bales, and many commission houses in New Orleans estimate it as high as *two hundred thousand Bales*. I have been an eyewitness to the destruction on the Banks of the Mississippi. From the mouth of the ["Ohio" *canceled*] Arkansas to Vicksburg, a distance of about 200 miles, I saw but one plantation that was ["not" *interlined*] under water. Three plantations were pointed out to me which had produced 1500 Bales[.] This year, they will not make a ["single" *interlined*] Bale! !

157

Other estates below Vicksburg have likewise seriously suffered.

The country so far is generally healthy, though sickness is apprehended when the great flood of waters subside.

Crops of sugar have never been known to be more promising than at present. If no casualty intervenes the crop will be one of the largest ever made in the State. Many cotton plantations in this vicinity have been converted during the past and present year into sugar estates.

I hear the Texans are much chagrined at the anticipation of the rejection of the Treaty. I saw two Georgians travelling in the west; they speak in terms of the utmost indignation of Mr. [Senator John M.] Berrien[']s course. They say the State is sure for Polk.

I should have mentioned that the crops of cotton, where above water, were never more promising.

I send letters to the [New York] Journal of Commerce over the signature of "*Manhattan*," some of which you may probably see.

I leave tomorrow on a steamer for St. Louis, on my return to New York, which place I expect to reach in 2 or 3 weeks.

I may probably embrace another opportunity of writing to you again before my return. I have the Honor To Remain Your very Sincere friend and Devoted Humble Serv[an]t, Alex. Jones.

ALS in ScCleA.

To Thomas O. Larkin, U.S. Consul, Monterey

Department of State
Washington, June 24th 1844

Sir, Your letters of the 10th, 11th, 12th & 16th of April and two letters of the 20th April, *not numbered*, have been received.

Your nomination was confirmed by the Senate and a new Commission sent to you on the 3rd of February last.

Orders have been given to the Despatch Agent of this Department to transmit to you, care of Messrs. William Appleton & Co. Boston, a Seal, press, Flag and the Arms of the U. States.

Authority is given to you to take from the office & to open all letters addressed by the Department to the Consulate at Monterey, previous to your appointment, as also those to San Francisco, should Mr. A[lbert] M. Gilliam, appointed U.S. Consul there, not have reached his post, when this letter is received by you.

The interesting information which you give respecting the arrival at New Helvetia of Lieu[tenan]t [John C.] Fremont & his party, and the sufferings which they have undergone, was immediately ordered to be published & your letter submitted to the Secretary of War for his perusal.

In making your official statement of American Commerce you will embrace such portion only of the Department of Upper California, as may be nearer to you, than to the residence of any other U.S. Consul in that Department. It is gratifying to the Department to learn that the taking of Monterey by Com[mo]d[o]re [Thomas Ap Catesby] Jones has produced no serious injury to our Country, or left a bad impression respecting it in California.

Agreeably to your request, permission is given to you to leave Monterey, when your business demands it, provided a faithful & competent person, for whose official acts you will be held responsible, is left by you to discharge the Consular functions.

In respect to the losses sustained by Isaac Graham & other American Citizens by reason of their arrest & imprisonment by armed officers & Soldiers of Mexico, the Department has been informed by Gen[era]l W[addy] Thompson ["late" *interlined*] U.S. Minister at Mexico, that he had effected an arrangement by which the amount previously agreed upon by the Mexican Government to be paid in these cases, should actually be paid. I am, Sir, Respectfully, Your obedient Servant, J.C. Calhoun.

LS in CU, Bancroft Library, Larkin Collection; FC in DNA, RG 59 (State Department), Consular Instructions, 11:249–251; PC in Hammond, ed., *Larkin Papers*, 2:143–144.

From Thomas O. Larkin

Consulate of the United
States, Monterey, June 24 1844

Sir, I have the honour to inform you that I have received my commission as Consul for this Port, from the President of the United States, by and with the advice of the Senate, under date of the twenty ninth day of January 1844.

I have had, the honour to inform the Department in the month of April of my commission as before given by the President, and acknowledged by the President of Mexico, with the corresponding Exequatur of this Government, the second commission has not been accompanied with the Exequatur; I beg leave to ask if it should be sent to me.

There has been appointed as U.S. Consul, Mr. Albert M. Gilliam, for the Port of San Francisco; the Port of San Francisco, is not a Port of entry, foreign vessels only going there by special licence of the Government of California, but not allowed by the Government of Mexico; Monterey is the only Port of Entry in California. Foreign vessels are fined for going into any other port before entering here, here only they pay their duties. There is therefore no occation to have but one United States Consul in California, and perhaps my commission had better be made out to that effect, all of which I leave to the wisdom of the Department.

There has been no American Ship of war on this coast for some time. As there are always vessels laying at anchor at Callao, I beg leave to recommend, that one should be constantly kept on here. I believe the same has always been recommended by our Commadores who have visited us. The American trade is on the increase in California, and may need protection in times of trouble. Sir I am with much respect, your most obedient servant, Thomas O. Larkin.

LS (No. 8) in DNA, RG 59 (State Department), Consular Despatches, Monterey (M-138:1), received 8/31; variant FC in CU, Bancroft Library, Larkin Collection; PC in Hammond, ed., *Larkin Papers*, 2:144–145.

To ALPHONSE PAGEOT, [French Minister to the U.S.]

Department of State
Washington, 24th June, 1844

Sir: I have the honor to inform you that the additional article agreed upon on the 15th of April last, to the convention for the surrender of fugitive criminals, of the 9th of November, 1843, between the United States and France, has been submitted by the President to the Senate of the United States, and was duly approved by that body on the 15th instant, with certain amendments defining more explicitly the crimes therein mentioned.

I hasten to communicate to you, for the information of your Government, a copy of the resolution of the Senate above referred to, and avail myself of the occasion to offer you renewed assurances of the distinguished consideration with which I am, Sir, your obedient servant, J.C. Calhoun.

FC in DNA, RG 59 (State Department), Notes to Foreign Legations, France, 6:81 (M-99:21).

From R[omulus] M. Saunders, [Representative from N.C.]

Raleigh, June 24, [18]44

My dear Sir, I have not since my return had the opportunity of mingling very much with our people—but as far as I have had the means of doing so, there exist on the part of the democratic party the best feeling. On the Texas question, the efforts of the Whigs is to divert the public mind from the main question—to raise false charges thus as they hope to silence the present feeling. Their only hope seems to be, that the thing will blow over. Some of our friends have thought you ought to be notified of what is passing—that you might give it the proper denial. I can[']t say, I consider it as necessary—but I have written the enclosed, that you can do as you shall see fit—and I of course shall be governed by your wishes in any reply you may make.

What do you infer from the answer from Mexico? Has any thing further been received as to the disposition of England?

I start to day on a tour in fulfillment of some political appointments in the East. We propose having a large mass meeting in Charlotte on the 23[rd]—as you will be invited, that might be a fit occasion for your coming out for Polk & adding any thing else you might think necessary. Y[ou]rs respectfully, R.M. Saunders.

[P.S.] Since writing I rec[eive]d the enclosed from Mr. [James A.] Black—which I think it best to enclose.

[Enclosure]

R.M. Saunders to J.C. Calhoun

June 24, '44

My dear Sir, I find it industriously circulated, that you went into the State department with the design of so managing the Texas question as to have the Treaty rejected—and that your object in keeping up the present excitement is to further your designs of effecting a dissolution of the Union. To shew that such is your purpose, reference is had to certain resolutions adopted at some of the public meetings in South-Carolina, avowing a wish for a dissolution should the annexation of Texas ultimately fail. I think it due to you to state these charges, that you may if so disposed give them a denial & exposure. Very respectfully, R.M. Saunders.

[Enclosure]

James A. Black, [Representative from S.C.], to R.M. Saunders

Raleigh, 22 June 1844

Dear Gen[era]l, I submit a rough draft of a letter of enquiry, which I wish you to put in such form as your better judgement may dictate, and forward to Mr. Calhoun. I am quite sure that such an answer as he can and will give, will be of service to our party and ["Country" *canceled*] the country.

As a matter of course, you will make the questions, such as you think proper, or you can mearly [*sic*] write him, so that he can have an opportunity to speake out, on the Union, Texas & the Tariff. On all these subjects he is right and his sentiments will be approved by the Southern people. Could all the People know truly Mr. Calhoun's views & feeling on these poients[?] the Whigs would be confounded. Your ob[edien]t Ser[van]t, James A. Black.

[Enclosure]

[By James A. Black, for R.M. Saunders to John C. Calhoun,
    rough draft]

Raleigh, June 1844

D[ea]r Sir, An attempt is now being made by the Whigs of this State, to make the an[n]exation of Texas, a question of Dis Union on the part of the South; ["And" *altered to* "and"] in proof of this they refer to a few excited meetings in South Carolina, and Mr. [George] Mc-Duffie[']s Speaches [*sic*] against the Tariff.

You are aware that the publick mind has been poisoned [*sic*] against your State, ["State" *canceled*] and yourself, ever since the Nullification movement, in which, instead of meeting you in argument it was found more conveniant [*sic*] to oppose both ["you & the State" *interlined*] by misrepresenting ["both" *canceled*] your motives and actions. I am anxious to meet this slander at once, & from authority, at least as far as you are conserned [*sic*], and so far as you can speak for your State. Will you on the receipt of this give me your ["views in" *canceled*] answers to the following questions, with liberty to publish and use them[?]

1st. Do you not beli[e]ve the Union necessary to insure Constitutional liberty and to secure to the people the blessings of Self government?

2nd. Do you not beli[e]ve the Union established on such principles as secures it from the attacks of Partizans and Fanaticks come from what quarter they may?

3rd. Do you not think ["that" *canceled*] all adgitation [*sic*] at this time on the Subject of the Tariff on the part of the South badly timed?

4th. Can the an[n]exation of Texas in any way endanger the Union?

5th. Do you not beli[e]ve that the an[n]exation of Texas, necessary to the safety of the South and and [*sic*] imperiously demanded to secure the Union from foreign influence ["?" *canceled*] and interference?

6th. Do you wish at this time a Southern Convention?

ALS with Ens in ScCleA.

From Ja[me]s W. Schaumburg, "for himself & the Estate of N. Cox," and H[enry] D. Gilpin, "for himself & the Estate of S. Elkins," Philadelphia, 6/24. They remind Calhoun of claims on the Mexican government which have been pending for many years and of which they are anxious to obtain settlement. They hope that a new convention will be made between the U.S. and Mexico. LS in DNA, RG 59 (State Department), Miscellaneous Letters (M-179:104, frames 595–596).

From Ernest Schwendler, U.S. Consul, Frankfort, 6/24. He congratulates Calhoun on his appointment, "which has been greeted with the highest satisfaction by all the States of our happy union." He discusses several small matters and adds that at Frankfort "the manufacturing and commercial communities are anxiously awaiting the decision of the fate of the treaty pending between the United States and the States of the German Zollverein, which is indeed a subject of importance to them." ALS (No. 35) in DNA, RG 59 (State Department), Consular Despatches, Frankfurt on the Main, vol. 1 (M-161:1), received 9/7.

To [FELIPE ARANA], "The Minister for Foreign Affairs of the Argentine Confederation"

Department of State
Washington, 25th June, 1844

Sir: The President of the United States having thought proper to name William Brent, Jr. their Chargé d'Affaires to the Argentine Confederation, I have the honor of announcing the same to Your Excellency and of praying you to give credence to whatever he shall say to you on my part. He knows the concern our Republic takes in the interest and prosperity of the Argentine Confederation, our strong desire to cultivate its friendship and to deserve it by all the good offices which may be in our power. He knows, also, my zeal to promote these by whatever may depend upon my Ministry. I have no doubt that Mr. Brent will so conduct himself as to meet your confidence, and I avail myself with pleasure of this occasion of tendering to you assurances of my high and distinguished consideration. (Signed) J.C. Calhoun.

CC in DNA, RG 84 (Foreign Posts), Argentina, Instructions, vol. 15. NOTE: EU's, possibly in Brent's handwriting, read "Rec[eive]d 22d July 1844" and "delivered to Felipe Arana The Minister of foreign affaires at Buenos Aires on the 16th[?] Nov. 1844."

From A[DOLPH] E. BORIE and Others

Philadelphia, 25 June 1844

Sir, The subscribers are holders of Certificates of Mexican Indemnity of which the payments were to be made to the Agent of the United States in Mexico in regular quarterly instalments of five per cent. We have been informed that the fourth instalment due on the 30th of April was not paid. Under these circumstances we respectfully and earnestly request the interposition of our government to obtain a compliance by Mexico with the terms of her agreement. The long period given for the entire payment and the small amount of each instalment were acceded to at the instance and for the benefit of Mexico; and a failure to comply with these terms is not only a violation of the stipulated arrangement but a most serious injury to the interest and property of the Claimants, whose just demands were originally so long postponed, and who have at least a right to expect that their awards will now be punctually paid. We earnestly solicit and confidently hope for the prompt interference and aid of the government. Very respectfully Your ob[edien]t Serv[an]ts, A.E. Borie, H[enry] D. Gilpin, Pr. Ls. Laguerenne, Lewis Waln, J. Fisher Leaming, James Nevins, S. Nevins.

LS in DNA, RG 59 (State Department), Miscellaneous Letters (M-179:104, frame 606); CC in DNA, RG 84 (Foreign Posts), Mexico, Instructions, vol. 5.I.

From SERENO E. DWIGHT, "Private"

Washington, June 25th, 1844
My dear Sir, Should you, after reading the inclosed statement [the application of 6/24 by Mary Dwight, the widow of the Rev. Timothy Dwight, for a Revolutionary pension], deem it proper for you to suggest your own opinion, respecting the case, to Mr. [James L.] Edwards of the Patent [*sic*; Pension] Office, I shall be much gratified with your doing so. If you judge otherwise, I shall be satisfied. In either case, I am With very high respect & regard, Your friend & obed[ien]t serv[an]t, Sereno E. Dwight.

ALS with Ens in DNA, RG 15 (Veterans Administration), Revolutionary War Pension and Bounty-Land Warrant Application Files, 1800–1900, W21025 (M-804:878, frames 666–667, 636–637, and 630–631). NOTE: An AEI by Calhoun reads: "Submitted for the consideration of Mr. Edwards. I am not sufficiently informed nor have I time to make myself so to venture an opinion as requested; but if Mr. Edwards should think there are sufficient grounds for it, I would be glad to see the claim allowed in so meritorious a case."

From BEN E. GREEN

Legation of the U.S. of A.
Mexico, June 25th 1844
Sir, I have the honor to send you (no. 1 & 2) copies of a note [of 6/23] from Mr. [José M. de] Bocanegra, and my reply [of 6/24].

The Report of the Committee, proposing to double the direct taxes, (which I sent you by last mail) has been rejected by the Congress. That body is now engaged in considering the proposition of Gen[era]l [Anastasio?] Parrodi, for a forced loan; but as yet nothing has been done. A commissioner sails in this packet to England &

France, to ask for aid. I have the honor to be Very Respectfully Your ob[edien]t Ser[van]t, Ben E. Green.

[Enclosure: State Department translation]

J[osé] M. de Bocanegra to B[en] E. Green, Charge d'Affaires of the U.S.

National Palace
Mexico, June 23, 1844

The Undersigned, Minister of Relations, has the honour to address the Chargé d'Affaires of the United States, with the object of informing him, that it appears from the public papers of that ["country" *changed to* "Republic"], that the Executive has assigned, and has ordered sea and land forces, to proceed, to prevent the Supreme Government of Mexico, from using its imprescriptible and well known rights, in occupying the territory of Texas with its own troops; which assertion is proved by the arrival of the frigate of war, belonging to those States, having anchored off the Isla Verde, in sight of Vera Cruz, and her commander having declared that other forces were to follow.

Such circumstances could not but attract the attention of the most Excellent President; and in consequence, he desires to know, in a clear and decisive manner, whether the troops which Mexico is now sending upon Texas, will be opposed by those of the United States, either on sea or on land; in order that he may regulate his conduct accordingly, as His Excellency is about to ["act" *canceled and* "operate" *interlined*] in compliance with his duty, for the occupation of the said territory, as an integrant portion of the Mexican Nation; and he would regret that any force of the United States should appear to oppose him, as such an act would be a declaration of war against Mexico, which would find herself under the necessity of repelling force by force, on seeing herself thus outraged, and the treaties which have bound together the two Republics, broken.

The Undersigned informs Mr. Green, that he has received express orders from His Excellency the President, to ["receive" *canceled and* "obtain" *interlined*] from ["the" *canceled*] him, the ["necessary" *interlined*] explanations, ["necessary" *canceled*] as to what has been published by the ["news" *interlined*] papers of the United States, and is confirmed by the Commander of the frigate, anchored off Isla Verde, as stated in this note, considering the circumstances and the serious and important nature of this affair.

The Undersigned repeats to Mr. Green the assurances of his most distinguished consideration. J.M. de Bocanegra.

[Enclosure]
Ben E. Green to J[osé] M. de Bocanegra

Legation of the U.S. of A.
Mexico, June 24th 1844

The undersigned, Chargé d'affaires of the U.S. of A. (ad interim) has this moment had the honor to receive the note of H.E. J.M. de Bocanegra, of yesterday's date, stating that, it appears, ["from" *interlined*] the public newspapers, that the executive of the U.S. has sent forces, by sea and land, to prevent the supreme Govt. of Mexico from occupying with its troops the territory of Texas; that this rumour is confirmed by the U.S. Frigate of War, anchored at Isla Verde, the Captain of which has said that more forces are to follow; and finally that H.E. the President wishes to know, clearly & explicitly, whether the troops, which Mexico may send against Texas, will be opposed by land or sea, by the forces of the U.S.

The undersigned regrets that he has received no communications from his Govt. on this subject, and is therefore unable to answer this enquiry, as clearly and explicitly, as he would wish. He will lose no time however in submitting the note of H.E. Mr. Bocanegra to his Govt., & in obtaining a reply. He is also in daily expectation of hearing from his Govt. His next despatches may enable him to give the desired information, and if so, he will immediately communicate it to H.E.

In the mean time, the undersigned, actuated by a sincere & frank desire of giving to H.E. all the information he possesses, begs leave to call to mind a note, addressed to the late Minister of the U.S., Mr. [Waddy] Thompson [Jr.], on the 23d of August last; in which H.E. Mr. Bocanegra himself first originated with this legation the question of the annexation of Texas to the U.S., accompanying his communication with a direct threat of war, in case the U.S. should determine on the measure referred to. That measure is now the subject of consideration in the Senate of the U.S. and the undersigned has reason to believe, that it is true, that forces have been prepared by his Govt., both by land & sea, to meet any contingency, which may arise, all which however, as the undersigned believes, has been done, as a defensive precaution, made necessary by the oft repeated threats, with which H.E. Mr. Bocanegra, in the name of the Mexican Govt., has thought proper to menace the U.S.

The undersigned avails himself of this occasion to renew to H.E. Mr. Bocanegra, the assurance of his distinguished consideration. (Signed), Ben E. Green.

ALS with Ens and State Department translation in DNA, RG 59 (State Department), Diplomatic Despatches, Mexico, vol. 12 (M-97:13); variant FC in DNA, RG 84 (Foreign Posts), Mexico, Despatches; draft with En in NcU, Duff Green Papers (published microfilm, roll 5, frames 606–607, 603–604); PEx with Ens in Senate Document No. 1, 28th Cong., 2nd Sess., pp. 77–78; PEx with Ens in House Document No. 2, 28th Cong., 2nd Sess., pp. 76–78.

From JOHN W. HOLDING

Washington, June 25th 1844

Sir, I respectfully request that you will cause to be laid before the Attorney Gen[era]l of the United States—If not Improper—for His Legal opinion the claim of the American Ship Good Return that is now Pending against the Late Government of Colombia, In accordance with the Treaty Between the U.S. and Spain for the year 1798—and before Colombia had one Particle of Political Existance.

It is to be observed that the said ship was never within the jurisdiction of Colombia.

I Particular desire this for my own Government, Having heard frequently, subaltern Reports adverse to the Propriety of the direct Protection by the U.S. and If such should Prove to be the case, I ["would" *interlined*] like much to be apprized of the fact. I Have the Honor to be Most Respectfully Your Ob[edien]t Servant, John W. Holding.

ALS in ScCleA.

From W[ILLIAM] S. MURPHY

Legation of the United States
Galveston Texas, 25th June 1844

Sir, Your despatch No. 18 of the 11 ult[im]o was received on the 15th Inst. and expecting to see the President [of Texas, Samuel Houston] in a few days, I deemed it best to have an informal conversation with his Excellency on the subject, you refer to, before I addressed a note [to] the Sec[re]t[ary] of State [Anson Jones]; in as much as the reply of the Secretary to my note, will not be given without the previous instructions of the President. I am also confident, that I can make a satisfactory arrangement with the President, in a private interview, and effect thereby, in less time, the object of my Government. I have the honor to be your ob[edien]t Serv[an]t, W.S. Murphy.

ALS (No. 31) in DNA, RG 59 (State Department), Diplomatic Despatches, Texas, vol. 2 (T-728:2, frame 361).

From JOSEPH RAY

Washington D.C., 25 June 1844

Sir, I have the honour to acknowledge the receipt of your letter of the 21st Ins[tan]t and now take the liberty of bringing my case before you at greater length than it has hitherto been, in order that you may see its justice, and after an examination give such instruction to our Minister in Brazil in regard to it as in your opinion it may demand.

As the shortest mode of putting you in possession of the facts, I send enclosed copy of a communication (No. 1) made by Mr. Norvall on my behalf to the Department of State in 1830, together with a copy of the instructions of the Department to Mr. [Ethan A.] Brown enclosing documents to support the claim. No. 2, also copy of a correspondence with Mr. [William] Hunter in 1837, 1839 and 1840 No. 3, also copy of a letter to Mr. [George H.] Proffit dated 8 January last to which letter I was not favoured with a reply. On my reappointment to the Consulate of Pernambuco in 1836, I was the bearer of a letter from the Department to Mr. Hunter calling his attention to my claim and by a reference to my correspondence with that Gent[lema]n you will perceive that up to 1840 he had not presented it.

Despairing of having my case presented to the Brazilian Government I dispatched an Agent to Rio who received on 4th January 1843 from Mr. Hunter, the Documents and papers relating to my claim. I petitioned and obtained leave to sue the National Treasury, and enclosed you have a certified Copy No. 4, of the proceedings of the suit, consisting of the Libel setting forth my demand for property sequestered, and the reply of the Procurador Fiscal, who not dissenting to the justice of the claim, alledges that it is barred by a law passed in October 1841 by which all claims on the Brazilian Govt. from 1826 not demanded before 1st January 1843, shall be null and void. No. 5 Copy of the law. It is under these circumstances that I submit my case for your consideration in order that I may not be deprived of the means of redress. There is one point in my case not brought fully to view in the letter of Mr. Norvall which I now take the liberty to mention, to wit, my illegal imprisonment by the Brazilian Authorities. In 1825 by instructions from Rio I was ordered to retire from the Brazilian Empire, the reason assigned being that I had sheltered some of the Liberal party and aided them in leaving the Country and that I had endeavoured to save the life of a Citizen of the United States implicated with others, by offering money to one of the Authorities. I think it well to inform you that the persons implicated in political offences have all long since returned to the country and many fill the highest offices under the Government. The Imperial decree specified that I should be allowed a reasonable time to settle my business. The President of the Province only granted the short period of fifteen days. I was then incarcerated in Fort Brum, where I was kept about seventeen days, and without any previous notice was conducted on board a vessel to sail immediately for the United States. It was after my departure that the Brazilian Authorities under the pretext that I was owing duties to the Government, amounting to nineteen thousand four hundred mil reis sequestrated and placed in the hands of Administrators, the whole of the debts due to my house[,] the Merchandize in my stores as well as my private property in my town and Country houses. I was engaged in large Mercantile operations, and had to my Consignment frequently twelve or thirteen vessels. By the Certificate to be found in the legal proceedings No. 4, you will see that the Administrators acknowledge a balance due to my house of One hundred and fifty three thousand mil reis, and estimating the Merchandize in my Stores and my private property at Two hundred thousand mil reis, which makes the amount, calculating the value of the mil rei in 1826 which was 50d St[erlin]g and the value of the mil rei in 1843 being 25½d Sterling, is equivalent to £77,000 Sterling say Seventy seven thousand Pounds Sterling or Six hundred and eighty thousand mil reis at the present time, whereby with the Interest thereon, and damages for illegal imprisonment, and the breaking up of my commercial establishment, is the claim for which I now seek indemnification.

In my view of the matter the law of 1841 is unjust, and such as our Government I feel convinced will not submit to. It is in the power of no Government by any such law to avoid the just demands against it by the Citizens of another country more especially where these demands have arisen from the seizure of property and for other unjust and illegal acts. I am very desirous that this long protracted business should now be brought to a close. I therefore respectfully request that Instructions be given to our Minister at Rio to urge my claim, without submitting to any further unnecessary delay. I shall be prepared to furnish the necessary proofs to establish it as well to show the illegal and oppressive course pursued by the Brazilian Government towards me. I am very respectfully Sir Your ob[edien]t Servant, Joseph Ray.

ALS in DNA, RG 76 (Records of Boundary and Claims Commissions and Arbitrations), Miscellaneous Claims Records: Brazil Convention, January 27, 1849, claims 1–38; FC in DNA, RG 84 (Foreign Posts), Brazil, Despatches, 11:[110–113].

From B.W. Richards, Philadelphia, 6/25. Richards recommends George M. Totten, a civil engineer, to Calhoun as a gentleman of intelligence, integrity, good character, and professional ability. ALS in DNA, RG 59 (State Department), Applications and Recommendations, 1837–1845, Totten (M-687:32, frames 512–513).

From ALFRED SCHÜCKING, "(Personal)"

Washington, June 25th 1844

Respected Sir: In the employment of persons for public trusts of whatever grade I believe it due to the public and to the functionary representing the public, that some certainty should exist as to the degree of responsibility attaching to the character of the employed. Not only because I have asked you to be employed as bearer of certain despatches to Europe—an honour and favour at your discretion for which I should be exceedingly grateful—but because I am anxious to avail myself of this opportunity to place on a solid foundation your good opinion of me—you will pardon me, if I stand forward as the exponent of my own humble merits in this respect; as—after the departure of the Baron de Raumer, who is well acquainted with my family—I know of no one else to perform this service for me, and as, being of foreign parentage, naturally less can be known of my personal circumstances and family connections, on which by reason of their moral and intellectual influence, I believe the most absolute republican may generally rest some just presumption of a man's character.

I would remark that my family in Germany is one of much consideration, my father having been, until removed for his liberal and independent action on the late accession of the notorious "duke of Cumberland" to the throne of Hanover, a District judge in that kingdom, and being pretty extensively known as a historical and philosophical writer—a work of his now in press is the history of Johannes Huss, one of the first German reformers and precursor of [Martin] Luther. My elder brother, Levin Schücking, lately married to the Baronness [*sic*] de Gall, one of the most distinguished ladies and lady-authoresses of Germany, is at present one of the editors of the often quoted "Augsburg Gazette" and well-known throughout Germany as one of the most popular writers of the day. You will find his name referred to (though in the usual manner of that print, of rough shoed [*sic*] criticism) in the leading article of the number of the "foreign Quarterly Review" which I beg leave herewith to communicate, as also in the letter of Dr. [John G.] Flügel, American Consul at Leipzig, herewith presented. My father is spoken of in another letter enclosed, from A. D[udley] Mann Esq. American Consul at Bremen.

I am conscious, that as to the private or public respectability of my name in this country I have done nothing to forfeit the entire respect of all those, who know me—among whom I reckon particularly the citizens of German birth, to whom I am more extensively known.

My family in Europe through more than a century filled honourable public stations, and faithfully served their country, in so much that one branch of them were rewarded with the degree of nobility, which they retain to this day. As a matter of curiosity allow me to enclose a copy [*not found*] of a letter from Frederic the Great of Prussia to one of my immediate ancestors, who had dedicated to him a work on the division of Poland in 1772.

Having thus ventured to engage your attention with matters entirely personal to me, I beg leave in conclusion to say, that whatever trust you may now or in future see fit to honour me with, will, I hope, not be misplaced, save when it transcends my capacity. I have the honour to be Sir, very respectfully Your most obed[ien]t Serv[an]t, Alfred Schücking.

ALS in ScCleA.

From W[illia]m J. Armstrong, Secretary, American Board of Commissioners for Foreign Missions, New York [City], 6/26. He thanks Calhoun for the passport recently sent for the Rev. H[enry] M. Scudder and asks that one now be sent for Edward Breath, a "missionary printer" who has worked for the last three years among the

Nestorians in Persia. The U.S. having no diplomatic agency in Persia, the protection of the British embassy was until recently extended to the American mission. The Russian ambassador there has offered to extend his protection to the mission if proof of American citizenship is provided. Breath's physical description is enclosed. ALS with En in DNA, RG 59 (State Department), Passport Applications, vol. 31, no. 2266 (M-1372:14).

From Burr & Smith, Warren, R.I., 6/26. This firm renews a recommendation it made several years ago that William Mayhew, Jr. be appointed U.S. Consul at the Bay of Islands, New Zealand. LS in DNA, RG 59 (State Department), Applications and Recommendations, 1837–1845, Mayhew (M-687:22, frames 507–509).

To A[ndrew] P[ickens] Calhoun, [Marengo County, Ala.]

Washington, 26th June 1844

My dear Andrew, It is now more than six[?] months since I have heard from you, although I answered your last letter promptly and requested you to let me hear from you early. I begin to be uneasy[?] and fear that something is the matter and shall be much more so, if I do not hear from you shortly.

The crop, by this time must be nearly made. I hope it promises well, & that the health of the place is, as usual good.

I had a letter from your mother [Floride Colhoun Calhoun], a few days since. She says that all are well & ["that" *canceled*] crops good. In her two last letters, she made special enquiries about you & the family, and said she had not heard from Margaret [Green Calhoun] for a long time. I wish you to say so to her, and, also, that I hope she will write to her before long.

I have been much engaged, so much so, indeed as to have little leisure for correspondence, which will account for my writing you less frequently & fully than I otherwise would. But as it is, I write more than two letters to you for your one.

John [C. Calhoun, Jr.] left here with Patrick [Calhoun] for St. Louis about 3 weeks since. The object is ["to" *canceled*] an excursion with a detachment of the U. States dragoons towards the Rocky

173

mountains for the benefit of his health. I fear his lungs are affected. He coughs much although he looks still well, & is free from fever. The doctors advised, that it is the best thing, that can be done for him. Patrick has a command in the detachment, which suits the arrangement. I heard from them at Louisville. John's health was better. I feel very uneasy about him. If he should not be benefitted by the tour[,] I fear his case will ["be" *canceled and* "prove" *interlined*] desperate. I suppose you have heard of the death of your Aunt Maria [Simkins Colhoun]. She died in child birth. Your uncle James [Edward Colhoun] is inconsolable I understand.

Mr. [Thomas G.] Clemson has been appointed Chargé to Belgium and I expect him here on his way by the 1st Aug[us]t. I found he was so anxious to visit Europe, & to spend a few years ["there" *interlined*], that I thought it was better to gratify him. The Mission is a respectable one, & within one day[']s journey of Paris. He is delighted with the prospect. The pay is $4,500 as outfit, & the same for annual salary.

I expect to return ["early" *interlined*] in Aug[us]t to Fort Hill on a visit, & hope to be able to spend six or seven weeks at home. I would be glad, if you & your family would meet me there, & spend the warm season there ["with us" *interlined*]. It would be very gratifying to me to see you all, & it would afford an opportunity to make some arrangement about our affairs, which will be indispensible. Do not fail to write me, & let me know, if I may expect you & your family. If you should write any time after the 1st Aug[us]t, address to Pendleton.

I have little to add on political subjects, beyond what you will see in the papers. I fear Texas will be lost to the Union. Both England & France will make a great pressure on its Executive to withdraw the proposition for annexation. I regard the Presidential election, as very doubtful. I remain in the [State] Department with great reluctance, but do not see how [I] can leave it without loss of character so long as annexation is a pending question.

My love to Margaret [Green Calhoun], & kind regards to Miss Eliza [M. Green]. Kiss the children [Duff Green Calhoun and John Caldwell Calhoun] for their Grandfather. I hope they continue to improve & grow finely. Your affectionate father, J.C. Calhoun.

ALS in NcD, John C. Calhoun Papers. NOTE: This letter is badly faded.

To R[OBERT] B. CAMPBELL, U.S. Consul, Havana

Department of State
Washington, June 26, 1844

Sir: The recent insurrectionary movements in Cuba, have attracted the serious attention of the Government and much interest is felt as to the causes which may have produced them as well as the probable consequences to which they may lead.

As your position at Havana affords you greater facilities for acquiring correct information on all the subjects, than are enjoyed by our Consuls elsewhere, I have to request that you would, as early as practicable, institute such inquiries, and make such investigation as may promise to afford to the Department the information it desires. This information embraces

1. The causes generally which may have given birth to the insurrectionary spirit which has lately displayed itself in different parts of the Island.
2. The Agents who are known or supposed to have been employed in exciting the blacks to rise on their masters.
3. The probable designs and objects of these agents.
4. The parts which Foreigners may have taken in these disturbances including our own citizens and what countenance they have may received, if any, from the English or other residents, and if such countenance has been given what course has been adopted by the authorities of the Island in regard to them.
5. The probable extent to which the slave Trade is carried on in Cuba, and whether it is encouraged or winked at by the Government, or by Foreigners resident on the Island.

A minute and detailed statement of facts and circumstances calculated to elucidate these points, would be very desirable, together with all such general information which you may be able to obtain going to shew the rise, progress and results of these movements, the number of prosecutions & convictions, the character of the culprits who may have been arrested or punished in consequence of them and the present state of feeling and opinion in the Island in respect to the projects and policy of Great Britain or of any other Foreign nation in regard to Cuba.

These facts and circumstances accompanied by your own views of the subjects proposed will be very acceptable to the Department and it is hoped you will be able to communicate them at an early day. I am &c, J.C. Calhoun.

FC in DNA, RG 59 (State Department), Consular Instructions, 10:252–253.

From Robert B. Campbell

Consulate of the United States of America, Havana
June 26th 1844

Sir, I had the honor to forward to you some time since a copy of a communication of the 12th of June 1844 from the Capt. Gen[era]l [Leopoldo O'Donnell] giving an account of the trial of the Corporal by whose order the American seaman Michael Murphy was shot. On receiving that communication and ignorant of all evidence justificatory of the Corporal I felt indignant at a punishment so slight, for a crime as I supposed so great, and a cruelty so wanton. I waited on the Capt. Gen[era]l in person and asked a copy of the testimony adduced before the Court. He manifested every disposition to concede every thing his duty permitted, but stated the impossibility of officially granting my requisition, as it would be expressly against the law and no judge would feel under an obligation to obey his order to furnish me copies, or permit me to take them. Through personal influence I was permitted access to the records and from an examination of the evidence on behalf of the Corporal I find the testimony of the Capt. of the Port to be as follows, which for your better information I herewith annex.

"A boat belonging to the American Brig Mary Pennell manned by the sailors of her crew called Michael Murphy and John Scott were warned repeatedly by the sentry of the guard of this Captaincy to shove off the said the said [*sic*] boat, (according to the orders which I have given to that effect) after landing the passengers which they may have: but the Corporal of the Regiment of Cuba Manuel Martines Commandant of said post, having observed that they paid no attention, he drew near to make them understand as well as he could, that they should obey the order, but the aforesaid Murphy raised an oar to strike the Corporal with it, who seized it and endeavoured to shove him off but scarcely had he let it go, when he attempted to strike him with it, and that though he seized his sabre he could not use it, for being knocked with the blade of the oar he fell in the water. Immediately several foreign boats drew near and their sailors also endeavoured to strike him with their oars, in this circumstance he ordered the Sentinel to support him, and to fire which he did, the result being that the said Michael Murphy was mortally wounded." This testimony appears to be supported by the evidence of other Spaniards, but as their character and standing were unknown to me I deemed it useless to make any other extracts. I have

176

the honor to be with considerations of very great respect y[ou]r mo[st] ob[edien]t Ser[van]t, Robert B. Campbell.

LS and duplicate LS in DNA, RG 59 (State Department), Consular Despatches, Havana, vol. 19 (T-20:19), received 7/5.

To T[HOMAS] G. CLEMSON, [Edgefield District, S.C.]

State Dept., 26th June 1844

My dear Sir, I received yours enclosing a letter to your attorney [J.B. Crockett] at St. Louis, which, after reading, I franked & forwarded to him. Since my last to Anna [Maria Calhoun Clemson], I have received a letter from Mr. [Henry W.] Hilliard our Charge at Brussels, which informs the Department, that he resigns his place to take effect on the 12th Aug[us]t. He was requested in answer to his letter requesting to be recalled to remain 'till his successor should arrive. As he expresses great anxiety to be recalled & to return early, I think you had better come on at once (as soon as you can make your arrangement) & take your departure in time to reach Belgium before he leaves. It would be of great service to you in the discharge of your official duties. ["It" *canceled.*] As an additional inducement to come on early, it would afford you time to read the correspondence, connected with the Belgian Mission, in the Dept., which would be of great aid to you. It would be the best preperation [*sic*] you could make. You could spend a week or ten days with great advantage.

I enclosed a note to Anna from Mrs. [Isabella Middleton?] Huger in reference to a nurse she has & ["which" *canceled and* "who" *interlined*] would suit her well. I hope she has received it.

I write in great haste, & in the midest [*sic*] of business, and can add no more, but that I am well.

Kiss the children [John Calhoun Clemson and Floride Elizabeth Clemson] for their Grandfather. I am anxious to see them. Love to Anna. Your affectionate father, J.C. Calhoun.

ALS in ScCleA.

From Tho[ma]s G. Clemson

Cane Brake[,] Oakland P.O.
Edgefield Dist[rict,] June 26th 1844

My dear Sir, Your favour of the 4th inst. came to hand as usual a long time after date. However late it was very acceptible [*sic*] & the information you give very satisfactory.

It affords us great pleasure to hear you speak so sanguinely of John[']s [John C. Calhoun, Jr.'s] recovery by going to the West. When in Missouri I saw several persons who had gone & returned from S[an]t[a] Fe & one of those persons then said to me that he believed restoration from confirmed consumption sure, to one who would take the trip. The living on animal flesh entirely he thought highly beneficial. Besides the purity of the atmosphere is highly extolled. That there are differences of Atmospheric purity can hardly be doubted and the accounts of the *looming* as frequently seen on the prairies is extraordinary. Dr. [James H.] Relfe [Representative from Mo.] has experience and I am happy to find he speaks so certainly. On enquiry of every person who knows this place I find that they speak with confidence as to its health & Mrs. Mowbley [*sic*; Lucretia Simkins Mobley] who lives half mile distant & who was born a few steps from where I reside speaks confidently of its health & indeed of that of the settlement & at all events it is said there is seldom if ever that there is fever before August or September & then only a few cases which are not confined to any particular locality. Mr. [Francis W.] Pickens I understand says the health is undoubted & persons here about think this countrey as healthy as any countrey in the State not excepting the mountains. Col. Hurt [*or* "Hunt"] who lives at Oakland P.O. 2 miles hence selected that place for health. Mr. Smith who lives at Mt. Willing speaks very confidently &c. &c.—so that I do not think there is danger to be apprehended from our staying here at least until August.

I should be pleased if Anna [Maria Calhoun Clemson] & the children [John Calhoun Clemson and Floride Elizabeth Clemson] would go to Pendleton & have expressed myself to that effect but she will not leave without I go & it would seem impossible for me to leave[;] there is so much to be done & that particularly if I leave for Europe.

We have had abundant rains latterly & the crops of every description save oats are looking finely. With regard to oats they were never more inferior[;] many do not pretend to cut them[.] As for my own part I can not otherwise than be satisfied with mine[.] I have been

178

cutting for a week and have not half done & tho the grain may not be as heavy as they are usual[l]y on this land still the crop is fine & by far the best that I have heard of. Mr. Mowbley [*sic*; John Mobley] my next neighbour makes few or none[.] His fall grain is no better than his spring oats & both as I have stated a failure. My corn crop is remarkably well looking[;] some of it has been laid bye for six weeks. My cotton crop is as good as my neighbours['], but the stand is inferior & I think that on that account I shall make less than I should have done had the stand been better. The weather thus far has been pleasant & far from hot. All persons hereabout concur in the belief that the cotton crop will be very large without accident. It is said that cotton never was more forward or promising. I regret to see the price of cotton so low. I hope you sold your cotton when prices were higher.

If I should go to Europe[,] as it appears almost certain now that I shall[,] it will be necessary for me to make some arrangements to meet some payments that will fall due next fall & winter. I had concluded upon writing Mr. [Franklin H.] Elmore [President of the South Carolina State Bank] to know if I could make an arrangement with the bank for that institution to pay the amounts which will be due before March when your note with Andrew[']s [Andrew Pickens Calhoun's] will fall due. But as I understood you to say, at the time of settlement, that if March did not suit me that you would make arrangements any time previous. I wrote Andrew last Winter on the subject but I have not received any answer upon the subject. I am not desirous of troubling you about the matter if it can be avoided & speak of it now rather to do what is agre[e]able to yourself if possible with me & should feel at liberty under any circumstances to present your note to the bank without having consulted you upon the subject. I already owe the bank $1500 which will fall due in January[;] To A[rthur] Simkins $3000, due in Jan[uar]y 1st[;] To Griffin[']s estate 500 & 000 dollars [*sic*; $500.00] for negro purchased last fall & a further sum of $550 dollars for Bill Laurence due in Jan[uar]y provided they give me a good tittle [*sic*]—making in all a sum of nearly $6000. Those sums will fall due in January except that to Griffin[']s—& I have no other means of meeting them than with yours & Andrew[']s joint note. If you will have the goodness to give me counsel on the subject you will oblige me very much.

Anna wrote Mrs. [Floride Colhoun] Calhoun a few days since on the subject of the carriage & horses[.] I should be sorry if she did not give her assent, because I think the establishment very cheap & difficult to equal. My neighbour Mr. Smith has just left here with

179

his family & his carriage made something on the plan of mine cost in Edgefield $450 dollars & is decidedly inferior in every respect & tho almost new it has been at the carriage makers several times since he has had it in use. When he saw mine he was disheartened with his. My Horses are sound, very gentle & work any where you put them. I mention the subject again merely because I think they would suit you & you would find it difficult to procure so complete & good an establishment at the same cost. When Anna was in Edgefield one of ["the" *interlined*] horses had a galled shoulder & in starting showed fractious symptoms & behaved as he did when we rode to Aiken. I have driven them since & before & truer & better conditioned horses would be difficult to find. Mrs. Calhoun was at Edgefield when Anna was there & may fear the horses are restive or badly disposed which is not the case.

Your letters to Mr. Packenham [*sic*; Richard Pakenham] have already had a very good effect upon the question of slavery & have done more for the question than any thing that has transpired in a long time. I have heard several speak in the same way. I look for Lord Aberdeen[']s answer with a good deal of anxiety. I regret on your account that the treaty [for the annexation of Texas] failed in the senate but I have no fear for the ultimate success of the project, & so far as [Thomas H.] Benton is concerned he ought to be crucified for his conduct. I do not think that the nomination of [James K.] Polk & [George M.] Dallas [is] calculated to unite the party with warmth & I should not be surprised if the Election was very close if not in favour of [Henry] Clay. However my opinion is not of much value on account of my being so much in the rear of *Saturday night*, for our mail continues to reach us two weeks after date.

Our family are all well & I think my own health better than it has been in a long time.

Anna sends much love. Your affectionate son, Thos. G. Clemson.

[P.S.] I presume that it would not do for us to leave for the North without further advices on the subject of the mission? Before I leave for the North I wish to go to Clarkesville in Georgia. How had I better go on to Washington? T.G.C.

ALS in ScCleA.

From James F. Cooper, [Superintendent of the U.S. Branch Mint], Dahlonega [Ga.], 6/26. Cooper requests to know whether the appointment of Isaac L. Todd as Assayer of the Dahlonega Branch Mint has been confirmed by the Senate. He encloses to Calhoun a "memorandum [*not found*] of a deposite standing to your credit in the mint." (A Clerk's EU indicates that Todd's nomination, made during the recess of 1843, was not sent to the Senate.) ALS in DNA, RG 59 (State Department), Applications and Recommendations, 1837–1845, Todd (M-687:32, frames 476–477).

From Edward Everett, London, 6/26. Because of the lenient practices adopted in granting passports to U.S. citizens, Everett reports that [Gerard] Koster, guilty of fraud in the U.S., has obtained a passport in his own name and another in a false name. This is the only case in which deception was used to obtain a passport in the 1,100 issued since Everett's appointment. LS (No. 149) with Ens in DNA, RG 59 (State Department), Diplomatic Despatches, Great Britain, vol. 52 (M-30:48), received 7/19; FC in DNA, RG 84 (Foreign Posts), Great Britain, Despatches, 8:312–314; FC in MHi, Edward Everett Papers, 49:303–306 (published microfilm, reel 23, frames 152–154).

From John Brown Francis, [Senator from R.I.], Providence, 6/26. He has heard that the U.S. Consul at the Bay of Islands, New Zealand, has left that place with the intention of resigning. If so, Francis recommends William Mayhew [Jr.] to be the new Consul. Mayhew acted as U.S. Vice-Consul there for "a considerable time" some years ago and has since been engaged in business with the Bay of Islands. ALS in DNA, RG 59 (State Department), Applications and Recommendations, 1837–1845, Mayhew (M-687:22, frames 503–506).

To the Governor of Maine [Hugh J. Anderson] and the Governor of Mass. [George N. Briggs], 6/26. Calhoun transmits copies of the letter of the British Minister [Richard Pakenham] of 6/10, concerning the disposition of land grants along the Maine-New Brunswick border in accordance with the fourth article of the Treaty of Washington. FC in DNA, RG 59 (State Department), Domestic Letters, 34:273–274 (M-40:32); PC in House Document No. 110, 29th Cong., 1st Sess., p. 44; LS with En (to Anderson) in Me-Ar; PC (to Briggs) in Jameson, ed., *Correspondence*, p. 599.

From Louis Mark, New York [City], 6/26. "I have herewith the honor to inclose my Consular Bond certified by the District Attorney to be signed by sufficient securities which I trust will be satisfactory." (A Clerk's EU reads: "Write to Mark—informing him as he has failed to explain, he is at liberty to resign, or otherwise he will be superseded—Bond returned." Another EU reads: "A private letter written by Mr. [Francis] Markoe at Ch[ie]f Cl[er]k's [Richard K. Crallé's] request.") ALS in DNA, RG 59 (State Department), Consular Despatches, Munich, vol. 1 (T-261:1).

To John Y. Mason, Secretary of the Navy, 6/26. William M. Blackford, U.S. Chargé d'Affaires in New Granada, has requested that a warship be ordered to pick him up at Cartagena about 12/15 and convey him to the U.S. for a leave of absence. If such an arrangement will not harm the public service, Calhoun will appreciate compliance with the request. LS with En in DNA, RG 45 (Naval Records), Letters from Federal Executive Agents, 1837–1886, 6:[183] (M-517:2, frames 391–393); FC in DNA, RG 59 (State Department), Domestic Letters, 34:261–262 (M-40:32).

From J[OHN] Y. MASON

Navy Department, June 26, 1844
Sir, I have the honor to request, that letters of introduction and recommendation to our Ministers at London and Paris may be furnished to Commander L[evin] M. Powell and Lieutenant A[ndrew] A. Harwood, of the U.S. Navy. These officers are ordered to Europe by the Department to enquire into and examine the improvements that have been made in the construction of cannon, shells, and shot, and all other matters relating to ordnance for sea service.

If similar letters, commending the object of their visit, could be obtained from the British and French Ministers at Washington, they would no doubt be of much advantage to these officers, who propose sailing on the 1st July in the steamer from Boston to Liverpool. I am very resp[ectfully] Y[ours] &c, J.Y. Mason.

LS in DNA, RG 59 (State Department), Miscellaneous Letters (M-179:104, frame 611); FC in DNA, RG 45 (Naval Records), Letters Sent by the Secretary of the Navy to the President and Executive Agencies, 1821–1886, 4:539–540 (M-472:2, frames 651–652).

From W[illia]m Musser & Co., Philadelphia, 6/26. They ask whether any information has been received at the State Department about the status of their claim on the government at Montevideo. LS in DNA, RG 59 (State Department), Miscellaneous Letters (M-179:104, frames 610–611).

From SETH T. OTIS

United States Consulate

Basel (Switzerland) June 26th 1844

Sir, On the 8th inst. I had the honor to receive from the hands of Messrs. Jon D. Bugbee & Tho[ma]s G. Casey your two letters [*not found*] under the respective dates of April 29th & May 9th last, addressed "To the Respective Diplomatic & Consular Agents Abroad" in which you state, that these two Gentlemen visit Europe for the purpose of arresting a man by the name of Gerard Koster charged with having committed extensive frauds in the United States, and you request all convenient attentions in their behalf.

Knowing that this man *Koster*, was in this Confederacy, I proceeded at once to discharge my duties in this important matter, in accordance with my "General Instructions" in the absence of a Minister of the United States. But I regret to say, that up to this time, my best exertions have proved unavailing in procuring his arrest. This has arisen from the fact that no Treaty exists between the United States & Switzerland, relative to the delivering up of Criminals—as also from the weak & imperfect Laws of this Country—together with the very apparent willingness of the high authorities of the Canton in which Koster at present stays—to *protect him* whilst in their Territory. Yet I am happy to state, that in my official interviews & applications to the High Government of Switzerland, as also with those of several of the adjoining Cantons, the Authorities have manifested the best possible disposition to bring this man to justice. I here copy ["an" *altered to* "a"] portion of the closing remarks of the Reply to my Demand from the Canton of Berne, which I think are equally applicable to all of the other Cantons alluded to, they are as follows. "Your Honor intimates that in a reciprocal case—on the request of the proper Government—the authorities of the United States will also not hesitate to furnish the requested help & co-operation for the finding out & giving up of Criminals.

According to all that has been said, it seems certainly without the least doubt, that Mr. Gerard Koster has committed in North America considerable frauds for which he is liable to be punished severely, and although there exists no Treaty between the Swiss Confederation and the United States of North America for the mutual deliverance of Criminals, we yet consider it the interest of all States & Nations that such crimes do not escape the punishment they deserve, and therefore do not hesitate to inform you, as a Reply to your Note, that we shall order the arrestation of Mr. Koster provided you be responsible for all the costs & consequences it may produce here.

As to the deliverance of Mr. Koster, we are also willing to grant it, so soon as a note from the Minister of the Exterior in the United States of North America ["is Received," *interlined*] giving assurances that the reciprocity will be insured to us."

To this communication I immediately replied; thanking them for the offer made, guaranteeing them harmless from the consequences of an arrest, & reiterated my conviction that my Govern[men]t would speedily comply with their offer.

Thus Sir you will readily perceive how this matter stands, and what high ground I have been compelled to take, as a last resort to secure the arrest & delivery of Koster to the tribunals of Justice in the United States.

I am perfectly aware that I have made these declarations without authority from my Govern[men]t, And without knowing whether they would approve of my course, but certainly with the belief that the necessity of the case required it, and that my Government would gladly avail herself of the ["proffered" *interlined*] opportunity to obtain & bring to justice one of the chief of *Scoundrels.* And when I saw this man, & experienced his *Brigandly* hurls of *Defiance*—and reflected upon the magnitude of his offences—the deadening effects such frauds produce in the Commercial World—confidence destroyed—Individuals, withered & crushed under their blighting influence; and the temptation for others to still follow in his train, unless he was brought to a speedy punishment, I could not consistently with my feelings of duty to my Country, do less than I have in this instance and I have not hesitated to use *all* my official authority & Personal influence to bring him to justice; and I cannot but believe my Govern[men]t will approve of my course & grant the required request, & agree to reciprocate with this Government such favors. And thereby show to the World, her high devotion to the principles of Justice. (See 2nd Sheet)

2nd Sheet of No. 7.

Should my Govt. now make the required request from the High Government of Switzerland as also from the Presidents & Councils of each of the Cantons in the Confederacy, it would I think certainly result in the arrest & delivery of Koster. The High Govt. would at once *advise* (for they have no power to *compel*) all the Cantons to deliver him up, the most of them would cheerfully do so, & the others would not longer dare to protect him under the trivial Pleas now set forth by them. Believing that my Government will be willing ["to" *interlined*] make the request, I herewith enclose an authenticated copy of the declaration of the President of the Augusta Insurance & Banking Co. [William M. D'Antignac] upon which ["a" *interlined and one word altered to* "declaration"] of fraud may be based. I do not deem it necessary to send other papers, but will here add a list of the entire frauds as represented to me by Messrs. Bugbee & Casey viz.

Augusta Insurance & Banking Co. Georgia		$70,500.00
Bank of Brunswick	do	73,000.00

Messers. B[ugbee] & C[asey] Represent the above named Institutions only, but add that the following frauds have ["also" *interlined*] been committed by Koster—

Mechanics Bank of Augusta	about	[$]40,000.00
Augusta Branch, Bank of the State of Georgia	do	45,000.00
Bank of St. Marys at Columbus	do	20,000.00
Sundry Individuals	do	50,000.00
Making a Total of about		$298,500.00

of which Amount *Fifty one thousand Pounds* Sterling have already been traced, as having been invested by Koster in Bills of exchange on Liverpool & London, & for which *he Received the cash.*

I would also here remark that Koster has several American Passports—which he uses as Occasion may require, two of them were obtained (under false representations of course) from our Minister Mr. [Edward] Everett in London. I also authenticated for him on the 11th day of May last an American certificate of citizenship, so he claims to be an *American*, although evading her Laws.

In closing this communication I cannot Omit to mention the fact—that the circumstances attending this case seem to open the way very clearly for a treaty between the two Governments relative to the delivery of criminals, & that I presume a thing so important among all civilized nations; will not be overlooked by my Government at this time.

Confidently Relying upon an early & favorable reply to this communication, Messrs. Bugbee & Casey will await here the returning steamer, for the same. I have the Honor to be Sir with unfeigned Respect Your Ob[edien]t Serv[an]t, Seth T. Otis, Consul.

P.S. I am happy to add, that I have just learned from our secret agents, that a secret arrangement has been made between the Police of the Canton of Solothurne (the one in which Koster is) and those of Berne, by which Koster is to be delivered to the latter on the night of the 28th inst. and by them to be imprisoned, subject to the request of the Secretary of State of the United States, as before stated.

Should the Police prove successful in this matter, we shall feel that Koster's return to the United States is moral[l]y certain. With this belief, Mr. Casey has gone to Paris, to effect an arrangement through our Minister Mr. [William R.] King, with the French Police, for the safe transmission of Koster through France to Havre. S.T. Otis.

ALS (No. 7) with En in DNA, RG 59 (State Department), Consular Despatches, Basle, vol. 1 (T-364:1), received 7/19; CC in DNA, RG 84 (Foreign Posts), France, Instructions (C8.1). NOTE: Otis was a native of N.Y. and a merchant in the then small town of Chicago when appointed to his Consulship in 12/1843. He held the post until 12/1845.

From S[tephen] P[leasonton], Fifth Auditor [of the Treasury], 6/26. He returns an account relayed to him a day or two ago. In order to understand it, one must revert to an account dated 1/13/-1840, under which Henry Middleton, former Minister to Russia, owed more than $12,000 to the U.S. Middleton claims that his indebtedness should be reduced by more than $5,000; but of that sum only $336.38 can be allowed. His account dated 6/13/1844 claims expenses in London and while traveling, but these seem to be questionable. After crediting the $336.38, suit has been initiated against Middleton for $11,743.69. FC in DNA, RG 217 (General Accounting Office), Fifth Auditor: Letters Sent, 5:137.

To J[ames] W. Schaumburg and H[enry] D. Gilpin, Philadelphia, 6/26. "I have received the letter which you addressed to me on the 24th instant, upon the subject of the claims against the Mexican Government represented by you, and in reply I have to state that your suggestions have been taken into respectful consideration." FC in DNA, RG 59 (State Department), Domestic Letters, 34:262 (M-40:32).

To John Tyler, Jr., 6/26. In reply to Tyler's letter of 6/18 enclosing a letter [of 6/7] from Charles S. Robinson to the President, Calhoun states that the State Department can furnish [Hallam Eldredge, attorney and agent for the Beauvais family,] with a letter of introduction to the U.S. Consul at Amsterdam or the U.S. Chargé d'Affaires at The Hague. However, the Department cannot give Eldredge "any appointment or official character whatever that would be likely to be of use to him in prosecuting the claim in question." FC in DNA, RG 59 (State Department), Domestic Letters, 34:260 (M-40:32).

From John Walker

Mrs. Gassaway[']s, number wanting
Pen[n]sylvania Avenue, June 26th[?] 1844

Sir, I am a native of Bermuda. There is a Tradition in my Country, for all the living actors are dead, and there is no record that I can come at to prove the fact but it is a Fact so well known at the time and so generally believed at the Present, that it admits not of a doubt! that about the close of the American Revolution, General [George] Washington was distressed for gun Powder and a set of men in Bermuda beguiled the Governor, opened the public Magazine[,] took out the Powder, and connveyed it to General Washington, and General [Nathanael] Green[e], which enabled them to fight the momentuous Battle which so singularly closed that Great Strife[.]

Had those Persons come over with the Powder, they would have been included in the general Peace, and become Citizens but they acted for base Lucre—remained in the Colony, and incurred the opprobrium of Traitors. They have ever since by holding the offices, and assuming Power, tyran[n]ized over the People; and kept them in Poverty and Ignorance, that they may rule.

Under these circumstances the Americans can but admire the Treason, while they dispise the Traitors! My Father had no hand in the affair, but I have been robbed of my Property, and so oppressed by these same People that I have applyed to the crown for redress, and am now in correspondence with the Brittish Ministers on the Subject.

Having been forced to take my Family to this country for personal Protection, where we mean to remain, and hearing there is, or was a Fund arrising out of the above Transaction, called the Bermudian Fund, and believing the American Government would be willing to relieve itself of any obligation if such Fund really exists, and as I have suffered wrong from the same Hands that it may be thought the assets are due to, but knowing that none of the de[s]cendents of such Persons would dare make a claim nor would I, to forfeit the Pleasure of my sovereign; but would receive any thing that may be due; and leave the matter under all the Circumstances to your Pleasure[.] I have the Honor to be Honorabl[e] Sir your very obedient Servant, John Walker.

ALS in ScCleA.

From HENRY WHEATON, "(Private)"

Berlin, 26 June, 1844

My dear Sir, I took the liberty of writing you a private Letter on the 12 June on the subject of the Sound-Duties & the Navigation treaties with Denmark, the Hanse Towns, &c. That Letter, & all others marked *private*, are intended to be considered as strictly so, & not to be placed on the files of the Department.

Since my last Letter, I learn that the Commercial Convention concluded here on the 25 March last with the German Zollverein encounters much opposition ["to its ratification" *interlined*] by the Senate on various grounds, & among others on the ground that (if ratified) we shall be bound by our Treaty of 1815 with G[reat] Britain to make reductions of duties on her linens, silks, &c. similar to those we have stipulated with Germany for the like articles. Mr. [Edward] Everett has communicated to me his Despatches, addressed to the Department, giving an account of his conferences with Lord Aberdeen on that subject. Baron [Heinrich von] Bulow has also mentioned to me that the Prussian minister in London had written to him to the same effect; but Baron B[ulo]w seemed to suppose that it was hardly possible our Senate could refuse to ratify *upon that ground*, as our Treaty of 1828 with Prussia (art. 5) contains the same Stipulation with the 2d article of the British Convention of 1815, & we persisted in maintaining for ten years the differential duties on French wines stipulated by Mr. [William C.] Rives' Convention with France of 1831, (art. 7,) notwithstanding the remonstrances of the Prussian Government which claimed to be placed on an equal footing in respect to the wines of Prussia. The correspondence between the Department & [Friedrich Ludwig,] Baron von Roenne has never been transmitted to this Legation, but he informs me that both Mr. [John] Forsyth & Mr. [Daniel] Webster maintained that Prussian wines were not entitled to be imported on payment of the same duties with French wines, as France had *purchased* the reductions stipulated in favour of her wines by abandoning her pretensions set up under the 8th article of the Treaty for the cession of Louisiana, & by stipulating to impose upon our *long-staple* Cottons the same duties as on *short-staples*.

I also learn that Mr. Webster had a correspondence with the Portuguese minister at Washington relating to a similar question arising under our Treaty with Portugal, but as the public documents were formerly received with great irregularity at this Legation, I have never had the advantage of seeing that correspondence, if indeed it was communicated to Congress & printed, of which I know nothing.

The Zollverein would therefore be very much dissatisfied if the Convention of March 25th should be rejected upon such a ground, & it might even lead to consequences extremely injurious to the future commercial relations between the United States & Germany. But I think the Prussian cabinet would very much prefer that we should extend the same reductions in favour of British manufactures to a rejection of the Convention, as it might be extremely difficult, if not impossible, to reconcile the discordant views of the different German States composing the Zollverein to any new arrangement which our Senate would be willing to ratify. And even supposing G[reat] Britain to be entitled, under our existing engagements with her, to be placed on the same footing with the Zollverein in respect to the articles mentioned in the Convention of the 25 March, I do not perceive that this forms any conclusive objection to the ratification on our part; since by the provisions of that Convention both Parties are at liberty to extend the same concessions to other Powers, with or without equivalents, the Prussian cabinet would probably make no complaint if we should ratify & ["to"(?) *canceled*] extend the reductions stipulated in favour of German manufactures to any or all other nations. On the other hand, should we refuse to ratify on that ground, they might consider themselves justly entitled to complain, as we are bound to know the nature & extent of our own previous engagements with other Powers. I therefore indulge the hope, that if the Senate is not disposed to ratify at present, the whole matter may be suffered to lay over until the next Session, in order that the necessary explanations may be given on this point. I have already shewn in my Letter of the 10th April, to which I beg leave to refer you, how the principal advantages stipulated in favour of our staple articles ["may" *canceled*] by the Convention may be secured to us, even if the Zollverein should avail themselves of the faculty reserved to both Parties of extending those advantages to other Nations; & will only add that the Convention was not intended by either Party to establish permanent systems of differential duties in the two Countries, but only by mutual reductions to set the example ["of ot(?)" *canceled*] to other nations which might gradually lead to a more liberal system of commercial intercourse between all. I have the honour to remain, my dear Sir, very truly your faithful friend, Henry Wheaton.

ALS in ScCleA.

From John Macpherson Berrien, [Senator from Ga.], Carlisle, Pa., 6/27. Berrien asks that Calhoun inform him if Homer Virgil Morel is a prisoner of Mexico. If so, Berrien asks "if this Government can, and will feel authorized to make any, and what efforts for his release? May I ask the favor of a reply to this, *directed to me at the American Hotel, New York*." ALS in DNA, RG 59 (State Department), Miscellaneous Letters (M-179:104, frame 643).

To A[DOLPH] E. BORIE and Others, Philadelphia

Department of State
Washington, 27th June 1844
Gentlemen, I have to acknowledge the receipt of your letter of the 25th instant, relative to the failure of the Mexican government to pay the 4th instalment due under the Convention of the 30th of January 1843 and requesting the aid of this Government for the purpose of securing the punctual payment ["of" *interlined*] those instalments in future. In reply, I have to inform you, that the Minister of the United States [Wilson Shannon] who is about to proceed to Mexico has been fully instructed upon the subject. I am, Gentlemen, Your Obedient Servant, John C. Calhoun.

FC in DNA, RG 59 (State Department), Domestic Letters, 34:263–264 (M-40:32). NOTE: Other addressees were H[enry] D. Gilpin, P[ierre?] L. Laguerenne, Lewis Waln, J. Fisher Leaming, James Nevins, and S. Nevins.

From F[RANCIS] M. DIMOND

United States Consulate
Vera Cruz, June 27, 1844
Sir, I have the honour herewith to transmit a despatch rec[eive]d by the last mail from our Legation at Mexico.

By the next opportunity I shall be able to transmit the document relative to the condemnation of the Schooner Vigilant.

We understand, Congress has refused, Santa Anna, the four millions he asked for, only consenting to grant one million, and as many Soldiers as he takes for the invasion of Texas, he must leave that number of militia under arms which he will not agree to. Respectfully referring you to our Chargé d'Affaires for particulars as I have not the means of gathering the truth here I have the honour to be Sir most Respectfully Your ob[edient] Serv[an]t, F.M. Dimond.

ALS (No. 227) with En in DNA, RG 59 (State Department), Consular Despatches, Veracruz, vol. 5 (M-183:5), received 7/16.

To Edward Everett, [London], 6/27. Calhoun introduces "Commander L[evin] M. Powell, of the United States' Navy, who has been ordered to Europe by the Navy Department to enquire into and examine the improvements that have been made in the construction of cannon, shells, and shot, and all other matters relating to ordnance for sea service." LS in MHi, Edward Everett Papers (published microfilm, reel 20, frame 534).

To Edward Everett, 6/27. Calhoun introduces Lt. A[ndrew] A. Harwood, U.S. Navy, who has been ordered to Europe to examine improvements in naval ordnance. LS in MHi, Edward Everett Papers (published microfilm, reel 20, frame 535).

From Geo[rge] W[illia]m Gordon

Consulate of the United States
Rio de Janeiro
27th June 1844

Sir, Herewith I enclose a duplicate of the Statement [dated 6/12] in relation to the trade and navigation between the United States and Brazil, which accompanied my despatch dated, 12th June 1844, and numbered 3.

If any copies of the "Senate Document, No. 217" containing, "Information in relation to the abuse of the flag of the United States in subservience to the African Slave trade, and the taking away of Slaves, the property of Portuguese subjects;" are in the possession of the Department, or can be conveniently obtained, I should be greatly obliged if you will direct that one be sent to me. I have the honor to be, Sir, Most respectfully, Your obedient Servant, Geo. Wm. Gordon, Consul United States.

ALS (No. 4) with En in DNA, RG 59 (State Department), Consular Despatches, Rio de Janeiro, vol. 7 (T-172:8), received 8/18. NOTE: Gordon's statement contained tabulations of the commerce between Brazil and the U.S. for 1843; the number of American and foreign vessels engaged in the Brazil trade; and a demonstration of the increase in U.S.-Brazilian trade from 1840 to 1843. Gordon

(1801–1877), a native of N.H. and a former Postmaster of Boston, had been appointed Consul at Rio de Janeiro by President Tyler in 1843.

From ALLEN A. HALL

Legation of the United States
Caracas, June 27th, 1844

Sir, I have the honor to acknowledge the receipt of your despatches, numbered 18 and 19.

I regret to be obliged to acquaint you, that the Congress of Venezuela adjourned without making the requisite appropriation for carrying into effect the adjustment, which I had concluded with this Government, of the claim in the case of the Brig Morris. Such a result was wholly unexpected to me. I had not believed, for a moment, that Congress would assume the responsibility, after what had passed, of refusing, or omitting, to make the appropriation. The adjustment was concluded very nearly three months ["prior" *interlined*] to the close of the session. In a day or two after it had been agreed upon, the Secretary of State for Foreign Affairs [Juan Manuel Manrique], as it appears from the Journal, announced it officially to the House of Representatives, and "urged the speedy despatch of the business"—"encareciendo el pronto despacho de este asunto." This, I *suppose*, was the sum of the efforts of the Executive Department to get the appropriation passed. You will perceive from Mr. Manrique's note [of 6/11] that it was not even taken into consideration! owing, as he says, to the numerous and important subjects of a domestic nature which engrossed the attention of Congress for the two or three last months of the session. If you could but know, or if it were fit in me to describe to you the nature, object, scope and tendency of the "numerous and important subjects" referred to by Mr. Manrique, you would smile at the gravity with which he thence deduces the "impossibility," during a space of seventy five days, of the case of the Morris being so much as considered.

Mr. Manrique having assured me in his note that the Executive had caused the appropriation to be "strongly recommended" to Congress, and that its failure had occasioned him "great concern," I chose to *assume* in my reply [of 6/14], that he had put them in possession of all the information necessary to enable them duly to appreciate the importance of the appropriation, and the responsibility they would incur by omitting to make it. I do not *know*, however, whether this assumption be well founded or not. The failure may be fairly ascribed to characteristic, Spanish-American want of activity and energy in both Departments of the Government, combined, no doubt, with a positive repugnance to pay this particular claim, and others of a similar character which they are well aware will be forthwith presented. Mr. [William M.] Blackford writes me, that the chances of getting an appropriation by the late Congress of New Granada of their proportion of the Morris indemnity were so utterly hopeless, that, at the pressing instance of the Executive, he agreed to postpone the signing of the Convention until Congress should adjourn. I greatly fear that these claims never can be fairly and equitably adjusted without a resort to co-ercive measures on the part of the United States.

My rejoinder to Mr. Manrique's note was written with the view of inducing the Executive, if practicable, of taking the responsibility of directing the money to be paid, although Congress had failed to make the requisite appropriation. I accordingly hinted very plainly at the unpleasant consequences that might ensue if the indemnity were not paid now; but you will remark that, while I pointed out what, under all the circumstances, the Government of the United States *might* be abundantly justified in doing, I carefully abstained from venturing an opinion as to what they *would* do. Before this reaches you, the Congress of the United States will most probably have adjourned. By the time they meet again in December, I shall have brought under the consideration of this Government all the residue of the claims of our citizens against the late Republic of Colombia, and then, with the facts and merits of each case before him, together with a knowledge of the disposition manifested in the interim by the States which formerly composed that Republic, to afford a fair and satisfactory indemnification, the President may perhaps have no difficulting [*sic*] in deciding whether the United States will not consult their dignity by either promptly enforcing the payment of the claims, or as promptly abandoning their further prosecution.

I am sorry to perceive increasing indications of the danger which hangs over the public tranquillity here. Within the last fortnight, a band of forty or fifty armed men have been marching with impunity from village to village in this province (they approached within twenty miles of Caracas) seizing horses and arms wherever they could be found—breaking open prisons and setting free the inmates—and calling out "Liberty forever! Death to the Oligarchy! Down with the Government!" Caracas was in a panic. The Governor called out the militia—guards were stationed around the arsenal—a run was made upon the Banks—and patrols on horseback watched over the safety of the City by night. The band I hear have dispersed—they were not taken. The people generally among whom they passed, manifested no eargerness [*sic*] to join them, and none to capture them. I attach no importance to the movement, except as it indicates the wretched state of things at present existing in this country. I am wholly unable to perceive any guaranty whatever for the preservation of peace and order. The Government possess neither moral nor political power, nor can they reckon upon the support of public opinion in the event of disturbances breaking out. I cannot say I believe there is imminent danger of a revolution, but I certainly ["should" *interlined*] not be surprised at the occurrence of such an event during the present year. I have the honor to be, Sir, with great respect your ob[e]d[ien]t serv[an]t, Allen A. Hall.

ALS (No. 36) with Ens in DNA, RG 59 (State Department), Diplomatic Despatches, Venezuela, vol. 2 (M-79:3), received 7/22.

From Rob[er]t Monroe Harrison

United States Consulate
Kingston, Jamaica, 27th July [*sic*; June] 1844

Sir, I do myself the honor to enclose you two Papers which are worth your perusal, as they clearly shew the ruin and misery that has befallen this fine Colony, by the insane measures persued towards it by the British Government.

The person who is employed to print the vile Pamphlets written in this place to create Insurrection &c in Cuba and elsewhere, has promised to reserve one for me which shall be forwarded to you as soon as I get it and if I am not wrongly informed, will be found, to be of a most dangerous character. With great respect I have the honor to be Sir your Ob[edien]t and most humble Servant, Robt. Monroe Harrison.

LS (No. 291) with Ens in DNA, RG 59 (State Department), Consular Despatches, Kingston, Jamaica (T-31:9), received 7/30. Note: Harrison enclosed copies of the Kingston *Morning Journal* of 6/21 and 6/25, containing articles on the economic distress in Jamaica caused by emancipation. On the issue of 6/21, Harrison wrote: "The Editors of this Paper are men of Colour, one a bright mulatto and the other a *Samboe* and have contributed more to produce the wretched state of things described in the letter by the Patriot underneath, than most men in England or the Colonies; they are both Honorable Members of the

Assembly, hold several offices, care nothing now for their own colour, by whom they have been elevated to their present greatness, and [*one word altered to* "invariable"] folly [*sic*] that line of policy which brings most to their Coffers. I hope the Honor[ab]le Secretary of State will find time to look over the letter of the *'Patriot.'* " On the issue of 6/25 Harrison wrote: "I hope the Hon[orab]l[e] Secretary of State will read this as will shew him the working of the "Free labour System" as detailed by the advocates of Emancipation. I wish the Fanatics of the north to come here and Judge for themselves."

From J[ohn] Y. Mason, [Secretary of the Navy], 6/27. In reply to Calhoun's letter of 6/26, he states "that Commodore [David] Conner has been authorized to send a vessel of war to Carthagena, by the 15th Dec[embe]r next, if it can be done without injury to the public service, for the purpose of conveying Mr. [William M.] Blackford, our Chargé d'Affaires at Bogota, to a port in the United States." LS in DNA, RG 59 (State Department), Miscellaneous Letters (M-179:104, frame 642); FC in DNA, RG 45 (Naval Records), Letters Sent by the Secretary of the Navy to the President and Executive Agencies, 1821–1886, 4:540 (M-472:2, frame 652).

From Rob[er]t Mills

City [of] Washington, June 27, 1844
Dear Sir, Congress at its last session appropriated $23,000 "for the erection of a Marine hospital at Key West in the Territory of Florida," under the charge of the Secretary of the Treasury. May I ask you to recommend my professional services to the Secretary [George M. Bibb], to carry into effect the requisitions of the act[?] I have made several designs, and closed several contracts for the Department for Marine hospitals, and given satisfaction. Being well acquainted with Southern habits and wants I may be useful in arranging the Key West hospital to suit its requirements. Two of the Hospitals designed by me were built to the South. With sentiments of high respect I have the honour to salute you, Robt. Mills, Architect.

ALS in DNA, RG 59 (State Department), Applications and Recommendations, 1845–1853, Mills (M-873:60, frames 448–449). NOTE: An AEI by Calhoun reads: "Submitted for the consideration of the Sec[re]t[ar]y of the Treasury. I have long known Mr. Mills & believe him to be well qualified for what he proposes to undertake."

To Daniel Parker, Acting Secretary of War, 6/27. "Having occasion to inspect, in full, the proceedings of the Court of Inquiry which recently investigated the conduct of Captain P[hilip] St. George Cooke while in command of the escort to traders on the road to Santa Fé, I will thank you to send me the proceedings . . . ." LS in DNA, RG 94 (Adjutant General), Letters Received (Main Series), 1844, C-unregistered (M-567:283, frames 856–857); FC in DNA, RG 59 (State Department), Domestic Letters, 34:264 (M-40:32).

From D[aniel] Parker, Acting Secretary of War, 6/27. He transmits the proceedings requested by Calhoun in the court of inquiry for Capt. P[hilip] St. G[eorge] Cooke and reminds Calhoun that the opinion of the court was sent to him by the Secretary of War [William Wilkins] on 4/24. LS in DNA, RG 59 (State Department), Miscellaneous Letters (M-179:104, frame 649); FC in DNA, RG 107 (Secretary of War), Letters Sent Relating to Military Affairs, 1800–1861, 25:348 (M-6:25); draft in DNA, RG 94 (Adjutant General), Letters Received (Main Series), 1844, C-unregistered (M-567:283, frames 858–859).

From D[ANIEL] PARKER

War Department, June 27, 1844
Sir, In the absence of the Secretary of War [William Wilkins], I respectfully transmit herewith a copy of a letter [of 5/27 to T. Hartley Crawford] from A.M.M. Upshaw Esq: Chickasaw Agent, just submitted to the Department by the Commissioner of Indian Affairs.

Believing the subject will claim the early attention of the Executive on the return of Judge Wilkins, I deem it proper to submit a copy to the Department of State at this time.

The volume of Indian Treaties[,] p. 626, shows that we have had a treaty of peace and friendship with the Camanches and Witchetaws since the 19 of May 1838. I believe the Witchetaws are considered a lawless and roving band. I have the honor to be Very respectfully, Your Obed[ient] Serv[an]t, D. Parker, Act[in]g Sec[retar]y of War.

LS with En in DNA, RG 59 (State Department), Miscellaneous Letters (M-179:104, frames 630–632); FC in DNA, RG 107 (Secretary of War), Letters Sent Relating to Military Affairs, 1800–1861, 25:348 (M-6:25); CC in Tx, Andrew Jackson Houston Papers. NOTE: The En discloses that two boys missing from Texas since Feb. or March last, when their family was murdered by Indians, are now living among the Wichitaw Indians "within the Chickasaw District of the Choctaw Nation" [in the U.S. Indian Territory]. Upshaw recommends that a force be sent to reclaim the boys and capture the murderers.

To William Wilkins, Secretary of War, 6/27. Calhoun refers Wilkins to a letter of 3/4 from the State Department to the War Department asking that an inquiry be made into the accusation that a U.S. Army officer protected "persons concerned in an assault upon [James Bourland] the Collector of Red River in Texas." Calhoun asks that the result of the investigation be communicated to the State Department so that it "may be communicated to the Chargé de'Affair[e]s of Texas accredited to this Government." FC in DNA, RG 59 (State Department), Domestic Letters, 34:264–265 (M-40:32).

From D[aniel] Parker

War Department, June 27, 1844
Sir, In answer to your communication of this day [to William Wilkins], I have the honor to transmit herewith copies of two letters of William Armstrong Esq. Acting Superintendent of Indian Affairs West, and Choctaw Agent, and a report [of 6/27/1844] of the Adjutant General of the Army [Roger Jones], which contain all the information required, and not embraced in the letter of the Secretary of War to the Department of State, on the 11th of May 1843, so far as it can now be furnished by this Department. I have the honor to be Very respectfully Your Obed[ient] Serv[an]t, D. Parker, Act[in]g Sec[retar]y of War.

[Enclosure]
W[illia]m Armstrong to T. Hartley Crawford, Comm[issione]r of Ind[ian] Affairs

Washington, 12th August 1843
Sir, I communicated to you some time since [on 4/16/1843] the seizure and detention of a large quantity of goods belonging to citizens of the United States by [James Bourland] the Collector of Customs in Texas in the district on Red River opposite Fort Towson [in Indian Territory]. The history of the transaction as far as I know is this. The steam boat Fort Towson ascending Red river with a cargo of merchandise was unable to reach her destination for want of water—she unloaded at what is called Boyerly [*sic*; Bryerly] landing in Texas, there is a warehouse at this point and none on the Choctaw side opposite—there is also shoals at this place which frequently makes it necessary for boats to lay up for a rise of water or store their freight. The Fort Towson reached this landing and stored, as was

customary—she returned and on her way up again called for the goods—they were refused on the ground that the Collector who was then present had them in charge. Upon this the Captain of the boat [Joseph Scott] confined the Collector and had the goods reshipped—there were a number of citizens of Texas present, some of whom aided in putting the goods aboard. I am well acquainted with Captain Bo[u]rland the Collector have not seen him since this Affair took place, but know that he has expressed himself at Doaksville in the Choctaw nation as being perfectly satisfied that no fraud was intended by the landing of the goods in Texas—that they were stored under the circumstances stated—And also plainly marked and intended for traders in the Indian country and for the garrison of Fort Towson.

As to the Commanding Officer at Fort Towson [Lt. Col. Gustavus Loomis] sending a guard to protect the boat—this was after the goods were reshipped and the boat laying some five or six miles higher up on the Choctaw side of Red river unable to get up for want of water. The Commanding officer at Towson fearing a rescue might be attempted sent a guard to protect the public property belonging to the United States. I have no idea that he knew anything of the retaking of the goods until after it was all over. Very respectfully Your mo[st] ob[edien]t Serv[ant], Wm. Armstrong, Acting Sup[erintenden]t W[estern] T[erritory].

LS with Ens in DNA, RG 59 (State Department), Miscellaneous Letters (M-179:104, frames 633–641); FC in DNA, RG 107 (Secretary of War), Letters Sent Relating to Military Affairs, 1800–1861, 25:348 (M-6:25); CC with Ens in Tx, Records of the Texas Republic Department of State, U.S. Diplomatic Correspondence; FC in Tx, Records of the Texas Republic Department of State, Copybooks of Letters Received from Texan and Foreign Representatives, vol. 2-1/98, pp. 527–530. NOTE: Jones's enclosed report contained copies of correspondence between himself and Gen. Zachary Taylor in March and April, 1844, relating to the *Fort Towson* affair.

From James Thomson, New York [City], 6/27. Thomson asks to be appointed to some "vacant consulate in the north of Europe." He reminds Calhoun that some months ago he received many recommendations for appointment at Glasgow. These were seriously considered by the President [John Tyler] and it was indicated that another application would be welcome. ALS in DNA, RG 59 (State Department), Applications and Recommendations, 1837–1845, Thomson (M-687:32, frames 422–423).

R[ichard] K. Cralle to Commander Charles Wilkes, 6/27. "The Department having no knowledge of the Writer of this letter, or of the circumstances of his app[ointmen]t, it is respectfully submitted to Commander Wilkes for his perusal, with a request that it may be returned accompanied with such explanations as he is enabled to give." The above note was written on a letter of 1/15/1844 to the Secretary of State from John C. Williams in Apia [Samoa]. In his letter Williams states that he has been exercising the duties of U.S. Consul at Apia since he was appointed by Wilkes when the U.S.S. *Vincennes* was there. He expresses "much diffidence arising chiefly from not having received despatches of any kind informing me whether I am appointed by Government or not." ES on ALS (received 6/27/1844) in DNA, RG 59 (State Department), Consular Despatches, Apia, Samoa, vol. 1 (T-27:1).

From EDWARD EVERETT

London, 28 June 1844
Sir, I transmit herewith a copy of a note of this day, addressed to Lord Aberdeen on the subject of the export duty levied on timber at St. John's, in virtue of an act of the Colonial legislature of New Brunswick.

I do not find among the papers accompanying your despatches numbered 87 and 90 [of 5/16 and 5/28] the statement from our consul at St. John's [Israel D. Andrews] referred to in Governor [Edward] Kent's letters. In consequence I presume of the absence of that document, the evidence of the relinquishment of the "stumpage," for cutting timber on the Crown lands of the province, is less positive than might be wished. That such relinquishment is a part of the measure is certainly implied in the preamble of the colonial act, and in the debate in the legislative council. I have however thought it best to state it only as a matter which had been represented to the American government.

While I was preparing the note to Lord Aberdeen, I had an opportunity of conversing informally with Lord Ashburton on the subject. He expressed a decided opinion that the duty in question did not violate the treaty, and that the clause which provides for equality of treatment for American timber and that of the Province authorizes its imposition. At the same time he was equally of opinion, that if by a repeal of the "stumpage" for cutting timber on the crown lands, or by an exemption of Province timber from duty, for the present year, it was made to operate, in fact as a discrimination against the timber of the United States, it was an unfair evasion, which ought to be enquired into by the home government. I ought to add, that these views were formed by Lord Ashburton, on the first impression of the case as stated in conversation, and the expression of them should be considered as wholly informal. It is by no means impossible, that upon investigating the subject, he would view the matter as we do.

To save the time which would be required to copy the printed argument transmitted with your despatch Nro. 87, I have sent it to Lord Aberdeen with the papers accompanying my note of this day. I beg leave to request that another copy may be procured & forwarded to me, to be placed on the files of the Legation. I have retained a list of the signatures, so that it is not necessary that they should be transcribed. I am, sir, with great respect, your obedient servant, Edward Everett.

Transmitted with despatch 150.
Mr. Everett to the Earl of Aberdeen, 28 June 1844.

LS (No. 150) with Ens in DNA, RG 59 (State Department), Diplomatic Despatches, Great Britain, vol. 52 (M-30:48), received 7/19; FC in DNA, RG 84 (Foreign Posts), Great Britain, Despatches, 8:315–317; FC in MHi, Edward Everett Papers, 49:325–327 (published microfilm, reel 23, frames 163–164); PC with En in House Document No. 110, 29th Cong., 1st Sess., pp. 19–23.

From BEN E. GREEN

Legation of the U.S. of A.
Mexico, June 28th 1844

Sir, I send you (nos. 1 & 2) copies of a note [of 6/25] received from Mr. [José M. de] Bocanegra [Mexican Minister of Foreign Affairs], & my reply [of 6/26], closing the correspondence. I hope that what I have written will be approved by the President [John Tyler]. I have thought it best, with a full knowledge of the position of things here & on the advice of those, on whom I could depend, to write this much. But I do not wish to continue it further. I have therefore not even noticed the singular position taken by Mr. Bocanegra, that Texas, although independent de facto, has no *right* to her independence, because *she is a rebel colony*! A strange argument this to come from a republican minister on the American continent.

Gen[era]l [Anastasio?] Parrodi's proposition for a forced loan has been rejected by the Congress. They now propose to raise money by increasing the duties. This of course will fail, for their Tariff is already so high that there are no importations. I have the honor to be Very Respectfully Y[ou]r ob[edien]t Serv[an]t, Ben E. Green.

[Enclosure: State Department translation]
J[osé] M. de Bocanegra to B[en] E. Green

National Palace
Mexico, June 25, 1844

The Undersigned, Minister of Foreign Relations and Government, has received the note, which the Charge d'Affaires ["ad interim" *interlined*] of the United States, was pleased to address to him, under date of the 20th instant, in reply to one from this Department of the 12th, in which, that gentleman continues to support as legal, the annexation of the territory of Texas to the United States, which the Executive of those States proposes to effect, by means of a treaty concluded and settled, between itself, and the so-called Government of Texas.

The Undersigned ["in and" *interlined*] after the second note, which he addressed ["to the American Legation," *interlined*] upon this important subject, considered in proper order, the acknowledgement of the independance of Texas, by the United States; and then had the honour to combat the principles advanced by Mr. Benjamin Green, as being contrary to natural right, to the rights of nations, and to international law, by convincing reasons, leaving no room for a moment's doubt as to the justice and reason ["of Mexico in this" *canceled*] with which Mexico protests against this act, ["the subject" *canceled*] resting entirely upon a fact, but incapable of destroying her rights, to that integrant portion of her territory. It would therefore appear, that this subject should not have been again touched but as it seems, from the note, to which this is an answer, that the Chargé d'Affaires of the United States invites the Supreme Government of Mexico, to make an express ["and decided" *interlined*] declaration, apart, and confined especially to the recognition of Texas by other powers, it becomes the duty of the nation, in whose name and behalf, the Department of Foreign Relations, now speaks, to declare as it now does declare, affirm, and maintain, that though the said powers have acknowledged Texas as independent of the mother country, this act can give no right whatsoever, to the usurpers of that territory, as they were really and truly neither more nor less than [*one word canceled*] rebellious colonists; and it can in no way affect injuriously, the incontestible rights of Mexico, as the natural right, cannot be destroyed by the law of nations, the civil law, and the international law.

The Undersigned indeed guided by the feelings produced by cool and judicious criticism, finds the incontrovertible doctrines already advanced by him ["as flowing from the law of nations," *interlined*] supported and confirmed in the last note, from Mr. Green, and in no wise opposed; while on the contrary he admits the views advanced in proof, that the recognition applies merely to the fact, and does not destroy nor even weaken the right, which a mother country has over her possessions, without adding any weight to his assertion, as regards the existence of a contradiction, in adducing the time of the recognition of the independance of Mexico by Spain.

This fact itself, affords to the Undersigned, the strongest proof—Mr. Green knows, that the independance of Texas, and her annexation to the United States, are not in the same line, are not the same thing, and consequently cannot be brought on a par with each other. In the first case, a fact, one of the many events, which the physical and social course of things present, is offered for consideration, without, attempting to classify it in any way, especially as the interests of others are involved, which must be taken into view and respected; and in the second case, the question turns upon legal capacity and dominion, which is possessed without any contradiction; Such as Mexico holds over Texas, ["which" *changed to* "a"] territory ["which" *interlined*] belongs to her, and has been quietly and peaceably possessed by her.

Mr. Green in his first note of the 23 of May, declares, as the only cause "that His Government in concluding the treaty of annexation of Texas to the United States, was ["not" *canceled*] actuated by no feelings of disrespect, or indifference, to the honour and dignity of Mexico; and that this measure had been forced upon it, in self defense in consequence of the policy adopted by Great Britain, in reference to the abolition of slavery in Texas;" and he subsequently enters upon the question of the acknowledgement of independance ["as the principal point," *interlined*] as shewn in his note, which the Undersigned is now answering, obliging him to make the present explanation, and to insist again, upon what has been so often established.

His Excellency the Constitutional President of the Republic, faithful to his duties, and consistently with his sentiments of the ["highest" *canceled*] most exalted patriotism, will never allow the Republic, to be despoiled, of that which belongs and has belonged to it. Those very nations which Mr. Green cites, including the United States of

America, have assented to the principles advanced by Mexico; and whilst recognising the independance of Texas, have declared that Mexico may recover what is her own, that she may employ her arms for the attainment of her lawful ends, and that supported by her own forces, she may without contradiction, vindicate her ["rights" *canceled*] constantly acknowledged and reserved rights. They acted thus in the very case offered as an example by the American legation, with regard to Spain; and the presentation of this case, instead of weakening the rights of the Mexican nation, strengthens them to such an extent, that her most firm reliance in this question is upon her recognition made by other powers, upon the grounds of the fact and the right, the principles on which nations have at the same time established her political existence.

Mexico does not, therefore change her protests, nor retire from her incontrovertible rights; on the contrary she repeats and and again [*sic*] presents these, protests, reserving and vindicating those rights so that nothing may be alleged against her hereafter, on the grounds of toleration, ["omission" *canceled*] remissness or consent.

The Undersigned repeats to Mr. Green the assurances of his most distinguished consideration. J.M. de Bocanegra.

[Enclosure]

Ben E. Green to J[osé] M. de Bocanegra

Legation of the U.S. of A.

Mexico, June 26th 1844

The undersigned, Charge &c, has had the honor to receive the note of H.E. J.M. de Bocanegra, dated June 25th, in which H.E., avoiding both horns of the Dilemma, in which the example and precedent of Mexico have placed him, half admits and half denies that Texas is a sovereign nation; and finally concludes, that although she is sovereign and independent, her independence and her annexation to the U.S. are not one and the same thing.

It has been the object of the undersigned in continuing this correspondence, to satisfy H.E., by the authority & example of Mexico herself, that Texas is a sovereign and independent nation: that, being sovereign and independent, she has an undoubted right to annex herself, by Treaty, to the U.S.; and that the latter have an equal right to receive her, if they think proper. The undersigned had hoped that when it was made manifest to H.E. that the grounds taken by him are contrary to the principles & practice, which Mexico herself has always maintained, the question would then be put to rest. But when he sees that even the authority of Mexico is unavailing to convince H.E., he deems it useless to continue the correspondence.

As to the question of *right*, which H.E. raises; all the Govts., which have acknowledged the independence of Texas, have thought it beyond the sphere of their duty to discuss this question. They have recognized her on the broad principle of *fact*, as is usual in such cases: on the principle laid down by all writers on international law, that every country which governs itself by its own authority and laws, is sovereign; the *fact* being presumed to carry with it the preexisting *right*. The undersigned, therefore, deems it improper and unnecessary for him to discuss the right of Texas to her independence. He now leaves this matter with his Govt., and in taking leave of it for the present, he avails himself of the occasion to renew to H.E. Mr. Bocanegra, the assurances of his consideration. (Signed) Ben E. Green.

ALS (No. 9) with Ens and State Department translation in DNA, RG 59 (State Department), Diplomatic Despatches, Mexico, vol. 12 (M-97:13); variant FC in DNA, RG 84 (Foreign Posts), Mexico, Despatches; draft with En in NcU, Duff Green Papers (published microfilm, roll 5, frames 618–621); PC with Ens in Senate Document No. 1, 28th Cong., 2nd Sess., pp. 79–82; PC with Ens in House Document No. 2, 28th Cong., 2nd Sess., pp. 78–81.

From J[AMES] HAMILTON, [JR.]

Oswichee Bend [Ala.,] June 28th 1844
My Dear Sir—Before this reaches you you will in all probability see the Resolutions adopted at a public meeting of the Citizens ["at" *canceled and* "in" *interlined*] this County in reference to a Southern Convention. Since the nomination of [James K.] Polk & the abuse which has been heaped upon yourself I have not the smallest hope that the South will have either the spirit or forecast to sustain such a measure. Altho I believe such a Convention by its moderation & Patriotism would save the Union, secure the annexation of Texas & carry the Democratic nomination.

You have never informed me what interest we ought to feel in this last ["measure" *interlined*] beyond the hope that annexation might be one of its results in case of success. I really feel at a loss to conjecture what our moves ought to be under the overwhelming majority which the joint power of [Henry] Clay and [Martin] Van Buren have organized & concentrated against us—in Congress on the Annexation Question.

["Our" *canceled.*] The friends of Annexation in Congress ought not to have adjourned without providing for an An[n]exation Convention to ["have" *canceled and* "to" *interlined; sic*] meet in Philadelphia in Aug[u]st—to have co[u]nteracted by a concentrated expression of public sentiment the weighty decision of Congress on the ["annexation" *canceled*] Question against us.

I see a Rumor of your intention to quit at an early day the Department of State. ["C" *canceled.*] Let me beg of you not to do this prematurely, as in the next six Months it is absolutely impossible to predict what new aspect the Annexation Question may assume affording you the occasion of great public usefulness & distinction. Bide your time. Great events may be coming on.

I never despaired however so much of the Country. Between the blind servility of the Whigs of the South to Mr. Clay & the expectation of the Democrats that every evil is to be remedied by the presidential election the South is prostrate & undone.

Messrs. [J. Pinckney] Henderson & [Isaac] Van Zandt inform me that they never received the Letter I enclosed you *for them* to be delivered in the first instance to Mr. [Isaac E.?] Holmes [Representative from S.C.].

I have transmitted a *duplicate* which I beg leave to request you to pardon my enclosing to you. I beg you to transmit it to Mr. Van Zandt as it contains a protest against the unjust preference given to Mr. [Frederick] Dawson's claims.

Let me hear from you directed to Charleston, where I shall be on the *15th July* on a visit of a few Days. Should you be coming South nothing would gratify me so much as to meet you there on that day. I have more to say to you than a Letter can record. I remain My Dear Sir With sincere esteem faithfully & respect[full]y Yours, J. Hamilton.

P.S. In case of your absence, I have requested your Cheif [*sic*] Clerk [Richard K. Crallé] to open this letter, when he will be so good as to send the Enclosed letter for Messrs. Van Zandt & Henderson to them, and to forward this sheet to yourself, wherever you may be. J.H.

ALS in ScCleA. Note: This letter was addressed to Calhoun in Washington with a note reading: "If Mr. Calhoun should have left Washington, the Cheif Clerk of the Department will please open this letter." An AEU by Calhoun reads: "Gen[era]l Hamilton[,] to be answered at Charleston by the 10th Inst."

From Henry W. Hilliard

Legation of the United States
Brussels, 28th June 1844

Sir; I have the honor to inform you that the discussion in the Belgian Chambers upon the tobacco question has, at length, been brought to a close. I stated in my last despatch, that the project of the law submitted by the Minister of Finance had been rejected by the Chamber of Representatives, and that other propositions were under consideration. These were brought to a vote in that body some days since and the enclosed project was adopted by a large majority and sent to the Senate. After a short discussion in the Senate, it was unanimously adopted in that body, and now only wants the Royal sanction to become a law. This, I have no doubt, it will receive, and it will become obligatory, immediately, according to the provisions of the second article. In examining the project which I enclose, it will be necessary to observe, in order to estimate the amount of duties, that a kilogramme is about 2¼ lbs. Avoirdupois, and that the charges are made in francs.

I am very much gratified at this result, not only because it relieves me from all apprehension as to the application of a retro-active principle to American interests, but, because the new law will, in my opinion be found to operate favorably to our trade in this article. There exists on the part of the Belgian Government a sincere and strong disposition to cultivate liberal commercial relations with us, and our affairs here are, at this time, in a state of the highest prosperity. It has become a subject of remark that the influence of the United States is powerful here and that the Belgian Government has shown a decided disposition to favor our country. If it should occur to you that any change in the commercial relations of the two countries may be made to our advantage, this may be easily arranged by treaty. The Brussels papers of this morning report a circumstance which occurred at Antwerp some days since, which is somewhat amusing, and which shows what a narrow escape a new importation of American tobacco has made from the provisions of the new Tariff. The law upon tobacco being upon the point of discussion in the Senate, the three masted ship, James H. Shepherd, Capt. Redman, being in the river with 700 hogsheads of tobacco from New Orleans, consigned to a merchant in Antwerp; the ship, that it might hasten its arrival was towed up before the town by a steamboat from Flushing and having quickly entered the basin will proceed immediately to discharge its cargo.

I have nothing farther of interest to communicate at this time, except to say that the Chambers are about to adjourn. I have the honor to be, Sir, Very respectfully, Your obedient servant, Henry W. Hilliard.

LS (No. 21) with En and State Department translation in DNA, RG 59 (State Department), Diplomatic Despatches, Belgium, vol. 2 (M-193:3), received 7/19.

From James B. Martin "of Texas," Wheeling [Va.], 6/28. He encloses to Calhoun a letter from S[hadrach] Penn, Jr., Editor of the St. Louis *Reporter*, and other documents concerning a confession by [William] Mason [in the case of the murder of Antonio José Chavis]. Martin believes those convicted to be innocent and asks that a pardon or a respite be granted. Martin wrote on the address page of this letter "To be read with haste." ALS in DNA, RG 59 (State Department), Petitions for Pardon and Related Briefs, 1800–1849, no. 292A.

To HENRY MIDDLETON

Department of State
Washington, June 28, 1844
Sir, I have the honor to transmit to you, enclosed, copies of a Communication addressed by [Stephen Pleasonton] the 5th Auditor of the Treasury to this Department, dated the 26th Inst. and of your account [as U.S. Minister to Russia] as settled by the accompting officer of the Treasury of date the 13th of January 1840.

The letter of the Auditor above referred to will explain to you minutely the present state of your accounts with this Department, which appear to have been audited and adjusted agreeably to the rules established in such cases. Under these circumstances I can perceive no grounds which would justify the interference of the Head of the Department. I am, Sir, your obed[ient] Ser[van]t, J.C. Calhoun.

FC in DNA, RG 59 (State Department), Accounting Records: Miscellaneous Letters Sent, 1832–1916, vol. for 2/1–9/30/1844, p. 272. NOTE: Middleton, a former Governor of S.C., had been Minister to Russia during 1820–1830 and a "Unionist" leader during the Nullification period.

From Henry Morris, Clerk, Treasury Department, 6/28. He asks that Calhoun consider the case of Robert Bell, a U.S. citizen imprisoned in Cuba "upon suspicion of having taken part in an insurrection of the slaves of that Island." ALS with Ens in DNA, RG 59 (State Department), Miscellaneous Letters (M-179:104, frames 657–661).

From A[LPHONSE] PAGEOT

Legation of France in the U. States
Washington, June 28, 1844

Sir, I have received the letter which you did me the honour to write to me, on the 24th of this month, and with it, the copy of the Resolution, whereby the Senate has introduced some amendments in the additional article, signed on the 15 of April, last to the Convention for the surrender of criminals, concluded at Washington on the 9th of November 1843. I have this day transmitted that Resolution to my Government.

As the Convention of November 9th leaves to each Government, the care of determining the forms to be observed in the surrender, I am charged Sir to request you, to inform me of the dispositions which the Federal Government may make on this subject. As regards France, the King's Government will limit itself to a request, that the demand for surrender be officially made, through a diplomatic channel, and should be accompanied by an order for arrest, or by some judgement, such as a warrant, verdict, true bill, or indictment, clearly stating the nature of the acts with which the individual demanded stands charged, as well as the nation to which he belongs. Accept Sir the assurance of my high consideration, A. Pageot.

State Department translation of LS (in French) in DNA, RG 59 (State Department), Notes from Foreign Legations, France, vol. 12 (M-53:8, frames 709–711).

To HENRY WHEATON, [Berlin]

Department of State
Washington, 28 June 1844

Sir, It is with regret I have to inform you that Congress adjourned without final action on the part of the Senate on the Treaty with the German Customs Union.

The Treaty was transmitted to the Senate accompanied by the appropriate documents on the 29th of April and was referred to the Committee on Foreign Relations. It was reported without amendment on the 30th of May to the Senate; but recommitted on the first of June on motion of the Chairman [William S. Archer] and reported back on the 14th of June[,] accompanied by a written Report against advising and consenting to its ratification; and, finally, laid on the table on the 15th inst., two days preceding the adjournment. I herewith transmit a Copy of the Report of the Committee together with an extract from the Journal of the Senate containing an account of its action thereon. The want of time for discussion and due deliberation at so late a period of the Session, was, no doubt, the motive for laying it on the table, but its effect must be to defeat the Treaty unless the time stipulated for the exchange of ratifications should be prolonged. Such a result would be deemed unfortunate, and no effort on our part should be wanting to prevent it; unless, indeed, you should find a decided disinclination on the part of the Zoll-Verein States against it; which will hardly be the case, should it be thought the Senate would advise its ratification in the event the time should be prolonged.

Whether it would or not, it is impossible to say with certainty. No vote has yet been taken calculated to test its opinion on the merits of the Treaty; nor is there anything by which the sentiment of any of its members can be ascertained except the Report of the Committee on Foreign Relations[,] consisting of five. It doubtless speaks the opinions of a majority of its members.

Their objections to the Treaty may, however, be regarded as embracing the leading arguments against it, and on which those opposed to it would mainly rest their advice as to its ratification. On their validity and force, the fate of the Treaty, should the time be prolonged, would probably depend. Under this impression I have examined them with care, and must say[,] they appear to me to be neither insuperable nor formidable. The two leading objections urged in the Report are, the want of "Constitutional competency" to make it, and the "unequal value of the stipulated equivalents." It relies mainly on the former to support the conclusions to which it comes. Indeed, it says that it is "upon that single ground" it advises that the Treaty be rejected. In support of its denial of the Constitutionality of the Treaty it states that it is "an innovation on the ancient and uniform practise of the Government to change duties laid by law"; that "the Constitution, in express terms, delegates the power to Congress, to regulate Commerce and to impose duties, and to no other["]; and that the "control of trade and the function of taxing belong, without abridgement or participation, to Congress." It is on these grounds the Report concludes that the Treaty is unconstitutional and ought to be rejected. If the conclusion be legitimate its ratification would be hopeless, and it would be idle to endeavour to prolong the time stipulated for an exchange of ratifications. The question then arises, Is it so? With all due deference I must think the Report greatly errs as to a part of its premises, and wholly as to its conclusions. So far is the Treaty from being "an innovation on the ancient and uniform practice of the Government," in stipulating "to change duties laid by Law" as is asserted in the Report, it may be safely affirmed that, in this respect, it is in strict conformity with the habitual practise of the Government. There are numerous instances of the kind. Among them may be cited the Treaty with Great Britain in 1815, which is relied on by the Earl of Aberdeen to claim for his Government the same privileges stipulated in this in favor of the Zoll-Verein States, should the Treaty be ratified. In that case an Act of Congress was passed to carry its stipulations to change the duties into effect. A still more ancient and memorable example may be cited in the case of the Treaty by which Louisiana was obtained. In that it was stipulated expressly, that exclusive and important commercial privileges should be extended to France and Spain during twelve years—and these stipulations, materially affecting duties and imposts, were subsequently carried out by Act of Congress. To these may be added the more recent case of our Treaty with France in 1832 when the like principle and practise prevailed. It is unnecessary to adduce further examples. There is an entire and numerous class (I refer to the reciprocity treaties) which almost invariably contain stipulations changing the existing laws regulating commerce and navigation, and duties laid by Law. So well is the practise settled that it is believed it has never before been questioned. The only question, it is believed, that was ever made, was, whether an Act of Congress was not necessary to sanction and carry the stipulations making the change into effect. You will see by the President's [John Tyler's] Message, transmitting the Treaty to the Senate, that he is of the opinion that it is; and that he, accordingly, announced to the Senate that, when it was ratified, he would transmit the Treaty and accompanying documents to the House for its consideration and action.

The conclusion to which the Report comes against the Constitutionality of the Treaty seems to me not less erroneous. It is, indeed, true, as it says, that the Constitution delegates to Congress the power of regulating commerce and laying duties; but the question still remains, does that inhibit the Treaty-making power from making commerce and duties the subjects of Treaty stipulations—or, to express it in more general terms, does the delegation of a power to Congress exclude it from being the subject of the Treaty-making power? If such be the case then that power would be limited in its operation to the reserved powers, to the entire exclusion of the delegated; that is to the separate and peculiar powers reserved to the States and the people, to the exclusion of those delegated to the Union, among which are included all those appertaining to our foreign relations. If this be a true view of the subjects confided to the Treaty-making power, it may be truly said that its exercise has been one continued series of habitual and uninterrupted infringement of the Constitution. From the beginning and throughout the whole existence of the Federal Government it has been exercised constantly on commerce, navigation, and other delegated powers to the almost entire exclusion of the reserved which, from their nature rarely ever come in question between us and other nations. The Treaty-making power has, indeed, been regarded to be so comprehensive as to embrace, with few exceptions[,] all questions that can possibly arise between us and other nations, and which can only be adjusted by their mutual consent, whether the subject matter be comprised among the delegated, or the reserved powers. So far, indeed, is it from being true, as the Report supposes, that the mere fact of a power being delegated to Congress excludes it from being the subject of Treaty stipulations, that even its exclusive delegation, if we may judge from the habitual practise of the Government, does not, of which the power of appropriating money affords a striking example. It is expressly and exclusively delegated to Congress; and yet scarcely a Treaty has been made of any importance which does not stipulate for the payment of money. No objection has ever been made on this account. The only question ever raised in reference to it is, whether Congress has not unlimited discretion to grant or withhold the appropriation?

But as untenable as is the "single ground" on which the Report advises the rejection of the Treaty, its other objection, "the unequal value of the equivalents stipulated," which it adds as a make-weight, is not less so. In making out its alleged inequality, it limits the advantages on our side to the reduction of the duties on lard and tobacco, excluding entirely the stipulations against increasing the present low duty on rice, and against the imposition of any duty on cotton; while on the side of the Zoll-Verein States, it enumerates, at large, the various articles which we stipulate to admit at reduced rates. In both it omits to give the quantity of each article imported into the respective countries, and the rates of the old duties, which are indispensable elements in estimating whether the equivalents are of equal value or not. Had the Report taken them into its estimate it would have found that the loss of revenue of the Zoll-Verein States on tobacco alone, in consequence of the stipulated reduction would have exceeded by many thousand dollars, the entire loss of revenue on our part, on all articles of theirs which are stipulated to be admitted on reduced duties. Without going farther and enlarging on the many advantages, we would have derived from the Treaty, this of itself is sufficient to show, that the Report even in the limited view it takes in estimating the equality of the stipulations has fallen into error. Such are the objections taken by the Report to the Treaty. The President after due deliberation cannot believe that they are such as are calculated to present any insuperable or formidable obstacles to its adoption; and cannot but hope that if the period for the exchange of ratifications could be extended so as to afford sufficient time for discussion and decision on its merits, that the Senate would advise and consent to its ratification. Under this impression he instructs you to use your best endeavours to have the period so extended as to allow sufficient time for the exchange of ratifications should the Senate advise and consent to it during the next Session of Congress which will terminate on the 4th of March 1845—unless, indeed, you should find as before observed, a decided disinclination on the part of Prussia and the other Zoll-Verein States. In that case, you will not from motives of delicacy insist on the extension. Should there be no such disinclination manifested, it is left entirely to your discretion to decide what steps should be taken in order to effect the object.

I avail myself of the opportunity to assure you, that the President places a high estimate on the industry[,] ability and skill with which you have conducted the negotiation that terminated in the formation of the Treaty. I have the honor to be, with high consideration, Your Obedient Servant, J.C. Calhoun.

LS (No. 57) with Ens in DNA, RG 84 (Foreign Posts), Germany, Instructions, 1:285–300; FC in DNA, RG 59 (State Department), Diplomatic Instructions, Germany, 14:75–83 (M-77:65); CC in NNPM, Wheaton Papers.

To Henry Wheaton, "Private"

Washington, 28th June 1844

My dear Sir, The omission of the Senate to act ["finally" *interlined*] on the treaty with the ZollVerein States is at once a subject of deep regret & mortification; regret on account of the advantages it promised to both parties, and which it is feared may be lost, & mortification, on account of the effects it may have ["on" *interlined*] the standing of the government abroad. The cause, to which it is to be attributed, is doubtless the same, as that to which the defeat of the Texian treaty may be, ["attributed," *canceled*] excepting in the former, the operation of the protective interest. But, I do not think, that of itself would have ["been" *interlined*] sufficient. You will see, that it is not even alluded to in the Report of the Committee. The true cause in both cases, I believe to be, the bearing, which it was feared it would have on the Presidential election. Mr. [Henry] Clay's friends, who are a decided majority in the Senate felt confident of his election, under the old issue, as it stood, when Congress met, & ["they" *canceled*] were averse to admit any new question to enter the issue. Their attempt to prevent it has been in vain, and will prove unwise, even in a party point of view. The Texian question has entered deeply into ["it" *canceled and* "the issue" *interlined*], & I have no doubt, that growing out of the ZollVerein treaty will also. Nor would I be surprise[d], if he should be beaten, in consequence of the part, which his friends in the Senate have acted, as weak, personally, as the candidate opposed to him [James K. Polk] is, comparatively.

I cannot but hope, that the treaty would be sanctioned by the Senate, should the time be prolonged, to the next session, when the Presidential [election] will be over, and the party ["motives" *interlined*] which have led to laying the treaty on the table, shall have passed away. I am strengthen[ed] in this opinion, from the very inconclusive reasons assigned by the Committee on foreign relations for its rejection, & which I feel confident, the Senate will never sanction, whatever may be the fate of the treaty.

Under this impression, you have been instructed to have the time so extended, as to afford the Senate an opportunity at the next session to act finally on the Treaty, unless there should be a decided disinclination on the part of Prussia & other ZollVerein States to the extension, which I fear may be the case. If such should be the fact it strikes me, ["me" *canceled*] that it would be very indelicate, on our part, to press it. It would be doubly mortifying to us, & still more offensive to Prussia & the other states of the league, if it should be rejected ["if we" *canceled*] should ["we" *interlined*] press, against their inclination, the extension of the time for the exchange of ratifications.

Let what may be the fate of the treaty, you can lose no reputation, as an able & successful negotiator. In making the treaty, you have effected what could have been accomplished by few, and what, if it should ["be" *interlined*] consummated, would constitute an era in our commercial history. I cannot doubt, it would lead, by its consequences, to other & great changes in the commerce of the civilized world, and lay a solid foundation for an intimate & close commercial & political union between the United States & Germany, which I greatly desire, and which, I do not, doubt would be for the mutual advantage of both. With great respect yours truly, J.C. Calhoun.

ALS in NNPM, Wheaton Papers.

To John Macpherson Berrien, [Senator from Ga.], New York [City], 6/29. Calhoun acknowledges Berrien's letter of 6/27 about Homer Virgil Morel, a Texan prisoner taken in the battle of Mier. Calhoun replies that the U.S. government cannot interfere "officially" in Morel's behalf, but [Wilson] Shannon, the U.S. Minister to Mexico, will be instructed to use his influence for Morel's benefit. FC in DNA, RG 59 (State Department), Domestic Letters, 34:269 (M-40:32).

To WILLIAM M. BLACKFORD, [Bogotá]

Department of State
Washington, 29th June, 1844

Sir: Your despatches to No. 24, inclusive, have been received.

The Postal Convention signed by Mr. [Joaquin] Acosta and yourself on the 6th of March, last, has been approved by the Senate and ratified by the President, and a ratified copy is now transmitted for the purpose of being exchanged for the ratification of the Government of New Granada. A power authorizing you to make the exchange on the part of this government is also now sent, and a draught of a certificate of exchange. You will communicate the draught to the person who may be appointed by the New Granadian government to effect the exchange and request that it may be translated into

Spanish, if it should meet with his approval, and that a day may be named for the exchange.

When this is accomplished the certificates are to be signed and the one in Spanish will accompany the New Granadian ratification, and the one in English will be placed with ours.

As the Congress of New Granada has approved of the Convention, it is presumed that the exchange of the ratifications will take place without delay. You may consequently detain the messenger who takes this until after that event and send the ratification of that government by him on his return, together with such communications as you may have occasion to address to this Department.

In consideration of the circumstances mentioned by you, I am directed by the President to say that the leave of absence which you request is granted. In accordance with your suggestion, application has been made to the Navy Department for orders to a vessel of war to touch at Carthagena about the 15th of December, next, for the purpose of giving you a passage to the United States, and this Department has been informed in reply, that the Commander of the squadron in the Gulph of Mexico has been authorized to send a vessel for that purpose, provided it can be done without injury to the public service. I am, Sir, your obedient servant, J.C. Calhoun.

LS (No. 18) in DNA, RG 84 (Foreign Posts), Colombia, Instructions, vol. A2; FC in DNA, RG 59 (State Department), Diplomatic Instructions, Colombia, 15:88–89 (M-77:44); CC in DNA, RG 84 (Foreign Posts), Colombia, Despatches, vol. B4.

From R. C. Caldwell and Geo[rge] Willis

Pensacola [Fla. Territory,] June 29th 1844

Sir, We the undersigned your suffering fellow citizens take the liberty of enclosing for your attention a Hand-Bill and newspaper that by looking over them you may the better understand our object in appealing to the Government of the U. States. We have brought the subject to the notice of the President in our letter of the 28th inst. addressed to him, but fearing that since the adjournment of Congress he may not be at Washington & the subject being such as to require immediate action if it is the will of the Government to give us aid, we therefore have thought it proper and important also thus respectfully to address your Honor.

In our letter to the Pres[iden]t alluded to we informed him that on the 26th about noon a boat answering to the description of [Jonathan] Walker's was seen at sea beating to the eastward and being about ten miles south of Pensacola Bar—that on receipt of this intelligence we applied next day to the Naval Commandant at the Yard for assistance to capture said Boat and rescue the property—the U.S. Steamer Poinsett lying at the Yard manned & equipped for sea and we agreeing to furnish her fuel for the expedition—that the Commandant replied that he could not move in the matter at all—that he had no authority—that under no circumstances whatever could he employ any part of the public force for such a purpose. We respectfully request in our letter of the 28th to know from the Commander in Chief of the Navy of the U. States if it is so that we can promise ourselves no protection in life or property from the public force at hand and quite available, or if it is otherwise and the Naval Comm[an]d[an]t has not taken the proper view of his duty and authority that he be instructed accordingly for our future safety and also requested that as we have yet ["not" *interlined*] lost hope of recovering the property that the Poinsett or other available force be ordered in pursuit of the fugitive from justice who it may be is guilty of Piracy for it is by no means improbable that, if he (Walker) has indeed stolen these Negroes, at all he has committed the theft upon the high seas or from the Territory specially reserved to the jurisdiction of the U. States for Military or Naval purposes.

We regard the question of our receiving or not ["receiving" *interlined*] pub[l]ic aid in the rescue of our property under the circumstances as one that is by no means confined to ourselves but that materially affects the interests and safety of the whole South.

Your aid in the matter will be gratefully acknowledged by this entire community and especially by your suffering fellow citizens who subscribe themselves as they have the honor to be very respectfully Your Ob[edien]t Serv[an]ts, R.C. Caldwell, Geo. Willis, p[e]r Jos[eph] Quigles, Agent.

LS with Ens in DNA, RG 59 (State Department), Miscellaneous Letters (M-179: 104, frames 662–663 and 666–675). NOTE: Enclosed was a copy of the *Pensacola Gazette* of 6/29 containing an article on the abduction by Jonathan Walker of seven slaves belonging to Caldwell and Willis. Also enclosed was a handbill describing the slaves and Walker and offering a $1,700 reward for their capture and delivery at Pensacola. The Commandant of the Pensacola Navy Yard was Capt. E.A.F. Lavalette.

To J[AMES] ED[WARD] COLHOUN,
[Abbeville District, S.C.]

State Dept., 29th June 1844

My dear James, I enclose two notes [*not found*] from Mr. [John S.] Skinner, which may be of interest to you. I would suppose that your mountain estate would be still more favourable to sheep raising than any location in the western parts of N. Carolina, as the climate is more mild & the winter shorter. The N.C. experiment will test the capability of our mountain region for the purpose of sheep husbandry. Should it succeed it will add greatly to the value of your estate there.

I avail my self of the occasion to express my deep condolence to you under your severe affliction [in the death of Maria Simkins Colhoun]. I will not attempt to offer consolation. Your bereavement is too great for that. When the wound is so deep, nothing but a change of scene & the gentle hand of time can assuage the pain. You must not think of remaining alone at Millwood. The scenes around you will but serve to remind you of your loss, and convert your greif [*sic*] into settled gloom. Let me entreat you to make our House your home, at least for some months to come. It would, I know, add to the happiness of your sister [Floride Colhoun Calhoun] & the family, and confer a favour on me in my absence. I expect to be home in August and do hope on my return to meet you there.

I had a letter from Patrick [Calhoun] from St. Louis a few days since. He & John [C. Calhoun, Jr.] had reached there in safety and were preparing to set out on their excursion with a detachment of dragoons. John's cough was much as it was. The weather had not been favourable. There had been a deludge [*sic*] of rain, & the Mississippi & Missouri ["were" *interlined*] higher than they had been for years. I hope the excursion will restore John's health. If it should not, I fear his case will be hopeless. Yours affectionately, J.C. Calhoun.

ALS in ScCleA. NOTE: An EU on this letter reads: "J.C.C. enclosing Notes from Skinner about Sheep-walk in N. Carolina."

From EDWARD EVERETT

London, 29 June 1844

Sir, I mentioned in my despatch numbered 69 [in 1843] that I had applied to Mr. Washington Irving [U.S. Minister to Spain] to procure if possible from the archives of Spain the documents containing the evidence adduced by the Spanish government in 1790, in support of their territorial claims upon the North West coast of America, on occasion of the Nootka Sound controversy. My despatch Nro. 82 [of 2/2/1844] contains an account of the failure of that application. Accident has since enabled me to procure an authentic report of the whole progress of the negotiations between this country and Spain, which resulted in the Nootka Sound convention. This report appears to contain a reference to all the official documents and correspondence exchanged between the two governments on that occasion, and leaves no reason to think that the Spanish minister, the count Florida Blanca, entered into any detailed argument in support of their claims to the North West coast. He assumed (as appears from the documents published at the time) the latitude of 61 degrees north as their boundary, and maintained that this resulted from "treaties, demarcations, takings of possession, and the most decided acts of sovereignty exercised by the Spaniards from the reign of Charles II of Spain and authorized by that monarch in 1692." But there is no trace in the report above alluded to, of any attempt to support this proposition. The negociation did not take a turn requiring this to be done.

Among the proposals toward the adjustment of the controversy made by England, was that of agreeing to a limit beyond which Spain should abandon her pretensions to the north, and the 40th degree was offered as a reasonable boundary, which England would acknowledge.

Not the least curious part of the proceedings of England disclosed by this report is the attempt to enlist the United States against Spain in the conflict supposed to be impending. Lord Dorchester, the governor of Canada, who had signified his intention of returning to England the ensuing summer, was directed to remain in his government, where his experience and ability were judged to be of the greatest importance. He was ordered to embody the militia of the Province, in the event of a rupture with Spain; and to prevent any alarm, which this measure might occasion on the part of the United States, "he was instructed to cultivate, as much as possible, the friendship of the inhabitants of Vermont."

I quote at length the following somewhat interesting passage from the Report:

"As this was an occurrence (an alarm on the part of the United States) on every account to be deprecated, and against the possibility of which it behoved the wisdom of His Majesty's government to provide as certainly as the exigencies of the moment would permit, Lord Dorchester was directed to adopt every means in his power to influence the Americans in favor of the British nation; and to prevent them from being induced, by any representations of the court of Spain, or by any offers which might be held out to them by that Power, to join with her in the event of her contest with England. For this purpose, in addition to the friendly professions, which he had constantly held out to them since the peace [of 1783], he was instructed to explain to them the real nature of the Spanish Pretensions; by which an exclusive claim, as against all the world, was advanced by them to the possession and dominion of the whole western coast of America and the adjoining seas; a claim, which, if admitted, must of course operate as strongly and as disadvantageously against the Americans as against the English, and must put an end to the prosecution of their Fur Trade, which was become so material for the carrying on of their commerce to China. He was also directed to suggest the important consequences which might result from the navigation of the Mississippi being opened to them; advantages at least as great, as could possibly be expected from their becoming possessed of the Forts on the frontier of Canada; particularly when it was considered, that they might acquire the former, by the assistance of Great Britain, much more easily than they could hope to possess the latter, against her will, by the help of Spain."

The Report in question is contained in a volume of about three hundred pages, privately printed at the time for the use of the government and never published, entitled "a narrative of the negotiations occasioned by the dispute between England and Spain in the year 1790." Of this volume I have been able to purchase a copy for the Department, which I shall forward to Washington, as soon as I can get it bound. I am, sir, with great respect, your obedient servant, Edward Everett.

LS (No. 152) in DNA, RG 59 (State Department), Diplomatic Despatches, Great Britain, vol. 52 (M-30:48), received 7/19; FC in DNA, RG 84 (Foreign Posts), Great Britain, Despatches, 8:319–324; CC in DNA, RG 76 (Records of Boundary and Claims Commissions and Arbitrations), Records Relating to the U.S.-Canadian Border, Documents Relating to the U.S. Case, no. 152; FC in MHi, Edward Everett Papers, 49:329–335 (published microfilm, reel 23, frames 165–168).

To "John F. Brown" [*sic;* John Brown Francis], Providence, R.I., 6/29. "I have to reply to your letter of the 26th instant, that Mr. [John B.] Williams has not informed the Department of his having vacated the office of Consul of the United States at the Bay of Islands in New Zealand. Should the office become vacant, the recommendations of Mr. Ma[y]hew will receive respectful consideration." FC in DNA, RG 59 (State Department), Domestic Letters, 34:267–268 (M-40:32).

From JOHN HOGAN, "Private & Confidential"

Utica [N.Y.] June 29th 1844

My dear Sir, I am fearful that you are sorely an[n]oyed at my writing you so often. *My apology you know to[o] well for me to mention* therefore I take the liberty. Matters in this State begin to assume a more favourable aspect. Still the friends of Mr. [Henry] Clay say that they are sure of the State. My opinion is strengthening every day that we will defeat them in this State. We have moved with Napoleon's rapidity & have thrown such fear into the ["fear" *canceled*] minds of the friends of Mr. [Martin] Van Buren that they are comeing out from day to day in favour of Mr. [James K.] Polk & Mr. [George M.] Dallas. The great matter in controversy is the Texas question. It is a bitter pill consequently we have to labour with a then[?] double energy. As soon as we can get it settled down as an American and English question then we are safe. One of our difficulties is that some of the Ultra friends of Mr. Van Buren stand in the gap against us. That together with the influence of the Gen-[eral] Administration against us makes our task more onerous. Now another point I will touch. Gent[lemen] may say what they please, Your course & position has placed you at the head of all. *Let me here say that should I be consulted* on the subject of your leaving the Cabinet & going home, *I would* be most decidedly & unequivocally opposed to it. Now I will assign my reasons. The Administration now has character & respectability[,] who brought it there I will not say. The People of the United States look to you as I said to you in Washington. They now feel safe[,] they are at leisure & quietly slumbering but as soon as you leave they will become alarmed & uneasy & the danger to be apprehended is that all that has been done to elevate the Nation & correct some wrongs *would be all lost* & the U.S. would be in a most deplorable position. There would be no responsibility at Washington[,] no man that the country could look to in time of need & there would gather to Washington an extraordinary set of men who would in fact take into their hands ruthlessly the helm of Gov[ernment]. All that has been done in Washington has been done by yourself (& your *subjects* as *some* Gen[tlemen] in this State call us) and should you now leave all would be lost. I [k]now the feeling of many of your friends in this State is that you would leave the Cabinet. Mr. [Charles A.?] Clinton[,] Mr. [John L.H.] McCracken & others are of that opinion. Let me ask what would be gained by it[,] the *country probably ruined* in the Election of Mr. Clay. Now when men speak they know that the polar *Star* is in its orb therefore they are fearless. Now you have my poor opinion on that question.

You may be in favour of something else but I consider my duty to my friend demands of me my fearless & matured views ["of" canceled] arising from deep reflection. Now to my own matter & then I will stop. I beg here to be permitted to say that I stand as much chance of getting an appointment from Mr. Tyler as the *man in moon*. Should I get the appointment it will have to be got by the personal application of Mr. Calhoun as a favour to him to have Mr. Hogan get an office. I was told while in New York [City] on ["the" altered to "my"] return home that a BrotherinLaw of the President[']s by the name of Miller—(Dr. [John G.] Miller) I believe said to some of our friends that the President would [appoint?] an[y] Gent to office that Mr. C[alhoun] desired. *Do not understand me as wishing to corner you in this matter* (as the Wall St. bankers say). I assure you that I feel a more lively interest in the appointment than I otherwise should owing to the fixed & boasted determination of the friends of Mr. Van Buren that at all hazards they would defeat Hogan in his purpose with the President. I wrote Mr. [Robert J.] Walker a day or two since. I am about getting his speech published here & sending about 5000 through the State. I hope your health is as vigorous as heretofore for *depend upon* what I say to you, *Your responsibility to Your Country has but just begun* and any effort on your part to divest yourself of that responsibility would be viewed by the country with alarm. I hope Mr. Pekins [*sic*; Francis W. Pickens] & Mr. [George] McDuffie will not go to[o] far in South Carolina. For *Heaven's sake let them be more discreet*. South Carolina should be mute when her Son holds the helm of State or when a Gent[leman] is at the head of affairs that is claimed by the whole Union. If those Gent[lemen] do not cease their inflam[m]atory proceedings in South Carolina they will ruin *us all now and for ever*. When matters are comeing around by the help of their friends as fast as time can bring them to the very point that they desire *why* will they overthrow us in our success[.] You can well say my dear Sir "Save me from my friends." They overdo the matter & when it come[s] to the point they fly from the track & run after some butterfly or other and leave their friends (or your friends) to fight the battle in other States single handed. I say again that if Mr. McDuffie & Mr. Pekins do not cease their inflam[m]atory proceeding they will ruin *yourself* & *your friends.* I am Sir your Ob[edien]t Ser[vant], John Hogan.

ALS in ScCleA.

From JA[ME]S HOWLAND 2ND and Others

New Bedford, 6 mo[nth] 29 1844

The undersigned, Masters, Ship owners, and Underwriters of New Bedford, Mass: (the 3d port in the United States in point of Tonnage of sea going vessels) would respectfully represent to the Honorable the Secretary of State that from years of actual experience, and from information [*missing word*] fully ["relyed" *altered to* "relied"] on, they are satisfied the location of the Head Quarters of our Consulate at the Bay of Islands, New Zealand, is every way most objectionable, and ruinous to our interests. Such are the gross immoralities of the place, that it is an outrage to the feelings of any honorable or respectable man, to reside there. They would therefore most respectfully suggest to the honorable Secretary, the high propriety, and in fact, almost absolute necessity of requesting the present worthy Incumbent to fix himself at the Metropolis of the Colony, the city of Auckland, and further they are fully satisfied that American interists would be greatly served by extending the jurisdiction of said Consul over the Feegee Islands, a group distant about 4 or 5 days sail, and where American ships are often wrecked, and the property destroyed, which frequently might be saved, had the Consul a right to interfere. [Signed:] Jas. Howland 2nd[,] Pres[id]ent Bedford Com[mercia]l Ins[urance] Company, R.R. Crocker Sec[retar]y [Bedford Commercial Insurance Company], Geo[rge] Howland Jun[io]r Pres[iden]t Whaling Ins[urance] Co., T.H. Howland Sec[retar]y W[haling] I[nsurance] Co., S. Minihew Pres[iden]t Mutual Marine Ins[urance] Co., W[illia]m H. Taylor Secr[etar]y [Mutual Marine Insurance Company], Tirel[?] Perry Pres[iden]t Pacific Ins[urance]

Company, Atkins Adams, Daniel Wood, Theron[?] Allen Pres[iden]t Merchants Insurance Co., Hathaway & Luce, Robert Gibbs, Edw[ar]d Merrill, John Coggeshall, Charles Grinnell, Gibbs & Penney, Richmond & Wood, William H. Wood, J.M. Richardson, C.S. Tobey, David Brayton, Cooke & Snow, Fred[eric]k Parker, Edmund Gardner, Edwin C. Jones, Laurence Grinnell, Asa F. Lawton, W[illia]m P. Grinnell, Hamlin & Gibbes[?], Benj[ami]n B. Howard, Benjamin Cushman, Ichabod Handy, Wilmot Luce, Benjamin Price, Hiram Nickerson, Gardner T. Lawton, W[illia]m C. Swain, W[illia]m P. Howland, James D. Thompson, David Baker, W[illia]m Howland 2d, Alexander Gibbs, J.B. Congdon, Reuben Nye, Paidon Tillinghast, Joseph S. Tillinghast, Pope & Morgan, Jno. Pope, W[illia]m Watkins, Thomas Watkins, John A. Macomber, Luther Little, Henry F. Eastham, George H. Clark, S.W. Rodman.

ADS in DNA, RG 59 (State Department), Consular Despatches, Bay of Islands and Auckland, New Zealand, vol. 1 (T-49:1). NOTE: A Clerk's EU reads "Rec[eive]d at Dept. with Mr. [John B.] William's letter of the 22nd July 1844."

To J[ohn] Y. Mason, Secretary of the Navy, 6/29. W[illiam] Musser & Co. of Philadelphia have enquired of the State Department about the status of their claim against the "Monte Videan government" for gunpowder belonging to them and appropriated by that government. Has any information been received from Commodore [Daniel] Turner [commander of the U.S. Navy Brazilian squadron] that will enable Calhoun to answer? LS in DNA, RG 45 (Naval Records), Letters from Federal Executive Agents, 1837–1886, 6:187½ (M-517:2, frames 401–402); FC in DNA, RG 59 (State Department), Domestic Letters, 34:268–269 (M-40:32).

From PASCHAL P. POPE and Others

Boston, June 29 1844

Sir, We understand that by the latest intelligence from Mexico, the April instalment of the indemnity, under the Convention of 30 Jan[uar]y 1843 was not paid but had been deferred.

We are claimants under that Convention and the awards granted in our favor are in the hands of Gover[n]ment, and we ask leave to call your attention to the subject, and with the hope ["that" *interlined*] the Gover[n]ment will make a prompt and efficient interposition to enforce the performance of the agreement made by Mexico.

The Interest and three of the instalments have been received, and it is only through the Gover[n]ment that the residue can be collected.

It was at the special request of Mexico, and to accommodate her that the instalments were reduced to such small amounts; taking five years for the payment of the awards, under the assurance on her part, and the confidence of that of our Gover[n]ment of their being punctually met. We are Sir Your Mo[st] ob[edient] Servants, Paschal P. Pope, Ozias Goodwin, W[illia]m Oliver, Bates & Co., C[harles] Bradbury.

LS in DNA, RG 59 (State Department), Miscellaneous Letters (M-179:104, frames 664–665); CC in DNA, RG 84 (Foreign Posts), Mexico, Instructions, vol. 5.I.

From [FRIEDRICH LUDWIG, Baron Von] ROENNE

Berlin, June 29th 1844

Sir—I have the honour to inform you that His Majesty the King of Prussia has appointed me, President of the New Department of Commerce (*Handelsamt*) which he has just created by Decree of the 7th of this month. His Majesty will without delay, appoint my successor, who will have the honour to present to the President of the United States, my letters of recal[l]. It is needless for me Sir, to express to you my deep regret, at quitting a country, in which I have passed the happiest years of my life. I beg the President [John Tyler], as well as you Sir, to preserve the remembrance of me; and I have the honour to be, with the most profound respect, Your Most obedient Servant, Roenne.

State Department translation of ALS (in French) in DNA, RG 59 (State Department), Notes from Foreign Legations, Prussia, vol. 1 (M-58:1), received 8/3; PC (in English) in Gunter Moltmann, "Eine Deutschland-Korrespondenz John C. Calhouns aus dem Jahr 1844," *Jahrbuch fur Amerikastudien*, vol. XIV (1969), pp. 162–163.

From STAFFORD & BARTLETT

New Orleans, 29th June 1844

Sir, Legal proceedings have been instituted against the Schooner "Cabot," by the U. States District attorney here, on the ground that said schooner brought from "Sabine Lake" a Cargo of Texas Cotton, without stopping at "Sabine ["port" *interlined*]" on the Sabine river, on the Texas side, and depositing her papers with the American Consul resident there, and paying him the fees prescribed by law for American vessels arriving at a foreign port from the United States. As the commerce between this place and particularly that portion of Texas having for its outlet the Sabine river is daily increasing, and promises, in a few years, to be of great magnitude, it is very desirable that we should know, *with the utmost certainty*, what advantages are secured us in the navigation of the Sabine river by the treaty of 1819; and what course it is *absolutely necessary* that we should pursue to enjoy those advantages, unalloyed by the trammels of legal quibbles. We may be wrong, but we apprehend the treaty to mean that the vessels of the contracting parties shall respectively navigate the Sabine river without paying either tribute. The case to which we want to call the attention of your honor is this: The Schooner Cabot left here for "Sabine Lake," at our instance, for a cargo of Texas Cotton. The Captain sailed from hence without clearing his vessel at the Custom House, which was not required, it being in the view of the Collector a domestic port for all commercial intents and purposes—and pursued his course directly to the lake where his Cargo was waiting for him in the stream on board of a Steam boat, flats & Keel boats—without touching or stopping on his voyage at either bank of the river. In returning, he was commanded off "Sabine Port" to come to and deposit his papers, and pay a duty of one Dollar per ton, which he refused to do; believing as he did, and as we do, that the treaty never contemplated any such exactions; but that its ostensible object was an uninterrupted navigation of that river by the vessels of the contracting powers without let or hindrance. If such was not the object of the treaty—and we have had the misfortune, in common with thousands of other merchants—to misunderstand its letter, contex[t] and spirit, to whom can we so safely appeal for its just interpretation as to your honorable self; and who, it is natural to suppose, will more cheerfully give the desired information.

In consequence of the real or supposed dereliction of duty on the part of the Captain of the "Cabot," the United States District attorney has bound him in a recognizance of seven hundred and fifty dollars, thus harrassing him, and rendering the trade to us, his sureties, both odious and onerous.

Fearful that we have not been sufficiently explicit in our exposition of this case we will venture to ask a few simple questions viz:

Can an American vessel leave New Orleans for the Sabine river, ["or" *interlined*] Sabine lake for a cargo of Texas Cotton, *to be delivered on board of her from boats in the stream,* without clearing hence, entering at an intermediate Texas Port, and again clearing at that intermediate port on her return[?] Are not the waters of the Sabine in the United States?; And have we not as much right to bring Texas Cotton from thence, in the way before described, without paying the Texas government tribute, as we have to bring it from ["the" *canceled and* "our" *interlined*] towns on the "Red River," through which we now receive at least two thirds of the entire crop of eastern Texas, without any thing further being exacted by our government of the Steam boats which bring it, than to regularly enter it at the custom house in like manner with other dutiable produce.

We are emboldened to address you these few remarks from the assurances of some of your best known friends here that they will not only elicit your early consideration, from their importance, but receive as prompt a response as the nature of your arduous and multifarious duties will permit. We have the honor to be Very Respectfully Your obed[ient] Humble S[er]v[an]ts, Stafford & Bartlett.

LS in DNA, RG 59 (State Department), Miscellaneous Letters (M-179:104, frames 676–678).

From G[EORGE] F. USHER

Commercial Agency of the U. States
Cape Haytien, June 29th, 1844
Sir, I have the honor to acknowledge the receipt of Your communication of the 17th Ult. granting my request to visit the U. States. I shall return in the vessel which brings this, and my permanent place of residence, while there, will be at Bristol R. Island.

I have appointed Benjamin P. Hunt Esq. an American Gentleman residing here, to be Acting U.S. Commercial Agent, at this place, during my absence.

I also herewith transmit my semi-annual returns, ending on the 30th day of June.

As far as I can learn, the political excitements which have prevailed for some time past, have subsided; and the whole Island appears now to be tranquil; but without the certainty of continuing so for any great length of time. I have the honor, Sir, to be, with the greatest respect, Your Very Ob[edien]t S[er]v[an]t, G.F. Usher, U.S. C[ommercial] Ag[en]t.

ALS (No. 17) with Ens in DNA, RG 59 (State Department), Consular Despatches, Cap Haitien, vol. 7 (M-9:7, frames 134–138), received 7/17.

From SHEPARD CARY, [Representative from Maine]

Augusta [Maine,] June 30th 1844
Dear Sir, Prior to my leaving Washington it was in agitation to obtain an able editor to take charge of the Spectator during the pending Presidential canvass. I find that many of our New England friends are anxious that Mr. [George M.] Weston the present editor of the [Augusta] Age, should obtain that place. I have conversed with him upon that subject & find that he may be induced to take the place if ["it should" *canceled*] if it should be deemed advisable at Washington. Mr. Weston is decidedly the ablest editor that is at the head of a democratic paper in New England, & surpassed by, but few in the Union, & probably by none of his age. I have no hesitation in saying, that ["that" *canceled*] it would be a great acquisition to our strength if his services could be obtained for that purpose. You may expect to hear further from Mr. Weston in a short time[.] Very respectfully Your ob[e]d[ien]t Serv[an]t, Shepard Cary.

ALS in ScCleA. NOTE: An AEU by Calhoun reads: "Mr. Cary of Maine[,] relates to emp[l]oying Mr. Weston as editor of the Spectator."

To a COMMITTEE at Charlotte, N.C.

WASHINGTON, June 30, 1844
GENTLEMEN: I am honored by your note of the 15th inst., tendering to me in the name of the republican party of Mecklenburg County, an invitation to a barbacue at Charlotte, on the 23d of July next. I regret that my official duties here, compel me to decline its acceptance, as strong as is the inducement, which the occasion and the place hold out to accept. I am highly flattered by the cordiality of your invitation, and the grounds on which you placed it. There is nothing which I have more at heart, than to see restored and placed in the ascendancy in their full vigour the old principles of the Republican party. My conviction is deep and of long standing, that

on it the duration of our glorious political system depends. It is that alone which can resist the fatal tendency to consolidation, which for many years has marked the progress of our Government, and which has been accomplished by increasing confusion, corruption and loss of confidence, as it approaches nearer and nearer to its consummation. It has been my destiny to stand in opposition to this fatal tendency a large portion of my political life, often under the most trying circumstances. If it is ever to be arrested it must be speedily done. It will soon be too strong to be resisted. Much will depend on the approaching contest. Should the Republican party succeed, and should they in good faith, earnestly and early commence the great work of bringing back the government to the original principles and policy of the party, the hopes of the founders of our political system may still be realized, our liberties preserved, and our free, popular, federal institutions be ever the admiration of the world. But if not, it is to be feared, the opposite will be our doom.

In conclusion, I offer the following sentiment:

The Republican Party: May it succeed in the coming election, and may its success be followed by the restoration and firm establishment of its original principles and policy. With great respect, I am, &c., &c., J.C. CALHOUN.

PC (from the Charlotte, N.C., *Mecklenburg Jeffersonian*) in the Charleston, S.C., *Mercury*, August 9, 1844, p. 2; PC in the Richmond, Va., *Enquirer*, August 13, 1844, p. 2; PC in the Washington, D.C., *Spectator*, August 13, 1844, p. 3; PC in the Camden, S.C., *Journal*, August 14, 1844, p. 2; PC in the Edgefield, S.C., *Advertiser*, August 14, 1844, p. 2; PC in the Raleigh, N.C., *North Carolina Standard*, August 14, 1844, p. 3; PC in the New Orleans, La., *Courrier de la Louisiane*, August 15, 1844, p. 3; PC in the Anderson, S.C., *Gazette*, August 16, 1844, p. 2; PC in the Columbia, S.C., *South-Carolinian*, August 22, 1844, p. 2; PC in the Greenville, S.C., *Mountaineer*, August 23, 1844, p. 1; PC in the Pendleton, S.C., *Messenger*, August 30, 1844, p. 1; PC in *Niles' National Register*, vol. LXVI, no. 27 (August 31, 1844), pp. 439–440. NOTE: The committee addressed by Calhoun consisted of W[illiam] J. Alexander, B. Morrow, C[harles] G. Alexander, J[oseph] W. Hampton, C[harles] J. Fox, P.C. Caldwell, C.T. Alexander, T.L. Hutchison, John Walker, and J[ennings] B. Kerr.

To JOHN W. "NISBETT" [*sic*; NESBITT] and Others, Philadelphia

WASHINGTON, 30th June, 1844

GENTLEMEN: I have been honored by your note of the 17th June, inviting me, in the name of the Democratic citizens of the First Congressional District [of Pa.], to unite with them in the celebration of the approaching anniversary. I regret to say that my official duties will not permit me to accept.

I feel myself much flattered by the considerations which have led to the compliment, and more especially to that which applies to my native State. As lofty as is her spirit, her patriotism is not less so. If she is intrepid in defence of her rights and safety, she is not less so in defending those of the whole Union. Whenever the common peace and safety are in danger, she is ever found in the front rank in their defence, and among the boldest to maintain them. To me she has been the kindest of mothers, and I would be the most ungrateful of sons not to feel pleasure whenever I hear her name honored.

Permit me, in conclusion, to offer the following sentiment:

Pennsylvania, the Keystone of the Federal Arch: Our Union is safe, so long as she remains true to the original principles and creed of the Republican party.

With great respect, I am, &c., J.C. CALHOUN.

PC in the Washington, D.C., *Spectator*, July 12, 1844, p. 3; PC in the Edgefield, S.C., *Advertiser*, July 24, 1844, p. 2; PC in the Jackson, Miss., *Southern Reformer*, August 3, 1844, p. 3. NOTE: Besides Nesbitt, this letter was addressed to Thomas McCully, B[enjamin] M. Evans, and John Thomson, the name of William Harleson being accidentally omitted. At the Independence Day observance in Philadelphia, the committee responded to Calhoun's toast with another: "Hon. John C. Calhoun: The unterrified and able champion and defender of the honor and interests of his native State—the high-spirited mother has just cause of rejoicing in the gallant bearing of the patriotic son."

From GEORGE H. PROFFIT

Legation of the United States
Rio de Janeiro, 30th June 1844

Sir, I have the honor to transmit herewith marked (No. 1) a copy of the deposition [of 3/29/1844] of the Supercargo, officers and others of the Brig "Isabella" of New York, alledging that the said brig had been fired at by a British Brig of war supposed to be the Frolic—No. 2 my note [of 4/17] to [Hamilton Hamilton] the British Minister—No. 3 His reply [of 4/24], transmitting a letter from Sir Thomas Pasley, another from Captain [W.A.] Willis, Commander of the Frolic, and also a letter from Lieutenant [Caesar C.] Powell acting Commander of the Frolic when the cause of complaint is said to have occurred.

I have reason to believe that the British Lieutenant in his anxiety to distinguish himself in discharge of a duty so imperatively enjoined, imagined very much of the strange conduct of the "Isabella," and on the other side our merchant Captains generally manifest no great hurry to show their colours, especially to British Cruisers. The contradictions in the statements of the parties are unaccountable, and as I am convinced that no insult was intended to the American flag, I did not deem it necessary to say any thing more on the subject.

No. (4) is a copy and translation of a decree [of 6/22/1843] and note [of 4/24/1844] received from [Ernesto F. França] the Minister for Foreign Affairs, informing me that the Barque "Mary" had been given up to Captain [Benjamin D.] Clark. I think this claim for the Mary had been transferred to ["the" *canceled*] Brazilian subjects, and therefore this favorable result.

No. (5) is a translation of a note [of 4/1844] from the Minister for Foreign Affairs informing me that he had received the Commands of H.M. the Emperor [Pedro II] to express to me his Majesty's gratification on being informed of Commodore [Daniel] Turner's attentions to the Brazilian Minister near the Argentine Confederation. I transmitted to Commodore Turner a copy of the Minister's note.

I have reason to believe that this Government is engaged in preparing a new Tariff of duties, and that it is nearly completed. It is of course strictly secret, but I feel confident that American products are favored to as great an extent as is possible on a general increase of duties. I have done all in my power by conversations with those having charge of the measure to show the liberality of the United States towards Brazilian productions, and flatter myself that my representations have not been without effect: nevertheless I have no doubt but that the Minister Resident of Brazil [Gaspar José de Lisboa] at Washington has informed his Government that the admission of Coffee free of duty, is much more the result of *party* interests, than a conviction of its propriety as the true policy of our Government, especially as a duty on coffee passed the House of Representatives when our present Tariff was before Congress, and as the late Secretary of the Treasury [John C. Spencer] recommended the laying of a duty on that article as being not only just and proper, but actually necessary to meet the public expenditure.

The late Minister for Foreign Affairs who is a member of the Legislature, put some important questions to the present Minister in a debate which took place a few days before the dissolution of the Chambers. "I wish to know" said he, ["]what policy will be pursued by the Ministry in the negotiations of the new Treaties which will shortly have to be made? Will British manufactures &c be admitted upon the same terms with American productions? Will this Government allow England to tax our Coffee &c. at the enormous rates now imposed, and yet admit her productions on the same terms as the products of the United States which take our Coffee free of duty?" The Minister maintained a guarded silence, but the questions have been echoed by the public prints, and this delicate subject may yet be the cause of much trouble.

I presume that the American Minister at London has informed you of the meaning of the terms "Brazil must treat on the principles of humanity" so often repeated in speeches and alluded to in the public journals. If England supposes that Brazil will consent to a gradual emancipation of her slaves, and fall into the British scheme of *"philanthropy,"* she is, to say the least of it, much mistaken. No public man dare mention approvingly such a policy in this Country, and I doubt much the Safety of any man's life who would be so hardy as to propose such an in[n]ovation on the institutions of this Country—certainly no citizen of Brazil dares openly advocate it. I have the honor to be, Sir, Your obedient Servant, George H. Proffit.

ALS (No. 12) with Ens in DNA, RG 59 (State Department), Diplomatic Despatches, Brazil, vol. 12 (M-121:14), received 9/20; FC in DNA, RG 84 (Foreign Posts), Brazil, Despatches, vol. 102; FC in DNA, RG 84 (Foreign Posts), Brazil, Despatches, vol. 11.

From HENRY WHEATON

Berlin, 30 June, 1844

Sir, I have the honor to enclose an official copy of a Treaty of Commerce & navigation between the Kingdoms of Prussia & Portugal, concluded here on the 20th February last, & since ratified by both parties. The ratification was accompanied with a Declaration relating to the Oporto wine trade, signed by the ministers of the two Powers, a copy of which is annexed.

[Friedrich Ludwig,] Baron von Roenne, having been definitively appointed President of the Board of Trade recently erected here, will not return to the U. States, & it is understood that Baron [F.] von Gerolt, now Prussian minister in Mexico, will be appointed his successor at Washington.

The proposition for an increase in the present duties on the importation of foreign ["manufactured" *canceled*] iron, into the German Zollverein, has been adopted by all the associated states, & will be carried into effect on the 1st of September. It is thought that the menacing & irritating tone assumed by Lord Aberdeen, in his late Note to Baron de Bülow, which you will have seen published in the newspapers, has contributed to produce this result in the councils of the Zollverein.

Since my last report on the subject of the Danish Sound-Duties, the negotiations, long since commenced by the Prussian Government, for a reduction, modification, or abolition of these Duties, have been continued without any satisfactory result. Denmark still continues to oppose a passive, but persevering, resistance to every proposition of this nature. The most recent projet brought forward has in view the redemption of the Duties by the other three maritime powers of the Baltic, Russia, Sweden & Prussia, who might afterwards collect in their ports an amount of tonnage-duties, or duties of importation & exportation of merchandize, equal to the interest of the capital advanced by them for this purpose; & thus the inconvenience, delay & expense of collecting the duties at Elsinore might be avoided. Besides the intrinsic practical difficulties of carrying into effect this plan, the Russian Court does not appear to feel sufficient interest in the question to join in adopting it, whilst political motives, in its view, of a higher order, induce it to conciliate Denmark with a view to future contingencies of great importance. Even if the other obstacles were surmounted, there would still remain the difficulty of settling the rate of the duties, & consequently the amount of capital necessary to redeem them, as the Danish Government still objects to reverting to the ancient standard of one *per centum ad valorem*, as fixed by the Treaty of Christianopel. I have the honor to be, Sir, with the highest consideration, Y[ou]r ob[e]d[ien]t Serv[an]t, Henry Wheaton.

LS (No. 253) with Ens (in French and German) in DNA, RG 59 (State Department), Diplomatic Despatches, Germany, vol. 3 (M-44:4), received 8/3; FC in DNA, RG 84 (Foreign Posts), Germany, Despatches, 4:138–140.

JULY 1–15, 1844

◻

Business of every sort, foreign and domestic, kept the Secretary of State at his desk. The most important item of business transacted under his jurisdiction, however, he did not learn about for many weeks. On July 3, near Macao, the American Commissioner Caleb Cushing signed for the first time a treaty of peace, amity, and commerce with a representative of the Emperor of China, an act of large and only partly foreseeable portent.

On July 2 Calhoun took time to reply to an old South Carolina friend, John R. Mathewes, who had plied him with advice about how to deal with perfidious Britain. Calhoun agreed with Mathewes about the imperial craftiness of the mother country, which at the moment was manifesting itself in particular in hostility to the "wealth & strength" of the Southern States of the American Union, and indicated something of the steps he intended to pursue in response.

There was a great deal of political correspondence received and sent. Calhoun had to pay some attention to a perennial problem—unrest among South Carolina supporters for whom his current cooperation with the national Democratic party was insufficient. This was the summer in which that problem, manifested as "the Bluffton movement," would become acute. Now was not the time for separate State action, and friends in the State had to be encouraged to hold the line.

Calhoun was pleased with the Democratic nominees in the national campaign. The nomination of James K. Polk, he thought, had broken the domination of the corrupt New Yorkers over the party machinery (especially since the aged hero, General Andrew Jackson, had at last lost his enthusiasm for Martin Van Buren). The Vice-Presidential nominee, George M. Dallas of Pennsylvania, was an old friend, personally, and politically from Calhoun's own campaign two decades ago. "My friends every where will give the ticket a hearty support," Calhoun wrote on July 14 to Francis Wharton, one of the numerous talented young men that he regularly encouraged, "and I have a strong hope it will succeed."

◻

From Geo[rge] Brown

Commission of the U. States Hawaii
Honolulu, July 1, 1844

Sir, I last had the honor of addressing the State department on the 4th of May since which, there has been no vessel for the coast by which I could forward.

The Hoikaika arrived from Mazatlan [Mexico] on the 4th Ult., bringing the sad news of the death of your predecessor [Abel P. Upshur], and other distinguished individuals, by the accident on board the Princeton, which threw a gloom over all the faces of their fellow countrymen here. The loss is a very serious one, and must be deeply felt, and while, I congratulate the President and country, upon having secured the services of one so able to fill the situation of the head of the State department, I must deplore the occasion that has made those services necessary.

On the 30th May, I received from the State department, despatch, "No. 2" dated November 22d/43 enclosing a letter from the President for [Kamehameha III] the King of these islands which I immediately forwarded to [Gerrit P. Judd] the Secretary of State for Foreign Affairs, with the note, marked "A." The answer to said note is marked "B."

On the 9th Ult., the U.S. Ship Levant arrived from Tahiti, she brought news of a battle having taken place, at that island, between the French and Tahitians, in which two hundred of the latter were killed, and of the former twenty six killed, and forty wounded.

It is an unfortunate affair, & more so, as we learn by the last arrival that the doings of Admiral [Abel] Du Petit Thouars are disapproved of, by his Government, and that the internal sovereignty of the Society Islands is to be restored to the Queen [Pomare]. The Levant leaves for Monterrey and Mazatlan on the 5th inst.

Since my last despatch, I have visited the island of Kauai, the most fertile of the group. I landed at Hanalei on the north side of the Island and visited all the towns and harbors on the island. The harbor of Hanalei is a very good one, during all the months in the year, except December & January, and with some expense laid out on it, might be made perfectly good & safe during the whole year. The Country round is very fertile, and produces very fine coffee. There are two extensive coffee plantations commenced there; one by Mr. [Charles] Titcomb, an American, the other by Mr. Bernard a Frenchman. Over one hundred thousand trees have been planted, and appear in a very flourishing condition. There are thousands of acres on the north side of Kauai that are well adapted to the raising of Coffee. The people on Kauai appear to be a pretty independent set, and very lazy, especially on the north side.

At Koloa on the South side they are rather more industrious and appear willing to work. At Koloa are the principal Sugar plantations. There are four, belonging to Mess. [William] Ladd & Co., [Charles] Tobey, [John] Lindsey and [D.H.] Goodale, all Americans. The prospect is that there will be near five hundred tons of sugar produced this year. Mess. Ladd & Co. have the only Sugar mill. The Government has a number of acres planted with cane, but it has been badly managed and is worth but little. There are no harbors on the South side of Kauai, but two or three open roadsteads which are generally safe anchorages.

While I was at Kauai, some three or four Americans applied to me complaining of injustice shewn them by the native authorities, but on examination, I found them to have been in the wrong almost always. In one case however, where a man was tried for assault and battery, and fined, I found that the Judge had not shewn proper fairness in the examination of witnesses, and on stating that fact to him, he very frankly told me that it might have been so, and that the man should have another trial. From what I have seen in regard to the Hawaiian courts of Justice, I am inclined to think that they rather lean towards foreigners, than otherwise. It is presumed that the Belgian Company if it goes into operation, will locate their people on Kauai.

Considerable excitement has taken place here lately, in regard to the Government of these islands, requiring all foreigners who hold office under it, to take the oath of allegiance. In the case of Mr. Thompson, who has heretofore been sheriff, and who is an American, he has resigned his office rather than do so, and the office has been given to an Englishman, who had not the same scruples. Mr. Thompson had also the appointment of Auctioneer, from the Governor of Oahu, the license for which expiring on the 30th June, the Governor has refused to renew, although Mr. Thompson is very acceptable to the merchants here.

The law allows, the appointment of only two auctioneers on the payment of five hundred dollars annually. This law is a bad one, and probably will be annulled ere long, and another one made, opening the auctioneers licenses to all, & fixing a duty on Sales at Auction.

There is no doubt, but that Mr. Thompson, has been refused his license as auctioneer, because he declined taking the oath of allegiance; indeed Mr. Judd acknowledged as much to me in a conversation I had with him. I told Mr. Judd that I could have no possible objection to any American taking the oath of Allegiance, who thought proper so to do, and that I had no doubt, that my Government would be pleased to have any of their citizens, serve the King of Hawaii, who could be useful to him, but that I protested against any one, being persecuted for refusing so to do. He denied that any one had been persecuted, though he did not deny, that if Mr. Thompson had taken the oath of Allegiance, he would have received the appointment of Auctioneer, but contended that the Governor, had a right to appoint whom he pleased. I did not think it worth while to make any difficulty about it, or to go into an official correspondence on the Subject, as I was in hopes that Mess. [William] Richards & [Timoteo] Haalilio, would soon return, when I trust affairs will be better managed.

Some of the Americans here are quite indignant at the action of Mr. Judd and the Governor, in this affair, or rather that of the former, (who is undoubtedly the moving spring,) and have expressed themselves in strong language. They appear to think, I ought to interfere, but I could see no reason for so doing, except by verbal remonstrances which appear to have had no effect, as I understand another Auctioneer, who is an Englishman, has been appointed to day, and has taken the Oath of Allegiance.

There are some Americans here, who ought to know better, who are in the habit of speaking in derogatory terms of this Government and people, and who have been here for many years past, when this people were in a state of barbarism, cannot divest themselves of their former contempt of the race. These men in former days, were considered the elite of the foreigners, and were deadly opposed to the missionaries, and their efforts at civilizing this people; and from being unsuccessful in their opposition, have become soured, and discontented with the present order of things. These men, at the head of whom, is a man by the name of [Stephen] Reynolds, are continually, using their exertions to degrade & lower the Government by abuse and ridicule, but so far as I have been able to perceive, with but little success, unless in the eyes of new Comers. I do not think however that Mr. Judd, especially since he has connected with him Mr. [John] Ricord as Attorney General, has used the conciliatory policy that it beho[o]ved him to do. I look forward to a better state of feeling on the return of Mr. Richards.

I have been applied to by some two or three Sailors, who have been discharged from the hands, of [William Hooper] the Commercial Agent here, for redress. They complain that having been left on his hands sick, by the masters of the vessels, in which they left the United States, he has discharged them from the support the laws of the U. States allow them; and contend, that he is obliged to keep them, although recovered from their sickness. I enquired of Mr. Hooper, the state of the case, and found that he had supported the men, untill they had been pronounced well by the Doctor, and afterwards, untill American vessels, had in vain endeavored to procure seamen to ship on board, they preferring to remain on shore, to be supported by the U. States, Government, rather than ship for a voyage. I found also, that some of them, had refused offers of work on Shore, while others were employed, and earning from one to two dollars per day as mechanics, while their board had been paid by the American Consulate. I was therefore compelled to uphold Mr. Hooper in his conduct, and to dismiss the complainants, with the advice to ship on board American vessels as soon as possible. Some of them have already shipped on board the Levant, finding they can no longer be supported in idleness.

I trust you will at the earliest opportunity, inform Mr. Hooper whether his conduct is approved of, and give him explicit directions for the future.

The British Corvette Modeste left this place for the Columbia river on the 11th June, as soon as she could get ready, after the arrival of the Hoikaika. I presume orders from England arrived by that vessel, as I understood from the Admiral before he left, that the Modeste would remain here untill she was relieved by another man of war.

I beg to call your attention to my despatch "No. 7" Nov[embe]r 17 [1843] whe[r]e I speak of the advantage to be derived ["to" *altered to* "by"] the U. States by having a hospital for seamen here, and a Naval Surgeon residing here. A good deal could be saved by such a plan.

I enclose my accounts up to June the 6th, and have this day drawn on the department at thirty days sight for the balance $105.14 say one hundred & five dollars, fourteen cents, in favor of Mess. C[harles] Brewer & Co.

I shall leave this, for the island of Hawaii next week, and shall be absent a month or six weeks. There are a number of Americans residing on that island, and my object is to see the whole and listen to all their complaints, though as yet I have found but little cause for complaint. I have the honor to be with great respect Y[ou]r very Ob[edien]t S[ervan]t, Geo. Brown.

ALS (No. 14) with Ens in DNA, RG 59 (State Department), Diplomatic Despatches, Hawaii, vol. 1 (T-30:1, frames 87–94), received 11/13.

From Fred[eric]k Dabney (for Charles W. Dabney, [U.S. Consul]), Fayal, [Azores], 7/1. He encloses semiannual returns. The U.S.S. *Constitution* arrived at Fayal on 6/16 with Henry A. Wise and family on board. This visit highly gratified Dabney, and he expresses a wish that more U.S. warships will visit Fayal. LS (No. 95) with Ens in DNA, RG 59 (State Department), Consular Despatches, Fayal, vol. 3 (T-203:3), received 8/18.

From [TIMOTEO] HAALILIO and WILLIAM RICHARDS

Washington, July 1st 1844

Sir, The undersigned Commissioners from [Kamehameha III] the King of the Sandwich Islands, had the honor to address a communication to the Secretary of State of the United States under date of December 14th 1842, in which they requested the government of the United States to acknowledge the Independence of the Sandwich Islands under their present Sovereign.

They received a reply to their communication under date of December 19th of the same year, which taken in connection with the subsequent acts of the President and Congress of the United States, was considered by the commissioners, as a full, though not a direct and formal recognition of Independence.

In more recent negotiations of the undersigned with some of the governments of Europe they met with some embarrassment in consequence of doubts expressed by those Governments whether the Independence of the Islands had been fully recognized on the part of the United States.

The undersigned therefore feel the necessity of making the inquiry, whether the Government of the United States consider their various acts in relation to the Sandwich Islands as a full and perfect recognition of Independence.

The undersigned avail themselves of this occasion to assure the Hon. Mr. Calhoun, of the high consideration with which they have the honor to be His Obedient Servants, Haalilio, William Richards.

LS in DNA, RG 59 (State Department), Notes from Foreign Legations, Hawaii, vol. 1 (T-160:1). NOTE: No written reply to the above has been discovered.

From G[ARDINER] G. [and] S[AMUEL S.] HOWLAND, JOHN JACOB ASTOR, and PETER HARMONY

New York [City,] 1 July 1844

Sir, The undersigned having learned with regret, as well as surprise, that there had been a demur[?] on the part of the Mexican Government in the payment of the April Instalment of the Mexican Indemnity, beg leave respectfully to request that you will on the part of the Government of the United States take such measures as made [*sic*] be deemed judicious in exacting a prompt Compliance with the Contract as we as holders of the Scrip feel it particularly oppressive that any further delay should take place after the many & great sacrafices that have been made in order to secure the amount awarded. With great respect Your Ob[edien]t Serv[an]ts, G.G. [and] S. Howland, John Jacob Astor & Son, p[e]r Wm. B. Astor, Peter Harmony By L.S. Sharer[?], att[orne]y.

LS in DNA, RG 59 (State Department), Miscellaneous Letters (M-179:105, frames 4–5).

From C. Edwards Lester, U.S. Consul, Genoa, 7/1. He encloses his semiannual returns. U.S. trade with Genoa has declined during the past six months. Lester feels that more U.S. goods should be carried in U.S. ships. American tobacco is being brought into Genoa and should be brought to other Italian ports as well. LS (No. 61) with Ens in DNA, RG 59 (State Department), Consular Despatches, Genoa, vol. 3 (T-64:3), received 11/18.

To PASCHAL P. POPE and Others, Boston

Department of State
Wash[ingto]n, 1st July 1844

Gentlemen, I have to acknowledge the receipt of your letter of the 29th Ultimo, relative to payments by the Mexican Government under the Convention of the 30th of January, 1843, and to inform you, in reply, that the Minister of the United States [Wilson Shannon] who is about to proceed to that Country has been fully instructed upon the subject. I am Your Obedient Servant, John C. Calhoun.

FC in DNA, RG 59 (State Department), Domestic Letters, 34:271 (M-40:32). NOTE: Besides Pope, the addressees of this letter were Ozias Goodwin, W[illia]m Oliver, Bates & Co., and C[harles] Bradbury.

From J[OHN] A. ROBINSON

Consulate, U.S. of America
Guaymas [Mexico], July 1st 1844
Sir, I herewith enclose semiannual return of fees collected at this Consulate to this date amounting to $24.

During the same period no American vessel has arrived or departed from this Port.

In consequence of the late interception of mails I enclose you copy of my communication under date of 8th May relating to the affairs of the late Mr. Sumner Grimes.

I beg to call your attention to the enquiries contained in my communication No. 4 Nov[embe]r 13, 1843 as this Consulate stands in much need of the information and documents referred to.

The removal of the former Governor Gen[era]l [José] Urrea, has had the effect of restoring peace to this Department [of Sonora] and business is gradually reviving. I remain very respectfully Y[ou]r ob[edien]t Serv[an]t, J.A. Robinson, Consul.

LS (No. 7) with Ens in DNA, RG 59 (State Department), Consular Despatches, Guaymas, Mexico, vol. 1 (M-284:1), received 9/21. NOTE: Robinson's letter of 5/8 concerned unsuccessful efforts to recover the property of Grimes, a U.S. citizen who died at "the Angelos."

From ALFRED SCHÜCKING

Washington, July 1st 1844
Sir: Permit me to avail myself of my earliest facility to return to you with the expression of my deepest obligation the enclosed sum, which, as may be in your recollection, you loaned me more than a year ago. My official salary ($800) for which, I believe, I am indebted to the good opinion of the President [John Tyler], affording but a scanty support for a household, its narrowness must be my excuse for not discharging before so late a date an obligation, contracted under circumstances on your part of personal kindness towards a then entire

stranger, which if anything could have added to my previous share of public respect for you—a respect such and so unique as in my opinion it has fallen to the lot of few American Statesmen to enjoy in your and *even my* native country—were so well calculated to strengthen it by private experience.

Being naturally disqualified for the begging importunities of an office seeker, I have only to regret that my abilities—however humble I conceive them to be—my classical attainments and particularly my linguistic acquisitions (of which there is for example such a striking want in the Department of State) can find no ample and more suitable sphere of useful service than in the *lowest* grade of a subordinate accountant—rather calculated to diminish than to increase my consideration with the German public. I ought also to have the benefit of the consideration, that I am *peculiarly* liable to be ousted on the installation of Henry Clay in March next—a contingency from the curse of which heaven may save this country! Such is the fervent prayer of thousands in the United States and of Your most obedient grateful servant, Alfred Schücking.

ALS in ScCleA.

From W. W. T. Smith

Consulate of the U.S.
Port La Vaca, Matagorda Bay Texas
July 1st 1844

Hon. Sir, Enclosed I transmit you, Consular return of American Vessels No. 3 and also Consular Statement of Fees No. 3. I will address you shortly on the causes which are operating to destroy our Commerce and are destroying it in Texas and transferring the same to European nations principally to England. In the mean time I will remark that the Texas Tariff will most probably be abolished in the course of the next year and if so that it will operate most favorably on our Commerce. Hon. Sir I am very respectfully your obedient servant, W.W.T. Smith, U.S. Consul.

ALS (No. 13) with Ens in DNA, RG 59 (State Department), Consular Despatches, Texas, vol. 1 (T-153:1), received 10/21.

To William C. Anderson, U.S. Marshal, St. Louis, 7/2. Calhoun informs Anderson that, in the face of new evidence, the President

[John Tyler] has granted a second reprieve to John McDaniel and Joseph Brown in order to allow time for investigation into the recently acquired evidence. This action should not be taken to indicate that the men will eventually be granted a pardon. FC in DNA, RG 59 (State Department), Domestic Letters, 34:277–278 (M-40:32).

From ISRAEL D. ANDREWS

Consulate of the United States of America
Saint John, New Brunswick, July 2d 1844
Sir, I beg leave to hand You two copies of "An Act Imposing Duties for raising a Revenue" passed [on 3/25/1844] by the late House of Assembly—together with two copies of a Table of the Imperial and Provincial duty payable on all articles imported into the Province of New Brunswick.

It may be proper for me to inform you that the rate of the Provincial Duty is altered Yearly by the House of Assembly with the advice and consent of the Council. I have the honor to be Sir, Your Ob[edien]t Serv[an]t, Israel D. Andrews, Consul.

ALS (No. 16) with Ens in DNA, RG 59 (State Department), Consular Despatches, St. John, vol. 1 (T-485:1), received 12/16.

From GEORGE BATES, "Private"

Boston, July 2, 1844
Dear Sir, I had the pleasure of getting home on Saturday and yesterday I met our friend Mr. [Abbott] Lawrence. Mr. L[awrence] expresses and feels, I have no doubt the highest personal respect for you and it may be truly said no man in this community who thinks for himself, does not feel that you have always been actuated by the purest motives of patriotism and disinterestedness in all your public acts. We all regret, that we cannot have the satisfaction of casting our votes for you at the coming Presidential election. Had it not been for the miserable policy and chicanery of selfish politicians, the People would have elected you President by an over whelming majority. I consider the people to have been cheated out of their rights in this as they have been in many other things. As affairs now stand, who can tell who is to be our next President?

I enclose a note [*not found*], which I have just received from Mr. Lawrence. One thing may be said of the Manufacturing Interests—while Mr. L[awrence] is making not less than $200,000 per Annum and others, *Agents*, Presidents, Treasurers &c. &c. selected from the richest families are receiving large and princely Salaries, the laborers, and Small Stockholders often get, but small wages and smaller dividends. The great Salaries have to be paid firstly—however now and for some time past the dividend[s] have been very handsome. I am with with [*sic*] the truest Sentiments of respect your ob[edien]t Serv[an]t and friend, George Bates.

ALS in ScCleA.

From GEO[RGE] BROWN

Honolulu, July 2d 1844

Dear Sir, I assure you it was with emotions of no unpleasant kind, that I heard that the President had been pleased to call upon you, to fill the office made vacant by the sad death of Mr. [Abel P.] Upshur, and I trust you will find your new situation as pleasing to yourself, as I have no doubt it will be profitable to the country.

The object of my addressing you at the present time is, to request of you, at your earliest convenience after having read my despatches, to return me a short answer approving of my conduct, *if you do so.* I have now been here nearly a year, and I have not received a word from the department either approving or disapproving of my actions, and I feel a little uneasy. I am a young diplomatist, though not a young man, and it would cheer me, some thousands of miles from my home and friends, to know that my conduct meets the approbation of the President and yourself.

I am well aware that this out of the way place, is but of little importance in comparison to the nations of Europe, which must command the most of your valuable time but I do hope a spare moment may be found ere long, to throw away upon me.

I have mentioned in my despatch of the 1st inst. which accompanies this the affair of Mr. Thompson. I have been rather in favor of Americans, who can, by holding office under this Government, be of service to it, taking the oath of allegiance to the King. *Some foreigners* must at present hold *certain* offices here, as there are not natives of sufficient information to be entrusted with them. I have therefore thought it *good policy*, to favor the plan of giving those offices to Americans, (as we have a paramount interest here,) rather than let them get into the hands of Englishmen and other foreigners, of which there are but few if any ["here" *interlined*] who are fit for any thing, trustworthy.

Some of my countrymen are very much opposed to this plan, being very short sighted as I conceive, letting their feelings run away with their policy, and if such feelings should have the sway & influence they desire, it will not be long ere many influential offices will be in the hands of Englishmen, who ["would" *interlined*] scruple not in taking oaths of allegiance to the Old Nick, were they to be gainers thereby. May I ask of you to give me your ideas on this matter as soon as convenient. I of course have not stirred in this matter except in the back ground, but you may be assured that it is of importance to keep the King [Kamehameha III] under the influence he is at present. I mean due[?] influence. Should others get hold of him, anarchy, confusion, drunken[n]ess and debauchery would prevail, and these poor natives would fast go to destruction & disappear.

There are a number of important questions touched upon in my former despatches, to which I would respectfully call your attention, as I am afraid that in the changes the department has met with, they may have escaped the notice due. Wishing you much health[,] happiness and prosperity I have the honor to be with much respect Y[ou]r ob[edien]t S[ervan]t, Geo. Brown.

ALS (Private) in DNA, RG 59 (State Department), Diplomatic Despatches, Hawaii, vol. 1 (T-30:1, frames 96–98), received 11/13.

From P[ETER] CARR

Charlottesville Virginia, July 2, 1844
Dear Sir, An acquaintance not indeed, as intimate as I could desire, a devotion to similar principles as ardent as a zealous disciple can cherish, and a common sympathy in the same great cause of deliverance, induce me to address myself to you personally on a subject, in regard to which, it might be thought by some, more appropriate to approach you through the medium of a mutual friend. But my acquaintance with you, & my appreciation of your character, both admonish me, that an immediate communication with you, and a

frank avowal of my wishes, whilst such course is best suited to my own disposition, will also be of a character which will meet with your approbation.

It has been my wish for some time past, to spend a year or fifteen months in foreign travel, with a view, in some degree, by personal observation, to inform myself of what the great Swedish Chancellor [Axel Oxenstierna] held in such light estimation, when he sent his son forth upon his travels. I have thought that if I could attain my object with the aid, which the favor of the Government would confer, it would both render my purposes, more agreeable in their accomplishment, and at the same time enable me to bring whatever indifferent capacities I may be blessed withal, to the service of the Government, and that Department of it over which you have the honor to preside. If, I am informed correctly, the post of Chargé d'affaires to Portugal is vacant—That is a situation, which if not inconsistent with the interests of the Government, it would give me pleasure to fill—yet if the Govt. shall have already designated any gentleman as an incumbent of that office; then one which would place me in the same, or like grade, in contact with European manners and civilization for a short period, would gratify my wishes, & in some measure advance my prospects. I do not in this matter, pursue a course adopted doubtless by many others. My character, I may flatter myself, without any ascription of vanity, is sufficiently well known to yourself to dispense with what w[oul]d be very easy of accomplishment, the endorsation [*sic*] of any number of friends in my behalf.

I much fear, from what information has reached me, that Texas may be lost to us—God forbid! if however, our fears should be realized, it will be a consolation that you have done all that a Statesman could, to avert the calamity, & a proud reflection, to be able hereafter to say to friend and foe alike, "Thou canst not say, I did it." In the contest in which the Republican party is engaged, Virginia is secure. Your friends have every where, throughout the old Commonwealth, borne themselves bravely, and if there was a fortress to be stormed, have been generally selected to lead on the assault. Here in Albemarle [County], we have been for the time repulsed. A combination of untoward circumstances has temporarily defeated us, but we shall rally unsubdued, and undismayed. Your friends will do their whole duty by the great cause. They throw themselves into the breach with great ulterior objects in view—and after next November, *we* should hear of no National Conventions of any character. There is not that purity, disinterestedness, and freedom from cabal,

245

and intrigue, the bane of all free governments, to commend them to Republicans.

Hoping to hear from you at your earliest leisure—I remain with sentiments of profound respect Yours, P. Carr.

ALS in ScCleA. NOTE: Peter Carr was Thomas Jefferson's nephew and had been Jefferson's secretary. Peter Carr's son, Dabney Smith Carr, was at this time the U.S. Minister to Turkey.

From W[ILLIA]M HOOPER

U.S. Commercial Agency
Sandwich Islands
July 2d 1844

Sir, I have the honor to enclose to you my half yearly returns of arrivals and departures at these Islands, and a statement of Fees received by the Vice Com[mercia]l Agent at Maui and at this Office for the same period.

My accounts for the quarter terminating on the 30th Ult[im]o have been forwarded to the Fifth Auditor and show a balance in my favour of thirty three hundred and sixteen doll[ar]s 93/100, for which I have drawn on the State Department at 30 days sight.

On examination of the returns herewith, it will be perceived that within the past six months there has touched at these Islands upwards of *fifty thousand tons* of American Shipping. The number of disabled seamen discharged is, of a consequence proportionably large as will appear by the Quarterly "Statement of cases of relief" herewith.

Within the month past I have discharged some six or eight seamen who had recovered from Sickness, and become "able bodied" but, who refused to embrace opportunities which were offered them to proceed to sea and gain their own livelihood. To this they make loud complaints, and demand that being legally discharged they are entitled and ought to be supported until an opportunity offers to send them as passengers direct to the U. States. I take no heed of their complaints so long as they can from any source obtain the means to furnish them with their daily bread.

The opportunities for sending seamen, really disabled, from these islands direct to the U. States, are very rare, and to this, in part, may be attributed the great expense of this Agency.

I would respectfully suggest that the Government Store ships that may hereafter touch here have orders to take off all destitute Am[eri-can] Seamen.

I would respectfully enquire if it is the intention of Government that Seamen, other than Citizens of the United States, who may become disabled on board of Am[erican] ships, are to be supported at the expense of Government?

It has not been the Custom of this office so to do, and as some complaints have been made I desire to be particularly instructed on that point.

If foreign Seamen are to be supported under the circumstances named, my opinion is, that one half of the whole appropriation made by Congress for the support of destitute seamen in foreign Countries will be absorbed by this office alone.

Whale ships on leaving the United States generally have their full quota of foreigners. On the voyage out they touch either at the Western, or Cape de Verd[e] Islands, and receive on board from two to five Portuguese.

During the first six months of their cruise in the Pacific they loose by desertion some six or eight of their original crew, these are replaced by deserters from English, French and Bremen Ships or by natives of some of the islands in this ocean. The question is, shall these foreigners in the event of their becoming disabled, be assisted by the Consulate? I have always declined to assist them at the expense of government, but have usually insisted that the master of the vessel leave such a sum of money as in the opinion of a Physician would be required to support the man until he recovered his health.

In discharging *sick* seamen from whale ships it has been my practice to demand of the master, the seaman's share of Oil, or its equivalent in money, in addition to the three months advance wages. The money thus received is appropriated for their support, when exhausted, they are supported at the expense of Government.

Masters of whale ships object to paying off their men when discharged on the ground, first, that the tenor of their shipping articles is such that the seamen ought not to be paid off until after the ship shall have procured a cargo of Oil and returned to the United States. To this I reply that the act of Congress of Feb. 28, 1803 clearly indicates that when seamen are discharged they must be paid off—that I know no difference, so far as my duties are concerned, between Merchant vessels and whale Ships and that I cannot allow any agreement entered into between owners of vessels and seamen to contravene any of the acts of Congress.

They object too, on the ground that other Consuls do not demand it! I am aware that such is the case at one or two of the Consulates in this ocean, but I doubt, very much, of the propriety of their receiving Seamen as *destitute* when they have property in the shape of Oil on board of the Ship from which they are discharged. In the discharge of other than sick seamen I pursue the course as marked out by the 5th Sec[tion] of the act of Congress of July 20, 1840.

As a general thing, crews of whale ships take up in foreign ports as much of their earnings as possible and it is the policy of the owners of whale ships that they should so do in order that the entire Cargo of Oil may fall into their hands, paid for, on its arrival in the U. States. To this end, owners put on board a large quantity of Clothing etc. which is advanced and charged to the seamen at high prices and by them converted into money at an enormous discount.

The evils arising from this practice of advancing crews of whale ships in foreign ports are so many as to induce the belief that the true interest[s] of seamen require some legislative interposition to check it, or, rather that there should be some marine laws enacted applicable particularly to the whaling service.

The frequent accidents which happen on board of whale ships, and the length of time which those vessels remain at sea, suggests the idea that from motives of humanity their owners should be required to put on board a Surgeon, as is the case in the English, French, and Danish whaling service.

The extra expense attending this, and also the expense which might fall on the owners in consequence of the passage of any law requiring that their Ships be manned *at all times* by at least three quarters Am[erican] *Seamen* instead of Islanders of the Pacific, might be made up to them in the way of a small bounty on the vessels engaged in the business.

The French, although they avail themselves of the skill and perseverance of Americans as ["ship" *canceled*] *masters* of some of their whale ships, are very particular in having their crews composed wholly of Frenchmen. The French are very successful and their fleet is increasing rapidly.

It has been suggested that the number of Am[erican] Seamen discharged at these Islands disabled is so great, as to render it highly desirable that the U.S. Government establish a Hospital here. Aside from its being opposite to the policy which the Government have heretofore pursued in these matters, I question very much if the benefits arising therefrom would be at all commensurate with the great expense attending the erection of buildings etc. The men now receive as much attention as they would in any Hospital, and at a very moderate expense. They are also in charge of persons who do not permit ardent spirits to be used on their premises.

I have to inform the Department that neither this office nor that at Maui have ever been furnished with a Flag or Coat of Arms. With Sentiments of the highest Consideration I have the honor to be Sir, Y[ou]r Mo[st] Ob[edien]t H[um]ble S[er]v[an]t, Wm. Hooper, Act[in]g U.S. Com[mercia]l Agent.

ALS (No. 35) with Ens in DNA, RG 59 (State Department), Consular Despatches, Honolulu, vol. 2 (M-144:2), received 11/13.

Geo[rge] W. Hopkins, [Representative from Va.], Powhatan County [Va.], to [Richard K. Crallé], 7/2. Hopkins wishes to ascertain the probability of Congress being called into an extra session later in the year, as he plans to set out soon for the Southwest "to lend my aid to the canvass in that quarter." He wrote a letter yesterday to Calhoun asking his opinion, but decided not to send it because "there might be some indelicacy in putting such a question to him as a member of the Cabinet . . . ." He discusses his own opinions on the annexation of Texas and requests that Crallé "throw together in your vigorous and condensed style the prominent points in *your own view* in which this Texas question should be cast out upon the public feeling." ALS in ScCleA.

To C[HARLES] J. INGERSOLL, [Philadelphia?]

State Dept., 2d July 1844

My dear Sir, It is not contemplated to remove the Consul at Buenos Ayres [Amory Edwards] at present. The application of Mr. Moss for the place will be put on file and will be duely considered should a vacancy occur.

The concerted & active interference of the English & French Governments against the Annexation of Texas cannot be doubted. I do hope the information of what they are doing may be received in such a form as to enable the President [John Tyler] to lay it before Congress.

As far as I can learn the South is becoming very excited & united on the subject. I see [Orestes A.] Brownson's quarterly has a short, but very good article on the subject. Yours truly, J.C. Calhoun.

ALS in PHi, Ingersoll Papers; PC in Jameson, ed., *Correspondence*, p. 599.

TO WILLIAM M. McPHERSON, U.S. Attorney, [St. Louis]

Department of State
Washington, 2nd July 1844

Sir, In consequence of representations recently made by several individuals to the President, and especially of a deposition of Or[r]in P. Rockwell taken on the 20th of April last, of a confession made to him in the jail at Independence, Mo. by William Mason, (see "St. Louis Transcript" of 20th June) the Executive has been induced to grant a further reprieve until the 16th of August next to John Mc-Daniel and Joseph Brown, now under sentence of Death at St. Louis for murder. It is not, however designed, by this interference, to creat[e] any hop[e] of the ultimate pardon of these men, but merely that time may be allowed to examine into the credibility of Rockwell, and to ascertain whether the confident assertions, contained in letters addressed to this Department, of a great change in public sentiment favorable to the prisoners, is founded in fact. I have therefore the honor to call your attention to these points, and to r[e]quest that you will institute proper inquiries to obtain the information desired, to be reported to this Department as soon as practicable. I am, Sir, respectfully Y[ou]r Ob[edien]t Serv[an]t, John C. Calhoun.

FC in DNA, RG 59 (State Department), Domestic Letters, 34:275 (M-40:32); LS offered for sale by Charles Hamilton, New York City, in catalog for Auction No. 120 (1979).

Francis Markoe, Jr., [State Department], to Louis Mark, "Private," [New York City], 7/2. Markoe writes to Mark at the request of [Richard K.] Crallé, Chief Clerk of the State Department, "to inform you, that as you had entirely failed to make the explanation you had been officially called upon to make, you were now at liberty to resign the Consular office [in Bavaria and the Prussian Rhine provinces] recently conferred upon you, and by so doing, save the Department from the painful duty devolved upon it, of superseding you. Your Consular bond is, by the Secretary's direction, returned to you. I cannot forbear to add that Mr. Crallé expressed great reluctance at making this communication." CC in DNA, RG 59 (State Department), Consular Despatches, Vienna, vol. 1 (T-243:1).

To James B. Martin, Wheeling, Va., 7/2. Calhoun acknowledges Martin's letter of 6/28 and informs him in reply that the President [John Tyler] has granted a second respite [to last until 8/16], to

John McDaniel and Joseph Brown. This respite is to allow for investigation of new evidence in the case and should not encourage hope of an ultimate pardon. FC in DNA, RG 59 (State Department), Domestic Letters, 34:275–276 (M-40:32).

To J[OHN] R. MATHEW[E]S, [Clarkesville, Ga.?]

Washington, 2d July 1844
My dear Sir, if every Southern man could be made to see & feel as you do, we would be safe & become a great & wealthy people. No people have a greater source of prosperity & strength; & yet from not understanding our advantages & rights we permit our wealth & strength to be exhausted without scarcely an effort to resist the robbery, or to raise a cheering voice to sustain those, who stand up in opposition to it.

I concur, in most of the views you take, and stand prepared to push the correspondence with the British Government to the utmost limits, embracing most of the points you suggest, if an opportunity should offer. I had hoped to draw out a full correspondence by my letters to Mr. [Richard] Pakenham. They were in part written with that view, and were intended to lay the foundation of a long & full correspondence, and I doubt not, what was intended would have been accomplished, had the Senate done its duty & ratified the [Texas annexation] Treaty. Their neglect to do so, I fear, will not only lose Texas to the Union, but also defeat my aim in reference to the correspondence. Had the treaty been ratified my last letter to Mr. Pakenham, which he transmitted to his Govt., would not have been left without a reply, which would have brought on, what I intended. As it is, it will not be answered, as I infer ["from I learn" *canceled*] from Mr. P[akenham]'s conversation recently. His Government is content to leave to our Senate the defence of its cause, and is too wise, when it can be avoided, to carry on a correspondence, in which they see they have but little to gain. I regret it. It will, I fear be difficult to get another opportunity so favourable to bring out our cause so fully & favourably before the world. I shall omit none, which may afford a decent pretex[t] for renewing the correspondence.

The course of the Senate has united England & France in concerted & active interference to prevent annexation, and it is greatly to be feared, they will succeed. The present plan is to use their efforts with the Texian govt. to withdraw the proposition for annexation, with an understanding, that it is never to be renewed. To induce it to take the step, Mexico is to be forced to recognize Texas without the condition of abolishing slavery. Nothing I fear can defeat the plan, except resolute resistance on the part of the people of Texas, if even that can. Yours truly, J.C. Calhoun.

ALS in DLC, John C. Calhoun Papers; PEx in H.E. von Holst, *John C. Calhoun* (Boston: Houghton, Mifflin and Company, 1882), p. 241 (erroneously cited to a PC in the Charleston, S.C., *Mercury*, November 28, 1860).

To S[hadrach] Penn, Jr., St. Louis, 7/2. Calhoun informs him, in answer to a letter relative to John McDaniel and Joseph Brown, that the President [John Tyler] has granted a second respite to those men while new evidence is being investigated. No hope of an eventual pardon is to be taken from this act. FC in DNA, RG 59 (State Department), Domestic Letters, 34:276–277 (M-40:32).

To WILSON SHANNON, [Mexico City]

Department of State
Washington, 2nd July, 1844
Sir, The Letters addressed to this department a copy of which you will receive herewith, are from persons interested in the awards under the Convention with the Mexican Republic of the 30th of January, 1843. They set forth the disappointment experienced by those persons in consequence of the failure of Mexico to pay the last instalment due under that Convention and call upon this government to require from her punctual payment in future. You will accordingly press the subject upon the attention of the Mexican government and represent in strong terms the just grounds of complaint on our part for her failure to comply with the provisions of the Convention of 1843, especially when it is considered that the United States entered into it for the purpose of accommodating Mexico. I am, Sir, your obedient servant, J.C. Calhoun.

LS (No. 3) with Ens in DNA, RG 84 (Foreign Posts), Mexico, Instructions, vol. 5.I; FC in DNA, RG 59 (State Department), Diplomatic Instructions, Mexico, 15:306–307 (M-77:111). NOTE: Enclosed were copies of letters to Calhoun from John Baldwin and others, 6/19/1844; from Richard S. Coxe and others, 6/20/1844; from A.E. Borie and others, 6/25/1844; and from Paschal P. Pope and others, 6/29/1844.

From JA[ME]S SHAW

Consulate of the United States
Belfast (Ireland), July 2nd 1844

Sir, I feel it to be my duty to acquaint you, that, from certain information which I have received, I have every reason to believe that *Linens* have been sent forward from this district, to a *considerable extent*, with the view of being introduced into the United States without payment of duty.

The course adopted I believe to be, that the packages are shipped at Liverpool, as if intended for *Montreal* or *Quebec*. I have the honor to be, Sir, Y[ou]r most obedient Servant, Jas. Shaw.

ALS (No. 15) in DNA, RG 59 (State Department), Consular Despatches, Belfast, vol. 1 (T-368:1), received 7/22; CC in PHi, James Hamilton Papers, Letterbook of the Collector of the Port of Philadelphia, 1844.

To Prof[esso]r [BENJAMIN] SILLIMAN, [Yale College]

State Dept., 2d July 1844

Dear Sir, I mentioned to the President [John Tyler] yesterday the subject of yours & Mr. [James Luce] Kingsley's letters; and I am authorised to say, no removal is contemplated at this time ["of the removal" *canceled*] of the officer in question. I communicate the fact without wishing my name to be mentioned in connection with it, except to the collector himself. I never interfere, except in very special cases, beyond the limits of my Department. Were it to be known that I did in any case, it would subject me to great inconvenience & no small responsibility, which I do not desire to incur. My opinion is known to be opposed to the proscriptive policy. Truly, J.C. Calhoun.

ALS in CSmH, Huntington Manuscripts. NOTE: The letters to which the above is a reply have not been found, but they presumably referred to the Collector of Customs at New Haven, James Donaghe.

To H[ENRY] W. CONNER, [Charleston]

Washington, 3d July 1844

My dear Sir, I have entire confidence in your friendship and disinterestedness, and shall always receive with attention any suggestion, or advice you may favour me with.

No one can be more deeply impressed with the magnitude of the present crisis, than I am; or be more disposed to make sacrafices to meet it. As long as I have served the publick and as desireous as I am to spend the rest of my days in quiet & retirement, I shall not hesitate to remain ["at my post" *interlined*], and do battle for our principles & the safety of the South and the Union, so long as there is a prospect, that I can be of any ["service" *canceled*] substantial service to the great cause. As to the suggestion in the article you enclose in reference to the gubernatorial Chair [of S.C.], I must beg to be excused. It is a post of high honor, but in no respect would suit me. If I can be of any service to the cause, it would be in another sphere.

I am rejoiced to see the people of the State & South so much alive to their true interest. We only want union among ourselves to redress all our wrongs. If we could unite the South, every thing we desire could be effected; and I am happy to say, that there is now a better prospect of union, than there has been since the election of Gen[era]l [Andrew] Jackson in 1828. I regard the defeat of Mr. [Martin] V[an] Buren's nomination and the prostration of his wing of the party, a great step towards it. They have been the real cause of the corruption, & defeat & distraction of the party. They kept us divided & the whole party under dictation by party machinery & drill. Among its first fruits, I place the change of tone in the Richmond Enquirer & the politicks of Virginia. So long as she was hitched to the N[ew] York Car, through the influence of the Enquirer, it was impossible to unite the South, or to make any decided resistance to the usurpations & abuses of the General Government. Another and great cause operating to unite us is the Texan question. It will do more to break down the whig party in the South & west, than any event which has occurred for many years. It is also doing much to unite the South & west. Their union would give them a preponderance in the Government, and be followed by a revolution in our politicks, of a highly salutary character.

Thus thinking, I am not disposed to encourage any seperate action, *at this time*, on the part of the State or the South. I am of the impression, that it is the worst moment, which could be selected to make any such. It would weaken us greatly in other quarters on the Texian question; it would endanger the election of [James K.] Polk & strengthen the prospect of [Henry] Clay, & lose us the control hereafter, let what party succeed. It would throw Polk, if he should be elected, back into the hands of the V[an] B[uren] wing of the party, &, if Clay should be elected, it would give the same wing the lead in opposition to his administration. It would, in a word, place us in a minority of the party, let what will happen.

With this impression, I am of the opinion, that our true course, *at present is*, to do nothing, that may tend to the loss of Texas, or to weaken the hold we have on the party. Yours truly, J.C. Calhoun.

ALS in ScC, John C. Calhoun Collection (published microfiche of Charleston Library Society manuscripts, 51–22); photostat of ALS in DLC, Henry Workman Conner Papers.

To EDWARD EVERETT, [London]

Department of State
Washington, 3d July, 1844

Sir, I take pleasure in transmitting to you, by the direction of the President of the United States [John Tyler], a copy of a joint resolution of Congress, passed at its recent session, tendering the thanks of that body to the British Authorities at Gibraltar, and to the Commander, Officers, and crew, of Her Britannic Majesty's ship "Malabar," for the generous zeal displayed by them in endeavoring to save from destruction [at Gibraltar] the American steam frigate "Missouri," and in preserving the lives of her officers and crew; and also for the kindness and hospitality shown to the ship's company of that unfortunate vessel. I have to request that you will communicate it to Her Majesty's Government, through the proper channel, accompanied by a note conveying the President's high appreciation of the conduct and character of those who participated in these Offices of humanity, so honorable to themselves and so well calculated to promote those friendly feelings between the citizens and subjects of the respective countries which it is alike the earnest desire and the interest of both to strengthen and perpetuate. I am, Sir, respectfully, your obed[ien]t serv[an]t, J.C. Calhoun.

LS (No. 96) with En in DNA, RG 84 (Foreign Posts), Great Britain, Instructions, 8:296–301, received 7/30; FC in DNA, RG 59 (State Department), Diplomatic Instructions, Great Britain, 15:201–202 (M-77:74). NOTE: As Secretary of State, Calhoun received much correspondence from the U.S. Consul at Gibraltar, Horatio Sprague, about efforts to raise the *Missouri,* which correspondence is not included in this publication.

From GEORGE HEFFERMAN

Campechey [Yucatan], July 3d 1844

Honorable Sir, I send this by the American Brig Adams (Captain Smith Naturelized Citizen of the U. States) bound to Newyork informing that the Said brig is owned in this place by two foreingers Don Pablo Pasqual and Captain Barranda a Spaniard the latter goes in her to N. york. She is held in the Name of an American at New Orleans who is in the habit of Doing this Kind of Business that Should be Stop[p]ed; Mr. L[eonard] R. Almy [U.S. Consul] is here from Laguna Bound to New Orleans I Sup[p]ose to account of the outrage Commit[t]ed by the House of Messers. Guteras Brothers & Co. at Laguna which house is in Charge of one of the Partners (an English Malato or a Couloured Gentelman). Reports Says the Case is to wit The Schooner Richard St. John was purchased by the Firm of J.W. Zachrie & Co. of N. Orleans in their Name for Messers. Guteras & Co. of Laguna and an American by the Name of Captain Cox put in Charge of her and Sent with a Cargo to Laguna. Whean she arrived Mr. Johnson the English partner of Guteras & Co. order Mr. Boyland to take Com[man]d of the Schooner and turn Capt. Cox out without having Power of attorney from Mess. Zachries to Do So. Capt. Cox Refused to Deliver the vessel up to any Foreinger. Mr. Johnson Sent an armed force of Englishmen Irish & Dutch & Spaniards on board hauled Down and trampled on the American Flag & turned Capt. Cox & Crew ashore Took possession of the Schooner. The *names* of the Pirates are as follows which is here bin Mentioned in Public—Mr. Huberter—Mr. Pike[,] Mr. Brown—Mr. Boylan—Mr. Aubrey—Mr. Elyes about twenty English Sailors and Captains & Mates all Principal[l]y in the Employ of the House of Guteras & Co.

I have not the least Doubt of your hearing also of the forsible Posses[s]ion Taken by an English by Name Robert Christian of Mr. Jonas P. Levy's Property amounting to about 3000$ up to Present Date which is over ten months. Mr. L[evy] has not nor Cannot Get Justice done to him by the authoritys nor Consuls—also Mr. L[evy] has bin compelled to Pay to Mexico Dutys on Free good to a Large amount which he Cannot get back. Mr. L[evy] is Brother to Commander U[riah] P. Levy U.S. Navy and Much Respected in Laguna as a merchant.

It is here reported that five American Seamen has bin Shot by General Pedro Ampudia at Tabasco. Enclosed I Send you the Remarks of the Campechanas on the awful Death of [Francisco] Se[nt]manat.

It is hoped Some protection will be sent on this Coast for we Americans. Excuse this in haste Your Very Respectfully Ob[edient] Ser[van]t, George Hefferman.

ALS with En in DNA, RG 59 (State Department), Consular Despatches, Campeche, vol. 2 (M-286:1), received 7/30. NOTE: Hefferman enclosed a printed circular entitled "Voz De La Naturaliza," protesting the execution of Sentmanat. A Clerk's EU, dated 8/16, reads "Respectfully referred to the Secretary of the Treasury [George M. Bibb] for his perusal & return."

To Henry Morris, Treasury Department, 7/3. "I have to acknowledge the receipt of your letter of the 28th Ultimo with its enclosures, in relation to the imprisonment of Mr. Robert Bell, at Carderas [sic, Cardenas, Cuba], and to state, in reply, that the case of Mr. Bell will receive proper attention." FC in DNA, RG 59 (State Department), Domestic Letters, 34:282–283 (M-40:32).

From J[AMES] C. PICKETT

Legation of the U. States
Lima, July 3rd 1844

Sir, On the 17th ultimo, the Prefect of Lima, Don Domingo Elias, promulgated a decree renouncing his allegiance to the Supreme Director and investing himself with "supreme authority" (his own words). And he published at the same time, a proclamation, in which he charges the Director with selfishness and incompetency and insinuates against him, dishonesty, cruelty and cowardice. This change has been effected without any disturbance, every body seeming to acquiesce in it, through good will or apathy or policy. Even the Lima militia, called National Guards, who swore they would die for [Manuel Ignacio de] Vivanco, when he left the city seven months ago, to join the army, transferred themselves without a moment's hesitation to the Prefect, who has been acknowledged by the authorities of the Department generally, as Supreme Chief.

It is rather difficult to account satisfactorily, for Elias's defection.

It may be that he is influenced by an honest and disinterested zeal for the public welfare; or that he is merely used as a tool by the military men who are his supporters; or that he is endeavoring to propitiate Gen[era]l [Ramon] Castilla, whom he has much reason to fear. He is wealthy and respectable and influential, but not being military can hardly be actuated by ambitious motives, unless he is mad, as well as weak and vacillating; for he cannot but know that he will be kicked out of power by his epauletted co-revolutionists, as soon as they have made the use of him they wish to make. His object is, he says, to convene a Congress and then to retire to private life, and this may be so, and his intentions may be very pure; but after having supported Vivanco through thick and thin, with money and service, for fifteen months, making himself the instrument to carry into effect, his harsh, illegal and arbitrary measures; and after publishing almost daily to the world, through the Press, that he (Vivanco) was the great man of the country, its idol and savior and regenerator, and all that is patriotic, chivalric and noble; and then, all at once, and without deliberation apparently, to abandon him at his utmost need, and not only to abandon, but to denounce and vilify him, certainly gives some room to doubt his (Elias's) disinterestedness; and it cannot be very uncharitable to suppose, that a view to his own interest as well as his country's may have influenced his conduct, in some degree. Those who undertake to justify or palliate it, assert that Vivanco had become dissatisfied with him and threatened him, and had even gone so far as to say that he would have him shot, should he have reason to suspect his fidelity; and this may be true, but no proofs have been published. It would be fortunate for Peru ["though," *interlined*] I have no doubt, if Mr. Elias could remain quietly at the head of affairs. He is disposed I believe, to be just—is said by those who know him well, to be honest about money matters and he would not plunder and peculate, as almost all do here that can. I speak of the Peruvian chiefs.

Now, since the revolution of the 17th there are three contending parties in arms, in Peru, each one arrayed against the other two; besides the party of the constitutional President (Mr. Menendez) still in exile in Chile, who has not however, any active partisans and but few of any kind; from which it may be inferred that the Peruvians feel but little solicitude for the fate of their Constitution; nor need they feel much, for they have had four or five, and when even nominally in force, they have been violated and trampled upon with but little ceremony and treated as though they were only so much waste paper.

This very complicated and critical state of things has made it necessary, that the foreign agents ["at Lima," *interlined*] should take into consideration what course it would be proper to pursue, for the protection of the persons and property of their fellow-citizens and subjects, and of neutral commerce. For this purpose some conferences were held which resulted in the adoption of two papers called (not much to my taste) *protocols*, in which is indicated the policy that will be adhered to during the present crisis. Copies of them are inclosed.

As it was of much importance that there should be uniformity of action, I became a party to those papers which were signed by all the diplomatic agents here. You will perceive that they are very moderate and guarded and only temporary in their character, for as soon as the country shall be tranquillized or any one of the factions shall get the ascendency, they will cease to be applicable. They have been resorted to distinctly on the ground that there is not at present, (as is notorious) a general government in Peru or a government of any kind capable of giving adequate protection to foreign residents, ["in Peru" *canceled*] even if disposed to give it.

The almost continual vexations to which, under the names of blockades and embargoes, neutral commerce has been subjected in Peru, since the downfall of the constitutional government in 1842, ought not, in my opinion to be any longer tolerated. It surely cannot be contended, that three or four or a dozen independent and irresponsible chiefs—some of them in their principles and conduct but little better than banditti—should all be recognised as heads of governments, merely because they style themselves *supreme*, their only title to the exercise of power, being that they command a few hundred ragamuffins—Indians and samboes—with arms in their hands. Yet this humiliation must be submitted to, unless the principles of the protocols shall be maintained, and every upstart ruffian of a day will then have it in his power to vex, annoy and paralyze neutral commerce, at his pleasure. So low has the military character fallen here, that the commanders of blockading vessels of war, acting under orders emanating from something like a respectable government, have engaged in smuggling, using their ships as receptacles for smuggled merchandise and participating, without doubt, in the profits. This I know from unquestionable authority, to have been frequently done.

I enclose copies of two letters to me [dated 6/25 and 6/28], from Captain [James] Armstrong, now commanding the Pacific Squadron. This I do, not for the purpose of justifying the course I have taken, but merely to furnish additional proof of the state of things here and of the necessity that existed for doing something for the protection of our commerce. It is very certain that he would not have promised his coöperation so unhesitatingly, if the propriety of the measures resorted to had been questionable.

I have now said more than enough, perhaps; but having pursued a line of conduct somewhat unusual as well as somewhat peremptory, it is proper that I should given [*sic*] my reasons for it. I have done so, and trust that they will be satisfactory: But it is difficult, without residing in this country and being an eye-witness, to form an idea of the abject and miserable condition to which it is reduced and of the disorder, anarchy and profligacy that prevail. What has been done by the foreign agents will be approved, not only by their fellow-countrymen residing in Peru and on this coast, but also by almost all reflecting and patriotic Peruvians. The object has been, not to usurp or impair or suspend a single right belonging to the Peruvian nation, but to restrain the licentiousness and violence of the tyrants and ruffians, by whom Peru is oppressed, plundered and enslaved. Even Mr. Elias himself admits that what has been done by the protocols is just and proper, although the exercise by him of sovereign power (which he claims to possess) is restricted in several important particulars.

I will add to what I have said, that I am not an admirer of protocols. I do not like either the name or the thing. By them three or four powerful European governments aim at ruling not only ["all" *interlined*] Europe, but the whole world. It is not my intention to sign another, unless something, now unforeseen and unapprehended should occur, which would make it not only a matter of expediency to do so, but of duty. On the recent occasion, the protocols were approved by General [Tomás C.] Mosquera, the Minister Plenipotentiary of New Granada, which is a conclusive proof, that the adoption of them was justifiable and proper, for he is devoted to the rights and independence of the Spanish American states and is a distinguished and experienced man. Should the European diplomatic agents be disposed to resort habitually to this mode of procedure, I cannot be their coadjutor, and should they evince a disposition to govern Peru by protocols or to put into practice on this coast, any new principle of international law, they will assuredly not have either my co-öperation or my acquiescence. Of this I perceive no symptom, however: But diplomatists are fallible as well as other people (and in a greater degree perhaps) and much indulgence in protocol-making might lead eventually, to pretensions and assumptions not originally contemplated. I have the honor to be, with great respect, Sir, Your most Ob[edien]t Servant, J.C. Pickett.

P.S. July 5th. It is stated in the foregoing despatch that there are three parties in arms in Peru. It appears, however, that there are four or five, and there may be still more. Gen[era]l [José Rufino] Echenique, who commands twelve or fifteen hundred men, 150 miles from Lima, and who was supposed to be acting in concert with Mr. Elias, condemns what the latter has done and says that he will not abandon Vivanco, but that he will not take any active part in the contest going on and will remain where he is; which means probably, that he intends to join the strongest side whenever that is ascertained, or that he will set up for himself, should he see any prospect of success.

A colonel Beltran also, it is said, is preparing to make war for himself or for somebody else, in the North. In this state of things, it does not appear to be possible to recognise the existence of a *bona fide* Peruvian government, even *de facto*, and there is really no such thing; though ordinary business must from necessity, be transacted with the government at the capital (Lima).

ALS (No. 96) with Ens in DNA, RG 59 (State Department), Diplomatic Despatches, Peru, vol. 6 (T-52:6, frames 504–538), received 10/6. NOTE: Pickett enclosed translations of Elias' decrees of 6/17 and of Elias' correspondence with other Peruvian generals. Pickett also enclosed copies, in French, of the diplomatic protocols of 6/20 and 6/27 designed to govern the activities of foreigners in Peru.

From SETH SWEETSER

United States Consulate
Guayaquil [Ecuador], 3d July 1844
Sir, I have the honour to inclose herein, the orriginal account with good and sufficient vouchers, "for the relief and support of distressed American seamen," in this Port for the last six months; during which period, the Yellow Fever, has raged in the city to a greater or less degree. This melancholy pestilence, having caused a want of seamen from its dreadful ravages among them, that the crews of the Whale Ships at Tumbes and Payta, encouraged by the high wages to sailors, have in many cases deserted their ships, and come to this place to seek high wages—but they have generally fallen early and unhappy victims to the Fever. This, will in some degree, account

for the heavy outlay we are called upon to make, for this useful, but unhappy class of our fellow citizens.

I have this day drawn on your on your [*sic*] department, for disbursements made by me, during the last six months; ending 30th June, "For the relief, and support of distressed American Seamen," in this Port; in favour of James J. Fisher Esq. or order at sixty days after sight, for the sum of $988.83—Nine hundred eighty eight dollars and eighty three cents, as p[e]r account herewith; which, please to protect and charge under the proper head, as p[e]r advice.

During the last three months, my attention and services have been directed almost exclusively, to the claims of our citizens, against the Ecuador; growing out of the Convention of Bogota, dated Nov. 25, 1829, by which, it was stipulated to pay the owners of the Brig Josephine, and Schooner Ranger: [*partial word canceled*] and the Convention referred to, was approved by General [Simon] Bolivar, then chief Magistrate of Colombia. I have great hopes ere long of being able to bring this ["long" *canceled*] protracted negotiation, to a final and satisfactory conclusion.

The Government of the Ecuador at the request of the French Consul, have granted the priviluge of a depot, for coals and other materials, for the line of Steamers they talk of establishing on the coast, to run between Lima and Panama; calling at *Puna* (an island in the mouth of this river) for coals, passengers, treasure, and correspondance.

I beg leave to call your attention, and through you, that of His Excellency the President's, to my communication[s]; dated Nov. 3d 1843 and Jan[uar]y 30, 1844, duplicates of which, you will find inclosed for your information, and government. I Remain Sir, Your Obedient Servant, Seth Sweetser.

LS and duplicate with Ens in DNA, RG 59 (State Department), Consular Despatches, Guayaquil, vol. 1 (T-209:1), received 12/30.

From WADDY THOMPSON, [JR.]

Washington, July 3, 1844

Sir, Richard Harrison Esquire of Florida has requested me to present his name to you as an applicant for the office of U.S. Attorney for the Middle District in Florida. Mr. Harrison is the son of the late Doctor Harrison of Greenville who I believe was known to you. I do not know any young man of finer talents, more unexceptionable character nor one more universally beloved and respected. He has resided in Florida for the last four years and has a high standing in his profession. I believe that his appointment would give general satisfaction and am very sure that it would be gratifying to your numerous friends in Florida. Mr. Harrison is my near relation and I am therefore restrained from saying more on the subject. I have the Honor to be with Great Respect Y[ou]r ob[edient] Ser[vant], Waddy Thompson.

ALS in DNA, RG 59 (State Department), Applications and Recommendations, 1837–1845, Harrison (M-687:14, frames 752–754).

From Benj[amin] W. S. Cabell

Bridge Water[,] Pitt[sylvani]a [County, Va.,] July 4th 1844
Dear Sir, At the instance of a beloved friend, and truly worthy relative of mine, Col. Edward A. Cabell, whom I have known from his early boyhood, and who, as well in adversity as in prosperity, has preserved a spotless purity of life and character—I, who have been for many years your *unwavering friend* and ardent supporter, venture, with becoming diffidence, to ask a favor at your hands. I ask you for a Clerkship, in your Department, for William Cabell, son of Col. Edward A. Cabell. I am a stranger—and intend to live and die a stranger, to the language of a courtier. Yet, if I had the ability to impart to you, all the facts and circumstances which impel me to address you in behalf of this young gentleman, and his family, who are people of taste, feeling, sensibility, and honor, I should present such an appeal, as would throb your generous bosom with delight, at the opportunity afforded you of extending to a young, talented, and worthy member of it, your patronage and protection.

Amidst the recent revulsions in the business of the country, Col. Edward A. Cabell, who is among the most modest and amiable, as he is among the most honorable men living, has been bereft of a fortune, caused, to a considerable extent, by a too generous confidence in friends, for whom he endorsed, without a wish or expectation of profit. His Father, G[rand] Father and G[reat] G[rand] Father, lived and died ["and died" *canceled*] in the (now) County of Nelson on James River, his birthplace, esteemed, respected, beloved and honored. His own domicile after his marriage, was in Amherst [County]. His wife was Mary Garland, daughter of David S. Garland, for many years a friend and associate of President [John]

Tyler, in the General Assembly of this Commonwealth, in both houses of which he served with distinguished usefulness. He also represented the Albemarle district in Congress. Mrs. Cabell is esteemed by the wide circle of her acquaintance among the most talented and amiable ladies of her day. They have five promising children. William, the eldest son, has just graduated, and possessing qualities and qualifications the necessary presages of future usefulness, is now prepared to enter into business. He is anxious to obtain a situation sufficiently profitable to enable him with a *truly fillial piety* to aid his parents in the education of his brothers. Col. Cabell, is now a Clerk in one of the public Offices, ["and" *canceled*] residing at Washington, and is dependent upon the income derived from a very inadequate salary, for the support of his family. He has many amiable and wealthy relatives in his native Country, who, deeply mortified at seeing a man of his standing laboring in a subordinate clerkship for a bear support, have generously proffered him assistance. But animated by a just pride, his feelings revolt at the idea [of] dependence—and he prefers a more *scanty living*, earned by the sweat of his brow. Col. Cabell was bred to the law, and made a respectable figure at the bar. Unfortunately in the days of his prosperity, he relinquished a profession, which, if he had continued to pursue, would have proved the best resource for him, in the day of calamity. He is a man highly esteemed and beloved, by numerous relatives and friends, among the most respectable and influential people in Virginia. Pardon Sir I pray you my importunity, when I beseech you, to extend your patronage to his son William, whom I doubt not you will find worthy of it. Be pleased Sir to confer *a Clerkship* on him—and thus enable him to support himself and to spare something for the assistance of his parents, so lately, suddenly, and unexpectedly reduced from affluence to comparative penury. Bred in the school of *high* and *nice honor*, you will find William Cabell, honest, faithful, and grateful.

I take the liberty of enclosing [*not found*] for your perusal, a letter addressed to me by Col. E.A. Cabell, and of course only intended for my own eye, and one written some time past by Mrs. Cabell, addressed to the President. These letters will disclose to you, more fully than I have been able to do, the reasons for my application to you, in behalf of young Mr. Cabell. If, after the perusal of these letters, in addition to the contents of my letter—I refer you to my highly respected friend Richard K. Cralle Esq[uir]e Chief Clerk in your Department.

And now in conclusion, with devotional fervour, I invoke upon your head, the constant protection and blessing of the Supreme Ruler and Gove[r]nor of the Universe, and pray that, in all your doings in the *great trusts* devolved upon you, you may be guided by a *wisdom* from on high; and that the results of your arduous labors may redound to your own honor—and to prosperity and Glory of our beloved Country. With high esteem & Respect I am Sir y[ou]r Ob[edient] S[ervan]t, Benj. W.S. Cabell.

ALS in ScCleA. NOTE: An AEU by Calhoun reads: "Gen[era]l B.W.S. Cabell[,] Applies for a clerkship for W. Cabell."

From FLORIDE [COLHOUN] CALHOUN

Forthill, July 4th 1844

My Dear Husband, I was disappointed at not receiving a letter from you when Mr. [Richard F.] Sim[p]son [Representative from S.C.] came. He brought one from Martha [Calhoun] Burt, and the things she was so good as to get for me. [Martha] Cornelia [Calhoun] was delighted with her dress, and breastpin. She needed the dress, as she has been wearing the same one to Church, ever since she has been in mourning [for Maria Simkins Colhoun]. I could not get any thing worth having at the Village [of Pendleton]. The stockings were very acceptable, as I have not purchased for her, or myself, a pair of [bla]ck silk stockings for several years. They ask three and four dollars [a] pair for them at the village. I did not see among the things a twisted green silk shawl, I gave Patrick [Calhoun], to have dyed a black. Do inquire for it, I should dislike very much to loose [sic] it. You must recollect it, it was like the one I gave Mrs. [Sophia Maria Green] Chappell. You brought them to me, from Washington the year before Andrew [Pickens Calhoun] married his first wife [Eugenia Chappell], and as Anna [Maria Calhoun Clemson] had been staying with Mrs. Chappell, you told me to give her one of them. It is striped all over as broad as my hand, and large leaves in the stripes. I have no doubt but you would know it if you were to send to the Dyers. If you cannot hear of it, write Pat about it. I was glad to receive John[']s [John C. Calhoun, Jr.'s] letter, he appears delighted with his journey [to the West], and is already better. I hope Pat, and himself, will write me as soon as they arrive, as I shall be very anxious about them until I hear again.

Anna has written me, to go down immediately, and take Cornelia, and William Lowndes [Calhoun], with me, as she cannot think of going [abroad], without seeing us once more, but I wrote her it was impossible for me to go, as my horses could not stand the journey, and William Lowndes, has been so sick for three weeks that I could not leave him. He is still so weak that he can hardly go about, but is mending very rapidly. The Doctor has discontinued medicine, and giving him tonicks. I hope he will be well enough to go to school when the Teacher comes. I have not heard from James [Edward Calhoun], for some time. His Uncle [James Edward Colhoun] wrote me he intended taking him to Edgefield with him. I wrote him to be up in time to commence with the New Teacher.

Mr. Fred[e]ricks says I must tell you, he is getting along remarkably well on the plantation. He has finished the big bottom, and going over the cotton for the last time. All the wheat is thrashed. The Negro[e]s have been very well until lately, none have been ill, excepting one of Nancey[']s children. It had worms. Mrs. [Margaret Hunter] Rion has managed it without sending for a Doctor, and it is getting better. I have had to break up the Negro[e]s raising chickens, as I could not get along until I did it. I expected to have had some dif[f]iculty about it, but had not, as they knew I could not avoid it. You will have to buy flitches for the plantation, as they have had no milk since you left home. I understand bacon is as low as three cents a pound in Augusta. You had better see about it soon. If I had not come as soon as I did, all our hams would have been ruined. Mrs. Rion had packed them in salt, and as it was had to feed a great many to the Negro[e]s. I had them all well washed in soapsuds, dried and hung up again. I hope the rest will be safe. You do not mention the receipt of my letter respecting Mr. [F.M.] Adams, he wishes if you can, conveniently to settle for the Boys[']s] schooling. I wrote you, if you did not come home soon, to send me a check for 50, and out of it I would settle with Mr. Adams, and keep the rest myself, as I shall require it. I was affraid you did not get my letter, or you would have sent the money on by Maj. Sim[p]son. Write me in answer to this letter when you think you will be at home, several persons have asked me, but I could not say. I observe through the papers, that your health is good. I do not place much faith in the health of Washington in summer. I must conclude as it is late. All join me in love. Your affectionate Wife, Floride Calhoun.

ALS in ScCleA.

From FLORIDE [COLHOUN] CALHOUN

Forthill, July 4th 1844

My Dear Husband, I write immediately on receiving your letter, in, order to say, I have received the check for 50 dollars, and will pay Mr. [F.M.] Adams immediately. [Martha] Cornelia [Calhoun] received a long and interesting letter from John [C. Calhoun, Jr.], he appears perfectly enchanted, with the country he has passed through. I also got two letters from Anna [Maria Calhoun Clemson], again, urging me to go down [to Edgefield District]. I have written her it will not be in my power to go. I am sorry she has set her heart so much on my going. William Lowndes [Calhoun's], fever has left him I hope. He looks very badly. Anna wrote me to get her carriage and horses. I would not make use of them, if she were to make them a present to me. It is an expence I do not wish you to incur this year, as ours will answer very well for some time yet. But I wrote her if her cook pleased her I would like you to buy him. She did not say one word about him. As to selling our Carriage, and horses I could not I believe give them away. The carriage is strong, and the horses are looking very well again. Cudy [Martha Maria Colhoun] told me just now she hea[r]d My Brother, James [Edward Colhoun] was to be up in a few days, I am glad to hear it as James ought to be here. The New Teacher has arrived. Mr. [Richard F.] Sim[p]son is to deliver the oration, and I understand there is to be a barbacue at the Village [of Pendleton], crowds of persons are to be there.

John writes he wishes his winter clothes sent on to him. I will have them put up carefully, and sent you by Anna, with directions where to send them. I tryed my best to make him take them with him. Cornelia, and William Lowndes, join me in love. Your affectionate Wife, Floride Calhoun.

ALS in ScCleA.

From C[ALEB] CUSHING

Macao, 4 July 1844

Sir; I have the pleasure to inform you that a Treaty of Peace[,] Amity and Commerce between the United States and China was concluded and signed yesterday by the Imperial Commissioner and myself, at Wang-hia, a village in the vicinity of Macao.

This Treaty is in all respects one eminently favorable to the United States, and will, I am confident, promote the commerce of both countries, at the same time that it unites them by ties of sincere and cordial friendship, and gives to the United States a position alike honorable and independent in China.

I am not able to make up my despatches and transmit the Treaty by this conveyance. Indeed the conveyance itself is a precarious one in point of time, as well as in other respects. I shall embrace the earliest opportunity, however, to transmit the Treaty, and the particulars of the negociations, by some vessel going directly to the United States.

When the correspondence reaches home, you will perceive that I have for the present waived going to Peking for the sake of at once concluding a favorable Treaty with Kiyeng, deeming this the more important object. I am With great respect Your Ob[edien]t Ser-[van]t, C. Cushing.

ALS (No. 69) and duplicate with En in DNA, RG 59 (State Department), Diplomatic Despatches, China, vol. 2 (M-92:3), received 1/5/[1845]. NOTE: This despatch was addressed to A[bel] P. Upshur. Cushing enclosed a copy of a circular he issued on 7/4, presumably for the information of Americans in or near China, announcing the signing of the treaty.

From F[rancis] M. Dimond

United States Consulate
Vera Cruz, July 4, 1844

Sir, I have the honour herewith to transmit the parts of seven Registers of vessels sold at this port the last year.

I last had the honour to address you by the U.S. Frigate Potomac under date of the 27 ult[im]o, and by Mr. [Isaac D.?] Markes I sent a despatch from Mr. [Ben E.] Green who had other documents from that gentleman.

I observed in my last respects that Congress had refused Gen[era]l Santa Ann[a] the Four million dollars and the 30,000 Troops—since however they have complied with his demand.

The instalment due the U.S. on the 30th April is yet unpaid and the Cutter which is here for it will return next week without it.

My own impression is they will keep it back until they know the Fate of the Treaty now before the Senate of the U.S.

Of the persons who accompanied Gen[era]l Samana [*sic*; Francisco Sentmanat] on his expedition against Tabasco[,] 27 have been shot and the Capt. of the vessel will share the same fate—the Crew I understand will be pardoned. I presume the particulars you will have rece[ive]d from our Consul at Tabasco. I have the honour to be Sir very Respectfully your Ob[edient] Serv[an]t, F.M. Dimond.

ALS (No. 228) in DNA, RG 59 (State Department), Consular Despatches, Veracruz, vol. 5 (M-183:5), received 7/25.

From W[illia]m P. Duval, "Private"

Palatka Florida, July 4th 1844

My dear Sir, The very trying circumstances, in which your position has placed you, have awakened (and it [is] to be hoped) effectually, the spirit and patriotism, of the great mass of our citizens. The recent action of the senate on the treaty with Texas, shews what ["what" *canceled*] sacrifices will be made of the national ["interest," *interlined*] by party drill, under the tactics of unprincipled leaders—woe, woe, to our country, unless the great democratic party shall speedily come to its resque. I yet believe if the democracy throughout the union, will act in concert, and with energy, & judgement, they will be triumphant. It seems to me, that Mr. [Henry] Clay may be defeated and if Mr. [John] Tyler and his friends, should cordially support Mr. [James K.] Polk, he will defeat the minions, of England, who are now exerting all their influence & power, to degrade their own country, and place us under the dictation of Great Britain. Nothing short of a war with England, will put down the native traitors of this nation—trade, commerce, and speculation, have corrupted our cities—they have extended their baneful influence, deep, & wide, thro' the land. War at all times is an evil, but it is a necessary one for us. The cankers of a long war are often felt, even after years of succeeding peace. The cankers of a long peace are more dangerous, because, they strike at the vital principles, on which freedom, and patriotism, is based. The scars & bruises of war, are on the surface, the p[l]otting[?], intrigues—and silent workings of unprincipled men, in days of peace, when the public mind, is slumbering in security— are the moments, when the unwatched enimies, the demons of our land, fasten on the lungs of liberty, producing inward decay—never manifested, until disease & corruption has struck deep into the heart of the constitution. War is necessary to unite and save our country, no sacrifice is to[o] great to accomplish this end—and this war should

269

be with England. There are at this moment more foreign enimies, and native traitors in the United States, than at any period since the revolution. England will leave nothing unattempted to circumscribe, limit, and cripple our power and resources. She is our natural enimy, and her interference in American affairs ought, and should be arrested, at all hazzard. It is evident to me, that the influence of England is rappidly increasing throughout the union, congress is deeply imbued, with British feelings, & many of the members are better representatives of her interest, than of our own. We have the option to become vassals of great Britain, or by war to rally the people and overthrow her influence, and expose our secret enimies, and traitors, to the odium of public opinion.

I had intended if the treaty with Texas ["had" *canceled and then interlined*] been confirmed to remove to that country, but if it is to be under the control of England—which now is almost certain, I cannot go there. My son in law Doct[or] W[illia]m D. Price with his family removed to Texas last may, and has settled at Galveston under the full belief that it would be annexed to the United States. I would have been gratified, to have gone there as Charge d'Affaires, but I never asked for the office, as that sort of solicitation, is repulsive to my pride & principles. I believe however that I could [do] more to promote the influence, & interest of the United States, than almost any other, that could be selected. My personal acquaintance with many of the the citizens of Texas—The services of two gallant sons in defence of her cause—one of whom was murde[re]d by Santa Anna in cold blood—my popular manners, and the facility of becoming acquainted with men, would give me decided advantage over most men. I say this without any expectation of being selected for this service, as I know the station has been recently filled. I expect to remain in Florida and will pursue my profession[.] With sentiments of sin[c]ere esteem I remain your friend, Wm. P. Duval.

[P.S.] I should like to have your opinion as to the probability of ever reannexing Texas, to the United States[.]

ALS in ScCleA.

From Benj[ami]n C. Foster, Buenos Ayres, 7/4. Foster reports that Calhoun can expect copies of certain letters within a short time. ALS in DNA, RG 59 (State Department), Miscellaneous Letters (M-179:105, frames 73–74).

From [Bvt. Maj. Gen.] Edmund P. Gaines, "Head Quarters, Western Division," New Orleans, 7/4. Gaines writes in behalf of Hallam

Eldredge of Binghamton, N.Y., who seeks "an agency abroad" from the State Department as a bearer of despatches "primarily to the service of the public and secondarily to afford relief to some indigent heirs residing in this country who are entitled to an estate or its proceeds from one of the Germanic States." Eldredge is a graduate of Yale College and is a student of law "with one of the first lawyers in New York." LS in DNA, RG 59 (State Department), Applications and Recommendations, 1837–1845, Eldredge (M-687:10, frames 95–97).

From Alex[ande]r Hamilton, Jr., Liverpool, 7/4. "I have the honor to tender to you my resignation as Secretary of the legation of the United States at Madrid." ALS in DNA, RG 59 (State Department), Diplomatic Despatches, Spain, vol. 34 (M-31:34), received 7/27.

From W[illia]m C. Anderson, "Marshal," St. Louis, 7/5. "The originals & Duplicates of the President's [John Tyler's] Respite of David McDaniel and Thomas Towson until the 21st day of June 1845, are received, and their contents have been duly communicated." ALS in DNA, RG 59 (State Department), Petitions for Pardon and Related Briefs, 1800–1849, no. 292B.

To BARING BROTHERS & CO., Bankers of the United States, [London]

Department of State
Washington, 5 July 1844
Gentlemen, Mr. Thomas G. Clemson, appointed Chargé d'Affaires of the United States to Belgium, is authorized to draw upon you for the amount of Salary as it may become due, from and after the 17th day of June 1844, at the rate of four thousand five hundred dollars per annum; and for the Contingent expenses of the Legation, not to exceed five hundred dollars per annum.

You are requested to honor his drafts accordingly. For your security his signature is annexed. I am, Gentlemen, Your Ob[edien]t Servant, J.C. Calhoun.

FC in DNA, RG 59 (State Department), Accounting Records: Miscellaneous Letters Sent, 1832–1916, vol. for 2/1–9/30/1844, p. 286. NOTE: Clemson's signature does not appear on this document although a place is marked for it to be written. This is typical of letters written in behalf of newly appointed diplomats, most of which are not included in this publication.

From RICH[AR]D H. BELT

U.S. Consulate
Matamoros, Mexico
5th July 1844

Sir, I have the honor to acknowledge receipt of your letter dated the 21st May last informing me of my appointment to the Consulate at this place and for the honor conferred upon me I beg leave to tender my acknowledgements.

Since my communication to the Department on the 1st June, you will perceive by the 2 Proclamations herewith enclosed that the Armistice with Texas is declared at an end, and that hostilities will be again resumed. From a gentleman who arrived here a few days since from the interior, I learned that the Mexicans are busily engaged in opening roads &c for the passage of their troops to Texas; they are also throwing up and repairing the embankments which environ this City. Steps I understand have also been taken to enrol and organise the militia in this neighborhood. From the observations I have made I am induced to believe that should the invasion occur, it will be in a short time.

The Comanche Indians have become very troublesome in this neighborhood; they have nearly entire possession of the Country lying between the Rio Grande and Nueces Rivers, and recently their incursions have been extended to the Mexican side of the Rio Grande in this vicinity. In one of their recent irruptions they killed 3 Mexicans and carried off several women. Although there are between 500 and 1000 troops quartered here, no effectual measures have been adopted to check their depredations which they are committing with perfect impunity. The authorities have taken no notice of them, further than the publishing of the enclosed document. The landing places of goods for this City are distant from it some 20 or 30 miles, and the travelling to the ["City" *canceled*] Shipping is attended with danger as the Indians have been seen immediately on the rout[e].

I transmit, herewith, a list of U.S. vessels that have entered this port from the 5th February to 30th June (inclusive) 1844, accompanied by a list of the fees received at this Office during the same period.

Enclosed I also transmit you a statement of the importations and exportations at this port for the years 1842 and 1843, from which you will perceive that nearly the entire trade has been carried on in vessels belonging to the United States.

Owing to the exceeding dullness of trade at present importations have nearly entirely ceased. I remain with respect Y[ou]r Ob[edien]t S[ervan]t, Rich[ar]d H. Belt.

ALS (No. 4) with Ens in DNA, RG 59 (State Department), Consular Despatches, Matamoros, vol. 4 (M-281:2), received 8/12.

To EDWARD EVERETT, [London]

Department of State
Washington, 5th July, 1844

Sir: I have the honor to acknowledge the receipt of your despatches to No. 147, inclusive.

The President [John Tyler] is perfectly satisfied with the manner in which you have presented the case of the American vessel "Washington," seized by British Colonial Authorities for having been found fishing within the Bay of Fundy, and with the argument on the main question contained in your note to the Earl of Aberdeen of the 25th of May last, involving the interpretation to be given to the provisions of the Convention of 1818.

The case of the "Rebecca," an American vessel captured on the coast of Africa in 1816, mentioned in your despatch No. 132, has been duly examined, and after a careful consideration of the facts of the case, so far as they have been obtained, and of the papers connected with it, the Department agrees with you in opinion that Captain [Jonathan] Brown, in accepting the compromise with the captors in 1818, has waived whatever claim he may have had against the British Government. It will, therefore, be unnecessary to take any further steps in the prosecution of this case.

With reference to your despatch No. 134, acquainting me with the favorable reception given by the British Government to your recent application for the pardon of certain American prisoners [from the Canadian insurrection] in the British Penal Colonies, I have to state that the President is much gratified with the promptitude and liberality evinced by Her Britannic Majesty in extending pardon to the misguided individuals in behalf of whom your several applications have been made. The suggestion in the latter part of the same letter, relative to the expediency of making some provision for the assistance of such of the released prisoners as may return to the United States via London, is one in which I would cheerfully concur, were the means of carrying it into effect within the control of the Department. The appropriations of funds from which all its disbursements are made, as well as that expended under the immediate direction of the President, are specific in their character, and cannot legitimately be diverted from the objects to which they were intended to be applied. If an advance were made from any of these funds—(as for instance that for the Relief and protection of distressed American Seamen, to which it is likely Consul [Thomas] Aspinwall will charge the allowance which you have advised him to extend to Dresser and Wright,)—the Accounting Officer of the Treasury would not pass the account, and the officer making the advance, would probably only be able to obtain a reimbursement of the amount, by applying to Congress. Whilst, therefore, the Department fully appreciates the humane and laudable motives which have prompted your conduct on the occasion, it regrets that it is not within its power to avail itself of your suggestion.

I send to you, herewith, copies of the two despatches (No. 76 and 79,) which have failed to reach you. The former is intended merely to complete your file—the directions contained in the latter are still operative. I am, Sir, respectfully, Your obedient servant, J.C. Calhoun.

LS (No. 97) in DNA, RG 84 (Foreign Posts), Great Britain, Instructions, 8:302–307, received 7/30; FC in DNA, RG 59 (State Department), Diplomatic Instructions, Great Britain, 15:202–204 (M-77:74). NOTE: The case of the ship *Rebecca* had been the subject of considerable correspondence not included in this publication between Calhoun and F.G. Cameron of New York City.

To G[ardiner] G. and S[amuel S.] Howland and Others, New York [City]

Department of State
Washington, 5th July 1844

Gentlemen, I have to acknowledge the receipt of your letter of the 1st Instant adverting to the failure of the Mexican government to pay the last instalment due to claimants under the Convention of the 30th January 1843, and requesting that measures may be adopted towards requiring from that government a prompt fulfilment of its contract. In reply I have to inform you that the Minister of the United States [Wilson Shannon] who has just set out for that Country has been amply instructed upon the subject. I am, Gentlemen, Your Obedient Servant, John C. Calhoun.

FC in DNA, RG 59 (State Department), Domestic Letters, 34:283 (M-40:32). NOTE: The other addressees were John Jacob Astor and Peter Harmony.

From D[aniel] Jenifer, [U.S. Minister to Austria], Vienna, 7/5. "A Courier from the British Embassy intending to leave this [city] for London in a day or two, I avail myself of the opportunity to forward statements of the value of Imports and Exports of the Austrian Empire from 1831 to 1840 inclusive, with remarks relating to the internal resources, industry and general condition of the Empire as connected with foreign Governments and its own Provinces. Also a comparative view of the Tariff laws of Austria and the States of the Zoll Verein, by which it will be seen that, with a much lower rate of duty upon Imports, the internal condition of the latter has rapidly improved and the revenues increased whilst the former has made but slow advances in either." Jenifer appended a 38-page "statement" containing statistical tables and commentaries upon the economy of the Austrian Empire. He also enclosed a printed circular and an English-language translation of it, concerning import and export duties of the Austrian Empire. LS (No. 23) with Ens in DNA, RG 59 (State Department), Diplomatic Despatches, Austria, vol. 1 (T-157:1, frames 261–283), received 9/3.

Louis Mark, "care of Gerding & Kunkelman," New York [City], to Francis Markoe, Jr., State Department, 7/5. Mark acknowledges Markoe's letter of 7/2 and hopes that his second bond recently transmitted will be accepted as proof of his worthiness to fill the office of U.S. Consul to Bavaria and the Prussian Rhine provinces. Although the offices are not financially rewarding, he would hate to lose them. He reminds Markoe of his assistance in negotiating the proposed U.S. treaty with the countries of the Zollverein and believes that [Henry] Wheaton's opinion of Mark should be accepted. Mark hopes that [Richard K.] Crallé's health has improved. Mark was delighted recently to hear of Markoe's probable promotion. ALS in DNA, RG 59 (State Department), Consular Despatches, Vienna, vol. 1 (T-243:1).

From W[ILLIA]M S. FLANAGAN, "Private"

Skaneateles, Onondaga Co[unty,] N.Y.
July 6, 1844

D[ea]r Sir, No earthly power can prevent the Election of Mr. [Henry] Clay. The people owe him a debt & they will discharge it by making him President. The State of New York will give a larger Majority for him than they did for Gen[era]l [William Henry] Harrison. Polk men may tell you that this State will go for [James K.] Polk—believe them not for it is not so. The writer of this knows you well publicly & has seen you at Washington—is your friend and hopes & desires that you will take Such a course towards Mr. Clay, that Mr. Clay[']s friends can after his 4 Y[ea]rs are out bring you forw[ar]d as their Candidate. You have many & Strong friends Scattered over this State who in due time will give you your Station in this republic. You killed off that old Pest [Martin] Van Buren. A man like yourself or Mr. Clay cannot be Politically killed. Your acceptance under John Tyler of office has hurt you Some—it is no honor for any man to take office under a traitor.

Your Station will not allow you to understand things as they are. I charge nothing for this. You may profit by it or you may not—as you please. Truly yours, Wm. S. Flanagan.

ALS in ScCleA.

To [ALBERT JOSEPH GOBLET], Minister of Foreign Affairs of Belgium

Department of State
Washington, 6th July, 1844

Sir: The President having thought proper to permit Henry W. Hilliard, who has for some time resided near the Government of Belgium, in the character of Chargé d'Affaires of the United States, to return to his country, I have directed him to take leave of Your Excellency, and to avail himself of the opportunity which will thus be afforded him, to repeat to you the assurances of the friendly sentiments entertained by the President towards the Government of Belgium, and of his desire to preserve and improve the relations of harmony and good understanding now so happily subsisting between the two Countries.

I avail myself, with pleasure, of this occasion, to offer to Your

Excellency assurances of my high and distinguished consideration. (Signed) J.C. Calhoun.

FC in DNA, RG 84 (Foreign Posts), Belgium, Instructions, 1:267.

To Charles Graebe, [Cassel], 7/6. Graebe is informed that he has been appointed U.S. Consul for Hanover and Hesse Darmstadt. [He was already Consul for "Hesse Cassel."] FC in DNA, RG 59 (State Department), Consular Instructions, 10:254.

From G.S. Oldfield and H.N.[?] Tucker, Baltimore, 7/6. These two merchants and shipowners recommend Joseph A. Scoville of New York for appointment as U.S. Consul at Marseilles if that position should become vacant. "Mr. Scoville has been for many years engaged in Mercantile Business and possesses general Commercial Information amply qualifying him to fulfil the duties of the Office with credit to himself and advantageously for the Country." LS in DNA, RG 59 (State Department), Applications and Recommendations, 1837–1845, Scoville (M-687:29, frames 572–573).

To [ALFRED] S[C]HÜCKING, [Washington]

State Dept., 6th July 1844

D[ea]r Sir, The testimonials, in reference to your character & standing, & and [sic] that of your family accompanying your note of the 25th June, are very satisfactory.

I regret that the place you hold is so unequal to your merit & qualifications; and hope an opportunity may offer to place you in a more eligible situation.

The small sum I advanced to you, & which you returned in your note of the 1st Inst. put me to no inconvenience, and I did not expect you to return it, unless it was perfectly convenient to you. With great respect I am & &, J.C. Calhoun.

[P.S.] I return the testimonials.

ALS in RNR.

From John Southgate, Norfolk, Va., 7/6. He asks for information about the present status of an award to the late Joseph Seaward by the government of Colombia. ALS in DNA, RG 59 (State Department), Miscellaneous Letters (M-179:105, frames 18–19).

From L[ewis] Warrington "for the Sec[retar]y of the Navy," 7/6. He acknowledges Calhoun's letter of 6/29 concerning the claim of William Musser & Co. for 600 kegs of gunpowder "converted to its own use by the Government of Monte Video." In response he encloses two documents [an order of 1/24/1844 from the Navy Department to Commodore Daniel Turner to enquire into the matter, and Turner's reply of 4/16, stating that he would do so in a few weeks]. LS with Ens in DNA, RG 59 (State Department), Miscellaneous Letters (M-179:105, frames 13–15); FC in DNA, RG 45 (Naval Records), Letters Sent by the Secretary of the Navy to the President and Executive Agencies, 1821–1886, 5:2 (M-472:3, frame 43).

From W[ILLIA]M WILKINS, [Secretary of War]

[Washington, July 6, 1844]

The camp equipage and rockets will be supplied.

The necessary transportation will also be furnished. Of the propriety of this order I am not very well satisfied. I make it in accordance with the request of the Sec[retar]y of State, and for the purpose of avoiding delay under the impression that it may give aid in the work of demarkation of the [Northeastern] Boundary Line.

This order is to go no further than to allow the transportation to Hancock Barracks, ["or" *interlined*] the place, ["it is presumed," *canceled*] where the party engaged upon the work will assemble.

I make the order now a special one, because, in strictness, I am under the impression that the Transportation should be charged to the *specific civil* appropriation and not to the appropriation for the Q[uarte]r Master department. Wm. Wilkins.

ALS in DNA, RG 92 (Quartermaster General), Consolidated Correspondence File, Boundary, Northeast Survey. NOTE: This letter is a reply to and is written on Calhoun's letter of 6/17 to Wilkins. A lengthy endorsement of 7/6 by Winfield Scott declares that the two Lieutenants requested from the Topographical Engineers cannot be furnished, but he offers to supply 2nd Lieutenants if the difference in compensation can be "made up to the officers of the line." He refers the request for rockets, transportation and subsistence to the Army departments involved. Another endorsement on 7/6 from Th[omas] S. Jesup, Quartermaster General, reads "It is for the executive to decide whether the military appropriations can be applied to a service entirely civil. If transportation & camp equipage be furnished by the quarter masters department the regulations must govern as to the amount or quantity; but neither can be allowed without the order of the Sec[retar]y of War."

From JOHN B. WILLIAMS

[Washington, July *ca.* 6, 1844]

Sir: I have the honor to apprize you that it is generally rumoured, that, the English are casting a longing eye, and in addition the French, on the Fegee Islands, and other Islands east, and west of them; with the intention of Colonizing them. A Colonial paper in a recent publication, represents the Fegee's in most glowing Colors. Their inordinate desire for grasping being prevalent in the long continued extasy of eulogies, and superabundant adaptation of these Islands, which are mentioned as growing spontaneous; such ["products" *interlined*] as Coffee, Cotton, Sugar Cane, and many other luxuries.

Were the English to assume the Government of these Islands, it would directly and materially interfere with the American Commerce, which is very extensive, and spreading in extent—rapidly; and is attended with great profit; and subsequently would result as a great resource to the United States.

Were the nations mutually to unite to this effect; that neither should usurp their national rights of Government over any of the South Sea Islands, the subsequent results would necessarily prove far more advantageous to each as a nation, than for either seperat[e]ly to posses[s] the Government reins.

The English for some time have had a strong desire for levying national Claims on the Fegees, and Islands to the east and west of the group.

The interest of the American merchants are most intimately and extensively connected with the freedom of these Islands.

The United States, could not bestow a more liberal act on their people in the South Seas, than the frequent visits of Ships of War, among the Islands; more especially to the Fegees, and the Islands east and west of them, for the protection of our Commerce and Flag, which is not unfrequently prostituted by unprincipled Foreigners, as well as our own Citizens, to cover a wicked and immoral trade; mercenarily, and strictly forbidden by the principles of philanthropy.

Our vessels are not unfrequently beholden to the naval forces of other nations, on that Station for propugnation and Shield; whilst cruising and trading among those obdurate and androphagus people. Unprincipled Europeans, and I regret to add some of my own Countrymen adequate in their vicious propensities, sowing seeds of discord amongst the natives, thereby impeding our Commerce in their progress of trade with them. Frequent complaints have been made to me, through letters and otherwise.

The natives in their primitive simplicity are easily seduced. I have the honor to be Sir Your most Obedient Servant, John B. Williams.

ALS in DNA, RG 59 (State Department), Consular Despatches, Bay of Islands and Auckland, New Zealand, vol. 1 (T-49:1).

From ROBERT B. CAMPBELL

Consulate of the United States of America, Havana
July 7th 1844

Sir, I have the honor to acknowledge the receipt on yesterday, of your Official communication of the 20th of May last enclosing a communication from the Hon. W[illiam] B. Calhoun [Representative from Mass.] in relation to the arrest and imprisonment of Mr. Henry J. Cavalier, also the communication of the Hon. H.Y. Cranstoun [*sic*; Henry Y. Cranston, Representative from R.I.] and others relative to the imprisonment and treatment of Mr. Bisbey [*sic*; William Bisby]; to which subjects and all of a similar character my attention is directed by the Department of State.

Mr. Cavalier, in whose behalf Mr. W.B. Calhoun addresses the department has not ["been" *interlined*] mentioned by me to the Dept. as his case required no comment. He was arrested, detained a short time, and gave bail for his appearance when called for and released. This information is derived from others than Mr. Cavalier, as he made no application to this Consulate. Mr. Bisbey whose case has already been the subject of a communication from the State Department to this Consulate, and of a correspondence between myself and the Executive of this Island (which correspondence has been forwarded to you at Washington accompanied by a communication from me) is now in Matanzas under the eyes of the Consul at Matanzas awaiting his trial, which I fear cannot be accelerated. Tis true I am personally acquainted with the President of the Military tribunal in Matanzas, but I presume Mr. [Thomas M.] Rodney [the U.S. Consul there] is equally so, and doubtless being on the Spot will have it more in his power to aid and assist him, than I can have at this distance, his efforts will be aided by Capt[ai]n [W.H.] Gardner of the U.S. Brig Lawrence now in this Port, who at my request is on the eve of departure for Matanzas to cooperate ["to cooperate" *canceled*] with the Consul in his exertions in behalf of any Americans who may be in prison. Fortunately for all parties in the limits of this Consulate, the Government has shewn every disposition to conciliate & even grant demands which have been made doubtingly. I have felt all the delicacy of my situation, requiring me to interfere in the execution of established laws for the internal police of the Island, at a time of occupying an official station which in the opinion of Mr. [Henry] Wheaton and perhaps of this Gov[erno]r; only entitles me to the privileges of a Commercial Agent. I have received no such intimation but such has been the language held[?] to the Consul Gen[era]l of the British Government in relation to himself.

It is superfl[u]ous to say that I shall at all times do all in my power to carry out the wishes of the Dept. and aid our resident Citizens.

By the British steamer arrived this day from Vera Cruz, I have received authentic and undoubted information that the Mexican Congress have voted an army of thirty thousand men, and four million of dollars at the request of the President for the invasion of Texas. Notwithstanding this appropriation, and encreased army it is not believed that Santa Anna seriously contemplates such an invasion, but only designs firmly and permanently to establish his power. The Steamer also brings intelligence that the attempted invasion of Tabasco by [Francisco] Sentmanat from N. Orleans has ended in the arrest & execution of himself and thirteen of his followers a portion of whom were Americans. I have the honor to be Y[ou]r Mo[st] Ob[edien]t S[ervan]t, Robert B. Campbell.

ALS in DNA, RG 59 (State Department), Consular Despatches, Havana, vol. 19 (T-20:19), received 7/24.

From SHEPARD CARY, [Representative from Maine]

Houlton (Maine), July 7th 1844

The interest that myself and other citizens of this portion of the State have in the surrender of the bonds and monies in the possession of the Government of the Province of New Brunswick, denominated the "Disputed territory fund" induces me to trouble you again upon that Subject.

You will perceive by reference to the Treaty of Washington that it is agreed by the contracting parties, that the Government of New Brunswick shall pay over to the Gover[n]ment of the United States for the benefit of Maine and Massachusetts, all monies and deliver ["up" *interlined*] all bonds in the possession of the Gover[n]ment of New Brunswick within six months after the ratification of the Treaty, which stipulation has not been complied with and *will not* be complied with, unless the British Minister directs the latter Government to do so, for the reason, that the monies have been squandered, and it is not the intention of that Government to account for them or pay them over if ["they" *canceled and* "it" *interlined*] can by any means avoid it.

The greater portion of the monies & bonds that constitute said fund, was abstracted from individuals without the form of law, the circumstances connected with which are in substance as follows. I, with others, obtained permits from the States of Maine & Massachusetts to cut timber upon lands owned by said States lying upon the waters of the Aroostook river and Massachusetts & Maine were paid for the timber so cut, which timber if *cut upon American territory* was free from duty or tax by the laws of Great Britian [*sic*] on going into the British Province of New Brunswick. But for sake of plundering us, New Brunswick laid claim to the ownership of the lands upon which we had cut the timber, seized it and would not relinquish their claim to it, unless we would give bonds to them, to pay One dollar and sixty cents per ton duty, which bonds we allowed to have put in suit and resisted the payment of, upon the ground that the timber was cut upon the territory of Maine & Massachusetts. After contending against the payment of the bonds from one to two years, at great expense and vexation, we compounded by paying forty cents per ton with interest and costs of prosecution, the Provincial Government agreeing to recommend to the Home Government to have the bonds delivered up; since which we have not been able to get up our bonds, or get from the Government of New Brunswick any satisfaction upon that subject. Many of the parties to those bonds were compelled to deposit the amounts thereof in money with individuals residing in New Brunswick who became sureties with them, and cannot withdraw the money so deposited, until the bonds can be got up and the sureties thereby released.

The Government of New Brunswick has never ["rendered" *inter-*

lined] a *correct* account to the Government of the United States, of the monies belonging to said fund, and does not intend to turn over to our Government those bonds on which they have collected twenty five per cent, as such a step would shew the falsity of ["the account" *interlined*] they have rendered.

I had a conversation with one of the Executive Council of New Brunswick last fall, in relation to the bonds and was informed by him, that the United States had not appointed an agent to demand the surrender of the bonds and that they would remain in the possession of their Government until a demand was made.

Now if it can be so arranged with the British Minister, that I can be appointed an agent to demand the surrender of the bonds and monies, ["and" *canceled and* "or" *interlined*] an account of the monies appertaining to that fund, accompanied by a request from the British Minister to the Governor of New Brunswick, to pay them over to me, we may obtain them, but unless some one is so empowered who is conversant with all the transactions, we shall have endless trouble and vexation in obtaining what has been unjustly withheld from us.

Hoping that this subject will receive your favorable consideration, allow me to subscribe myself with the highest respect & consideration Y[ou]r Very Ob[e]d[ient] Serv[an]t, Shepard Cary.

ALS in DNA, RG 76 (Records of Boundary and Claims Commissions and Arbitrations), Letters and Miscellaneous Documents Relating to the Maine-New Brunswick Boundary Dispute, 1824–1850, no. 300.

From Stewart Newell

United States Consulate
Sabine, Texas
July 7th 1844

Sir, In my No. 18 I had occasion to call your attention, to continued acts of Gen[era]l [William S.] Murphy towards me, and enclosed a number of Documents, as testimony of the manner, in which I have allways endeavoured, to discharge my duty, and have never heard of any complaint being made, until Gen[era]l Murphy opened the War upon me and has been the instigator of the Affidavits published, and to refute which, I refer the Department, to the documents forwarded, and which I beg leave may be permitted, to be placed on File.

Gen[era]l Murphy, continues to display The Flag of the Legation, and to Wear an Official dress, on all occassions that offers, and to inform the Public, of his being still the Minister of the U.S. until his successor arrives. Under the Influence which such appearances, and statements, give to his acts, Gen[era]l Murphy continues to injure the Consul of the Port of Galveston [Archibald M. Green], and myself, by misrepresentations of the worst Character, among which, he, stated a few days since, that Mr. Green, and myself, were leagued together, to defraud the Owners of the Steam Boats "Scioto Belle," and "Col. Woods," out of their Property, and appropriate the same, to our own use.

That I was appointed *Vice Consul*, by Green, and for that purpose, and that I, only held my Commission, so long as Mr. Green thought proper, and was not Appointed by the President.

The Department will readily perceive, the extent of Mischief, that would arise, under such statements by the Chargé, had he, been continued, and I could have done no less, than ask an investigation, into the whole matter, but I presume, the Rejection & Recall, of Gen[era]l Murphy, does not now, permit such a course. He, has endeavoured to injure me, in private and in Public, but cannot do so, with those who know me. Should however, any of his Reports have reached the Department, relative to me, I trust the Department, will not give them more weight, than entitled to, and which the Wilful perjuries of [James J.] Wright, and [James W.] Wood, referr[e]d to, instigated by Gen[era]l Murphy, will show, to what extent, he, Murphy will go, to ruin others, and sacrifice them, *to his*, private revenge.

I beg leave to inform the Department, that J.J. Wright, is now in New Orleans (as informed from good authority,) furnished with means, from this place, by Two persons from the U. States, to purchase a Suitable vessel, to engage in some illicit Trade, either Smuggling, or to be occupied in introducing Slaves, from the W. Indies, into Louisiana, and Texas, and that said Wright, Cleared the Steamer Scioto Belle, on or about the 7th day of Feb[ruar]y 1844, with a false Manifest, and bound for, and arrived and entered in a Texian Port, and that said Wright, in my opinion, has been guilty of the Crime of Perjury, in having made an Oath, to the same, at time of Clearance from New Orleans, knowing the same, to be a false Manifest.

Also, that said Wright knowingly and Wilfully, made Oath before me, of the genuineness, and correctness, of a Book purporting to be the Log Book, of said vessel, but which, by Affidavits of E[dward] Jones, and Peter D. Stockholm, forwarded with *No. 18*, to the Department, will show, was known to said Wright, to be untrue.

Under instructions contained in Letter dated May 1st, from Department, I have reported James Wood, and have felt it my duty, to do the same, as to Wright.

James Wood I am informed, is now on his way to Wheeling Va. where he is to meet his family, having left Texas a few days since. I have the honor to be most Respectfully Your Ob[edien]t Servant, Stewart Newell.

ALS (No. 19) in DNA, RG 59 (State Department), Consular Despatches, Texas, vol. 1 (T-153:1), received 7/20. NOTE: An AEI by R[obert] S. C[hew], Clerk in the Consular Bureau, reads: "Certificate enclosed relative to J.J. Wright having cleared the Steamer Scioto Belle under false manifest &c, sent to U.S. Dist[rict] Att[orne]y N. Orleans July 26th 1844."

From F[RANCIS] M. DIMOND

United States Consulate
Vera Cruz, July 8th 1844
Sir, I have the honour herewith to transmit the Returns for this Consulate up to the 30th June 1844, which I hope will be found correct.

Accompanying my last respects I had the honour to enclose parts of Seven Registers of vessels sold at this port the last year and I have now the honour to transmit the other Seven halves.

We have had no arrivals from the United States for the last month. All appear to look anxiously for the fate of the Treaty in the Senate of the U. States. I have the honour to be Sir most Respectfully Your Ob[edient] Servant, F.M. Dimond.

ALS (No. 229) with Ens in DNA, RG 59 (State Department), Consular Despatches, Veracruz, vol. 5 (M-183:5), received 7/31.

To Theophilus Fisk, Portsmouth, Va., 7/8. "It is the President's [John Tyler's] wish that you should repair to Washington without delay, for the purpose of taking charge of important despatches for Europe, of which you will be made the bearer." FC in DNA, RG 59 (State Department), Diplomatic Instructions, Germany, 14: 84 (M-77:65).

From DENIS GAHAGAN

New York [City,] July 8th 1844

Sir, The undersigned respectfully desires to call the attention of the Hon[orab]l[e] the Sec[retary] of State to the following statement, in the view that it may call for some action of the part of his Government, to indemnify the undersigned, for losses sustained in the sale of $8,850, United States Treasury Certificates under Mexican Convention.

The undersigned was compelled to sell above am[oun]ts of certificates for a sum less than $1600, under the following circumstances. He rec[eive]d an award of $12,042, 25th Feb. 1842, from the Umpire under the commission with Mexico receiving from his attorney the late F[rancis] S[cott] Key, $9,600 in above mentioned certificates, the sum due after deducting expences &c. After trying the two best markets in the United States for the sale of these securities, and holding on to them as long as possible, the above mentioned sale was made, as the certificates were made negociable by the United States, and issued in a form to make them in a measure valueless to the claimant, and previous to the last arrang[ement] with Mexico, whereby they are now being paid in installments of cash.

The undersigned or the public could have had no knowledge of the value the United States and Mexico chose to place by their last arraingement upon these securities, as the wording of them precluded the idea.

The undersigned regrets that the same value was not stamped upon the face of these securities, when he received them, as was given them in the construction that the Hon[orab]l[e] Dan[ie]l Webster placed upon the Treaty under which they were issued, in his Official Letter of 26 July 1842 to the Hon[orab]l[e] Sec[retary] of the Treasury, giving instructions in regard to the payment of the Mexican indemnity.

The undersigned is therefore again Compelled to become a petitioner to his Government for redress after he had before waited Ten Years for Justace and then not realize a sum for his losses and privations in Mexico sufficient to pay the expences and trouble of his original Claim.

The undersigned beleives that in appealing to his Government through the present Head of the department of State, he will be entertained with such advice as may be beneficial to him, or informed if a Claim founded upon above considerations would be prosecuted against Mexico. The undersigned has the honour to be Very Respectfully Your Ob[edien]t Ser[van]t, Denis Gahagan, 80 Wall St., New York.

ALS in DNA, RG 59 (State Department), Miscellaneous Letters (M-179:105, frames 19–21).

From WILLIAM B. GOOCH

East Baldwin, Me., July 8th 1844

Sir, I arrived in Boston on the 1st inst. and should have immediately visited Washington, but receiving a letter that my family were sick, I deemed it important for me to return home without delay. Since my arrival, I have been unable to write on account of my own illness until this morning.

In my last letter to the Department of State, I informed you that it was important for me to return to the United States, & that I had requested Captain [Thomas W.] Freelon of the U.S. Ship Preble, to appoint some suitable person to supply my place until an appointment should be made by Government, deeming it of the utmost importance that we should have some capable person to represent our commercial interests at Aux Cayes, in this unsettled state of the Island [of Haiti]. Dr. [Richmond] Loring an American Gentleman, was selected by Captain Freelon as the best qualified among the few Americans at Aux Cayes, for the office.

I appointed Dr. Loring Vice Comm[ercia]l Agent during my absence a few months last year, & on my return, found my accounts in so unsatisfactory a state that I thought I could not again trust him with the Agency, should I wish to be absent, or recommend him as capable to discharge the duties of the office; but in this unsettled state of the place & his being well acquainted with the Creole dialect and of a fearless character, & particularly, as he will have a Clerk to keep the Books of the Agency, (being qualified in other respects;) my views are in accordance with Captain Freelon[']s, & it is no object for any person in this Country to receive the appointment, as the emoluments of the office will but little more than pay the expenses of a single person without a family.

I feel under deep obligations for the confidence reposed in me by my Government & I trust that confidence has not been abused, & if I have the same assurance from the Department that I have received from shipmasters who have visited the port where I have been located, & more especially of the merchants since my return, I shall feel amply compensated for all my labours & the many privations I have had to suffer, from the Island being in a state of revolution for the past two years, & my exertions have been perhaps, as great, or greater, for the protection of my countrymen & their property during this time, than almost any other Consular Agent of the U.S.

The health of my family requires that I should remain with them for the present, & [I] must request to be discharged from serving my government any longer as Comm[ercia]l Agent at the port of Aux Cayes, having been assured by the merchants at Boston & New York that if I should I [sic] again have to leave on account of my health, the services I have already rendered the commercial interests of my Countrymen, will be favourably noticed by Government. I wish to have my Bond in possession of Government (if my conduct has been satisfactory;) returned, if it is the usual practice. I am my dear Sir, with high regards your obedient and devoted Servant, William B. Gooch.

ALS in DNA, RG 59 (State Department), Consular Despatches, Aux Cayes, vol. 2 (T-330:2).

From A[RCHIBALD] M. GREEN

Consulate of the U. States of America
at Galvezton, Republic of Texas
8th July 1844

Sir, I have the honor to acknowledge the recei[p]t of yours of the 20th June which informs me that my several letters, to No. 37 inclusive have been received.

My application for a leave of absence this summer, made to the Department, through the medium of Mr. Thomas Green, having been granted me; but at the same time being informed, through the same source, that it was the wish of the Department, that I should remain at my post until the arrival of Gen[era]l [Tilghman A.] Howard, Ch[arg]e d'Affaires to Texas ["should arrive" *canceled*].

I have concluded to remain should Gen[era]l [William S.] Murphy leave for the United States—And think proper to leave the books and papers of the Legation in my charge, without an order to that effect—notwithstanding my great desire to be with my family this summer.

On the evening of the 5th Inst. Gen[era]l Murphy was taken very sick and is now confined to his bed.

By this mail I send to the Department the *Civilian* of the *Third* (3) and 6th July and the Evening *News* of the sixth—containing articles which I beg leave to call ["the" *canceled*] to your notice. I have the honor to be very Respectfully Y[ou]r Ob[edien]t S[ervan]t, A.M. Green, Consul U. States.

ALS (No. 42) in DNA, RG 59 (State Department), Consular Despatches, Galveston, vol. 2 (T-151:2), received 7/20.

From Rob[er]t Monroe Harrison

United States Consulate
Kingston, Jamaica, 8th July 1844
Sir, I do myself the honor to inform you that I a few days past addressed a letter to His Excellency [James Bruce] Lord Elgin the Governor, informing him that *Six Seamen* had deserted from the "United States" Ship "Preble" at "Aux Cayes" [Haiti] with the Launch, a number of Muskets, ammunition, and sundry other articles.

And as it was supposed ["they" *altered to* "that"] they could or have already landed on the East part of this Island, I requested his Excellency to be good enough to instruct the Inspector Gen[era]l of Police, to direct his subordinates in the Out Ports to be on the "Qui Vive" to arrest them, should they make their appearance.

Herewith I have the honor to enclose you His Lordship[']s answer [of 7/6], and as my requisition was perfectly simple, and in which I was fully borne out in making, according to the Laws and usages of all nations; I am surprised beyond measure to find he could not take upon himself to decide at once, without refer[r]ing to H[er] M[aj]esty's] Attorney General as in the mean time, these men may arrive and get away before that officer[']s opinion can be had.

From this procrastination on the part of His Excellency I have every reason to believe, that difficulties will be thrown in the way in securing the men in question should they come here. And as this is not likely to be the only instance of men deserting from "American" vessels of war and taking refuge here, it might be well if you would be pleased to instruct me as early as possible as to what cooperation or assistance I have a right to demand from the local authorities of this Colony.

I am myself by no means ignorant of the Courtesy due to my Government in these respects, but as an American Consul's opinion here, carry little weight, unless he can make a *grand display*, it is therefore not in my power to do much of a useful nature for my Country at any time, without some authority in writing from you. With profound respect I have the honor to be Sir Your Ob[edien]t and most humble Servant, Robt. Monroe Harrison.

P.S. The laws of nations on Existing Treaties, are not much read, or even known here by those, who ought to be conversant in such things. English law is all they care about which in their opinion, should predominate and take cognizance of all things either on land or sea, regardless of the flag of the nation under which crimes may be committed; they therefore usurp to themselves what the *"Romans"* were want [*sic*] to do in their best days, and have only to say, *I am an Englishman*! ! !

Please to give Course to the letter to Gen[era]l [James] Semple [Senator from Ill.], as I do not know his address. R.M.H.

LS (No. 294) with En in DNA, RG 59 (State Department), Consular Despatches, Kingston, Jamaica, vol. 9 (T-31:9), received 8/10. NOTE: A State Dept. Clerk's EU reads "Nothing to be done 'till Mr. Harrison is again heard from."

From CHRISTOPHER HUGHES, "Private"

The Hague; 8th July 1844

My dear Sir, I have been applied to by one of my Friends & Colleagues—the Minister of Hanover—at this Court—to assist him in having certain papers legalised at Philadelphia; and I take the liberty of putting my letter to Mr. J[oseph] R. Ingersoll, under cover to you, for greater security, as it contains the original Document.

I shall be greatly obliged to you, if you will have my letter forwarded to Mr. Ingersoll, and[?] *franked*; & I pray you, my dear Sir, to excuse the liberty I take and the trouble I give you.

I have nothing whatever, of any sort of public interest, to communicate to you! Every thing is peaceful and prosperous in this country; and as far as *we* are concerned, every thing is perfectly conciliatory & satisfactory. In this quiet & comfortable state of things I can see no sort of use, or object, in importuning you with long & pointless Despatches.

My Friend, Mr. J.R. Ingersoll writes me—on 27th May—informing me of the prompt & amiable manner, in which, you had acquiesced in the understanding, that I might make a short visit to the U. States— on my private affairs. I need not say, how sincerely obliged, I feel to you, my dear Sir; and how grateful I am to the President [John Tyler], for this renewed proof of his kind & friendly disposition to- wards me; which, in fact, is only a continuation—on the part of Mr. Tyler, of the most friendly & flattering sentiments of kindness & ac- commodation, whenever & wherever, my wishes & my interests have been concerned—since the day—on which—I had the honour to make his personal acquaintance! And I beseech you, my dear Sir—to as- sure the President of my very grateful sense of his *uniform* kindness to me. I am sure, he will believe in the sincerity of my thanks, & accept them, in the same spirit of kind feeling, in which, I respectfully give them. Nor are my thanks the less sincere, and the less cordial, from the fact of my having given up all intention of visiting the United States, this year; of which change in my plans, I think it proper, to advise you & the President. I am, my dear Sir, most re- spectfully, your faithful servant, Christopher Hughes.

ALS in ScCleA.

To Richmond Loring, Aux Cayes, 7/8. Calhoun sends Loring his appointment as U.S. Commercial Agent and encloses documents re- lated to the office. FC in DNA, RG 59 (State Department), Con- sular Instructions, 11:252.

Francis Markoe, Jr., [State Department], to [Louis Mark, New York City], 7/8. "I rec[eive]d today y[ou]r letter of the 5th inst. and placed it in the hands of the Secretary of State, who remarked that the bond wh[ich] was returned to you had nothing to do with the matter ["in question" *interlined*], the true issue between you & the Govt. being upon the former bond, which purports to be signed by a respectable firm in New York, which firm declare they did not sign it, ["or sanction it in any manner" *canceled*], & were indeed en- tirely ignorant of its existence. The Secretary of State submitted, y[ou]r letter to me to the President [John Tyler], who willing to give you every opportunity to vindicate y[ou]r character, has al- lowed you for that purpose till the 15th prox[im]o at wh[ich] period, if the required explanations shall not, have been rec[eive]d, & prove satisfactory you will be dismissed ["from office" *interlined*]. With this indulgence the Secretary, will of course expect you not to leave the U. States, until your difficulties ["with the Govt. are" *interlined and* "are" *canceled*] settled ["one way or another" *canceled*]." Rough draft in DNA RG 59 (State Department), Consular Instructions, Vienna, vol. 1 (T-243:1).

To William Musser & Co., Philadelphia, 7/8. He acknowledges their letter of 6/26 concerning a claim against the government at Montevideo. The latest information is that Commodore [Daniel] Turner wrote the Navy Department on 4/16 that he would attend to the claim soon. FC in DNA, RG 59 (State Department), Domestic Letters, 34:286–287 (M-40:32).

From JOHN NELSON

Attorney General's Office, 8th July 1844
Sir, The Treaty with France providing for the surrender of persons accused of the crimes therein enumerated, and fleeing within the jurisdictions of the United States and France respectively, prescribes as well the mode and manner, as the evidence upon which such surrender shall be made.

The mode and manner prescribed is:

"Requisitions made in the name of the respective parties through the medium of their respective Diplomatic Agents."

The evidence upon which it is to be done is:

"Only when the fact of the commission of the crime shall be so established, as that the laws of the country in which the fugitive or the person so accused shall be found, would justify his or her apprehension, and commitment for trial if the crime had been there committed."

With reference to the mode and manner to be pursued, as preliminary to the surrender, there can be no difficulty. The Treaty is explicit on the subject, and the suggestion contained in Mr. [Alphonse] Pageot's note [of 6/28] is accurately conformed to it.

In regard to the degree of evidence, which may be required to establish the fact of the commission of the crime, of which the person demanded may be accused, there is much difficulty. No rule more explicit or certain than that contained in the Treaty itself can indeed be prescribed. Cases as they occur, will necessarily depend upon the laws of the several States in which the fugitive may be arrested or found. That which may be sufficient to justify the apprehension and committement in one State, may not be regarded as sufficient in another. All that can be stipulated for therefore is, that in every case that may be presented to this Government, all proper and lawful means will be used to bring about the surrender demanded. In practice there will be found no difficulty, whilst an attempt to particularize might exclude the very means of redress most effectual to accomplish the object in the view of the contracting parties.

Upon principle, I do not think that a mere warrant for the arrest of an accused party, *without the evidence upon which it was granted,* would be sufficient to justify the imprisonment of a citizen.

A *Verdict* would—so also an Indictment and True Bill ought, I should think, to be regarded as *prima facie* evidence of guilt. But as I remarked before, this will depend on the law of the jurisdiction, in which the accused party may be found, and must be referred to the judgment of the United States officer, whose aid may be invoked in execution of the Treaty.

The provisions of the Treaty with England on this subject are more full, though substantially the same with those in the Treaty with the King of the French. To shew the liberal principles upon which that Treaty has been carried into execution, I beg leave to refer to my opinion, in the case of Christina Cochrane, a printed copy of which is enclosed.

In view of the whole subject, I am of opinion, that whilst the mode of making the demand may be stipulated and that suggested by Mr. Pageot is unexceptionable, it is impracticable to prescribe any rule of evidence more definite, than that contained in the Treaty itself. Its provisions can be effectuated only by a *bona fide* effort in every case to arrest and surrender the guilty accused. I have the honor to be Very respectfully Sir Your obedient Servant, Jno. Nelson.

LS in DNA, RG 59 (State Department), Miscellaneous Letters (M-179:105, frames 24–26); FC in DNA, RG 60 (Justice Department), Opinions of the Attorney General, F:189–190.

To [FRIEDRICH LUDWIG], Baron Von ROENNE, [Berlin]

Washington, 8th July 1844

My dear Sir, As much as I would have been gratified with your return to the United States, I take too deep an interest in whatever concerns you, not to congratulate you on the cause, which prevented it. I regard the appointment you hold [President of Department of Commerce], as a distinguished mark of the favour and confidence of your Souvereign. The office may be fairly considered as one among the most important at this highly commercial era, when the extension of its trade has become a prime object of policy with every civilized nation. Your commercial alliance is conclusive proof of the deep interest which the German States take in promoting and extending their trade.

I have long regarded a more intimate commercial and political connection between the United States and Germany, as of great importance to both. The Germans and their descendants constitute a very important element in our population. As great as it now is, it is destined to be much greater still, in consequence of the vast annual addition by emigration, to be accompanied by a strong and growing sympathy between the two countries.

I regard the Treaty negotiated by Mr. [Henry] Wheaton as the first step towards a more intimate Union and greatly regret the omission of the Senate to act finally on it, at the late Session. I hope, however, it will not involve the loss of the treaty. I cannot think, that it originated in any settled opposition to it. On the contrary, I am of the impression, it may be traced to causes of a temporary character, connected with the pending presidential election. No doubt the protective policy had some agency in it; but I do not think that of itself, so powerful as it is, would have been sufficient to delay the action of the Senate.

I highly appreciate the character and services of Mr. Wheaton. I have known him long, and would take much pleasure in meeting his wishes. The President [John Tyler] had made his selection [of William R. King] for the mission to Paris before I arrived at Washington.

I am much obliged to you for the opportunity of forming the acquaintance of Professor [Friedrich] von Raumer. I hope he will find his tour in the United States agreeable. I regret, that the time he has prescribed for his visit will be too short to afford him full opportunity to become acquainted with the country and its institutions.

Permit me, in conclusion, to say, that I reciprocate to the full your kind feelings, and place a very high value on your good opinion and friendship. I do not know whether the people will ever call on me to take the command of the Vessel of State; but if they should, I would feel it to be my duty to change the steerage in several important particulars. With the highest regard and esteem, yours truly, J.C. Calhoun.

Transcript by Professor Gunter Moltmann of an ALS in Deutsches Zentralarchiv, Historische Abteilung II, Merseburg, German Democratic Republic (the former Geheimes Staatsarchiv, Berlin), Rep. 92, Nachlass Friedrich Ludwig von Rönne, no. 3; PC in Gunter Moltmann, "Eine Deutschland-Korrespondenz John C. Calhouns aus dem Jahre 1844," in *Jahrbuch fur Amerikastudien*, vol. XIV (1969), pp. 164–165. NOTE: Calhoun addressed his letter to "Baron de Roenne." The letter appears to have been received on 9/18/1844.

From A[MBROSE] H. SEVIER, [Senator from Ark.]

Little Rock, July 8th 1844

Dear Sir, I have understood that Mr. [Grandison D.] Royston, the [U.S.] district attorney for Arkansas has resigned his office. This intelligence I did not receive until a day or two since.

I can recommend the appointment of Solon Borland, a gentleman of the highest respectability, and well qualified for the office. He resides in Little Rock, and has been recommended by many of our prominent friends. Do me the favour to attend to this immediately, and don[']t let the President [John Tyler] neglect it.

All things are going on well here. Your friend, A.H. Sevier.

ALS in DNA, RG 59 (State Department), Applications and Recommendations, 1837–1845, Borland (M-687:2, frames 705–706).

To CHARLES S. TODD, St. Petersburg

Department of State
Washington, 8th July, 1844

Dear Sir: I transmit to you, enclosed, an extract from a private letter [to me], dated 20th of June, last, just received from F.N. [*sic*; Franklin H.] Elmore, Esq[ui]re, of Charleston, South Carolina, who is desirous of obtaining, for practical purposes, certain information of the process now generally in use in Russia for separating gold from its ore. As answers in detail to the inquiries he prefers will probably prove useful, and indeed highly important to the mining interest in the Southern portion of the United States, where every day is developing new springs of mineral wealth, allow me to enlist your good offices in procuring, from the most authentic sources within your reach, the information sought for. It is possible this object may be attained by an informal application to Count [Karl Robert] Nesselrode; but, if not, you will adopt any other measures that may appear to you to promise success in its accomplishment. Of the result of your inquiries you will be pleased to apprize this Department. I am, Dear Sir, with great respect, Your obedient servant, J.C. Calhoun.

LS with En in DNA, RG 84 (Foreign Posts), Russia, Letters Received, vol. 4337; FC in DNA, RG 59 (State Department), Diplomatic Instructions, Russia, 14:65 (M-77:136); FC with En in DNA, RG 84 (Foreign Posts), Russia, Instructions, 4406:26–28.

To HENRY WHEATON, [Berlin]

Department of State
Washington, 8th July, 1844

Sir: I transmit to you with this despatch, ratified copies of two Conventions for the mutual abolition of the droit d'aubaine, and taxes on emigration, between the United States of America on the one part, and the Grand Duchy of Hesse, and the King of Würtemberg, respectively, on the other parts—the former concluded and signed by you at Berlin on the 26th of March, and the latter, on the tenth of April, of the present year, which have been approved and ratified by the President [John Tyler], by and with the advice and consent of the Senate of the United States.

Mr. Theophilus Fisk has been selected, on this occasion, as bearer of despatches to you, and will take charge of this despatch, and of the ratified copies of the Conventions referred to above, which he will be directed to proceed to Berlin, immediately, for the purpose of placing in your hands.

I transmit, at the same time, special powers from the President authorising you to make the exchange of the ratifications of these Conventions. The ratified copies to be received in exchange for those sent, herewith, will be brought home by Mr. Fisk, who, it is presumed, will not be detained for any length of time for that purpose. I am, Sir, Your obedient Servant, J.C. Calhoun.

LS (No. 58) in DNA, RG 84 (Foreign Posts), Germany, Instructions, 1:309–311; FC in DNA, RG 59 (State Department), Diplomatic Instructions, Germany, 14:83–84 (M-77:65).

From C.L. Coles, New York [City], 7/9. He states that Philip A. de Creny, U.S. Consul at St. Pierre, Martinique, is a person of low character, no education, and colored parents. De Creny allowed his name to be used by a citizen of Martinique in a fraudulent business buying products in the U.S. Many people suffered by this illegal activity. De Creny denies that his name was used with his permission, but he now partakes of the profits of the scheme and lives with his supposed former partner. Coles asks that de Creny be replaced. Several other people can testify to the correctness of this statement. ALS in DNA, RG 59 (State Department), Consular Despatches, St. Pierre, vol. 2 (T-431:2).

To Theophilus Fisk

Department of State
Washington, 9th July, 1844

Sir: The President has selected you as a bearer of despatches from this Department to Henry Wheaton, Esq[ui]re, the Minister of the United States, at Berlin. These despatches, and a large package containing important public papers, are to be delivered without delay, and you will, therefore, proceed, with them in your charge, to New York [City], and embark in the first or quickest conveyance for the nearest and most convenient port, on the route for your place of destination. Upon arrival at Berlin, you will immediately deliver to Mr. Wheaton the package committed to your care, and the despatches, and return to the United States by the first opportunity, unless detained a short time by him, bringing with you such letters and papers, as shall be entrusted to you by him.

Your compensation will be $6 a day from the time of your leaving this city until your return, and all your necessary travelling expenses actually incurred, of which you will keep a regular account, to be sustained by vouchers where they can be procured. This allowance must not be understood to include your expenses during your detention at Berlin. The sum of $500 will be advanced to you on account. I am, Sir, respectfully, Your obedient Servant, J.C. Calhoun.

FC in DNA, RG 59 (State Department), Diplomatic Instructions, Germany, 14:84–85 (M-77:65).

From J[ohn] W. Holding, Washington, 7/9. Based upon his conversations with officials in Bogota, New Granada, Holding proposes that the State Department issue instructions to its diplomatic representatives there to compromise in the case of the *Good Return* claims. Holding suggests that the New Granadan government honor the claims upon terms "Payable in gold; in 6, 7, 8 or more years, with Interest Semi Annually." ALS in DNA, RG 59 (State Department), Miscellaneous Letters (M-179:105, frames 26–28).

From C[harles] Morris, [Commodore, U.S. Navy], 7/9. "By a gentleman recently returned from the Paccific I learn, the French Government has made an agreement to have a vessel leave Callao on the 23d of each month, for Panama. These vessels return again to Callao, & persons seldom have to wait at Panama for a passage longer than ten or fifteen days. By remaining six or eight leagues from the city they are in a healthy situation." LS in DNA, RG 59 (State Department), Miscellaneous Letters (M-179:105, frame 28).

From JOHN NELSON

Attorney General's Office, 9th July 1844
Sir, The laws of the United States do not provide for the case upon which you have asked my opinion. The only Acts of Congress which relate at all to the subject of maintaining peace on our frontiers, are those of the 20th of April 1818, and of the 10th of March 1838, which are designed to guard against hostile invasions of the territories of powers with whom the United States are in amity.

The invasion of the Custom House in Texas by citizens of Arkansas, and the violent abstraction therefrom of property, under a claim of title, however much to be dis-approved and condemned, constitute under the laws of the United States no ground of claim against this Government.

The case may be regarded in two points of view: *First,* as governed and to be dealt with under our own laws; and *Secondly,* as controlled by the laws of the Republic of Texas. Under neither, do I think this Government can rightfully interpose.

First: under our own laws: The violence complained of was perpetrated by citizens of the State of Arkansas, acting under no public authority, and clothed with no public trust. They were mere private trespassers, for whose lawless acts this Government cannot be held responsible. As such trespassers they may be obnoxious to a double prosecution; the one civil; the other criminal. But both must be instituted in the tribunals established by the law; the first by action for the recovery of the goods abstracted or for their value which may be brought by the Texian Collector in either the State or Federal Courts in which he would be entitled to recover damages commensurate to the injury sustained. The criminal proceeding, if sustainable, must be prosecuted in the local Courts of Arkansas. I have said *if sustainable*, because I am not sufficiently familiar with the criminal code of that State, to enable me to express a positive opinion on the subject. At the Common Law it is quite clear, that an agreement between two or more, entered into within the jurisdiction of the State, to commit an unlawful act, would be indictable as a conspiracy, and assuming that law to obtain in Arkansas, the prosecution against the perpetrators of the wrong complained of, may be supported in her Courts. These are remedies however as you will perceive that this Government has no power to advance. They must be left to the pursuit of the parties injured.

What may be the grade of the offence alleged to have been committed, under the laws of the Republic of Texas, I have no means of ascertaining.

If the injury under her system would be a mere trespass, it can be prosecuted for only when an opportunity may be available within her own territory, unless the parties choose to have recourse to the tribunals in Arkansas for redress. If on the other hand, the offence be criminal under her system, the parties implicated may be punished wherever found within the jurisdiction of her laws. If demanded as fugitives, this Government has no authority to deliver them up for trial, in the absence of Treaty stipulations to that effect.

As to pecuniary indemnity, if proper to be made at all, it can be provided for only by Treaty stipulation. But I confess I do not perceive any principle upon which such indemnity can be demanded or accorded. I have the honor to be Very respectfully Sir Your Obedient Servant, Jno. Nelson.

LS in DNA, RG 59 (State Department), Miscellaneous Letters (M-179:105, frames 32–34); FC in DNA, RG 60 (Justice Department), Opinions of the Attorney General, F:191.

To William Nelson, U.S. Consul, Panama, 7/9. A letter of 3/15 was previously sent to Nelson informing him of his replacement. This letter introduces J[eremiah] A. Townsend who is to succeed Nelson as Consul. FC in DNA, RG 59 (State Department), Consular Instructions, 11:254.

To William Nelson, Panama, 7/9. "I have to inform you that . . . Congress, has made no provision at its last Session, for the continuance of the [U.S. Despatch] Agency at Panama." FC in DNA, RG 59 (State Department), Domestic Letters, 34:290–291 (M-40: 32).

From JOHN NORVELL, [former Senator from Mich.]

Detroit, July 9, 1844

My Dear Sir, A commission for J. Humphrey as Marshal for the District of Michigan, superseding that of Colonel Joshua Howard; was yesterday received by the District Judge of the United States. It is presumed that the commission was intended for Levi S. Humphrey, there being no J. Humphrey in this State, and Levi S. Humphrey having been a delegate from this State to the late Baltimore Tyler Convention.

Your aversion to the policy of removals from office for mere differences of political opinion, justifies the conclusion that the present removal has been effected without your concurrence. Colonel Howard has discharged the duties of Marshal with capacity, integrity and fidelity. He has, so far as his course has come within my daily observation, been quiet and inoffensive in the expression of his political opinions. His term of office does not expire, by limitation, until next spring. Without, therefore, giving any opinion touching the competency or fitness of the person appointed to succeed Colonel Howard, I must be permitted to say, that, in my judgment, neither the public interest, nor any political object favorable to Mr. Tyler or the democratic party, will be subserved by the change.

The limitation of the terms of office to four years, deaths, resignations, and the creation of new offices, afford all the necessary opportunities to any new administration for the bestowal of patronage upon its friends. Experience, honesty and fitness are, I know, in your judgment, the proper qualifications for public station. The abuse of the power of removal and appointment is daily becoming more and more a crying evil, and must end in driving high-spirited and honorable men from office, and in the substitution of servility and ignorance in their stead.

I do, therefore, most sincerely trust, that you will set your justly great influence against the continuance of this corrupting policy, and, as far as your Department is concerned, aid in arresting its alarming progress.

I am with you on all the great political questions of the day, remaining firm in the democratic faith, in favour of your Texian treaty, against a high protective tariff, against any national bank, for a strict construction of the constitution, and against abolition in all its moods and tenses: And, therefore, you will not suppose me influenced, in the preceding remarks, by any consideration adverse to the republican cause, or the public welfare. I have the honour to be, Very truly and respectfully, Your friend & most ob[edien]t serv[an]t, John Norvell.

ALS in ScCleA.

From T[homas] M. Rodney

Consulate of the United States of America
Matanzas [Cuba], July 9, 1844

Sir, I have the honour to enclose the correspondence & such testimony as I have been enabled to collect in relation to the treatment of Samuel Moffatt & William Bisby; persons of the first respectability who are well acquainted with the facts have called at this consulate and declared to the truth of the statement made in my Note of the 4th of June to the Government of Matanzas, but are afraid to put their names to paper least it might become known to the Authorities, and end in their imprisonment and loss, and I must ask of the Department, in no case, to allow the names of those who have testified in this matter to be made public as it would surely end in their imprisonment and ruin.

I have not been able to obtain the written statement from the prisoners, who are still in confinement, without any prospect of immediate release; they solemnly declare in relation to the charge of bribery, that while they were in the stocks they were treated with some kindness by the person who had charge of them, that he would sometimes allow them to take one leg out and stretch and work it for the purpose of circulating the blood; that on their keepers being changed they observed to the new one, that if he would treat them as well as his predecessor had done, they would give him something when their trial was over; on this is predicated the charge of bribery, and the excuse for taking them to prison in chains: had I the power to send for persons and papers I feel assured I could place the Lieut[enan]t Governor of Cardenas in no enviable position as regards veracity.

There are two other native Americans, Thomas Savage, and John Thompson, respectable young men, Engineers, confined since the 9th day of May last but as they have received no worse treatment than other prisoners I have thought it worse than useless to make any application to the authorities.

I feel keenly for these four young men who are now confined in the same prison with 1200 blacks at the worst season of the year and I fear if not shortly released, will through disease and sickness end their days in jail.

Mr. [Maurice] Hogan was acquitted and released on the 4 Inst.

I hear of the arrival at Havana on the 1st Inst: of the U.S. Brig Lawrence, but though I have written to our Consul Mr. [Robert B.] Campbell I cannot hear whether she will visit this port or is the bearer of any instructions in relation to matters here. I have the honour to be, Sir With hig[h] respect, Your obed[ien]t Serv[an]t, T.M. Rodney.

[Enclosure]
Theodore Phinney to T.M. Rodney, Copy

[Undated]

Sir, In compliance with your request to give you some information respecting the treatment of William Bisby and Samuel Moffort [sic], one an engineer the other a carpenter, were both employed on my estate called "Senora."

About the 25th of March last William Bisby was taken up on the declaration, as was said, of a black man belonging to me, but after a day or two was set at liberty. After which a man by the name of Contrera to satisfy his revengeful feelings against Bisby, had Nicolas the black man mentioned above flogged in such a terrible manner that he fainted several times, but still denied that Bisby had said any thing to him, to implicate himself; the next day Nicholas was again taken out to be flogged and told that he would be flogged to death unless he confessed that Bisby was in the, as they called it, Conspiracy, and finding no other way to save his life, he by indication said all that he thought would save him from being further tormented and Bisby and Moffort were again taken up, and put in close confinement each with both feet in the stocks, on the sugar estate of Mr. Blain, not being allowed to see or have communication with any one. After some two or three weeks during which they were kept in the stocks, they were sent to Cardenas about 6 miles distant, with a parcel of negroes tied like felons, and there put in a room with a number of negroes and chained to the floor not being allowed to have any communication with any one of their friends, until Bisby was taken dangerously ill, when from the urgent solicitude of his friends he was taken and put into a small room, still it was with the greatest difficulty any of his friends could obtain permission to see him or supply him with the proper medicine and nourishment.

The black man Nicholas when he was called upon to ratify what he had said of Bisby denied all that he had said, and declared he did not know what he did say and that he, Bisby had never said any thing to him with respect to raising[?] on the white inhabitants.

And so far am I from believing that Bisby had any thing to do, as it respects the Conspiracy against the white inhabitants of the Island [I] feel assured from the knowledge I have of him that had he even suspected any such movement he would have risen from his bed at any hour of the night to have given me information, and believe that his imprisonment has resulted in the fiend like disposition of revenge of the before mentioned Contrera.

Sam[ue]l Moffort has suffered as much and perhaps more than Bisby and from the same testimony and if you can do any thing for their relief you will confer the greatest obligation on dear sir your ob[e]d[ien]t S[ervan]t, signed *Theodore Phinney.*

LS (No. 21) with Ens in DNA, RG 59 (State Department), Consular Despatches, Matanzas, vol. 4 (T-339:4), received 7/23. NOTE: Rodney also enclosed to the State Department copies of his correspondence with Antonio Garcia Oña, Governor of Matanzas, and affidavits of Henry J. Cavalier, dated 6/30, and Robert Hiton and Daniel Downing, dated 7/1, describing the conditions of confinement of Bisby and Moffat at the Cardenas jail.

From C.D. Arfwedsen, U.S. Consul, Stockholm, 7/10. He encloses his semiannual returns. "You will observe from the same, that no American vessel has during that time visited our port or any other in my District. All the trade between Stockholm and the United States has been carried on in foreign vessels. . . . The intercourse with the United States seems not to be very lively in 1844, and I do not believe that any improvement in this respect will take place before the winter sets in. All American goods are extremely low in this market . . . . Iron which is the only article sent from hence to the United States, is likewise very cheap . . . ." ALS (No. 35) with En in DNA, RG 59 (State Department), Consular Despatches, Stockholm, vol. 2 (T-230:2), received 9/3.

To Rich[ar]d H. Belt, U.S. Consul, Matamoros, 7/10. Belt's despatches 2 and 3 have been received, and the Mexican decree re-opening trade at Taos, which he sent, has been published. FC in DNA, RG 59 (State Department), Consular Instructions, 11:255.

From ROBERT B. CAMPBELL

Consulate of the United States of America, Havana
July 10th 1844

Sir, During my residence here as Consul, many instances have oc-curred of English Sailors shipped in the States on American Vessels for a specific time or designated voyages, deserting their vessels, vio-lating their contracts, and taking refuge in English Men of War under the British flag. In all these cases preceding an occurrence of the present month, they have without exception and with little trou-ble been given up to me on demand, and restored by me to their Vessel. Under existing orders from the board of Admiralty, Her Majesty's Naval Officers have no discretion and are compelled by a sense of duty, and a spirit of obedience to retain all British seamen without regard to their previous contracts who find their way on board an English Man of War, as you will perceive by the copy [of] a letter from the Commanding Officer of the Illustrious the flag ship on the North American station. Thinking it possible that the State Department may not be furnished with a copy of the Admiralty Order on which the action of Capt. [John] Erskine is predicated I herewith enclose a copy of so much as relates to the immediate in-terest of our Merchantment [*sic*] and Men of War, by which you will perceive that the former may be subjected to the most serious in-convenience, and the latter to unpleasant collisions, ["for," *canceled*] from my opportunities of observation I find that many foreigners are employed in our service, and great abuses are practised in the pro-tections that are given them as American Citizens. Instances of the last, occurring to such an extent that I have seen more than half of an entire crew, who had no conception of the names under which they had shipped or by which they were designated in their protections. I have the honor to be with great respect y[ou]r mo[st] ob[edien]t Ser[van]t, Robert B. Campbell.

LS with Ens in DNA, RG 59 (State Department), Consular Despatches, Havana, vol. 19 (T-20:19), received 7/23. NOTE: Campbell enclosed an extract from the Royal Navy's "Station order Book" relating to the protection of British seamen and a copy of Erskine's letter of 7/5.

From W[ILLIAM] S. FULTON, [Senator from Ark.]

Little Rock, July 10th 1844

Sir, It gives me pleasure to recommend Dr. Solon Borland of our State, for the office of United States Attorney, which is vacant since the resignation of G[randison] D. Royston Esq[ui]r[e]. To a highly cultivated mind and talents of the first order, Dr. Borland, unites both energy and intrepidity of character, and great zeal and perseverance in the prosecution of business. He has qualified himself for the legal profession; and I assure you, that his appointment could not be otherwise than satisfactory. I solicit the office for him; & beg you to present him most favorably to the President. I am most respectfully Your ob[edien]t S[ervan]t, W.S. Fulton.

ALS in DNA, RG 59 (State Department), Appointments and Recommendations, 1837–1845, Borland (M-687:2, frames 707–708).

From JA[ME]S GADSDEN, "Private"

Richmond, July 10, [18]44

My Dear Sir, After I left you I had a long conference with E[li S.] Davis formerly of So[uth] C[arolina] now of La Grange Tennessee. You know him as well as I do. His being an agent from a Company with authority to make proposals to induce others to finish the Memphis & La Grange Road, is a political farce, got up by himself to divert attention from his real designs. I have penetrated what he is after—$100,000 have been appropriated for the Navy Yard at Memphis—and he is ready to put his hand into a share of that plunder. I have been active in promoting that appropriation, as the entering wedge to the completion of our own line of Rail way from Charleston to Memphis. Knowing the interest you feel in this project[?], I have, in the hurry of an hour[']s detention here thought it advisable to write you this scrawl. The 100,000 Dollars ought & I have no doubt will be exclusively spent under the direction of the

Navy Department, & therefore I feel desirous that the President [John Tyler] should not be mislead by political considerations to pervert any portion of the fund from the grand object for which appropriated.

I think however in connection with the Navy Yard, we may direct attention to the Rail Road connection between Charleston & Memphis. The two projects are intimately connected, and if by any Governmental action you can make them legitimately play on each other, you may advance the success of both. I think and repeat that the Naval appropriation should be expended under the direction of the Naval Department & not permitted to be distributed among partizans or political agents. But if the Government in its judgement should deem it advisable to raise a Commission of examination, under the act, of not only the location but on the military connections by Rail Ways & other channels of communication & should think proper to associate Citizens in the Commission I should be gratified on being named on the Commission. My examination of the Country, my knowledge of the Route and of all the advantages to flow from the connection being formed are my recommendations. My motive is to bring the whole subject & under the authority of a Report to the notice of the Government & the country.

Will you reflect on it, confer with the Secr[etary] of Navy [John Y. Mason] & Com[modor]e Warrenton [*sic*; Lewis Warrington], on whose Bureau will devolve the duty of examination; and see whether such a commission may not be reared. I have no other desire of being associated with it, than that of imparting at once to a Committee all the information I have on the subject, and of stimulating that Committee, as one of its members to such a Report as may effect our objects.

Don[']t permit the Governmental appropriation to be frittered away in rewards to pretended political friends. The President may, as he has been, be played upon.

Davis is at home a W[h]ig. Memphis & the neighbourhood, I know from undoubted authority to be W[h]ig, and Davis with the W[h]igs in Washington was on their side. Yours truly, Jas. Gadsden.

ALS in ScCleA.

To "Dennis" [*sic*; Denis] Gahagan, New York [City]

Department of State
Washington, 10th July 1844

Sir, I have to acknowledge the receipt of your letter of the 8th Inst., requesting this department to prosecute a claim against the Mexican government on account of losses which you say you have sustained by a sale of certificates received from the Treasury Department as a Claimant under the Convention with [the Mexican] Government of the 11th of April, 1839, for this department cannot comply with your request inasmuch as by the sale of the certificates you relinquished all your rights against Mexico growing out of the award in your favor. I am Sir Your Obedient Servant, John C. Calhoun.

FC in DNA, RG 59 (State Department), Domestic Letters, 34:293 (M-40:32).

From David Henshaw, "Private"

Boston, July 10, 1844

Dear Sir, I have understood that G[eorge] M. Weston of Augusta Maine has been applied to, to assist in the Editorial department of the Spectator at Washington during the present presidential campaign: and I have been requested to write to some one of our political friends concerning him; and hence the liberty I take in addressing this letter to you.

My personal knowledge of Mr. Weston is not very intimate. But he has the reputation of being a man of ability; and the editorial department of the Augusta Age, under his charge, certainly justifies this reputation. He is entirely sound on all the points of the democratic creed, and has been steadily opposed to the continued claims of Mr. [Martin] Van Buren. I think he would be a highly valuable aid to the cause in the position of Editor of the Spectator. I am dear sir with the highest respect Your Ob[edien]t Ser[van]t, David Henshaw.

ALS in ScCleA.

To HENRY W. HILLIARD, [Brussels]

Department of State
Washington, 10th July, 1844

Sir: Your despatches to No. 20, inclusive, have been received.

Referring to despatch No. 14, from this Department, in which I communicated the wish expressed by the President [John Tyler] that you would remain at Brussels until the arrival of your successor, for reasons of public policy, which were therein explained, I have now the honor to inform you, that, as Mr. Thomas G. Clemson, who has been appointed by the President to succeed you, will probably be able to reach Bruxelles some time in August, no material interest will be likely to suffer by the short interval, and you are, therefore, permitted to close your mission on the 12th of August, the period on which you have fixed as that which will be most convenient to you, or as soon after the receipt of this despatch, as circumstances may allow. Of the exact date of your taking leave, you will inform the Department, and the Bankers of the United States, who will be desired to settle your accounts accordingly. You will, as a matter of course, in case of your departure before Mr. Clemson's arrival, leave for him, in the custody of some trustworthy person, the archives, books and property of the Legation, as well as all the despatches from this Department to you, and a record or drafts of your letters to the Department, together with all your correspondence with the Belgian Government.

I transmit, enclosed, a letter [of 7/6] addressed to [Albert Joseph Goblet] the Minister of Foreign Affairs of Belgium, with an office copy of the same, informing him of your recall; which you will present in the usual form, and accompany by assurances to His Excellency of the sentiments of friendship entertained by this Government towards that of Belgium.

In accepting your resignation, the President has directed me to convey to you his entire approbation of the manner in which you have discharged the public duties placed in your care. I am, Sir, respectfully, Your obedient Servant, J.C. Calhoun.

LS (No. 16) with En in DNA, RG 84 (Foreign Posts), Belgium, Instructions, 1:263–267; FC in DNA, RG 59 (State Department), Diplomatic Instructions, Belgium, 1:51–53 (M-77:19).

From LUCIUS LYON, [Representative from Mich.]

Detroit, July 10, 1844

Dear Sir, Col. Edward Brooks, who will hand you this, is Collector of the Customs at this place and has heard that among other changes here it is in contemplation to remove him and put some other man in his place.

This I think would be bad policy, so far at least as Col. Brooks is concerned; and, as I do not know the Secretary of the Treasury [George M. Bibb], I desire to say to you, as I have said to the President [John Tyler], that Col. Brooks is an active and influential supporter of the present Administration, and that neither the friends of Mr. Tyler nor the friends of Col. [James K.] Polk can gain any thing by his removal at present. The only party that could gain by such a change would be the whigs. With great respect, I am, Dear Sir, very truly Yours, Lucius Lyon.

ALS in DNA, RG 56 (Secretary of the Treasury), Applications for Appointment as Customs Service Officers, 1833–1910.

To ALPHONSE PAGEOT, [French Minister to the U.S.]

Department of State
Washington, 10th July, 1844

Sir: With reference to your letter of the 28th ultimo, acknowledging the receipt of that addressed to you by this Department on the 24th of the same month, and in answer to your request to be made acquainted with the intentions of this Government as to the forms to be observed in the surrender of fugitive criminals pursuant to the provisions of the Convention of the 9th of November, 1843, between the United States and France, I have the honor to transmit to you a copy of a communication [dated 7/8] just received from the Attorney General of the United States [John Nelson], to whom your letter has been submitted for his consideration. Concurring in the views therein taken of this subject, and seeing no objection whatever to the course of proceeding proposed to be adopted on the part of the King's Government, as explained in your note, to give effect to the stipulations of the Convention, I beg you to accept renewed assurances of my distinguished consideration. J.C. Calhoun.

FC in DNA, RG 59 (State Department), Notes to Foreign Legations, France, 6:81–82 (M-99:21).

From C[HARLES] S. TODD

Legation U.S. America

St. Petersburg, $\frac{28\ \text{June}}{10\ \text{July}}$ 1844

Sir, As your Despatch No. 15 [of 5/11] authorized me, if an occasion should call for it, to make the necessary explanations to the Russian Government in relation to the recent Treaty of Annexation and with that view my attention was specially directed to the Correspondence on that subject, I have the honor to enclose a copy of my note of 17/29 June to [Woronzow Daschkoff] the [acting] Minister of Foreign Affairs transmitting the Documents as being the most suitable mode of complying with the wishes of the President.

I could not doubt but that it was the object of your Despatch to have these documents brought to the notice of the Imperial Ministry and as the mode was confided to my discretion I supposed my note to the Minister of Foreign Affairs would be the most appropriate for the attainment of that object. Such is the state of society at this Court that an occasion for this explanation would rarely occur even were not the Imperial Family at the Country Palace of Tsarskoè-celo and the Emperor secluded from intercourse with the Diplomatic Corps in consequence of the distressing illness of the Grand Duchess Alexandra. In the actual condition of things an occasion must be sought and my note effects this object while I do not profess to seek it. I have placed the communication on the ground of voluntary confidence rather ["than" *interlined*] upon an explanation of what is not requested to be explained. A copy of the note from Count Woronzow Daschkoff expressing his acknowledgements for the receipt of the Documents is herewith enclosed. This acknowledgement is included in a note requesting me to transmit the originals of the letters from the President to the Emperor referred to in my note of 15/27 June.

I take the liberty of enclosing, under cover to the Department, the result of my enquiries for Mr. Elliott [*sic;* Jonathan Elliot] who is charged by the House of Representatives with the collection of authentic information as to the Funding System, Banks, Revenue and Finances of other Countries. In order to obtain the most satisfactory information I have been compelled to refer to some recent publications in the Russian Language which I have transmitted to Mr. Elliott in the hope that he may be able to procure a translation. I have the honor to enclose a recent Journal published here in German, containing the speech of Mr. Vrontchenko, successor to Count Cancrere in the direction of the Department of Finances, delivered before the Board of Trade. The Treatise on Banks published in 1840 in Russian, herewith forwarded to Mr. Elliott, gives an accurate statement of every thing connected with that subject and I have added a valuable work, also in Russian, as to the Balance of Russian Trade of 1842, that for 1843 not being published.

The Revenue of the Empire is derived from the following sources— (computed for 1843)—

Capitation Tax on Serfs	Silver Roubles	20,000,000
Tax on peasants in lieu of personal service		16,000,000
Customs for St. Petersburg		15,868,904
Salt Tax		14,500,000
Brandy do.		36,500,000
Stamp do.		2,000,000
Mint		2,105,000
Tax on Merchants certain p[e]r c[en]t on their Capital		1,500,000
do. on private Mining in Siberia		2,000,000
218 poods of Gold from Government Mines in Siberia @ 12,000 S.R. per each pood		2,616,000
	S.R.	93,089,904

This is independent of the Customs received at other ports of the Empire. The public debt is estimated at 300,000,000 S.R.—or $225,-000,000.

I have been gratified to learn by a letter from Mr. [Edward] Everett that in a conversation with the Emperor, the latter expressed himself as entirely satisfied with Maj. [George W.] Whistler and the American Engineers employed in his service, adding that he had a great deal of work for them in his Empire and he hoped they could be induced to remain for many years.

It is anticipated that there will be an increased number of American Vessels in port this year, the importation of sugar, thus far, having been very profitable. Many of the ships, however, will be compelled to return in part in ballast—or in deals to ports in France for a Cargo—or to New Castle and thence to the Continent with coal; if such be permitted by the English Navigation Acts.

A note from the Grand Master of Ceremonies of $\frac{19 \text{ June}}{1 \text{ July}}$ of which a copy is enclosed, announced that the Imperial Court went into mourning for twelve days on account of the death of the Duke of Angouleme. I have the honor to be with high Consideration & Esteem Your ob[edien]t Ser[van]t, C.S. Todd.

P.S. 1/13 July. I have just procured & have the honor to enclose a copy of the recent speech of the Minister of Finance published in French and contained in the ["supplement to the" *interlined*] Annual Report of the Minister of the Interior.

ALS (No. 46) with Ens in DNA, RG 59 (State Department), Diplomatic Despatches, Russia, vol. 14 (M-35:14), received 8/21; FC in DNA, RG 84 (Foreign Posts), Russia, Despatches, 4406:220–222.

From HENRY WHEATON

Berlin, 10 July, 1844

Sir, Enclosed is an official copy of the Royal Cabinet-Order, by which the modifications in the existing duties on the importation of *Iron* into the *Zollverein*, proposed at the Congress held here last summer, are to be carried into effect on the 1st of Sept. next.

The Cabinet-Order also contains certain alterations in the duties imposed by the present Tariff on sugar.

The origin of the measure in respect to the increase of the duties on *Iron*, will be found fully explained in my former Despatches, Nos. 235 & 236. It constitutes an exception to the general principle, by which no alterations in the Tariff, unless by Treaty with foreign Powers, can regularly be made, during the triennial period for which it is established, & at the end of which it is subject to revision, & may be altered by the unanimous consent of all the associated States. The execution of the measure has been, for some time, suspended by the veto of Bavaria, who wished to supply herself with *rails* for the extended rail-roads which are being constructed in that Kingdom, before the increased duties went into effect.

The foreign countries, which will be principally effected by the measure, are G. Britain, Sweden & Belgium. A vast quantity of iron is imported into Germany from the first mentioned of those countries, but the augmentation of duties will have much less effect upon the amount of importation than was calculated at the time when the measure was first proposed, in consequence of the recent rise in the prices of British Iron, growing out of the increased demand at home & abroad. As mentioned in my last Despatch, the menacing tone assumed by Lord Aberdeen, in his recent correspondence with

[Heinrich Ulrich Wilhelm,] Baron Bülow, has probably contributed to determine the councils of the Zollverein to carry this measure into effect without further delay.

The Cartel, for the mutual delivery of military deserters, between Russia & Prussia, which had expired by its own limitation, has been recently renewed with some modifications. The stipulations of the new Cartel are not retroactive, & do not extend to authorize the extradition of the deserters who had come over, in immense numbers, from the Russian-Polish territory, during the period when the operation of the Cartel was suspended. This will not be a popular measure in Germany, where the Russian Government & nation are heartily detested; but the continuance of the actual state of things had become intolerable even for Prussia herself, as it was found extremely burthensome to provide employment for the unfortunate Russian & Polish deserters, whose numbers were added to the inhabitants of the frontier provinces where the natural increase of population is constantly pressing against the means of subsistence. It remains to be seen whether any equivalent concessions have been obtained by Prussia from the Russian Government, in respect to commercial intercourse between those provinces & Poland, which is very much obstructed by the fiscal system adopted by Russia, with the view of protecting her manufacturing establishments carried on by the great proprietors by the labor of their serfs. It seems probable, however, that the influence of these proprietors is too powerful to allow any considerable relaxation of the prohibitive Tariff hitherto maintained by the Russian Government as a fundamental principle of policy. I have the honor to be, with the highest consideration, Sir, Y[ou]r Ob[e]d[ien]t Serv[an]t, Henry Wheaton.

LS (No. 254) with Ens in DNA, RG 59 (State Department), Diplomatic Despatches, Germany, vol. 3 (M-44:4), received 8/3; FC in DNA, RG 84 (Foreign Posts), Germany, Despatches, 4:140–143.

From Charles Bracken, New York [City], 7/11. He asks to be considered for appointment as [U.S.] Marshal in Wisc. Territory, from which post, he has heard, the incumbent is to be removed. Bracken signs himself as being of Iowa County in that Territory. ALS in DNA, RG 59 (State Department), Applications and Recommendations, 1837–1845, Bracken (M-687:3, frames 2–3).

To William Hogan, Boston, 7/11. "Your letter of the 6th instant, applying for a Consular appointment, has been duly received. The President [John Tyler] having left this city a few days ago, I have only to state, in reply, that your communication will be sent to him, at Old Point Comfort, by the mail of today for his consideration and decision." FC in DNA, RG 59 (State Department), Domestic Letters, 34:295 (M-40:32).

From JOHN NELSON

Attorney General's Office, July 11, 1844
Sir, The only provisions of the acts of Congress which relate to the case of Captain [Samuel S.] Thomas and his mate [of the *Zebra*] are those contained in the 4th and 5th Sections of the act of the 3d of March 1825, neither of which as you will at once perceive, upon referring to them, authorizes the trial of the parties accused in any court of the United States, for the homicide alledged to have been committed in a Foreign port. The 5th section on the contrary has been most cautiously so worded, as to leave to the Foreign jurisdiction the exclusive cognizance of such cases; providing as it does for a particular class of offences, in which that supposed to have been committed by Captain Thomas and his mate, is not embraced. I have the Honor to be, very respectfully, Sir, Your obed[ien]t Serv[an]t, Jno. Nelson.

LS in DNA, RG 59 (State Department), Miscellaneous Letters (M-179:105, frames 47–48).

To Wilson Shannon, [U.S. Minister to Mexico], 7/11. Calhoun relays information received from Tampico about the estate of Patrick M. McCarthy, a U.S. citizen who died there. It is alleged that excessive and illegal charges were made against the estate by the court that assumed the administration of the estate, in violation of a treaty with Mexico that puts the estates of U.S. citizens on the same footing as those of Mexican citizens. Shannon is to inquire into the matter and to make any representations to the Mexican government that he may deem necessary to induce it to respect the treaty in this instance. LS (No. 4) in DNA, RG 84 (Foreign Posts), Mexico, Instructions, vol. 5.I; FC in DNA, RG 59 (State Department), Diplomatic Instructions, Mexico, 15:307–308 (M-77:111).

To H[ENRY] WHEATON, [Berlin]

Washington, 11th July 1844

My dear Sir, I received yours of the 12th June by the Great Western yesterday.

There is no one to whom I would confide with more ["readiness" *interlined*] the subjects to which it refers, than to you, if it was advisable to commence the negotiation in reference to them at this time. Without having examined them or formed an opinion whether they should become a matter of negotiation, I am decidedly of the impression, they should not at this time, & under existing circumstances.

The fate of the Texian & Zoll verein Treaties is sufficient admonition ag[ai]nst entering on other negotiations, and into other treaties, untill the result of the election is known and who shall hold the reins of government the next four years after the fourth of March. Both were made under circumstances, which, one would have supposed, would ensure their approval by the Senate.

I was selected & nominated by the President [John Tyler] in reference to the pending negotiations, and it was so understood by the Senate. My nomination was unanimously & promptly confirmed with the knowledge that I had early avowed my opinion, that Texas ought to be annexed to the Union. My appointment was hailed with approbation on all sides, accompanied by urgent requests from both parties to accept, which I did with great reluctance and only in obedience to the call of the Government & Country. And yet, this very treaty, to negotiate which I was appointed under these circumstances, was rejected by a large majority of the Senate, although not an objection has been made to its details or provisions which is not groundless in fact, and acknowledged so to be by the impartial on all sides. What adds to the extraordinary character of the transaction is the fact, that it was rejected by the united votes of the friends of Mr. [Henry] Clay & Mr. [Martin] V[an] Buren, both of whom had used their best efforts to effect the same object while Secretary of State!

The case of the ZollVerein treaty is not less strong or strange. You are too well acquainted with the steps taken through a long course of years to prepare the way for the negotiation, which you conducted with so much success; and yet, this treaty too is laid aside by the party, who took the lead in urging the negotiation, on the most flimsy pretex[t]!

With these facts before me, which but too clearly show, that the attachment to party has, to a great extent, absorbed the love of country, I hold that it would be undignified & wrong for this administration to enter on any other negotiation of any importance, at least till after the next election. It would be but to expose itself to additional mortification & the Government to farther discredit in the eyes of the world. I would, indeed, with this impression retire forthwith from the Department, did I not feel it to be a duty to remain, so long as there is any hope, that I may contribute to the successful termination of two measures, in which I take so deep an interest. I regard the result of the Presidential election as doubtful. Should Mr. Clay be elected, he would find it difficult to resist the rally, which would be made ag[ai]nst his policy. With great respect Yours truly, J.C. Calhoun.

ALS in NNPM, Wheaton Papers.

From W[illia]m Wilkins

War Department, July 11th 1844
Sir, My answer to your communication of the 17th ult[im]o was delayed at first, by temporary absence.

There is some difficulty in the case you present, in relation to the application of army funds to a civil work for which, it is understood, there is a distinct and specific appropriation.

The Quartermaster General has been directed to furnish the proper transportation of Lieutenant [James L.] Donaldson and his detachment from this place to the point where Major [James D.] Graham's party assemble. The order in this case is a special one, to place the detachment in position to become useful on the work for establishing the [Northeastern] boundary line under your direction, and it is presumed that all further transportation, extra-pay and other expenses, will be charged to the specific civil appropriation.

The detachment will receive their usual allowances of subsistence, camp equipage &c.

The rockets required by Major Graham have been ordered, and all details and facilities afforded as far as practicable. Very respectfully, Your Obed[ient] Serv[an]t, Wm. Wilkins, Secretary of War.

LS with En in DNA, RG 59 (State Department), Miscellaneous Letters (M-179: 105, frames 45–46); FC in DNA, RG 107 (Secretary of War), Letters Sent Relating to Military Affairs, 1800–1861, 25:362 (M-6:25); draft in DNA, RG 92 (Quartermaster General), Consolidated Correspondence File, Boundary, Northeast Survey. NOTE: Wilkins enclosed a copy of an order of 11/29/1839 from Secretary of War J[oel] R. Poinsett relating to the payment of transportation allowances to officers engaged in civil works.

From Geo[rge] M. Bibb, Secretary of the Treasury, 7/12. He acknowledges receipt of correspondence from [J.C. de Figaniere e Morão] concerning high tariff duties imposed on Portuguese wines under the Tariff of 1842 and agrees that those duties were unjustly charged. Customs officers will be informed of this decision and excess duties refunded. Bibb adds that this decision applies only to duties charged under the Tariff of 1842. LS in DNA, RG 59 (State Department), Miscellaneous Letters (M-179:105, frames 49–51); FC in DNA, RG 56 (Secretary of the Treasury), Letters to Cabinet and Bureau Officers, 1842–1847, 4:401–403.

To Peter A. Brinsmade, 7/12. Calhoun notifies Brinsmade of his appointment as U.S. Consul at Hawaii in the Sandwich Islands, where he is already Commercial Agent. Calhoun transmits official documents, discusses minor matters of business, and encloses a letter of this date to J.C. Jones. FC in DNA, RG 59 (State Department), Consular Instructions, 11:256–257.

To Franklin Chase, U.S. C[onsul], Tampico, 7/12. Calhoun acknowledges receipt of Chase's despatches 47 through 51. Wilson Shannon, U.S. Minister to Mexico, has been instructed to look into the excessive court costs levied on the estate of the late U.S. citizen Patrick M. McCarthy. According to treaty, the administration of estates of U.S. citizens in Mexico is to be at the same cost as that of Mexican citizens. FC in DNA, RG 59 (State Department), Consular Instructions, 11:258.

To THOMAS G. CLEMSON, "Appointed Chargé d'Affaires of the United States to Belgium"

Department of State
Washington, 12th July, 1844

Sir: The President of the United States, by and with the advice and consent of the Senate, having appointed you Chargé d'Affaires near the King of the Belgians, I transmit to you, with this despatch, the following papers, which will be found necessary or useful to you, in the discharge of the duties of the mission to which you have been appointed:

1. Your Commission;
2. A special passport for yourself and suite;
3. A letter of Credit on the Bankers of the United States in London, authorizing them to pay your drafts for your salary as it becomes due, with the Contingent expenses of the mission, actually incurred, which, however, are limited to the sum of five hundred dollars per annum. In availing yourself of this authority, you will be careful not to exceed, in the amount drawn for, the sums to which you may be entitled, in account with the United States, at the respective dates of your drafts. You will designate in your drafts the accounts upon which they may be drawn, stating particularly whether they are for salary or for contingent expenses. And if you draw for both, you will name the respective amounts which are chargeable to each account.
4. A letter of credence addressed to the Minister of Foreign Affairs of Belgium, with an office copy of the same;
5. A set of printed personal instructions prescribed by the Department of State for the government of all the diplomatic representatives of the United States abroad;
6. A printed list of the diplomatic and Consular agents of the United States in foreign countries.

Your compensation, as fixed by law, is at the rate of four thousand five hundred dollars per annum, with an outfit equal to a year's salary, and a quarter's salary for your return to this Country. Your salary will commence on the day of the date of your commission, the 17th day of June, of the present year. For your outfit you will draw on this Department.

It is probable that your predecessor, Mr. [Henry W.] Hilliard, will have left Brussels before your arrival. He has been instructed, in that event, to leave the archives and property of the Legation in the hands of some proper person, who will deliver them to you, upon application for them. They are believed to be in good condition, and they, as well as the series of books allowed by the Department, for the use of the Legations will, no doubt, be found complete. I am, Sir, respectfully, Your obedient Servant, J.C. Calhoun.

FC (No. 1) in DNA, RG 59 (State Department), Diplomatic Instructions, Belgium, 1:53–55 (M-77:19). NOTE: Clemson's commission, dated 6/17/1844 and signed by President John Tyler and Calhoun, is in ScCleA. Clemson's special diplomatic passport, dated 7/6 and signed by Calhoun, is at Fort Hill, Clemson, S.C.

From WILLIAM DAUGHERTY

Woodstock, Shenandoah [County,] Virginia
July 12th 1844

Hon. Sir; I perceive from the public prints, that the Hon. Mr. [Henry W.] Hilliard, our Chargé De Affaires at Brussells, has sent in his resignation and I presume a successor is to be appointed.

In view of this, I deem it alike my duty & pleasure to present to the consideration of the Department—the name of Alexander Anderson Esq. of this place, as eminently worthy of that station. And I feel an assurance that I am consulting the interest of my country in pressing his claims upon our Government for honourable promotion.

Mr. Anderson is a lawyer of distinction and has ever been an ardent & devoted republican. True, he has filled no conspicuous offices either in the General or State Governments—but the sole reason is—that he has never sought them. With him the post of honour has been the private station.

Upon the accession of Mr. [John] Tyler to the Presidency, some of Mr. Anderson's friends, without his knowledge took occasion to present his name for the office of Judge of Iowa Territory—but the appointments had gone out in advance of their application.

A pledge was however given by the Executive that the wishes of his friends should be gratified at some future period. That pledge has not as yet been redeemed—& I rejoice that such is the case—now that an occasion presents itself when the Executive may confer upon an individual every way meritorious—an honour worthy of himself.

To the people of Shenandoah—the Executive is indebted for many evidences of their regard & attachment in by gone days—& more especially to the immediate relatives of Mr. Anderson—who sustained him in opposition to Jno. Randolph for the Senate of the U.S. And even at a later period the "old Tenth Legion" has evinced no ordinary degree of attachment to Mr. Tyler for his firmness & devotion to the principles of his early life.

Since however the Texas Question has been mooted, I venture the assertion that no people throughout the confederacy can be found who have taken a deeper interest in & who will adhere more firmly to this great national measure than the Republicans of Shenandoah.

In this aspect of things there is a fitness in the promotion of Mr. Anderson for he was the first of her sons to advocate this cause, immediately after the battle of San Jacinto. To his efforts much of the present feeling is attributable. And although He looks for no other reward than the convictions of duty & the approbations of his immediate friends—Yet I am humbly of opinion the Executive would alike consult his own dignity & the interests of our common country— by tendering to Mr. Anderson this appointment or some one of kindred honour & emolument. Whether Mr. A[nderson] would accept I know not—having had no consultation with him on the subject—but that fact can be readily ascertained at the proper period by dropping him a line.

I feel that I have discharged an agreeable duty in presenting his name to your consideration & should feel myself under weighty obligations in the event of having been the successful instrument in procuring for a distinguished friend a station in the gift of his Government, which would receive from its incumbent as much honour as it could possibly reflect upon him. Very Respectfully Your Obed[ien]t Servant, William Daugherty.

ALS in DNA, RG 59 (State Department), Applications and Recommendations, 1837–1845, Anderson (M-687:1, frames 149–152). NOTE: A Clerk's EU reads "Acknowledged—place already filled."

To Edward Dixon, [Alexandria, D.C.?], 7/12. Calhoun transmits to Dixon a package to be delivered to [William M.] Blackford, U.S. Chargé d'Affaires in New Granada. Dixon will be "governed by his [Blackford's] directions in regard to the length of your abode in that City [Bogotá] and you will bring with you on your return to the United States such communications as he may have occasion to send." Dixon's travel expenses will be paid by the State Department, and he will receive the sum of $6 per day from his departure until his return. "The expenses attendant upon your sojourn in" Bogota will not "be considered as travelling expenses." Dixon's courier's passport is herewith transmitted. FC in DNA, RG 59 (State Department), Diplomatic Instructions, Colombia, 15:90–91 (M-77:44).

To J.C. Jones, California, 7/12. Calhoun has learned that Jones has failed to surrender to P[eter] A. Brinsmade the records of Jones's former consular post in the Sandwich Islands. He requests Jones to turn over the records to Brinsmade as soon as possible. FC in DNA, RG 59 (State Department), Consular Instructions, 11:257.

From ROBERT LEBBY

James Island, St. Andrews Parish So. Ca.
12th July 1844

Sir: At a late meeting of the Agricultural Society of this Parish, a Circular from the Hon. W[hitemarsh] B. Seabrook President of the State Society was rec[eive]d: calling the attention of the local Societies on the Seaboard, to the propriety of adopting immediate measures, for the introduction of the Sea Island or long staple cotton into the markets of China; thereby creating a competition, in the manufacturing of the raw materials, by the ingenious inhabitants of that empire, with the Spinners of Great Britain. As Chairman of the Committee to whom the subject was referred, allow me the honor to request of you, (if not contrary with the usages of your Office) a copy of the treaty lately entered into between China & Great Britain, with any other information in your possession, that will enable us to carry out a measure which promises to be so advantageous to the Sea Island Planters of South Carolina. Likewise your views, and and [*sic*] any suggestions you may do us the honor to make, with any commercial documents, that will enable the Committee to make a full and comprehensive report. I have the honor to remain with much respect Your Fellow Citizen, Robert Lebby, M.D.

ALS in DNA, RG 59 (State Department), Miscellaneous Letters (M-179:105, frames 51–52).

From John McFerran, Wheeling, Va., 7/12. McFerran greatly desires to receive information about the progress of the State Department in investigating the operation of the Bankruptcy Act. ALS in DNA, RG 59 (State Department), Miscellaneous Letters (M-179:105, frames 52–53).

To JOHN SOUTHGATE, Norfolk, Va.

Department of State
Washington, 12th July 1844

Sir, I have to acknowledge the receipt of your letter of the 6th inst. The claim to which it refers is presumed to be that on the late Government of Colombia on the case of the Schooner Ranger which was adjusted by the Convention between Mr. [Thomas P.] Moore and the Minister for Foreign Affairs of that Republic of the twenty fifth of November, 1829. The amount of the claim as recognized in that Convention was five Thousand one hundred and thirteen dollars and fifty nine Cents with Interest at six per Cent from the second of August, 1825, until paid. That Republic separeted soon after the date of the Convention into the three states of which it was composed. This made it necessary to demand payment of those States according to the proportions of the debts of Colombia which they severally assumed. Fifty per Cent was accordingly demanded of the Republic of New Granada through the Chargé d'Affair[e]s of the United States accredited to that Government and in 1837, the New Granadian Congress appropriated four thousand three hundred and Twenty one dollars for the payment of its share of the indemnification due in the case of the Ranger. This sum is believed to have been paid in the course of the summer of 1839, by the authorities at Santa Martha to Mr. Robinson [*sic*; T.W. Robeson,] the Consul of the United States at that place, who remitted the amount to Mr. Fred[eric]k Vincent of Norfolk. It appears that with a letter from this Departm[en]t to Mr. [James] Semple, Chargé d'Affaires of the United States at Bogota of the 4th of September, 1838, a power of attorney from Augustus Martin[,] John Bushill[,] and William B. Manning to Frederick Vincent and another power from Mr. Vincent to Mr. Semple and Mr. Gooding of Bogota in relation to this case was transmitted. It also appears from Mr. Semple[']s despatches that Mr. Robinson remitted the money to Mr. Vincent in obedience to Mr. Semple's directions. The Republic of Venezuel[a] was accountable for twenty eight and a half per Cent of the claim. This was demanded through Mr. [John G.A.] Williamson, the Chargé d'Affairs of the United States at Caracas and an appropriation for its payment was made during the Session of the Congress of that Republic of 1838–1839. From a letter of this department to Mr. Vincent of the 5th of March 1839, it appears that the expediency of his executing a power of Attorney authorizing some person at Caracas to receive the money from the Venezuelan government was suggested.

It is understood that he complied with the suggestion by empowering Mr. Williamson for that purpose. The money was received by Mr. Williamson in the course of the summer of 1839, and remitted to Mr. Vincent by a bill of exchange which was contained in a sealed letter from Mr. Williamson to him. Mr. Williamson[']s despatch transmitting that letter through this Department, bears date the 6th of August, 1839. The precise amount paid by Venezuela is not mentioned in any paper in the Department but may easily be computed from the data given above. The balance of the claim amounting to twenty one and a half per Cent is still due by the Republic of Ecuador. I am, Sir, Your Obedient Servant, John C. Calhoun.

FC in DNA, RG 59 (State Department), Domestic Letters, 34:297–299 (M-40:32); PC in Jameson, ed., *Correspondence*, pp. 600–601.

From S[TEPHEN] H. WEEMS

U.S. Consulate
Guat[emal]a, July 12, 1844
Dear Sir, I would not think of calling your attention to the subject of this letter, were I not fully satisfied in my own mind of the national benefit that it would secure to the U.S. to raise our Diplomatic character in this country, where commerce with the U.S. is considerable & might be much more so—the annual produce of this State alone in cochineal amounting to nearly a million of dollars, at once show the capabilities of the country.

As consul, my powers limited, I have already found considerable difficulty in treating with Govt., questions constantly arising that are frequently beyond my authority to decide—as the accompan[yin]g correspondence will prove. This is the more so, as for several years our Commercial Treaty has expired, & it is a source of surprise to this country that it has not been renewed.

England, France, Belgium, & the H[anse] Towns are represented here by their Consul-Generals with full Diplomatic powers.

Having been resident in this Country for several years & also represented the U.S. here as Consul, I naturally feel anxious for the appoint[men]t of Diplomatic Agent, which would put me on the same footing with the representatives of European nations. Should therefore your views on this subject coincide with mine, my present object is to solicit your powerful influence to be nominated to the appoint[men]t & what ever steps you may think right to pursue I shall ever feel grateful for your interest in this matter.

Requesting your indulgence for the liberty I have taken—I have the honor to be Dear Sir Y[ou]r V[er]y ob[edien]t H[umbl]e S[ervan]t, S.H. Weems, Consul.

ALS in DNA, RG 59 (State Department), Consular Despatches, Guatemala City, vol. 1 (T-337:1), received 8/27.

From [Commander] Charles Wilkes, [U.S. Navy], Washington, 7/12. Wilkes encloses a copy of a letter previously sent to the State Department "in answer to your enquiries relative to Mr. John C. Williams whom I appointed as U.S. Consul at the Samoan Group of Islands." The En is dated 11/10/1839 and is from Wilkes to John Forsyth, [former Secretary of State]. Wilkes explains that numerous whaling vessels stop at the Samoan Islands for various reasons. The presence of a U.S. Consul there would be very helpful to them. Williams is a Polynesian, "the son of the well Known Missionary," and is very influential with the Samoan Chiefs. Wilkes hopes that the appointment will be confirmed. ALS with En in DNA, RG 59 (State Department), Applications and Recommendations, 1837–1845, Williams (M-687:34, frames 272–275).

To WILLIAM WILKINS, Secretary of War

Department of State
Washington, 12th July, 1844

Sir, I will thank you to communicate to this Department any information which may be in the possession of the Department of War in regard to the number and description of the arms taken by orders of Captain P[hilip] St. George Cooke of the Dragoons from the Texan force under the command of Colonel [Jacob] Snively, and, also, in regard to the disposition which was made of those arms. I have the honor to be, Your obedient servant, J.C. Calhoun.

LS in TxDaHi, Howard Collection; FC (dated 7/11) in DNA, RG 59 (State Department), Domestic Letters, 34:296 (M-40:32).

From an UNKNOWN PERSON

Eutaw, Greene Co[unty] Ala., July 12th [18]44

My dear Sir: A native of South Carolina, and for many years ["while in Carolina," *interlined*] one of your warmest supporters—you must know, that I feel deeply in relation to every ["ever" *canceled*] event that concerns you—or Carolina—or the South. As I do not design to place my name to what I may here write (for it is not necessary) it will be no violation of modesty, to say to you, that among us here, you are the favourite above all other men—and we look to you—and to you only—for assistance in bringing us out of the difficulties which now surround us. We expect you to devise and to assist in executing the ["pla" *canceled*] plan, by which we may be relieved from the present Tariff—and by which proper and secure guards may be placed around our slave property—and *slave population*. But the object of this communication is to say, that our cause is being now much injured, by the meetings in Carolina, which speak of "Texas with or without the Union."

This is taken hold of here by the Whig prints, and Whig Orators, and it helps much, to weaken our argument in favour of the annexation of Texas. Mr. [Thomas H.] Benton makes the charge of Disunion against certain persons, and if the Spectator at Washington contradicts and repels this charge, the Mercury at Charleston does not copy the articles.

The truth is—if we can hold still, and prevent the force which the charge of Disunion might have on the election of [James K.] Polk & [George M.] Dallas until after they are elected—we shall then be able to do something ["for our relief" *interlined*]—but if the subject of the Tariff should be pressed too far, at the present, and our Carolina friends should insist too warmly on "annexation with or without the Union"—it may have a tendency to defeat our Candidates for the Presidency. I am fully apprized of the fact, that these meetings in Carolina, have not been got up at your instance, or by your advice—*but can you not through your many discreet and influential friends there, stop them for the present?*

Our object here is to do every thing, to prevent the succession of Thomas H. Benton.

He professed in his late speech, that he had "pulled the Devil out from under the blanket." The only Devil which we could see in his speech was his arrogant egotistic self, anxiously ["and" *canceled*] labouring with all his malignant jealousy, to injure *certain persons*, (who in genius, talent and purity stand infinitely above him) and to

325

ingratiate the North and anti-slave States of the West, so as to obtain their support for the Presidency in 1848. Does not every sagacious, thinking man see this?

I would, that South Carolina, ["would" *canceled*] should say nothing for the present, about Disunion, or Nullification. That filthy reptile—Benton, is fired with envy and jealousy, and he well knows the effect that these words have in a certain quarter.

Your friends here, are not only anxious that every wish you may have should be fully gratified, but they would freely *shed* their blood, in defence of ["your" *interlined*] fair fame and reputation.

I have the honor of a personal acquaintance with you—but delicacy forbids that I should here make myself known.

My great anxiety for the success of our cause, has induced me to make these suggestions. With high consideration &c. Ever yours &c. [Unsigned.]

ALU in ScCleA.

From B[ENJAMIN] ANDREWS

Cleveland, Ohio, July 13th, 1844

Sir, Should the Department desire the services of a bearer of Despatches to the government of Mexico I beg leave respectfully to suggest the name of *Charles M. Gidings** Esq. [*Marginal interpolation*: "*No relation to (Joshua R.) Gid(d)ings the representative from this Dist. a different sort of a man altogether."] of this City. He is a gentleman who is favourably known in this community, and is a person every way well qualified, by business capacity, for a proper and satisfactory discharge of the duties of the service. Our Minister, Mr. [Wilson] Shannon, while he was in this City, prior to his leaving for Washington, expressed to Mr. Gidings his desire that, should ["the" *interlined*] government need the services of such an officer, he (Mr. G[idings]) might be appointed. Permit the undersigned to express the hope that the Hon. Secretary may bear the subject in mind; and, should occasion require, give Mr. G[idings] the opportunity of serving the Department in this capacity. I have the honor to be Sir Your most ob[edien]t Serv[an]t, B. Andrews P[ost] M[aster].

ALS in DNA, RG 59 (State Department), Applications and Recommendations, 1837–1845, Gidings (M-687:12, frames 648–649).

From D.C. Campbell, Macon, Ga., 7/13. He recommends [Thomas M.] Griffin as highly suitable for appointment as U.S. Marshal for "this District." ALS with En in DNA, RG 59 (State Department), Applications and Recommendations, 1837–1845, Griffin (M-687:13, frames 642–645).

To J.C. de Figaniere e Morão, [Portuguese Minister to the U.S.], Philadelphia, 7/13. Calhoun encloses a copy of a letter [of 7/12] from [George M. Bibb], Secretary of the Treasury, "on the subject of duties upon the wines of Portugal." FC in DNA, RG 59 (State Department), Notes to Foreign Legations, Portugal, 6:73–74 (M-99:80).

From W[illiam] H. Freeman

Consulate of the United States
Island of Curacao &c, July 13, 1844
Sir, I have the honor to inform you, that in answer to my application in January last to this Government (which was then referred to the general Government at Surinam) urging upon them the entire release of American Whalers frequenting this Colony from all harbour dues and port charges—I have received notice under date of the 9th Inst. of the following ordinance emanating from Surinam upon that subject viz, "Translation" "That all American Whalers frequenting Curacao, for the purpose of refitting, replenishing stores, and refreshing their crews, shall hereafter be released from the payment of any Port charges or Harbour dues of whatever nature excepting Pilotage—and in case of it being necessary to sell any part of their cargoes to defray their outlays, or expenses, they shall be liable to pay the duties on imported goods only (1% on the value thereof) for that portion so sold, and even then they shall be released from the usual Port charges." This, Sir, is only one of the many advantages I shall be enable[d] to procure for our Marine by an Official residence here. (The above information in regard to Whalers has been received in this Colony at least some seven weeks, and was not communicated to me until repeated and pressing verbal enquiries of the Governor by me, as to the action of the Government General on that subject, owing to his (the Governor's) desire not to address me in any official capacity.)

I cannot here but state to your department the very embar[r]assing situation in which I am placed in, in many respects from the want of an Exequatur—referring you to my last letter dated June 22nd No. 10. The fact is also now commonly known here, of there having been goods, American property, lately exposed for sale at Bonaire (a dependency of this Government; and some twenty five miles to windward of Curacao) which said goods have been pilferred by boats from that island from an American Barque ship wrecked on the Rocas' some few weeks ago, and for which goods I can make no claim upon this Government for those concerned, owing to the want of an Exequatur upon my Commission appointing me Consul of the U. States for Curacao, its Dependencies &c. Had I had the late Governor a[d] i[nterim] to confer with upon this subject, I should have had every aid given me in his power, but the present Governor, a military man, evinces hostility to this office for which I am unable to account, and though he does not directly interfere with me, yet, will not Officially assist me in any way, where I may call upon him for such Aid as circumstances may require, situated at such a distance as the Mother Government is from the Dutch West India Colonies, and no consul admitted at any of them excepting at Curacao, then evidently refusing to have one there, when the Government of the U. States sends one of its own Citizens to displace a Dutch subject may seem somewhat strange.

I cannot here, however, enter at length into the necessity of some authorised agent in at least one of their West India possessions being recognised, who can have in his proper sphere some jurisdiction over all, but the trade being a valuable one should be fostered and protected. (I am in no way concerned therein beyond my Office as Consul.)

I have sent to Mr. [Christopher] Hughes, the Chargé d'Affaires in Holland, a copy of the Curacao Gazette containing the Governor a.i. Official recognition, and have no reply ["to" *altered to* "from"] him beyond the letter, a copy of which, marked A. I sent the Department in June last; the Governor however has repeatedly assured me that he had while in Europe an "Understanding["] with him, Mr. H[ughes] upon the subject; this, however informal ["its" *altered to* "it"] may seem to me for a Governor of a Colony to have acted with our chargé, I only state in order that it may partly appear as a reason, why as yet I am induced to believe no application has ever been made in my behalf, and I hope most confidently that the Government of the U. States—through such channel as to them may seem fit, will take measures to have me properly reinstated in this Office.

I shall make my half yearly returns in a few days, as I am only awaiting from the Custom House (the only resource I have) the report to me of the value of Cargoes brought in, in American Bottoms. I have the honor to be Your ob[edien]t Serv[an]t, W.H. Freeman, U. States Consul.

LS (No. 11, Duplicate) in DNA, RG 59 (State Department), Consular Despatches, Curacao, vol. 2 (T-197:2).

From BEN E. GREEN

Legation of the U.S. of A.
Mexico, July 13th 1844

Sir, I have the honor to send you files of the Diario del Gobierno, and the Courier Francais of the 10th July, in which you will find a correspondence of the French, Spanish & English Ministers with the Mexican Govt., on the subject of [Francisco] Sentmanat's expedition to Tabasco. It is truly curious, and the note of the French Minister [Isidore Alleye de Cyprey] of the 27th June is perhaps the most remarkable document ever addressed to any Govt. After having published the first part of the correspondence, the Mexican Govt. sought to suppress this note of the French Minister. It was perhaps for this purpose that they resorted to the decree, which you will find in the Diario of the 5th of July, and to which I beg leave to call your attention. It is surprising what little sensation this attack on the liberty of the press has caused in a country called a Republic.

The French Minister, however, making as it were an appeal from Santa Anna to the people of Mexico, published his note in the Courier Francais. Santa Anna immediately ordered the number containing it to be stopped and sent orders to the Post Office to intercept those sent to the interior. But he was too late. The papers had been sent to the interior before they appeared in the city; and the note of the Baron having thus been made public, the Mexican Govt. thought proper to publish it with an answer. Accordingly in the Diario of the same day (the 11th,) appeared an answer signed by the Minister of War. But at one o'clock on the following day, the original had not been received by the Baron. The singularity of thus publishing a diplomatic note 24 hours before the original was received by the Minister most interested, as well as the improper use made of the name of the British Minister, has afforded much amusement to the Foreign Residents of Mexico (not English). Mr. [Charles] Bankhead was much and justly incensed at the manner, in which his *good friends* sought to get out of their difficulties by throwing the load on his shoulders; & informs me that he has written them a very sharp note on the subject. I was well pleased to see the British minister receive this back-handed blow from this Govt., for his Govt. has deserved it.

To add to the amusement, which all this has caused, the Mexican Govt. after the *diario*, containing the reply of the Minister of War, had been distributed, discovered that they had made a great mistake, in noticing the fact of Sentmanat[']s being a Mexican. They therefore caused a second edition, with corrections, to be printed the next morning, and by order of the most Excellent Gen[era]l Santa Anna, Constitutional President, the subscribers to the paper were forced to return the first copies, in exchange for the revised and improved edition of the following day. I send you both editions.

Having got into a difficulty by shooting those men without any form of trial, they now hope to get out of it, *by* trying them, *after having shot them,* & by making it appear that they were all citizens of the U.S. Accordingly, the declaration of one Don Bernardo Othon, on the subject, given the 11th July, was published in the Diario of last evening. I recommend it to your notice. I have the honor to be Very Respectfully Your ob[edien]t Serv[an]t, Ben E. Green.

ALS (No. 12) in DNA, RG 59 (State Department), Diplomatic Despatches, Mexico, vol. 12 (M-97:13), received 8/25; variant FC (dated 7/12) in DNA, RG 84 (Foreign Posts), Mexico, Despatches.

From J[AMES] HAMILTON, [JR.]

Savannah, July 13[t]h 1844

My Dear Sir, I have only a moment to say that some private business will take me on to New York on Monday next the 15[t]h and that for the gratification of seeing you I shall be at your office on the arrival of the Mail on Thursday & remain 24 hours with you. I pray you even if you designed leaving in a day or two to wait my arrival as I have much of importance to say to you & the President [John Tyler] respecting our yet securing the annexation of Texas to the Union. We must not be foiled. No one understands the Country better than myself or can exercise more influence in it whenever that Prince of Brigands & scoundrels [Samuel] Houston goes out of power which thank God will be on the first day of Dec[embe]r. In the mean time if he is disposed to go wrong we must check mate him.

I shall leave for Texas early in the Autumn to play a strong hand with a sword in it "if need be."

God bless you. Yours ever, J. Hamilton.

P.S. I leave this place to night for Charleston to take the Wilmington Steamer on Tuesday Ev[enin]g.

I need not say how highly I applaud the noble & heroic conduct of President Tyler on the ["Presidential" *canceled and* "Texian" *interlined*] *Crisis* ["which it may well be called" *interlined*]. If my vote could make him President he should next to yourself have it in preference to any other man in the U.S.

Charleston, July 14[t]h 1844

My Dear Sir—I came on in the Mail Boat last Ev[enin]g and found on my arrival your gratifying favor of the 9th inst.

As I shall so soon see you I reserve for our interview a full conference on the points which you notice.

I leave tomorrow but will haul up for one day in Richmond for the purpose of seeing some of my friends there.

Expect me however on Thursday on the arrival of the Mail from the South. I remain My Dear Sir with sincere esteem faithfully Yours, J. Hamilton.

ALS in ScCleA. NOTE: An AEU by Calhoun reads "Gen[era]l Hamilton."

From JOHN HOGAN, "Private"

Utica N[ew] York, July 13th 1844

Dear Sir, I received a letter by yesterday[']s mail from Gen. [Antonio de] Aycinena the Consul Gen[eral] from Guatamala in which he says that he has not yet received any Communication from his Gov[ernment] and from the tone of his letter it would seem that from some Cause or other difficulties had again broken out in Guatamala[;] I suppose the prompting of the English interest in that Country. From the letter I received I take it for granted that the Gen. is much disap[p]ointed and dispairs. Therefore I can look no longer to that Country. I now leave the matter and I am fearful that my prospects are over. Should I be forgotten by my friends ["at Washington" *interlined*] as the indication ["now" *interlined*] is I have one consolation *that on my part there has been nothing left un-*

done honourable that lay in *my power* to do for the advancement of my friend that I have not urged with energy[;] of ["the" *canceled*] Course the Van Buren men leave no stone unturned in this State to effect my Defeat and I fear that their influence has prevailed. I hope that Mrs. Calhoun & family are well & that your own health improves as the Season advances. I am Sir with the greatest respect your Ob[edien]t Servant, John Hogan.

ALS in ScCleA.

From Anson Jones, Secretary of State, Washington, [Republic of Texas], 7/13. "Mr. Isaac Van Zandt, who has for some time been accredited to the Government of the United States, in the character of Chargé d'Affaires of the Republic of Texas, being about to return to his country, I have directed him to take leave of your Excellency at the proper time, and to embrace the opportunity which will thereby be afforded him to convey to your Excellency the expression of the friendly sentiments entertained by the President [Samuel Houston] towards the United States, and of his desire to preserve and improve the relations of harmony so happily subsisting between the two countries." LS in DNA, RG 59 (State Department), Notes from Foreign Legations, Texas, vol. 1 (T-809:1), received 9/11.

From DILLON JORDAN, "Confidential"

Pensacola, July 13th 1844

My dear Sir, I have the honour to inform you, that about ten months since I addressed a letter to Hon. David Levy [Yulee], requesting him to inform the President of the United States, that I would approve the dismissal from office of Eben[ezer] Dorr the Marshal for the District of West Florida. About the 30th May last I addressed a letter to the President requesting him not to remove from office the said Dorr exclusively because I had requested it (in the absence of any charges against him by others). My aversion to removals ["from office" *interlined*] but for *dishonesty*[,] *incapacity* or *political abuse* of its influence, prompted me upon discovering an apparent improvement in his conduct to address that letter to the President. But since then circumstances have transpired which satisfy me that this amendment in his deportment is only temporary, and assumed in anticipation of the expiration of his present term of office which will occur shortly. I am now perfectly convinced, that he is still personally unfriendly ["to" *canceled and* "towards" *interlined*] Walker Anderson E[s]q[ui]r[e] my District Att[orne]y one of the most accomplished scholars, a perfect gentleman and the most amiable of men, and also towards myself. Under other circumstances the personal feelings of a Marshal in regard to the Judge & District Att[orne]y would be a matter of but little importance—but it is otherwise in a Country like this. A portion of our population is composed of the most desperate and unprincipled of men, exiled by their crimes and profligate habits from the old States; in dealing officially with such ["gentl" *canceled*] men, the situation of the Judge and District Attorney is sometimes one of much peril, and at such a crisis to be attended by an officer on whose personal friendship we have no reliance is exceedingly unpleasant.

In addition to the bond generally required of U. States Marshals for the faithful performance of their duties, the Act of Congress passed in 1828 Sec. 8th requires the Marshals appointed for the Territory of Florida to give another in the penalty of $10,000 conditioned for the faithful performance of their duties as Executive officers of the Territory. This last mentioned *Bond* has not yet been given by the said Dorr altho he has been in office nearly four years, and altho he has been requested by me to give it on pain of my suspending his functions as a Territorial officer.

The fact being communicated to me that the offices of Deputy and assistant Marshals through out this District were filled by gentlemen of the Whig party, I protested against this monopoly of office by any political party, and respectfully requested him to remove some and substitute Democrats so as to make an equal distribution among gentlemen of different politics. At this reasonable proposition he became very indignant & rudely and discourteously refused. I thereupon made of my own accord the distribution.

I must therefore in justice to the District Attorney, the people of this District, and myself request you to renew to the President my desire for the instant removal of the said Dorr—or if His Excellency prefers it (as his term will soon expire) that he be not reappointed. The District Att[orne]y and myself would recommend as Successor to said Dorr, Florentia T. Commyns. He is a just[,] firm[,] upright and honourable man, well qualified in every respect, and a man who can give the most unquestionable Security. Walter C. Yonge of Walton County would also make a good Marshal should the President have any objection to Commyns. As I have reason to fear that some of my communications to Washington City have never reached their destination, you will please do me the Kindness to advise me of your receipt of this.

Wishing for the sake of our beloved Country that you may be blessed with uninteruppted health, and that no combination of circumstances may induce a change of your position unless it be to one of more extended power, I have the honour to be Most respectfully Your ob[edient] S[ervan]t, Dillon Jordan, Judge of the United States for the District of West Florida.

P.S. You will find embraced in this, a copy of my note [of 6/7/-1843] to said Dorr requesting him to give bonds as required by law—with which request he has never complied. I have the honour to be Most resp[ectfull]y Your Ob[edient] S[ervan]t, Dillon Jordan, Judge &c.

ALS with En in DNA, RG 59 (State Department), Applications and Recommendations, 1837–1845, Dorr (M-687:9, frames 420–424). Note: An AEU by Calhoun reads "Judge Jordan." A Clerk's EU reads "His commission expires 13th September 1845."

From WILLIAM R. KING

Legation des Etats Unis
Paris, 13th July 1844

Sir, I have the honor to inform you that I arrived in Havre on the 7th, and at this place, on the 10th of last month. As soon as the necessary arrangements could be completed I sought an audience of the King [Louis Philippe] in order to present my letter of Credence. The 1st of July was appointed for this purpose, and accordingly, on that day, I repaired to Neuilly where the Court resides at this moment. In presenting the letter of the President [John Tyler] to His Majesty the King of the French, I made the brief Address, a copy of which (A.) is subjoined. Nothing could be more cordial than the reply and reception of the King. He reciprocated very warmly my assurances of national and personal good will, and acknowledged with marked sensibility the just tribute which I paid to the virtues of his family. Referring to my allusion to the assistance rendered to the United States at the period of their revolutionary struggle, he observed that the recollection of it afforded him great satisfaction, and added, in emphatic words and manner, that he ever considered America the natural ally of France. Much more to this purport and in this strain, the King delivered in very good English, expressed in warm and well chosen terms. I was afterwards presented to the Queen and to the Duke de Nemours, by whom I was received with equal Kindness and consideration. The next day, I received an invitation for myself and Secretary of Legation [John L. Martin] to dine with his Majesty on the fourth of July, a compliment which derived its chief value from the selection of the day. On that occasion, after dinner, the King, in a familiar conversation, broached the subject of Texas, and asked why the Treaty had been rejected by the Senate, the news of which had just been received. I seized this opportunity to assure him that the rejection was caused by political considerations of a domestic nature; that the object would, in my opinion, be prosecuted with unabated vigor; that it was my firm belief that a decided majority of the American people were in favor of the measure, which would certainly be consummated at no distant period. Thereupon the King frankly observed that it was his desire to see Texas remain an independent state, and spoke of commercial advantages secured to France by treaty with that republic. I replied that the interests of France, which were purely commercial, were totally distinct from those of England, and that they would be promoted by the annexation of Texas to the United States. His Majesty admitted that the colonial possessions of Great Britain in North America involved that power in political considerations which did not affect France, with reference to this question, and he finally assured me, or gave me, at least, distinctly to understand, that in any event, no steps would be taken by his government, in the slightest degree hostile, or which would give to the United States just cause of complaint. This declaration I consider of no small importance, for although a constitutional monarch, the King of the French is no cypher, but substantially his own prime minister, and a minister moreover, who does not hold his place by the uncertain tenure of a fluctuating majority in the Chamber of Deputies.

In the course of the conversation, his Majesty informed me that his emphatic advice to the Mexican government, ["had been," *interlined*] as the best policy for that state and for others, to acknowledge at once the independence of Texas. Among other topics, the King took occasion to observe that some anxiety had been felt by the French government with regard to supposed designs of the United States upon the Sandwich islands. I promptly reassured him upon this subject, with the declaration that the interests of the United States in the Pacific being purely commercial, nothing more was desired by them than to prevent any European power from acquiring a preponderance in that quarter, which might prove detrimental to

American navigation, so extensive and so valuable in the South Seas.

A few days after, I requested of M. [François P.G.] Guizot, Minister of Foreign Affairs, an interview for the purpose of holding a free conversation upon topics interesting to the two countries. He expressed a corresponding desire, but upon the plea of numerous engagements, requested a postponement of the conference, until next week, to which as I had no specific proposition to communicate, I was constrained to defer. Indeed, the conversation which I have had in a higher or rather the highest quarter, makes me less solicitous about the delay, though I shall omit no proper steps to obtain an early interview, and an explicit understanding, the result of which I shall not fail to transmit by the first opportunity.

The general impression in the best informed circles here, is that England, at this moment, exerts a marked influence upon the councils of the French government, and particularly upon the mind of M. Guizot, who is the ruling spirit, of the Cabinet, as well as the ablest expounder and defender of its principles and policy in the tribune. Still the policy of the King is essentially pacific and conservative, and, I am persuaded, that however much he or his ministers may desire to maintain a cordial understanding with the Cabinet of St. James, that disposition, as the King assured me, will not proceed to the extent of acts hostile or unfriendly to the United States in reference to the Texas question. Indeed, domestic embarrassments and European questions, among which those of Algiers and Morocco preponderate at present, necessarily indispose the governments both of England and France, from involving themselves in active difficulties in remote quarters, whatever may be the feeling with which they, and particularly the former, contemplate any measure calculated to augment the territory and power of the United States. About the time of my arrival, much was said about a joint protest of France and England against the annexation of Texas to the United States, and indeed Mr. [Ashbel] Smith the Chargé d'Affaires of the former republic, informed me that he had reason to believe that such a step had been taken. I have not been able to satisfy myself that such a document exists, and, indeed, what I have gathered, leads me to the opposite conclusion. If it does, and I shall not hesitate to ask M. Guizot the question, however much it may be regretted, as proof of the malign influence exerted by Great Britain upon the councils of the French government, in a matter which concerns the latter so remotely, it should be regarded as of little weight after the assurances of the King to which I have referred, and the other considerations upon which I have touched.

The intervention of this Legation was appealed to by the agents of the Banks of Columbus, ["in" *canceled*] Georgia, and Apalachicola, which had been swindled to the amount of about 300,000 dollars by a certain Gerard Koster, who has taken refuge in Switzerland, where he sets his victims at defiance. Under these circumstances I deemed it my duty to apply to the government of Switzerland, through its representative at this court, for the arrest, detention, and ultimate delivery upon the production of satisfactory evidence, of Gerard Koster. Although there is no Treaty of Extradition between the governments of the United States and Switzerland, I did not hesitate to assure [G. de Tschann] the Swiss Chargé d'Affaires, that *in* the United States, criminals had been delivered, under analogous circumstances, and that the same comity would, doubtless, be extended to Switzerland. In giving this qualified assurance, without which there was little or no hope, that my request would be complied with, the well known case, among others, of the individual who stole the jewels of the Princess of Orange ["was in my mind;" *interlined*] and the engagement is only that the State governments will do for the government of Switzerland what has been, or may be done, for other countries with which the United States have no Treaty for the mutual surrender of criminals. I abstain from further details in this place, as the whole transaction is sufficiently explained in my ["ltt" *canceled*] letter to the Chargé d'Affaires of the Swiss Confederation, a copy of which (B.) together with his answer (C) is subjoined. I addressed also a communication to the French government, ["(D)" *interlined*] requesting permission, should my application to the government of Switzerland be complied with, to transport Koster through France, and also his arrest and detention should he take refuge in the French territory, in order to give time and opportunity for the further proceedings which would, in that case, become necessary. An answer to this communication has not yet been received, but I have assurances, that one will promptly be sent. I shall not fail to keep you advised of the progress of this important and delicate affair.

I have the honor to acknowledge the receipt of your despatch No. 2 and in accordance with its instructions, I have applied to the French government for the Exequaturs of Francis M. Auboyneau and Joseph W. Fabens appointed Consuls of the United States ["for the" *canceled*] the former for the port of La Rochelle in France, and the latter for that of Cayenne in French Guiana.

Mr. [Henry] Ledyard, our late Chargé d'Affaires at this court, left Paris on the 11th for Havre, whence he intends to embark for the United States, with his family on the 10th of August. It gives me great pleasure to bear testimony to the very efficient and creditable manner in which his duties have been performed and to the favorable impression which he has uniformly made upon the authorities of this country, as well as upon his fellow citizens generally. His deportment towards myself won my entire regard, and I shall ever feel a lively interest in his welfare and that of his amiable and estimable family.

In conclusion I respectfully request that I may be promptly and sufficiently advised of everything which may enable me to be of service to the country in my relations with this government, which always looks to the minister of the United States for the earliest and most authentic information from his government. I have the honor to be very respectfully your obedient servant, William R. King.

LS (No. 1) with Ens in DNA, RG 59 (State Department), Diplomatic Despatches, France, vol. 30 (M-34:33), received 8/3.

From Louis Mark, New York [City], 7/13. "Immediately on my return here having been informed by you that the first Bond I gave was informal and objected to, I had the inclosed one signed by proper Securities and certified by the District Attorney and I trust that it will be accepted and recorded as a proper security. Relative to the first Bond and any other Charges against me, I trust as I have been appointed at various times by three Presidents, and confirmed by three different Senates as a Consul of the United States, no Charges against me will be admitted or acted [upon] on the bare assertions of any Persons, but that Proof will be required of them, and I am confident you will find them all to originate in Calumny or Error." ALS in DNA, RG 59 (State Department), Consular Despatches, Vienna, vol. 1 (T-243:1).

Louis Mark, New York [City], to Francis Markoe, Jr., [State Department], 7/13. Mark promises to obtain evidence concerning the charges made against him recently. [Henry] Wheaton will write to the State Department when he learns of the attacks made on Mark's character. Mark returns his second bond, feeling that this is necessary since he has acted as Consul already. He has been ill and can write no more. ALS in DNA, RG 59 (State Department), Consular Despatches, Vienna, vol. 1 (T-243:1).

From J[ohn] Murphy, U.S. Consul, Cork, 7/13. He encloses his consular returns. He has not yet received any reply to his letter of 5/3, and still retains possession of the parcel mentioned in that letter [of communications from Thomas Fitnam to Daniel O'Connell]. LS (No. 17) with Ens in DNA, RG 59 (State Department), Consular Despatches, Cork, vol. 1 (T-196:1), received 8/23.

From C.A. Murray, [U.S. Consul], Gothenburg, [Sweden], 7/13. He transmits his semiannual consular returns. "There has been no American vessel in the Port during the first half of this year, the foreign vessels becoming, it appears, with every year more Successful rivals with the Americans." ALS with Ens in DNA, RG 59 (State Department), Consular Despatches, Gothenburg, vol. 1 (T-276:1), received 9/9.

To Charles S. Sibley, U.S. District Attorney, Tallahassee, Fla. Territory, 7/13. "I herewith transmit extracts of certain communications [from Governor Richard K. Call] to this department affecting your official character, and have to request, that you will, without unnecessary delay, furnish me with such explanations as the nature of the complaints therein preferred seems to require." FC in DNA, RG 59 (State Department), Domestic Letters, 34:299 (M-40:32).

From W[illia]m Wilkins, War Department, 7/13. In reply to Calhoun's note of yesterday, he states that he does not have any information in regard to the number and description of the arms taken by Capt. P[hilip] St. George Cooke from the Texas force of Col. [Jacob] Snively. The arms have been deposited at Fort Leavenworth. He encloses a copy of an order issued today "to obtain for you all the information required by your note." LS with En in DNA, RG 59 (State Department), Miscellaneous Letters (M-179: 105, frames 55–58); FC in DNA, RG 107 (Secretary of War), Letters Sent Relating to Military Affairs, 1800–1861, 25:363–364 (M-6:25); CC in DNA, RG 107, Letters Received, Registered Series, 1801–1860, S-25 (M-221:135).

From Ben E. Green

Legation of the U.S. of A.
Mexico, July 14th 1844

Sir, I have the honor to send you a speech of Don José Julian Tornel, brother of the late Minister of War [José M. Tornel], to which I beg leave to call your attention. I informed you some time since of the quarrel between Santa Anna and Gen[era]l Tornel. Santa Anna was so much incensed against Tornel, for the occurrences of Puebla, that he would not receive him for a long time after his return to the Capital. This vindictive attack on the U.S. was a kind of peace offering offered up on the shrine of Santa Anna's deep rooted hatred of the U.S., and the next day, the Gen[era]l went to the palace of Tacubaya, & after being made to wait three hours in the antechamber, by way of mortification and penance, was kindly received, pardoned and invited to dine.

The speech of D[o]n José Julian Tornel is but a repetition of the slanders, which Santa Anna and his creature, the other Tornel, commenced many years ago, & have repeated up to this time. They began by the proclamation of the Congress of Vera Cruz (Santa Anna's stronghold) against Mr. [Joel R.] Poinsett, and have been continued ever since. This system of abusing the U.S. and exciting prejudices on the part of Mexico against us has been the cover, under which Santa Anna has hid his own daring ambition. That ambition has finally reached the Dictatorship and the "Constitutional Presidency" (what satire lurks in that title of Constitutional President) but satiety has not yet followed success. Power still more absolute is before him, and by the same means, he hopes to lead his countrymen, from hating us, to hate our republican institutions and to invest him with imperial and absolute power. That his efforts have been more than partially successful, you will see from Gen[era]l [Waddy] Thompson's despatches of the 28th June, in which he says: "I am now satisfied that I was in error in saying that the feelings of any of these people are friendly to me—the feeling is universally and strongly otherwise"—and of the 30th July, in which he says: "The Mexicans hate us with the hatred of a Spaniard, bitter & unchangeable. The rights of American citizens of every grade & character are subject to constant outrage."

This "bitter and unchangeable hatred" has been excited by Santa Anna and his partisans, of whom the most conspicuous for rancorous falsehood is Gen[era]l Tornel. Unfortunately it is, as Gen[era]l Thompson describes it, strong and nearly universal, and ["unfortunately" *canceled*] I have no hopes of a change for the better, so long as Santa Anna retains his present unlimited power. He has caused and seeks to continue it. The very force loan, which he exacted to pay the claims of our citizens, was intended to exasperate the Mexicans against us; for the Diario of the time, by his order as I have no doubt, defended the forced loan by saying, that the previous administration of [Anastasio] Bustamente had engaged to pay those claims, & that although they were unjust, the national honor required that the engagement should be complied with, and the avarice of their neighbours of the north satisfied, by resorting to the odious measure of forced loans.

In this model Republic there is no one who dares to speak or write the truth. The report of the Committee of Congress, which I sent you some time since, was most remarkable for boldness, notwithstanding the anxious disclaimer of all intention to blame Santa Anna. But the spirit of that report was soon smothered. The day after its publication, Santa Anna summoned the generals and military men to a consultation at Tacubaya, and the arrogance of the Congress was at once checked by the mere announcement of a consultation of Generals.

I send you nos. 1[,] 2[,] 3[,] 4 & 5, copies of several notes from the Minister of F. Relations, and my replies. My reply (No. 5) to Mr. [José M. de] Bocanegra's note of the 8th July has not yet been sent, for the same day it was written, a rumour arrived here by the way of Campeachy that the Senate had rejected the Treaty. The allusion to aspiring intriguants, who have sought to divert attention from themselves by slandering the U.S., is a direct blow at Santa Anna, and the reference is so plain, that every one in this country will understand it. I am afraid therefore that he would reply in such angry and insulting terms as would lead to serious consequences. He calculates largely, I know, on our party divisions, which he thinks are so great that our Govt. may be insulted and our national honor & character attacked with impunity. I hope that the next news from the States will show him that he has overestimated the evil of party amongst us and undervalued our national spirit. If the news by the next mail will warrant it, I will send this note to Mr. Bocanegra. The previous correspondence has been published by the Mexican Govt., and I presume this also will be. If it is, I am in hopes that it will have a good effect (not indeed with the present Govt., for of them I hope for nothing good) with the people, both by removing the prejudices now so generally entertained against us, & by reconciling them to the independence & annexation of Texas. I think it desirable that the Mexican people should be, if possible, undeceived in some way. For they now almost universally believe the stories propagated by Santa Anna, through such instruments as Tornel, & think that we are the cause not only of their frequent revolutions, & consequent deplorable condition, but that our Govt. has directly fomented the revolution of Texas, & intends to do the same with California, & all their northern provinces.

My object has been, if possible, to put a stop to the present movement against Texas, and for this purpose I have, on all proper occasions in my intercourse with these people, used the language & arguments contained in this note (no. 5).

I send you the Diario of the 2d July, in which you will find another projet for raising money by taxing the rents of houses. This is the measure, which meets with most favour, because the burden thus reaches the clergy and the foreigners. I do not see that our Treaty positively exempts our citizens from this tax, although its avowed object is a foreign war. The bill has passed the Chamber of Deputies; but the Senate seems disposed to reject it. If it does Santa Anna will send his soldiers to turn the senators out and close the doors.

I send you also the continuation of the correspondence about the Tabasco affair; a slip containing the ["last" *interlined*] note of the Spanish Minister, and the Diario of various dates containing documents in relation to this subject, which with France begins to assume a threatening aspect. I have the honor to be Very Respectfully Your ob[edien]t Serv[an]t, Ben E. Green.

[Enclosure: State Department translation]
J[osé] M. de Bocanegra to Ben E. Green

Mexico, July 2, 1844

The Undersigned, Minister of Relations, has received the note dated the 24 of June last, from Mr. B.E. Green Chargé d'Affaires of the United States, in answer to one from this Department, relative to the military and naval forces, destined by the Government of the United States, to prevent the recovery of Texas by Mexico; in which Mr. Green states that he has received no instructions on that subject, and consequently cannot answer the question as clearly and expressly as he could wish.

Mr. Green nevertheless enters at length into the subject and at the end of his note refers to the letter from the Undersigned of the 23 of August last. If that note be cited by Mr. Green, in order to apply it to the case of the explanations demanded, it appears that those explanations are given in the affirmative sense. The Undersigned must therefore repeat, in order to remove all misapprehension, in a matter so delicate and serious, that Mexico, in her said note, did not declare war, but did declare, that she should justly regard, as equivalent to a declaration of war, the annexation of Texas to the United States; on grounds which were afterwards set forth, and which have been reproduced without variation.

To regard an act as a declaration of war, is not the positive act of declaration of war; it is, if the actual state of the negotiation be considered, to prevent any injury, which war might occasion.

Mexico has endeavoured to avoid all cause of ill feeling on the part of the Government of the United States. Such has been her course, and with this object, she has frankly and honourably declared, in what light she would regard, the annexation of Texas. It is not Mexico, therefore which declares the war; others wish to make war on her, and in this unfortunate event, the consequences will not rest upon her responsibility. The Undersigned repeats this view, by express order of the Constitutional President, in order to correct that formed by Mr. Green, to whom he renews the assurances of his distinguished consideration. J.M. de Bocanegra.

[Enclosure: State Department translation]
J[osé] M. de Bocanegra to B[en] E. Green
National Palace Mexico, July 2, 1844
The Undersigned, Minister of Foreign Relations and Government, has received the note from Mr. Green Chargé d'Affaires *ad interim* of the United States of America, dated the 26th of June last, in answer to one from this Department, both relating to the projected annexation of Texas to the United States; and he observes in it ["that" *interlined*] the American Legation insists that the recognition of the so called Republic although it be of the fact, supposes a right; an assertion with which the Undersigned cannot conform.

Although a question which has been already ["discussed" *interlined*] in former communications should not be resumed, yet as Mr. Green declares, as already said, that the recognition of a fact, presupposes a right, the Undersigned, adhering to the words of Mr. Green, conceives that the idea can only be defined, by adopting and admitting the view exposed by the Undersigned on this subject. Nations in the case in question, acknowledge the fact, and nothing more; to this they confine themselves; and is it not true, that even the United States, have done what ["the" *interlined*] other ["nations" *interlined*] did on the subject of the independance of Texas? Is it not clear, that they have all left the rights of Mexico untouched, as regards this integrant part of her territory; and that respecting, as they have those rights, they have acknowledged and do acknowledge, the perfect right of Mexico, over that Department? It follows therefore, as an obvious and natural deduction, that the Executive of the United States, has violated all the conventions, by signing the treaty of annexation of Texas; thus acting upon proceedings entirely at variance with the general principles of right, and the special principles of its own Government.

The American Legation will allow the Undersigned, before concluding, to make one observation, drawn from the very nature of things; he means to say, that the independance proclaimed in Texas, with very few exceptions was not proclaimed by Mexicans, as he has already had the honour to remark to Mr. Green; but was proclaimed by natives of the United States, some of them adventurers, and the others speculators in lands, neither of which classes of persons, could appropriate to themselves, a territory, belonging to Mexico, in full and absolute dominion; that consequently no one had the right to act in the manner in which they acted; being foreign adventurers; and that ["this" *interlined*] act is a real usurpation, and their independance is an occurrence accompanied by particular circumstances, which as they are not common, may be styled exceptional and unexampled; for which and for other reasons, sufficiently manifest, it cannot be compared with what has occurred in all ages, in each Continent. Bands of persons assembled for the purpose of robbing others of their property, should not, and cannot enjoy the privileges peculiar to Sovereignty; the law classifies them, and places them in their proper line.

Mr. Green concludes by declaring, that he leaves this matter to his Government. The Government of the Undersigned has declared in its previous communications, that although this discussion had been brought properly to an end between this Department, and the American Legation, yet it could not do less, than enter upon it, after it had been brought forward again by that Legation. The policy of Mexico in this serious affair is fixed, and is frankly declared. The Undersigned has express orders from the Constitutional President of the Republic, to repeat the oft-repeated protests on its part, which maintain its rights in safety; insisting especially upon what has been already clearly set forth, at length, in fulfilment of the sacred duties imposed by the nation, on the Executive.

The Undersigned avails himself of this opportunity to repeat &c, J.M. de Bocanegra.

[Enclosure]
Ben E. Green to J[osé] M. de Bocanegra

Legation of the U.S. of A.
Mexico, July 4th 1844

The undersigned, Chargé d'affaires ad interim of the U.S. of A., has this moment had the honor to receive the note of H.E. J.M. de

Bocanegra dated the 2d inst. The undersigned was in hopes that this unpleasant subject was at an end, at least so far as he was concerned. But the remark of H.E. that the Independence of Texas was declared (with few exceptions), by natives of the U.S., adventurers and speculators in lands, seems intended to cast an indirect imputation on the countrymen of the undersigned, and he feels called upon to notice it.

H.E. must remember that those "natives of the U.S." went to Texas upon the invitation and under the laws of Spain and Mexico herself, that they left their native country, that they carried with them their families and their fortunes, & settled both in Texas, not however with a view to usurpation, but upon the invitation of Mexico and for her benefit. They ceased to be citizens of the U.S. & became "colonists" of Mexico, with her consent and at her solicitation. They went to Texas under the confederated form of Govt. When a consolidated Govt. was substituted in its stead, they declared their independence. Many natives of the U.S. went to their assistance. But this was nothing new in American history. Many doubtless left the U.S. for Texas for purposes of gain, but most of those, who went to her assistance, were led thither by the same spirit, which rallied Commodore [David] Porter and other countrymen of the undersigned around the standard of Mexico, in her contest with Spain.

Writers in international law say, that "*to give a nation a right to make an immediate figure in the great society of nations, it is sufficient that it be really sovereign and independent,*["] *that is, that it govern itself by its own authority and laws: and that "the rights of every nation, which does so govern itself are naturally the same as those of any other nation.*"

The undersigned expected that, the *fact* being admitted, the mere citation of this well known rule would be sufficient to establish the *right* of the sovereignty of Texas. He therefore forebore in his note of the 26th ult[im]o to notice the grounds, on which H.E. sought to exclude Texas from the benefit of this well established principle, to wit; because she was a revolted colony ("Pues que no eran sino colonos sublevados.")

The undersigned was silent on this point from a motive of delicacy, which he trusts will be properly appreciated by Mr. de Bocanegra. He knew that it could not but be unpleasant to H.E. to have the example of Mexico again thrown as a stumbling block in his way.

H.E. says that Texas has no *right* to her independence. Why? Because she is a revolted Colony. The argument is unfortunate, and it is certainly the first time that the undersigned has ever heard it advanced on the American continent, and by a Republican Minister. He deems it unnecessary to undertake to refute it. For to do so would be to imply a doubt, not only of the right of Mexico to throw off her dependence on Spain, but also of the right of the U.S. to do the same in regard to England. Both are "revolted colonies," the one of Spain and the other of G.B.: and the undersigned deems their *right* to their independence too clear to need argument from him to support it. He deems it not only unnecessary but improper for a representative of one of the American Republics (all of which were originally *revolted colonies*) to undertake to refute an argument which denies their *right* to independence, and calls their actual independence an usurpation. Their right is as clear as the noonday sun: needs only to be stated to be admitted; and the undersigned expected that a Mexican Minister would be the last to call it in question. For the undersigned at least, it is a settled question; settled by the authority of his own country and of Mexico. Whatever arguments, therefore, ingenious casuistry may advance to prove that *revolted colonies* have no *right* to independence; that the U.S. in declaring their independence, *usurped* the dominions of the King of England; and that [Miguel] Hidalgo, [José M.] Morelos and [Augustín de] Iturbide, in achieving the independence of Mexico, violated the divine right of the King of Spain, and usurped his territory, the undersigned begs leave to pass them by in respectful silence, and to decline the discussion.

Texas presents a parallel case with Mexico and the U.S. The very terms of H.E.'s argument affirm it. The very terms of that argument, tested by the whole history of the American continent, prove that the ground taken is untenable. For that, which H.E. applies, as a stigma to Texas, was common to all American States and to Mexico herself. They were all revolted colonies.

The undersigned renews to H.E. Mr. Bocanegra the assurance of his distinguished consideration. (Signed) Ben E. Green.

[Enclosure: State Department translation]
J[osé] M. de Bocanegra to B[en] E. Green
National Palace Mexico, July 8, 1844
The Undersigned, Minister of Foreign Relations and Government, had the honour to receive the communication dated the 4th instant, from the Chargé d'Affaires of the United States of America, and its contents oblige him not to leave it unanswered.

If Mr. Green has flattered himself, that the discussion would have been terminated on his part, the Undersigned has exposed clearly and decisively, in his preceding notes, that although he was desirous to conclude it, yet he could do no less than continue it, in order to sustain the dignity and integrity of the Republic, which the American Legation has attacked, by presenting the affair at one time on the grounds that the policy of its Government, in order to maintain slavery in the United States, obliged it to sign the treaty of annexation; then denying the rights and dominion of Mexico over that Department; then asserting that the United States are fully authorised to treat with Texas. This variable course which has been given by Mr. Green to the principal question, namely as regard the treaty above mentioned, has forced the Ministry to take into consideration, each of these points, and to answer on each, in order to place in a clear light, the justice of the course of Mexico, through the replies given to the arguments adduced by the Legation.

In the last note of the 4th instant, to which the Undersigned is now replying, the Chargé d'Affaires appears in the character of a defender, and as if he were a representative of the Independance proclaimed by the colonists, and adventurers ["of" *canceled*] who came into Texas. This remarkable circumstance, against which the Undersigned has express orders to protest, as he does protest, (*rechazar*) as also against the errors in which the Charge d'Affaires will permit me to tell him he has fallen, again force the Undersigned to rectify the statements of facts, which are cited, in order to overthrow the rights attempted to be deduced from them, as they have been leading ["him" *interlined*] from position to position, ever since the Chargé d'Affaires began this correspondance.

Mr. Green asserts that the natives of the United States were invited by the Laws of Spain and Mexico; that they left their country, and established themselves in Texas, not with the object of usurpation &c. This assertion indeed wants exactness, as it assumes what does not exist; it assumes that Mexico invited colonists to those territories, whilst it appeared[?] by ["authentic and well known" *interlined*] documents that the colony solicited and founded by [Stephen F.] Austin, had a contrary origin, and Mexico in the annals of her independance, has it set forth, in a historical and invariable manner, An act ["of so much generosity, so much" *canceled*] so generous, so hospitable, so worthy of gratitude, and from which the nation has received no benefit, cannot be cited in the terms employed with regard to it by Mr. Green; and much less, considering that a small number of families has never been allowed to place itself above the general mass of the nation. Is there any system of legislation which gives a fraction the superiority over the whole?

Mr. Green says, that the colonists went to Texas, under the federal system, and declared their independance when a consolidated system was substituted for the other. This proposition is entirely destitute of foundation. The permission to colonise, was obtained under an absolute system of Government; they submitted to it freely and spontaneously; and as Mexico did not adopt federal institutions until October 1824, ["the erro" *canceled*] it is manifestly erroneous to assert ["that" *interlined*] the Colonists went to Texas under the federal form of Government; and the merit claimed for them ["on this grounds," *interlined*] on account of their insurrection, is in consequently destroyed.

Austin in his character of a colonist, and the families which he brought with him, were obliged to follow the lot of the nation, of which they became a very small part; they were necessarily to submit to its laws, and to follow the changes which the majority makes. This is a principle of law, constantly observed, and is essential to a Republic.

As regards those who left the United States for Texas, who as the American Legation confesses, came to the aid of the colonists, led by the same feeling which induced Commodore Porter to take part with Mexico, the Undersigned does not discover the identity asserted by the American Legation. The officer here named, was in the service of the nation, in the Mexican navy; and he was under the obligation to defend its rights. Those who have gone to Texas, with views of self interest, and in order to aid the usurpation, can never be regarded as other than adventurers, introduced into the Republic, in the most illegal manner, and therefore deserving to be treated with all the severity of the laws, and as cooperating with the usurpers. The intentions assigned by Mr. Green to the colonists, are contradicted by subsequent acts, and their perfidious conduct places them in evidence; nor can the convention avail them, as it cannot shield them from the operation of the invariable fundamental law of every society, that the minority cannot place themselves above the majority.

It is thus demonstrated, by the history of the period, and the circumstances under which Austin obtained the permission to colonise in Texas, that it began under an absolute system of Government; that after the independance of Mexico had been secured the imperial Government ["was" *interlined*] then recognised; that federal forms did not begin to be in force until the year 1824; and it being on the other hand it is unquestionable, that the submission yielded to the Spanish Government, as well as to the Mexican, involved no condition, and did not leave them at liberty to withdraw from the nation to ["which they had" *changed to* "whose sovereignty"] they had submitted, it follows naturally that their insurrection could never be regarded otherwise than as a scandalous act, and a usurpation against Mexico. Consequently, the doctrine of the writers on international law, which Mr. Green cites, is ["not" *interlined*] applicable to the case, from what has been here shewn and proved.

The Undersigned has previously said, and he now repeats, that the occurrence of the attempted independance of Texas, is connected with circumstances such and of so exceptional a nature, that there is no parity between ["them" *canceled and* "it" *interlined*], and those which have occurred at other times, in both continents; and arguments cannot be deduced from the one, applicable to the other.

The Undersigned and the nation, in whose name he has the honour to speak, will always apply the term of insurgents to colonists, who have, with the most notable bad faith, usurped this integrant part of the territory of Mexico, violating all rights, even those of hospitality; he will in like manner recognise ["as such" *interlined*] those adventurers, who have since introduced themselves, and in the land speculators; regarding them all, merely as authors and fomenters of the rebellion.

The Undersigned, after minutely examining the facts in question, finds no analogy, nor anything in common, between the insurrection of Texas, and the independance of Mexico; and Mr. Green will permit him to repeat, that ["there is a difference between" *interlined*] proclaiming ["independance" *canceled and* "emancipation," *interlined*] and obtaining it; by obtaining emancipation, the right of sovereignty is obtained, and cannot be disturbed, even by the mother country; as occurred in fact, with respect to Mexico; other nations leaving her, to sustain herself by her own forces, and declaring that Spain may regain her dominion, by her forces. It is therefore clear, that no one has denied to the nation, on which an ["insurgent" *interlined*] colony depends, the power to reduce it, to its former dependance. This was the case with regard to the United States of America. Nor can it be said, that this is not a Republican principle, as that condition does not exclude justice, or the respect due to rights; on the contrary he who is most just, is the best Republican.

Can the Hidalgos, Morelos, Iturbides, and other illustrious champions of Mexico, who with their own forces and resources, succeeded in giving liberty to their nativeland, be placed on a par with the [Mirabeau B.] La Mars, [Samuel] Houstons ["and" *interlined*] Sniveleys [*sic*; Jacob Snively], who had no title to legitimate their entry, and insurrection.

Mexico, guided by the fundamental maxims of right, cannot conceive, nor can it ever be proved to her in a certain and positive manner, that the complete dominion which she acquired over the department of Texas, has been lost by a reunion of foreigners, who have attempted to withdraw it, from obedience to her Government, and to break the unity of the nation, by shaking all the rights and conventions of society. Mexico, like all other nations, in her situation, preserves her legitimate dominion, in spite of the rebels, who endeavour to seperate themselves from the legitimate and recognised Government. Force has been, and continues to be the ultimate and effective means, which has always been employed in the civilised world, to reduce to order, those who attempt to subvert order. There is nothing strange in the conduct of the Mexican Republic.

On this has Mexico founded her protests; she again insists upon them; and as the American legation may be supposed to have urged this point, only in order to sustain the Independance of Texas, which the Mexican Government does not and cannot admit, Mexico remains in ["the" *interlined*] legal position, in which she has stood, and in the enjoyment of the perfect right, which has constantly remained ["to her" *interlined*] untouched, without having suffered any wound, to her dignity and integrity.

The Undersigned repeats to the Chargé d'Affaires of the United States the assurances of his distinguished consideration. J.M. de Bocanegra.

[Enclosure]

Ben E. Green to J[osé] M. de Bocanegra

Legation of the U.S. of A.
July 12th 1844, Mexico

The undersigned, Charge d'Affaires ad interim of the U.S. of A., has had the honor to receive the note of H.E. J.M. de Bocanegra, dated 8th July, & must be permitted to express his surprise that Mr. de Bocanegra should charge him with the latitude which this correspondence has taken. For it is evident from the correspondence itself, that he has only followed H.E. from point to point, from position to position, and, one by one, exposed the fallacy of his arguments by the simple example of Mexico. The sole object of the undersigned has been to show that Texas is a sovereign and independent nation; for this position being once established, the right of the U.S. to conclude the Treaty of annexation, which has given rise to this correspondence, follows as a necessary consequence.

Mr. de Bocanegra first advanced the singular doctrine that recognition by the mother country could alone give sovereignty to a colony, which had thrown off its allegiance. The fallacy of this position was made apparent by the example of Mexico. H.E. then shifted his ground; half admitted and half denied the sovereignty of Texas; admitted the fact and denied the right, and did so on the ground that revolted colonies had no right to independence. The example of Mexico again surprised H.E., who now again shifts his position, & denies the sovereignty of Texas on the ground that the minority have no right to rule the majority. No one will admit the truth of this principle more readily than the undersigned. But he is unable to see in what manner it is applicable to the present case. For the right, which Texas claims, is not to govern Mexico but simply to govern herself. And even if this principle were applicable the example of Mexico and the U.S. would again prove fatal to H.E.'s argument. For they, a minority, declared their independence of Great Britain & Spain a large majority, and their *right* has as yet never been questioned at least on this side of the Atlantic.

The undersigned must be permitted to inform H.E. Mr. Bocanegra, that he made no mistake in saying that the Colonists of Texas went thither at the invitation of Mexico, and under the Federal form of Govt. For the great majority of them went thither under the colonization laws of the States of Coahuila & Texas, enacted March 24 1825, after the adoption of the Federal system. It is H.E. who has fallen into an error, in supposing that when the undersigned spoke of the colonists of Texas, he referred only to Austin, who, it is true, went to that country under the imperial Govt., but who was only the Pioneer of Colonization in ["that country" *canceled and* "Texas" *interlined*]. The undersigned referred to those, who followed him, & who went thither under the law above referred to, to the great body of them, & not to one man. He did not however refer to this circumstance ["for the purpose" *interlined*] of justifying the revolution of Texas. His sole object, in referring to the history of that colony at all, was to vindicate his Govt. from the charge that it had fostered and was responsible for that revolution.

The undersigned begs leave in conclusion to offer some remarks not inappropriate to this occasion. Since he has been in this country, he has observed that his Govt. and his countrymen are the daily objects of the most virulent abuse, the most false and detestable calumniation. Nor is this evil spirit of recent growth. Since the first establishment of diplomatic relations between the U.S. and Mexico it has been at work. Aspiring intrigants, bad & dangerous men, dangerous alike to the internal peace & foreign interests of Mexico, have sought to create jealousies and ill feeling towards the U.S., wishing to divert attention from their own misdeeds, and to escape punishment, by fixing the public eye on another object. Unfortunately their efforts have been but too successful. Mr. de Bocanegra is well aware of the many rank calumnies and slanders of the U.S., which daily teem from the Mexican press, and which have even found their way into the official newspaper, which, as we have been officially informed, is under the immediate direction & supervision of the Mexican Ministry.

Knowing the feelings, which by such men and for such purposes, have been so industriously and so effectually sown in the public mind of Mexico, the undersigned saw with surprise and regret that H.E. Mr. Bocanegra had gone out of his way to remark, in his note of the 2d July, that the independence of Texas was declared (with few exceptions) by natives of the U.S. The undersigned could not but see this remark of the minister of F. Relations was calculated indirectly to strengthen the erroneous impressions & prejudices, which have been propagated by the men and for the purposes above referred to, and to give a *casi* semi official authority to their falsehoods. He must suppose that Mr. de Bocanegra overlooked, through inadvertence, the effect which this remark was likely to have. For he can not suppose that the minister of F. Relations would lend his official character to give weight to calumnies, which he knows to be false. The Records of the Ministry of F.R. will prove their falsity. The Minister of F. Relations ought to know the truth, and the undersigned is bound to presume that he does.

Recurring to the history of the past we find that Spain, before the revolution adopted the policy of peopling Texas with *colonists.* The object, as the undersigned believes was to bring thither a population, which would put a stop to the ravages of the hostile indians. After the revolution the Mexican United States by a law of the state of Coahuila & Texas, enacted March 24, 1825, adopted and continued the same policy. The colonists, who embraced the *invitation* thus held out, were principally natives of the U.S. and the north of Europe.

The disturbances, which soon afterwards took place in Texas, could not fail to attract the attention of the Govt. of the U.S., which soon foresaw what, in the natural course of things, would be the result; and so early as the 15th March 1827, warned Mexico of the collisions which would inevitably ensue. On the 25 Aug[us]t 1829, it again called the attention of the Mexican Govt. to the fact, that most of the grants, which had been made in Texas, were already in the hands of Americans & Europeans; to the want of confidence and reciprocal attachment between the Mexican Govt. and the inhabitants of Texas; to the fact that this want of confidence had in the short space of five years displayed itself in no less than four revolts, one of them having for its avowed object the independence of the country; to the hazard of dismemberment, to which the extensive confederacy of Mexico was exposed by the frequent revolutions, to which she was subject; and finally to the probability that the first successful blow would be struck in Texas.

Thus the Govt. of the U.S., so far from being responsible for any of the circumstances, which led to the revolution of Texas, so early as 1827, pointed out to Mexico the results likely to ensue as the natural & necessary consequences of her own policy, and forewarned her of her danger.

The result has verified the prediction. Texas, having the example of Mexico and the U.S. before her eyes, declared her right to govern herself, as was to have been expected. She declared her independence, & successfully repelled the army sent to subdue her. She effectually sustained by force of arms the right, which she claimed, and having shown her ability to realize and establish as a *fact* the *abstract right* to independence, which she asserts, the world admits & Mexico, who set her an example, ought not to deny, she was received into the society of Sovereign and independent nations.

As a sovereign and independent nation she applied for the benefit of admission into the American Union. This was at first refused her, perhaps owing to that regard, with which the Govt. of the U.S. has always treated Mexico. The U.S. have now waited eight years for Mexico to reconquer Texas. She has not done so, nor attempted it, and it is now proposed to grant to Texas the admission into the American Union, which she desires.

But Mexico claims that she has a right to reconquer Texas, and that the U.S. have therefore no right to consider Texas as a sovereign state. The undersigned by no means admits the deduction. The U.S. admitted the right of Spain to reconquer Mexico; but long before Spain relinquished this right, the U.S. not only treated with Mexico, as sovereign both de jure & de facto, but proposed also to purchase of her this very portion of territory, over which Spain then asserted the same rights that Mexico now does. They did so in 1827, and in 1829, on the very eve of a Spanish invasion.

The undersigned avails himself, &c &c, Ben E. Green.

ALS (No. 10) with Ens and State Department translations in DNA, RG 59 (State Department), Diplomatic Despatches, Mexico, vol. 12 (M-97:13), received 8/25; variant FC in DNA, RG 84 (Foreign Posts), Mexico, Despatches;

draft with Ens in NcU, Duff Green Papers (published microfilm, roll 5, frames 659–662, 631–634, and 646–653); PEx with Ens in Senate Document No. 1, 28th Cong., 2nd Sess., pp. 82–91; PEx with Ens in House Document No. 2, 28th Cong., 2nd Sess., pp. 81–90.

From RICE W. PAYNE

Warrenton, Va., July 14, 1844

Sir, Having with some difficulty, so far mastered my feelings as to be willing to present myself to you in the unpleasant, and self-humiliating character of an applicant for office, I have taken the liberty of addressing to you this note. In doing so, I venture to ask at your hands a favor which I could not bring myself to do in person, although I had an opportunity of so doing whilst in Washington a few days ago, under circumstances perhaps somewhat favorable, had I felt disposed to speculate upon the acquaintance, or friendship of those who are favorably known to you[.]

With no claim whatever upon you—perhaps, without even the slight recommendation of an unforgotten acquaintance, I yet make bold to ask at your hands, some public appointment within your control—such as a consulate, or that of bearer of despatches to a Foreign Government. My highest wishes would be gratified in making a trip in some public capacity like this, to China, South America, or any court of Europe.

Of my qualifications for such an office, I need not speak. I could easily furnish, if required, satisfactory testimonials of character, standing &c, from many who are well known to you in public, and private life. It may not be improper to state, that I was graduated at the University of Va. and that I have since then, carefully cultivated my acquaintance with the modern languages of Europe, especially the French and Italian.

Having chosen the law as my profession, I have found, from a few years' experience of the practice, that it has ceased in a great measure, to be profitable, save to those of extensive personal popularity, or of commanding legal talents. And, impressed as I am, with a sense of unfitness, from education and association, for most of the hardier pursuits of life, I feel in some degree justified, in thus presenting my case to your consideration. And I beg leave at least, to add, that you are one of the few, at whose hands I would, or could under any circumstances short of actual want, ask the bestowal of the patronage of office[.]

Be pleased, Sir, to acknowledge the receipt of this—and permit me to subscribe myself, With great respect yours &c, Rice W. Payne.

ALS in ScCleA.

From S[HADRACH] PENN, JR.

St. Louis, July 14 1844

D[ea]r Sir, I feel that justice requires that I should address you again in reference to John McDaniel and Joseph Brown; men that I regard as unfortunate, and thus far the victims of [William] Mason, who turned State[']s evidence against them. Mason's original statement was made when he was in fear of being executed at once, and with a view to save himself from the fury of what may be properly termed a mob, and he adhered to that statement publicly to save himself, (as he was persuaded it was necessary to do so,) and moreover with a view to preserve a sort of character for consistency and truth, which he never was entitled to as was shown by the evidence adduced on the trial. He was, in fact, proved to be infamous from boyhood. Besides, I fully credit the statement or affidavit of [Orrin P.] Rockwell, that Mason confessed that he was the murderer of Charvis [*sic*; Antonio José Chavis], and committed the deed when the McDaniels were striving to prevent it. In the absence of Mason's testimony neither of the men arraigned could have been found guilty of the murder of Charvis—and looking to the infamy of Mason, his peculiar position, and the total absence of any proof (except the testimony of Mason) that any one of the prisoners shot Charvis, I must say the propriety of Executive interposition appears to me to be obvious.

But in addition to this, the Court seemed to have resolved on the conviction of the prisoners. Every point made was decided against them, and Judge [John] Catron, particularly, spoke of them as land pirates and scoundrels, and I am informed by a member of the bar that he refused to give the ordinary instruction, that if the jury doubted as to their guilt they should be acquitted. I was only present some two hours during the trial of J. McDaniel, but in that short time I saw enough to convince me ["that" *interlined*] Judge Catron had resolved on their conviction. Indeed it cannot be truly said that the trials were conducted[?] according to the usual forms of justice; and the impression is now becoming general that Mason was the real murder[er]. Public opinion has undergone a great change, whatever you may hear to the contrary, and I feel confident that a final pardon of the unfortunate men, McDaniel and Brown, would be agreeable to a large majority of the public.

Recollect that the ["Masons" *canceled and* "McDaniels" *interlined*] were acting under the authority of Texas; that it was their purpose to convey Charvis to Texas; that nothing beyond a division of his money could have been claimed by the men, and such a division was coerced. What possible object could the ["Masons" *canceled and* "McDaniels" *interlined*] have to take his life under such circumstances.

I understand the District Attorney here [William M. McPherson] has been active in endeavoring to keep up the excitement against the McDaniels, but without success; that he has acted as Deputy Marshal, and proved excessively rigid—preventing them from being visited by respectable men. These facts are mentioned to enable you to put a proper estimate on any communication he may may [*sic*] make on the subject.

It is proper that I should say neither of the McDaniels nor Brown know me personally; that I can neither be actuated by personal friendship nor motives of interest. My only desire is to prevent the infliction of unjust punishment. It is only for this purpose that I have interested myself in their behalf.

Generally I am disposed to discredit a man who turns States' evidence, and when he is proved infamous and unworthy of credence on oath, I cannot believe him. This is the case of Mason, on whose testimony, backed by the over-rigid and arbitrary conduct of the senior Judge the convictions were had.

A long respite would at least seem to be necessary. One of a month affords no time, at this distance from the seat of Government, for such inquiry and investigation, as are necessary, if further developments are deemed necessary to enable the President to act humanely and understandingly in the cases referred to. The McDaniels have no relatives here—no friends—save such as have been made so by sympathy for them. All they can expect is that Mr. [James B.] Martin will act for them, and he must, as a comparative stranger act under disadvantages, in eliciting information and facts in their behalf. A respite of four or five months would give him time to act. I therefore earnestly recommend a long respite, previous to the expiration of which I feel confident the propriety of pardoning them will be admitted. With great respect I am Yours Truly, S. Penn, Jr. [P.S.] This is for the President as well as yourself. S.P., Jr.

ALS in DNA, RG 59 (State Department), Petitions for Pardon, Tyler Administration.

To F RANCIS W HARTON, [Philadelphia]

Washington, 14th July 1844
My dear Sir, I have been so incessantly engaged with my official duties untill recently, as to compel me, in a great measure, to neglect my private correspondence, which will, I hope, satisfactorily explain, why I have delayed so long to ack[n]owledge yours of the 31st May.

I regard the nomination of Mr. [James K.] Polk to [be] the best, that could be made under all the circumstances. It has done much by freeing the party of the dangerous control of what may be called the New York Dynasty. Another four years of its control, after the restoration, would well near have ruined the party and country. A more heartless and selfish body of politicians have rarely ever been associated together. I was much gratified with Mr. [George M.] Dallas' nomination [for the Vice-Presidency]. My friends every where will give the ticket a hearty support; and I have strong hope it will succeed. The intelligence, as far as my information extends, is favourable . . . .

PEx in Jameson, ed., *Correspondence*, p. 601.

From W[illia]m C. Anderson, St. Louis, 7/15. He acknowledges receipt of a respite for John McDaniel and Joseph Brown until 8/16. The respite was received at 5 o'clock the evening before their scheduled execution. Anderson has also received his appointment to be U.S. Marshal and will inform the State Department of his acceptance or nonacceptance of that office as soon as possible. ALS in DNA, RG 59 (State Department), Petitions for Pardon and Related Briefs, 1800–1849, no. 292B.

From R[ichard] S. Blennerhassett, St. Louis, 7/15. Blennerhassett takes the opportunity afforded by [James B.] Martin's visit to Washington to send Calhoun his opinion of the conviction of the men involved in the capture, robbery, and murder of the Mexican trader [Antonio José] Chavis. Blennerhassett was a defense counsel for all of the men capitally charged except for John McDaniel. He asserts that "judicial outrages" were committed during the trials. Blennerhassett reported the details of the trials to Supreme Court Justice "McLane" [*sic*; John McLean] who agreed that the defendants did not receive a fair trial. In addition, public sentiment in the region has shifted in favor of the convicted men. "Many, very many respectable men have from the beginning doubted the policy and propriety of convicting those men on the testimony of such a man as [William] Mason the informer and I cannot after the most dispassionate review of the whole case come to any other conclusion than that Mason's evidence as to the *Actual Killing* & the circumstances immediately preceding it was *false*." U.S. District Attorney [William M.] McPherson has used the trials for political purposes and cannot be trusted to report the true state of opinion in the community. ALS in DNA, RG 59 (State Department), Petitions for Pardon, Tyler Administration.

To William Brent, Jr.

Department of State
Washington, 15th July, 1844

Sir: A copy of the instructions to Mr. [Harvey M.] Watterson on his departure for Buenos Ayres as Special Agent of the United States, herewith enclosed, will give you a full view of the relations between the two countries at that time. Nothing has since occurred to change them. No answer has been received from the Buenos Ayrean government to the note which was addressed to General [Carlos Maria de] Alvear by Mr. [Daniel] Webster on the 4th of December, 1841, on the subject of the Falkland Islands. Its long continued silence, added to the contents of the note of its Minister for Foreign Affairs to Commodore [Charles] Morris of the 14th of August, 1842, may be regarded as proof of its implied assent to the proposition contained in Mr. Webster's note. If that government, however, should make to you any communication upon the subject of the Falkland Islands in reference to the acts of Captain [Silas] Duncan there in 1832 [in capturing alleged pirates], you will say that the Government of the United States has determined to suspend any further discussion of that subject until the pending controversy between Buenos Ayres and Great Britain in regard to the Islands, shall be settled.

The suspension of the question in reference to the Falkland Islands involves of course a suspension of the claims of the citizens of the United States growing out of the seizure of their sealing vessels there, if, indeed, any claim could be preferred against that government on their account, without implying that Vernet's authority was lawful. The obligation to make amends for an improper exercise of jurisdiction, would seem to be inseparable from the right of jurisdiction itself.

The particulars of the other claims are mentioned in the list and statement which you will receive from Mr. Watterson. You will endeavor to induce that government at least to acknowledge them. There should be no reluctance on their part to do this from an apprehension that the government of the United States would require payment upon terms which would be inconvenient to Buenos Ayres. There is reason to believe that a feeling of this sort has hitherto retarded the adjustment of the claims of our citizens as well on that government as on those of other Spanish American States. We are willing to grant any reasonable accommodation in point of time for the satisfaction of the claims, taking into consideration the waste to which the resources of that country have been subjected by civil and foreign wars. If, however, we omit to require an acknowledgement of the claims or even delay it much longer, it might be inferred that we mean to abandon them or to assume them ourselves, which cannot be done without allowing it to be supposed that aggressions may with impunity be committed upon the persons and property of citizens of the United States.

The power with which you are furnished authorizes you to conclude a Convention upon the subject of claims. So far, however, as their aggregate amount can be ascertained from materials in this Department, it would scarcely be sufficient to warrant that proceeding. The most eligible course, therefore, would be for you to settle the claims singly, by an arrangement with the Minister for Foreign Affairs, beginning with that which may appear to be the fairest in point of principle and the best supported by proof.

A reciprocal treaty of commerce with that government is in many respects desirable, but especially to equalize the tonnage duties on vessels of the United States in the ports of that country with those on vessels of Great Britain and of the Argentine Republic itself, which, it is understood, are subjected to a moiety only of those which are exacted from ours. You will accordingly embrace an early opportunity to sound the Buenos Ayrean government upon this subject, and if you should find its disposition to be favorable, you may intimate that it would be agreeable to this government to receive its overtures through the diplomatic representative of Buenos Ayres in the United States, and that the negotiation should be carried on at Washington. If, however, they should decidedly prefer Buenos Ayres as the seat of the negotiation, your power will enable you to act for that purpose, but it is not deemed advisable that you should sign a treaty until you shall receive further instructions from this Department.

There is reason to suppose that it is the intention of the government of Paraguay, whose territories are conterminous with those of the Argentine Confederation, to deviate from the policy which it has hitherto pursued, to cultivate friendly relations with other powers and to encourage foreign commerce. You will accordingly endeavor to acquire authentic information in regard to that country, which you will transmit to this Department. I am, Sir, your obedient servant, J.C. Calhoun.

LS (No. 1) in DNA, RG 84 (Foreign Posts), Argentina, Instructions, vol. 15; FC in DNA, RG 59 (State Department), Diplomatic Instructions, Argentina, 15:6–8 (M-77:10).

From Silas E. Burrows, Montevideo, 7/15. Burrows asks that damages of $4,600 be sought for him from the government of Argentina for storm damage to his ship, the *Herald*, while it was illegally in the custody of that government. According to Burrows, U.S. Consul [Amory] Edwards [at Buenos Ayres] encouraged the seizure of the *Herald*. He refers Calhoun to letters from [Harvey M.] Watterson for information on the case. ALS in DNA, RG 76 (Records of Boundary and Claims Commissions and Arbitrations), Miscellaneous Claims Records: Buenos Ayres, 1816–1849, received 11/14.

To R[ICHARD] K. CALL, Governor of Fla. Territory

Department of State
Washington, 15th July 1844

Sir, I have had the honor to receive your letters of the 22nd May, and 2nd and 3rd of June last, with accompanying papers, complaining of certain malversations in office of Charles S. Sibley, Attorney of the United States for the Middle District of Florida. With regard to the first specification, the aiding and promoting malicious prosecutions to gratify personal and political animosity, I can only state that this department is not the proper authority to which application should be made in the first instanc[e]. A Court of Justice, in my opinion is the proper tribunal to examine and pronounce upon this charge, and to it recourse ought first to be had by the parties aggrieved. The other two allegations, charging Mr. Sibley "with high misdemeanors in compromising various criminal prosecutions," &c. and "with official impropriety in receiving pay, in the name of fees, from defendants in criminal Cases, as an inducement to dismiss proceedings against them after indictments found," &c, are of a character to challenge inquiry. A copy of the papers preferring these charges will accordingly be transmitted to Mr. Sibley, with a request that he furnish to this Department, without unnecessary delay, such explanations as the nature of the complaints seems to require. You will be furnished with a copy of his explination [*sic*] and if additional evidence should be required you will be apprized of the steps which will be taken to obtain it. I am, Sir, with great respect Your Obedient Servant, John C. Calhoun.

FC in DNA, RG 59 (State Department), Domestic Letters, 34:300–301 (M-40:32); PC in Carter, ed., *Territorial Papers*, 26:932–933.

From EDWARD EVERETT

London, 15 July 1844

Sir, I duly received your despatch Nro. 87 [of 5/16] transmitting among other papers a copy of a letter from Mr. Shepard Cary of the 11th of May addressed to yourself, on the subject of a boom across the mouth of the Aroostook river, within the Province of New Brunswick; and instructing me to use my best efforts, in my informal conferences with members of Her Majesty's Government to procure the assent of the crown to the act of the legislature of New Brunswick for incorporating the company formed for the support of the aforesaid boom.

Thinking it best in reference to a matter of this kind, to apply directly to Lord Stanley, I addressed a note to him on the 4th instant asking an interview, and left it at the Colonial Office; but from some accident it failed to reach him.

On the 10th I addressed him another note briefly indicating the subject on which I wished to confer with him and enclosing a copy of Mr. Cary's letter.

I have received a note in reply, of which I transmit an extract of all that pertains to the matter in hand. As it is marked "private," you will be pleased to regard it in that light.

Lord Stanley alludes to the possibility that the act for incorporating the proprietors of the boom may be thought by the Law Officers of the Crown, to conflict with the provisions of the Treaty of Washington. I own I do not see how this can be the case. Nor was I aware before, that any similar act had been disallowed by the home Government last year. Mr. Cary states that the Governor of New Brunswick refused his official approbation to a similar act of the colonial legislature at the last session, because it did not appear to have been sanctioned by the State of Maine, and this is the only act relative to the establishment of a boom, of which I have received any information.

I should not be surprized if Lord Stanley had reference to the act relative to the duty on timber exported from St. John's, which was disallowed by the Home Government as being inconsistent with the Treaty of Washington—but which certainly bears no resemblance to the present act. I am, sir, with great respect, your obedient servant, Edward Everett.

Transmitted with Despatch 160.

Extract from a note of Lord Stanley to Mr. Everett, dated 12th June 1844, marked "Private."

[Appended]

St. James's Square
12 July 1844

My dear sir, I hope you will believe that if I had received your note of the 4th instant, asking to see me, to which you advert in that of the 10th, you would not have been left so long unanswered. I will endeavour to ascertain how the mistake has arisen.

I believe that there is no question but that the act to which you refer is desired by the Inhabitants of Maine as well as by New Brunswick. It is at present under the consideration of the government, but an act which appears to me to be similar was referred last year to the Law officers of the Crown and was disallowed on their report that it was repugnant to the stipulations of the Treaty of Washington. It will probably be necessary to consult them again on the present act. . . .

LS (No. 160) with En in DNA, RG 59 (State Department), Diplomatic Despatches, Great Britain, vol. 53 (M-30:49), received 8/3; FC in DNA, RG 84 (Foreign Posts), Great Britain, Despatches, 8:338–341; FC in MHi, Edward Everett Papers, 49:379–381 (published microfilm, reel 23, frames 191–192).

From F[e]r[dinand] Gardner, U.S. Consul, Villa da Praia, St. Jago, Cape Verde Islands, 7/15. Gardner encloses shipping returns of American vessels visiting St. Jago, a statement of fees collected in the previous six months, and a statement of the accounts of the Consulate. He repeats information contained in his last despatch concerning the expiration of the Portuguese concession permitting a storehouse at St. Jago for the use of the U.S. African Squadron. "The Vessels of the Squadron are now all on the Coast, and I have no late news from them." ALS (No. 69) with Ens in DNA, RG 59 (State Department), Consular Despatches, Santiago, Cape Verde Islands (T-434:3).

To WILLIAM B. GOOCH, East Baldwin, Maine

Department of State
Washington, July 15th 1844
Sir, Your letter No. 17 of the 4th May last, informing the Department, for reasons stated, of your being compelled to resign the office of U.S. Commercial Agent at Aux Cayes, & to return to the U. States, and enclosing Copies of the correspondence between yourself & Capt. [Thomas W.] Freelon of the U.S. Ship "Preble," relative to the appointment of a suitable person to act as Commercial Agent, until the pleasure of the Government is known, has been received, as also your letter dated 8th Inst. at East Baldwin, Maine.

The President [John Tyler] has accepted your resignation & in view of the great importance of having at this time, the Commercial interests of the U. States represented at Aux Cayes, he has already appointed Richmond Loring Esq[ui]r[e], as your Successor.

The Department is pleased to see by your letter of the 8th Inst. that you have given so great satisfaction to your Countrymen, in protecting their persons & property.

It is not the practice of the Department to surrender the Bonds of Consuls & Commercial Agents, who resign. The one given by you cannot therefore, be returned. I am, Sir, Respectfully, Your obedient Servant, J.C. Calhoun.

LS in ScU-SC, John C. Calhoun Papers; FC in DNA, RG 59 (State Department), Consular Instructions, 11:259.

From E[lisha] Hathaway, Jr., [U.S. Consul], Hobart Town, 7/15. He encloses his semiannual consular returns and reports that no

American vessels have called there since his despatch of 4/1. ALS (No. 3) with Ens in DNA, RG 59 (State Department), Consular Despatches, Hobart, vol. 1 (T-127:1), received 2/22/1845.

From Tho[ma]s H. Holt, St. Louis, 7/15. Holt takes the opportunity afforded by the visit to Washington of Capt. [James B.] Martin to send Calhoun a statement in favor of granting executive clemency to John McDaniel and [Joseph] Brown, convicted of the murder of Antonio [José] Chavis and sentenced to be hanged. Holt represented [Nathaniel H.] Morton, [William J.] Harris, and [John A.] McCormick, convicted of larceny in the Chavis affair. He believes that the chief witness against the men, William Mason, committed perjury. He further states that a letter from President John Tyler and from Calhoun seeking information on the case has been used by [William M. McPherson] the U.S. District Attorney *against the Administration.* McPherson is "anxious for their execution, and . . . has pursued them, with the most *unrelenting hostility.*" ALS in DNA, RG 59 (State Department), Petitions for Pardon, Tyler Administration.

Francis Markoe, Jr., [State Department], to Geo[rge] W. Morton and James T. Bache, [New York City], 7/15. "The Secretary of State has directed me to transmit to you enclosed a communication addressed to Louis Mark, Esq. and to desire you to read, before delivering, it to him." Copy in DNA, RG 59 (State Department), Consular Despatches, Vienna, vol. 1 (T-243:1).

Francis Markoe, Jr., to [Louis Mark, New York City], 7/15. Markoe returns to Mark his substitute Consular bond which he recently transmitted for the second time to the State Department. No bond will be accepted on Mark's behalf until he has satisfactorily explained the controversy concerning his first bond. "["He" *canceled and* "The Secretary" *interlined*] refers you to my last letter of the 8th inst. written by his command & bids me to add that if you do not explain, or resign, by the 15th prox[im]o, you will most certainly be dismissed from ["the" *interlined*] office of Consul for Bavaria & the Prussian provinces of the Rhine. In the interim he ["will" *canceled and* "wishes to" *interlined*] receive no communication from you except such as may be to the point." Rough draft in DNA, RG 59 (State Department), Consular Despatches, Vienna, vol. 1 (T-243:1).

To J[AMES] K. POLK, Columbia, Tenn.

Washington, 15th July 1844
My dear Sir, This will be handed to you by Mr. [Isaac S.] Ketchum of Michigan, to whom I take pleasure in introducing you. Mr. Ketchum is a gentleman of very respectable talents and of great worth, and devoted to the success of the Republican cause. He is disposed to take a decided & Zealous part in the approaching election, & from his extensive acquaintance & the general este[e]med [*sic*] in which he is held I have no doubt can render efficient aid. With great respect yours truly, J.C. Calhoun.

ALS in DLC, James K. Polk Papers (Presidential Papers Microfilm, Polk Papers, roll 27). NOTE: Calhoun's letter was enclosed by Ketchum to Polk in a letter written at Lexington, Mo., on 9/16/1844.

From Pedro de Regil y Estrada, [U.S. Consul], Merida, Y[ucatan], 7/15. He reports that the U.S. barkentine *Henry Leeds* of Baltimore anchored near Sisal on 7/11. Her cargo was removed except for that portion consisting of breadstuffs and shoes. These articles remained on board because their importation into Yucatan is forbidden. H[enry] A. Holmes, captain of the *Henry Leeds*, has complained that the U.S. had no notice of the commercial regulations of Yucatan. Regil y Estrada had sent to the State Department a copy of the 1840 *Reglamento de Comercio Para El Estado de Yucatan* on 12/14/1843 and encloses another copy with the present despatch. ALS (No. 4, in Spanish) with En in DNA, RG 59 (State Department), Consular Despatches, Merida, vol. 1 (M-287:1, frames 61–114), received 8/17.

From Pedro de Regil y Estrada, Merida, Y[ucatan], 7/15. The U.S. Chargé d'Affaires at Mexico City has repeatedly requested Regil y Estrada's commission as U.S. Consul [so that an exequatur may be secured]. His commission was sent at a time when communication was disrupted and he never received it. In accordance with the wishes of the Yucatan government he has fulfilled his consular duties without a commission. He now requests a duplicate commission from the State Department. ALS (No. 5, in Spanish) in DNA, RG 59 (State Department), Consular Despatches, Merida, vol. 1 (M-287:1, frames 115–116), received 8/17.

From A[BRAHAM] RENCHER

Lisbon, Legation of the U. States
July 15th 1844

Sir, I received on the 26th of June last your Despatch, (No. 6) inclosing me a letter from W[illiam] H. Taylor, agent for the owners of the Ship Miles and cargo. I received about the same time your Despatch (No. 5) informing me of your appointment by the President, by and with the advice and consent of the Senate, as Secretary of State. The latter came by a merchant ship from New York which I suppose to be the cause of the delay in its transmission. I had previously received through other channels satisfactory information of your appointment, and I thought myself therefore justified in addressing to you my last despatch. But as the information was not official, I did not feel myself at liberty to indulge in the expression of the sincere pleasure which the information afforded me and to congratulate the country, as I now do, upon an event so auspicious to her honour and interest both at home and abroad.

I have not thought it advisable to press the claim of the owners of the ship Miles and its Cargo to a decision at present. I have thought I would best promote the success of the claim by deferring it till after the adjustment of the existing difficulty between the Government of the United States and that of Portugal. If the bill reported to Congress to reduce the duty upon the wines of Portugal, and to refund duties overpaid under the Treaty of 1840, as understood by Portugal, should become a law, the Government of Portugal will be in a better temper towards the claims of the citizens of the United States. I have been somewhat induced to this course by the fate of the claims submitted and urged by my predecessor [Washington Barrow], the justice of some of which appeared to me very imposing, and yet he spoke very hopelessly of their success. In a few weeks I hope to be informed of the action of Congress and of the final disposition of this subject, and whatever may be the result, I shall lose no time in urging the Portuguese Government to a decision upon this claim as well as others and shall do all in my power to obtain for them a favourable consideration.

The court at present is at Cintra where the Queen [Maria II] has been since the first of June last. Most of the *Corps Diplomatique* are absent from Lisbon. Some of them are at Cintra, and others are gone to other parts of the kingdom or to the adjoining countries. The same may be said of the nobility and other persons of wealth residing in Lisbon. This must be rather for recreation than health, as the city appears perfectly healthy. I expect however to follow the course of fashion and remove to Cintra, especially as it may be expected of me to yield this much to Her Majesty's ta[s]te for the scenery of Cintra and the pleasant amusement of donkey riding.

Things have continued quiet in Portugal since the fall of Almeida. The newspapers in opposition to the administration continue to be very violent. They have abundant food with which to feed the spirit of discontent in the embarrassed condition of the finances and the general prostration of trade. There are other causes of dissatisfaction. The present first minister of the Government [Antonio José de Sousa?] is a man of undoubted talents, but he has risen from comparative obscurity by the force of talent, and by means which many consider not very creditable to him. The nobility and those who attach great importance to noble birth and hereditary distinction, and who are yet sincerely attached to the Sovereign and her government, would notwithstanding favour any popular movement which would hurl from power one so wanting in what they consider of so much importance. The adherents of Don Miguel are still considerable & always ready to oppose the Queen's Government and those who administer it. The unsettled condition of Spain is not without its influence upon the affairs of Portugal. From the contiguity of the two kingdoms a popular vibration in the one communicates its impulse to the other. Even foreign diplomacy is not altogether inactive. The greater powers will seek a controling influence over the smaller. From this spring rival interests. Those who think themselves out of favour with the powers that be, will fan the flame of opposition to the administration of those who are in. Looking, therefore, to the past and considering all these i[n]fluences, I can hardly hope the present tranquility of Portugal will be of long continuance.

A French frigate arrived here yesterday and departs in a few days to join the Squadron off Gibraltar under the command of the Prince de Joinville. Evidently the two great powers of France and England are watching each other in that qua[r]ter very carefully, and not without some degree of jealousy. England can not be very contented under the controlling influence which Louis Philippe now exerts over the affairs of Spain. Believe me to be With high consideration Y[ou]r ob[edien]t Servant, A. Rencher.

LS (No. 4) in DNA, RG 59 (State Department), Diplomatic Despatches, Portugal, vol. 14 (M-43:13), received 8/21; CC in DNA, RG 84 (Foreign Posts), Portugal, Despatches, vol. 1841–1847.

From L.M. Shreve, St. Louis, 7/15. Shreve writes in behalf of pardons for [John] McDaniel and [Joseph] Brown, sentenced to be hanged for the murder of the Mexican trader [Antonio José] Chavis. He mentions as extenuating factors "the testimony on which they were convicted, [by William] Mason a notorious liar, and two half breed Mexicans," and "the Character of *Chavis* the avowed enemy of American citizens save when spying and trading amongst us." Shreve thinks that a commutation of their sentences to a prison term would serve justice, but he has heard that Calhoun believes the President has only the power to pardon, not to commute sentences. ALS in DNA, RG 59 (State Department), Petitions for Pardon, Tyler Administration.

From J. G. Syz

Philadelphia, July 15th 1844

Sir, The federal directory of the Republic of Switzerland having learned that a treaty has been concluded between the United States of North America and the Customs Union of Germany by which treaty the productions of german manufacture Shall enjoy certain privileges on their importation into the United States, invites me to give it Some information upon the Subject, and also whether the productions of Switzerland imported under the Same flag as those of Germany would not be placed on the Same footing with the latter.

The directory remarks that the United States having till now always recognised the principle on the one Side, that the flag covers the merchandise, and on the other the principle of a just reciprocity in reguard to granting commercial facilities, there is certainly no country in Europe, which is entitled to greater commercial facilities on the part of the United States, than Switzerland, a country which offers at once a rich & entirely free market for the productions of the United States.

I would therefore beg leave to request you for Such official information upon this Subject as may tend to enlighten the question. With Sentiment of the highest reguard I have the honor to be, Sir Your obedient Servant the Consul of the Swiss Confederation, J.G. Syz.

ALS in DNA, RG 59 (State Department), Notes from Foreign Consuls, vol. 2 (M-664:2, frames 393–395).

JULY 16–31, 1844

◫

"But the Session of Congress having been brought to a close, and the present being the Season of the year when the least public business is transacted," wrote the British Minister to Calhoun on July 22, "it occurs to me that you may now feel at leisure to proceed to the consideration" of the largest subject of difficulty pending between the two great Anglo-Saxon powers: "a satisfactory arrangement respecting the Boundary of the Oregon or Columbia Territory."

Negotiations had been scheduled last February. A few days before they were to begin Secretary of State Upshur had been killed in the explosion on the Princeton. *The matter had been waiting. In the meantime it had become considerably more difficult, since it had become an issue in the American Presidential election campaign now underway. Thus Pakenham, the British Minister, launched a round of talks which was to occupy himself and Secretary of State Calhoun for the next several months.*

Though Calhoun would doubtless have liked to have been home for a bit during the growing season, Pakenham's business made this impossible, as did the absence of his Chief Clerk, Crallé, in Virginia on pressing family matters, and the absence of the vacationing President. It also would have been well if Calhoun could have been at home to reckon at first hand with "an uneasy & restless spirit" evident, as a Charleston correspondent wrote on July 24, among some of the stronger Southern rights men of South Carolina. The spirit became a public and national event on the last day of July during public proceedings at Bluffton. At these proceedings there was a call for early employment of nullification against the tariff of 1842, to be followed if necessary by stronger measures. And there was an evident dissatisfaction with Calhoun's more deliberate and tactful policy. The discontent was spreading, but could be and would be confined.

The Secretary could never get far away from the question of Texas and the related question of Mexican relations, and doubtless the Texas and Mexican despatches, hurried from Vera Cruz and Galveston to New Orleans and thence to Washington, were the first he opened. The new U.S. representative in Texas sent his first despatch from Galveston on July 27. He had arrived in the middle of a devastating yellow fever epidemic. It was a favorable sign, however, when Old Hickory's nephew wrote the Secretary of State from Nashville on July 29, enclosing a copy of the aging Jackson's letter to his protegé, Sam Houston, now President of the Texas Republic, warning him, in terms with which Calhoun could entirely agree, of the perfidy of Great Britain, and urging against betrayal of Texas's future with the Union of the States.

Ⅱ

To [GEORGE M.] BIBB, [Secretary of the Treasury]

16th July [1844]

Dear Sir, This will be handed to you by Col. [Edward] Brooks, formerly of the Army, but now collector of the Port of Detroit, to whom I take pleasure in introducing you.

He is a gentleman of high honor & respectability, & I do not doubt an excellent officer. I enclose you a letter [of 7/10] which the Col. Brought me from Mr. [Lucius] Lyon, member of Congress from Michigan & a very worthy man. With great respect yours truly, J.C. Calhoun.

ALS in DNA, RG 56 (Treasury Department), Applications for Appointment as Customs Service Officers, 1833–1910.

From D[ABNEY] S. CARR

Legation of the U.S.
Constantinople, [July] 16th 1844

Sir, I learn from a private letter of Mr. [William] Boulware, our Chargé d'Affaires at Naples, to one of the Gentlemen of this Legation, that on the 28th of June (the date of his letter) the sloop of War Plymouth was there on her way to the Black sea. But for a private letter from Mr. [David] Henshaw to me, since he left the Navy Department, I should have known nothing of the intention of sending this vessel here, till now, and as she will probably be at the Dardanell[e]s in a few days, she would have been detained there, God knows how long, waiting for a Firman to authorize her coming up. Luckily however, immediately on the receipt of Mr. Henshaw's letter, I applied for a Firman for her and, in consequence, hope to have it with the Consul there by the time the Plymouth gets there. I mention this that the Navy Department may hereafter know that when they are about to send a vessel to pass the Dardanell[e]s, they should give early notice to the Legation here. It may be well to apprize the Department also, of what seems not to be known to it, that no vessel of war carrying more than ten guns is allowed to pass the Dardanell[e]s, unless she be a vessel intended to be attached to the Legation. I have had to insinuate that such is to be the case in this instance. I shall do what I can to procure permission for her to proceed to the Black Sea; but have little hope of success, as the Turkish Government has, heretofore, been deaf to all such applications for armed vessels and the Russian Government is also very jealous of any such entering that sea. I am truly glad however that this vessel is coming here, as nothing has so good an effect here as the exhibition of *power*. It is worth all the diplomacy. The same letter from Mr. Boulware mentions that the Frigates Cumberland and Columbia were at Naples on their way to Smyrna, and it is most grateful to myself and all the Americans in this Eastern part of the world to hear this. Our Commerce with Smyrna is already valuable, and with it, and this, and other places in this region is, I think, with a wise attention on the part of our Government, destined to a considerable increase. In this view, the display of our flag in the Levant, in an imposing form and frequently, is most desirable. I hope hereafter the Navy Department will make the Mediterranean Squadron cruize up in these parts as far as Smyrna, or up to the Dardanell[e]s, and always, when the Squadron comes up there, that a vessel, of the allowed number of guns, may be sent up to this place. It would be a great deal better than hugging around Port Mahon. I have the honor to be with great respect Your very ob[edien]t Serv[an]t, D.S. Carr.

LS in DNA, RG 59 (State Department), Diplomatic Despatches, Turkey, vol. 10 (M-46:12), received 9/3.

From A[rchibald] M. Green, [U.S. Consul at] Galveston, 7/16. He reports the death of William S. Murphy, U.S. Chargé d'Affaires, on 7/13 and his burial with all proper honors on that day. Green asks that Calhoun notify Murphy's wife and family of his death. ALS (No. 43) in DNA, RG 59 (State Department), Consular Despatches, Galveston, vol. 2 (T-151:2), received 8/16.

From John W. Holding, Washington, 7/16. Holding seeks a final settlement of the issue of the *Good Return* claims against Colombia. He requests that, when the State Department has drafted instructions to the U.S. Legation at Caraças, a copy of them be sent to him at Baltimore. He also requests the State Department "to forward a like Intimation by the Special Messenger to Bogota." ALS in DNA, RG 59 (State Department), Miscellaneous Letters (M-179:105, frame 65).

To Dr. ROBERT LEBBY, James Island, St. Andrews Parish, S.C.

Department of State
Washington[,] 16th July 1844

Sir, I have received the letter which you addressed to me on the 12th instant, (as chairman of a committee of the agricultural Society of the Parish of St. Andrews,) and lose no time in transmitting to you an abstract of the first eight articles of the commercial treaty of 8th October, 1843, between Great Britain and China, and a printed copy of the General Regulations of Trade therein referred to. To the information contained in these papers, I can only add that the new China Tariff makes no discrimination between different qualities of raw cotton imported into that Empire.

This article is admitted to entry at either of the five ports named in the first article of the Treaty upon the payment of a specified duty of 24¼ pence Sterling per cwt. without reference to kind, quality, or origin. I am, Sir, respectfully Your Obedient Servant, John C. Calhoun.

FC in DNA, RG 59 (State Department), Domestic Letters, 34:304 (M-40:32).

To [James] "McDowal" [*sic*; McDowell], Gov[erno]r [of Va.], 7/16. "I take the liberty of presenting to you, the name of Francis Wharton Esq. of Philadelphia, for the place of Commissioner of your State for Pennsylvania for acknowledging deeds & taking depositions. He is a young lawyer of high standing & distinguished talents. I would be much gratified with the success of his application." ALS in Vi, Executive Papers.

To H[arvey] M. Watterson, [Buenos Ayres], 7/16. "Mr. William Brent, Jr. having been appointed Chargé d'Affaires of the United

States to Buenos Ayres, you will deliver to him the books and papers appertaining to the Legation of the United States in that City. Your functions as special agent of the United States will cease on the day when Mr. Brent shall be received in his official character by the Buenos Ayrean Minister for Foreign Affairs [Felipe Arana]." FC (No. 5) in DNA, RG 59 (State Department), Diplomatic Instructions, Argentina, 15:10 (M-77:10).

From J[AMES] E[DWARD] BOISSEAU

New York [City,] July 17 /44
My dear Sir, I rec[eive]d your letter this day, enclosed $86.88 on a/c of loan made Patrick [Calhoun] when in N.Y. Patrick made a mistake in rendering amo[un]t to you; it was 230 Doll[ar]s, 150 Doll[ar]s on his arrival, and 80 Doll[ar]s a day or two before his departure.

Please request Patrick when you see him to purchase with the balance 143$ that ["which" *interlined*] would be most desirable to his Mother [Floride Colhoun Calhoun], & present it to her with my love.

I desire to visit Carolina the coming winter, if so I will most assuredly accept of your kindness, & be with your family once more, for whose welfare I hope I shall always take an interest in.

I shall be much please[d] to see any member of your family in N.Y., & give them every attention in my power.

There have been quite a number of arrivals from Car[olina] & Georgia within two or three days, we are much engaged at present. I see by the last arrival the cotton market is more animated which has caused a small advance here.

I hope John [C. Calhoun, Jr.] & Patrick may have a pleasant trip [to the West] & one which may prove advantageous to ["them" *interlined*].

I am in health; as to my business I have no reason to complain; as regards its prosperity I have nothing to communicate that w[oul]d interest.

Give my love to your family when you write to them. I remain your friend, J.E. Boisseau.

ALS in ScCleA.

To [Henry Bowen], the Secretary of State of R.I., 7/17. "The Secretary of State of the United States being desirous of obtaining certain statistical information from authentic sources, not contained in the returns of the last Census, has to request, that you will be pleased to furnish this Department with copies of such printed 'Prison Reports,' as may shew the number and sex of Convicts white and colored for the years 1840, [18]41, [18]42, [18]43, & 1844 in the State of Rhode Island." If no printed reports containing this information are available, it should be furnished in tabular form. LS in ScU-SC, John C. Calhoun Papers.

From D[ABNEY] S. CARR

U.S. Legation
Cons[tantino]ple, 17th July 1844
Sir, I presume the Department is aware that, heretofore, the Sublime Porte has declined to hold any official correspondence or intercourse with persons appointed by other Governments to act as Consuls at Constantinople. Respect has been paid by it to certain official acts of such persons—such as passports &c., but they would never acknowle[d]ge them or grant them Exequaturs for this Port. By the enclosed note, from the head of the Bureau of Passports, you will see that Mr. [George A.] Porter, the acting Secretary of this Legation, who is also our Consul here, is distinctly recognized as Consul. I presume the same has been done in regard to the Consuls of the other Powers. This is one of the many evidences, daily occur[r]ing, of the giving way of ancient prejudices among this people and of approach to civilized usages.

I am happy to inform you that there is a prospect of an increase of trade between this place and the U.S. The Brig Lion, from Boston, recently came up here from Smyrna, bringing most of her outward Cargo, Consisting of Beef and Pork, N[ew] E[ngland] Rum, Coffee, and cheap Domestics. She found the market here better than at Smyrna, and found no difficulty in getting a full freight (chiefly of wool) for the U.S. She is a vessel of 235 Tons and her freight home will be $2,500. She will be back here in January. Another American vessel is daily expected here, and from all I can learn, it requires only a wise attention on the part of our Government to build up a valuable trade with this place. If our duty upon the coarse wool of this Country were slightly reduced it would insure, at all times, full freights for our return vessels. The chief obstacle, heretofore, to the establishment of a good trade with this part of the world and the U.S. has been the want of a return Cargo.

The Navy Department has ordered a vessel of war, the Plymouth, up here and into the Black Sea, with a view of gaining information on the subject of extending our trade into that Quarter. That Department was not aware I presume, that no vessel of war could pass the Dardanell[e]s without a Firman, or if it was aware of the fact, it was probably supposed that a Firman could be procured immediately on application; for I have received no instructions to apply for one, and the Porte takes a long time to think (or thinks it does) about every thing of this sort. I applied, on my own responsibility, two weeks ago (when I heard by accident, that the Plymouth was Coming here) for a Firman and have not got it yet, though I expect to get it in a few days. As for getting her permission to go into the Black Sea, there is no hope of it. It would not be granted to any nation for an armed vessel. I hope the time is not distant when the Civilized maritime powers—the U.S. taking the lead, will say to this people, and all others, that no such obstructions will be allowed on the great highways of nations. Till then, the Navy Department need not send armed vessels upon such cru[i]zes in these parts. I have the honor to be with great respect Your ob[edien]t Serv[an]t, D.S. Carr.

LS (No. 15) with En in DNA, RG 59 (State Department), Diplomatic Despatches, Turkey, vol. 10 (M-46:12), received 9/3; FC in DNA, RG 84 (Foreign Posts), Turkey, Despatches, C:138–139.

From ANNA PEYRE DINNIES, "Private"

Saint Louis, 17th July 1844
Dear Sir, Vivid as are my recollections of yourself, dear as are the associations they awaken, and familiar as I am with your public career, I know of no less powerful motive than the one that now impels me, which could have induced me to attempt recalling myself to your memory. But there are periods, in the history of every one, which it is pleasant to recollect; The incidents and the friends of youth and early manhood ere the vicissitudes of Life have blunted their sensibilities, or the crowding events of after years, given to the mind a sterner, colder tone, then come upon the Heart in all their pristine strength and freshness. I have presumed to flatter myself that the name of *my father*, and the memory of his attachment to

you, will be one of these; and you must be aware, Sir, that at no period of your life have you ever possessed a friend more devoted to you, both in your public and private relations than William L. Shackelford.

Perhaps, my own childish recollections of yourself and family, would long since have faded into forgetfulness, had they not been too deeply impressed upon my heart, by my father's conversations and encomiums, for the lapse of years, or the changes of Life to eradicate! But, be this as it may, it is pleasant for me to Know that, they have not; and often in this far land, when I have heard your name uttered by the lips of Strangers, and your talents and your virtues the theme of admiration and *of prophecy*, my heart has bounded at the thought that I too had a *right* to Know and love the subject of so honorable a reputation. But I will not let my feelings lead me longer into playing the egotist; they have already, perhaps, carried me farther than you may like, but I will state directly the subject of this Letter. I have been particularly requested to address you with the view of interesting ["you" *interlined*] in behalf of Mr. John McDaniel, and of soliciting you to exert your powerful influence with the President to obtain his pardon! Oh, Sir, I am sure you would do this, *unrequested* did you Know all the mitigating circumstances of the case; but of course you will learn them through the documents now being prepared to forward to Washington; and it is but left for me to entreat your attention to them as speedily as possible! Public opinion has changed very greatly since the condemnation of the unfortunate man took place, and his own conduct, united with the facts since developed, induce most persons to hope he will be pardoned. To you, I will not quote Portia's appeal, nor talk of Mercy as the attribute of Deity vested in the Executive which it is so glorious to exercise. McDaniel is a *South Carolinian*, and I have even been told that he was once a denizen of your house hold! These circumstances Sir, render my application to you almost unnecessary, although I trust they also make it excusable, for they must by touching your own sensibilities, teach you to sympathise with *mine*. Oh, if it be possible to obtain a pardon for him, dear Sir, do it! Let not a native of our proud, chivalric State perish on a scaffold in a distant land! He is innocent—I am sure he is innocent of the foul crime attributed to him—for he has been proven to possess too many lofty traits of character, to permit us to suppose for a moment, that the ignoble passions which could alone have led to the perpetration of this horrible murder, can tarnish their beauty.

I would be most happy to present my husband to your acquaintance! To him, like myself and many, *many* others, your withdrawal from the Presidential canvass has occasioned much disappointment. But I trust you do not always, My dear Sir, mean like Codrus, to sacrifice yourself for what *you* consider the best interests of your country! There are too many wise men who differ with you on this point, for us to concede to you the usual clearness that distinguishes your decissions [*sic*]. May I hope that I have succeeded in arousing some pleasant reminiscences of other days, and that you will do me the favour to acknowledge this Letter. Very respectfully and affectionately Yours, Anna Peyre Dinnies.

[P.S.] If your family are in Washington pray recall me to the memories of such who Knew me when a child.

ALS in ScCleA. NOTE: This letter appears to have been hand-delivered to Calhoun, perhaps by Dinnies' husband, John C. Dinnies. Anna Peyre Dinnies, a native of Georgetown, S.C., was an essayist under the pseudonym "Moina" and author of a volume of poetry.

To EDWARD EVERETT, [London]

Department of State
Washington, 17th July, 1844

Sir: Your despatches to No. 148, inclusive, have been duly received at this Department.

I transmit to you, herewith, a printed document (No. 278,) containing a report from this Department, in answer to a resolution of the House of Representatives of the 4th ultimo, requesting the President to communicate to that body certain correspondence between the Government of the United States and that of Great Britain relating to the duties levied by the latter on rough rice imported into the United Kingdom from this country. It is matter of surprise that your note of the 18th of October last, on a subject which has been so fully discussed, and must now be so well understood, should yet remain unanswered. The present is supposed to be a favorable conjuncture, of which it is hoped you will not fail to avail yourself, for pressing this claim upon the British Government. The delays which have arisen on its part, in the settlement of this question, are calculated to excite dissatisfaction in the mind of the President [John Tyler] as well as of those immediately interested, and he regards with painful feelings the obvious reluctance of Her Majesty's Ministers to satisfy a demand so clearly founded in justice. I am, Sir, respectfully, Your obedient servant, J.C. Calhoun.

LS (No. 98) in DNA, RG 84 (Foreign Posts), Great Britain, Instructions, 8:308–309, received 8/5; FC in DNA, RG 59 (State Department), Diplomatic Instructions, Great Britain, 15:204–205 (M-77:74).

Francis Markoe, Jr., to Messrs. Gerding, Kunkelman & Co., New York [City], 7/17. "The Secretary of State has desired me to place the enclosed communication for Mr. Louis Mark, under cover to you, & to request you to read ["it" *canceled*] & deliver it, & to inform ["the Govt." *canceled*] him whether Mr. Mark has left the U.S." (The enclosed communication was probably Markoe's letter of 7/17 to Mark.) CC in DNA, RG 59 (State Department), Consular Despatches, Vienna, vol. 1 (T-243:1).

To R[obert] M. Hamilton, U.S. Consul, Montevideo, 7/17. Calhoun acknowledges receipt of Hamilton's despatches 80 through 88. The observations on the "Political, Moral, and Commercial Condition of Paraguay," enclosed in No. 82 [of 12/19/1843 to Abel P. Upshur], have been read with great satisfaction and submitted to the President [John Tyler]. William Brent, Jr., has been appointed Chargé d'Affaires to Argentina and will soon report to his post. FC in DNA, RG 59 (State Department), Consular Instructions, 11:260.

To [Philip C. Johnson], the Secretary of State of Maine, 7/17. In order to obtain information not furnished by the returns of the last census, Calhoun requests "copies of such printed 'Prison Reports' as may shew the number and sex of Convicts white and colored for the years" 1840–1844. If no printed reports are available, a tabular statement will be acceptable. LS in Me-Ar.

From W[illia]m M. McPherson,
U.S. District Attorney

St. Louis, 17 July 1844

Sir, Your letter of 2d July directing me to make enquiries as to the character and credibility of O[rrin] P. Rockwell, and also as to the alleged change in public opinion favorable to the prisoners convicted of the murder of [Antonio José] Chavis, was duly received. I now address you in reply.

I am not personally acquainted with Rockwell but his name and character have been notorious throughout this State & Illinois for the last three years; he is a Mormon and among Mormons the most depraved, and said to be always ready for the commission of ["almost" *interlined*] any act known in the catalogue of crime. It is generally believed here, that as the tool of Joe Smith he attempted the assassination of Governor [Lillburn W.] Boggs. I am satisfied that Rockwell[']s evidence unless corroborated by other testimony would not weigh a feather with any jury in this State. I send you herewith the letters of Governor [Thomas] Ford, and others of the most respectable citizens of Illinois, relative to Rockwell's character & credibility, and to which I refer in confirmation of my opinion.

As to the change in public opinion favorable to the prisoners, mentioned in your letter, I can only say that it appeared to be *news* to almost every person with whom I conversed on the subject.

Being desirous to comply with your directions, immediately on the receipt of your letter, I addressed a note to the Grand Jury of St. Louis County then in session—and another to Merit Tillery Esq[ui]r[e] a highly respectable citizen of Clay County and a near neighbour and friend of the McDaniel family, requesting such information as they could furnish on the subject. I enclose you those notes and the answers thereto. I had thought of proceeding to interrogate others of our respectable citizens, but I found from conversation, that most of them although they approved the convictions were opposed to giving any expression of opinion in cases involving life, and many seemed to think that four trials in a court of justice, and the verdicts of four different juries composed of intelligent men ought to be more conclusive than any thing they could say in the matter. These suggestions coming as they did from various quarters, induced me to suspend my enquiries by letter & therefore I wrote none others on the subject.

The day before I received your letter, I saw two letters addressed to the McDaniels—one from a brother and the other from their friend Fitzgerald who visited Washington in the Spring in behalf of the prisoners. The McDaniels were advised in both letters, that public opinion was so strong against them in Clay County, that if they were pardoned they had better not return to that County.

From all I can learn I am satisfied, that those persons who wrote letters relative to public opinion, either wrote upon a subject of which they were ignorant, or they stated *what they knew to be false*.

I regret that any undue means have been resorted to, or any circumstances placed before the President in a way calculated to deceive that officer in the exercise of a delicate power. I will allude to some of them. I learn that articles which have appeared from time to time, in the St. Louis Transcript, and in the Evening Gazette, newspapers published in this city, have been laid before the President as worthy of his consideration. The Transcript is edited by Mr. Shreeve [L.M. Shreve?] a young lawyer of this place, whose partner (Mr. Wright) appeared as counsel for McDaniel, and from the time his partner was employed as counsel in the case, Shreeve espoused their cause, through the columns of his paper. Shreeve is also a frequent visitor at the cell of Doct[o]r [Joseph R. De] Prefontaine, where he doubtless collects many of his facts. Doct[o]r Prefontaine, was convicted as one of the party concerned in the robbery of Chavis and who is now undergoing his punishment in the jail of this County, has for months past been a regular contributor of the Evening Gazette, and is most probably the author of all the articles published in that paper in their behalf. One of those articles in the Gazette of the 16th (yesterday) professing to give the purport of the Mexican testimony has scarcely the semblance of truth about it.

On the trial of David McDaniel the counsel for the defense were trying to prove the prisoner[']s age, to show his youth, I remarked to his counsel that I would *admit* the defendant[']s own statement as to his age—the defendant then stated that he was *twenty four* years of age, and yet, I am informed, that it has been stated to the President that he, David, was only nineteen. I do not mention this to prejudice the case of David, but only to show the disposition to impose upon the President.

Other matters, and other influences that have been brought to bear on this case might be alluded and explained but I forbear.

I do not believe that in forty trials the result would be changed. [William] Mason, the witness, is no doubt a scoundrel; but I believe that every disinterested man who listened to his examination, and cross examination, in the different trials, and when he was kept for hours upon the witness' stand, and all the ingenuity of able counsel exercised in their efforts to entrap him, and then heard the corroborating testimony of the Mexican Witnesses, but were satisfied that in those cases he told the truth. But take McDaniel's own published statement of the affair, apply it to the law, and still it is murder.

I have in the foregoing endeavoured to comply with your requirement, although it imposed upon me an unpleasant duty. I had hoped, that I should never again have occasion to refer to those cases; but individual feeling shall never make me shrink from the performance of official duty.

My wish is that the President may not be imposed upon in this matter; if he pardons the prisoners, John McDaniel & Joseph Brown, he must do it as an act of *Mercy*, and not upon ["any" *interlined*] extenuating circumstances, for none exist. Very Respectfully Your Obedient Servant, Wm. M. McPherson, U.S. District Attorney.

P.S. If Col. Weston F. Birch late [U.S.] Marshal of Missouri is ["now" *canceled*] in Washington, I refer you to him in support of the statements here made by me.

[P.P.S.] Since the foregoing was written & copied I have met with Doct[or] Hope of Alton [Ill.], who informed me that the statement of young Combs as to the Cruelty of Chavis to the Texian Prisoners has been presented as matter in extenuation. Combs speaks of Chavis without giveing his Christian name. ["and" *canceled*] the Chavis family is a numerous one and I learn that Antonio José Chavis was two hundred miles from the scene of cruelty. Col. Birch can inform you of the facts. Wm. M. McPherson.

LS in DNA, RG 59 (State Department), Petitions for Pardon and Related Briefs, 1800–1849, no. 292B; CC in DNA, RG 59 (State Department), Petitions for Pardon, Tyler Administration, Cases 153, 154, 159, 160, 161, 166. Note: A Clerk's EU reads "Copies sent to the Pres[ident] 30th July 1844 at Old Point Comfort or Norfolk." The second postscript is in McPherson's own hand.

Francis Markoe, Jr., [State Department], to Louis Mark, [New York City?], 7/17. "The Secretary of State has just read in the [New York] Herald of the 16th inst. a paragraph stating that you were going out in the Britannia as bearer of despatches to ["the Ministers" *canceled*] London, Paris, & Berlin. This notice" has surprised Calhoun, who directed Markoe to "remind you that the indulgence wh[ich] has so far been extended in your case, has been coupled with the condition of your remaining in the U.S. until you sh[oul]d have made ["satisfactory" *interlined*] explanations of your conduct, or resigned your office ["& that" *interlined*] if you violate these conditions, ["it will be his duty" *canceled*] y[ou]r commission will be ["promptly" *canceled and* "instantly" *interlined*] revoked, ["& an official notice of the fact made public" *canceled and* "& so announced" *interlined*]." Rough draft in DNA, RG 59 (State Department), Consular Despatches, Vienna, vol. 1 (T-243:1).

From Geo[rge] W. Morton, New York [City], 7/17. Morton acknowledges the receipt of a letter from Francis Markoe, Jr., written to Louis Mark by Calhoun's direction, informing Mark that he must explain by the 15th of August the circumstances connected with the execution of his first Consular bond. Having known Mark since childhood, Morton feels that "it is utterly incomprehensible to me how he could possibly present a bond to the Department not executed by the obligors therein named." Morton will begin to investigate the matter. Since Mark sailed for Europe from Boston on 7/15, he will not be able to furnish the requisite explanation by the deadline mentioned in Markoe's letter. Morton hopes that "the Secretary of State will delay any action against Mr. Mark until I can hear from him." ALS in DNA, RG 59 (State Department), Consular Despatches, Vienna, vol. 1 (T-243:1).

From Whitemarsh B. Seabrook

Hot Springs, Virginia, July 17th '44
My Dear Sir, There are two routes to this place, of which the better one is through Winchester. After stopping at the warm springs, the finest bath in America, this, the white, salt & red, you proceed with out detention to New bern, 40 miles from the last spring. On the following morning the stage from Fincastle, the regular line to Tennessee, will take you to rogersville or Greenville in that State. I believe that at either place you will be detained one day. The latter, therefore, being distant only 25 miles from the Warm Springs in No[rth] Ca[rolina] is the proper place for you to rest, which, from the roughness of the road, I know from experience you will greatly need. At the Warm Springs you will be obliged to stop one day, to which I presume you would not object.

Every one to whom I have mentioned the probability of your passing this way, has expressed a desire to see you. Of all our distinguished fellow citizens you are personally perhaps the least known. I request you therefore most earnestly to ["take" *interlined*] this route. The road as far as the Red Sulphur is uncommonly fine, & the scenery highly romantic. In 4 days from Washington, via Winchester or Charlott[e]sville, you will reach the White Sulphur. I shall go to the White on the 20th inst.—there to remain until the 1st of August. I shall then proceed to the Salt with a view of sojourning there until about the middle of the month. It would greatly gratify me to accompany you as far as the Warm Springs, No[rth] Ca[rolina]. Respectfully yours & &, Whitemarsh B. Seabrook [later Governor of S.C.].

ALS in ScCleA.

To WALKER ANDERSON, U.S. Attorney, Pensacola

Department of State
Washington, 18th July 1844

Sir, In a letter dated at Pensacola, on the 20th of January last, addressed to the Secretary of the Navy by Commander J[oseph] Mattison of the United States brig "Bainbridge," he says, "I have delivered into the Custody of the United States Marshal of this district, the two American Citizens (S[amuel] S. Thomas, Master, and J[oseph] R. Curtis, mate, of the brig "Zebra," of North Yarmouth, Maine, imprisoned at the Island of Haiti, on a charge of murdering the Captain of an English vessel in that port) "whom I released from prison at Praires in December last, together with the *documentary evidence taken in the case by the Haytian authorities,* and confided to my care." I have to request, if indeed you are not already in possession of the documentary evidence referred to, that you will apply to the Marshal for it, and that you will forward it as soon as possible, to this department, where it is necessary in order to an examination, and full understanding of the facts of the case. I am, Sir, respectfully, Your Obedient Servant, John C. Calhoun.

FC in DNA, RG 59 (State Department), Domestic Letters, 34:307 (M-40:32).

From BARING BROTHERS & CO.

London, 18 July 1844

Sir, We have the honor to receive the letter with which you have been pleased to favor us under date 22 June, & shall attend to the instructions you give us as to the manner of rendering our Accounts hereafter.

We now beg leave to furnish the inclosed extract for the quarter ending the 30 Ult. shewing a balance due to the Executive of £13363.17.11 ... p[er] that day, & dependencies to the debit [£]-3909.15.2 ... as detailed thereon & we place these items to the credit & debit of your Department on the new Account. We send a copy of this account, with the required vouchers, to the 5th Auditor's Office as usual. We have the honor to be, Sir, Your most obedient Humble Servants, Baring Brothers & Co.

LS with En in DNA, RG 59 (State Department), Accounting Records: Letters from London Bankers, 1790–1848, received 8/3; "Duplicate" with En in the same file, received 9/3. NOTE: Enclosed was an account of the U.S. Treasury with Baring Brothers & Co. showing disbursements from 4/1/1844 through 6/30/1844 for salaries and contingent expenses of U.S. officials throughout Europe.

From MOSES BENJAMIN

United States Consulate
[Demarara,] British Guiana
18th July 1844

Sir, I have the honor to forward herewith the usual half Yearly Consular Returns for this Consulate ending 30th June and including the neighbouring Port of Berbice.

The Returns for the last six months exhibit a diminution in number of Vessels engaged in the direct Trade with the United States as compared with the last Half Year 1843 of *Twenty five:* a strong evidence of the unprofitable character of the Trade encumbered as it is with the onerous Tariff of Colonial Import Duties copy of which for the present Year was forwarded the Department of State in May last, together with a "Copy of Regulations of the Agricultural & Commercial Society" recently established here. Duplicate copies of these documents are forwarded by the present conveyance also a Paper containing the Half Yearly Report of the Seaman[']s Hospital and some valuable "Meteorological Observations" which may be useful to the Surgeon General of the United States.

I take leave here to acknowledge receipt of the Circular from the Department of State of 1st April 1844—Announcing your appointment as Secretary of State of the United States. I have the honor to be Very respectfully Sir, Your most Obed[ien]t Humble Se[r]v[an]t, Moses Benjamin.

LS (No. 49) with Ens in DNA, RG 59 (State Department), Consular Despatches, Demerara, vol. 2 (T-336:2), received 9/2.

From Geo[rge] M. Bibb, Secretary of the Treasury, 7/18. He encloses printed copies of the instructions [of 7/16] to customs house officers concerning import duties to be charged on Portuguese wines and refunds of excess duties heretofore charged. LS with En in DNA, RG 59 (State Department), Miscellaneous Letters (M-179: 105, frames 67–68); FC in DNA, RG 56 (Secretary of the Treasury), Letters to Cabinet and Bureau Officers, 1842–1847, 4:403.

From C[ALEB] CUSHING

Macao, 18 July 1844

Sir: By the Convoy, which is to sail for New York on the 20th, I propose to send to you a copy of the Treaty signed by me at Wang-Hia, with some remarks thereon, together with a duplicate of the letter which I addressed to the Department by the overland mail (No. 69 of 4 July 1844) announcing the fact of the conclusion of the Treaty; also a despatch acknowledging yours of the 29th February. The Treaty, with all the correspondence immediately appertaining [to] it, as also Duplicates of my previous correspondence, and sundry miscellaneous matters, will be despatched either by the Ann Eliza or the Sappho, both of which vessels are getting ready with all expedition to sail for the United States in ten or fifteen days. It is *probable* that the Ann Eliza & the Sappho will reach home before the Convoy, as the latter is a slow vessel, and starts so short a time before them; but on the other hand it is *possible* that the Convoy may arrive first; for which ["reason" *interlined*] I transmit by her a copy of the Treaty. I am very solicitous that the President should obtain the Treaty or its contents before the commencement of the next session of Congress; and therefore I embrace all the opportunities of writing which occur.

I am getting the Treaty and its documents ready with all possible despatch but Tsiyeng having been taken sick, was obliged to return to Canton before the Tariff was completed, which has occasioned delay.

You may inquire why I send the Treaty by the Cape of Good Hope rather than by the overland ["mail" *interlined*]. I do so 1. Because it is a so much cheaper mode; 2. Because it is on the whole safer; & 3. Because it is at this season quite as expeditious. Letters mailed here ["after the very beginning" *interlined*] of July cannot reach Bombay earlier than for the October mail from Bombay; which will probably reach the U.S. in December, not before. I am Very respectfully Your ob[edien]t S[er]v[an]t, C. Cushing.

ALS ("Private") in DNA, RG 59 (State Department), Diplomatic Despatches, China, vol. 2 (M-92:3), received 1/6/1845. NOTE: This letter was addressed to John Nelson.

From EDWARD EVERETT

London, 18 July 1844

Sir, A debate of some interest took place in the house of commons on the evening of the 16th, on the subject of the suppression of the Slave Trade. It arose on a motion of Lord Palmerston for the production of the returns of the number of negroes landed for the purpose of Slavery on the Islands and continent of America from 1815 to 1843. The motion, it may be supposed, was little more than formal, and made chiefly for the sake of the opportunity which it afforded Lord Palmerston of addressing the house generally, on the course pursued by the past and present ministry in reference to measures for the Suppression of the Slave Trade.

After the speeches of Lord Palmerston and Sir Robert Peel, Commodore [Charles] Napier put to the first naval Lord of the Admiralty the question, "what instructions had been given to British cruizers on the American coast, and whether if an English vessel saw a vessel hoisting the American flag, she would have any right to board her, not to search her, but to ascertain whether she was *bona fide* an American vessel?"

To this question Sir Robert Peel interposing replied, "that he hoped his gallant friend would not give any particular explanation, as to the nature of the instructions issued to British cruizers. The government of the United States had declined to state the nature of the instructions issued to their cruizers, conceiving that the publication of those instructions might defeat the object for which they were issued; and he thought the government of this country ought to adopt a similar course." Sir Robert Peel then observed, that the most satisfactory information had been received from the British Officers commanding cruizers on the African stations, in reference to the cordial cooperation of the Squadrons of the two nations.

Commodore Napier, not satisfied with Sir Robert Peel's explanation and statement, renewed his question in the following terms: "If a British Cruizer, not being in sight of an American cruizer, fell in with a vessel hoisting the United States' flag, would the commander of the British cruizer be justified in boarding such a vessel?"

To the interrogatory thus renewed, Sir Robert Peel replied that "he must decline giving an answer till such a case as that put by the honorable and gallant officer occurred. He had no doubt, that under those circumstances, a British cruizer would give a good account of such a vessel."

These quotations are taken from the [London] "Times" of the 17th. Notwithstanding the general correctness of the reporters of the London press, occasional errors are of course unavoidable; and I think it probable there is some inaccuracy in the language ascribed to Sir Robert Peel, as to the Government of the United States having declined to state the nature of the instructions issued to their cruizers for the reason assigned. I suppose the fact to be, that the British Government was desirous for the reason given, that the instructions of the two governments should not be published to the world, and that the government of the United States acquiesced in this course.

It is proper, however, to state on this point, that Lord Aberdeen a short time since informed me, that they were about to submit to parliament a full report of all the instructions, (as I understood him) which had at any time been given to their cruizers employed for the suppression of the Slave Trade, including, of course, those now in force. This he said was rendered necessary by the modification of the system recently determined upon, and the substitution of a more vigilant watch of the coast of Africa for the previous plan of cruizing on the coasts of the countries to which slaves are transported. Lord Aberdeen said he apprized me that the publication of the instructions now in force would perhaps shortly take place, as the Government of the United States might otherwise be surprized at their appearance, after the opinion expressed on the part of England, that, for the present, the instructions of the two governments had better not be divulged. I am, sir, very respectfully, your obedient servant, Edward Everett.

LS (No. 164) in DNA, RG 59 (State Department), Diplomatic Despatches, Great Britain, vol. 53 (M-30:49), received 8/3; FC in DNA, RG 84 (Foreign Posts), Great Britain, Despatches, 8:347–351; FC in MHi, Edward Everett Papers, 49:400–404 (published microfilm, reel 23, frames 202–204).

From A[rchibald] M. Green, [U.S. Consul at] Galveston, 7/18. Green states that Texas is in the grip of a stifling heat wave that has caused and is causing numerous deaths. Although only two cases of yellow fever have occurred, many more are expected unless the heat breaks soon. "The mercantile operations are very small, there being but a small quantity of Cotton to dispose of so late in the season." ALS in DNA, RG 59 (State Department), Consular Despatches, Galveston, vol. 2 (T-151:2), received 8/16.

From J[AMES] C. PICKETT

Legation of the U. States
Lima, July 18th, 1844

Sir, I have the honor to acknowledge the receipt of despatches Nos. 19 and 20, from the Department, which came to hand on the 13th instant. No. 18 has not yet been received.

I am instructed in despatch No. 20, to propose to the government here, that the specie that may be taken from Peruvian ports, for the purpose of defraying the expenses of vessels of war of the United States, may be exempted from the export duty, if the inquiries to be first made should result in an opinion, that a request for the boon, officially made would be granted.

The export duty on silver coin is, at Lima, five per centum—on gold, one, and the former is required for our ships of war, gold not answering the purposes. It has been proposed to the government heretofore, that this duty should not be exacted, but the proposition was not favorably considered, and I am very certain that it will not be, if renewed. The offer to reciprocate the measure would not effect the object, as Peru would derive no practical advantage from the reciprocation. I will ascertain, however, if any thing can be done.

I informed you in my last (sent by the frigate "U. States") that another revolution took place here on the 17th of June, Don Domingo Elias[,] Prefect of the Department having renounced his allegiance to the Supreme Director, whose lieutenant ["he" *interlined*] was, and declared himself *supreme*; and that general or colo[nel Rufino] Echenique, commanding a force of 12 or 15 hundred, 150 miles off, had decided to remain neutral though not to abandon the Director: But he marched suddenly against Lima, two weeks ago, assigning as a reason for so doing, Elias's refusal to furnish him with money and clothing for his troops, as he had promised to do—so Echenique alleges. But upon arriving within five or six leagues of the city, with about a thousand men, he found that considerable preparations had been made for defence; whereupon he retired to the Andes, whence he had come, giving as a reason for this retrograde movement, his unwillingness to shed the blood of his fellow-citizens. He asserts that he did not approach the capital as an enemy, but as a neutral and friend, and with no object but to procure supplies for his troops; and this may possibly be true, for considering that he is a Peruvian chief he enjoys a pretty fair reputation. He had the supreme command here two or three weeks, just before [Manuel Ignacio de] Vivanco came to Lima in April 1843, and gave very general satisfaction.

I think that, very probably, the spirit so unexpectedly displayed by the Limenians, on hearing of his approach, somewhat influenced his determination to retire, peaceably. He did not expect to meet with any resistance, whereas he found three thousand men in arms on the side of the Prefect.

The secret of the misunderstanding between Elias and Echenique, is pretty clearly this: They had agreed to abandon Vivanco, from contempt for him and for the purpose of propitiating Castilla, each intending to place himself at the head of the government in this city; but Elias got the start and proclaimed himself supreme chief, without consulting Echenique, at which the latter took offence and refused to co-operate any further with his ally, who is not the man, he says, to produce a fusion of all the parties, and to secure the welfare of the country—meaning perhaps, that he himself is.

The condition of a country must be almost hopeless when two men like Elias and Echenique, who are called patriots and are considered to be persons of honor and probity, do not hesitate, from personal pique and jealousy, to involve it in the horrors of a civil war, and to the senseless and savage conflict now going on in the South, to add another to be waged in and near the capital. What is to be expected then of those who have no claims either to patriotism or to honor or probity, and scarcely to common honesty? as is the case with a vast majority of the Peruvian functionaries. It seems that the public men here, the moment they become public, take leave of every sentiment of honor, consistency and good faith, and no amount of duplicity, treachery and villa[i]ny excites the least surprise, when perpetrated by them. I have the honor to be, Sir, with great respect, Your very Ob[edien]t Servant, J.C. Pickett.

ALS (No. 97) in DNA, RG 59 (State Department), Diplomatic Despatches, Peru, vol. 6 (T-52:6, frames 538–540), received 12/30.

To J. G. S y z, Consul of the Swiss Confederation, Philadelphia

Department of State
Washington, 18th July, 1844

Sir: In reply to your note of the 15th Instant, I have the honor to inform you that there is no Treaty existing between the United States and the Custom's Union of Germany, Congress having adjourned without any final action of the Senate upon the Treaty lately concluded at Berlin, which had been laid before that Body, at its late Session, for its advice and consent. I am, Sir, with great Consideration, Your obedient Servant, J.C. Calhoun.

FC in DNA, RG 59 (State Department), Notes to Foreign Legations, German States, 6:94–95 (M-99:27).

H[ARVEY] M. WATTERSON to John Tyler

Buenos Ayres, July 18th 1844

Dear Sir, I have just been shown a letter from Senator [Benjamin] Tappan [of Ohio], dated Washington City April 4th, to [Amory Edwards] the Consul in this City, who is his nephew, stating that he had seen Mr. Calhoun and informed him *"that as Mr. Watterson would be rejected"* (these are his words) he would be pleased if Mr. Calhoun would give the aforesaid Consul power to prosecute the claims of our citizens, Mr. Halstead[']s most especially, against this Government. The words in italics are all he says in reference to myself, and as I have not received a line from any of the Tennessee delegation in Congress, I take ["it" *interlined*] for granted that they have been waiting for the action of the Senate ["previous to writing" *canceled*] and thinking the chances were in favor of my rejection, they did not wish to communicate bad news in advance. This is the only inference I can draw from their silence. The question now with me is, on what ground have I been rejected? Is it because they did not deem Buenos Ayres a country of sufficient importance to authorize the *enormous* expense of four thousand five hundred ["dollars" *interlined*] in order to keep up diplomatic relations with it? (This was my fear, you will recollect, when you were kind enough to tender me my present appointment.) Or has it been done through the influence of the Tennessee Senators, both of whom are my bitter enemies—one of them (Col. [Ephraim H.] Foster ["& myself" *interlined*]) having once been the warmest the most intimate personal friends? Or has it been done from a sincere conviction of my unfitness for the Office? If upon the latter ground, I shall be truly mortified, and ["will my" *canceled and* "my" *interlined*] only consolation will be, that my old constituents, who have never failed to sustain me—that the entire Democracy in Tennessee, with Old Hickory at their head, think otherwise. And now a word in regard to the Consul, in the event

I have been rejected, and no other person confirmed. I have already written you two letters in regard to his conduct in the Administration of the Estate of Andrew Thorndike, an American Citizen, who died intestate in this City, two or three years ago. Lest you may not have received them, I will again ["briefly" *interlined*] give you the facts: The estate was worth at the lowest sum twenty thousand Silver dollars—so says every American in Buenos Ayres that I have talked to on the subject—the Consul administered upon it—sold it—and wrote to the heirs in the United States, (which letter I have seen and read) that it brought fifteen thousand & some hundreds of dollars, which amount he was ready to pay over to any person authorized to receive the same. Such a person, Timothy Thorndike, of Boston, brother to the deceased made his appearance here, about the 1st of February last. Mr. Edwards was absent—having taken a trip to Patagonia. When he returned, he told Mr. Thorndike that in Twenty days he would pay over the money. The twenty days expired—& no money. He kept promising from ["time" *canceled and* "day to day" *interlined*] for two months and still no money. Mr. Thorndike appealed to me. I satisfied ["myself" *interlined*] that Mr. Edwards had squandered ["that" *canceled*] nearly the whole estate & frankly told him, that if he did not settle the matter, it would cost him his office, that I would feel it my duty to write to the President on the subject and I was certain he would remove him. To all this he replied he was not afraid of it—offering at the same time some miserable reason, why he delayed payment. I then told him that he had acted illegally from the beginning—that the sale was null and void—& that I would see Gov. [Juan M.] Rosas and have the property ["returned" *interlined*] to the heirs. This alarmed the purchasers and among hands, in order to get undisputed titles, they assisted the Consul in raising four thousand dollars, which sum he paid to Mr. Thorndike and obtained a clear receipt. This is a simple statement of the facts in the case, and now it is for you to say whether such additional power shall be con confer[r]ed [*sic*] upon him as was asked of Mr. Calhoun by his ["beautiful" *canceled*] uncle, Senator Tappan. I have written to you on this subject, because it is my duty to do so and not that I have the slightest unkind feeling toward him. On the contrary, he has been and is ["now" *interlined*], so obliging, so accommodating to me, that I would almost [*one word altered to* "permit"] him to rob me without saying a word against it.

The vessel by which I send this letter was advertised to sail to morrow, but the Capt. has just called to see me and says, that he will sail in one hour. This I regret, as I intended to write you in regard to some other matters—Paraguay in particular. I have several Official documents from that Country which I shall transmit to the Secretary of State by the next vessel which sails for the United States. Nothing would gratify me more ["pleasure" *interlined and then canceled*] than to ["receive instructions to" *interlined*] visit Paraguay. Excuse blotches, interlineations &c. as I have not time to read over, much less copy this letter. Yours truly, H.M. Watterson.

ALS in DNA, RG 59 (State Department), Diplomatic Despatches, Argentina, vol. 5 (M-69:6), received 10/15.

To Henry A. Wise

Department of State
Washington, 18 July 1844

Sir, I transmit a copy of a letter dated the 25th of last month, and of its accompaniments, addressed by Mr. Joseph Ray to this Department upon the subject of a complaint of his, against the Brazilian Government. The following are the material facts in the case.

Mr. Ray was a member of the commercial firm of Ray and Bryan, which transacted an extensive business at Pernambuco at the period of the rebellion in that Province headed by [José da Costa] Carvalho in 1824. In the progress of the hostilities of the one party against the other, he gave refuge in his house to members of both, for the purpose of screening them from personal violence with which they were threatened by their adversaries. It appears, however, that although the Imperial party availed themselves of the asylum offered by Mr. Ray, they made the fact of his showing the same humanity towards the party of Carvalho, the groundwork of a representation to the Government at Rio de Janeiro that he had improperly tampered with the politicks of the country, and had taken part with Carvalho. This charge was followed by a formal decree of the Emperor, banishing Mr. Ray from his dominions. Against the justice of this decree he appealed in a petition to the Emperor himself, which Mr. [Condy] Raguet acting Chargé d'Affaires at Rio de Janeiro, communicated to the minister for Foreign Affaires with a note of the 22d of June 1825. The Minister replied in a note of the —— of August, 1825, that Mr. Ray's banishment could not be revoked and that under the circumstances, it was considered a mild measure. The decree of banishment required the Governor of Pernambuco, to allow Mr. Ray a reasonable time to adjust his affairs, but only fifteen days were allowed him for that purpose. He accordingly complied with the decree and returned to the United States. On the 8th of May 1826, he addressed a letter to Mr. [Henry] Clay, then Secretary of State, setting forth the circumstances of his banishment and requesting the interposition of this government for the purpose of obtaining redress therefor. No answer appears to have been returned to that letter, and as no instructions were given to the Chargé d'Affaires at Rio de Janeiro upon the subject, it is presumed that the legality of the banishment was not doubted or that it was considered inexpedient to contest it. This part of the case (although the measure adopted against Mr. Ray would seem to have been sincere [sic] and unmerited,) may consequently be considered to have been settled at that time and no disposition is at present entertained to ["re" interlined] open the same. It further appears, however, that, on the 27th of August, 1826, a Mr. Mendonça of Pernambuco, who was a surety on some unpaid Custom House bonds of the house of Ray and Bryan obtained an attachment upon all the property of that house at Pernambuco, and an order, represented to have been illegal, which resulted in the closing of their Compting House and the transfer of their Books, debts, and other property to Commissioners for the purpose of collecting the debts and disposing of the property at the pleasure of the Commissioners.

The Documents do not show what were the proceedings of the Commissioners nor whether the attachment was judicially resisted by the house of Ray and Bryan. With a despatch from this Department of the 18th of November, 1830, Mr. [William] Brent, then Chief Clerk, transmitted to Mr. [Ethan A.] Brown, Chargé d'Affaires of the United States at Rio de Janeiro, the papers in relation to the Case and said in the despatch that it was the wish of the Secretary of State [Martin Van Buren] that he should employ his good offices as far as that could be properly and advantageously done, towards obtaining from the government of Brazil the indemnity to which Mr. Ray might be found entitled. Nothing appears to have been done by Mr. Brown with reference to this instruction until the 25th of April, 1833, when that gentleman had an interview with the Minister for Foreign Affairs, with whom he had left the papers on the 23d of that month. The particulars of the conference you will find in Mr. Brown's No. 46 of the 6th of May, 1833. Its result, was an opinion on the part of Mr. Brown that the subject was too delicate a one to be moved at that time. He accordingly requested the Minister to return the papers, and says in his despatch that he anticipated the approbation of the department in regard to the course which he had taken. Nothing further however appears to have been written to him upon the subject, and it is not mentioned in his subsequent despatches.

No special instructions were given to Mr. [William] Hunter in relation to Mr. Ray's case until the 7th of Oct[obe]r, 1836, when the latter having been reappointed Consul at Pernambuco, Mr. Hunter was directed to apply for his Exequator, and to take an early opportunity to exert his good offices in favor of Mr. Ray's claim on the Brazilian Government.

The receipt of this instruction was acknowledged by Mr. Hunter in a postscript of the 3d of January, 1837, to his despatch No. 48 of the 19th of December, 1836.

In his No. 49, of the 17th of January, 1837, Mr. Hunter expresses an unfavorable opinion of the Claim but does not assign any reasons therefore. He had returned the papers to Mr. Ray in order that a statement of the case might be prepared and remarks that he presumed the purport of his instructions would be complied with if he were to present the claim to the Minister for Foreign Affairs with a note requesting for it the favorable consideration of that Government and stating that, in so doing, he acted under the instructions of his own Government requiring him to interpose his good offices in Mr. Ray's behalf.

No further instructions were given to Mr. Hunter in regard to the case and consequently the view which he had taken of it, and the construction which he had placed upon the instructions already given were neither expressly confirmed nor disapproved by the department. He next mentions it in his despatch No. 76 of the 27th of May, 1838. He repeats his unfavorable opinion of the claim but again omits to give his reasons. He mentions that he had received the statement which he had advised Mr. Ray to have prepared, and that he would *soon* give it all its chances of favor, but that unless otherwise instructed, he could not do more.

It does not appear from Mr. Hunter[']s despatches that he ever carried into effect the intention which he here expresses. From a letter which he addressed to Mr. Ray under date, the 20th of July, 1840, it seems that he deemed it advisable in the then state of Brazil and of our other business with that Government, not to drive Mr. Ray's affair to what he terms a hasty and dangerous result; and that consequently, with some other cases, he had thought it for the good of all concerned, to hold it back for a while. Mr. Ray accordingly despatched an agent to Rio de Janeiro, who on the 4th of January,

1843, withdrew from Mr. Hunter's custody the documents in relation to the case. He then applied for and obtained leave to sue the National Treasury of Brazil. The attorney of the Government alledged that the suit was barred by a law passed in November, 1841, which provided that all claims upon that government originating in transactions from the year 1826 and not presented prior to the 1st of January, 1843, should be null and void.

In consequence of this Mr. Ray has again applied for the interposition of his own Government. The grounds on which he relies are that Mendonça[']s liability for him was, as he alleges, for an amount little exceeding nineteen thousand milreis, and that the Custom house bonds on which Mr. Mendonça was surety, were not actually due at the time the proceedings under the sequestration were begun, that the property seized, was of a value more than ten times the amount of the liability, and that the seizure resulted in a complete stoppage of the business of the House of Ray and Bryan.

If the seizure was not warranted by the law, it must be imputed to vindictiveness on the part of Mr. Ray's personal enemies or commercial rivals, or to a desire in the Imperial Authorities at Pernambuco to show their zeal by adding the punishment of Confiscation to that of banishment which the Emperor had decreed; for so far, the effect of the attachment has been tantamount to a confiscation. If this were so, it would be an aggression upon the rights of Mr. Ray for which the most ample atonement should be required by this government.

It appears, however, that the assignees in whose charge the property of Ray and Bryan was placed, themselves acknowledge a balance due that House of one hundred and fifty three thousand milreis after the settlement of the demands against the house. If this be so, it was due from the Brazilian Government itself, and of course the effect of the statu[t]e of limitations would be but to prevent that Government from paying its acknowledged debt. But in no view can the sufficiency of this plea, under the circumstances, be admitted by this government, for it may be with strict propriety said that the claim had in fact been demanded of the Brazilian Government at the period of the interview between Mr. Brown and the Minister for Foreign Affairs adverted to above. If the demand was not more early made of that Government by Mr. Ray himself or by his private agent, it is but fair to suppose that this may have been owing to a supposition on his part that his own Government had undertaken the exclusive prosecution of the claim from the period of the instruction to Mr. Brown of the 18th of November 1830, with a copy of which, it seems Mr. Ray was furnished. Even if the terms of the instruction may not have warranted such an inference, the omission or delay to seek justice for himself may probably be fairly ascribed to a mis-apprehension of the instructions of this Government.

The department is of opinion that the hesitation of both Mr. Brown and Mr. Hunter in this matter should in part at least be ascribed to their viewing the case as a whole, to their blending the banishment with the sequestration or attachment. If the instructions to them had been more explicit, and if from their tenor they could have inferred that it was meant they should have discriminated be-tween the political and the judicial part of the case, it is quite prob-able that the subject would have been long since again, at least, formerly presented to that Government.

You will accordingly lose no time in taking this course. You will represent that the Government of the United States is convinced that Mr. Ray has been wronged by the proceedings under the seques-tration. It would have been desirable that the judicial tribunals of Brazil should have afforded him relief, but as his application through that channel has failed, this government deems itself bound to inter-fere in his behalf. It is of opinion, that if it should not be competent for the Executive branch of the Brazilian Government to grant relief, the act of limitation, barring the legal prosecution of Mr. Ray's claims, should be so modified as to permit him to apply to the courts of Justice for a decision of his case.

It would seem from the letter of the Brazilian minister for Foreign Affairs to Mr. [João Francisco] Lisboa, a translation of which is now enclosed, that the existing Brazilian authorities, are far from harbour-ing ill will or resentment towards Mr. Ray on account of the circum-stances attending his banishment, that he made himself generally acceptable to them while he last held the Consulate at Pernambuco and left a strong impression in his favor. It is hoped, therefore, that your interposition in his behalf will be well received, and that it will be brought to the prompt and successful issue which his misfortunes certainly entitle him to expect. I am Sir Your Obedient Servant, J.C. Calhoun.

LS (No. 6, "Duplicate") in DNA, RG 84 (Foreign Posts), Brazil, Instructions, vol. 2; FC with En in DNA, RG 84 (Foreign Posts), Brazil, Despatches, 11:105–[113]; slightly variant FC in DNA, RG 59 (State Department), Diplomatic In-structions, Brazil, 15:106–113 (M-77:23).

JOHN C. CALHOUN, JR. to [James Edward Calhoun, Pendleton]

Fort Des Moines July 19th 1844
Sacks & Fox nation[,] Iowa Te[rrito]ry

My dear brother, We arrived here a few days ago, after a long journey of more than 2,500 miles by the route from Washington, during which time, we have seen every variety of climate, soil, vegetation, and society. I have not more than recovered from the fatigues of the journey, but still feel, that it would not be acting properly to delay longer, as I know, that you are all anxious to hear from us. Just before starting from St. Louis, I wrote to Sissy [Martha Cornelia Calhoun], and gave her a brief description of our trip up to that time, and therefore will not make a recapitulation, but will commence where I left off.

We left Saint Louis on the 21st of last month, after purchasing, ammunition, guns, two double barrells, two brace pistols, two bowie knives, three horses, & a servant.

The steamboat we left Saint Louis in, was the Lancet, a pleasure boat bound for St. Anthonys falls, we had a fine band of music on board, and a great many Creole ladies, some of whom were very beautiful, they danced once or twice, but we were so much fatigued that we could not take a part. The Mississippi was very full, higher by several feet than it was ever known before, by the oldest inhabitants, it was ten miles broad at St. Louis, which is situated 1,750 miles above the mouth, thus giving you some idea of the magnitude of the river.

The scenery on the upper Mississippi is truly picturesque, the part of the river called upper, begins above the mouth of the Missouri, where the river entirely changes its character, from a mud[d]y, it becomes a beautiful limpid stream, at this place, the shore rises to a great height, it is one solid wall of limestone, ranging from 3 to 4, and sometimes 500 feet high, the shore is the most beautiful on the Illinois side, in the ["County" *interlined*] of Calhoun. From this place, nothing of interest hapenned until we got to Quincy on the Illinois side, here, just a[s] we were going to land, a steamboat the El Dorado coming down the river, ran against us, breaking in the side of the vessel, and so disabling her, as to cause considerable delay, which gave us time to walk about the city, which is one on the neatest on the river, we found after our return to the boat, that the other boat, had purposely struck our boat, there being some bad feeling between the two Captains. From Quincy we started for Nauvoo, and arrived there after dark, it was the evening after the Governor [Thomas Ford] had sent to ar[r]est Joe Smith, and the City in consequence in a great state of excitement, a large number of us being anxious to see the Prophet, begged the Captain of the boat to wait two or three hours for us, and in a few minutes after, found ourselves in an omnibus, rowling rapidly through water street, and soon our horses were drawn up before the door of the Hotel, kept by the Prophet himself, at first he thought we were spies sent by the Governor, so he kept 300 men armed round the house, and sent his Marshall to disperse us, but upon telling him the purpose of our visit, he invited us to the drawingroom, where he soon joined us, he gave us a full description of his difficulties, and also an exposition of his faith, frequently calling himself the Prophet, in the course of conversation.

Nauvoo in Hebrew signifies the beautiful, & in this case I think fully deserves the name, for its site is said to be the most beautiful in the Western World, it is on a level plain, extending back for 3 miles, and then rises into high bluffs. A few days after leaving Nauvoo, we arrived at Fort Madison Iowa Territory, where we remained 8 days, and spent a pleasant time, while there we received several invitations to parties, at one time we received a note signed the ladies of Fort Madison inviting us to a large Fair and party given by them. On the 3d of July we mounted our horses and started for this place, the distance from Madison here is 200 miles, which is all one Pra[i]rie, there being all together not more than 20 miles of timber, you cannot imagine how much the first pra[i]rie struck me, one has not an idea of the immensity of the Earth[']s surface until he sees one; from F[or]t Madison to this place there is a continual rise, at first gradual, then becoming very rowling. Soon after you ascend the sum[m]it of the bluffs of the river, you strike the timber, which after passing through a very narrow strip of timber you come to the edge of the first pra[i]rie which is generally flat, and extends for 30 miles without a rise, covered with grass about knee high, the effect is very singular at ["or over" *interlined*] the line of vision it looks like water and I frequently immagined I was approaching the ocean. We would have started for the far west before this, but after Joe was killed, the Governor made a requisition to the Gover[n]ment for 700 Dragoons, so we have to remain to see what orders come from the ["Sectary" *altered to* "Secatary"; of War], in that case we will not start until 2 weeks at the lowest calculation. A day or two ago a boat arrived from below, which is the second ever been here, we took a sail up as far as the mouth of Beaver river, 8 miles above this, it is the first boat that has ever been above this. There are three tribes of Indians here, the Fox and Sacks & Ioways, the two former are very powerful, but the latter though now small, was once a very formidable tribe, the whole amount of the three tribes are 3,800, their boundary extends 30 miles below, and on the east, while on the west are the Sioux or Dahcotah's, the most powerful tribe as far as numbers are concerned in the United States. The Indians here are quite wild, and not one of them can speak English, except good morning, which they say whether you meet them in the morning or at night, when they drink each others health, they say How, they are in our rooms almost every day. I went with [Lt.] Pat[rick] Noble [Jr.] a few days ago to some of their vil[l]ages, we visited the village of Appenense, Kirkirk, Hardfish, and Kish-Kiikosh, the latter is a great brave & chief and his likeness you can see, among the celebrated ["Fox" *interlined*] Indians, he is successor of Black-Hawk, there are two sons of the latter chief here, they are very fine looking men, and considered brave. There is a great deal of game about 50 miles above, such as, bear, deer, Antelope, Bison, Elk, and a few wild horses, the Indians are daily coming in loaded down with meat, I saw an Elks horn a few days ago, measuring 7 ft. some inches in length; & before I forget it, I must tell you a *big* but true fish story—while at Madison, I saw a boy about your size, catch a blue-cat with a hook and line, weighing 65 pounds, and measuring 6 ft. in length, this is what I saw, now I will tell you what I heard, it was that cats are frequently cought in the Mississippi, in weight 200 lbs., jacks are also cought in length from 12 to 15 ft. Pat says you must remember him to his brothers and sisters, & tell them to write to him. I must conclude as my pen is bad and it is getting late.

Pady [Patrick Calhoun] & Pat send their love to you and Willy [William Lowndes Calhoun]. Give my love to *Kate* [Catherine Floride Townes] & Eugenia [Calhoun] & tell them, they must write to me. Direct your letters to St. Louis. I remain, your ever devoted brother, John C. Calhoun, Jr.

ALS in ScU-SC, John C. Calhoun Papers. NOTE: Joseph Smith's arrest and subsequent murder occurred not long after the above-described visit to Nauvoo.

From [Governor] R[ichard] K. Call, Tallahassee, [Fla. Territory], 7/19. Call reminds Calhoun of the charges he has preferred against U.S. Attorney Charles S. Sibley, and wishes to know what course the State Department intends to pursue in the matter. (A Clerk's EU reads: "Copy of this sent to Mr. Sibley, Oct[obe]r 25, 1844.") ALS in DNA, RG 59 (State Department), Applications and Recommendations, 1837–1845, Sibley (M-687:30, frames 105–107).

From F[RANCIS] M. DIMOND

United States Consulate
Vera Cruz, July 19th 1844

Sir, The U.S. Cutter Woodbury being on the point of sailing for New Orleans, affords me a moment, respectfully to say, that the Governor of this City, has just rec[eive]d intelligence through the Mexican Consul at New Orleans, via Campeache, that the Treaty had been rejected by the Senate of the U.S., and has dispatched a messenger with the news to Mexico [City].

We are without any arrivals from any part of the States for nearly a month. I have the honor to be Sir most Respectfully Your Ob[edient] Servant, F.M. Dimond.

ALS (No. 230) in DNA, RG 59 (State Department), Consular Despatches, Veracruz, vol. 5 (M-183:5), received 7/30.

To J.C. de Figaniere e Morão, [Portuguese Minister to the U.S., Philadelphia?], 7/19. Calhoun encloses a copy of a letter of 7/18 from [George M. Bibb] Secretary of the Treasury, with a printed copy of instructions to customs officers about lower duties to be charged on Portuguese wines in future and refunds of excess duties heretofore charged. FC in DNA, RG 59 (State Department), Notes to Foreign Legations, Portugal, 6:74 (M-99:80).

From Gerding & Kunkelman, New York [City], 7/19. They acknowledge the receipt of a letter from Francis Markoe, [Jr.,] for Louis Mark, which they were requested to read and deliver. They state that they received a letter of 7/16 from Mark in Boston in which he reported that he was leaving the U.S. on the Britannia. They therefore return Markoe's letter. "Mr. Mark brought us letters of introduction from very respectable german houses interrested in the Zoll Verein treaty and in his last letter held out strong hopes of his succeeding to bring said treaty to a satisfactory conclusion." LS in DNA, RG 59 (State Department), Consular Despatches, Vienna, vol. 1 (T-243:1).

From JOHN HOGAN, "Private"

Utica N[ew] York, July 19th 1844
My dear Sir, Our Supreme Court of this State is now in Session in
this City & has been for two weeks. As a matter of course the Lawyers from all parts of the State are also here. Amongst them is
B[enjamin] F. Butler[,] Mr. [Martin] Van Buren[']s drill Sergeant
at the Baltimore Convention. He called on me yesterday at my office & remained with me for an hour or two. As a matter of course
we entered at once into your merits & that of others and on the
Presidential Election. He feels a little sour towards you but I think
that I answered all of his objections. He insisted that your friends
were the ones that caused the defeat of Mr. V[an] B[uren] that the
friends of the other Gent[lemen] could have been quieted. In reply
I said that Mr. V[an] B[uren's] friends were bound by every consideration to have supported you for the Presidency that you were
entitled to it at their hands for the noble and magnanimous course
you pursued toward the Administration of Mr. V[an] B[uren] in
1837. When his Ad[ministration] was sinking of its own weight
you step[p]ed in with your Gigantic tallent & took Mr. V[an] B[uren]
& his friends from the gutter and that the understanding was *as I
knew* that you were to be supported for the Presidency in 44. He
then replied that in consequence of Mr. V[an] B[uren's] defeat the
party were anxious to reinstating him in 44 & that you could then
claim their support. I then reminded him of the tyrannical course
of his friends at the meeting of Congress that not *One of your friends*
got a single favour and that if we would have given Mr. V[an]
B[uren] a support we had but little prospect of fair play[,] that we
had no disposition to do any thing but justice and that we would do
at all events. I said to him that he for one had but little to say to
you or ought not for that I had no doubt you did not entertain a single
hostile feeling toward him. Neither did I think that you did *toward
any Gent* for that he[,] Mr. B[utler,] as well as myself knew too
well your high toned mind that you were far above that low bitterness that some other Gent[lemen] were possessed of. He then enquired of me if I got my (*great*) appointment as he understood that
I was to be appointed a Minister to some of the South American
States. To which I replied that I had not & that it was doubtful with
me whether I should. He then replied that that was the course in
most cases pursued toward those at the north who contended &
sustained at great Sacrafice the interest of Gent[lemen] at the South
but Closed by saying that he hoped I would not be disap[p]ointed.

At all events I put him in better humour. He mentioned before he left that he thought that the manner that the Texas question was presented at the North would embarrass us much in the Election but he expressed his firm opinion that we would carry this State. I had a conversation with Judge [Samuel] Nelson & Judge [Greene C.] Bronson of the Supreme Court. They both say that matters look well in this State and appear satisfied with the result. But [*ms. torn;* "let"?] me here say to you that we do not stand any too well in this State. There exists some sourness yet. The friends of Mr. [Henry] Clay are doing all that men are capable of to give Mr. C[lay] the Electoral Vote of this State. I hope Mrs. Calhoun was well when you last heard from home. I fancy you have Scalding weather now at Washington. I hope our friends in South Carolina will keep cool as she now should step in as Peace Maker in my opinion. I am Sir your Ob[edien]t & humble Servant, John Hogan.

ALS in ScCleA.

From C[HARLES] J. INGERSOLL

Forest Hill, Philad[elphia], July 19, [18]44
Dear Sir, In a letter to the Trenton N[ew] Jersey celebration of the 4 July I touched on the Senate's action on the Texas question, as in that herewith [*not found*] to the Phila[delphia] City dinner party an English aspect of the subject is cursorily presented. In either a speech or written publication I intend to treat what Col. [Thomas H.] Benton calls the President's [John Tyler's] appeal to the people—probably in a speech[,] for I am constantly desired to address the people of my district, who, as far as my party is concerned, I find cordially unanimous for my reelection, which I don't believe that even the tornado of native Americanism can prevent if I consent to it. I am sincerely y[ou]rs, C.J. Ingersoll.

ALS in ScCleA.

To [James McM. Shafter], the Secretary of State of Vt., 7/19. Calhoun requests that he be provided with copies of "Prison Reports," showing "the number and sex of Convicts white and colored" for the years 1840–1844. LS in Vt, Correspondence of the Secretary of State.

From M[ark] Alexander, [former Representative from Va.]

Park Forest
Mecklenburg C[oun]ty [Va.]
July 20, 1844

My dear Sir, I have recently read a portion of Mr. [William C.] Rives' speech upon the subject of the Tariff, lately delivered in the Senate of the U.S. to see the ground he takes to justify his change of opinion.

It was not surprising to find, according to the new doctrine of Mr. [Henry] Clay and his followers, by discriminations, retaliation &c. that Mr. R[ives] should claim the power under the treaty-making power, and that clause of the constitution which regulates commerce with foreign nations and among the several States, in order, to justify the Treaty he made with France some years since, by which, for an inconsiderable reduction of duties upon sea Island cotton and rice, her wines and silks were introduced at a much lower duty into this country.

I thought then this feature of the Treaty was improper, and infringed upon the rights of Congress, in assuming to regulate by Treaty, the revenue feature of the govt. which originates with the house of representatives. If we admit this doctrine, the whole power of lowering or raising duties, may be taken from the Congress of the U.S. and transferred to the Minister, President and Senate. The power of protecting domestic manufactures as Mr. R[ives] says, can be as effectually done in this way, as any other, and, as the treaty becomes the supreme law of the land, (no money provision being necessary to carry it into effect), it may be done without consulting the representatives of the people. It is true, the Treaty with France, and the [German] one recently laid aside by the Senate, contemplates a reduction of the imposts, but the principle is the same, and supposing the manufacturing party in power, they may go upon the other extreme, and favor the protective system both at home and abroad, by discriminations. I do not know what party caused the late treaty to be laid upon the table, or postponed, but presume it was the Tariff party, as, in this case, it was rather against their interest. But we can expect no advantages from foreign nations in this way, and the very small reduction of the duty on cotton and rice with France, never enhanced the price of those articles in this country. The capacity of the country is always capable of producing them to such an extent, as ["always" *canceled*] to bring the price to

403

the relative value of other agricultural productions. I am clearly of opinion, they should be confined to that clause of the constitution, in their arguments, under which taxes and imposts are raised, in order, more effectually to put them down. Mr. [Martin] V[an] Buren, I think, began to favor this mode of protection, by discrimination, as getting round the constitutional difficulty. Nor, do I think, the power to regulate commerce with foreign nations and among the several States, gives to Congress a right to impose duties with a view to protect domestic manufactures. The power to regulate commerce is one thing, and has been confined to the manner in which foreign vessels should trade with us, as to its tonnages[,] crew &c. but I believe, has never extended to the articles on board, which come under the revenue clause, and is a very different power. I believe it to be a sound decision in constitutional law, in our govt. and may be found in Judge [John] Marshall's opinions, that a power to do any act, must be shewn to exist, under one clause of the constitution, and not under various and different clauses.

It seems to me, it would be well for some leading paper either in Washington or this State, to place this subject properly before the public, to prevent the party from being divided upon it. We are now likely to agree in our principles, and it is all important, that no new theories should separate us.

Having been defeated upon the Texas question by the Senate, in their devotion to Mr. Clay, seeing the abolition feeling has been gotten up, I am now reconciled to it, and think it best for her and the U. States, if she can be independent of Foreign powers with her southern institutions, to remain as she is. She will be a protection to us, and we to her against northern fanatics. And, if she were annexed, when she comes to be admitted into the Union, we, I see very clearly are to have the Missouri ["question" *interlined*] raised again, notwithstanding the compromise; and if she is to come in with restrictions, and to be cut down to one slave State only, it seems to me, more wise for her to remain and grow up with our Southern principles. She will be free from the operation of the Tariff policy, as an isolated republic, when, if brought into the Union, she may be placed in reference *to us*, pretty much as Louisiana is upon the sugar duty. I have no doubt, in the course of time, the North and the West will be more in favor of her admission, than the South, should she maintain her established government. I think it incumbent upon the U.S.[,] England, and France, to secure her independence, even of Mexico. And with their guarantee, she may be the happiest Republic in the World.

I hope you will continue in the Adm[inistratio]n until you see whether any thing can be done, to save us from the danger and misrule with which we are threatened. I am, with sincere respect & friendship, Y[ou]r ob[edien]t S[er]v[an]t, M. Alexander.

ALS in ScCleA.

T[HOMAS] BALTZELL and Others to [John Tyler] the President of the United States and [John C. Calhoun] Secretary of State

Tallahassee, July 20, 1844

Sir, We have been informed that during the temporary absence of C[harles] S. Sibley Esq. U.S. Dist[rict] Atto[rney] for this District, the gentleman he left in charge of his business has received a letter from the State Department addressed to Mr. S[ibley] enclosing extracts of charges of "stifling prosecutions" for private ends & "pecuniary considerations" of being bribed to dismiss prosecutions or entering nolle prosequis & receiving five dollars in one case for so doing &c &c. We are told the names of his accusers & the witnesses & the names of the cases are left blank in the document communicated by the Dept. We have known Mr. Sibley for years having been engaged in active practice at the bar with him. His conduct & character have been without reproach & ["now" *interlined*] for the first time we have heard imputations of the kind alluded to; & which we believe to be wholly unfounded & unjust. But we deem it due to Mr. Sibley & his friends—to the bar of this District the integrity of which is assailed through him, & to the cause of truth & public justice that these charges should be rigidly investigated & that all the original letters[,] communications[,] affidavits & other papers referring to ["these" *altered to* "them" *and* "charges" *canceled*] be submitted to the judge of this District to be laid before the next Grand jury of this District to the end that the authors sustain them by legal proof or meet the consequences due to a calumnious & false accusation. We are assured this course is in accordance with the wishes of Mr. Sibley's relatives who in his absence act for him & that he will approve of it. If the Govt. deem it best to designate any other tribunal or a Committee of disinterested individuals to make a preliminary investigation here *for its action,* we are assured its action will be entirely satisfactory. We trust however that no steps prejudicial to

Mr. Sibley will be taken till the matter has been fully & openly investigated. Very respectfully Your Ob[edien]t Serv[an]ts, T. Baltzell, Simon Towle, Joseph Branch, John P. DuVal, Tho[mas] H. DuVal, R.W. White.

LS in DNA, RG 59 (State Department), Applications and Recommendations, 1837–1845, Sibley (M-687:30, frames 108–110). Note: Appended to this LS is the statement: "The undersigned citizens of Leon County respectfully Concur in the foregoing," followed by 22 signatures.

From R[ICHARD] K. CRALLÉ

Lynchburg [Va.,] July 20th 1844

My dear Sir: I am much gratified to inform you that Mrs. [Elizabeth Morris] C[rallé], who was seriously ill for ten days before my arrival, has safely passed the ordeal, and is now doing well. As a Father and a Husband you can justly appreciate the feelings which such an event so naturally enginders—and I shall therefore say nothing of them. One anxiety, however, succeeds another. I am apprehensive my absence may, in some measure, embarrass your own movements; and I write to request you would inform me, as nearly as you now can, of the day when you wish to leave Washington. You will not, of course, before the arrival of Mr. [Thomas G.] Clemson, (which if I remember aright) you expected would be about the last of the present month. He will not probably depart on his mission before the 10th or 15th of August—and I suppose you will not take your southern trip before his departure. But the time he will be delayed in Washington is *Conjectural*; and I would be much obliged to you to let me know on the receipt of this, what stay he will make, and at what time you would desire me to return. I make the request because, (though I would be glad to remain here until Mrs. C[rallé] is well enough to accompany me) I would not wish to be absent from the Department a day, after you leave for the South. Mrs. C[rallé] is now walking about—having passed her accouch[e]ment nearly two weeks since. She is doing so well that in three weeks more I might venture, I think, to move her. But I had rather return for that purpose, than be absent from my place while you are gone.

There is much excitement here, and in the adjoining Counties on the subject of the election. Both parties are enthusiastic, and exerting their utmost energies. On the part of the Democrats the unison on [James K.] Polk is perfect, the President [John Tyler] having no friend that I have heard of. The whole force of the Party will concentrate on Polk; and from all I hear Virginia may be regarded as certain. Many of your friends who went off in 1840 have returned to the Party, and are doing yeoman's service. To the zeal and influence of the State Rights men alone can the success of the Party in the State be attributed. This has drawn on them the bitterest denunciations of Clay's friends—and you are held responsible for the mischief. I am glad of this—for it will serve to identify you with the Party more thoroughly than any other course things could take. As to [Thomas H.] Benton, he is most cordially cursed on all sides by the Democrats—for the Texas question which, when I was last here, was rarely mentioned[,] is now the absorbing topic in all circles—public and private. I never before witnessed as much enthusiasm as now prevails among the Republicans here. A large meeting was held the night before the last where the utmost zeal and interest were exhibited. The Chief speaker, heretofore your enemy, was truly eloquent as well as able in defence of the Treaty, and handled the subject with much tact and efficiency. I was *casually* present, and could not resist the loud & repeated calls to address the meeting; though I expressed my unwillingness to appear before the public, holding the relation I did to the Government. I confined myself chiefly to the two Treaties, and am told produced some effect on the Whig portion of the meeting; which I think probable, as I was angrily interrupted by the Leader of that Party in the midst of my remarks—a circumstance that produced intense feeling, tho' I did not deign [*one word canceled*] to notice it myself. The truth is the whole country is profoundly ignorant of the facts attending the Treaties—and when I stated a few only, the meeting manifested the strongest feelings of indignation. Several *countrymen* were present, and I have since received an invitation to address a large meeting of the People of Campbell [County] to be convened for that purpose. I thought it, however, more prudent to decline, as it might subject the administration to censure.

Your letter to Pakenham is bitterly denounced by the Whigs, and proudly extolled by the Democrats, as the ablest State Paper ever issued from the Department. Even the more moderate of the Whigs admit the correspondence to be triumphant—and acknowledge that Pakenham was fairly driven from the field. Your friends here are very anxious to see you; and I much wish you would come this route on your way to the Springs. It is the best route—and I should be much gratified if you would take it, instead of the mountain route. They have long desired to see you (both Parties) for both have joined in their public invitations. Why not come?

Let me hear from you—direct to New London, Campbell County Va. With the highest esteem and affection I am yours &c, R.K. Crallé.

ALS in ViU, Richard Kenner Crallé Papers.

From A[RCHIBALD] M. GREEN

Legation of the U. States
in Charge of the Consulate
Galvezton, July 20th 1844

Sir, I have the honor to report to you that Gen[era]l [William S.] Murphy late Cha[rg]e d'Affair[e]s of the U. States to this Republic, died at this place on the 13th inst. at 1:30 O'clock A.M.

On the day succeeding his death I addressed a note to Lt. Com-[man]d[an]t John A. Davis of the Sch[oone]r Flirt requesting him to order two of the Officers of that vessel to take an inventory of the archives of the Legation and also of his private affects [*sic*] before they were handed into my custody; and I enclose herewith to the Department copies of the inventory and memorandum made by the Officers appointed for that purpose.

I find among the papers left by Gen[era]l Murphy, many rough draughts of letters upon public subjects that have not been copied into either of the Record books of the Legation, nor have the Despatches from the Department of State from the 27th Oct[obe]r 1843 to the date of your last number, been placed upon the records.

Much time and labor will therefore be necessary to make the records of the Legation complete.

Since the death of the late Chargé d'Affair[e]s, much of my time has been occupied in recording his correspondence, and in consequence of my anxiety to make the records complete in this particular, I am compelled to defer my own Consular report until the next boat.

A despatch bearer (Captain [Noverto] Galan) from Mexico arrived at the seat of Govt. of Texas about a week since in the absence of President [Samuel] Houston, who was at his private residence on the Trinity River. I understand that the despatch was immediately transmitted to Gen[era]l Houston by the Secretary of State [Anson

Jones], and I have not yet been able to obtain any authentic information of its purport.

I have addressed a communication [of 7/19] to the Secretary of State (a copy of which I herewith transmit) and availed myself of the occasion to request information of the nature of the despatch.

As soon as I can gather any authentic information upon the subject, I shall immediately report it to the Department.

I regret that it is not in my power to give to the Dept. any relyable information on the subject of this despatch by this opportunity, and in the absence of such I can merely give you the rumours that are in circulation at the seat of Government, in relation to the despatches.

It is suggested by some who profess to enjoy the confidence of the Govt. that it is a proposition of some kind for the recognition of the independence of Texas, provided she will enter into a stipulation to remain seperate, free, and independent and form no treaty of annexation with the U. States; And it is further reported that this proposition has been made through the interposition of the English Minister to Mexico [Charles Bankhead].

These are mere rumours, and when tis considered that those who have put them in circulation have, up to this time, had no better opportunities of learning the true character of these despatches, than the public at large, but little reliance is to be placed in their truth. I have the honor to be With much Respect Y[ou]r ob[edien]t S[ervan]t, A.M. Green.

ALS (No. 2) with Ens in DNA, RG 59 (State Department), Diplomatic Despatches, Texas, vol. 2 (T-728:2, frames 363–369), received 8/16. NOTE: In his letter of 7/19 to Anson Jones, Green states that a Mexican despatch bearer recently arrived in Washington, Texas, with despatches from the Mexican government to that of Texas. Green asks "to be made acquainted with such parts of the subjects of those despatches as may be interesting to" the U.S. government.

From A[RCHIBALD] M. GREEN

Legation of the U. States
in Charge of the Consulate
at Galveston, Texas
20th July 1844

Sir, I have the honor to report that during a conversation in my office with Her Brit[a]n[nic] M. Consul (Mr. [William] Kennedy) at this Port he remarked that he had just rec[eive]d a letter from the Hon[ora]ble Secretary of State of Texas [Anson Jones], in which he expressed much solicitude that he (Mr. K[ennedy]) would be appointed Ch[arg]e d'Affair[e]s on the part of the British Government to *fill up* the *vacancy* which *had occurred*; from which I infer that Mr. Elliott [*sic*; Charles Elliot] is recalled and a new appointment will take place.

There is no diplomatic representative in the Govt. at this time, and Mr. Elliott[']s movements have been rather misterious, no one knows where he is, at the present time.

Whilst I understand he is expected by his government to return home.

By the last arrival from Washington I learn, and indeed I understand from the Consul before named, that the object and purport of the despatches born[e] to this Govt. by Capt. Gallan [*sic*; Noverto Galán] from the Mexican Govt. were merely to apprise Texas that the Armistice was terminated and though none positively know the true object—yet I think this last rumour the most probable.

A french Brig of War, Defron[?] brought Despatches from the Govt. at home, she is now at anchor off the Bar and is to leave this, for *Vera Cruz*.

I send you a couple of newspapers. I have the honor to be most Respectfully Y[ou]r Ob[edien]t S[ervan]t, A.M. Green.

ALS (No. 3) in DNA, RG 59 (State Department), Diplomatic Despatches, Texas, vol. 2 (T-728:2, frame 370), received 8/16.

From Andrew Hammond, P[ost] M[aster], Jackson, Ark., 7/20. He writes to request a pardon or reprieve for John and David McDaniel, his "unfortunate relatives" who were convicted of murder. Hammond's father, J.B. Hammond, "was raised in Pendelton & Pickens S.C.," and his uncle Joseph Grisham is doubtless acquainted with Calhoun. "David McD[aniel] has professed religion and I think that if they are pardoned they will make honorable and worthy citizens." ALS in DNA, RG 59 (State Department), Petitions for Pardon and Related Briefs, 1800–1849, no. 292B.

From Mariano D. Papy, Tallahassee, 7/20. He has received Calhoun's letter informing Charles S. Sibley of charges made against him by a person whom Calhoun did not name. Sibley is at Apalachicola with his family but will return in a few weeks; then he will answer the charges. Papy assures Calhoun of the confidence of the community in Sibley's integrity. Certain enemies, notably Governor

[Richard K.] Call, have probably made these charges out of malicious anger or prompted others to do so. Papy describes at length court procedures in Fla. Territory in order to exculpate Sibley of charges of bribery. He is confident that Calhoun will take no steps prejudicial to Sibley's interests until Sibley has answered the charges and hopes that the names of the accusers will be furnished to him. Two ALS's in DNA, RG 59 (State Department), Applications and Recommendations, 1837–1845, Sibley (M-687:30, frames 112–125).

From E[DWARD] PORTER

> Consulate of the United States
> Frontero de Tabasco, 20th July 1844

Sir, On the eight[h] of June instant, the Schooner W.A. Turner of New Orleans [John] Petit master appeared off this Port with Francisco Sentmanat[,] the former Governor of this State and Fifty of his followers on Board the Schooner, which was pursued[,] driven a Shore & Fired into by the National Vessels of this Government.

Sentmanat & his Men Succeeded in Landing and passed through the Woods up the Country where they surrendered to the Government Troops on the promise of being pardoned by their laying down their Arms. Ex Governor Sentmanat being the only person that Fired a Single Shot on the occasion. He was taken prisoner and Shot[,] his Head cut off & Fried in boiling oil[,] put on a Spike[,] hung up in an Iron Cage & exhibited in the public Square for days. Thirty eight of the Men that were promised pardon were shot after being confined a few days "without any Tryal" among them was three native Citizens of the United States, James McDuffy, Manwell Musselman & Ramon Riemeres and Six that claimed Citizenship by naturalisation. The remainder of those unfortunate Men with all the sailors[,] the Mate and two native American passengers that came on the Schooner are now Incarsarated [*sic*] in a Miserable prison in Tabasco where it is Feared by us that Contagion will Terminate the work of destruction commenced by the Governor General [Pedro de] Ampudia.

The Schooner was pillaged of every thing moveable She possessed and then Burned by the officers and Men of the National Vessels of this Government.

Captain Petit has made his escape by the influence of a few thousand dollars to the Governor "agreeable to information."

I went up to Tabasco where the Men were Confined to render them all the Assistance in my power but found I could do little or nothing for their releace [*sic*] Governor Ampudia was so hostile to all and every thing touching the United States.   I have the Honour to Rema[i]n Your Most obedient Servant &c &, E. Porter.

ALS (No. 8) in DNA, RG 59 (State Department), Consular Despatches, Tabasco, vol. 1 (M-303:1, frames 220–222), received 9/23; CCEx in ScCleA.

From Alex[ander] Tod

Alexandria, 20th July 1844

Sir, I have the honor to refer to my communication of this date announcing the decease at Malta of Mr. John Gliddon U.S. Consul for Egypt.

In awaiting the pleasure of the U.S. Government as to the nomination which this event involves, I take the liberty to solicit from His Excellency the President, the honor of this appointment, for which I trust to be duly qualified.

I have for sometime past exercised the functions of Pro-Consul for Alexandria and the adjacent coast of Egypt, and my efforts have been directed to the desirable object of seeking to establish a commercial communication between the two Countries, which, although Rivals in their leading articles of Export, may still present the elements of an interchange of commercial commodities; and in consequence, the visit in 1843 of two Merchant Ships of the U.S. the "Cambridge" & "Effort" with the certainty of at least the same number this year the "Minerva" & "Ganges" all of which loaded or will load complete return Cargoes for the U.S. will prove to Your Excellency that these efforts have not thus far been unattended with success.

As the chief of a British Commercial House here, the relations I have the honor to hold with the Vice-Roy's Govt. are amicable and suited to the functions of the appointment now solicited, in the representation here of a great commercial Country.

During the period of my Pro Consulship, the U.S. Frigate "Congress" Capt. [Philip F.] Vo[o]rhees visited Alexandria, & the Commander and Officers, should they have now returned to the U.S., will I doubt not vouch for the satisfactory state of your Consulate's relations with the Vice-Roy's Govt. which it would be my aim to perpetuate, no less than to uphold inviolate the rights & interests of the U.S. citizens, should I be honored by the President with the appointment of U.S. representative here. I have the honor to be Sir, Your most obedient Servant, Alex Tod.

ALS in DNA, RG 59 (State Department), Applications and Recommendations, 1837–1845, Tod (M-687:32, frames 460–462), received 8/20.

To [Isaac] Van Zandt, "Wednesday," [7/20?]. "I would be glad to see you if you can make it convenient to call before 3 o[']clock." Photostat of ALS in TxU, Isaac Van Zandt Papers.

From Ja[me]s T. Archer, Tallahassee, 7/21. Archer has learned with great surprise that charges of "the gravest character" have been made against Charles S. Sibley, U.S. District Attorney for Middle Fla. Archer has long been on terms of intimacy with Sibley and considers him one of the most respectable and worthy people of his acquaintance. Archer believes that some "great mistake" was made in listening to any charges against Sibley. When Sibley returns to Tallahassee, the charges will be answered; until then Archer hopes that no action will be taken by the State Department. ALS in DNA, RG 59 (State Department), Applications and Recommendations, 1837–1845, Sibley (M-687:30, frames 126–128).

From JOHN A. BRYAN

Hicksville, Ohio, 21st July 1844

Dear Sir: You may remember my mentioning to you the design of the President [John Tyler] to app[oin]t me as Chargé d'Affaires to Peru. This is to be done on the first of the ensuing month. I have suggested to him, by letter, that the proper papers be forwarded to me at Columbus in this State, where I will be on the first of the month. It may be necessary for me to come to Washington again, tho' I am now preparing for an early departure on receipt of the Commission and instructions. I have been gathering up some smattering of the Spanish language, preparatory to an entrance upon my duties, and have my private matters so arranged as to enable me ["to" *interlined*] leave for my destination very shortly.

I make this communication to you, my Dear Sir, that, so soon as the instructions shall be in readiness, I may either receive them at Columbus, or come to Washington for that purpose.

With an ardent wish for the continuation of your health and happiness, Believe me, faithf[ull]y & Sincerely y[ou]r friend, John A. Bryan.

ALS in DNA, RG 59 (State Department), Applications and Recommendations, 1837–1845, Bryan (M-687:3, frames 546–547).

To J[ames] Ed[ward] Colhoun, [Abbeville District, S.C.]

Washington, 22d July 1844

My dear Sir, I have complied with your request, both in respect to Mr. [John S.] Skinner & the [Washington] Spectator. As soon as the ["Editor of the" *interlined*] latter shall send in his account to me, which I requested him to do by note, I will pay it, and transmit it to you.

I am affraid [*sic*], I shall not be able to leave this [city] before the mid[d]le of next month. It is a little uncertain, whether I will take the route by Charleston & Augusta, or by the Virginia Springs. I do not think, I shall have time to visit Dahlonega, as you suppose.

Mr. [Thomas G.] Clemson & Anna [Maria Calhoun Clemson] arrived here safely and will remain here some 8 or 10 days. They and the children [John Calhoun Clemson and Floride Elizabeth Clemson] are well.

I hope you will find travelling favourable both to your health & sperits. Your affliction has been great, but you are too young yet to [*one word canceled*] retire from the part assigned you in the drama of life. While health & strength remain we have duties to perform; and we ought not to permit the greif [*sic*] caused by the incidents & afflictions that life is subject to, to prevent us from performing them.

You must be sure to make your arrangement, so as to spend all or much of your time with us, while I shall be at home, which I hope may embrace the greater part of the month of September.

Mr. Clemson & Anna join their love to you. Yours affectionately, J.C. Calhoun.

ALS in ScCleA. NOTE: Colhoun's "affliction" was the death of his wife, Maria Simkins Colhoun, in April.

From GEORGE R. GLIDDON

Philadelphia, 22nd July 1844

Sir, I have intended, for the last two months, to address the Department of State on a subject to me and my family connexions, of painful interest, but I delayed, in the hope that I might have been spared the melancholy duty.

As the Department is probably aware, owing to a dispatch forwarded from Alexandria about last March, my Father, John Gliddon, U.S. Consul in Egypt, had been compelled to leave that Country in April; with the faint hope of seeking, in change of air to Malta and Italy, relief from an overwhelming malady.

Previously to his departure, he left the affairs of the U.S. Consulate in charge of my brother-in-law, Mr. Alexander Tod, his "locum tenens" at Alexandria; who also takes charge of the U.S. Consular agency at Cairo, properly and carefully represented by my brother, W[illia]m A. Gliddon. The interests of the United States suffer not the slightest detriment from my Father's, I had hoped, temporary absence.

My letters, however, by this packet, desire me "to relinquish all hope" of my Father's recovery; as, on the 18th June at Malta, his life was fast ebbing, without a shadow of expectation that "he could recover."

Under these circumstances it beho[o]ves me, to reflect upon the prospective arrangements of the United States' Government, in regard to the Consulate at Alexandria; and I cannot but hope, that the Department will kindly take into consideration my Father's faithful services, as an honorary officer, during fourteen years, and my own for eight of that period, when, as his bereaved Son, I endeavor to execute his testamentary behests.

Premising, that no *American Citizen* is a *resident* of Egypt, where, (spite of my disastrous efforts,) owing to the absence of direct intercourse with this Country, the duties of the Consul are restricted to the protection of Travellers, the reception of occasional Ships of War, and similar official details, I cannot conceive, that any local Egypto-*European* claimant can present to the United States the guarantees, which, for so long a period, have been afforded by the family of *John Gliddon*—while it seems improbable, that any *American Citizen* should seek for an office, which, in the absence of a *Salary* (by no means required under the present system,) can only lead him into certain expenses, without any definite prospective advantages; thus compelling the incumbent to depend entirely upon his own individual resources. Nor does Egypt, in the range of U.S. diplomacy, possess such importance as to warrant an expenditure, in the shape of a Stipend adequate to the wants of a Consul—(at least $2500, per annum,)—that can be more advantageously devoted to more vital interests.

It is the expressed wish of my Father, that the United States' Government be solicited, not to take away, without cause, from his name and children, the long cherished honor of the American Consular Office—the more particularly, as he leaves members of ["his" *interlined*] family personally as efficient, and pecuniarily-speaking more so than, of latter years, he has been, to support the dignity of the Office. And, I would fain indulge the hope, that the writer is Sufficiently known to the Department, to be deemed trustworthy, when, as a son, he adds his testimony to the dying wish of the parent.

My own Career is so changed, and my intentions are so unsettled, that I cannot avail myself of the Vacancy created by my Father's demise; and, therefore, my own personal interests cannot now be advanced by my seeking, for myself, the post of Consul at Alexandria, of which I should be proud to be the incumbent, were I in Egypt. Yet, I may be permitted to share with my Father, the honorable wish, that the Consulate should not pass away from our name and family.

To provide, therefore, for all eventualities, permit me, Sir, in my Father's name, and in my own, to place on the records of the State Department, in the probable event of John Gliddon's decease, the *application* of my brother-in-law, Mr. *Alexander Tod*, Merchant resident at Alexandria, for the honor of the U.S. Consulship of Alexandria; which he undertakes to conduct on the same dignified principles, and in the same efficient manner, that it is my pride to look back upon, during my Father's long administration of the interests of the United States in Egypt.

Mr. Tod will require no further allowance from the United States, than that which the Government, since 1837, has bonified to my Father, for the expenses of Dragoman, Janis[s]ary &c. &c.—a sum, that has always been kept within the limits of $500 per annum. Mr. Tod, without extra allowance of any kind, will undertake to ["keep" *interlined*] up the indispensable U.S. consular Agency at Cairo, and to be *responsible* for its efficient administration. My brother, W[illia]m A. Gliddon, formerly in this Country, and of late years resident of Cairo in our family domicile, will be in every way qualified to protect all American interests, under Mr. Tod's supervision.

In this method, we hope, that the official interests of the United

States can be advantageously reconciled with our own wishes, without even the inconvenience of alterations—and our Egyptian houses may still be distinguished with the emblems, and surmounted with the banner of the U. States.

My brother-in-law, Mr. Alexander Tod, came from Scotland to Egypt in 1828, and is now about thirty four years of age. Eighteen years' residence in Egypt and the Levant, with the prior advantages of a liberal education, have combined to render him familiar with European and Oriental languages, customs &c. &c. while his talents, amenity of character, and highmindedness as a gentleman, have endeared him to our family, and have rendered ["him" *interlined*] beloved and respected by the Government, the Europeans, and the Natives of Egypt.

In 1834, Mr. Tod founded, at Alexandria, a house of mercantile business; which, under his active management, ranks among the first, being very influential in its ramifications, and highly respected in Egypt and in Europe; where his connexions are those of the highest standing. He is agent for Baring Brothers & Co., and of other powerful English and Parisian banking establishments. Totally disconnected from the Egyptian Government, his house enters yearly into the largest operations of the export and import traffic of the Egyptian market. He is rapidly acquiring wealth; and is both able and desirous of doing full honor to the American Consulate; at the sametime, that his intimate relations with our family name, interests and affairs, have familiarized him with all the details and routine of official etiquette and consular duties. In Mr. Tod the United States' Government would have a faithful servant, whose position and qualities as a man would do credit to any appointment.

I have so high a confidence in the favor of the United States' Government towards my family, that I do not deem it necessary to produce *testimonials*, at present, in behalf of Mr. Tod, unless such were called for by the Government; but, at any time, I can present the most satisfactory. The Hon[ora]ble Caleb Cushing, the Commander and Officers of the U.S. Frigate "Congress," and numbers of American Travellers can testify to the ability and promptitude of Mr. Tod, to obtain for them the greatest facilities of the Pasha's Government, no less than to offer to all of them his personal good offices and hospitalities.

With regard to the *Bonds*, that may be required by the Department, in the event of the Government's consenting to the transfer so ardently desired by the applicants, it will be my part to present, in Mr. Tod's favor, every appropriate guarantee.

Such, Sir, is the object of the present petition, which a mournful necessity alone impels me to prefer to the Department, whose indulgence towards my anxious appeal I most respectfully and fervently solicit.

Premature is this application, until there be positive assurances, that the present incumbent has sunk into the cold and silent grave; but the nature of my advices are too poignantly precise for me to doubt, that, ere this, the doom is sealed, which severs me for ever from a Father, such as it is not generally the lot of filial gratitude to deplore—while my own somewhat bitter experience of "the ways of the world" renders it imperative on me, not [to] allow a chance of my being forestalled in the application.

Having thus respectfully submitted, Sir, to your notice and consideration the facts, which induce me to trouble your complaisance, and unwillingly trespass on your time, with interests perhaps out of the order of official correspondence, I would crave permission to leave all further action of mine in abeyance, until I may be in possession of more definite advices; when, in the too-probable contingency I dread, I shall take the liberty of acquainting the Department of State of the necessity, for transmitting relative instructions to my Father's assigns in Egypt. With every sentiment of respect and high consideration, I have the honor to be, Sir, Y[ou]r mo[st] ob[e]d[ien]t & obliged Serv[an]t, George R. Gliddon, formerly U.S. Consul for Cairo—Egypt.

ALS in DNA, RG 59 (State Department), Applications and Recommendations, 1837–1845, Tod (M-687:32, frames 463–469). NOTE: An AEU by Calhoun reads "Mr. Gliddon desires the appointment of Mr. Tod to the Consulate of Egypt on the death of his father, the present Consul."

From J[ohn] Y. Mason, [Secretary of the Navy], 7/22. In response to a letter of 7/16 [*not found*] Tattnal F. Daniell's name will be placed on the register of applicants to be considered for appointment when there is a vacancy in the Marine Corps. FC in DNA, RG 45 (Naval Records), Letters Sent by the Secretary of the Navy to the President and Executive Agencies, 1821–1886, 5:7 (M-472:3, frame 45); FC in DNA, RG 45 (Naval Records), Miscellaneous Letters Sent by the Secretary of the Navy, 34:18 (M-209:13).

From R[ICHARD] PAKENHAM

Washington, 22d July 1844

Sir, In the Archives of the Department of State will be found a note which I had the honor to address on the 24t[h] February last to the late Mr. [Abel P.] Upshur, expressing the desire of Her Majesty's Government to conclude with the Government of the United States a satisfactory arrangement respecting the Boundary of the Oregon or Columbia Territory.

The lamented death of Mr. Upshur, which occurred within a few days after the date of that note, the interval which took place between that event and the appointment of a Successor, and the urgency and importance of various matters which offered themselves to your attention immediately after your accession to office, sufficiently explain why it has not hitherto been in the power of your Government, Sir, to attend to the important matter to which I refer.

But the Session of Congress having been brought to a close, and the present being the Season of the year when the least public business is usually transacted, it occurs to me that you may now feel at leisure to proceed to the consideration of that subject. At all events it becomes my duty to recall it to your recollection, and to repeat the earnest desire of Her Majesty's Government that a question on which so much interest is felt in both Countries, should be disposed of at the earliest moment consistent with the convenience of the Government of the United States. I have the honor to be, with high Consideration, Sir, Your obedient Servant, R. Pakenham.

LS in DNA, RG 59 (State Department), Notes from Foreign Legations, Great Britain, vol. 22 (M-50:22); PC in the Washington, D.C., *Daily National Intelligencer*, December 12, 1845, p. 1; PC in *Niles' National Register*, vol. LXIX, no. 17 (December 27, 1845), p. 260; PC in Senate Document No. 1, 29th Cong., 1st Sess., pp. 141–142; PC in House Document No. 2, 29th Cong., 1st Sess., pp. 141–142; PC in Crallé, ed., *Works*, 5:419–420.

From N[ATHAN] B. PALMER, "Private"

Indianapolis (Ia.), 22nd July 1844

De[a]r Sir, In a speach made in this city by Hon. Thomas Ewing of Ohio on the 20th Inst., and in an elaborate argument against the annexation of Texas to the U.S. he took occasion to advert to the correspondence between yourself & Mr. [Richard] Packenham [*sic*], and affected to quote, so much of your letter to that Gentleman as took the position, that in a State of Slavery the labouring portion of mankind would be much better conditioned and happier than in the character and attitude of freeman.

Mr. Ewing qualified this by saying, that in this instance it was true you confined the application to the African race, but stated that you had over & over again made the like statements in the Senate of the U.S. in general terms, and without such restriction in your remarks to the coulered population.

The whole tenour of Mr. Ewing's remarks on this point, was most obviously intended to convince his Auditory, that the leading men in the Democratic party, and yourself in particular, held to principals looking to a System of Slavery, embracing the entire labouring population, without regard to colour.

Believing that Mr. Ewing is mistaken in his statement, in relation to your avowals in the Senate, and that neither you nor any other of the leading men in the Democratic party entertain such views, or any principals leading thereto, and being aware also, of the injurious consequences to our party, which would result from permit[t]ing statements of this sort, from a Gentleman, who has oc[c]upied so many high and important stations as has Mr. Ewing to pass without contradiction and such merited rebuke as the extr[a]ordinary character of the propagated slander would seeme to require, I have thought proper, (altho a stranger to you), to ask that you will have the goodness to a[d]vise me, as early as convenient, whether Mr. Ewing[']s] statement is well founded or otherwise. Very respectfully Your Most Ob[edien]t Servant, N.B. Palmer.

ALS in ScCleA. NOTE: AEU's by Calhoun read "Mr. Palmer[,] Refers to remarks of Mr. Ewing" and "Mr. Palmer[,] refers to Mr. Ewing[']s misrepresentations at Indianapolis."

From Sam[uel] S. Sibley and James D. Westcott, Jr., Tallahassee, 7/22. In behalf of C[harles] S. Sibley, U.S. District Attorney for Middle Fla., they ask that he be furnished with full copies of all letters and documents containing charges against him and that these copies be forwarded soon, in order that they will be in Tallahassee when he returns. These copies are desired only for the purposes of defending him and prosecuting the instigator of the charges if they are disproved. The signers are Sibley's brother and brother-in-law, respectively. (A Clerk's EU indicates that this request was received on 7/28 and that the copies requested were mailed on 7/29. In the same file are copies of the extracts that were sent.) LS with Ens in

DNA, RG 59 (State Department), Applications and Recommendations, 1837–1845, Sibley (M-687:30, frames 129–135).

From G[ilbert] L. Thompson

New York [City,] July 22d/[1844]
Respected Sir, It is well that I came to this place. There is every reason to beli[e]ve that the letter of Gen. Santa Anna which purports to have come via New Orleans was written in this City.

I shall be detained longer than anticipated; if Convenient be pleased to say to the Hon. Sec[retar]y of the Navy [John Y. Mason] that I am absent with your knowledge and wish. Respectfully Your Ob[edien]t S[er]v[an]t, G.L. Thompson.

ALS in ScCleA.

From John B. Williams

Salem [Mass.,] July 22, 1844
Sir, I have the honor herewith to send you a *memorial* [of 6/29], transmitted to me, from New Bedford, Signed by the Pres[i]d[en]ts of Ins[urance] Companies, and the merchants of that place—requesting my location to be at Auckland N[ew] Z[calan]d; and of the utmost importance of including the Fegee Islands in the Consulate of New Zealand—which, in a previous communication to the Department, I have recommended. Were my location at Auckland I could have daily and weekly intercourse with the Colony, and the adjacent groups of Islands, intimated in a previous letter. The English and in addition the French for some time have had a Strong desire for levying national claims on the Fegees. The interest of the American merchants as I have antecedently stated are most intimately and extensively connected with the *freedom* of these Islands, and it is highly necessary that a Ship of war should occasionally cruise in that qua[r]ter, to afford that protection to our Commerce which is greatly needed. The Commerce of the United States in that region is very extensive and rapidly increasing. Our Ships trading at the Islands are not unfrequently interrupted in their progress of trade by unprincipled men residing among the natives; and frequent com-

plaints have been made to me. I know of no part of the world where the presence of a Ship of *war* ["is" *interlined*] so often required. Should the alterations be made a new Seal would be required (both large & small)—And I have the honor to inform you that the Consulate is *deficient* of a Flag, it is requisite that *three* or *four*, together with a boat "flag," should be furnished, as it is quite impossible to replace them at New Zealand. I beg respectfully to apprize ["you," *interlined*] that on a former occasion I informed The Hon. The Secretary of State of the United States, of the appointment of W[illia]m Mayhew Esq. as vice Consul during my absence. I have the honor to be Sir Your most Obedient Servant, John B. Williams, Consul U.S.A. [Bay of Islands, New Zealand.]

ALS with En in DNA, RG 59 (State Department), Consular Despatches, Bay of Islands and Auckland, New Zealand, vol. 1 (T-49:1). Note: A Clerk's EU reads "Respectfully referred to the Secretary of the Navy [John Y. Mason] for his perusal, with the request that it may be returned."

From A. Calderon de la Barca, Washington, 7/23. He asks when and where he will be granted an opportunity to present his credentials as Spanish Minister to the U.S. He assures Calhoun of his respect. ALS (in Spanish) in DNA, RG 59 (State Department), Notes from Foreign Legations, Spain, vol. 11 (M-59:13, frame 982).

From W[illia]m M. D'Antignac

Office of the Augusta Insurance &
Banking Company, [Ga.,] July 23rd 1844
Sir, I take the liberty of addressing you upon a subject not only of importance to this institution, but some what national in its character. In May last you were apprized of the stupendous frauds committed by one Gerard Koster upon several of the Banks of this city & kindly furnished our agent J.D. Bagbee, with all the documents then deemed necessary to his arrest in Switzerland. Upon Mr. Bagbee's arrival there, he met with the zealous & able co-operation, of the American Consul S[eth] T. Otis Esq. who made an official demand upon the Government, for the arrest & surrender of Koster. Our agent furnishes us with the following copy of the Government reply to Mr. Otis.

"Your Honor intimates that the Minister of the Exterior (Mr.

Calhoun) has given to the Consuls, a special commission to request proper measures to be taken for the arrestation and deliverance of the said Koster, by those states & Governments wherever he may be found. At the same time you intimate, that in a reciprocal case on the request of the proper Government, the Authorities of the United States of North America, will not hesitate to furnish the Requisite help and co-operation for the finding out & giving up of criminals."

"According to all that has been said, it seems, certainly, without doubt, that Mr. Gerard Koster has committed, in North America, immense frauds, liable to be punished very severely. And although there exists no treaty between the Swiss Confederation, and the United States of North America for the mutual deliverance of criminals, we consider it the interest of all Nations or States, that crimes do not escape the punishment they merit; and, therefore, do not hesitate to inform you, as a reply to your communication, *that we shall order the arrestation of Mr. Koster, provided you be responsible for all the costs & consequences, it may have here.*"

"As to the deliverance of Mr. Koster we are also, willing to grant it, as soon, as by a Note, the Minister of the Exterior of the United States of North America" (meaning our Secretary of State) "*gives assurance that the Reciprocity will be insured to us.*"

Mr. Otis having given the requ[ested?] guaranty for costs & consequences, it remains for Your Excellency to determine whether you can consistently address a note of request to the High Government of Switzerland, or to the Government of any one of the Cantons of the Swiss Confederation, where the said Koster may be found, that they will surrender him to the United States at the same time promising reciprocity on the part of this Government, in similar cases.

It is not for me to do m[ore?] than advert to the great benefit which would result to the commercial portion of the Union, by such mutual surrender of absconding criminals.

In the hope that it will comport with your views of official duty to furnish the desired communication, I have but to request that it be forwarded to Mr. Otis, by the steamer of the first pr[o]x[i]mo, As dispatch is all important to the arrest of this swindler. I have the honour to be most Resp[ect]fully Y[ou]r Ob[edien]t Serv[an]t, Wm. M. D'Antignac, President.

P.S. It will be seen from the accompanying certificate that Gerard Koster, is a citizen of the United States.

ALS with En in DNA, RG 59 (State Department), Consular Despatches, Basle, vol. 1 (T-364:1).

From John W. Fisher, [U.S. Consul], Pointe-à-Pitre, Guadeloupe, 7/23. Fisher transmits his quarterly returns. He comments on the "Gross neglect, of the Different Collectors of the Ports in the United States, of Clearing Foreigners with American Protections." His physician has advised him to leave immediately for the U.S., and he has appointed three Vice-Consuls to act during his absence. He hopes that this arrangement will meet the approbation of the State Department. ALS (No. 7) with Ens in DNA, RG 59 (State Department), Consular Despatches, Guadeloupe, vol. 2 (T-208:2), received 8/12.

From John G. Gunn, Sam[ue]l B. Stephens, J.W. Sprott, A.K. Allison, R.C. Gibson, G. Stilworth[?], J.L. Tompkins, J. Ferguson, Jr., Isaac R. Harris, "Clerk, Sup[erio]r Court, G[adsden] C[ounty]," and J.T. Seegar, "P[ost] M[aster], Quincy, Florida," Quincy, 7/23. The signers testify to the integrity of [Charles S.] Sibley and disparage charges recently made against him. They request that Calhoun postpone any action on the matter until Sibley can be heard from and also request that he or his friends be furnished with the names of those who have accused him. "This request is from citizens of diverse political sentiments." LS in DNA, RG 59 (State Department), Applications and Recommendations, 1837–1845, Sibley (M-687:30, frames 136–137).

To JOHN MCFERRAN, Wheeling, Va.

Department of State
Washington, 23d July 1844

Sir, I have duly received your letter of the 12th Inst. and ["have" *interlined*] in reply to state, that the resolution of the House of Representatives requesting the President to obtain certain information relative to the operation of the late Bankrupt law, has been referred to this Department; but as no appropriation was made to meet the expenses which would necessarily attend this service, and as the contingent fund of this—were it properly applicable to this purpose—is at present inadequate, no steps have yet been taken with the view of obtaining the information desired. Nor is it likely that any thing can be done until some pecuniary provision is made by Congress, so that the Department may be enabled to act in the matter. I am, Sir, with great respect Your Obedient Servant, John C. Calhoun.

FC in DNA, RG 59 (State Department), Domestic Letters, 34:311–312 (M-40:32).

To SETH T. OTIS, U.S. Consul, Basel

Department of State
Washington, 23rd July 1844

Sir: I have received and read with interest your communication No. 7 dated the 27th Ultimo on the subject of Gerard Koster, a criminal, who having obtained by fraud, a large sum of money from various Bank[s] and individuals in the State of Georgia, made his escape to Europe in the month of March last, and has taken refuge in the Canton of Soluere, where, it appears arrangements were made for his arrest, and detention in the Canton of Berne, to the Custody of whose police he was to be delivered.

It seems that the condition upon which the arrangement to deliver Koster up to the U.S. was made, was an assurance on your part that the authorities would be held harmless from the consequences of the arrest, and that you were convinced your Government would speedily comply with the offers that had been made by those authorities. It also seems that these assurances were given on a proposition from the high Government of Switzerland that Koster should be delivered up, provided the U. States, in a reciprocal case, would not hesitate upon the request of the proper Government to furnish when so requested all help and Coöperation for the finding out, and delivering up of Criminals taking refuge within our jurisdiction. To your assurances, given upon this proposition it was replied that the high authorities would order the arrest of Mr. Koster provided the U. States became responsible for all the costs & consequences that act would occasion, and the delivery would be granted so soon as a note from the Secretary of State of the U. States of America would be received giving proper assurances that reciprocity, in like cases, would be insured to Switzerland.

I am directed by the President [John Tyler] to instruct you to say that there exists every disposition on his part to comply with the whole arrangement as thus proposed by the high authorities of Switzerland for the detention and delivering up of the criminal

Koster, but that he regrets extremely at the same time to add that under the form of our Government the object in contemplation can be effected by no other means than a Convention, providing for the mutual delivering of criminals fugutive from justice, and he directs me further to say that for the purpose of forming such a convention due authority will be given to the minister of the U. States in Paris [William R. King], who will be invested with full power to enter into & to negotiate a Convention with any person furnished with like powers on the part of the high Government of Switzerland for the mutual extradition of criminals, fugutive from justice in certain cases.

The President hopes that the sincere desire he feels to confirm the arrangement, & the prompt adoption, on his part, of the only means by which it can be effected will be taken by the high authorities as a fulfilment of the arrangement, and that they will feel justified in delivering up Koster & by so doing fulfil the ends of justice in this case of enormous fraud.

The Zeal you have shown on this occasion merits the approbation of this Department. I am &c, J.C. Calhoun.

P.S. It is to be understood that the authority to be given to Mr. King to conclude the convention will be made contingent upon the delivery of Koster.

FC in DNA, RG 59 (State Department), Consular Instructions, 10:255–257; CC in DNA, RG 84 (Foreign Posts), France, Instructions (C8.1).

From R[ICHARD] PAKENHAM

Washington, 23 July 1844

Sir, It has been represented to Her Majesty's Government that the Naval force of the United States on the Lakes Ontario, Erie, and Huron, at this moment considerably exceeds that to which Great Britain and the United States reciprocally restricted themselves by the agreement entered into in April 1817.

It is true that not long ago while Her Majesty's Canadian Dominions were threatened with invasion from parties unlawfully organized within the United States, Great Britain did maintain, in Her own defence, a Naval Force exceeding the amount stipulated in the agreement, but explanation was given of the necessity of that departure from the existing engagement, which appeared to satisfy the Government of the United States, and when a change in the attitude and disposition of the People on the frontier was sufficiently evident to enable the British Government to feel security against aggression the British Force was reduced to the limits prescribed by the agreement of 1817.

At the present moment there are happily no circumstances on either side to justify or require any departure from the strict fulfilment of that agreement, and it therefore becomes by all means desirable that it should be fulfilled to the letter by both the Contracting Parties.

In addition to the information which had reached Her Majesty's Government respecting an undue increase of the Naval Establishment of the United States on the Lakes, I have observed in the Newspapers of this Country an Advertisement stating that proposals would be received at the Bureau of Ordnance for the supply of a quantity of cannon Shot and Shells for the Naval Service of the United States, of which a proportion including a number of 32 Pounder Chambered Guns is to be delivered at certain places on the Lakes—whereas by the agreement of 1817 it is provided that the armament to be used on board the vessels of the limited Tonnage allowed by the same agreement shall be 18 Pound Cannon.

This circumstance will I am sure appear to you, Sir, still further to justify the desire of Her Majesty's Government to receive satisfactory explanation as to the intentions of the United States Government with reference to the fulfilment of the agreement of 1817. I have the honor to be with high consideration, Sir, Your obedient Servant, R. Pakenham.

LS with Ens in DNA, RG 59 (State Department), Notes from Foreign Legations, Great Britain, vol. 22 (M-50:22).

To Stephen H. Preston, Marshal, Mich., 7/23. "I have to reply to your letter of the 16th instant [*not found*] that at present there are no vacancies and no new appointments are likely soon to be made in the offices of Chargés d'Affaires, Congress having failed to make the necessary appropriations for outfits, &C. Your letter will be laid before the President [John Tyler] on his return to Washington. Should you, under these circumstances, wish to withdraw the letter of application to my predecessor, it will be enclosed to you. The 'petition' to which you refer has not been received at this Department." FC in DNA, RG 59 (State Department), Domestic Letters, 34:310–311 (M-40:32).

From NATHAN RANNEY

Saint Louis, July 23 1844

D[ea]r Sir, Col. [Thomas H.] Benton who is doubtless the the [sic] most bitter enemy you have on earth is now destined to fall. It was thought that his black hearted conduct towards the lamented [Dr. Lewis F.] Linn—(& since the death of this Hon. Senator, towards the bereaved family[)] would have destroyed him in Missouri at first— but that enormity would have been passed over by his leaders had not the violent opposition he made to the "Annexation Treaty["] defeated that patriotic measure and done great injury to the prospects of the nominees of the Baltimore Convention. He is now considered our worst enemy. He calls me [( ]who for 26 years have voted the Democratic ticket) a traitor & a Whig, and thousands of other better democrats than himself he denounces in the same manner. He is now in the Western part of the State trying to make fair weather with the people but the thing is impossible. Our election is near at hand and the matter will be s[oon] settled. I have a written statement of 5 pages from Mrs. [Elizabeth Relfe] Linn giving me all the particulars of Col. Benton[']s course towards her late husband, showing how he exerted all his powers secretly to injure the favorite Senator of Missouri and not only so—showing how he followed with a persecuting spirit Governor [Daniel] Dunklin for refusing his Benton[']s counsel and advise touching the Senatorial office. Mrs. Linn and the Orphan Children forbid Col. Benton in the most explisit and most solemn manner to announce the death of Senator Linn in the U.S. Senate— but this was disregarded, & not only so but the opportunity was seized upon to state a falsehood in relation to the family which was calculated to wound their feelings most painfully.

You do not know me but I have often seen you in the U.S. Senate & refer to Senators [James] Buchanan & [Levi] Woodbury as to the probability of my statements being true. Yours with great respect, Nathan Ranney.

ALS in ScCleA. NOTE: An AEU by Calhoun reads "Mr. Ranney[,] relates to the conduct of Col. Benton towards Dr. Linn."

From Sam[uel] S. Sibley, Tallahassee, 7/23. Sibley encloses a letter addressed to the President [John Tyler] and Secretary of State [dated 7/20 from Thomas Baltzell and others of Fla. Territory]. "The requests made in the enclosed—the suggestions therein made, and indeed the language employed in the paper [in defence of Charles

S. Sibley], are in compliance with my wishes expressed to the few of our leading citizens of both parties who have signed it." ALS with En in DNA, RG 59 (State Department), Applications and Recommendations, 1837–1845, Sibley (M-687:30, frames 108–111).

From R. C. CALDWELL and GEO[RGE] WILLIS

Pensacola, July 24th 1844

Sir, We feel it our duty to apprise you at this the earliest practicable date of the return of our Negroes which were the subject of our Letter of the 28th Ult. to His Excellency The President [John Tyler] and of our Letter of the 29th Ult. to Your Honor.

The Man "Walker" was captured in his Whale-boat with the Seven Negroes by a Wrecker from Key West on the 8th inst. and is now secured in the Jail of this County to await his trial—And the Negroes are again in our possession.

We are induced to believe from what the Negroes tell us (of course from their memory) that the boat which the Packet-sloop reported on the 27th Ult. off Pensacola Bar was the Boat of the said Jonathan Walker and if so that there is scarcely room for a doubt that the "Poinset[t]" could have overhauled her in a few hours, and have saved us the delay, trouble and expense to which we have been subjected by the application for the services of that vessel being refused. As our present misfortune is however an evil past being remedied we are chiefly solicitous for the action of the Government so that we may entertain the hope of succor in any similar emergency that may occur in future. We have the Honor to be Very respectfully Your Ob[edien]t Serv[an]ts, R.C. Caldwell, Geo. Willis, p[e]r Jos[eph] Quigles, Agent.

P.S. We see by the Newspapers that his Excellency the President is absent from the City of Washington. As Above, R.C.C., G.W. p[e]r J.Q.

LS in DNA, RG 59 (State Department), Miscellaneous Letters (M-179:105, frames 75–77); PC in Carter, ed., *Territorial Papers*, 26:934–935. NOTE: A Clerk's EU reads "Respectfully referred to the Secretary of the Navy [John Y. Mason] for perusal."

From H[ENRY] W. CONNER

Charleston, July 24, 1844

My Dear Sir, I duly rec[eive]d your letter of the 3rd & am happy to say the policy you recommend meets with general concurrence in Charleston & with few exceptions I think throughout the State. In Colleton & in Edgefield Districts there is some evidence of an uneasy & restless spirit & a few persons in each of these districts it is to be feared are bent upon violent courses & if the spirit of discontent is not soon checked there is danger that it may extend to other parts of the country & do harm at least abroad. To ardent & impetuous persons delay is always irksome & in addition to the delay now rendered proper by circumstances[,] the delicacy of our position at the present moment forbids the ["public" *interlined*] discussion of any definite plan of action for the future & in the abscence of such plan that description of persons seem to consider it as equivalent to an intention to submit altogether. I am apt to think that this is the motive that induces most of the disaffection that we see in the news papers & elsewhere.

I would suggest therefore whether it might not be a wise precaution for you to admonish some of your leading friends in those districts & elsewhere against all premature & inconsiderate action as being calculated to defeat ["to" *canceled*] a well timed & efficient plan of action on the part of the South at a future day. I am aware of objections that may present themselves to your indicating too pointedly at the present moment any very precise course of action for the future but I am fearful that unless something is done to give to public sentiment a right direction it may take a wrong one. Excitement is very contagious & the elections now approaching, it may extend itself farther than we expect. Hence my motive for writing you. As regards myself my great solicitude is that South Carolina may do nothing to injure herself either with the democratic party or the other States but to be prepared whenever the contest does come to bring a strength & influence unimpaired by any previous action on her part seperately to bear upon it. Mr. [George] McDuffie told me when here that he had yielded the convictions of his own mind to the judgment & advice of others—meaning yourself I believe, & would direct his efforts no farther than to produce union amongst the Southern States. I am not quite sure sure [*sic*] however that he has not transcended the limits prescribed to himself. A meeting at which he was to speak was to have been held at Edgefield tomorrow I believe but his ill health has caused a postponement

I learn. The feeling is very strong in that quarter & some intemperate expression would no doubt have been given to it.

The substantial & considerate portion of the community composing the majority I am satisfied are at present averse to any action on the part of S.C. that would place her in a false position either in reference to the present or the future but this fact will be better known probably at home than abroad for the two leading democratic papers of the State are mostly with the movement[?] party & give expression to their views. Very truly yours, H.W. Conner.

ALS in ScCleA. NOTE: The two newspapers referred to in Conner's last paragraph were apparently the Charleston *Mercury* and the Edgefield *Advertiser*.

From C[harles] H. DuPont, Quincy, Fla. Territory, 7/24. DuPont has heard that charges "of a grave character" have been preferred against Charles S. Sibley, U.S. District Attorney for Middle Fla. DuPont hopes that Sibley will be given time to answer those charges before any action is taken. Sibley's character "as an officer & gentleman stands unimpeached before this community." ALS in DNA, RG 59 (State Department), Applications and Recommendations, 1837–1845, Sibley (M-687:30, frames 138–139).

From EDWARD EVERETT

London, 24 July 1844
Sir, Considerable inconvenience is occasionally experienced at this office by applications for passports made by persons who leave America without any passport or other evidence of citizenship. The general instructions to the diplomatic agents of the United States imply, that passports should be granted only on the faith of some evidence, that the persons in whose favor they are applied for are entitled to them, because it is directed that a "record containing the name and voucher of American citizenship of the persons to whom they are given should be kept in the office of the legation."

Were this regulation enforced, it would deprive a very considerable number of our countrymen of passports. It very frequently occurs that they are applied for by individuals, who leave home without any voucher of citizenship—occasionally by persons unable to furnish any adequate reference in this country. In such cases, where there is no ground to suspect the individual to be a subject of a foreign power, unable to obtain a passport from his own minister, his request is complied with, and the word "presumed" is entered in the passport book in the column of vouchers.

This practice is certainly loose and objectionable. The passport being an official certificate of citizenship, ought not to be granted on a low degree of presumption. I found it however the established usage of the Legation, and it could not be departed from, without subjecting many of our travelling countrymen to inconvenience.

The reasons most frequently assigned by applicants for passports for their omission to procure them in America are 1s[t] that they were informed or led to think, that they could be procured by asking for them at this office, and 2d that the individual did not, on leaving the United States, propose to visit the continent.

A partial remedy for the existing evil would no doubt be found in a public notice from the Department, apprizing all persons going abroad of the nature of the existing regulations and recommending them to provide themselves with passports or other evidences of citizenship. Even if not wanted in reference to visiting the contient, they may be useful in other respects to the American traveller in England. I am, sir, very respectfully, your obedient servant, Edward Everett.

LS (No. 167) in DNA, RG 59 (State Department), Diplomatic Despatches, Great Britain, vol. 53 (M-30:49), received 8/21; FC in DNA, RG 84 (Foreign Posts), Great Britain, Despatches, 8:355–357; FC in MHi, Edward Everett Papers, 49:436–438 (published microfilm, reel 23, frames 220–221). NOTE: A Clerk's EU on the LS reads "For notice relative to passports, see Madisonian of 27 or 2[8?]th of Aug[us]t 1844."

To Moses C. Good, U.S. Dis[tric]t Att[orne]y, Wheeling [Va.], 7/24. Calhoun sends Good a certificate from Stewart Newell, U.S. Consul at Sabine, Texas, concerning the illegal activities of James Wood, captain of the ship *Col. Woods*. According to Newell, Wood has left Texas to return to his home at Wheeling. Good is authorized· to proceed against Wood and to recover penalties assessed against him. FC in DNA, RG 59 (State Department), Consular Instructions, 11:263.

From ROB[ER]T MONROE HARRISON

American Consulate
Kingston Jam[aic]a, 24th July 1844

Sir, I herewith have the honor to enclose you further communications [of 7/22] from His Excellency the Governor [James Bruce] concerning the deserters from the U. States Ship Preble; by which he now from some cause best known to himself, wishes to make it appear that on receiving my letter of the 3rd *inst.* he lost no time in complying with the requisition therein contained.

And as regards the affidavits which Mr. Attorney General has mentioned as *necessary*; I consider it merely as an excuse to evade the delivery of the men in question; because in such cases it is not only un[n]ecessary; but if it was otherwise, I could not do it as the Preble is not here.

In case of desertion from a Merchant vessel, the exhibition of the Shipping Articles is all that is required, and surely more could not be required of a Ship of War.

But as I yesterday received information from "Manzanilla de Cuba" that three of the deserters alluded to, with the launch, had been arrested at that place, and held subject to the orders of our Consul or nearest Consular Agent; and this without any requisition on my part; I am at a loss to account for the non-appearance of the others at Manzanilla, unless they have been landed elsewhere or made away with. In all probability however, they may have come to this Island in the first instance; and hearing I was on the look out; three of them may have left for Manzanilla (which being a small place, and out of the way, they might run less risk of detection;) while the others concluded as it is supposed, to remain in this Island.

The conduct of these Magistrates and those of this place, as regards this affair cannot fail to strike you, as it has me and others, to whom the circumstance has been made known: and I therefore trust that it is unnecessary to reiterate to you the necessity of furnishing me as speedily as possible, with your instructions, should a similar case of desertion occur from our Men of War and Merchantmen. With great respect I have the honor to be Sir Your ob[edien]t & most humble serv[an]t, Robt. Monroe Harrison.

P.S. Since writing the above, I have been confidentially informed that the sudden change in His Excellency's opinion, (or conduct), has been owing to his having been referred to the 10th article of the [1842] Treaty between the two Governments [of the U.S. and Great Britain] concerning the delivery of persons guilty of crimes and escaping to either country. In consequence of which, an Express was sent off to me, and reached my house at *precisely two in the morning,* making *twenty one days* since I first communicated with him on the subject.

LS (No. 296) with En in DNA, RG 59 (State Department), Consular Despatches, Kingston, vol. 9 (T-31:9), received 8/15.

From [JOHANN GEORG Von] HÜLSEMANN

Legation of Austria
Washington, July 24 1844

Sir, The note which I addressed to Mr. [Daniel] Webster on the 31 of August 1842, requesting that the collectors of the Custom houses, should be instructed, to admit the wines of Austria *imported in bottles,* at 15 cents per gallon, like the wines of Sicily, not having produced that result as yet; I have to request you Sir, to take into consideration, that the 8th Section of the 5 article [of the tariff law of 1842; "which" *interlined*] lays a duty of 20 cents per gallon, on *Austrian* wines, imported *in bottles,* and a duty of 15 cents on Sicilian wines, imported in bottles, is evidently contrary to the 7th article of the treaty, existing between Austria and the United States; and I doubt not that your Government will do justice to this claim, and that the Secretary of the Treasury, will at the same time order the restitution of whatsoever may have been paid in excess on such importations.

I avail myself of this occasion Sir to repeat the assurances of my very high consideration. Hulsemann.

State Department translation of ALS (in French) in DNA, RG 59 (State Department), Notes from Foreign Legations, Austria (M-48:1); CC (in English) in DNA, RG 56 (Secretary of the Treasury), Letters Received from Executive Officers, Series AB, vol. 1844, no. 29.

From J[AMES] G. LYON

Mobile, July 24, 1844

Sir, I understand that the office of agent of the Creek Nation of Indians on the border of Arkansas is vacant. Will you ["to" *altered to* "do"] me the favor to offer my name to the President [John Tyler] as an applicant for the office, refer[r]ing him to the Hon[ora]bles D[ixon] H. Lewis, A[rthur] P. Bagby & James E. Belser [Senators and Representative from Ala., respectively] &c. My residence in this country since 1814 has given me an opportunity ["with" *canceled*] of acquiring a thorough acquaintance with the Indian character, & more especially with the Chocktaws[,] Chickasaws & Creeks—and I would willing accept the office of a post for either of those tribes with an assurance that the duties should be faithfully performed. I remain Truly Y[ou]r friend, J.G. Lyon.

ALS in DNA, RG 59 (State Department), Applications and Recommendations, 1837–1845, Lyon (M-687:20, frames 387–388).

From JOHN MCDANIEL

St. Louis Prison, July 24, [18]44
Dear Sir: My friends forward you some affidavits in relation to the verasity of O[rrin] P. Rockwell by the same mail in which this goes. There is one, also, substantiating, to some extent, the affidavit of Rockwell.

Were *time* allowed me, I feel well assured that I could have facts developed which would make my innocence appear to you *palpably plain.* These facts *do* exist, and they exist in such a form that they *can* be brought to light.

Since my condemnation my friends have not been allowed more than six or eight days at a time to act in; therefore it has been impossible to effect much. For your kindness in investigating my case I feel myself under deeper obligations than words can express. I am Your Most Ob[edien]t Serv[an]t, John McDaniel.

ALS in DNA, RG 59 (State Department), Petitions for Pardon and Related Briefs, 1800–1849, no. 292B. NOTE: An EU on the address page, not in McDaniel's handwriting, reads "In haste!"

To THOMAS M. RODNEY, U.S. Consul, Matanzas, [Cuba]

Department of State
Washington, July 24 1844
Sir, Your communication of the 9th Ult., with its enclosures, has just been received at the Department, & I take the earliest opportunity

to advise you of the receipt, at the same time of a despatch from the U.S. Consul at the Havana [Robert B. Campbell] dated the 7th instant informing the Department that at his request, the U.S. Brig Lawrence, commanded by Capt. Gardiner [*sic*; William H. Gardner], was then on the eve of departing for Matanzas to coöperate with you in your exertions in behalf of our citizens imprisoned there. I need scarcely add that this Govt. expects such remonstrances to be made with the proper authorities and such other energetic measures to be taken as will lead to a speedy & fair trial of these persons, as well as to the promotion of their comfort until the final decision of their cases. I am &c, J.C. Calhoun.

FC in DNA, RG 59 (State Department), Consular Instructions, 10:257; transcript in DLC, Carnegie Institution of Washington Transcript Collection.

From H[ENRY] WHEATON, "(Private)"

Berlin, 24 July, 1844

My dear Sir, Your despatch of the 28 June relating to the Treaty with the Zollverein has been received. I cannot write you *officially* in answer until I have ascertained the intentions of the other Parties, but I entirely concur in your views as to the delicate manner in which the subject must be treated here. I have already spoken with [Heinrich Ulrich Wilhelm,] Baron Bulow, who appears *personally* to have no objections to extending the time for the ratifications but seems to doubt what may be the disposition of some of their Allies. As it will be necessary for Prussia to consult her co-states, he desired me to hand him a written Note ["on the Note" *canceled*] on the subject which would clearly shew the state in which the Senate left the Convention when it adjourned. This Note I shall frame from your excellent Despatch, & accompany it with such verbal explanations as may be necessary. After all, the consent of the Zollverein to extending the time for ratification may be considered extremely doubtful; as, whatever may be thought on your side of the water, the concessions made by them are considered here as more than equivalent to those made by us. The consent of some of their States was only obtained by great importunity on the part of Prussia, & by my fixing a peremptory term within which it was to be given, or the negotiations to be broken off. Those of the States who think their interests have not been sufficiently provided for, would perhaps prefer to let the present Treaty drop, & renew the negotiations in the hope of obtaining better terms. Such golden opportunities should not be let pass, & it will prove very unfortunate if our distracted councils should ultimately defeat a measure from which so much good might have been derived.

Please to present my best thanks to the President [John Tyler] for his approbation of my services as expressed in your despatch.

I have also to thank you for the very kind expressions contained in your private Letter. The warm & constant friendship with which you have so long honoured me induces me to take this occasion to impart freely my thoughts & wishes respecting my own position in the public service. I will not, therefore, conceal from you that I was somewhat dissapointed [*sic*] at not having received the mission to Paris. It has, however, occurred to me that if the President is disposed to consider my public services as founding a claim to promotion, an opportunity might occur to give effect to this disposition should Mr. Jennifer [*sic*; Daniel Jenifer] leave the mission at Vienna, as I am told is his intention. I wish, however, that it may be distinctly understood that it is only on the supposition that the ["miss" *canceled*] Austrian mission will be vacated, that I make this suggestion, as I do not wish any man to be *removed* in order to make room for me. Nor should I be willing to be recalled from this post until actually nominated to, & confirmed by, the Senate for Austria.

So far as depends on my exertions, all the principal objects of this mission have now been fulfilled; but the Austrian empire opens a new field, in which my diplomatic experience might be utilized for the public interest. As my transfer to that post would make a vacancy here, this mission might then be given to some other friend whom the President might think fit to notice, as I presume it would be a matter of indifference to such person whether he was sent to Berlin or Vienna.

The whole subject is, however, confided entirely to your discretion to act as you may think best for my permanent welfare. I am ever truly your, faithful friend, H. Wheaton.

ALS in ScCleA.

To George M. Bibb, Secretary of the Treasury, 7/25. Calhoun transmits to Bibb a copy of a translation of a note [of 7/24] from Chevalier [Johann Georg von] Hülsemann to the State Department "on the Subject of [tariff duties on] Austrian wines." LS with En in DNA, RG 56 (Secretary of the Treasury), Letters Received from

Executive Officers, Series AB, vol. 1844, nos. 28 and 29; FC in DNA, RG 59 (State Department), Domestic Letters, 34:349–350 (M-40:32).

From HENRY W. HILLIARD

Legation of the United States
Brussels, 25th July 1844

Sir; I have the honor to inform you that the Tariff of Differential duties has been adopted by the Belgian Senate, and as I anticipated has received the signature of the King [Leopold I]. I forward the law as published in the official paper.

I am much gratified too, to be able to inform you that by an "Arrêté Royal" just issued, the flag of the United States is assimilated to the Belgian flag, so far as the direct trade between the two countries is concerned. The Ministry have thus promptly redeemed the pledge which they some time since gave me, and the system will be found I hope to operate greatly to the advantage of our trade.

I repeat what I have heretofore given as my view of the state of our affairs here, they are upon an excellent footing, our trade is sought, and our influence is felt. It is a source of great satisfaction to me to be able to leave our affairs in so prosperous a condition. I have impressed the Government with the conviction that we desire to cultivate commercial relations with them, upon fair and liberal terms, and have endeavored to save from the application of high duties, those great staples which we produce and in which we are so much interested. Cotton, you will perceive, is to enter Belgium subject to a duty merely nominal while our tobacco enjoys some peculiar priveleges and escapes the severe measure which threatened it.

Col. [William H.] Daingerfield, the Chargé d'Affaires of Texas, accredited at the Hague and instructed also to open diplomatic relations with this Government returned to Brussels some days since, after an absence of some months to ascertain the disposition of the Belgian Government at this moment. In a despatch, dated the 28th December last, I stated the result of his former application. He has met with no better success now for in an interview with the Minister of Foreign Affairs, he was informed by Count [Albert Joseph] Goblet that his Government was apprehensive any recognition of Texas now would be offensive to the Government of the United States, with which they were upon excellent terms. Col. Daingerfield, of course, declined pressing the matter further. I was certainly amused, when he informed me of the result of the interview, and informed him that when we were ready to take Texas, we should not regard a circumstance of that sort as at all in the way.

I forward my account and vouchers for the last quarter. I have the honor to be Sir, Very Respectfully Your obedient servant, Henry W. Hilliard.

LS (No. 23) in DNA, RG 59 (State Department), Diplomatic Despatches, Belgium, vol. 2 (M-193:3), received 8/21.

To WILLIAM R. KING, [Paris]

Department of State
Washington, 25th July, 1844

Sir: You will find, enclosed, copies of a letter [dated 6/26] with accompanying papers, which has just reached this Department from [Seth T. Otis] the Consul of the United States at Basle, relative to the case of a person named Gerard Koster, who is charged with having defrauded certain banking institutions and sundry individuals in Georgia of large sums of money, and who has since fled from this country and taken refuge in one of the Swiss Cantons. It appears from Consul Otis's letter, that in answer to his application for the arrest and surrender of Koster, willingness has been evinced on the part of the constituted authorities of Switzerland to arrest the fugitive in question, and to deliver him up for trial in this country, upon the receipt of a communication from the Secretary of State of the United States assuring them of the reciprocal surrender in like cases, of persons charged with the commission of criminal offences in Switzerland, who may escape to the United States. The Consul is mistaken in supposing it within the competency of this Department to give such an assurance in the absence of any conventional stipulations between the two Governments on the subject, and he will accordingly be so informed, as well as of the purport of the instructions hereinafter given to you with reference to this matter.

The occurrence of this case, and other considerations which will readily suggest themselves to you, have rendered it desirable that this Government should, without any unnecessary delay, enter into an arrangement with the Swiss Confederation for the mutual surrender of criminals, fugitive from justice, and seeking an asylum either in the United States or Switzerland, upon the respective requisitions of the contracting parties or their authorized agents. I am therefore directed by the President [John Tyler] to authorize and empower you to negotiate and sign a Convention between the United States and that Confederation for the giving up of criminals, fugitive from justice, in certain cases. Similar arrangements, as you are aware, have already been made with France and Great Britain, printed copies of which I send you herewith. The object of these stipulations is the same, but the provisions of the latter are somewhat more full, and perhaps of more easy application in practice. You will take them as a guide in preparing your projet; and it might be well to add to the list of crimes therein designated, such others (carefully excluding those of a political character,) as may in your opinion be properly embraced in it, and especially those with which Koster is charged. A special power is also enclosed.

If there is a diplomatic representative of the Swiss Confederacy at Paris, you will immediately after the receipt of these instructions, open a communication with him on the subject of this letter, and invite him, if not already possessed of the requisite powers to enter upon the negotiation of such a Convention, to apply to his Government for them. I cannot doubt that they will be promptly granted and transmitted to him, and that you will find no difficulty in agreeing upon a conventional arrangement with him which will be beneficial to both countries. If these anticipations are well-founded, you will, when effected, forward to this Department the Convention, as signed, to be submitted to the President for his consideration and approval, and to be laid before the Senate, at its next session, for its constitutional advice and consent as to its ratification.

I have only to add in conclusion that these instructions are predicated upon the presumption that Koster will be surrendered to the pursuing parties by the Swiss authorities. Should his delivery be refused, it will be unnecessary to take any further steps in the negotiation. I am, Sir, respectfully, Your obedient servant, J.C. Calhoun.

LS (No. 3) with Ens in DNA, RG 84 (Foreign Posts), France, Instructions (C8.1); FC in DNA, RG 59 (State Department), Diplomatic Instructions, France, 15:5–7 (M-77:55). NOTE: Among the Ens was a copy of Calhoun's instructions to Otis, dated 7/23, in reply to Otis' despatch No. 7, dated 6/26.

To J[ohn] Y. Mason, Secretary of the Navy, 7/25. "Mr. William Brent, Jr., appointed Chargé d'Affaires of the United States to Buenos Ayres, contemplates proceeding thither by the way of Rio de Janeiro, for which last port he will embark in a merchant vessel. As he would prefer a conveyance in a ship of war of the United States from Rio de Janeiro to Buenos Ayres, I will thank you to give the necessary orders for that purpose to the commander of the squadron on the Brazil station." LS in DNA, RG 45 (Naval Records), Letters from Federal Executive Agents, 1837–1886, 7:19 (M-517:2, frames 449–450); FC in DNA, RG 59 (State Department), Domestic Letters, 34:313 (M-40:32).

From ROBERT G. SCOTT

Richmond, July 25th 1844

Dear Sir, A succession of engagements to meet which will employ me for the next month at the least, deprives me of the opportunity & pleasure of saying personally to you, some things in favor of my estimable friend Mr. Washington Greenhow. His friends, & not he, nor upon his motion or suggestion, wish to procure for him some employment by the government. Recently the health of Mr. Greenhow has been much impaired, & a trip abroad, would I feel assured, not only tend to its restoration, but at the same time, if in the service of the country, would afford him a suitable opportunity, to shew his aptitude & capacity for the useful & honorable discharge of any the highest & gravest duties of such service. Indeed in the form of a letter, I can not adequately express to you, how high an estimate I place on the ability & character of this gentleman. A devoted friend as I know him to be, a perfect & accomplished gentleman of the Southern school—A noble high minded man—An accomplished scholar & writer—A genuine State right Republican of the Jeffersonian school, possessing a firmness & unshakiness of purpose, enabling him at all times & under all circumstances, to maintain calmly & decidedly his opinions & his purposes, I declare to you, that I should consider the acquisition of the services of such a man as every way desireable for the public interests.

I have but to repeat, that I wish I could be with the friends of Mr. Greenhow, & *speak* to you all I feel for & towards him. I know & appreciate the difficulties that may attend his being taken at once into the country's service, yet I hope some vacancy may occur, if none such now exists, to fill which you may call Mr. Greenhow. With assurances of my high respect & esteem I am yours &c, Robert G. Scott.

ALS in ScCleA. NOTE: Scott sent this letter "care of Mr. [John S.] Caskie."

From Simeon Toby, "President, Insurance Company of the State of Pennsylvania," Philadelphia, 7/25. He wishes to know if any information has been received from U.S. representatives in Ecuador, New Granada, and Venezuela concerning the long-standing claims for the *Josephine*. These claims were fully explained to Secretary of State [Daniel] Webster in 10/1842. He encloses a letter to Seth Sweetser, U.S. Consul at Guayaquil [Ecuador], concerning the matter. ALS in DNA, RG 59 (State Department), Miscellaneous Letters (M-179:105, frames 78–80).

From Geo[rge] M. Bibb, Secretary of the Treasury, 7/26. "I have the honor to return herewith, the letter [of 7/2] addressed to the Department of State by [James Shaw] the U.S. Consul at Belfast, Ireland, referred to this Department, the necessary instructions having been given to the officers of the Customs, consequent on the information communicated by the Consul" [concerning the smuggling of linens into the U.S.]. FC in DNA, RG 56 (Secretary of the Treasury), Letters to Cabinet and Bureau Officers, Series B, 4:405.

From W[ILLIA]M M. BLACKFORD

Legation of the U.S.
Bogotá, July 26th/44

In my Despatch No. 22 [of 3/8] I stated some facts, in relation to the insidious efforts, now making by the British Government, to obtain a footing upon the Mosquito Coast and promised to collect further information upon the subject. In a conversation with the Secretary of Foreign Affairs, I requested him to give me a few notes of the origin & progress of this extraordinary and unprovoked aggression upon the territorial rights of New Granada, which he promised to do, and, accordingly, handed me, a few days since, a statement, carefully drawn up from official documents in his office. Instead of making it the basis of a despatch, I deem it better to transmit, herewith, a translation of the whole statement, for your perusal.

A settlement on the Mosquito shore, by a European nation, is of infinite importance, when considered in reference to the contemplated canal across the Isthmus, of which it will be the key on the Atlantic side. The newspapers will have informed you that a Consul General has been sent there, & that San Juan de Nicaragua has been again blockaded by a British squadron.

I have the honor to transmit a circular despatch, received from the Secretary of Foreign Relations, (marked A) on the rights and privileges of Consuls, together with a copy of my answer (marked B). As there was no instance alleged of a Consul of the United States having assumed privileges to which he was not entitled, and as I was aware of the secret motives and object of the movement on the subject, I deemed it necessary to answer the note in as decided a manner as courtesy would permit, and to forward extracts of the correspondence to the several consuls for their information and government.

There would be many advantages attending a better definition of the rights, duties and immunities of Consuls in this country, and, should the Department think fit to entertain the overture, made by the Secretary, for a Convention to that effect, I respectfully call its attention to the one now in force between Spain and France, which might serve as a model. It will give me pleasure to carry into effect the instructions of the Government, upon the subject, to the best of my ability.

Mr. [Lino de] Pombo has resigned his appointment as Commissioner to negotiate a Treaty with the United States, as you will perceive by the correspondence between the Secretary of Foreign Relations & myself, (marked C. D.) herewith transmitted.

I beg leave to call your attention to the communication (marked E.) from Mr. [Marios] Espinel, Chargé d'Affaires of Ecuador near this Government. As it was at the instigation of this gentleman—acting, as he said, under the orders of his Government—that I applied for authority to enable me to treat with him, I was not a little surprized at the decision announced by his note. I hope you will approve the character of my answer (marked F).

I await, with impatience, the decision of the President, touching the naval demonstration recommended in my last Despatch. Subsequent reflection has served but to strengthen the conviction of its necessity, and as the late concentration of the Squadron in the Gulf will render its execution more easy, I hope to hear that the measure has been determined on.

I have succeeded in settling a claim upon this Government of the owners of the schooner "Ranger," for a balance due them under the Convention of 25th Nov[embe]r 1829, in the case of the Josephine and Ranger. I enclose a statement of the claim as settled. The money will be paid in September next. As I hold a power of Attorney, I will receive the sum & remit in such manner as the owners may direct.

I have the honor to enclose the receipt of Mr. [William] Gooding for the eleventh Instalment of the "By-chance" Indemnity. The last Instalment is payable on the 1st prox[im]o.

There is no news of the slightest interest. The primary election for the Presidency took place last month & passed off very quietly. The colleges meet in about ten days. The two prominent candidates are the Generals, Mosquera and Borrero—but it is thought the scattering votes may prevent either from having a majority, and thus devolve the election upon Congress—in which event, I have little doubt, Mosquera will be chosen. I entertain no apprehension of any disturbance, let the result be what it may. All parties seem to admit that it is, comparatively, unimportant who is President—whilst the preservation of peace and order is of the highest importance to the prosperity of the country.

I indulge the pleasing hope that my application, contained in despatch No. 24, for a Leave of absence, has been favorably considered by yourself & the President.

I have dates from New York to the 4th June, and letters from my family to the 23 May, but, I regret to say, not a line from the Department. I am, therefore, in ignorance of the views of the President and yourself in relation to the Convention about the mails which I concluded with this Government. I have the honor to be, with high respect, Your Ob[edien]t Ser[van]t, Wm. M. Blackford.

ALS (No. 26) with Ens in DNA, RG 59 (State Department), Diplomatic Despatches, Colombia, vol. 10 (T-33:10, frames 234–273), received 9/14; CC with En in DNA, RG 84 (Foreign Posts), Colombia, Despatches, vol. B4. NOTE: Blackford enclosed a 56-page memorandum on British encroachments upon the Mosquito Coast, a region of disputed ownership. In order to increase their local influence, the British had recently recognized "an independent Indian power" nominally ruled by an Indian king of the Mosquito tribe, but in fact controlled by British residents.

From G[eorge] M. Dallas, [Philadelphia], 7/26. Dallas asks that Calhoun examine the claim of Jacob Idler against the government of Venezuela and do what he can to secure an indemnity for Idler, an aged man with no means of support. ALS in DNA, RG 59 (State Department), Miscellaneous Letters (M-179:105, frames 80–81).

From BEN E. GREEN

Legation of the U.S. of A.
Mexico, July 26th 1844

Sir, I have the honor to send you a copy of a communication [of 7/3] just received from Mr. [John] Parrott, our consul at Mazatlan, on the subject of the *"Menudeo"* decree of the 23d Sept. 1843; also a note [of 7/24], which I addressed to the Mexican Govt. immediately on the receipt of Mr. Parrott's communication. The French Minister received a similar communication from his consul in Mazatlan, by express, some eight days before Mr. Parrott[']s letter reached me. He immediately sent a note to the Govt. on the subject, which was referred to the Minister of Hacienda. The same will be done with mine. It will go to the Minister of Hacienda and there it will stay, until France sends a fleet to bring Santa Anna to his senses.

I beg leave to call your attention particularly to this decree. If enforced, it will not only cause a greater sacrifice of American interests than all the previous outrages of Mexico put together, as Gen[era]l [Waddy] Thompson [Jr.] has already informed the Department, but it will utterly ruin our citizens engaged in commerce in Mexico. I have the honor to be Very Respectfully Your ob[edien]t Serv[an]t, Ben E. Green.

ALS (No. 13) with Ens in DNA, RG 59 (State Department), Diplomatic Despatches, Mexico, vol. 12 (M-97:13), received 8/25; FC (dated 7/25) in DNA, RG 84 (Foreign Posts), Mexico, Despatches; draft (dated 7/25) with En in NcU, Duff Green Papers (published microfilm, roll 5, frames 689–690 and 681–682). NOTE: In his note of 7/24 Green protested that the "interpretation and extension" given to the decree of 9/23/1843 applied to wholesalers regulations meant to apply only to retailers. He considers the enforcement of that decree as indicated a violation of article 3 of the 1831 treaty of amity and commerce between the U.S. and Mexico.

From R[OBERT] M. T. HUNTER

L[l]oyds, Essex [County, Va.,] July 26, 1844

My D[ea]r Sir, The friends of Mr. Washington Greenhow (former editor of the Petersburg Republican) are exceedingly desirous to obtain some appointment abroad for him. I have had a letter from [James A.] Seddon in relation to him who expresses the strongest desire to see the post of chargé des affaires to some of the South

American or minor European governments confer[r]ed upon him. I believe no appointment could be more generally gratifying to your friends in Va. than such a nomination of Greenhow. I have not enough of personal acquaintance with Mr. G[reenhow] to speak advisedly of his qualifications but such are the representations of some of our friends on this subject that I cannot doubt for a moment his entire fitness for such a post so far as education[,] high character and general intelligence can adapt one of his years to such a place. Mr. Greenhow[']s importance to our friends in this State has been such as to entitle him to our gratitude. He fought the battle for you in this State until the Baltimore convention and conducted the paper without a cent of salary as Mr. S[eddon] has informed me. You will probably hear from Mr. Seddon himself on the subject of this appointment. Greenhow knows nothing of our application. His friends[,] alarmed for his health which is declining and anxious too to secure him a place whose opportunities and emoluments could be both improving and useful to him[,] have moved in the matter of their own accord. He is poor and the salary would be something to him. But we desire the place for him more on account of the opportunities for improvement and a more enlarged experience which it would give him.

Your friend[s] here have been gratified by Mr. [James K.] Polk[']s declaration to run no more after the first term. I incline to think that the growing popularity of the one term principle will perhaps secure such a result even should he change his mind. The signs in favor of his election seem to be increasing, but I confess that the course of the Southern Whigs on the subject of Texas has been such as to give me a distrust for all the usual elements of calcu[la]tion upon political events. There is one idea thrown out by Mr. [Henry] Clay in his letter which is much used in the South. [Thomas H.] Benton too has used it. I mean the suggestion that Texas will afford as many non slave holding as slave holding States. This cannot be so. What is the southern bou[n]dary of our own Territory and what the ["prob-able" *canceled*] northern boundary claimed by Texas[?] Should you have any document on this subject I would be greatly obliged to you to send it to me. Mr. [Littleton W.] Tazewell said two months ago that there would not be time for the people to take the Texas fever before the Presidential election and therefore he hoped less than others for its assistance in that contest. But he says the day will come when no Southern man will find pardon for those who defeated the Treaty. I did not hear but such I learn were his sentiments. I incline to think there is some truth in this. The question will be felt in the Presidential election but not to so great an extent as we had hoped. But Benton[']s extraordinary course has contributed to postpone the Texas question. He will meet his reward I hope.

If the Baltimore convention could have been magnanimous enough to have given us yourself ["as the" *interlined*] candidate, the Texas question would have been felt in all its force. But it is useless to speak of the past. There is a future still before us which I trust your friends will improve. My nephew (Mr. [Muscoe R.H.] Garnett) has ["nearly" *interlined*] prepared a review of your speeches which I would like to get in the Democratic Review if it be not too warm for that latitude. I have not yet examined it however. Perhaps Mr. [Richard K.] Cralle has some connexion with that review ["and through" *canceled and* "if so" *interlined*] its insertion might be procured through him. Most sincerely your friend, R.M.T. Hunter.

ALS in ScCleA. Note: An AEU by Calhoun reads: "Mr. Hunter[,] relates to Mr. Greenhow."

From J[ohn] Y. Mason, [Secretary of the Navy], 7/26. As Calhoun requested in his letter of yesterday, Mason has ordered Commodore [Daniel] Turner to provide a passage to William Brent, Jr., Chargé d'Affaires to Argentina, in a public vessel from Rio [de] Janeiro to Buenos Ayres. LS in DNA, RG 59 (State Department), Miscellaneous Letters (M-179:105, frame 83); FC in DNA, RG 45 (Naval Records), Letters Sent by the Secretary of the Navy to the President and Executive Agencies, 1821–1886, 5:10 (M-472:3, frame 47).

To Balie Peyton, U.S. Dis[tric]t Att[orne]y, New Orleans, 7/26. Calhoun sends Peyton documents relative to James Julian Wright, captain of the steamer *Scioto Belle*. Wright has falsely declared his cargo to customs agents at New Orleans and is suspected of having kept a false log book aboard the ship. Peyton is instructed to proceed against Wright, who is known to be at New Orleans at present. FC in DNA, RG 59 (State Department), Consular Instructions, 11: 264.

From T[homas] M. Rodney

Consulate of the United States of America
Matanzas, July 26, 1844

Sir, Presuming that the views of the Department have undergone some change since the 4th of May last in relation to dispatching a ship of war to this port I shall avail myself of the leave of absence granted me on the 6th day of April last and return to the United States in the only vessel for my neighbourhood for perhaps some months. The business season is entirely over and I leave but two registers in the office.

The Duties of the office during my absence will be performed by Cha[rle]s P. Traub Esq[ui]re a gentleman of high character and ability who has on a former occasion officiated in the same capacity, and for whose official acts I hold myself responsible.

On my arrival in the United States I will do myself the honour to call at the Department at the earliest possible moment. I have the honour to be Sir With high respect Your obed[ien]t Serv[an]t, T.M. Rodney.

LS in DNA, RG 59 (State Department), Consular Despatches, Matanzas, vol. 4 (T-339:4), received 8/10.

To Sim[e]on Toby, President of the Insurance Comp[an]y of the State of Penn[sylvani]a, Philadelphia

Department of State
Wash[ingto]n, 26th July 1844

Sir, I have to acknowledge the receipt of your letter of yesterday. The communication for Mr. Seth Sweetzer [*sic*] which accompanied it, has been forwarded. An application has been received from him for authority from his Government to negotiate with the Government of Ecuador an adjustment of the claim in the case of the Josephine, and of others. It is not, however, deemed expedient to give that authority to any person at present. The Chargés d'Affaires of the United States at Bogota and Caracas have not apprised the Department of any result in the negotiation for the balance claimed of New Granada and Venezuela in the case of the Josephine. Their particular attention shall again be invited to the subject. I am, Sir, Your Obedient Serv[an]t, John C. Calhoun.

FC in DNA, RG 59 (State Department), Domestic Letters, 34:314 (M-40:32).

From John C. Bennett, Louisville, Ky., 7/27. "I take the liberty of enclosing you a communication to Governor [Wilson] Shannon, our Minister to Mexico. Will you have the goodness to enclose it to him? If so, you will confer a great favor on a warm and old political friend." ALS in DNA, RG 59 (State Department), Miscellaneous Letters (M-179:105, frame 90).

From EDWARD EVERETT

London, 27 July 1844

Sir, On the 25th instant Lord Aberdeen laid upon the table of the House of Peers the instructions for the cruizers employed for the suppression of the Slave Trade, drawn up by a commission consisting of Dr. [Stephen] Lushington, Mr. Bandinell [*sic*; James Bandinel] of the Foreign Office, Captain [Joseph] Denman of the Royal Navy, long in command on the African station, and Mr. [Henry C.] Rothery, a solicitor of the Treasury, whose name appears in my correspondence relative to the indemnification of the owners of the "Tigris" and "Seamew." The instructions recommended by this commission were, of course, submitted to the government to be revised, and are now issued by authority. They form a large volume in folio, in the usual form of the parliamentary documents. I shall take care to procure a copy for the department by the first opportunity. They comprize a complete code of directions for the guidance of British cruizers, in reference to every case for which it is possible to provide before hand.

In submitting these instructions to the House of Peers, Lord Aberdeen spoke at some length upon the general subject of the suppression of the Slave Trade. He observed that notwithstanding all that had been effected much still remained to be done. There was reason to think that till the last three years an annual number of slaves varying from 90,000 to 100,000 had been exported from Africa. The average for the last three years was 28,000, having risen from 17,000 in 1842 to 38,000 in 1843. The increase the last year was to be ascribed to the necessity of removing a portion of the force usually employed in watching the coast of Brazil to the river Plate, in consequence of the "senseless war" between Buenos Ayres and Monte Video; and to the change in the governor generalship of Cuba. During General Valdez'[s] administration of that office, the number of slaves imported into the Island had been reduced as low as 3000; but instead of his receiving the support of his government, positive orders had been sent him from Madrid to relax in his measures for putting a stop to the trade and he had finally been recalled. The responsibility of the continuance of the Slave Trade now rested with the governments of Brazil and Spain. Those governments had entered into engagements with England to co-operate in the total suppression of traffic in slaves which they must be prepared to fulfil. Lord Aberdeen mentioned with satisfaction that the marquis de Viluma, during his brief term of office as prime-minister of Spain, had sent an order to Cuba directing that severe punishment should be inflicted on persons carrying on the trade: an order which would have the force of law till the meeting of the cortes. There is an appearance of inaccuracy, in the report of this part of Lord Aberdeen's remarks.

In reference to the co-operation of the cruizing officers of the United States Lord Aberdeen expressed himself in the following terms:

"He had to mention another circumstance, which was calculated to increase his hopes of success. He alluded to the active co-operation and good understanding which existed between Her Majesty's cruizers on the coast of Africa and the Squadron of the United States. The officers employed by the government of the United States had co-operated cordially and actively with Her Majesty's officers, and there could be no doubt that the greatest possible advantage would arise from the existence of that good understanding. This was more important, because there was a slight difference of opinion between the two governments, as to the construction of certain claims made respectively by the two governments, as to the mode in which interference to put down the Slave Trade should be carried on; but this difference of opinion was rendered altogether innocuous, by the conciliatory spirit and friendly dispositions existing on the part of the officers engaged in the suppression of the Trade. Had a different spirit prevailed inconveniences might certainly have arisen from the different views taken by the two parties respectively. He had also reason to know that the French government had recently shewn a disposition to take a more active part than heretofore, in the suppression of the Slave Trade by her cruizers. With the co-operation of the United States and of the French cruizers, there was now a better prospect that our exertions would be crowned with success."

In my despatch Nro. 164, I adverted to a change of system which had been determined upon by this government vizt. "the substitution of a more vigilant watch of the coast of Africa for the previous plan of cruizing on the coasts of the countries to which slaves are transported." Lord Aberdeen dwelt upon this change of plan in the conclusion of his speech on the 25th instant, and its probable advantages. He added, however, that it was not intended altogether to withdraw their cruizers from the coast of Brazil. The force there would be diminished, in order that the force employed on the coast of Africa might be rendered efficient for its purpose; but still the force kept up on the coast of Brazil would be sufficient to capture any slave vessel, which might happen to escape from the coast of Africa.

Nothing material fell from the members of the House of Lords who followed Lord Aberdeen in the discussion. I am, sir, with great respect, your obedient servant, Edward Everett.

LS (No. 168) in DNA, RG 59 (State Department), Diplomatic Despatches, Great Britain, vol. 53 (M-30:49), received 8/21; FC in DNA, RG 84 (Foreign Posts), Great Britain, Despatches, 8:358–363; FC in MHi, Edward Everett Papers, 49:442–447 (published microfilm, reel 23, frames 223–225).

From John Fine, Ogdensburgh, N.Y., 7/27. He asks that Calhoun submit to [George M.] Bibb [Secretary of the Treasury] for presentation to President [John Tyler] a petition recommending reappointment of David C. Judson as Collector of Customs at Ogdensburgh. Judson has held several public offices in N.Y. including those of both Representative and Senator in the State General Assembly. A recent inspection of his Collection district resulted in a report that his district "was the best managed of all." (An AEI by Calhoun reads: "Submitted for the consideration of the Sec[re]t[ar]y. The writer of the letter Mr. Fine was formerly a member of Congress and is a very worthy citizen." An EU reads "make out new Comm[issio]n.") ALS in DNA, RG 56 (Secretary of the Treasury), Applications for Appointment as Customs Service Officers, 1833–1910, Judson.

From BEN E. GREEN

Legation of the U.S. of A.

Mexico, July 27th 1844

Sir, With much regret, I have seen by New Orleans papers received yesterday, that a letter of mine to Mr. [William S.] Murphy has found its way into the Texas papers. I expected that it would be used with the Texan Govt.; but had no thought of its being made public. This practice of publishing diplomatic correspondence can not be too much condemned. It materially impairs the usefulness of diplomatic agents, and renders their position, in cases like this, any thing but pleasant. I am on the best & most cordial terms with Mr. [Charles] Bankhead. He is a gentleman of information, an agre[e]-able companion, and personally I esteem and like him. As the diplomatic representative of G. Britain, however, I deem it my duty to inform myself of his views, and to communicate them to my Govt. and my colleagues. The cordiality existing between us affords me the best opportunity of obtaining that information. But I fear that the publication of this letter will make him much more guarded in his intercourse with me for the future.

I send you more of the correspondence about the Tabasco affair. The opinion has generally prevailed here for some time, that the William Patterson, who figures in this tragedy, is a detestable scroundrel who has been in the employ of [Pedro de] Ampudia, as a spy & doer of dirty work generally: that he was sent to New Orleans by Ampudia, to entice [Francisco] Sentmanat back to Tabasco, whence he had fled, with a view to get hold of him and shoot him; and that the application made by Mr. Bankhead in favor of this Patterson was intended to conceal the part he had taken in entrapping Sentmanat, in order to shield him from the vengeance of the friends of the latter. The reference made in Mr. Bankhead's note to the services, which Patterson had rendered to the Mexican Govt., is made use of by some to implicate him as a party to this unclean transaction. But I know Mr. Bankhead too well, & believe him to be too much the gentleman to lend himself to any such purposes. He has been imposed upon and without knowing anything of the man or the circumstances, made the application upon the data furnished him by the party interested.

I am much gratified to see by the N. Orleans Picayune of the 15th June, and 9th July, just received, that the purposes of Sentmanat were not publicly known in New Orleans, as asserted by the Mexican Govt., & press, until after his departure. The Mexican Govt. were well informed upon the subject so early as the first of May; and it appears from testimony of one Bernard Othon, published by the Mexican Govt. (which I have already sent you) that the Mexican Consul in N. Orleans, instead of endeavouring to put a stop to the expedition, connived at it. This man Othon is well known here, and is considered a villain capable of any crime. Patterson's reputation is little better. These men, Othon and Patterson, ["were then, it appears, the accomplices and instigators of this expedition" *canceled*] and Mr. Arrangois, a gentleman, whom I am sorry to find in such bad company, were then, it appears, the accomplices & instigators of this expedition, which has given Santa Anna so much pleasure, and the Mexican press under his control another occasion for charging the U.S. with fitting out piratical expeditions to rob and plunder Mexico.

I did not interpose for the Americans engaged in this affair, because I knew that my interposition under the then existing circumstances, would do them more harm than good, if innocent, and if guilty, they were not entitled to protection from me. Besides I knew that it was too late to save their lives; and that Santa Anna would seize the occasion to heap insult and abuse upon the U.S., and to exasperate the Mexicans still more against us, by charging us with not only fitting out piratical expeditions against Mexico, but endeavouring afterwards to protect those pirates against the consequences of their crime. Insulting charges of this nature have been made over and over with impunity, and I have thought better, if possible, to avoid giving occasion for a renewal of them, until our Govt. shall be in disposition to answer them in such a manner as will prevent a repetition of them.

In the Diario of the 23d July is published by authority a letter of Gen[era]l Ampudia, very insulting to the French and Spanish Ministers. As if to add force to this insult, a copy of the letter was sent to the English Minister, as a *mark of the particular respect and consideration*, which he had merited of H.E. the President. See communication of the Minister of War, dated 28th July, in the Diario of the 24th.

[Ignacio] Trigueros, the Minister of Hacienda, was last night accused in the Congress of embezzlement of the public funds. The accusation was passed over to the Gran Jurado. I have just learned that Santa Anna has been all day engaged sending couriers to the different departments, *on dit*, with instructions to the generals to *pronounce* against the Congress. I have the honor to be Very Respectfully Your ob[edien]t Serv[an]t, Ben E. Green.

ALS (No. 14) with En in DNA, RG 59 (State Department), Diplomatic Despatches, Mexico, vol. 12 (M-97:13), received 8/25; FC in DNA, RG 84 (Foreign Posts), Mexico, Despatches; draft in NcU, Duff Green Papers (published microfilm, roll 5, frames 697–700).

From T[ilghman] A. Howard, [U.S. Chargé d'Affaires to Texas]

Galveston Texas, 27 July 1844

Sir, I left Washington City on the 18th of June, came by way of Indiana, remained four days with my family, arrived at Orleans on the 14 inst. left that city on the 17th on the Texian Brig Rover, (there being no other vessel then leaving known to me) and after a boisterous passage of ten days, I arrived here on yesterday.

You will doubtless have been informed before this reaches you of the death of Gen. [William S.] Murphy, who died on the 12th, of yellow fever.

Our Consul, Col. [Archibald M.] Green, is now sick of the same disease, and the epidemic is very prevalent in this city.

Understanding that President [Samuel] Houston is sick on Trinity river, and there being no present means of conveyance to Houston I have accepted an invitation to spend a few days at the residence of a gentleman residing a few miles west of this, which may explain the reason of what might, unexplained, seem, an improper delay on my part, in presenting my credentials and forwarding to my government the evidence that I had entered on the duties of my mission. I am, with great respect, Your very ob[e]d[ien]t servant, T.A. Howard.

ALS in DNA, RG 59 (State Department), Diplomatic Despatches, Texas, vol. 2 (T-728:2, frames 372–373), received 8/23.

From John Tyler, Jr.

Fortress Monroe [in Va.] July 27th 1844

Dear Sir: In relation to the presentation of M. [Angel] Calderon de La Barca, the President [John Tyler] desires me to say to you, that he will be in Washington in the course of ten or twelve days, but that if the presentation should be considered necessary before that time M. Calderon will have to come to this place. The President does not deem it important for you to accompany him, unless convenient to do so, inasmuch as a letter of presentation from you will answer every purpose. I have the honor to be Y[ou]r very ob[edien]t Ser[van]t, John Tyler, Jr., P[rivate] Secretary.

ALS in DNA, RG 59 (State Department), Miscellaneous Letters (M-179:105, frame 89). NOTE: A Clerk's EU reads "Information com[municate]d to M. Calderon 30 inst."

From Benj[amin] W. S. Cabell

Bridge Water[,] Pitt[sylvani]a [County]
near Danville [Va.] July 28th 1844

Dear Sir, It appears to me to be proper to return you my cordial thanks for your favor of the 12th inst. It was all, that, under the circumstances, I could have desired. I abhor proscription, and it was only I assure you, because I was led to suppose there was, or was likely to have been about the time I addressed you, a *vacancy* that I presumed to ask for an appointment for a truly meritorious young man [William Cabell]. His name however is now before you, and, if a suitable occasion presents itself, I am sure you will not overlook him.

We are in the midst of the Presidential Canvass, and the whigs, are moving Heaven and Earth to get up another "Harrison *Fuss.*" They are decidedly in advance of the Republican Party, in the publication of every thing calculated to promote their cause. My old colleague V. Witcher, never a nul[l]ifier by name, yet a *seceder* at that day, has become [a] U.S. Bank man—Tariff, according to [Henry] Clay[']s interpretation of it in his Georgia letter, goes for Distribution—and, like Gen[era]l Waddy Thompson, is out and out against annexation—*now*—and forever.

The course of the States Rights party of Georgia—and indeed, of the Southern Whigs, with a few exceptions, at the last session of Congress, but far more, that of the States right party of my native State, to which in the darkest hour of its fortunes I was proud to belong, has not only been witnessed with amazement, but with the most awful vaticinations, for the future fate of my Country.

Will you send me the Texas Treaty, together with every speech and Document relative to it. We have not had either [Thomas H.] Benton's or [Robert J.] Walker[']s speech in reply. Great stress was laid at our Court, on an acknowledgement of the Independence of

Mexico by old Spain, in the Treaty of Cordova. I remember that there was an effort to obtain a recognition of the Independence of Mexico, and to place Iturbide, or some other Bourbon, on the throne— but I supposed it was quashed by the Spanish Cortes, then in permanent session. Where facts depend upon the record, we have not, oftentimes, the record to refer to.

You will have seen Gen[era]l Thompson[']s speech in the National Intelligencer. His location, and position in the Whig Party give weight, in the estimation of many to his views on annexation. If his Speech has been reviewed effectively, send ["it" *interlined*; to] me if you please. If it has not, the subject is worthy of your notice, on account of its direct bearing on the Treaty, just negociated by you. As to my own part, I regard annexation, as equivalent to a new Declaration of the Independence of the Southern States— and the loss of the Treaty—finally—(ie. unless ratification shall be forced by the force of public sentiment[ )]—as a deadly blow, at that Independence, and of the Liberty, which it guarantees.

I have addressed you with the frankness and freedom of an old acquaintance. I have revered your character so long, that I forgot that you could have known nothing of me. I beg you to believe that I am not disposed to trespass upon your time, by drawing you into a correspondence. But I want authentic information, to aid me in such efforts as I may have it in my power to make, before the people of Pittsylvania &c in vindicating the Treaty—and have therefore taken the liberty to apply at once for it, at Head Qua[r]ters.

We have not yet seen Mr. [George] McDuffie[']s final answer to the Protectionists in his Speech in the S[enate] U. States. I hope he will draw out at length, and have the speeches he made at Rich-[mon]d and Petersburg, published, for the benefit of his political friends. He is so powerful in his illustrations, which he has so great a facil[i]ty[?] for adapting to the comprehension of plantation men, that he ought ["to" *interlined*] run out the practical operation of those principles which he assails, and shew *how* they *tax* the people. Shew them what they have to pay upon Iron, Salt, Sugar, and cotton, & wool[l]en goods—and then estimate the *annual levy* upon the Southern States, over and above, what ought to be required ["to pay" *interlined*] for an economical administration of the finances. A hint from you might ["set" *canceled and* "induce" *interlined*] him to encounter the labor of put[t]ing the whole subject, in a *form tangible* to the *mass* of *readers*. The complex character of the subject, puts the possibility of doing this, beyond the *resources* of the generality of speakers. May the Almighty continue to bless you with corporeal and intellectual health—and prosper you both as a private & a public man. With high esteem & Respect Y[ou]r Ob[edient] S[ervan]t, Benj. W.S. Cabell.

ALS in ScCleA. NOTE: An AEU by Calhoun reads: "Mr. Cabell[,] wants Texan treaty & Doc[umen]ts." A second AEU by Calhoun reads: "Wants the Tex[a]n treaty & all the speeches & Do[cumen]ts con[cerne]d with it."

From F[RANCIS] W. PICKENS

Edgewood [near Edgefield, S.C.] 28 July '44
My dear Sir, I have just rec[eive]d yours in relation to my going to Nashville &c. I had rec[eive]d a very kind and flattering letter of invitation from the Committee alluding to my having been at College in Tenn: &c., but I had answered declining. It is the sickley season, and my children are small, & I have no human being to whom I can trust them, so much so that it makes me uneasy to be absent for a night. But I have written [Franklin H.] Elmore & if he will go I will nevertheless go on too, as you request it. I have promised to address a mass meeting in Augusta [Ga.] on the 6th August & can go directly on from there. I was invited to meet the young men's Democratic convention at the Indian Springs Geo[rgia] 25th inst: & would have done so but that some young men got up a dinner at this place to [George] McDuffie for 26th & I was obliged to stay. But he has declined from illness.

I have not seen him or heard from him but understand he says he will raise the "banner of Disunion if only three men follow him" &c. Now if such moves as this are to be made at this peculiar juncture we are ruined—all disaster & defeat will be put upon So[uth] Ca[rolina]—& you might as well strike your name & fame from the annals of the country. He used this language in Charleston and some of the best men were alarmed at it. Now that we have just got Va. seperated from N.Y. for the first time in 15 years, I think we have every prospect of uniting the South & if *that is once done we can right* ourselves in one year. The gre[a]t source of our difficulty and betrayal has come from the union of Va. with N.Y. politicians. However I have no time to go into these things now. I deeply regret to hear what you say as to [Samuel] Houston & Texas. If that is so it will end in a war which we cannot avoid much longer.

Perhaps you may have seen garbled accounts in the Whig papers of Augusta & Hamburg of some of my recent speeches. Perhaps too the Pres[i]d[en]t [John Tyler] has seen them or the [Washington] Madisonian. If so I hope they will not notice any thing said as to the President. I have not contradicted any thing they have said however false in their account.

You know they have brought out violent & bitter opposition to me [for reelection to the S.C. Senate] by F[rancis] H. Wardlaw & this has been the cause of the attacks of the whigs of Hamburg. It makes no impression here but is made up for the Geo[rgia] market, & Wardlaw has ruined himself by lending his name. There are 2600 voters in the Dist[rict] & it is thought he may get 400—& 320 of them whigs about Hamburg.

Tell Mr. [Thomas G.] Clemson I sent Mr. Van [*manuscript torn; name illegible*] by his place the other day & all were well & doing well. We have for the first time this summer just had a fine rain last night[;] it is too late for old corn it being somewhat out of roasting-ear. I never had such a prospect for cotton, although the lice have injured it much in places. It is opening very much. This is very early. Some are picking now in the neighbourhood below this. I have not heard a word from Cousin Floride [Colhoun Calhoun] since she left although she borrowed a horse and saddle from me for the cook to ride up on, & the Driver was to come immediately back with them. Truly, F.W. Pickens.

ALS in ScCleA.

From [FRIEDRICH LUDWIG, Baron Von] ROENNE, "Private"

Berlin, July 28th 1844

My dear Sir, I informed you some time ago, that a Board of Trade would be erected of which I was to be the President. Knowing the great interest you have always kindly taken in the affairs of my country, I beg leave now to inform you, that the new Department has since been erected under the title of "Handels-Amt" and that the King [Frederick William IV] has appointed me the President of the Department. There is to be a Council of Trade besides, but this is to be no Department at all, only when I report to the King about commercial matters some of the other Ministers ought to be present and we thus form the Council of Trade in which the King decides upon my report. I hope this new institution will prove beneficial to the developement of our commerce and industry. I regret, that the Senate have not ratified our treaty, but hope that our relations will nevertheless continue as friendly as they were when I resided in the U.S. The new Department will, I trust, contribute to promote the intercourse between Germany and America and I hope our joint efforts will place it upon a firmer basis. Every body must see at once that two great countries with a vast population, the one of which has all sorts of raw products while the other has all sorts of cheap manufactures, and both of which are unrestricted by any consideration of colonial policy, seem to be destined by nature to trade with each other. There is one subject which is much in the way of the full developement of the commerce of certain provinces of Prussia. Mr. [Henry] Wheaton will write to you on the subject and I beg leave strongly to recommend it to your consideration. The shipping and commercial as well, as the planting interests of the U.S. are deeply concerned in the question.

The attempt to assassinate the King has created a general feeling of disgust, it was an isolated fact, a fellow who for misconduct had been turned out of Office by his own fellow-citizens (he was Burgemaster in a small town, was elected for that place and not reelected) asked the King repeatedly for a place of some kind or other, which was refused, whereupon, to revenge himself, he made the attempt against the life of the King. Such things are, however, deeply to be deplored, they undermine the respect for the Monarchy and our people are not ripe for self-government, nor do they wish it; the poor Queen too, the best of women, made a narrow escape; they proceeded, however, immediately on their journey; today there was a general thanksgiving, the churches were crowded to excess.

I beg you, my dear Sir, to believe me most truly & sincerely, your most obed[ien]t serv[an]t, Roenne.

ALS in ScCleA; PC in Gunter Moltmann, "Eine Deutschland-Korrespondenz John C. Calhouns aus dem Jahre 1844," in *Jahrbuch fur Amerikastudien*, vol. XIV (1969), pp. 163–164; PEx in Jameson, ed., *Correspondence*, p. 964.

From John J. Browne, Paterson, N.J., 7/29. Browne asks that Calhoun attempt to obtain the release of U.S. prisoners in Cuba. ALS in DNA, RG 59 (State Department), Miscellaneous Letters (M-179: 105, frames 97–98).

To W[illia]m M. D'Antignac, President, Augusta Insurance and Banking Co., Augusta, Ga., 7/29. "In reply to your letter of the 23rd inst. I have to state that previous to its receipt such instructions as the Department conceived to be proper in regard to the arrest of Gerard Koster were transmitted to the U.S. Consul at Basle [Seth T. Otis]." FC in DNA, RG 59 (State Department), Consular Instructions, 10:257.

From A[NDREW] J. DONELSON,
"private—confidential"

Nashville, July 29, 1844

Sir, Having seen the letter which Col. [James] Gadsden addressed to Gen[era]l [Andrew] Jackson after conversing with you in relation to the difficulties yet in the way of attaching Texas to our Union, it was my intention at that time to write to you, mentioning that no time had been lost in addressing to [Samuel] Houston a letter warning him of the designs of Great Britain—but I was taken ["from" *interlined*] home by engagements which have occupied me until now.

That you may be fully apprized of what has been done, I think it best to send you a copy of the letter to Houston, which he will have received by the time you get this. If Houston could be induced to rely with any confidence on the success of the nominations of Messrs. [James K.] Polk and [George M.] Dallas I should suppose the advice offered him by the Gen[era]l would be controlling.

The danger is that he may not be able to stand up before his own people if the guarantee promised by England & France is accompanied by terms otherwise very favorable to Texas. But of this accident we must run the risk, relying on the justice and force of those views which sustain the policy of the measure of annexation, and which we are sure must prevail as soon as the people of the United States understand the magnitude of the mischief which will result from the location of British influence on that frontier.

The [Henry] Clay party in this State have as perfect an organization as they had in 1840, and it will require the union of every Democratic interest to break it down. The State is becoming almost an encampment. My belief is that the Democratic Party will gain the victory, but that to do so, much must be done that the lovers of good order must regret. We shall be obliged to encourage the association of military companies, and adopt all other honorable means of breaking the chain of such *array* as was adopted by the Whigs in 1840 and as they yet maintain.

I was gratified to hear from Col. Gadsden that you felt a deep interest in the success of Polk. I am very respectfully y[ou]r ob[edi-en]t ser[van]t, A.J. Donelson.

[Enclosure]

Andrew Jackson to Gen. Sam Houston, "Private, Confidential"

Hermitage, July 19th 1844

My Dear Sir, The great interest I take in the success of the propo-sition to annex Texas to the United States, induces me again to ad-dressy [*sic*] you.

The rejection of the treaty by the Senate, filled me with regret: but the effect of this movement brings the subject directly to the at-tention of the people, and we shall in the course of a few months be enabled to understand what their verdict will be. There is every reason now to believe that discussion and reflection are strengthen-ing the views of the politicians who favour annexation, and that Mr. Clay weakened by his position in this respect will be defeated by a large majority. So confident am I that this will be the case that I am anxious you should be prepared for it, and not take any course for Texas which may create new embarrassments in the negotiation or Legislation which will be necessary to carry into effect the measure of annexation.

Let me say to you as a friend, anxious for the preservation of your fame, and incapable of deceiving you, that you ought on no account to let go the position you have taken as the friend of an-nexation. Great Britain is aiming at the overthrow of the Republican System. She will omit no opportunity to prepare herself for the contest which is yet to come—a contest which is to decide the great question, whether the liberal principles fostered by the United States, are to be received or rejected by the other nations of the Earth. All the skill of her diplomacy, all her energies at home and abroad, are directed therefore to undermine the prosperity of the United States, and sow the seeds of disunion and discord among their people.

In such a contest as this, I want you to be on the side of your native land, on the side of Liberty and the representative principle which is the only shield that liberty now has in the world.

You have won a great name on the fields of St. Jacinto. You will ["still" *canceled*] win a still greater by showing to England and France that you are not to be caught by their diplomacy—That you are not to be estranged from the policy which is to give to Texas the flag of freedom and make her a part of the great system which is ulti-

461

mately to unfetter the human mind and give to man in every quarter of God[']s earth civil and religious liberty.

Great Britain, my friend, will tempt you in a thousand ways, and she will be aided by emissaries from this country as hostile as she is to the true interests of the United States and of Texas. Believe them not—trust them not—spurn them from your confidence as long as there is a hope that annexation will have the sanction of our people.

If contrary to my belief Mr. Clay's counsels are to be uppermost in this Country, it will then be time enough for you to decide what movement is best for Texas. If the hope of union with the United States is cut off the omen will be a bad one for the cause of human rights, but you will not be responsible for it, and your efforts then to promote the happiness of your own citizens, however disastrous they may be to the United States, will have the sanction of patriotism and duty.

Great Britain will give up for the present the scheme of abolition— she will surrender almost every thing to disappoint the proposition of annexation, to the United States. But depend upon it she will deceive you. On whatever terms you may make an alliance with her, in less than three years you will find yourself called on to give up ["not only" *interlined*] your soil and negro's, but your liberty. Her present power cannot be maintained if the doctrine of equal rights and of Government by the people is not subverted: The contest is between the British Constitution and the American Constitution, and if Texas is in alliance with her, she must take part against us.

As I stated before, suspend action; wait for further developements from the people of this Country and you may do much not only for yourself but for millions yet unborn.

I make these suggestions knowing your attachment to your native land. And I do it with the freedom which a long friendship alone can justify. I cannot hope to live but a short time more, but with the blessing of God many more years are reserved for you: and you may do much to influence the result of the great contest to which I have adverted. Remember what I tell you. Resist British alliance—Oppose her policy—denounce her intrigues! The lovers of freedom throughout the world will thank and honour you!

Adopt her suggestions—embrace her offer to pay your national debt and give you her protection! Texas becomes an instrument in the hands of monarchy to break down the experiment of popular Government, and Houston her gallant and honored *hero* becomes a subordinate character in a remote colony.

I am growing weaker every day, but have had strength to dictate this letter to my nephew M[a]j[o]r Donelson, in whose handwriting it is.

Farewell—May God bless you and your amiable Lady & Son and may you live to see Texas a star in the galaxy of our Union and a noble accession to the cause of popular liberty is the sincere prayer of your old friend, Andrew Jackson.

ALS with En in ScCleA; PC in Jameson, ed., *Correspondence*, pp. 964–965.

From John P. DuVal, Tallahassee, 7/29. DuVal praises Charles [S.] Sibley, U.S. District Attorney for Middle Fla., against whom charges have been preferred by an unknown person. DuVal is sure that the charges are inspired by an office-seeker. He hopes that Calhoun will not be "the innocent cause of doing injustice to a worthy man." ALS in DNA, RG 59 (State Department), Applications and Recommendations, 1837–1845, Sibley (M-687:30, frame 140).

From W[illia]m B. Hodgson

Lebanon Springs N. Y[or]k, July 29, 1844

Sir, Mr. [George R.] Gliddon, who is now in Philadelphia, has informed me of the extreme illness of his father [John Gliddon], the actual Consul of the U. States, in the Pachalick of Egypt. He painfully anticipates his father's decease, and desires the appointment of Mr. Alexander Tod, as his successor at Alexandria, and that of his brother William Gliddon, at Cairo. Mr. Tod is the brother-in-law of Mr. Gliddon.

He thinks, that in consideration of my late official relations to the Government, in Turkey, Egypt and Barbary, a representation to yourself, Sir, on this subject, would be indulgently received.

In my official report to the Department of State, in the year 1835, and now on file, I presented a detailed account of our Consular system in the Levant, and of the persons administering that system. This report was made under secret and special instructions. It bears large testimony to the estimable characters ["of" *canceled*] official and private, of our Consuls Mr. John Gliddon at Alexandria and Mr. George R. Gliddon at Cairo. I will not now, either add to or substract from, that testimony.

Whilst I was in Egypt, I had the advantage of knowing personally, Mr. Tod and Mr. William Gliddon. They are both highly honorable gentlemen, and what is important in our foreign representation, they are superior to the littleness, which characterizes natives of that country—the Levantines.

My report expresses the opinion, with corresponding facts, that the Barbary Consulate of Tripoli, ought to be abolished, and the salary transferred to Alexandria. To this latter place, our citizens throng. In Tripoli, there has not been an American vessel or citizen, in twenty years. For all purposes of national advantage, we might as well have a salaried Consul at Timbuctoo. I have the honor to be Sir, with great respect Y[ou]r Ob[edien]t Ser[van]t, Wm. B. Hodgson.

ALS in DNA, RG 59 (State Department), Applications and Recommendations, 1837–1845, Tod (M-687:32, frames 470–472). Note: An AEU by Calhoun reads "Mr. Hodgson in favour of Mr. Tod." Daniel S. Macauley was U.S. Consul in Tripoli during 1831–1849. Hodgson, a Virginian, had been Dragoman of the U.S. legation in Turkey during 1832–1836. He had been appointed by John Tyler in 1842 to be U.S. Consul for Tunis, but apparently had not been confirmed by the Senate.

From Stewart Newell, *"Now at Galveston"*

Consulate of the U. States
Port of Sabine, July 29th 1844

Sir, I have the honor to report to you, the arrival at this place, of the Hon. A.T. [*sic*; Tilghman A.] Howard, Charge de Affaires of the U. States to Texas. He arrived on the 25th inst., but owing to the existence of an Epidemic, resembling in its Character Yellow Fever, he, immediately left, for a more healthy location, about nineteen miles, distant on the Sea Shore.

I was absent to Sabine, at the time of his arrival, and returned to Galveston via Sabine, yesterday Evening, in time only, to see, the last Earthly honors paid, to my deceased friend, A[rchibald] M. *Green* Esq[ui]r[e], the Consul for the U. States at this Port. He was taken ill of the prevailing Fever, on the 23d, in the Afternoon, and died at my residence in this City. Although I, was absent, yet, my Wife, and family, nursed him, day and Night, until he departed this life yesterday, (Sunday) at 6 A.M. He was attended by Three of the best Physicians our City admits of, and who, are not only regular

Graduates, but have been very successful, in the Treatment of the diseases of the Country.

Mr. Green, had been treating his first sym[p]toms, with some Medicine, upon his own judgement, and seem[e]d in his usual good spirits, until the 22d, the day on which the U.S. Sch[oone]r Flirt left the Harbour. He with several others, accompanied the vessel, outside the Bar, some 4 or 5 Miles and returned in the Pilot Boat, much exposed, to an Intensely hot Sun, which no doubt, contributed to render the Attack, more violent. Every care, and attention, that friends, much attach[e]d to him, could render was cheerfully bestowed, notwithstanding which, he died, much regretted, by all who knew him.

The Consulate at Sabine, requireing attention, only about three Months in the year, and Mr. Green, not having appointed a Vice Consul, I have taken charge of the Consulate at Galveston. Not having a knowledge of any one, in whom I could place the Responsibility, I have determined to perform the duties, until the pleasure of the Department is known, and as I have not yet seen Gen[era]l Howard who arrived in the City, this Morning, from his residence, and left in one hour after for Washington, *Texas* I had not an opportunity of communicating with him.

The Books & Papers of the Legation are in the Office of the Consulate, until Gen[era]l Howard's pleasure, is known, relative to them. I have the honor to be most Respectfully Y[ou]r Ob[edien]t Serv[an]t, Stewart Newell.

ALS (No. 20) in DNA, RG 59 (State Department), Consular Despatches, Texas, vol. 1 (T-153:1), received 8/23.

From THOMAS C. REYNOLDS, "(Private)"

Petersburg Va., July 29th 1844
Sir, I am taking a great liberty in thus addressing you, & on such a subject as the one I am about to introduce: but as the paper which I edit is considered the organ of your ["party" *altered to* "friends" *and then canceled*] friends in this State, I hope my motives will be appreciated & form my excuse.

You are doubtless aware that systematic attempts are now made in this State & elsewhere to represent you as unfriendly to the existence of the Union. The ["idea" *canceled and* "accusation" *interlined*], however preposterous, is repeated so often, that even those who first advanced it, knowing it to be false, have repeated the lie so often that they begin to believe it themselves. It is unquestionably injuring the States Rights cause, & your own position in this State, and several persons, (among others, a prominent leader of the Whig Party, who does not forget that he is a Southerner), have urged me to write to you & obtain from you, (if possible, also for publication) a letter containing your views on the subject (as far as ["they" *canceled*] concerns the accusation so impudently made). I have the honour to be Honourable Sir very truly yours, Thomas C. Reynolds, Editor of Petersburg Republican.

ALS in ScCleA. Note: An AEU by Calhoun reads "Mr. Reynolds, ["Charges" *canceled*] relates to charge of[?] my[?] being a Disunionist." Thomas C. Reynolds (1821–1887), a native of S.C., was graduated from the University of Va. in 1842. He was subsequently Governor of Missouri under the Confederate States.

To Samuel S. Sibley, [Tallahassee, Fla. Territory], 7/29. "I have to acknowledge the receipt of the letter of the 22nd instant, signed by yourself and Mr. [James D.] Westcott [Jr.], and herewith enclose a copy of such portions of the papers to which you therein refer as affect the official character of Mr. [Charles S.] Sibley, the rest being of a nature not to require the attention of this Department." FC in DNA, RG 59 (State Department), Domestic Letters, 34:316 (M-40:32).

From W. Thomson, Somerville, N.J., 7/29. "Herewith I send the memorial of Henry Dolliver, respecting his claim on the Mexican Government. He has heretofore communicated with the Department of State on the subject and he was advised to send a memorial on the subject that there might be the foundation laid for the Government to act on." Dolliver's memorial is dated 7/30 [*sic*] and sets forth the circumstances of the seizure by Mexican authorities of the cargo of the schooner *Lady of the Lake*. ALS with En in DNA, RG 76 (Records of Boundary and Claims Commissions and Arbitrations), United States and Mexican Claims Commissions, U.S. Board of Commissioners, Established by an Act of Congress of March 3, 1849.

From [Commander] CHARLES WILKES, [U.S. Navy]

Washington City, 29th July 1844
Sir, I have the honor in answer to your note to state that the Person[']s name is David Whippy formerly of Nantucket but now a resident of the Feejee Islands. He resides on the Island of Ovalou at the town of Livuka, it is the best harbour in the Group for the resort of our Ships where they may obtain all the supplies of these Islands.

Of David Whippy's character I must bear the fullest testimony of and again express to you my conviction he is a very suitable person for the situation of Vice Consul. With great respect I am Your ob[edien]t Se[rvan]t, Charles Wilkes.

ALS in DNA, RG 59 (State Department), Consular Despatches, Bay of Islands and Auckland, vol. 1 (T-49:1).

From Walker Anderson, U.S. District Attorney for Western Fla. Territory, Pensacola, 7/30. In reply to Calhoun's letter of 7/18 requesting copies of documentary evidence taken in the case of two U.S. seamen [Samuel S. Thomas and Joseph R. Curtis] accused of murdering a British sea captain in Haiti, Anderson encloses a copy of the only testimony taken in the case. ALS with En in DNA, RG 59 (State Department), Miscellaneous Letters (M-179:105, frames 108–111).

From H[ENRY] BAILEY, "Private"

Charleston, 30th July, 1844
Dear Sir, At a meeting of the Committee of Vigilance &ca, on the subject of Texas, which was held last evening, Col. [James] Gadsden, a member of the committee, presented & read a letter he had just received from General [Andrew] Jackson, a copy of which he placed at the disposal of the Committee. Whereupon it was resolved, that the copy should be sent to you, for reasons which will appear upon its perusal. I have now the honor to inclose it to you conformably to the instructions of the Committee, & am further instructed by them to say to you, that they concur fully in the views of General J[ackson].

The Committee have appointed a sub committee to prepare an

address to the people of Texas, & they would be glad if you would suggest any other mode of action by the Committee in furtherance of the object of their appointment. The general impression seems to be, that it would be best to merge our operations in those of the democratic party, inasmuch as the election of the democratic candidates for the Presidency [James K. Polk] & Vice-Presidency [George M. Dallas] seems to us the most efficient means at this time of promoting the annexation of Texas; & the Committee, being embar-[r]assed in this respect, by their original appointment, which was by a public meeting of the Citizens "without distinction of parties," we see nothing that we can do which would be useful, & fear that any movement might embar[r]ass the election.

As I am writing I will take the opportunity to say, that some symptoms have recently been exhibited here, & elsewhere, of a disposition to agitate the ["mode" *canceled and* "subject" *interlined*] of resistance to the tariff, by nullification, or other State action, Southern Convention, & the like; and this disposition has received some (perhaps unintentional) countenance from the answers of our representative Mr. [Isaac E.] Holmes to certain inquiries propounded to him through the newspapers. My opinion is that this feeling meets with no sympathy from the great majority of Mr. Holmes constituents; & I think I might venture to say with confidence that 9/10ths of the democratic party in Charleston, are of opinion, that sound policy & good faith both require, that for the present we should confine our attention to the election of Mr. Polk, & Mr. Dallas; & that all agitation of modes of resistance, although professedly with a view to future action only, are exceedingly unwise & pernicious, tending to impair the success of our efforts for the election of these gentlemen, to put in question our good faith in relation to the pledges we gave when we accepted their nomination, & finally to render more difficult, & less probable, that union among the Southern States, from which alone any effectual & beneficial relief can be expected from the evils we labor under. Under these circumstances measures I think will be taken to set the party here right, in so far as its position may be misunderstood in consequence of Mr. Holmes letter; but as union among ourselves is all important we shall endeavor to have the correction made by Mr. Holmes himself. We are so accustomed however to find wisdom in your views & success in your recommendations, that I should be very glad, if you could spare the time, to favour us with your suggestions as to the course which it is adviseable for us to pursue in the present state of affairs. With great respect Your Ob[e]d[ien]t Serv[an]t, H. Bailey.

468

[Enclosure]
Andrew Jackson to Col. Ja[me]s Gadsden

Hermitage, July 19, 1844

My Dear Sir, Your favor from the City of Washington D.C. of the 8th inst. has been received and duly considered. I have wrote to Gen[era]l [Samuel] Houston as strong a letter as I was, in my feeble health capable of doing, & hope it may have the desired effect. Was I with him I am sure, I could stimulate him to resist both British and French influence. But I am, and have been fully apprised of the depressed situation of Texas and made use of the strongest language in my letter to A[aron] V. Brown [Representative from Tenn.], "that the golden moment to regain Texas must not be lost, or we may lose her altogether, or have to take her at the point of the bayonet" which will cost us oceans of blood & millions of dollars—and in order to open the eyes of some of my friends in the Senate, I enclosed an extract of a confidential letter from the highest functionaries of Texas, stating the real situation of Texas—that in case of a rejection by the United States, Texas would have to look to England and France for relief &c &c. Therefore some of the Senators who profess to be warmly in favor of reannexation voted against the treaty with all this information before them.

The speeches of the Whig Senators in congress and their Assurance to the Mexican Minister [Juan N. Almonte], that the treaty would be rejected, were well calculated to rouse Gen. Santa Anna to again raise money and threaten the invasion of Texas. This under the advice of England will be done to alarm Texas and to induce her to come into the measures of France and England, and may have the effect to compel Texas, rather than to be conquered, to make the arrangement with England and France. The last accounts from Mexico are, for the raising of a large army to invade Texas[,] the General appointed[,] and his requisition 30,000 men and three millions of dollars. To prevent this invasion, what ought, or can the United States do. Something must be done or Texas is irretrievably gone, either conquered, or under the protection and guidance of England and France. This will require energy in the President [John Tyler]— the President ex officio being charged *to see the laws faithfully executed.* The treaty of 1803 with France lay the United States under certain obligations to the people inhabiting Louisiana, Texas being a part. This treaty is the supreme law of the land, and in future treaties by the United States the consent of France, and the people of Texas not given could [not] be binding, but must be received, as a nul[l]ity, and altho Texas became part of the Mexican Confederation under their Constitution of 1824 that Confederation by usurped power & despotism was put down, and the attempt to coerce Texas into that measure Texas resisted. The battle of San Jacinto made her independent; her first act after this, was to demand to be annexed to the United States. To have taken her into the Union was what our national faith was bound to do, by the Treaty of 1803; and now under that treaty, which is still the supreme law of the land, our national honor is bound in good faith to protect them in their rights, liberty and religion, and no further treaty by the United States with any other power can exonerate the United States from this solemn obligation. Here is the stand I would now take with Mexico, and the whole world, and notify Mexico that an invasion now before Congress had acted finally upon the subject would be resisted as a violation of the obligations of the Treaty with France of 1803 ceding the country to the United States. This would be a bold but righteous move under the treaty of 1803; one that could be well sustained under every principle of well settled international law, and would now be sustained by the whole democracy of the Union. If Texas is not sustained by some bold move of the United States, she will, nay must succumb to this threatened invasion by Mexico. This will be secretly councilled by Great Britain. Had I strength, I think I could clearly show that the rights secured to the inhabitants of Texas under the Treaty of cession to us by the treaty of 1803 are still obligatory on the United States, and the inhabitants of the ceded Territory has done no act to forfeit those vested rights, and having demanded admission, we are bound to receive her, and protect her in her rights, liberties and religion as altho she never had been ceded to Spain. Was I now at the head of the Executive Department of the Government, this is the ground I would assume, and act on, viewing treaties with Spain and Mexico as nullities, and of none effect, and could not be without the consent of France, and particularly the citizens inhabiting the territory ceded to us. Ours is a much stronger claim than Mexico ever had to Texas.

You can ponder these crude ideas, consult with your learned friends, and if you find substantial ground in them to fix our ebenezer upon, you can arrange, and give them to Mr. Calhoun whose capacious mind will grasp them and present them to the Executive for consideration. *Something must be done to keep up the drooping spirits of the Texans, until our election is over or she may resign herself, into the net set for her by England and France.* What must the curses be, I say, loud & strong, that must fall upon those Senators who have sacraficed ["their" *altered to* "the"] safety and best interests of our country, by voting against the Treaty to obtain for Mr. [Henry] Clay the abolition votes of the north and east. The Key to our future safety happiness and prosperity being presented to us in peace and honor, to be rejected by an American Senate shews the deepest kind of treachery to the best interests of our country.

The whole democratic States ought to hold meetings and instruct by resolutions their Senators and representatives to vote for speedy re-annexation of Texas, and the Legislatures that may be in session— and if it is true that Mexico is providing a large army to invade Texas, Congress should be called, our democratic members prepared with a law based upon the treaty of 1803 to receive the Texans into the Union, and to protect and defend them agreeable to the stipulations of the Treaty ceding it by France to the United States. But my dear Gadsden, I must close; it has been a severe task to write thus much. My shortness of breath since I had the pleasure of seeing you, has increased with great costiveness and of course debility. Let me hear from you. The political horizon is brightening here, and is bright every where, as far as heard from friends sanguine every where. Keep up the Texean feeling, and we may yet save Texas from the jaws of the Lion. Present me and my family's respectfully to Mrs. [Susanna Hort] G[adsden] and receive yourself our best wishes, your friend Sincerely, signed, Andrew Jackson.

ALS with En in ScCleA; variant PC in Boucher and Brooks, eds., *Correspondence*, pp. 241–242. NOTE: An AEU by Calhoun reads "Mr. Bailey[,] Enclosing Gen[era]l Jackson's letter to Col. Gadsden."

To R[ichard] K. Call, [Governor of Fla. Territory], Tallahassee, 7/30. "I have the honor to inform you that, at the request of Messrs. Samuel S. Sibley and James D. Westcott[,] Ju[nio]r, of Tallahassee, I have furnished them with a Copy of such portions of the papers transmitted by you to this Department as affect the official character of Mr. Charles S. Sibley, and with the names of the signers." FC in DNA, RG 59 (State Department), Domestic Letters, 34:316 (M-40:32); PC in Carter, ed., *Territorial Papers*, 26:936.

From Isaac Chase, U.S. Consul, Cape Town, 7/30. He encloses "a rough sketch of the Island of Ichaboc." This island is a very good place for procuring guano, and Chase recommends that U.S. whalers take a cargo of guano and thus the owners of the whalers can make a double profit. The prohibition on importing salted beef, pork, fish, and oil has been removed; whalers could therefore sell their oil in Cape Town if they so desired. LS (No. 94) with En in DNA, RG 59

(State Department), Consular Despatches, Cape Town, vol. 3 (T-191:3), received 1/13/1845.

From F[RANKLIN] H. ELMORE

Charleston, July 30, 1844

My Dear Sir, Mr. [John] H[e]art goes to Washington & I had intended to write to you very fully by him, but I have been away until a few days since & have had so much to do that I could not be as full as I desired. I must only sketch.

First. I found on my return a very fermented feeling—a fretful temper—disposed to commence agitation & carry it to the point of immediate resistance to the Tariff. I think I have had the good fortune to change the feeling & perhaps directed it more safely. At any rate our friends are by no means so impetuous. If you could find time to give some of us ["such" *canceled*] a letter containing your views in such a shape that we could show it, it would perhaps be well. The idea is industriously urged by the Whigs here under the lead of [Richard] Yeadon[']s paper (the Courier) that your opinions have undergone a change as to State action, as a principle—and that your views are against action of the State, at any time & under any circumstances. I would suggest that a word or two from you on this point would be well at this time.

Col. [Louis T.] Wigfall of Edgefield was here a few days ago. He is very excited & represents his District as equally so—that [George] McDuffie & [Armistead] Burt are equally so—and that since [James K.] Polk[']s unlucky letter he thinks they will break all bounds, denounce him & begin agitation for immediate action by the State. I can hardly think so. Wigfall is himself too much inclined for such a course to be a good judge of what others think. Still I mention these things that you may judge what is best & if you think advisable advise with them. The ground of our Legislature in 1842 is strong & it is perfectly consistent with it that we wait the events depending on the coming election.

I rec[eive]d a letter from Col. [Francis W.] Pickens this morning on the subject of the trip to Nashville. He can go & I wrote immediately to urge him to do so. It is impossible for me to do so. I never regretted more my inability to do any thing—but my private affairs are in such a condition, in connexion with our [Nesbitt] iron works company that it is impossible for me to go there. [Former] Gov.

472

[Pierce M.] Butler whose time is limited here, has arranged for settling our business & it is of such a pressing, paramount nature, that I cannot avoid the appointment. Mr. McDuffie will I fear not be able to go. His health is much impaired & his Physicians advise quiet.

I will write you more fully in a few days, of what is doing. Very truly Yours, F.H. Elmore.

ALS in ScCleA; PEx in Boucher and Brooks, eds., *Correspondence*, pp. 242–243. NOTE: An AEU by Calhoun reads: "Mr. Elmore[,] On political subjects."

From BEN E. GREEN

Legation of the U.S. of A.
Mexico, July 30th 1844

Sir, I have the honor to send you the finale of the correspondence about the Tabasco affair. The subject now goes to the French and Spanish ["Govts." *interlined*], & there is little room to doubt what will be their course. You will see, by the note of the British Minister, that an Irishman has also been shot first and tried afterwards. Mr. [Charles] Bankhead has information that this man was engaged by [Francisco] Sentmanat to go to Tabasco, to work upon his plantations as a carpenter, and that he knew nothing of Sentmanat's revolutionary purposes. It is strange that I have received no communication from our consul in Tabasco [Edward Porter] upon the subject. I have written to him for information, but have as yet received no answer.

I send you (nos. 1 & 2), a note [of 7/24] to the Minister of Foreign Relations, protesting against the failure to pay the indemnity; and his reply [of 7/27].

I send you also the Diario del Gob[iern]o, of the 27th of July, containing a decree, relating to passports. I beg leave particularly to call your attention to the 8th art., by which fugitive slaves are invited to Mexico, and taken under the protection of the Mexican Govt. The Diplomatic Corps are to have a meeting tomorrow, to take this decree into consideration. I will inform you immediately of the result.

On dit, that in a few days Santa Anna will resign the "*Constitutional Presidency*," and that there will be a *pronunciamento* to make him Dictator, and to do away with the Congress & the representative system. I mark in the newspapers whatever is worth your attention. I have the honor to be Very Respectfully, Your ob[edien]t Serv[an]t, Ben E. Green.

P.S. In the Diario of the 27th July, is a report from the Minister of Hacienda to the Congress, a curious document, in which Santa Anna very modestly asks to be empowered to *levy taxes*, as he may think useful and proper. Ben E. Green.

ALS (No. 15) with Ens in DNA, RG 59 (State Department), Diplomatic Despatches, Mexico, vol. 12 (M-97:13), received 8/25; FC in DNA, RG 84 (Foreign Posts), Mexico, Despatches; draft in NcU, Duff Green Papers (published microfilm, roll 5, frames 705–706); PEx with Ens in Senate Document No. 81, 28th Cong., 2nd Sess., pp. 16–17; PEx with Ens in House Document No. 144, 28th Cong., 2nd Sess., pp. 16–17. NOTE: In his letter of 7/24 to Jose Maria Ortiz Monasterio, Acting Mexican Minister of Foreign Affairs, Green protests the failure of the Mexican government to pay the April 30 instalment due to the U.S. under their Jan. 31, 1843 Convention with Mexico. Monasterio states in reply on 7/27 that Green's letter was referred to the Treasury Department whose response will be forwarded when received.

From BEN E. GREEN, "Private"

Legation of the U.S. of A.
Mexico, July 30th 1844

D[ea]r Sir, That you may know what the diplomatic corps in Mexico think of [Francisco] Sentmanat's expedition, and the Tabasco tragedy, I send you ["the" *canceled*] a copy of a note to Mr. Oliver, the Spanish Minister, & his reply. As this was a private note to me, I send it to you in a private letter. I do not wish it to find its way into the newspapers. Very truly Your ob[edien]t Serv[an]t & friend, Ben E. Green.

Mr. Green to Mr. Oliver.

D[ea]r Sir, I have just received files of the N.O. papers. In the N[ew] O[rleans] Picayune, of the 15th June, and 9th July, I meet the following

(Extracts)

It seems from this that the assertion made by the Mexican Govt. and press, that this affair was publicly known in N.O. before Sentmanat sailed, is false. It also appears from the declaration of one Bernard Othon, published by the Mexican Govt., that the Mexican Consul in N.O. was himself an aider and abettor, an accomplice, if not an instigator of this expedition. I trust that Mr. Arrangois will be able to prove the falsehood of this Othon's declaration, & thus wash his hands

of the disgraceful and almost criminal connivance, attributed to him, by the Mexican Govt., in this transaction. Yours truly, Ben E. Green.
Mr. Oliver to Mr. Green.

Monday, 29th July
My dear Sir, I thank you for the extracts from the Picayune Journal that you had the goodness to send me by your much esteemed letter of this morning.

I join with you in the opinion that all this horrible ["transaction" *canceled*] affair has been connived at, if not excited by the agents of this Government, in order to get rid of Sentmanat. Yours very truly, P.P. de Oliver.

ALS in ScCleA.

From C. F[REDERICK] HAGEDORN

Philadelphia, July 30th 1844
Sir, I take the liberty of applying to Your Excellency in behalf of the Bavarian Government, who are very anxious to receive all possible information, in regard to Canal Steam Navigation; which they intend to introduce on the new Canal which unites the River Danube with the Rhein. My request to Your Excellency is therefore, that you will have the graet courtesie to cause such information to be given to me, that would enable me to convey the most minute information in regard to the application of Mr. [William W.] Hunter[']s propeller, & Machinery ("which according to what I have le[a]rned from people capable of judging is the best adapted for Canal Navigation") to the Government of Bavaria.

The desire of introducing all useful and practicable inventions of this country on the Continent of Europe, where they are sure of being duly appreciated, will I trust plead an appology for the liberty I have taken in ad[d]ressing Your Excellency. I remain with the highest regard Your Excellency[']s very obedient Servant, C.F. Hagedorn, Bavarian Consul.

LS in DNA, RG 59 (State Department), Notes from Foreign Consuls, vol. 2 (M-664:2, frames 397–399); CC in DNA, RG 45 (Naval Records), Letters from Federal Executive Agents, 1837–1886, 7:31 (M-517:2, frames 471–473).

From T[ILGHMAN] A. HOWARD

City of Houston, Texas
July 30 1844

Sir, I came from Galveston to this city yesterday, and in addition to the melancholy contents of my letter of the 27th it is now my painful duty to ["announce" *canceled*] communicate the death of Col. [Archibald M.] Green, our consul at Galveston. He died on the 28th of yellow fever.

It is very important that a successor be appointed at an early day. With great respect I remain Your very ob[e]d[ien]t servant, T.A. Howard.

ALS in DNA, RG 59 (State Department), Diplomatic Despatches, Texas, vol. 2 (T-728:2, frame 373), received 8/23; autograph copy in DNA, RG 84 (Foreign Posts), Texas.

To R[OBERT] M. T. HUNTER, [Lloyds, Va.]

State Dept., 30th July 1844

My dear Sir, I would be much gratified to have it in my power to contribute to meet Mr. [Washington] Greenhow's wishes. I highly appreciate his worth & qualifications, & the strength of his claims on myself & party; & yet I can scarcely venture to hold out any hope either to him or his friends.

The claims on the part of Mr. [John] Tyler's political & personal friends ["on him" *interlined*] are pressing; and it is naturally to be expected, that he would give them a preference, especially as many of them have had their expectations excited for a long time. It is difficult under such circumstances to press any one ["of my friends" *interlined*] on him successfully however great his qualifications. Acting, as I suppose, under the force of the circumstances alluded to, he makes most of his appointments on his own responsibility without consulting the appropriate Department. This, however, is in strict confidence.

What I have said goes on the supposition, that there may be a vacancy of the place of chargé [d'Affaires]. I have no reason to think, that will be the case shortly; and if there should be one, there can be no outfit till one is voted by ["the Senate" *canceled*] Congress at the next session; so that on the whole, the prospect is not enycouraging [*sic*].

The idea, that Texas will afford as many ["slave" *canceled and* "non" *interlined*; slave] holding States, as slave holding is perfectly idle. The Southern boundary of the U. States, in that quarter, is the Arkansaw river, west of the 100th longitude, from London. The compromise line is the 36th latitude. The part of Texas north of it is a small zone of worthless land. [Thomas H.] Benton was so conscious of it, that his proposition was to form two non slave holding States, lying west of the Two eastern to be slave holding, & to be extended quite down to the Gulf [of Mexico]. [Robert J.] Walker & others of our friends here, who attend to the progress of events, as connected with the election, are very sanguine of the success of [James K.] Polk & [George M.] Dallas. They count 11 States as certain for them & not more than 4, or 5, or 6, at the utmost, for [Henry] Clay. Of the 11 they do not include Louisiana, Georgia, Tennessee[,] Indiana, N.C.[,] Maryland, or New Jersey. I think the result doubtful; but if we are defeated Benton[,] [Martin] V[an] B[uren] & [Silas] Wright are the responsible party.

There has been a very respectable review of my volume of Speeches in the Democratick [Review] already. I doubt, whether it would publish another. Would ["it" *interlined*] not be better to publish your Nephew's [Muscoe R.H. Garnett's] in the Southern Literary Messenger? The point to make a favourable impression is Virginia. I would rather have her support, than any three in the non slave holding. Yours truly, J.C. Calhoun.

[P.S.] If it should be published in the Messenger I would be obliged to your Nephew to send me a number containing it. J.C.C.

ALS in ScCleA; PEx in Jameson, ed., *Correspondence*, pp. 602–603.

From Nathaniel McLean, Cincinnati, 7/30. He has heard that the office of the First Auditor has been made vacant by the death of the incumbent. McLean asks Calhoun to place McLean's name before President [John] Tyler as an applicant for the position. The President is acquainted with McLean, and, for that reason, McLean submits no recommendations; if necessary, however, they will be forwarded immediately. ALS in DNA, RG 59 (State Department), Applications and Recommendations, 1837–1845, McLean (M-687:21, frames 426–428).

From Stewart Newell, U.S. Consul at Sabine, Galveston, 7/30. He asks that he be appointed U.S. Consul at Galveston, an office that was promised to him in 1838 before the appointment of E[lisha] A. Rhodes. Newell feels that his experience as Consul at Sabine, his

knowledge of the Galveston Consulate, and the promise earlier referred to all entitle him to the appointment he requests. ALS in
DNA, RG 59 (State Department), Applications and Recommendations, 1837–1845, Newell (M-687:24, frames 140–143), received 8/23;
ALS (Duplicate, No. 21) in DNA, RG 59 (State Department), Consular Despatches, Texas, vol. 1 (T-153:1), received 11/23.

To President [JOHN TYLER]

Department of State
Washington, 30th July 1844
D[ea]r Sir, I have the honor to forward to you several papers of late
date renewing the application in behalf of [John] McDaniel and
[Joseph] Brown, who unless pardoned or reprieved will be hung at
St. Louis, on the 16th proximo. I also send copies of counter testi-
mony recently received here. These documents will enable you to
form a judgment as to the propriety of commuting their sentence.

As a mere measure of precaution to enable me to carry into effect
your decision, *should it be favorable* to the prisoners—but not as
indicating any opinion in the case—I enclose a blank sheet to be
signed by you, *in the event*, and returned to this Department, to be
subsequently prepared and transmitted to the United States Marshal
for the district of Missouri upon the receipt of the usual direction.
I have the honor to be dear Sir, Your Obedient Serv[an]t, John C.
Calhoun.

FC in DNA, RG 59 (State Department), Domestic Letters, 34:318 (M-40:32).

To John B. Williams, U.S. Consul, Bay of Islands, [New Zealand],
"now at Salem, Mass.," 7/30. In reply to Williams's letter of 7/22,
the State Department has no objection to Williams's suggestion that
his consular residence be moved from Bay of Islands to Auckland,
but to accomplish this, Williams's old commission must be revoked
and a new one issued. In the interest of trade with the Fiji Islands,
Calhoun wishes Williams to appoint David Whippy to be a Consular
Agent at Levuka, "on the Island of Ovelon [*sic*; Ovolau]." FC in
DNA, RG 59 (State Department), Consular Instructions, 11:265–266.

From FERNANDO WOOD, [U.S. Despatch Agent]

New York [City,] July 30, 1844
Dear Sir, Information has been communicated to me of the intention of the two Mexican Steamers now in this harbour to ship 200 Seamen, and that some preparatory arrangements for that purpose have been made to effect that object. It being contrary to the laws of nations &c. for one nation to allow the ships of war of another to recruit men for hostile purposes against a nation with which it is on terms of peace—and as those Mexican steamers evidently desire those men to be used against Texas I have felt it my duty to inform you of the facts.

I am in possession of the facts in this case and can take effectual means to prevent it, if so empowered or desired by the authorities. Very truly &c, Fernando Wood.

ALS in DNA, RG 59 (State Department), Miscellaneous Letters (M-179:105, frames 103–105). NOTE: A Clerk's EU's indicate that this letter was received and answered on 8/2.

From D. C. CAMPBELL

Macon Geo[rgia,] July 31st 1844
Dear Sir, I have been requested by the gentlemen whose names are attached to the enclosed invitation and by several other of the prominent Democrats of this vicinity urgently to request your acceptance of it. The meeting will unquestionably be large. From 15 to 30,000 are expected. The present Whig Party of Georgia, the former nullifiers of the State[,] are urging upon their opponents the charge of disunion in consequence of their devotion to the cause of Annexation of Texas to the American Union. It is impossible to foretell what will be the result of this effort.

It is in your power to a greater extent than any other to arrest it. Your presence here on that occasion is also desirable for several other reasons. If it be possible will you be with us? You will receive a most cordial welcome. Be pleased to let us hear from you at your earliest convenience[.] Respectfully Y[ou]r ob[edien]t Ser[van]t, D.C. Campbell.

[Enclosure]
From H[enry] G. Lamar and Others
Macon, Geo[rgia], July 30, 1844
Dear Sir: It has been determined by the Democracy of this [Bibb

County] and several of the contiguous counties, to hold a State Mass Convention in this City, on Thursday, the 22d day of August next. From the central position of this place, the facilities of access to it, and the deep interest which the momentous questions involved in the pending Presidential canvass, have excited in the public mind, it is expected the assemblage will be unsurpassed by any that has been heretofore convened in the State.

To you, it need not be said, a crisis has arrived in the affairs of our country, which should call into exercise, the talents, the intelligence, the wisdom, and the firmness of every friend of constitutional liberty. We beg leave, then, respectfully and urgently, to invite you to be present on that occasion, to participate in the deliberations and counsels of the Convention; and there to lend your aid in the maintenance of those great Democratic Principles which alone can secure the perpetuity of the Union and the purity of its Republican institutions. With great respect and regard, We are your Obedient Servants, H.G. Lamar, James Smith, John Lamar, S[amuel?] M. Strong, W[illia]m Green, A[bner] P. Powers, D.C. Campbell, Committee of Invitation.

ALS with En (printed circular) in ScCleA. NOTE: An AEU by Calhoun reads: "Invitation to a mass meeting at Macon Georgia."

From RICH[AR]D S. COXE

New York [City,] July 31, 1844

Sir, Since my arrival at this place my friend and connexion Mr. John Warren has received a letter from his brother in law Mr. [John A.] Robinson, who has for many years resided at Guaymas on the Western Coast of Mexico. He writes that he has suffered heavy losses recently from the illegal seizure of his property by the Mexican General [José] Urrea, and that although part of it has been restored through the exertions of General [Waddy] Thompson still he is a heavy loser. Mr. R[obinson] is the American Consul at Guaymas & probably your Department may contain a statement of the case and of the proceedings of Gen[era]l Thompson in relation to it. These arbitrary and lawless proceedings of Mexican functionaries are the fruitful source of difficulties between the two governments and strong and energetic measures should be adopted to prevent and redress them. It is not in my power to give you a detail of the injuries inflicted in this instance upon the rights of an American Citizen, nor unless you are already in possession of this information can I ask you to do more than to give Mr. [Wilson] Shannon instructions to afford Mr. Robinson such aid, and to appeal to the Mexican government in such terms as he shall after full inquiry into the facts think expedient & proper.

You will oblige me very much if you will in your next despatch to Mr. Shannon draw his attention to this case in an especial manner. Very respectfully Yours &c, Richd. S. Coxe.

ALS in DNA, RG 59 (State Department), Miscellaneous Letters (M-179:105, frames 114–116).

To G[EORGE] M. DALLAS, Philadelphia

Department of State
Washington, 31st July, 1844

Sir: I have the honor to acknowledge the receipt of your letter of the 26th instant upon the subject of Mr. Jacob Idler's claim against the Venezuelan government.

It appears from the letters hitherto addressed to him by this Department and to the representatives of the United States at Caracas, that as the claim originated in a contract with that government, it has been deemed inexpedient and contrary to the uniform policy of this Government to engage in an official negotiation upon the subject. There is, however, reason to apprehend from the course of the Venezuelan government in regard to other cases, that no amicable negotiation would have hastened a favorable result. Consequently, although I sympathize in the privations to which Mr. Idler has been subjected, I see no way in which he may expect relief unless some general arrangement for the adjustment of all the old claims on Colombia and the States of which it was composed, could be made. I have the honor to be, Sir, Your obedient servant, J.C. Calhoun.

LS in ScU-SC, John C. Calhoun Papers; FC in DNA, RG 59 (State Department), Domestic Letters, 34:319–320 (M-40:32).

From R[OBERT] M. HAMILTON

Consulate of the United States
Montevideo, July 31st 1844

Sir, I have the honor to transmit herewith, the Half Yearly Returns, and Statement of Fees, of this Consulate, from the 1st January to 30th

June present year, inclusive, and also those of my Consular Agent at the Port of Maldanado, in blank, there having been no Arrivals to, or departures from, that Port, in consequence of its being closed by the Order of General [Manuel] Oribe, Commander in Chief of the Argentine Army, who at present occupies the place.

This City is Besieged as heretofore by the Forces of Governor [Juan Manuel de] Rosas, whereby the produce of the Country is completely cut off; Provisions from the United States are frequently arriving, and fully supply the Market, the returns, (in Specie) are remitted to Buenos Ayres, for the purchase of Hides, Wool & & & & for the United States, and thus the Metal[l]ic Currency is gradually withdrawn from this place.

The Argentine Blockading Squadron have recently prohibited the Fishermen from supplying the City, and have thus cut off, in the absence of fresh Beef, a very essential article of support.

The Government are about raising Funds by additional taxes, one of which, on Doors, & Windows, will no doubt place a large Amount at its disposal monthly, and from all appearances, another six months continuance of the present state of this disastrous War, may be anticipated. The U.S. Ship "Boston" is near this port, Officers, and Crew, all well.

I am happy to state, that our political relations with the Belligerents in this quarter, continue to be on the most amicable footing, and that our Citizens located in this Territory, observe the strictest Neutrality. I have the honor to be Sir with the utmost respect, Your very Obedient Servant, R.M. Hamilton, United States Consul.

ALS (No. 90) with Ens in DNA, RG 59 (State Department), Consular Despatches, Montevideo, vol. 4 (M-71:4), received 10/18.

From WILLIAM R. KING

Legation des Etats Unis
Paris, le 31st July 1844

Sir, In my first despatch I had the honor to state that I had requested and obtained the promise of an interview with Mr. [François P.G.] Guizot, the Minister of Foreign Affairs, for the purpose of conferring with him upon topics interesting to my government. A week or ten days having elapsed without hearing further from him, and being somewhat anxious to have an explicit understanding with him upon topics of no small importance, I reiterated my request in writing, whereupon the twentieth of July, was appointed for the desired interview. I commenced the conversation with Mr. Guizot by observing that I wished to confer with him upon a subject in which the government and people of the United States felt a deep interest—the annexation of Texas. I remarked that on my arrival here, I was met by rumors that the government of France had united with that of England in a formal protest against the proposed annexation; that, convinced that such a step did not comport either with the interests or policy of France, I had attached little or no importance to rumors so improbable, which I had even dismissed from my mind after the assurances, received in my conversation with the King, which I had the honor to communicate in my last and first despatch; that nevertheless subsequent information of a character and from a source, which I did not feel myself authorized altogether to disregard, had reached me, which had induced me, reposing entire confidence in the well-known frankness of His Majesty's government, to put an end to conjecture, by seeking information from a source upon which I could ["ent" *canceled*] altogether rely. With considerable animation if not some impatience, Mr. Guizot at once assured me that no such step as that referred to had been taken; that on this subject France had acted for herself and in connection with no other power; that the French government did, indeed, desire to see the independence of Texas maintained, but that I might be assured, its action whatever that might be would be entirely independent of that of England whose interests in relation to this question were different from those of France, which were purely commercial. I expressed my gratification at these assurances, remarking that a movement such as that which had been, I was happy to learn, erroneously imputed to the French government, would have seriously impaired the friendly, nay, I might also say affectionate feelings entertained for the French nation by the American people, a result which no one would have regretted more than myself. Mr. Guizot then observed, with evident allusion to the rejection of the Treaty by the Senate—"but the subject of annexation is at an end." I told him, at once, that I owed it to frankness to say, that I by no means considered it so; that public opinion was all-powerful in the United States, and that whoever might be called to administer the government, must be controlled by it; that, according to my belief, a large majority of the American people were in favor of the proposed annexation, not from a desire to obtain more territory, but from a pervading conviction that it was necessary to the security of the country. To his enquiry if this feeling was not confined to one of the great political parties, I replied—certainly not—though more general with that called the democratic. He then asked me if my government would be satisfied with a guarantee of the independence of Texas without conditions. To this query, I replied that I could give no assurances on this point, upon which I was not instructed, but that it was of such vital importance to us that no foreign power should obtain a preponderance in Texas, that we should view with great distrust any movement calculated to place that republic under foreign and particularly British influence; that, England, having once refused to unite with France and the United States to urge upon Mexico the acknowledgement of the independence of Texas, was a circumstance calculated to excite suspicion of her views and intentions. I added that Mexico was known to be very much under her control, and it was not to be disguised, that, whether impelled by that influence or not, the Mexican ["was"(?) *canceled*] Republic was hostile to the United States, and indeed, to France also; that so great had been the emigration to Texas from the British dominions, of late years, as to threaten, should it continue, to give, sooner or later, a predominating influence to ["the" *canceled*] England in that wide region, and I observed that he must see the necessity on our part of guarding against such control, for the security of the peculiar property of the South, to say nothing of the exposed situation of New Orleans, the great emporium and outlet of the West, should a hostile power spring up in its immediate vicinity. Leaving the subject of Texas Mr. Guizot enquired whether the slave population of the United States increased rapidly. I replied, more rapidly in proportion than the white, a proof that the slaves were well-["fed" *canceled*] treated, well-fed, and not overworked. He then asked if they seemed contented with their situation. I replied that a more contented and cheerful population of laborers did not exist either in Europe or America, and to this conclusion, every intelligent, inquiring and unprejudiced traveller had come. He made no comment upon this whereupon I rose and took my leave with the remark that I would communicate to my government the substance of the conversation which I had had the honor to hold with him, and which could not fail to prove highly satisfactory.

I will take this occasion to express my confidence that the course of the American government upon the important question which was the principal subject of my conference with Mr. Guizot, will not be influenced by rumors of dangers from abroad which do not exist, and which if they were real, it would be our true policy to face with a calm but firm aspect. However desirous France may be to see the independence of Texas preserved, her opposition, if assurances from the highest sources may be relied upon, will not assume ["a hos" *canceled*] an unfriendly attitude, nor will that of England proceed to the extremities which have been so fearfully paraded in certain quarters. However earnest her resistance to the annexation of Texas to the United States, and I am by no means disposed to underrate it, I have no idea that Great Britain will ["for this object," *interlined*] hazard the employment of any arms, besides those of diplomacy, a cheap instrument if it prove successful. I have been much gratified to find a healthy state of feeling upon this subject among our countrymen abroad of all parties, whose patriotism seems to expand as they recede from the sphere of domestic conflicts of opinion. They look upon this question as one involving considerations of national dignity and power, and they feel that it would be folly as well as weakness to be deterred from the right course by the frowns, the menaces, or even the hostile acts of any foreign power. This much I thought it my duty to say.

I transmit herewith a copy of a letter (A.) with its enclosures from [G. de Tschann] the Chargé d'Affaires of the Swiss Confederation, at this court, from which it appears that the Federal Directory, in the case of Gerard Koster, had already taken the steps requested in my application, upon the demand of [Seth T. Otis] the American Consul at Basle. A copy of my reply (B.) is also subjoined. I would suggest the propriety of instructing me to present to the government of Switzerland, through its representative in Paris, the thanks of the President for ["the" *canceled and* "its" *interlined*] prompt, honorable, and friendly action in this case, involving property of our citizens to so large an amount; as well as assurances of the disposition of the American government to reciprocate in every proper and practicable manner. The case of Koster gives an opportune character to the disposition expressed by the Federal Directory of the Swiss Confederation for the negotiation of a Convention for the mutual surrender of criminals between the two republics.

Koster has not yet been arrested, but the most active means have been employed to attain that object, with what prospect of success I have not the means of judging. I have received assurances from the French government, that proper steps will be taken for his arrest and detention should he take refuge in France. I have the honor to be very respectfully your obedient servant, William R. King.

LS (No. 2) with Ens in DNA, RG 59 (State Department), Diplomatic Despatches, France, vol. 30 (M-34:33), received 8/22.

From JOHN LAMAR

[Macon, Ga., July 31, 1844]

Dear Sir, Permit me most respectfully to join in the desire expressed by our friend Col. [D.C.] Campbell, that you will if possible attend the Mass Meeting, here. Your friends in Geo[rgia] are extremely anxio[u]s to see you & as you have never visited this section of Geo[rgia] a fit opportunity is now presented, in which your presence will add much to the interest of our meeting[.] Most Truly yours, John Lamar.

ALS in ScCleA. NOTE: This was written on the back of Campbell's letter of 7/31 to Calhoun. John Basil Lamar, a planter, had been briefly Representative from Ga. during 1843 and was killed in action with the Confederate army in 1862.

From Stewart Newell, [U.S. Consul at] Sabine, 7/31. He encloses a letter [of 7/21] from W[illia]m C.V. Dashiell, Collector of Customs at Sabine, "relative to the charges, contained in Affidavits, of J[ames] J. Wright & J[ames W.] Wood, against me," and asks that it be placed on file in the State Department. ALS (No. 22) with En in DNA, RG 59 (State Department), Consular Despatches, Texas, vol. 1 (T-153:1), received 8/23.

AUGUST 1–15, 1844

Ⅲ

A good deal of the Secretary's attention had to be devoted to routine official business. And a good deal also had to be devoted to the reading and sending of letters about the developments in South Carolina that were already national news as "the Bluffton movement." The raising anew of the idea of nullification, in the midst of an election campaign in which such important matters as Texas and the tariff were involved, was in Calhoun's view, inappropriate. He wrote on August 7 to a nephew by marriage in Abbeville: "It seems to me that this is the most unpropitious period, which could possible [sic] be selected to agitate the subject of seperate action. It is not possible, that it can do any good at present, & cannot but do harm. If it should be attempted it will prove an entire abortion, to the great injury of those concerned; to the State, & to the cause, and prevent the possibility of resorting to it [nullification] hereafter, when circumstances may be more favourable . . . ."

It was time to renew his campaign against British presumption to regulate the rights and morals of American slaveholders. For Calhoun, the defense of slavery and the defense of American rights and nationality were entirely coincidental. On August 7 he wrote at length to the U.S. Minister in London, providing the arguments to initiate a diplomatic refutation of the British refusal to deliver up indicted criminals who had escaped from the United States to their colonies when the fugitives were slaves. The President, on August 13, found this despatch to be "clearly right" and "well argued."

A second initiative was taken with a long despatch to the new American Minister to France, William R. King, on August 12. Here Calhoun outlined the American position on Texas and on British interference there, and laid bare for the other powers of the world the hollowness of British antislavery philanthropy, the end result of which could only be to destroy the most effective competitors for British colonial produce. The despatches to Everett and King "are both calculated to make a strong impression," Calhoun told his son-in-law.

◫

CIRCULAR Relating to Passports

Department of State
Washington, August, 1844

As citizens of the United States going to foreign countries, may be subjected to inconvenience for the want of sufficient evidence of their national character, the Secretary of State deems it proper to give notice that passports will be granted by him, *gratis*, to such citizens, on his being satisfied that they are entitled to receive them.

To prevent delay in obtaining a passport, the application should be accompanied by such evidence as may show the applicant to be a citizen of the United States, where that fact is not already known to the Department of State, and with a description of his person, embracing the following particulars, viz:

Age   years; stature   feet   inches; forehead   ; eyes   ; nose   ; mouth   ; chin   ; hair   ; complexion   ; face   .

When the applicant is to be accompanied by his wife, children, or servants, or females under his protection, it will be sufficient to state the names and ages of such persons, and their relationship to the applicant, as one passport may serve for the whole.

Certificates of citizenship, or passports granted by the different States and municipal authorities in the United States, are not recognised by the officers of foreign governments, and for the want of necessary official information as to those authorities, the ministers and consuls of the United States in foreign countries cannot authenticate such documents.

It is proper to add that persons who leave the United States without certificates or other evidence of their citizenship, expecting to be furnished with passports by the diplomatic agents or consuls of the United States, residing in the country to be visited, are always liable to be disappointed in obtaining them, as these documents are only properly granted on the faith of some evidence that the individuals in whose favor they are applied for, are entitled to them. Such testimony, it is sometimes difficult, if not impracticable, to procure among strangers; and it is therefore recommended to every citizen of the United States who purposes going abroad, to furnish himself, before leaving home, with the necessary passport.

PC in the Washington, D.C., *Madisonian*, August 28, 1844, p. 2; PC in the New York, N.Y., *Herald*, August 30, 1844, p. 1; PC in the Charleston, S.C., *Mercury*, September 4, 1844, p. 2.

From ALBERT M. GILLIAM

Cincinnati Oh[io,] August 1844

Sir, Having upon the twenty sixth day of July, in the year eight hundred and forty three received from his Excellency John Tyler, President of the United States the appointment of Consul of the United States of America for the Port of San Francisco in California Mexico.

And having duely in person at the City of Mexico through our resident Minister the Hon. W[addy] Thompson obtained the usual Exequatur of the Government of Mexico, of date the second of December eight hundred and forty three—I upon the eighth of January following took my departure from the City of Mexico for my destined post by an inland journey by the way of the citys of Largos, Zacatacas, Durango and Caneles, intending the Port of Mazetland [*sic*] on the Pacific Ocean as the port of my embarcation for San Francisco California.

But discovering by the time of my arrival at Caneles, a distance of two thousand miles from the City of Mexico, that in consequence of the continued internal wars of the Arpache and Camanche Indians with the Northern Departments of Mexico, as well as added to the almost insurmountable difficulty and dangers of traverling through a country of it self peopled by theaves and highway rob[b]ers prejudiced against American foreigners.

I therefor upon my arrival at Caneles having from that place an additional charge of two small children my nephews determined to returne to the United States, and accordingly upon the twelfe of July last, embarked from the port of Tampeco Mexico for the City of New Orleans La.—where I arrived upon the twen[ty] first of the same month—but not there having delayed longer than to pass from one Steamer to another—I have therefor, upon my arrival at Cincinnati taken the earliest opportunity of forwarding to your honour of the State Department of the United States, this my letter of resignation of the appointment of Consul at the port of San Francisco in California Mexico, of which I have had the distinguished honour of

489

receiving from his Excellency President Tyler—and to me it shall ever be a source of much regret that difficulties and change of condition so obtruded as to prevent my having rendered some service to my country.

Hoping that this my letter of resignation will suffice, I hope the liberty I have taken of retaining my Commission will be excused— but if that should be required, it shall with pleasure be forwarded, upon my having been informed of the demand on my arrival at my home of Lynchburg Virginia. I am Sir Very Respectfully Your Obedient Servant, Albert M. Gilliam.

ALS in DNA, RG 59 (State Department), Consular Despatches, Acapulco, vol. 1 (M-143:1). NOTE: Clerks' EU's read "Rec[eive]d Sep[tembe]r 2" and "Resignation accepted Aug. 1, 1844."

Thomas Baltzell, Tallahassee, [Fla. Territory], to President [John Tyler] and Secretary of State [John C. Calhoun], 8/1. Baltzell expresses his entire confidence in the integrity of Charles S. Sibley, U.S. District Attorney for Middle Fla. Baltzell hopes that the ridiculous charges preferred against Sibley will be speedily and completely disproved. ALS in DNA, RG 59 (State Department), Applications and Recommendations, 1837–1845, Sibley (M-687:30, frames 200– 201).

To John [J.] Brown[e], Paterson, N.J., 8/1. Calhoun informs Brown[e] that the attention of the government has already been called to the cases of U.S. citizens imprisoned in Cuba "and that further measures will be taken on the arrival of the minister [Angel Calderon de la Barca] recently appointed to the United States by the Spanish Government, who is expected shortly." FC in DNA, RG 59 (State Department), Consular Instructions, 10:258.

From John I. De Graff, [former Representative from N.Y.], 8/1. De Graff has heard that a new U.S. Marshal is to be appointed for the Western District of N.Y.; he therefore recommends Edward H. Walton for that appointment. Walton is very well qualified to fulfill the duties and is a very worthy Democrat whose appointment would gratify numerous friends of Calhoun. ALS in DNA, RG 59 (State Department), Applications and Recommendations, 1837–1845, Walton (M-687:33, frames 532–533).

From R[obert] C. Ewing, Richmond, Missouri, 8/1. He asks that he be considered for appointment as U.S. Marshal. The appointment offered by President [John Tyler] to W[illiam] C. Anderson was declined by that gentleman. Ewing was recommended by several members of the Missouri and S.C. Congressional delegations prior to Anderson's appointment, and Ewing calls these recommendations to Calhoun's attention. ALS in DNA, RG 59 (State Department), Applications and Recommendations, 1837–1845, Ewing (M-687:10, frames 364–366).

From A.P. Gibson, U.S. Consul, St. Petersburg, 8/1. He encloses his returns for the first half of 1844. The majority of vessels trading directly or indirectly from the U.S. to his post bring cargoes of sugar. Exports from Russia to the U.S. are diminishing and, in Gibson's opinion, will continue to do so until the trade between the two countries will be "of very trifling importance" to what it once was. ALS (No. 93) with Ens in DNA, RG 59 (State Department), Consular Despatches, St. Petersburg, vol. 6 (M-81:4), received 9/19.

From Jayme P. Inneranty, San Juan de los Remedios, [Cuba], 8/1. Inneranty asks that a U.S. Consulate be established at San Juan de los Remedios, formerly an agricultural district, but becoming more actively engaged in commerce every year. It will be useful to U.S. vessels trading with that country if a consulate is established there. He asks to be considered as an applicant for the position if a consulate is established. ALS in DNA, RG 59 (State Department), Applications and Recommendations, 1837–1845, Inneranty (M-687:17, frames 69–71), received 8/27.

From J[AMES] C. PICKETT

Legation of the U. States
Lima, Aug. 1st, 1844

Sir, No official notification of your having accepted the appointment of Secretary of State, has yet reached me; but as letters and newspapers received in this city, shew clearly that you have, it appears to be proper to address you as such.

The following is an extract of a letter dated at Panama, the 15th of April last and written by an intelligent British subject residing at that place:

"From the sudden interest shewn by the French Government

about the Isthmus, the natives are afraid France has views of seizing it, and indeed, taking into consideration, the line of packets established by the French Government between Callao and this, at an expense of 1300 dollars per month, when it is well known the French have no correspondence of any importance—the arrival of a French consul here and the claim made by the Chargé in Bogotá, who alleges the privilege of Messrs. Salomon & Co. to be still in force, notwithstanding the period stipulated for the work being finished, has expired without any thing whatever being done, and the evident desire of the French consul to pick ["a" *canceled and* "some" *interlined*] quarrel with the authorities—all these things look rather suspicious."

Whether the writer of this extract wrote in any degree, under the influence of anti-gallican prejudices or not, I am unable to say, not being acquainted with him. Be this as it may, however, it is undoubtedly true, that the attention of the French government has been attracted to the Isthmus, in a very remarkable manner, within the last twelve months.

For some time past, the utility and practicability of a ship-canal across the Isthmus to connect the two oceans, have been much discussed in England and in France, and the government of the latter sent two engineers some months ago, to make surveys and examinations with reference to artificial communications of all kinds. What the opinion of those engineers may be, I do not know; but my own is, that the idea of a ship-canal is at present, and will be, for a century to come, altogether chimerical and illusory. I do not consider the project to be achievable, at an expense of less than 25 or 30 millions of dollars; or that the canal, if made, would yield a reimbursing dividend, for [*three or four words canceled and* "a very long time," *interlined*] if ever. A different opinion seems to prevail however, in Europe, and many dissertations have been written, of late, to prove that the canal can be easily made—at a moderate cost, and that it would be of vast importance to the commercial world. But after having read the ablest of those publications, it appears to me that they emanate generally, from persons, who, however learned and ingenious they may be and well-informed in other respects, have but an imperfect knowledge of the Isthmus and of the intertropical regions of this continent, and of the many obstacles in the way of such an undertaking—(the construction of a ship-canal) the enervating climate, deluging rains, excessive heat, disease, the difficulty of procuring laborers, materials, supplies, &c. &c.

A ship-canal across the Isthmus will never be made, I think, by private individuals. The enterprise is too gigantic for private means, and those who embark in it in good faith, will lose their time and their money, in all probability. Two or three or more, opulent governments might unite and construct it, for the benefit of all mankind, and if it did not answer public expectation, the loss being divided among millions, would not be felt. But nations do not unite for such disinterested and beneficent purposes, and the idea of such a union would be still more chimerical, perhaps, than that of a ship-canal.

I am rather inclined to believe, that should its engineers recommend the construction of a canal or of a road merely, across the Isthmus, the French government is somewhat disposed to have the direction of the work, when in progress, should it be commenced, and the control of it, when completed. To accomplish this, it would only be necessary to take the Isthmus under its protection, as it has taken Tahiti. But the British government, which has its eye upon every spot on the globe, of any consequence, would not consent to a French occupation, I suppose, unless it were first agreed, that Great Britain might look where she pleased for an equivalent—to Cuba or the Californias, for instance.

It appears to me that the importance of the Isthmus of Panama, both commercial and political, has been in general, much overrated; but nevertheless, the occupation of it by a European power, whether as protector or as sovereign proprietor, would be, without doubt, prejudicial to the interests of the United States. I have the honor to be, with great respect, Sir, Your very Ob[edien]t Servant, J.C. Pickett.

ALS (No. 98) in DNA, RG 59 (State Department), Diplomatic Despatches, Peru, vol. 6 (T-52:6, frames 541–544), received 12/6.

To T[HOMAS] C. REYNOLDS, [Petersburg, Va.]

State Department, August 1, 1844

Sir: I duly estimate your motives for giving me the information you have; but the charge of being unfriendly to the Union, is so utterly unfounded, and so obviously circulated for mere electioneering purposes, that I cannot think it worthy of serious refutation on my part. The whole tenor of my long public life contradicts it, and every friend and acquaintance I have, knows it to be false. My life has been devoted to the service of the Union, and the constant and highest object of my ambition has been to preserve and perpetuate it, with our free, popular, federal system of Government.

But according to my opinion, justice, equity, and a strict adherence to the Constitution, are the bases of our Union, and they who most firmly maintain them, are its best and truest friends; and not those who most vociferously cry out disunion, and at the same time embrace those, who not only openly avow their opposition to the Union, but push, with all their zeal, measures, which they must know will, if successful, end in its destruction. With great respect &c., J.C. Calhoun.

PC (from the Petersburg, Va., *Republican*) in the Washington, D.C., *Spectator*, August 6, 1844, p. 3; PC in the Washington, D.C., *Daily Madisonian*, August 7, 1844, p. 2; PC in the Charleston, S.C., *Mercury*, August 8, 1844, p. 2; PC in the Charleston, S.C., *Southern Patriot*, August 8, 1844, p. 2; PC in the Norfolk and Portsmouth, Va., *American Beacon & Daily Advertiser*, August 9, 1844, p. 2; PC in the Milledgeville, Ga., *Federal Union*, August 13, 1844, p. 2; PC in the Richmond, Va., *Enquirer*, August 13, 1844, p. 2; PC in the Edgefield, S.C., *Advertiser*, August 14, 1844, p. 2; PC in the Raleigh, N.C., *North Carolina Standard*, August 14, 1844, p. 3; PC in the Anderson, S.C., *Gazette*, August 16, 1844, p. 3; PC in the Pendleton, S.C., *Messenger*, August 16, 1844, pp. 2–3; PC in *Niles' National Register*, vol. LXVI, no. 25 (August 17, 1844), p. 402; PC in the Columbus, Ohio, *Ohio State Journal*, August 20, 1844, p. 2; PC in the Camden, S.C., *Journal*, August 21, 1844, p. 2; PC in the Columbia, S.C., *South-Carolinian*, August 22, 1844, p. 2; PC in the Concord, N.H., *New-Hampshire Patriot and State Gazette*, September 9, 1844, p. 1; PC in the Jackson, Miss., *Southern Reformer*, September 14, 1844, p. 2.

To T[homas] M. Rodney, U.S. Consul, Matanzas

Department of State
Washington, August 1st 1844

Sir, The inclosed extract of a letter from [William H. Gardner] the Commander of the U.S. Brig Lawrence, addressed to the Secretary of the Navy[,] is transmitted to you with the request that you will inform this Department without delay whether any privaleges have been afforded to the subjects of Great Britain, or to the Citizens or subjects of any other power imprisoned at Matanzas which have been denied to Citizens of the U.S. If it be found that any such privaleges have been extended immediately demand in the name of this Government the extension of the same to our Citizens. I am &c, J.C. Calhoun.

FC in DNA, RG 59 (State Department), Consular Instructions, 10:258; transcript in DLC, Carnegie Institute of Washington Transcript Collection.

From GEO[RGE] M. BIBB, Secretary of the Treasury

Department of the Treasury, August 2d 1844
The note of the Chevalier [Johann Georg von] Hülsemann, the diplomatic representative of Austria, which you did me the honor to communicate, has been considered.

Treaties are to be observed and fulfilled, with the most Scrupulous good faith, according to their spirit, meaning & intent. The words of each contracting party are to be taken in all cases most strongly against him, & most favourably for the party contracted with, so that the essense of the treaty be not evaded, by adhering to the letter & sticking in the bark, by subtilities & refinements.

The treaty between the United ["States" *interlined*] and Austria concluded on the 27th day of August 1829 is the Supreme law of the land. In the ["proviso(?) to the" *canceled*] 5th paragraph of the 8th Section of the Act of the Congress of the United States, of the 30th August 1842, laying the duties upon wines it is provided "That nothing herein contained shall be construed or permitted to operate so as to interfere with Subsisting treaties with foreign nations."

The Congress therefore manifested the desire & intent to observe the treaty with Austria.

Instructions to the collector[s] of the customs, will be forthwith issued, to admit the wines of Austria imported, into the United States, in bottles, at fifteen cents per gallon. Very respectfully yours &c, Geo. M. Bibb, Secretary of the Treasury.

ALS in DNA, RG 59 (State Department), Miscellaneous Letters (M-179:105, frames 118–119); FC in DNA, RG 56 (Secretary of the Treasury), Letters to Cabinet and Bureau Officers, Series B, 4:430–431; CC in DLC, John G. Hülsemann Papers (Toner Collection).

To T[HOMAS] G. CLEMSON, [Philadelphia?]

Washington, 2d Aug[us]t 1844
My dear Sir, Nothing of importance has occurred since you left. I had a letter from Mrs. [Floride Colhoun] Calhoun. The sickness had abated, and all going on well. Yesterday I received one from Col. [Francis W.] Pickens. He had just heard from [your place,] the Canebrake. All were well & things going on well. They had fine

rains at the Village of Edgefield. To day I had one from John [C. Calhoun, Jr.], dated at Fort Desmoines. He gives a fine picture of the country around. His cough was better. Patrick [Calhoun] was unwell with chills & fever, but not severely. My cold is abated a good deal, & I hope to be clear of it in a few days. My general health is good.

I enclose you several letters.

I hope you found your Mother [Elizabeth Baker Clemson] & sister [Elizabeth Clemson Barton] & her family well.

I miss you, Anna & the children much, although I have had a good deal of company.

Jane informed me, that the stages refused to take the ticket you left her. I took it from her, & gave her $2.50 to take her by the rail road, as the stages had left. I enclose the ticket, though I presume it can be of no further use.

I again bid you ["all" *interlined*] farewell with my prayers for a safe & pleasant voyage, an agreeable residence abroad, and a safe return home.

You & Anna must not fail to write to me from N[ew] York [City]. Kiss the children for their Grandfather. Your affectionate father, J.C. Calhoun.

ALS in ScCleA.

From C[ALEB] CUSHING

Macao, 2 August 1844

Sir: I have the honor to remit to you herewith by the barque Sappho and the favor of Augustine Heard Esquire, one of the originals of the Treaty of Wang-Sheah, together with the Tariff, which is to be considered as annexed to and a part of the same.

The Treaty, as I informed the Department in my despatch of the 8th instant, numbered seventy two, was executed in English & in Chinese, four copies of each language, of which two were retained by Tsiyeng & two by myself. The distance of the United States from China—& the possibility of one of the copies being lost by perils of the sea on so long a voyage, dictated this precaution. And I shall embrace the best means which offer, by some other conveyance, to transmit to Washington the duplicate which remains in my possession, in the hope that one or the other may reach the President before the commencement of the next session of Congress. I am Very respectfully Your ob[edien]t Ser[van]t, C. Cushing.

ALS (No. 81) in DNA, RG 59 (State Department), Diplomatic Despatches, China, vol. 2 (M-92:3), received 12/6; slightly variant FC in DNA, RG 84 (Foreign Posts), China, Despatches, 5:125–126; PC in Senate Document No. 67, 28th Cong., 2nd Sess., p. 76; PC in the Washington, D.C., *Daily Madisonian*, April 3, 1845, p. 2.

From F[rancis] M. Dimond

United States Consulate
Vera Cruz, 2 Aug. 1844

Sir, I have the honour herewith to transmit several Documents from our Legation at Mexico and Consul at Mazatlan [John Parrott].

We have nothing new of Inter[e]st at this point. A French man of war arrived yesterday with the British mail from Havana—the British Steamer having met with a serious accident on a reef between this & Cuba.

Respectfully referring you to communications from Mr. [Ben E.] Green accompanying this I have the honour to be most Respectfully your Ob[edient] Serv[an]t, F.M. Dimond.

ALS (No. 231) in DNA, RG 59 (State Department), Consular Despatches, Veracruz, vol. 5 (M-183:5), received 8/25.

From Edward Everett

London, 2 August 1844

Sir, I duly received by the "Britannia," the steamer of the 16th ultimo, your despatches Nos. 96 and 97, making the series complete to the last number inclusive.

The general intelligence which will be conveyed to America by the steamer of the 4th is not without interest.

The operations of the French Army in Morocco are a matter of great anxiety to the French and English Governments. I lately had an interview with Lord Aberdeen in the course of which he stated to me, that he was satisfied with the reasonableness of the French demands on the Emperor of Morocco. Their precise nature I did not ask; they are represented to be, in general terms, satisfaction for the past and security for the future. The most difficult point is no doubt the last named. The indomitable chieftain Abd-el-Kadr, who has given the French so much trouble in Algeria has taken refuge in Morocco where he endeavors, by skilful appeals to the national fanaticism, to rouse the population to a general war against the European invaders. France does not demand that Abd-el-Kadr should be excluded from Morocco, but that if an asylum be granted to him, it should be in a part of the empire, where he cannot harrass the French possessions. It is doubtful whether the government of the Emperor is sufficiently strong, to enable him to carry into effect an agreement on this subject, even if he can be brought to feel the necessity of making one. Lord Aberdeen informed me, that the British Government had directed their Consul General, Mr. Drummond Hay to repair to the Emperor's residence, and to exhort him, in the most earnest manner, to comply with the demands of the French; and Sir Robert Wilson the Governor of Gibraltar crossed the straits some time since, no doubt to promote the same object.

The probability is that the Emperor of Morocco will undertake to do whatever is required of him; but it is by no means certain that he will be able to restrain his subjects. Many of the tribes which roam the desert in his dominions owe him but a nominal allegiance, and the ascendancy, which Abd-el-Kadr has acquired over the Musulmans of Algeria, may be extended to their brethren of Morocco. Should this take place, nothing is more likely or more consonant with the Oriental character and manners, than the subversion of the ruling dynasty and the founding of a new one in the person of this formidable chieftain. Such an event would be followed by a war with France of a most serious character and doubtful result. But it is useless to speculate at length on these contingencies.

Great sensibility has been excited here by the return to London of Mr. [George] Pritchard lately Consul at Tahiti, from which place he was removed to some other similar post in the Pacific, at the instance of the French Government, who took umbrage at his alleged interference with their proceedings in that quarter. It seems that before he had left Tahiti, at the moment of embarking he was arrested and confined by the French Commandant on a charge of being engaged in exciting the natives to revolt, and the islands themselves placed in a state of siege. Such is the general nature of the transaction, as related in the French and English papers, with great differences in detail and coloring, on the opposite sides of the channel. Mr. Pritchard succeeded in making his escape and is now here.

The affair has been the subject of explanation in both houses of parliament, and has been spoken of by Sir Robert Peel and Lord Aberdeen as an outrage on the part of French of a most serious character. As it occurred, however, under the temporarily assumed Sov[e]reignty over the Society Islands, which had already been disavowed by France, the means of adjustment are obvious without necessarily exciting the national sensibility.

Lord Aberdeen observed in the house of Lords last evening in making a statement on the subject, that though he was sure the French Government would regard the event, with as much concern as the English, "he could not but fear, that it will prove a godsend to the enemies of peace between the two countries, and he had no doubt but they would turn it to good account in forwarding their views."

Lord Aberdeen observed, in the course of our interview, that he thought the situation of Cuba very critical. The Governor General seems determined to give full scope to the Slave trade, and by that and other ways the population has been thrown into a state of general alarm and partial insurrection. I alluded to the apprehensions which existed in the minds of some persons, that the disorders in Cuba were stimulated by England, with an eye eventually to the possession of the island. Lord Aberdeen did not consider this imputation as needing a serious denial; and added that fortunately they had had it in their power to give to the Spanish Government very satisfactory proofs that they harbored no such designs.

Lord Aberdeen said that he was informed by Mr. [Richard] Pakenham that there seemed to be a disinclination at Washington to enter upon the discussion of the Oregon boundary question: that he was rather surprised at this, considering the manner in which the subject had been alluded to by the President in his communications to Congress; but that he felt himself no anxiety to urge the subject, if there was an indisposition to engage in the negotiation, on the part of the United States, and that he had written to Mr. P[akenham] accordingly. I am of course without instructions which enabled me to make any reply to these observations.

An attempt was made on the 26th July, to assassinate the King of Prussia [Frederick William IV], by firing at him with a pistol loaded with two balls, just as he was on the point of stepping into his carriage to start for Silesia. One of the balls slightly grazed the king's breast; the other passed within a few inches of the queen's head who was already in the carriage. It was an act of private revenge, on the part of an individual named Tscheck, formerly burgomaster of a small town called Storkow, and removed from that office for some misconduct.

The Overland mail from India has arrived with news from China to the 20th April. I have a private letter from Mr. [Caleb] Cushing of the 28th March; but as you can hardly fail to have later advices from him directly, I need not trouble you by repeating its contents. I see in the morning papers in an extract from the "Friend of China of April 20" the following statement:

"There is a report very currently circulating in Canton, that Keying is appointed Governor of the two Kwangs. The appointment is made in order, it is said, to prevent the French and American Missions proceeding north." I am, Sir, with great respect, Your obedient Servant, Edward Everett.

P.S. I was in an error in saying that Mr. Pritchard escaped from Tahiti. He was set at liberty by the French authorities, on the application of the Commander of an English Steamer, on condition of leaving the island.

LS (No. 171) in DNA, RG 59 (State Department), Diplomatic Despatches, Great Britain, vol. 53 (M-30:49), received 8/22; FC in DNA, RG 84 (Foreign Posts), Great Britain, Despatches, 8:366–373; FC in MHi, Edward Everett Papers, 49:481–488 (published microfilm, reel 23, frames 242–246).

From J[OSEPH] R. FLANDERS

Fort Covington [N.Y.], Aug. 2, 1844

Dear Sir, I notice in a New York paper, that the name of W[illiam] L. Mackenzie has been sent on to the Treasury Department, by Mr. [Cornelius P.] Van Ness, for an appointment in the Custom House at New York, but that in consequence of objections which have been interposed, his name has been withdrawn for the present.

I am personally acquainted with Mr. Mackenzie, and consider him an honest and deserving man. He has been unfortunate, it is true, and is now, with a large and dependent family, in necessitous circumstances; but that he is guilty of any crime, other than political, or of any moral delinquency, I have seen no cause to believe. He engaged in an attempt to free Canada from Colonial dependence, from honest and patriotic motives, as I am thoroughly convinced, and though he failed, and is outlawed by the British government, that circumstance will not, I am sure, to your just and discriminating mind, render conduct dishonorable and censurable, which success would have made praiseworthy and glorious. Mr. Mackenzie may have been imprudent, but that he was sincere and devoted, the steadfastness with which he has adhered to the cause in which he enlisted, the sacrifices which he he [*sic*] has made, and the sufferings which he has endured, conclusively prove. And though he may have done things which you cannot [*ms. torn; two or three words missing*] trust you will "pardon [*ms. torn; three or four words missing*] spirit of liber[*ms. torn.*]

The only objection which I have seen stated, to Mr. Mackenzie's receiving an appointment under the Federal Government, is that he is a British outlaw. Mr. Mackenzie is an American citizen and having been allowed to become such, it appears ["to me" *interlined*] that he is entitled to all the rights of citizenship, & that no difference ought to be made between him and other citizens, in appointments to office, provided he possesses equal or superior personal qualifications. And the fact that the British Government treats him as an outlaw, for a political offence, not impeaching his moral character, in the estimation of our government and people, should not be allowed to operate against his employment in official station. If we are to regard a British decree of outlawry in such a case, to the restriction of the rights of an American citizen, we in effect allow foreign laws and decrees to operate within our jurisdiction, upon those subject to our authority and under our protection. I think this as wrong in principle, as the doctrine that we have no right to treat with Texas for annexation, though independent in fact and by recognition, merely because Mexico obstinately claims Texas as a rebellious subject, whose allegiance she will persevere in demanding.

Mr. Mackenzie is a true friend of our form of government, and is ardently attached to those principles, as applicable to the construction of the Constitution, and the practical administration of its powers, for which you have so ardently contended. I saw him in New York [City] last summer, and had a lengthy and free conversation with him, in which he avowed himself a whole-hearted democrat, of the State Rights School, and [*ms. torn; one or two words missing*] admirer of yourself. I am aware that [*ms. torn; two or three words missing*]nstance will not influence you [*ms. torn; three or four words missing*] think it consistent with your duty to interest yourself in behalf of Mr. Mackenzie; and I only mention it, to satisfy you that I am not recommending to your attention an enemy to our institutions, or to the republican cause to which you are attached.

If you can reconcile it to your views of duty to promote the appointment of Mr. Mackenzie, should his name again be presented to the Treasury Department, you would, in my estimation, aid a worthy and competent citizen, and I need not assure you, that to me, and many other of your and Mr. Mackenzie's friends, it would be considered a personal favor, which would entitle you to our especial acknowledgments.

I am gratified that, in making this communication, I ask what it is in the power of a man to grant, whose character I esteem, and even venerate, as I do that of Judge [George M.] Bibb. The part he took as a Senator, in the South Carolina Controversy, has endeared him to me as one of the best men of our country, and whose name is still more cherished, with those of [George M.] Troup, [Littleton W.] Tazewell, and other choice and ["faithful" *canceled and* "devoted" *interlined*] spirits, who have kept the faith, from the fact that many of that spartan ["band," *interlined*] who resisted federal encroachment in 1832, are now, alas! in the ranks of the consolidationists, and foremost in sustaining those schemes of plunder which they had so gallantly resisted at the former period.

I owe you an apology for troubling you so often with my applications, but I trust the fact that I ask nothing for myself, And can be actuated by no selfish motive, will obtain for me your favorable consideration. I am, with the highest respect, Your obedient servant, J.R. Flanders.

ALS in ScCleA.

From [Jean Corneille, Chevalier] Gevers, Chargé d'Affaires of the Netherlands, New York [City], 8/2. Gevers requests a reply to his note of 6/14 to Calhoun inquiring if the Executive could take any action to remove the discriminating duty upon Java coffee. Gevers has learned that a U.S. duty on wines from Portuguese colonies has been removed because it violated treaties of reciprocity between the U.S. and Portugal. He hopes that the similar situation regarding Java coffee will be redressed. ALS in DNA, RG 59 (State Department), Notes from Foreign Legations, Netherlands, vol. 2 (M-56:2, frames 177–179).

From GEORGE R. GLIDDON, "Private"

Philadelphia, 2nd Aug[us]t 1844
Dear Sir, The kind and flattering approbation, which your confidential favor of the 28th ultimo bestows on my trifling labors, and the interest you express in respect to the progress of Hierological discoveries, prompt me to wait on you with the enclosed Boston Paper, as containing, in a short compass, the *latest* African results, entirely confirmatory of those doctrines you have so long sustained. By establishing that *Meroe*, in the fabled Ethiopia, is of very *modern* date (1500 years later than the *last* of some *40* Memphite Pyramids) [Karl Richard] *Lepsius* has captured the last stronghold of the *African* theorists—while his discoveries prove, that its civilization proceeded from *Caucasians*, from the remotest hour to the present day!

I am hard at work on a paper, that will throw some unexpected light on the "Cosmogony of *Moses*"; wherein I shall condense *new* views, at any rate, on Ethnography and Chronology. I think, that we can demonstrate, that the *Negro*, the *Malay*, the *Mongolian*, and the American *Indian*, Races of Man are entirely omitted in the Book of Genesis; although the three first Races are found on Egyptian Monuments, as existing *anteriorly* to Moses' day—the 15th Century B.C. while, without straining Scripture, we can show, that *Moses* never intended to speak of others than the grand divisions of the *Caucasian* Race—*symbolized* in "Shem, Ham and Japheth."

Of course I avail myself of the latest discoveries; and, if I cannot succeed in building a *Castle* I shall erect a Martello Tower that will survive a good deal of cannonading. When ready, in the course of this Autumn, I shall have the honor of submitting it to your consideration. In the interim, I shall not fail to forward anything *new* on ethnographical themes to me accessible, that may be worthy of your perusal.

I seize this opportunity to express my sincerest and most respectful sentiments of gratitude for the protection you vouchsafe to my pending petition to the State Department, and still more for the promptness, with which so much consolation was conveyed to, Dear Sir, with profound respect, Y[ou]r ob[e]d[ien]t & truly obliged Serv[an]t, George R. Gliddon.

ALS in ScCleA.

From ALLEN A. HALL

Legation of the United States
Caracas, August 2nd, 1844

Sir, Herewith you will receive a copy and translation of the note [of 7/13] which Mr. [Juan Manuel] Manrique, after a month's delay, addressed to me in reply to my communication to him of the 14th of June in relation to the failure of Congress to appropriate, at its last session, the sum agreed to be paid by the Government in the case of the Brig Morris. The Government, as you will observe from Mr. Manrique's note, strongly deprecates any interruption of the amicable relations subsisting between the two countries, and most confidently expresses the opinion that, Congress, when it meets again, in January next, will, at an early day thereafter, make the requisite appropriation. I am obliged to believe that the appropriation will be made accordingly; never the less, I think the Government of the United States ought to be prepared to blockade La Guayra immediately, in the event of its not being made at the next session of the Venezuelan Congress. As there appeared to be nothing in this last note of Mr. Manrique calling for reply from me, I contented myself with acknowledging its receipt and informing him that I would forward a copy for the consideration of my Government.

I am glad to be able to advise you that order and quiet continue to be maintained in this country, and that the elections, so far as heard from, have passed over without the occurrence of any of the anticipated popular outbreaks. The Government, however, deemed it expedient to concentrate several hundred troops in this City with a view to repress any attempt at revolution that might be made. The general result of the elections is yet unknown. It is believed that the party friendly to the Government have prevailed in almost all the provinces, though in the City of Caracas they sustained a signal defeat. I have the honor to be Very respectfully your ob[e]d[ien]t serv[an]t, Allen A. Hall.

ALS (No. 39) with Ens in DNA, RG 59 (State Department), Diplomatic Despatches, Venezuela, vol. 2 (M-79:3), received 8/30.

From MEMUCAN HUNT

Galveston, Texas, August 2, 1844

My Dear Sir, The announciation of the death of A[rchibald] M. Green Esq[ui]r[e] U.S. Consul at Galveston will have been announced to you doubtless before this reaches you. It gratifies me to say that he was very highly esteemed in this city both in his official and private relations ["of" *canceled*].

R[obert] D. Johnson Esq[ui]r[e] of this city, now Post Master, and formerly President of the county court desired me to apply to Gen[era]l [Tilghman A.] Howard, U.S. Char[g]é d'Affa[i]res, to give him the acting appointment ["of Consul" *interlined*] with the hope of getting it confirmed by the Executive of the U.S. Should the President appoint a citizen of Texas Consul there is no gentleman better qualified in the City of Galveston than Mr. Johnson, & it affords me pleasure to recommend ["to" *canceled and* "him to you" *interlined*] as a gentleman, & capaple [*sic*] of discharging the duties. Previous to Mr. Green[']s appointment Governor [Thomas W.] Gilmer [of Va.] had promised to procure the appointment for Mr. Johnson, letters to the effect of which Mr. Johnson now has, but certain old associations of Mr. Green's father & the [*sic*] caused the application of the latter to be successful. The gentleman superceded ["by" *canceled*] by Mr. Green [Elisha A. Rhodes] is one of the best men and one of the best officers in the station he oc[c]upied your government had in its service. How so good a man and excellent ["an" *interlined*] officer should have been removed I have always been at a loss to conjecture. He always performed his duty & manifested, to my knowledge, a benevolence to his countrymen, unusually great for a Consul, but this is characteristic of him in private life. He owns no real estate in Texas—any property in which he may be indirectly interested ["in" *canceled*], is in the name of his son William [Rhodes]. I mention this as it has been intimated that the al[l]egation that he owned real estate in Texas was used as the grounds and cause of his removal, but no one but a citizen of Texas can hold real estate in Texas ["without" *canceled*] with the exception of cert[a]in government scrip which was sold in the years 1836 & 1837. Colo[nel] Rhodes is still a citizen of the U.S.A., but is residing at this place, he is now near fifty years old, has a large family and is poor. I have known him since I was 12, or 15 years old ["and" *interlined*] an honester or better man I do not believe lives. His correspondence with the Department over which you preside will evidence his capability, & should your Government appoint a citizen of your own country, & not Judge Johnson, Consul at this place, it would be very gratifying to me to Colo[nel] R[hodes] get the ["appoin" *canceled and* "appointment" *interlined*]. I hope you will excuse the liberty I take in expressing my earnest solicitude that Colo[nel] Rhodes be appointed. Should he receive the appointment I shall ["look" *interlined*] upon it as a personal favor from you to me, & I know your government could not be better represented by any one in that office. His son is an ardent advocate of annexation & is one of the most tallented young men in Texas—he is in his 22 year and is really second to but few men in the Republic as a speaker—his father's appointment as Consul will promote annexation more ["than" *canceled*] than the appointment of any other man, so far as respects the continued steadfast desire of Texas for the measure ["on the part Texans" *canceled*].

We are very much pleased with your Minister Gen[era]l [Tilghman A.] Howard, from the slight acquaintance we have made ["with" *interlined*] him.

The yellow fever has been raging here with great violence. One fifth of the grown male population have di[e]d, viz. of 500, or 580—100, or 125 have di[e]d. I was very ill with it, but am restored to health.

We feel great interest for the success of Colo[nel] Polk over Mr. Clay in the country. (In haste) I have the honor to be your friend & s[er]v[an]t, Memucan Hunt.

P.S. I should be very glad to hear from you.

ALS in DNA, RG 59 (State Department), Applications and Recommendations, 1837–1845, Johnson (M-687:17, frames 365–368). NOTE: Hunt, a native of N.C., had been Minister to the U.S. and Secretary of the Navy for the Texas Republic.

To Louis Mark, 8/2. He is informed that President [John Tyler] has directed the revocation of his commission as U.S. Consul "for the Kingdom of Bavaria & the Prussian [Rhine] Provinces," and his duties as such shall cease upon receipt of this letter. FC in DNA, RG 59 (State Department), Consular Instructions, 10:258–259.

To John Y. Mason, Secretary of the Navy, Washington, 8/2. Calhoun transmits to Mason a copy of a letter of 7/30 to Calhoun from C. F[rederick] Hagedorn, Bavarian Consul at Philadelphia, in which Hagedorn solicits information from the U.S. government on canal steam navigation and upon [William W.] Hunter's propellers and machinery. If Mason can provide Calhoun with the information he will transmit it to Hagedorn. LS with En in DNA, RG 45 (Naval Records), Letters from Federal Executive Agents, 1837–1886, 7:31 (M-517:2, frames 470–473); FC in DNA, RG 59 (State Department), Domestic Letters, 34:350–351 (M-40:32).

From Winslow Turner, Plattsburg, Missouri, 8/2. Turner states that he taught David McDaniel years ago and found him to be a "youth of good character and fair promise." McDaniel's father was a respectable and wealthy man who emigrated from S.C. Turner hopes McDaniel will be granted a pardon. ALS in DNA, RG 59 (State Department), Petitions for Pardon and Related Briefs, 1800–1849, no. 292B.

TO FERNANDO WOOD

Department of State
Washington, 2nd Aug[us]t 1844

Sir, I have received your letter of the 30th Ultimo, relative to a supposed intention of the two Mexican Steamers now in the harbor of New York, to ship two hundred American Seamen.

If you can, without applying to the United States' district attorney [Ogden Hoffman], and without attracting too much public attention to the subject, defeat this project, I see no reason whatever why you should not employ any "effectual means" within your control to do so. There can, however, be no objection to the enlistment of a few additional men for the navigation of these vessels, if it be necessary. I am, Sir, respectfully Your Obedient Servant, John C. Calhoun.

FC in DNA, RG 59 (State Department), Domestic Letters, 34:321 (M-40:32).

FROM T[ILGHMAN] A. HOWARD

Legation of the United States
Washington, Texas, 3 Aug. 1844

Sir, I arrived at the seat of Government on the 1st and was yesterday accredited. In the reply of the Secretary of State [Anson Jones] to my address, he expressed the hope of a still closer union between the two countries; and on my presentation to President [Samuel] Houston, the satisfaction evinced by him when I stated, at some length, the state and character of the annexation question in the United States, left me to conclude, that no change of policy in regard to it need be apprehended at present, so far as Texas is concerned.

A few days since a Mexican officer arrived at the seat of this government, with dispatches from Gen. [Adrian] Woll, complaining of the alledged perfidy of the "people of Texas" in reference to the alledged armistice. It was addressed in such form as not to recognize any subsisting government, or public functionary in Texas, and declares the armistice at an end from the 11 of June last.

The reply of Gen. Houston, I understand is addressed to Santa Anna, and will probably be published in a few days. I will forward you a copy at the earliest moment.

I transmit herewith a paper entitled "the Civilian & Galveston Gazette" of the 13 July containing an article of considerable interest, entitled "Reflections on the reconquest of Texas" by Don Juan de Dios Canedo.

In travelling through Texas, I have found a very general sentiment prevailing in favor of annexation, and it is due to President [John] Tyler that I should add, that a very lively feeling of gratitude is cherished towards him throughout the Republic

The vacant Consulate in Galveston I have already adverted to in a former note, and I now only have to remark that I have taken care to leave the archives in safe hands to await the appointment, by the president, of a successor to Col. [Archibald M.] Green. Several gentlemen have been spoken of, namely Judge [Robert D.] Johnson, Temple Doswell and Col. [Elisha A.] Rhodes the former Consul. Their full names, will of course, be forwarded by themselves or friends, should they all become applicants. Judge Johnson is postmaster at Galveston. They all appear to be men of fair standing.

In reference to the appointment allow me respectfully, and confidentially to say, that there are more interests than American interests at Galveston, and the strong feelings, in many quarters, for European interests, render it necessary that our Consul should be American in every sense. I have the honor to be, faithfully, Your Ob[e]d[ien]t serv[an]t, T.A. Howard.

ALS with En in DNA, RG 59 (State Department), Diplomatic Despatches, Texas, vol. 2 (T-728:2, frames 374–382), received 8/26; autograph copy in DNA, RG 84 (Foreign Posts), Texas.

From W[illia]m M. McPherson

St. Louis, August 3d 1844

Sir, About the 18th of July last I addressed a letter to President [John] Tyler in anticipation of a vacancy in the office of U.S. Marshall for this District and in that case urging the *Reappointment* of Col. W[eston] F. Birch to that office.

In that letter I stated that I would forward such evidence of approval as would show that the appointment would be acceptable to the people of Missouri.

Ill health and professional engagements have prevented so far my complying with this promise but I intend to make it good.

It is generally understood here that Col. [Thomas H.] Benton procured his rejection to gratify personal malice and this impression is calculated to make the ["appointment" *altered to* "reappointment"] more acceptable ["th" *canceled*] to the whigs & *liberal* Democrats.

I herewith send you an article from [the *New Era*] a leading whig paper of this city[;] it expresses the views of every Lawyer who has any business to transact with the marshall regardless of Politics.

I believe every member of the Bar[,] Judge or Clerk will say that Col. Birch is the best officer ever appointed in Missouri.

It is very important that a marshall should be appointed before the first Monday in September as the District Court meets at that time. In hast[e] Respectfully, Wm. M. McPherson, U.S. District Attorney.

ALS with En in DNA, RG 59 (State Department), Applications and Recommendations, 1837–1845, Birch (M-687:2, frames 367–374).

From Alanson Nash, "Counsellor at Law," New York [City], 8/3. Nash asks on behalf of William Bestwick and other U.S. citizens who served on board Mexican vessels that the captains of those vessels be forced to pay the men for the time that they served the Mexican government. He recommends that Calhoun detain a Mexican vessel now in New York harbor and force the aforesaid payments to be made. ALS with Ens in DNA, RG 59 (State Department), Miscellaneous Letters (M-179:105, frames 120–123).

From R[ICHARD] PAKENHAM

Washington, 3 August 1844

Sir, Her Majesty's Government have been informed by Her Majesty's Consul at Galveston that on the 22 and 26 of May last very efficacious assistance was rendered by the Commander of the United States Sloop of War "Vincennes," to two British merchant Vessels, the "Cybele" and the "Cato," whilst in great peril in Galveston Roads.

I am instructed to make known to you, Sir, and to request that you will have the goodness to communicate to Commander [Franklin] Buchanan, the high sense which Her Majesty's Government entertain of that Officer's timely and able assistance on this occasion.

Her Majesty's Government have peculiar gratification in acknowledging generous acts of this description, which are so honorable to the parties who perform them, and so well calculated to promote those feelings of international friendship and good will which it is ever desirable to cherish and uphold between the two Countries.

I discharge an agreeable duty in thus fulfilling the Instructions which I have received from Her Majesty's Government upon this subject. I have the honor to be, with high consideration, Sir, your obedient servant, R. Pakenham.

LS in DNA, RG 59 (State Department), Notes from Foreign Legations, Great Britain, vol. 22 (M-50:22); CC in DNA, RG 45 (Naval Records), Letters from Federal Executive Agents, 1837–1886, 7:33 (M-517:2, frames 476–477).

From Sam[uel] S. Sibley, Tallahassee, 8/3. He transmits a compiled statement of all criminal cases in the Superior Court of Leon County, Fla. Territory, during its 11/1843 and 4/1844 terms and of the dispositions of those cases. He sends also notes and memoranda about all cases that were dismissed or not prosecuted, giving fuller information than the statement. He hopes that these will prove to the satisfaction of everyone that Charles S. Sibley, U.S. District Attorney for Middle Fla., is innocent of any allegations that he abused his office or accepted bribes in return for dropping prosecutions. (EU's indicate that this letter was received on 8/14 and that a copy was sent to [Richard K.] Call.) ALS with Ens in DNA, RG 59 (State Department), Applications and Recommendations, 1837–1845, Sibley (M-687:30, frames 141–204).

From [President] J[OHN] TYLER

Old Point [Comfort, Va.] Aug. 3, 1844
D[ea]r Sir, I send under cover Mr. [Angel] Calderon's [de la Barca] credentials [as Spanish Minister to the U.S.] which, in consequence of my absence for two or three days at my farm [in Charles City County, Va.], were not presented until this morning.

You will please do whatever is necessary to consummate his recognition.

I send you also ["three" *canceled and* "a" *interlined*] private letter from Mr. [Caleb] Cushing ["one of" *canceled*] which contains a suggestion as to negociating with Japan of which I think favorably.

I hope to be with you during this or early next week. Truly y[ou]rs, J. Tyler.

ALS in ScCleA.

To [ROBERT J.] WALKER, [Senator from Miss.]

State Dept., 3d Aug[us]t 1844
My dear Sir, B[enjamin] W.S. Cabell of Danville Virginia, a highly respectable man, requests me to send him a copy of the Texas Treaty, and such other documents as might be of use in the Canvass. I have sent him the President's message with all the Documents published by the Senate, and have written to him, that I would write to you, to send others, if you had them. I hope you will send him such as you can spare & which you may think will be of the greatest use, for that meridian. I am sure he will make good use of them. He is going to take the Stump actively.

I enclose you a letter from a respectable citizen of Dahlonega Georgia, the Seat of the mint.

If a certified extract from the [Senate] Journal containing Mr. [Henry] Clay's vote on the establishment of the branch mint there, and a few hundred copies of his speech, or rather speeches, in opposition to it could be struck off & sent to Mr. [Joseph B.] Varnum, they would have, I doubt not, a powerful effect against him. It is a heavy voting part of the State, & ["which" *canceled*] has the deepest interest in the mint. Truly, J.C. Calhoun.

ALS in ScU-SC, John C. Calhoun Papers.

From R[ICHARD] K. CRALLÉ

Lynchburg [Va.,] Aug[us]t 4, '44
My dear Sir: I was much pleased to receive your letter enclosing the packet within which I transmit to Mr. [Robert] Greenhow under cover with this. The contents are unknown to me, but may be of interest and importance to him.

You speak of entering into the Oregon negotiation. Though the Party which has disgraced the Country and perilled its interests are unworthy of passing judgement on your labour, your own character and the public weal require you to carry out your original purposes. It is expected that you should settle the question in regard to Oregon; and I am frequently interrogated as to your views and purposes in respect to it. Justly indignant at the course pursued by the Senate on the Texas Treaty, I was unwilling to see you again placing yourself before that body; but passion, however justly aroused, is a bad Counsellor—and I am glad to see that you propose to take the matter in hand. Whatever the Senate may have designed or wished in the rejection of the Treaty, so far as you are concerned, the blow, (if any were meditated) has signally failed of its aim. I have not heard, even in this hotbed of Federalism, a solitary reflection on your motives[,] your patriotism and disinterestedness. The worst of the Whigs speak respectfully and even kindly. [Thomas H.] Benton in *"the Missourian,"* as I see, has roused the ire of [Thomas] Ritchie— and while he purposed your destruction, has done you a great service. I am told that R[itchie] is taking an open stand in your favour; and for the future will act as becomes the organ of the Republican Party in Virginia.

I need not say aught of party politics here. The greatest excitement and enthusiasm prevails on both sides; but the Whigs are certainly failing. Their opponents are becoming daily more sanguine— and I have never seen the Party more thoroughly roused. Public meetings are held every day of the week—and strong and stirring addresses are made. Tho' invited to many I have declined to accept of the invitations. Yet I cannot see [*one word canceled and another altered to* "how"] to avoid addressing the People of this Town next week, so general and urgent has been the call. I will deliberate on it—as the Court will be in session, and many persons from a distance be present.

I have just received a note from my wife who is in the country, with some letters enclosed to me from you. She expresses the fear, it hastens my departure earlier than we expected. Important private business, and her feebleness will detain me until Saturday or Monday next—and I shall be in Washington on Wednesday the 14th inst. at farthest. If Mrs. [Elizabeth Morris] C[rallé] be unable to travel the whole distance, I will leave her at her sister's (Mrs. Bolling[?]) seven miles above Richmond, for I wish to see you before your departure.

One of the letters enclosed in your last was from Mr. [Jean

Corneille] Gevers [Dutch Minister to the U.S.], who has not received the decision of the Secretary of the Treasury [George M. Bibb] in his case. He writes for it very urgently, so as to communicate the result by the next Steamer. In great haste I am, dear Sir, most truly yours, R.K. Crallé.

ALS in ScCleA. NOTE: An AEU by Calhoun reads "Crallé."

From J[ames] L. DeWitt, New York [City], 8/4. He solicits appointment as U.S. Consul at Laguna, Mexico. He worked with a previous Consul there, [Charles] Russell, for several years and is well acquainted with the duties required. DeWitt plans to make Laguna his permanent residence. ALS in DNA, RG 59 (State Department), Applications and Recommendations, 1837–1845, DeWitt (M-687:9, frames 157–159); Abs in DNA, RG 59 (State Department), Consular Instructions, Ciudad del Carmen (M-308:1).

From JOHN W. HOLDING

Baltimore, 4th Aug[us]t 1844

Sir, I Have made some arrangements through which, I Intertain some assurance of closing the claim of the A[merica]n Ship *Good Return* upon time. If the Secretary of State will authorize, the Legations, comprehending the late Gov[ern]ment of Colombia to Exersise their judgments, upon the merits of the case to meet the settlem[en]t so made by convention with the U.S., In conformity to such Intimation I would consider It as a very great favor. I am Induced to solicit this from a Knowledge of the fact, that this claim, is the only one arising out of a similar character that the Legation of the U.S. in Colombia, has at any time, received, [and] taken charge of; as admissiable for the direct Interferance of the Gov[ern]ment, and this Claim Has received the attention of Gen[era]l Harrison, [Thomas P.] Moor[e, former U.S. Minister to Colombia], [Robert B.] McAfee, and [James] Semple [former U.S. Chargés d'Affaires to New Granada].

I Particularly desire this concideration, for the Purpose of adding some small value to the settlem[en]t so made; wherein If It is found by Private agreement and the Payment made in the domestic Bonds of the country, It would not pay the Expenses Incurred. I Have claims similar to those of Com[man]d[e]r Daniels and others, that the Late Secretary of State [Abel P. Upshur?], commended to the friendly Interferance of the Gov[ern]ment, and feel Perfectly satisfyed, But I do most certainly think under all circumstances that some little Exception might, and ought to be Intertained, to justify this simple solicitation.

A Gentleman will leave this in a few days for Ven[e]zuela; and could the Department feel justifyed in granting this Special favor It will be received in this City. I Have the Honor to be Most Respectfully Your most Ob[edien]t Servant, John W. Holding.

ALS in DNA, RG 59 (State Department), Miscellaneous Letters (M-179:105, frames 136–137).

From C[HARLES] J. INGERSOLL, [Representative from Pa.]

Forest Hill, Philad[elphia], Aug. 4, '44

Dear Sir, Such paragraphs as I have marked in the Newspapers sent with this letter seldom if ever appear in the Swabian Mercury or in letters from Vienna without authority.

If what it states is true, as I believe, the influence of England has failed to prevent Austria following Prussia in a liberal tendency towards our staples.

And I agree entirely in the view taken by the leading Article in the Newspaper I send you—written by I do not know who, perhaps [Francis J.] Grund—that Prussia, Austria and Russia, instead of aiding England in her designs on the U.S. are, on the contrary, spontaneously about enacting a continental system of exclusion against British manufactures which ["system" *interlined*] due encouragement from us will establish beyond all resistance.

If so, what a vast opening for the tobacco, rice, cotton, and eventually flour, flesh, Indian corn, timber, iron, fish—in short almost every thing we have, including cotton twist and other manufactured cotton.

Fourteen years ago, at the French revolution of 1830 I moved resolutions in the Legislature of this State having this commerce in view, and throughout all Mr. [Martin] Vanburen's administration I was constantly trying to convince him and my friend [John] Forsyth [then Secretary of State] that the way to remove all our English troubles is to deal less with her[,] our rival in every thing and more with continental Europe, our rival in almost nothing, that in this way all causes of hostility are removed and vast sources opened of incalculable commercial prosperity, the exports of the southern States permanently increased and the navigation & manufactures of the northern with them.

Cotton alone may be made to do all this. It is the talisman.

I am glad to learn from Mr. [David] Levy [Yulee, Delegate from Fla. Territory] that you think of treating the question of the extradition article in the English Treaty, which I promised him to try & undertake during the leisure of this summer but I am afraid it will be frittered away in party politics and other idleness.

Extradition, a necessary arrangement between conterminous nations, Canada or Mexico and the U.S., for instance, when carried over the Atlantic as in [John] Jay's treaty with England, and with several new concessions superadded by [Daniel] Webster's treaty, is, in my opinion, cont[r]ary to the laws of nations and to first principles of national independence.

As respects our slaves and the English law on that subject it is a concession wholly without equivalent or reason.

I have always thought that the Executive should denounce the stipulated reservation[?] of the article and also of that for joint occupation of Oregon. I am very truly y[ou]rs, C.J. Ingersoll.

ALS in ScCleA.

From ALBERT SMITH

Boundary Line
Moose River [Maine]
Aug[us]t 4th 1844

Sir: I deem it my duty to acquaint ["you" *interlined*] with the progress, the present season of the joint survey of that part of the Boundary Line described in the Treaty of Washington of Aug[us]t 9th 1842, which is required by said Treaty to be surveyed. In the early part of last January the British Commissioner [Lt. Col. James B.B. Estcourt] and myself ["meet" *altered to* "met"] at the City of Washington, where a plan of operations was arranged and mutually agreed upon by us, for the present season, by which the line of Boundary would have been completed to the head of Halls Stream at the North Western Corner of New Hampshire.

It was stipulated that we should meet with our respective parties at the height of Land, upon the Canada and Kennebec road on the first day of June.

This agreement it was impossible for me to fulfil. For, notwithstanding all my efforts to obtain an appropriation for the Survey at the early part of the late session of Congress, it was not made until the seventeenth day of June. I immediately addressed a Communication to Maj. James D. Graham of the U.S. Top[ographical] Engineers, who, as you are already aware had been appointed by the President, the head of the Scientific Corps, and director of such scientific operations on the part of the American Commission as should be deemed proper by the Commissioner, stating succinctly the arrangements of the Commissioners, in regard to the work, and expressing my anxiety to have our parties upon the line at the earliest possible period.

To that distinguished and excellent officer had been assigned the duty of giving the necessary instructions to the American Engineers and Surveyors, for carrying into effect the arrangements of the Commissioners, with the care of all the Instruments of the Commission on our side.

In my communication of the 17th of June, I stated to Maj. Graham, that the Commissaries would make the utmost despatch in placing upon the line, the proper supplies, Tents, &c—and requested him, immediately to give the necessary directions to the American Engineers to be upon the Line as early as possible.

Mr. [Alexander W.] Longfellow did proceed to the Line early in July under instructions from Maj. Graham and entered upon the duties assigned him. On the 20th of June, I left Washington and arrived in Boston on the 24th. The supplies were purchased in that City, and shipped with all possible dispatch, to St. John N[ew] B[runswick] and to Augusta Maine. They were thence transported to the different points on the Boundary Line for which they were destined—excepting the portion assigned for the survey of a part of the line under the immediate observation of Maj: Graham, which I directed to be stored at the Grand Falls of the St. John, to await his orders.

I remained in Boston some ten days hoping to meet him, when I went to Portland.

In the mean time I sent a party of twenty men to this point, with the supplies to await orders—and two Civil Engineers with their assistants arrived here about the same time, by my directions. After remaining at Portland until the 24th July, I left for this point where I arrived on the 28th. I found here the British Commissioner waiting to proceed with our operations. My men and the Civil Engineers before named were also encamped upon the height of Land—without any scientific Instruments to prosecute the work of the Survey. I have received no communication from Maj: Graham since I left Washington. Under these circumstances I felt bound to communicate to you the facts in the Case. I have not the least doubt that Maj: Graham will be able to give the most satisfactory reasons for the delay, and trust that by increased diligence and energy we shall be able to make up for the lost time. I have the honor to be Sir, most respectfully Your ob[e]d[ien]t Serv[an]t, Albert Smith, U.S. Com[missione]r.

N.B. Since the above was written I have rec[eive]d the pleasing intelligence from Maj. G[raham] by a letter from Boston under date July 27, that he is on his way to the line; & assigning, as a reason for his ["delay" *canceled*] detention, the fact that the Sec[retar]y of War, *being absent,* he was unable to obtain the supplies for the detachment of Artillery placed under his orders, or the necessary supply of rockets. I exceedingly deplore the circumstance, both on account of the expense which has been thereby incurred, & the delay of the work. A.S.

LS in DNA, RG 76 (Records of Boundary and Claims Commissions and Arbitrations), Letters Received by the Department of State Concerning the Northeast Boundary Line. NOTE: The postscript is in Smith's handwriting.

To Leonard R. Almy, New Orleans, 8/5. Because the Mexican government has refused to grant Almy an exequatur he will be unable to perform his duties as U.S. Consul at Laguna, Carmen Island. Almy is instructed to deposit his seal and records with the Collector of Customs at New Orleans. FC in DNA, RG 59 (State Department), Consular Instructions, 11:267.

From [Angel] Calderon de la Barca, Old Point Comfort [Va.], 8/5. He states that he delivered his credentials [as Spanish Minister to the U.S.] to President [John Tyler] this morning. He announces that he is going to remain with his family in New Port, for which place he will depart tomorrow, until he "can find a Convenient house to hire in Washington." ALS in DNA, RG 59 (State Department), Notes from Foreign Legations, Spain, vol. 11 (M-59:13, frame 983).

From Henry Y. Cranston, [Representative from R.I.], Newport, 8/5. Cranston repeats an earlier request that Calhoun attempt to procure, through the U.S. representative in Havana, the release of

William Bisby from prison. From his knowledge of Bisby's character, Cranston feels that there is no possibility that Bisby is guilty of committing the crime [of promoting slave insurrection] with which he is charged. LS in DNA, RG 59 (State Department), Miscellaneous Letters (M-179:105, frames 141–142).

From Edward Everett, London, 8/5. Everett transmits a letter of 8/2 from the Earl of Aberdeen informing him that an upcoming report from the Governor of New Zealand will deal with duties charged on alcoholic beverages imported into the Bay of Islands before New Zealand came under British control. The report will cover the case of [Nathaniel L.] Rogers [& Brothers] previously referred to Everett. LS (No. 172) with En in DNA, RG 59 (State Department), Diplomatic Despatches, Great Britain, vol. 53 (M-30:49), received 9/3; FC in DNA, RG 84 (Foreign Posts), Great Britain, Despatches, 8:373–374; FC in MHi, Edward Everett Papers, 49:495–496 (published microfilm, reel 23, frames 249–250).

From P.J. Farnham & Co., Salem, Mass., 8/5. They ask for any recent information concerning their claim against the British government for the seizure of the *Jones* on the coast of Africa. LS in DNA, RG 59 (State Department), Miscellaneous Letters (M-179:105, frame 140).

From W[ILLIAM] H. FREEMAN

Consulate of the United States
Island of Curacao, August 5th, 1844
Sir, Enclosed, I have the honor to send you the returns of this Consulate from the 1st January to 30th June inclusive of the current year—No. 2. By it, you will perceive that the number of American vessels frequenting this Island is gradually increasing; not having as yet been formally recognised by the Government of Holland, I am unable to make any returns from Bonaire; I trust however that the steps that it may please the Government of the U. States to take with Holland for an Exequatur for me, will soon place me in a situation to do so. The foreign Commerce with this Island and its Dependencies, is solely American, and I flatter myself that I have done, during my residence here, much, towards fostering the same; my sole attentions being directed to my Official duties. I have drawn upon you at thirty days

sight, this date, favour of Hymen L. Lipman for One hundred and nine Dollars, Seventy four Cents for disbursements and commission on the same, as per account rendered the "Fifth Auditor of the Treasury Department" which please honor.

May I solicit of the Government another "Flag" to replace the present one now too much worn for use? By forwarding the same to Messrs. J. Foulke and Sons, Merchants, New York, they will see that it comes to hand. I have the honor to be Your Ob[edien]t Serv[an]t, W.H. Freeman, U. States Consul.

LS (No. 12) with Ens in DNA, RG 59 (State Department), Consular Despatches, Curacao, vol. 2 (T-197:2), received 10/21.

To [Johann Georg von] Hülsemann, [Austrian Chargé d'Affaires in the U.S.], 8/5. Calhoun states that Hülsemann's note of 7/24 was received and referred to the Secretary of the Treasury. He encloses a copy of the Secretary's reply [of 8/2] stating that U.S. collectors of customs will be instructed to admit Austrian wines, imported in bottles, at a duty of fifteen cents per gallon. FC in DNA, RG 59 (State Department), Notes to Foreign Legations, German States, 6: 96 (M-99:27).

From J[oseph] R. Ingersoll, [Representative from Pa.], Philadelphia, 8/5. Ingersoll requests that an enclosed document be forwarded to C[hristopher] Hughes, U.S. Chargé d'Affaires at Brussels. "I had the pleasure of seeing Mr. [Thomas G.] Clemson last evening and learning that his family was in good health. Mrs. [Anna Maria Calhoun] C[lemson] was not within when I called with the ladies of my family to pay our respects to her this morning." ALS in DNA, RG 59 (State Department), Passport Applications, vol. 32, unnumbered (M-1372:15).

To "James G." [*sic*; James B.] Martin, Wheeling, Va., 8/5. Calhoun informs Martin that papers renewing a request that [John] Mc-Daniel and [Joseph] Brown (two prisoners scheduled to be executed in St. Louis on 8/16) be pardoned were sent to President [John Tyler] some time ago, but nothing has since been heard from Tyler. If a favorable decision reaches the State Department within a few days, it will be immediately forwarded. FC in DNA, RG 59 (State Department), Domestic Letters, 34:324–325 (M-40:32).

To Alanson Nash, New York [City], 8/5. "I have to acknowledge the receipt of your letter of the 3rd instant, accompanied by a petition of William Bestwick to the President [John Tyler], praying the President[']s interposition for the purpose of obtaining his discharge from service as a ship carpenter on board the Mexican war steamer Guadaloupe, and the recovery of wages alleged to be due him in that character. The case appears to be one in which the Courts of Justice alone can with propriety interfere as between the petitioner and the Commander of the vessel." FC in DNA, RG 59 (State Department), Domestic Letters, 34:323–324 (M-40:32).

To R[ichard] Pakenham

Department of State
Washington, 5th Aug[us]t, 1844

Sir: I have received the letter which you did me the honor to address to me, by direction of Her Majesty's Government, on the 3d instant, informing me that very efficacious assistance was rendered on the 22d and 26th of May last, by the commander of the United States' sloop of war "Vincennes" to two British merchant vessels, the "Cybele" and the "Cato," whilst in great peril in Galveston Roads; and requesting me to communicate to Commander [Franklin] Buchanan the high sense which Her Majesty's Government entertains of that officer's conduct on the occasion.

I will take pleasure in transmitting to Commander Buchanan, through the proper channel, a copy of your letter to this Department, conveying, in terms so obliging, the acknowledgments of the Queen's Government; and I avail myself of this opportunity to renew to you assurances of my distinguished consideration. J.C. Calhoun.

FC in DNA, RG 59 (State Department), Notes to Foreign Legations, Great Britain, 7:22–23 (M-99:36).

From R[ichard] Pakenham

Washington, 5 August 1844

The Undersigned Her Britannick Majesty's Envoy Extraordinary and Minister Plenipotentiary, has been instructed to communicate to the Secretary of State of the United States the enclosed extracts from reports which have been received from Her Majesty's Commissioners and Her Majesty's Consul at Rio de Janeiro, relative to the participation of American Vessels in the Slave Trade.

Important information upon this same subject was communicated to the Minister of the United States in London by a Note from [Lord Aberdeen] Her Majesty's Principal Secretary of State for Foreign Affairs, dated 22 November 1843, which note will doubtless have been transmitted by that Minister to His Government.

Her Majesty's Government entertain the hope that the Government of the United States will be disposed to adopt decided measures to put a stop to the abuses which have thus been brought to their knowledge, and which tend so materially to defeat the combined efforts of the two Governments for the prevention of the Trade in Slaves.

The Undersigned takes advantage of this opportunity to renew to Mr. Calhoun the assurance of His high consideration. R. Pakenham.

LS with Ens in DNA, RG 59 (State Department), Notes from Foreign Legations, Great Britain, vol. 22 (M-50:22).

From L[ewis] Warrington for [John Y. Mason], Secretary of the Navy, 8/5. Passed Midshipman Edward A. Barnett has recently been ordered to Hong Kong "as U.S. Naval Storekeeper" and will proceed by the overland route to China. Joseph Lewis will accompany Barnett as his clerk, and Lewis can be "the bearer of any despatches you may desire to send to the United States Embassy at China." LS in DNA, RG 59 (State Department), Miscellaneous Letters (M-179: 105, frame 143); FC in DNA, RG 45 (Naval Records), Letters Sent by the Secretary of the Navy to the President and Executive Agencies, 1821–1886, 5:14 (M-472:3, frame 49).

From W[illia]m H. Brockenbrough, [later a Representative from Fla.], Tallahassee, 8/6. He testifies that charges against Charles S. Sibley, U.S. District Attorney for Middle Fla., are "ridiculous" and that Sibley's character is unspotted. Brockenbrough suggests that documents containing the charges should be sent to the U.S. District Judge of Middle Fla. to be laid before a grand jury, which can then investigate the accusations and "prefer indictments" against either Sibley or his accuser. ALS in DNA, RG 59 (State Department), Applications and Recommendations, 1837–1845, Sibley (M-687:30, frames 214–217).

From William Clark, Gettysburg, Adams County, Pa., 8/6. He asks that Calhoun send to him copies of "a pamphlet of the Tariff containing the duties on imports of goods into the U.S." and a similar pamphlet showing duties charged on British imports. He adds, "I am 50 years of age, have always been a Democrat & will rejoice *Sir* to have it in my power to cast my suffrage for you at any time." ALS in DNA, RG 59 (State Department), Miscellaneous Letters (M-179: 105, frames 144–145).

To J[ames] L. DeWitt, New York [City], 8/6. DeWitt's letter of 8/4 is acknowledged. The President [John Tyler] is now absent from Washington, but will be informed of DeWitt's application for office. FC in DNA, RG 59 (State Department), Consular Instructions, 11:267–268.

To JOHN W. HOLDING, Baltimore

Department of State
Washington, 6th August 1844

Sir, Your several letters including that of the 4th instant, upon the subject of the claim against the late Republic of Colombia in the case of the ship Good Return, have been received. In reply I have to state that the opinion which I expressed to you orally at this Department a short time since, has undergone no change. The case affords no ground for any interference of this Government. I am, Sir, your Obedient Serv[an]t, John C. Calhoun.

FC in DNA, RG 59 (State Department), Domestic Letters, 34:327 (M-40:32).

From W[ILLIA]M HOOPER

United States Com[mercia]l Agency
Sandwich Islands
August 6th 1844

Sir, I have the honor to transmit, herewith, a copy of a letter received at this Agency from [Jules Dudoit] the French Consul for these Islands, announcing that the Protectorate of France had been conditionally granted to the Islands of "Wallis," "Fortouna" and the "Gambier" group in this Ocean.

I also enclose [published] copies of the Award of J[ohn] Ricord,

Att[orne]y general for His Hawaiian Majesty, on the meaning of "Lord Aberdeen's letter" etc. and "report upon the Rules of precedence and etiquette" to be observed at His Majesty's Court. With Sentiments of the highest Consideration I have the honor to be, Sir, Y[ou]r Mo[st] Ob[edien]t S[er]v[an]t, Wm. Hooper, Act[in]g U.S. Com[mercia]l Agent.

ALS (No. 36) with Ens in DNA, RG 59 (State Department), Consular Despatches, Honolulu, vol. 2 (M-144:2), received 12/16.

To [FRIEDRICH LUDWIG], Baron Von ROENNE, [Berlin]

State Dept., 6th August 1844

Sir, Your communication of the 29th of June announcing, that the King of Prussia had withdrawn you from your long residence near this Government to place you at the head of the important commercial Department recently created by his Majesty, has been received with mingled feelings of regret and pleasure; regret at parting with one, so much esteemed for his social virtues and respected for his eminent talents and dignified deportment, as publick functionary—and pleasure, at hearing that his great worth was duly appreciated by his Souvereign.

Be assured, Baron, that your memory will be cherished by all who had the happiness to know you in private, or official life, and by none more than by myself.

Accept, Sir, my sincere respect and lasting regard. J.C. Calhoun.

Transcript by Professor Gunter Moltmann of recipient's copy in Deutsches Zentralarchiv, Historische Abteilung II, Merseburg, German Democratic Republic (the former Geheimes Staatsarchiv, Berlin), Rep. 92, Nachlass Friedrich Ludwig von Rönne, No. 3; FC in DNA, RG 59 (State Department), Notes to Foreign Legations, German States, 6:97 (M-99:27); PC in Gunter Moltmann, "Eine Deutschland-Korrespondenz John C. Calhouns aus dem Jahre 1844," in *Jahrbuch fur Amerikastudien*, vol. XIV (1969), pp. 165–166.

From Cha[rle]s S. Sibley, Tallahassee, 8/6. He sends a letter from Leslie A. Thompson, former Auditor of Public Accounts of Fla. Territory, testifying that Sibley's practices as U.S. District Attorney for Middle Fla. are in conformity with those of all of his predecessors in that office. Sibley apologizes for not writing in more detail at present, but his return from a distant city has "occasioned me such

illness, that since my arrival, I am scarcely able to attend to business."
He feels no bitterness that such ridiculous charges have been preferred against him and has no desire to know the name of the instigator of those charges. ALS with Ens in DNA, RG 59 (State
Department), Applications and Recommendations, 1837–1845, Sibley
(M-687:30, frames 205–213); PC in Carter, ed., *Territorial Papers,*
26:938–939.

From H[ARVEY] M. WATTERSON

Special Agency
[Buenos Ayres,] Aug. 6, 1844

Sir, By the Ship "La Plata," which sails this day for Philadelphia, I
have transmitted to you the laws establishing the political Administration of the Republic of Paraguay—also the message of the President of that Republic [Carlos Antonio Lopez] to the National
Congress.

I received many facts from the late Paraguay Minister in Buenos
Ayres, which conclusively satisfy my mind, that Paraguay is destined
to be at no distant period, one of the most important states of South
America. She now contains near a million of inhabitants—a number
almost double that of the thirteen states, composing the Argentine
Confederation. Brazil, Peru, Bolivia, and Chili, have acknowledged
her independence, and it is confidently believed that England and
France will follow suit in a very short time. She is more anxious that
her independence should be acknowledged by the United States than
by any other nation. Her people have formed the impression, that
ours is the most perfect government on earth, and they are desirous to
cultivate with us the most intimate relations. I was assured by the
Paraguay Minister that an Agent from the United States would be
received with open arms.

I have just been informed by Señor Don Felipe Arana, [Argentine]
Minister of Foreign Affairs, that orders have been given at the custom
House in this City to "clear out coasting vessels laden laden [*sic*]
with merchandize for Paraguay; and to allow the reshipment of all
flour and wheat now in bond, in coasting vessels bound to Santa Fe,
Entre Rios, Paraguay, and ports in the Oriental State not occupied
by the enemy." This is the first step towards the free navigation of
the Rio De La Plata, and you have only to glance at the Map to satisfy
yourself, how immensely important to us in a commercial point of

view, will be the free navigation of this noble river and its tributary streams, which water one of the finest portions of the Globe. Very Respectfully, H.M. Watterson.

FC in DNA, RG 84 (Foreign Posts), Argentina, Correspondence with Embassy Officials.

To A[RMISTEAD] BURT, [Representative from S.C., Abbeville]

State Dept., 7th Aug[us]t 1844

My dear Sir, I learn by letters from Charleston, that there is some disposition to agitate the subject of the seperate action of the State at this time, and an impression that your District is still more inclined to it, and yourself & [George] McDuffie both ["disposed" *interlined*] to favour it. It is added, that he avows his determination to come out openly for disunion, if he should have to stand alone. My informants do not believe the rumours, and I feel assured that they cannot be true.

It seems to me, that this is the most unpropitious period, which could possible [*sic*] be selected to agitate the subject of seperate action. It is not possible, that it can do any good at present, & cannot but do harm. If it should be attempted it will prove an entire abortion, to the great injury of those concerned; to the State, & to the cause, and prevent the possibility of resorting to it hereafter, when circumstances may be more favourable, & when no other remedy but interposition can reach the disease.

On a survey of the whole ground, it seems to me, that the great point, towards effecting of which all our efforts ought to be directed, is to unite the South. I cannot but ["think" *interlined*] that circumstances are very favourable, and that with wisdom & prudence it may be effected, let the Presidential election terminate as it may. If [Henry] Clay should be defeated, the whig party will lose its head & disperse, when the Southern portion will have no alternative but to rally on Southern grounds. But, if he should succeed, his policy will be such, as to force off his Southern supporters to a great extent, & throw them into our ranks; and that will be greatly aided by the disappointment, which a large majority of the Southern Whig leaders are doomed to experience in reference to office, & the utter impossibility of Clay maintaining himself, if elected. His fall ["will" *canceled and* "would" *interlined*] be certain.

In addition, there are other & powerful causes at work to bring about the union of the South. The great cause, which has heretofore caused & continued it, is the position occupied by Virginia from 1829 (the election of Gen[era]l [Andrew] Jackson) untill the defeat of Mr. [Martin] V[an] B[uren] by the Baltimore ["election" *canceled and* "convention" *interlined*]. Instead of standing at the head of the South, which is her natural position, she was hitched to the N[ew] York Car, through the influence of Mr. [Thomas] Ritchie & the [Richmond] Enquirer. Events have forced her again into her natural position, which will, with the causes above stated, contribute powerfully to unite the South, and will certainly bring about that desirable result, if not counteracted by our imprudence.

Without it we can do little, but with it every thing. We may, if sufficiently united in our own State, prostrate the Tariff by State interposition; but that ["would" *canceled and* "could" *interlined*] not reach abolition, a danger at least as formidable. To meet that, the union of the South is indispensible; and that makes the distinction between 1832 & the present time. Then we had to contend with the Tariff alone; but now with that & abolition; and to decide judiciously on our course, regard must be had to both. We have now a prospect of acting with effect against the latter by annexing Texas; but to do that Mr. Clay must be defeated & Mr. [James K.] Polk elected, which of itself is a sufficient reason why we should do nothing at present, calculated to weaken him & strengthen Mr. Clay.

I understand an idle rumour has been put into circulation, that I have changed my opinion relative to nullification. So far is that from being true, time & experience have but confirmed me in its truth and importance. I hold it impossible for our system to last without it; but that with it, ["it" *interlined*] may be ["among" *canceled and* "one of" *interlined*] the most durable Govts., that has ever been established. I think too highly of it to ["put it" *canceled*] appeal to it, except when there is a prospect, that the appeal may be successful as in 1832.

I understand also, that it is insinuated, that I am influenced in my course, by having my eye fixed on 1848. Those who may think so, if there be any, know little of me. I am incapable of being influenced by such considerations, as my whole life proves.

Let me add in conclusion, I hope that you & McDuffie will both discontinue any attempt at a seperate move on the part of the State at this time.

We have little knew [*sic*] beyond what you will see in the papers. Our information in reference to the disposition of France ["on the

Texan question" *interlined*] is favourable. We have nothing to apprehend from her.

I hope your crops are fine & the District healthy. My love to Martha [Calhoun Burt] & Eugenia [Calhoun] should she be with you. With great respect yours truly, J.C. Calhoun.

ALS in NcD, John C. Calhoun Papers.

From D[ABNEY] S. CARR

U.S. Legation
Cons[tantino]ple, August 7th 1844

Sir, Your No. 8 forwarded by way of London came to hand by the last French steamer from Marseilles in the good time in which every thing sent by that route reaches here.

I send herewith a Translation of a new regulation, just received from the Sublime Porte, in relation to the passage of the Dardanelles, which it will be well to have published in Washington and also in some paper in each of our large ports, especially New York and Boston.

You will have learned probably before this reaches you, of the death of the American Consul, Mr. [John] Gliddon, at Alexandria, in Egypt. His son-in-Law Mr. [Alexander] Tod had been left in charge of the Consulate and he is a Gentleman so highly qualified in every respect, for the office, that I hope he will be appointed to it, unless an American of as good qualifications can be got to take it; which I presume cannot be.

He writes under a late date that Mehemet Ali the Vice Roy of Egypt and one of the great men of the day has recently shown strong symptoms of alienation of mind and that it is daily expected at Alexandria that Ibrahim Pacha, his son or rather his step-son, will be Called to take charge of the Government. The Plymouth sloop of war and Frigate Cumberland were at Smyrna the other day. Their appearance in these parts has had the finest effect. The latter has gone to the Coast of Syria and thence to Tangiers. The former is daily expected here and I deem it of the highest importance to our interests in this Quarter to keep her here as long as possible. She ought to be stationed here. I have the honor to be With great respect Your ob[edien]t Serv[an]t, D.S. Carr.

527

LS (No. 16) with En in DNA, RG 59 (State Department), Diplomatic Despatches, Turkey, vol. 10 (M-46:12), received 9/19; variant FC in DNA, RG 84 (Foreign Posts), Turkey, Despatches, G:140–141.

To EDWARD EVERETT, [London]

Department of State

Washington, 7th Aug[us]t, 1844

Sir: Some time in September last, a gang of seven negroes, in East Florida, robbed the son and daughter of a citizen of the territory of the name of [John H.] Geeren, and plundered his house in his absence; and, after murdering him, while in pursuit of them, escaped to Nassau, in New Providence. The Grand Jury of the Judicial District, after full investigation, returned bills of indictments against each of them for robbery and murder. Requisition was made in due form by the Secretary of State, through the British Minister at Washington, and transmitted to the Marshal of that portion of the territory, who was authorized to receive the criminals. He repaired to Nassau; and, on application, the Governor of the Bahamas issued his requisition to the Chief Justice of the Colony, who, acting with the Associate Judges, in open Court, refused to deliver up to justice the fugitives, on the ground, that the evidence offered was not such as was required by the act of Parliament for giving up criminals, fugitives from justice, in certain cases. The Court remarked, in delivering its opinion, that: "An indictment, *per se*, can never be received as evidence. It is not enough for us to know, that the American jury thought the parties guilty. We ought to know the *grounds* upon which they thought them guilty. What may constitute the crime of murder in Florida, may be very far from doing so according to the British laws, or even to the laws of the Northern States of America. By issuing a warrant, then, to apprehend the parties, in virtue of these indictments, we might be doing so on evidence which would not justify their apprehension by the British laws, and should thereby be proceeding in direct violation of the act."

The President, in compliance with calls from the two Houses, transmitted to Congress all the correspondence and documents connected with the case, of which a copy is enclosed, with a copy of the speech of Mr. [David] Levy [Yulee], the Delegate from the territory, on a motion to refer the message and documents to the Committee on Foreign Relations, to which I would refer you for more full information. The message, with the documents, was referred to the committee. No report was made; but, it is understood, one will be at the next session.

You will see, by reference to the documents, that the crimes committed by the fugitives were wanton and atrocious. The affair, connected with the refusal to deliver the fugitives up, has caused much feeling and excitement, especially in that portion of the Union. The remarks of the Court leave little doubt, that it is its opinion, that the case does not come within the 10th article of the treaty [of 1842], on the ground that the crimes charged of murder and robbery being committed by slaves, escaping from the authority of their masters, do not constitute murder and robbery according to the laws of Great Britain. No other meaning can be attached to the remarks which accompanied the objection taken against receiving the authenticated copies of the bills of indictment found by the grand jury, which were offered in evidence.

It is very desirable to know, before any further step is taken, whether the Government of Great Britain intends to support the ground taken by the Court, as clearly intimated in its remarks. If so, it would be idle to discuss the question whether the authenticated copies of the bills of indictments found by the grand jury, was sufficient evidence of the crimes charged to justify the commitment of the fugitives under the provisions of the 10th article, or to take any further step to have them surrendered, in this or any other case of fugitive slaves, be their crime what it may, or under whatever circumstances committed. There can be none stronger than this, whether regarded in reference to the atrocity of the crimes, or the circumstances under which they were committed. When it is ascertained, whether the Government of Great Britain intends to support the grounds indicated by the Court or not, we, on our part, will be prepared to decide what course it will be proper for us to adopt.

According to that ground, the acts charged as murder and robbery must be such as to constitute those crimes not only according to the laws of Florida, but also to constitute them such by the laws of Great Britain; or, rather, in this case, of the Bahama Islands. After a careful examination of the subject, I cannot regard it as tenable; on the contrary, I hold it to be clearly inconsistent with ["the" *interlined*] provisions of the article and the plainest dictates of reason. The body of the article is in the following words: "It is agreed that the United States and Her Britannic Majesty shall, upon mutual requisitions by them or their Ministers, Officers, or Authorities respectively made, deliver up to justice all persons who, being charged with the crime of murder, or assault with intent to commit murder, or piracy, or arson, or robbery, or forgery, or the utterance of forged papers, committed within the jurisdiction of either, shall seek an asylum, or shall be found within the territories of the other." Such is the body of the agreement. Nothing can be more clear. The persons to be delivered up to justice; the crimes charged for which they are to be delivered up; within whose jurisdiction they must be committed, and within whose territories the fugitives shall be found, are all so clearly specified, as to preclude the possibility of doubt. It comprehends *all persons, charged* with the crimes of murder, robbery, &c., &c., committed within *the jurisdiction* of the party making the requisition, and *found* in *the territory* of that on whom the requisition is made. That these words are broad enough to comprehend the case under consideration is beyond doubt; and of course the only possible question which can be made is, whether it is not taken out by the proviso which immediately follows. The material portion, and that on which the construction of the residue depends, is in the following words: Provided "that this" (the delivery up to justice), "shall only be done upon such evidence of criminality as, according to the laws of the place where the fugitive or person so charged shall be found, would justify his apprehension and commitment for trial, if the crime or offence had there been committed." It is too plain to require proof, that it relates to the evidence on which the fugitive is to be given up to justice, exclusively, without intending to restrict, or change, the body of the agreement. That having clearly specified, who were to be delivered up to justice, on the requisition of either party, it became necessary, in order to give effect to the agreement, to specify on what evidence it should be done; and to do that accordingly is the sole object of the proviso. It specifies that it shall be done on such evidence of criminality as would justify his apprehension and commitment for trial by the laws of the place where the fugitive is found, had the crime *charged* been there committed; that is, if the crime *charged* be murder or robbery, as in this case, on such evidence as would justify apprehension and commitment for trial for murder or robbery at the place.

Taking the body of the agreement and proviso together, it would seem to be unquestionable, that the true intent of the article is, that the *criminality* of the act charged should be judged of by the laws of the country within whose jurisdiction the act was perpetrated; but that *the evidence* on which the fugitive should be delivered up to justice, should be by the laws of the place where he shall be found. Both are to be judged by the laws of the place where they occur; and properly so; as they are paramount within their respective limits. And hence it is expressly specified in the body of the agreement, that the crime charged must have been committed within the jurisdiction of the party making the requisition; and, in the proviso, that the evidence, on which the fugitive shall be delivered up, shall be such as is required to apprehend and commit for trial according to the laws of the place where he is found. That this is the true construction, is confirmed by the fact, that it reconciles the proviso with the body of the agreement; while the opposite, which would judge of the criminality of the act, not by the laws of the place within whose jurisdiction it was committed, but by those of the place, where the fugitive was found, would not only essentially change what is clearly specified in the body of the agreement, but make it absurd. If such had been the intention of the parties, instead of reading as it does, it ought to have read as follows: It is agreed that the United States and Her Britannic Majesty shall, upon mutual requisitions by them or their Ministers, &c., &c., respectively made, deliver up to justice all persons, who, being guilty of (not charged with) the crimes of murder, &c., &c., &c., &c., according to the laws of the place where the fugitive is found (not committed within the jurisdiction of the party making the requisition,) shall seek an asylum, or shall be found in the territories of the other. Such an agreement would have been manifestly absurd; and yet, as absurd as it would be, it must be so worded, to make it agree with that construction of the proviso, which would judge of the criminality of the act by the laws of the place where the fugitive was found, and not by that where the act was committed. If it be against a fundamental rule of construction to give such a construction to one part of an agreement, as to make it inconsistent with another, when it is possible to avoid it, what shall be said of a construction, which shall give to a proviso, such a construction, as would render the body of the agreement absurd, when another would reconcile the two and give effect to every word of both? If there should be an irreconcilable difference between them, the subordinate should surely yield to the principal—the proviso to the body of the agreement.

But such a construction of the proviso would not only be irreconcilable with the body of the agreement, but would, as I have stated, be inconsistent with the plainest dictates of reason. No act committed in one country, however criminal according to its laws, is criminal according to the laws of the other. Crimes, in a legal sense, are local; and are so only because the acts constituting them are declared to be so by the laws of the country where they are perpetrated. Great

Britain cannot by her laws make an act committed within the jurisdiction of the United States criminal within her territories, however immoral of itself; and *vice versa*. The proposition is too clear to require illustration, or to be contested; but if that be admitted, it must also be admitted that the criminality referred to in the proviso is to be judged of by the laws of the place within whose jurisdiction the act was charged to have been perpetrated, and not where the fugitive is found.

Against this but one position can be taken in defence of the ground indicated by the Court of the Bahama Islands; and that is, to admit our construction of the proviso to be correct, but to maintain, that, while the criminality of the act must be judged of by the laws of the place, where it was charged to have been committed, it must, at the same time, be such as would constitute the crime charged, by the laws of the place where the fugitive was found. To this two answers may be given, either of which is conclusive. In the first place, it may be replied, that it is a pure assumption unwarranted by any thing whatever, either in the proviso, or the entire article. It is not only not expressed, but is not necessary to give to any word in the article its full and proper meaning, or to reconcile any apparent conflict among its provisions. And in the next, that it would be impossible to give such a construction to the proviso, without greatly restricting the plain meaning of the body of the agreement. Instead of subjecting *all* persons to be delivered up to justice who are charged with the crimes of murder, &c., &c., &c., committed within the jurisdiction of the party making the requisition, and found in the territories of the other, it would subject *only those* to be delivered up who were charged with acts constituting the crimes of murder, &c., &c., &c., by the laws *of both* countries, in direct contradiction to the express provisions of the body of the agreement, and against the plain intent of the proviso, as has been shown, and the fundamental rule of construction which requires that the different parts of an agreement should be so construed, if possible, as to reconcile all, and give effect to each.

I might go further, and show, that the position is against the plain and literal meaning of the proviso itself, but I deem it unnecessary to add to the force of the reply already advanced against it. Indeed, it might be shown, that, if admitted, it would not sustain the ground indicated by the Court. In order to do that, it would be necessary to assume, that according to the laws of Great Britain, a slave is justified in killing and robbing, if it be necessary to effect his escape and secure his liberty. Without pretending to be conversant with her laws, I feel assured I hazard nothing in asserting that there is no such law either in Great Britain or the Bahama Islands, or any other of her numerous colonial possessions. No doubt there are laws in all, which justify homicide, if committed in resistance to unlawful restraint; but none that do, where the restraint is lawful. That is the broad and fundamental distinction in the penal code of all countries, between justifiable homicide and murder, where death ensues in consequence of resistance to restraint. By it, this case must be tested, if the ground indicated by the Court of the Bahama Islands be admitted, and not by the incidental circumstance, whether this or that restraint be lawful or not, by the laws of both countries. Each has the right to determine for itself what restraints its welfare and safety may require to be imposed on the acts of the individuals of which it is composed, and that must be determined in reference to circumstances, that are almost infinitely varied, not only in relation to the two countries as a whole, but also to the various States, Territories, Colonies, and dependencies of which they are composed. They are in consequence greatly diversified, and would be found, on examination, very different in reference to most of the crimes enumerated by the 10th article of the treaty; and which would lead to great confusion and uncertainty, if any other rule of judging of criminality be admitted, but the broad and fundamental one above stated. Tested by that, this case would be embraced by the article, even according to the restricted standard indicated by the Bahama Judges. There is no doubt that the restraint from which these fugitives were escaping, when the acts charged were perpetrated, was imposed by the laws of Florida, and, of course, was a lawful restraint, and the homicide committed by them, murder; and so, there is little doubt, it would have been declared, even by the Bahama Court, in any other case of restraint made lawful by the acts of Florida, except the one in question.

This brings up two very grave questions. On what principle can such a distinction be made, and is the Government of Great Britain prepared to make it? I can imagine but one, and that is, that the form of restraint implied under the name of domestic servitude; that is, of one man holding another under subjection and commanding his labor without his consent, is so repugnant to the moral code, that it cannot be made lawful, although sanctioned by laws of the country where it exists. But it cannot be, that Great Britain, who is more responsible than any other country for the extent of that form of servitude on this continent, and which has but so recently abolished it, with so little benefit to herself or those liberated, in her own possessions, is prepared to adopt and act on such a principle, and thereby place, as far as its operation may extend, this country, Russia, Spain, Brazil, and all others not prepared to follow her example, in a state of national outlawry in reference to herself, against the authority of all ages, and of the great expounders of international laws, and it may be added, of the Bible itself, which, as often as it is mentioned, no where discourages such servitude, or pronounces it to be repugnant to morals or religion. It cannot be, that she is prepared to adopt a principle, which, if carried out in practice, would not only be subversive of the right of one man holding in subjection and commanding the labor of another without his consent, but equally so, of one People or Nation holding another, or one portion of one People or Nation holding the other, in subjection and commanding their labor without its consent. It cannot be, but she must see, that the principle tends to the subversion of all human authority, and that it contains within itself the germ of universal anarchy; and must, if carried out in practice, react with destructive fury on her political institutions, and burst the bonds, which hold in servitude under her subjection, so large a portion of the human race.

But, be that as it may, it is at least certain, that she cannot but know, that the treaty never would have been ratified, had we believed, that she would adopt the principle, or so construe the 10th article, as to exclude from its operation fugitive slaves, charged with the crime of murder, robbery, or any other of those enumerated, who might seek an asylum, or be found in her territories. Certain it is, that no Senator from the slave holding States would have knowingly voted for a treaty embracing a principle, which would stamp such a stigma on their constituents and institutions, and exclude them from almost all the advantages they could hope to derive from it. It might be added, nor any Senator vote for it who regarded the honor of his country, or the sacred obligations of the Constitution, which makes it the duty of the Federal Government to extend equal protection to all the members of the Union. The subject, indeed, was not passed over without notice, while the treaty was before the Senate. During the discussion, it was objected to the article, that it was so worded, intentionally, as to exclude from its operation cases of this description. It was replied, that the portion of the article objected to was copied verbatim from Jay's treaty of 1794, made long before England had contemplated the abolition of slavery in her possessions, and when there could be no intention of the kind. It was added, that treaty had never received an interpretation that would warrant such a construction. The reply quieted all apprehension, and the treaty received the vote of a large majority of the slave holding States. Without them, it would not have been ratified.

Such we believe to be the true construction of the 10th article of the treaty, in reference to this most important point, and such was the expectation under which the treaty was ratified. It is full time, that we should know what construction the Government of Great Britain intends to adopt in relation to it; and whether our just expectation is to be realized or not. You are, accordingly, hereby instructed by the President [John Tyler] to bring the subject, without any unnecessary delay, to its attention in strong, but respectful, terms, and to urge it to come to an early decision. Be that what it may, it is very desirable, that we should know it before the meeting of Congress at its next session, when the subject will doubtless claim the attention of both Houses. I am, Sir, very respectfully, Your obedient Servant, J.C. Calhoun.

LS (No. 99) in DNA, RG 84 (Foreign Posts), Great Britain, Instructions, 8:310–328, received 9/2; FC in DNA, RG 59 (State Department), Diplomatic Instructions, Great Britain, 15:205–216 (M-77:74); CC in DNA, RG 233 (U.S. House of Representatives), 28A-E1; PC in House Document No. 114, 28th Cong., 2nd Sess., pp. 1–7.

From JOHN W. HOLDING

Baltimore, 7th Aug[us]t 1844
Sir, Your favor under date of the 6th Instant is received—and is now before me In which ["In which" *canceled*] I am Informed that the Gov[ern]ment of the U.S. can give no Interference to favor the claim-[an]ts, In the case of the Ship Good Return—as formally Expressed in the Department of State. I must confess that I did not so comprehend the Secretary of State, but that He could ["not" *interlined*] extend His Instructions beyond those of His Predecessors—and I cannot say what those Instructions were.

Inasmuch as the Property was on Board of an American Ship, and under the Protection of the American Flag, and Specifically guarded by Treaty Stipulations, Between Spain, and The U.S., I did [not?] think that an Insult thus offered to the national Honor, would Prove of so little consequence as to Pass Entirely unnoticed, and unworthy of the least concideration by a Party at the time, and since an Indifferent commentary to the Predijuce [*sic*] of Indiv[id]ual Interests of citizens of the U.S. But It appears In this I am mistaken. The very high opinion I Have ever Intertained of The character, and abilities of Mr. Calhoun to comprehend and decide in all matters regarding Public Law, and In[di]vidual rights, compells me Patiently submit, However I might and did most ardently desire some better notice in this matter to the contrary notwithstanding. I Have the Honor To be with great consideration &c &c &c, John W. Holding.

ALS in DNA, RG 59 (State Department), Miscellaneous Letters (M-179:105, frames 147–148).

From T[ILGHMAN] A. HOWARD

Legation of the United States
Washington, (Texas,) 7th August 1844
Sir, I have the honor to transmit herewith, the copy of a letter received by me, on yesterday from the Hon. Anson Jones, Secretary of State &c. dated the 6th instant, also copies of several documents refer[r]ed to in his communication by the letters A & B, besides a copy of a letter [of 8/6] to him from the Secretary of War of this Republic [George W. Hill].

Accompanying which, will also be found, a copy of my reply [of 8/6] to the letter of Mr. Jones.

The uncertainty of any regular or speedy communication between this point and [New] Orleans, via Galveston, and the necessity that I should ["lay" *canceled and* "transmit" *interlined*] the information communicated, to you without delay, have induced me to send an express to Fort Jessup, and through the aid of Gen. [Zachary] Taylor, to have the despatches forwarded from that point. A copy of my letter [of 8/6] to Gen. Taylor is herewith enclosed.

I had prepared other communications, which I expected to forward by the usual course of the mails, but I avail myself of this opportunity of hastening their transmission.

On last evening the President [Samuel Houston] did me the honor to visit me, and we had an interview of several hours. He expressed great dissatisfaction that his ministers [Isaac Van Zandt and J. Pinckney Henderson] had not exacted stronger guarantys of the United States, before going into the treaty of annexation, and made strong expressions in reference to its effect upon the relations of the two countries. He seemed to be impressed with the opinion, that I would have the power, if I chose to exercise it, to order the military to take up a suitable position for the defence of Texas, if the requisition should be made by her Executive. He showed considerable passion. I heard all he had to say, and respectfully replied to him in the spirit & temper of my reply to the Secretary of State, who was also present at the interview. We parted with perfect courtesy &, I trust, cordiality, and I shall labor to prevent any misunderstanding, and to preserve the present friendly relations of the two countries.

It will be seen that I have left the way open for instructions from my ["own" *interlined*] government, and it will afford me great pleasure to receive & conform my conduct to them. I have the honor to be, most truly, Your most Ob[e]d[ien]t serv[an]t, T.A. Howard.

[Enclosure]
Anson Jones to Tilghman A. Howard

Department of State

Washington [Texas,] Aug[us]t 6th 1844

The Undersigned, Secretary of State of the Republic of Texas has the honor to transmit, herewith, to Gen. Howard, Chargé d'Affaires of the United States, near this Government, the copy of a communication from the Hon. G.W. Hill of this date, with accompanying documents A. and B. containing the information that Mexico is about to recommence active hostilities against this country.

The Undersigned is aware that Gen. Howard has already been informed of the efforts making by Gen. Santa Anna to raise funds in Mexico and an Army of thirty thousand men for the subjugation of Texas, and that troops in considerable numbers have already been moved towards our South western frontier under the command of Gen. [Valentín] Canalizo of the Mexican Army, an Officer appointed to carry this object into effect.

The information now in possession of this Government leads the Undersigned to the conclusion, that Mexico, intends either to renew a system of predatory warfare against Texas, or else to make a formidable attempt for its conquest, and that whichever alternative she may have concluded to adopt she has been induced to her course by the negotiations pending between Texas and the United States on the subject of Annexation.

In view of these facts, and adverting to the assurances given to this Government by Gen. [William S.] Murphy, Chargé d'Affaires of the United States, on the 14th of February, and by Mr. Calhoun, Secretary of State on the 11th of April last, the Undersigned by direction of His Excellency the President [Samuel Houston] has the honor to request that Gen. Howard, will as early as convenient take the necessary steps to cause to be carried into effect these assurances, and to extend to Texas the aid which the present emergency requires.

The Undersigned embraces, with great pleasure, this occasion to present to Gen. Howard the assurances of his distinguished consideration and regard. Anson Jones.

[Enclosure]

T.A. Howard to Anson Jones

Legation of the United States
Washington [Texas], 6th August 1844

The undersigned Chargé d'Affaires of the United States, near the government of the Republic of Texas, has the honor to acknowledge the receipt of the communication of the Hon. Anson Jones Secretary of State of this Republic, of this date, together with its accompanying documents.

The undersigned is aware of the incipient steps which have ["been" *interlined*] taken by the Chief of the Mexican government, with the alledged purpose of invading and subjugating Texas; but how far the preparations have gone he is not informed. He has no reason, however, to doubt the information communicated by the Hon. Secretary—on the contrary, he has received similar information from other quarters. How far the relations of Texas & the United States, may have excited the Mexican government to additional efforts to reconquer Texas, & hastened the renewal of hostilities, the undersigned has no means of judging. Whatever may be the cause, it cannot but be the subject of universal regret throughout Christendom, that a war of the character which has marked the relations of Texas & Mexico, since the Revolution of 1836, should not be brought to a close.

If, however, the recommencement of this conflict has been owing to negotiations between the governments of the United States and Texas, and if the United States have given "assurances to extend to Texas the aid which the present emergency requires," by which the undersigned supposes is meant, military aid, in repelling the anticipated invasion by Mexico, the obligations thus incurred ought to be, and he doubts not, will be observed by his government.

The undersigned has taken occasion to re-examine the letters of the late Gen. Murphy of the 14th of February last, and of Mr. Calhoun, Secretary of State of the United States of the 11th of April ensuing; he has also turned his attention to the letter of the Hon. John Nelson Secretary of State *ad interim* to Gen. Murphy of the 11th of

March 1844 and of the Hon. Isaac Van Zandt of the 17th of January of the same year. The letter of the Hon. Mr. Nelson, it will be seen, limits very much the assurances given by the Hon. Mr. Murphy, and discloses in explicit language the constitutional limitations under which the Executive of the United States must act in regard to the military power of the country.

The question, then, is mainly left to rest upon the letter of the Hon. Mr. Van Zandt of the 17th of January and the answer of Mr. Calhoun of the 11th of April 1844. Mr. Van Zandt submits the following inquiry to the Secretary of State, (Mr. [Abel P.] Upshur): "Should the president of Texas accede to the proposition of annexation, would the President of the United States, after the signing of the treaty, and before it shall be ratified and receive the sanction ["of the other branches" *interlined*] of both governments, in case Texas should desire it, or with her consent, order such number of military and naval forces of the United States, to such necessary points or places upon the territory or borders of Texas, or the Gulf of Mexico, as shall be sufficient to protect her against foreign aggression?" Mr. Calhoun, after refer[r]ing to the orders given to the naval & military forces gives the assurance, that should the exigency arise *during the pendency of the treaty of annexation*, the president would deem it his duty to use all the means placed within his power by the Constitution to protect Texas from invasion.

The undersigned assures the Hon. Secretary of State, of the disposition of his government to fulfil all her obligations to Texas, and of the deep interest felt both by the government and people of the United States, in whatever concerns her welfare; to which he will add his own anxious wish, to preserve the most perfect faith towards both the government & people of Texas: But he is not able to perceive, that an assurance given, that the military power should be used so far as it constitutionally might, to repel invasion *during the pendency of the treaty*, to which alone, both Mr. Calhoun & Mr. Van Zandt seem to have had reference, would raise an obligation on the president of the United States, to interpose by affording military aid to Texas in the present emergency.

In communicating this opinion to the Hon. Secretary of State, the undersigned is happy to know, that he addresses one, who is familiar with the fundamental laws & government of the U. States, which prescribe certain rules of action for every public functionary.

Nevertheless, as the subject is one of great moment, and is entitled to the consideration of the government of the United States—and as the facts communicated are important, he will transmit as speedily as practicable, this correspondence with the accompanying documents to his government, and await her instructions.

The undersigned with the most unfeigned pleasure takes this occasion, to present to the Hon. Mr. Jones the assurance of his distinguished consideration & esteem.   T.A. Howard.

ALS (Confidential) with Ens in DNA, RG 59 (State Department), Diplomatic Despatches, Texas, vol. 2 (T-728:2, frames 382–390), received 8/26; autograph copy with Ens in DNA, RG 84 (Foreign Posts), Texas; PEx with Ens in Senate Document No. 1, 28th Cong., 2nd Sess., pp. 24–29; PEx with Ens in House Document No. 2, 28th Cong., 2nd Sess., pp. 24–29; PEx with Ens in *Congressional Globe*, 28th Cong., 2nd Sess., Appendix, pp. 2–3; PEx with Ens in the Washington, D.C., *Globe*, December 6, 1844, p. 1; PEx with Ens in the Washington, D.C., *Daily National Intelligencer*, December 7, 1844, p. 2; PEx with Ens in the Washington, D.C., *Daily Madisonian*, December 7, 1844, p. 3; PEx with Ens in *Niles' National Register*, vol. LXVII, no. 15 (December 14, 1844), pp. 231–232; PEx with Ens in Crallé, ed., *Works*, 5:356–363. NOTE: Attached to Jones's letter to Howard of 8/6 were three documents not transcribed above: a letter of 8/6 to Jones from G[eorge] W. Hill, Texan Secretary of War and Marine; an extract of 7/21/1844 from John C. Hays, "Comm[an]d[in]g So[uth] western frontier," to Hill; and a translation of a letter of 6/19 from Adrian Woll to Sam Houston. In his letter to Gen. Taylor, labelled "Confidential," Howard requested Taylor's aid in the prompt transmission to Calhoun of the enclosed documents because "they relate to an anticipated invasion of Texas by Mexico."

From C[OLIN] M. INGERSOLL, "Private"

New Haven, Aug. 7, [18]44
My Dear Sir, You will I trust excuse the liberty I take in soliciting a favour at your hands which you may find it in your power to do me. I am somewhat desirous of taking a sea voyage and to be absent three or four months from the U.S. and supposing that despatches are often sent from the department to our Ministers near the Foreign Courts, I am prompted to express a wish to you, that you would suggest my name to the President, should an opportunity present itself, as the Bearer of any special despatches the Government may wish to send.

The Democracy of Connecticut I am happy to assure you is fully aroused to the importance of the next election, and the universal sentiment is, to overcome the opposition, and save the land from ruin. The feeling with us is far different from what it was before the Convention which met at Baltimore.   We thought then Mr. [Martin] V[an] Buren would be the candidate of the Dem[ocratic] party and with him for a *leader* (if one who despises the term may use it) every one, almost, felt that we were doomed to defeat, in spite of the tactics of party. It is perhaps a melancholy reflection to the Christian Patriot of this country that the people are governed more by their feelings than by reason or moral reflection. The man that is of them—whose heart beats to theirs—who is known to be open, generous, and bold, they prefer to the mere diplomast whose blood creeps lazily through his veins. They will rally around the man who possesses personal popularity, though bad reputation, rather than support another who though he has no stain upon his character, has no one element of popularity—without feeling—and cold as a block of ice. The issues made up at the National Convention, the Democracy of Connecticut will stand by. The Tarriff question is beginning to be understood and I shall be surprised if our people consent much longer to submit to be robbed by this unjust system of Taxation. I look upon the battle of 1844 as between the people and *corporations*, if the latter prevail, individual rights will be swallowed up, and should that time ever come, which heaven forbid, then we must have a Revolution, or sink into abject slavery. The daring iniquities of Banks and manufacturing establishments that we submit to, it seems to me, would in any other country justify a resort to violence. But here the *Ballot* is our weapon—"the Ithuriel spear of Freeman." The Political signs are auspicious and gratifying, and I hope if we are victorious in the fall, truth will follow the victory. Still I cannot say that I have the fullest faith that when we get into power we shall use it as we should. There are those who call themselves Republicans who have not the moral courage to cast off the bondage of Corporations and act for the general good, there are yet too many joined to their idols, to hope for that freedom which it is presumed the pilgrims saw in "clear dream and solemn vision." Among the other questions which now are agitated in this State, there is none more popular with the Democracy than the Texas question, at the mention of the name at our meetings, the welkin rings. The secret circular movement will have no influence with us. A Connecticut family [Moses Austin's] founded the colony of Texas—A Connecticut Legislature first acknowledged its independence as a nation, and I believe Connecticut will be found with the other States in favor of its reannexation to the U.S.

But sir I am troubling you perhaps with an idle waste of words. Excuse me for writing you in so plain and familiar manner as I have above, my admiration for the man, has led me unconsciously to write him as I would an old friend and confidant. Accept assurances of my high respect and consideration, and believe me Very Truly Your servant, C.M. Ingersoll.

ALS in ScCleA.

From JAMES B. LONGACRE

Philad[elphi]a, Aug. 7, 1844

Sir, After my interview with you on the 1st inst. I learned at the Treasury Department, that there would probably be no action in relation to the appointment of Engraver to the Mint in this City, untill after the return of the President [John Tyler] to Washington.

Some of the gentlemen, on whose testimonials of character and ability, I place peculiar value, are at this time out of the City: and it will require some four or five days longer, before I can obtain their letters; which as soon as received, I will forward to your care.

In the mean time if it should be thought expedient to act on the appointment, I have concluded to send you my application together with the enclosed testimonies, which I hope in such case, may be sufficient to induce a favourable consideration of my claims to attention.

Mr. [Thomas] Sully, is too well known in the arts of the country to require any comment on the value of his commendation.

Mr. [John F.] Watson, is the well known author of "The Annals of Philadelphia." His communication is addressed, (as you will perceive) to the Secretary of the Treasury [George M. Bibb].

Mr. [John] Sartain, I need scarcely say, is at the head of his department in art in this country, as a mezzotint engraver.

The note of Mr. Bradford is addressed to the President which he will no doubt fully appreciate.

While I wish to escape the charge of egotism if possible, the very circumstance of my application, seems to require that I should say something of what I have done, or can do, as an artist: and I have the less hesitation on the subject, as there is no one equally competent to give the information—and I have the example of Leonardo da Vinci as a precedent.

I was born in the State of Pennsylvania, in which I have always lived. In my professional pursuits, I was the pupil of the late Mr. [George] Murray of the house of Murray, Draper, Fairman, & Co. I am acquainted with, and have successfully practised the various processes of engraving on copper, steel, silver and gold: I am familiar with the use of the graver in almost every form; with the steel and diamond points; with *roulettes, punches* and *dies*: with the modes and menstruums used in etching on steel, copper, and gold. I have also practised in design, and drawing from the life, from statuary, and from *alto* and *basso-relievo*; and although I have been most employed in portraiture—I have executed works in various other departments of art—such as ornamental dies, subjects in architecture, Landscape and Natural History.

At the present time I am employed on a private order in engraving medallions on gold; and the study of Numismatics has been a favourite pursuit with me, independently of my professional employment. I am with sentiments of most sincere respect, Your Obedient Servant &c, James B. Longacre.

ALS in DNA, RG 56 (Secretary of the Treasury), Applications for Positions as Assistant Treasurers and Mint Officers, 1836–1898. NOTE: Longacre received the appointment solicited.

From HENRY WHEATON

Berlin, 7 Aug., 1844

Sir, Your Despatch, No. 57 [of 6/28], has been duly received, & I have framed from it an official note to [Heinrich Ulrich Wilhelm,] Baron de Bülow, a copy of which will be transmitted to the Department with the answer, as soon as the latter shall be received.

The Hanoverian *Chargé d'Affaires* at this court has just communicated to me the intention of his Government to augment the present duties on the importation of raw *tobacco* into the Kingdom of Hanover. He, at the same time, expressed to me their desire to negotiate with us for the admission of our tobacco, & other agricultural productions, into that Kingdom, on the most favorable footing. In return for these concessions, they will only require a reduction of the duties now levied by us on the article of *linens*, that being the chief article of manufacture they export to the United States.

In reply to this overture, I merely stated that I would communicate it to the Department, but could not expect to receive any specific instructions upon the subject until the fate of the Convention with the Zollverein States was determined by the Senate.

Should that Convention be ultimately ratified, I think I am not mistaken in anticipating that Hanover will not be the only European

Country that will come forward to negotiate with us on the same basis. Mr. [Chretien-Frederic] Engelhardt, the French Commissary for the Portendic affair, & who is also employed in the commercial negotiations between his Government & the Zollverein, recently informed me that he should advise Mr. [Francois P.G.] Guizot to open a negotiation with us, on a similar basis, the moment the Convention of the 25 March was ratified. As the opinion of Mr. Engelhardt is known to have great weight with his Government in all commercial questions, I have no doubt it will be followed in this instance.

I perceive nothing in our existing Treaties with France, under which she can claim, without adequate equivalents, the same advantages which are conceded to the German Zollverein by the Convention ["of the 25 March," *interlined*] as our Convention with France, of 1800, has long since expired, & there is nothing in the existing Treaty of 1822, under which she can set up such a claim.

The Prussian & Belgic Governments have become involved in a war of commercial retaliation, in consequence of the German Zollverein States having imposed an additional duty upon raw & manufactured iron imported from Belgium. The latter power has now retaliated by imposing, upon Prussian vessels, entering the ports of Belgium, the same tonnage duties which are levied upon all foreign vessels not belonging to favored nations, & by revoking the exemption hitherto enjoyed by Prussian vessels, in common with other nations, of the tolls payable on the Scheldt, under the Treaties for the separation of Belgium from Holland.

The origin of this controversy may be traced to a decree of the Belgic Government, by which the same favors were extended, without any equivalent, to the silks & wines of the Zollverein States, which had been previously granted by Belgium to the silks & wines of France, for an equivalent concession on the part of the latter Power. This decree had been issued by the Belgic Government, in the hope that some reciprocal advantages would be granted by the Zollverein States; but, this hope having been disappointed, the decree was revoked, & the revocation was followed, on the 21 June, by an ordinance of of [*sic*] the Zollverein States, imposing extraordinary duties on Belgic iron. This again led to the ordinance of the 29 July, by which the existing duties on Prussian navigation have been considerably augmented in Belgium. I have the honor to be, with the highest consideration, Sir, Y[ou]r Ob[e]d[ien]t Serv[an]t, Henry Wheaton.

LS (No. 256) in DNA, RG 59 (State Department), Diplomatic Despatches, Germany, vol. 3 (M-44:4), received 9/3; FC in DNA, RG 84 (Foreign Posts), Germany, Despatches, 4:144–148.

From H[ENRY] W. CONNER, "Private"

Charleston, August 8, 1844

Dear Sir, What I most fear'd when I wrote you a short time since has come to pass—a portion of the democratic party in Colleton [District] have determined upon a seperate & distinct action on the part of the State & their course is embarrassing in the extreme & in all respects singularly unfortunate at this time. In Charleston with few exceptions, all are opposed to precipitate actions of any kind & I think it is so mostly throughout the State but it so happens that the decomocratic [*sic*] papers of the State are in that interest & give utterance only to the sentiments of the movement party & their voice is abroad I doubt not ["is" *canceled*] taken to be the voice of South Carolina & necessarrily produces its injurious effects.

Your friends in Charleston are extremely anxious to see & be councilled by you in the present peculiar state of things & have learned that you may probably pass this way sometime about the middle or last of this month. We entreat that you stop amongst us a day or two (the city is perfectly healthy) & give your friends an opportunity of conferring with you. Myself & several others whose business will take them away shortly would be glad to know about what time we may expect you as we wish to be here at that time.

There never was a time when your councils were more needed to the State than just now. Very truly y[ou]rs &c, H.W. Conner.

ALS in ScCleA.

From W[ILLIAM] D. PORTER

Charleston, 8 August 1844

Respected Sir, I should not venture to trouble you with this letter, were it not that I feel that my position as President of the Young Men's Democratic Association of Charleston, imposes it upon me as a duty to seek your advice concerning the position we should occupy in the present state of ["appro"(?) *canceled*] affairs. You must of course have observed the ground recently taken by the Mercury & by Mr. [Robert Barnwell] Rhett & his friends at Bluffton. I have every reason to believe that the majority of our Young Men of the City look upon the step of these gentlemen as rash & uncalled for—and that they look with all confidence to your wisdom & patriotism to suggest to them safer & more prudent counsels. I shall be happy to receive your views as to the course ["which" *canceled*] we should pursue, the more particularly as this issue has been unexpectedly forced upon us, & will certainly involve the most serious consequences. I am, Sir, very respectfully Your most obedient Servant, W.D. Porter.

ALS in ScCleA.

From FERNANDO WOOD

New York [City,] August 8 1844

Sir, I have the honour to enclose a memorial [of 6/13] for the appointment of Roland Dubs Esq. ["to" *interlined*] the vacant Consulate at Maracaybo Venezuela. He is a resident ["here" *altered to* "there"] and a gentleman ["of" *interlined*] standing and respectability who would faithfully discharge the duties.

Our commerce with that place is gradually becoming very important and the necessity of a representation of the government and a protector for our vessals is quite evident. I hope your attention at an early day will be given to the subject, and Mr. Dubs be appointed. Very Respectfully Your ob[e]d[ien]t Ser[van]t, Fernando Wood.

ALS with En in DNA, RG 59 (State Department), Applications and Recommendations, 1845–1853, Dubs (M-873:24, frames 456–458).

From Geo[rge] M. Bibb, Secretary of the Treasury, 8/9. In response to the letter [of 4/21] from Chevalier [Jean Corneille] Gevers, forwarded by Calhoun to the Treasury Department, Bibb reviews U.S. treaties with the Netherlands and the provisions of the tariff of 1842 as they relate to Java coffee imported into the U.S. in Dutch vessels. He concludes that a 20 per cent duty on such coffee contravenes the 1839 reciprocity treaty. That portion of the tariff law is thus unconstitutional because it contradicts a pre-existing treaty. "The task of declaring such enaction by the Congress to be void because of such repugnance to the Constitution, & to a previously subsisting & continuing treaty, howsoever delicate & responsible to be undertaken by the head of this department, is one from which I shall not shrink, when so presented by the diplomatic accredited agent of a foreign nation, and involving the good faith of the government of the United States." He will order Customs Collectors to refund duties paid upon Java coffee imported in Dutch vessels and to cease collecting such duties. With regard to that portion of Gevers's note relating to Dutch merchants obliged to pay customs duties at rates altered while they were at sea, Bibb states that he has no authority to reimburse them or to modify rates charged. ALS in DNA, RG 59 (State Department), Miscellaneous Letters (M-179:105, frames 156–164); FC in DNA, RG 56 (Secretary of the Treasury), Letters to Cabinet and Bureau Officers, Series B, 4:412–418.

From John E. Carew

Charleston S.C., 9 August 1844
Dear Sir, The "Young Men[']s Democratic association" of Charleston, So[uth] Ca[rolina], deeply sensible of the vitally important position of political affairs, as now presented by the antagonist parties of the United States; and having been accustomed to regard your opinions, and counsel with the most profound respect and consideration, respectfully request that you will, (as far as may be compatible with your sense of propriety) indicate the course which in your judgment, you may deem it expedient for the Democratic party of South Carolina to pursue in reference to the great questions now before the people.

It is perhaps, Sir, not out of place to inform you that our association has adopted as its motto—"Free Trade[,] Low duties—no debt—separation from Banks, Economy—retrenchment—and a strict adherence to the Constitution," sentiments which it regards as the condensed text of your political life, and which if triumphant, must preserve Liberty and the Union, and carry your already honored name down to a distant and grateful posterity. I have the honor to be your Very Re[s]p[ectfu]l & Ob[edien]t Servant, Jno. E. Carew, Ch[airman,] Corresp[ondin]g Com[mittee].

ALS in ScCleA. NOTE: Carew became editor of the Charleston *Mercury* in 1847.

To EDWARD EVERETT, [London]

Department of State
Washington, 9th Aug[us]t, 1844

Sir: It is with much satisfaction that the President [John Tyler] perceives, from despatches recently received from Mr. [Caleb] Cushing, that the most marked attention and kindness have uniformly, throughout Mr. Cushing's progress towards his destination, been shown, on the part of the British authorities, to him, and to his suite, as well as to Commodore [Foxhall A.] Parker and the officers of the Frigate Brandywine, at Bombay and Poona, where, more especially, the conduct of Sir George Arthur, Sir Robert Oliver, and other persons in authority, was such as to make a strong and grateful impression. I am accordingly directed by the President to instruct you to convey to the British Government his high sense of the courtesy and hospitality of Her Majesty's officers in this instance, which he trusts will be reciprocated whenever an occasion may be offered.

With reference to that part of your despatch, No. 153, which recalls the attention of this Department to the wish of Her Britannic Majesty's Government, that applications for exequâturs for Consuls at the British colonial possessions should be accompanied with information whether the persons appointed are already at their posts, you are informed, that, since the receipt of your No. 58, in the postscript of which the same subject is mentioned, the suggestion has been acted upon as far as it was in the power of the Department to act; and that it will continue to be borne in mind in future.

The accompanying papers, a list of which is enclosed, embrace all the applications in favor of American Citizens imprisoned at Van Diemen's Land, which have been received at this Department since the date of my despatch No. 94.

With respect to the proposal of Mr. Samuel Deacon, communicated in your No. 162, to sell to this Government a complete set of the "London Gazette," from 1665 to 1834, I have to state, that the contingent fund of this Department is too limited to warrant such an expenditure for our Library. The price at which the set is held, appears to be high, though it would certainly be valuable for purposes of reference. I will cause to be communicated to the Joint Committee on the Library of Congress a copy of Mr. Deacon's letter to you, of the 13th ultimo, with the view of obtaining their decision upon his offer. I am, Sir, respectfully, Your obedient Servant, J.C. Calhoun.

LS (No. 101) with Ens in DNA, RG 84 (Foreign Posts), Great Britain, Instructions, 8:335–342, received 9/2; FC in DNA, RG 59 (State Department), Diplomatic Instructions, Great Britain, 15:218–219 (M-77:74).

From Ben E. Green, Secretary of Legation and Chargé d'Affaires ad Interim, Mexico, 8/9. He discusses arrangements for paying to him his salary. ALS (retained copy) in NcU, Duff Green Papers (published microfilm, roll 5, frame 735).

To ALLEN A. HALL, [Caracas]

Department of State
Washington, 9th August, 1844

Sir: Mr. John W. Holding, who is understood to be the representative of the claim on the late government of Colombia in the case of the ship Good Return, has requested that a special instruction might be addressed to you upon the subject. I informed him that I could not go further than repeat the instructions of my predecessors.

The instruction of Mr. [John] Forsyth to Mr. [James] Semple upon this subject has already been communicated to you. Herewith you will receive a copy of the letter of Mr. [Henry] Clay to Mr. [Beaufort T.] Watts of the 8th of January, 1827. You will consider these as your instructions in relation to the case. I am, Sir, your obedient servant, J.C. Calhoun.

LS (No. 20) in DNA, RG 76 (Records of Boundary and Claims Commissions and Arbitrations), Miscellaneous Claims Records: Colombia, 1818–1825; FC in DNA, RG 59 (State Department), Diplomatic Instructions, Venezuela, 1:48 (M-77:171).

From JAMES WISHART, "Private"

St. Clairsville [Ohio,] Aug[us]t 9th 1844

My Dear Sir, In order to relieve you from any additional burden which a correspondence with me might impose on you, I have, within the last year made an effort to secure a southern correspondent among your reputed friends but have now abandoned the fruitless effort.

I have waited until our nominations were made to ascertain the temper of the Bentonians who are anti Texas and rule our political destinies in this county. Rule or ruin is still their object, and in order to defeat a friend of yours who is on the ticket I look for the overthrow of the whole ticket this fall. They declare openly their intention to open the campaign for [Thomas H.] Benton immediately after the present election is over. It is believed they secretly desire the defeat of [James K.] Polk although they profess to go for him. The indecision of those who profess to be with us has given them more than their usual control and although they can carry nothing of their own, they are strong enough to defeat us. The same congress candidate who represented this district last winter [Joseph Morris] is again nominated. He will be elected in the district. We have men greatly his superior in every respect, but they are powerless as things now stand.

Until 1832 I was popular and possessed more influence than any other in the county. From then til now wrongs[,] injustice and oppression have pursued me. Circumstances beyond my control will compel me to leave my present ["position" *altered to* "location"] unless you have the influence to secure for me a temporary appointment. It is with extreme reluctance and dif[f]idence I prefer this request, and should your compliance subject you to any embarrassment or inconvenience, I beg that you do not, on my account, incur either. This is the first application ["of the kind" *interlined*] I have ever made to any one, and you are the only one I can bring myself to make it to, ["now" *interlined*] and it would be very difficult for me to find language to express my sensations in addressing such a request to you.

We shall carry Polk and Texas even should our local ticket fail. Very Respectfully, James Wishart.

ALS in ScCleA.

From Jesse Atkinson, Tallahassee, 8/10. He encloses a deposition "of John C. Hall, taken by me on yesterday . . . upon interrogatories Submitted by" Charles S. Sibley. It is to be added to other documents comprising Sibley's defense against charges made against him. ALS with En in DNA, RG 59 (State Department), Applications and Recommendations, 1837–1845, Sibley (M-687:30, frames 218–221).

From John Baldwin, "Mansion House," New York [City], 8/10. He has heard rumors that Mexico will not make any more payments on her indemnity to the U.S. unless the U.S. renounces any intention of annexing Texas at any future time. Baldwin asks Calhoun to inform him if this rumor is founded in fact, in order that he can find some way to save himself from ruin because of Mexico's faithlessness. ALS in DNA, RG 59 (State Department), Miscellaneous Letters (M-179:105, frames 166–167).

From Charles H. Delavan, U.S. Consul, Sydney, Nova Scotia, 8/10. He informs Calhoun of the British detention of the U.S. fishing schooner *Argus* "for an alleged trespass on the fishing ground." From the evidence that Delavan can gather, the *Argus* was far from land when the seizure occurred. He hopes that the vessel will be released when his evidence is presented to the Attorney General at Halifax. ALS in DNA, RG 59 (State Department), Consular Despatches, Sydney, Canada, vol. 1 (T-490:1), received 8/27.

To J[OHN] W. HOLDING, Baltimore

Department of State
Washington, 10th Aug[us]t 1844
Sir, Your letter of the 7th inst. has been received. I inform'd you in Conversation that in any despatches to the representatives of the United States at Caracas or Bogota, upon the subject of the claim in the case of the Good Return, I could not go further than my predecessors, but was willing to repeat the orders which they had given. I at the same time remarked that I considered the case a hopeless one and I understood that you had determined to abandon it. As it appears, however, that you desire a repetition of the orders which have heretofore been given upon the subject, a letter to Mr. [Allen A.] Hall, the Chargé d'Affaires of the United States to Venezuela, has accordingly been prepared and is contained in the accompanying package, which I will thank you to forward by the opportunity to which you have referred. I am, Sir, Your Obedient Servant, John C. Calhoun.

FC in DNA, RG 59 (State Department), Domestic Letters, 34:329 (M-40:32).

From T[ILGHMAN] A. HOWARD

Legation of the United States
Washington (T[exas,]) August 10 1844

Sir, I have the honor to transmit herewith, a letter [of 7/30] from a highly respectable gentleman [Oscar Farish], recommending Robert D. Johnson as a suitable person to fill the vacancy occasioned by the death of Col. [Archibald M.] Green, in the Consulate at Galveston. Mr. Farrish [*sic*] is the brother in law of Col. Green. I have the honor to be very truly Your friend & servant, T.A. Howard.

ALS (No. 5) with En in DNA, RG 59 (State Department), Diplomatic Despatches, Texas, vol. 2 (T-728:2, frames 391–393), received 10/20; autograph copy in DNA, RG 84 (Foreign Posts), Texas.

From F[RANCIS] W. PICKENS

Covington Geo[rgia,] 10 August '44

My dear Sir, I am thus far on my way to Nashville, but have been so disappointed about stages &c—that I fear I cannot get there in time for the meeting the 15th. But I shall go on at any rate as I am started & see the leading men. [Franklin H.] Elmore could not come but met me in Augusta. He shewed me your letters & seems to be with us fully and yet the [Charleston] Mercury moves strangely. I assure ["you" *interlined*] it is ruining us in this State with our best friends. I was with Col. J[ohn H.] Howard of Columbus last night and you know he is a nullifier, yet he says the Mercury is killing us in Geo[rgia]. They say if we lose the State it will be from the course of some of our friends in So[uth] Ca[rolina]. Judge Dyer a *whig* from Augusta told me last night that a letter had been rec[eive]d in Augusta which stated that Mr. [Robert Barnwell] Rhett had split from you and had said you were bought off by the Presidency. Something of the same kind was said a week ago at Edgefield by Col. [Louis T.] Wigfall who is for Disunion open.

I asked Elmore expressly what Rhett was doing &c—he told me *he knew nothing of him.* This may all be exag[g]erated—but there must be something wrong somewhere. I see by a letter published from the White Sulphur Spring[s] Va. in the Mercury that the same idea is suggested of your "deserting your old friends" &c and if so another must be look[ed] to to save the State &c. I wrote you sometime since but rec[eive]d no answer. I seriously believe that many of the whigs of this State are desirous to run you immediately after this Election is over[,] let who will be elected.

I shall take the highest ground at Nashville ag[ain]st the Tariff, but at the same time ag[ain]st all seperate action of the State at present—that we will wait the result of the Fall Elections, & if ag[ain]st us we will organize with our Rep[ublican] brethren of the South who have fought the battle with us in good faith, and consult freely as to the grounds of conserted action.

As to the Tariff of 1842, without ["and" *canceled*] an inflated currency it cannot stand. Without a Bank (& they cannot get that in the present state of the country) it must fall. [Henry] Clay cannot sustain his Adm[inistration] 6 months upon the Tariff of 1842. Va. seperated from N[ew] York will now give us a united South & I believe we can right the Gov[ernment,] let who will come in. If we are to split with some of our rash friends we must do so firmly but mildly, & we must take ground soon or the injury will be perpetrated. Our cause will in reality be thrown back instead of advanced.

I do not know whether to write from Nashville or not as Mr. [Thomas G.] Clemson wrote you [were] going to Pendleton this month. If s[o I] will return by Clark[e]sville [Ga.] & Pendleton to see you a few days. In haste but truly, F.W. Pickens.

ALS in ScCleA; variant PEx in Boucher and Brooks, eds., *Correspondence*, pp. 243–244.

To S[tephen] Pleasonton, Fifth Auditor

Department of State
Washington, 10 Aug[us]t 1844

Sir, I have had under consideration the statement of the claim of Mr. Henry Middleton [of S.C.], late Minister to Russia, presented by you.

With respect to the first item, for his expenses at London in the year 1820, for thirteen weeks, at £70 per week, on a special mission there by order of the Department of State, when on his way to St. Petersburgh, including his travelling expenses from Liverpool to London and from London to St. Petersburgh, I have to remark, that Mr. Middleton was at the time in receipt of his salary as Minister to Russia, and that he was not entitled to charge the expenses of his journey from the United States to St. Petersburgh. If, in consequence of taking London in his way he was subjected to expenses that would not otherwise have accrued, allowance should be made therefor upon the fact being shown. Also, for any expenses during his detention in London over what would have accrued at St. Petersburgh, had he been in the latter city, and the additional expense which he may have incurred in travelling to St. Petersburgh at an unfavorable season of the year, in consequence of his detention in London.

The second item, being a claim for contingent expenses for four years and seven months at a fixed rate per annum, being that of the average of several preceding years, is not presented in a shape to allow the exercise of a proper discretion, being without the necessary specification of items. I cannot therefore direct its allowance.

The item for expenses of attending the coronation of the Emperor Nicholas, as stated in his letter of the 22d Ultimo, amounting to $511, may be allowed, similar allowances having been made to Ministers of the United States at other courts.

I do not feel authorised to allow the fourth item, for salary of an acting Secretary of Legation, such allowance being prohibited by the act of the 1st of May, 1810, to persons not duly appointed; and as it appears that the salary of a Secretary of Legation was paid during the whole period for which the claim is made, with the exception of nine days. It appears to me, that Congress, alone, is competent to allow such a claim. I am Sir, Your obedient Servant, J.C. Calhoun.

FC in DNA, RG 59 (State Department), Accounting Records: Miscellaneous Letters Sent, 1832–1916, vol. for 2/1–9/30/1844, pp. 335–[336].

From RAMON LEON SANCHEZ

Consulate of the United States
Cartagena, 10th August 1844
Sir, I accompany herewith, Copies of a Communication received from the Governor of this Province dated 31 July Ultimo, and of a Recent Resolution of the Executive of this Republic, respecting the Custom introduced in all the ports on this Coast, of the Consuls hoisting the Flags of their respective nations, at their several residences, and the manner in which such a Custom, is to be regarded. I also accompany Copy of my answer to the Governor under date of 1 August.

The practice of hoisting the Flags, was introduced as early as the establishment of Consuls in all the ports of Colombia, and has been

Continued in ["all" *interlined*] the ports of the three Republics, that emerged out of the former. In all the Republics in Spanish America, the custom prevails of using the Flag, and I believe that it also prevails in the ports of several of the Kingdoms in Europe.

It certainly is the most respectable and proper insignia to denote the residence and office of the Consul. The Executive of New Granada does not object to the Continuation of this Custom, but clearly stipulates that the Flag, shall not protect the houses whereat they are hoisted, from the jurisdiction of the Country, nor from being entered and searched by the the [*sic*] local Authorities. I don[']t Know how far this doctrine will agree with international law, but I think, it will be subject to very great abuses, in Countries so frequently disturbed by civil wars, during which, in most instances, very little regard is paid to the Laws of the Country by the rival parties, and no security given to the persons and property of foreigners, but, what is extorted by the dread, of incurring a heavy responsibility, towards the Government of their respective Countries.

Heretofore in all the political troubles in this Republic, the Flags of the different Consulates, have been, most sacredly respected by the Chiefs and partisans of the Contending parties, because until now, there existed a tacit admission of the immunity of the Consulates, and no authority has ever questioned it. In such a crisis, the Consulate has always served as an asylum for the citizens, of the country it represents, and they have always found it a place of Safety, when no other existed.

If this inviolability of the Flag is annulled, and the Consulates, liable to be entered and searched by the local Magistrates, under any circumstances, then the protection, heretofore granted to our citizens, will be in future, but nominal, since it will be impossible for the Consulate to protect, when it has no means of protecting—especially in revolutionary times, when the country is divided into factions, neither, respecting, or observing any law. The inviolability of the Archives and public papers, which, ["it" *canceled*] is said to be, one of the Consular privileges, will be but a chimera, since, at any time, his office may be invaded under any pretext, and the Consul himself imprisoned upon any specious charge.

During the time of civil war, Consuls are obliged, to come, often, in collision with the authorities, in defending the rights of their fellow citizens, and may often, in so discharging their duties, fall under the displeasure of the Said Authorities, and in these Countries, every opportunity of that sort is apt to be embraced, to annoy & humiliate a foreign agent.

The preceding remarks, can of course have no other tendency, but to Show, how far Consuls will be at the mercy of Factions, and often perhaps at that of the Constituted authorities of the State, if the doctrine laid down by the Granadian Executive is of an absolute character, and to be enforced under all circumstances.

It is clearly established and understood that Consuls are not Diplomatic agents, and therefore not entitled to the rights[,] privileges and immunities enjoyed by Public Ministers; yet, all writers upon international law agree, that they are entitled to some privileges and exemptions, and some, advocate their absolute independence of the jurisdiction of the Country. In Countries where a well organized and Settled Government exists, it appears prudent to limit the rights and privileges of foreign Consuls, as much as possible, but such a policy is very questionable when applied to States, subject to periodical Convulsions, every five or Ten Years. States too, in which the Maladministration of Justice, is proverbial, and the solemn decission of whose High Courts, have been from its gross and palpable injustice, laid aside, by the Governments of France and Great Britain, on very recent occasions—The first in the Case of Consul Barrot at this place, and the Second, that of Acting Consul Russel, at Panama.

I respectfully submit these remarks to the Consideration of the Government, declaring that I am not at all disposed to contend for any right that may not be either clearly defined by Written law or well established by usage, but at same time, I do not like to relinquish any right[,] privilege or immunity clearly and distinctly belonging to the Office of Consul. In the absence of Treaty Stipulations, there is no other guide, but the international Law.

I have communicated on this subject with Mr. [William M.] Blackford, Chargé d'Affaires of the U.S. [at] Bogota.

I wish particularly to record, that I advocate no priviledges, but what are accorded by law to Consuls. My wish is to Know exactly what these privileges are, or rather if the view of the Granadian Governm[en]t on this point is correct and Conformable with the idea entertained on the same subject by the U.S. Government. I have the honor to be Sir Your mo[st] Obed[ien]t Serv[an]t, Ramon Leon Sanchez.

ALS (No. 37) with Ens in DNA, RG 59 (State Department), Consular Despatches, Cartagena, vol. 4 (T-192:4), received 9/14.

From Cha[rle]s S. Sibley, Tallahassee, 8/10. He defends himself against charges of misconduct in office that have been preferred by Governor Richard K. Call and by two others. Sibley informs Calhoun that an indictment against Call for obstructing navigation [on the St. Marks River] was issued by order of a grand jury. The evidence submitted by Sibley should remove from the minds of Calhoun and of President [John Tyler] any suspicion that Sibley is guilty of any misconduct. (A Clerk's EU reads: "Copy of this sent to Gov[erno]r Call. See letter to him of 22d Oct[obe]r 1844.") ALS in DNA, RG 59 (State Department), Applications and Recommendations, 1837–1845, Sibley (M-687:30, frames 227–245).

From Albert Smith, U.S. Com[missione]r, Moose River, Maine, 8/10. "It being deemed indispensable to a proper prosecution of the Boundary Survey, under the Treaty of Washington, to have a large Transit Instrument—and a large Telescope, those Instruments, were ordered by Maj. J[ames] D. Graham, the head of the American Scientific Corps, last December. They have recently arrived from England, & their cost is $1274.81—for which a Bill has been presented to me for payment. They are now in use upon the line. Am I authorized to pay the Bill?" ALS in DNA, RG 76 (Records of Boundary and Claims Commissions and Arbitrations), Letters Received by the Department of State concerning the Northeast Boundary Line.

From ISAAC VAN ZANDT

Legation of Texas
Washington, August 10th 1844

Sir, After an examination of the facts stated in the letter (a copy of which you did me the honor to show me) from A.M.M. Upshaw Esq., Chickasaw Agent, of the 27th of May, last, to the Commissioner of Indian Affairs [T. Hartley Crawford], concerning the two boys captured by the Indians on the Trinity River within the territory of Texas, and now represented to be among the Wichitaw Indians within the United States, I deem it my duty formally, but most respectfully to request, (that you may be pleased to communicate the same to His Excellency the President of the United States [John Tyler]) that such orders may be given by the proper Department to the proper Indian Agent or Military authorities of the United States, as may be necessary to secure the delivery of the two boys and their return to their own country, as provided in the 33rd Article of the Treaty of 1831.

I avail myself of this occasion to renew to you the assurance of

my distinguished consideration. Isaac Van Zandt, Cha[r]gé d'Affaires of the Republic of Texas.

LS in DNA, RG 59 (State Department), Notes from Foreign Legations, Texas,
vol. 1 (T-809:1); FC in Tx, Records of the Texas Republic Department of
State, Letters and Dispatches Sent by the Texas Legation in Washington,
1:528–529; CC in Tx, Records of the Texas Republic Department of State, U.S.
Diplomatic Correspondence; FC in Tx, Records of the Texas Republic Department of State, Copybooks of Letters Received from Texan and Foreign Representatives, vol. 2–1/98, p. 532; PC in Senate Document No. 14, 32nd Cong.,
2nd Sess., pp. 125–126. NOTE: On the LS is an AES of 8/14 by Tyler that
reads: "Let the proper directions be given by the Secretary of War [William
Wilkins] to the Officer in Command."

To [THOMAS G. CLEMSON, Paris?]

State Dept., 12th Aug[us]t 1844
My dear Sir, I wrote you and enclosed my measure, and franked a
package to you from Mr. [Francis] Markoe [Jr.] and mailed in time
to reach N[ew] York the evening before you sailed. I hope you received them in time. I now enclose a package from Gen[era]l
[James] Hamilton [Jr.] put under cover to Mr. [William R.] King
[U.S. Minister to France] who I presume will receive it before you
arrive at Parris [*sic*].

I received a letter yesterday from Mr. [James Edward] Boisseau
& ["one from" *interlined*] Mr. Mason of Boston after their return
from the Argo[?], and was happy to learn, that you had so fine a start
and were all in such good sperits. I hope you may find the voyage
agreeable throughout. I shall be anxious to hear of your arrival at
Paris.

Nothing new since I last wrote. I had a letter from home & one
from Willey [William Lowndes Calhoun] dated at Millwood, after
the return of himself & his uncle [James Edward Colhoun] from
Glen's Springs. All were well at home; and Willey writes that his
health & that of his Uncle's had improved.

I have been exceedingly engaged in preparing dispatches for the
Steamer for the last 8 or 10 days; and have just finished. I send out
by her two very important ["ones" *interlined*] to Mr. [Edward]
Everett [U.S. Minister to Great Britain] and one to Mr. King. That
to the latter & one of the two to Mr. E[verett] are very long; and I
think they are both calculated to make a strong impression. ["The"
canceled.] One ["of those to Mr. E(verett)" *interlined*] is on the

subject of the seven slaves in Florida, who after escaping from their masters and murdering & robbing in their way took shelter in Nassau, whence they were demanded and refused to be given up under the Ashburton treaty. The question involved is, whether it is a case within the provisions of the treaty. That I think I have established beyond controversy. The one to Mr. King relates to Texas & presents I think some very interesting views in relation to it, which I think will be felt in Europe.

My health remains good, though I have not yet got entirely clear of my cold. I expect to leave between this & the 20th Inst. for home & may be gone 5 or 6 weeks.

My love to Anna [Maria Calhoun Clemson] & the children [John Calhoun Clemson and Floride Elizabeth Clemson]; and prayers for the health & hap[p]iness of you all. I rec[eive]d your's & her letter, written the day before you sailed. Your affectionate father, J.C. Calhoun.

ALS in ScCleA; variant PC in Jameson, ed., *Correspondence*, pp. 605–606.

To EDWARD EVERETT, [London]

Department of State
Washington, 12th August, 1844
Sir, While I was engaged in preparing my Dispatch No. 99 [of 8/7] relating to the extradition of the fugitive slaves, who after committing murder and robbery in Florida, escaped to Nassau in the Bahama's, it became necessary for me to look into the correspondence in relation to the case, when for the first time, Mr. [Abel P.] Upshur's dispatch No. 69 and yours in answer to it, No. 90, came under my notice.

You conclude your dispatch by informing the Department, that if you should receive the instructions alluded to in your conversation with the Earl of Aberdeen, that you would lose no time in forwarding them to Washington, and that if, after a reasonable interval you should not hear from him, you would again call his attention to the subject of his (Mr. Upshur's) dispatch No. 69. Since then, the Department has neither received the instructions alluded to, nor heard from you in reference to the subject.

The object of addressing you now is, to call your attention to the subject. It is regarded as one of deep interest, and involving a very important principle.

In your account of the conversation between yourself and the Earl of Aberdeen, in reference to the subject of Mr. Upshur's dispatch, you state, that he remarked in reply to your observation in reference to the views of the laws of nations applicable to such cases as the Creole, which were maintained in his dispatch, that he doubted whether the instructions given to the colonial authorities enjoined them to adopt a course in conformity with those views; adding, "that it was impossible for Her Majesty's Government to make the slightest compromise on the subject of slavery; and that where slaves were found within the British jurisdiction, by whatever means, or from whatever quarter, they were ipso facto, free."

If it be the meaning of his Lordship, that Her Majesty's Government cannot make the slightest compromise of the principle that where slaves are found within the British jurisdiction, that they are by the fact itself made free, as is to be inferred he did from the latter part of his remarks, we have no desire or intention to controvert it. The laws of Great Britain declare the fact to be so, and we do not question her exclusive and absolute right of legislation on that or any other subject within her own jurisdiction.

But if it be his meaning, that a vessel of the United States having slaves on board and passing from one of their ports to another, would cease to be under the jurisdiction of the United States and be within that of Great Britain, if she should be carried into the waters or harbour of one of her adjacent colonies, by the force of the elements or by the revolt of the slaves on board taking possession of the vessel after overpowering the crew and murdering the commander, as in the case of the Creole, or by any other overruling and irresistible necessity, so as to subject the slaves on board to the operation of the Act of Parliament for the emancipation of slaves within the British dominions, then it would be the assertion of a principle, which we maintain to be in direct conflict with the laws of nations, with the admission of Lord Ashburton in his correspondence with Mr. [Daniel] Webster in negotiating the Treaty of Washington, and the express understanding under which that Treaty was accepted and ratified. While we admit the full and absolute right of Great Britain to legislate for her own subjects within her own dominions, we never can admit, that she can by any act of hers change the laws of nations, or divest us of a particle of right, which we can justly claim under them. Nor can we admit, that our vessels, when forced into her waters under the circumstances above stated, cease to be under our jurisdiction or come under hers, so as to change the relations of the parties on board or to divest them of their property. In such cases the higher laws of humanity, by the consent of all civilized nations, intervene and overrule the municipal laws of the place, at least to that extent; not to insist, as we might, that the duties of good neighbourhood require, that each should, as far as possible, so regulate its own affairs as not to interfere with the rights and convenience of the other.

I cannot believe, that his Lordship, when he said that Her Majesty's Government could not make the slightest compromise, on the subject of slavery, could intend to extend the remark to cases of this kind; and I am happy to have my belief strengthened from his reply to your remarks subsequently made, alluding to an expression used by Lord Ashburton in his correspondence with Mr. Webster in reference to the point immediately in question.

All we ask is, that such instructions shall be given to those exercising authority in the colonies in our immediate neighbourhood, enjoining them that in executing the Act of Parliament for abolishing slavery within the British dominions, that they shall conform to the assurances given by Lord Ashburton in the correspondence above referred to and the principles of the laws of nations in such cases. It is England and not we, that has made the change in the condition of the negro portion of her population, which has led to the difficulty; and we have a right to insist, that she shall adopt such proper precautions, as to prevent the change from injuriously affecting our rights or security. I am, Sir, with great respect Your obedient Servant, J.C. Calhoun.

LS (No. 102) in DNA, RG 84 (Foreign Posts), Great Britain, Instructions, 8:343–349, received 9/2; FC in DNA, RG 59 (State Department), Diplomatic Instructions, Great Britain, 15:219–222 (M-77:74); PC in Jameson, ed., *Correspondence*, pp. 603–605. NOTE: An FC of Upshur's despatch no. 69 to Everett, dated 11/28/1843, can be found in DNA, RG 59 (State Department), Diplomatic Instructions, Great Britain, 15:177–183 (M-77:74). The LS of Everett's no. 90 in reply, dated 2/27/1844, is in DNA, RG 59 (State Department), Diplomatic Despatches, Great Britain, vol. 52 (M-30:48).

From EDWARD EVERETT

London, 12th August 1844

Sir, On the 5th instant the original of despatch Nro. 76, dated 24th January, was delivered to me by Mr. J. Morrison Harris, just arrived in England from an extensive tour on the Continent. This is the despatch accompanying Mr. [Joseph Rodney] Croskey's Commission as Consul at Cowes in the Isle of Wight; which being supposed to be lost, a copy of the despatch and of the Commission were transmitted to me some time since from the Department.

Mr. Harris observed, by way of explanation of the delay, that he had received the despatches with the impression, that its contents were of no importance. He further stated that he had, at the same time, received despatches for several of the Continental legations, which he supposed to contain newspapers only, none of which, if I understood him rightly, he had been able to deliver in person.

I also received on the 5th instant the original of despatch Nro. 79, of the 9th March with its enclosures. Of this despatch also a copy had lately been forwarded to me, on the supposition that it was lost. It was received at Liverpool by the "Great Western," on the 4th instant and had externally a somewhat worn appearance.

I am led by the delay in the reception of these despatches to suggest to the Department the expediency of transmitting its communications exclusively by the Letter-bags forwarded by the regular mail steamers. Although in the winter season in which the steamers sail but once a month, a little time may occasionally be saved by the transmission of despatches by a fast sailing vessel, I believe it will be found, in the long run, that nothing is to be gained in that respect.

In reference to the practice of entrusting parcels to travellers, with a view to their convenience as bearers of despatches, I would would [*sic*] respectfully express the opinion that it is liable to some serious objections. It rarely happens in these cases that parcels are promptly delivered. In the majority of the cases where parcels have been thus forwarded, no serious inconvenience has probably resulted from the delay; but it ought not, I think, to be assumed of any of the communications which the Government makes to abroad, that their punctual transmission is a matter of entire indifference.

In the present case no little anxiety was caused to the Consul at Cowes by the delay of his Commission. It was the subject of frequent correspondence between us, and awakened doubts whether there was not an error in the newspaper account of his appointment. By the delay in the transmission of despatch 79, an act of becoming acknowledgment for the handsome conduct of the British Consul at Gonaives [Haiti], directed by the Department early in March, failed to be made till the end of July.

Even when the parcel consists only of newspapers forwarded to the foreign Ministers, the delay is not altogether a matter of indifference. They form one of the sources, in some cases perhaps the only source, from which the Minister derives his knowledge of Executive communications to Congress, of the doings of that body, and other important matters of public intelligence. They are consequently looked to with interest; their delay is attended with disappointment and their loss with inconvenience.

In one or two cases which have fallen under my notice, Passports have been granted to travellers as Bearers of despatches to whom nothing of the nature of a despatch has been furnished, beyond a letter of introduction to the Minister. Without presuming to call in question the expediency of an occasional act of accommodation of this kind, I would observe that the unnecessary multiplication of passports of Bearers of despatches is of itself an evil. It impairs the respect with which such a passport ought to be treated; and thus tends to deprive those, who really take charge of the Public despatches and thereby gratuitously render an important public service, of that consideration at the Custom-house which they would otherwise enjoy, and which forms the only compensation they receive for their trouble.

In one case a good deal of inconvenience arose, in consequence of a person, who had been furnished with a few newspapers and a passport as a Bearer of despatches, having presented himself in that capacity and passed the Custom-house, in advance of the gentleman entrusted with the letter-bag. The unusual circumstance that two persons thus accredited came in the same steamer, appears to have awakened suspicion. The first had been expedited; but the second was subjected to a more than usually rigorous examination. The loss of time thus occasioned was the cause of a series of delays, which retarded the delivery of the despatches in London, for more than forty eight hours.

I hope the freedom with which I have expressed my views on this subject—exclusively one no doubt for the discretion of the Head of the Department—will be excused on the ground, that I can be influenced by no considerations but the respectability, and efficiency of the public service; and that from the nature of the case, the inconveniences of the existing practice can come to the knowledge of the Department, only from the representations of the Ministers abroad. I am, Sir, with great respect, Your obedient Servant, Edward Everett.

LS (No. 175) in DNA, RG 59 (State Department), Diplomatic Despatches, Great Britain, vol. 53 (M-30:49), received 9/3; FC in DNA, RG 84 (Foreign Posts), Great Britain, Despatches, 8:377–382; FC in MHi, Edward Everett Papers, 50:17–22 (published microfilm, reel 23, frames 277–280).

To [JEAN CORNEILLE], Chevalier GEVERS

Department of State
Washington, 12th Aug[us]t, 1844

Sir: With reference to the letter addressed to you from this Department on the 29th of May last, relative to the duties levied in United States' ports on coffee imported from Holland, I have the honor to acquaint you that a copy of the correspondence on this subject was communicated to the Chairman of the Committee of Foreign Affairs of the House of Representatives on the 30th of the same month, and that on the 7th of June a report was made to the House in which the committee express their opinion "that all duties collected upon coffee imported from Holland since the passage of the act of 1842, should be refunded, and that hereafter no duties should be collected on the coffee of Holland which are not laid on the coffee of the most favored Nations." A bill in conformity with these views was at the same time submitted. It was read a first and second time, and committed to a Committee of the Whole House on the State of the Union; but owing probably to the pressure of other business, or to some cause of which I am not advised, no further legislative proceedings appear to have been had upon the subject. Printed copies of the report and bill referred to are herewith transmitted.

During the session of Congress, in a conversation on the subject with the Comptroller of the Treasury, he stated to me that he was disposed to regard the claim favorably. His view of it, however, upon being subsequently submitted to the Acting Secretary [McClintock Young], with whom the ultimate decision then rested, was not concurred in.

Always desirous that the most liberal construction should be given to the conventional stipulations between the United States and the Netherlands, I deemed it expedient upon the appointment of a new Secretary of the Treasury to present your application for reconsideration; and I have now the pleasure of transmitting to you the copy of a letter just received at this Department from that functionary, containing his decision on the subject, which will doubtless be found to be satisfactory.

Your suggestion relative to refunding to certain merchants of the Netherlands the import duties levied in the ports of the United States on cargoes shipped before the provisions of the existing American tariff were known abroad, has also received due' attention, and been considered in the most friendly spirit; but the Secretary [George M. Bibb] is of opinion, as you will perceive from his letter of the 9th instant, that the twenty-fifth section of the act, under the provisions of which the charges referred to have been made, "has the force of a positive rule, leaving him no discretionary power to substitute another."

I avail myself of this occasion to renew to you the assurance of my high consideration. J.C. Calhoun.

FC in DNA, RG 59 (State Department), Notes to Foreign Legations, Netherlands, 6:35–36 (M-99:75).

From HENRY W. HILLIARD

Legation of the United States
Brussels, 12th August 1844

Sir; In obedience to instructions conveyed to me in your despatch of the 7th June, I waited upon the Minister of Foreign Affairs some days since and had a conversation with him respecting the payment of the indemnity due from the Belgian Government to American citizens for losses sustained in the destruction of the entrepôt at Antwerp.

I informed him that it was the earnest wish of the Government of the United States that the claims of its citizens should be promptly paid, and that it hoped, these claims, so just in themselves and so warmly pressed by the parties interested, would be no longer delayed. Count [Albert Joseph] Goblet assured me that the matter was proceeding with all possible expedition and that the interests of citizens of the United States were by no means overlooked. I contented myself with urging the subject upon his attention and requesting on the part of the Belgian Government as little delay as possible.

During the interview to which I have just referred, Count Goblet expressed some anxiety to be informed of the present state of the question of the annexation of Texas to the United States. I replied that the subject was at present under consideration, and would give it as my opinion frankly that at no distant day the annexation must take place. He asked me what effect the recognition of the independence of Texas by the Government of Mexico would probably have upon the question. I replied that it seemed to me that it would facilitate the arrangement, as the only objection now urged to this step by many public men in our country was, that it would give offence to a neighbour at peace with us. He then asked if Mexico should make the recognition of the independence of Texas the condition that the latter Government would never consent to annexation to the United States, whether this would dispose of the question. I replied that it seemed to me very improbable that the Government of Texas would accept a recognition from Mexico upon such terms; that it was believed by many to be the wish of the British and French Governments to settle the question upon this basis, and that I should be happy to know if he believed this opinion well founded: he replied that his information was derived from M. Guerra, a former President of the Mexican Senate and at this time charged with diplomatic powers to this Court. I observed that it seemed to me strange that Mexico should so warmly oppose the wish of Texas to annex herself to the United States when it was an admitted fact that the territory could never be re-conquered by Mexico. Count Goblet remarked that Mexico probably wished to interpose some independent power between herself and the United States, in order to check any further encroachments upon her boundaries; to which I replied in a pleasant way that I thought we might content ourselves there without seeking to go further south. He seemed to think this not very probable, saying that the superiority of the population of the United States to that of neighbouring countries rendered it almost certain that the last would give way before it.

I was interested in this conversation and it seemed to me to disclose the true views of the Mexican Government. If I may venture to express an opinion at this time it is that Mexico has been advised to re-commence hostilities against Texas in the most vigorous way that she may not seem to acquiesce in the recognition of the independence of her former province, and that certain European powers may have the opportunity of interposing their good offices and bringing about a reconciliation between the two Governments based upon the express understanding that Texas shall continue to exist as an independent power. This is my conviction and I am persuaded that events will prove that I have not misjudged the question.

Your despatch of the 10th July covering a letter of recall addressed to the Minister of Foreign Affairs has been received; and while I should be happy to await the arrival of Mr. [Thomas G.] Clemson that I might render him some service in entering upon the duties of his mission, I fear it will be necessary for me to leave before he reaches here. In that event I shall leave everything in order, together with a full letter giving such suggestions as may be useful to him in his new position.

He will find a good disposition here on the part of the Government and people, towards him as the Representative of the United

States and will, I trust, find the residence in every respect as agreeable as it has been to me.

I expect, in a few days, to take leave of the King, and of the Minister of Foreign Affairs, and will hereafter inform you of the day of the delivery of my letter of recall.

I cannot forbear expressing to you my great satisfaction at receiving the approbation of the President for my official course; I have certainly endeavored in a high sense to do my duty in my position, and the only reward which I ask for it besides my own consciousness of the fact is the approbation of my Government. I have the honor to be, Sir, Very respectfully, Your obedient servant, Henry W. Hilliard.

LS (No. 24) in DNA, RG 59 (State Department), Diplomatic Despatches, Belgium, vol. 2 (M-193:3), received 9/3.

From JOHN S. JENKINS

Vera Cruz, August 12th 1844
Sir, Having understood, from the very best authority, that [Leonard R. Almy] the present "Consul" at "Laguna," will not be recognised, by the "Government" of this Country, on account of the personal hostility, entertained towards him by many influential persons of that port, and that consequently, some person not obnoxious, to the authorities, will have to be appointed; I have been encouraged by the advice and recommendation, of many friends, to make application for the post. Having resided and done business, in "Columbia" S.C. for nearly twelve years; any gentleman, in that portion of the State will be enabled to testify, to my probity and capacity—in especial, I respectfully refer you to the Messrs. [Wade] Hampton, Pierce Butler, [William C.] Preston, Doctor "John Fisher" and Peyton M. Southall; who have long been acquainted with me. My friend, Mr. Francis M. Dimond, the present Consul, for this port, who leaves in a few days, to visit his family in Bristol R.I., will be the bearer of this Communication, and can also speak as to fitness for the office. It may not be amiss to add that in the prosecution of my business, I have lately resided in "Laguna" and understand thoroughly the disposition and Customs of the population. Should you deem proper to consider favourably my application—I will endeavour in every manner, to deserve your good opinion, and to sustain the fair name of our com-

mon Country. With Sentiments of the highest respect I Remain Your Ob[e]d[ien]t Servant, John S. Jenkins.

ALS in DNA, RG 59 (State Department), Applications and Recommendations, 1837–1845, Jenkins (M-687:17, frames 228–229). NOTE: The writer of this letter is *not* John S. Jenkins, the N.Y. author who published *The Life of John Caldwell Calhoun* in 1850.

To WILLIAM R. KING, [U.S. Minister to France]

Department of State
Washington, 12th Aug[us]t, 1844

Sir: I have laid your despatch No. 1 before the President [John Tyler], who instructs me to make known to you, that he has read it with much pleasure, especially the portion which relates to your cordial reception by the King [Louis Philippe], and his assurance of friendly feelings towards the United States. The President, in particular, highly appreciates the declaration of the King, that in no event any steps would be taken by his Government in the slightest degree hostile, or which would give to the United States just cause of complaint. It was the more gratifying, from the fact, that our previous information was calculated to make the impression, that the Government of France was prepared to unite with Great Britain, in a joint protest against the annexation of Texas, and a joint effort to induce her Government to withdraw the proposition to annex, on condition, that Mexico should be made to acknowledge her independence. He is happy to infer from your despatch, that the information, as far as it relates to France, is, in all probability, without foundation. You did not go further than you ought in assuring the King, that the object of annexation would be pursued with unabated vigor, and in giving your opinion, that a decided majority, of the American people were in its favor, and that it would certainly be annexed at no distant day. I feel confident, that your anticipation will be fully realized at no distant period. Every day will tend to weaken that combination of political causes, which led to the opposition to the measure, and to strengthen the conviction, that it was not only expedient, but just and necessary.

You were right in making the distinction between the interest of France and England in reference to Texas, or rather, I would say, the apparent interests of the two countries. France cannot possibly have any other than commercial interest in desiring to see her preserve her separate independence; while it is certain, that England looks beyond, to political interests, to which she apparently attaches much importance. But in our opinion the interests of both against the measure, is more apparent than real; and that neither France, England, nor even Mexico herself, has any in opposition to it, when the subject is fairly viewed and considered in its whole extent and all its bearings. Thus viewed and considered, and assuming, that peace, the extension of commerce, and security, are objects of primary policy with them, it may, as it seems to me, be readily shown, that the policy on the part of those powers, which would acquiesce in a measure so strongly desired by both the United States and Texas for their mutual welfare and safety, as the annexation of the latter to the former, would be far more promotive of these great objects, than that which would attempt to resist it.

It is impossible to cast a look at the map of the United States and Texas, and to note the long, artificial and inconvenient line, which divides them, and then to take into consideration the extraordinary increase of population and growth of the former and the source from which the latter must derive its inhabitants, institutions, and laws, without coming to the conclusion, that it is their destiny to be united; and of course that annexation is merely a question of *time* and *mode.* Thus regarded, the question to be decided would seem to be, whether it would not be better to permit it to be done now, with the mutual consent of both parties, and the acquiescence of ["the" *interlined*] three Powers, than to attempt to resist and defeat it. If the former course be adopted, the certain fruits would be the preservation of peace, great extension of commerce by the rapid settlement and improvement of Texas, and increased security, especially to Mexico. The last, in reference to Mexico, may be doubted; but I hold it not less clear than the other two.

It would be a great mistake to suppose, that this Government has any hostile feelings towards Mexico, or any disposition to aggrandize itself at her expense. The fact is the very reverse. It wishes her well, and desires to see her settled down in peace and security; and is prepared, in the event of annexation of Texas, if not forced into conflict with her, to propose to settle with her the question of boundary and all others growing out of the annexation, on the most liberal terms. Nature herself has clearly marked the boundary between her and Texas by natural limits too strong to be mistaken. There are few countries whose limits are so distinctly marked; and it would be our desire, if Texas should be united to us, to see them firmly established, as the most certain means of establishing permanent peace between the two countries, and strengthening and cementing their friendship.

Such would be the certain consequence of permitting the annexation to take place now with the acquiescence of Mexico; but very different would be the case, if it should be attempted to resist and defeat it, whether the attempt should be successful for the present or not. Any attempt of the kind would, not improbably, lead to a conflict between us and Mexico, and involve consequences in reference to her and the general peace, long to be deplored on all sides, and difficult to be repaired. But should that not be the case, and the interference of another Power should defeat the annexation for the present, without the interruption of peace, it would but postpone the conflict, and render it more fierce and bloody, whenever it might occur. Its defeat would be attributed to enmity and ambition on the part of that Power by whose interference it was occasioned, and excite deep jealousy and resentment on the part of our People, which would be ready to seize the first favorable opportunity to effect by force, what was prevented from being done peaceably by mutual consent. It is not difficult to see how greatly such a conflict, come when it may, would endanger the general peace, and how much Mexico might be the loser by it.

In the mean time, the condition of Texas would be rendered uncertain, her settlement and prosperity in consequence retarded, and her commerce crippled, while the general peace would be rendered much more insecure. It could not but greatly affect us. If the annexation of Texas should be permitted to take place peaceably now, as it would without the interference of other Powers, the energies of our People would, for a long time to come, be directed to the peaceable pursuits of redeeming and bringing within the pales of cultivation, improvement, and civilization, that large portion of the continent, lying between Mexico, on one side, and the British possessions on the other, which is now with little exception, a wilderness with a sparse population, consisting, for the most part, of wandering Indian tribes. It is our destiny to occupy that vast region; to intersect it with roads and canals; to fill it with cities, towns, villages, and farms; to extend over it our religion, customs, Constitution, and laws; and to present it as a peaceful and splendid addition to the domains of commerce and civilization. It is our policy to increase by growing and spreading out into unoccupied regions, assimilating all we incorporate. In a word, to increase by accretion, and not through conquest by the addition of masses held together by the cohesion of force. No system can be more unsuited to the latter process, or better adapted to the former, than our admirable Federal System. If it should not be resisted in its course, it will probably fulfil its destiny, without disturbing our neighbors, or putting in jeopardy the general peace; but if it be opposed by foreign interference, a new direction would be given to our energy much less favorable to harmony with our neighbors, and to the general peace of the world. The change would be undesirable to us, and much less in accord with what I have assumed to be primary objects of policy on the part of France, England, and Mexico.

But, to descend to particulars; it is certain, that while England, like France, desires the independence of Texas, with the view to commercial connections, it is not less so, that one of the leading motives of England for desiring it, is the hope, that, through her diplomacy and influence, negroe slavery may be abolished there, and ultimately, by consequence, in the United States, and throughout the whole of this continent. That its ultimate abolition throughout the entire continent is an object ardently desired by her, we have decisive proof, in the declaration of the Earl of Aberdeen delivered to this Department, and of which you will find a copy among the documents transmitted to Congress with the Texan treaty. That she desires its abolition in Texas, and has used her influence and diplomacy to effect it there, the same document with the correspondence of this Department with Mr. [Richard] Pakenham, also to be found among the documents, furnish proof not less conclusive. That one of the objects of abolishing it there, is to facilitate its abolition, in the United States, and throughout the continent, is manifest from the declaration of the abolition party and societies, both in this country and England. In fact, there is good reason to believe, that the scheme of abolishing it in Texas, with the view to its abolition in the United States and over the continent, originated with the prominent members of the party in the United States; and was first broached by them in the so-called World's Convention, held in London in the year 1840, and through its agency brought to the notice of the British Government.

Now, I hold, not only that France can have no interest in the consummation of this grand scheme which England hopes to accomplish, through Texas, if she can defeat the annexation; but that her interests, and those of all the continental Powers of Europe, are decidedly and deeply opposed to it.

It is too late in the day to contend that humanity or philanthropy is the great object of the policy of England in attempting to abolish African slavery on this continent. I do not question but humanity may have been one of her leading motives for the abolition of the African slave trade; and that it may have had a considerable influence, in abolishing slavery in her West Indian possessions; aided, indeed, by the fallacious calculation that the labor of the negroes would be at least as profitable, if not more so, in consequence of the measure. She acted on the principle, that tropical products can be produced cheaper by free African labor and East India labor, than by slave labor. She knew full well the value of such products to her commerce, navigation, navy, manufactures, revenue, and power. She was not ignorant, that the support and the maintenance of her political preponderance depended on her tropical possessions, and had no intention of diminishing their productiveness, nor any anticipation that such would be the effect, when the scheme of abolishing slavery in her colonial possessions was adopted. On the contrary, she calculated to combine philanthropy with profit and power, as is not unusual with fanaticism. Experience has convinced her of the fallacy of her calculations. She has failed in all her objects. The labor of her negroes has proved far less productive, without affording the consolation of having improved their condition.

The experiment has turned out to be a costly one. She expended nearly one hundred millions of dollars in indemnifying the owners of the emancipated slaves. It is estimated that the increased price paid since by the people of Great Britain for sugar and other tropical productions in consequence of the measure, is equal to half that sum; and that twice that amount has been expended in the suppression of the slave trade; making together two hundred and fifty millions of dollars as the cost of the experiment. Instead of realizing her hope, the result has been a sad disappointment. Her tropical products have fallen off to a vast amount. Instead of supplying her own wants and those of nearly all Europe, with them, as formerly, she has now, in some of the most important articles, scarcely enough to supply her own. What is worse, her own colonies are actually consuming sugar, produced by slave labor, brought direct to England, and refined in bond, and exported and sold in her colonies as cheap, or cheaper, than what they can produce there; while the slave trade, instead of diminishing, has been in fact carried on to a greater extent than ever. So disastrous has been the result, that her fixed capital vested in tropical possessions, estimated at the value of nearly five hundred millions of dollars, is said to stand on the brink of ruin.

But this is not the worst. While this costly scheme has had such ruinous effects on the tropical productions of Great Britain, it has given a powerful stimulus, followed by a corresponding increase of products, to those countries which have had the good sense to shun her example. There has been vested, it is estimated, by them, in the production of tropical products, since 1808, in fixed capital, nearly four thousand millions of dollars, wholly dependent on slave labor. In the same period, the value of their products have been estimated to have risen from about seventy-two millions of dollars annually to nearly two hundred and twenty millions, while the whole of the fixed capital of Great Britain, vested in cultivating tropical products, both in the East and West Indies, is estimated at only about eight hundred and thirty millions of dollars, and the value of the products annually at about fifty millions of dollars. To present a still more striking view[:] Of three articles of tropical products, sugar, coffee, and cotton, the British possessions, including ["the" *interlined*] West and East Indies, and Mauritius, produced, in 1842, of sugar only 3,993,771 pounds, while Cuba, Brazil, and the United States, excluding other countries having tropical possessions, produced 9,600,000 pounds; of coffee, the British possessions produced only 27,393,003, while Cuba and Brazil produced 201,590,125 pounds; and of cotton, the British possessions, including shipments to China, only 137,443,446, while the United States alone produced 790,479,275.

The above facts and estimates have all been drawn from a British periodical of high standing and authority [*Interpolated:* "Blackwood's Magazine for June, 1844"], and are believed to be entitled to credit. This vast increase of the capital and production on the part of those Nations, who have continued their former policy towards the negro race compared with that of Great Britain, indicates a corresponding relative increase of the means of commerce, navigation, manufactures, wealth, and power. It is no longer a question of doubt, that the great source of the wealth, prosperity, and power of the more civilized Nations of the Temperate Zone, especially Europe, where the arts have made the greatest advance, depends, in a great degree, on the exchange of their products with those of the tropical regions. So great has been the advance made in the arts, both chymical [*sic*] and mechanical, within the few last generations, that all the old civilized Nations can, with but a small part of their labor and capital, supply their respective wants, which tends to limit, within narrow bounds, the amount of the commerce between them, and forces them all to seek for markets in the tropical regions and the more newly settled portions of the globe. Those who can best succeed in commanding those markets, have the best prospect of outstripping the others in the career of commerce, navigation, manufactures, wealth, and power.

This is seen and felt by British statesmen, and has opened their eyes to the errors which they have committed. The question now with them is, how shall it be counteracted? What has been done cannot be undone. The question is, by what means can Great Britain regain and keep a superiority in tropical cultivation, commerce, and influence? Or, shall that be abandoned, and other Nations be suffered to acquire the supremacy, even to the extent of supplying British markets to the destruction of the capital already vested in their production? These are the questions which now profoundly occupy the attention of her statesmen, and have the greatest influence over her councils.

In order to regain her superiority, she not only seeks to revive and increase her own capacity to produce tropical productions, but to diminish and destroy the capacity of those who have so far outstripped her in consequence of her error. In pursuit of the former, she has cast her eyes to her East India possessions; to Central and Eastern Africa, with the view of establishing colonies there, and even to restore, substantially, the slave trade itself, under the specious name of transporting free laborers from Africa to her West India possessions, in order, if possible, to compete successfully with those, who have refused to follow her suicidal policy. But these all afford but uncertain and distant hope of recovering her lost superiority. Her main reliance is, on the other alternative, to cripple or destroy the productions of her successful rivals. There is but one way by which it can be done, and that is, by abolishing African slavery throughout this continent; and that she openly avows to be the constant object of her policy and exertions. It matters not how, or for what motive, it may be done; whether it be by diplomacy, influence, or force; by secret or open means; and whether the motive be humane or selfish—without regard to manner, means, or motive—the thing itself, should it be accomplished, would put down all rivalry, and give her the undisputed supremacy in supplying her own wants and those of the rest of the world; and thereby more than fully retrieve what she has lost by her errors. It would give her the monopoly of tropical productions, which I shall next proceed to show.

What would be the consequence, if this object of her unceasing solicitude and exertions should be effected by the abolition of slavery throughout this continent, some idea may be formed, from the immense diminution of productions, as has been shown, which has followed abolition in her West India possessions. But as great as that has been, it is nothing, compared to what would be the effect, if she should succeed in abolishing slavery in the United States, Cuba, Brazil, and throughout this continent. The experiment in her own colonies was made under the most favorable circumstances. It was brought about gradually and peaceably, by the steady and firm operation of the parent country, armed with complete power to prevent or crush at once all insurrectionary movements on the part of the negroes, and able and disposed to maintain to the full the political and social ascendancy of the former masters over their former slaves. It is not at all wonderful, that the change of the relations of master and slave took place, under such circumstances, without violence and bloodshed, and that order and peace should have been since preserved. Very different would be the result of abolition, should it be effected by her influence and exertions, in the possessions of other countries on this continent, and especially, in the United States, Cuba, and Brazil, the great cultivators of the principal tropical products of America. To form a correct conception of what would be the result with them, we must look, not to Jamaica, but, to St. Domingo, for an example. The change would be followed by unforgiving hate between the two races, and end in a bloody and deadly struggle between them for the superiority. One or the other would have to be subjugated, extirpated, or expelled, and desolation would overspread their territories, as in St. Domingo, from which it would take centuries to recover. The end would be that superiority in cultivating the great tropical staples would be transferred from them to the British tropical possessions.

They are of vast extent, and those beyond the Cape of Good Hope possessed of an unlimited amount of labor, standing ready, by the aid of British capital, to supply the deficit which would be occasioned by destroying the tropical productions of the United States, Cuba, Brazil, and other countries cultivated by slave labor on this continent, so soon as the increased price, in consequence, would yield a profit. It is the successful competition of that labor, which keeps the prices of the great tropical staples so low, as to prevent their cultivation with profit in the possessions of Great Britain, by what she is pleased to call free labor. If she can destroy its competition, she would have a monopoly in those productions. She has all the means of furnishing an unlimited supply—vast and fertile possessions in both Indiés; boundless command of capital and labor, and ample power to suppress disturbances, and preserve order throughout her wide domains.

It is unquestionable, that she regards the abolition of slavery in Texas, as a most important step towards this great object of policy, so much the aim of her solicitude and exertions, and the defeat of the annexation of Texas to our Union, as indispensable to the abolition of slavery there. She is too sagacious not to see, what a fatal blow it would give to slavery in the United States, and how certainly its abolition with us would abolish it over the whole continent, and thereby give her a monopoly in the productions of the great tropical staples, and the command of the commerce, navigation, and manufactures of the world, with an established naval ascendancy and political preponderance. To this continent the blow would be calamitous beyond description. It would destroy in a great measure, the cultivation and production of the great tropical staples, amounting annually in value to nearly three hundred millions of dollars— the fund which stimulates and upholds almost every other branch of its industry; commerce, navigation, and manufactures. The whole, by their joint influence, are rapidly spreading population, wealth, improvement, and civilization over the whole continent, and vivifying, by their overflow, the industry of Europe, thereby increasing its population, wealth, and advancement in the arts, in power, and civilization.

Such must be the result, should Great Britain succeed in accomplishing the constant object of her desire and exertions, the abolition of negro slavery over this continent; and towards the effecting of which she regards the defeat of the annexation of Texas to our Union so important. Can it be possible that Governments so enlightened and sagacious as those of France and the other great continental powers can be so blinded by the plea of philanthropy, as not to see what must inevitably follow, be her motive what it may, should she succeed in her object? It is little short of mockery to talk of philanthropy, with the examples before us of the effects of abolishing negro slavery in her own colonies, in St. Domingo, and the Northern States of our Union; where statistical facts, not to be shaken, prove, that the freed negro, after the experience of sixty years, is in a far worse condition, than in the other States, where he has been left in his former condition. No; the effect of what is called abolition, where the number is few, is not to raise the inferior race to the condition of freemen, but to deprive ["him" *canceled and* "the negro" *interlined*] of the guardian care of his owner, subject to all the depression and oppression belonging to his inferior condition. But, on the other hand, where the number is great, and bears a large proportion to the whole population, it would be still worse. It would be to substitute, for the existing relation, a deadly strife between the two races, to end in the subjection, expulsion, or extirpation of one or the other, and such would be the case over the greater part of this continent, where negro slavery exists. It would not end there; but would in all probability extend, by its example, the war of races over all South America, including Mexico, and extending to the Indian, as well as to the African race; and make the whole one scene of blood and devastation.

Dismissing, then, the stale and unfounded plea of philanthropy, can it be, that France and the other great continental Powers, seeing what must be the result of the policy for the accomplishment of which England is constantly exerting herself, and that the defeat of the annexation of Texas is so important towards its consummation, are prepared to back, or countenance her in her efforts, to effect either? What possible motive can they have to favor her cherished policy? Is it not better for them, that they should be supplied with tropical products, in exchange for their labor, from the United States, Brazil, Cuba, and this continent generally, than to be dependant on one great monopolizing Power for their supply? Is it not better, that they should receive them at the low prices, which competition, cheaper means of production, and nearness of market would furnish them by the former, than to give the high prices, which monopoly, dear labor, and great distance from market would impose? Is it not better, that their labor should be exchanged with a new continent, rapidly increasing in population, and the capacity for consuming, and which would furnish, in the course of a few generations, a market nearer to them, and of almost unlimited extent for the products of their industry and arts, than with old and distant regions, whose population has long since reached its growth?

The above contains those enlarged views of policy which, it seems to me, an enlightened European statesman ought to take, in making up his opinion on the subject of the annexation of Texas, and the grounds, as it may be inferred, on which England mainly opposes it. They certainly involve considerations of the deepest importance, and demanding the greatest attention. Viewed in connection with them, the question of annexation becomes one of the first magnitude, not only to Texas and the United States, but to this continent and Europe. They are presented, that you may use them on all suitable occasions, where you think they may be with effect, in your correspondence, where it can be done with propriety, or otherwise. The President relies with confidence on your sagacity, prudence, and zeal. Your mission is one of the first magnitude, at all times, but especially now; and he feels assured, nothing will be left undone on your part to do justice to the country and the Government in reference to this great measure. I have said nothing as to our right of treating with Texas, without consulting Mexico. You so fully understand the grounds on which we rest our right, and are so familiar with all the facts necessary to maintain them, that it was not thought necessary to add any thing in reference to it. I am, Sir, very respectfully, Your obedient servant, J.C. Calhoun.

LS (No. 4) with Ens in DNA, RG 84 (Foreign Posts), France, Instructions; FC in DNA, RG 59 (State Department), Diplomatic Instructions, France, 15:8–23 (M-77:55); CC's in DNA, RG 84 (Foreign Posts), in files for Russia, Germany, Netherlands, Spain, and Texas; PC in Senate Document No. 1, 28th Cong., 2nd Sess., pp. 39–47; PC in House Document No. 2, 28th Cong., 2nd Sess., pp. 38–45; PC in *Congressional Globe*, 28th Cong., 2nd Sess., Appendix, pp. 5–7; PC in the Washington, D.C., *Globe*, December 6, 1844, p. 2; PC in the Washington, D.C., *Daily National Intelligencer*, December 9, 1844, p. 1; PC in the Washington, D.C., *Constitution*, December 10, 1844, p. 2; PC in the Washington, D.C., *Daily Madisonian*, December 11, 1844, pp. 2–3; PC in *Niles' National Register*, vol. LXVII, no. 16 (December 21, 1844), pp. 247–249; PC in the Columbus, Ga., *Times*, December 25, 1844, p. 2; PC in the London, England, *Times*, January 2, 1845, p. 3; PC in the New York, N.Y., *National Anti-Slavery Standard*, January 2, 1845, p. 1; PC in *Hon. J.C. Calhoun's Letter to the Hon. W.R. King* (Charleston: printed by Walker & Burke, no date), an 8-pp. pamphlet; PC in Adolphe Jollivet, *Documents Americains, Annexion du Texas, Emancipation des Noirs, Politique de l'Angleterre* (Paris: de l'Imprimerie de Bruneau, 1845), pp. 7–27; PC in *De Bow's Review*, vol. IX, no. 1 (August, 1850), pp. 184–191; PC in Horace Greeley, *A History of the Struggle for Slavery Extension or Restriction in the United States . . .* , pp. 37–40; PC in Crallé, ed., *Works*, 5:379–392; PC in Frederick Merk, *Slavery and the Annexation of Texas* (New York: Alfred A. Knopf, 1972), pp. 281–288. NOTE: Copies of Richard Pakenham's letter of 4/19 to Calhoun and Calhoun's reply of 4/27 seem to have been enclosed with this letter to King.

From John L. Lafitte, Baltimore, 8/12. He renews his previous application for appointment to be the U.S. Consul at Foo-Chow-Foo, China, because a "large operation" in connection with China has been proposed to him. ALS in DNA, RG 59 (State Department), Applications and Recommendations, 1837–1845, Lafitte (M-687:19, frames 7–8).

To Henry Middleton, 8/12. "I have received your letter of the 22d Ultimo, in relation to charges in your account as Minister to Russia. I have given to it, in connection with a statement from the Fifth Auditor [Stephen Pleasonton], full consideration, and enclose a copy of my letter [of 8/10] to the Fifth Auditor, communicating the result thereof." FC in DNA, RG 59 (State Department), Accounting Records: Miscellaneous Letters Sent, 1832–1916, vol. for 2/1–9/30/1844, p. 334.

To John Baldwin, New York [City], 8/13. "I have to acknowledge the receipt of your letter of the 10th instant, and to inform you that[,] according to the official information in this Department[,] the rumor of which you speak has no foundation." FC in DNA, RG 59 (State Department), Domestic Letters, 34:331 (M-40:32).

From Joseph Carroll, David Henderson, James Lewis, and Alvah Post, New York [City], 8/13. These seamen [former crewmen of the brig *Hope*] petition for compensation for time lost from employment while they were detained as witnesses against Cornelius F. Driscoll, accused of engaging in the illegal African slave trade. After giving testimony in Rio de Janeiro on 1/16/1844, they were sent on 1/23 aboard a U.S. warship to New York City, and have been lodged in the city jail from 5/31 until the completion of their testimony today. They have received compensation for the period since 5/31, but not for the period between 1/23 and that date. LS in DNA, RG 59 (State Department), Petitions for Pardon, Tyler Administration, Unnumbered Cases.

From F[RANCIS] M. DIMOND

United States Consulate
Vera Cruz, Aug. 13, 1844

Sir, The Brig J. Huntington leaving suddenly only affords me a moment to enclose you a dispatch rec[eive]d from our Charge [in Mexico City] by the last mail.

As the U.S. Ship Falmouth left Norfolk on the 20th ult[im]o we are hourly expecting her.

The two last instalments due are not yet paid.

I purpose sailing in the Barque Ann Louisa for New York on the 18 inst. appointing L[ewis] S. Hargous Esq. to act for me in my absence.

The Commander in Chief of the Army for Texas report says declines the honour. I have the honour to be Sir most respectfully your Ob[edient] Serv[an]t, F.M. Dimond.

ALS (No. 232) in DNA, RG 59 (State Department), Consular Despatches, Veracruz, vol. 5 (M-183:5), received 9/7.

From [President] JOHN TYLER

August 13th, 1844

Dear Sir, Your despatch [of 8/7] to Mr. [Edward] Everett, relative to felon slaves, is clearly right; and the subject is well argued. I suggest whether a full illustration of the principle might not have been impressively enforced by referring to the case of forgery of Bank Notes. We have no law to punish the forgery of the Notes of the Bank of England, or the public securities of England, and yet can it be doubted, that the forger would be delivered up by us.

As you write not only for Sir Robert Peel, but the Mass of mankind, I suggest the illustration. Its adoption, with others, such for example as may be drawn from the case of an impressed seaman, &c. &c., would make the paper unanswerable. Truly Your's, John Tyler.

LS in ScCleA; PC in Boucher and Brooks, eds., *Correspondence,* p. 244. NOTE: An AEU by Calhoun reads: "The President[,] relates to my dispatch to Mr. Everett."

To Lorenzo Draper, [U.S. Consul], Paris, 8/14. President [John Tyler] having appointed Robert Walsh to succeed Draper, Draper is to surrender the records of the post to Walsh. FC in DNA, RG 59 (State Department), Consular Instructions, 12:89.

From Gabriel G. Fleurot, Norfolk, 8/14. Fleurot asks that he be appointed U.S. Consul at St. Pierre, Martinique, in place of the incumbent [Philip A. de Creny] who he considers to be a man with business interests that conflict with his office. Fleurot mentions that he discussed his appointment recently with the President [John Tyler] while the President was at Old Point Comfort, Va. ALS in DNA, RG 59 (State Department), Consular Despatches, St. Pierre, vol. 2 (T-431:2).

To Robert L. McIntosh, 8/14. McIntosh is notified of his appointment to be U.S. Consul at Fuchowfou, China, and is sent documents relevant to the conduct of the office. FC in DNA, RG 59 (State Department), Consular Instructions, 10:259–260.

From R. A. Parrish

Newport R.I., 14 August 1844

Sir, I have written a hurri[e]d letter to the President [John Tyler] during a visit to this place, on the subject of the Peruvian Mission. As it is believed that he will take some action in reference to this appointment, on his return to Washington, I am induced to address it to your care, partly in order that it may escape any delay in the hands of his private secretaries, and partly (if your inclination and leisure permit) in order that you may peruse it.

The expressions you have kindly made of a disposition to aid my views, is my apology for troubling you in this, and should it be agreeable to you to add any thing to the weight of my application, I should be most happy. You are aware that many of the most respectable citizens of my State have solicited such an appointment for me, together with the whole *Penn[sylvani]a delegation* in Congress, and that many of the latter have had personal interviews with the Pres[iden]t and taken a warm and active interest in my behalf. Judge [William] Wilkins [Secretary of War] also, and Mr. [John] Nelson [Attorney General], have led me to believe that my appointment would receive their approbation. With the addition of your influence I can scarcely doubt of success, and be assured that any exertion of it in my favour will be duly remember[e]d and appreciated. Yours with great consideration very truly, R.A. Parrish, of Philad[elphi]a.

ALS in DNA, RG 59 (State Department), Applications and Recommendations, 1837–1845, Parrish (M-687:25, frames 222–224).

From George H. Proffit, Rio de Janeiro, 8/14. "Your letter informing me that the Senate of the United States had not confirmed my appointment [as U.S. Minister to Brazil], was handed me by Mr. [Henry A.] Wise on the 3rd Inst. I immediately asked an audience of leave, which was granted on the 10th Inst." ALS in DNA, RG 59 (State Department), Diplomatic Despatches, Brazil, vol. 12 (M-121: 14), received 10/4; FC in DNA, RG 84 (Foreign Posts), Brazil, Despatches, vol. 102.

To Alexander Tod, Alexandria, Egypt, 8/14. Tod is informed of his appointment as U.S. Consul. Documents relevant to the office are enclosed. FC in DNA, RG 59 (State Department), Consular Instructions, 10:259–260.

To Isaac Van Zandt

Department of State
Washington, 14th August, 1844

The Undersigned, Secretary of State of the United States, has the honor of transmitting herewith to Mr. Van Zandt, Chargé d'Affaires of the Republic of Texas, a copy of a note from the Secretary of War [William Wilkins, dated 4/24], covering a copy of an extract of the proceedings of the Court of Inquiry in the case of Captain [Philip St. George] Cooke, relating to the discharge of the duty assigned him for the protection of the caravan of the Santa Fe traders, through the territories of the United States to the Texian frontier, in May and June, 1843. The Court was ordered at the request of my immediate predecessor [Abel P. Upshur], in conformity to the intimation contained in his communication to Mr. Van Zandt of the 19th of January, last, in order to ascertain more fully and in the most authentic form the circumstances and facts connected with the proceedings of Captain Cooke and his command, in the disarming of the Texian force under the command of Colonel [Jacob] Snively. Mr. Van Zandt will find, on recurring to the extract, that the opinion of the Court is, that the place where the Texian force was disarmed was within the territory of the United States; that there was nothing in the conduct of Captain Cooke which was harsh or unbecoming, and that he did not exceed the authority derived from the orders under which he acted. It is proper to add that the Court consisted of three officers of experience and high standing; that the case was fully laid before it, and that its opinion appears to be fully sustained by the evidence.

There seems to be no doubt that Captain Cooke was sincerely of the opinion, that the Texian force was within the territory of the United States, and that the fulfilment of his order, to protect the trade made it his duty, under such circumstances, to disarm them. It is readily conceded, that the commander of the Texian forces, with equal sincerity, believed the place he occupied was within the territory of Texas. Which was right, or which wrong, can be ascertained with certainty, only by an actual survey and demarcation of the line dividing the two countries, between the Red and Arkansas Rivers.

With these impressions, the Undersigned is of the opinion that it is not either necessary or advisable to renew between the two governments the discussion on the question whether the Texian force was or was not within the limits of the United States, or the others heretofore brought into the discussion in connexion therewith. It could lead only to fruitless efforts to establish, what in the present state of information cannot be fixed with any certainty, to be followed by irritated feelings between two countries, whose interest it is to be on the most friendly terms.

In the hope, therefore, of closing this discussion and putting an end to this exciting subject, the Undersigned renews the offer of his predecessor contained in the communication above referred to; "to restore the arms taken from the Texian force, or to make compensation for them,["] and his assurance given at the same time, that "his government never meditated and will not sanction any indignity towards the government of Texas, nor any wrong towards her people, and will readily repair any injury of either kind, which may be made to appear."

The Undersigned has also the honor to transmit herewith a copy of a letter [of 6/27] from the [Acting] Secretary of War [Daniel Parker], covering communications from the Adjutant General [Roger Jones] and [T. Hartley Crawford] the Commissioner of Indian Affairs, giving additional information in reference to the outrage said to have been committed by citizens of the United States on [James Bourland] the Collector of the District of Red River in Texas and which has heretofore been a subject of correspondence between the two governments.

It would seem, on a review of all the evidence, that the outrage was the act of the captain of the Fort Towson [Joseph Scott] and the individuals who accompanied him, and that no officer of the United States, civil or military was implicated in it, either before, as advisers or aiders, or after, as abettors. The guard ordered down by the commandant of the garrison of Fort Towson [Lt. Col. Gustavus Loomis], seems to have been for the protection of the public property on board. Should, however, any fact hereafter come to light calculated to implicate anyone acting under the authority of the United States, it will be made a subject of special investigation.

The Undersigned admits that the outrage was one of an aggravated character; and also that according to the law of nations, it is the duty of government to prevent its citizens or subjects from injuring another government or its citizens or subjects, whenever it can; and when it cannot, that it should compel the offender to make reparation for the damage or injury, if possible, or to inflict on him exemplary punishment, or deliver him up to the offended State to be punished according to its laws in such cases, or make reparation itself for the injury. It is to be regretted that there is no law of the United States or treaty stipulation between them and Texas providing for punishing offenders of the kind, or delivering them up to the offended party to be punished according to its laws. In their absence, this Government has no power to deliver up the offenders in this case or to punish them for the offence, unless indeed the laws of the State of Arkansas make it penal for its citizens to enter into a combination or conspiracy to commit an unlawful act beyond its jurisdiction and within that of another State or country. If they do, the perpetrators of the outrage may be indicted and tried in the criminal Courts of the State, and orders will accordingly be given, if such should be the case, to the District Attorney of the United States for the State of Arkansas to institute criminal proceedings against them, with a view to their conviction and punishment.

As to the reparation to be made for the damage sustained by the Government of Texas, in consequence of the forcible seizing and taking away from its possession the goods introduced in violation of the revenue law, and for which Mr. Van Zandt has made in its name a demand for compensation equal to their estimated value, the Undersigned is instructed by the President [John Tyler] to state that it will require the sanction of Congress to make the compensation, as the Constitution of the United States provides expressly, that "No money shall be drawn from the Treasury but in consequence of appropriations made by law"; but that he will recommend the subject to that department of the government for its favorable consideration and action at the next session.

In order to enable him to present the subject fairly, Mr. Van Zandt will, of course, see that it will be necessary for his government to furnish this, with all the evidence which may be requisite to establish, authentically, the facts of the illegal introduction of the goods, their forcible seizure and taking away by the citizens of the United States and the amount of damage suffered in consequence; to be transmitted by the President to Congress with his [annual] Message.

The Undersigned avails himself of this occasion to offer Mr. Van Zandt renewed assurances of his very distinguished consideration. J.C. Calhoun.

FC in DNA, RG 59 (State Department), Notes to Foreign Legations, Texas, 6:71–74 (M-99:95); FC with Ens in Tx, Records of the Texas Republic Department of State, Copybooks of Letters Received from Texan and Foreign Representatives, vol. 2-1/98, pp. 523–530; CC in Tx, Records of the Texas Republic Department of State, U.S. Diplomatic Correspondence; PC in Senate Document No. 1, 28th Cong., 2nd Sess., pp. 109–111; PC in House Document No. 2, 28th Cong., 2nd Sess., pp. 106–108; PC in Crallé, ed., *Works*, 5:408–411.

To Robert Walsh, Paris, 8/14. Calhoun notifies Walsh of his appointment as U.S. Consul at Paris and sends him documents relevant to the office. FC in DNA, RG 59 (State Department), Consular Instructions, 12:89–90.

To William Wilkins, Secretary of War, 8/14. "I have the honor to transmit a note dated the 10th instant, addressed by Mr. [Isaac] Van Zandt, Chargé d'Affaires of Texas, to this Department, and to invite your attention to the President's endorsement thereon. The note being an original document I will thank you to return it and to inform me when the orders directed by the President are given, so that I may communicate the fact to Mr. Van Zandt." LS in DNA, RG 75 (Bureau of Indian Affairs), Letters Received by the Office of Indian Affairs, 1824–1880, Miscellaneous, 1844, S3683 (M-234:443, frames 328–330); FC in DNA, RG 59 (State Department), Domestic Letters, 34:332 (M-40:32).

From HENRY A. WISE

Rio de Janeiro, August 14th 1844
Sir, I duly rec[eive]d the last despatches from the Departm[en]t of State, consisting of my passport, power, instructions &c &c, on the morning of the 29th of May last, the day I sailed from the city of New York.

We arrived at Rio the 2nd of August, after a passage of sixty two days, lying by in all seventeen days at the places—Fayal, Madiera and Teneriffe—where we touched.

After communicating with Mr. [George H.] Proffit, I addressed, on the 5th inst., a note to Mr. [Ernesto Ferreira] França, the Minister and Sec[re]t[ar]y of State for foreign affairs, informing him of my arrival, inclosing to him the office copy of my credentials, and asking when it would be most agreeable to him for me to call upon him in person. He promptly replied on the 6th, that he would have the pleasure to receive ["me" *interlined*], Thursday the 8th at 11. A.M., at the Foreign Office. At the appointed time, Mr. Proffit accompanied me to the Foreign office where we were most kindly rec[eive]d by the Minister, who informed me verbally that he would communicate by note the appointment of his Majesty of the times of our audiences of leave and of reception. On the 8th he addressed me a note saying that the Emperor [Pedro II] would receive my credentials, on the 10th at 6 P.M., in the Palace of Bon Vista; at which time and place I was duly rec[eive]d and accredited with every mark of favor and respect towards the United States and the President. As my remarks to the Emperor on the occasion pointed somewhat significantly to the policy of my instructions, I herewith transmit a copy of them for your supervision, marked "A." Thus I have been duly recognized, and have entered upon the duties of my mission.

Very soon after my arrival here I regret to say a very extraordinary case *with the British Govt.* presented itself, which received my prompt attention. Capt. [P.C.] Dumas, of the American brig Cyrus of New Orleans, just arrived at Rio in a French vessel, has laid a complaint before [George W. Gordon] our Consul here of a most flagrant outrage, perpetrated, & repeated no less than three times, upon our Commerce on the Coast of Africa, by H.B.M. brigs of war the Heroine and the Alert, during the months of May and of June last. Capt. [Daniel] Turner, the Commander of our Squadron on this station, stated to me, on the 8th inst., the Complaint of Capt. Dumas, and at my request obtained for me an interview with him at the office of our Consul on the morning of the 9th. I took at once a memorandum of his statement. But as our Consul is proceeding regularly to take his affidavit and protest, and the depositions of a number of witnesses now here, and as I shall soon be enabled to communicate them in full and in proper form to the State Department, I will abstain from attempting to give the particulars at this time. As soon as the Consul prepares all the papers, I shall transmit them with a letter, and furnish Mr. [Hamilton] Hamilton, the British Minister here, with complete copies, in order that he may advise the British Govt. of the nature of the information of this outrage sent home by me to the United States. Without waiting for instructions in such a case, this course seems to me the most proper, and I trust it will be approved by the President and the Department of State.

As soon as my household arrangements become more settled, I shall enter fully upon the business of my mission to Brazil. Time has not afforded me the opportunity as yet to obtain any insight, into affairs here. But Mr. Proffit, who I must say has shown me every attention and seems to leave here with a large portion of esteem, is returning home immediately, and he can give you a much clearer view of matters than I can pretend to have acquired in so short a time. He tells me that there has been some anxiety for a short time past respecting a probability of war between this country and Buenos Ayres. It arose from rumors, and newspaper paragraphs and from the supposed objects of a visit to Rio by Gen[era]l Paez, late military commander in Monte Video, and from certain indications of Gen-

[era]l Guido, the Buenos Ayrean Minister here, all which Mr. Proffit will best explain in person. The mediation of England, France and Brazil is, perhaps, sought to end hostilities between Buenos Ayres and Monte Video; and it is surmised by some that the attempt will be made to reannex the latter country to Brazil. Nothing, however, is yet clearly developed, and when the true state of the case is known to me, the Department shall be duly advised.

I most reluctantly add a word touching my own affairs. Doubts expressed by Mr. Proffit have led me to fear that I may not be allowed the difference in exchange on my drafts for my *outfit*, which I have yet to draw and which necessity compels me to realize here. The reason, he says, why this difference may not be allowed on drafts for *outfit* as well as for *salary* is, that the outfit in its very nature is to be advanced in the United States. If there be any such rule as this I can only say that, after diligent inquiry for all information touching my accounts with the Govt., no notice of it was given me by the Department before my departure from the U. States; there is nothing of the kind intimated in my printed instructions on the subject, and I respectfully submit that, in any event, my case does not come within the reason of the rule, if there be any such rule & reason. Because the appropriation of my outfit was not made by Congress before the sailing of the frigate Constitution in which vessel I was ordered by Mr. [Abel P.] Upshur to ["sail" *altered to* "depart"], and because I had in fact drawn on the Govt. at home a sum exceeding my outfit by the sum of more than $500, and thus, at my own expense of 6 p[e]r cent interest on $5000 until the appropriation was made, saved the Govt. the difference of exchange on the sum of $9500. I obtained an order from the President to draw for a half year's salary, amounting to $4500, and I drew in favor of Corchoran & Riggs, brokers in Washington, for $5000 to be paid out of my outfit when appropriated, I paying them 6 p[e]r cent interest until the appropriation should be made. This in all equity should acquit me from further expense in realizing the balance of outfit, amounting to $4000, at the place of my mission. And, accordingly, I shall not hesitate to draw on the U. States for that balance of outfit, charging the difference of exchange here as in case of a draft for salary. And I trust that you will cause my account to be settled in accordance with the obvious justice of my case. I deem it proper thus to anticipate any and all cavil about any draft which I may make on the Govt., and to prevent the possibility of a protest which to me would be exceedingly unpleasant. I shall be scrupulously particular in my accounts & I ask nothing more than justice from the Government.

With the assurance of my highest regard and respect I have the honor to be Your ob[e]d[ien]t Serv[an]t, Henry A. Wise.

ALS with En in DNA, RG 59 (State Department), Diplomatic Despatches, Brazil, vol. 13 (M-121:15), received 10/7; FC (marked No. 1) with En in DNA, RG 84 (Foreign Posts), Brazil, Despatches, 11:77–81; autograph draft (incomplete) in Eastern Shore of Virginia Historical Society, Onancock, Va. (microfilm in NcU, Henry A. Wise Papers).

To WILLIAM M. BLACKFORD, [Bogota]

Department of State
Washington, 15th August, 1844
Sir: Your despatch No. 25 has been received. The result of the negotiation in the case of the brig Morris is to be regretted. The remedy you advise would no doubt prove effective but the President has no right to order a blockade and it cannot of course be resorted to without the sanction of Congress. The only measure that he can adopt is to order a naval force to the ports of New Granada and Venezuela, in the hope that its presence may give additional weight to your exertions in obtaining justice for our citizens. It is probable, therefore, that vessels of war of the United States will visit those ports after the next hurricane season. I am, Sir, your obedient servant, J.C. Calhoun.

FC (No. 19) in DNA, RG 59 (State Department), Diplomatic Instructions, Colombia, 15:89–90 (M-77:44); CC in DNA, RG 84 (Foreign Posts), Colombia, Despatches, vol. B4.

To H[enry] Y. Cranston, [Representative from R.I.], Newport, 8/15. Calhoun acknowledges Cranston's letter of 8/5 and informs him in reply that "no information has yet been received at the Department of the release of Mr. [William] Bisby from imprisonment but that the most constant and vigilant attention has been given to the condition of our unfortunate countrymen imprisoned in Cuba." FC in DNA, RG 59 (State Department), Domestic Letters, 34:332 (M-40:32).

To CALEB CUSHING, [Macao]

State Department
Washington, 15th Aug[us]t, 1844

Sir: The President [John Tyler] has taken into consideration your suggestion in your private letter to him, of the propriety of giving you authority to treat with Japan, should an opportunity offer. It is apprehended that little probability exists of effecting any commercial arrangement with that country; but as you think it may possibly be accomplished, a full power to treat with the Japanese authorities is herewith transmitted to you in accordance with your desire.

Your despatches to No. 40, inclusive, (with the exception of No. 18,) dated the 14th of March last, have been duly received and transmitted to the President. The industry, zeal, and ability which they evince, challenge his approbation, and lead him to indulge a sanguine hope that the principal objects of the mission will be ultimately attained.

With the most sincere wishes for your success, I remain, Sir, very respectfully, Your obedient servant, J.C. Calhoun.

FC (No. 9) in DNA, RG 59 (State Department), Diplomatic Instructions, China, 1:23–24 (M-77:38).

From Eben[ezer] Dorr, U.S. Marshal, Pensacola, [Fla. Territory], 8/15. Dorr does not have any information in regard to the two Americans, [Samuel S.] Thomas and [Joseph R.] Curtis, rescued from Haiti by the U.S. brig *Bainbridge*. He refers Calhoun to Commander J[oseph] Mattison [of the Navy]. ALS in DNA, RG 59 (State Department), Miscellaneous Letters (M-179:105, frames 233–234).

From Edward Everett, London, 8/15. As promised in his despatch of 7/27, Everett transmits to the State Department a copy furnished to him by Lord Aberdeen of the instructions to officers of British cruisers employed in suppressing the slave trade. LS (No. 177) with Ens in DNA, RG 59 (State Department), Diplomatic Despatches, Great Britain, vol. 53 (M-30:49), received 9/3; FC in DNA, RG 84 (Foreign Posts), Great Britain, Despatches, 8:383–384; FC in MHi, Edward Everett Papers, 50:34–35 (published microfilm, reel 23, frame 286).

To P.J. Farnham & Co., Salem, Mass., 8/15. "I have received your letter of the 5th instant, respecting your claim on the British Government in the case of the bark 'Jones'; and herewith transmit to you, in accordance with your request the copy of a despatch addressed to this Department on the 15th of June last, by Mr. [Edward] Everett, the Minister of the United States at London, and of the document therein referred to, which will put you in possession of all the recent information we have on the subject." FC in DNA, RG 59 (State Department), Domestic Letters, 34:333 (M-40:32).

From FRANKLIN GAGE

Consulate of the United States
Cardenas [Cuba,] 15th Aug[us]t 1844

Sir, I have this day had the honor to receive your communication dated April 25th 1844. I very much regret not having received it at an earlier date, as in that event my course in relation to American citizens imprisoned in this place would have been materially different. Since my communication these individuals have been removed from this place to Matanzas & I believe our Consul Mr. [Thomas M.] Rodney has made all necessary communications to the Department in regard to them. Their names are [William] Bisby, Moffatt [*sic*; Samuel Moffat,] Thompson and Savage.

The case of Bisby & Moffatt has been peculiarly ag[g]ravated; They were upon the evidence of a slave under the torture of the lash, about four months in the common Prison in Cardenas, confined in Stocks and Irons in the same apartment with Negroes, deprived of all assistance and comfort; attention not being paid even to the common decencies of life. Bisby whose health is delicate was treated with uncommon severity, being chained to the floor until it was thought he could no longer survive such severe treatment. I made application to see them but was peremptorily refused. They have since been in confinement in Matanzas without trial, and are obliged to pay their own expences, and I see no prospect of their being released without some interference in their behalf on the part of the Government.

Of the case of Savage and Thompson I am not so well informed, they being sent to Matanzas soon after their arrest. They are however closely confined in Matanzas with no prospect of release. From what I learn the Spanish Authorities are of opinion that our government will afford no protection to its citizens.

I have not the slightest doubt of the innocence of these individuals, and am confident they would be released or brought to a speedy trial should a demand be made from our Government to that effect.

I deem it proper to state that I have received no communication from our Consul in Havana [Robert B. Campbell] on the subject. I have the honor to be Sir Your mo[st] ob[e]d[ien]t Serv[an]t, Franklin Gage.

ALS (No. 8) in DNA, RG 59 (State Department), Consular Despatches, Cardenas, vol. 20 (T-583:1), received 8/31.

To the Rev[eren]d J[ohn] D. Gardiner, [Sag Harbor, N.Y.]

State department, 15 Aug[us]t 1844

My Dear Sir, It affords me great pleasure to state, that the President [John Tyler] has determined on appointing your Son Samuel [L. Gardiner to be] Collector of the Port of Sag Harbor, which I hope will put you at your ease in reference to the Education of your youngest son Calhoun; I trust he may one day do honor to you & the name he bears. With great Respect, yours truly, J.C. Calhoun.

Copy in ScCleA. Note: This copy was made by John D. Gardiner in the text of his letter to Calhoun on 12/6/1844.

To Allen A. Hall, [Caracas]

Department of State
Washington, 15th August, 1844

Sir: Your despatches of the 25th of May and 27th June, last, both numbered 36, have been received.

The failure of the Congress of Venezuela to make an appropriation for the purpose of enabling the Executive to comply with the arrangement between the Minister for Foreign Affairs [Juan Manuel Manrique] and yourself, in the case of the brig Morris, is to be regretted. The remedy which you advise would no doubt prove effective, but it cannot be adopted without the sanction of Congress. The only measure which the President can adopt is to order a naval force to the ports of Venezuela in the hope that its presence may give additional weight to your exertions in obtaining justice for our citizens. It is probable that such a force will visit those ports after the next hurricane season.

The subject of your despatch of the 27th of June is one of deep interest, and you may inform the government of Venezuela that the President will take it into serious consideration. I am, Sir, your obedient servant, J.C. Calhoun.

LS (No. 21) in DNA, RG 84 (Foreign Posts), Venezuela, Instructions, 1835–1853; FC in DNA, RG 59 (State Department), Diplomatic Instructions, Venezuela, 1:49 (M-77:171).

From J[ohn] P. Kennedy, Baltimore, 8/15. Kennedy requests Calhoun to forward an enclosed package, containing a private petition to the King of France [Louis Philippe], to the U.S. Minister at Paris, William R. King. (A Clerk's EU reads: "enclosure not rec[eive]d . . . .") ALS in DNA, RG 59 (State Department), Passport Applications, 1795–1905, vol. 32, unnumbered (M-1372:15).

From John M. Niles, [Representative from Conn.], Hartford, 8/15. James L. Belden of New Haven intends to make a communication to Calhoun. Niles testifies, on the basis of long acquaintance, to Belden's respectable character and to his public services as a magistrate, member of the Conn. legislature, and Postmaster of Wethersfield for many years. ALS in DNA, RG 59 (State Department), Applications and Recommendations, 1837–1845, DeWitt (M-687:9, frames 173–174).

To R[ICHARD] PAKENHAM

Department of State
Washington, 15th Aug[us]t, 1844

Sir, I have duly received your letter of the 5th instant, communicating to this Department, by direction of Her Majesty's Government, certain extracts from reports of Her Majesty's Commissioners and Her Majesty's Consul at Rio de Janeiro, relative to the participation of American vessels in the Slave Trade, and referring to a note, conveying information on the same subject, which was addressed to Mr. [Edward] Everett, the Minister of the United States at London, on the 22d of November last, by Her Majesty's Principal Secretary of State for Foreign Affairs.

I will not fail to take an early occasion of laying these papers before the President for his consideration, and with the view to the adoption of such measures as may be judged expedient by this Government for the repression of any abuses of this character that may be found to exist.

I pray you to accept the assurance of my distinguished consideration. J.C. Calhoun.

FC in DNA, RG 59 (State Department), Notes to Foreign Legations, Great Britain, 7:25–26 (M-99:36).

From L[ewis] Warrington for [John Y. Mason], Secretary of the Navy, 8/15. "I . . . transmit herewith the documentary evidence in the cases of Messrs. [Samuel S.] Thomas & [Joseph R.] Curtis received this day from Commander J[oseph] Mattison[,] late of the U.S. Brig Bainbridge." LS with Ens in DNA, RG 59 (State Department), Miscellaneous Letters (M-179:105, frames 184–232); FC in DNA, RG 45 (Naval Records), Letters Sent by the Secretary of the Navy to the President and Executive Agencies, 1821–1886, 5:16 (M-472:3, frame 50).

From H[enry] C. Williams, Washington, 8/15. Williams informs Calhoun that Senator [Alexander] Barrow of La. will "cheerfully support" in the Senate the nomination of Patterson Fletcher for appointment as U.S. District Attorney for middle Tenn. Barrow himself would recommend Fletcher but for a long-standing practice of never recommending any person for office. Williams believes that Fletcher's appointment would "be a good one and acceptable to the people of Tennessee." ALS in DNA, RG 59 (State Department), Applications and Recommendations, 1837–1845, Fletcher (M-687:11, frames 376–378).

AUGUST 16–31, 1844

〚〛

The situation of Texas remained potentially critical. Given the nature of Mexican politics and the several weeks required for news to reach Washington, rumor was bound to be rife and much anxiety had to be experienced by those in the United States who were officially responsible. Potentially, Mexico might launch hostilities against Texas at any time, either reprisals, a token invasion, or a major effort at reconquest. This would leave the executive branch of the federal government in a most difficult position, militarily and Constitutionally. To add to the discomfort, yellow fever was raging in Texas as never before, and word was received over a few days of it having carried off the three chief U.S. representatives there: William S. Murphy, the outgoing Chargé; Tilghman A. Howard, the newly-arrived Chargé; and Archibald M. Green, the experienced Consul at Galveston.

In the meantime, Calhoun had to be prepared for negotiations with the British Minister that would cover the whole ground of competing historical and legal claims to the vast northwestern territory of Oregon, as an effort was made to clarify the issues and inch toward a settlement. And he had to encourage his less hot-headed friends in South Carolina in their efforts to contain those "Bluffton" militants who were bound to be labelled elsewhere, including over most of the South, as reprehensible disunionists.

At the end of August Calhoun began to receive disturbing reports from Ohio friends. Thomas Ewing, a fiery partisan Whig orator, was regaling campaign crowds across the Old Northwest with the charge that John C. Calhoun, who was represented as the true and secret director of the Democratic party, was an advocate of slavery for the laboring class of white men. It was a tactic that constituted possibly the ugliest turn that sectional animosity had taken since the Hartford Convention. It was hard to imagine anything more destructive to the harmony of the Union if any significant number of Northerners could be persuaded to give credit to such defamation.

As August closed, Calhoun could gain relief from official and political pressures with the consoling thought that his daughter, son-in-law, and grandchildren had by now arrived at their post in Brussels, where experiences of delight and improvement awaited them such as were granted to relatively few Americans. (And such as he himself would never have.) On August 29 he wrote to Anna Maria, who by the time she received the letter would have seen Paris: "I will expect to hear from you often & fully; and you must give me your impressions, just as you feel them."

Ⅲ

From W[illia]m C. Barrett, "U.S. Attorney's Office," New York [City], 8/16. In the absence of U.S. District Attorney O[gden] Hoffman, Barrett encloses a petition [of 8/13] to Calhoun from Joseph Carroll and others and endorses the statements contained therein. Though no law allows for "the compensation of parties sent home as witnesses from a foreign port," Barrett believes that the claim is just and that the men may be "constructively" considered as "present in Court from the commencement of the voyage" from Brazil. (An EI by Calhoun indicates that this letter was referred to the Secretary of the Treasury.) ALS in DNA, RG 59 (State Department), Petitions for Pardon, Tyler Administration, Unnumbered Cases.

To [Henry Bowen], "the Secretary of State" of R.I., 8/16. Calhoun acknowledges receipt of a letter of 8/10 enclosing a statement of the convicts in the State prison during 1840–1844. "From the very limited number of convicts returned, it would appear that the clerk has misunderstood the enquiry, and reported only the number received during each year, instead of the whole number in prison each year." The statement is therefore returned "with a view to correction." LS in ScU-SC, John C. Calhoun Papers.

From Burr, Benedict, & Beebe, New York [City], 8/16. These attorneys support the claim for compensation contained in the petition of Joseph Carroll and other seamen to Calhoun [of 8/13]. ALS in DNA, RG 59 (State Department), Petitions for Pardon, Tyler Administration, Unnumbered Cases.

From R[ICHARD] K. CALL

Tallahassee, 16th August 1844

Sir, I have the honour to acknowledge the receipt of your letter of the 18th ultimo, and am at a loss to know how the following paragraph of that letter should be construed. "With regard to the first specification the aiding and promoting malicious prosecutions, to gratify personal and political animosity, I can only state that this Department is not the proper authority to which application should be made in the first instance. A Court of justice in my opinion, is the proper tribunal, to examine and pronounce upon this charge, and to it recourse ought first to be had by the parties aggrieved." If I comprehend the language in which this paragraph is expressed, it is your opinion, that I being the party aggrieved, must first have recourse to a Court of Justice, or in other words that I must first bring an action to ["remove" *altered to* "recover"] damages from Mr. [Charles S.] Sibley before the Department will take notice of a charge, supported by evidence, of culpable misconduct in office. If this be the true construction of that part of your letter, (and I am able to give it none other,) it appears to me that the Department has assumed a most extraordinary position. I charge this officer on evidence, (and if further testimony is required, I have pointed out the way by which it may be obtained,) ["of" *canceled*] with offences, of which if guilty every honorable man would say he should be removed from office. But the Department will not consider the evidence, supporting this charge, now before it, or collect other testimony, nor will it take any notice ["whatever" *interlined*] of this charge, until I shall have recourse to "a court of Justice," as though the offence could in any degree be lessened or mitigated by my failure to seek redress in Court. Now I have no hesitation in saying to you, that I shall never have such recourse, That I shall never ask a jury to give me pecuniary damages, for injustice or injury done to me by a public officer in his official station. I seek no such redress, but I desire to protect myself, and to protect others from similar injuries in future, and I call on the high functionaries of the Government whose duty it is to watch over the purity and dignity of ["its" *canceled and* "their" *interlined*] subordinates, to investigate the charge, and if true, to visit the offender with appropriate punishment. The District Att[orne]y of the United States represents his government. His official acts are the acts of his Government, and his official improprieties, when made known if not rebuked and punished, by the proper Department, must reflect on his Government the same dishonour, with which he has covered himself.

This appears to me to be the inevitable result in the present case. I therefore indulge the hope, that I am mistaken in the construction I ["have" *interlined*] given this part of your letter, and that the first charge and specifications I have preferred against the District Attorney, will receive a fair and impartial, ["trial" *canceled*] but a rigid investigation. The specification shews that there is nothing either complicated, or difficult in this investigation. I charged the Dist[rict] Att[orne]y with aiding and promoting malicious prosecutions against me. I have laid before you copies of two indictments for that purpose, prepared and signed by him. I have laid before you conclusive evidence, that all the material allegations contained in both these indictments are not only false, but that they were known by the District Attorney to be false, before, and at the time he prepared the indictments. These facts are known almost to this entire community, and in further support of them, I beg leave to refer you to Gov. W[illia]m P. Duval, Mr. Thomas H. Hagner and Mr. Simon Towle of Florida, now in Washington.

In support of the second charge which you have thought worthy of investigation, I beg leave to refer you to the enclosed copy of a correspondence between the District Att[orne]y and Mr. George K. Walker, and to the certificate of Doctor William Treadwell, and Mr. Edward Houston. The case of J[ohn] C. Hall mentioned in the letter of Mr. Walker was criminal in a eminent degree. The Defendant with a large knife attacked an unarmed man, gave him a deep and dangerous wound in the neck, and would, it is believed, have killed the unfortunate man, but for the interposition of a Gentleman present at the time, and whose testimony on the subject may be obtained if you desire it. This case was compromised, and the District Attorney received in consideration thereof, the sum of five dollars in violation of the following provision of the act of the Legislative Council, Approved 10th Feb. 1834. "Provided that in no case of criminal prosecution shall any fee be allowed to the District Attorney, when the prosecution fails by reason of any default in the indictment or a *nolle prosequi* is entered."

There are numerous other cases of the same, or even of a more aggrevated nature, which have occurred in the courts of this District; and of which I will here mention one. In the Leon [County] Superior Court, a noted prostitute was indicted for lewdness, and her conviction was certain, had she been brought to trial. But a married man whose mistress she was at the time, came forward, paid Mr. Sibley the same fees to which he would have been entitled for a conviction, and had the case dismissed.

The most positive proof of these facts can be procured, Should you deem in [*sic*] necessary.

I know not Sir, what *ex parte* testimony, Mr. Sibley may be able to obtain, but if the matter is openly investigated he will certainly be convicted of every charge I have preferred against him, and for the honour of the Government I trust the investigation will be made. I have the honour Sir to be Very Respectfully Your Obedient Serv[an]t, R.K. Call.

ALS with Ens in DNA, RG 59 (State Department), Applications and Recommendations, 1837–1845, Sibley (M-687:30, frames 246–255). NOTE: A Clerk's EU reads "Copy of this sent to Mr. Sibley, Oct[obe]r 25th 1844." Call's term as Governor of Fla. Territory had expired on 8/11.

To Edward Dixon, Warrenton, Va., 8/16. "I have to inform you that the vessel in which it is expected you will take passage for Carthagena as bearer of despatches to the Legation of the United States at Bogotá, is ready for sea. You will consequently repair hither without delay for the purpose of receiving the despatches." FC in DNA, RG 59 (State Department), Diplomatic Instructions, Colombia, 15:91 (M-77:44).

To Gabriel G. Fleurot, Norfolk, 8/16. "I have to reply to your letter of the 14th instant, that it has been laid before the President [John Tyler] and that his decision in reference to the application therein made will, when made known to the Department[,] be communicated to you." FC in DNA, RG 59 (State Department), Domestic Letters, 34:336 (M-40:32).

From [Jean Corneille, Chevalier] Gevers, New York [City], 8/16. Gevers acknowledges receipt of Calhoun's letter of 8/12 enclosing the favorable decision of [George M. Bibb] the Secretary of the Treasury regarding tariff duties on Java coffee. He expresses pleasure at the decision and gratitude to Calhoun for his assistance in the matter. LS in DNA, RG 59 (State Department), Notes from Foreign Legations, Netherlands, vol. 2 (M-56:2, frames 179–181).

To Albert Smith, Moose River, Somerset County, Maine, 8/16. Calhoun authorizes Smith to pay from the Northeastern boundary commission contingency fund the bill for the large "transit instrument" mentioned in his letter of 8/10. In the future the prior consent of the Secretary of State should be obtained for any such order. FC in DNA, RG 59 (State Department), Domestic Letters, 34:335–336 (M-40:32).

From ISAAC VAN ZANDT

Legation of Texas
Washington, D.C., August 16th 1844

The Undersigned, Chargé d'Affaires of the Republic of Texas, has the honor to acknowledge the receipt of the note of Mr. Calhoun, Secretary of State of the United States, of the 14th Instant, furnishing the decission [*sic*] of the Court Martial appointed for the trial of Captain [Philip St. George] Cooke; and additional information concerning the forcible rescue of certain goods from the Collector of Red River [James Bourland], with the opinions of the President of the United States [John Tyler] in relation thereto—also the documents enclosed therewith explanatory of the two cases refer[r]ed to. Copies of the same will, immediately, be transmitted to the Government of Texas for its information.

It is not deemed necessary, at this time, to add any thing further, in relation to the trial and acquittal of Captain Cooke.

The very just and proper views expressed by the Honorable Secretary of State concerning the outrage upon the Collector of Red River, and the willingness manifested by the President of the United States to make compensation for the injuries inflicted and damages done, will be very gratifying to the President of Texas [Samuel Houston], furnishing, as it does, renewed evidence, on the part of the Government of the United States, of a disposition to preserve the most friendly relations between the two countries, a disposition which the Undersigned is happy to assure the Secretary of State, is fully reciprocated by the Government of Texas.

The testimony refer[r]ed to, as necessary to be transmitted to Congress with the message of the President of the United States, will be furnished at the earliest day possible.

The Undersigned avails himself of this occasion to renew to Mr. Calhoun assurances of his very distinguished consideration. Isaac Van Zandt.

LS in DNA, RG 59 (State Department), Notes from Foreign Legations, Texas, 1836–1845, vol. 1 (T-809:1); FC in Tx, Records of the Texas Republic Department of State, Letters and Dispatches Sent by the Texas Legation in Washington, 2:[1]; FC in Tx, Records of the Texas Republic Department of State, Copybooks of Letters Received from Texan and Foreign Representatives, vol. 2–1/98, pp. 530–531; CC in Tx, Records of the Texas Republic Department of State, U.S. Diplomatic Correspondence; PC in Senate Document No. 1, 28th Cong., 2nd Sess., pp. 111–112; PC in House Document No. 2, 28th Cong., 2nd Sess., pp. 108–109; PC in Crallé, ed., *Works,* 5:412.

From W[illia]m Wilkins

War Department, Aug[us]t 16th 1844

Sir, I have the honor to acknowledge the receipt of your note of the day before yesterday.

You can communicate to Mr. [Isaac] Van Zandt that orders have been issued from this Department, in pursuance of the instructions from the President, for the liberation and return to their native country of the two Texan boys referred to in the note addressed to you under date of the 10th inst. by the Chargé d'Affair[e]s of Texas.

To secure the object of the instructions I have received, my orders have been issued to Mr. [William] Armstrong of the Choctaw Indian Agency, and also to the Commanding military officer presumed to be most convenient to the Indian district in which the boys are likely to be found.

I return herewith Mr. Van Zandt's note to you with the President's endorsement. I have the honor to be, Sir, With high respect Y[ou]r Ob[edien]t Serv[an]t, Wm. Wilkins, Sec[retar]y of War.

LS in DNA, RG 59 (State Department), Miscellaneous Letters (M-179:105, frame 235); ALS (retained copy) in DNA, RG 75 (Bureau of Indian Affairs), Letters Received by the Office of Indian Affairs, 1824–1880, Miscellaneous, 1844, S3683 (M-234:443, frames 331–332); FC in DNA, RG 107 (Secretary of War), Letters Sent Relating to Military Affairs, 1800–1861, 25:376 (M-6:25); FC in DNA, RG 75 (Bureau of Indian Affairs), Letters Sent by the Office of Indian Affairs, 35:421 (M-21:35).

From James L. Belden

New Haven Conn., August 17th 1844

Dear Sir, Understanding from my nephew Mr. James L. DeWitt that he has addressed you respecting the consulate at Laguna de Terminos [Mexico]—which is now vacant—I take the liberty of commending him to your favorable consideration for that ["Office" *canceled*] which I am encouraged to do from the Letters of the Hon. Ralph I. Ingersoll—and Jeremiah Day President of Yale College—who have kindly written you, ["and as in my" *canceled*] in my behalf—with their assurance that you might have confidence in ["any" *interlined*] statement which I should make respecting Mr. DeWitt—their Letters accompany this.

In commending Mr. DeWitt for this vacant Office I do it under the fullest conviction that he is qualified to perform all its duties acceptable to you, and give satisfaction to the Public. Mr. DeWitt return[e]d to this Country about a year since from Laguna De Terminos—a few months after the death of Mr. [Charles] Russell the late Consul—in whose Office he ["had" *canceled and* "was" *interlined*] employ[e]d for *several years*—in performing the duties of the consulate as well as a Clerk in the Mercantile House of Mess. Gutierrez Brothers & Co. of which Mr. Russell was a Partner. I have reason to beleive that about four years—Mr. DeWitt enjoy[e]d the Confidence of Mr. Russell—as well as of the Mercantile Establishment—and was entrusted with the management—correspondence and confidential part of their business.

His residence in Central America—improv[e]d the Knowledge he possessed of the ["Spanish" *interlined*] Language—which I have no doubt he understands and writes—with sufficient accuracy for all the purposes of business.

Mr. DeWitt is a Gentleman of *respectable talents*—with a ["fair" *canceled*] character fair and unblemished, in the prime of life—about ["forty" *canceled and* "thirty seven" *interlined*] years—been acclimated to the Climate—and in my opinion should he receive the appointment—would be faithful and diligent in performing the duties of the Office—would do honor to himself and the Country he would represent.

I again commend him to your consideration—and conclude by saying—that should he receive this appointment—it will be gratefully remember[e]d by his highly respectable connections and friends—and ["by" *canceled*] particularly by your Ob[edien]t Serv[an]t, James L. Belden.

ALS in DNA, RG 59 (State Department), Applications and Recommendations, 1837–1845, DeWitt (M-687:9, frames 162–164).

To T[homas] G. Clemson, [Brussels?]

State Dept., 17th Aug[us]t 1844

My dear Sir, I enclose a packet of letters from G[e]n[era]l [James] Hamilton [Jr.], with a note of mine a few days since, to the care of Mr. [William R.] King[,] our minister at Paris. I now enclose two letters, which I had put under cover to you at the Cane Brake, & which returned here by the mail of yesterday.

Nothing new has occurred here since my last. The elections are going on in Kentucky, Indiana, Illinois, Missouri, & Alabama, or rather the returns are coming in. The contest is close; but on the whole the indication is in favour of [James K.] Polk. Every State thus far has given an increased majority compared with the election of '42, when the whigs were so badly beatten.

I expected to have left Washington ere this for home; but have been detained by my official duties. I fear I shall not be able to leave for a week or 10 days yet. I had a letter from Mrs. [Floride Colhoun] Calhoun yesterday. All well & the crop fine; the best ever made on the place.

My health is still good, but I am not yet entirely free from my cold. I shall be anxious to hear from you, as soon as you arrive.

My love to Anna [Maria Calhoun Clemson] & kiss the children [John Calhoun Clemson and Floride Elizabeth Clemson] for their Grand father. Your affectionate father, J.C. Calhoun.

ALS in ScCleA.

From Jeremiah Day

Yale College, Aug. 17th 1844

Dear Sir, James L. Belden Esq[ui]r[e] of this city having occasion to make a communication to you on business, I take the liberty to state, that as he discharged the duties of a Postmaster [of Wethersfield] with fidelity for nearly thirty years; as well as of other important offices and stations in public life; and having, since his residence in this place, sustained a character of high respectability and exemplary integrity, I have no hesitation in expression [*sic*] my conviction, that whatever statements he may make to you, may be relied on, as strictly correct. I have the honor to be, With high regard, Your friend and serv[an]t, Jeremiah Day.

ALS in DNA, RG 59 (State Department), Applications and Recommendations, 1837–1845, DeWitt (M-687:9, frame 168).

From R[ALPH] I. INGERSOLL, [former Representative from Conn.]

New Haven, 17 August 1844

Dear Sir, James L. Belden Esq[ui]r[e] now a resident of this city, will make an application in behalf of his nephew Mr. James L. De-Witt, for a consulate appointment at Lagune De Terminos in Central America. Mr. DeWitt has formerly been the Clerk in the office of the late Consul Mr. [Charles] Russell deceased. The office is now vacant.

As Mr. Belden who makes the application is a stranger to you, I take the liberty to say, that he is a gentleman of the first respect-ability—was formerly and for many years Post Master of ["Wash-ing"(?) *canceled*] Wethersfield his former residence, which he re-signed (after holding it 29 years) on his coming to live here. He was also for several sessions a member of our State Legislature, and a Magistrate of the county where he resided. You may therefore rely with entire confidence on any statement that he make[s] to you. I am not acquainted with his nephew, but know that Mr. Belden is entitled to every confidence, & therefore commend his application to your favorable consideration. With great respect I am your ob[edien]t Serv[an]t, R.I. Ingersoll.

ALS in DNA, RG 59 (State Department), Applications and Recommendations, 1837–1845, DeWitt (M-687:9, frames 165–167).

From R[occo] Martuscelli, [Consul General of the Two Sicilies], New York [City], 8/17. Martuscelli complains about the delays he has encountered in receiving a satisfactory reply from the Secretary of the Treasury concerning the claims of Dacorsi and De Martino against the Collector of Customs of New York City. The two men objected to the method of valuation at that city of a shipment of macaroni from Naples. After an exposition of Dacorsi's and De Martino's complaint, Martuscelli states that, given the intransigence of the Secretary of the Treasury, he may be obliged to publish in local newspapers the correspondence between himself and the U.S. government on the matter. (In his translation from the French language, Robert Greenhow appended a note referring to Martuscelli's language: "The French word *'esquive'* here used in the original means literally *'to dodge'*—and is by no means a courteous expression.") CC (in French) and State Department translation in DNA, RG 59 (State Department), Notes from Foreign Legations, Two Sicilies, vol. 1 (M-55:1).

To Mrs. W[ILLIAM] S. MURPHY, Chilicothe, Ohio

Department of State
Washington, Aug. 17, 1844

Madam, It becomes my painful duty to communicate to you, intelligence of the death of your husband Gen[era]l W.S. Murphy. He died at Galvezton on the 13th of July. The enclosed copy of a letter received at the Department from the United States Consul at that place will inform you of the particulars connected with this melancholy event. Sincerely sympathising with you in your bereavement, I have the honor to be &, J.C. Calhoun.

FC in DNA, RG 59 (State Department), Consular Instructions, 11:270–271.

To ISAAC VAN ZANDT

Department of State
Washington, 17th August, 1844

Sir: I have the honor to acknowledge the receipt of your note of the 10th instant and to acquaint you in reply that it was referred to the Secretary of War [William Wilkins], who has informed me that proper orders have been issued from his Department for the liberation and return to their native country of the two Texan boys referred to in your note.

I avail myself of this occasion to offer you renewed assurances of my very distinguished consideration. J.C. Calhoun.

FC in DNA, RG 59 (State Department), Notes to Foreign Legations, Texas, 6:75 (M-99:95); FC in Tx, Records of the Texas Republic Department of State, Copybooks of Letters Received from Texan and Foreign Representatives, vol. 2–1/98, p. 532; CC in Tx, Records of the Texas Republic Department of State, U.S. Diplomatic Correspondence; PC in Senate Document No. 14, 32nd Cong., 2nd Sess., p. 126.

From Miss BETSEY HAWLEY

Darien, Connecticut, 18th Aug. 1844

Sir, I am about to address a letter to you in such a way, as that it will go into your hands, instead of into the hands of the clerks of the Department.

The reason of this is, that I have been repulsed there in a very improper manner, during the administration of some of your predecessors.

I am now very desirous to obtain the copy of a document which is at the Department of State, which interests me very highly as heiress to my brother's [Capt. Isaac P. Hawley's] estate, who died in a foreign country. And as I have been denied a copy of a document relating to the same subject, I have not the confidence to expect that the request I should wish *now* to make, would be granted me, unless you will take the supervision of the examination. A[l]tho' it is a document of great importance, yet it seems to me improper that I should be put to the necessity of hiring a person to go from here to examine the records, so long as provision is made at the expense of the public for such purposes. I can give such directions as that it may be found in a short time, and have to ask you, sir, whether I may be permitted to have a copy of that document upon my giving information where it may be found.

You will place me under lasting obligations, sir, if you will be so kind as to answer me without delay. I am, sir, with high respect, Your servant, Betsey Hawley.

[P.S.] Please address Miss Betsey Hawley[,] Darien Connecticut.

ALS in ScCleA. NOTE: On the address sheet of this letter, the writer appended the following: "This letter is not to be opened by any clerk at the Department, but is designed expressly for Mr. Calhoun's perusal."

From THOMAS O. LARKIN

Consulate of the U. States of America
Monterey California, August 18, 1844

Sir, The undersigned improves the opportunity of the Sloop of war Levant going to Mazatlan of writing to the Department.

General [Manuel] Micheltorena Commander in cheif in California has received orders to place everey port of California in the best state of defence in particular this town as the Mexican Government expect that the U.S. Senate would annex Texas to the Union in which case Gen. Santa Anna would immediately declare war. Fifteen or twenty guns that were on the fort of Mont[erey], many of them useless, Gen. Micheltorena has sent twenty five or thirty miles into the country and left not one on the fort. He has ordered all the people from fifteen to sixty years of age to be enrolled and to be called out once a week for drill.

There are in California from two hundred and fifty to two hundred and eighty Mexican troops and one hundred and fifty to two hundred California troops the latter cheifly boys, and I think nearly all forced into the line. There may be one thousand Californians fit to form a militia of whom nine tenths I think would refuse any call on them. The one hundred and fifty would dislike being called into severe service, while the two hundred and eighty might follow their General. The one thousand militia are within San Diego, and San Francisco eight or nine hundred miles, but few of this class have any interest in the present Government, and care but little who commands them.

For two months families have been moving from town, supposing that Com[m]odore [Alexander J.] Dallas would arrive here to take the place[;] in which case they had great fear of trouble with the two hundred and fifty Mexican troops in town supposing they would spend the first night in robbery and plunder. From the great order and quietness during the twenty four hours [in 1842] this town was under Com[m]odore [Thomas Ap C.] Jones, the people are not afraid of the next squadron, perhaps many are anxiously waiting its arrival as under present circumstances property is not secure. They therefore may well wish a change.

Gen. Micheltorena had orders to treat every American man of war with every respect and politeness which he has and will continue to do not only by orders from his Government, but from inclination. Americans living here are safer in my opinion in their property than the natives. I find every respect from Gen. Micheltorena and all in the country. There has this month arrived forty six American men, women and children, to settle in California[;] many more are preparing to leave the Oregon for this country.

The undersigned having seen a supposition that England may purchase California from Mexico begs leave to say that should such be the case, those of our country who take an interest in the Oregon should use every legal and fair means to effect an exchange of eight degrees of the country north of the Columbia for eight degrees in

California thereby taking in one of the finest countries in the world, and the best and most magnificent harbours known.

The undersigned would again call the attention of his Government to the marriages that are taking place among American and English emigrants in California who have come here by land from the U.S. There has now been several of these emigrants married by Mexican Alcaldes who have not that authority, as the ceremony can only be performed here by a Catholic Priest; as our countrymen are flocking into California from home more of these marriages may take place which among families of property in the future generations may cause perplexities before unknown to our laws. It has been allowed that Consuls can perform the ceremony of marriage between their countrymen in any part of the world if on board an American ship, as the ship in the harbour is as much under the jurisdiction of the U.S. as the City of Washington; it is therefore of much importance to many Americans in California and will be of more to their children to know if they can be married in their consular house.

The undersigned begs leave to call the attention of the Department of State to the importance of having one of our vessels of war more on this coast. The Levant remains here eight or ten days, the Warren is expected here in Sept. and is supposed will sail immediately. As the country is a thousand miles long and means of information from one end of the coast to another a month in passing, it is impossible for many to visit a man of war as she would have sailed before they know she had arrived. While we have five or six sail at Callao one could be kept six months in a year in California. The neces[s]ity is increasing yearly as the American trade enlarges in particular the whaling buissiness. It is said that one hundred sail will be on this coast next year, three hundred being this year on the N.W. Coast.

The undersigned takes this opportunity of asking you what releif he can give his countrymen in California who are not mariners by profession. There have arrived a few by water and many by the way of the Rocky Mountains. There is now a Native of the State of New Hampshire in this vicinity, crasy, and much in want of assistance. He is a man of good connexions, well educated, a good english and spanish scholar, has found his way from place to place and is now coming to me being sent by some alcalde as I have understood. I expect other cases of distress brought to my notice and craving my consular assistance. By instructions that I have, which are quite small [and] having no law books, I am unable to come to any conclusion on the subject.

The whaling business being now carried on by hundreds of American Ships on the N.W. Coast, and constantly increasing will bring to the coast of California many thousand American seaman [*sic*] taken down with the scurvy, or otherwise reduced by the severe duties of their profession. The undersigned begs leave to inform the department that for twenty years a few whalers have yearly visited California for provisions, and in most cases been allowed to sell four or five hundred dollars worth of goods from each ship to purchase supplies, by paying the duties on the goods sold when required, yet in some instances they have been refused—though the refusals have been very rare but this year the Collector has given six months notice that on no condition whatever shall a whaler be allowed to sell anything. The American whale ship Charles W. Morgan is now here, a full ship thirty-four months out, sickness on board and much in want of provisions. The Captain is thus brought suddenly under the new regulation six months being no time to inform the whaling interest of any change of laws. It becomes more severe on the Captain as when before here he had liberty to sell goods.

By the laws of Mexico vessels cannot trade within the Republic unless they enter all the cargo and pay the tonnage duties (this a whaler cannot do) yet as in California the priveledge has always been allowed for whalers to sell so small a sum as five hundred dollars paying the regular duties on the same. The benefit to a large class of people would be very great if our minister at Mexico could bring into effect some certain arrangement with the Mexican Government on this subject. It is almost the only way for the farmers to sell their produce of the kind required by the whalers. I have the honour to be Sir your most Obedient Humble Servant, Thomas O. Larkin.

LS (No. 9) with En in DNA, RG 59 (State Department), Consular Despatches, Monterey (M-138:1), received 11/13; variant FC in CU, Bancroft Library, Larkin Collection; PC in Hammond, ed., *Larkin Papers*, 2:204–207. NOTE: Larkin enclosed a copy of his letter of 8/14 to the U.S. Minister at Mexico City, explaining the effect of the prohibition of trade between Californians and American whalers.

From N.[?]O. Platt, New York [City], 8/18. "I take pleasure in adding my testimony to the capability and fitness of Mr. J[ames] L. DeWitt for the post of Consul at Laguna [Mexico]. The late Charles Russell Esq. was a particular friend of mine, and in all my commercial transactions with him both here, and at Laguna, I had an opportunity to become familiarly acquainted with Mr. DeWitt and hesitate not to say, that a more judicious appointment (I think) could not be made." ALS in DNA, RG 59 (State Department), Applications and Recommendations, 1837–1845, DeWitt (M-687:9, frames 169–170).

From JOSEPH PORTER

Boon[e]ville Mo., August 18th 1844
Mr. John C. Calhoun, Owing to the great and high estimation in which I hold you as a statesman, and a patriot you must excuse me for the present obt[r]usion. My first acquaintance, with you took place about ["a" *canceled*] the commencement of your struggle, with Gen[e]ral [Andrew] Jackson and his combin[e]d forces, upon the subgect of the Tariff. I thought you then right and I still think you right not onely upon that subgect, but every other qu[e]stion which has since followed. I was then Resider in a remote, part of Arkansas. You had know friends in that section, but my self and one other, Thomas [S.] Drew, who is now a candidate, for Governor [of Ark.], a declar[e]d state right partisan, of your stamp. The marks of his and my devotion to you and the principals to which you hold, may bee seen by the change that has taken place in that portion of Arkansas, in your favour. Wee both incur[re]d the sensur of a formadable ["party" *interlined*] for years on your ac[coun]t. Thank God I trust we have Triumpht. I am hear in Missouri, pushing fourth your clames, and bat[t]ling against, all charges prefard against you and the principles which you hold. Thomas [H.] Benton has been hear delivering stum[p] speeches, to the people, in opposition to Texas and on all occaisions both private and public he is defameing and impuneing your motives, as dangerous and corrupt. It is easy to sea the ground of his obgection to you. It is not principal, but a place, which he wishes to presearve. Thank Providence, his destiny is fixt. From what I can learn from the Retearns of the State Electione he will be Left out. The people in this State that is those that belonge to the Democratic and state right party ar[e] in favour of the Tr[e]aty proposed by you, and Mr. Benton minds me of the fabel of the rat who attempted to avenge him self by [g]nawing one of the Blacksmith's files which sune wore out his one teeth. In moveing from Arkansas, to this State I have Lost, your speeches, your debate with Mr. [Henry] Clay and Daniel Webster, at the extra session of [18]38. I will take it as ["a" *interlined*] great favour if you will but send it to me. You cannot confear on me a greater favour, than by sending

me all your speeches. I want Clay and Webster's speech, and your ancer to each[.] A part of your ancer, I have yet at memmory[.] I use Mr. Webster[']s, speech in part to prove the fact of your acting, with the minorrity on all those great and important qu[e]stions, which Time has proved the correctness of your position and that place and party, has not been the rule of your action, but country and principal[.] I have a son who will be 5 years old the 22 of this month, who I Cal[l] John C. Calhoun in honor of your self. ["I" *canceled*] Bebleaven that you have know friend upon Earth more devoted to you than my self, I think ["it" *interlined*] right for me to make my self known to you. Your friend, Joseph Porter.

[P.S.] You will observe the corner of this which is stained with Polkbury guce which was casu[al]ly[?] don[e] by one of my children w[h]ile I was wrighting these Lines.

ALS in ScCleA.

From W[illia]m Smith

Warrenton [Va.,] Aug[us]t 18, 1844
My dear Sir, Will you send me the annual statement of the Commerce & Navigation of the U.S. for last year—it is surely printed by this time.

I should be glad to get the various Tariffs of the U.S.[,] a document of the late Congress.

We shall certainly carry Va. ag[ains]t [Henry] Clay.

I am glad that you have provided so handsomely for [Edward] Dixon. Most Truly Y[ou]rs, Wm. Smith.

ALS in ScCleA. NOTE: Smith marked this letter "per Mr. [Edward] Dixon."

From James L. DeWitt

New York [City,] Aug[us]t 19th 1844
Sir, Your letter of the 6 inst. in reply to mine of the 4th—by some unaccountable circumstance—I did not receive until yesterday, and I now hasten to communicate the necessary testimonials, which I hope may prove satisfactory.

It was thought sufficient by my friends to enclose a few respectable references, without presenting a tedious array of names, accordingly

I acquiesced in their views, the weight of which I respectfully submit to your consideration. I have the honor to remain Very Respectfully Your mo[st] Ob[edien]t S[ervan]t, James L. DeWitt.

ALS with Ens in DNA, RG 59 (State Department), Applications and Recommendations, 1837–1845, DeWitt (M-687:9, frames 160–168).

From ALFRED KENDRICK

New Bedford [Mass.,] Aug. 19 1844

Sir, During the last session of Congress I handed to the Hon. Joseph Grinnell M.C. from Massachusetts a pamphlet describing certain tracts of land purchased by my father (John Kendrick) the original deeds of which according to 'Spark's Life of Ledyard' are or were, in the Sec[retary] of State[']s Office Washington; these lands are on the NW Coast of America, and as negociations are pending between our Government and that of Great Britain, I requested he would hand the pamphlet to you, for perusal, thinking that any thing that would serve to throw light on the subject, or to establish the American claims would be interesting to you. I would respectfully ask the favour of you (if the boundary agreed upon between our Government, and that of Great Britain, should leave those lands purchased by my father on the English side of the line) to solicit of the British Minister an allowance, on the behalf of the heirs of John Kendrick for those claims. I make this request of you Sir on account of my father having sailed under the sanction of Congress as you will see by his correspondence with Mr. [Thomas] Jefferson who was at that time Secretary of State. Nearly all his fortune was embarked in that expedition, which in consequence of his untimely death was lost to his family. That voyage which opened a trade, by which our country has been enriched, was attended with most disastrous effects upon our family; We lost our father and our fortune; The circumstances of his death were briefly these. Capt. [George] Vancouver an English discoverer and my father were verry warm friends. On my father's birth day he proposed firing a salute in honour of him; one of the guns of the [H.M.S.] Discovery was loaded with a canister of grape which could not be well drawn off, and by some mistake it was discharged which killed my father. An account of his death is given in 'Delano's Voyages,' I think on the 400 page. I make this effort with the hope if the lands fall into the hands of the British Government they will be willing to allow us something for that which was purchased and paid for by the head of our family. ["but if we cannot realise any thing from it, we must be content to struggle on with poverty the remainder of our days" *canceled.*] Respectfully Your Ob[edien]t S[e]rv[an]t, Alfred Kendrick.

P.S. When the pamphlet is no longer of any use to you please envelope and address to me at N[ew] Bedford Mass.

ALS in ScCleA.

From Ja[me]s Lewis

Washington City, Aug. 19 1844

Sir, Having been appointed by Edward Barnett of the U.S. Navy, who has received from the Secretary of the Navy [John Y. Mason] the appointment of Naval Store Keeper at Hong Kong, China, (under the late Act of Congress,) his clerk, and being anxious to accompany him on his route overland to his place of destination, I am induced to request of you to send by me certain despatches which I understand are prepared for the Hon. Caleb Cushing[,] Comm[ission]er &c.

Mr. Barnett is anxious that I should travel in company with him, as the journey is long & laborious & the presence of a friend will tend much to lighten it—and he will not take that route by himself. From a letter received from him this morning, I learn that there is no vessel to sail for China for a month to come[;] consequently the despatches will be detained.

My salary as Clerk is fixed by the Secretary of the Navy at $600.

It would probably take the whole of this to pay my expenses, which would leave me for the first year without a cent. I therefore would ask from the State Department the sum of Four hundred dollars to pay my extra expence of travel as the bearer of the despatches to Mr. Cushing and am willing to take that sum. I have the Honour, to be, your ob[edien]t Ser[van]t, &c &c, Jas. Lewis.

ALS in DNA, RG 59 (State Department), Accounting Records: Miscellaneous Letters Received.

To W[ILLIAM] D. PORTER, "Pres[iden]t of the Young Men's Demo[cratic] Asso[ciation of Charleston]"

Washington, 19th Aug[us]t 1844

Dear Sir, I delayed answering your letter [of 8/8] in the hope, that I would, ere this, have been in Charleston on my return home, and have seen and conversed with you and other friends on the subject to which it refers. In that, I have been disappointed. My official duties have detained me here, and it is now quite uncertain when they will permit me to leave.

I regret the movements to which you refer. I think the time every way unpropitious. No good can come from them and they may do much harm, and I so expressed myself to our delegation before they left for home. Our present policy is to do all we can to unite ["the South" *interlined*] and to avoid whatever may tend to divide her; and this whether we look for redress to Washington, or to the separate action of the State. It is not less essential to the ["success of the" *interlined*] latter, than the former, should we be compelled, which is not improbable, to resort to it finally. In my opinion, after a survey of the whole ground and full reflection, a premature movement now, on the part of the State, is calculated to defeat all hope of redress through either, and that it will in the end, should it be persisted in, endanger the safety of the entire South. In coming to this conclusion, I take into consideration its effects both in referrence to abolition and the Tariff. They are joint measures. The one strikes at our property itself, and the other at its proceeds.

On the other hand should the State act with prudence at present, and do nothing to divide or distract us, or the South, or endanger the success of the Republican party, I see much to hope, that we may redress our wrongs through one or the other, or both conjointly, let the election eventuate as it may. There is, to say the least, much to cheer us at present, if we take wisdom and prudence for our guides and not a gleam of hope, if we turn aside from their counsel, *as far as I can see*. In this I may be wrong; but my conviction is deep and sincere, and I shall be compelled to act in conformity to it. But I wish my friends all to understand, that my adherence to the great conservative doctrine of State interposition, and confidence in its ["efficency" *altered to* "efficiency"] when properly called into action was never stronger than at present. I entertain no doubt that the salvation of our Union and the permanency of our free institutions depend on it. There can be no delusion greater, than to hope to secure the one, or preserve the other, without it. As much as I value our Union and our glorious *Federal* system, in the same degree do I value State interposition, as the only means by which they can be saved. Thus thinking I would cheerfully lay down my life, if I know myself, in its support, if it should be necessary to establish it. One of the strongest objections I have, indeed, to the present agitation of the subject at this time in the State is, that it is calculated to weaken it. I value it too highly to put it to test, except when other means have failed and circumstances are favourable to a fair trial of its efficiency. Others of our friends may think that such is the case now; but they must know, that many, equally sincere, differ from them, and surely, that of itself is reason sufficient for desisting from pressing it now. I hold with them, we are bound to fulfil our pledges but surely time and circumstances are to be taken into consideration, when we are called on to act.

Let me advise moderation and forbearance. It is all important that the State should be kept united. Nothing would so much rejoice our opponents as disunion among ourselves.

I have a letter [of 8/9] from Mr. [John E.] Carew, the corresponding Sec[retary] of your association on the same subject, and I hope he will regard this as an answer to his letter as well as to yours.

I do not intend this for publication, but I hope you will show it to Mr. [Franklin H.] Elmore, Mr. [Henry] Bailey, Mr. Connor [*sic*; Henry W. Conner] and other influential friends, as well those, who differ from us, as those who may think with us, on the subject to which it refers. I do trust, that the Mercury will see the propriety of dropping the subject, at least till the election is over. If we can effect nothing else by the election of [James K.] Polk and the defeat of Mr. [Henry] Clay, we shall at least succeed in annexing Texas, which of itself is no small consideration—certainly enough to justify a suspension of the agitation of the subject of separate action for a few months. With great respect, I am &c &c, J.C. Calhoun.

Contemporary copy in LNHT, Colcock Family Papers. NOTE: An EU on the letter reads "Copy of a Letter from Mr. Calhoun to Mr. Porter, Pres[iden]t Demo[cratic] Asso[ciation] of Charleston."

From P[ETER] CARR

Charlottesville, Aug[us]t 20th 1844
Dear Sir, The aspect, which the Whig leaders in our old Commonwealth are attempting to give to the great contest, in which we are

engaged, induces me to address you a few lines, and to solicit of you, in reply, a full, and free exposition, of your views in regard to the matter of my communication. Our people here in Virginia, and I doubt not, throughout the borders of all the old Thirteen, are sincerely attached to the Union, which our own [George] Washington fashioned, and formed, and which [Thomas] Jefferson, and his compatriot worthies aided in perfecting. Unjust and partial legislation has doubtless had some effect in estranging the affections of many from that which was once, and will still continue to be, if its Government is rightly administered, the Ark of our common safety. The Whig party are well aware, that the attachment of the great masses of our population to the Union is deep, & abiding; and their leaders are seeking in default of other material wherewith to operate, to infuse into the popular mind the belief, that that portion of the Dem[ocratic] Republican party including your friends is hostile to its longer duration. It is a striking characteristic of the Southern people to be restive, & uneasy under the operation of laws which they believe unjust in their operation. As long ago, as the period of their colonial dependence, they were distinguished by Edmund Burke in the British House of Commons, as a people who "augured misgovernment at a distance, & snuffed the approach of tyranny in every tainted breeze." Should we not in view of the tremendous magnitude of the interests involved, deliberate, reason, protest, use all means, before resorting to what may be, "a critical, ambiguous, and bitter potion, to a distempered State." Should we not enter upon all matters of political controversy with associated Commonwealths, in a spirit full of candour and decency? I have always entertained the opinion in my short career, that much political wisdom was embodied in that single sentence of one of the mightiest of the sharpshooters of constitutional freedom—"Respect is due to the station occupied by our adversaries; and if a resolution must at last be taken, there is none so likely to be supported with firmness, as that which has been adopted with moderation."

Our State Convention of delegates from all quarters of the Commonwealth, will assemble in our Town on the 10th proximo. I hope to hear from you, in time to make known your views, in the present crisis, to our friends, who will convene in imposing numbers on that occasion. I remain Dear Sir, Yours truly, P. Carr.

ALS in ScCleA.

From George R. Gliddon, Philadelphia, 8/20. He reiterates his previous letters concerning the qualification of his brother-in-law,

Alexander Tod, to be U.S. Consul at Alexandria, Egypt. He now encloses recommendations from four prominent [European] residents of Egypt concerning the qualification of his brother, William A. Gliddon, to serve as Vice-Consul at Cairo. ALS with Ens in DNA, RG 59 (State Department), Applications and Recommendations, 1837–1845. Tod (M-687:13, frames 55–65).

From BEN E. GREEN

> Legation of the U.S. of A.
> Mexico, Aug[us]t 20th 1844

Sir, I have the honor to inform you that Mr. [José M.] de Bocanegra has retired from the Ministry of F[oreign] R[elations], and that Don Manuel C. Rejon is his successor. The latter is said to be a man of talent. In former days he was a Yorkino and a liberal in politics, but now he is whatever his own interest and the wishes of Santa Anna may require. Bad health is the reason assigned for Mr. de Bocanegra's retirement; but it is also more than probable that he sees difficulties ahead, in which he does not wish to be committed. During the correspondence with the French & Spanish Ministers about the Tabasco affair, he requested leave of absence on the same plea, of sickness. He was opposed to shooting [Francisco] Sentmanat's followers without trial, and equally opposed to the harsh tone used toward the French & Spanish ministers, in that correspondence. I regret his departure from the Ministry of Foreign Relations; for if his influence had been greater, the foreign relations of Mexico would have been much better conducted than they are & have been.

Since the arrival of the last packet from England, the movement against Texas has been pushed with fresh vigor. The idea of invasion by land has been abandoned, and it is now decided to attack by sea. The staff leave this city on the 25th to embark at Vera Cruz. Galveston is to be burned to the ground, and the war is to be one of extermination. The soil is to be purged of every drop of Anglo-Saxon blood. The decree of the 17th July 1843—the same, which legalized the massacres of Tabasco—is to be enforced in the same way in Texas, as soon as the Mexican army shall have gained possession! ! For the sake of humanity and their own character, it is to be hoped that they may not succeed.

I have at last received a communication from our consul in Tabasco [Edward Porter], of which I send a copy herewith. He states that the crew of the vessel are still in prison. Gen[era]l [Pedro de] Ampudia, however, says in a letter, published by order of the Minister of War, that they have been set at liberty. I called to ask the Minister of Foreign Relations whether they are still in prison, or have been set at liberty, as stated by Gen[era]l Ampudia. He promised to enquire into the matter, & inform me immediately how the case stands. As this was our first interview, the new minister took occasion to say a thousand civil things, with all those fine phrases, which, with a Mexican, say so much and mean so little; to all which I replied with equal cordiality, but, I fear me[?], with much more sincerity, wishing that nothing would occur to weaken the bonds that bind the *two sister Republics.*

I wrote some time since that the Legation was in want of stationary. Please cause to be sent out, by the first packet, a supply of pens, and letter, note and despatch paper: also two ledgers, one for recording notes to the Mexican govt., and the other for the despatches to the govt. at home. I have the honor to be Very Respectfully Your ob[edien]t Serv[an]t, Ben E. Green.

[Enclosure]
E[dward] Porter, U.S. Consul, to [Ben E. Green]

Consulate of the U. States
Frontera de Tabasco, July 20th [18]44

Sir, On the 8th of June last, the schooner W.A. Turner, of New Orleans, [John] Pettit Master, appeared off this Port with Francisco Sentmanat, the former Governor of this state, and fifty of his followers on board the schooner, which was pursued, driven on shore and fired into by the national vessels of this Govt. Sentmanat and his men succeeded in landing, & passed through the woods up the country, where they surrendered to the Govt. troops, on the promise of being pardoned by then laying down their arms; Ex-Gov[erno]r Sentmanat being the only person that fired a shot on the occasion. He was taken prisoner, and shot; his head cut off, fried in boiling oil, put on a spike, hung up in an iron cage, & exhibited in the public square for days.

Thirty eight of the men, that were promised pardon, were shot, after being a few days confined, without any trial. Among them were three native citizens of the U. States, James McDuffy, Manuel Mussulman and Ramon Ramirez, and six that claimed citizenship by naturalization. The remainder of those unfortunate men, with all the sailors, the mate and two native American passengers, that came on the schooner, are incarcerated in a miserable prison in Tabasco, where, it is feared by us, contagion will terminate the work of destruction commenced by Gov[erno]r Gen[era]l Ampudia. The schooner was pillaged of everything moveable she possessed, and then burned by the officers and men of the national vessels of this Govt.

Captain Pettit has made his escape by the influence of a few thousand dollars with the Governor, agre[e]ably to information. I went up to Tabasco, where the men were confined, to render them all the assistance in my power; but found I could do little or nothing for their release, Gov. Ampudia was so hostile to all and everything American. With sentiments & respects & &c &c, (signed) E. Porter, U.S. Consul.

ALS (No. 17) with En in DNA, RG 59 (State Department), Diplomatic Despatches, Mexico, vol. 12 (M-97:13), received 9/28; variant FC in DNA, RG 84 (Foreign Posts), Mexico, Despatches; draft in NcU, Duff Green Papers (published microfilm, roll 5, frames 767–770).

From W[illia]m M. Gwin, [former Representative from Miss.], "Private"

Vicksburg [Miss.,] August 20th 1844

My dear Sir, I rec[eive]d this morning the enclosed letter from General G[eorge] W. Terrell the Attorney General of the Republic of Texas. All except the first page is on private business. Altho General Terrell from his position & enthusiastic & enterprising character is well calculated to produce a decided effect in favor of any cause he espouses yet I should not attach much importance to his opinions on this question but for other & unerring indications that the feeling in favor of annexation is on the wane in Texas[.]

My intercourse with the citizens of that Republic is very great and I have been not a little surprised at the evident & great change in the opinions of those who were so ardent in favor of annexation. All they ask is for peace with Mexico & they intend to unfurl the banner of Free Trade & invite[?] commerce with the whole world. Our last chance is passed I fear to get that great Country[.]

I must plead the freedom with which you have always permitted me to express my opinions to you in making the following suggestion. Before Congress meets again the limitation put in the Treaty will have expired. The calling of an extra session of Congress is a fearful experiment. If I mistake not I was informed that the Texan Pleni-potentiaries had powers to extend the limitation put upon the period of ratification. If they have this power still, would it not be well to make the expiration of the treaty without ratification twelve instead of six months[?]

If [James K.] Polk is elected it will give him time to submit it to a new Senate or Congress which ever is deemed most adviseable, should the present Congress refuse to act. The authorities in Texas would not interfere with such a treaty while if it does not exist they may make other arrangements which will put annexation out of the question for ever. From that quarter we have all to fear[,] not from the people of the United States who will prove themselves in favor of annexation at the polls in November next. With sentiments of the highest respect I remain your friend & ob[edien]t Se[rvan]t, Wm. M. Gwin.

[Appended: Gwin to Richard K. Crallé:]

Private

My friend Cralle can use his discretion in showing the letter to Mr. Calhoun & its enclosure to the President [John Tyler]. I see from the papers that Mr. Calhoun contemplated about this period a visit to his family. While I was in Washington he expressed an anxious desire that I should go as chargé to Texas if Gen[era]l [William S.] Murphy's nomination should be rejected. The appointment of General [Tilghman A.] Howard arose I presume from some obligation that the President was under to him, unknown to Mr. Calhoun. The death of General Howard which I see announced in the papers will require the appointment of another chargé to that Republic. I think I could be of much service to this Government at this time in Texas. If the invasion takes place and the Texans experience reverses it will not be difficult for the Representatives of France & Great Britain to bring about a pacification on their own terms. My association with all of the principal men in Texas has been most intimate and at this juncture might be made useful to our Government if I occupied the station above named.

I leave it to you my good friend to have my name presented to the President or not as you think best. I have addressed a note to Mr. Calhoun at his residence ["on the subject," *canceled*] which with this note is all I have written on the subject. I shall name it to no one else[.]

I shall leave here in a day or two for Washington. If nothing more can be done I should like for the appointment to be kept open until I reach there[.] Very truly y[ou]r friend, W.M. Gwin.

[Enclosure]
G[eorge] W. Terrell to W[illia]m M. Gwin

Washington Texas, July 7th 1844

My Dear Doctor, It has been so long since I have heard any thing from you, that I fear I have almost lost a place in your recollection. It is with me very different—I never forget old friends. We had heard here that you were spoken of as the probable successor of Gen[era]l Murphy, and your friends here particulary [James] Reily, [Lewis M.H.] Washington and myself were greatly in hopes we should see you here in that capacity. We received news however yesterday that Gen[era]l Howard of Ind. has been appointed, which disappointed us much.

Annexation has failed! I am gratified—for I have been opposed to it from the beginning. Tom Benton like, I have stood "solitary and alone" in the Cabinet on that subject. The idea of merging our National existence in that of any other power, has been to me little less ["than" *altered to* "terrific"] than that of annihilation. I therefore heartily rejoice that the humbug has blown over, and as I sincerely hope, forever. This question being disposed of, we will set about, in good earnest, making another president for our little republic. My opinion is that Dr. [Anson] Jones will be elected, but as these things are always somewhat uncertain until they actually transpire—no certain opinion can be formed, as yet, as to the result.

I have a favour, of some importance to myself, to ask of you; which, although it will devolve upon you some trouble, I am confident you will attend to. I left in Vicksburg a trunk containing a great many papers, which are to me very valuable, and have never been able to get them. Dr. King got them in possession, and carried them to Judge Martin's before he died—and I suppose his family have them now. Will you do me the favour to get them, and have them put up so they will come in safety, and send them to me, directed to the care of [William Bryan] our Consul at New Orleans— if they are sent to him he will know what to do with them. There are many old manuscripts as well as news papers and other old political documents, which I had preserved ever since I first began to dabble in politics—the most however, my own writing—hence the value I attach to them—and feell much concerned on account of them. Do try and get hold of them all and send them to the Consul, and I shall be sure to get them. I have applied to half a dozen individuals to forward them, but never could get it done. As a last resort I determined to apply to you, believing that you would take upon yourself that much trouble for an old friend.

I have paid your taxes in this country for the years [18]42 & [18]43—amounting in all to something like $250—a part of which however was in old treasury notes. I am very hard run, as we poor devils who serve this republic, scarcely get enough to live upon, in the most common manner—nevertheless I told Col. Washington that I would raise enough all the time to keep your interests from suffering. Some of the lands belonging to the estate of Mrs. Gwin's first husband are involved in law, and are now before the Supreme Court which is now in Session. The suits were brought wrong, and my opinion is they will be lost on that account. I think you missed it by not employing me to attend to any suits that might arise out of those interests. When I found them in Court however, I found other gentlemen attending to them—and not having been spoken to, I did not feel myself at liberty to interfere.

Please make my kindest regards to your excellent lady, and accept for yourself assurances of the high respect with which I am Your friend, G.W. Terrell.

P.S. I am much rejoiced at the nomination of Polk for the Presidency—Hurra for old Tennessee.

ALS with En in ScCleA; PEx in Boucher and Brooks, eds., *Correspondence*, pp. 244–245.

From J[AMES] HAMILTON, [JR.], "(*Private & Confidential*)"

Savannah, Aug[u]st 20[t]h 1844
My Dear Sir, You have seen the movements in [Robert Barnwell] Rhett[']s Distr[ic]t. I cannot believe that he is acting in any feeling in opposition to your self which I understand he denies.

I deemed it important to let it be understood that I deem this no period (*at the present* moment) for separate action. I send you a paper which after reading be so kind as to send Mr. [Thomas G.] Clemson.

I leave for Macon to attend the great Mass meeting tomorrow an ac[count] of which I will give you from that place day after tomorrow. We must cultivate the Georgians & unite the South.

I hope you sent my last Letter to Mr. Clemson containing the Enclosures. I remain My Dear Sir With esteem Yours faithfully, J. Hamilton.

ALS in ScCleA.

From Henry LaReintrie, Baltimore, 8/20. He has previously asked Calhoun to recommend him for an appointment to be a Purser in the Navy. While he awaits a vacancy in that Naval rank, he offers his services to the State Department as a translator of Spanish and French. ALS in DNA, RG 59 (State Department), Applications and Recommendations, 1837–1845, LaReintrie (M-687:19, frames 140–142).

From LLOYD SELBY

Warrenton Miss., Aug. 20, 1844
Hon. Sir, With the view of furthering the cause of equal rights I ask of you if you please to furnish me with the vote in the Senate of the U.S. in June 1836 on the passage of a bill prohibiting the transmission of abolition documents by mail. It is alleged that [Henry] Clay voted with the north on that occasion.

I want the vote in such form that Clay[']s friends cannot deny its authenticity. I would thank you also for a copy of the [Washington Daily National] Intelligencer containing Gov. [William H.] Seward[']s letter to some persons in Vermont wherein he avowed ["it" *canceled*] the abolition of slavery as a part of Whiggery. The letter was written sometime in last June. Our cause looks well in this State. The tariff & the Texas questions are the principal ones agitated. Very Respectfully, Lloyd Selby.

ALS in ScCleA.

To Isaac Stone, New Orleans, 8/20. Calhoun informs Stone of his appointment as U.S. Consul at San Juan de los Remedios, Cuba, and encloses documents relevant to the office. Stone's exequatur will be applied for in Madrid. FC in DNA, RG 59 (State Department), Consular Instructions, 10:261.

From D[avid] Levy [Yulee, Delegate from Florida Territory], Washington, 8/20. Upon request of Charles S. Sibley, [Yulee] encloses copies of certain correspondence relevant to the charges against Sibley. The correspondence is among Sibley, [Richard K.] Call, and [Charles B.] Penrose, [Solicitor of the Treasury Department]. ALS with Ens in DNA, RG 59 (State Department), Applications and Recommendations, 1837–1845, Sibley (M-687:30, frames 256–275).

From Jos[eph] Grinnell, [Representative from Mass.]

New Bedford [Mass.,] Aug[us]t 21st 1844
Sir, I have the honor to hand you herein a letter [of 8/19] from Capt. Alfred Kendrick of this place, asking your attention to the claim of the heirs of John Kendrick to lands in Oregon, concerning which I sent you a printed Pamphlet last winter. I hope in the settlement of the boundary of this Territory you may succeed in obtaining some thing from the British Government for the relinquishment of this claim to the right of soil. Mr. Kendrick estimates its value at $50,000, but he will be content with any settlement you may make. With great respect &c, Your ob[edien]t Servant, Jos. Grinnell.

ALS with En in ScCleA. Note: An AEU by Calhoun reads "Mr. Grimball [*sic*] relates to the claims of the Heirs of Capt. Kendrick."

From [William Hogan]

Nashua N[ew] Hampshire, August 21, 1844
I have not had the honor, Sir, of hearing what the result ["was" *canceled*] of my application, through you, to the President, for another Consulate has been; I presume he has either forgotten or declines giving it altogether, if the former I have no doubt, Sir, but you will bring the subject to his recollection.

Since I have had the honor of writing to you last, I have thought much upon our present relations with Mexico, and every thing that has transpired since upon the subject, only confirms the truth of the report, which I have made to the State Department, and to which I would most respectfully ask your attention once more. By refference to my report, dated last March, at Vera Cruz, you will see that I informed our Government of the intentions of Santa Anna & Great Britain on the Texas question. The difficulties then apparently existing between England & Mexico were got up merely for effect, and while they were "corum publico," [*sic*; coram populo] quarrelling, England was engaging to furnish Santa Anna with money & his army with Officers for the sole purpose of subjugating Texas. While in Mexico, I satisfied myself fully upon the subject. I sounded Mr. [Waddy] Thompson [Jr.], then our Minister at Mexico, as to his views & finding them so entirely at variance with my own, as well as

with the facts of the case, I deemed it useless to have any further conversation with him, or even to let him know what I had done or intended to do in Mexico. I looked upon him as the dupe of Santa
Anna & [Charles Bankhead] the British Minister. They persuaded
him that England had no designs upon Texas & that Santa Anna
"cared nothing about it." My report stated the very contrary.
Events have proved that I was ["wright" *canceled*] right, and had
Mr. Upsher [*sic*; Abel P. Upshur] lived untill my return to Washington, we might have this day peaceable possession of Texas. He knew
me & gave me his full confidence upon the subject. He was satisfied
that I was the only man in this country, who could advantageously
treat with the Mexican Government upon that vexed question of
Texas. I satisfied him that by whatever name the Mexican Government was called, that in whatever form it treated with other
governments, it was itself, and *"de facto"* a mixed Government, *Ecclesiastical* & *Civil* or perhaps more truly speaking, a government both
Ecclesiastical & Military. I saw two great interests in that Country,
that of the Church & that of the State or Military; the latter almost entirely depended upon the former, both for means & men. The former
has every thing to lose in case of the success of the Texans ["we &" *canceled and* "in" *interlined*] war with Mexico; the latter nothing, but
the lives of a few wretches, who are almost an incubus upon society.
Knowing this to be a fact, I saw that the only mode of negociating,
was to commence with the Ecclesiastical Department, to satisfy them
that their Church, their immence wealth, theier [*sic*] almost incalculably valueable Jewels, precious stones, and enormous amount of
Gold, manufactured into Images, were even jeopardised ["with"
canceled and "by" *interlined*] a war with Texas, and the difficulties
were ended! Produce this alarm in the Church, & Santa Anna must
come to terms. Neither he, with all his Despotism, nor England with
all her intrigue, could induce Catholic Mexico, to move a hand or
foot against Texas. Santa Anna could not occupy his throne, twenty
days against the will of the Mexican Church. But the actual state
of things is, in a measure, concealed from the Ecclesiastical Department of the Government. Our Ministers have no authority to treat
with them officially, & even if they had, they do not know how. No
one but an Ecclesiastic, at some period of his life can do so.

When I returned ["from" *canceled and* "to" *interlined*] Washington
from Mexico, I did not intend remaining ten days. My sole object
was to advise with Mr. Upsher, and as he is no more, if you will permit me to go to Mexico now as bearer of Despatches & without any
authority from Government to commit it, pro or con, but to give you,

through Mr. [Wilson] Shannon, such information & such a clue to the arrangement of our difficulties, as I can furnish, at an expence of not more than six hundred dollars, to be spent in the payment of *my necessary expenses,* I will do more to facilitate your negociations with Mexico, in relation to Texas, than all the Ministers & all the Despatches, you can send to Mexico for the next ten years. This ["f" *canceled*] six hundred Doll[ar]s [*and here this incomplete manuscript ends.*]

ALU (incomplete) in ScCleA.

Receipted bill from Catharine Owner, Washington, 8/21. This document bills Calhoun for two weeks' board @ $10 per week and acknowledges his payment of $20. ADS in ScU-SC, John C. Calhoun Papers.

From William H. Stiles, [Representative from Ga.], Cassville, Ga., 8/21. Upon receipt of the news of the death of William Bee, "late one of the appraisers in the Custom House" in Savannah, Stiles asks that Calhoun recommend to President [John Tyler] that William Mackay of Savannah be appointed to fill that post. Stiles adds in a postscript "We have but little ["doubt" *interlined*] of being able to redeem Georgia from Federalism at the approaching Election." ALS in DNA, RG 56 (Secretary of the Treasury), Applications for Appointments as Customs Service Officers, 1833–1910.

From FRANCIS WHARTON

Philadelphia, August 21st, 1844
My dear Sir, On my return, yesterday, from a month's journey to the Eastward, I found your letters, & the enclosures on my table. I cannot tell you of my thanks for the kindness you have shown me. I hope I may live to show you under what strong ties of obligation you have placed me.

I have lately had a good deal of conversation with Mr. [George M.] Dallas & Mr. [Henry D.] Gilpin, who are very anxious about your position. The developements, or rather, the hints, in the Charleston Mercury, have gone a great way to leave in the minds of your friends in the North that you have neither part or lot in the wild movements in which Mr. [Robert Barnwell] Rhett is engaged. Mr. [Isaac E.]

Holmes' letter, & Mr. Rhett's speech, which I saw at the White Mountains, alarmed me exceedingly; ["and" *canceled and* "but" *interlined*] when I saw how blindly the movement was conducted, how it stumbled and groped along, I was clear that your countenance & guidance had been withdrawn. What good can we do now by throwing fire into our own camp? With *your* aid, as the acknowledged head of the States-rights party, the republicans will be guided into the right path, but without it, I fear they will run to ruin. On the question of a bank & the sub-treasury, both North & South are orthodox enough; and I am clear that on *that* point, at least, there is no fear. The tariff looks badly, I confess, & the leaders in Pennsylvania, (the interior) are playing a treacherous game; but we cannot too highly praise the boldness with which our New England friends have supported us. If we refuse to coöperate with the republican party, we will secure its defeat, & make probable its demoralization; if we act with ["it" *interlined*], if *you* act with it, warmly & urgently, if the ["su"(?) *interlined and then canceled*] majority is not obtained, the regeneration of the party will [be] brought about. I think of preparing a short article in the Democratic Review on the union of the States-rights & democratic parties, but I feel somewhat disheartened & turned back by the very unhappy manifestations in the Beaufort [S.C.] district. In what light may I look upon you in relation to so great an issue? If you will take the lead on the republican side, and no one else can take it, while you are in the way, if you will allow the people to look upon you as the head of a great national party, fraught with national measures, if, as the Rhett clique have withdrawn from ["th" *canceled*] your guidance, you will allow the republican party throughout the land, once more to proclaim you its leader, can we not know it, and be armed in the conflict by the consciousness of your presence?

Suppose I prepare an *editorial* for the Review on the subject of the union of the two sections, would it be the proper place to note & insert either from you or through you, any declaration or indication? With great respect, but with some anxiety, I am yours most devotedly, Francis Wharton.

[P.S.: "if we(?) could" *canceled.*]

ALS in ScCleA; PEx in Boucher and Brooks, eds., *Correspondence,* pp. 245–246.

From DAVID HUBBARD, [former Representative from Ala.]

Kinlock, Lawrence C[oun]ty Ala., 22d August 1844
Dear Sir, I have thought it not improper to mention to you that I attended the great "Union Democratic convention" at Nashville on the 15 August.

Gen[era]l [Lewis] Cass, was there, and spoke—His speech was good, able, and subtle. He intended to make the impression, "that the west & north west was through his friends earnestly engaged in promoting the election of [James K.] Polk & [George M.] Dallas." He denounced every attempt to dis[s]olve the Union, ["]come from whatever ["source" *canceled*], quarter of the union, by whomso-[e]ver made—whenever & wherever and for ["who(?), whatever" *canceled*] whatever cause." Mr. Mellville [*sic*; Gansevoort Melville] spoke next. He with much parade declared himself to represent "the great State of New York" and that she altho prefer[r]ing [Martin] Van [Buren]—would yet fight manfully for ["Dallas" *canceled*] Polk & Dallas," no one should be more active than Mr. Van Buren[']s friends & they too were for "Union and annexation." No one came from Penn[sylvania] or Ohio. Judge Bolling or Bolding [*sic*; James B. Bowlin, Representative] from Missouri & two or three from Louisiana[,] Arkansas, & many from Miss.—Thomas [F.] Marshall [former Representative] from Ky. & several others. The Tennesseans were merely passive in these "Union loving" demonstrations. I do not think that ["the" *canceled*] the prominent men encouraged any such movements.

I am led to this conclusion from the fact that "He at the Hermitage" [Andrew Jackson] is "out against [Thomas H.] Benton." I had the fact from a young Mississippian who called on him & to whom he said "he wished that Missouri would leave Benton at home since he had deserted her interests."

I believe that Polk will carry Tennessee by a greater vote than [Henry] Clay will get Ky. Polk will scarcely lose a western State ["except Ky." *interlined*] so far as I can judge from what I heard at Nashville.

I have written this much that you might hear. I write it in confidence. Having declined yourself a correspondence, I hope you will not think that *I* desire or wish to renew it; but I thought that some one ought to let you know what happened, and as no South Carolinian was there, I did not know whether you would receive any thing but a Newspaper account of the matter.

The mass[?] meeting was very large[,] 21,000 men were there in companies & camped as soldiers on the ground[;] 700 large baggage waggons & hundreds & thousands of men[,] women[,] children & servants. Gen[era]l Cass accustomed to look at crowds estimated the meeting to amount to 50,000 souls—An army—who neither fear England or Mexico. I have the honor to be Respectfully &C, David Hubbard.

ALS in ScCleA. NOTE: Gansevoort Melville, a brother of Herman Melville, toured Tenn., Ky., Ohio, and western N.Y. speaking for Polk's election. He was appointed Secretary of the U.S. Legation at London by Polk in 1845.

From Elihu Jefferson, Newcastle, Del., 8/22. Jefferson has heard that Nathaniel Wolf, U.S. Marshal for Del., is to be removed from office. If that is true, Jefferson asks that he be considered as a replacement. Calhoun is referred to testimonials already on file in the State Department. Jefferson will appreciate Calhoun's assistance in this matter. ALS in DNA, RG 59 (State Department), Applications and Recommendations, 1837–1845, Jefferson (M-687:17, frames 217–218).

From John L. Lafitte, Baltimore, 8/22. He has read in a newspaper that R[obert] L. McIntosh has been appointed a U.S. Consul in China. Lafitte supposes that this is the post for which he applied at "Foo-Chow-Foo." If so, he hopes that Calhoun will consider him for an appointment as Consul at either Ningpo or Shanghai. Lafitte refers Calhoun to several government officers for references. ALS in DNA, RG 59 (State Department), Applications and Recommendations, 1837–1845, Lafitte (M-687:19, frames 9–11).

From STEWART NEWELL, [Galveston]

Consulate of the United States
Sabine, Texas
Aug. 22d 1844

Sir, I, yesterday, enclosed p[e]r St[eam] P[ac]k[e]t "Republic," for New Orleans, the Returns of this Consulate, also Returns from Consulate, at Galveston, ending July 1st, and continued to 16th, being the last record of A[rchibald] M. Green Esq[ui]r[e], late Consul at Galveston, his sudden decease, having prevented him, making out, and forwarding the same.

I had hoped the painful duty, of reporting the ravages of disease, in the Official Ranks, of our Officers, had ceased, but am again called upon, and have the painful duty, to inform the Department, of the Death of the Hon. Tilghman A. Howard, who was taken ill, of the Fever of the Country, (called Congestive Fever) on the 13th inst., and died, on the 16th, near Washington, Texas. Thus has his useful labors, in behalf of his Country, and Government, been cut short, by the hand of Death, and his Country, Government, and Friends, left to mourn over his, untimely decease, and indeed it seems, as if a pestilence, had covered the Land. From every section of this Country, we have intelligence, of the Death of distinguished, and prominent Men. Only a few days since, the Hon. P[atrick] C. Jack, Judge of the adjoining district, to this, and long a resident of the Country, died with Fever, after an illness of 4 days. His Brother [William H. Jack], also, an eminent Lawyer, is now extremely ill, and yesterday, the Remains of Hon. Richard Morris, Judge of this District, was consigned, to thier last resting place. He died of Yellow Fever, after an illness of 5 days, at this place. He was a native of Virginia, and truly, an "Upright Judge."

I, received and forwarded, a few days since, to Hon. T.A. Howard, a despatch from Department of State, of U.S. ["Post" *interlined*] Mark[e]d 22d July, it had not reached him, before his decease, and is now, returned to me. Under the peculiar existing circumstances, I beg leave to ask, from the Department, what may be my duty, relative to the disposition of any despatches, that may arrive, at this place, addressed to the Hon. Chargé, he not having appointed any person, to act in his stead, under an emergency, in his Official matters, and sometime, will elapse, before a Successor will arrive.

I, am willing, to render any feeble aid, in my power, and shall take great pleasure, in forwarding the views, and wishes, of my Government, in any capacity, that may be required of me.

I beg leave to enclose, a Letter [of 8/9] received yesterday by Mail, from Gen[era]l Howard, and written only 4, days before his ["illness" *interlined*]. Also, one [of 8/3] from Thomas Barrett Esq[ui]r[e], Collector of Customs, at New Orleans. The latter, is interested in the result, of the Case of the St[eam] B[oa]t "Scioto Belle," and with whom, I, have not the pleasure of a personal acquaintance, but has no doubt, from enquiry, satisfied himself, of that, which he, has been pleased to refer to, as to my standing &C in New Orleans.

Gen[era]l Howard, mentions his, having reccommended Messrs. [Robert D.] Johnson, [J. Temple] Doswell & [Elisha A.] Rhodes (all permanent citizens of Texas) for this Consulate, to the consideration of the Department.

I deem it my duty to inform the Department, that Gen[era]l Howard, spent but 2 days, at this place, and had not an opportunity, of a personal acquaintance, with the applicants who importuned him. R.D. Johnson, has been a Magistrate, and now is Post Master for this place. Mr. Doswell, is a young Man, without the experience and energy requisite for a Consulate, and for E.A. Rhodes, formerly and now an Applicant, I refer the Hon. Secretary, to Letters Nos. 8, 9, & 18, of A.M. Green Esq[ui]r[e] to Department, the facts of which as set forth, being well known here. I have the Honor to be Most Respectfully Your Ob[edien]t Serv[an]t, Stewart Newell.

ALS (No. 25) with Ens in DNA, RG 59 (State Department), Consular Despatches, Texas, vol. 1 (T-153:1), received 9/16.

To R[ICHARD] PAKENHAM

Department of State
Washington, Aug[us]t 22d, 1844

Sir: The various subjects which necessarily claimed my attention on entering on the duties of my office have heretofore, as you justly suppose in your note of the 22d of July last, prevented me from appointing a time to confer with you and enter on the negotiation in reference to the Oregon Territory.

These have, at length, been despatched; and, in reply to the note which you did me the honor to address to me of the date above mentioned, I have to inform you, that I am now ready to enter on the negotiation, and for that purpose propose a conference tomorrow, at one o'clock, P.M., at the Department of State, if perfectly convenient to you; but, if not, at any other which it may suit your convenience to appoint.

The Government of the United States participates in the anxious desire of that of Great Britain that the subject may be early and satisfactorily arranged. I have the honor to be, With high consideration, Sir, Your obedient servant, J.C. Calhoun.

FC in DNA, RG 59 (State Department), Notes to Foreign Legations, Great Britain, 7:27 (M-99:36); PC in the Washington, D.C., Daily National Intelligencer, December 12, 1845, p. 1; PC in Niles' National Register, vol. LXIX, no. 17 (December 27, 1845), pp. 260–261; PC in Senate Document No. 1, 29th Cong., 1st Sess., p. 142; PC in House Document No. 2, 29th Cong., 1st Sess., p. 142; PC in Crallé, ed., Works, 5:420–421.

From R[ichard] Pakenham

Washington, 22 August 1844

Sir, I have had the honor to receive your Note of this morning's date, in which you signify your readiness to enter on the Negotiation in reference to the Oregon Territory, proposing to me to meet you in conference on that subject tomorrow at one o'clock.

In reply, I have the honor to acquaint you that I shall have great pleasure in waiting on you at the Department of State at the hour proposed.

Be pleased to accept the assurance of my distinguished consideration. R. Pakenham.

LS in DNA, RG 59 (State Department), Notes from Foreign Legations, Great Britain, vol. 22 (M-50:22); PC in the Washington, D.C., *Daily National Intelligencer,* December 12, 1845, p. 1; PC in *Niles' National Register,* vol. LXIX, no. 17 (December 27, 1845), p. 261; PC in Senate Document No. 1, 29th Cong., 1st Sess., p. 142; PC in House Document No. 2, 29th Cong., 1st Sess., p. 142; PC in Crallé, ed., *Works,* 5:421.

From R[ichard] Pakenham, Washington, 8/22. Pakenham renews a request for the refund of excess duties charged on British goods imported into the U.S. between 6/30/1842 and 9/1/1842. A stipulation of the U.S. tariff of 1842 allowing goods shipped from east of the Cape of Good Hope or beyond Cape Horn before 9/1/1842 to pay the lower duties in effect before the tariff of 1842, while charging full duties on goods shipped from Britain in the same period, conflicts, in Pakenham's opinion, with a provision of the U.S.-British convention of 7/3/1815. LS in DNA, RG 59 (State Department), Notes from Foreign Legations, Great Britain, vol. 22 (M-50:22); CC in DNA, RG 56 (Secretary of the Treasury), Letters Received from Executive Officers, Series AB, 1844, document no. 35.

From W[illia]m Wilkins, Secretary of War, 8/22. "The copies of documents which I have the honor to transmit herewith, will furnish you with the information requested in your letter of the 12th ultimo, respecting the number, description, and value of the arms, taken, by order of Capt. P[hilip] St. G[eorge] Cooke of the Dragoons, from the Texan force under the command of Colonel [Jacob] Snively." LS with Ens in DNA, RG 59 (State Department), Miscellaneous Letters (M-179:105, frames 244–248); FC in DNA, RG 107 (Secretary of War), Letters Sent Relating to Military Affairs, 1800–1861, 25:381

(M-6:25); CC in DNA, RG 107, Letters Received by the Secretary of War, Registered Series, 1801–1860, S-25 (M-221:135).

To G[eorge] M. Bibb, Secretary of the Treasury, 8/23. Calhoun refers for Bibb's decision R[ichard] Pakenham's letter [of 8/22] claiming reimbursement for excess duties charged on certain British goods imported into the U.S. under the tariff of 1842. LS with En in DNA, RG 56 (Secretary of the Treasury), Letters Received from Executive Officers, Series AB, 1844, documents no. 34 and 35.

To A[ndrew] J. Donelson, [Nashville],
"Private & confidential"

State Dept., 23d Aug[us]t 1844
Dear Sir, I have read the letter [of 7/19] of General [Andrew] Jackson to President [Samuel] Houston, enclosed in your's [*sic*] with deep interest. It is written with great power, and the appeal to his patriotism, honor & future fame cannot but have a powerful effect on him. But, I agree with you, that it will depend much on the prospect of Mr. [James K.] Polk's election, whether the appeal will prove successful or not. Should Mr. [Henry] Clay be elected, the door would probably be closed against the admission of Texas, and, if closed, she would be almost forced to seek the alliance of Great Britian [*sic*], however disasterous it might prove in the end to her, to the United States, &, I might add, to this Continent. No one, however segacious, can tell where the calamity would terminate. But, I trust, the good sense and patriotism of the American people, by defeating ["by defeating" *canceled*] Mr. Clay & electing Mr. Polk will avert the danger & disasters to which the madness of faction has exposed both countries. I think the prospect of his election is good. The people are becoming daily more sensible of the importance of the questions at issue, & the Republican party more Zealous & united. It has thus far, not only held its own, compared to the election of '42, when the whigs were so signally defeated; but has actually, either increased its majority, or diminished that of the whigs, in every State, where there has been a trial of strength. It proves, that ours is a growing cause; and I can see no reason, why the tide should turn before the election; but should it not, and the States which have not yet

voted, should do as well in proportion as those which have, Mr. Polk's election will be certain.

Before I received your letter with its enclosure, I received, a copy of the letter [of 7/19] addressed by Gen[era]l Jackson to Col. [James] Gadsden, alluded to in your's. The course of policy, which it suggests is marked by that boldness and decision, which so strongly characterizes the thoughts and action of the General. I deemed it to be my duty to bring it, as well as the one inclosed in your's, to the notice of the President [John Tyler]; and, accordingly, I losed [*sic*; lost] no time, after his return from Old Point Comfort in doing so. After bestowing on their contents the attention due to their importance, and the source from which they emanated, he is of the opinion, that his position is too weak for him to undertake so bold & decided a movement, and I must say, that my opinion concurs with his.

The question, what under all the circumstances of the case ought to be done is one of deep interest. It became a subject of conversation at the last meeting of the cabinet, but nothing was definitely decided on. The subject of calling Congress to convene, before the constitutional period, say the 1st Nov[embe]r, was alluded to, but it was thought advisable to wait for farther ["for farther" *canceled*] developements, and in particular from our Charge in Texas, Gen[era]l [Tilghman A.] Howard, who had just arrived, by the last accounts.

I am disposed to a decided course, and am of the impression, that honor as well as expediency, demands that we should defend Texas against Mexico, should she undertake to invade her, while the question of annexation is pending, as I still consider it to be. The treaty, it is true, is rejected, but Texas has not yet withdrawn her assent to be annexed, nor is the joint resolution moved by Mr. [George] McDuffie on the subject in the Senate, yet disposed of. Both parties, indeed, appealed to the people, before whom it may now be fairly considered as pending, and as constituting the leading question, now at issue, to be decided in the pending presidential election. It is, in my opinion, an insult to ["us" *interlined*] for Mexico, under such circumstances, to undertake to attack Texas for accepting our invitation to treat with her on the subject of annexation and entering into an agreement to that effect.

Thus thinking, I have thought, that Congress ought to be called to meet at a day earlier, than that fixed by the Constitution, so as to be prepared to act, if an invasion should take place, which, I presume, must be in Nov[embe]r if at all; but I find many of our best friends here object on the ground, that there is nothing to hope from Congress, & that the call might possibly affect injuriously the result of the Presidential election. That certainly would constitute a strong objection, if it be well founded; but according to my observation, when you are right, boldness is the best policy.

I am happy to inform you, that our intelligence from France is very favourable. She is opposed to the annexation on commercial principles, but we have strong assurances, through our minister [William R. King], that she will take no position hostile to us, and has not, as it has been rumoured, agreed to unite with England in a joint protest against the annexation.

Although I have marked this private & confidential, I can have no objection to your showing it either to Gen[era]l Jackson, or Mr. Polk. With great respect yours truly, J.C. Calhoun.

ALS in DLC, Andrew Jackson Donelson Papers; PC in St. George L. Sioussat, ed., "Selected Letters, 1844–1845, from the Donelson Papers," in *Tennessee Historical Magazine*, vol. 3 (June, 1917), pp. 139–141.

From [ROBERT MONROE HARRISON]

United States Consulate
Kingston Ja[maica,] 23rd Aug. 1844
Sir, I do myself the honor to inform you, that in consequence of the almost daily intercourse between this place and the Island of Cuba, we are put in possession of nearly every public, (and sometimes private) occurrence which takes place there.

And I deeply regret to inform you that, by our last accounts, the arrests of persons for treasonable practices, and Insurrectionary movements, still continue; and that, in almost every instance, documents have been found on these individuals tending to implicate a Man by the name of [David] "Turnbull," who is at the head of what is here called the "Court of Mixed Commission," for Africans *expected* to be captured and brought to this port under the Portuguese flag: and shewing, that he has, with the aid of Emissaries, and by the distribution of pamphlets, been at the bottom of all the attempts at Insurrection on the part of the negroes; who had for object the destruction of the entire white population of that Island, by the most cruel deaths; with the exception of the younger and more beautiful females, who were to be reserved for African lust.

That the said Turnbull, and others are endeavouring to produce the same state of things in America, I make not the least doubt. He has a press here where his pamphlets are got up; and as I occasionally employ the same printer to perform small jobs for me in the way of Official documents, he promised to let me see one of them; but, whether he thought it prudent to question his employer as to the propriety of doing so, or whether he wants a high price for the same; I cannot say, as I have not yet received it; and being much indisposed myself, at a few miles distance from Town, I cannot with propriety intrust anyone with a communication to him on the subject.

I have taken the liberty more than once to recommend to your predecessors in office the propriety of calling the attention of the State Governments, as well as the general Government to the reorganization and discipline of our Militia; but especially that of the Slaveholding States to the South: and I have been the more anxious on this point, because I feel certain that the time is not far distant when every white Inhabitant in those States, will have to shoulder his musket in defence of everything he holds dearest in life.

Your own gallant State, notwithstanding the known reputation of its citizens for courage; from the paucity of its numbers of white citizens compared to the Blacks, and the laxity of its Militia discipline, will be greatly exposed, and the worst consequences may result therefrom; and therefore, as you are much beloved, and have the greatest influence, with all classes in the said State, I trust that it may not seem like presumption on my part, if I take the liberty of advising you to recommend the Governor thereof, to be on the *quivive*: for, in the event of a successful insurrection of the Negroes in Cuba, our Southern States will be exposed to great danger; being, owing to the invention of Steam, at little more than a stone's throw from that Island.

Although England would be rejoiced to see the utter ruin and destruction of our Country, she will not aid Insurrection openly among us, unless assured of the neutrality or cooperation of faithless France, (that is to say, of Louis Phillip [*sic*], as I beleive the people of that country, are friendly towards us,) yet she will, by underhand means, do us equal injury.

A person by the name of "Daughtrey" went from here a short time since, to the United States, for the purpose, as it has been said, of examining into the nature of our prison discipline; but as he is one of the psalm singing Stipendiary Magistrates, and moreover the inseperable friend of that bad man "Turnbull," he may for aught I know, be one of his *clique*; and as we have here several hundreds of convict negroes, I have been told that he is also instructed to find out some place to locate them in. This, he attempted to do sometime ago at the Islands of Trinidad, as well as at Demerara but the authorities of those Colonies would not consent.

These savage negro felons are daily increasing in numbers, and it is now difficult to find places to secure them; independently of the enormous expense incurred for their support; so that I know not what the Colony will do, unless some pseudo-philanthropic Governor comes here, and turns them loose upon the community; as was done by the Marquis of Sligo, and the Earl of Malgrave.

As there are several black regiments in this, and other Islands; these wretches, might also, in the event of a war with the United States, be turned into one, and do as good service as the others. Being more intelligent than the Africans who compose the others, they might be made the Vanguard or forlorn hope in desperate occasions; and then woe to the Inhabitants where they landed—though neither Turnbull [*Marginal interpolation*: "This fellow is a regular Church-goer; and has just married the sister in law of His Lordship the Bishop—tho' a more villainous looking fellow was never seen."] or his Government would care about that.

If you should deem anything in this communication deserving attention, and communicate with any of the Governors of the Southern States, I pray you to caution them not to make public any information as derived from me; for it is a well known fact that the British Government have their paid Agents everywhere; and I should at once lose my situation; as our Government, from courtesy to foreign Courts, has always made it a point to remove Consular Agents, on any complaints being made against them by the Governors of Colonies belonging to said powers; the Consuls being simply informed, "that if they are not on terms with those with whom their official relations are to be had, they cannot be useful to their fellow citizens."

Under these circumstances, you will at once perceive Sir, that coupled with the fear of displeasing these petty Governments, the desire of of [*sic*] performing their duty faithfully, on the part of our unfortunate Consuls, prevents them in many places from reposing on beds of roses; and if they are not vexed by foreigners, their own Countrymen, I am sorry to say, seldom fail to do so: for the quarter part of the trading part of them, with whom I have the misfortune to be acquainted, have no more respect for the highest authority known under our Constitution, than they have for me!

Trusting that you will be pleased to pardon me for so long trespassing on your time, and also for breaking off from the subject, with which I commenced, I have the honor to be Sir With the highest respect Your ob[edien]t and most humble serv[an]t.

LU (No. 299) in DNA, RG 59 (State Department), Consular Despatches, Kingston, vol. 9 (T-31:9), received 9/25.

From O[GDEN] HOFFMAN

U.S. Attorney's Office

New York [City,] Aug. 23, 1844

Sir, I have received a communication [of 8/20] from Mr. L.E. Hargous, the Mexican Consul in this City, in which he complains of an advertisement published in a daily newspaper called the "Sun," in which the advertiser, James Arlington Bennett, asks the President of Texas "on what conditions five thousand volunteers from the United States will be received to defend that patriotic people against the designs of Mexico."

The Mexican Consul considers this an act of declared hostility against Mexico, and wishes me, as an officer of the United States, to take immediate measures against the offender.

The 6th section of the act of Congress passed on the 20 April 1818, (6th Vol. Laws U.S. p. 322) provides

"That if any person shall, within the territory or jurisdiction of the United States, begin or set on foot, or provide, or prepare the means for, any military expedition, to be carried on from thence against the territory or dominions of any foreign prince or state, or of any colony, district or people, with whom the United States are at peace, every person, so offending, shall be deemed guilty of a high misdemeanor, shall be fined not more than one thousand dollars, and be imprisoned not more than one year.["]

This case does not seem to come within this section or any other law of the United States; but I have thought it advisable to submit this application of the consul to the Department of State, and accordingly have the honor to transmit to you this communication, together with a copy of the publication which he deems a violation of the peaceful relations of the United States with Mexico. I have the honor to be, Sir Your ob[edien]t serv[an]t, O. Hoffman, U.S. Attorney, [transmitted] by W. Watson.

LS with Ens in DNA, RG 59 (State Department), Miscellaneous Letters (M-179:105, frames 249–262). NOTE: Hoffman enclosed a copy, in Spanish, of Hargous's letter to him and the New York, N.Y., *Sun*, of 8/15, containing Bennett's advertisement.

To WASHINGTON IRVING, [Madrid]

Department of State
Washington, 23rd August, 1844

Sir: I transmit, herewith, the Commission of Isaac Stone, of New Orleans, whom the President [John Tyler] has appointed Consul for the United States, for the Port of San Juan de los Remedios, in Cuba. On its receipt you will apply to the Spanish Government for an exequatur, which, when obtained, you will promptly transmit, with the Commission, to Mr. Stone, at the place for which he has been made Consul.

The practice, which has for some time prevailed in this Department, of requiring Consuls to remit to the Minister at Madrid funds sufficient to enable him to pay the sum charged by Spain upon the emission of their exequaturs, has been found, upon an experience of several years, to be so embarrassing, and, in some cases, so detrimental to the public service, that it will, hereafter, be dispensed with altogether. On the receipt, therefore, of Mr. Stone's Commission, and of all Consular Commissions, which may hereafter be communicated for a like purpose, you will yourself defray the amount of expense incurred, equal, it is understood, to the sum of $18.25. These items will be paid out of your contingent fund, and may be charged by you in your quarterly accounts.

You will take the occasion which this change in former instructions of the Department upon this subject presents, to protest against a tax so irksome to the officers of the United States, and so unworthy of a nation like Spain, with which the United States are upon terms of amity which their common interest requires to be unalterable. You will remind the Government of Spain that no charge whatever is exacted in this country from her Consular officers, nor from those of any other nation, for similar documents, nor for their promulgation, through the Journals which publish the official acts of the Government. The reason given to Mr. [Cornelius P.] Van Ness, in 1830, in an answer declining the proposition he made for such an exemption, viz., that these fees were of old established usage, and were acquiesced in by all foreign nations, is quite unsatisfactory; and I can not but feel confident that if a serious remonstrance be made upon your part, against this vexatious and petty exaction, it will be promptly abolished by Spain upon principles of courtesy, as well as of a strict and just reciprocity.

M. [Angel] Calderon de la Barca has arrived, and presented his credentials to the President on the 5th Instant.

Your despatches to No. 48, inclusive, have reached the Department. I am, Sir, respectfully, Your obedient Servant, J.C. Calhoun.

LS (No. 33) in DNA, RG 84 (Foreign Posts), Spain, Instructions, 1:499–503, received 9/23; FC in DNA, RG 59 (State Department), Diplomatic Instructions, Spain, 14:178–180 (M-77:142).

From STEWART NEWELL, [Galveston]

Consulate of the United States
Sabine, Texas
Aug. 23d 1844

Sir, I, had the honor to address the Department of yesterday's date, informing the Department, of the decease of Hon. T[ilghman] A. Howard, Chargé de Affaires, of the United States, to Texas, who was taken ill, of Congestive Fever, about 2 Miles from Washington Texas, on the 13th inst., and died on the 16th. Further particulars I have not yet heard. The Intelligence, came by Express from Washington, to Houston, and from the latter, to this place, by Steam Boat.

The Department, will please inform me, what may be the wishes, of the Government, as to any mark of respect, desired to be exhibited by the Government, &C &C, towards the remains, & if to be conveyed to this place, and forwarded to the United States, &C, &C.

I, have address[e]d a Letter, to the Department of State of Texas, to request, that the Effects of the late Chargé, may be forwarded to this Consulate, subject to the order of the Department, or friends of deceased, as may be proper. As soon as received, I will inform the Department of the fact.

The Archives of the Legation, had not yet, been forwarded, when informed of the decease of the Hon. Chargé, and are still in this Consulate, and under my Charge. I trust the Department will excuse the liberty, on my part, of referring to the situation of the Books, and other documents & matters, belonging to the Legation of the United States, left by one, of the late Chargés, in charge of a person resident at Austin, the late Capitol of Texas, and as I understand, subject to a charge of Eight dollars, p[e]r Month, for keeping them, and as I have been told, are much exposed to being injured, by the Weather, and being Stolen, or destroy[e]d by Fire, with the present uncertain, Frontier condition, of Texas, and distance, from the present seat of Govt. and not, in charge of a person responsible to the Govt. for thier safe keeping. Would it not be proper, to have the same, brought to

Washington the present seat of Govt., or to this place, for greater security. I beleive there is about 2 years payment, due upon the said Books &C, for keeping charge of them.

    I have also, to call the attention of the Department, to the movements of J[ames] J. Wright, lately in command of the St[eam] B[oa]t "Scioto Belle," and who, has been for sometime past, engaged in secretly getting up an expedition, of an improper character, and came to this place, a few days since, from New Orleans, to meet one of his Associates, in the matter, but, who had died the day before Wright arrived. The latter, left for New Orleans again, on the Steamer "Republic" on the 20th inst., and as it is supposed, to meet with expected funds, to carry out the object, and which I, have learned, is to fit out the fast sailing, and light draught, Schooner "Marie Antoinette" as a *Privateer*, Wright, having in his possession, *One Commission*, fully executed, by the Texian Government, about 2 years since, and 2 Blank Commissions, with authority of same date, to fill them up, and within the last few days, has been, and I am informed, *has* raised Money, and parties, to carry out the Plan. I have seen the Commissions referred to, whilst investigating the "Scioto Belle" matter, at Sabine, but believing them then, of no effect, did not speak or think of them again, but from the general character of the Man, and his suspicious movements, whilst here, I have been induced to watch him, and have every reason to think, *he has, or* will, succeed to some extent, and the Sabine, has been the place named, for a part of the operations, to be carried on, and I, have felt it my duty, to communicate these circumstances to the Department, as early as possible.

    I have not thought it proper, to address any communication to this Govt., on the subject, not knowing how far, I might be authorized to do so, upon that, or any other subject, until instructed by the Department. I have the Honor to be, Respectfully, Your Ob[edien]t Serv[an]t, Stewart Newell, U.S. Consul.

ALS (No. 26) with En in DNA, RG 59 (State Department), Consular Despatches, Texas, vol. 1 (T-153:1), received 9/16.

From STEWART NEWELL

Consulate of the United States
Galveston, Aug. 23d 1844

Sir, The Death of Hon. T[ilghman] A. Howard, having excited a general sympathy, in the whole community, and being an event, as unlooked for, as it is unfortunate, in its consequences, in the present state of affairs, pending between the Govts. of the U. States and Texas, and beleiveing it a duty, imperatively enjoined upon ["me" *interlined*] to communicate the fact, to my Government, by the first conveyance that can be commanded, and in consequence of there being no Vessel in Port, that can be obtained, the St[eam] Packet, having left two days since, and will not return to, and from this Port, to N. Orleans, in less than three or four weeks.

I have under these circumstances, and impressed with the importance, of the interests of my Government involved, in the immediate transmission of this intelligence, I have chartered, the only conveyance to be had, being a small Boat, and two men, to proceed from this Port, to the Port of Franklin La., or to the Balize, or S.W. Pass of Missi[ssi]ppi, or to either, that the Wind will permit, and as will most readily facilitate the transmission of this despatch, and have incurred an expence, of One hundred dollars, for the same, as a compensation, and the Govt., to make what further, compensation, the importance of the communication, and the readiness to perform the duty, and risk run by these Men, may be deemed proper, by the Department.

For the present compensation, to the Bearers of these despatches, I have drawn upon the Collector of the Port of New Orleans, having no funds in my hands, and trust my course, under the circumstances, may meet the entire approval of the Government, and the Hon. Secretary.

Permit me, under apparrently well founded, apprehensions, of an Invasion from a Mexican Force, by Land, and possibly, from a visit of the Mexican Government Steamers, off this Port, what course the Department, will require me, to pursue under the emergency, consequent upon such a case occurring. Having in my possession, the whole Archives of the Legation, and Consulate, to be preserved, and protected, as well perhaps, many of our Citizens, thier property, and Families, at present resident here, and the possibility existing, of the time that may elapse (before a Chargé may arrive,) permitting these apprehensions being realized, and whatever duty may be, assigned me, in the matter, ["neither" *interlined*] the Government, nor the Department, shall have reason to fear, a discharge of, *on my* part, promptly, and properly, as becomes my Flag. I have the Honor to be Most Respectfully Your Ob[edien]t Serv[an]t, Stewart Newell, [Acting] U.S. Consul [at Galveston].

ALS (No. 3) in DNA, RG 59 (State Department), Consular Despatches, Galveston, vol. 2 (T-151:2), received 9/16.

To R[ICHARD] PAKENHAM

Department of State
Washington, Aug[us]t 23d 1844

The Undersigned, Secretary of State of the United States, has the honor to acknowledge the receipt of a note addressed to him by the Right Honorable Mr. Pakenham, Her Britannic Majesty's Envoy Extraordinary and Minister Plenipotentiary, of the 27th of April last, stating that information had been received by his Government that two American citizens, charged with the murder of a British subject, master of the brig "Naiad," were, in the month of December last, delivered up by the Haytien Government to the Commander [Joseph Mattison] of the United States brig "Bainbridge," to be tried by the tribunals of this country.

In reply, the Undersigned has the honor to transmit, herewith, to the Right Honorable Mr. Pakenham copies of certain communications addressed to this Department by G[eorge] F. Usher, United States Commercial Agent at Port au Prince, in the Island of Hayti, together with other documents (numbered from 1 to 10 inclusive,) which present all the material facts in the case referred to.

From these and other papers, or *proces verbaux*, consisting of notes of examination of witnesses, depositions, warrants, decrees of courts, and other judicial proceedings, duly certified by the Haytien Authorities at Gonaives, it appears that on the evening of the 31st of July, 1843, Daniel Hays, master of the British brig "Naiad," in company with several other persons, came on board the United States' brig "Zebra," Samuel S. Thomas, master, then lying at anchor in the port of Gonaives; and, after some conversation with the said Thomas, (those who accompanied him in the mean time conversing apart with the crew,) left the vessel and returned to shore. That previous to this visit, Captain Thomas had been informed by the Commander of the British barque, "Eliza Killick," that Hays was endeavoring to excite his crew to mutiny, or to seduce them from his employment. That about 10 o'clock at night of the same day, Hays came alone in a boat alongside the "Zebra," and, being hailed and warned off by the Captain, retired. An hour afterwards he again approached the vessel as before, was again hailed, but returned no answer. At the same time one of the crew of the "Zebra," in a mutinous spirit, encouraged him to come on board, and proffered him assistance; but, the Captain promptly interfering, the boat again left the vessel, and returned to shore.

On the next day, August 1st, the master of the "Zebra" went on shore; and, after conferring with the consignees of his vessel, informed some of the authorities of the place of the facts, and solicited the aid of a guard; which not being granted, he employed the services of a Haytien to assist him in preserving subordination amongst his crew. At about 9 o'clock, P.M., of the same day, a person approached the ship in an open boat, as on the night previous, who proved to be Captain Hays, the master of the Brig "Naiad." He was hailed, but returned no answer. One of the crew of the "Zebra" again invited him to come on board, with promises of aid. He was warned to desist from his obvious purpose; and, being threatened, returned an answer of defiance, at the same time lifting something from the boat, and pointing it towards the deck of the "Zebra," as if in the act of firing. At this moment the Haytien on board, with or without orders, discharged his piece, and Hays fell mortally wounded.

The day after these events, Captain Thomas, his mate [Joseph R.] Curtis, and the Haytien, were arrested; and after an examination before the authorities at Gonaives, committed to prison, where they remained until the 12th of December, 1843, (frequent though unheeded applications being made in the mean time, by the United States' Commercial Agent at Port au Prince for their trial or discharge,) when, on the demand of the commanding officer of the United States' brig "Bainbridge," that they should either be brought to trial, or released, they were formally delivered up to him.

Such appear to be the principal and well established facts of the case. Other circumstances are also adduced in evidence which leave no doubt that Hays had corrupted the crew of the "Zebra"; that his object in those night visits was to take them to his own vessel then lying at the mouth of the harbor ready for sea; and that the act of killing being in self defence, was one of justifiable homicide.

The Undersigned is not disposed to controvert the principle asserted by the Right Honorable Mr. Pakenham in regard to the jurisdiction of independent States over offences committed within the limits of their respective territories. As a general rule, the principle is readily admitted; but the facts and circumstances attending the case under consideration would seem justly to constitute it an exception to such rule; and when the long confinement of the accused, the revolutionary state of the country, the unsettled condition of the Government within whose jurisdiction the offence is charged to have been committed, and the prospect of indefinite imprisonment arising from the intestine commotions of the Island prevalent at the time, are considered, the conduct of the Commander of the "Bainbridge" in demanding the trial or enlargement of the prisoners, seems to be warranted by the duty which every Government, under such circumstances, owes to its citizens.

The Undersigned, in reply to that part of Mr. Pakenham's note which suggests that the individuals charged with the offence should again be arrested and brought to trial, deems it proper further to remark that the courts of the United States have no jurisdiction in cases like the present, nor can an arrest be lawfully made. It may, however, be proper to state that, in the present case, the individuals charged with the murder were, on their landing at Pensacola, brought before a criminal court in the territory of Florida, duly arraigned, and upon an examination of the testimony certified by the Haytien authorities at Gonaives, fully acquitted and discharged from custody.

The Undersigned avails himself of the occasion to renew to the Right Honorable Mr. Pakenham the assurances of his high consideration. J.C. Calhoun.

FC in DNA, RG 59 (State Department), Notes to Foreign Legations, Great Britain, 7:28–32 (M-99:36); PC in Jameson, ed., *Correspondence*, pp. 606–609. NOTE: An appended "List of accompanying papers" indicates that copies or extracts of 10 letters were enclosed to Pakenham.

PROTOCOL by R[ichard] Pakenham and J[ohn] C. Calhoun

[Washington, August 23, 1844]

On the 23d of August 1844 a conference was held by appointment at the office of the Secretary of State in the city of Washington between the Hon. John C. Calhoun Secretary of State of the United States, and the Right Honorable Richard Pakenham, Her Brittanick Majesty's Envoy Extraordinary and Minister Plenipotentiary, both duly authorized by their respective Governments to treat of the respective claims of the two Countries to the Oregon Territory with the view to establish a permanent boundary between the two Countries westward of the Rocky Mountains to the Pacific Ocean.

The conference was opened by assurances on both sides of the desire of their respective Governments to approach the question with an earnest desire & in the spirit of compromise to effect an adjustment consistent with the honor and just interests of either party. The Plenipotentiaries then proceeded to examine the actual state of the question as it stood at the last unsuccessful attempt to adjust it.

This done the American Plenipotentiary desired to receive from the British Plenipotentiary any fresh proposal he might be instructed to offer on the part of his Government towards effecting an adjustment.

The British Plenipotentiary said he would be ready to offer such a proposal at their next conference, hoping that the American Plenipotentiary would be ready to present a proposal on the part of his Government. The conference adjourned to meet on Monday the 26th instant. J.C. Calhoun, R. Pakenham.

DS in DNA, RG 59 (State Department), Notes from Foreign Legations, Great Britain, vol. 22 (M-50:22); PC in the Washington, D.C., *Daily National Intelligencer*, December 12, 1845, p. 1; PC in *Niles' National Register*, vol. LXIX, no. 17 (December 27, 1845), p. 261; PC in Senate Document No. 1, 29th Cong., 1st Sess., p. 143; PC in House Document No. 2, 29th Cong., 1st Sess., p. 143; PC in Crallé, ed., *Works*, 5:421–422.

From S[tephen] P[leasonton]

Tr[easury] Dept., 5th A[uditor's] O[ffice]
August 23d 1844

Sir, Your letter of the 10 inst. was received at this Office together with a letter from Mr. [Henry] Middleton in relation to his accounts in my absence from this City.

I am sorry to perceive that Mr. Middleton has taken offence at a doubt I expressed in my letter to you of 26 June last that he was not employed on such a Special Mission at London as would entitle him to pay (for that was my meaning) as Mr. [Richard] Rush was then the Resident Minister and I might have added another reason for thinking so and that was that Mr. Middleton [in] making out his claims against the Government from time to time up to 13 Jan[uar]y 1840 never referred to this Mission as far as I know as forming any ground of claim Against the U. States. The extracts from his instructions and letters to the [State] Department contained in his letter do indeed shew that he was Authorized to confer with the British Govt. concerning deported slaves but still there is nothing to shew that the Govt. had promised or expected to pay him for this service.

Unless it shall appear that the Govt. promised him compensation in some form or other for this service I would respectfully submit whether it would not be a safer course and one more in accordance with usage ["not" *canceled*] to refer Mr. Middleton to Congress than to make an allowance in any shape upon a claim brought forward for the first time after a lapse of 24 years.

Mr. Middleton assumes the fact altogether incorrectly that I have rejected his several claims. He ought to know that in all claims of a contingent and discretionary nature it is the province of the Secr[etar]y of State to decide on the propriety of their allowance.

It has not been my practice nor can I exercise a discretion in cases of a contingent nature without usurping the Authority of the Secretary of State. [Signed:] S[tephen] P[leasonton].

FC in DNA, RG 217 (General Accounting Office), Fifth Auditor: Letters Sent, 5:157–158.

To HENRY WHEATON, [Berlin]

Department of State
Washington, 23rd August, 1844

Sir: I have received your despatch No. 238, dated on the 20th February last, enclosing copy of a communication from the Count de Bulow, proposing several alterations, both of form and substance, in the original projêt of a Convention between the United States and Prussia, with certain other German States, relating to the mutual delivery of fugitives from justice.

The President [John Tyler], to whom the subject has been submitted, does not perceive any sufficient objections to the alterations in the Convention suggested by the Prussian Minister of Foreign relations; and has directed me, in case I concur with him, to authorise you to meet the views of Count Bulow. The President has entire reliance upon your ability and good judgment, and it is his wish that you should proceed, without delay, to carry out and to complete the arrangements in view, in such form and manner as, in your opinion, will best advance the interest of both countries.

Your despatches to No. 255, inclusive, have been received. I am, Sir, respectfully, Your obedient Servant, J.C. Calhoun.

LS (No. 59) in DNA, RG 84 (Foreign Posts), Germany, Instructions, 1:313–316; FC in DNA, RG 59 (State Department), Diplomatic Instructions, Germany, 14:85–86 (M-77:65).

From HENRY A. WISE

Rio de Janeiro, August 23rd 1844

Sir, Since my last despatch [Manoel Alves Branco] the Minister of the Treasury has published the New Tariff of this Empire, dated the

12th of August 1844, and to go into effect the 11th of November 1844. It is just published and by the evening of this day I will have a translation completed ["and" *canceled and* "of the law and" *interlined*] of the comparative rate of duties, which, as the U.S. frigate United States sails in the morning, I make haste to send to you. Hereafter I may make further communication or commentary on this subject. Very hastily I have the honor to be y[ou]r humble serv[an]t, Henry A. Wise.

ALS with Ens in DNA, RG 59 (State Department), Diplomatic Despatches, Brazil, vol. 13 (M-121:15), received 10/6; ALS (retained copy) in DLC, Henry Alexander Wise Papers; FC (marked No. 2) in DNA, RG 84 (Foreign Posts), Brazil, Despatches, 11:82.

To [HENRY] BAILEY, [Charleston], "Private"

State Dept., 24th Aug[us]t 1844

My Dear Sir, I have delayed answering your letter [of 7/30], enclosing one from Gen[era]l [Andrew] Jackson to Col. [James] Gadsden, until it could be submitted for the consideration of the President [John Tyler], who has been absent till lately at Old Point Comfort [in Va.]. It was placed in his hands with another from Gen[era]l Jackson to President [Samuel] Houston, written in consequence of the letter from Col. Gadsden to Gen[era]l Jackson, the day after his return, and the subject was submitted to the Cabinet at its last meeting[.]

The opinion was unanimous, that the measure suggested was too strong for the position occupied by the President, and I have written to Maj[o]r [Andrew Jackson] Donelson, who enclosed me the Gen[era]l's letter to President Houston, to that effect.

My own opinion is, that ["the" *canceled*] honor as well as expediency, demands, that we should repel any invasion which Mexico may make during the pendency of the question of annexation. It is true the treaty was rejected by the Senate, but it is equally so, that the proposition for annexing is still undisposed of. The joint resolution offered by Mr. [George] McDuffie [Senator from S.C.] is yet to be acted on, and remains to abide the appeal made by both parties to the people, to be decided in the coming presidential election. It is also true, that Texas has not signified any intention of withdrawing her consent to be annexed. To attack her, under such circumstances, because she dared to accept our invitation to be admitted into the Union, is in my opinion an insult, which we would be in honor bound to repel.

With this impression, I have thought, that the meeting of Congress ought to be called at a period earlier, than that fixed by the Constitution, say 1st Nov[embe]r but many of our friends think it would be of no avail, and that it might have an injurious effect on the result of the presidential election. The question has not been yet decided, but the prospect is, that there will not be a call.

I entirely concur in the views you express in referrence to separate State action at this time, and have read the Charleston proceedings in referrence to it with pleasure. It will do good. I expressed myself in opposition to it, at this time, to our delegation before they left here. The point is now to let it die away without causing any soreness among our friends, or division in our ranks. There is ample cause for the indignation, that those, who took a different view have expressed at our oppression [*sic*]. A difference of opinion, as to the proper time for action, ought not to make any division in our ranks. That would be a great misfortune indeed.

I expected to be in Charleston before this, on my way home, but I have been compelled to take up the Oregon negotiation, which I fear will keep me at my post nearly all September. I have been much engaged of late and among other things, in preparing important dispatches in referrence to Texas, and points of importance between us and Great Britain, growing out of the abolition question.

I am happy to say that our intelligence from France is good. She is unfavourable to the annexation of Texas, on commercial grounds, but has given strong assurances, that she will not take grounds hostile to us, and that she has not agreed to unite with England in a joint protest against it, as has been reported.

You will see by the contents of this letter why I mark it private, but I do not intend that you should not show it to such friends as you may deem proper, or to state so much of the contents to your Committee [of Vigilance on the subject of Texas], as may relate to the discharge of their functions. Yours truly, J.C. Calhoun.

Contemporary copy in LNHT, Colcock Family Papers. Note: The manuscript copy transcribed above bears the following AEU: "Private[.] Copy of a Letter from Mr. Calhoun to Mr. Bailey Dated 24 Aug. 1844." An "ALS" of this letter was advertised for sale by Anderson Galleries, New York City, on 4/8/1907 as Item No. 27 in Catalog 533.

From C[ALEB] CUSHING

Macao, August 24th 1844

Sir: After the conclusion of the Treaty of Wang-Hiya, which, if ratified by both Governments, will have placed the political as well as the commercial relations of China & the United States on so favorable a footing, there remained sundry incidental questions for discussion, which immediately required my attention at Macao. Of these, I have given account in successive despatches, as the discussion of them arose; and I have now, I think, disposed of them all, some finally, and the rest so far as any disposition of them can at present be made.

It remained for me next to consider what other public objects in China demanded my attention, either in the execution of any express instructions from the Department, or in the discretionary discharge of such duties as might seem to be imposed on me by the general interests of the United States.

First among the objects of this class was the question of visiting Peking.

I have already detailed to you at length the considerations, which induced me, in my negociations with the Imperial Commissioner, to consent to waive, for the time being, the purpose of repairing to the Court.

In doing so, I obtained the engagement of Tsiyeng, that, in case the Minister of any other Power should be received at Court, the same privilege should be accorded to the Minister of the United States.

I supposed, at this time, that the French Minister would certainly proceed to Peking, whether opposed in this by the Chinese Court or not. I did not suppose that any Minister would be sent to Peking by Great Britain; because the military position of that government at Hong-kong and Chusan gives, to her, *peculiar* advantages & means of influence in China; whereas, if there were a British Minister at Peking, there would also as a matter of course be a French and a Russian Minister, who would thus, by diplomatic influence, balance & neutralise the now comparatively exclusive authority of Great Britain. But if, as I had anticipated would be the case, M. de Lagrenée [*sic*; Theodose-Marie de Lagrené] should, on his arrival in China, proceed without delay to the mouth of the Pih-ho, it would be the recognized right, as well as the duty, of the American Minister to do the same.

Simultaneously, however, with the arrival of M. de Lagrenée at Macao, came to me the report, in the French & English newspapers & by letters from Europe, of the speech of Mr. [Francois P.G.] Guizot in the French Chambre of Deputies, by which it appeared that the same considerations, which had led me to waive proceeding to Peking, had induced the French Government to give M. de Lagrenée positive instructions not to go to Peking, if the objects of his Mission could be accomplished without doing it.

In this state of facts, it became me, of course, to relinquish all present idea of visiting Peking.

This conclusion I came to with the less of regret, inasmuch as all the immediate and most substantive objects of proceeding to Peking had been effected at Macao. I had negociated a Treaty of Amity & Commerce to the full as advantageous as I could have hoped to obtain at Peking, and with great comparative economy of time & expense. Indeed, if I had proceeded to Peking, I could scarcely have completed my negociations there in season to lay the result before the present Congress.

Meanwhile, I had transmitted the special letter of the President of the United States to the Howang Tei [the Emperor], in one of the modes expressly provided for by the general instructions of the Department.

There was, however, a secondary object in proceeding to the North, independently of being accredited at Peking, namely, the inspection of the Ports of Hiya-mun ["(Amoy)" *interlined*], Fuchow, Ning-po, and Shang-hai, newly opened to foreign commerce. I made some preparations, indeed, to visit these Ports, as will have been seen by the letter, heretofore communicated to the Department, which I addressed to Tsiyeng on this subject. But I have been diverted from this purpose by considerations, which have induced me the rather to return to the United States.

I premise, that the Mission entrusted to me is, on the face of the Act of Congress which appropriated the funds for it, as well as by the tenor of the commissions & instructions ["for" *interlined*] constituting the Mission, a *special* one.

To be sure, it is in the power of Congress to make it a permanent one, by means of additional appropriations, or by otherwise indicating such a purpose. But I have no intelligence that any additional appropriations have been made by, or are in the contemplation of, the present Congress. On the contrary, I have reason to suppose that the Mission will be left to stand (at present at least) on the appropriation already made by the last Congress.

That appropriation is now exhausted by the salaries & other charges, to which it is subject under the orders of the Department. This consideration has appeared to me to dictate, that, unless overpowering considerations of public duty require me to remain longer in China, I should now return to the United States. That is to say, I do not conceive it to be just & proper for me, by my own act, without grave cause, and without any previous authorization of Congress, to create a new charge on the Treasury by continuing here as Minister of the United States. If, indeed, the negociations for the Treaty were still lingering, or in any other respect the interests of the United States were in peril, so as to constitute an imperious demand for the presence here of a Minister Plenipotentiary at this time, I should have felt myself justified in remaining, nay I should have deemed it my duty to remain, even at my own charge & risk, trusting for remuneration to the justice & equity of Congress. But no such immediate & ["permanent" *erased and* "paramount" *interlined*] exigency exists to detain me here, & to forbid my return to the United States.

On the other hand, I think the great objects of my Mission may be best promoted by the latter course.

I have transmitted to Washington one copy of the Treaty by the best means, which any unofficial opportunity of conveyance afforded, namely, by the bark Sappho. I have also transmitted despatches to the Department from time to time as occasion offered, in order to keep the Department fully advised of all my acts. But the great length of the voyage involves some degree of uncertainty as to the arrival of all these documents in the United States. The failure of the Treaty to arrive in season to be laid before Congress next winter would be a serious inconvenience, as the period for the exchange of ratifications is fixed at eighteen months from the date of the Treaty, which period expires on the 3rd of January 1846: too soon for the action of the next Congress. Even if the copy of the Treaty transmitted by Mr. [Augustine] Heard should arrive safely, still the failure of any part of the despatches would be inconvenient, in leaving unexplained, perhaps, things material to the understanding of the Treaty and to the intelligent action of the Senate. I have already heard of the loss of a mass of important matter placed by me on board the bark Convoy in July; that vessel having been stranded on the island of Luzon. The duplicate copy of the Treaty might be sent home by a bearer of despatches; but *lacunae* in the despatches can only be supplied by my own original drafts or by personal explanations on my part. In which point of view, I feel satisfied that, to meet all such contingencies, it cannot but be useful that I should myself be at Washington.

And, even if all the documents transmitted should seasonably arrive in the United States, yet in other respects personal explanations on many points which I cannot anticipate, and for which I cannot provide by my despatches, may prove acceptable either to the President of the United States or to the Senate; because the distance of China precludes the possibility of such explanations, when the case arises, being obtained by means of letters from and to the Department.

I have come to the conclusion, therefore, to repair immediately to the United States ["carrying with me the duplicate of the Treaty;" *interlined*] and in looking around for a direct & expeditious means of proceeding thither, I have decided to go by the way either of Mexico or of Panama.

To enable me to accomplish this purpose, Commodore [Foxhall A.] Parker has authorised ["Captain (John S.) Paine, in command of" *interlined*] the Perry, to convey me at once to the coast of Mexico, the Brandywine and St. Louis remaining for a while longer on the coast of China.

Mr. [Fletcher] Webster will also return immediately to the United States, probably by the way of the Red Sea. And he will render account of the archives & other public property in his charge.

I annex copies of a communication addressed by me to the Imperial Commissioner, acquainting him with my purpose to leave China.

I beg your attention to two points in this communication.

One is, the notice, which I have given to the Imperial Commissioner, that the Commander of the Naval Forces of the United States in the East Indies has authority to protect & superintend the rights & interests of the United States in China, in the absence of any diplomatic representative of the Government.

The other is, the authority given by me to Dr. [Peter] Parker to receive and translate, and then transmit to the United States, any communications for me from the Imperial Commissioner. This includes the reply of the Howang Tei ["(Emperor)" *interlined*] to the letter of the President of the United States, as well as letters which Tsiyeng may direct to me, in reply perhaps to mine of the 20th instant on the subject of Sherry and of Shu-Amias[?], and of the 23rd instant concerning my departure from China.

In taking this step, I beg not to be understood as intending to raise the implication that no need exists for a permanent diplomatic agent of the United States in China. On the contrary, the large & increasing commerce of the United States in China, the political importance there which that fact gives to, nay imposes on, the

United States, the magnitude & delicacy of the duties devolved on the Representative of the United States in China by the new relations of that Empire to the West, and the necessity of guarding in all respects the stipulations of the Treaty of Wang-Hiya, will undoubtedly require that that Representative shall be some person other than ordinary consuls, engaged in commercial affairs, having personal interests of their own which may be in conflict with those of their fellow-merchants, and for the same reason, (that of being themselves engaged in commerce), not enjoying the highest consideration of the Chinese Government.

I beg leave to add, in further justification of the step I have taken, that my distance from the seat of Government compels me to act without waiting to ask & receive the directions of the President; that for this reason my instructions appear to leave much to my own discretion; and that if, peradventure, the action of Congress, or that of the Senate in its own separate function, shall have been such as to suppose the longer continuance of the Mission, I shall, on my arrival at Washington, submit the whole matter to the disposition of the President. I am With the highest respect Your ob[edien]t s[er]-v[an]t, C. Cushing.

ALS (No. 91) with En in DNA, RG 59 (State Department), Diplomatic Despatches, China, vol. 2 (M-92:3), received 1/2/1845.

To the MINISTER for Foreign Affairs of Peru

Department of State
Washington, 24th August, 1844

Sir: Mr. James C. Pickett, who has been for some time accredited to Your Excellency as Chargé d'Affaires of the United States, being about to return to his country, I have directed him to take leave of Your Excellency and to embrace the opportunity which will thereby be afforded him to convey to Your Excellency the expression of the friendly sentiments entertained by the President towards the Republic of Peru, and of his desire to preserve and improve the relations of harmony so happily subsisting between the two countries.

I avail myself of this occasion to offer Your Excellency the assurance of my distinguished consideration. (Signed) J.C. Calhoun.

CC in DNA, RG 84 (Foreign Posts), Peru, Instructions (C8.14), 1836–1847.

From S [HADRACH] PENN, JR.

St. Louis, Aug. 24 1844

D[ea]r Sir, I perceive that it is rumored in the eastern papers that the President [John Tyler] will convene Congress earlier than usual. I think such a movement would have a happy effect, provided the Proclamation could be so prepared as to give the people a brief outline of ["the" *interlined*] views which influence the Executive. I take it for granted that England and France have tendered to Texas a treaty of guaranty, and report says the former has agreed to advance to Mexico four millions of dollars, to renew a war, not for her own benefit, but to drive Texas into the toils of England. It seems to me, under such circumstances, that the Government should not only declare its determination to adhere to the policy avowed by Mr. [James] Monroe as to foreign or European interference with the affairs of this continent, but plant itself on the treaty of 1803, and avow its purpose to protect the people of Texas. A Proclamation taking these positions and showing the extent to which Britain and France have already interfered, would kindle a flame throughout the nation—force those powers to desist and produce the happiest results. But to render the action of the President as effective as the crisis demands, for the good of the [*mutilation*: country,] he should publicly withdraw from [the can]vass for the Presidency. His warning would be heeded, if those disposed to sustain him could give the assurance that he had no object in view but ["the" *interlined*] prosperity, security and glory of the country.

In this State we have had a bitter local contest. I think the Legislature is anti-Benton by a small majority; and in a few days I shall make this statement in my paper [the St. Louis *Missouri Reporter*].

My assistant, Mr. [Samuel] Treat, has just returned from the Nashville Mass Convention, and he assures me that Col. [Thomas H.] Benton was there regarded a traitor to the party, and as laboring covertly for the defeat of [James K.] Polk & [George M.] Dallas. Mr. Treat saw Gen. [Andrew] Jackson & Col. Polk, and conversed with them, and with many other leading Democrats of the West and Southwest. Col. B[enton] was condemned by all, and I yet hope to see him defeated, at the approaching session of the Legislature. Yours Truly, S. Penn, Jr.

P.S. The Charleston Mercury is, I think doing mischief. I wish to see the present tariff law repealed or greatly modified, but it is not, in my opinion, to be effected by the course advocated by the Mercury.

ALS in ScCleA.

From D[A]N[IEL?] ROBERTSON

Norfolk, Aug[us]t 24th 1844

Sir, I take the liberty of addressing you on a subject which as a Commercial man, I feel some Interest in & commend the matter to your kind consideration. I am told that the present incumbent of the United States Consulate at St. Pierre's[,] Mart[iniqu]e [Philip A. de Creny], is about being displaced, on account of charges prefer'd against him which I regret to say are too well founded. Mr. G[abriel] G. Fleurot, of New York, Merchant in said Island, and now in this country, has made an application to the President for the office, & a personal one to you. In the furtherance of his views, I cannot, but think him deserving & well qualified to fill the same. My house enjoying a large share of the business emenating from the Islands of Mart[inique] & Guad[eloup]e I feel a pride that the nation should be properly & faithfully represented in the former Island. Such has not been the case for some time past. Within a few days I have learned that the President has tendered the appointment in question to a Mr. [Isidore] Guillet, a Gent[leman] no doubt fully qualified to fill the station, but being a man of family, & the remuneration so small, he has written the President to endeavour to give him something better. Should he have it in his power to grant his request, my object is to recommend to your favorable notice Mr. F[leurot] as a suitable person for the app[ointmen]t. With considerations of my highest regards I am Your very Ob[edien]t Serv[an]t, D[a]n[iel?] Robertson.

"P.S." During your visit here I had the honor of being presented to you by my brother in law Jno. Henderson.

LS in DNA, RG 59 (State Department), Applications and Recommendations, 1853–1861, Fleurot (M-967:17, frames 137–138).

From R[ICHAR]D F. SIMPSON, [Representative from S.C.]

[Pendleton] August 24 1844

D[ea]r Sir, The charleston mercury gives to day a rumor that a cabinet counsel had recommended a call of congress. I should be very glad to know the truth of the matter as far a[s] a prudent disclosure will enable you to give.

I have delayed writing for your opinion on several matters that I feel great solicitude about from hearing that you were expected home every week for a month past—and for the same reason have delayed giving you information of our political actings and doings. You are aware that the Whigs make a shew no where in the State but in my election District. I have now made a tour into all my District, and am satisfied I shall beat [William] Butler some thing like 1000 votes more that my majority before. The feeling in favour of Texas is so general here that Butler has been compelled to come into it and now in his speeches declares himself as much in favour of Texas as I or any one else. I have heard of no one who is clearly out in open opposition to the annexation but Gen[era]l [Waddy] Thompson [Jr.]. In a speech recently at a Barbacue at Chicks springs in Greenville [District] he asserted there was not a section of Land in Texas worth a groat that was not covered over with one if not more grants—and that he would not give a county in maine for the whole of Texas. That he has conversed with the President [John Tyler], Mr. Calhoun & Mr. [George] McDuffie in Washington and the reasons given for the Treaty were so futile as to induce a belief that some other object was aimed at by the leaders in Annexation and read a part of [Thomas H.] Benton[']s speech to prove that a dis[s]olution of the union was aimed at, and particularly that the leaders of the Democratic party in S.C. aimed at that. And asserted that if the Treaty had been confirmed we would now be at war with Mexico, England & France.

The Speech I could see, as well as ["hear" *interlined*] from the opinion of others fell still-born and such has been the effect of his course on that subject since his return from Washington and his Albany speech and letters, that even his old friends acknowledge that his influence is gone. It is confidently asserted that in Greenville [District] Butler cannot get more than 600 out of 1500 votes and that the Democratic party are very firm and decided. In our [Pendleton] District election [John] Maxwell, [Edward] Harleston[,] Maj. [John T.] Broyles, [James L.] Orr, & [John C.] Miller are certain of election [to the S.C. General Assembly], and the whole ticket would be but from the fact that we have two more candidates than the right number and from want of concert in the voters, in selecting the same 7 to run all over the election District.

I have taken the views expressed by you the evening before we left Washington so far as I could recollect them. And altho I found my friends here generally pretty warm they have quietly and very cordially come into them. In our discussions before the People I have refused to be led off by Butler to old issues but have kept him to the new ones which I find disarms him altogether. I have taken the grounds that this State should make no move now, but but [*sic*] wait the lead of some other State—that the Texas question was to us now the most important of all, particularly as the Slave question must rise or fall with it—and that it was really a Brittish and American question; That for this neither Nullification, nor cecession would answer—that a conciliatory course to unite the South was the true one—that nothing could be done during the pendency of the Presidential election. Unite on [James K.] Polk and [George M.] Dallas & if elected the political influence of the South would be to some extent restored. And that after the election and Texas admitted the prosperity of the South might be hoped to return. That the Tariff would cease to be serviceable to the manufacturers after two or three years more, then they must clamor for more—if Polk is elected they can't get it—if [Henry] Clay is and grants it—it will kill both him and the Tariff. At all events then will be the time to resist it when the South may be expected to make a united opposition that will be effectual.

I have not hesitated that the views I've expressed I learned from you. I therefore mention them with the hope if in any point I have mistaken your meaning you will do me the favour & yourself the justice to correct me. The only difficulty I have had in giving my friends satisfaction is in not being able to point to any ultimate course as a remedy. And on this point I would be much gratified to have your views. The truth is I have been long so thoroughly convinced of the extraordinary soundness and depth of your political opinions that I am not satisfied to drink at any other fountain.

[Robert Barnwell] Rhett & [Isaac E.] Holmes have given me some trouble to resist the imputations of disunion which Butler has endeavoured to fasten on our party in this State, the evidence for which he deduces from their writings and the Bluffton toasts. However he has not as yet been able to satisfy any but the Whigs of such design and I doubt whether they believe it.

I would be very much pleased to hear from you—to be instructed in any thing important for us to adopt. It would be very gratifying to be informed by yourself that your position in the cabinet was pleasant to you and that your enemies has failed to excite any prejudice against you in the mind of the President & his friends. Knowing that the Devil in the shape of Benton & [Francis P.] Blair is using his best efforts—I know you will pardon this solicitude ["for one" *interlined*] so much respected and so surrounded by spies.

Not only myself but many of your friends here are anxious to know whether it would meet your views to place you again in the Senate in December. Our great hope is that you may be continued in Polk[']s cabinet & therefore would not wish any step taken that would throw any obstacle to that result. This you may rely on, your State is anxious for your services for her all the time they are not employed for the General Government.

I take it for granted you have regularly your Familly and domestic news. With sentiments of great regard your ob[edien]t Serv[an]t, Rd. F. Simpson.

[P.S.] Our crops are pretty good and the examining committee [of the Pendleton Farmers Society] appointed to examine the different farms with a view to the 20$ premium for the best conducted farm, resolved upon as you will recollect a year ago, have been waiting your return to commence their visits, preferring if they could to have it that you should be at home when they visited yours. Next week however they have resolved to start.

ALS in ScCleA; PEx in Boucher and Brooks, eds., *Correspondence*, pp. 246–248.

From Isaac Van Zandt

Legation of Texas
Washington D.C., August 24th 1844

Sir, I have the honor to inform you that on the 15th of September, next, a Council will be held at Tawacono creek near the Brassos river, between Commissioners of Texas and the Commanche and other Indians who reside within and upon her limits, and that it is the desire of the President of Texas [Samuel Houston], that a Commissioner or Agent of the United States should be present at that time and place empowered to aid in promoting the reciprocally important object of effecting treaties with those tribes.

The place fixed upon for holding this Council is the same at which Gov. [Pierce M.] Butler attended in March 1843.

Although the time is fixed for the 15th of September, it is not thought probable that the Indians will generally assemble before the last of the month; and any Commissioner which might be dispatched by this Government would doubtless reach the place designated in time to aid in the objects contemplated.

Should a Commissioner or Agent be sent to attend this Council on the part of the United States, it is thought desirable by the President of Texas that he should be attended by a suitable escort, not that any danger is apprehended to the Commissioners, but for the purpose of making an impression upon the savages.

With renewed assurances of my distinguished consideration I have the honor to be Your Mo[st] Ob[e]d[ien]t Serv[an]t, Isaac Van Zandt, Chargé d'Affaires of Texas.

LS in DNA, RG 59 (State Department), Notes from Foreign Legations, Texas, vol. 1 (T-809:1); FC in Tx, Records of the Texas Republic Department of State, Letters and Dispatches Sent by the Texas Legation in Washington, 2:5; FC in Tx, Records of the Texas Republic Department of State, Copybooks of Letters Received from Texan and Foreign Representatives, vol. 2–1/98, pp. 534–535; CC in Tx, Records of the Texas Republic Department of State, U.S. Diplomatic Correspondence; PC in Senate Document No. 14, 32nd Cong., 2nd Sess., pp. 126–127.

From GEO[RGE] E. WATNESS & CO.
and Others

[New York City?, *ca.* August 24, 1844]

Sir, We the undersigned Merchants, doing business in the United States, ["& others," *interlined*] understanding that Mr. Gabriel Gaspar Fleurot, formerly of the city of New-York and now residing in the town of St. Pierre's, in the Island of Martinique, West-Indies, is desirous of obtaining the office of Consul for said port of St. Pierre's, and is about to make application there for to the proper authorities of the United-States, at Washington,

Would cheerfully recommend him for that Office, as a person who would fulfill all the duties of the office with honor to himself and the Country, and with due regard to the interests of foreign countries. He understands and speaks the french and English languages with equal facility and correctness having resided several years in the French West Indies, and professes [*sic*] in all respects the qualifications necessary for the Office of Consul. [Signed:] Geo. E. Watness & Co., Geo. A. Thomas, C.L. Cole, Lorenzo Jackson, Curtis & Lyman, Hennequin & Co., Auguste Davezac, Thomas M. Adams & Co., E. Lyman, Jr., Buck & Peters, Frederick R. Sherman, Coleman & Stetson, Capt. Cole [of the] brig Ann, Capt[ai]n Roberts, B[rig] Mary Cole, Capt. Sanford [of] Bangor [Me.].

LS in DNA, RG 59 (State Department), Applications and Recommendations, 1853–1861, Fleurot (M-967:17, frames 140–142).

From F[ITZWILLIAM] BYRDSALL, "Private"

New York [City,] August 25th 1844

Dear Sir, I am very desirous of obtaining a copy of [Representative from N.H., Edmund] Burke's Report upon the Rhode Island Suffrage Movement, which I am informed is now being printed at the Globe office. As I know of no better mode of procuring one than applying to you, I throw myself upon your kindness with the request, that you will forward me a copy, if you can with perfect convenience do so.

I cannot refrain from taking this oppertunity [*sic*], now that the National-Convention-Campaign is ended, to say a few words in relation to your political friends in this city. Having formed the only Calhoun organization that ever existed in this part of the Union, I may assume to have to [*sic*] some knowledge of its members. In regard to political intelligence and fidelity to any cause they espouse, they are not excelled by any body of democrats in the Union. It was for your State right and constitutional views of our system of Government, that we preferred you as our candidate, and such was our fidelity, that after your own Southern friends had hawled down the Calhoun flag, we still kept it up, untill you become [*sic*] a member of the Cabinet. We then rallied to the [John] Tyler Standard and have remained true to him untill his withdrawal, for which, as well as for his excellent letter, we feel both grateful and gratified, if for no other reason than that now we are *free* to go to the support of [James K.] Polk & [George M.] Dallas without any dishonor to ourselves. We are the last to leave any cause we pledge ourselves to support.

Upon yourself or the President we have no reflections to make, but we have been greatly chagrined at the deficiency of organization and tact of your Southern friends, as well as at the heartlessness of his professing friends. Each of you may well say, "save me from my friends!" You for the inefficiency of yours, and he for the perfidy of his.

After all, we have done much—there is great reason for gratulation. A political Dynasty [Martin Van Buren's] is broken down, a Texas candidate is nominated and our principles of Revenue tariff, District system of representation and strict construction of the constitution, are on the ascent toward ascendancy.

I should be much pleased to receive from you, your views of our political prospects as well as some hints as to the course to be pursued by your friends here. To what great point shall we direct our efforts?

With sentiments of the highest esteem I have the honour of subscribing myself Dear Sir Your obliged and Obedient Servant, F. Byrdsall, 28 Vandam St., New York.

ALS in ScCleA; PC in Jameson, ed., *Correspondence*, pp. 965–967.

From Miss Betsey Hawley, Darien, Conn., 8/25. She acknowledges Calhoun's letter [*not found*] in which he offered to supervise personally a search for a document requested by her. She thanks Calhoun for this offer and adds that it is her "only hope, (if I may judge from the manner in which business has been done at the Department by the clerks of some of your predecessors,) I should have, of having the business, correctly, thoroughly, & promptly, done." ALS in DNA, RG 59 (State Department), Miscellaneous Letters (M-179: 105, frames 271–272).

From F[RANKLIN] H. ELMORE

Columbia, August 26, 1844

My Dear Sir, Since I wrote you last I rec[eive]d yours of the 6 Aug[us]t & concurring entirely in the views it expressed, I showed it to several of your friends to prevent any misconception of your opinions. Events occurred after I wrote you wholly unexpected to me. Mr. [John A.] Stuart the Sen[io]r Editor of the Mercury has not been in Charleston, nor connected in any way with politics, so much as even to write a line for his paper for 14 months, until he suddenly threw off his inaction & with ["out" *interlined*] consultation that I can learn with any one out of the small circle in Beaufort, wrote that fiery Editorial which has caused so much excitement everywhere. I knew he was excited himself but I had no idea he would throw himself into such a position. Mr. [John M.] Clapp did not agree with him & felt fettered & embarrassed, but I fear even he now feels himself called on to stand up to the lead. In Charleston the effect was at one moment alarming—it produced in the old Union men a disposition to renew the old issues. Some of them thought ["it" *interlined*] a most favorable opportunity to force us from our State Rights principles & drive us either to a recantation or into a minority. They wished to join issue with the Mercury's leader & Mr. [Robert Barnwell] Rhett & cut them off & so weaken us who were left that if at any time hereafter we proposed to put the State on her sovereignty, that we would be unable to move. Col. [Christopher G.] Memminger's terms were 1. to join issue with Rhett & his friends & make his proposition a question of union or Disunion. 2d. That we should pledge ourselves that we would not under any circumstances make any move to put the State in action against the Tariff of 1842 during the whole term of the next Legislature. A public meeting was absolutely necessary, for either, he & those he could influence would take steps to bring the public mind to these points, or we must anticipate him. We had ascertained his views in a consultation of a part of our active men & as he would not recede & we could not concur with him, we took the lead & had our meeting & passed the Resolutions you have seen. So far I have heard no objections to our course & am in great hopes they will be satisfactory to allmost all our friends & go far to prevent any further divisions or to render them if inevitable less dangerous to the Union & good feeling of our Party. We so timed our proceedings as to send them to the great Macon [Ga., Democratic] meeting, which the state of my health & private affairs prevented my attending.

I have rec[eive]d letters from Mr. [James A.] Seddon [of Va.] & from [John H.] Howard of Georgia imploring us to turn aside the movements for State action. They said the measures proposed in South Carolina, were embarrassing them exceedingly & seemed to be exceeding apprehensive that we would cause their defeat in Va. & Ge[orgi]a. I hope they will be relieved by our Resolutions. I wrote to both to Seddon particularly & requested him to get Mr. [Thomas] Ritchie to notice & give our proceedings such an interpretation as would place us right before the Party.

I am very much obliged to you for the attention you gave my request about the weights & measures & also about the Russian process for the gold working. The latter, you say, if you obtain, you will send Dr. [William H.] Ellet [Professor in the South Carolina College]. If you will send it to me I will prefer it. The arrangement was made for that course with the Doct[o]r.

I found it impossible to go to Nashville & finding [Francis W.] Pickens was not going, I went up to the Augusta Barbacue on the 5 Aug[us]t to meet him to urge him to change his mind. I succeeded, but I fear he was too late after all for that meeting, as he was delayed two days at Madison in Georgia. Had it not been for that object I w[oul]d have staid away from Augusta & gone to Macon. My trip to Augusta nearly cost me an attack of fever & put it out of my power to risk going to Macon. I hope that our friends had there a good meeting. They expected much good to result from it. I was in Augusta on the 21st & found more confidence & hope in our friends.

They are daily getting in better spirits. The prospect for carrying Georgia I think *decidedly good.* The canvass is very active & the Whigs are put at no little disadvantage by their meeting at Madison & their openly espousing the Tariff. Col. Howard thinks our party will triumph.

I think it not improbable I shall go up to Greenville in a day or two & if I do & learn any thing of interest I will write. Yo[u]rs very truly, F.H. Elmore.

ALS in ScCleA; PEx in Jameson, ed., *Correspondence,* pp. 967–968. NOTE: The Charleston *Mercury,* August 21, 1844, p. 2, gives a full account of the proceedings, report, and resolutions of the Charleston mass meeting organized by a "Committee of 80" and addressed by Elmore. One of the resolutions adopted deprecated "as a great calamity any division and conflict amongst our brethren in this State" and called upon citizens "to forbear at present to resort to the sovereign action of the State to redress our grievances." Elmore, James Hamilton [Jr.], H[enry] Bailey, and James S. Rhett were elected delegates to a mass Democratic meeting to be held in Macon during August 22–23.

From GEO[RGE] W[ILLIA]M GORDON

Consulate of the United States
Rio de Janeiro
26th, August 1844

Sir, The object of this is to present to you, Captain P.C. Dumas, late of the Brig "Cyrus" of New Orleans.

Captain Dumas arrived at this port about the 1st of the present month from Cabinda in Africa, and came before me, as Consul of the United States, and made affidavit, that while lying at Cabinda, on the 2d day of June last, his vessel, the Brig "Cyrus" was boarded by an officer and boat's crew belonging to H.B.M. Brig of War "Alert," Captain [W.] Bosanquet, who searched his vessel, pulled down from where he had placed it, and trampled upon, the American Flag, forcibly entered his Cabin, broke open his trunk, and seized and carried away his Ship's Papers, and that thereupon he, Captain Dumas, abandoned his vessel to the British Government. And under date of the 22d instant, Captain Dumas entered his solemn Protest at this Consulate, against the said British Brig "Alert," her Commander, and all others whom it may concern—and declared that he now looks to the Government of the United States alone for redress.

Captain Dumas is furnished with copies of his own Affidavit and Protest, and of the depositions of several other witnesses who have appeared before me, and of certificates and other papers in relation to the case—all of which he will lay before you.

And I beg to add that by the next conveyance to the United States, duplicate copies of all the papers in relation to the case in my possession, will be forwarded to the Department. I have the honor to be, Sir, most respectfully, Your Obedient Servant, Geo. Wm. Gordon, Consul, United States.

ALS (No. 6) in DNA, RG 59 (State Department), Consular Despatches, Rio de Janeiro, vol. 7 (T-172:8), received 11/3; LS ("Duplicate") in *ibid.*, vol. 7, received 10/29.

From GEORGE HOUSTON and Others

New Castle [Del.,] Aug[u]st 26, 1844
Sir, Having understood Nathanuel Wolfe Esq[ui]r[e] Marshall for the Derstrict of Delawere would be removed from office—and that Elihu Jefferson is an applicant for that Situation, We the undersigned take great pleasure in saying that Mr. Jefferson, born and raised amoungst us, now resides in the Town of New Castle where the U.S. Courts are held—he is one of our most respectable democrats— has been Sheriff of this County, and is well qualified to discharge the duties of said office and we donot hesitate to say, in our opinion, his appointment would be a popular one and ["as" *interlined*] acc[e]ptable ["as" *canceled*] to the Democratic party as any one in the State. We therefore Respectfully and earnestly recommend his appointment—and we further say that Mr. ["Wolfe" *altered to* "Wolf"] is a voilent whig and is now useing all his influence for Mr. [Henry] Clay and that the interest of the Democratic party requires his Speedy removal. We are Verry Respecfully, Your ob[edien]t Ser[van]ts, George Houston, Giles Lambron, Isaac Grubb, E.B. Rigeston[?], H.G. Chase, J.L.[?] Caldwell, Isaac Grubb, Jr., Israel H. Fols.

[P.S.] The undersigned begs leave to inform the Sec[retar]y of State that the within Signers of this recommendation are respectable members of the Democratic Party. William H. Rogers, Aug. 26th [18]44.

[P.P.S.] I cheerfully endorse Mr. Roger's remark. Geo. Read Riddle [future Senator from Del.].

LS in DNA, RG 59 (State Department), Applications and Recommendations, 1837–1845, Jefferson (M-687:17, frames 219–221).

To WILLIAM R. KING, [U.S. Minister to France]

Department of State
Washington, 26th Aug[us]t 1844

Sir: I have the honor to acknowledge the receipt of your despatch No. 2, dated July 31st and to express my gratification at the result of your conversation with Mr. [F.P.G.] Guizot; especially that part of it which refers to the rumored protest of the French Government, conjointly with that of Great Britain, against the proposed annexation of Texas to the United States. Such a step, had it been taken by France, must have excited unkind feelings, and given to the United States just cause of complaint. The Government of the United States will confidently rely on the assurances of Mr. Guizot, and it is hoped that, neither separately, nor jointly with any other Power, will France adopt a course which would seem so little in accordance with her true interests, or the friendly relations which have so long subsisted between the two countries.

My reply to your first despatch, which was forwarded by the last steamer, renders it unnecessary for me to enlarge on the topics presented in your last. In regard to Mr. Guizot's inquiry respecting a proposed guaranty of the independence of Texas, your reply was well timed and judicious. The settled policy of the United States has been to avoid entering into such guaranties, except in cases of strong necessity. The present case offers no reasons to warrant a deviation from that policy. On the contrary it presents a strong additional reason why it should be adhered to, as such a guaranty would permanently defeat the proposed measure of annexation which both countries seem anxious to advance. A suggestion of the same purport was made to me by the British Minister here, Mr. [Richard] Pakenham, during a casual conversation, soon after I came into office; and he was promptly informed that the Government of the United States could not accede to such a proposition. I am, Sir, respectfully, Your obedient servant, J.C. Calhoun.

LS (No. 6) in DNA, RG 84 (Foreign Posts), France, Instructions; FC in DNA, RG 59 (State Department), Diplomatic Instructions, France, 15:24–25 (M-77: 55); CCEx in DNA, RG 46 (U.S. Senate), 28A–E3; PEx in Senate Document No. 13, 28th Cong., 2nd Sess., p. 3; PEx in *Congressional Globe*, 28th Cong., 2nd Sess., p. 62; PEx in the Washington, D.C., *Globe*, December 23, 1844, p. 2; PEx in the Washington, D.C., *Daily National Intelligencer*, December 24, 1844, p. 2; PEx in the Washington, D.C., *Daily Madisonian*, December 27, 1844, p. 2; PEx in the London, England, *Times*, January 15, 1845, p. 5. NOTE: The copy of this letter transmitted to the Senate, and thus the subsequent printed versions, omitted the last sentence referring to the British Minister.

From Eneas McFaul, Jr., Baltimore, 8/26. He renews his application for appointment to be the U.S. Consul at Laguna, Mexico. He has engaged in mercantile pursuits for years and is interested in establishing a business in Mexico. He is acquainted with "the business of the place" and is devoted to Southern and Democratic interests. Testimonials will be forwarded if necessary. ALS in DNA, RG 59 (State Department), Applications and Recommendations, 1837–1845, McFaul (M-687:21, frames 304–306).

PROTOCOL by R[ichard] Pakenham and J[ohn] C. Calhoun

[Washington, August 26, 1844]
On the 26th of August 1844 the second conference was held between the respective Plenipotentiaries at the office of the Secretary of State.

The British Plenipotentiary offered a Paper containing a proposal for adjusting the conflicting claims of the two Countries. The American Plenipotentiary declined the proposal. Some remarks followed in reference to the claims of the two Countries to the Territory, when it became apparent that a more full understanding of their respective views in reference to them was necessary at this stage, in order to facilitate future proceedings. It was accordingly agreed that written statements containing their views, should be presented before any further attempt should be made to adjust them.

It was also agreed that the American Plenipotentiary should present a statement at the next conference; and that he should inform the British Plenipotentiary when he was prepared to hold it. J.C. Calhoun, R. Pakenham.

[Enclosure]
Whereas the Proposals made on both sides, in the course of the last negotiation, had been mutually declined, Her Majesty's Government were prepared, in addition to what had already been offered on the part of Great Britain, and in proof of their earnest desire to arrive at an arrangement suitable to the interests, and wishes of both Parties, to undertake to make free to the United States, any Port, or Ports, which the United States Government might desire, either on the Mainland, or on Van-Couver's Island, South of Latitude 49°. R.P.

DS with En in DNA, RG 59 (State Department), Notes from Foreign Legations, Great Britain, vol. 22 (M-50:22); PC with En in the Washington, D.C., *Daily*

National Intelligencer, December 12, 1845, p. 1; PC with En in *Niles' National Register*, vol. LXIX, no. 17 (December 27, 1845), p. 261; PC with En in Senate Document No. 1, 29th Cong., 1st Sess., pp. 143–144; PC with En in House Document No. 2, 29th Cong., 1st Sess., pp. 143–144; PC with En in Crallé, ed., *Works*, 5:422–424.

From J[OHN] & J[OSIAH] STARLING

Portland [Maine,] August 26th 1844

Sir, We beg leave to lay before you the enclosed letter [of 8/19] from our Consul at Halifax [T.B. Livingston], and earnestly beg for your interference to see justice done us.

We are fishermen, and have but little property, and are wholly unable to pay the sum the Consul says is required, by the Court, to be secured ["secured" *canceled*], before we are permitted to have a trial of our Vessel.

Our Vessel was fifteen miles from any land, when she was seized; and, if the British construction of the Treaty is right, then no American can fish in the Bay of Fundy, even if he is fifty miles from any shore.

As well might we draw a line from Cape Florida to Cape Cod and say that meant three "marine miles from our shore" between these Capes.

It appears, from the Consul[']s letter, to be the determination of the English Government to condemn the Vessel, and all our Vessels, found within "three marine miles" of a line drawn from Cape to Cape. Our Vessel had two hundred and fifty quintals of Fish on board, and the Vessel was valuable to us, and to her Crew, who were turned on shore, without friends or means to help them home.

It appears that this seizure is made to settle the disputed construction of the Treaty, and we most confidently rely on the strong arm of our Government to defend and protect us in our honestly acquired property and peaceful industry. With great respect, We are, Sir, Your most Obedient Servants, J. & J. Starling.

LS with Ens in DNA, RG 59 (State Department), Consular Despatches, Halifax, vol. 5 (T-469:5); CC with Ens in DNA, RG 84 (Foreign Posts), Great Britain, Instructions, 8:407–414.

From Ro[bert] Tyler

No. 34, 7th Street [Philadelphia?]
[*ca.* August 26?, 1844]

My dear Sir, The enclosed letters of recommendation deserve the highest consideration. Mr. [Gabriel G.] Fleurot will himself explain to you the reasons of his application. The present incumbent [U.S. Consul in Martinique, Philip A. de Creny] it is very generally believed wishes to return home. I understand that the incumbent of this office has been accused of swindling, in truth that evidence can be adduced, going to establish this fact. I should be pleased if Mr. Fleurot, who seems an intelligent gentleman[,] could be gratified with this appointm[en]t. With respect Y[ou]r Ob[edien]t S[ervan]t, Ro. Tyler.

ALS with Ens in DNA, RG 59 (State Department), Applications and Recommendations, 1853–1861, Fleurot (M-967:17, frames 135–142). Note: Enclosed were letters of D[a]n[iel] Robertson to Calhoun, 8/24/1844, and Geo[rge] E. Watness & Co. and others to Calhoun, *ca.* 8/24/1844.

From C[aleb] Cushing

United States Brig Perry
August 27th 1844

Sir: I have the honor to inform you that I embarked at Macao this day, on board the United States Brig Perry, with the views expressed in my despatch of the 24th instant, numbered ninety one.

It is due to the Governor of Macao to state that, on occasion of my departure, the usual salute was fired by the Fort of S. Francisco.

Indeed, the authorities of Macao have testified a sincere disposition to treat the United States with hearty good will, on all occasions, during my residence at Macao. Reference is made to this subject in the correspondence communicated by my despatch of the 24th instant, numbered ninety two.

In this disposition, the Portuguese authorities at Macao have allowed all the stores needed for the squadron to be landed free of duty, and with other conditions as to storage & so forth convenient to Commodore [Foxhall A.] Parker.

Macao is, and will probably long continue to be, the residence of many Americans, especially of those, who, being in business at Canton, have families in China; for the climate of Macao is unexceptionably salubrious, which gives it an advantage over Hong-kong as a place of residence, the latter being very unhealthy; and although the residence of foreign ladies at Canton is no longer prohibited as formerly, and is indeed protected by the English & American Treaties, and several American ladies have resided there more or less of late, yet the prejudices of the Chinese, the limited space occupied by foreigners at Canton, and the frequency of disturbances there, all combine to render it not an agreeable place of abode, in comparison with Macao.

Under these circumstances, as well as from considerations of commerce, Americans resort to Macao in such numbers, as to cause it to be an object of importance in their behalf to maintain a good understanding with the Portuguese authorities; which, on the other hand, are impelled to encourage the resort of Americans, by the accessions these bring to the population, commerce, and prosperity of Macao.

I shall, hereafter, address to the Department a communication on the special subject of the political & commercial condition of Macao. I am Your ob[edien]t s⌊er⌋v⌊an]t, C. Cushing.

ALS (No. 95) in DNA, RG 59 (State Department), Diplomatic Despatches, China, vol. 2 (M-92:3), received 1/2/1845.

From LUCY MARIA MURPHY

City of Chillicothe [Ohio,] Aug. 27/44

The official document together with your letter, were duly received, containing the melancholy intelligence, of my beloved husband[']s [William S. Murphy's] demise. I am overwhelmed with greif [sic]. Thus have I been suddenly deprived, of one of the kindest, and most affectionate husbands, & six children, of one of the kindest of fathers. By the misterious Providence of God, just as his labours had closed in a foreign land, and we were hourly expecting him home.

He possessed a mind, "that was cast in nature's finest mould," with sensibility, & feelings, the most exquisite, & tender. How ardently he loved his country, and how faithfully, he executed the trusts committed, to his charge your honourable self, can render a testimonial.

Nothing remains for me now, but to implore the sustaining grace of God, to support me under this heavy bereavement, and only in *this*, & the healing influence of time, do I expect to find any releif [sic].

My son desires me to tender you, his highest regard, for affording him the opportunity, of seeing once more his beloved parent, and giving him an evidence, that he would be able to occupy his place, when he was no more.

I would present ["him" *interlined*] to your consideration, & if you can in your official Station, aid him, you will have the gratitude & pray[ers] of an afflicted Widow, & six fatherless children.

Enclosed, is a letter for Gen[era]l [Tilghman A.] Howard, making special enquiry, as to all the particulars of my late husband[']s illness, & what disposition was made of his effects. If you can obtain any information relative to it, or give us any advice, how to proceed in the settlement of his account, with the Treasury department, I shall feel truly thankful.

The enclosed letter, I would wish forwarded in a despatch, as the most safe & expeditious way.

And in conclusion, permit me to return my thanks, for your simpathizing regard. I trust the day is not far distant, when this nation, will award you that place, which your transcendant genius, & talent demand.

With sentiments of the highest regard, & in the depths of affliction, I subscribe myself truly yours, Lucy Maria Murphy.

ALS in DNA, RG 59 (State Department), Accounting Records: Miscellaneous Letters Received. NOTE: A Clerk's EU reads "The legal representative of Gen. Murphy will have to present an account and vouchers to the Fifth Auditor who will adjust it and the balance due, if any will be paid at the Treasury." Another Clerk's EU indicates this letter was answered on 9/2.

From S[tephen] P[leasonton], Fifth Auditor of the Treasury, 8/-27/"1845" [*sic;* 1844]. Pleasonton comments on [William] Wilkins's letter of 8/22 to Calhoun [*not found*], claiming compensation for office rent while he was U.S. Minister to Russia. Secretary of State [John] Forsyth disallowed this claim in 1836. More recently Secretary [Abel P.] Upshur also "rejected it on the ground that such allowance was not usual at the time Mr. Wilkins['s] account was settled and on the further ground that it would be improper to open an account after it was settled." FC in DNA, RG 217 (General Accounting Office), Fifth Auditor: Letters Sent, 5:159.

To [Certain U.S. MINISTERS and CHARGÉS D'AFFAIRES]

Department of State
Washington, August 27, 1844

Sir, I enclose herewith a copy of a Despatch [of 8/12] recently addressed by this Department to Mr. [William R.] King our Minister at Paris; and respectfully call your attention to its contents. It presents the views of our Government on the important subject of which it treats; and occasions may occur in your intercourse or correspondence where, with prudence and discretion, they may be used to advantage in vindicating the character and conduct, and sustaining the policy of the United States in reference to Mexico and Texas. I am Sir Your Obedient Servant, J.C. Calhoun.

LS with En in DNA, RG 84 (Foreign Posts), Germany, Instructions, 1:317–345. NOTE: Copies of this letter were sent to Edward Everett, Henry Wheaton, Washington Irving, Charles S. Todd, Daniel Jenifer, Henry A. Wise, Ministers to Great Britain, Prussia, Spain, Russia, Austria, and Brazil; and to Christopher Hughes and Thomas G. Clemson, Chargés d'Affaires to the Netherlands and Belgium, respectively. LS and FC versions can be found in DNA, RG 84 (Foreign Posts), in various files; FC versions are in DNA, RG 59 (State Department), Diplomatic Instructions, in several files. The version transcribed above is that sent to Henry Wheaton at Berlin. Edward Everett's copy concludes with the following paragraph: "You will also receive enclosed Packages addressed to our Ministers at the Hague, Berlin, St. Petersburg and Madrid, which I would thank you to cause to be forwarded to them by the first safe *private* medium which may offer." LS (No. 104) in DNA, RG 84 (Foreign Posts), Great Britain, Instructions, 8:353–403, received 9/2; FC in DNA, RG 59 (State Department), Diplomatic Instructions, Great Britain, 15:224 (M-77:74).

From W[illiam] W[ilkins, Secretary of War], 8/27. "I have the honor to lay before you" a letter received at the War Department from Brig. Gen. Z[achary] Taylor dated 8/9, with enclosed documents from the Texas government [concerning the announced renewal of hostilities by Mexico against Texas]. FC in DNA, RG 107 (Secretary of War), Letters Sent Relating to Military Affairs, 1800–1861, 25:384 (M-6:25).

To John B. Williams, U.S. Consul, Bay of Islands, [New Zealand], 8/27. Upon reconsidering Williams's request to move his post from Bay of Islands to Auckland, Calhoun states that Williams will not have to resign one commission and be issued another in order to relocate. If Williams thinks it advisable he is authorized to appoint a

Commercial Agent at Bay of Islands. Calhoun also encloses a certificate of appointment for a Commercial Agent for the Fiji Islands and with it a strong recommendation by President [John Tyler] of David Whippy for the post. FC in DNA, RG 59 (State Department), Consular Instructions, 11:271–272.

To William M. Blackford, [U.S. Minister to New Granada], 8/28. Calhoun states that Blackford's request for a leave of absence has been granted. "If it should be convenient, you may take passage in the United States brig Oregon, which has been ordered by the Navy Department to remain at Carthagena until your wishes upon the subject shall be known to her commander." FC (No. 20) in DNA, RG 59 (State Department), Diplomatic Instructions, Colombia, 15:90 (M-77:44); CC in DNA, RG 84 (Foreign Posts), Colombia, Despatches, vol. B4.

To J[ohn] Murphy, U.S. Consul, Cork, [Ireland], 8/28. Murphy's recent despatches and correspondence, with the exception of a letter dated 5/3, have arrived at the State Dept. FC in DNA, RG 59 (State Department), Consular Instructions, 12:93.

From WILSON SHANNON

Legation of the U.S. of A.
Mexico [City], August 28, 1844

Sir, I avail myself of this opportunity to inform you that I arrived in this city on the evening of the 26th Inst. after a long and tedious journey and after having been rob[b]ed and plundered on the road by an armed banditti of all the property I had about my person. This outrage was commit[t]ed in broad day light, on the public high way and within two miles of the City of Puebla, and while traveling not only under the implied but express promise of the public authorities that I should receive ample protection on my way to this city.

I have not yet been presented to the President [Santa Anna]. I will write you at large in a few days and give you all the information in my power in relation to matters here. Yours with great respect and esteem, Wilson Shannon.

ALS in DNA, RG 59 (State Department), Diplomatic Despatches, Mexico, vol. 12 (M-97:13), received 9/28; FC in DNA, RG 84 (Foreign Posts), Mexico, Despatches (C3.9).

From H[ENRY] WHEATON

Paris, 28 Aug. 1844

My dear Sir, I have the pleasure to acknowledge the recei[p]t of your Letter respecting the negotiations with the Hanse Towns & Denmark for a revision of the Reciprocity treaties of Commerce & Navigation & on the question of the [Danish] Sound Duties. I very cheerfully acquiesce in your views as to the inexpediency of our moving in those matters at present, & had I been aware of what had already occurred at Washington when I wrote should not have proposed it for consideration.

I am ["about to" *canceled*] availing myself of an interruption of business, & the absence of the Court & corps diplomatique to make a short excursion to France, where my family have been residing for some time past. As I shall always be within a distance of 5 days journey from my Post, & as my despatches will be regularly sent to me here from London, no inconvenience will occur to the affairs of the Legation by a short absence. I left no business behind me, & shall always hold myself in readiness to return should any thing occur to render my presence necessary. But as my stay here may possibly be protracted some what longer than I now intend, I beg leave to suggest the expediency of sending me a *leave of absence*, in case you deem it necessary in point of form, it being always understood that I shall return to Berlin whenever my presence there is necessary.

Enclosed is a Certificate [of 8/13] from a Mr. [Frederick] Diergardt, ["at"(?) *canceled*] a very respectable silk manufacturer at Viersen in the Prussian Rhine Province, well known to me, respecting one of the various imputations against Mr. [Louis] Mark, which Mr. M[ark] has sent to me with a request that I would transmit it to you. I have been very much grieved & mortified to find that he should have ["given" *interlined*] any cause for such dark suspicions & charges against his character, but as I have already communicated with Mr. [Francis] Markoe respecting his case, I forbear from any comment upon it at present, not doubting that full justice will be done him, in case he should be able to explain the more serious charge against him, & not wishing to screen him from the consequences of his own misconduct should he ultimately forfeit the confidence which has been reposed in him in consequence of my recommendation. I am, my dear Sir, ever truly, your faithful friend, H. Wheaton.

ALS with En in ScCleA. NOTE: The enclosed letter contradicts the charge published in newspapers in the U.S. that Mark had sought a bribe from German merchants to promote ratification of the Zollverein treaty by the U.S.

From R[euben] G. Beasley, [U.S. Consul], Havre, 8/29. "I transmit herewith a notice published on the Stade duties levied by the King of Hanover on the Commerce which is carried on with Germany & Prussia through his dominions. The view thus taken by the English journals is probably correct, and will serve as a guide in case our Government should judge it to be expedient to enquire into, and relieve our Commerce in that quarter from this charge upon it. This tax has probably been long submitted to by all nations like the [Danish] Sound dues." LS (No. 213) with En in DNA, RG 59 (State Department), Consular Despatches, Havre, vol. 4 (T-212:4), received 9/19.

To A[NNA] M[ARIA CALHOUN] CLEMSON, [Brussels?]

State Dept., 29th Aug[us]t 1844

My dear daughter, I suppose you will be surprised to learn by the date of my letter, that I am still at Washington, so late in the month of August; and still more so, to hear, that I shall not be able to leave probably 'till the mid[d]le of next month. I found, after I had prepared the dispatches, which were necessary before I left, that I could not postpone the Oregon question, 'till after my return from home, as I expected when you left, and I accordingly entered on that difficult subject ["about a week since" *interlined*]. Very little progress has yet been made, and I fear it will detain me here the greater part of the month of September.

In consequence of my being expected at home ere this, I have not heard from there since the 16th Inst. They were all well at that time. There is nothing new since I wrote you last. The elections are going on with great zeal, & the prospect is, that [James K.] Polk will be elected.

My own health is good; which I am rather surprised, at considering how much I have to do, and how anxious I am to return home.

I have heard nothing of Patrick [Calhoun] & John [C. Calhoun, Jr.] for a long time.

You will, my dear daughter, long ere you have received this, have arrived at Havre, after, I hope, a safe & pleasant voyage, & seen Paris with all its curiosities & wonder. I shall be exceedingly anxious to hear from you & to know what impression France & Paris have made on you. I will expect to hear from you often & fully; and you must give me your impressions, just as you feel them.

I hope you & Mr. [Thomas G.] Clemson & the children [John Calhoun Clemson and Floride Elizabeth Clemson] stood the ["journey" *canceled and* "voyage" *interlined*] well, and that you are all in fine health & sperits. Say to Mr. Clemson, I have heard nothing about his place, & that I remitted his check to John [Ewing] Bonneau & am informed by him, that he has taken up his note in bank, the bank making the discount, or rather taking off the interest, that would be be [*sic*] due on it.

You must excuse this short & hasty letter. I write in the midest of continued inter[r]uption, and it is the last day & last hour by which it can go by the steamer.

May the blessings of a Kind Providence rest on you all. Kiss the dear children for their Grandfather. Your affectionate father, J.C. Calhoun.

ALS in ScCleA.

From SETH SWEETSER

United States Consulate
Guayaquil, 29 August 1844
Sir, Having received from his Excellency the Minister of Foreign Affairs at Quito a letter of which the following is a translation[:]

"Republic of Ecuador"
Foreign Office, Quito, 27 May 1844
Sir, It is with pleasure this government are informed of your determination to visit the Capital with the object of settling the Claims of the Citizens of the U.S. relative to the Josephine and the Ranger.

I can assure you that this business shall be brought to a settlement in a manner satisfactory.

Meantime waiting the pleasure of seeing you I subscribe myself with great regard Your obed[ien]t Serv[an]t, signed Benigno Malo. Seth Sweetser Esq[ui]re &ca &ca &ca.

And having in my possession thro' the Department of State at Washington, all the public and private documents relative to our Claims on the Ecuador, in the case of the Josephine and the Ranger, I deem it my duty to go up to Quito the capital of this Country, to carry out the views of our government; And to this end, I have drawn on the Department of State, at Sixty days after sight for Five hundred dollars in favor of Ja[me]s H. Causten Esq. or order for and on account of disbursements and expences attendant on so long and tedious a journey across the Chimborazo [mountains] at this inclement season of the year.

Waiting the needful instructions from the Department, and your acceptance of the enclosed, I have the honor to be, with renewed assurances of my high consideration Your obed[ien]t Serv[an]t, signed Seth Sweetser.

CC in DNA, RG 59 (State Department), Consular Despatches, Guayaquil, vol. 1 (T-209:1), received 1/2/1845.

To S[tephen] H. Weems, U.S. Consul, Guatemala, 8/29. With regard to Weems's suggestion that the U.S. establish a Diplomatic Agency at Guatemala, Calhoun informs Weems that it is thought inexpedient to do so at this time. However, Weems is requested to send a full report on the political, commercial, and social institutions of Guatemala in order that the matter may be considered with the best possible information at hand. FC in DNA, RG 59 (State Department), Consular Instructions, 11:272–273.

From W[illia]m Wilkins, Sec[retar]y of War

War Department, August 29th 1844
Sir; I have given my attention to the proposition upon which we conversed yesterday, and which is made the subject of the letter of the date of the 24th inst. addressed to you by Mr. [Isaac] Van Zandt, the Chargé d'Affair[e]s of the Republic of Texas, and now have the honor to say to you.

That, two unsuccessful attempts have been made by our Government, one in the spring and the other in the fall of last year, at the instance of the Texian authorities to negotiate in conjunction with them and form a Treaty with the Cumanche and other Indians residing upon the limits of Texas.

The character of those Tribes, and their wild and roaming habits do not encourage the hope that any renewed attempts at negotiation will be more successful than those hitherto made. Still, Sir, if the

Foreign Relations, or any diplomatic considerations may render, in your opinion, another effort to be necessary or politic, I shall promptly carry out your wish by directing all the appropriate military arrangements.

Col. [Pierce M.] Butler, the Agent of the Cherokees, is at present absent from his post in South Carolina.

Should the proposed measure be adopted, I would endeavor to execute it by constituting the Captain, to whom the command of the Cavalry escort would be given, the Agent or Commissioner to join in the negotiation on behalf of our Government.

The Head Quarters of the First Regiment of Dragoons is at Fort Leavenworth on the Missouri River in the 2d Military Department commanded by [Bvt.] Brig. Gen. [Mathew] Arbuckle.

Two Companies of it are stationed at Fort Gibson, on the Arkansas river, and one company at Fort Washitau near Red River [in the U.S. Indian Territory].

Capt. [Nathan] Boone commands one of those companies at Fort Gibson, and might, probably, be selected as a fit person to execute the purpose you have in view.

I shall wait to be informed of your wish. I return Mr. Van Zandt's letter. I have the honor to be, Sir, With high respect, your ob[edien]t ser[van]t, Wm. Wilkins, Sec[retar]y of War.

LS in DNA, RG 59 (State Department), Miscellaneous Letters (M-179:105, frames 282–283); FC in DNA, RG 107 (Secretary of War), Letters Sent Relating to Military Affairs, 1800–1861, 25:388–389 (M-6:25).

To W[illia]m Wilkins, Secretary of War

Department of State
Washington, Aug[us]t 29th 1844

Sir: I have the honor to acknowledge the receipt of your note of this date referring to our conversation of yesterday in relation to the suggestions contained in the letter of Mr. [Isaac] Van Zandt addressed to this Department some days since.

In reply, I can only repeat to you, what I said on yesterday, that, upon laying the letter of Mr. Van Zandt before the President [John Tyler], he expressed a wish that some Indian Agent or officer of the United States, should be ordered, with a detachment of Dragoons, to attend the proposed meeting of the Texan Commissioners and Cumanche Indians for the purpose of ascertaining whether it is practicable to secure by negotiation, friendly relations with that Tribe. I have the honor to be, with high respect, Sir, Your ob[edien]t Serv[an]t, J.C. Calhoun.

LS in DNA, RG 107 (Secretary of War), Letters Received, Registered Series, 1801–1860, S-574 (M-221:134); PC in Senate Document No. 14, 32nd Cong., 2nd Sess., pp. 129–130.

From Woolsey & Woolsey, New York [City], 8/29. They enclose an invoice for $23.92 for the barrel of crushed sugar ordered by Calhoun on 8/22. As directed, they have drawn on D. Thompson, Cashier of the Bank of America, for the amount. LS with En in ScU-SC, John C. Calhoun Papers. (Found with the above documents is the draft mentioned, which has been endorsed by Thompson to R[ichard] Smith, "Cash[ie]r," [Washington].)

From HIRAM CUMMING

Washington, Aug[u]st 30th/44

Respected Sir, As you will perceive by the Prospectus enclosed I am about establishing a new Democratic paper at Baltimore having been earnestly solicited so to do by several leading democrats of that city which with the Empire State Democrat which will remain under my control will zealously support you for the presidency in 1848 should you be a candidate for that distinguished office at that time. If you are sufficiently acquainted with my character to warrant you in giving me a letter to some of your friends in that place your favor will be kindly appreciated and if ever in my power duly reciprocated[.] With great respect I remain your very obedient Servant, Hiram Cumming.

P.S. Since writing the foregoing ["I" *canceled*] Gen. Tyson [*sic*; Nathan Towson] called on me with whom I have had a conversation in regard to the campaingn of 1848 and should you wish any further knowledge of me I refer you to him[.] Yours &c, H. Cumming.

ALS with En in ScCleA. NOTE: Enclosed is a prospectus for a newspaper called *The Maryland Democrat and Baltimore Daily Advertiser,* to be published daily and weekly in support of the acquisition of Texas and the "great principles of the Democratic creed."

Cha[rle]s H. Haswell, Cold Spring, Putnam County, N.Y., to John Y. Mason, Secretary of the Navy, 8/30. "I have just been advised of the receipt of an order by a friend of mine from the Mexican Government, for 70 24 pounder & 15 each 8 & 10 inch Guns (100 in all) & 27000 shot." An AEI by Mason reads "Resp[ectfull]y referred to Sec[re]t[ar]y of State for perusal. J.Y.M." ALS in ScCleA.

From S[TEPHEN] H. PRESTON

Marshall Michigan, August 30th 1844
Dear Sir, Your letter of the 16th instant [*not found*], enclosing to me the application for a diplomatic appointment was duly received. Here, perhaps all further correspondence ought to end, since you give very little encouragement in regard to obtaining an office in either of the departments, and add "I would not advice [*sic*] any friend who can support himself respectably by his own means or exertions to look to office." While I behold thousands who are rich seeking office and resorting to every species of chicanery to obtain it I cannot persuade myself to believe that in my present situation domestically and pecuniarily I shall be considered impertinent in offering my services to my country in some suitable capacity. And if I am left to choose in what capacity I most desire, it is employment in the diplomatic corps. As a citizen of Michigan, where I have resided ever since & before it was admitted into the Union, I likewise, with a due respect for the doctrine of *State Rights* as well in the distribution of offices as in other matters cannot believe myself impertinent, since the State has no citizens employed either at Washington or in the diplomatic corps and let it be understood that during the entire service of Gen. [Lewis] Cass in the War dept. & as Minister to France he hailed from Ohio. I recently saw a statistical table of the distribution of the offices among the several States in the National Intelligencer of the 20th of Aug. which convinces me to renew the application, especially since I have been recommended by a strong petition of my neighbors. I do not ask the removal of any incumbant; but the post at Pera & Galata near Constantinople or at Caraccas in Venezuela would suit me. As I said in my former communication, I aspire to nothing higher than Chargé d'Affaires, unless it be Minister resident at Constantinople. I have had free access to the public documents & the 3 vols. on Commercial Regulations in your friend Gen. [Isaac E.] Crary's office and he will inform you of my fitness to disgarge [*sic*] the duties of the office sought.

I am sick of mere politicks & desire to abandon the political arena to others. However that you may know what my principles are, I send you the number of the Expounder, containing the ["constitution of the" *interlined*] democratic association for this Town. Respectfully Your Ob[edien]t Servant, S.H. Preston.

[P.S.] This is my last effort to obtain any thing from this administration & perhaps I ought here to say that I voted the democratic ticket in 1840, never having voted any other.

ALS in DNA, RG 59 (State Department), Applications and Recommendations, 1837–1845, Preston (M-687:26, frames 572–574). NOTE: Stephen H. Preston (1810–1883) was editor of the Marshall *Democratic Expounder* in Calhoun County, Mich.

R[ichard] K. Crallé to E[dward] Stubbs, "Fiscal Agent," [State Department], 8/30. "The Secretary of State finds himself constrained" by a recent act of Congress "to dispense with the further services of the Extra Clerks in the Department, for the present." A few exceptions for work in progress are specified. ALS in DNA, RG 59 (State Department), Miscellaneous Letters from Congressional Committees, 1801–1877.

From ROBERT I. ALEXANDER and Others

St. Clairsville O[hio], Aug. 31, 1844

Dear Sir, On the 19th of this month the whigs held a mass meeting in this place, and among others, were addressed by the Hon. Thomas Ewing of this State, who, in reference to yourself, made in substance, the following statement—"that John C. Calhoun had in his letter to [Richard] Pakenham laid down this monstrous proposition[,] *that the true or natural condition of the labouring portion of the community was that of Slavery.* It is true (Mr. Ewing continued) that Mr. Calhoun in that letter was speaking of the black population of the South; but I have often, on the floor of the Senate, heard him lay down the broad and general position *that the best and most natural condition of the labouring community, was that of Slavery.*"

Not believing that you ever did on the floor of the Senate or elsewhere utter any such sentiment, nor that you ever entertained such, we have deemed it proper to address you this note, so that you may, if you consider it of sufficient importance, correct the error in a public manner, by a letter to us on that subject.

Some of us heard Mr. Ewing on the occasion alluded to, and we suppose that he has made the same statement in various parts of the State. With great respect, yours, &c., Robert I. Alexander, A. Patton, E.G. Bryson, John C. Tidball, William P. Simpson, William Wilkins, J.M. Mitchell, James Wishart.

LS in ScCleA; PC in the Charleston, S.C., *Southern Patriot,* October 1, 1844, p. 2; PC in the Washington, D.C., *Daily Madisonian,* October 5, 1844, p. 2; PC in the Edgefield, S.C., *Advertiser,* October 9, 1844, p. 2; PC in the Pendleton, S.C., *Messenger,* October 11, 1844, p. 3. NOTE: The ms. of this letter is in Alexander's hand.

From Geo[rge] M. Bibb, Secretary of the Treasury, 8/31. In response to Calhoun's communication in relation to the petition of Joseph Carroll and others, he states that "No act of the Congress of the United States has provided for compensation in such cases." ALS in DNA, RG 59 (State Department), Petitions for Pardon, Tyler Administration, Unnumbered Cases; FC in DNA, RG 56 (Secretary of the Treasury), Letters to Cabinet and Bureau Officers, Series B, 1842–1847, 4:437.

To R[OBERT] B. CAMPBELL, U.S. Consul, Havana

Department of State
Washington, Aug[us]t 31st 1844

Sir, In consequence of the absence from his post of [Thomas M. Rodney] the U.S. Consul for Matanzas, I transmit to you a copy of a letter received at the Department from [Franklin Gage] our Consul at Cardenas, dated the 15th instant in relation to the outrages committed upon our Citizens now imprisoned at Matanzas.

These cases have formed the subject of several communications from the Department to you & other Consuls of the U.S. in Cuba. In those communications you were instructed to interpose with the Authorities, in the most urgent manner, in behalf of the unfortunate persons arrested, and one of the most especial objects in directing such interposition was to cause a speedy and fair trial to be given them. In this, the Government of the United States has been greatly disappointed: but it is the President's determination to see that our fellow Citizens who have been so long incarcerated, apparently upon the most frivolous grounds, shall receive that protection to which they are entitled, and which this Government is bound to extend to them.

He therefore directs me to instruct you to express to the proper authorities the surprise occasioned by the unwarrantable procrastination of the trial of these individuals, and to demand in the name of the Government of the United States, that their cases shall be immediately brought before the proper tribunal and that no delay may be made in the disposition of them further than a fair and impartial trial may render necessary.

In communicating to the authorities the substance of this letter, which you will lose no time in doing, you will request, but not in a manner which may be calculated to cause offence, a prompt answer to the demand it conveys. This you will of course, transmit to the Department without delay. I am &c, J.C. Calhoun.

FC in DNA, RG 59 (State Department), Consular Instructions, 10:263–264.

To Philip A. De Creny, U.S. C[onsul], St. Pierre, Martinique, 8/31. Calhoun notifies De Creny that Gabriel G. Fleurot has been appointed to succeed him as U.S. Consul at St. Pierre. De Creny is to surrender to Fleurot the archives and records of the Consulate. FC in DNA, RG 59 (State Department), Consular Instructions, 12:94.

From HENRY F. FISH

Salisbury, Litchfield Co[unty]
Conn: 31 August 1844

Sir, Some two months gone, I had the honor to present to you letters from Judge [Samuel] Church, and Prof: [Benjamin] Silliman, commending me to your favorable notice, as competent to discharge the duties of a Consul, should any vacancy exist.

During my stay in Washington, I was so far honored by your confidence, as to have the Consulship at Maracaibo offered to me, but it resulted, that no vacancy did really exist.

When I took my leave of you soon after, you kindly remarked to me, that my petition was on file in the Department, and that it would receive your favorable notice, in event of any vacancy.

Emboldened, Sir, by these evidences of your good intentions toward me, and learning that the Consulship at Galveston, Texas, is vacant, I respectfully solicit from you this appointment; always deferring, however, to such considerations of policy or public service, as may induce a decision adverse to this, my humble request. With profound respect, Your Very Humble Servant, Henry F. Fish.

ALS in DNA, RG 59 (State Department), Applications and Recommendations, 1837–1845, Fish (M-687:11, frames 280–282). NOTE: An AEU by Calhoun reads "Mr. Fish. See the President about app[ointmen]ts tomorrow."

To Gabriel G. Fleurot, [Norfolk], 8/31. Calhoun notifies Fleurot of his appointment as U.S. Consul at Martinique and sends him documents relevant to the office. Fleurot's exequatur has been applied for in Paris. FC in DNA, RG 59 (State Department), Consular Instructions, 12:93–94.

To Isidore Guillet, Richmond, 8/31. Calhoun notifies Guillet of his appointment as U.S. Commercial Agent at St. Thomas [Virgin Islands] and encloses relevant documents. FC in DNA, RG 59 (State Department), Consular Instructions, 10:264–265.

From W[ILLIA]M IRVING

Newyork [City,] August 31st 1844

Sir, There is now Lying in the Port of Newyork two armed Steam Ships of the Republick of Mexico to be repaired and are now enlisting a Crew for the express object to Aide the invasion of Texas and in fact these two vessele is the life & soul of the expedition and Gen[era]l Santa Anna can not invade Texas without them the Question

I wish to submite to your consideration is if Mexico has not paid the instalments due to the U. States by Treaty has not the Gover[n]ment a right to attach said Vesseles and hold them as Collateral security for the payment, of moneys due the U. States till paid and if so it would end the war of Mexico aga[i]nst Texas. I am Respectful[l]y Yours, Wm. Irving.

ALS in ScCleA.

To William R. King, [Paris], 8/31. "The disposition recently evinced by the Swiss Confederacy to arrest and deliver up to justice the notorious Gerard Koster, could not fail to meet with the President's [John Tyler's] approbation. He has accordingly directed me to instruct you, as I now do, to convey to that Government, through its diplomatic representative in Paris, his high sense of the friendly feeling manifested on that occasion by the Swiss Confederacy towards the Government and People of the United States." LS (No. 7) in DNA, RG 84 (Foreign Posts), France, Instructions; FC in DNA, RG 59 (State Department), Diplomatic Instructions, France, 15:25– 26 (M-77:55).

From WILLIAM R. KING

Legation des Etats Unis
Paris, le 31 August 1844

Sir, Although I have nothing to communicate with regard to American affairs, I cannot let the steamer depart, without presenting some very brief observations upon events which are exciting the public mind in Europe. It is not my design to inform you of what may be read in the newspapers, yet it is not easy to communicate anything besides, for with the publicity that prevails where the press is free, but little escapes the notice of those vigilant sentinels.

The affairs of Marocco & Tahiti have seriously impaired the cordial understanding which but recently subsisted between England and France. The indignation excited in the former country; by the news of the arrest and expulsion of the British Consul was heightened by the language employed by Sir Robert Peel and Lord Aberdeen, just before the adjournment of Parliament, language, especially that of Sir Robert, not characterized by their usual prudence and reserve. On the other hand, the disavowal of the act of Admiral Dupetit Thouars in taking possession of these islands in the Pacific, which was generally attributed here to the demands of England, left the popular mind of France in a very unpropitious ["condition" *canceled*] temper for the concessions required to satisfy the British government. The offensive tone of the English press increased this indisposition, which was yet more aggravated by the jealousy manifested with regard to the designs of the French against Marocco. At this critical juncture, the leading journal in London published some letters from British officers in the Mediterranean, criticizing severely the operations of the French in bombarding Tangiers, and reflecting gratuitously and most unjustly upon the courage and conduct of the Prince de Joinville and the fleet under his command. These ungenerous strictures from such a source have excited the popular mind in this country to the highest pitch, and rendered a satisfactory solution of the Tahiti question more difficult than ever.

Nevertheless I think that an adjustment will be effected. The two governments are sincerely desirous ["of" *canceled*] for the maintenance of peace, and where this is the case, an accommodation is rarely impracticable. England is represented at this court by a mild and discrete man, the brother of the Duke of Wellington. He is sensible of the difficulties of the French government, and does everything in his power, to smooth the path to a reconciliation. Commercial interests, too, which have now a predominating influence upon public policy, demand the preservation of peace. Moreover, the wounded pride of France has been not a little soothed by the signal advantages just achieved by French arms in Marocco, which has improved sensibly the popular temper.

One effect however, must be the result of late events. The cordial understanding, *l'entente cordiale,* which has long since ceased to exist between the two nations is now also interrupted between their governments. They will scarcely continue to harmonize in their European policy, and much less with regard to American questions. That of Texas has almost disappeared from their horizon, having been absorbed by topics of nearer interest and more urgent importance. To annoy or to thwart the United States, the French government will no longer be disposed to follow in the wake of England. Whatever may be the preferences of Mr. [F.P.G.] Guizot, to maintain himself he will be constrained to avoid even the appearance of that subserviency to British policy with which he has been so bitterly reproached and the suspicion of which has hurt him and his government so seriously and deeply in popular estimation. Of this effect the United States will have no reason to complain.

I have the honor to acknowledge the receipt of your despatch No. 3 of the 25th July with its enclosures. The government of Switzerland having through its representative at this court [G. de Tschann], expressed its willingness to comply with my application for the arrest, detention, and ultimate delivery of Gerard Koster, I shall not fail to carry out your instructions by putting myself in prompt communication with that gentleman, for the purpose of negotiating with him a convention for the mutual surrender of criminals, fugitives from justice, with the qualifications and precautions which you prescribe. I have the honor to be very respectfully your obedient servant, William R. King.

LS (No. 3) in DNA, RG 59 (State Department), Diplomatic Despatches, France, vol. 30 (M-34:33), received 9/19.

To Tho[ma]s M. Rodney, U.S. Consul, Matanzas

Department of State
Washington, Aug[us]t 31, 1844

Sir: I transmit to you a copy of a letter received at the Department from [Franklin Gage] the U.S. Consul at Cardenas, dated the 15th inst., in relation to the outrages committed upon our citizens now imprisoned at Matanzas.

These cases have formed the subject of several communications to you from the Dept. In those communications you were instructed to interpose with the authorities, in the most urgent manner, in behalf of the unfortunate persons arrested, and one of the most especial objects of those instructions was to cause a speedy and fair trial to be given them. In this the Govt. of the U.S. has been greatly disappointed; but it is the President's determination to see that our fellow citizens who have been so cruel[l]y and inhumanly incarcerated apparently upon the most frivolous grounds shall receive that protection to which they are entitled & which this Government is bound to extend to them. He therefore directs me to instruct you to express to the proper authorities the surprise occasioned by the unwarrantable procrast[inat]ion of the trial of these individuals, and to demand in the name of the Govt. of the U.S. that their cases shall be immediately brought before the proper tribunal & that no delay may be made in the disposition of them farther than a fair and impartial trial may render necessary.

In communicating to the authorities the substance of this letter, which you will lose no time in doing, you will request, but not in a manner which may be calculated to give offence, a prompt answer to the demand it conveys. This you will of course transmit to the Department without delay. I am &c, J.C. Calhoun.

FC in DNA, RG 59 (State Department), Consular Instructions, 10:262–263.

From JAMES WISHART

St. Clairsville [Ohio,] Aug[us]t 31st [18]44

My Dear Sir, Ex-Secretary [of the Treasury Thomas] Ewing is now stumping ["the" *interlined*] State for the whigs. On the 19th they had a gathering at this place which was a failure. 1840 cannot be repeated. The object of this letter is to inform you of a charge against yourself which is, I presume, intended to be spread far and wide in the north and west. Mr. Ewing stated in substance as I am informed what is contained in the letter [of today's date, from Robert I. Alexander and others] to which my name with others is signed. The whigs ["are" *interlined*] representing you as the democratic party or the pivot on which it turns, with the view to hold you responsible for all the errors either of practice or doctrine held by it. And there is a class of democrats who are pleased to have your name connected with every thing that is unpopular at the north or west, for purposes which I doubt not you understand.

That you do not hold the doctrine attributed to you by Ex Secretary Ewing I feel certain, from the fact that in your reply [of 2/6/-1837] to Mr. [William C.] Rives on the subject of Slavery you said you could not be driven into a defence of the dogmas of Sir David Filmore [*sic*; Sir Richard Filmer]. Your friends here deem the subject to which we have refer[r]ed an important question and if permit[t]ed to go uncontradicted would destroy your ["character" *canceled*] popularity in the free States. We hope therefore that you will give Mr. Ewing such a rebuke as will check the spirit ["of" *interlined*] slander and defamation resorted to by the whigs and their *secret allies* here and elsewhere. With sentiments of true & high Respect, James Wishart.

ALS in ScCleA.

SEPTEMBER 1–15, 1844

◫

The Republic of Texas, independent for eight years by reason of its own valor, had accepted an invitation to treat with the United States for annexation. A treaty had been concluded, but after several months had been rejected by the Senate. Yet everyone knew that the issue of annexation was not dead and would be resumed in a few months when the Presidential election had been decided (in November) and Congress reconvened (in December).

The administration of which Calhoun was the chief officer under the President had extended Texas the invitation of the Union, which had been postponed in its consummation, but was still pending. It was well understood that negotiation with the United States was likely to bring upon Texas renewed military attack from Mexico; indeed hostilities had been sporadic since Texan independence in 1836. What was the moral obligation of the United States in regard to the defense of Texas while annexation was pending? What was the Constitutional power of the President, Congress being out of session, to fulfill any military necessities that might arise?

These difficult questions were taken up by Calhoun in a despatch to the American minister in Mexico City, Wilson Shannon, on September 10. For some time the information received in Washington from many quarters had been pointing toward a renewal of hostilities by Mexico. Possibly it was hoped that a strong despatch might act as a deterrent. Undoubtedly, when its contents were conveyed to the Mexican authorities, it would leave as little room as possible for encouraging doubts on the part of those authorities. "There can be no longer any doubt that Mexico intends to renew the war against Texas, on a large scale; and to carry it on with more than savage ferocity," Calhoun wrote. The President has considered this situation carefully and has arrived at a decision, dictated by honor and humanity, that he will "use all his Constitutional means" in the case of an invasion.

Writing the next day again to Shannon and reviewing the vexing matter of the many claims of Americans against the Mexican government, which had been delayed and disregarded, Calhoun instructed Shannon that in dealing with the Mexican authorities "it is proper that

688

*you should adopt a tone and manner which shall indicate, unequivo-
cally, the fixed determination of the United States to maintain, at all
hazards, their just rights and dignity."* It was the strongest tone that
Calhoun himself had yet taken toward any power during his five
months in the State Department.

In the midst of these matters, the Oregon negotiation went forward. An obviously well-prepared Calhoun, who as always was ready
to do battle for the rights of the Union and any and all parts of it,
delivered an extended statement of the American position on Oregon
to the British Minister on September 3, which was replied to on the
12th. Calhoun even found time on the 13th to write to the American representative in Copenhagen some suggestions about the Danish
Sound Dues, a long-standing and perennial problem in international
relations.

Ⅲ

To Dr. [SAMUEL GEORGE] MORTON, [Philadelphia]

State Dept., Sep[tembe]r 1844
Dear Sir, I am under great obligation to you for your Crania AEgyptiaca, transmitted through Mr. [George R.] Gliddon. It is a subject,
in which I take much interest, as well as whatever relates to Egyptian antiquities.

My engagements have hitherto prevented me from perusing it.
I shall devote my first leasure to it; and expect to derive much information & pleasure from it.

In a casual conversation with the President [John Tyler], a short
time since, the subject turned on ancient Egypt. I alluded to your
work, among other things. He expressed much curiosity on the subject, & I am sure you would oblige him much, if you should have a
spare volume, by transmitting it to him. I feel assured you will excuse me for making the suggestion. With great respect yours truly,
J.C. Calhoun.

ALS in ScU-SC, John C. Calhoun Papers. NOTE: Morton wrote to Calhoun on
[*ca.* May 9, 1844] transmitting a copy of his *Crania Aegyptiaca* (see *The Papers
of John C. Calhoun,* 18:463).

From Jonathan Elliot, Washington, 9/2. He proposed to [Abel P.] Upshur, late Secretary of State, that Elliot publish "an edition of the American Diplomatic Code, bringing all our foreign treaties down to the present time. The work will now make 3 vol[ume]s. I believe I proposed for 500 copies at 5 dollars per volume full bound in the best binding, and very best style of printing & paper. I desire, in this note, to renew the proposal." ALS in DNA, RG 59 (State Department), Miscellaneous Letters (M-179:105, frames 295–296).

From S[elah] R. Hobbie, [Assistant Postmaster General], 9/2. "I have the honor to inform you, that the appointment of Daniel Collins to be Postmaster at Marietta, Georgia, was ordered, this day, immediately on receiving the letter of recommendation, submitted by you, from the Rev[eren]d Isaac W. Waddel, dated 27 ult. [*not found*]." LS in DNA, RG 59 (State Department), Acceptances and Orders for Commissions, 1837–1844.

From S[elah] R. Hobbie, Post Office Department, 9/2. "In reply to your request accompanying the letter of S. Mansfield Bay, Esq.," Hobbie informs Calhoun that Abraham Fulkerson was appointed Postmaster of Jefferson City, Cole County, Mo., on 8/6/1844. LS in DNA, RG 59 (State Department), Miscellaneous Letters (M-179:105, frame 292).

To John Nelson, Attorney General, 9/2. Calhoun relays a request from the British Minister, [Richard] Pakenham, for a warrant under the extradition provision of the treaty of 1842, and asks Nelson's opinion "as to the legality of the arrest, and the proceedings under it." Also, the President [John Tyler] "desires your opinion" in a case referred by [Ogden] Hoffman, U.S. District Attorney [at New York City on 8/23] "involving an alledged breach of neutrality as respects Mexico." LS in DNA, RG 60 (Justice Department), Letters Received in the Office of the Attorney General, 1813–1849, 1844, no. 1679.

PROTOCOL by R[ichard] Pakenham and J[ohn] C. Calhoun

[Washington, September 2, 1844]
On the 2d of September 1844 the third conference was held at the office of the Secretary of State, according to appointment. The Ameri-

can Plenipotentiary presented a written statement of his views of the claims of the United States to the portion of the Territory drained by the waters of the Columbia River, marked A & containing his reasons for declining to accept the proposal offered by the British Plenipotentiary at their second conference. J.C. Calhoun, R. Pakenham.

DS in DNA, RG 59 (State Department), Notes from Foreign Legations, Great Britain, vol. 22 (M-50:22); PC in Senate Document No. 1, 29th Cong., 1st Sess., p. 144; PC in House Document No. 2, 29th Cong., 1st Sess., p. 144; PC in the Washington, D.C., *Daily National Intelligencer,* December 12, 1845, p. 1; PC in *Niles' National Register,* vol. LXIX, no. 17 (December 27, 1845), p. 261; PC in Crallé, ed., *Works,* 5:424–425. NOTE: The statement presented by Calhoun to Pakenham is dated 9/3.

From Albert Smith, Commissioner, Boundary Line, Moose River, Maine, 9/2. He requests that $10,000 be placed to his credit in the Merchants Bank at Boston, because this season's portion of the appropriation for running the boundary line is almost exhausted. He estimates that a total of $25,200, itemized under six distinct categories, has been expended thus far. A more nearly exact statement is impracticable, because Smith has about 150 men at work along 300 or 400 miles of the line. He receives drafts constantly and sometimes unexpectedly, and "it would be very annoying to be without funds to meet them." (EU's indicate that this letter was received and answered on 9/9 and that a requisition was issued on the same day.) ALS in DNA, RG 59 (State Department), Accounting Records: Miscellaneous Letters Received.

From T[homas] L. Smith, Register, Treasury Department, 9/2. He requests that Calhoun prepare and transmit as soon as convenient the usual estimates of appropriations that will be needed for the fiscal year that will end on 6/30/1846. PDS in DNA, RG 59 (State Department), Letters Received from the Fifth Auditor and Comptroller, 1829–1862.

To SETH SWEETSER, U.S. Consul, Guayaquil, [Ecuador]

Department of State
Washington, 2d Sept[embe]r 1844
Sir, Your drafts, dated 31st December 1843, One for $473.37 and one for $289.63 were presented on the 12th July, and could not then be

paid, as, the Fifth Auditor [Stephen Pleasonton] reported that the state of your account did not justify such payment. They have been, again, presented this day, and upon inquiry at the Auditor's office it has been ascertained, that, upon the settlement of your account to the 31 December, last, the balance in your favor was, only $30.07, the sum of $653.10 having been suspended for explanation, for which the Auditor had written to you on the 16th of July, last. It has been ascertained from the Auditor that one of the causes of the suspensions, requiring explanations, was, that vouchers for expenses consequent upon the death and burial of American seamen, bore, for signatures, the names of the seamen for whom they appear to have been incurred.

I have, under the circumstances, been reluctantly compelled to decline paying your drafts.

You will, without delay, render the necessary explanations in relation to your accounts; and will be particularly cautious, hereafter, not to draw upon the Department without having previously transmitted accounts and vouchers in proper form. You will thus secure to your drafts due honor, the want of which not only tends to the loss of your own credit, but of that of the government of which you are an agent. I am, Sir, respectfully Your obed[ien]t Servant, J.C. Calhoun.

LS in PHarH, Samuel W. Pennypacker Papers, Scrapbook.

From HENRY A. WISE

Rio de Janeiro, Sept[embe]r 2nd 1844

Sir, I reserve for a separate despatch the inclosed copies, numbered 1 & 2, of a correspondence with the Minister & Secretary of State for foreign affairs, Mr. [Ernesto Ferreira] França who tenders to the U. States through me, the grateful acknowledgements of His August Majesty, the Emperor of Brazil, for the "generous offices" and "polite attentions" of Mr. [James C.] Pickett, U.S. Chargé at Peru, and of Capt. [Cornelius K.] Stribling, in command of the frigate "United States," to S[eno]r [Miguel C.] Lima, Ex-Chargé of Brazil at Peru, on his return passage to this court. In such a case I did not hesitate to return the answer which I enclose, and which I hope will be approved by the President. He will please to observe I have intimated that he himself will take further notice of this compliment.

In connection with this subject, and in testimony of the good understanding now here existing between the Empire of Brazil and the U. States, I deem it my duty to remark upon another manifestation of confidence and respect by the Brazilian authorities, which, though paid to our Navy specially, belongs to our nation. Since my arrival, our countrymen have been animated by a proud display of U. States Naval force at this port. When the Constitution anchored in the harbor she found the Raritan and Congress frigates and the brig Pioneer at their moorings. Shortly after, the brig Bainbridge, belonging to the station, and the sloop of war Cyane and the frigate United States, bound home from the Pacific, arrived and thus there was in port a fleet of the U. States, consisting of 4 frigates, 1 sloop of war and 2 brigs. This, though purely accidental, had a finer effect than could be readily imagined at home, and tended to confirm my previous convictions that Congress and the Executive could do nothing more essential to promote our commerce, respect for us abroad and our peace with all the world, than to appropriate and apply all the Naval expenditures which can be liberally but economically spared, to keep as many frigates and sloops of war as possible *in active commission.* The Neapolitan prince [Louis, Count of Aquila], nearly allied to the crown of this Empire by his marriage with the princess Januaria [sister of Emperor Pedro II], and lately appointed High Admiral of the Brazilian Navy, visited, in great state, all the Naval forces in port, with the practical view of inspecting the different systems of all. So pleased was he with the perfect order, neatness and discipline of our ships, particularly with the symmetry, beauty and order of the frigate Congress under the command of Capt. [Philip F.] Voorhees, that another visit to them was made by the Minister of Marine, who was so struck by our Naval excellence that when ["lately" *canceled*] soon thereafter the Congress & Raritan sailed, for the purpose of cruising on this station, several officers, of the grades of Lieutenants & Midshipmen, belonging to the Brazilian Navy, were, with the consent and approbation of Capt. [Daniel] Turner, sent in those ships, to observe and learn their construction, practice and discipline. This preference of our service was a distinguished compliment well earned by the ability and efficiency of Commodore Turner and the officers and crews under his command. They are distinguished for all that adorns gentlemen, officers and seamen. Without disparagement to the service or ships of any other nation, I believe that ours may proudly compare with the best of them, and Americans at least claim that they have won from the Minister of Marine of Brazil the palm of excellence from all others in this port. The papers of this city have delicately & properly noticed this compliment. The "United States," the Cyane and the Pioneer have sailed for home, and the Constitution will in a few days sail for India. The Raritan and Bainbridge are cruising on the coast, the Congress has returned and will soon be the only ship remaining in port. I trust our Naval force on this station will not be reduced, as it has a good effect upon the national mind, fond of a display, here, and for the sake of our most important general commerce and for the reason of the Slave trade and the abuses and insults of our flag which that trade induces in these seas.

The Russian Minister requests me to inclose the within letters, and I have the honor to remain Your ob[e]d[ien]t Serv[an]t, Henry A. Wise.

ALS with Ens in DNA, RG 59 (State Department), Diplomatic Despatches, Brazil, vol. 13 (M-121:15), received 10/29; FC (marked No. 4) in DNA, RG 84 (Foreign Posts), Brazil, Despatches, 11:85–87.

To Messrs. Burr, Benedict & Beebe, New York [City], 9/3. Calhoun acknowledges their letter of 8/16 "together with the petition of Joseph Carroll and others praying that compensation be allowed them for loss of time incurred during a voyage from the Port of Rio Janeiro to New York, as witnesses against Cornelius F. Driscoll." In answer Calhoun encloses a copy of a letter from the Secretary of the Treasury on the subject. FC in DNA, RG 59 (State Department), Domestic Letters, 34:360 (M-40:32).

From Geo[rge] W[illia]m Gordon, U.S. Consul, Rio de Janeiro, 9/3. He transmits numerous legal documents concerning the case of [British outrage against] Capt. P.C. Dumas and the American brig *Cyrus* of New Orleans. Certified copies of these documents have also been furnished to U.S. Minister to Brazil Henry A. Wise at his request. ALS (No. 7) with Ens in DNA, RG 59 (State Department), Consular Despatches, Rio de Janeiro, vol. 7 (T-172:8), received 10/-29; LS ("Duplicate") and CC in *ibid.*; PC's of Ens in Senate Document No. 300, 29th Cong., 1st Sess., pp. 10–39.

From M[ordecai] M. Noah

New york [City,] Sep[tembe]r 3, 1844

Dear Sir, Admiral Espina commanding the Mexican Steam Frigates in this port, received Despatches by the Acadia from the Mexican Minister at London [Don Tomás Murphy], directing him forthwith to sail for Vera Cruz, for the purpose of urging his Government to expedite the marching of the troops towards Texas, prior to the meeting of congress at Washington; and in case the Steam Frigates now under repair in this harbour, were not ready for Sea, to repair in person with his despatches by the nearest route. Accordingly Admiral Espina took the Cars last evening for New Orleans direct. One Steam Frigate is ready, & the other will be completed I learn in two weeks, when directions are given to sail for Vera Cruz, where they are to be reinforced by another Steam Frigate from England, with additional supply of arms & ammunition. This information I received confidentially from a friend, Mr. Delmar, Spanish interpreter to the Admiral, and I hasten to communicate the same to you, under the impression that it may be serviceable to the Government. With sincere regard, I am Dear Sir, very truly your friend, M.M. Noah.

ALS in ScCleA. NOTE: Noah was a newspaper editor and author who had held several appointive offices.

To R[ICHARD] PAKENHAM

Washington, 3d Sept[embe]r, 1844

The Undersigned American Plenipotentiary declines the proposal of the British Plenipotentiary, on the ground that it would have the effect of restricting the possessions of the United States to limits far more circumscribed than their claims clearly entitle them to. It proposes to limit their northern boundary by a line drawn from the Rocky Mountains along the 49th parallel of latitude to the northeasternmost branch of the Columbia river; and thence down the middle of that river to the sea—giving to Great Britain all the country north, and to the United States all south of that line, except a detached territory extending on the Pacific and the Straits of Fuca, from Bulfinch's Harbor to Hood's Canal. To which it is proposed, in addition, to make free to the United States any port which the United States' Government might desire, either on the main land, or on Vancouver's Island, south of latitude 49°.

By turning to the map hereto annexed, and on which the proposed boundary is marked in pencil, it will be seen that it assigns to Great Britain almost the entire region, on its north side, drained by the Columbia river, lying on its northern bank. It is not deemed necessary to state, at large, the claims of the United States to this territory;

and the grounds on which they rest, in order to make good the assertion that it restricts the possessions of the United States within narrower bounds than they are clearly entitled to. It will be sufficient for this purpose to show that they are fairly entitled to the entire region drained by the river; and to the establishment of this point, the Undersigned proposes, accordingly, to limit his remarks at present.

Our claims to the portion of the territory drained by the Columbia river may be divided into those we have, in our own proper right, and those we have derived from France and Spain. We ground the former, as against Great Britain, on priority of discovery and priority of exploration and settlement. We rest our claim to discovery, as against her, on that of Captain [Robert] Gray, a citizen of the United States, who, in the ship Columbia, of Boston, passed its bar and anchored in the river, ten miles above its mouth, on the 11th of May, 1792; and who afterwards sailed up the river twelve or fifteen miles, and left it on the 20th of the same month, calling it "*Columbia*," after his ship, which name it still retains.

On these facts our claim to the discovery and entrance into the river rests. They are too well attested to be controverted. But they have been opposed by the alleged discoveries of [John] Meares and [George] Vancouver. It is true that the former explored a portion of the coast through which the Columbia flows into the Ocean, in 1788, (five years before Captain Gray crossed the bar and anchored in the river,) in order to ascertain whether the river, as laid down in the Spanish charts, and called the St. Roc, existed or not: but it is equally true, that he did not even discover it. On the contrary, he expressly declares, in his account of the voyage, as the result of his observations, that "*we can now safely assert that there is no such river as that of the St. Roc as laid down in the Spanish charts*"; and as if to perpetuate his disappointment, he called the promontory lying north of the inlet where he expected to discover it, Cape *Disappointment*, and the inlet itself *Deception* Bay. It is also true that Vancouver, in April, 1792, explored the same coast; but it is no less so that he failed to discover the river, of which his own journal furnishes the most conclusive evidence, as well as his strong conviction that no such river existed. So strong was it, indeed, that, when he fell in with Captain Gray shortly afterwards, and was informed by him that he had been off the mouth of a river in latitude 46 degrees 10 minutes, whose outlet was so strong as to prevent his entering, he remained still incredulous, and strongly expressed himself to that effect in his journal. It was shortly after this interview that Captain Gray again visited its mouth, crossed its bar, and sailed up the river, as has been stated. After he left it, he visited Nootka Sound, where he communicated his discoveries to [Juan Francisco de la Bodegay] Quadra, the Spanish Commandant at that place; and gave him a chart and description of the mouth of the river. After his departure, Vancouver arrived there in September, when he was informed of the discoveries of Captain Gray, and obtained from Quadra copies of the chart he had left with him. In consequence of the information thus obtained, he was induced to visit again that part of the coast. It was during this visit that he entered the river on the 20th of October, and made his survey.

From these facts, it is manifest that the alleged discoveries of Meares and Vancouver cannot, in the slightest degree, shake the claim of Captain Gray to priority of discovery. Indeed, so conclusive is the evidence in his favor, that it has been attempted to evade our claim on the novel and wholly untenable ground that his discovery was made not in a national, but private vessel. Such and so incontestible is the evidence of our claim, as against Great Britain, from priority of discovery, as to the mouth of the river, crossing its bar, entering it and sailing up its stream, on the voyage of Captain Gray alone, without taking into consideration the prior discovery of the Spanish navigator [Bruno] Heceta, which will be more particularly referred to hereafter.

Nor is the evidence of the priority of our discovery of the head branches of the river and its exploration less conclusive. Before the treaty was ratified by which we acquired Louisiana in 1803, an expedition was planned at the head of which were placed Meriwether Lewis and William Clark, to explore the river Missouri and its principal branches to their sources; and then to seek and trace to its termination in the Pacific, some stream, *"whether the Columbia, the Oregon, the Colorado, or any other which might offer the most direct and practicable water communication across the continent, for the purpose of commerce."* The party began to ascend the Missouri in May, 1804, and in the summer of 1805 reached the head waters of the Columbia river. After crossing many of the streams falling into it, they reached the Kooskooskee, in latitude 43°34′—descended that to the principal southern branch, which they called Lewis—followed that to its junction with the great northern branch, which they called Clark; and thence descended to the mouth of the river, where they landed and encamped on the north side, on Cape Disappointment, and wintered. The next spring they commenced their return, and continued their exploration up the river, noting its various branches, and tracing some of the principal; and finally arrived at St. Louis in

September, 1806, after an absence of two years and four months.

It was this important expedition which brought to the knowledge of the world this great river, the greatest, by far, on the western side of this continent, with its numerous branches, and the vast regions through which it flows, above the points to which Gray and Vancouver had ascended. It took place many years before it was visited and explored by any subject of Great Britain, or of any other civilized Nation, so far as we are informed. It as clearly entitles us to the claim of priority of discovery, as to its head branches, and the exploration of the river and region through which it passes, as the voyages of Captain Gray and the Spanish navigator, Heceta, entitle us to priority in reference to its mouth and the entrance into its channel.

Nor is our priority of settlement less certain. Establishments were formed by American citizens on the Columbia as early as 1809 and 1810. In the latter year, a company was formed in New York, at the head of which was John Jacob Astor, a wealthy merchant of that city, the object of which was to form a regular chain of establishments on the Columbia river and the contiguous coasts of the Pacific, for commercial purposes. Early in the spring of 1811, they made their first establishment on the south side of the river, a few miles above Point George; where they were visited in July following, by Mr. [David] Thompson, a surveyor and astronomer of the Northwest Company, and his party. They had been sent out by that company to forestall the American Company in occupying the mouth of the river; but found themselves defeated in their object. The American Company formed two other connected establishments higher up the river; one at the confluence of the Okenegan with the north branch of the Columbia, about six hundred miles above its mouth; and the other on the Spokan[e], a stream falling into the north branch some fifty miles above.

These posts passed into the possession of Great Britain during the war which was declared the next year: but it was provided by the first article of the treaty of Ghent, which terminated it, that *"all territories, places, and possessions whatever, taken by either party from the other, during the war, or which may be taken after the signing of the treaty, excepting the islands hereafter mentioned, (in the Bay of Fundy,) shall be restored without delay."* Under this provision, which embraces all the establishments of the American Company, on the Columbia, Astoria was formally restored, on the 6th of October, 1818, by agents duly authorized on the part of the British Government to restore the possession, and to an agent duly authorized on the part of the Government of the United States to receive it;

which placed our possession where it was before it passed into the hands of British subjects. Such are the facts on which we rest our claims to priority of discovery, and priority of exploration and settlement, as against Great Britain, to the region drained by the Columbia river. So much for the claims we have in our own proper right to that region.

To these we have added the claims of France and Spain. The former we obtained by the treaty of Louisiana, ratified in 1803; and the latter by the treaty of Florida, ratified in 1819. By the former, we acquired all the rights which France had to Louisiana, *"to the extent it now has (1803) in the hands of Spain, and that it had when France possessed it, and such as it should be after the treaties subsequently entered into by Spain and other States."* By the latter, His Catholic Majesty *"ceded to the United States all his rights, claims, and pretensions"* to the country lying west of the Rocky Mountains, and north of a line drawn on the 42 parallel of latitude, from a point on the south bank of the Arkansas, in that parallel, to the South sea; that is, to the whole region claimed by Spain west of those mountains, and north of that line.

The cession of Lousiana gave us undisputed title west of the Mississippi, extending to the summit of the Rocky Mountains, and stretching south between that river and those mountains to the possessions of Spain; the line between which, and ours, was afterwards determined by the treaty of Florida. It also added much to the strength of our title to the region beyond the Rocky Mountains, by restoring to us the important link of continuity westward to the Pacific, which had been surrendered by the treaty of 1763, as will be hereafter shown.

That continuity furnishes a just foundation for a claim of territory, in connection with those of discovery and occupation, would seem unquestionable. It is admitted by all that neither of them is limited by the precise spot discovered or occupied. It is evident that, in order to make either available, it must extend, at least, some distance beyond that actually discovered or occupied; but how far, as an abstract question, is a matter of uncertainty. It is subject, in each case, to be influenced by a variety of considerations. In the case of an island, it has been usually maintained in practice to extend the claim of discovery or occupancy to the whole. So likewise in the case of a river, it has been usual to extend them to the entire region drained by it; more especially in cases of a discovery and settlement at the mouth, and emphatically so when accompanied by exploration of the river and region through which it flows. Such, it is believed, may be affirmed to be the opinion and practice in such cases since the discovery of this continent.   How far the claim of continuity may extend in other cases, is less perfectly defined; and can be settled only by reference to the circumstances attending each.   When this continent was first discovered, Spain claimed the whole, in virtue of the grant of the Pope; but a claim so extravagant and unreasonable was not acquiesced in by other countries, and could not be long maintained. Other Nations, especially England and France, at an early period, contested her claim.   They fitted out voyages of discovery, and made settlements on the eastern coasts of North America.   They claimed for their settlements, usually, specific limits, along the coasts or bays on which they were founded; and, generally, a region of corresponding width, extending across the entire continent to the Pacific Ocean. Such was the character of the limits assigned by England in the charters which she granted to her former colonies, now the United States, when there were no special reasons for varying from it.

How strong she regarded her claim to the region conveyed by these charters and extending westward of her settlements, the war between her and France, which was terminated by the treaty of Paris, 1763, furnishes a striking illustration.   That great contest which ended so gloriously for England, and effected so great and durable a change on this continent, commenced in a conflict between her claims and those of France, resting on her side on this very right of continuity extending westward from her settlements to the Pacific Ocean; and on the part of France on the same right, but extending to the region drained by the Mississippi and its waters, on ground of settlement and exploration.   Their respective claims which led to the war, first clashed on the river Ohio, the waters of which the colonial charters, in their western extension, covered; but which France had been unquestionably the first to settle and explore.   If the relative strength of these different claims may be tested by the result of that remarkable contest, that of continuity westward must be pronounced to be the stronger of the two.   England has had, at least, the advantage of the result; and would seem to be foreclosed against contesting the principle, particularly as against us, who contributed so much to that result; and on whom that contest and her example and pretensions, from the first settlement of our country, have contributed to impress it so deeply and indelibly.

But the treaty of 1763 which terminated that memorable and eventful struggle, yielded, as has been stated, the claim and all the chartered rights of the colonies beyond the Mississippi.   The seventh article establishes that river as the permanent boundary between the possessions of Great Britain and France on this continent. So much as relates to the subject, is in the following words: *"The confines between the dominions of His Britannic Majesty, in that part of the world, (the continent of America,) shall be fixed irrevocably by a line drawn along the middle of the river Mississippi, from its source to the river Iberville, and from thence, by a line drawn along the middle of this river, and the lakes Maurepas and Pontchartrain to the sea,"* &c.

This important stipulation, which thus establishes the Mississippi as the line *"fixed irrevocably"* between the dominions of the two countries on this continent, in effect extinguishes, in favor of France whatever claim Great Britain may have had to the region lying west of the Mississippi. It, of course, could not affect the rights of Spain; the only other Nation which had any pretence of claim west of that river; but it prevented the right of continuity, previously claimed by Great Britain, from extending beyond it, and transferred it to France. The treaty of Louisiana restored and vested in the United States all the claims acquired by France, and surrendered by Great Britain under the provisions of that treaty to the country west of the Mississippi, and, among others the one in question. Certain it is that France had the same right of continuity, in virtue of her possession of Louisiana, and the extinguishment of the right of England by the treaty of 1763 to the whole country west of the Rocky Mountains and lying west of Louisiana, as against Spain, which England had to the country westward of the Alleghany Mountains, as against France. With this difference, that Spain had nothing to oppose to the claim of France, at the time, but the right of discovery; and even that England has since denied; while France had, opposed to the right of England, in her case, that of discovery, exploration, and settlement. It is, therefore, not at all surprising that France should claim the country west of the Rocky Mountains, (as may be inferred from her maps,) on the same principle that Great Britain had claimed and dispossessed her of the regions west of the Alleghany; or that the United States, as soon as they had acquired the rights of France, should assert the same claim, and take measures immediately after, to explore it with a view to occupation and settlement. But since then, we have strengthened our title by adding to our own proper claims and those of France, the claims also of Spain, by the treaty of Florida, as has been stated.

The claims which we have acquired from her, between the Rocky Mountains and the Pacific, rest on her priority of discovery. Numerous voyages of discovery, commencing with that of Moldonado, in 1528, and ending with that under Galiano and Valdes, in

1792, were undertaken by her authority along the northwestern coast of North America. That they discovered and explored not only the entire coast of what is now called the Oregon Territory, but still further north, are facts too well established to be controverted at this day. The voyages which they performed will, accordingly, be passed over at present, without being particularly alluded to; with the exception of that of Heceta. His discovery of the mouth of the Columbia river has been already referred to. It was made on the 13th of August, 1775; many years anterior to the voyages of Meares and Vancouver, and was prior to [James] Cook's, who did not reach the northwestern coast until 1778. The claims it gave to Spain of priority of discovery were transferred to us, with all others belonging to her, by the treaty of Florida; which, added to the discoveries of Captain Gray, places our right to the discovery of the mouth and entrance into the inlet and river beyond all controversy.

It has been objected that we claim under various and conflicting titles, which mutually destroy each other. Such might, indeed, be the fact, while they were held by different parties; but since we have rightfully acquired both those of Spain and France, and concentrated the whole in our hands, they mutually blend with each other, and form one strong and connected chain of title, against the opposing claims of all others, including Great Britain.

In order to present more fully and perfectly the grounds on which our claims to the region in question rests, it will now be necessary to turn back to the time when Astoria was restored to us under the provisions of the treaty of Ghent; and to trace what has since occurred between the two countries in reference to the territory, and enquire whether their respective claims have been affected by the settlements since made in the territory by Great Britain, or the occurrences which have since taken place.

The restoration of Astoria took place under the provisions of the treaty of Ghent, on the 6th day of October, 1818; the effect of which was to put Mr. Provost [*sic*; John B. Prevost], the agent authorized by our Government to receive it, in possession of the establishment; with the right at all times to be reinstated and considered the party in possession, as was explicitly admitted by Lord Castlereagh, in the first negotiation between the two Governments in reference to the treaty. The words of Mr. [Richard] Rush, our Plenipotentiary on that occasion, in his letter to Mr. [John Quincy] Adams, then Secretary of State, of the 14th of February, 1818, reporting what passed between him and his Lordship, are: *"That Lord Castlereagh admitted, in the most ample extent, our right to be reinstated, and to be the party in possession, while treating of the title."*

That negotiation terminated in the convention of the 20th of October, 1818, the third article of which is in the following words:

"It is agreed, that any country that may be claimed by either party on the northwest coast of America, westward of the Stony Mountains, shall, together with its harbors, bays, and creeks, and the navigation of all rivers within the same, be free and open, for the term of ten years from the date of the signature of the present convention, to the vessels, citizens, and subjects, of the two Powers: it being well understood, that this agreement is not to be construed to the prejudice of any claim which either of the two high contracting parties may have to any part of the said country, nor shall it be taken to affect the claims of any other Power or State to any part of the said country; the only object of the high contracting parties, in that respect, being to prevent disputes and differences amongst themselves."

The two acts, the restoration of our possession and the signature of the convention, were nearly contemporaneous, the latter taking place but fourteen days subsequently to the former. We were then, as admitted by Lord Castlereagh, entitled to be considered as the party in possession; and the convention which stipulated that the territory should be free and open for the term of ten years, from the date of its signature, to the vessels, citizens, and subjects of the two countries, without prejudice to any claim which either party may have to any part of the same, preserved and perpetuated all our claims to the territory, including the acknowledged right to be considered the party in possession, as perfectly during the period of its continuance, as they were the day the convention was signed. Of this there can be no doubt.

After an abortive attempt to adjust the claims of the two parties to the treaty in 1824, another negotiation was commenced in 1826, which terminated in renewing, on the 6th of August, 1827, the third article of the convention of 1818, prior to its expiration. It provided for the indefinite extension of all the provisions of the third article of that convention; and also that either party might terminate it at any time it might think fit, by giving one year's notice, after the 20th of October, 1828. It took, however, the precaution of providing expressly that *"nothing contained in this convention, or in the third article of the convention of the 20th of October, 1818, hereby continued in force, shall be construed to impair, or in any manner affect, the claims which either of the contracting parties may have to any*

703

part of the country westward of the Stony or Rocky Mountains." That convention is now in force, and has continued to be so since the expiration of that of 1818. By the joint operation of the two, our right to be considered the party in possession, and all the claims we had to the territory, while in possession, are preserved in as full vigor as they were at the date of its restoration in 1818, without being affected or impaired by the settlements since made by the subjects of Great Britain.

Time, indeed, so far from impairing our claims, has greatly strengthened them since that period; for since then the treaty of Florida transferred to us all the rights, claims, and pretensions of Spain to the whole territory, as has been stated. In consequence of this, our claims to the portion drained by the Columbia river, the point now the subject of consideration, have been much strengthened, by giving us the incontestible claim to the discovery of the mouth of the river by Heceta, above stated. But it is not in this particular only that it has operated in our favor. Our well-founded claim, grounded on continuity, has greatly strengthened during the same period, by the rapid advance of our population towards the territory; its great increase, especially in the valley of the Mississippi, as well as the greatly increased facility of passing to the territory by more accessible routes; and the far stronger and rapidly swelling tide of population that has recently commenced flowing into it.

When the first convention was concluded in 1818 our whole population did not exceed nine millions of people. The portion of it inhabiting the States in the great valley of the Mississippi, was probably under one million seven hundred thousand; of which not more than two hundred thousand were on the west side of that river. Now, our population may be safely estimated at not less than nineteen millions, of which, at least eight millions inhabit the States and Territories in the valley of the Mississippi, and of which upwards of one million are in the States and Territories west of that river. This portion of our population is now increasing far more rapidly than ever, and will, in a short time, fill the whole tier of States on its western bank.

To this great increase of population, especially in the valley of the Mississippi, may be added the increased facility of reaching the Oregon Territory in consequence of the discovery of the remarkable pass [South Pass] in the Rocky Mountains, at the head of the La Platte. The depression is so great, and the pass so smooth, that loaded wagons now travel with facility from Missouri to the navigable waters of the Columbia river. These joint causes have had the effect of turning the current of our population towards the territory; and an emigration estimated at not less than one thousand, during the last, and fifteen hundred, the present, year, has flowed into it. The current thus commenced, will no doubt continue to flow with increased volume hereafter. There can, then, be no doubt now that the operation of the same causes which impelled our population westward from the shores of the Atlantic across the Alleghany to the valley of the Mississippi, will impel them onward with accumulating force across the Rocky Mountains into the valley of the Columbia; and that the whole region drained by it is destined to be peopled by us.

Such are our claims to that portion of the territory, and the grounds on which they rest. The Undersigned believes them to be well-founded, and trusts that the British Plenipotentiary will see in them sufficient reasons why he should decline his proposal.

The Undersigned Plenipotentiary abstains, for the present, from presenting the claims which the United States may have to other portions of the territory.

The Undersigned avails himself of this occasion to renew to the British Plenipotentiary assurances of his high consideration. J.C. Calhoun.

FC in DNA, RG 59 (State Department), Notes to Foreign Legations, Great Britain, 7:32–47 (M-99:36); FC in DNA, RG 84 (Foreign Posts), Great Britain, Instructions, 9:99–133; PC in the Washington, D.C., *Daily National Intelligencer,* December 12, 1845, pp. 1–2; PC in *Niles' National Register,* vol. LXIX, no. 17 (December 27, 1845), pp. 261–263; PC in the London, England, *Times,* December 29, 1845, p. 5; PC in Senate Document No. 1, 29th Cong., 1st Sess., pp. 146–153; PC in House Document No. 2, 29th Cong., 1st Sess., pp. 146–153; PC in *Oregon: The Claim of the United States to Oregon, as Stated in the Letters of the Hon. J.C. Calhoun and the Hon. J. Buchanan . . . to the Right Hon. R. Pakenham* (London: Wiley and Putnam, 1846), pp. 3–14; PC (dated 9/13) in Crallé, ed., *Works,* 5:427–440.

From A.M. Bouton, Newark, N.J., 9/4. "Your Friend A.M. Bouton has an Interest in knowing whether the clames [*sic*] awarded by our Commis[s]ioners against the Mexican Government are about to be adjusted—or whether he must abandon all hope of obtaining his just due." ALS in DNA, RG 59 (State Department), Miscellaneous Letters (M-179:105, frames 305–306).

From Henry Dolliver, Somerville, N.J., 9/4. "I observe by the Papers That Santa An[n]a is withholding the Instalment of the Indemnity due this Conntry on the 1st of May last, untill he shall Ascertain whether the treaty of annexation Has been Ratified: for such

Ratification would make the United States a party to The war betwe[e]n Mexico and Texas and the Occurrence of war between two nations abrogates All treaty stipulations. Have the goodness to Inform me when Conveant [*sic*] what your Opi[ni]on is Respecting our Relations with Mexico at present and w[h]ether you think thear is any Provibility [*sic*] of my gitting any Part of wh[a]t they Robbed me of." ALS in DNA, RG 59 (State Department), Miscellaneous Letters (M-179:105, frames 306–307).

From THEOPHILUS FISK

Berlin Prussia, Sept. 4, 1844

Sir, I have the honour to inform you of my safe arrival at the place of my destination. I should have written yesterday, but having travelled for several successive days and nights, I omitted the performance of that duty until today.

Mr. [Henry] Wheaton being at Paris with his family, I delivered the despatches to Mr. [Theodore S.] Fay in the same good order in which they were received. The Minister from Hesse being unavoidably absent, I shall necessarily be detained here for three or four weeks. Mr. Fay caused him to be written to instantly upon my arrival, which will hasten his return. The other Minister will by appointment, receive his treaty on Monday next, when he will immediately communicate with his government; an answer may be expected in two or three weeks at farthest. Mr. Fay assures me that there shall be no effort spared to expedite my return at the earliest possible period.

I have to thank your kindness ten thousand times for conferring upon me a duty so delightful. It has been to me a source of unbounded delight. A sense of the great obligation you have imposed, will cease but with life.

I have every where been treated with the most respectful consideration during my journey. The expression "I am an American," has been sufficient on all occasions to elicit the kindest courtesy. I am prouder than ever of our own blessed land.

Allow me again and again to express my deep sense of gratitude, and to subscribe myself With perfect respect Your ob[edien]t ser[van]t, Theophilus Fisk.

ALS in DNA, RG 59 (State Department), Diplomatic Despatches, Germany, vol. 3 (M-44:4), received 10/22.

From David Hoffman, Philadelphia, 9/4. Hoffman, as the lawyer for some U.S. citizens holding "the late Mexican Indemnity scrip," encourages Calhoun to take action to insure the payment by Mexico of the overdue installment of that indemnity. Hoffman hopes that the matter will "be as speedily and as cogently urged as the wants of my constituents really demand." ALS in DNA, RG 59 (State Department), Miscellaneous Letters (M-179:105, frames 307–309).

To Eneas McFaul, [Baltimore], 9/4. Calhoun notifies McFaul of his appointment as U.S. Consul at Laguna de Terminos, [Carmen Island, Mexico], and encloses documents relating to the performance of the office. FC in DNA, RG 59 (State Department), Consular Instructions, 11:282.

From J[OHN] Y. MASON, [Secretary of the Navy]

Navy Department, September 4, 1844

Sir, The communication of the Right Hon. R[ichard] Pakenham, addressed to you on the 23d July ult[im]o which you did me the honor to refer to me for perusal, is herewith returned.

I have the honor to submit the following remarks: I am not aware that the U.S. Naval force on the lakes Ontario and Huron exceeds that to which Great Britain and the United States reciprocally restricted themselves by the agreement entered into in April 1817.

By an Act of Congress, approved September 9, 1841, an appropriation was made by Congress "for the construction or armament of such armed steamers or other vessels for defence, as the President may think ["most" *interlined*] proper, and as may be authorized by the existing stipulations between this and the British government."

On the 27th November, 1841, Mr. Secretary [of the Navy Abel P.] Upshur addressed to the President of the Board of Navy Commissioners an order to take the necessary measures for constructing one steamer for defence on Lake Erie. These measures were taken, and a steamer, called the Michigan, is lately completed at Erie [Pa.], on Lake Erie, of 498 tons burthen, with an armament of two eight-inch Paixhan guns and four thirty-two-pounder carronades. Her armament is on board, and the ship is ready for a cruise. In consequence of the remonstrance of Her Britannic Majesty's Minister, I have ordered her commander not to leave the port of Erie on a cruise, until he shall receive further orders.

You will perceive that the orders were given for the construction of this vessel at a time when the British Government had in commission a larger force than that authorized by the agreement of April, 1817. But there is nothing on the records of the Department to show that there was a purpose of disregarding the restrictions of that agreement. I have reason to believe that Her Majesty's Government has still in commission on the Northwestern lakes a much larger force, both in number and tonnage, than that authorized by the agreement. I transmit copies of two letters received on that subject. The vessels mentioned in the letter of Passed Midshipman [Dillaplain R.] Lambert as in commission and commanded by Officers of the Royal navy, are borne on the navy list of the Royal navy, published by authority of the Admiralty; and although they are reported to be pierced for a larger number of guns, they appear by the list to mount only one gun each. But the restriction is as imperative as to tonnage and number, as to armament. It is worthy of remark, that at the date of the agreement between the two Governments, steamers were in use to a very limited extent, as passenger vessels, and perhaps not at all as ships of war. The restriction as to tonnage would probably not have been adopted, if their use had been anticipated. No effective steamer for any purpose, it is believed, would be built of a tonnage of one hundred tons.

I would respectfully suggest that this consideration would justify a revision of the agreement on the subject; and also, that, if it is considered that the British vessels are not inconsistent with the agreement, by reason of the armament being limited to one gun each, the armament of the steamer Michigan can be readily reduced to that number.

The advertisement for cannon, shot, and shells has been made by the Bureau of Ordnance and Hydrography by my direction, in pursuance of a policy adopted for many years, and in execution of laws of Congress. That policy has been, gradually to collect materials, ordnance, and munitions, on our entire seaboard and lake frontier. The contemplated purchases of the present year do not exceed the proportion to which the Northern frontier is entitled, in pursuance of the system adopted; and the measures taken have had no reference to any anticipated disturbances with Great Britain. How far that Government, in its wise forecast, has made similar preparations for circumstances which may render them necessary, I am not advised, and have not enquired, as the agreement of 1817 does not impose any restriction on such supplies. I have no reason to believe, that the appropriations made by Congress for cannon and munitions were influenced by any considerations which threaten the peace which happily subsists between Great Britain and the United States. The advertisement has been made to execute in a regular course these laws of Congress. I have the honor to be, very respectfully, Sir, Your obedient Servant, J.Y. Mason.

LS with Ens in DNA, RG 59 (State Department), Miscellaneous Letters (M-179:105, frames 297–303); FC in DNA, RG 45 (Naval Records), Letters Sent by the Secretary of the Navy to the President and Executive Agencies, 1821–1886, 5:21–23 (M-472:3, frames 52–53).

From JOHN NELSON

Attorney General's Office, Sept[embe]r 4th 1844
Sir, The application of L.E. Hargous, the Mexican Consul in the City of New York, for the prosecution of James Arlington Bennett for an alledged violation of the relations subsisting between the United States and the Republic of Mexico, cannot be gratified. The act complained of, is in conflict with no provision of any of our Statutes and cannot be made the subject of a criminal procceding. I have the Honor to be, very respectfully, Sir, Your obed[ien]t Serv[an]t, Jno. Nelson.

LS in DNA, RG 59 (State Department), Miscellaneous Letters (M-179:105, frame 309); FC in DNA, RG 60 (Justice Department), Opinions of the Attorney General, 1818–1844, F:192.

From R[ichard] Pakenham, Washington, 9/4. He transmits for the information of the U.S. government a copy of "the Instructions recently issued for the guidance of Her Majesty's Naval Officers employed in the suppression of the Slave Trade." LS in DNA, RG 59 (State Department), Notes from Foreign Legations, Great Britain, vol. 22 (M-50:22).

To W[ILLIA]M WILKINS, Secretary of War

Department of State
Washington, Sept. 4th 1844
Sir: I have the honor to acknowledge the receipt of your note of the 22d ult[im]o, in referrence to your claim against the Government, for expenditures incurred while Minister Resident at St. Petersburgh

[*sic*]. The well established rule of the Department, at the time when the claim was first made, did not admit of its allowance; and acting on this rule my predecessors[,] Messrs. [John] Forsyth and [Abel P.] Upshur, decided against it. Office-rent at the period referred to, was not allowed except to our Ministers at London and Paris, and this rule has been invariably adhered to, except in the cases to which you refer, of Messrs. [Cornelius P.] Van Ness and [John H.] Eaton. The reasons which induced Mr. [Daniel] Webster to adopt a different rule in these cases are unknown to me. I cannot however concur with him in its propriety, as it tends, directly, to open anew long settled accounts, & I have invariably declined to act upon it, in the cases submitted to my decision. I have the honor to be respectfully Your ob[edien]t Ser[van]t, Jno. C. Calhoun.

FC in DNA, RG 59 (State Department), Domestic Letters, 34:363–364 (M-40: 32); PC in Jameson, ed., *Correspondence,* pp. 609–610.

To William Wilkins, Secretary of War, 9/4. "I will thank you for a copy of the orders which the Department of War may have issued or may issue to the person appointed to be present, on the part of the United States, at the negotiation in Texas with the Camanche Indians." LS in DNA, RG 107 (Secretary of War), Letters Received, Registered Series, 1801–1860, S-577 (M-221:135); FC in DNA, RG 59 (State Department), Domestic Letters, 34:362 (M-40:32).

From Cuyler W. Young, Halcyondale, Ga., 9/4. "Understanding there is likely to be a vacancy in the office of Consul for the port of Havana in the Island of Cuba, I avail myself of this occasion to apply through you to his Excellency, the President [John Tyler], for the appointment to supply the said vacancy." ALS in DNA, RG 59 (State Department), Applications and Recommendations, 1837–1845, Young (M-687:35, frames 308–309).

From Vespasian Ellis, "Office of the Old School Democrat," St. Louis, 9/5. "Under all the circumstances of the case, & especially in consideration that the ring leaders [John McDaniel and Joseph Brown] in the affair of the Charvis [*sic*; Antonio José Chavis] murder, have been executed I am free to recommend the pardon of the residue." ALS in DNA, RG 59 (State Department), Petitions for Pardon, Tyler Administration.

To Franklin Lippincott, [Woodbury, N.J.?], 9/5. Calhoun notifies Lippincott of his appointment as U.S. Consul at Cien Fuegos,

Cuba, and encloses relevant documents. Lippincott's exequatur has been applied for in Madrid. FC in DNA, RG 59 (State Department), Consular Instructions, 10:266.

To R[ICHARD] PAKENHAM

Department of State
Washington, Sept[embe]r 5, 1844

Sir: The note which you did me the honor to address to me, of date the 23d of July last, in which you state that it had been "represented to Her Majesty's Government that the naval force of the United States on the Lakes Ontario, Erie, and Huron, at this moment, considerably exceeds that to which Great Britain and the United States reciprocally restricted themselves by the agreement entered into in April, 1817," was promptly referred, for consideration, to the Honorable Secretary of the Navy [John Y. Mason], a copy of whose reply [of 9/4] I have now the honor to transmit herewith. With high consideration, I have the honor to be, Sir, your obedient servant, J.C. Calhoun.

FC in DNA, RG 59 (State Department), Notes to Foreign Legations, Great Britain, 7:48 (M-99:36).

From S[hadrach] Penn, Jr., St. Louis, 9/5. Penn informs Calhoun that he has signed a petition for the pardon of the prisoners at St. Louis convicted of complicity in the murder of Mexican trader [Antonio José] Chavis. The executions of [John] McDaniel and [Joseph] Brown have satisfied justice and many citizens of St. Louis have united to request pardons for the remaining convicts. ALS in DNA, RG 59 (State Department), Petitions for Pardon, Tyler Administration.

From W[illia]m Wilkins, Secretary of War, 9/5. "I respectfully transmit herewith, copies of the orders and instructions that have been given by this Department [to Bvt. Brig. Gen. Mathew Arbuckle and Capt. Nathan Boone], to ensure the attendance of a detachment of the Army and a representative from the Indian Department, during the Texian conference for a treaty with the Camanche Indians." LS with Ens in DNA, RG 59 (State Department), Miscellaneous Letters (M-179:105, frames 311–315); FC in DNA, RG 107 (Secretary of

War), Letters Sent Relating to Military Affairs, 1800–1861, 25:391 (M-6:25); draft in DNA, RG 107, Letters Received, Registered Series, 1801–1860, S-577 (M-221:135); PC with Ens in Senate Document No. 14, 32nd Cong., 2nd Sess., pp. 127–129.

To Geo[rge] M. Bibb, Secretary of the Treasury, 9/6. "I have the honor to enclose herewith an extract of a letter [of 7/13] received at this Department from the Hon. Dillon Jordan, Judge of the United States for the Western District of Florida, complaining that the Marshal of the United States for that District, has not complied with the requirements of the Law in referrence [*sic*] to his bonds." FC in DNA, RG 59 (State Department), Domestic Letters, 34:366 (M-40:32).

From GEORGE BROWN

Commission of the United States
Honolulu, Septe[mbe]r 6, 1844

Sir, I last had this honor on the 1st of July, since which I have visited the island of Hawaii, having left this on the 9th July and returned on the 11th of August. I visited the port of Kauihai, crossed the island, passing through Waimea to Laupahoihoi, from thence by boat to Hilo, visited the Volcano of Kilauea, and returned to Hilo, from which port I embarked on my return. My intention on leaving this, was to have visited all the ports, and mission stations of the island, but was prevented by an accident which happened to me by falling on the wet grass, a dislocation of my left wrist. It is slowly recovering. I found the island of Hawaii in many parts, in the interior, and on the north side, very fertile; but a large proportion of the island, is nothing but but [*sic*] lava on its surface, and will not for centuries to come be fit for cultivation. Indeed some of the eruptions of late years, have destroyed thousands of acres of fine lands. There are considerable herds of cattle, on the island, both wild and tame; the former belonging to the King [Kamehameha III], the latter to private individuals. I saw near Waimea a herd of 2200 head, belonging to an American of this Place (Mr. [William] French), which were in very fine condition. Some of the land about Hilo is very rich, producing excellent sugar cane; and the coffee trees grow very luxuriantly.

The harbor of Hilo is a most excellent one, and if it was in the hands of a nation, capable of bearing the expense of building a breakwater for a short distance, (there is a reef for a foundation,) it might be made one of the best and safest in the Pacific. At some times it is inconvenient for landing goods on account of the surf, but I understand never dangerous. I found a number of Americans on the island, but had no complaints from them, except that they could not get land for cultivation, of which there are hundreds of thousands of acres, now useless. This will be remedied in time, I think, as at present these people are in the unenviable situation of "the dog in the manger"; They will neither work themselves, or allow others the wherewithal to work upon.

On the 16th Ult. the Frigate Carysfort Lord George Paulet arrived here from Tahiti via Raiatea, at the latter place having landed the Queen of Tahiti. There had been several skirmishes taken place at Tahiti, between the French and Tahitians, in which, the latter had always been beaten, but the former had suffered considerably. It is to be presumed that the affairs at that island will soon be arranged. They were at last accounts in a sad state.

Lord George was not at all well received by the authorities here, but even with rudeness, which was in bad taste. I found him a very gentlemanly man, and if he had not fallen, at his first visit, into the hands of the clique he did, I have no doubt would have been very popular, instead of the reverse.

I dined on board the Carysfort on the 26th Aug. Prince Albert[']s birth day, and was treated with every kindness and consideration. She left here on the 4th inst. for Hilo, which place she leaves for St. Blas & Mazatlan on the 20th and a vessel leaves here on the ["10th" *altered to* "11th"] to carry to her, dispatches, by which I shall forward this.

I forward my quarterly account to this date and have drawn this day, on the department for $300, three hundred dollars, the balance of ditto, in favor of Mess. C. Brewer & Co. thirty days sight, which please honor. I have also drawn another bill for the like sum $300 in favor of same individuals, payable at *ninety days date, when my next quarter is due*, which also please honor & place to my account when paid. This place is so far from home, that I find sometimes, a want of money before the time, when the quarter is out.

The two enclosures A & B are the only official notes that have passed since my last, except one from Dr. [Gerrit P.] Judd Secretary of State, enclosing me a Code of Etiquette, established by this Government (a copy of which I forward,) and some others to which I refer below, & which you will find in a seperate dispatch, enclosed with this.

I forward by the Corvo, which sailed to day for the U. States, a file of the Polynesian, up to date, addressed to the department.

I am sorry to say that it has been necessary for me to enter into a correspondence, of not a pleasant nature, with the Sec[re]t[ar]y of State. The importance of which demands a seperate dispatch, to which I beg to refer you. I have the honor to be with the greatest respect Y[ou]r Very ob[edien]t S[ervan]t, George Brown, Commissioner.

ALS (No. 15) with Ens in DNA, RG 59 (State Department), Diplomatic Despatches, Hawaii, vol. 1 (T-30:1, frames 98–101), received 12/19.

To Edward Everett

Department of State
Washington, 6th Sept[embe]r, 1844

Sir: It would seem from a perusal of the papers which accompany this despatch, that an outrage has recently been committed by the British cutter "Sylph," on the American fishing schooner "Argus," William Doughty, Master, off the coast of Cape Breton, much in character with some of those which have from time to time been made the subject of remonstrance by this Government. Instructions in cases analogous to the one now under consideration having already been given by this Department to the Legation of the United States at London, it is not deemed necessary to repeat them at this time, for the purpose of expressing the views of this Government, or of pointing out the course which you will be expected to pursue in presenting the case of the "Argus" to the notice of the British Government. I am, Sir, respectfully, Your obedient Servant, J.C. Calhoun.

LS (No. 105) with Ens in DNA, RG 84 (Foreign Posts), Great Britain, Instructions, 8:404–414, received 10/1; FC in DNA, RG 59 (State Department), Diplomatic Instructions, Great Britain, 15:225 (M-77:74). NOTE: Enclosed with this were copies of a letter of 8/26/1844 from J[ohn] & J[osiah] Starling to the Secretary of State and of depositions of Edward Doughty and Joshua Doughty.

To J[ohn] Y. Mason, Secretary of the Navy, 9/6. "This Department will have occasion to send a Bearer of Public Despatches [Duff Green] to our Legation at Mexico [City]," who will be ready to leave Washington early next week. Calhoun hopes that "some public vessel at Pensacola may be held in readiness to convey him to Vera Cruz with the least possible delay." LS in DNA, RG 45 (Naval Records), Letters from Federal Executive Agents, 1837–1886, 7:67 (M-517:2, frames 512–513).

From Albert C. Ramsey, York, Pa., 9/6. He transmits a letter for [William R.?] King and asks that Calhoun forward it. By doing this Calhoun "would confer a favour on the son of your old friend William Ramsey of Carlisle and on an humble but warm admirer of yours." ALS in DNA, RG 59 (State Department), Miscellaneous Letters (M-179:105, frames 335–336).

To Isaac Van Zandt

Department of State
Washington, 6th September, 1844
Sir: I have the honor to transmit to you herewith, copies of the orders and instructions [of 8/31] issued by the Department of War to Brigadier General M[athew] Arbuckle and Captain Nathan Boone, in reference to the proposed negociation with the Comanche tribe of Indians. With high consideration, I have the honor to be Sir, Your obedient servant, J.C. Calhoun.

FC in DNA, RG 59 (State Department), Notes to Foreign Legations, Texas, 6:75 (M-99:95); FC with Ens in Tx, Records of the Texas Republic Department of State, Copybooks of Letters Received from Texan and Foreign Representatives, vol. 2–1/98, pp. 535–537; CC with Ens in Tx, Records of the Texas Republic Department of State, U.S. Diplomatic Correspondence; PC in Senate Document No. 14, 32nd Cong., 2nd Sess., p. 127.

Tho[ma]s Barrett to Geo[rge] M. Bibb, Secretary of the Treasury

Collector[']s Office
New Orleans, 7th Sept[embe]r 1844
Sir, I have the honor to inform you that there arrived here this morning a Special Bearer of Despatches, from Galveston, Texas.

He was despatched by Mr. S[tewart] Newell, U.S. Consul at Sabine (now at Galveston), with important Despatches for his Government—also with the melancholy news of the death of Gen: Tilghman [A.] Howard U.S. Chargé d'Affair[e]s after an illness of only three days.

There is a report in the city, that ten thousand men had landed at Rio Grand[e], from Mexico for the invasion of Texas. The bearer does not mention anything of it—but states that a vast number of families were moving from Texas. The alarm has spread and they fear to be invaded both by land and from the Sea coast.

I have the honor to transmit you herewith Copy of a letter received by me from Mr. Newell who is now at Galveston. With high respect I have the honor to be Your Ob[edien]t Serv[an]t, Thos. Barrett, Collector.

[Enclosure]

Stewart Newell to Thomas Barrett, "Collector of Customs at Port of New Orleans"

Consulate of the United States
Sabine, Texas
August 23d 1844

Sir, The Official ranks of the United States being again invaded, and the death of our Chargé d'Affair[e]s having occurred, in the person of Hon. T[ilghman] A. Howard, after an illness of only 3 days, at Washington—I deemed it of sufficient importance, to our Government have Chartered a small boat (the only conveyance to be had) for the purpose of transmitting despatches to the Department of State relative to this matter and others of great importance and have drawn upon you for $100, As compensation to the bearer of the Despatches enclosed to your care, and which you will please forward immediately by such conveyance *as you* may think best.

The Govt. Paper of Texas, announces the preperation on the part of Mexico for an Invasion, as certain and speedy, of which I also inform the Department.

I am without instructions how to act in an emergency of this kind, and have no means of quick communication from here, to the U. States. Will it be deemed under the circumstances improper to permit the Revenue Sch[oone]r Vigilant under the Brave and Energetic [William B.] Taylor to proceed to Sabine, or this Port, and remain for the purpose of transmitting Despatches, until the reply, and Instructions are received from the Department as to the present situation of Affairs, if the Vigilant cannot be permitted to remain at Galveston, I could always employ a person, at small expence to proceed to Sabine, with communications for the Government.

In having *drawn upon you*, for the amount of Compensation, to bearer of Despatches, it was under the peculiar circumstances existing. *No* Minister here, I discharging, the duties of two Consulates, Negotiations broken off or interrupted, and *deemed by the Govt.* so important, News of an Invasion and not being provided with Instructions to meet these *all* important events, I feared the injury our Govt. might sustain, if I *hesitated* and *decided* upon the risk of approval or disapprobation and choosed, as *I* think the lesser evil Governed by my usual determination, to do what, *I* conceive to be my duty, at *all hazards,* as I am ever ready to do, upon all occasions, that involves the character of my Government, and her Flag, under which I have the Honor to Act.

Should the Government not approve of my course, and justify the expence incurred, and shall notify you, or I of it, you shall not lose by it, as *I* will at any Sacrifice refund to you. (sign'd) Stewart Newell, U.S. Consul.

LS with En in DNA, RG 59 (State Department), Consular Despatches, Texas, vol. 1 (T-153:1), received 9/16.

Arabella E. Donahoo, "wife of [the] Rev. James T. Donahoo," Werts Grove, Franklin County, Ohio, to [John] Tyler, 9/7. She informs Tyler that her brother, Robert W. Turner, formerly Sheriff of Victoria County in Texas, is now a prisoner in the castle at Perote. She asks that Tyler use his influence to obtain the release of her brother. (An EU indicates that this letter was submitted to the attention of the Secretary of State. Another EU directs that an answer be made, indicating the President's concern in this case and his continuing efforts to obtain the release of Mexican prisoners.) ALS in DNA, RG 59 (State Department), Miscellaneous Letters (M-179: 105, frames 339–341).

G. Walker, Hamburg [S.C.], to Mrs. [Floride Colhoun] Calhoun, Pendleton, 9/7. Walker presents a bill totalling $50.75 for sugar, "Java Coffe[e]," and "Sperm Candles." These items have been forwarded to Pendleton "by direction of Hon. J.C. Calhoun" and "I hope will please." A shipment expected from Charleston has not yet arrived. ALS in ScU-SC, John C. Calhoun Papers.

From Tho[ma]s Wilson and W[illia]m S. Peterkin, Baltimore, 9/7. They discuss a debt owed to the former firm of Wilson & Peterkin by G[ilbert] K. Fitzgerald, a U.S. citizen who died in Santa Marta [New Granada] on 9/12/1838. Since Fitzgerald's death, Wilson has corresponded with the U.S. Consul at Santa Marta, T[homas] W. Robeson, about the payment of the debt from the proceeds of the settlement of Fitzgerald's estate. They have received only sparse information and no payment. Documents returned from the State Department yesterday arouse suspicions that Robeson has appropriated to himself proceeds of Fitzgerald's estate. They ask for the assistance of the State Department. LS with Ens in DNA, RG 59 (State Department), Consular Despatches, Santa Marta, vol. 1 (T-427:1).

From Sam[ue]l James Douglas, [Superior Court Judge for the Middle District of Fla. Territory], Jerusalem, Southampton [County], Va., 9/8. Douglas defends the conduct of the U.S. District Attorney in his district, Charles S. Sibley, finding Sibley to be "both consciencious & laborious." He explains why he believes Sibley has behaved properly and complied with usual practices in regard to pleas of *nolle prosequi* entered in his court. If Sibley is dismissed, Douglas recommends either James T. Archer or D.P. Hogue for the post. ALS in DNA, RG 59 (State Department), Applications and Recommendations, 1837–1845, Sibley (M-687:30, frames 288–291).

From M[ORDECAI] M. NOAH, "Private"

New york [City,] 8 Sep[tember] 1844
Dear Sir, Public opinion in this section, is not in favour of an Extra Session of Congress, unless there are powerful considerations of public safety that call for it; and our political friends are also apprehensive, that any obstacles thrown in the way of the Presidential Canvass, may have an injurious effect, and if this result should occur, there are some who would endeavour to fix the responsibility upon you. Still they think, that a call of Congress at an earlier period than the commencement of the Session, say Nov. 11 would be productive of good results, and would be in time for any action on Mexican affairs, without taking any one away from the political field. Rely upon it, that England has marked out the Campaign in Texas which will be discreet & forbearing. The heads of the proclamation on entering into the territory, have been drawn out by the British Minister in Mexico [Charles Bankhead], and are exceedingly pacific, inviting the Planters & others to continue their occupations, and guarenteeing protection of persons & property, renewing the same offer of the Constitution tendered originally to Gen. [Stephen F.] Austin, and declaring their intentions to change nothing but the flag, and thus allay all apprehensions & prevent opposition. Indeed the Contemplated invading forces, and the

unprotected position of Texas render defence hopeless.   Mexico has no intention to retain possession of Texas; we can have it, but we must purchase it of her; England is in favour of the independence of Texas and a commercial treaty.   Mexico has no interest in seconding the views of England; she would rather arrange with us for the purchase & fix the boundary.   [Anson] Jones I think has been elected President.   He & [Samuel] Houston understand the ulterior views of Mexico, and I think will do little on the defensive.

The nomination of Silas Wright [for Governor], has infused new energies in the party.   The moneyed interest anxious to preserve the credit of the State, and having great reliance on his discretion, will support him.   He will carry in [James K.] Polk & [George M.] Dallas, and thus secure their election; but if he accepts he does it most unwillingly, as he thinks it will interfere with any prospects he may have for the succession.   By nominating [Addison] Gardiner with him as Lt. Gov., I think [Martin] Van Buren has assured him, that Polk will offer him the Dept. of State, and that he can place himself on the line of succession without incurring the Executive responsibilities of this State, if he will consent to serve, and in this V[an] Buren will be seconded by [Francis P.] Blair, [Thomas H.] Benton, & [Andrew] Jackson; but the important officer of Governor of this great State, must not be made the stepping stone for any ambitious objects.   Wright once pledged to the State by his accepting the nomination must retain the office at least during the term, and he will be required to remain in it.   Mr. Polk if elected, will have but few Cabinet changes to make, the ["position" *canceled and* "condition" *intor lined*] of the South, admonishes him to be exceedingly cautious & delicate in any steps, calculated to shake his position in that section of the union, and at the same time he cannot forget that the errors of his friends in this State, lead to the overthrow of 1840.   If he is discreet & cautious, his administration will be successful.   I am glad that you are not mixed up in the present injudicious movement in S.C.; you have only to maintain your old position & uniform decleration, *Liberty & Union* and your opponents will not be able to reach you.   Sincerely y[ou]rs, M.M. Noah.

ALS in ScCleA; PEx in Boucher and Brooks, eds., *Correspondence*, pp. 248–249.

From Isaac T. Preston, New Orleans, 9/8.   He recommends Frederick A. Sawyer for appointment to be the U.S. Chargé d'Affaires in Texas as successor to the late [Tilghman A.] Howard.   Sawyer is a lawyer of fine talents and "prepossessing manners" who has traveled extensively in Texas.   Preston is confident that Sawyer's distinguished friends in Texas will be pleased if he is granted the appointment. ALS in DNA, RG 59 (State Department), Applications and Recommendations, 1837–1845, Sawyer (M-687:29, frames 379–380).

From H[ARVEY] M. WATTERSON

Special Agency of the United States
Buenos Ayres, Sept. 8, 1844

Sir, Since my arrival in this city nothing has afforded me such high gratification as the many evidences I have received of the friendly feeling of the government of Buenos Ayres toward that of the United States and its citizens. Whilst the citizens of other nations are looked upon with jealousy and even hatred, ours are regarded as friends and *countrymen.* This happy state of things has been produced by the prudent and manly Conduct of our naval and other officers, who, in no instance, have taken part in the civil wars which unfortunately afflict this country—on the contrary they have invariably adhered, both to the letter and spirit of their instructions, and maintained the strictest neutrality.

To give any thing like a correct account of the origin and progress of the existing War between Buenos Ayres and the Oriental Republic, would be a task of much difficulty and but little interest. Every insignificant *guerrilla* is magnified into an important battle, and *both* parties never fail to claim a most splendid victory.

About eighteen months ago, the City of Monte Video, containing at that time near fifty thousand inhabitants, was besieged by six or seven thousand Buenos Ayrean troops, commanded by *General* [Manuel] *Oribe,* who claims to be the legal President of that Republic. Skirmishes between the two armies are of almost daily occurrence, unimportant in their results but evincing a savage cruelty, unwarranted and unsanctioned by the principles of civilized warfare. Monte Video is defended by some three thousand Frenchmen, one thousand Italians, fifteen hundred negroes, and less than five hundred *natives!* A few months since the French Admiral demanded that his countrymen should either lay down their arms or take off the badges of their nationality in which latter event he would consider them beyond the pale of his protection. Between these alternatives they did not hesitate a moment. To a man they tore off their French badges, and forthwith unfurled the Oriental flag, said it waved over the country of ["the" *altered to* "their"] adoption and they would defend it to the last extremity. Should he capture Montevideo, General Oribe has threatened death to all these *"savage Unitarian foreigners"* and there is but little doubt, that he would execute it with as little hesitancy, as he would *lazo* and slaughter so many wild cattle. With a knowledge of this fact staring them in the face, it will be no easy work to successfully storm the City, as doubtless all are firmly resolved upon victory or *death* (if it must come) at the point of the bayonet. This barbarous war seems to be just as far from its termination, at this time, as it did when I first sat foot on the shores of South America. Indeed it is doubted by some of the best informed men in the country, whether it is the policy of Governor [Juan M.] Rosas, to terminate hostilities *immediately* even were it in his power. He is compelled to maintain ["an" *altered to* "a"] standing army, and whilst they are employed against the *enemy* in the Banda Oriental, there is no danger that their arms will be turned against *him at home*; and consequently he is more firmly seated in power, than if peace reigned throughout the provinces of the Rio De La Plata. The partial blockade which has been placed upon the port of Monte Video, operates less to the prejudice of our commerce than almost any other nation, as the introduction of flour[,] rice &c. are not prohibited. For more than two years, the intervention of England and France, for the purpose of putting a stop to this war, has been confidently predicted, still no intervention has taken place, neither do I believe that either of those governments will interfere, further than their own interests prompt them.

I have been repeatedly assured by Señor Don Felipe Arana, Minister of Foreign Affairs, that all the claims of our citizens against this Government, which, upon examination, are found to be just, will be promptly paid. This examination I have never *pressed*, for the reason, that since 20th April last I have been daily expecting to receive intelligence of either my rejection or confirmation by the Senate of the United States, as Charge De Affair[e]s—intending in the event of my confirmation, to bring to the immediate notice of this Government several claims of long standing and urge their payment. I knew it was perfectly idle to press the settlement of these claims whilst my nomination was pending, as there would not ["have" *interlined*] been wanting pretexts to stave off action until it was ascertained, that my nomination was confirmed. I perceive from the newspapers, that the Senate, after keeping my nomination before them more than four months, at length rejected it, and confirmed that of W[illia]m Brent Jun[ior]. I trust that Mr. Brent will be able to settle in the most satisfactory manner, all questions between the two Governments. I am

greatly deceived if it is not the sincere desire of Gov. Rosas to cultivate with the United States the most friendly relations. Very Respectfully Your Ob[edien]t S[er]v[an]t, H.M. Watterson.

ALS in DNA, RG 59 (State Department), Diplomatic Despatches, Argentina,
vol. 5 (M-69:6), received 12/11; variant FC (dated 9/10) in DNA, RG 84
(Foreign Posts), Argentina, Correspondence with Embassy Officials.

To A.M. Bouton, Newark, N.J., 9/9. Calhoun acknowledges
Bouton's letter of 9/4 and states in reply that the information in the
State Department relative to the claims "on the Mexican Government,
to which you refer, is not sufficient to enable me to express an opinion,
as to the probability of their being adjusted." FC in DNA, RG 59
(State Department), Domestic Letters, 34:369 (M-40:32).

From George Brown, [U.S. Commissioner to the King of Hawaii],
Honolulu, 9/9. Brown states that John Wiley, a U.S. citizen resident
in Honolulu, was convicted of rape without any evidence having been
produced in his trial. Wiley claimed through William Hooper, U.S.
Commercial Agent in Honolulu, the right to a trial by a jury composed of foreigners. This claim was based on a promise made by the
King [Kamehameha III] to Brown at their first interview. Many letters have passed between Brown and [Gerrit P.] Judd, Secretary of
State of the Sandwich Islands, concerning this case. Judd has taken
the advice of [John] Ricord, a U.S. citizen acting as Hawaiian Attorney General, in refusing the requested jury trial. Brown has been
forced, after many unsuccessful attempts to change this decision, to
request an audience with the King. This audience has not yet been
granted. Ricord has publicly talked of the decision he would make
in the case, and he did indeed render the verdict, although he was
not judge in the case. Brown was instructed when he first came to
Hawaii to regard the rights of U.S. citizens and to insist that they be
placed on a footing of equality with the most privileged nations.
Until this occurrence, nothing of importance had deprived U.S. citizens of any privileges. Brown asks that he be upheld in his position
on this matter. He requests an early answer to be forwarded through
Mazatlan. "Unless the U. States should be willing to give up the
point at once there is but one way to settle it—by letting these people
know *in terms not to be mistaken*, the determination to be placed on
a par *in every respect*, with the most favored nations." ALS (No.
16) with Ens in DNA, RG 59 (State Department), Diplomatic Despatches, Hawaii, vol. 1 (T-30:1, frames 101–132), received 12/19.

To Henry Dolliver, Somerville, N.J., 9/9. "Your letter of the 4th instant has been received. It would not be proper for me to comply with your request for my opinion on the Subject of the relations between the United States and the Mexican Republic." FC in DNA, RG 59 (State Department), Domestic Letters, 34:369 (M-40:32).

From N[ATHANIEL] B. ELDRIDGE, [later a Representative from Mich.]

Lapeer Mich., Sept. 9th [18]44

Sir, I am desirous of learning a fact which I can not get in so satisfactory a manner as from yourself.

It is, did President [James] Madison signe the bill, which was passed by Congress in 1816, rechartering a United States Bank? Or did he permit it to become a law without his signature?

You will, by an answer, gratify myself as well as many others, and perhaps furnish me with an argument against our common enemy, the Whigs.

I have every facility for knowing, and have no hesitency in saying, that this State is beyond a doubt, safe for [James K.] Polk & [George M.] Dallas by a large majority. I have the honour to be Your Most Ob[edien]t Serv[an]t, N.B. Eldridge.

ALS in ScCleA.

From CHA[RLE]S GRAEBE

Consulate of the United States
Hesse Cassel, 9th Sept[em]b[er] 1844

Honorable Sir, Since my last respectfull one No. 32, I did receive merely the Honorable Secretary Circular of 1st April.

The refusal of the Senate, to advise the ratification of the treaty, agreed on, between the United States and the ZollVerein, has produced in the latter, a bitter feeling against, the U. St[ates] nourisched by rather harsh ["feeling" *canceled and* "expressions" *interlined*], of its press.

Far from allowing myself official[l]y, an opinion on this non-ratification I still consider it my duty, to lay the public opinion, in regard of the probable effect, which this treaty if ratified, would have had, before the Honorable Secretary.

The ZollVerein as a body, is more an exporting, than an importing country, the only advantage which therefore could have accrued to the United States, by the treaty, would have been if the ZollVerein would admit our principal produces, as Cotton, rice, tobacco, at a lower rate of duty, than those, being of the growth of other countries, whereby alone a corresponding increase in the consumption thereof, in the ZollVerein could be produced, which however has not been done, nor is ["it" *interlined*], I have reason to believe, the intention of the ZollVerein.

The proposed reduction of 1½ rixdahler per quintal on the duty of tobacco, being of the growth of the United States, is in my humble opinion, not only insufficient of producing any increase in the consumption thereof in the ZollVerein; but leaves the same unfavorable taxation of U. St[ates] tobacco against those from South america & Westindies, as stated in my last respectfull report No. 32, dated 25th January last, as the duty on our tobacco will even after the proposed reduction, amount to an advalorem rate of about 50%, whereas the other kinds would continue of paying merely about 25% ad valorem, and as long as this is not equalized, no increase in the consumption of our tobaccos could be expected.

The duty on rice, was few years ago reduced by the ZollVerein from 3 to 2 rixdahlers, but this reduction has been a general one, and not a favor, granted only to the U.St[ates], and whereby the lower qualities from the Eastindies, have principal[l]y been benefited by, whose consumption has owing to their low price, been nearly doubled in the ZollVerein, whereas the one ["from" *canceled*] of rice from the United States, has remained nearly stationary or has even decreased, and only a differential reduction of duty, in favor of our rice, could have benefitted our planters.

The promise of the ZollVerein, not to lay any duty on Cotton, amounts, according to my humble opinion to nothing, because they can never do so, without destroying thereby their spinning establishments.

The price of Hogs lard is in the interior of the ZollVerein as low as in the Western countries, none has therefore, nor will be imported from the U.St[ates], and the proposed reduction of duty thereon by the ZollVerein, is considered by its mercantile community, merely as a sham concession.

The advantages which the U.St[ates] could have gained by the

724

treaty would according to my humble opinion, have been mere nothing, and the ["advantages" *altered to* "disadvantages"] very large.

The export of goods from the ZollVerein to the United States, amounts, according to the reports of the Verein, annual[l]y to about 15 Million prussian rixdahlers, on which the reduction of duty, which the United States, would have been obliged to make, averages about 10% making a total of 1½ Million rixdahlers, what their goods would have paid less, than if the same goods had arrived from other countries, which by such advantages, would natural[l]y have continual[l]y increased. The highest importation of tobacco into the ZollVerein, has amounted according to official report to 248,748 quintals, of which not more than 200,000 quintals, were of the growth of the U.St[ates], the loss in the receipt of duties thereon, would have amounted, in reducing the same 1½ rixdahlers per Cwt., to the Zoll-Verein in utmost of 300,000 rixdahlers, whereas the annual sacrifice of the United States would have amounted at least 1½ Millions of rixdahlers, equalizing nearly to the whole amount of tobacco, taken from us by the ZollVerein.

The treaty if ratified, would have besides this direct loss, have also altered entirely our commercial relations with Germany, the Zoll-Verein possesses only seaports, in the Baltic; and nine tenths of its importation and exportations take place, through the ports of the Netherlands and the Hanseatic towns, the latter being the free ports of Germany, where our vessels can resort and deposit their cargoes at a trifling charge and without the least molestation.

Prussia whose constant aim, is, to be one of the great powers, and to extend through the ZollVerein, her ascendency over the smaller german governments, has ever been anxious, to extend for this purpose, the Verein to the North sea, which by the refusal of Hanover and the Hanseatic towns has been, as yet, frustrated, the treaty with the United States if ratified, would have assisted Prussia therein, as the vessels of the Hanseatic towns, having participated so far with those of our country, in the car[r]ying of our produces, ["to their ports" *interlined*] and by being excluted from the benefit of the treaty, they having no other employ for their vessels, would have been forced to join in self defence the ZollVerein, who would have established her custom houses in the Hanseatic towns and subjected their ports and the rivers Elbe & Weser to their regulations, forcing thereby, Hanover and the other few governments as Oldenburg and Mecklenburg to become likewise members of the ZollVerein. This not intended result, from the part of the U.St[ates], of the treaty would have been, if ratified, that the ZollVerein had extented all over Germany, with the exception of Austria; and their avowed purpose being to raise a revenue, the ZollVerein would soon have increased the duty on our produces, tobacco and rice; which being considered by the same, articles of luxury, whereon it was the best to lay a heavy tax.

To prevent which, it is in my humble opinion, of the highest importance, ["to the U.St(ates)" *interlined*] that the Hanseatic towns, should remain free ports and not subject to the ZollVerein; that the United States, should even stipulate in futur[e] treaties with any of the german governments, that our produces coming through any hanseatic port, should be admitted at the same rate of duty as if having ["been" *interlined*] imported direct into a port of such contracting part, no matter if brought to the Hanseatic towns in one of ours or their vessels.

The whole population of the three hanseatic towns, consists merely of about 250,000 inhabitants, their competition in the car[r]ying trade from the United States, can therefore never be so large, as the benefit which the United States, must always experience, in finding their ports open to our vessels, and admitting their cargoes at a trifling duty, and free from all the vexatious regulations, which monarchical governments always car[r]y with them. So long as the Hanseatic towns, remain independent and their ports free, so long have we not to fear that the ZollVerein, will impose any prohibitif duty on our produces; they must have them; their soil and the climat[e] does not allow them to raise Cotton and rice; and it is general[l]y believed, that the growth of tobacco in the ZollVerein, has been car[r]ied there, already to the highest possible extend; the cultivation requires in Germany too much manure, which they cannot produce cheap enough. The United States have therefore not to fear any decrease, in the consumption of their tobacco, if even the ZollVerein should increase the duty thereon; the germans will rather miss a meal than their pipe or segar.

The german newspapers being under censorship, their articles bear therefore in some way an official character, and their harsh articles on the U.St[ates] and against our federal government, bespeak in some manner, the opinion of the authorities of the ZollVerein, wherefore I have consider it my duty, of laying, my respectfull view, drawn from experience and the knowledge of the trade between the United States and Germany, before the Honorable Secretary, representing the bearing and probable effect, which the treaty, would have had, if ratified, of the correctness of which, the H[onora]ble Secretary will be the best judge, and I beg leave of subscribing The

Honorable Secretary most obed[ien]t servant, Chas. Graebe, United States Consul.

ALS (No. 33) in DNA, RG 59 (State Department), Consular Despatches, Hesse-Cassel, vol. 1 (T-213:1), received 10/5.

To David Hoffman, Philadelphia, 9/9. Calhoun acknowledges Hoffman's letter of 9/4 and assures him that "the suggestions which it contains have been taken into respectful consideration." Calhoun also assures Hoffman that the unpaid installments due by the Mexican government under the convention of 1/30/1843 have received and will continue to receive, the "Serious attention of the Executive." FC in DNA, RG 59 (State Department), Domestic Letters, 34:371 (M-40:32).

To Ogden Hoffman, U.S. Attorney for the Southern District of N.Y., [New York City], 9/9. "I have to acknowledge the receipt of your letter of the 23d Ult[im]o, and of its accompaniments. The case has been duly considered, and the Executive concurs with you, in the opinion that it is not provided for by any law of the United States." FC in DNA, RG 59 (State Department), Domestic Letters, 34:371 (M-40:32).

To W[illia]m H. Newman, New York [City], 9/9. "I have the honor to inform you that the Consul of the United States at Sydney, in Nova Scotia, having appointed a Consular Agent at St. John's[,] Newfoundland, it is at present not deemed expedient, to appoint a Consul for that Port." FC in DNA, RG 59 (State Department), Domestic Letters, 34:368–369 (M-40:32).

From F[RANCIS] W. PICKENS

Edgewood, 9 ["August" *canceled and* "Sept." *interlined;* 18]44
My dear Sir, After great trouble and exhaustion I arrived at home yesterday from Tenn: I came accross from Athens [Ga.] to Pendleton under an expectation I would meet you there. But when I got there I found you were not expected and I heard one of my children was very ill—so I came directly through & did not see your family.

Although I did not get to Nashville in time for the great Convention yet I flatter myself I got [there] in time to do some good. I attended other meetings and addressed the people &c. I saw delegates from every State in the valley of the Miss: and I can assure you that *all is right* in that quarter. There is deep excitement and great activity, and what is best the canvass is conducted on our principles. I went over the whole ground as to measures & men with [James K.] Polk (at whose ["who" *canceled*] house I spent two days) and there are no disguises. *Every thing* is *perfectly satisfactory.* I wish I could have seen you. There is no connection at all with the N[ew] York managers *& no correspondence even.* ["Benton" *canceled*; Thomas H.] Benton is off—and he is denounced every where. I was at [Andrew] Jackson's a day &c—& he conversed perfectly free with me upon all points. He tells me Benton will never be with us again— and says "thank God! the party can do without him." He sent a message to Benton by his particular friend Judge Boldin—to the same effect but even stronger. Jackson says he is deranged by the explosion of that gun. *Polk is entirely untram[m]eled* and is determined if elected to do all he can to reform the Gov[ernment] & the 1st thing is to reduce the Tariff of 1842 to a revenue measure entirely & upon the principles of the compromise act—2d to introduce strict economy—3d acquire Texas at all hazzards. He will plant himself upon these measures and look firmly to posterity to do him justice and without the slightest reference to *temporary power* as he has announced his determination not to look to re-election. He will look to integrity & qualifications solely for office and none, will be removed except for deficiency in those points. I found him exceedingly friendly and we were very free—but of course I mention these things to you alone. None of the old leaders are in council with him—*this I know.* He answers no committees & writes to none but very general letters & in particular cases. The information is that every State in the valley will certainly go for him except K[en]t[uck]y & Ohio—and the probabilities are that the latter will go with us—particularly since [John] Tyler's withdrawal.

Our friends are determined to fight every inch of ground for K[en]t[uck]y & with some reasonable hopes so they tell me. ["Ken" *canceled*.] Tenn. is deeply excited & from what I see & hear will go for us. They are in full discussion upon the Tariff there & I addressed them exactly as I would a So. Ca. audience—they are with us in feeling. All we want is prudence and judgement amongst ourselves to secure the fruits of a complete victory, & if we should be defeated, to organise a powerful opposition upon sound principles, and with the certainty of success. In 1832 we had no bearing with the Rep[ublican] party as Jackson had led them off & we had none with the National Rep[ublican] party as they were ag[ain]st us on principle, but now we are forcing the discussion upon our issues with the whole Democratic party & they are just coming up to us. We have every prospect of having a combined & powerful union, & with the unsound portion of the party thrown off; now under these circumstances it is madness & folly, & worse *unpatriotic*, to seperate ourselves and throw off those who are with us in feeling and principle. All your friends in Nashville[,] Shelbyville & Huntsville[,] Ala: conversed with me freely & anxiously. I stop[p]ed in Huntsville on my return, and the whole population from what I could learn are determined to move for you early after the Election. Judge [J.C.] Thompson, Col. [James W.] McClung, Mr. Clements [*sic;* Jeremiah Clemens] are all your friends and they are the *leaders* about Huntsville. I told them when they moved to call the people together, & commence by set[t]ing forth that "we the people are determined to manage the next presidential Election for ourselves alone, & therefore nominate you as the people's candidate" &c. They will move in all North Ala: exactly where I want the move to commence[,] in the heart of the old Jackson ranks. *Your friends* in Nashville say they can get at least *50,000* people to meet ["you" *interlined*] in Nashville at any time. From full conversation and from what I have seen of the West I am satisfied that you ought to visit that *country next May.* Go early before any public move is made for you. I know you can do much. I never saw men so devoted to our cause than they are there, and I had such crowds of gentlemen to call even on me that I talked myself perfectly hoarse every night. I know, all they want is light. All our ideas are new to them & they seize them with the greatest eagerness. They are a shrewd people & patriotic. The only thing I had to contend ag[ain]st was the sensativeness, that I feared, might be created in the breast of other gent[lemen] from distant States, from the excessive desire manifested to hear from *So. Ca.* to the exclusion of attention to others. I therefore rather avoided speaking when I could. I saw this feeling distinctly shewn in Mr. [Gansevoort] Melville of N[ew] York. But I could utter no sentiment on the Tariff too strong for those people, & they are all becoming [*sic*] to understand it thoroughly.

I think we have now every prospect of carrying the election. If N[ew] York goes with us of course Polk is elected, but even if not & N[ew] Jersey & Tenn: go still he is elected without N.Y. If [Henry] Clay is defeated of course he is done, and will no longer be a disturbing force in the South. I think all our prospects are better than I have seen them for years. I am sure a calm & dignified course in yourself will give you the complete command of the future—and you know I have generally spoken my candid sentiments to you. I think things have developed now clearly who were your sincere friends & those who were so merely from selfish considerations.

I wrote you from Geo[rgia] & would have done so from **Tenn:** but expected to meet you on my return.

I found my family quite well, the child having recovered. The country [is] very dry—cotton cut off one half—no crops at all from here to Huntsville[,] Ala.—& there very triffling—so in Tenn: except corn—heard the worm was ruining South Ala. & Miss:—a great deal of sickness—saw at Huntsville Mr. Lyon, Andrew's [Andrew Pickens Calhoun's] neighbour, he says there was sickness in the Canebreak for the first time. Crop very fine—Andrew the best farmer in the State &c &c. I heard from Dr. [Frederick W.] Symmes in Pendleton as I passed through that there had been 33 cases of fever at your place & James [Edward Calhoun] & Cousin F[loride Colhoun Calhoun] had been sick but both entirely well now.

I find this State perfectly calm & united out of Beaufort, and the only contrary appearance is exhibited in the Mercury.

I heard [George] McDuffie was for Disunion, but saw him for a few moments in Abbeville as I passed and he did not talk that way to me. I do not think he has any definite ideas. He seemed to deprecate the recent moves in Beaufort & Colleton as far as I could understand him, yet I confess he seemed more confused than I ever saw him. There were several present, amongst them Judge [David L.?] Wardlaw, & I denounced the mad schemes of ["every"(?) *canceled*] those who were crying for seperate action. I afterwards took McD[uffie] one side to talk freely with him & told him what I had heard of him—he denied it—& yet seemed indefinite—said he prefer[r]ed ["cessessi" *canceled*] cesession [sic] to Nul[l]ification & that was all the idea he suggested. His health is much improved.

I suppose the Oregon question is before you by this. Very truly, F.W. Pickens.

ALS in ScCleA; PEx in Jameson, ed., *Correspondence*, pp. 968–971.

From T[ruman] B. Ransom, President, Norwich University, [Vermont], 9/9. He acknowledges receipt from the State Department of 18 vols. of documents of the 3rd Session of the 27th Congress for the University library. He closes "With many cherished recollections of the pleasing interview I had with you in Company with Col. [Thomas H.] Seymour [Representative] of Ct., just pending the Democratic nomination for the Presidency." [Ransom was subsequently killed in action in the Mexican War.] ALS in DNA, RG 59 (State Department), Miscellaneous Letters (M-179:105, frame 344).

From ISAAC VAN ZANDT

Legation of Texas
Washington City, ["August" *canceled and*
"September" *interlined*] 9th 1844

Sir, I have the honor to inform you that since the date of my last note, in reply to yours, in relation to the arms taken from Colonel [Jacob] Snively's command, I have received further instructions from my Government respecting the same; and now announce to your Excellency the acceptance of the offer made by you on the part of your Government. As it is not probable that the arms could be returned in the order in which they were taken, compensation will be received for them. Their value &C, as I understand, having been communicated to the Department of War of the United States, I hope you will inform me at what time your Government will be in readiness to discharge the demand.

I avail myself of this occasion to offer to you renewed assurances of my distinguished consideration. Isaac Van Zandt, Chargé d'Affaires of the Republic of Texas.

LS in DNA, RG 59 (State Department), Notes from Foreign Legations, Texas, vol. 1 (T-809:1); FC in Tx, Records of the Texas Republic Department of State, Letters and Dispatches Sent by the Texas Legation in Washington, 2:5–6; FC in Tx, Records of the Texas Republic Department of State, Copybooks of Letters Received from Texan and Foreign Representatives, vol. 2–1/98, p. 538; CC in Tx, Records of the Texas Republic Department of State, U.S. Diplomatic Correspondence; PC in Senate Document No. 1, 28th Cong., 2nd Sess., p. 112; PC in House Document No. 2, 28th Cong., 2nd Sess., p. 109; PC in Crallé, ed., *Works*, 5:413.

From ——

[Washington] 9 September 1844

Mr. Calhoun, Is it true, that the British Government have collected at Jama[i]ca, Coal Sufficient for 50 Steamers for 4 years. And that they have there an army of 30,000 blacks, officered by white men. If this be so, can there be a doubt, but they meditate an attack on either New Orleans or Charleston, to stir up the blacks and desolate the Southern States and thereby carry out their *avowed purpose* of abolishing slavery throughout the world.

Pretext with England is not wanted. Expediency is all sufficient with them. And does America, and the Land of [George] Washington see this, and supinely look on, without raising a shield, a Broad Shield, behind which the fair daughters of the South may repose in safety, and before which her Sons may *fight forever*, or crush the instigators of such calamity and Crime. I wish you w[oul]d bring this subject before the Cabinet to see what the actual state of the case is and what is best to be done under the Circumstances. [Signed:] Y[ou]r friend.

ALU in DNA, RG 59 (State Department), Miscellaneous Letters (M-179:105, frames 341–342).

From A[mos] M. Alexander, Clerk of the Superior Court of Wakulla County, Newport, Fla. Territory, 9/10. Alexander forwards to Calhoun a copy of a grand jury presentment against R[ichard] K. Call. He hopes that this will be additional evidence of the innocence of [Charles S.] Sibley, U.S. District Attorney for Middle Fla., of the "foolish charges" made against him. The enclosed presentment dated 5/14/1844 charges the [Tallahassee] Railroad Company with obstruction of navigation on the St. Marks River by "the piers of the old Bridge at the rail road," which bridge is called a "public nuisance." Call is cited as the President of the Railroad Company, and the grand jury directs indictments to be made against him. Appended is an AES by A[ndrew] Denham [foreman of the grand jury], stating that the District Attorney was opposed to the prosecution against Call. ALS with En in DNA, RG 59 (State Department), Applications and Recommendations, 1837–1845, Sibley (M-687:30, frames 76–79).

From J[ohn] S. Barbour, "Private"

Catalpa [Va.] Sep[tembe]r 10th 1844

My Dear Sir, Do you remember that in the winter of 1832'3, whilst the compromise was in agitation, that the Committee met on a Sunday morning, (from necessity) that Messrs. [Felix] Grundy & [William C.] Rives appeared at the Capitol (they were members of the

Committee) and in leaving the Committee for their respective Churches, each said "we ["can't stay but we" *interlined*] will concur in anything that Mr. Calhoun agrees to."

In one of my publick speeches I have said so. I do not wish to call your name, nor any other persons on a question of that kind. But the fact is as clear to my perception as if of this moment[']s occurrence.

It has not been denied. I do not know that it will be. So many odd things happen that we can scarce guess what may come next.

Do you remember my enclosing to you at the session of 1842–3 a letter from Mr. Rives to me, in which he responds to my question "Is there anything to forbid your support of Mr. Calhoun?" And in his response he speaks of you in the strongest terms of cordiality & respect, refers to what I knew of his ancient[?] opinions of you & reminds me of them. That letter I sent you, & on meeting you in Washington in Feb[ruar]y 1843, you said to me that the expressions in that letter were in perfect coherence with Mr. Rives' conduct to you *of late* in the Senate.

I do not think you ever returned me Mr. Rives' letter. If you did I have mislaid it, never dreaming of the possibility for its use.

I encountered Mr. [Valentine W.] Southall recently & the popular verdict was so decisive, that he is muttering under his defeat, various complaints. And a few days since Gen[era]l [William F.] Gordon of Alb[emarl]e told me Mr. Rives had said as much to him as he said in his letter to me, *and authorised him to make it known.*

I am to address the people of Centreville next Saturday. Those of Warrenton next Tuesday the 21st and I have a most pressing solicitation to be at Amelia the 27th Sep[tembe]r to meet Mr. [Benjamin W.] Leigh, Mr. Rives & Mr. [Alexander H.H.?] Stuart. Mr. [Lewis E.?] Harvie of Amelia implores me to be there & I must obey his wishes for reasons that are of weight on my judgement & my friendship.

In extreme haste, y[ou]rs faithfully, J.S. Barbour.

[P.S.] "All is well" in this quarter. Nothing will make greater surprise than the terrible defeat that awaits the Whig party. J.S.B.

ALS in ScCleA.

[To George M. Bibb, Secretary of the Treasury], 9/10. A register of letters received by the Secretary of the Treasury indicates that a letter of 9/10 from Calhoun was received on 9/11. The letter apparently enclosed a letter from S[olomon?] Cohen, Savannah, [to Calhoun?], recommending G. Cohen for appointment as Naval Agent at

Savannah. Entry in DNA, RG 56 (Secretary of the Treasury), Registers of Letters Received, 1834–1872, 11:C-788.

From Geo[rge] M. Bibb, Secretary of the Treasury, 9/10. "I have the honor to acknowledge the receipt of your letter of the 26th inst. [*sic*; 8/26; *not found*] with the applications of Messrs. Lafayette Caldwell and Andrew B. Calhoun for appointments as Lieutenants in the Revenue Marine, and in reply have to inform you that no vacancy exists at present. Should any occur it will afford me pleasure to submit the names of the above gentlemen to the President [John Tyler] for his consideration." LS in DNA, RG 59 (State Department), Miscellaneous Letters (M-179:105, frame 347); FC in DNA, RG 26 (U.S. Coast Guard), Revenue Cutter Service: Letters on Revenue Cutters and Boats, 4:282.

From Geo[rge] Brown

Honolulu, 10th Sept[embe]r 1844

Sir, I was informed by Mr. Wiley [*sic*; Robert C. Wyllie] H.B.M. Consul that it would be necessary to have my dispatches at his office at nine oclock tomorrow morning and I I [*sic*] have worked until midnight to get them ready. They are not in so good condition as I could wish, but the duplicates shall be in better order. This affair, which they refer to, has given me a great deal of vexation, and I have done all in my power to keep off the evil day. I have been all along congratulating myself, that I had escaped so far, coming into collission with the present managers of this Government, while the British Consul Gen[era]l has been in hot water the whole time, that he has been here. I was in hopes that Mess. [William] Richards & [Timoteo] Haalilio would have returned long ere this, and that better counsels, would then prevail. At present, the King [Kamehameha III] is completely under the guidance of [Dr. Gerrit P.] Judd, and Judd completely under the thumb of [John] Ricord. Every body is disgusted. They appear (Judd & Ricord) ["to think" *interlined*] that this nation is second to none on earth, and the airs they have put on, have made them appear ridiculous. Dr. Judd is not a bad man, far from it. I believe he has the interests of this people much at his heart, but he has little experience and Ricord who is a designing if not unprincipled man has got him entirely under his control. My object in addressing you this private letter, is to beg of you to forward an answer to my Dispatches as soon as possible, as should this Government adhere to their present decision, I shall be very anxious to know from the Department, what to do, and whether my conduct is approved of. You may judge how uncomfortable I must be at such a distance from home with the certainty of its being *at least* five months before I can hear from you. If this was a country in Europe where I could hear in fifty or sixty days, it would be far different. I am surrounded by Americans, all anxious to know whether this affair is to be settled, according to the King[']s guarantee or not, and of course feeling great interest in the decision.

The subject has become public talk, through the means of Ricord, and Dr. Judd. I was told by a gentleman to day that he was in the foreign office & that Judd, wanted him to read some of the documents, a Queer way of conducting business. Unless you was here yourself, you cannot imagine what a singular state of society this is. Every body knowing every body's business. Compared to other affairs that must take up much of your valuable time, this may appear to you of small moment, but I assure it is important to American interests here, and if this Govt. gains the day in this, there is no knowing how far they may proceed in other matters, full as important.

The surest way I think will be to send me dispatches via New Orleans, Vera Cruz and Mexico, directed to the care of our Consul at Mazatlan, but duplicates might be sent via Panama, and Valparaiso. Excuse me for troubling you with a private letter on this subject, but knowing your willing attention to all matters relating to the interests of your countrymen ["I" *interlined*] have taken the liberty. No news from U. States since 1st April and nothing from the department since Jan[uar]y which was in the shape of newspapers by the way of Cape Horn. Very respectfully Y[ou]r most ob[edien]t S[ervan]t, Geo. Brown.

ALS (Private) in DNA, RG 59 (State Department), Diplomatic Despatches, Hawaii, vol. 1 (T-30:1, frames 132–133).

To R[OBERT] M[ONROE] HARRISON, U.S. Consul, Kingston, Jamaica

Department of State
Washington, September 10th 1844
Sir: It has been incidentally intimated to the Department that the British Government is making preparations for the support at Jamaica

of a Naval and military force of a very unusual and extraordinary extent, and I feel it to be my duty to urge upon you the importance of exercising your utmost vigilance in regard to the movements hinted at, and to keep the Department constantly advised of every occurrence calculated to induce the belief that the intimations we have received are not groundless. I am, Sir, Your obed[ien]t Serv[an]t, J.C. Calhoun.

LS in DNA, RG 84 (Foreign Posts), Kingston, Instructions and Miscellaneous Correspondence; FC in DNA, RG 59 (State Department), Consular Instructions, 12:95.

To OGDEN HOFFMAN, U.S. Attorney for the Southern District of New York, [New York City]

Department of State
Washington, Sept. 10th 1844

Sir: The Department of State has received information from Several qua[r]ters, that the Mexican Government has two armed Steamships in the port of New York, and that the Commanders are enlisting crews, and procuring Military Stores and equipments, in that city and elsewhere. The object of this note is to call your attention to the Subject, and to urge the Strictest Scrutiny in regard to their proceedings. No doubt is entertained that the object of these preparations, is the invasion of Texas; and it is important that our laws of neutrality Should be Strictly observed. It may be well, therefore, that you institute enquiries, and use your best exertions to ascertain, whether the existing laws have been violated, and if so, to take immediate Steps to bring the offenders to justice. In order to afford a clue to your investigations, I enclose you extracts from two letters just received at the Department. With high respect &c, Jno. C. Calhoun.

FC in DNA, RG 59 (State Department), Domestic Letters, 34:373 (M-40:32); PC in Jameson, ed., *Correspondence*, p. 610.

From W[ILLIA]M HOOPER

U.S. Commercial Agency
Oahu, Sandwich Islands
September 10th 1844

Sir, Refer[r]ing to my communication of Feb[ruar]y last (No. 33) you will notice that I then stated that I did not apprehend that any exclusive privilege would ever, by treaty, be granted to the subjects of any nation by the gover[n]ment of these Islands.

The events of the past week, however, prove that I was mistaken in the opinion then expressed. On examination of the correspondence which has taken place between the Governor of this Island and myself, (copies of which are herewith enclosed, marked A B C D,) relative to the case of John Wiley, accused of committing a crime [rape] against the laws of this country, you will perceive that the Governor refused to grant me the privilege of nominating a jury of foreigners— a privilege, which by the III Art. of the treaty made in Feb[ruar]y last between this country and Great Brittain, is allowed the British Consul. The reasons for my *demanding* of the Governor the right of nominating Jurors in this case are fully set forth in my letters to him, to which I refer you.

In order that the Department may fully understand this subject I deem it necessary to state that, after Wiley was unjustly condemned by a common native Judge to pay a fine of fifty dollars, he applied to me for advice. I recommended him to submit his case to a jury, and left him his choice that it be composed of an equal number of natives and foreigners, or of foreigners alone. He preferred the latter, and I immediately called on the Governor for the purpose of nominating twelve foreigners to sit as jurors.

The Governor hesitated about arranging the business and finally referred me to Mr. [Gerrit P.] Judd the Sec[retar]y of State, as is ["his" *interlined*] custom to do in all cases which are not perfectly clear to him. I immediately proceeded to the Secretary's office and observed to him that as the Governor did not appear to understand the nature of the III Art. in the English Treaty which secured to Consuls the right of nominating Jurors in certain cases, I had come for the purpose of arranging the business with him. He made no objections whatever to my proposition, but remarked that he wished the jury composed of respectable men, and set down and aided me in filling out the list.

The following day, he together with Mr. [John] Ricord the Attorney General, called at my office, professedly on some other business, but in reality to say to me that as there was no treaty existing between the U. States and the Gover[n]ment of these Islands which granted to its Consuls the right of nominating jurors in certain cases, it would not be allowed in the case of Wiley. I replied to them, that treaty or no treaty they might feel assured that under all the Circumstances, the Gover[n]ment of the United States would never consent that its Citizens, resident here, should not be on an equal footing with the subjects of other nations.

They spoke of the impropriety of allowing consuls to select jurors—that they might bribe them unbeknown to the Governor, and in that way, all laws would be set at naught. I observed to them that, that should have been thought of before signing the treaty submitted by the English Consul General; but it did not appear that any objection was then made.

Mr. Judd remarked, that he was not aware at that time that the Independence of the Islands had been acknowledged by the three powers, and the manner in which the treaty was laid before the Gover[n]ment was such as to induce the belief that it *must* be signed.

Mr. Ricord observed that by refusing the Gover[n]ment of the United States the privilege which was granted to England, it would probably become a subject of discussion between the two gover[n]-ments, and he had not a doubt that it could be presented to my gover[n]ment in such a light, as not only to induce it to forego the privilege, but be instrumental in breaking up the English Treaty.

I then observed to them that if they wished the obnoxious article in the English treaty expunged, they should seek some other way than by insulting the Gover[n]ment of the U. States—that the more honorable way of affecting [*sic*] it would be to grant the privilege claimed, and place the Gover[n]ment on an even footing with other nations, and then beseech its good offices with the British Gover[n]ment.

After the gentlemen left, I immediately addressed a note to the Governor, of which please see Copy A—his answer and my reply will explain themselves. After the receipt of his final answer (D) I deemed it my duty to lay the business before Mr. Commissioner [George] Brown.

On the day of the trial I appeared at Court and there wrote the protest (E) against the jury as impanneled by the Governor, and informed Mr. Ricord, who in this case, as indeed, in all others acts as Judge, Att[orne]y General, reporter, &c, that Mr. Wiley would make no plea. This he considered as equivalent to a withdrawal of the appeal, and dismissed the case retaining the fine as exacted by the native Judge.

From a twelve years residence at these Islands and an intimate acquaintance with native character I am fully persuaded that it would not be safe, in important cases, to trust ["to" *interlined*] the verdict of a jury composed of natives: Although they might be perfectly honest, yet circumstantial evidence, or the wishes of any particular chief, would influence them quite as much as proof to the point—and in cases w[h]en[?] the jury were composed of half foreigners and should one of them be well versed in the native language, he would manage, the native part to suit his own views.

Under all ["the" *altered to* "these"] circumstances, therefore, I trust that the Gover[n]ment will see the importance of demanding of His Hawaii[a]n Majesty, *unconditionally*, all the privileges which are now secured to Great Brittain and France, and I trust too, they will demand that a new trial be granted Wiley, in order that justice may be rendered him.

I have to observe, in Conclusion, that in a conversation which I had with *Mr. James J. Jarvis*, now a naturalized Hawaii[a]n, ["and an officer in the Govt." *interlined*] he remarked to me, that "this gover[n]ment would never give up the point." So also the Governor has been made to say to me, that an "Angry letter," to use his own words, must come from the Govt. of the U. States before this Govt. would grant what I claimed. With Sentiments of the highest Consideration I have the honor to be Sir, Your Mo[st] Ob[edien]t S[er]v[an]t, Wm. Hooper, Acting U.S. Com[mercia]l Agent.

ALS (No. 37) with Ens in DNA, RG 59 (State Department), Consular Despatches, Honolulu, vol. 2 (M-144:2), received 1/2/1845.

To TILGHMAN A. HOWARD, [Washington, Texas]

Department of State
Washington, September 10th 1844
Sir, The Despatch No. 1 [of 8/7], transmitted through General [Zachary] Taylor, enclosing a copy of your Correspondence with the Secretary of State of the Republic of Texas [Anson Jones], has been laid before the President [John Tyler], who has given to it, that deliberate Consideration which its importance claims.

He approves of the Construction, which you placed on the letter [of 3/11] of Mr. [John] Nelson, acting Secretary of State *ad interim*, to Mr. [William S.] Murphy, and on mine [of 4/11] to Mr. [Isaac]

Van Zandt, in relation to the assurances, to which the Texan Secretary of State refers in his letter, to which yours is a reply. But he instructs you to assure the Government of Texas, that he feels the full force of the obligation of this Government to protect Texas pending, the question of annexation, against the attacks, which Mexico may make on her, in consequence of her acceptance of the proposition of this Government to open negotiations on the subject of annexing Texas to the United States. As far as it relates to the Executive Department, he is prepared to use all its powers for that purpose; but the Government of Texas is fully aware, that they are circumscribed by the Constitution within narrow limits, which it would not be possible for the President to transcend. All that he can do is, to make suitable representations to the Mexican Government against the renewal of the war, pending the question of annexation, and the savage manner, in which it is proposed to conduct it, accompanied by appropriate protests and indications of the feelings with which he regards both; and to recommend to Congress to adopt measures to repel any attack which may be made.

In execution of the first, a communication [of 9/10] (a copy of which is enclosed) has been addressed to our Minister in Mexico [Wilson Shannon], and forwarded to him by a special Messenger, which, it is to be hoped, will not be without effect in arresting her hostile movements. You will give a copy of it to the Texan Government, and you will assure it, that when Congress meets, the President will recommend the adoption of measures to protect Texas effectually against the attacks of Mexico, pending the question of annexation. He hopes these measures will prove satisfactory to the Government of Texas; and that no serious invasion will be attempted, at least before the meeting of Congress.

I enclose a copy of a Despatch to our Minister at Paris [William R. King], which you may show to President [Samuel] Houston and the Secretary of State. It will doubtless be satisfactory to learn, that France is not disposed, in any event, to take a hostile attitude in reference to annexation. A despatch of a subsequent date to the one, to which the enclosed is an answer, gives a conversation between Mr. [F.P.G.] Guizot and our Minister, equally satisfactory, as that with the King. He stated in reply to a question on the part of our Minister, that France had not agreed to unite with England in a protest against annexation.

I am happy to add, in conclusion, that the indications of public sentiment are highly favorable to the cause of annexation; and that we may now look forward with much confidence to the consummation of that great measure; at no distant period. I am, Sir, respectfully Your Obedient Servant, J.C. Calhoun.

LS (No. 3) in DNA, RG 84 (Foreign Posts), Texas; FC in DNA, RG 59 (State Department), Diplomatic Instructions, Texas, 1:102–103 (M-77:161); CCEx in Tx, Records of the Texas Republic Department of State, Letters and Dispatches Sent by the Texas Legation in Washington, vol. 1; PC in Senate Document No. 1, 28th Cong., 2nd Sess., pp. 38–39; PC in House Document No. 2, 28th Cong., 2nd Sess., pp. 50–51; PC in *Congressional Globe*, 28th Cong., 2nd Sess., Appendix, p. 5; PC in the Washington, D.C., *Globe*, December 6, 1844, p. 2; PC in the Washington, D.C., *Daily National Intelligencer*, December 9, 1844, p. 1; PC in the Washington, D.C., *Daily Madisonian*, December 9, 1844, p. 3; PC in *Niles' National Register*, vol. LXVII, no. 15 (December 14, 1844), p. 234; PC in Crallé, ed., *Works*, 5:377–379.

From ALEX[ANDE]R JONES

Baltimore, September 10th 1844
12 oclock, M. (Night)

Respected Sir, I have just arrived in this city, on my second trip to the West, and expect to leave at 7 A.M. tomorrow for Wheeling, having left New York this morning. You will have seen by my hastily written letters ["in" *canceled*] published in the [New York] Journal of Commerce, the route I pursued in my late journey, as well as the objects which to some extent engaged my attention. I have, also, since my return written an article or two over the same signature in defence of Free Trade, the last in yesterday[']s paper, being, a Breif [*sic*] Review of Mr. [Daniel] Webster[']s speech lately delivered at Albany.

I am ["at" *interlined*] present on a flying visit to Tennessee; in part to see some relations, and in part to look for something to do. My first trip proved more interesting than profitable. I expect, however, to return to New York [City] in all the month of October.

I was gratified in my journey through the west to find your freinds [*sic*] both strong, numerous & respectable. Free Trade has made & is still making greater progress among the Grain growing farmers of the west than most people suppose, and much more than I had anticipated. It is on this ground I think mainly rest[s] your popularity in that quarter, ["west" *canceled*] especially in Missouri & Illinois. I look upon the latter as decidedly a *"Calhoun State."* Over the whole west & South West, you have leading[,] strong and influential friends.

In Louisiana, you were, & would be again if necessary, the strongest Democratic Candidate before the people. And I presume much, the same feeling exist[s] in Mississippi & Alabama.

I think the prospects of Col. [James K.] Polk's election almost as settled in his favour. I trust, if he succeeds, he will toe the mark on free Trade, Texas &C.

While travelling on the upper Mississippi, stopping at Galena [Ill.] &C, circumstances transpired which led me to believe, that ["a" *canceled*] considerable bands of smugglers, are in a very clandestine manner, introducing Contraband Goods, such as sewing silks and other Goods, by the way of Lakes Huron & Superior, from thence across an unsettled country to the Mississippi ["River" *interlined*] in the neighborhood of St. Anthony[']s Falls [Minn.], thence down that River to St. Louis &C. I have not time, to state all the facts in confirmation of my statement.

I am perfectly satisfied, however, were it necessary, I could convince the Secretary of the Treasury [George M. Bibb] that, that quarter of the country requires vigilant & watchful care. Look at & examine that part of the country on a map. ["With" *interlined*] its thinly populated character, the facility of getting goods, through the Lakes especially Lake Superior, the extreme western point of which, reaches within comparatively a short distance of St. Anthony[']s falls, situated also in an unguarded & almost unsettled country & yet open, for ["a large" *canceled*] Steam Navigation continually (all the mild season of the year) from thence to New Orleans.

I am told it is sometimes customary for the Secretary of the Treasury to employ private, or confidential guards, in protecting the Revenue Laws, at a moderate salary. I do not know if this be the case. But should he have such authority & think that part of the ["require" *canceled*] country requires looking after by an active & industrious agent in the service of the Department, I should feel much obliged to him, to be so employed. Having visited that section, or at least a part of it, I could at any moment be prepared to enter upon such service, & discharge its duties, with all the fidelity, industry, and energy ["that might" *canceled*] in my power, & in such a manner as I trust would be useful & satisfactory to the Government.

I have not mentioned this subject to anyone, save yourself, or do I expect to do so. If you think favourably of my ["rep" *canceled*] report & suggestion, I will feel extremely, and much obliged to you, if you will call upon *Judge Bibb*, and bring the subject matter of my letter before him, and give it such direction, as you may think best.

In the meantime, I shall be happy ["to" *canceled*] to receive a line from you, on this or other matters, while I have the Honor to Remain Your very Ob[edien]t & Humble Serv[an]t, Alex[ande]r Jones.

P.S. In writing to me, please address your letter to me, at *Nashville Tennessee*, with an endorsement, requesting ["your" *canceled*] it, "*to be kept till called for.*" Y[ou]rs, A.J.

ALS in ScCleA.

To WILSON SHANNON, [U.S. Minister to Mexico]

Department of State
Washington, Sept[embe]r 10th 1844

Sir, There can be no longer any doubt that Mexico intends to renew the war against Texas, on a large scale; and to carry it on with more than savage ferocity. The loan she has authorized, and the expensive preperations she is making, by land and sea, are sufficient proofs of the former; and the orders of the Commander of the Army of the North, General [Adrian] Woll, issued the 20th day of June last, and the Decree of Santa Anna, General of Division and Provisional President of Mexico, on the 17th day of June, 1843, of the latter. The decree makes the Generals in Chief of Divisions of the Army, and Commandant General of the coast and frontier responsible for its exact fulfilment. It was under that responsibility, it would seem, that General Woll, to whom the Texan frontier was assigned, issued his order of the 20th of June. After announcing that the war was renewed against Texas; that all communications with it must cease, and that every individual, of whatever condition, who may have communication with it, shall be regarded as a traitor, and as such, ["be punished according to the articles of war," *interlined*] the order announces, in its third article, that "Every individual who may be found at the distance of one league from the left bank of the Rio Bravo will be regarded as a favourer and accomplice of the usurpers of that part of the national Territory, and as a traitor to his Country," and after a ["]summary military trial," shall be punished accordingly. And in its fourth article it also states "that any individual, who may be embraced within the provisions of the preceeding article, and may be rash enough to fly at the sight of any force belonging to the Supreme Government, shall be pursued until taken, or put to death."

In what spirit the decree of the 17th of June, which the order is intended exactly to fulfill, is to be executed, the fate of the Party under General [Francisco] Sentmanat at Tabasco, affords an illustration. They were arrested under it, and executed without hearing or trial, against the indignant remonstrances of the French and Spanish Ministers near to the Government of Mexico; who in vain invoked the voice of humanity, the sacred obligations of the Constitution, and the sanctity of Treaties, in behalf of their countrymen who were executed under this illegal and bloody decree.

If the Decree itself was thus enforced in time of peace on the subjects of friendly powers, and against the remonstrances of their ministers, some faint conception may be formed of the ferocious, and devastating spirit in which the order of General Woll is intended to be executed against the inhabitants of Texas, and all who may, in any way, aid their cause, or even have communication with them. It was under a decree similar to that of the 17th of June 1843, and issued by the same authority on the 30th of October 1835, but which was not so comprehensive in its provisions, or so bloody and ferocious in its character, that the cold blooded butchery of [Col. James W.] Fannin and his Party, and other Texan prisoners was ordered by Santa Anna in his invasion of 1836.

That decree was limited to foreigners who should land at any port of Mexico, or arrive by land, being armed, and having hostile intentions, or who should introduce arms and munitions of war to be used at any place in rebellion, or placed in the hands of its enemies. As savage and outrageous as its provisions were, the order of General Woll, intended to carry out that of June 1843, goes far beyond. It embraces every individual, who may be found east of a line drawn three miles east of the Rio del Norte, without distinction of age or sex; foreigner or Citizen; condition or vocation. All of every description, whether they resist or surrender, are to be treated as Traitors; and all who flee, to be shot down. The war is intended; in short; to be one of utter extirpation. All that breathe are to be destroyed or driven out; and Texas left a desolate waste; and so proclaimed to the world by Mexico, in advance of her projected invasion.

The first question which presents itself for consideration on this statement of facts is, shall we stand by and witness, in silence, the renewal of the war by Mexico and its prosecution in this blood thirsty and desolating Spirit? In order to answer it fully and satisfactorily, it will be necessary to enquire first into her object for renewing the war at this time.

There can be but one, and that is, to defeat the annexation of Texas to our Union. She knows full well that the rejection of the

Treaty has but postponed the question of annexation. She knows that Congress adjourned without finally disposing of it; that it is now pending before both Houses, and actively canvassed before the People throughout the wide extent of our Union; and that it will in all ["probability" *interlined*] be decided in its favor, unless it should be defeated by some movement exterior to the country. We would be blind not to see that she proposes to effect it by the projected invasion; either by conquering and subjecting Texas to her power, or by forcing her to withdraw the proposition for annexation, and to form commercial and political connexions with some other Power, less congenial to her feelings, and favorable to her independence; and more threatening to hers and our permanent welfare and safety. Of the two the latter is much the more probable. She once attempted conquest, but signally failed, although the attempt was made, under the lead of her most skilful and renowned General at the head of a well appointed army, consisting of her best disciplined and bravest troops, and while Texas was yet in her infancy without a Government, almost without means, and with an inconsiderable population. With this example before her, she can scarcely hope to succeed now, under a leader of less skill and renown, and when Texas has settled down under a well established Government, and has so greatly increased in means and population. It is possible she may be overrun, but to expect to hold her in subjection with her present population, and means, at the distance of more than twelve hundred miles from the City of Mexico, with a difficult intermediate Country, destitute in a great degree of resources, would be extreme folly. The very attempt would exhaust her means, and leave her prostrated. No; the alternative is to drive out the inhabitants and desolate the Country, or force her into some foreign and unnatural alliance; and this, the ferocious and savage order of General Woll shows, is well understood by Mexico, and is, in reality, the object of her policy.

Shall we stand by and permit it to be consummated, and thereby defeat a measure long cherished, and indispensable alike to the safety and welfare of the United States and Texas? No measure of policy has been more steadily or longer pursued; and that by both of the great Parties in to which the Union is divided. Many believed that Texas was embraced in the cession of Louisiana, and was improperly, if not unconstitutionally surrendered by the Treaty of Florida in 1819. Under that impression and the general conviction of its importance to the safety and welfare of the Union, its annexation has been an object of constant pursuit ever since. It was twice attempted to acquire it during the Administration of Mr. [John Quincy] Adams;

once in 1825, shortly after he came into power, and again in 1827. It was thrice attempted under the administration of his successor General [Andrew] Jackson, first in 1829 immediately after he came into power; again in 1833, and finally in 1835, just before Texas declared her independence. Texas herself made a proposition for annexation in 1837 at the commencement of Mr. [Martin] Van Buren's administration, which he declined; not however on the grounds of opposition to the policy of the measure. The United States had previously acknowledged her independence, and the example has since been followed by France and Great Britain. The latter, soon after, her recognition, began to adopt a line of policy in reference to Texas, which has given greatly increased importance to the measure of annexation, by making it still more essential to the safety and welfare both of her and the United States.

In pursuance of this long cherished and established policy, and under the conviction of the necessity of acting promptly in order to prevent the defeat of the measure, the present administration invited Texas to renew the proposition for annexation, which had been declined by its predecessor. It was accepted; and as has been stated, is now pending. The question recurs, shall we stand by quietly, and permit Mexico to defeat it, without making an effort to oppose her? Shall we, after this long and continued effort to annex Texas, now, when the measure is about to be consummated, allow Mexico to put it aside perhaps forever? Shall the "golden opportunity" be lost never again to return? Shall we permit Texas, for having accepted an invitation tendered her at a critical moment, to join us and consummate a measure, essential to theirs, and our permanent peace, welfare, and safety, to be desolated; Her inhabitants to be butchered or driven out; or in order to avert so great a calamity, to be forced against her will, into a strange alliance, which would terminate in producing lasting hostilities between her and us, to the permanent injury, and, perhaps, the ruin of both?

The President [John Tyler] has fully and deliberately examined the subject, and has come to the conclusion, that honor and humanity, as well as the welfare and safety of both Countries, forbid it; and that it ["is" *interlined*] his duty during the recess of Congress, to use all his constitutional means in opposition to it; leaving that body when it assembles to decide on the course, which, in its opinion, it would be proper for the Government to adopt.

In accordance with this conclusion, the President would be compelled to regard the invasion of Texas by Mexico, while the question of annexation is pending as highly offensive, to the United States. He entertains no doubt, that we had the right to invite her to renew the proposition for annexation; and she, as an independent state, had a right to accept it, without consulting Mexico, or asking her leave. He regards Texas, in every respect, as independent as Mexico; and as competent to transfer the whole or part of Texas as she would be the whole or part of Mexico. To go no further back, under the [Mexican] constitution of 1824, Texas and Coahuila were members of the Federation, formed by the United States of Mexico. Texas; with Coahuila, forming one state, with the right guarantied to Texas, by the constitution, to form a separate state, as soon as her population would permit; The several states remained equal in rights, and equally independent of each other, until 1835, when the constitution was subverted by the military, and all the states which dared to resist subjugated by force, except Texas. She stood up manfully and bravely in defence of her rights and independence, which she gloriously and successfully asserted on the battle ground of San Jacinto in 1836, and has ever since maintained. The constitution of 1824 made her independent, and her valour and her sword have maintained her so. She has been acknowledged to be so, by three of the leading Powers of Christendom, and regarded by all as such, except Mexico herself. Nor has she ever stood, in relation to Mexico, as a rebellious Department or Province, struggling to obtain independence after throwing off her yoke; much less as a band of lawless intruders and usurpers without Government or political existence, as Mexico would have the world to believe. The true relation between them is, that of having been, independent members of a Federal Government, but now subverted by force; the weaker of which has successfully resisted, under fearful odds, the attempts of the stronger to conquer and subject her to its power. It is in that light we regard her; and in that, we had the right to invite her to renew the proposition for annexation, and to treat with her for admission into the Union, without giving any just offence to Mexico, or violating any obligation, by treaty or otherwise, between us and her. Nor will our honor, any more than our welfare and safety, permit her to attack Texas, while the question of annexation is pending. If Mexico has thought proper to take offence, it is us who invited a renewal of the proposition, and not she who accepted it, who ought to be held responsible; and we as the responsible Party, cannot, without implicating our honor permit another to suffer in our place. Entertaining these views, Mexico would make a great mistake, if she should suppose, that the President would regard with indifference the renewal of the war, which she has proclaimed against Texas. Our honor and our interests are both involved.

But another and a still more elevated consideration would forbid him to look on with indifference. As strong as are the objections to the renewal of the war, those to the manner in which it is to be conducted, are still more so. If honor and interest forbid, a tame acquiescence in the renewal of the war, the voice of humanity cries aloud against the manner of conducting it. All the world have an interest, that the rules and usages of war, as established between civilized nations in modern times, should be respected; and are in duty bound to resist their violation, and to see them preserved. In this case that duty is preeminently ours. We are neighbours, the nearest to the scenes of the proposed atrocities, most competent to judge from our proximity, and, for the same reason enabled more readily to interpose. From the same reason also our sympathy would be more deeply wounded by viewing the mingled scenes of misery, which would present themselves on all sides, and hearing the groans of the suffering; not to mention the dangers to which we would be exposed, in consequence, on a distant and weak frontier, with numerous and powerful bands of Indians in its vicinity.

If any thing can add to the atrocity, with which it is proclaimed the war will be waged, it is the bold fiction, regardless of the semblance of truth, to which the Government of Mexico has resorted in order, to give colour to the decree of June 1843, and the orders of General Woll. Finding nothing in the conduct of the Government or People of Texas to justify their bloody and ferocious character, it has assumed in wording them that there is no such Government or Community as Texas; that the individuals to be found there are lawless intruders and usurpers, without political existence, who may rightfully be treated as a gang of pirates, outcasts from Society, and as such not entitled to the protection of the laws of nations or humanity. In this assumption, it obstinately persists in spite of the well known, and excepting the Government of Mexico, the universally admitted fact, that the Colonists of Texas, instead of being intruders and usurpers, were invited to settle there first under a grant, by the Spanish Authority, to Moses Austin, which was afterwards confirmed by the Mexican Authority; and subsequently by similar grants from the state of Texas and Coahuila, which it was authorized to issue by the constitution of 1824. They came there as invited guests; not invited for their own interests, but for those of Spain and Mexico; to protect a weak and helpless province from the ravages of wandering tribes of Indians; to improve, cultivate and render productive, wild and almost uninhabited wastes, and to make that valuable, which was before worthless. All this they effected, at great costs, and with much danger and difficulty, which nothing but American energy and perseverance could overcome; not only unaided by Mexico but in despite of the impediments caused by her interference.

Instead of a lawless gang of adventurers, as they are assumed to be by the Government of Mexico, these invited colonists became, in a few years, a constituent portion ["of one" *interlined*] of the members of the Mexican Union; and proved themselves to be the descendants of a free and hardy race by the bravery and energy with which they met the subverters of the constitution of 1824, and successfully preserved their independence. This done, they gave a still higher proof of their descent by establishing wise and free institutions, and yielding ready obedience to laws of their own enacting. Under the influence of these causes they have enjoyed peace and security, while their industry and energy, protected by equal laws, have widely extended the limits of cultivation and improvement over their beautiful Country. It is such a People, living under a free and well established Government, and on whose soil "no hostile foot has found rest," for the last eight years, who have been recognized and introduced, as one of its members, into the family of Nations; that Mexico has undertaken to treat as a lawless banditti; and against whom, as such, she has proclaimed a war of extermination, forgetful of their exalted and generous humanity when during the former invasion, they spared the forfeited lives of him, who ordered, and those who butchered in cold blood, the heroic Fannin and his brave associates, regardless of plighted faith. The Government of Mexico may delude itself by its bold fictions, but it cannot delude the rest of the world. It will be judged and held responsible, not by what it may choose to regard as facts, and to act upon as such, but what are in reality facts, known and acknowledged by all save herself.

Such are the views which the President entertains in reference to the renewal of the war, after so long a suspension, and under existing circumstances; and the barbarous and bloody manner in which it is proclaimed it will be conducted.

He instructs you accordingly, to address, without delay, to the proper Department of the Mexican Government, a communication, in which you will state the views entertained by him in reference to the renewal of the war, while the question of annexation is pending, and the manner in which it is intended to be conducted; and to protest against both in strong language, accompanied by declarations, that the President cannot regard them with indifference, but as highly offensive to the United States.

You are also instructed to renew the declaration made to the Mexican Secretary by our chargé d'Affaires [Ben E. Green] in announcing the conclusion of the Treaty, that the measure was adopted in no spirit of hostility to Mexico, and that if annexation should be consummated, the United States will be prepared to adjust all questions growing out of it, including that of boundary, on the most liberal terms. I am, Sir, respectfully Your Obedient Servant, J.C. Calhoun.

LS (No. 6) in DNA, RG 84 (Foreign Posts), Mexico, Instructions, vol. 5.I; FC in DNA, RG 59 (State Department), Diplomatic Instructions, Mexico, 15:309–319 (M-77:111); CC's in DNA, RG 84 (Foreign Posts), files for Russia, Germany, France, Spain, Netherlands, Sweden, Brazil, Great Britain, and Texas; PC in Senate Document No. 1, 28th Cong., 2nd Sess., pp. 29–34; PC in House Document No. 2, 28th Cong., 2nd Sess., pp. 29–34; PC in *Congressional Globe*, 28th Cong., 2nd Sess., Appendix, pp. 3–4; PC in the Washington, D.C., *Globe*, December 6, 1844, pp. 1–2; PC in the Washington, D.C., *Daily National Intelligencer*, December 7, 1844, p. 2; PC in the Washington, D.C., *Daily Madisonian*, December 9, 1844, p. 2; PC in *Niles' National Register*, vol. LXVII, no. 15 (December 14, 1844), pp. 232–233; PC in the Jackson, Miss., *Mississippian*, December 25, 1844, pp. 2–3; PC in Crallé, ed., *Works*, 5:364–373. NOTE: The bloodthirsty orders of the Mexican General Woll on 6/20/1844, and Santa Anna's decree of 6/17/1843, referred to in Calhoun's first paragraph, are printed in Crallé, ed., *Works*, 5:373–375.

To J[ohn] & "T." [*sic*; Josiah] Starling, Portland, Maine, 9/10. Calhoun acknowledges their letter of 8/26 concerning the seizure of their ship by a British cruiser. Information about the case has been communicated to the U.S. Minister at London [Edward Everett], "with instructions to bring the Subject to the notice of the British Government." FC in DNA, RG 59 (State Department), Domestic Letters, 34:372–373 (M-40:32).

From DAVID STEWART, [later a Senator from Md.]

Balt[im]o[re], Septem[ber] 10 1844

Mr. Francis R. Gillm[e]yer of this City apprizes me that the Consulate at Galveston is vacant, and that he is desirous of receiving an appointment to that station.

Mr. Gillm[e]yer has occasionally been in correspondence with the President but at the same time requested this letter to yourself to avouch the necessary qualifications. I have known him for a long time, have great confidence in his integrity and think him well qualified to discharge the Consular functions. I beg therefore to present him to your favorable regard, And remain very truly and faithfully, Y[ou]r Ob[edien]t Servant, David Stewart, No. 20 St. Pauls Street.

LS in DNA, RG 59 (State Department), Applications and Recommendations, 1837–1845, Gillmeyer (M-687:12, frames 754–756).

From Isaac Van Zandt

Legation of Texas
Washington D.C., September 10th 1844
The Undersigned Charge d'Affaires of the Republic of Texas presents his respects to Mr. Calhoun, Secretary of State of the United States, and has the honor to acquaint him that his resignation has been accepted and permission given him to return home, and respectfully to request that he may be informed at what time it will be convenient for Mr. Calhoun to receive him for the purpose of delivering his letter of recall.

Mr. Calhoun is further informed that, after the Undersigned shall have taken his leave, ["that" *canceled*] Mr. Charles H. Raymond, the present Secretary of Legation, in pursuance of the instructions of the Secretary of State of Texas [Anson Jones] made by order of the President [Samuel Houston], will assume the duties of this Legation as "Acting Chargé d'Affaires,["] until a Successor shall be appointed. The Undersigned takes pleasure in commending Mr. Raymond to Mr. Calhoun and doubts not he will merit his confidence.

In closing this his last official note, the Undersigned, with pleasure, avails himself of the occasion to tender to Mr. Calhoun his most sincere thanks for the zeal and ability which he has at all times displayed in the promotion of every measure (consistent with the honor and integrity of his own government) calculated to advance the prosperity and happiness of the government and people of Texas; and to assure him that his efforts will be duly appreciated by them; and at the same time to acknowledge, with a high sense of the obligations they impose; the frequent manifestations of kindness and confidence with which Mr. Calhoun has favored him, personally, during their official intercourse, and to express the ardent hope that his life

751

may be as prosperous and happy as it has been useful and distinguished, and that he may continue to receive the honors due the gifted and patriotic. Isaac Van Zandt.

LS in DNA, RG 59 (State Department), Notes from Foreign Legations, Texas, vol. 1 (T-809:1); FC in Tx, Records of the Texas Republic Department of State, Letters and Dispatches Sent by the Texas Legation in Washington, 2:6–7; FC in Tx, Records of the Texas Republic Department of State, Copybooks of Letters Received from Texan and Foreign Representatives, vol. 2–1/98, pp. 538–539; CC in Tx, Records of the Texas Republic Department of State, U.S. Diplomatic Correspondence; PC in the Washington, D.C., *Daily Madisonian,* September 14, 1844, p. 2; PC in the Washington, D.C., *Spectator,* September 17, 1844, p. 3.

To [ISAAC] VAN ZANDT, Texan Chargé d'Affaires to the U.S.

Department of State
Washington, 10th September, 1844

The Undersigned, Secretary of State of the United States, presents his respects to Mr. Van Zandt, Chargé d'Affaires of the Republic of Texas, and has the honor to inform him that he will be ready to receive him, for the purpose stated in his note of the present instant, tomorrow, at half after ten o'clock, at the Department of State.

The Undersigned cannot permit the occasion to pass, without bearing testimony to the zeal, fidelity and ability with which Mr. Van Zandt has ever discharged his official duties, combined with a courtesy and candor, which made his intercourse with the Department and the Government very acceptable and agreeable.

The Undersigned is highly gratified to learn that his course in reference to the important questions which have been the subject of discussion and negotiation between the United States and Texas, ["during the period" *erased*] since he has occupied his present situation, has been so acceptable to Mr. Van Zandt. If they have all been satisfactorily adjusted, it is because neither sought any undue advantage for his own country at the expense of the other, while both were careful to protect the rights of their own—the only way in which negotiations ought ever to be conducted, but which unfortunately for the peace of the world, is too often departed from in practice.

The Undersigned cannot close this note, without expressing his earnest desire that the great measure of annexation, the most important subject of their negotiation, may yet be consummated, to the mutual freedom, safety and happiness of both countries. Be it when it may, both will owe a debt of lasting gratitude to Mr. Van Zandt, for his important agency in effecting it.

The Undersigned, in conclusion, reciprocates most sincerely the kind personal wishes of Mr. Van Zandt. J.C. Calhoun.

LS in Tx, Andrew Jackson Houston Papers; FC in DNA, RG 59 (State Department), Notes to Foreign Legations, Texas, 6:75–76 (M-99:95); FC in Tx, Records of the Texas Republic Department of State, Letters and Despatches Sent by the Texas Legation in Washington, 2:7–8; FC in Tx, Records of the Texas Republic Department of State, Copybooks of Letters Received from Texan and Foreign Representatives, vol. 2–1/98, p. 539; CC in Tx, Records of the Texas Republic Department of State, U.S. Diplomatic Correspondence; PC in the Washington, D.C., *Daily Madisonian*, September 14, 1844, p. 2; PC in the Washington, D.C., *Spectator*, September 17, 1844, p. 3.

From F[RANCIS] R. GILLMEYER

Baltimore, Sept. 11, 1844

Sir, I am desirous of procuring from the President the appointment of *Consul* to the Port of Galv[e]zton Texas—which I understand is now vacant—and at which place I intend establishing myself. I flatter myself possessed of the ability &c to fill the station with credit to the department and to myself and my views upon several subjects affecting the rights of the South being in accordance with your own I take the liberty of writing you this Communication as also of procuring the letter [dated 9/10] of the Hon. D[avid] Stewart which accompanies this and to which have the goodness to reffer. Your ob[edien]t S[ervan]t, F.R. Gillmeyer.

ALS with En in DNA, RG 59 (State Department), Applications and Recommendations, 1837–1845, Gillmeyer (M-687:12, frames 752–756).

From J[ohn] Y. Mason, [Secretary of the Navy], 9/11. "I have the honor to acknowledge the receipt of your letter of the 6th inst. and to state in reply that orders will be given to Lieut[enant Henry H.] Bell, of the Steamer Union, now at Pensacola, to take the bearer of despatches [Duff Green] on board, and proceed to Vera Cruz without delay, touching at Galveston." LS in DNA, RG 59 (State Department), Miscellaneous Letters (M-179:105, frame 350); FC in DNA, RG 45 (Naval Records), Letters Sent by the Secretary of the

Navy to the President and Executive Agencies, 1821–1886, 5:25 (M-472:3, frame 54).

To WILSON SHANNON, [U.S. Minister to Mexico]

Department of State
Washington, 11th September, 1844

Sir, The frequent and pressing appeals made to this Department by the claimants under the Treaty with Mexico of the 30th of January, 1843, make it necessary to urge on the Mexican Government a prompt compliance with its stipulations. At the date of our latest advices the instalments due on the 30th of April and the 30th of July, last, had not been paid; nor so far as it appears, were there any arrangements in progress with a view to their liquidation. This want of punctuality on the part of Mexico is alike injurious to the honor and the interests of our citizens. These claims have been long due, though recognized only at a comparatively recent date; and it cannot be expected that the government of the United States should longer look with indifference on the virtual denial of justice to their citizens. The exhausted state of her Treasury may have, heretofore, furnished some grounds of excuse; and looking to that, the Government of the United States has refrained from pressing the subject as urgently as the rights of the claimants and the express stipulations of the treaty warranted. But this forbearance seems to have had no other effect than to encourage that disregard of her engagements which has uniformly marked her conduct towards this country for some years past. You will, therefore, on the receipt of this despatch, should the instalments in arrear be still unpaid, address a note immediately to the proper officer of the government, calling his prompt attention to the subject, and urging, in the most decided language, the necessity of a strict compliance with the stipulations of the treaty. You will also avail yourself of the occasion to protest, in the most positive terms, against the past neglect of the government to discharge punctually its treaty obligations, and to remonstrate, in advance, against a like neglect in future; giving it plainly to understand that, while the Government of the United States will only ask of other governments what is clearly right, it will not forget that its own dignity and self respect forbid it to submit to what is clearly wrong.

It has been the common practice of the Mexican functionaries in their correspondence with our Ministers, not only to vaunt the claims of their own government to punctuality and a strict observance of treaty stipulations, but, at the same time, to cast unmerited imputations on the motives and conduct of ours on questions involving our national faith and honor. Should Mexico seek, in these insulting and groundless imputations a pretext to justify its total disregard of engagements solemnly entered into with this Government, you will repel the charge in a spirit becoming the dignity of your country; and show, from the history of the past, that her pretensions as regards herself, are as little entitled to credit as her accusations against us. In no instance has the Government of the United States ever failed to comply strictly with its treaty engagements; while Mexico, on the other hand, has, in repeated instances, utterly disregarded the faith of Treaties. Her order of expulsion of the 14th day of July, 1843, directed in the first instance exclusively against the citizens of the United States; her decree of the 23d of September, 1843, unjustly and arbitrarily closing the doors of our retail merchants at Mazatlan and other places, and her more recent failure to pay the instalments under the Treaty of the 30th of January, 1843, not to mention others, are so many flagrant examples of this. Her whole conduct, indeed, for some time past, has been characterized by outrage and insult, and in your intercourse and official correspondence with her officers it is proper that you should adopt a tone and manner which shall indicate, unequivocally, the fixed determination of the United States to maintain, at all hazards, their just rights and dignity. I am, Sir, with high respect, Your obedient servant, J.C. Calhoun.

FC (No. 7) in DNA, RG 59 (State Department), Diplomatic Instructions, Mexico, 15:320–322 (M-77:111); PEx in Senate Document No. 81, 28th Cong., 2nd Sess., p. 17; PEx in House Document No. 144, 28th Cong., 2nd Sess., pp. 17–18; PEx in Senate Document No. 85, 29th Cong., 1st Sess., pp. 17–18.

Isaac Van Zandt, Washington, to Anson Jones, Secretary of State [of Texas], 9/11. Van Zandt acknowledges Jones's letter of 7/13 accepting his resignation; he has been ill and will leave Washington as soon as possible. "I had hoped to be able to give the subject of the movements of the United States troops and Navy more attention than I have been able to do. Mr. [Charles H.] Raymond has seen Mr. Calhoun several times on the subject, and Mr. Calhoun has been kind enough to call at my room frequently, but it was impossible, owing to my feeble state, to discuss the matter at any length." [Tilghman A.] Howard, U.S. Chargé d'Affaires to Texas, will be "fully instructed so Mr. Calhoun informed me." Van Zandt has informed Calhoun that Raymond will be Acting Chargé d'Affaires. LS in Tx, Records of the Texas Republic Department of State, U.S. Diplomatic Correspondence.

From FRANCIS WHARTON

Philadelphia, September 11th 1844

My dear Sir, I wrote you a letter some time since, and though I do not know whether you are in Washington, I am going to write you another. I have been for some time considering the propriety of establishing a weekly paper in this City, based on the plan of the ["London" *interlined*] Examiner or Spectator, designed to be both political and literary. Mr. [Henry D.] Gilpin & Mr. C[harles] J. Ingersoll, whom I have consulted, both consider the plan to be judicious, & likely, if placed in enterprizing hands, to be of great benefit to the republican party. I am half involved as editor, but before taking any step, I am anxious to consult with you. If it is got up here, under the patronage of the established party leaders, it will be soon [Martin] Van-Burenized & Silas Wrighted. There will be no helping it. They will control the subscription list, & contribute the capital. Mr. Ingersoll will hand in a tariff article, and in it will go, and Mr. Gilpin will load us with anti-Texas squibs, which we will have to fire. We will be prevented from taking the republican stand, advocating the States-rights party, rallying under *your* name, and what is worse, we will be hunkerized & Albany regency-ized till we settle into a weekly edition of the Pennsylvanian.

For such a cause, I have no taste. It is my ambition to fall into other ranks, and it would give me the greatest pleasure to devote, unrepayed, my time to the dissemination of your views in the Northern States. I believe it could be done with success. I see great need for an organ which would do so [*one word canceled and* "north" *interlined*] of the Potomac. I am fully confident of the ability of myself, and those who would be associated with me, to put the matter firmly & attractively, before the public. If we mean to move, however, we must be started. If we do not lean, primarily, upon the North for subscribers, we must lean on the South. Could not twenty gentlemen, who will contribute fifty dollars apiece, ["as shareholders," *interlined*] for the establishment of such an organ [be found]? A paper coming out weekly, under such auspices, with such declared views, at two dollars and a half a year, could, I am sure, run up a large & active list of subscribers. I have consulted with the publisher of the Pennsylvanian, who thinks that as a financial matter, the plan would succeed; and with some government, & more personal, patronage, its success would be certain. Allow me, therefore, to ask your consideration to ["the" *canceled and* "its" *interlined*] practical bearings. With great attachment, I am yours sin[cerely?,] Francis Wharton.

[P.S.] I send one or two English papers on the same plan.

ALS in ScCleA; variant PC in Jameson, ed., *Correspondence*, pp. 971–973.

From W[ILLIA]M WILKINS, [Secretary of War], *"Unofficial"*

Washington, Sep[tember] 11, '44

D[ea]r Sir, Upon examination I find I cannot make the arrangement that would be agreeable to you in reference to the Arms taken from the Texians by Capt. [Philip St. George] Cooke. I know not how I could authorize the issuing of a warrant for the purpose you suggested.

The proceeds of the sales of our condemned Arms are not kept as a distinct fund—but go into the *general mass* in the Treasury.

I write this note informally, presuming it will answer in your conversations with Mr. [Isaac] Van Zandt. Faithfully yours, Wm. Wilkins.

ALS in DNA, RG 59 (State Department), Miscellaneous Letters (M-179:105, frame 349).

To ROBERT I. ALEXANDER and Others, St. Clairsville, Ohio

State Department, Sept. 12, 1844

Gentlemen: I have received your letter of the 31st August, informing me that the Hon. Thomas Ewing, on the 19th August, at a Whig Mass meeting held at St. Clairsville, made the following statement: "That John C. Calhoun had in his letter to Mr. [Richard] Packenham [*sic*], laid down in [*sic*] this monstrous proposition, that the true and natural condition of the laboring portion of the community was that of slavery. It is true (Mr. Ewing continued) that Mr. Calhoun in that letter was speaking of the black population of the South; but I have often, on the floor of the Senate, heard him lay down the broad and general position, that the best and most natural condition of the laboring community was that of slavery.["]

Had I not as high authority as your names to furnish for the fact, I would not have believed that Mr. Ewing, or any man of any standing, having the least regard to character, would have ventured to make a statement before a public audience so utterly destitute of the shadow of truth. But on your high authority, I am constrained to believe he made it.

A regard to my character compels me to notice it; and I accordingly pronounce it to be utterly false. I laid down no such proposition as he asserts I did, in my letter to Mr. Pakenham, in the abstract, or in reference to the black population of the South, or any which can fairly be construed into it. I did, indeed, assert, that their condition there, was far better than that of the free blacks in the non-slaveholding States and that I conclusively proved by the late census. Nor did I ever lay down the proposition in the Senate, or any where else, that the best and most natural condition of the laboring community was that of slavery, or any thing like it. The whole is a calumny, utterly destitute of foundation.

So far from ever having entertained such an abominable sentiment, my whole life has been devoted to endeavoring to uphold our free popular system of government, and resisting the course of policy advocated by Mr. Ewing and his party; and which, I firmly believe, is calculated to subvert the liberty of the people, and reduce the laboring class of this country to the wretched condition, to which they have been reduced by the same policy in England, where it has existed so long and in such high perfection. It is my devotion to what I regard as the cause of our unburdened and unshackled industry, and opposition to measures that must end in enslaving the laboring population of our country, if persisted in, which constitute my offence in his eyes and those associated with him; and not the base doctrine, which he falsely attributes to me. Do with this as you may think proper. With great respect, I am, &c., J.C. Calhoun.

PC in the Charleston, S.C., *Southern Patriot,* October 1, 1844, p. 2; PC in the Washington, D.C., *Daily Madisonian,* October 5, 1844, p. 2; PC in the Edgefield, S.C., *Advertiser,* October 9, 1844, p. 2; PC in the Anderson, S.C., *Gazette,* October 11, 1844, p. 2; PC in the Pendleton, S.C., *Messenger,* October 11, 1844, p. 3. NOTE: The committee addressed by Calhoun consisted of Robert "J."

[*sic*; I.] Alexander, A. Patton, E.G. Bryson, J[ohn] C. Tidball, W[illiam] P. Simpson, W[illiam] Wilkins, J.M. Mitchell, and J[ames] Wishart.

From John C. Bennett, "Hampton, Rock Island County, Illinois," 9/12. He encloses several "packages" for [Wilson] Shannon and hopes that Calhoun will frank and forward them. "It is generally supposed here that the Democratic majority in November will exceed that of August, and that [James K.] Polk and [George M.] Dallas will carry the State triumphantly." ALS in DNA, RG 59 (State Department), Miscellaneous Letters (M-179:105, frames 357–358).

From BEN E. GREEN

Legation of the U.S. of A.
Mexico, Sep[tember] 12th 1844

Sir, I have had the honor to receive your despatch of the 3rd June (no. 4), and learn with much regret and mortification that my draft, in favour of Messrs. Hargous & Bros. could not be paid, and that I was not entitled to draw for the salary of a Chargé d'affaires. I was led to take a different view of the case, from knowing that extra salary was allowed to our consul here, who acted on a former occasion, as chargé d'affaires ad interim, and from that clause in the instructions to Ministers, which relates to their absence from their respective posts.

Had I supposed that this difficulty would arise I never would have consented to remain in charge of the Legation; for the cost of living in Mexico is such as can not be conceived in the U. States, where everything is so much cheaper, and, apart from my salary, I had no means of supporting that decent appearance, required of the representative of our country. With rigid economy I have had to spend much more than my salary as Secretary of Legation, and I trust that as soon as my claim can be admitted and paid, it will be done. I have the honor to be Very Respectfully Your ob[edien]t Serv[an]t, Ben E. Green.

ALS in DNA, RG 59 (State Department), Diplomatic Despatches, Mexico, vol. 12 (M-97:13), received 11/3; FC in DNA, RG 84 (Foreign Posts), Mexico, Despatches; draft in NcU, Duff Green Papers (published microfilm, roll 5, frames 804–805).

To Duff Green, 9/12. Calhoun notifies Green of his appointment to be U.S. Consul at Galveston, Republic of Texas, and encloses documents related to the conduct of the office. PDS in DLC, Duff Green Papers; FC in DNA, RG 59 (State Department), Consular Instructions, 11:273–274.

From J[AMES] HAMILTON, [JR.]

Oswichee Bend [Ala.,] Sept. 12[t]h 1844

My Dear Sir, Your kind favor of the 28[t]h ult[im]o I received a few Days since. I am gratified that my Bluffton Letter accords with your own views of sound policy. I think [Robert Barnwell] Rhett is injuring the cause by premature action, for it is quite obvious, that he ["has" *interlined*] neither the sympathy nor support of the other ["Southern States" *canceled and* "portions even of South Carolina" *interlined*], in his ill timed move.

I am gratified to hear you say, that [James K.] Polk[']s prospects are rising for I concur with you in the opinion that his election & [Henry] Clay[']s defeat will be a revolution in itself. The tariff & High expansion *party can* rally under no other man.

I am sorry I could not attend the Nashville Convention. I think I might have done some good in cementing the Union between the South & West. I found on my return a most urgent Letter from the Committee to attend, accompanied by a very complimentary one from a ["most"(?) *canceled and* "Mr." *interlined*] Southhall [*sic;* J.J.B. Southall] of the Committee to which I have replied not at any great length but to some effect ["(I hope)" *interlined*] on the great work of conciliation between ["Tennessee & So. Carolina" *canceled and* "the West & ("So. Ca." *canceled*) South," *interlined*] or rather between Tennessee & South Carolina. I think I have given [Thomas H.] Benton a dose of arsnec [*sic*]—and whilst I have not named him— "He who runs may read." Whether they will publish or not I know not but I think they will.

I am very much gratified that France has withdrawn from the foolish *position* she was at first disposed to occupy in reference to Texas. This I suspect has arisen from some ill will that has ["arisen" *canceled and* "taken place" *interlined*] between herself and G[reat] B[ritain]. I do not believe the Republican Party ["in France" *interlined*] will allow the two countries to remain ["much" *interlined*] longer at peace.

I have no doubt My Dear Sir that Mexico will make a most formidable invasion of Texas this winter and that in consequence of the Annexation Question ["for which our own Govt. is responsible" *interlined*]. What are we to do? The Govt. of the U.S. would be powerless without the assent of Congress & this is hopeless. I see no other hope for the ["Country" *canceled and* "Texas" *interlined*] but for the brave spirits of the South to rush to the *rescue*. What in the strictest confidence are your views on the subject? *They shall never be quoted.* I feel the strongest disposition to make a dash if I could see my way clearly.

I think the Crop of (Ala.) will not be equal to the one she made last Year. The cotton has shed a good deal from the ["late" *canceled and* "Aug(u)st" *interlined*] Rains.

Should Mr. G[azaway] B. Lamar ["call" *canceled*] of Savannah now in Alexandria D.C. call on you, you can speak to him without reserve. He is a true Southron. A Man to be relied on and a firm friend of yours.

As the within Letter relates to some *public business*, I will thank you to forward it for me under your frank to ["West Po" *canceled*] New York. I remain My Dear Sir with esteem very Respect[full]y & faithfully Yours, J. Hamilton.

P.S. Direct your reply to *Savan[n]ah* where I shall be in about 10 *Days* or a *fortnight*, as I shall have to go to look after my Rice Crop.

I shall leave early in Nov. as soon as it is safe to ["visit Texas, in consequence of" *canceled*] visit Galveston & Houston where my Letters inform me the Yellow fever prevails to a dangerous extent, which nothing but frost will check. You may rely on it that the moment I get there, I will give such a direction to public affairs as may be in conformity to ["your" *canceled*] President [John] Tyler[']s views & your own. I can carry the country in the direction we desire against ["Tyl"(?) *canceled*; Samuel] Houston. But my friends will be in power ["& he will be out of Power on the 1s(t) Dec." *interlined*] & we will ["take" *canceled and* "carry" *interlined*] matters with a rush. Houston goes out of office on the 1st Dec. and I will aid Gen[era]l [Tilghman A.] Howard in getting a ["new" *interlined*] treaty through which before President Tyler goes out of office will check mate the Whigs & yet give his administration I hope the renown of annexation.

What do you think of Waddy Thompson[']s Eulogium on Santa Anna? And that too in the presence of Ladies! ! ! Of the Mexican Chieftian [*sic*] I think the same may be said as was said of Ceasar Borgia, "That he never spared a Man in his wrath or a Woman in his lust."

If the Nashville Committee publish my Letter I do not see well how Benton can refrain from calling ["me" *interlined*] personally to account, as I give him the lie direct on his charge of Disunion against *So. C.* If he does I mean to make up the issue with him with the hope of punishing him for his brutality to [George] McDuffie.

P.S. Should Mr. Crawley [*sic*; Richard K. Crallé] open this Letter he will be so kind as to forward the enclosed to New York & this Letter to Mr. Calhoun wherever he may be.

ALS in ScCleA; PEx in Boucher and Brooks, eds., *Correspondence*, pp. 249–251. NOTE: On the address sheet of this letter Hamilton wrote: "In case of Mr. Calhoun's absence from Washington ["Mr. Crawley" *canceled*] the Chief Clerk of the Depart[men]t of State will be pleased to open this Letter."

To T[ILGHMAN] A. HOWARD, Washington, Texas

State Dept., 12th Sep[tembe]r 1844

My dear Sir, I regret, that the bearer of your dispatch [Duff Green] has been detained here as long as he has. It was owing, in part, to the indisposition of the President [John Tyler], who was, in consequence, prevented from attending business for nearly a week, and partly to the pressure of my duties, in consequence of having the Oregon negotiation on hand. When your dispatch was received, I was in the midest of it, preparing a paper containing a statement of our rights to the Territory, which I had to finish before I could take up the subject of your dispatch.

I hope things remain in a satisfactory state in Texas. The indications here, I regard as very favourable in reference to annexation. You will have seen, that Mr. [Henry] Clay has been compelled to come out with a third letter, and to take ground on the side of annexation. It was too late and will do him no good, but will help the cause. Our friends regard [James K.] Polk's election, as almost certain, and think that we have a fair prospect of a majority in the Senate after the 4th March. If such should be the result of the election, I would not be surprised, if a joint resolution, embracing the provisions of the Treaty, should be passed before the 4th March next.

I hope to hear from you frequently & fully. With great respect I am yours truly, J.C. Calhoun.

ALS (Private) in DNA, RG 84 (Foreign Posts), Texas; PC in "Some Letters of Tyler, Calhoun, Polk, Murphy, Houston, and Donelson," *Tyler's Quarterly Historical and Genealogical Magazine*, vol. VI, no. 4 (April, 1925), pp. 232–233.

NOTE: The address leaf of this letter contains an AEI by A[ndrew] J. D[onelson], Howard's successor as U.S. Chargé d'Affaires to Texas, that reads, "Private letter from Mr. Calhoun to Mr. Howard, opened by mistake as forming a part of the public letters left with Mr. [Elisha A.] Rhodes."

PROTOCOL by R[ichard] Pakenham and J[ohn] C. Calhoun

[Washington, September 12, 1844]

On the 12th of September 1844, the fourth conference was held at the Office of the Secretary of State, when the British Plenipotentiary presented his statement [of 9/12] marked D—counter to that of the American Plenipotentiary marked A [and dated 9/3] presented at the preceding conference. J.C. Calhoun, R. Pakenham.

DS in DNA, RG 59 (State Department), Notes from Foreign Legations, Great Britain, vol. 22 (M-50:22); PC in the Washington, D.C., *Daily National Intelligencer*, December 12, 1845, p. 1; PC in *Niles' National Register*, vol. LXIX, no. 17 (December 27, 1845), p. 261; PC in Senate Document No. 1, 29th Cong., 1st Sess., p. 145; PC in House Document No. 2, 29th Cong., 1st Sess., p. 145; PC in Crallé, ed., *Works*, 5:425.

From R[ICHARD] PAKENHAM

[Washington, September 12, 1844]

The Undersigned British Plenipotentiary has studied with much Interest and attention the statement [of 9/3], marked A, presented by the American Plenipotentiary, setting forth the grounds on which He declines the proposal offered by The British Plenipotentiary as a compromise of the difficulties of the Oregon Question. The Arrangement contemplated by that proposal would, in the estimation of the American Plenipotentiary have the effect of restricting the possessions of the United States to limits far more circumscribed than their claims clearly entitle them to.

The claims of the United States to the portion of Territory drained by The Columbia River are divided into those adduced by the United States in their own proper right, and those which they have derived from France and Spain.

The former as against Great Britain they ground on priority of discovery and priority of exploration and settlement.

The claim derived from France, originates in the Treaty of 1803, by which Louisiana was ceded to The United States with all its rights and appurtenances as fully and in the same manner as they had been acquired by the French Republic—and the claim derived from Spain is founded on the Treaty concluded with that Power in the year 1819 whereby His Catholick Majesty ceded to the United States, all His rights, claims, and pretensions to the territories lying East and North of a certain line terminating on the Pacific in the 42 Degree of North Latitude.

Departing from the order in which these three separate claims are presented by the American Plenipotentiary the British Plenipotentiary will first beg leave to observe with regard to the claim derived from France that He has not been able to discover any evidence tending to establish the belief that Louisiana as originally possessed by France—afterwards transferred to Spain, then retroceded by Spain to France, and ultimately ceded by the latter Power to the United States extended in a westerly direction beyond the Rocky Mountains. There is on the other hand strong reason to suppose that at the time when Louisiana was ceded to the United States its acknowledged Western Boundary was the Rocky Mountains. Such appears to have been the opinion of President [Thomas] Jefferson, under whose auspices the acquisition of Louisiana was accomplished.

In a letter written by Him in August 1803, are to be found the following words, "The Boundaries (of Louisiana) which I deem not admitting question, are the high lands on the Western side of the Mississippi, inclosing all its waters, the Missouri of course, and terminating in the line drawn from the North West Point of the Lake of the Woods to the nearest source of the Mississippi as lately settled between Great Britain and the United States."

In another and more formal document, dated in July 1807, that is to say, nearly a year after the return of [Meriwether] Lewis and [William] Clark, from their expedition to the Pacific, and 15 years after [Robert] Gray had entered the Columbia River, is recorded Mr. Jefferson's opinion of the impolicy of giving offence to Spain, by any intimation that the claims of the United States extended to the Pacific—and we have the authority of an American Historian, distinguished for the attention and research which He has bestowed on the whole subject of the Oregon Territory, for concluding that the Western Boundaries of Louisiana, as it was ceded by France to the United States were those indicated by nature, namely the high lands separating the waters of the Mississippi from those flowing into the Pacific.

From the acquisition then, of Louisiana, as it was received from France, it seems clear that the United States can deduce no claim to Territory west of the Rocky Mountains. But even if it were otherwise and if France had ever possessed, or asserted, a claim to Territory west of the Rocky Mountains, as appertaining to the Territory of Louisiana, that claim whatever it might be was necessarily transferred to Spain when Louisiana was ceded to that Power in 1762, and of course became subject to the provisions of the Treaty between Spain and Great Britain of 1790, which effectually abrogated the claim of Spain to exclusive dominion over the unoccupied parts of the American Continent.

To the observations of the American Plenipotentiary respecting the effect of continuity in furnishing a claim to territory the Undersigned has not failed to pay due attention, but He submits that what is said on this head may more properly be considered as demonstrating the greater degree of interest which the United States possess by reason of contiguity in acquiring territory in that direction than as affecting in any way the question of right.

The Undersigned will endeavour to shew hereafter that in the proposal put in on the part of Great Britain the natural expectations of the United States on the ground of contiguity have not been disregarded.

Next comes to be examined the claim derived from Spain.

It must indeed be acknowledged that by the Treaty of 1819, Spain did convey to the United States all that she had the power to dispose of on the North west Coast of America—North of the 42 Parallel of Latitude, but she could not by that transaction annul or invalidate the rights which she had by a previous transaction acknowledged to belong to another Power.

By the Treaty of 28th October, 1790, Spain acknowledged in Great Britain certain rights with respect to those parts of the Western Coast of America not already occupied.

This acknowledgment had reference especially to the Territory which forms the subject of the present negotiation. If Spain could not make good Her own right to exclusive dominion over those Regions, still less could she confer such a right on another Power, and hence Great Britain argues that from nothing deduced from the Treaty of 1819, Can the United States assert a valid claim to exclusive dominion over any part of the Oregon Territory.

There remains to be considered the claim advanced by the United

States on the ground of prior discovery and prior exploration and settlement.

In that part of the Memorandum of the American Plenipotentiary which speaks of the Spanish Title it is stated that the Mouth of the River (afterwards called the Columbia River) was first discovered by the Spanish navigator [Bruno] Heceta—the admission of this fact would appear to be altogether irreconcileable with a claim to priority of discovery from any thing accomplished by Captain Gray. To one, and to one only, of those Commanders can be conceded the merit of first discovery. If Heceta's claim is acknowledged, then ["Captain" *interlined*] Gray is no longer the discoverer of the Columbia River. If on the other hand preference is given to the achievement of Captain Gray, then Heceta's discovery ceases to be of any value. But it is argued that the United States now represent both titles, the title of Heceta and the Title of Gray, and therefore that under one or the other, it matters not which, enough can be shown to establish a case of prior discovery as against Great Britain. This may be true as far as relates to the act of first seeing and first entering the mouth of The Columbia River, but if the Spanish claim to prior discovery is to prevail, whatever rights may thereon be founded are necessarily restricted by the stipulations of the Treaty of 1790, which forbid a claim to exclusive possession.

If the act of Captain Gray in passing the Bar and actually entering the River is to supersede the discovery of the entrance, which is all that is attributed to Heceta, then the principle of progressive or gradual discovery being admitted, as conveying, in proportion to the extent of discovery, or exploration, superior rights, the operations of [George] Vancouver in entering, surveying and exploring, to a considerable distance inland, the River Columbia, would, as a necessary consequence supersede the discovery of Captain Gray, to say nothing of the act of taking possession, in the name of His Sovereign, which ceremony was duly performed, and authentically recorded, by Captain Vancouver.

This brings us to an examination of the conflicting claims of Great Britain and the United States on the ground of discovery, which may be said to form the essential point in the discussion, for it has above been shewn that the claim derived from France must be considered as of little or no weight, while that derived from Spain in as far as relates to exclusive dominion is neutralized by the stipulations of the Nootka Convention.

It will be admitted that when the United States became an independent Nation they possessed no claim, direct or indirect to the Columbia Territory. Their Western Boundary in those days was defined by the Treaty of 1783. Great Britain, on the contrary, had at that time already directed Her attention to the North West Coast of America, as is sufficiently shown by the voyage and discoveries of Captain [James] Cook who in 1778, visited and explored a great portion of it from Latitude 44° Northward.

That Great Britain was the first to acquire what may be called a beneficial interest in those Regions, by Commercial intercourse will not, either, be denied—in proof of this fact we have the voyages of the several British subjects, who visited the Coast and adjacent Islands previously to the dispute with Spain, and that Her Commerce actual as well as prospective in that part of the world was considered a matter of great national importance, is shewn by the resolute measures which she took for its protection when Spain manifested a disposition to interfere with it.

The discoveries of [John] Meares in 1788, and the complete survey of the Coast and its adjacent Islands from about Latitude 40° Northwards, which was effected by Captain Vancouver in 1792, 1793 and 1794 would appear to give to Great Britain, as against the United States, as strong a claim on the ground of discovery and exploration Coastwise, as can well be imagined; limited only by what was accomplished by Captain Gray at the mouth of the Columbia, which as far as discovery is concerned forms the strong point on the American side of the question.

In point of accuracy and authenticity it is believed that the performances of Cook and VanCouver stand preeminently superior to those of any other Country whose vessels had in those days visited the North west Coast, while in point of value and importance surely the discovery of a single Harbour although at the Mouth of an important river cannot, as giving a claim to territory, be placed in competition with the vast extent of discovery and survey accomplished by the British navigators.

As regards exploration inland, entire justice must be done to the memorable exploit of M.M. Lewis and Clarke, but but [sic] those distinguished travellers were not the first who effected a passage across the Oregon Territory from the Rocky Mountains to the Pacific—as far back as 1793, that feat had been accomplished by [Sir Alexander] Mackenzie, a British subject. In the course of this expedition Mackenzie explored the upper waters of a River since called Fraser's River, which in process of time was traced to its junction with the sea, near the 49 Degree of Latitude, thus forming in point of exploration a counterpoise to the exploration of that part of the Columbia which was first visited by Lewis and Clark.

Priority of settlement is the third Plea on which the American claim proper is made to rest.

In 1811 an Establishment for the purposes of trade was formed at the South side of the Columbia River, near to its mouth by certain American Citizens. This Establishment passed during the war into the hands of British subjects, but it was restored to the American Government in the year 1818, by an understanding between the two Governments—since when it has not however been in reality occupied by Americans. This is the case of priority of settlement.

The American Plenipotentiary lays some stress on the admission attributed to Lord Castlereagh then Principal Secretary of State for Foreign Affairs, that "the American Government had the most ample right to be reinstated, and to be the party in possession while treating of the title." The Undersigned is not inclined to dispute an assertion resting on such respectable authority—but He must observe, in the first place, that the reservation implied by the words "while treating of the title" exclude any inference which might otherwise be drawn from the preceeding words, prejudicial to the title of Great Britain, and further that when the authority of the American Minister is thus admitted for an observation which is pleaded against England, it is but fair that on the part of the United States credit should be given to England for the authenticity of a Despatch from Lord Castlereagh to the British Minister at Washington which was Communicated verbally to the Government of the United States, when the restoration of the Establishment called Astoria, or Fort George was in contemplation, containing a complete reservation of the right of England to the territory at the Mouth of the Columbia (Statement of the British Plenipotentiaries, December 1826).

In fine, the present state of the question between the two Governments appears to be this—Great Britain possesses and exercises in common with the United States a right of joint occupancy in the Oregon Territory, of which Right She can be divested, with respect to any part of that Territory, only by an equitable partition of the whole between the Two Powers.

It is for obvious reasons desirable that such a Partition should take place as soon as possible, and the difficulty appears to be in devising a line of demarcation which shall leave to each Party that precise portion of the Territory best suited to its interest and convenience.

The British Government entertained the hope that by the proposal lately submitted for the consideration of the American Government that object would have been accomplished.

According to the arrangement therein contemplated the Northern Boundary of the United States West of the Rocky Mountains, would for a considerable distance be carried along the same Parallel of Latitude, which forms their Northern boundary on the Eastern side of those Mountains, thus uniting the present Eastern Boundary of the Oregon Territory with the Western Boundary of the United States from the 49th Parallel downwards.

From the point where the 49th Degree of Latitude intersects the North Eastern Branch of the Columbia River called in that part of its course McGillevray's River, the proposed line of Boundary would be along the middle of that River, till it joins the Columbia, then along the middle of the Columbia to the Ocean, the navigation of the River remaining perpetually free to both Parties.

In addition Great Britain offers a separate territory on the Pacifick possessing an excellent Harbour, with a further understanding that any Port or Ports whether on VanCouvers Island, or on the Continent South of the 49th Parallel, to which the United States might desire to have access, shall be made free Ports.

It is believed that by this arrangement ample justice would be done to the claims of the United States on whatever ground advanced, with relation to the Oregon Territory. As regards extent of Territory they would obtain acre for acre, nearly half of the entire territory to be divided—as relates to the navigation of the principal River they would enjoy a perfect equality of right with Great Britain, and with respect to Harbours, it will be seen that Great Britain shows every disposition to consult their convenience in that particular. On the other hand were Great Britain to abandon the line of the Columbia as a frontier, and to surrender Her right to the navigation of that River, the prejudice occasioned to Her by such an arrangement would beyond all proportion exceed the advantage acoming to the United States from the possession of a few more square miles of Territory. It must be obvious to every impartial investigator of the subject that in adhering to the line of the Columbia, Great Britain is not influenced by motives of ambition with reference to extent of Territory but by considerations of utility, not to say necessity, which cannot be lost sight of and for which allowance ought to be made, in an arrangement professing to be based on considerations of mutual convenience and advantage.

The Undersigned believes that He has now noticed all the arguments advanced by the American Plenipotentiary in order to shew that the United States are fairly entitled to the entire Region drained by the Columbia River. He sincerely regrets that their views on this subject should differ in so many essential respects.

It remains for Him to request that as the American Plenipotentiary declines the proposal offered on the part of Great Britain, He will have the goodness to state what arrangement He is, on the part of the United States, prepared to propose for an equitable adjustment of the question—and more especially that He will have the goodness to define the nature and extent of the claims which the United States may have to other portions of the Territory, to which allusion is made in the concluding part of His statement, as it is obvious that no arrangement can be made with respect to a part of the Territory in dispute, while a claim is reserved to any portion of the remainder.

The Undersigned, British Plenipotentiary has the honor to renew to the American Plenipotentiary the assurance of his high consideration. R. Pakenham.

DS in DNA, RG 59 (State Department), Notes from Foreign Legations, Great Britain, vol. 22 (M-50:22); PC in the Washington, D.C., *Daily National Intelligencer*, December 13, 1845, p. 2; PC in *Niles' National Register*, vol. LXIX, no. 17 (December 27, 1845), pp. 263–264; PC in the London, England, *Times*, December 29, 1845, p. 5; PC in *Oregon: The Claim of the United States to Oregon, as Stated in the Letters of the Hon. J.C. Calhoun and the Hon. J. Buchanan . . . to the Right Hon. R. Pakenham* (London: Wiley and Putnam, 1846), Appendix, pp. 3–8; PC in Senate Document No. 1, 29th Cong., 1st Sess., pp. 153–158; PC in House Document No. 2, 29th Cong., 1st Sess., pp. 153–158; PC in Crallé, ed., *Works*, 5:440–449.

From G[reen] B. Samuels, [former Representative from Va.], Woodstock, [Va.], 9/12. "It is a matter of some concern to me to be informed at what precise date or dates the 9th & 10th Articles of the amendments to the Federal constitution became parts of that instrument." He would like a satisfactory official statement of the time. ALS in ScCleA.

To [U.S. MINISTERS and Certain CHARGÉS D'AFFAIRES]

Department of State
Washington, Sept[embe]r 12th, 1844

Sir, I herewith transmit to you a copy of a Despatch [of 9/10] to the Honorable Wilson Shannon our Minister at Mexico in order that you may be possessed of the views of your Government in regard to Texas, and the proposed invasion by Mexico. The Despatch is also designed as a reply; incidentally, to the appeal made by Mexico to the Ministers of Foreign Powers. I am, Sir respectfully Your Obedient Servant, J.C. Calhoun.

LS with En in DNA, RG 84 (Foreign Posts), Great Britain, Instructions, 8:417–436. NOTE: Copies of this letter were sent to Edward Everett, Minister to Great Britain; William R. King, Minister to France; Charles S. Todd, Minister to Russia; Henry Wheaton, Minister to Prussia; Daniel Jenifer, Minister to Austria; Henry A. Wise, Minister to Brazil; Washington Irving, Minister to Spain; Dabney S. Carr, Minister to Turkey; Christopher Hughes, Chargé d'Affaires to the Netherlands; Thomas G. Clemson, Chargé d'Affaires to Belgium; George W. Lay, Chargé d'Affaires to Sweden; William W. Irwin, Chargé d'Affaires to Denmark; William Boulware, Chargé d'Affaires to the Two Sicilies; Robert Wickliffe, Jr., Chargé d'Affaires to Sardinia; and Abraham Rencher, Chargé d'Affaires to Portugal. LS and FC versions can be found in DNA, RG 84 (Foreign Posts), in many files; FC and Abs versions are in DNA, RG 59 (State Department), Diplomatic Instructions, in many files. One copy of this letter was dated 9/10; two were dated 9/13. The version transcribed is that addressed to Edward Everett at London.

From [ISAAC VAN ZANDT]

Fellers, [Washington,] 12th Sept. 1844

Mr. Van Zandt[']s compliments to Mr. Calhoun and returns the the the [*sic*] communication made to him and wrong dated, with the proper alteration, also the letter to Gen[era]l [Tilghman A.] Howard which Mr. C[alhoun] had the kindness to submit for his perusal.

[P.S.] (*Confidential*)

The last note of Mr. V[an Zandt] to Mr. C[alhoun; "as they contain no" *canceled*] and the reply of Mr. C[alhoun] as they contain no secrets of state would it not be well to give them to the Madisonian that they may be published with the Speeches of Mr. V[an Zandt] and the President [John Tyler.] It would be but justice to Mr. C[alhoun] that the people of Texas should be fully informed of his untiring efforts in their behalf as also those of the President?

["I suppose" *canceled*] the speeches will be published today most likely.

ALU in ScCleA.

771

F[RANKLIN] H. ELMORE to
R[ichard] K. Crallé

Char[les]t[o]n, Sep[tember] 13, 1844

My Dear Sir, I rec[eive]d at Columbia the other day yours of 23rd ult[im]o. I was absent when it reached here & it was sent to meet me there. You will see it in the [South-]Carolinian [newspaper of Columbia], for [the editor, Alton H.] Pemberton to whom I showed it begged it out of me & in the present state of things I thought it not altogether inadvisable to let him have his way.

Our movement here to which you refer has I think settled every thing. All it failed to do is done by Judge [Langdon] Cheves' letter, which is a good report for our Resolutions. It is a noble letter & will be circulated every where by us.

Will you do me one favor—a particular one. Gen[era]l [Waddy] Thompson [Jr.] told me there was in a treaty between Mexico & England, a stipulation of Mexico to abolish slavery, or if abolished, never to permit its reestablishment. I mentioned it in your presence to Mr. Calhoun & I think you corroborated the fact. Will you do me the *special favor,* to inform me *as soon as you can* if this is so, or how the fact is—The date of the treaty, the article & its bearing, or a copy of the article. I have a very special reason for wanting it & *as soon as* possible too.

One word more—I have two letters in regard to the [Washington] Spectator. Duff Green writes & proposes to take a hand—so does Mr. [William A.] Harris. The latter is a man to whom nobody can object. Our friend Green I fear could not give much weight to a paper. ["His" *altered to* "The"] idea seems to be to buy out the Madisonian & unite it with the Spectator. Now if Harris will take them, I have no doubt the proprietors of the Spectator would readily release the interest they have to any permanent arrangement with Mr. Harris. I fear his idea of their raising $2,000 to pay him a Salary would not be likely to be done. The press they would I have no doubt give, but no more I fear. Will you think of this—if you please talk with Mr. Calhoun & [John] Heart confidentially & let us know the best plan of action?

I will write to [Robert Barnwell] Rhett, to Heart & to both Gree[n and] Harris, but to you I look for the consideration of the *whole matter* & some feasible plan to make the press & materials of the paper available. Write me soon on this—but *on the treaty* matter as soon *as possible.*

Has the British Govt. ever noticed Mr. Calhoun[']s second letter to Mr. Packenham [*sic*] or followed up the correspondence in regard to the Slavery question? In the greatest haste Y[ou]rs truly, F.H. Elmore.

ALS in ScCleA. NOTE: Crallé's letter of 8/23, mentioned in the first paragraph above, has not been found in either ms. or printed versions.

From Rob[er]t Monroe Harrison, U.S. Consul, Kingston, J[a-maic]a, 9/13. He informs Calhoun that "Her Majesty's Schooner Pickle arrived here yesterday from St. Juan de Nicaragua, bringing the news of the raising of the Blockade by the British Squadron at that place. It is to be supposed that the affair which caused it, has been so arranged as to cause this movement." LS (No. 303) in DNA, RG 59 (State Department), Consular Despatches, Kingston, vol. 9 (T-31:9), received 10/23.

From W[ILLIA]M HOGAN

Boston, Sept. 13th 1844

I understand, Sir, that the Consulate of Antwerp is now vacant, by the resignation of Mr. [Francis J.] Grund, recently appointed to that office. I think his Excellency, President [John] Tyler, will have no objection, to give me that office, if you think proper to nominate me, though I should much prefer your sending me to Mexico with Despatches, which I had the honor of mentioning to you in a previous letter[.] Very Respectfully Yours, &c., Wm. Hogan.

ALS in ScCleA.

To TILGHMAN A. HOWARD

Washington, September 13th 1844

Dear Sir, I yesterday forwarded to you by a Special Messenger, Lieut[enant] George Stevens, a copy of a Despatch [of 9/10] to our Minister, at Mexico, Gov. [Wilson] Shannon, the original of which will be delivered to him by Gen[era]l [Duff] Green, who having been detained here a day, furnishes me the opportunity of transmitting to you the enclosed paragraph, which, since the departure of Mr. Stevens, it has been thought advisable to add to the original Despatch.

It is probable that you will not have delivered the copy before this reaches you, as Gen[era]l Green leaves here tomorrow direct for Vera Cruz, *via* Galveston. In this case you can annex the enclosed as the *concluding paragraph* of the Despatch, immediately preceeding the signature. If, however, you shall have delivered the copy, it would be proper to hand the paragraph to President [Samuel] Houston, and inform him that it should be so annexed so as to make it a full and correct copy of the original. With high respect I am, dear Sir, Your obedient Servant, J.C. Calhoun.

LS (Unofficial) in DNA, RG 84 (Foreign Posts), Texas; PC with En in Jameson, ed., *Correspondence*, pp. 612–613. NOTE: The enclosure, as printed by Jameson, reads: "You are requested to renew the declaration made to the Mexican Secretary by our Charge d'affaires, in announcing the conclusion of the Treaty—that the measure was adopted in no spirit of hostility to Mexico, and that if annexation should be consummated, the United States will be prepared to adjust all questions growing out of it, including that of boundary, in the most liberal terms."

To W[ILLIAM] W. IRWIN, Copenhagen

Department of State
Washington, 13th September, 1844

Sir: The attention of this Department has been again called to the subject of the Danish Sound Dues. The information respecting these dues on file here, is not sufficient; and I now write for the purpose of obtaining from you whatever may be necessary to render that information complete. On the receipt of these instructions you will proceed to examine the subject, and to procure and transmit hither, at as early a moment as practicable, every thing in relation to the Sound Dues which may be within your reach. As a satisfactory mode of imparting the kind of knowledge which is sought, it is suggested to you to make out, or cause to be made out, in a tabular form, statements showing the number of American vessels and the amount and kind of American property, which, (since 1783, the period when, it is believed, our commerce first entered the Baltic), has passed, annually, through the Sound and Belts—the amount of tonnage—the dues exacted, and all other taxes and impositions, of every description, arising directly, or indirectly, out of the enforcement of this toll, and a comparative view of the commerce of other nations trading to the Baltic, within the same period. You will also furnish copies of the different tariffs which have been in force, and point out the various discriminations which have affected, and still affect, favorably or unfavorably, the trade and commerce of the United States. In this connection, it may be proper to remark that the rates per centum of the duties laid upon different articles of commerce may be equal, but, at the same time, by laying high duties upon some articles and low duties upon others, there may be an advantageous discrimination in favor of one and a disadvantageous discrimination in regard to the other.

The Sound duties are, as you know, regarded, by the Northern Powers of Europe, in the same unfavorable light that they are by the United States. Prussia is interested in their modification or suppression; they being held by her to be the chief obstruction to the full developement of the Baltic trade, and more especially of the direct trade of the United States with the States composing the German Custom's Union which must pass through the Prussian ports of the Baltic.

You will make no formal communication to the Danish Government upon this subject, but if it should become necessary to apply to it for any information which you think may prove useful, you are at liberty to state, if necessary, that the object of the application is to enable you to answer inquiries which your Government has made in regard to the Sound dues.

As bearing upon the subject under consideration, I have directed copies to be made, and forwarded to you with this despatch, of a correspondence between Mr. Steen Billé, the Diplomatic Representative of Denmark, near this Government, and Mr. [Daniel] Webster, then Secretary of State, respecting the negotiations between England and Denmark, which resulted in the Convention of ["August" *interlined*] 1841, by which the former power obtained a reduction of the duties on those articles in which her trade was chiefly interested.

Your despatches to No. 29, inclusive, have been received, with the exception of No. 12. I am, Sir, respectfully, Your obedient Servant, J.C. Calhoun.

FC (No. 12) in DNA, RG 59 (State Department), Diplomatic Instructions, Denmark, 14:42–45 (M-77:50); PC in Jameson, ed., *Correspondence*, pp. 610–612. NOTE: Appended to the FC was a list of the documents Calhoun enclosed. These were: Billé to Webster, 8/1/1841; Billé to Webster, 6/20/1842; and Webster to Billé, 6/27/1842.

To R[OBERT] A. MAXWELL, Pendleton

Washington, 13th Sep[tembe]r 1844
Dear Sir, The debt of Mr. [Thomas G.] Clemson to the estate of Mr. [James C.?] Griffin, to which you refer in your note, will be paid punctually, when it falls due. I hope to be in Pendleton before the time it will; but, if I should not, I will remit the amount by a check on Charleston. With great respect I am & &c, J.C. Calhoun.

ALS in TxU, John C. Calhoun Papers.

From EUSTIS PRESCOTT, "Private"

New York [City,] 13th Sept[embe]r 1844
My Dear Sir, I have taken the liberty to give F.W. Hatch of New Orleans, a letter of introduction to you, he is a very respectable and independant young Merchant, who has engaged but little in politics, and I am convinced will be a valuable auxiliary, for it is by the young men that the next conflict must be sustained. Mr. Hatch thinks of retiring from business, and would I believe be pleased to receive the appointment of Treasurer of the [New Orleans] Mint—should the present incumbent be removed. I can with great confidence recommend him for the office, he has been a uniform friend of the President [John Tyler]. Mr. Hatch is anxious that Dr. [Isaac?] Stone should succeed the present Surgeon of the [New Orleans] Marine Hospital who is stated to be a warm friend of Mr. [Henry] Clay. I would also recommend Dr. Stone, he is a very popular Democrat, and a warm friend of yours.

Many changes ought to be made in New Orleans previous to the election, if we are not to be opposed by the Officers of Government, but I am reluctant to urge the matter on the President, if however he should change the District Attorney, I trust our friend [William A.] Elmore may be remembered.

It is my intention to be in New Orleans in Oct[obe]r and I hope to have the pleasure of seeing you *en route.*

I had the pleasure of seeing Mr. [Thomas G. Clemson,] Mrs. [Anna Maria Calhoun Clemson] & Master [John] Calhoun Clemson the morning of embarkation. I very much regretted not to have known earlier that they were in the city to have tendered my services and introduced my Wife & Daughter to them. Mrs. Clemson and you little grandson are I think very much ["I" *canceled*] like you. I trust they have had a very pleasant passage.

I am still anxious to spend two years abroad, and then return to this city, as a permanent residence. I know the South will be safe, and that our contest must be carried on vigor[o]usly from this point. At length the northern press are becoming just to you, and we shall not have the same difficulties to contend with, as some years since. It is unfortunate that some of our South Carolina friends cannot have a little patience, our cause is gaining friends every hour and must be successful.

The contest in this State will be very warm, but as the Democratic party are now united I believe they will be succes[s]ful. The Whigs are however rich and will not spare money, speeches or songs. A large majority of ["the" *changed to* "our"] party are in favor of the annexation of Texas & the occupation of Oregon, these must become great popular questions.

Mr. Clemson remarked to me that Mr. [Christopher] Hughes would return from the Hague, that is somewhat of a mercantile mission, and if there is no hope of obtaining the Consulate at Liverpool, possibly the President might favor me with that appointment. I have been in Holland & know something of its commerce which ought to be more extended with us, and I think might be—altho I know not the precise character of our treaty with that Government. It would afford me much pleasure to be placed in a situation to cooperate with Mr. Clemson in extending our commercial relations.

The loss of my eldest son has rendered my family averse to returning to New Orleans, and I shall probably close my business there this winter, if however you do not see a prospect of my obtaining any foreign appointment, I should be very willing to accept a respectable appointment in New Orleans which would not interfere with the closing of my affairs and which I could resighn in the spring if desirable. I however have such entire confidence in your friendship that I leave the matter entirely with you. I am rather too proud to be an Applicant for office, or make my wishes known to any public man but yourself.

Do you see the [New York] Journal of Commerce, it is vigorously sustaining the cause of free trade. With great respect I remain Dear Sir Yours very sincerely, Eustis Prescott.

ALS in ScCleA.

From ROBERT B. CAMPBELL

Consulate of the United States of America, Havana
Havana, Sept. 14, 1844

Sir, I flatter myself we have at last arrived at a period when we see the approaching termination of the vexatious difficulties and persecutions to which foreigners and others who have unfortunately been suspected of aiding in kindling the torch of servile incendiarism have been subjected. Bisbee and Mofford [*sic*; William Bisby and Samuel Moffat] in favor of whom public sympathy has been so generally and deservedly excited in the United States have been released on bail. I have no fear that they will receive further molestation. Theirs have been cases (as many other foreigners and subjects of the Government) of great hardship. Those hardships have grown in some instances out of the peculiar character of the Tenientes of particular sections, who it seems have been able when called upon by proof *true* ["and" *altered to* "or"] *false* to acquit themselves in the estimation of the Capt. Gen[era]l of cruelty or unnecessary severity.

In most instances however these cruel and long continued imprisonments have their origin in the institutions and usages of the country. In criminal cases where conviction would be followed by death or long incarceration the party accused cannot be bailed, at his arrest he is not permitted to be informed of the charges against him or the name of the accuser. An officer called a fiscal whose duties are those of both a grand juror and solicitor in our country, examines witnesses, records their evidence and finally reports to the court before which the case is to be tried (in these late cases a military court).

The party accused is then brought before the court and for the first time he learns the cause of arrest. The court hand the accused the names of some twenty or thirty officers from which he chooses his defender. The officer selected is subjected to severe penalties upon failing to do all that his talents and ingenuity suggest to obtain an acquittal of the party. The exculpatory evidence is here taken, the accuser and witnesses are confronted with the accused the fiscal still acting for the Government. Upon this evidence the decision of the Court is made. That decision is reported to the Capt. Gen[era]l for approval or rejection, it is handed by him to an assessor selected by the crown as a law adviser and now for the first time the Capt. Gen[era]l can act officially, action at any earlier period of the trial would be extra official and upon his own responsibility, ["a reposibility" *canceled*] a responsibility rarely assumed in important cases. He approves the sentence or objects and sends the case back for revision. It is thus perceived that without a change of their institutions in times like those recently passed, all persons against whom charges may be made are subjected to greivous sufferings and long continued incarceration. Mr. Savange [*sic*; Thomas Savage] another American citizen acting as engineer on the Island has also been released upon his personal pledge to be forthcoming if called for. This last gentle-[man] from the slender testimony against him would have been discharged earlier if I could have offered sufficient bail. He does not complain of other cruelty and unkindness save his long confinement and detention from his business. The remonstrances which were made in the earlier cases having produced a great amelioration of the treatment of those subsequently arrested.

Mr. [John] Thompson is the only remaining American imprisoned at Matanzas, his case not being yet tried. These different Americans have been subjected to the expence of purchasing daily rations, the food allotted to prisoners being unac[c]eptable and perhaps insufficient.

There are now in prison at Matanzas awaiting and in progress of trial sixteen hundred coloured persons bond and free. Twenty four whites embracing four Englishmen & a few subjects of other countries, the remainder Spaniards. There have been thirty nine executions among which was one white (Spaniard) the ballance coloured, among those executed the most conspicuous was a coloured Dentist named Dodge, said to be a man of large fortune and Placido a coloured poet of more reputation than any other native poet of the Island.

The question has been frequently asked me by Americans whether redress in the shape of compensation for time lost, suffering endured and expenses incurred, is to be obtained from this Government. Will you do me the favor to send me special instructions on the subject. Although the arrests have neither been made within the limits of this Consulate or of persons living in it, I have done all in my power for their liberation and am disposed to do the same to obtain the most ample redress. Justice however compels me to admit that arrests however wrongful have been made under some shadow of law and at a period of great excitement and alarm imaginary or real. I have the honor to be y[ou]r mo[st] ob[edien]t Ser[van]t, Robert B. Campbell.

LS in DNA, RG 59 (State Department), Consular Despatches, Havana, vol. 19 (T-20:19), received 10/2.

From ROBERT B. CAMPBELL

Consulate of the United States of America, Havana
Sept. the 14th 1844

Sir, By the Schooner Warrior sailing this evening for Charleston, an opportunity is afforded me of communicating to the Department of State two affidavits taken in my office in relation to the most gross and unauthorised outrage, and ["an" *canceled*] indignity offered the American Flag on board the American Brig Cyrus of New Orleans P.C. Dumas master, of a character which must excite in the breast of the most peace loving American citizen, a feeling of indignation and resentment, that can only be appeased by the most ample atonement in redress and apology. The Cyrus cleared at this office on the fifteenth day of January last, her papers all complete, with an assorted cargo consisting of merchandize of various kinds as will be perceived by the accompanying receipt of her master dated January 3d 1844. It does not become me to make further comment on this transaction, than to say I have no cause to doubt or suspect the truth of the accompanying affidavits, That the Cyrus has made other voyages to the coast of Africa, that she is not a vessel which would be considered as suited for a slaver, and so far as I know has never been suspected. Justice to my countrymen demands of me to add that I do not beleive any of them in this City have in ["any" *interlined*] manner participated during my residence here in the odious, inhuman and piratical traffic of the slave trade. I have the honor to be with very great respect y[ou]r most ob[edien]t Ser[van]t, Robert B. Campbell.

LS with Ens and duplicate in DNA, RG 59 (State Department), Consular Despatches, Havana, vol. 19 (T-20:19), received 10/2.

To T[HOMAS] G. CLEMSON, [Brussels]

State Dept., 14th Sep[tembe]r 1844

My dear Sir, I am, you will see, still detained here, contrary to my calculation & desire; but expect to leave certainly between the 20 & 25th Inst. for home.

I have been much engaged between the Oregon negotiation; preparing dispatches, & the ordinary duties of the office. The Steamer, which takes this, takes also for you a copy of a dispatch [of 9/10] (sent to day by a special messenger) to our minister at Mexico. I ["had" *canceled*] transmitted to you by the last steamer a copy of a dispatch to Mr. [William R.] King at Paris. Both have been sent to all our Diplomatick agents in Europe, where it was supposed an explanation of our motives, in reference to Texas would be of service.

There has been a good deal of sickness at Fort Hill owing to the severity of the drought and the low state of the River; but no deaths. All were well the last accounts. It is thought the cotton crop will be cut very short, compared to what had been expected, by the long continuance of the drought. I have not heard from your ["crop" *canceled and* "place" *interlined*]. Our Alabama crop is very good, according to last accounts.

The political prospect is good. I hold [Henry] Clay's defeat and [James K.] Polk's election almost certain; and, as far as I am informed, there is no danger, that the latter will fall under the influence of [Thomas H.] Benton, or that wing of the party. He, indeed, appears to have lost cast[e] with the party.

Nothing has occur[r]ed since my last to Anna [Maria Calhoun Clemson] worth relating.

If you got my measure, I would be glad, if an opportunity should offer, that you would send me a broad cloth coat & ["a pair of" *interlined*] pantaloons, both black, and a waist coat of the same, or some suitable colour. Also a pair of boots & ["one of" *interlined*] shoes.

You have, ere this, ["have" *canceled*] been some time in Paris, & will I presume be in Brussels before it can reach its destination, to which place, I have accordingly, addressed it. I shall be very anxious to hear from you and learn the impression, which Europe and especially Paris has made on Anna.

I hope you all continue well, and have enjoyed yourselves much.

My love to Anna, & Kiss the dear children [John Calhoun Clemson and Floride Elizabeth Clemson] for their grandfather.

My health continues good, although I have been working hard. Your affectionate father, J.C. Calhoun.

ALS in ScCleA; variant PC in Jameson, ed., *Correspondence*, pp. 613–614.

From J[AMES] HAMILTON, [JR.], "(*Private & Confidential*)"

Oswichee Bend [Ala.,] Sept. 14[t]h 1844

My Dear Sir, Since writing you day before yesterday my Letters and Papers from New Orleans, reached me by last Evening['s] Mail.

I find, that Gen[era]l [Tilghman A.] Howard has fallen a victim to the fatal pestilence that is now scourging Texas.

The news of his death, ["when" *canceled and* "whilst" *interlined*] reflecting on the situation of the Count[r]y on my Pillow ["last night" *interlined*] it occurred to me, that at this particular juncture I might as his Successor be useful to both count[r]ies.

If the President [John Tyler] & yourself should concur in these views, I will without hesitation accept the appointment.

I think, if I went to the Country, as the Representative of the U.S. I would go there, with an influence which would enable me to place the Question of Annexation, *where* the President & yourself might desire to see it placed. Indeed, without indulging, in an inordinate self love, I think I could check mate my friend Capt. Elliott [*sic*; Charles Elliot, British Chargé d'Affaires in Texas,] & form just such a new Treaty, as the President & yourself might desire, or induce the Congress of Texas, to ["call a convention of the People to" *interlined*] make such a Declaratory Manifesto on the subject of their Union with the U. States, as might be deemed expedient. I think I at least see *one way* in which Annexation may be accomplished, before President Tyler retires from office. After all he has done and I may ["say" *interlined*] *suffered* by the infamous hostility of a majority in the Senate, I sincerely desire for his administration the renown of this acquisition.

It is true, that my relations with [Samuel] Houston are unfriendly, from the rabid jealousy, which he has cherished from my apprehended influence in the Country. That is to say, *they are unfriendly behind my back*. In my presence he is the most supple scycophant [*sic*] you can imagine. I can manage him however. But my *bona fide* ["power" *interlined*] will be with his Successor & with the Congress. He goes out of office just about the time I should reach Texas.

In one word if you think with me that I can be useful and President Tyler desires my service, you are at liberty to act for me as you deem best. I rely however if my appointment is prevented by causes beyond your Control, that this Letter will rest in the confidence of our *private friendship*, as I do not desire, to appear as a Candidate for, ["office" *canceled and* "public employment" *interlined*].

In the event of your absence I have authorized Mr. Crawley [*sic*; Richard K. Crallé] to open this Letter & if he deems the em[er]gency sufficiently urgent to hand ["it" *interlined*] *confidentially* ["this communication" *canceled*] to the President that he may act as he thinks proper.

I ought not to conceal from you that in the event of Texas being *in flagrante Bello* (which I deem almost certain) I might render *her* & the U.S. some service. Indeed if need be after I go there, I could resign my appointment, & if desirable go to the head of her Army, that is to say, if it did not commit, or *compromit* rather ["the" canceled] *our own Govt.* I do not deem it it [*sic*] improbable that by the time I could the next month reach New Orleans, that the only mode of my going promptly to Galveston would be in a diplomatic Capacity in one of our armed vessels, as the two Steamers in N. York belonging now to the Mexican service will doubtless bring up off Galveston, and lay that port under Blockade—waiting the arrival of an army of Invasion for a Combined attack by Sea & Land. You may rely upon it that as long as I should be an agent of the *Govt. of the U.S.* I will endeavour to act with the highest discretion with an implicit obedience to my Instructions. If I become a General officer in the Texian Army then I will go *thorough stitch to the knife handle.*

It is possible from the active part I have taken, in sustaining Annexation if the appointment were given me by the President my ["appointment" *canceled and* "nomination" *interlined*] might stick a little in the Senate. But it would only be for a time. [William C.] Rives[, William S.] Archer [Senators from Va.] & [John M.] Berrien [Senator from Ga.] will think & ponder twenty times before they go against me. I should feel myself complimented by the opposition of [Thomas H.] Benton.

To conclude My Dear Sir this long Winded Epistle on the most unpropitious of all themes *oneself* I trust you will pardon the additional vanity of my remarking, ["that" *canceled*], if I was Diplomat enough to induce her Britannic Majesty[']s Govt., in the face of the steady & u[n]mitigated War of all the abolitionists in England ["It" *canceled*] strenuously & acrimonieously waged against me for three years to recognize the Independance of Texas, I should indeed be a miserable Dabbster if I could not induce her to settle ["the" *canceled and* "on favorable (*"terms" canceled*) conditions the" *interlined*] terms on which she will become *one & indivisible* with the U. States.

I see by the papers that Gen[era]l [Adrian] Woll has probably *actually* crossed the *Rio Bravo.* Let me earnestly entreat you ["not to" *canceled*] to suggest to the President not to call Congress together at this incipient stage of the Invasion. Painful ["as" *interlined*] it is yet [we] will have to wait until fire & sword have made some progress in the Country to arouse that sympathy on the part of the people of the U. States, which would cooerse [*sic*; "the" *canceled*] Congress to sanction the interposition of our Govt. A Call of Congress *now* would have the same termination as the sequel of the

Treaty. Depend on it you must wait for the active & irresi[s]table[?] sympathy of the U.S. before you act which suffering & desolation will alone ["call forth" *interlined*]. My opinions must be taken as sincere when I have a Plantation Crop & Negroes to be destroyed & plundered on the Brasos.

Be so kind as to write me *immediately,* ["D" *canceled*] *in duplicate.* Direct one Copy to the Oswichee *Post office, via Columbus—* the other to Savannah Geo[rgia]. Ever My Dear Sir with sincere esteem faith & respect Your ob[edien]t Ser[van]t & friend, J. Hamilton.

ALS in ScCleA.

From Geo[rge] M. Keim, U.S. Marshal, Philadelphia, 9/14. He submits the statistics requested in Calhoun's letter of 7/23. Keim has no clerk; "the researches, in the absence of any former inquiry, being intricate and voluminous, I took the liberty to employ a person capable to the task and beg leave herewith to tender his charge for services." ALS in DNA, RG 59 (State Department), Accounting Records: Miscellaneous Letters Received.

To Richard Pakenham, 9/14. Calhoun acknowledges receipt of Pakenham's note of 9/4, "accompanied by a printed copy of the instructions recently issued for the guidance of Her Majesty's Naval Officers employed in the suppression of the slave trade." FC in DNA, RG 59 (State Department), Notes to Foreign Legations, Great Britain, 7:49 (M-99:36).

F[rancis] W. Pickens, Edgewood, [Edgefield District, S.C.], to J[ames] Edward Colhoun, Calhoun's Mills, Abbeville District, S.C., 9/14. After commenting on local matters, Pickens discusses the political situation. "You know I went to Nashville at the urgent request of Mr. [John C.] Calhoun & others. My trip was very troublesome & dreary. I saw [Andrew] Jackson & [James K.] Polk and delegates from every State on the waters of the Miss., and addressed immense crowds. I never saw such intense excitement in my life. We shall carry every State in the West, South & North West except K[en]-t[uck]y and many of our friends think they will carry that. But what is best for us, the battle is fighting upon our principles. I could utter no sentiment too strong on the Tariff for those people. Since [Silas] Wright's nomination for Gov[ernor] we shall carry N[ew] York, & since [John] Tyler's withdrawal N[ew] Jersey is certain & I think

Ohio. There is now every probability that Polk will be elected by a large majority. [Thomas H.] Benton is off entirely from us & the N[ew] Yorkers have no correspondence with Polk. He is entirely untrammeled, and from the position of Benton & the N[ew] York tacticians will be forced to fall back upon us & our principles. I went over every inch of ground with him & I assure you *all is safe for us.* The only difficulty in our position is the mad & reckless moves made by Mr. [Robert Barnwell] Rhett. I seriously believe they are made deliberately to injure Mr. Calhoun. This is the first time that the Rep[ublican] party have ever fairly canvassed upon our principles in reference to the Tariff. In 1832 Jackson led them off & we had no hearing. But it is entirely different now. Besides the abolition question & Texas have sprung up since 1832, & considering the issues England has tendered connected with these questions we have no right to separate ourselves at present from the slave-holding States. It would be under existing circumstances fatal to us. We must wait events. I have not heard a word from Mr. Calhoun in a long time." ALS in ScU-SC, Francis W. Pickens Papers.

From Geo[rge] R. Chapman, Tahiti, Society Islands, 9/15. He announces the death of U.S. Consul Samuel R. Blackler. Before his death Blackler appointed Chapman to be Acting Consul but was unable to inform the State Department of that action. Chapman was recognized as Acting Consul by Tahitian authorities on 9/11. He hopes the State Department will approve his appointment. ALS in DNA, RG 59 (State Department), Consular Despatches, Tahiti, Society Islands, French Oceania (M-465:2, frames 192–193).

From J[AMES] HAMILTON, [JR.], "*(Private)*"

Oswichee Bend [Ala.,] Sept. 15[t]h 1844

My Dear Sir, I forgot in my Letter, yesterday to say to you, that I shall be in Charleston on the 5[t]h Oct. and remain there on business until the 10[t]h. If you should be coming South at that time, you will be sure to *meet me there*, and whether I go to Texas in a diplomatic capacity or not I should like to have a full[,] free & unreserved conference with you on the subject of the best course we have to take at the South, in relation to that Country, should she be seriously beleagu[e]red by Mexico, which I deem now *inevitable.*

I hope you will not consider me as at all importunate on the subject of the Texian Mission but from the hold I have on all the people of worth in that Country I believe whether it be at peace or in the jaws of war I could render some service, if protected under the sover[e]ignty of our own Country. My object would be to be in Washington by the 1st Feb[ruar]y with a new Treaty ["to cooperate in its ratification" *interlined*] or a Declaratory Manifesto of the people ["of Texas" *interlined*] which I think would compel an act of Congress annexing the two Countries.

If my appointment should be made I would suggest that it be announced as *Chargé* D'Affaires ["to" *canceled*] and *special envoy* to Texas, to *mark* the *importance* of *my Mission.* For considering the post I have before held a Chargé to Texas is a little below my Mark. But a crisis invests any ["post of" *canceled and* "Station with" *interlined*] importance, ["&" *canceled*]—where ["high" *interlined*] public service is to be rendered.

If I do go I hope I may make a *Coup* for President [John] Tyler['s] administration & for myself. For you may rely upon it, Annexation is to be accomplished *now* in Texas in the *first instance* & in Washington ["afterwards" *interlined*]. *One hour*[']s conversation between us, will I think fix this matter. I will carry with me every man of influence in Texas.

I believe until a nomination has been ratified by the Senate the Appointee can neither draw his Salary or outfit. I will thank you to apprize me ["of" *canceled and* "how" *interlined*] this matter stands, that I may provide for my expences out of my own means in case of my *appointment.*

If you answer this Letter on or before the *23d inst.* be so kind as to direct to Oswichee P. O. *via Columbus* Geo[rgia], if after to Savannah where I shall be on the 1st Oct.

God bless you my Dear Sir[,] Ever your friend, J. Hamilton.

ALS in ScCleA.

From JOHN HOGAN

Utica N.Y., Sept. 15th[?] 1844

My Dear Sir, With this letter you will receive the result of the [State] election in Maine. That Election is an index to Mr. [Henry] Clay's prospects in November. No one now can doubt what the result will be and as I said to you some time ago this State will give her vote to [James K.] Polk and [George M.] Dallas. The nomination of Mr. [Silas] Wright [for Governor] draws into the contest all the friends of Mr. [Martin] Van Buren. There were two or three causes for his nomination which weighed strongly in his favour at the State Convention in this State. They are as follows[:] Mr. Wright did not wish to be in the U.S. Senate when the question would come up as to the Annexation of Texas. I have no doubt he was fearful that should he in the Senate pursue the same course he has done it would prove his overthrow (as no doubt it would). Therefore he was anxious to be out of that Body the coming session. Another cause in my opinion is that the present Governor [William C.] Bouck inclines to be opposed to him (Mr. W[right]) together with a strong minority of the Democratic Party in this State. The principal cause of Bouck['s] defeat was his want of talent and decision and other things combined produced his defeat as well as the nomination of Mr. W[right]. Our man Judge [Addison] Gardiner the Candidate for Lieut. Gov. is in a great measure as able a man as Mr. W[right] and I believe would poll more votes at this Election were he the Candidate for Gov[erno]r. With our Lieut. Gov. we will be able to keep the other Gentlemen in check and we may get a U.S. Senator probably Judge Gardiner himself. There is another point in this matter which I will not pass over in order to put you in possession of the whole ground. Mr. Wright will meet with a bitter opposition in the Office of Gov[erno]r from the friends of Gov. Bouck who will watch him closely and will If possible defeat him. My own opinion is from the distracted state of the Party in this State and from the position of her internal improvements && and the great swarm of office seekers which will crowd around Mr. W[right] when elected the chances are his election of Gov[erno]r at this time will prove prejudicial to his *future prospects*. There will be as many as 12 applicants for Every Office and he must ["necessaliry"(?) *canceled and "necessarily" interlined*] disappoint 11 of them who will return to their homes embittered against him. Combining this with the opposition of Bouck's friends you need not be surprised If Mr. W[right] has mistaken his future interest. I understand that the opposition to his administration is already organizing. Now to my mind our position in the Melee is to keep quiet and let these Gent[lemen] place themselves in a hostile attitude towards each other and in the course of 2 years we can step in and take with us which ever of those interests we think proper and by that means carry the State with us. I thought it was due to you to know the true position of matters in this State and our future prospects.

Now I will take the liberty of refer[r]ing to another subject and one too of vital interest to the U.S. I mean with regard to our Foreign relations. You must have noticed the hostile attitude France is placing herself in, towards England in the South Sea and the Mediterranean. I see by the London Morning C[h]ronicle, and the London ["Times" *interlined*] that are occasionally sent me that the English people are becoming bitterly sore towards France. The debates in the English Houses of Lords and Commons evinces a sensitiveness that is unusual for English Statesmen. The Ministry endeavour to evade an issue as much as possible but one would think they will be unsuccessful. One thing is certain that England cannot hazzard a conflict with France or any other Country until Mr. [Daniel] O[']Connell and the Irish People are conciliated and that conciliation cannot take place short of yeilding [*sic*] to the Irish People their demands which the People of England will never concede short of coercion. Therefore England is not prepared for a collision with France or any other European Power. In my opinion there has not been a period for 20 years in our Diplomatic intercourse with Europe when we required more able Statesmen at those Courts than we do at present. Had we such a *one* at the Court of St. James who understood the English People England would be compelled to with[h]old her interference in the Slavery and Texas questions by properly directing her attention to her own internal affairs in keeping an eye to the movements of Mr. O[']Connell in Ireland[,] the imprisonment of whom is well worthy of attention for, rest assured that, that is a tremendous weapon now in Europe and likely to become still more so for the reason that England could do nothing better calculated to embroil her with the Catholic Countries of Europe than her treatment at this time of Ireland and O[']Connell. I will point it out to you. The people of Ireland have always been, in a measure dependent on the Catholic Countries of Europe for protection. Therefore there has always existed a strong sympathy between the People of Ireland and France[,] Spain[,] Portugal[,] and Austria and in fact all the Catholic Countries of Europe, and whatever Louis Phillip[e] may be disposed to do he will be compelled for his own interest to adopt such measures as will be best calculated to aid the People of Ireland. O[']Connell is now looked upon by the Catholics of Europe as a Martyr for his Religion and you understand mankind too well to doubt the frenzy that such a feeling is capable of producing and rest assured If a war should break out between England and France that those feelings will be the moving cause and he who has studied the History of the past knows well how readily men will immolate themselves in such a contest, and then England's complicated and precarious affairs on the Continent adds still more to her embarrassment.

There is no doubt that England was desirous to form what she was pleasured to call an Anti Slavery League in Europe the object of which is too apparent to need further comment.

Our Minister at St. James [Edward Everett] is a Gentleman of handsome literary acquirements but from all that I can gather he is much better adapted for that pursuit than for a Diplomatist and especially too when our all depends upon the skill of our Representatives.

You no doubt have noticed the embarrassed position England is placed in with regard to Spain, the French interest has at length predominated by driving [Baldomero] Espartero from the Regency of that Country. Has not Spain some claim upon Texas[?] If so then why not through the Spanish Minister or through our Minister at Paris Mr. [William R.] King procure from Spain a release of their claim upon Texas If such a claim exists and why is not this the time to negociate that matter. You see England is making strenuous efforts to regain her influence in Spain. My opinion is that she cannot for the simple reason that France is preparing to bring about a Different result and to my humble mind now is the Golden hour. England to sustain herself must endeavour to draw Austria into her measures but will be unsuccessful for Prince Metternich is too able a Statesman to be entrapped in any such movement simply because it would involve him in difficulty with all the uneasy Spirits of Austria and the [Italian] Carrabonara [*sic*; Carbonari] Party is still secretly in existence and to be added ["to" *interlined*] that all the Literary Institutions of Austria are strongly disposed to push for a Republican form of Government and there is no Statesman in Europe who dreads that Spirit more ["than" *interlined*] Prince Metternich does. This brings me to another point[,] what class of Gent[lemen] have we at the Court of Vienna. Of all men in the U.S. Mr. [Daniel] Jenifer is least calculated for that Station at this juncture, it is true he may understand the Tobacco matter but at this time that does not weigh a feather in the Scale. To my mind there is no Gent[leman] in the U.S. better calculated for that station than Gen. [Lewis] Cass. His vast knowledge [of] the conflicting European interests[,] his commanding position with the King and People of France, render him at this time an important Representative for our vast interests in Europe. I have no doubt he could be prevailed upon under the circumstances to accept the appointment. It is true that Mr. [Daniel] Webster caused a breach between him and the President [John

Tyler]. Surely that could be healed and should the General go there it would be well in *other respects* which it would not be necessary for me to mention at present. With Mr. King at Paris & General Cass at Vienna and another Gent[leman] of the same class at London depend upon it much could be done and a much better Treaty could be got than Mr. [Henry] Wheaton['s] Zollverein Treaty which was rejected by the Senate. You know too well the bitter enmity that exists between Russia & England and I have no doubt that Russia If properly informed would ["any" *canceled and* "render no" *interlined*] assistance to England in her trouble, as for Prussia she is like ["the" *canceled*] a mere appendage to Austria & Russia.

Inclosed I send you an article written by a celebrated German Statesman which goes far to confirm my opinions. I purpos[e]ly got this Copied that you would be enabled to lend it. I am Sir with great respect your ob[edien]t Servant, John Hogan.

ALS in ScCleA; PEx in Boucher and Brooks, eds., *Correspondence*, pp. 251–252.

From R[OBERT] WICKLIFFE, JR.

Legation of The United States
Turin, Sep[tember] 15th 1844
Sir, I have the honor to acknowledge the receipt of your despatches of the 30th May and of the 17th of June last, Nos. 4 and 5. I had availed myself of the retirement of the Court to the Country to make a rapid visit to Genoa and to learn as much as possible in the time I could command, of our commerce with that Port. Your despatches reached me at that City and upon their receipt I immediately returned to ["this" *canceled*] Turin. Upon my arrival I ascertained that His Majesty [Charles Albert] had not yet returned to town. I addressed a Note to the First Secretary of State for Foreign Affairs, requesting to know the most agreeable manner in which the letter of M. [John] Tyler could be communicated to His Majesty. Count Solar de la Marguerite in reply informed me that by enclosing the letter to him, he would make it his duty to conduct it to its high destination. This I did accordingly and have his note acknowledging its receipt.

Although contrary to the interests of our commerce, yet I am pleased to find by your despatch No. 5 [of 6/17], that the opinion which I had ventured to express, with regard to the question of the Protests of American Captains, has met with your authoritative Sanction. The course which you instruct me to pursue is the one which I had already marked out for myself. I shall use every exertion to procure some modification of the laws of this Kingdom upon that subject, but at the same time will strictly observe your caution not to vex and annoy this government with unreasonable importunity in pressing my views. I have addressed a Note to the Minister for Foreign Affairs, suggesting the propriety of establishing the laws of this country, so as to meet the proffer of reciprocity made by the Act of Congress upon this point or if that should not be agreeable respectfully requesting him to propose some other plan by which the mutual commerce of the two countries may be relieved from the unnecessary taxes[,] restraints and inconveniences at present imposed. As soon as I receive his response, I will send you copies of my letter and his reply. I am duly impressed with the importance of the subject and hope if not to succeed at least to merit your approbation by the promptness with which I will attend to it.

I have also a communication to send you on another subject, which I will forward by the first person whom I can entrust as a special Messenger to Paris. I also take the liberty to suggest, once for all, that if at any time you have any thing to communicate to this Legation, which you do not wish to be known by the Government here, that it is very unsafe to trust the sanctity of the Post or to rely on the security of Cypheres, & that it should be sent at least from Paris by an accredited Courier.

There is at present no Consul at Florence. The former incumbent M. Ambrosi [*sic*; James Ombrosi] was dismissed more than two years ago and Mr. Edward Gamage appointed in his place As late as the middle of July, although appointed so long ago ["Mr. G(amage)" *interlined*] had not arrived and the general impression seemed to be that he would not come at all. Despatches[,] Circulars & Documents however come addressed to him as Consul in that City from the Department and from this circumstance I presume you are under the impression that Mr. Gamage ["is" *interlined*] at his post. The profits of a Consul at Florence are very small & not of themselves any inducement for a person to undertake its duties. The policy of having foreigners in such stations is obviously bad and I respectfully suggest that some new person should be appointed. Although we have not a great deal of commerce with Florence, yet there is a large number of American Citizens who visit and many who reside in that City and the presence of a Consul may be often necessary to facilitate their [*mutilated word*] and to protect their rights. Unless a mercantile man can be induced to take the place, I believe although I do not know it, that either Mr. [Horatio] Greenough or Mr. [Hiram] Powers would accept it. They are both located in Florence with their families—both are men of character[,] integrity and industry— both would discharge the duties conscientiously & faithfully if they undertook them and both as artists would perhaps be aided in their Profession by the Protection which the [*one word altered to* "Consular"] office bestows. Mr. Greenough speaks of returning to America but as Mr. Powers will continue indefinitely there, he would be more likely to accept it. My apology for mentioning this subject is that there is no American Representative nearer to Tuscany than myself.

I avail myself of this occasion to renew to you the assurances of my most distinguished Consideration, R. Wickliffe, Jr.

ALS (No. 10) in DNA, RG 59 (State Department), Diplomatic Despatches, Sardinia, vol. 4 (M-90:5), received 10/22.

SEPTEMBER 16–30, 1844

◫

The determination which the Tyler administration had taken to stand up to any Mexican employment of force against Texas began to receive some concrete implementation. Much of the latter part of September was spent in investigating the activities of two Mexican warships which were fitting out and recruiting in New York. On September 16 Calhoun wrote to Andrew J. Donelson urging his immediate acceptance of the post of American Chargé in Texas to succeed Tilghman A. Howard, who had been felled by fever a few days after his arrival. Besides being an experienced soldier and lawyer, Donelson enjoyed the added advantage, providing reassurance to the Texans, of being the nephew of Andrew Jackson. On the 17th Donelson was informed that the War Department was taking direct measures to counter rumored Mexican incitement of the Indians against Texas.

The Oregon negotiations continued, but having carried them about as far as they could be for the moment, Calhoun was beginning to give thought to a trip home. In his last days in Washington he took time to follow up his earlier despatch to Edward Everett in London on the fugitive slave question. And to express to an Alabama friend, David Hubbard, his optimism about the political situation. It seemed likely that the Democrats would win the Presidency and achieve a remedy for the burden of the tariff. If so, Polk's "administration will mark a great and salutary era in our political history . . . . and give renewed vigour to the Constitution & the Union."

Calhoun's old ally, the peripatetic and indefatigable Duff Green, had been named U.S. Consul at Galveston and entrusted with the delivery of important despatches to the American Minister in Mexico City. Before the end of September he was in Texas and already scouting out new routes to the Pacific, suitable for a future railroad. Meanwhile, on September 28, the President returned from a sojourn at the Virginia springs, leaving Calhoun free to depart Washington. Richard K. Crallé was to be Acting Secretary of State. On about the 28th Calhoun headed south, to spend a month in Carolina.

◫

From Ezra Conant, Bridgewater, Mass., 9/16. Conant asks if a rumor is true that [Henry L.] Ellsworth is to be removed as Commissioner of the Patent Office. Conant and many of his acquaintances have had unpleasant dealings with Ellsworth, and they feel that his removal would be "salutary." He asks for an early answer. ALS in DNA, RG 59 (State Department), Applications and Recommendations, 1837–1845, Conant (M-687:6, frames 149–150).

From D[avid] Conner, [U.S. Navy], Philadelphia, 9/16. "Herewith I transmit the book containing an account of Spanish discoveries on the N[orth] W[est] coast of America which I mentioned to you on the morning I had the honor of seeing you at the Navy Dept. When you have done with it I will thank you to return it to me, as I do not believe another copy is to be procured in the U. States." ALS in DNA, RG 59 (State Department), Miscellaneous Letters (M-179: 105, frame 364).

To "Maj[o]r" A[NDREW] J. DONELSON, [Nashville]

State Dept., 16th Sep[tembe]r 1844
My dear Sir, The mail of yesterday brought the melancholy intelligence of the death of General [Tilghman A.] Howard, our Charge at Texas; an event, which may be justly regarded, under present circumstances, as a publick misfortune.

The state of things in Texas is such, as to require, that the place should be filled without delay, and ["to select" *interlined*] him, who under all circumstances may be thought best calculated to bring to a successful decision, the great question of Annexation, now pending before the two countries. After full deliberation, you have been selected, as that Individual; and, I do trust, my dear sir, that you will not decline the appointment, however great may be the personal sacrafice of accepting. That great question must be decided in the next three or four months; and whether it shall be favourably or not, may depend on him, who shall fill the Mission now tendered to you. I need not tell you how much depends on its decision, for weal or woe to our country, and perhaps to the whole Continent. It is sufficient to say, that viewed in all its consequences, it is one of the very first magnitude; and that it gives an importance to the Mission, at this time, that raises it to the level with the highest in the gift of the Government.

Assuming, therefore, that you will not decline the appointment, unless some insuperable difficulty should interpose, and in order to avoid delay, a Commission is herewith transmitted, without the formality of waiting your acceptance, with all the necessary papers. You will be entitled to an outfit of $4,500 and a salary of an equal amount, commencing with your acceptance. There is no outfit appropriated, as no vacancy was anticipated; but application will be made to Congress to make an appropriation when it meets. In the mean time, the President [John Tyler] has ordered, that a quarter's salary should be advanced, which you will find done by a draft on N[ew] York. I hope it may be sufficient for the present. It was all that could be done. If, by any possibility, you should be prevented from accepting, which, I trust, will not be the case, you will please return the draft.

You will find, also, enclosed a copy of the dispatch, with its enclosures, forwarded a few days since to the late Charge, by a special Messenger. They are transmitted to you, in order to put you in advance, in possession of the views of the Government, in reference to the threatened invasion of Texas by Mexico. They are for your own eye; but you are at liberty to show them to General [Andrew] Jackson and to consult with him on the subject.

I shall be anxious to hear from you, at the earliest period, and take the liberty of wishing you, in anticipation of your acceptance, much success in your Mission. As I expect to leave this [city] for my residence in South Carolina, before your answer can reach here, I must request you, in addition to your official letter addressed to the Department, to address a private letter to me at Pendleton, South Carolina. With great respect yours truly, J.C. Calhoun.

ALS in DLC, Andrew Jackson Donelson Papers, series 2; autograph draft in ScCleA; PC in Jameson, ed., *Correspondence*, pp. 614–615. NOTE: Andrew Jackson Donelson (1799–1871) was a nephew and former secretary of Andrew Jackson, a graduate of West Point second in his class, and a Nashville lawyer. Donelson's AEU on the letter reads: "Rec[eive]d after my return from Mississippi[,] ans[were]d 4 [*sic*; 2] Oct."

From HOPKINS HOLSEY

Athens Ga., Sept. 16th 1844

D[ea]r Sir, In a public discussion held in the Town-Hall of this place, some time in July last, after a high eulogium upon Henry

Clay[']s political character by one of his friends, I felt bound to state the results of my personal observation in regard to his opinions on the *Constitutional power* of Congress to abolish slavery in the ["federal" *canceled*] district of Columbia, which were—that, previous to 1839, he had entertained the opinion that Congress did possess the power— ["and" *interlined*] that this continued to be his opinion down to his celebrated speech in 1839, in which he turned a political somerset upon this question utterly at variance with the *consistent*, dignified, and elevated character attributed to him. Gales and Seaton's Register of debates confirms my recollection of his course on the Constitutional question in 1836. Some of his leading friends here still deny the record upon the authority of a letter in possession of one of them from Mr. Clay himself. So far as I can learn its contents they rely chiefly upon a statement made by him of his course on the resolution introduced by you in 1837, for the purpose of shewing *that he then denied the Constitutional power.* This however if the record of 1836 be true, as it most certainly is, would in fact admit the ["alleged" *interlined*] change in his position, and would only make up an issue with me as to the *time* of his conversion. I have before ["me" *interlined*] the Register of Debates, the resolutions of '37, Mr. Clay[']s speech of 1839, and also a letter from him dated 2nd Inst. (still later than the one upon which his friends here rely) addressed to the Editor of the Lexington (Kentucky) Observer and Reporter. Now, my dear Sir, well remembering the deep interest you have ever taken in every thing which concerns the South, as also the conspicuous part you bore in relation to the subject of Abolition in all its phases, I have taken the liberty to appeal to you for your recollection of facts, ["and also your opinion," *interlined*] as to Mr. Clay[']s ["opinions" *canceled and* "position" *interlined*] on ["this subject" *canceled*] the *constitutional power* of Congress to abolish Slavery in the federal ten miles square, at the respective periods of '36—'37—'39—and *the present time.* As I have publicly demanded the publication of a letter which his friends are using to disprove my allegations, and as they may possibly defer their answer untill a period ["which" *canceled*] which might prevent a reply before our Congressional elections, on the first Monday in October next, I have thought it prudent to be prepared for the emergency by having your recollections and views of Mr. Clay[']s position in relation to the Subject before mentioned, ready to be used at a moment[']s warning, should it be your pleasure to give them, and to permit them to be published. I am, Sir, With very great Respect Your Ob[edien]t Serv[an]t, Hopkins Holsey.

ALS in ScCleA.

From THOMAS O. LARKIN

Consulate of the United States
Monterey California, Sept. 16, 1844
Sir, The undersigned has the honour to inform the Department that every thing in this consulate is quiet. There has been some preparation on the part of his Excellency the Gov[erno]r to put Monterey in a state of defence supposing his government would declare war against the U.S. in case Texas was annexed to the Union. We have heard the an[n]exation did not take place. All warlike preparations are therefore postponed.

The General in command of this department has about two hundred and fifty Mexican soldiers and perhaps one hundred Californian soldiers, the most of whom are in this town with two Colonels, four Lieut. Colonels and about twenty other commissioned officers. Last month private letters reached here from the city of Mexico, that this Commander was to be superceded, when some of the officers in command called out their troops who were with them and denounced the new Gen. binding themselves to serve Mexico under no other Commander but the present one Manuel Micheltorena. The people of this place ["where" *altered to* "were"] in much alarm, expecting a sack of the town to take place by the Soldiers. The affair is however hushed up.

The Government of California is in the hands of Gen. Micheltorena, whose resources are from the Custom House, most of which arising from the duties on some yearly Vessels from Boston being in all 80 to 90,000$ p[e]r year. Of late years many English[,] German & American goods are brought here from Mazatlan having there paid the duties, thereby causing less duties to be paid in California, leaving the Gen. much in want of funds. He has therefore nul[l]ified the Mexican Tariff publishing this year a law forbid[d]ing after six months any Foreign goods being introduced in California without payment of the duties, which is to be the same whether from a Mexican or Foreign port—however they may once have been rec[eive]d by a Mexican Collector of the Custom House.

Foreign goods of any kind are entered in the Custom House of Monterey by paying the duties put on and valued by this Collector. By the Mexican Tariff very many goods are prohibited, but all are entered here. With this the Department will receive the new law of the Gov. Gen. of California.

Last month for several days there were reports in and about Monterey that the the [*sic*] wreck of a Vessel had been seen by many people on various occasions. We were expecting at the time a Boston Vessel and supposed it was her, or a Whaler. In connexion with the Gov. Gen. Manuel Micheltorena the Undersigned sent out two Boats & twelve English and Americans with sufficient provissions for the occasion. They were gone 8 or 10 days bringing back proof that it was a Whaler off the coast many days fishing under short sail and topmast &c down.

The Undersigned cannot give too much praise to Gen. Micheltorena for his promptness and liberality in sending out this expedition, when he had not sufficient funds for his Troops the next pay day— Mexico having entirely failed in furnishing him in funds. He at all times shows a good disposition towards Foreigners in California.

The Undersigned takes this opportunity of inquiring if the expence incurred by him in the expedition above named, or if there should be a reason for another of the kind; will be defrayed by the Department. Such occasions however will be extremely rare on this coast. I am with much respect your most obedient, Thomas O. Larkin.

LS (No. 10) with En (in Spanish) and State Department translation in DNA, RG 59 (State Department), Consular Despatches, Monterey, California (M-138: 1), received 12/16; slightly variant FC in CU, Bancroft Library, Larkin Collection; PC with En in Hammond, ed., *Larkin Papers,* 2:228–230. NOTE: Larkin enclosed a printed copy of Micheltorena's decree of 7/30/1844 altering the customs regulations of the port of Monterey.

From Thomas McGuire, [U.S. Consul], Glasgow, 9/16. He complains of the great number of merchants in Scotland who ship goods to the U.S. without obtaining a Consular certificate to their invoice. This practice is so widespread that, although the amount of exports to the U.S. "has been double that of the corresponding period last year," "a great falling off has taken place in the number of my certificates to Invoices." ALS (No. 10) in DNA, RG 59 (State Department), Consular Despatches, Glasgow, vol. 3 (T-207:3), received 10/5.

From Foxhall A. Parker, "U.S. Frigate Brandywine, Boca Tigris," 9/16. Parker informs Calhoun of the death of Thomas W. Waldron, U.S. Consul at Hong Kong. The treaty recently negotiated by [Caleb Cushing] has been "confirmed and certified to by the Emperor." Since the treaty has been made public in China, Parker has furnished a copy of it to the U.S. Consul at Canton [Paul S. Forbes], "in order that they [American merchants] may govern themselves accordingly." LS with Ens in DNA, RG 59 (State Department), Diplomatic Despatches, China, vol. 2 (M-92:3), received 1/21/1845.

From L[ouis] W. Tinelli, [U.S. Consul], Oporto, 9/16. Tinelli has learned that the U.S. Consul at Antwerp has either resigned or been recalled. If this is true, he asks that he be considered as a replacement in that position. Tinelli's position at Oporto is not lucrative, and his growing family demands that some more dependable financial support be found. He hopes that his experience as Consul to Oporto will qualify him for the position that he solicits. ALS (No. 19) in DNA, RG 59 (State Department), Consular Despatches, Oporto, vol. 1 (T-342:1), received 10/22.

T. HARTLEY CRAWFORD to Maj. W[illia]m Armstrong, "Act[in]g Sup[crintenden]t [of] Ind[ia]n Affairs, Choctaw Agency West of Arkansas"

War Department
Office [of] Indian Affairs
September 17, 1844

Sir, Information has this day been communicated through the Secretary of State to the War Department, that ["there is reason to apprehend" *interlined*] the Mexican Government or some of its citizens, are inciting the Wild Indians on the borders of the United States & Texas to acts of hostilities against both.

This is a grave and serious matter to which your most vigilant attention is requested. Ascertain by diligent and cautious enquiry how the facts are, leaving no expedient unemployed which shall enable you to fathom the designs of Mexico or her Citizens, and to understand the true state of things in reference to the information we have received, and make report of all you learn immediately to this Office.

You are also specially directed to be wide awake on this subject, that you may detect any intention on the part of Mexico or her Citizens to engage the border Indians in future hostilities against the United States or Texas, or both, or any attempt at executing such an intention by stirring up these Savages to acts of plunder or blood ["or to any hostile movements or demonstrations on the part of the Indians themselves," *interlined*] against the Citizens of either or both, and to report from time to time and without delay to this Office.

I shall send a copy of this letter to each of the Agents and Sub Agents in the Western Territory, to save time, instead of requesting you to instruct them to an observance of its contents.

This is a delicate affair, which will require the exercise of prudence and discretion—and one of which it will be well to speak little. At the same time you are authorized to confer fully with the Military Commanders or Officers near you, who will probably be instructed on the subject from the proper Department of the Government. Very respectfully Your Ob[edien]t Serv[an]t, T. Hartley Crawford [Commissioner, Office of Indian Affairs].

CC in DNA, RG 59 (State Department), Miscellaneous Letters (M-179:105, frames 369–370). NOTE: A Clerk's EU indicates this document was received by the State Department from the War Department on 9/18.

To A[NDREW] J. DONELSON, [appointed Chargé d'Affaires to Texas]

Department of State
Washington, 17th September, 1844
Sir: Annexed hereto is a copy of a despatch [of 9/10] recently forwarded to the late Chargé d'Affaires of the United States to Texas [Tilghman A. Howard], which, should you accept the appointment conferred on you by the President [John Tyler], will be regarded as if directed to yourself. The package containing the original, and other papers, was delivered to Lieutenant George Stevens, who, as special messenger, was instructed to deliver it into the hands of the Chargé, General Howard. It is not improbable that, owing to the untimely death of General Howard, and the absence of any representative of the United States at the seat of the government of Texas, Lieutenant Stevens may return it to this Department. To obviate the inconvenience which might arise from such a state of things, I forward herewith a copy of the despatch and accompanying papers.

Since the date of the despatch to Mr. Howard, information has been received at this department, through Major [Pierce M.] Butler, Agent for the Cherokee Indians, that Mexican Commissioners or agents of the Mexican Government, are employed in instigating the

Indian Tribes on our south western frontier to acts of hostility against our citizens and those of Texas residing in their respective neighbourhoods. This, if true, is in direct violation of the Treaty of Amity between the two countries of the 5th of April, 1831, a printed copy of which I herewith forward to you, calling your attention, at the same time, to its 33d article.

There seems to be but little doubt as to the correctness of the information communicated by Major Butler, and the President instructs and authorizes you, in case the Government of Texas should apply to you to fulfil the Treaty obligations of the United States, to maintain peace and harmony among the several Indian nations who inhabit the lands adjacent to the lines and rivers which form the boundaries of the two countries, and to restrain, by force, all hostilities and incursions on the part of the Indian nations living within our boundaries, and if you should, upon examination, consider the grounds sufficient to warrant such application, to make requisition on either or all of the commandants of the forces at Forts Jesup, Towson and Washita, for such portions of their respective commands as may be deemed necessary for the purpose, to be marched and stationed at such points, as you may, on consultation with the Texan authorities, deem best adapted to secure the object, either within the limits of the United States, or, if requested by the government of Texas, within its limits, it being understood that the objects are limited to the fulfilment of our treaty stipulations.

I herewith enclose copies of the orders which have been issued by the proper Department to the several officers in command at the respective posts, to comply with your requisition. You will take care, in making the requisitions, to have a sufficient force at the respective stations to protect them and the public property against the dangers to which, in your judgement, they may be exposed. I am, Sir, with high respect, Your obedient servant, J.C. Calhoun.

[First Enclosure]

L[orenzo] Thomas to Brig. Gen. Z[achary] Taylor, Commanding 1st Dept., Fort Jesup, La.

Adjutant General's Office
Washington, September 17, 1844

Sir: The General-in-chief has received instructions, through the Department of State, from the Executive, to hold the troops now between the Red and Sabine rivers ready to march, in case of a requisition being made by the United States chargé d'affaires residing near the Government of Texas, to such point within our limits or those of Texas as the said chargé may designate, in order to restrain any hostile incursion on the part of the border Indians, as required by the provisions of existing treaties.

You will please to take such preliminary measures as may be deemed necessary to put the greater part of the forces under your command, designated above, in march for the above purpose at short notice.

Should the apprehended hostilities with the Indians alluded to break out, an officer of rank, probably yourself, will be sent to command the United States forces placed in the field, and who will receive hence further instructions for his government. I have the honor to be, sir, your obedient servant, L. Thomas, Assistant Adjutant General.

[Second Enclosure]

L[orenzo] Thomas to Brig. Gen. M[athew] Arbuckle, Commanding 2nd Dept., Fort Smith, Ark.

Adjutant General's Office
Washington, September 17, 1844

Sir: The General-in-chief [Winfield Scott] has received instructions, through the Department of State, from the Executive, to hold the troops within your department, at Forts Towson and Washita, ready to march, in case of a requisition being made by the United States chargé d'affaires residing near the Government of Texas, to such point within your limits or those of Texas as the chargé may designate, in order to restrain any hostile incursion on the part of the border Indians, as required by the provisions of existing treaties.

You will please take such preliminary measures as may be deemed necessary to put those troops in march for the above purpose at short notice.

It is understood that any requisition that may be made upon Forts Towson and Washita will leave at least one company at each of those posts, to guard the same.

Should the apprehended hostilities with the Indians alluded to break out, an officer of rank will be sent to command the United States forces placed in the field, and who will receive hence further instructions for his government. I have the honor to be, sir, your obedient servant, L. Thomas, Assistant Adjutant General.

FC (No. 1) in DNA, RG 59 (State Department), Diplomatic Instructions, Texas, 1:104–106 (M-77:161); PC in *Congressional Globe*, 28th Cong., 2nd Sess., Appendix, pp. 4–5; PC with Ens in Senate Document No. 1, 28th Cong., 2nd Sess., pp. 36–38; PC with Ens in House Document No. 2, 28th Cong., 2nd

Sess., pp. 36–38; PC with Ens in the Washington, D.C., *Globe*, December 6, 1844, p. 2; PC with Ens in the Washington, D.C., *Daily National Intelligencer*, December 7, 1844, p. 2; PC with Ens in the Washington, D.C., *Daily Madisonian*, December 9, 1844, p. 3, and December 11, 1844, p. 2; PC with Ens in *Niles' National Register*, vol. LXVII, no. 15 (December 14, 1844), p. 234; PC in Crallé, ed., *Works*, 5:376–377. NOTE: Texts of the two Ens are taken from the Senate Document cited.

From J[AMES] H. HAMMOND,
[Governor of S.C.]

Silver Bluff, 17th Sept. 1844

My Dear Sir, I do not know how far it may clash with any rules you have laid down for yourself or with any of the delicacies of your position, to interfere with the disposition of the petty offices which it is in the power of the President [John Tyler] to bestow. I write for the purpose of soliciting your interest in the disposal ["of" *interlined*] one in which I feel great interest myself, but if it will occasion any embarrassment to you to exercise your influence in the matter I know too much of such matters to urge it for a moment, or to feel in the least hurt if you decline to do it. My brother M[arcus] C.M. Hammond graduated at West Point in 1836 & remained in the Army until 1 Jan[uar]y 1843, serving in Florida several campaigns & at Fort Gibson. He married in 1842 a Miss Davi[e]s of Georgia (step-daughter of Wyatt Starke) & partly on that account & partly because of his health, very reluctantly & against my wishes resigned his Commission. He has regretted it I believe almost ever since & has been anxious to return to ["it" *canceled and* "the Army" *interlined*]. A vacancy has just occurred by the death of Maj. [Peter] Muhlenberg [Jr.] Paymaster & he has applied to fill it. Of his qualifications I need say nothing. As to his character in the Army, he can bear the strictest scrutiny. Gen. [Winfield] Scott is as well acquainted with him & his position as he probable [*sic*] was with any of his subordinates & may be appealed to. He is now planting in Burke Co[unty] Geo[rgia]. But his tastes & feelings have been formed at West Point & in the service. You may judge how he is likely to succeed at cotton.

As I never expect to ask or to hold a Federal appointment it is not in the power of the Government & those administering it to confer any favor on me so great as the appointment of my brother to this vacancy, & I am sure that it would please you to see me gratified by it.

I would give a great deal for a few hours conversation with you on political matters. I *must* speak you know in November [to the S.C. General Assembly]. I do not think I shall recommend any *specific action,* but I mean to state the facts of our present position in as plain & strong language as I can And notwithstanding all I see in the papers & hear from those who I *know* are not your *friends,* I am still confident that I shall say nothing but what you will approve.

I am almost beginning to think there is a chance for [James K.] Polk. Any body against [Henry] Clay should be the motto of the South. Yours sincerely, J.H. Hammond.

ALS in ScCleA.

From R[OBERT] M. T. HUNTER

[Lloyds, Va.?] Sept[embe]r 17th 1844
My dear Sir, I have not had time before to inform you of our proceedings in the Charlottesville [Democratic] convention. Of the general result the papers of course ["have" *interlined*] informed you. Your friends had a private meeting and appointed a committee to ascertain as soon after the election as possible Mr. [Thomas] Ritchie[']s probable course in relation to you. Should he not give satisfactory pledges they are to write us letters privately and we have promised to convene in Richmond to decide upon our course. We have also determined to establish a review (if possible) in Richmond—[Washington] Greenhow and [William M.] Overton to be the editors. The latter I do not know but he is said to be eminently qualified. The control of the review will of course be in the hands of our central committee—we will establish this if we can. I presume that we might fairly count upon some support from the other Southern States as it will be devoted to Southern interests. Your friends at that convention were numerous, talented and enthusiastic. Of Eastern Virginia we are safe but we have not as much strength in the West. We have some of our (Calhoun) speakers on a short trip over the mountain but they will not remain long enough to make as permanent an impression as we desire. Our friends in Richmond think that Ritchie is leaning towards us. Some attempts have been made to supplant the Enquirer which (as we believe) he has traced

to the [Thomas H.] Benton faction. Our friends opposed and put them down. As some proof of his leaning this way—He selected Millson of Norfolk (an old and devoted friend of yours) to write the address. He also selected me to write the tract on the Theory of our government which has appeared in the last no. of the Democratic Review. This shows a conviction that the battles of the South are to be fought upon our ground. Still we must not be deluded by mere appearances. We will know how the matter stands before we arrange definitively for the next campaign. I at least ought to be cautious for there is now pretty full evidence that I was *arranged out* of ["th" *canceled*] Congress. Still I am ready to forget and forgive all if they will only do even tardy justice to you.

I am now engaged in the canvass and will do all that my health permits until it is over. Your friends have manly fought the battle.

There was a pamphlet sent you by Gov[erno]r [Lewis] Cass on the subject of the right of search written by a member of the French chamber of deputies about two years ago. If you have it I should be very glad to get it. If not it was translated by [John L.] Martin for the Spectator when he edited it and perhaps [John] Heart could search it up. It would be very useful to us in the Texas question. Very sincerely your friend, R.M.T. Hunter.

P.S. Please do not mention any thing about the meeting of your friends. We bound ourselves to tell no one unless we would be personally responsible for him and if it were to get out without our being able to account for it it might beget suspicion.

ALS in ScCleA.

From R[occo] Martuscelli, [Consul General of the Two Sicilies], New York [City], 9/17. Martuscelli reminds Calhoun that he has not yet received an answer to his letter to Calhoun of 8/17. LS (in French) in DNA, RG 59 (State Department), Notes from Foreign Legations, Two Sicilies, vol. 1 (M-55:1).

From W[illia]m H. Richardson, Secretary of the Commonwealth [of Va.], Richmond, 9/17. "Your letter of the 17th July last was necessarily referred to the Superintendent of the Penitentiary, whose report [*not found*] has just been received and is herewith enclosed." FC in Vi, Executive Letterbook, 1839–1844, p. 394.

From Edm[un]d C. Watmough, Philadelphia, 9/17. "I saw at Mr. [George M.] Dallas' a Map of Texas which appears to be printed under the direction of the State Department. I should like very much to have one of those Maps, at the period it would be exceedingly useful. If I have made an unreasonable request I hope you will pardon me." ALS in ScCleA.

To FRANCIS WHARTON, [Philadelphia]

State Dept., 17th Sep[tembe]r 1844
My dear Sir, I have been prevented by my numerous and weighty engagements from acknowledging your note of the 21st Aug[us]t at an earlier period.

The excitement in a portion of [South] Carolina, to which you refer has gradually subsided, and will give no farther trouble. I had to act with great delicacy, but at the same time firmness in relation to it.

In reference to the subject touched on in yours of the 11th Inst. I have no doubt of the great necessity for such a Journal, as you suggest in Philadelphia, and I would rejoice to see you at the head of such an one; but I apprehend that there would be difficulty in obtaining the patronage from the South, which you intimate. It would be difficult to make those, who have the means, realize the necessity of establishing such a paper by funds to be drawn from other States, especially in a place so populous and wealthy as Philadelphia. Add to this the great pressure from exceedingly low prices of their agricultural products, under which our planters have been labouring for many years, and I should think the prospect hopeless.

Although I cannot hold out hope for support from the South, yet, I trust, there may be found sufficient local support of a sound character to sustain an able, honest and respectable paper in your city. Your present Journals are woefully deficient; quite below the standard of New York, Boston, Richmond and Charleston. The evil ought to be removed, and I am sure would be, if you were placed at the head of a paper, with a respectable list of subscribers. Can you not rally a sufficient number of the respectable portion of your citizens for the purpose, especially the younger part? I do not know a State or City, which requires to have its politicks elevated to a higher standard, than Pennsylvania and Philadelphia. In none is the contrast greater between the individual character of its people and that of its government.

I am of the impression, that the defeat of [Henry] Clay and the election of [James K.] Polk is almost certain. It will be a marked event in our political history. It will be the last of Clay; and when he disappears from the publick stage, the Whig party will disperse and new political combinations must follow. It will be a new departure, from which many are destined to date their fall or elevation. My own impression is, that it will prove auspicious to the cause of sound principles and correct policy. Mr. Clay has been a great disturbing power in the harmonious and regular movements of our Government, especially in the southern and western portion, where the influence of his personal character has been the most felt. He has done much to distract the South, and to keep the West out of its true position. These reflections, if correct, go to show the great importance of able and honest Journals to give the proper direction at such a juncture.

I write you freely and you must regard what I have written to be intended for yourself.

PC in Jameson, ed., *Correspondence*, pp. 615–617.

From Geo[rge] M. Bibb, Secretary of the Treasury, 9/18. In response to Richard Pakenham's request for reimbursement of certain duties charged on British goods imported into the U.S. under a provision of the tariff law of 1842, Bibb finds that no violation of the U.S.-British trade agreement of 7/3/1815 occurred because the goods in question were not "like" goods imported from south of Cape Horn or the Cape of Good Hope. Pakenham's request is therefore denied. ALS in DNA, RG 59 (State Department), Miscellaneous Letters (M-179:105, frames 317–332); FC in DNA, RG 56 (Secretary of the Treasury), Letters from Cabinet and Bureau Officers, Series B, 1842–1847, 4:452–460.

To Capt. David Conner, U.S.N., Philadelphia, 9/18. "I return to you the Journal of the Voyage of the Spanish Schooners Zetil and Mexicana, which you were so kind as to send me with your letter of the 15th [*sic*; 16th] inst., as I find upon enquiry that a copy of the work is in the Library of the Department." FC in DNA, RG 59 (State Department), Domestic Letters, 34:380 (M-40:32).

From THEO[DORE] S. FAY

Berlin, 18 Sept., 1844

Sir, I beg to address you as Chargé d'Affaires, *ad interim,* during the absence of Mr. [Henry] Wheaton in Paris.

[Heinrich Ulrich Wilhelm,] Baron Bülow has just informed me that the time for the ratification of the Convention, of the 25 March, with the Zollverein, will not be prolonged, all the replies of the States, yet received, tending the same way. As to the reported measures of retaliation, none are *yet,* upon the *tapis.* Against such measures, hereafter, he would not answer, but expressed the assurance that the Zollverein would be always ready to treat with the U. States in their mutual interests. It is plain that Baron Bülow himself, as well as the States of the Customs' Association, regards our refusal immediately to ratify the Convention, as a slight, & is unwilling to subject himself ["to" *interlined*] the possibility of another similar one.

I am authorized by Mr. Wheaton to acknowledge your Despatch, No. 58, of 8 July last, brought by Mr. [Theophilus] Fisk, with ratified Copies of the Conventions for the mutual abolition of the *droit d'aubaine,* &c between the U. States on the one part, & the Grand Duchy of Hesse & the Kingdom of Würtemberg, on the other parts, & enclosing special powers to Mr. Wheaton. Mr. Fisk reached Berlin the 4th inst. The Minister of the Grand Duchy of Hesse was absent, for probably about three weeks. I immediately informed him of Mr. Fisk's arrival.

The Minister of Würtemberg required ten or twenty days to have prepared his ratified Copy.

I hope Mr. Fisk may leave Berlin for Washington, between the 1st & 15th of October. I have the honor to be, with the highest consideration, Sir, Y[ou]r Ob[e]d[ien]t Serv[an]t, Theo. S. Fay.

ALS (No. 21) in DNA, RG 59 (State Department), Diplomatic Despatches, Germany, vol. 3 (M-44:4), received 10/22; FC in DNA, RG 84 (Foreign Posts), Germany, Despatches, 4:152–153. NOTE: Fay (1807–1898) was Secretary of the U.S. Legation in Berlin during 1837–1853. Previously he had been active in literary circles in New York City. His sentimental and melodramatic novel, *Norman Leslie* (1835), had been very popular and had drawn the devastating ridicule of Edgar Allan Poe. Fay was subsequently U.S. Minister to Switzerland and remained in Europe the rest of his life.

From Geo[rge] W[illia]m Gordon

Consulate of the United States
Rio de Janeiro, 18th Sept. 1844

Sir, I have the honor herewith to transmit a certified Copy of a deposition of two American Seamen, by names John Fairburn, and James Gilliespie, lately passengers in the American Brig "Monte Video" Capt. [J.L.] Pendleton from the coast of Africa to Victoria in Brazil.

The deposition states among other things that the said Brig "Monte Video," was fitted into a Slaver at Victoria, and furnished with water and provissions accordingly; whence she sailed on the 9th of August last, thus fitted and provissioned, under American colors, in charge of her American Master, (Pendleton) and crew, for Cabinda in Africa, having on board also as passengers, a Portuguese Master and crew—And that on her arrival at said Cabinda, she was to be delivered to other owners to whom she had been sold, and by them, as the deposers fully believe, to be used for the purposes of the Slave Trade.

Having advised with [Henry A. Wise] His Excellency the Minister of the United States at this Court, I have sent said Deposers to New York in the Barque "St. Joseph," Capt. Neill, to sail from this port tomorrow, and by the same conveyance have advised the United States Marshall of the District of New York thereof, and have requested him to hold them in custody until he receives your instructions in the premises.

The Brig "Monte Video" formerly belonged to New York, and was owned by Capt. Alex[ande]r Riddell of that City, and it is probable that Capt. Pendleton and the American portion of his crew, after ["the" *interlined*] Brig shall have been delivered upon the coast of Africa, will return to that port. Should their destination become known at this Consulate, information thereof will immediately be communicated to the Department of State.

Capt. Joshua M. Clapp, late of the Brig "Ganneclifft,["] referred to in the deposition, took passage at this port on the 10th August last in the Brig "Hershell," Adams [master], bound for Boston. The Italian boy's name is supposed to be Francis Oliver—he speaks English.

The accompanying Deposition also further states, that at Victoria there is an individual by name Souto, who claims to be & exercises the privileges and duties of American Consul, and that said Souto, is deeply interested in the Slave trade, and is the general Agent or Consignee of Slave Vessels visiting that port.

A copy of this Deposition has been placed in the hands of His Excellency Mr. Wise and being fully pursuaded that ["neither" *interlined*] said Souto, or any one else, is authorized by the President to act as Consul of the United States at that place, I have respectfully asked the particular attention of Mr. Wise to this portion of the deposition, and he has already expressed to me his intention of addressing this Government on the subject. And I would add that from all the information I can obtain, I am entirely pursuaded that no United States Consul is needed at the aforesaid port of Victoria for the furtherance of any honest purposes or lawful American trade. I have the honor to be, Sir, Most respectfully, Your Obedient Servant, Geo. Wm. Gordon, Consul, United States.

ALS (No. 8) with Ens in DNA, RG 59 (State Department), Consular Despatches, Rio de Janeiro, vol. 7 (T-172:8), received 11/11.

To C[HARLES] H. RAYMOND, [Texan Chargé d'Affaires ad interim to the U.S.]

Department of State
Washington, 18th September, 1844

Sir: The note addressed to this Department by the Honorable Mr. [Isaac] Van Zandt, late Chargé d'Affaires of the Republic of Texas, dated on the 9th inst., has been referred to the Honorable Secretary of War [William Wilkins] for his decision, and I have the honor to inform you that it is not considered within the competency of the Government without further legislation on the part of Congress, to carry out the arrangement proposed in reference to the arms taken from Captain [Jacob] Snively's command by the orders of Captain [Philip St. George] Cooke. The proceeds of the sales of the condemned arms have gone according to law with the general mass of receipts into the Treasury, and of course are not subject to be drawn out by warrant without an appropriation for that purpose. Under these circumstances, it is deemed advisable to await the meeting of Congress, when the subject will be brought specially to its consideration, and the necessary appropriation asked to complete the arrangement proposed. I have the honor to be, Sir, Your obedient servant, J.C. Calhoun.

FC in DNA, RG 59 (State Department), Notes to Foreign Legations, Texas, 6:77 (M-99:95); PC in Senate Document No. 1, 28th Cong., 2nd Sess., p. 112;

PC in House Document No. 2, 28th Cong., 2nd Sess., pp. 109–110; PC in Crallé, ed., *Works*, 5:413–414.

To Seth Sweetser, U.S. Consul, Guayaquil, [Ecuador], 9/18. Sweetser's drafts for $473.37 and $289.63 have been paid despite the imperfect statements and vouchers which he presented to the State Department. "The 5th Auditor [Stephen Pleasonton] reports that he has written to you upon the subject, and the object of this letter is to inform you, that unless satisfactory explanations, be made forthwith, suit will be instituted upon your Consular Bond for the amount paid beyond what is properly accounted for; and the further duty will devolve upon me of recommending to the President your removal from office." FC in DNA, RG 59 (State Department), Consular Instructions, 11:274–275.

From Charles P. Traub

Consulate of the United States of America, Matanzas
Matansas [Cuba], 18 Sept[em]b[e]r 1844
Sir, I have the honor to acknowledge receipt of the Departments letters [to Thomas M. Rodney] of 24th July and 1st Ult[i]mo, the latter accompanied by Extract of letter of Capt. W.H. Gardner of U.S. Brig Lawrence. In reply I beg to state that since the departure of the Lawrence our citizens have enjoyed the same liberty that the most favored english have, and that on the 10th inst[an]t Mr. Thom-[a]s Savage was acquitted & released and Sam[ue]l Moffart [*sic*] and W[illia]m Bisby were released under bail (given by Mr. T. Phinney). This security is given for their appearance if call[e]d for, and if they should not be forthcoming Mr. P. will be fined from 50 to 200$ for each one.

John Thompson is the only one now remaining in confinement, his trial not having yet come on, but I have been assured by the president of the military commission that it shall be hastened as much as possible.

Several of the english prisoners have come out on same conditions, the Brittish Consul going their security and paying all their costs & expenses while in confinement. The general treatment of the prisoners since their confinement in Matansas is good, and they only complain of the injustice in taking them up on such feeble testimony and their long confinement without trial—the english prisoners had the

freedom of the yard of the Jail some days before the americans otherwise there has been no difference in their treatment. I have the honor
to be with much respect Your ob[edien]t s[er]v[an]t, Charles P.
Traub.

ALS in DNA, RG 59 (State Department), Consular Despatches, Matanzas, vol.
4 (T-339:4), received 10/4.

From G[EORGE] F. USHER

Commercial Agency of the U. States
Cape Haytien, Sept. 19th, 1844
Sir, I have the honor to inform You of my arrival at this place, and
that I have resumed my official duties.

The Press forwarded to Boston has been received here.

As far as I can learn, the Political and military affairs of these
people have become quite tranquil. The President [Philippe] Guerrier is making the Cape his temporary residence; but left however,
a few days since to make a visit toward the Spanish part, to return
here again. I have the honor, Sir, to be, Most Respectfully, Your
Very Ob[edien]t S[er]v[an]t, G.F. Usher, U.S.Com[mercia]l Ag[en]t.

ALS (No. 18) in DNA, RG 59 (State Department), Consular Despatches, Cap
Haitien, vol. 7 (M-9:7, frame 138), received 10/6.

From E[ben] R. Dorr, U.S. Consul, Valparaiso, 9/20. He transmits a recent report by the Chilean Minister of Foreign Relations
"wherein the position taken by this government in relation to the
pending [U.S.] claim in the case of the Macedonian is distinctly set
forth." ALS (No. 25) with En in DNA, RG 59 (State Department),
Consular Despatches, Valparaiso, vol. 3 (M-146:3), received 1/25/-
1845; FC in DNA, RG 84 (Foreign Posts), Chile, Despatches, vol.
B-3-D1.

From A. FOLSOM

Boston, Sep[tembe]r 20/44
Sir, Agreeable to your suggestions I take this course to lay before the
executive my solicitations for the interference of the American Gov-

ernment in enforcing my claim on the Haytien Govt. for losses sustained and occasioned by the late revolutions of 1843 & 44.

As the American Govt. has no accredited agent in Hayti, and as the french Consul General residing there has kindly offered to take charge of my claim (with whom I will deposit my documents) and use his influence in collecting the same, provided he should be officially charged by the American Govt., I therefore beg you to forward me an *official* letter to him to that effect, or obtain one from the representative of the french government residing at Washington which may probably answer the same purpose.

As all moral influence would be lost on that government without a demonstration of physical force, I beg you to give instructions to the commander of a man of war to go there for that purpose and confer with the French Consul General as to the most effectual means of obtaining payment of my claims.

Owing to the troubled state of that country—the importance of the American trade—and the manifest intentions of the french government of obtaining a permanent footing there, I think it of the first importance that this Govt. should keep there in permanence a Man of War as well to protect our trade and citizens, as to prevent any arrangement unfavourable to our commerce, should negotiations be entered into, as probably must soon be the case, between the French & Haytien governments. I remain Dear Sir Yours Very Respectfully, A. Folsom.

P.S. As I expect to leave for Jeremie Hayti in about ten days, your *kind* and *early* attention to the letters to the French Consul will much oblige yours &c, A.F.

[P.P.S.] Please direct to the care of Messrs. B.C. Clark, Merchants[,] Boston.

ALS in DNA, RG 59 (State Department), Miscellaneous Letters (M-179:105, frames 388–390).

From B[enjamin] D. Heriot, Navy Agent's Office, Charleston, 9/20. "My Commission as Navy Agent on the Charleston Station, will expire on the 4th October, ensuing. I have held the appointment for eight years, and would respectfully solicit your kind offices, in procuring my reappointment. For the manner in which my duties have been performed, I would beg to refer to [Aaron O. Dayton] the Fourth Auditor." LS in DNA, RG 59 (State Department), Applications and Recommendations, 1837–1845, Heriot (M-687:15, frames 125–126).

PROTOCOL by R[ichard] Pakenham and J[ohn] C. Calhoun

[Washington, September 20, 1844]
At the fifth conference held at the Office of the Secretary of State on the 20th of September the American Plenipotentiary delivered to the British Plenipotentiary a statement [of 9/20] marked B in rejoinder to His counter statement [of 9/12] marked D. J.C. Calhoun, R. Pakenham.

DS in DNA, RG 59 (State Department), Notes from Foreign Legations, Great Britain, vol. 22 (M-50:22); PC in the Washington, D.C., *Daily National Intelligencer*, December 12, 1845, p. 1; PC in *Niles' National Register*, vol. LXIX, no. 17 (December 27, 1845), p. 261; PC in Senate Document No. 1, 29th Cong., 1st Sess., p. 145; PC in House Document No. 2, 29th Cong., 1st Sess., p. 145; PC in Crallé, ed., *Works*, 5:425.

TO RICHARD PAKENHAM

Department of State
Washington, Sept[embe]r 20, 1844
The Undersigned, American Plenipotentiary, has read with attention the counter-statement of the British Plenipotentiary; but without weakening his confidence in the validity of the title of the United States to the territory, as set forth in his statement, marked A. As therein set forth, it rests, in the first place, on priority of discovery, sustained by their own proper claims, and those derived from Spain through the treaty of Florida.

The Undersigned does not understand the counter-statement as denying that the Spanish navigators were the first to discover and explore the entire coasts of the Oregon territory; nor that [Bruno] Heceta was the first who discovered the mouth of Columbia river; nor that Captain [Robert] Gray was the first to pass its bar, enter its mouth, and sail up its stream; nor that these, if jointly held by the United States, would give them the priority of discovery which they claim. On the contrary, it would seem that the counter-statement, from the ground it takes, admits such would be the case, on that supposition; for it assumes that Spain, by the Nootka Sound Convention in 1790, divested herself of all claims to the territory, founded on the prior discovery and explorations of her navigators; and that she could consequently transfer none to the United States by the treaty of Florida. Having put aside the claims of Spain by this assumption, the counter-statement next attempts to oppose the claims of the United States by those founded on the voyages of Captains Cooke [*sic*; James Cook] and [John] Meares, and to supersede the discovery of Captain Gray, on the ground that [George] Vancouver sailed further up the Columbia river than he did; although he effected it by the aid of his discoveries and charts.

It will not be expected of the Undersigned that he should seriously undertake to repel what he is constrained to regard as a mere assumption, unsustained by any reason. It is sufficient, on his part, to say that, in his opinion, there is nothing in the Nootka Sound Convention, or in the transactions which led to it, or in the circumstances attending it, to warrant the assumption. The Convention relates wholly to other subjects; and contains not a word in reference to the claims of Spain. It is on this assumption that the counter-statement rests its objection to the well-founded American claims to priority of discovery. Without it there would not be a plausible objection left to them.

The two next claims on which the United States rest their title to the territory, as set forth in Statement A, are founded on their own proper right; and cannot possibly be affected by the assumed claims of Great Britain, derived from the Nootka Convention.

The first of these is priority of discovery and exploration of the head waters and upper portion of the Columbia river by [Meriwether] Lewis and [William] Clarke [*sic*]; by which that great stream was first brought to the knowledge of the world, with the exception of a small portion near the ocean, including its mouth. This the counter-statement admits; but attempts to set off against it the prior discovery of [Alexander] Mackenzie, of the head waters of Frazer's river—quite an inferior stream, which drains the northern portion of the territory. It is clear that, whatever right Great Britain may derive from his discovery, it can, in no degree, affect the right of the United States to the region drained by the Columbia; which may be emphatically called the river of the territory.

The next of these, founded on their own proper right, is priority of settlement. It is not denied by the counter-statement, that we formed the first settlements in the portion of the territory drained by the Columbia river; nor does it deny that Astoria, the most considerable of them, was restored under the third article of the Treaty of Ghent, by agents on the part of Great Britain, duly authorized to make the restoration, to an agent on the part of the United States, duly authorized to receive it. Nor does it deny that, in virtue thereof, they have the right to be reinstated and considered the party in possession, while treating of the title, as was admitted by Lord Castlereagh in the negotiation of 1818; nor that the convention of 1818, signed a few days after the restoration, and that of 1827, which is still in force, have preserved and perpetuated until now all the rights they possessed to the territory at the time, including that of being reinstated and considered the party in possession, while the question of title was depending, as is now the case. It is true, it attempts to weaken the effect of these implied admissions—in the first place, by designating positive treaty stipulations as *"an understanding between the two Governments"*: but a change of phraseology cannot possibly transform treaty obligations into a mere understanding. And in the next place, by stating that we have not, since the restoration of Astoria, actually occupied it; but that cannot possibly affect our right to be reinstated, and to be considered in possession, secured to us by the treaty of Ghent, implied in the act of restoration—and since, preserved by positive treaty stipulations. Nor can the remarks of the counter-statement in reference to Lord Castlereagh's admission weaken our right of possession, secured by the treaty and its formal and unconditional restoration by duly authorized agents. It is on these, and not on the denial of the authenticity of Lord Castlereagh's despatch, that the United States rest their right of possession, whatever verbal communication the British minister may have made at the time to our Secretary of State; and it is on these that they may safely rest it, setting aside altogether the admission of Lord Castlereagh.

The next claims in which our title to the territory rests, are those derived from France, by the treaty ceding Louisiana to the United States, including those she derived from Great Britain by the treaty of 1763. It established the Mississippi as "the irrevocable boundary" between the territories of France and Great Britain; and thereby the latter surrendered to France all her claims on this continent west of that river; including, of course, all within the chartered limits of her then colonies, which extended to the Pacific Ocean. On these, united with those of France, as the possessor of Louisiana, we rest our claim of continuity, as extending to that ocean, without an opposing claim, except that of Spain, which we have since acquired and, consequently, removed, by the treaty of Florida.

The existence of these claims the counter-statement denies, on the authority of Mr. [Thomas] Jefferson; but, as it appears to the Undersigned, without adequate reasons. He does not understand Mr. Jefferson as denying that the United States acquired any claim to the Oregon territory by the acquisition of Louisiana, either in his letter of 1803, referred to by the counter-statement, and from which it gives an extract, or in the document of 1807, to which it also refers. It is manifest, from the extract itself, that the object of Mr. Jefferson was, not to state the extent of the claims acquired with Louisiana, but simply to state how far its unquestioned boundaries extended; and these he limited westwardly by the Rocky Mountains. It is, in like manner, manifest from the document, as cited by the counter-statement, that his object was not to deny that our claims extended to the territory, but simply to express his opinion of the impolicy, in the then state of our relations with Spain, of bringing them forward. This, so far from denying that we had claims, admits them by the clearest implication. If, indeed, in either case, his opinion had been equivocally expressed, the prompt measures adopted by him to explore the territory after the treaty was negotiated, but before it was ratified, clearly show that it was his opinion, not only that we had acquired claims to it, but highly important claims which deserved prompt attention.

In addition to this denial of our claims to the territory on the authority of Mr. Jefferson, which the evidence relied on does not seem to sustain, the counter-statement intimates an objection to continuity as the foundation of a right, on the ground that it may more properly be considered, (to use its own words,) as demonstrating the greater degree of the interest which the United States possessed by reason of contiguity in acquiring territory in a westward direction. Contiguity may, indeed, be regarded as one of the elements constituting the right of continuity, which is more comprehensive, and is necessarily associated with the right of occupancy, as has been shown in statement A. It also shows that the laws which usage has established in the application of the right to this continuity, give to the European settlements on its eastern coasts, an indefinite extension westward. It is now too late for Great Britain to deny a right on which she has acted so long; and by which she has profited so much; or to regard it as a mere facility, not affecting, in any way, the question of right. On what other right has she extended her claims westwardly to the Pacific Ocean, from her settlements around Hudson's Bay? or expelled France from the east side of the Mississippi, in the war which terminated in 1763?

As to the assumption of the counter-statement, that Louisiana, while in the possession of Spain, became subject to the Nootka Sound Convention, which, it is alleged, abrogated all the claims of Spain to the territory, including those acquired with Louisiana, it will be time enough to consider it, after it shall be attempted to be shown, that such, in reality, was the effect. In the mean time, the United States must continue to believe, that they acquired from France, by the treaty of Louisiana, important and substantial claims to the territory.

The Undersigned cannot assent to the conclusion to which, on a review of the whole ground, the counter-statement arrives; that the present state of the question is, that Great Britain possesses and exercises, in common with the United States, a right of joint occupancy in the Oregon territory, of which she can be divested only by an equitable partition of the whole between the two Powers. He claims, and he thinks he has shown, a clear title on the part of the United States to the whole region drained by the Columbia; with the right of being reinstated and considered the party in possession, while treating of the title, in which character he must insist on their being considered, in conformity with positive treaty stipulations. He cannot, therefore, consent that they shall be regarded, during the negotiation, merely as occupants in common with Great Britain. Nor can he, while thus regarding their rights, present a counter-proposal, based on the supposition of a joint occupancy merely, until the question of title to the territory is fully discussed. It is, in his opinion, only after a discussion which shall fully present the titles of the parties respectively to the territory, that their claims to it can be fairly and satisfactorily adjusted. The United States desire only what they may deem themselves justly entitled to; and are unwilling to take less. With their present opinion of their title the British Plenipotentiary must see, that the proposal which he made at the second conference, and which he more fully sets forth in his counter-statement, falls far short of what they believe themselves justly entitled to.

In reply to the request of the British Plenipotentiary, that the Undersigned should define the nature and extent of the claims which the United States have to the other portions of the territory, and to which allusion is made in the concluding part of statement A, he has the honor to inform him, in general terms, that they are derived from Spain by the Florida treaty, and are founded on the discoveries and exploration of her navigators; and which they must regard as giving them a right to the extent to which they can be established, unless a better can be opposed. J.C. Calhoun.

FC in DNA, RG 59 (State Department), Notes to Foreign Legations, Great Britain, 7:49–56 (M-99:36); FC in DNA, RG 84 (Foreign Posts), Great Britain, Instructions, 9:135–[146]; PC in the Washington, D.C., *Daily National Intelli-*

gencer, December 13, 1845, p. 2; PC in *Niles' National Register,* vol. LXIX, no. 17 (December 27, 1845), pp. 264–265; PC in the London, England, *Times,* December 29, 1845, pp. 5–6; PC in Senate Document No. 1, 29th Cong., 1st Sess., pp. 158–161; PC in House Document No. 2, 29th Cong., 1st Sess., pp. 158–161; PC in *Oregon: The Claim of the United States to Oregon, as Stated in the Letters of the Hon. John C. Calhoun and the Hon. J. Buchanan . . . to the Right Hon. R. Pakenham* (London: Wiley and Putnam, 1846), pp. 14–19; PC (dated 9/29) in Crallé, ed., *Works,* 5:450–456.

MORGAN L. SMITH to John Tyler, President

New York [City,] Sept. 20th 1844

On the application of friends from N. York I had the honour to be appointed Consul for the port of Velasco Texas in March 1843. As this port has little or no com[m]erce the non perform[a]nce of the duties of that office has subjected no one to inconvenience. Under these circumstances together with the fact that it has no emoluments but on the contrary is attended with considerable expense will I trust be a satisfactory apology for not hitherto entering upon its duties.

If Texas should be invaded by the Mexicans the duties of consul at that place might be important for the protection of American property. Under these circumstances I would respectfully request your Excellency to permit me to enter upon the duties of that office on my arrival in that country *next month.* An intimation through the State department or any other medium addressed to me at Velasco Texas will receive prompt attention. I have the honour to be your Excellency[']s ob[edien]t Serv[an]t, Morgan L. Smith.

ALS in DNA, RG 59 (State Department), Consular Despatches, Texas, vol. 1 (T-153:1).

To "The President" [JOHN TYLER]

State Dept., 20th Sep[tembe]r 1844

Dear Sir, I enclose various applications to you to be appointed Consul at Liverpool. Most of the applicants are known to you and nothing need be said on my part in reference to their application.

The application of Mr. [Eustis] Prescott may, however, be considered an exception. I do not know whether you are acquainted with him or not. I have known him for many years. He is a gentleman of great worth and I do not doubt, if he should be elected [*sic*], will [fill] the office well.

To the list of the applicants I must add that of Mr. [Francis] Markoe [Jr.] of this office. You know him well. He long filled the Consular Bureau in this Department in a highly satisfactory manner and I doubt not would discharge the duties of the Consulate at Liverpool with great credit to himself & the country, should he be selected. I need scarcely add that his appointment would be very acceptable to me not only on his own individually [*sic*] merit, but because of his near connection to my lamented friend Mr. [Virgil] Maxcy. With great respect yours truly, J.C. Calhoun.

ALS in ScU-SC, John C. Calhoun Papers.

From James M. Broom, Philadelphia, 9/21. He asks that Calhoun provide him an introduction to the U.S. Consul at Glasgow so that he can obtain information about a private matter. "I am too much shocked in my feelings, even at this late day, to realize the death of our mutual friend [Virgil] Maxcy, to whom I owe the pleasure of a personal acquaintance with you." ALS in DNA, RG 59 (State Department), Miscellaneous Letters (M-179:105, frames 395–396).

From J[ames] Hamilton, [Jr.]

Oswichee Bend [Ala.,] Sept. 21st 1844

My Dear Sir, Perceiving by the papers that you were last week to leave Washington for Pendleton, I write to say to you, that after learning the intelligence of Gen[era]l [Tilghman A.] Howard[']s death (the late Chargé to Texas) I wrote you directed to Washington, that if you concurred with me in opinion (and I would only accept it from so believing), I would consent to take the appointment as his successor & go with all convenient dispatch to Texas to form a new Treaty or obtain such a declaratory Cartel from the people of that Country in Convention or in their Congress as might induce Congress ["at their next Session" *interlined*] by act to admit Texas into the Union more especially as at that time the Presidential Question will be taken out of the shambles.

I write this Letter under the possible contingency of your not having received my Letter directed to Washington.

Be so kind as to direct to me at Savannah for which I shall leave in a [*partial word canceled and* "week" *interlined*]. I remain My Dear Sir With esteem faithfully & respect[full]y Yours, J. Hamilton.

ALS in ScCleA. NOTE: AEU's by Hamilton on the cover sheet of this letter, which was addressed to Calhoun in Pendleton, read: *"via Augusta"* and "Should Mr. C[alhoun] not have reached Pendleton the P[ost] M[aster] is requested to retain this Letter until he arrives."

To Governor [JAMES H.] HAMMOND, [Barnwell District, S.C.]

State Dept., 21st Sep[tembe]r 1844
My dear Sir, The vacancy to which you refer [in your letter of 9/17] was filled some time since. Had it remained opened [*sic*] I would have laid your brother's [Marcus C.M. Hammond's] name before the President [John Tyler] with pleasure.

I would be glad to see and converse with you on many subjects, general & particular, and hope I may be able to meet you, while on my visit to the State. I hope to be able to leave next week for my residence in Pend[l]eton, and to spend the whole of the month of October there. I cannot now fix the day, or I would make an appointment for you to meet me at Aiken; but that may be done on my return, unless you should be able to make it convenient to make me a visit at Fort Hill, where I would be very glad to see you.

I think the defeat of [Henry] Clay & the election of [James K.] Polk pretty certain. Yours truly, J.C. Calhoun.

ALS in DLC, James Henry Hammond Papers.

From TH[OMAS] S. HINDE

Mount Carmel, Wabash County
Illinois, Sept. 21st 1844
Dear Sir, To this *point*, it is probable you may recollect some twenty years ago, I called your attention as a suitable place for fixing the Western National Armory. Having a water power yet un[i]mproved calculated to drive 300 pair of five feet burrs [millstones]—in the Center of the Ohio & Mississippi Valley. The Northern Capitalists, have seized on all the important points on the lake tributaries, & have

been endeavoring to divert all the Southern trade *north.* The recent floods have tried the western streams & left the Great Wabash to realize my anticipations; having ascertained that its highest rise has never exceeded 24, while the Ohio has exceeded 60 feet—& other streams more. To the Southern Cities (as at all Seasons of the year the trade can go *South,* when obstructed by lakes and canals by ice) the flour market is all important, and as I hold the *Key* or connecting point (as the principal proprietor) of the northern and Southern trade of the richest and most productive valley of the Great West, I wish to dispose of it to Capitalists who will improve the Sites & take off the productions of the country—and as this ["country" *interlined;* is] now situated, I cannot effect the object as we have no Capitalists in this region, & wishing to dispose of my interests & lands[,] farms &c already prepared for a Company, I wish in the decline of life to employ myself in publishing a vast deal of Western manuscript which I have had accumulating on my hands for the last 30 or 40 years or more, I should be glad to meet with Capitalists who may feel it their interest, to take a part or the whole of it off my hands.

My attention was a few days ago, called to this Subject and concern, by the arrival of an agent from Richmond Va., who was looking out for a flouring Establishment as suggested where the *Wheat* might be had from about the same latitude, as the Richmond *brand* meets with no competition in foreign or *home* markets.

As the Richmond *Capitalists* are looking out for such Establishments, it occurred to my mind that those of Charleston might find it equally advantageous to obtain sites for such Establishments, & might add for Cotton and Woolen Establishments & indeed *Iron* as it is an abundant coal region, and as to timber unequalled on the White rivers by any part of Creation.

I have therefore taken the liberty Sir of addressing you this note on the Subject, which if deemed of sufficient importance to attract the attention of any of your friends in the South, that you will please to transmit it to any one you may think propper. I had intended visiting Charleston this winter, hoping that a Southern tour might recruit my health—And should a correspondence be opened from that region may (if I can) visit that region. I have furnished a sketch of the *causes* & *effects* of the Great *Western floods* to the Editors of a paper at Washington, but doubtful (from the state of things) of them being published. *This point* is a *"pioneer[']s choice"* in anticipation of such events—& those anticipations have been realized. I think from the very nature of things, that the Southern cities ought to be seeing some of the places, calculated for flouring establishments before they are wholly engrossed by Northern Capitalists. An early attention therefore to this matter may be necessary as I wish to arrange matters, for a quite different sphere of action—my time and my pen may be employed suitably to the decline of life and an enfeebled constitution. I am Sir with Great respect your fellow Citizen & ob[edien]t Serv[an]t, Th. S. Hinde.

ALS in ScCleA. Note: An AEU by Calhoun reads "Mr. Hinde, possesses extensive water power on the Wabash which he wishes to sell."

To Ogden Hoffman, [New York City]

Department of State
Washington, Sept. 21st 1844

Sir: A communication was addressed to you by this Department Sometime since [on 9/10], calling your attention to the conduct of the Mexican Government, in fitting out, as has been represented to this Department, two Steam Vessels of war in the Port of New York, against the provisions of the Acts of Congress of the 20th of April 1818, and the 10th of March 1838—and requesting your prompt attention to the Subject. It is a Source of equal surprise and regret, that no notice of this communication has been received at this Department. The subject is one of high importance, involving at once the power of the Country & the Supremacy of its laws; and in the discharge of my duties I cannot too earnestly urge it on your consideration. One of these Vessels, I am to day informed, has already sailed from the port, destined, as there is strong ground to believe, against the Territory, and citizens of a country, [Texas,] with which the United States are at peace. You will pardon me, therefore, in again Calling your attention to the Subject, with a view to such information, as may enable the Executive to decide what course it ought to pursue, in maintaining the Laws of the Country & the honor of the Republic. The case is deemed of so much importance, that the Department has thought itself authorized to employ the professional Services of the Hon. John McKeon [former Representative from N.Y.] to aid you in the investigation; and a communication has this day been addressed to him to that effect, & he is desired to See and Cooperate with you. I am &c, J.C. Calhoun.

FC in DNA, RG 59 (State Department), Domestic Letters, 34:401–402 (M-40:32); PC in Jameson, ed., *Correspondence*, pp. 617–618.

To JOHN MCKEON, New York [City]

Department of State
Washington, Sept. 21st 1844

Sir: Information has been received at this Department from various quarters, which leaves little doubt that the Mexican Government is now engaged in fitting out two Steam Vessels of war in the Port of New York, against the provisions of the Acts of Congress of the 20th April 1818 and the 10th March 1838. This Department is informed that the commanders of these Vessels, have given orders for large Supplies of Shot, Shells &c, and are enlarging the number and calibre of the guns on board, enlisting Seamen and purchasing munitions of war generally, to be used it is apprehended against the citizens and Territory of the Republic of Texas, with whom the United States are at peace.

Under these circumstances the Department considers itself called upon, to institute an enquiry into the facts of the case; and relying on your zeal, patriotism, energy and intelligence, I have to request that you see and consult with the United States District Attorney [Ogden Hoffman], if he should be in the City, and cooperating with him[,] you will immediately take such steps as may Seem expedient, in order to ascertain the facts and report them to this Department. If the District Attorney Should be absent, you will yourself promptly adopt such measures as may appear to you necessary and proper to Secure the desired information. Our laws of neutrality Should be strictly observed by, and enforced against all nations as involving the public peace and National honor.

I have to day learned that one of these vessels has been permitted to leave the port without question or Scrutiny, and that the other is on the eve of Sailing. You will therefore perceive the necessity of immediate action, in order that the Executive may be enabled to adopt Such measures, as the circumstances of the Case may warrant, and the laws demand. I am &c, J.C. Calhoun.

FC in DNA, RG 59 (State Department), Domestic Letters, 34:402–404 (M-40:32); PC in Jameson, ed., *Correspondence*, pp. 618–619.

From A[lbert] Schumacher, Baltimore, 9/21. Schumacher transmits "a Commission from the Senate of the free and hanseatic City of Hamburg appointing me their Consul General" for the U.S. He requests that the commission be presented to the President and returned with an exequatur. ALS in DNA, RG 59 (State Department), Notes from Foreign Consuls, vol. 2 (M-664:2, frame 399).

From WILSON SHANNON

Legation of the U.S. of A.

Mexico [City,] Sept. 21st 1844

Sir, I had the honor to inform you, by my note of the 28th ult[im]o, of my arrival in this city, and the disagre[e]able occurrence that I encountered on the road.

A short time before my arrival, Mr. [José M. de] Bocanegra had retired from the State Department, and Don Manuel C. Rejon had been appointed in his place. The retirement of Mr. Bocanegra is said to have been voluntary.

On the 27th ult[im]o I addressed a note to the Secretary of Foreign Relations, informing him of my arrival in this city, and desiring to be informed of the time and place, at which I could be permitted to present my letters of credence to the President of the Republic [Santa Anna]. I was advised in due time that I would be received by the President at his palace at Tacubaya, on the first instant. I accordingly attended, in company with Mr. [Ben E.] Green [Secretary of the U.S. Legation], at the time and place designated, & was received by the President with all the courtesy and respect that I could have desired. (See nos. 1, 2 & 3, accompanying this despatch.)

On my way to this city the stage remained one night at the castle of Perote, which afforded me an opportunity to visit the Texan prisoners confined at that place. I called on the Governor of the castle, & although it was after night and the prisoners were locked up in their rooms, he very kindly permitted me to visit them. They were confined in six rooms, and some of them were in a wretched condition, being almost naked. They manifested a strong desire to be liberated, and solicited my interference in their behalf. I assured them that whatever I could do in their behalf without compromitting my Govt. should be done with great pleasure. Shortly after my arrival here I drew up a letter addressed to the President asking, as a personal favour the liberation of all the Texan prisoners, and appealing to his liberality and generosity in their behalf. Immediately after having been presented to the President, I embraced the occasion to hand him this letter, with the request that he would give it an early and favourable consideration. In a few days I received a reply couched in friendly terms, but indefinite & ambiguous in relation to the discharge of the Texan prisoners. I addressed the President a second communication, asking a private interview; to which he replied that he would be pleased to see me on the 12th instant at 12 o'clock. Mr. Green and myself attended at the hour appointed, were well received and had a private interview with the President, which resulted in his agreeing to release all the Texan prisoners on the 16th Instant; that being the day of Mexican independence. Orders to that effect were immediately issued, and on the day named the Texan prisoners were all liberated. There were one hundred & four confined in the castle of Perote, ten in Vera Cruz, three in Mexico, one in Puebla and two in Matamoros, making in all one hundred and twenty, who had formerly been citizens of the U.S., and who have friends & relations in that country.

As the friends and relations of those unfortunate men, in the U. States, will no doubt be highly gratified to hear of their liberation, I send you a list of their names (marked no. 4) for publication.

Gen[era]l Santa Anna desired me to say to the President [John Tyler] that he wished to cultivate the most amicable relations with the U. States, that the interest of Mexico and that country was the same, and that he hoped his liberation of the Texan prisoners would be received by the President and people of the U. States as an evidence of his liberality and friendly disposition (nos. 5 & 6 relate to the release of the Texan Prisoners).

The instalments, which fell due on the 30th of April and 30th of July last, under the Convention of the 30th January 1843, were paid to the agent of the Govt., appointed to receive and transmit the same, on the 27th ult[im]o—(see no. 7)—I am inclined to believe that this Government will hereafter be more prompt in meeting its engagements under the above named treaty than it has heretofore been, and if it should turn out otherwise, it will be owing to a real inability to raise the means. I am advised that it was with the utmost difficulty that this Govt. was able to raise the money to pay the two last instalments. The truth is there is no money in the Treasury, and the large military establishment, kept up by the Govt., and which must be paid, absorbs the revenues as fast as they come in. But as Santa Anna is desirous to avoid a rupture at this time with the U.S., I am inclined to think that every exertion will be made on the part of this Government to meet the future instalments as they become due.

I have been unable to find a copy of the Convention of the 30th Jan. 1843 on the files of this legation. It is important that I should have one. I have therefore to ask you to transmit me a copy by the first opportunity.

On the 7th instant I requested the appointment of Plenipotentiaries on the part of this Govt., to treat in relation to the two amendments proposed by the Senate of the U. States to the Convention of the 20th Nov[embe]r 1843; and have received assurances that it would be done in a short time. In relation to this business I can only say that I have strong hopes that it will be satisfactorily arranged in time for the early action of Congress at the next session. (See nos. 8 & 9.)

No. 10, accompanying this despatch relates to the estate of Patrick McCarthy, who recently died at Tampico; to which I have, as yet, received no reply.

Nos. 11, 12, 13, 14, 15 & 16 relate to the claim of a Mr. Bensley [manager of the North American Circus Company] for the return of [Thomas A. Farrington] his apprentice boy taken and detained by the Governor of San Luis Potosi, without any color of right, and without any circumstances to mitigate the outrage.

I have thought it prudent to delay bringing to the consideration of this Government the other matters, with which I have been charged, until the final action of the President in relation to the Texan prisoners. I shall lose no further time in the disposal of all the business, with which I have been entrusted. I find Mr. Green a young man of fine talents and acquirements, and his services invaluable.

The President has at his disposal at this time a large military force and is daily increasing it. The avowed object of this force is the reconquest of Texas. It is however publicly said in this city, and by many well informed men believed, that the President does not intend to send his forces into Texas; but that his object is different, and personal in its character. It is well known that he has difficulties with the Congress, and it is believed that he w[oul]d be glad to get rid of that body. He left this city on the evening of the 12th instant for Mango de Clava, his private residence, and in the mean time [Valentín] Canalizo, his devoted friend, has been appointed to act as President. If any demonstrations are made towards putting down the Congress, they may be expected in the absence of Santa Anna, and consequently near at hand.

While President Santa Anna is amusing the public mind with the idea of the reconquest of Texas, it is not probable that any proposition will be made, or would be entertained by this Government, which looks towards the relinquishment on the part of Mexico of her pretended claim to that territory. The time must soon arrive however, when the war against Texas must be recommenced and prosecuted, or openly and publicly abandoned.

I send you herewith an extract from the Diario del Gobierno [official newspaper] of the 14th inst.; being a circular, in relation to passports, issued by this Govt., as *addenda* to the passport regulations issued on the 22d of July last, a copy of which was forwarded at the time to the Department by Mr. Green. Believing that many of the provisions of this circular are in violation of the Treaty existing between the U. States and Mexico, and oppressive and injurious to our citizens, I feel myself called upon to enter my protest, in the name of the Govt. of the U.S., against the same.

By the accompanying report of the Minister of Hacienda, you will see that the Executive has proposed to the Congress to close, against foreign vessels, all the Ports of Mexico, except Vera Cruz, Tampico, Campeche and Acapulco. It is generally thought however that the measure will not be carried in the Congress. I have the honor to be Very Respectfully Your ob[edien]t Serv[an]t, Wilson Shannon.

LS (No. 2) with Ens in DNA, RG 59 (State Department), Diplomatic Despatches, Mexico, vol. 12 (M-97:13), received 11/4; FC in DNA, RG 84 (Foreign Posts), Mexico, Despatches (C8.9); PC in Senate Document No. 81, 28th Cong., 2nd Sess., pp. 17–20; PC in House Document No. 144, 28th Cong., 2nd Sess., pp. 18–20; PEx in Senate Document No. 85, 29th Cong., 1st Sess., p. 17.

From WILSON SHANNON, *"Private"*

Legation of U.S. of A.
Mexico [City], Sept. 21, 1844
D[ea]r Sir, I do not know that the public interest will require the appointment of a bearer of dispatches to this legation during this fall or coming winter but if such should be the case I would recommend Dr. Jno. Dunham of St. Clairsville Ohio as a suitable person to be appointed. I do not know that Dr. Dunham desires the appointment but if he should he will signify to you his willingness to accept. He is the Editor of the St. Clairsville Gazett[e] and has always been your warm and devoted friend, and is a gentleman of high standing and moral worth. His appointment I know would be highly gratifying to your friends in eastern Ohio. Yours with great respect and esteem, Wilson Shannon.

ALS in ScCleA. NOTE: An AEU by Calhoun reads "Gov[erno]r Shannon."

To A. P. DUVALL and Others

Washington, 22d Sept. 1844
Gentlemen: It will not be in my power to attend the mass meeting to be held in the vicinity of Georgetown [Ky.], on the 5th Oct. by the

Democratic party. My public engagements will not permit it.

Although I cannot be present, you have my best wishes for the success of the great cause, which it is intended to advance. Much depends on the result of the elections now pending. The questions at issue are great and numerous; and on their decision the future policy and destiny of the country will in no small degree turn. With great respect, I am &c., J.C. Calhoun.

PC in the Washington, D.C., *Constitution*, November 8, 1844, p. 2. NOTE: Other members of the committee addressed included G.W. Johnson, R.M. Johnson, J. Pratt, J.A. McHithern, and W. Johnson.

To D[AVID] HUBBARD, [Lawrence County, Ala.]

Washington, 22d Sep[tembe]r 1844

My dear Sir, I am much obliged to you for the information, which you gave me of the occurrences at the Mass meeting at Nashville. It is the fullest and most satisfactory I have received. Much of it is very signi[fi]cant, and all confirmatory of what I have heard from other sources.

I regard the election of [James K.] Polk, as being now in a great measure certain. The cause of Texas and free trade is now gain[in]g daily, and, with it, the strength of Polk. The Whigs are clearly much alarmed; and will have cause to be still more so, as the election approaches.

I cannot but think, that the prospect is now fairer to return to the good old Republican doctrines of '98; to reform the Government; restore the Constitution, and throw off the burthen, which has been weighing down the South; exhausting her means & debasing her sperit, than it has been since 1828. That hope & that alone keeps things quiet at present. The Tariff of 1842, and the treachery of the [Thomas H.] Benton, [Martin] V[an] Buren ["&" *canceled*; "Wright's" *altered to* "Wing"] of the party have excited deep indignation in the South; and a too general distrust of the Northern portion of the party, who would all along ["have" *interlined*] been true, had it not been for the portion to which I refer. They now look forward to Mr. Polk's administration, should he succeed, to apply a remedy. If he should realize their expectation, of which I have much confidence, his administration will mark a great & salutary era in our political history; but, if not, there is great reason to fear, that distrust will become widely spread and that a large portion of the people will cease to look to the General Government for relief. Thus thinking, I cannot, but look to his success and the course of his administration with great interest, ["with" *canceled and* "and" *interlined*] a strong hope & desire, that it may realize the ["hope" *canceled*] expectation of the patriotick, and give renewed vigour to the Constitution & the Union.

I was not aware, that our correspondence had been suspended, leaving me in your debt; but, if ["it" *interlined*] be the case, I am still more indebted to you for your letter, as its renewal. I am always happy to hear from you and place much reliance on your judgment & friendship. With great respect yours truly, J.C. Calhoun.

ALS in ScU-SC, John C. Calhoun Papers; photostat of ALS in DLC, George Washington Campbell Papers; photostat of ALS in T, David Hubbard Papers.

From Edm[und] F. Brown, "Agency, Notarial, and Conveyancing Office," Washington, 9/23. A Kentuckian has informed Brown that some of the public advertisements have been ordered to be published in the Maysville, Ky., *Advocate* and in the Louisville, Ky., *City Gazette*, "both of which papers have been *dead* a considerable time." The Frankfort, Ky., *Yeoman* is a good, liberal, widely circulated Democratic newspaper that has "uniformly given Mr. [John] Tyler's Administration a 'fair hearing.'" Brown asks Calhoun to consider its claims "to such patronage as you may have to bestow." ALS in DNA, RG 59 (State Department), Miscellaneous Letters Received Regarding Publishers of the Laws.

From O[GDEN] HOFFMAN

U.S. Attorney's Office
New York [City], Sept. 23d 1844

Sir, I have the honor to acknowledge the receipt of your letter of the 21st inst., calling my attention to your letter of the 10th inst., which directed my notice to the conduct of the Mexican Government, in fitting out, as reported to the Department of State, two steam vessels of war in this Port.

I sincerely regret, that through some inadvertence your letter of the 10th instant was not formally acknowledged, although I gave instructions to have it acknowledged, shortly after its receipt, but the pressure of other official duty, prevented my personal attention to the subject. The wishes of the Department, however, as expressed in that letter, received my prompt attention. Immediately on the receipt of your communication of the 10th inst., I had an interview with Mr. A[lanson] Nash, a lawyer of this city, who, as I understood, had, from some private retainer, watched the movements of the Mexican officers, and who proposed to obtain and furnish me with some definite information, upon which I might institute immediate legal proceedings. I have been, since that time, in daily communication with Mr. Nash, and he has daily promised to procure a person or persons, who would make an affidavit, shewing that American citizens had enlisted as seamen on board the two Mexican vessels now in this Port, in violation of the second section of the Act of 20th April 1818, but no such affidavit has yet been obtained, nor have I been able to procure any person to make such affidavit. I have every reason to believe that Mr. Nash is most anxious to furnish me with the necessary proof. I also secured the services of other persons to aid me, in watching the movements of these vessels, and in fact, I have adopted every means, within my power, to ascertain whether the existing laws have been violated and if I can obtain the slightest legal evidence of such violation, I have been and am most anxious to maintain the laws of the country and the honor of the republic.

I also felt myself justified in employing one of our most active Deputy Marshals to assist me in carrying out the wishes of the Department, and I am informed by him that he was yesterday (Sunday) watching both vessels, and that they are both in our waters, but apparently in a condition to sail.

I will still continue the strictest scrutiny in regard to the proceedings of the vessels, and the moment I obtain any reliable information, I will adopt immediate proceedings. My efforts, thus far, have been to procure some evidence whereby proceedings could be instituted under the act of the 20th April 1818, but your letter of the 21st inst. having called ["my" *interlined*] attention to the Act of 10 March 1838, and to the supposed violations of the provisions of that act by the two Mexican vessels, a different po[licy?] from that which I proposed to follow, has been pointed out. The provisions of the Act of 1838 are very broad, and refer to "*any vessels*, prepared for any military expedition or enterprise, against any foreign prince or State &c with whom the United States are at peace." But these general and broad terms appear to be qualified by the reference in this Act to the provisions of the 6[th section] of the Act of 20 April 1818.

The 6th section thus referred to provides for the punishment of any person who "shall, within the Territory of the United States, begin to set on foot or provide, or prepare the means for any military expedition or enterprise, to be carried on from thence against the

Territory &c of any foreign state &c with whom the United States are at peace."

The facts much [*sic*] be such as would warrant a prosecution under the latter section, before a seizure of the vessel can be had under the 1st section of the Act of 1838, and I have always entertained doubts whether the 6th section of the Act of 1818 was applicable when the military expedition or enterprise was not begun and commenced by foreigners or our own citizens on their own account, within the jurisdiction of the United States, and have thought that it had no reference to a foreign public vessel duly commissioned, and sailing under the flag of a sovereign prince with whom we are at peace and amity; and in case any wrongs may be committed by such public vessel "the questions to which such wrongs give birth," are, in the language of Judge [John] Marshall, in the case of the Schooner Exchange vs. McFaddon and others "rather questions of policy than of law, that they are for diplomatic rather than legal discussion" (7 Cranch 146.) I am by no means certain that I am right in this construction of the statute, but as the subject is one of delicacy, involving nice points in the law of nations, and as I can find no case reported, where there has been a seizure or detention of a public armed ship under the provisions of this act, I would respectfully ask your opinion on the subject, or that of the Attorney General of the United States. I shall, however, be governed by any instructions from you, and shall most cheerfully, do all in my power to accomplish the desires and wishes of the Department.

I addressed a letter, this morning, to Hon. John McKeon requesting his aid and co-operation as suggested in your letter; but to my regret I find that he has left the city for Nashville Tennessee, and that he will not return for some weeks. I am, Sir, with great respect Your Ob[edient] Ser[van]t, O. Hoffman, U.S. Att[orne]y.

LS in DNA, RG 59 (State Department), Miscellaneous Letters (M-179:105, frames 402–404).

From WILSON LUMPKIN

Athens [Ga.] Sep[t]. 23d 1844

My dear Sir, An apology for my long silence, might indicate the appearance of an assumed consequence on my part, which I do not feel.

You are doubtless better advised upon all subjects connected with the discharge of the duties of your present station, than to need the suggestions of your personal or political friends, who like myself live in absolute retirement. But secluded as I am, I read[,] reflect & feel a very deep interest in the passing events of the day. So many extraordinary events have transpired since we last confer[r]ed together on the affairs of the Country, that I am at a great loss, in regard to coming Events. It is now obvious, to every one—that since the absolute withdrawal, of the names of the President [John Tyler] & yourself, from the presidential canvass, That the patriotic & wise measures of the administration, is more & more appreciated by the whole Country. The present generation, as well as posterity, will duly appreciate the importance of the Texas question, and award full & ample justice to the present administration, while the opponents of the measure, will remain standing monuments on the pages of history, for the slow unmoving finger of scorn to point at. I rejoice, that the Texas question, has enabled Mr. [Martin] Van Buren & some other temporising politicians to go into honorable retirement. But am still more gratifyed, in the hope, that Tom Benton, The Globe—with all that selfish mass of corruption, which has desolated the good old Republican party, may be swept over board, & driven from the ranks of the Patriots of the Country. The stigma which rests upon these monsters, can never be effaced. From a sense of duty, taking a view of things as they Exist, I go fully & zealously into the support of [James K.] Polk & [George M.] Dallas—It is the best I can do—The only present hope of deliverance, especially to our own beloved South.

A great battle, & long struggle yet lies before us, on the Texas question, & the inevitable incidental questions connected with that subject. Although [John M.] Berrien [Senator from Ga.], ridicules us for speaking of the present as *a great crisis,* be assured it will prove to be such. So far as has been laid before the publick, President Tyler & yourself, have in my humble opinion, acted with great wisdom & far seeing forecast, in your diplomatic correspondence with the govt. of Great Brittain, on the slave question. We have to meet this question, & now is the accepted time—and now (if ever) is the day of salvation.

You have taken the high ground, upon which you will be impregniable, in the Eyes of the civilized world, & that of posterity. We are not only a nation, but a great nation. We can only maintain peace & good relations, with our great Rival England—by a dignifyed self respect.

Ask nothing but what is clearly right, and submit to nothing wrong.

I deeply regret the death of Gen[era]l [Tilghman A.] Howard. I thought his appointment an excellent one, & considered his station a very important one, at the present moment. The triumph of the Enemies of annexation so far, must produce a powerful effect upon ["the" *interlined*] temper & wishes of many of the people of Texas. And the Agents & Emis[s]aries of other governments, as well as those of other wicked & mischievous associations, you may rest assured will not be idle. On our part, is required sagacity, firmness, prudence, and untiring vigilance. If Texas can be kept from commit[t]ing herself to others, & ["in" *canceled*] her good feelings towards us maintained—we have nothing to fear, as regards ultimate success. The people of our Union, will ere long—rally to their great interest. Let the Presidential election, go as it may—The slave holding States & Texas, must become one & indivisible.

Publick & private considerations still induce me to desire to visit Texas shortly (I have a son & his family there). Should I find the Country & other things as ["I" *interlined*] now anticipate—you may not be surprized, if I should finally determine to hazard my life, my little competancy—my all—in sustaining the principles & cause for which I have hitherto contended. Texas must not fall a prey, to Santa Anna & his allies in wickedness.

I think I could carry a Thousand men to Texas, with the spirit & means to defend the country, from whatever assaults might come.

With these views hastily thrown together, & frankly submitted— will you please to throw in my way such information, as you may feel at liberty—and which may be calculated, if prudently used—To benefit the U. States as well as Texas. If I could only be with you, I have a great many things to hear & learn, as well as say—upon the present aspect of the political affairs of our beloved Country.

I think Polk will get the vote of Georgia, but I am astonished beyond measure, to see the course of the Southern Whigs. They boldly sustain, the whole *chain* of measures, dictated by their leader [Henry] Clay. They are now fully committed to old fashioned Federalism, with all its new tricks & mummeries of Demagogueism. Polk[']s heart is right, & I trust he may be made the honored instrument, of righting many of the evils which we have witnessed. Gen[era]l [Andrew] Jackson[']s patriotism has been arroused to new life, upon the Texas question. The mist from before his Eyes, in regard to many of his old associates must be completely removed.

I trust Mr. Tyler may be spared, to hear & rec[e]ive the congratulations of his Countrymen, for the public services which he has rendered our Common Country. As Ever your friend & Servant, Wilson Lumpkin.

ALS in ScCleA.

From Florence McCarthy, New York [City], 9/23. McCarthy acknowledges a letter of 9/21 from the State Department to John McKeon. McKeon is now absent from the city, and McCarthy so informs Calhoun in order that other arrangements can be made "in relation to the subject ["matter" *interlined*] of said Communication as may be deemed advisable." ALS in DNA, RG 59 (State Department), Miscellaneous Letters (M-179:105, frames 400-402).

From R[ichard] Pakenham, 9/23. He calls to Calhoun's attention claims presented to the State Department in 1/1844 in behalf of several British merchants engaged in the woollen trade to the U.S. [These merchants maintain that large quantities of their goods were illegally and fraudulently seized and auctioned off in 1839 by the then Collector of the Port of New York, Jesse Hoyt, according to numerous enclosed documents. The claims have been prosecuted in the courts without success.] Pakenham calls for the national government to extend "to the aggrieved Parties complete redress and compensation for the injuries which they have suffered from the evil practices of official Servants of the United States." LS with Ens in DNA, RG 59 (State Department), Notes from Foreign Legations, Great Britain, vol. 22 (M-50:22).

From ROBERT G. SCOTT

Richmond, September 23rd 1844
Dear Sir, The vacancy in the Consulship at Liverpool occasioned by the death of [James Hagarty] the late incumbent, you will have shortly to fill. Pardon me for recommending for this station, William Maury esq[ui]r[e] of Liverpool a citizen of the United States, as every way eminently distinguished by mercantile experience & high character for this office. I entertain no doubt, that the public interest will be secured & advanced by his appointment. I am with senti-

ments of sincere attachment & respect yours very truly, Robert G. Scott.

ALS in DNA, RG 59 (State Department), Applications and Recommendations, 1837–1845, Maury (M-687:22, frames 454–455).

From "ALIENUS"

[Alexandria, D.C., published September 24, 1844]
Sir: Deign to look down from your high station *in office*, UNDER John Tyler, and answer two plain questions, addressed to you by one who was your friend, when the parasites around you *now* were your bitterest revilers.

Did you put your official seal to a Loco Foco party publication to give it weight and importance certifying as to the commission of magistrates who took Mr. [Henry] Clay's recognizance, when he was challenged [in 1841?] by Mr. [William R.] King, of Alabama, to fight a duel? And did you refuse a Whig to certify, under your official seal, certain *facts*, which it was thought important to have certified?

Do you suffer John Tyler to put *his* own friends into office, Andrew Jackson Donelson and all, and to keep your's out of office, although the appointments are strictly in your department?

Be assured, sir, your present position, and your public course for some time past, require explanation, to *old friends* out of South Carolina as well as in that mighty State. [Signed:] Alienus.

PC in the Alexandria, D.C., *Alexandria Gazette & Virginia Advertiser*, September 24, 1844, p. 2.

From J[OHN] S. BARBOUR

Catalpa [Va.] Sep[tembe]r 24th 1844
My Dear Sir, I have some reason to believe that the newspapers have misrepresented the truth when they assert the abuse of you by Mr. [William C.] Rives [Senator from Va.] at Winchester in his speech made there the first of this month.

I shall learn with certainty in a few days & will as soon as I do hear inform you of it. I hope that he is misrepresented. In my remarks at Orange I only stated that I w[oul]d not believe it until compelled to do so, "for if I had heard it I should rouse myself up & ask if I was not dreaming."

Everything depends in this election upon the vote of New York[;] if that is secure then the Cause of the Country is safe. With Great Respect y[ou]rs faithfully, J.S. Barbour.

ALS in ScCleA.

To George M. Bibb, Secretary of the Treasury

Department of State
Washington, 24th Sept[embe]r 1844

Sir, I have the honor to communicate a correspondence between this Department and the late and present British Ministers accredited to this Government [Henry S. Fox and Richard Pakenham], relative to grievances alleged to have been sustained by certain British subjects engaged in the importation of Woolens into the United States. As the subject appertains to your Department I herewith submit the same with all the papers relating to it for your consideration and decision.

The accompanying papers being originals, I will thank you to cause them to be returned when you shall no longer have occasion for them. I have the honor to be, Sir, Your obedient Servant, J.C. Calhoun.

LS in DNA, RG 56 (Secretary of the Treasury), Letters Received from Executive Officers, Series AB, 1844, document 39; FC in DNA, RG 59 (State Department), Domestic Letters, 34:383–384 (M-40:32).

From George Brown, Honolulu, 9/24. Brown encloses numerous documents concerning his contention that U.S. citizens accused of crimes in the Sandwich Islands are entitled to trial by a jury of foreigners. These enclosed documents were transmitted to Brown by the Foreign Office at Honolulu and include a letter from the King of Hawaii to the President [John Tyler], asking that Brown be recalled. Brown points out several passages in various communications that he considers to be both false and offensive. He asks that Calhoun reply as soon as possible and emphasizes that his course was chosen with a view to the rights of U.S. citizens resident in the Sandwich Islands. ALS (No. 18) with Ens in DNA, RG 59 (State Department), Diplomatic Despatches, Hawaii, vol. 1 (T-30:1, frames 220–316), received 2/15/1845.

From RICH[AR]D S. COXE, "Private"

Baltimore, Sept[embe]r 24th 1844

Dear Sir, I have thus far advanced on my way & hope to reach New York [City] this evening. In our conversation yesterday nothing was said on the subject of compensation, a matter which I am disposed to leave entirely to yourself but it would be convenient for me to have some funds in New York. If therefore you can remit me a draft on that place for $150 or $200 ["on account" *interlined*] you will much oblige yours with Great respect, Richd. S. Coxe.

ALS in DNA, RG 59 (State Department), Accounting Records: Miscellaneous Letters Received. NOTE: An AEI by Calhoun reads "Remit $150 out of the Foreign intercourse app[ropriatio]n." An AES by J[ohn] Tyler reads "approved." A Clerk's EU reads "Rec[eive]d from Sec[retar]y 25 Sep[tember] and remitted same day."

To FRANKLIN DEXTER, U.S. District Attorney, Boston

Department of State
Washington, Sept. 24th 1844

Sir: This Department learns through the public prints, that the house of Philo S. Shelton & Co. of Boston has contracted to supply the Mexican Government with a quantity of tents, and that the contract is understood to have been made through British Agency.

It is desirable that the truth of this statement should be ascertained. You will consequently make proper inquiries for that purpose, and communicate the result to this Department. Your attention is particularly requested to the laws of the United States passed for the purpose of maintaining our neutrality, and if you should have reason to beleive [*sic*] that any measures are in contemplation calculated to contravene them, you will institute proper process with a view to defeat these measures. I am Sir &c &c, Jno. C. Calhoun.

FC in DNA, RG 59 (State Department), Domestic Letters, 34:384–385 (M-40:32); PC in Jameson, ed., *Correspondence*, p. 619.

To ALEX[ANDE]R H. EVERETT, [Boston?]

Washington, 24th Sep[tembe]r 1844
My dear Sir, I have read with deep interest the Copy of the memorial on the present condition of the Island of Cuba. It indicates on the part of the author a thorough Knowledge of the subject and a sound & vigorous mind. I agree with you, that the present state of the Island requires, on our part, prompt & decided attention.

I have also read with much interest your pamphlet on Texas. It does you great credit, and, coming from the quarter it does, cannot but do ["yo" *canceled*] much good. It is strange that party feelings should so completely overpower the judgement. As far as interest is concerned, no portion of the Union has a deeper stake in the question of annexation, than New England[']s.

I am much obliged to you for the opportunity of perusing both the memorial & your pamphlet.

I regard the defeat of [Henry] Clay and the election of [James K.] Polk now almost certain. With great respect I am yours truly, J.C. Calhoun.

ALS in MHi, Everett-Peabody Papers. NOTE: Everett's "pamphlet on Texas" was probably his 23-pp. *A Letter on the Texas Question* (no place: no date), reprinted from the *United States Magazine and Democratic Review* of September, 1844.

From O[GDEN] HOFFMAN

U.S. Attorney's Office
New York [City], 24th Sept[embe]r 1844
Sir, I have just procured an affidavit, in relation to the two Mexican Steam Vessels, "Guadaloupe" and "Montezuma," now in this port, a copy of which, I have the honor to inclose for your perusal and consideration.

One of the persons, who aids me, in my exertions to watch the movements of these vessels, will I think, procure some additional testimony in a day or two, of which, I will immediately apprise you. Mr. [Alanson] Nash, the Lawyer, referred to, in my communication of yesterday, has applied to me, to secure the attendance of [Henry] Cook, (by whom the enclosed affidavit is made) as a witness for the Government, either by having him committed, or by requiring him to give Security for his appearance, but I deem it, to be my duty not to adopt any public proceedings in reference to those vessels, in the absence of instructions. I therefore respectfully request your early advice and instructions in the premises. I have the honor, to be Sir Very Respect[full]y Your obed[ien]t Serv[an]t, O. Hoffman, U.S. Attorney.

LS with En in DNA, RG 59 (State Department), Miscellaneous Letters (M-179: 105, frames 407–410). NOTE: Hoffman enclosed an affidavit, dated 9/24/1844, of Henry Cook, formerly a seaman aboard the *Montezuma*, in which he described the voyage of the vessel from Vera Cruz and its refitting at New York City.

To Tho[ma]s McGuire, U.S. Consul, Glasgow, 9/24. Calhoun states that James M. Broom, an acquaintance of Calhoun, will soon write to McGuire to obtain some information from Glasgow. Calhoun would appreciate any help that McGuire can render to Broom. FC in DNA, RG 59 (State Department), Consular Instructions, 12:97.

From SAM[UE]L MCLEAN

Consulate of the U.S.A.
Trinidad [Cuba], Sept[embe]r 24th 1844
Sir, On the 24th of August I received a letter dated Cienfuegos the 22nd Aug[us]t from a Dr. Elias Wolf a naturalized citizen of the United States, who has been for some years past acting as agent for the San Fernando mines, (owned by Citizens of the U.S.) situate about twenty miles from Cienfuegos and near the town of Villa Clara.

In his letter he complains of being arrested on suspicion of being concerned in the late conspiracy of which you have been advised. At the last accounts from him, he was confined as a prisoner to his room (his family being with him) waiting until his health would enable him to be sent under guard to Villa Clara to undergo an examination before the milatary commission sitting in that town. He was on the eve of embarking for the U.S. when he was arrested, and complains very much, and if innocent with justice, of the detention, and the expense incident thereto. I wrote to the Governor of Cienfuegos on the receipt of Dr. Wolf[']s letter, intimating my expectation of his being released without any unnecessary delay. In his answer he informed me that the order for the Doctor[']s arrest emmanated from a higher authority than his own, but expressed a desire to promote my wishes to the extent of his power. Thus the matter stands at this time, and I would have deffered writing to you on the subject until I could have done so more definitely, but that it becomes necessary for me to make arrangements for returning to the U.S. as soon as possible, being informed that I have been superseded in my office at this place. This information was only received by me a few days since (and that not officially) and I think I have just cause of complaint against the Department for not informing me of the matter, but allowing me to remain here during *the dull and sickly season,* when the receipts of the office will not pay house rent; thereby becoming the mere "locum tenens" for a person who did not think proper to subject himself to poverty and disease, but gladly avails himself of my services in the mean time.

Should the person appointed not arrive before I leave I will take care to place the business in the hands of one well qualified to fill the duties of the office.

The appointment as it appears in the Madisonian, was approved of by the Senate on the 15th or 17th of June, ample time has been allowed for my being *officially* advised of it. I have the honour to be Sir Your most ob[edien]t Serv[an]t, Saml. McLean.

ALS (No. 47) in DNA, RG 59 (State Department), Consular Despatches, Trinidad, Cuba, vol. 2 (T-699:2), received 10/23.

To [ROCCO] MARTUSCELLI, Consul General of the Two Sicilies, New York [City]

Department of State
Washington, 24th September, 1844
Sir: Your notes of the 18th [*sic*; 8/17] ultimo and 17th instant have been duly received at the Department of State. A reply, to the former, would have been promptly made, had not delay, in its translation, occasioned by the pressure of more important business, prevented its being brought to my attention at an earlier period. The latter simply reminds the Department that an answer is due to the former.

I am, now, under the unpleasant necessity of saying, that your note is every way exceptionable. Its tone and language are so discourteous, that the Department can not insult the Secretary of the Treasury [George M. Bibb] by referring it to him, and I therefore return it to you. And I take this occasion to add, that if you can not use more courtesy in your communications, your correspondence with this Department must cease. I am, Sir, with due consideration, Your obedient Servant, J.C. Calhoun.

FC in DNA, RG 59 (State Department), Notes to Foreign Legations, Italian States, Greece, and Turkey, 6:71–72 (M-99:61).

PROTOCOL by R[ichard] Pakenham and J[ohn] C. Calhoun

[Washington, September 24, 1844] The 6th Conference was held on the 24th of Sept[embe]r when the British Plenipotentiary stated that He had read with due attention the statement [of 9/20] marked B presented by the American Plenipotentiary at the last conference but that it had not weakened the impression previously entertained by Him with regard to the claims and rights of Great Britain as explained in the paper lately presented by Him marked D. That reserving for a future occasion such observations as he might wish to present by way of explanations in reply to the statement last presented by the American Plenipotentiary, He was for the present obliged to declare with reference to the concluding part of that statement that he did not feel authorized to enter into discussion respecting the Territory North of 49 Parallel of latitude which was understood by the British Government to form the Basis of Negotiation on the side of the United States as the line of the Columbia formed that on the side of Great Britain. That the proposal which he had presented was offered by Great Britain as an honorable compromise of the claims and pretensions of both Parties, and that it would of course be understood as having been made subject to the condition recorded in the protocol of the third Conference held between the respective Plenipotentiaries in London in Dec[embe]r 1826. J.C. Calhoun, R. Pakenham.

DS in DNA, RG 59 (State Department), Notes from Foreign Legations, Great Britain, vol. 22 (M-50:22); PC in the Washington, D.C., *Daily National Intelligencer*, December 12, 1845, p. 1; PC in *Niles' National Register*, vol. LXIX, no. 17 (December 27, 1845), p. 261; PC in Senate Document No. 1, 29th Cong., 1st Sess., p. 145; PC in House Document No. 2, 29th Cong., 1st Sess., p. 145; PC in Crallé, ed., *Works*, 5:425–426.

From E[DWARD] PORTER

Consulate of the United States of America
at Guadalupe de Frontera
Department of Tabasco, Sept. 24th 1844

Sir, I had the honour of a[d]dressing you on the 20th of July passed Concerning our Citizens and Sailors that are still incarscerated in a loathsome prison in the Town of Tabasco. Sickness and Con[ta]gion is wasteing them away. There is not nor can there be any accusation brought against them save that they Ship[p]ed on board the Schooner W.A. Turner bound for Ballize Honduras. When at Sea [Francisco] Sentmanat & his Confidants assumed the Control of the Schooner and brought her to this Coast where she was fired into and driven ashore by Vessels of war of the Mexican Government.

Our Citizens and Sailors had no foreknowledge of the the [sic] intentions of Sentmanat to Carry them here.

I have applied to the Governor of this State in their behalf and solicited to know their intentions towards the Sailors & passengers but cannot get any reply on the Subject. I have the Honour to remain Your Most ob[edien]t Serv[an]t &c &c, E. Porter.

ALS in DNA, RG 59 (State Department), Consular Despatches, Tabasco, vol. 1 (M-303:1, frame 226), received 12/12.

From CLEMENT C. BIDDLE

Philadelphia, 25th September, 1844

My dear Sir, Understanding that Joshua Clibborn, Esquire, of New York, is an applicant for the appointment of the Consulate at Liverpool, become vacant by the decease of Mr. Haggerty [sic; James Hagarty], the warm regard I feel for Mr. Clibborn must be my excuse for addressing you in his behalf.

Mr. Clibborn, in my opinion, is eminently qualified to fill this important office. His thorough knowledge of business, liberal education, and for many years extensive commercial transactions, conducted always with integrity and ability, have won for him the lasting respect and attachment of many leading merchants, with whom he has been brought into close connexion, in our principal Atlantic seaports. These gentlemen, I am informed, will present to the Department of State their testimony of the spotless integrity of Mr. Clibborn's mercantile character, his perfect and familiar acquaintance with commercial concerns, and consequent admirable fitness for the consular appointment at so important a port as Liverpool.

Mr. Clibborn resided many years in this city, and is well known and esteemed by our old and respectable citizens. I myself have known him from my infancy, and can truly say, I never knew a more liberal and warm hearted man. I have had much intercourse with him, am indebted to him for many kindnesses, and enjoy high pleasure from his conversation and correspondence.

Mr. Clibborn, moreover, has strong claims on his political friends; for he always has been a firm and decided, but liberal, democrat of the oldest and best school. Colonel [James] Monroe appointed him Consul at the port of Antwerp during his administration. At that time Mr. Clibborn was at the head of an extensive commercial establishment in Antwerp; and in all his intercourse there with his countrymen, private and public, he enjoyed their confidence and support. And to you, my dear Sir, I may be permitted to add, that Mr. Clibborn is an ardent and able advocate of the soundest principles of political economy; a science whose fundamental doctrines have received their fullest illustration and most logical enunciation from your own enlightened and vigorous pen and tongue; and respecting the practical truth and importance of which, Mr. Clibborn has been convinced by long, careful, and intelligent observation and experience.

I must not omit to state, that Mr. Clibborn's wife was born in the State of Georgia, and is the only child of the late Major [Benjamin] Fishbourne, the favorite aid de camp, and who served with the highest distinction under General [Anthony] Wayne, in his brilliant and successful campaign in South Carolina and Georgia at the close of our Revolutionary war. After that war, on the establishment of the Federal Government, General [George] Washington, as some evidence of his estimation of the military services of Major Fishbourne, appointed him Collector of the port of Charleston in your own republican and patriotic State. With the highest respect and consideration, believe me always, my dear Sir, most truly and faithfully yours, Clement C. Biddle.

ALS in DNA, RG 59 (State Department), Applications and Recommendations, 1837–1845, Clibborn (M-687:5, frames 504–506).

From Ja[me]s T. Brady

New York [City,] Sept[embe]r 25th 1844
Dear Sir, When a number of our Democratic Young men in this city interested themselves to have you nominated for the Presidency, I was very glad to give them my hearty coöperation. My approval of your political creed in its principal features commenced many years ago, and although I did not then, and do not at this time fully concur in your views about Slavery, it was my sincere conviction that you would if elected to the Presidency administer this government on a system of sound principles, and with salutary measures.

My exertions in your behalf though by no means so effective as I wished to render them, were made from mere admiration of your political, and personal character, without any acquaintance with you personally, ["and" *canceled*] or the slightest desire, or hope to advance my own interests. There can be no objection to my making under these circumstances and in view of your present position, a declaration which might otherwise appear egotistical, or interested.

My special purpose in addressing you is not to avow my own partiality for you as a public man, but to mention to you the kind effort in your behalf during the recent political movement, of one whose friendly interest in your prosperity might otherwise remain unknown to you. I allude to Major Augustus A. Nicholson of the Marine Corps who at a very early period in the movement to which I refer wrote to me urging such efforts for your advancement as it might be in my power to make. In the spirit with which this was done he manifested a very strong desire that you should obtain from the American People the preferment to which he like myself considered you entitled.

I dare say that his partiality for you remains like mine unchanged. I have no doubt too that like mine it is utterly free from any feeling except that which an American Citizen of the Democratic Republican faith should entertain for a Champion of its principles whom he believed to be honest, and faithful. It is in reference alone to your efforts for these principles, and the strict adherence to the ways of truth, and independence which has in my judgment marked your political career, that I have formed my estimate of your character, or been stimulated to advocate your cause. In short I thought more of the faith, than even of the Champion, and in desiring to see you elevated, considered more the good of the people, than your gratification. I know that you will appreciate aright the sentiments I here utter. Do not I beg suppose that this letter is designed to draw from you any letter. It is a voluntary act on my part, and I should be sorry if it deprived you of any more time than you occupy in its perusal. Yours truly, Jas. T. Brady.

ALS in ScCleA.

To J[AMES] ED[WARD] COLHOUN, [Abbeville District, S.C.]

State Dept., 25th Sep[tembe]r 1844
My dear Sir, I find on enquiry, that your brother [John Ewing Colhoun, Jr.] was mistaken; and that there has been no dividend of the old United States Bank since 1834.

I am glad to hear so good an account of your mountain land; and will with pleasure avail myself of every opportunity of letting it be known, where ["it" *interlined*] would likely be of service to you, that you would sell.

I had a letter from your sister [Floride Colhoun Calhoun] at Glenn Springs [S.C.]. She says, that James [Edward Calhoun] had greatly improved, & that her health was better.

I expect to leave for home on the 28th & to be there early in October. You must be sure to make us a visit while I am there, which will be all the month of Oct[obe]r & the early part of Nov[embe]r I hope.

I have been very much employed. My health is good, although there is much sickness in Washington. Yours Affectionately, J.C. Calhoun.

ALS in ScCleA.

From RICH[AR]D S. COXE

New York [City,] Sep[tembe]r 25, 1844
Sir, I reached this place between 11 & 12 O'clock last night, and proceeded at an early hour this morning upon the business of my mission. Unfortunately I find that Mr. [John] McKeon is not in town

and is not expected to return for several weeks. I have called twice at Mr. [Ogden] Hoffman's office, but have not been so fortunate as to find him in.

Under these circumstances I have been compelled to resort to such sources of information as I could employ without awakening suspicion. So far I have learned that the Mexican vessels have advanced very far towards the completion of their refitment, that they have materially augmented their effective strength in munitions of war, and have also increased the numerical strength of their crews. That they are now in a situation which would enable them in a very short time to be ready for sea, but will probably unless some apprehension be awakened not sail for some considerable time. The impression is that they are not adequately supplied with funds.

The information thus furnished me does not come in such a shape that it can be made the foundation of legal proceedings, but if proper means are employed this can probably be effected. The individuals with whom I am in communication learn what they know from the representations & assurances of others. It may be necessary to resort to the immediate actors or those who have personal knowledge of the facts.

If you can transmit me a general letter authorising me to call upon the various officers in the employ of the government, civil and military, to point out the particular subjects to which inquiry should be directed, and to employ the means which they have at command to pursue this investigation, and to apprise them that in this business I am acting on behalf of and under instructions from the government, I have little doubt that I could soon ascertain the precise state of the facts as they exist, and thus furnish the information requisite to enable the government to determine upon the course to be pursued.

This authority I especially wish at this time to authorise me to communicate with the Collector & other officers of the Customs and Capt. [Silas H.] Stringham in command at the Navy Yard. Governor [Cornelius P.] Vanness [sic] is not at present in the City or I would without this formal authority at once communicate with him. With Capt. Stringham I am not personally acquainted and should therefore request that Judge [John Y.] Mason would address him in general terms on the subject referring him to me for the details.

My impression is very strong from what I have already heard that the facts which can be substantiated will exhibit a clear case of a violation of our neutrality but every consideration demands that a solid foundation should be laid before any decisive action is had upon the subject. I need scarcely add that no exertion on my part shall be omitted to justify the confidence you have reposed in me.

Any communication to me addressed to the care of John Warren Esq[ui]r[e] Wall Street will be promptly received. Very respectfully Yours &c, Richd. S. Coxe.

ALS in DNA, RG 59 (State Department), Miscellaneous Letters (M-179:105, frames 420–421).

To EDWARD EVERETT, London

Department of State
Washington, Sept. 25th 1844

Sir, Mr. [Robert J.] Walker one of the Senators of Mississippi, submitted for the consideration of the Senate, near the close of the last Session of Congress, the two following resolutions.

Resolved, That the President be requested to inform the Senate, whether the Parliament of Great Britain has passed any act extending its criminal jurisdiction to the United States, so as to subject any portion of their citizens, or persons within their limits, to its penalties, for acts done within the same, and to communicate a copy of said act, if any such there be, together with any information he may possess, as to the means, which may have been adopted to carry its provisions into effect.

Resolved, That he be also requested to inform the Senate, whether the Government of Great Britain has issued circulars to its diplomatic or consular agents, to collect information, as to the condition of any portion of our population, and, if so, to transmit to the Senate a copy thereof, if in his possession, together with any information he may possess as to the object of issuing the same.

They were laid on the table without being acted on, as it may be presumed from the want of time. They will probably be renewed at the next session and adopted.

The immediate object of this despatch is to obtain the information requested by the resolutions, in order to have the means of answering the call, should it then be renewed and adopted.

On examining a collection of the Statutes of Parliament, I can find but one act (the 6th and 7th of Victoria,) entitled "an Act for the more effectual suppression of the Slave trade" which would seem to come within the description of the first resolution. It is the one probably, which occasioned its introduction. It expressly extends the criminal jurisdiction of Great Britain to its subjects in foreign Countries, in all cases embraced within its provisions; and, as it may, of course, be inferred, to her subjects residing in the United States; but in order to remove all doubt upon that point, you will ascertain through the proper Department of the Government, whether her subjects, residing within the United States, are intended to be embraced in the provisions of the Act or not; and, if they are, you will obtain and transmit a copy of the same, published by the authority of the Government.

You will, in the next place, ascertain, who are intended to be embraced under the expression of British Subjects. Is it intended to be restricted to those only, who may be sojourning or residing temporarily in the United States, without intending to become citizens? or to all, who may have been born within the limits of the British dominions, including as well those, who have become citizens of the United States, as those that have not?

The 2nd Section of the 5th of Geo: 4th declares it to be unlawful for any person (except in special cases thereinafter specified) to deal, or trade in, purchase, sell, barter, or transfer, or to contract for the dealing or trading in, purchase, sale, barter or transfer of Slaves, or persons intended to be dealt with as Slaves; or to lend or advance, or become security for the loan or advance of money, goods or effects employed or to be employed in accomplishing any of the objects or contracts or in relation to the objects and contracts, which objects and contracts have hereinbefore been declared unlawful; or to become guarantee or security, or, in short to be in any manner engaged or concerned in buying, selling or dealing in Slaves.

The Act of the 6th and 7th Victoria, recites these provisions and declares that they shall extend to British subjects in foreign Countries, and adopts all the provisions of the Act of the 5th Geo: 4th, entitled "An Act to amend and consolidate the laws relating to the abolition of the Slave trade." The 10th Section of that Act declares that all persons offending against its provisions, and their procurers, counsellors[,] aiders and abettors, to be felons, and shall be transported beyond sea, for a term not exceeding ten years, or shall be confined to hard labour for a term not exceeding five years, nor less than three, at the discretion of the court, before which they may be tried and convicted. You will ascertain whether it is intended that British subjects in the United States, who shall any way be concerned in buying[,] selling or dealing in Slaves, as is declared in the 2nd Section of 5th Geo: 4th, and recited and adopted by the 6th and 7th

Victoria, as above stated, shall be liable to the penalties contained in the 10th Section of the former.

There is not a little uncertainty as to the object intended to be effected by the Act of the 6th and 7th Victoria, taken in connection with that of the 5th Geo: 4th. The object of both, as declared in their respective titles, is the suppression of the Slave trade; by which it is usually understood, the African Slave trade. That was unquestionably the object of the 5th Geo: 4th. But the object of the 6th and 7th Victoria (the act in question) would seem to be not so much the abolition of the Slave trade, as the abolition of Slavery itself, as far as British subjects in foreign countries are concerned. If reference be had to the reported debates on the Bill, while on its passage through the House of Commons, in order to ascertain its object, it would seem, by the declarations of its advocates, that it was to prohibit, indirectly, the Slave trade, by prohibiting British Subjects and British capital from being engaged in purchasing and employing Slaves in countries, where the African Slave trade is still permitted, in order to prevent thereby the increased stimulus, it was calculated to give that trade. If that is, in truth, its object, there can be no motive whatever for extending its provisions to the United States. They have long since effectually suppressed the trade. But, if that be not the object, you will ascertain what in fact is the object for extending the provisions of the Act to British Subjects in the United States.

You will also ascertain what measures have been adopted to enforce its provisions, and particularly what instructions have been given by the British Government to their Consuls or other Agents concerning that Act, or that of the 5th Geo: 4th. I enclose for your information a copy of a circular purporting to contain instructions to its Consuls in relation to the former Act, taken from one of the public journals. If any such circular has been issued or any other, you will obtain a copy, and transmit it to this Department, and also a copy of that issued under the act of the 5th Geo: 4th, referred to in the circular, if any such has been issued.

You will finally ascertain, whether it has issued a circular or circulars of the description referred to in the 2d resolution; and if so, obtain and transmit copies to the Department. We have no knowledge of any such, but it has been intimated from different quarters by the public journals, that a circular of the kind has been issued. It is probable, that these frequent intimations have led to the introduction of the resolution.

The British Government cannot take any just exception to the course adopted by this Government to get the information, which you have been instructed to obtain. The Act of the 6th and 7th Victoria, on its face, purports to extend its criminal jurisdiction to persons within our limits, and who while there are subject to our laws and entitled to our protection, and that not only gives our Government a right to obtain the information asked for, but makes it its duty to ask for it.

Should you ascertain, that it is intended to extend the provisions of the Act to British Subjects residing in the United States, you will, in an earnest manner, invite the attention of the British Government to the subject. We hold that the criminal jurisdiction of a nation is limited to its own dominions, and to vessels under its flag on the high seas; and that it cannot extend it to acts committed within the dominion of an other, without violating its sov[e]reignty and independence. Standing on this well established and unquestioned principle, we cannot permit Great Britain or any other nation, be its object or motive what it may, to infringe our Sov[e]reignty and independence by extending its criminal jurisdiction to acts committed within the limits of the United States, be they perpetrated by whom they may. All therein are subject to their jurisdiction, entitled to their protection, and are amenable exclusively to their laws.

It is not anticipated, that the British Government will deny or contest a principle so clear, and so unanimously acknowledged; and we must believe, until convinced of the contrary, that the Act passed without due deliberation, or taking into consideration its bearing on the Sov[e]reignty and independence of other Countries. It would, indeed, seem, if we are to judge from the debate as reported, that it passed the House of Lords without its attention being particularly directed to its provisions, and that of the Commons, after a very hurried discussion, just at the close of the Session, and little to the satisfaction of many of its members.

It is to be hoped that the Government of Great Britain, on having its attention invited seriously to the subject, will readily correct what would seem to be an inadvertance committed in the hurry of legislation. If in this we should be disappointed, it would be difficult to conceive what measure she could adopt more offensive to our dignity and rights, as an independent Country, or calculated more certainly to lead to serious consequences. I am, Sir, very respectfully Your Obedient Servant, J.C. Calhoun.

LS (No. 108) with Ens in DNA, RG 84 (Foreign Posts), Great Britain, Instructions, 8:437–455, received 10/16; FC in DNA, RG 59 (State Department), Diplomatic Instructions, Great Britain, 15:226–232 (M-77:74); PC in Jameson, ed., *Correspondence*, pp. 619–623. NOTE: Enclosed herewith is a copy of an article from the New York *Republican* of unknown date appending Lord Aberdeen's putative circular instructions of 12/31/1843 to British Consular agents in the U.S. on the subject of British enforcement of laws concerning the slave trade. The law extends British jurisdiction to all "British subjects, whether residing, or being, whether in any countries or settlements not belonging to the British Crown, or within the British dominions, Colonies or settlements."

From Geo[rge] W[illia]m Gordon

Consulate of the United States
Rio de Janeiro, Sept[embe]r 25th 1844

Sir, I have the honor herewith to communicate directions for Vessels approaching the "Island of Ichaboe," sometimes called "Guano Island," situated on the southwest coast of Africa. This island, I apprehend, is at present but little known to American navigators. It is only important for the large quantity of *Guano*, (excrement of birds,) which it furnishes, and which, for horticultural and farming purposes, has become an article of immense importation into Great Britain and other European nations; and may, at no distant day, be introduced extensively and with advantage into the United States. During the month of July last, it is said that upwards of one hundred and thirty vessels, mostly British, were loaded with this article at this island.

The Island is situated about three miles from the main-land; is difficult of approach, of bold, rocky shore, without any harbor, and exposed to heavy surf, and frequent fogs. It is but little more than a mile in circumference, without soil or the least sign of vegitation [*sic*], and covered with *guano* to the depth of twenty to thirty feet. The birds that inhabit it are a species of Penguin, their wings being a kind of fin, which enables them to fly but a short distance. They are said to be so numerous and tame, that it is difficult to walk about the island without treading upon them.

That part of the Continent near to which the island ["is" *interlined*] situated, is also barren, and destitute of fresh water. It seldom rains in that latitude, and vessels approaching the coast, during high winds from off shore, will often be covered with sand at the distance of fifty, or even a hundred miles from the land. I have the honor to be, Sir, Most respectfully, Your Obedient Servant, Geo. Wm. Gordon, Consul of the United States.

ALS (No. 11) with En in DNA, RG 59 (State Department), Consular Despatches, Rio de Janeiro, vol. 7 (T-172:8), received 11/21. NOTE: A Clerk's EU reads "published in Madisonian 26th Nov[embe]r '44."

To Ogden Hoffman

Department of State
Washington, Sept. 25, 1844

Sir, I have acknowledged the receipt of your letter of the 23d inst. and am gratified to learn from its contents that you have bestowed vigilant attention upon the case of the Mexican war Steamers. You will persevere in your endeavors to detect any violations of the Act of Congress of the 20th of April, 1818. At the date of the communication to you of the 21st inst., the fact that the duration of the Act of the 10th March 1838, was limited to two years, was overlooked. This makes it unnecessary to request the opinion of the Attorney General [John Nelson] upon the subject. Before you receive this, you will have learnt from a letter of which Mr. R[ichard] S. Coxe of this city was the bearer, that he has been retained as assistant Counsel, to cooperate with you. I am &c &c &c, John C. Calhoun.

FC in DNA, RG 59 (State Department), Domestic Letters, 34:389–390 (M-40:32).

From O[gden] Hoffman, U.S. Att[orne]y, New York [City], 9/25. Hoffman transmits to Calhoun "an additional affidavit [of Martin Tosney, dated 9/25] relative to the Mexican Steam vessels 'Montezuma' and 'Guadaloupe.'" (In the En, Tosney stated that the vessels are being refitted "to cruise against the subjects and citizens and property of one or more nations at peace with the United States, to wit the Republic of Texas.") LS with En in DNA, RG 59 (State Department), Miscellaneous Letters (M-179:105, frames 422–424).

From W[illia]m Hooper

U.S. Commercial Agency
[Honolulu,] Sandwich Islands
Sep[tember] 25th 1844

Sir, Since my respects of the 10th inst. (No. 37) Anthony Jenkins, a Citizen of the U. States, having been convicted by the Inferior, or Police Court of Honolulu, for a violation of one of the laws of this Country, and sentenced to pay the fine of 30$ or be imprisoned for eight months, he requested me to apply to the Governor for a trial by a Jury of foreigners. Application was accordingly made, and although not successful at first, yet the Governor finally yielded the point.

As the penalty attached to the offence charged against Jenkins is ["of" *canceled*] much less than that in the case of [John] *Wiley*, I have reason to think that in all cases which may hereafter arise, the privilege of a foreign Jury will be allowed. With Sentiments of the highest Consideration I have the honor to be, Sir, Y[ou]r Mo[st] Ob[edien]t S[er]v[an]t, Wm. Hooper, Act[in]g U.S. Com[mercia]l Agent.

ALS (No. 38) with Ens in DNA, RG 59 (State Department), Consular Despatches, Honolulu, vol. 2 (M-144:2), received 2/15/1845. NOTE: Hooper enclosed August and September 1844 issues of the Honolulu newspapers, *The Friend of Temperance and Seamen* and *The Polynesian*. The *Polynesian* of 9/21 contained an article on the Wiley affair and a letter from Hooper to the editor of the *Polynesian* describing the position of the U.S. legation on the matter. The Honolulu *Friend of Temperance and Seamen* of 9/4/1844, p. 84, contains the message: "If Mr. Herman Melville, formerly officer on board Am[erican] W[hale] S[hip] Acushnet, is in this part of the world, and will call upon the seamen's chaplain, he may find several letters directed to his address."

From DANIEL E. HUGER, [Senator from S.C.]

New York [City], Sept[embe]r 25th 1844
My dear Sir, It is reported here that the Consul of Liverpool [James Hagarty] is dead. If this be so, it would be very gratifying to the friends of Mr. Alfred Huger that he should be appointed. Mr. Alfred Huger has been unwell for some time past, and it is supposed that a continued residence in Europe would restore him to health.

As you know this gentleman, I will say no more on this subject than to request your attention to his claims. I have the honor to be with great respect yours &c, Daniel E. Huger.

ALS in DNA, RG 59 (State Department), Applications and Recommendations, 1837–1845, Huger (M-687:16, frames 523–524).

To Stewart Newell, U.S. C[onsul], Sabine, 9/25. The records of the Galveston consular post which came into Newell's hands at the death of A[rchibald] M. Green are to be surrendered to Gen. Duff Green on his arrival. Newell's claim for pay of [George C.] Brennen for copying State Department despatches cannot be allowed under an 1810 law. His claim for copying Galveston records damaged in the hurricane of 1842 will be paid on submission of proper evidence.

FC in DNA, RG 59 (State Department), Consular Instructions, 11: 277–278.

From John M. Patton, [former Representative from Va.], Richmond, 9/25. Patton asks that the appointment as U.S. Consul at Liverpool be conferred upon William Maury. Maury is the son of a former U.S. Consul at Liverpool [James Maury] and is well acquainted with the duties of that position. He is engaged in business with England and has extensive knowledge of the U.S.-English trade. Patton apologizes for troubling Calhoun with this matter. ALS in DNA, RG 59 (State Department), Applications and Recommendations, 1837–1845, Maury (M-687:22, frames 456–458).

From JOHN TYLER

[Charles City County, Va.?]
Sep[tember] 25, 1844

My Dear Sir; Your note advising me of your intention to leave for S. Carolina the last of the week, and expressing a desire to see me before your departure reached me last evening and I hasten to say that it is my intention to return to the City [Washington] on Friday or Saturday, which is as early as my arrangements here will permit, and yet My Dear Sir, with full knowledge of the severe labour to which you have recently been subjected I would not detain you a moment from that relaxation which is your due and to which you are so thoroughly entitled. If then you should desire to leave before Saturday communicate fully with Mr. [Richard K.] Crallé and I shall thus be placed in possession of your views and wishes.

There is a subject which I have thought of in the last few days as well worthy to claim our attention. As matters now are and are likely to stand without our interposition, the overland mail rout[e] to China has fallen into the hands of England and is likely to be engrossed by her. In view of enlarged commercial intercourse between us and China, this monopoly might be extremely inconvenient if not embarrassing. Should we not then take measures to guard against it by negociating with Egypt a free transmission of our mail, or by inducing her to stipulate with England upon the subject. A Treaty with her might also embrace other matters of interest to our trade. I regard the matter as one of much importance, and if you concur I will at an early day appoint a Diplomatic agent for the purpose. A conversation with Mr. Crallé would enable him to look up all information on the subject, and to communicate with you, if necessary, at your home. With true and sincere regard, John Tyler.

[P.S.] I would leave nothing undone which would lead to the good of the country. The early expiration of my term of service has no effect upon me, nor ought it.

ALS in ScCleA.

From FRANKLIN CHASE

Consulate of the United States of
America, Tampico, September 26th 1844
Sir, I have the honor to enclose to you herewith a Copy of the Decree of the Mexican Government, of the 21st August last, imposing an extra tax upon the owners and occupiers of real estate.

This extra tax is granted by the Legislature to this government for the purpose of being expended beyond the limits of the country, and also for the purpose of reconquering and preserving her territory, as is proved by the message directed by the chief of the Executive power [Santa Anna] to Congress on the 10th of June last, and from which the above mentioned extra tax originated.

Under these circumstances it is my humble opinion, that Citizens of the United States residing in this Country, are exempt from this impost, because it is a clear contribution for purposes of war. I have therefore advised my countrymen to refuse the payment of the amounts that may be designated, but in case they are called upon and forced by the authorities, to do it under protest in order to save their just rights.

The French, and Spanish Ministers have instructed their respective Consuls to refuse the payment of the before mentioned tax. Not having received any instructions from the Legation of the United States upon this subject, I trust that the course which I intend to pursue will have your approbation. I have the honor to be, with great respect, Sir, Your very, Obedient Servant, Franklin Chase.

ALS (No. 56) with En in DNA, RG 59 (State Department), Consular Despatches, Tampico, vol. 3 (M-304:2, frames 85–88), received 10/27.

From RICH[AR]D S. COXE

New York [City,] Sept[embe]r 26, 1844

Sir, I wrote you yesterday just as the mail was about closing informing you of what had transpired up to that time. During the afternoon I saw Mr. Thompson who had just arrived. This morning I met Mr. [Ogden] Hoffman with whom I had a long and satisfactory interview. He shewed me a copy of the letter he had written you & of the affidavits sent on. By tomorrow I hope that we shall be in possession of much further intelligence which will enable us to report to you more in detail.

The information already procured is perfectly satisfactory that a daring violation of the neutral rights of the United States has been perpetrated & already consummated. The ground is already laid upon which the government may determine as to the course which it will pursue. The testimony yet to be had will be only corroborative and more in detail. The necessity for prompt action is equally apparent. We have reason to believe that it is contemplated that these vessels shall sail on Tuesday next. They are nearly ready for sea.

In reference to the course proper to be adopted in this posture of the case, my own impression is that an order should be transmitted under the authority of the President [John Tyler] to the Mexican Commanders and Minister prohibiting them from sailing, and to the military and naval authorities not to permit their departure until the future decision of the President.

You must be aware that while we are compelled to rely upon such testimony as can be obtained confidentially and secretly, the testimony cannot be so full and so clear as it will be when we can enforce the attendance of witnesses before a judicial forum.

I have as yet not rec[eive]d a line from you since leaving Washington, and from leaving home in great haste shall be in want of funds.

I beg leave to add that I have rec[eive]d the most prompt and efficient aid from every individual to whom I have addressed myself. Very respectfully, y[ou]rs &c, Richd. S. Coxe.

ALS in DNA, RG 59 (State Department), Miscellaneous Letters (M-179:105, frames 431–432).

From Jos[eph] E. Garlington, Josiah Collins, and Charles P. Sanders

Clinton[,] Green[e] Co[unty,] Ala., Sept. 26/44

Dear Sir, The Democracy of this portion of our State having elected a mass meeting to be held at this place on the 26 Oct[obe]r next and chosen the undersigned a committee to invite their distinguished friends—are proud of the opportunity thus afforded of testifying their high regard for the patriot, and Statesman of the South who has so long and nobly defended those great principles of Republican liberty and manifested through all the great and trying emergencies he has been asked to pass the loftiest and most disinterested patriotism.

We can say naught expressive of the profound respect and admiration entertained by the Democracy of Alabama for your long and well tried services in the councils of this Nation.

Your name[,] your virtues and meritorious efforts in the maintainance of that beautiful feature of our Federative System—"equal rights" has been indellibly written in the hearts of your country men—and the brightest pages of our country[']s history will unfold to after generations the character of one the South justly appreciates and recognizes as an inflexible guardian of her rights.

Permit us farther to remark that your opinions on all the great questions of the day are no where more appreciated than in Alabama and it would afford the friends we represent unspeakable joy to meet and welcome you to this convention.

We are not unapprised of the fact that your distance from us and official engagements are likely to preclude us the pleasure of your company—as a feeble testimony of our respect and esteem we could not however forbear tendering you this cordial invitation to visit us—and in the event of your inability to visit us we will be pleased to hear from you.

Accept the assurances of our best wishes for your health & happiness. Your Ob[edien]t Servants, Jos. E. Garlington, Josiah Collins, Charles P. Sanders.

LS in ScCleA. NOTE: The writer of the above letter signed it for all three men. An AEU by Calhoun reads "Mr. Sanders[,] Invitation to a Mass meeting, Green County, Alabama."

From J[AMES] HAMILTON, [JR.], "(Private & *confidential*)"

Oswichee Bend [Ala.,] Sept. 26[t]h 1844

My Dear Sir, The Mail of yesterday brought me your short note of the 20[t]h inst. Your Letters directed to Savannah have not been received & therefore I shall be unable to reply to them until ["next" *canceled*] the last of the next week when I expect to be in Savannah. I write this ["to" *canceled*] in great haste to say that I will not be in Charleston until the 8[t]h or *10*[t]h *Oct.*—and therefore I can not hope to be there in time to see you. I trust on your return from Pendleton or your ["return on" *interlined*] way thro', that I shall have the gratification of meeting you, as I presume from public business your stay will be short in Pendleton.

I think Major Doneldson's [*sic*; Andrew Jackson Donelson's] appointment a very judicious one and rejoice that my Letter did not reach you in time that my name might not have come in competition with his and possibly thro' your friendship for me ["it would" *interlined*] have prevented the Pres[i]d[en]t [John Tyler] from doing what I presume he desired a gratifying thing to the Old Gen[era]l [Andrew Jackson]. I shall be in Texas by meeting of Congress say the 1st Dec. when [Samuel] Houston goes out, & will aid Doneldson all in my power in the accomplishment of the object of his Mission. *Because* I *wish* it *done* in *your administration of the Dept. of State*, [and] from his friendship for [James K.] Polk I presume he would be quite willing it should run into his administration if he is elected. He is however a Man of honor I really believe & will do his duty *under any* ["& all" *interlined*] *circumstances*.

I know I can carry annexation in Texas on a better Basis for both Countries than the late Treaty & ["in a form" *interlined*] far more likely ["than" *canceled*] to be adopted by our Congress. An official station under the U.S. would give me great additional influence[;] if therefore Doneldson should not accept & *my name in the first instance was in no degree brought into competition with his*, you may consider me at your disposal if you want my services. But I think Doneldson will accept & that Gen[era]l Jackson will scarcely permit him to decline.

If you should write me from Charleston be so kind as to direct to Savannah. God bless you My Dear Sir Ever sincerely & faithfully Yours, J. Hamilton.

P.S. I deeply regret my Dear Sir that my time will not permit me to visit Pendleton.

ALS in ScCleA. NOTE: An AEU by Hamilton on the cover sheet of this letter reads: "To kind attention of Mr. [Henry W.] Conner." The letter is addressed to Calhoun as Secretary of State, "Expected in Charleston."

To OGDEN HOFFMAN

Department of State
Washington, 26 Sept. 1844

Sir, I have to acknowledge the receipt of your letter of the 24th inst., accompanied by a copy of an affidavit of Henry Cook[,] a fireman on board of the Mexican Steamer Montezuma. In reply, I have to state in reference to the case of the Mexican steamers that if, after consultation with Mr. [Richard S.] Coxe[,] a doubt should arise on a point of law, you will state the point distinctly and transmit the same without delay for the opinion of the Attorney General [John Nelson]. In regard to facts, consulting with Mr. Coxe as you will on all occasions, you are much more capable of making up a correct opinion than the department at this distance. Mr. Coxe and yourself will therefore act conjointly on your own responsibility so far as evidence of facts is concerned, observing the rule to act in no case but on clear evidence, and at the same time not to permit the vessels to depart if the evidence be clear that it would be in violation of our neutral obligations. I am Sir &c &c, J.C. Calhoun.

FC in DNA, RG 59 (State Department), Domestic Letters, 34:390–391 (M-40: 32); PC in Jameson, ed., *Correspondence*, pp. 623–624.

From STEWART NEWELL

Consulate of the United States
Galveston, Sep[tember] 26th 1844

Sir, I have the honor, to inform the Department, that on the 24th Aug., ult., I despatched a communication No. 3, from this Consulate, conveying the intelligence of the Death, of Gen[era]l T[ilghman] A. Howard, who died, at Washington Texas, on the 16th Aug., of Fever, after an illness, of about 60 hours.

Owing to the Abscence [*sic*], of the regular Steam Packets, they leaving for the North, during the Months of June, to Oct., the communication by Sea, is almost entirely cut off, seldom a Vessel arriving, or departing, for a Port in the U. States. Under these circumstances, at my suggestion, the Collector of Customs at New Orleans, did me, the honor, to despatch the U.S. Rev[enue] Sch[oone]r "Woodberry [*sic*; Woodbury]," to this Port & arrived on 20th inst., subject to my orders, to convey despatches, to the U. States, should occassion require it, during the interim, above named, and by which, no addittional expence, to the Govt. is incurred, there being two Revenue Vessels, stationed off the Mississippi River, and which arrangement, may prove of service, in protecting, any commerce, that may arrive from the U. States, as well, as bear despatches, when necessary. I have been informed, that a Courier, passed over land, on his way with despatches, from Gen[era]l Wool [*sic*; Adrian Woll], Commanding the Mexican Forces, on the Rio Grand[e], to Washington Texas, but had not arrived, when the Mail last left, but think it probable, he may have arrived ere this.

I have addressed a Letter, to the Hon. Secr[etar]y of State [of Texas], Anson Jones, informing him, of the arrival of the "Woodberry," and her readiness to convey, any communications this Government, may have to make to the Government of the United States.

His Excellency, President [Samuel] Houston, has returned to Washington, in good health, and Hon. Anson Jones, is beyond a doubt, President Elect, by a majority of about *1500* votes, over Gen[era]l [Edward] Burleson.

Waiting Instructions, from the Department, I have the honor, to be, Most Respectfully, Your Ob[edien]t Servant, Stewart Newell.

ALS (No. 5) in DNA, RG 59 (State Department), Consular Despatches, Galveston, vol. 2 (T-151:2), received 10/17.

To T[homas] W. Robeson, U.S. Consul, Santa Marta, [New Granada], 9/26. Calhoun inquires about the death of a U.S. citizen, G.K. Fitzgerald, in Santa Marta in 1838, and about the administration of Fitzgerald's estate. The inability of creditors [Thomas Wilson and William S. Peterkin] to obtain satisfaction on a debt of $9,863.63 and Robeson's failure to report the matter to the State Department require explanation. Failure to provide explanation will result in Robeson's dismissal. FC in DNA, RG 59 (State Department), Consular Instructions, 11:279–280.

To [FRIEDRICH LUDWIG], Baron Von ROENNE, [Berlin]

State Department, 26th Sept. 1844

My dear Sir, I congratulate you, that the errection [*sic*] of a Department of trade has been completed by your government, and that you have been appointed its President. The arts and trade, two kindred pursuits, have assumed an importance, unknown in former times, and which is yet but in its infancy. I rejoice to see, that Germany is alive to what relates to both. These interests are the same. We have a deep interest in your prosperity commercial and political. There is not a point, on which our interests can come into collision. I am glad to say, in this connection, that there is a fair prospect, that the free trade interest will prevail in the pending election. I regard it as almost certain, that [Henry] Clay will be defeated and [James K.] Polk elected; when I hope a far freer commercial intercourse will follow between the our [*sic*] countries.

I have been so much occupied, on other subjects, that I have not had time to attend to the [Danish] Sound duties, to which you allude; but have taken measures to obtain all the necessary information to make myself fully acquainted with it.

I did not doubt, but that the attempt to ass[as]sinate the King [Frederick William IV], originated either in insanity, or some such motive as you have stated; and I would have been surprised had it not excited the indignation it has throughout his dominion. His conduct has justly made him the favourite of his people.

In conclusion, I beg you, my dear Sir, to believe me to be most truly and sincerely yours, J.C. Calhoun.

Transcript by Professor Gunter Moltmann of recipient's copy in Deutsches Zentralarchiv, Historische Abteilung II, Merseburg, German Democratic Republic (the former Geheimes Staatsarchiv, Berlin), Rep. 92, Nachlass Friedrich Ludwig von Rönne, No. 3; PC in Gunter Moltmann, "Eine Deutschland-Korrespondenz John C. Calhouns aus dem Jahre 1844," in *Jahrbuch für Amerikastudien*, vol. XIV (1969), p. 166. NOTE: This letter apparently was received 11/4/1844.

To Ramon Leon Sanchez, U.S. Consul, Cartagena, [New Granada], 9/26. Sanchez's letters nos. 36 through 38 have been received. In reply to no. 37, enclosing resolutions of the Executive of New Granada concerning display of consular flags, the U.S. government will comply with the resolutions. FC in DNA, RG 59 (State Department), Consular Instructions, 11:280–281.

To Silas M. Stilwell, U.S. Marshal, New York [City], 9/26. Calhoun answers Stilwell's letter of 9/24 [*not found*]. Stilwell is to pay $75 to B.B. Phillips for the latter's services and expenses "in procuring statistics from City Prison, Penitentiary, House of Refuge, Alms House, &c &c for the years 1840, 1841, 1842, 1843, and 1844." When Stilwell submits a receipted claim, the outlay will be refunded to him. FC in DNA, RG 59 (State Department), Accounting Records: Miscellaneous Letters Sent, 1832–1916, vol. for 2/1–9/30/1844, p. 394.

From FLETCHER WEBSTER

Office of the U.S. Mission
Macao, 26th Sept. 1844

Sir, I have the honour to enclose to you the translations of two notes received from the Chinese Commissioner.

One [dated 9/9/1844] is of an official notification of the ratification by the Emperor of China of the Treaty of the 3d of July.

The other [dated 9/9] is of an unofficial note to Mr. [Caleb] Cushing to the same effect.

It appears from the first that it is the intention of of [*sic*] the Chinese Government to put the Treaty into immediate operation at all the five Ports.

It is probable that before this shall be received the terms of the Treaty will have been made public by the Chinese. I have the honour to be with great respect Your obedient servant, Fletcher Webster.

ALS with Ens in DNA, RG 59 (State Department), Diplomatic Despatches, China, vol. 2 (M-92:3), received 1/21/1845. NOTE: Fletcher Webster (1813–1862), son of Daniel Webster, was secretary of Caleb Cushing's mission to China. He was subsequently killed commanding a Union regiment in the Civil War.

To G[EORGE] M. BIBB, Secretary of the Treasury, and J[OHN] Y. MASON, Secretary of the Navy

Department of State
Washington, 27th Sept. 1844

Sir, Mr. Ogden Hoffman[,] the Attorney of the United States for the Southern district of New York and R[ichard] S. Coxe Esq. of this City have been authorized and directed to make diligent inquiry in order to ascertain whether the two Mexican vessels now in the harbour of New York have taken in additional munitions of war or taken any other step which might bring them within the several acts of Congress passed to preserve the neutrality of the United States.

It might greatly facilitate the execution of their duties to have the cooperation of the officers at New York and its vicinity subject to the orders of your Department and I will thank you as early as practicable to give orders to that effect. When the orders are prepared, I will also thank you to transmit them to this Department to be forwarded under cover to Messrs. Hoffman & Coxe. I have the honor to be Sir &c &c &c, J.C.C.

FC's in DNA, RG 59 (State Department), Domestic Letters, 34:391–393 (M-40:32).

To Rob[er]t C. Ewing, U.S. Marshal, Richmond, Missouri, 9/27. "I enclose you the President's [John Tyler's] pardon of David McDaniel, Thomas Towsen [*sic*; Towson], Joseph R. De Prefontaine, Nathaniel H. Morton, W[illia]m J. Harris, and John A. McCormick, the receipt of which you will please acknowledge." FC in DNA, RG 59 (State Department), Domestic Letters, 34:387 (M-40:32).

To A. Folsom, Boston

Department of State
Washington, Sept. 27 1844
Sir: Your letter of the 20th instant, upon the Subject of your Claims against the Haytien Government, has been received. In reply I have to inform you that I cannot with propriety officially request the French Consul General in Hayti to interfere in your behalf, nor can the French Minister here. I have however held a conversation with M. [Alphonse] Pageot upon the Subject, as you will See by his note [of 9/27] to me, a copy of which is now enclosed. If you were to shew this to the Consul General, it would probably be sufficient for your purpose.

It is the duty of the Secretary of the Secretary of the [*sic*] Navy [John Y. Mason] to order vessels of war to Such Stations as he may think the public service requires. He is aware of the importance of their visiting Hayti from time to time, and will no doubt give orders to have Such visits repeated during the coming season; but I hope you may have your case adjusted through the arrangement made, without any aid of the kind. I am &c &c, Jno. C. Calhoun.

FC in DNA, RG 59 (State Department), Domestic Letters, 34:388–389 (M-40:32).

To George W. Gordon, U.S. Consul, Rio de Janeiro, 9/27. Gordon's despatches 3 through 5 have been received. His statement of trade between Brazil and the U.S. for 1843 and the information on Brazilian coffee and sugar exports for 1840–1843 have also been received, and copies have been given to William G. Lyford for publication. Calhoun sends Gordon a copy of Senate Document No. 217 relative to the abuse of the U.S. flag by ships engaged in the African slave trade. FC in DNA, RG 59 (State Department), Consular Instructions, 11:281.

From DUFF GREEN, "Private"

Velasco Texas, Sep[tembe]r 27th 1844
My dear Sir, The steamer Union, did not get under way until Monday morning. We had cloudy, stormy weather, and came to anchor off this place yesterday morning. The waves ran so high that we could not get a pilot or get on shore until this evening. Upon examining the boilers it was found that one of them was much crushed & heating so as to render it unsafe to raise steam, & the Capt[ai]n deems it unsafe to rely on the sails of the ship, (she being imperfectly rigged). He will therefore return to Pensacola, tommorrow; and I will proceed to Galveston: and there await a vessel to be sent to me from Pensacola. As this will delay my reaching Mexico, my stay there will not be so long as I had anticipated. I will endeavor to return so as to enable you to recieve [*sic*] Gov[erno]r [Wilson] Shannon's despatches before the Meeting of our Congress.

The Rumor here today is that Doctor Anson Jones is elected President by a small majority, but this is not a proof that the people are opposed to annexation. On the contrary, ["it" *canceled*] he and his friends pledged themselves in favor of annexation.

The people of middle and western Texas are not satisfied with the Treaty because it left the question of boundary open. I write this from the residence of Gen[era]l Thomas J. Green, who commanded the flotilla in the expedition against Mier, and he describes the [Rio] Grand[e] River as navigable for steam boats to the mouth of the Conchos, & up that river near Chih[u]a[h]ua, and he tells me that that [*sic*] a rail road of three hundred miles [*partial word canceled*] from that point will reach a navigable point on the Yiaqua [*sic*; Yaqui], emptying into the Gulf of California. He tells me that the navigation of the Rio Grande is equal to that of the Mississippi, and that of the Conchos equal to that of the Ohio. The Mexicans are now engaged in making a canal into the lagune near Matamoras, & that thirty miles of canal will give an inland communication from the Rio Grande to the Sabine, for steam boats, & seventy miles more will connect the Sabine, with the Mississippi River.

He describes the Valley of the Rio Grande west of that River as about fifty miles in width and of unexampled fertility. He thinks that nothing can prevent the occupation of that Valley by the Anglo Saxons; and that the best route to the Pacific is that indicated. You can ["see it(?)" *canceled*] trace [it] on Tanner[']s Map of Mexico. If he is correct, a steam boat can leave Pittsburg[h], and go to Chih[u]a[h]ua, and within three hundred miles of the navigable waters of the Gulf of California by making a canal of one hundred miles, without entering the Gulf. This is an important feature of the Texas question.

The health of Galveston is said to be restored. I write in haste. Yours truly, Duff Green.

ALS in DNA, RG 59 (State Department), Diplomatic Despatches, Special Agents, vol. 13 (M-37:13, frames 10–12), received 11/14. NOTE: An AEU by Calhoun reads: "Gen[era]l Green—Gives an account of a new route to the Pacifick by the Del Norte & Choncos."

To R[OBERT] M. T. HUNTER, [Lloyds, Va.]

Washington, Sept. 27th 1844
My dear Sir, I have entire confidence in the judgement and discretion of my friends in Virginia. Their position is one of great command. They have fought the present battle in Virginia. It has made them acquainted with the people and the people with them, and given them a stand and influence ["with" *canceled and* "in" *interlined*] the State, which, if they act together & be prudent & vigillant must given [*sic*] them its control.

From all I hear, I should think, Mr. [Thomas] Ritchie is well disposed. He ought to be treated with great delicacy & respect; and so long as there is any prospect of his acting in concert, all collision with him ought to be avoided. If he will go right, take his stand on the old platform of the Republican party and put Virginia at the head of the South, all will go right.

I expect to leave tomorrow for my residence in South Carolina, where I shall probably spend the month of Oct[obe]r. I have been much engrossed by the duties of my office since the adjournment of Congress. I have prepared in the time many and some of them very important dispatches. Our foreign relations, especially as it regards the South, have been much neglected by the Government for many years.

The general impression here, with our friends, is, that [Henry] Clay will be defeated & [James K.] Polk elected. Indeed, it is regarded by the great majority, that it is almost certain. Although I do not go as far, I think the prospect is highly favourable to our side.

I have, I think, the pamphlet of Gov[erno]r [Lewis] Cass to which you refer, but it is among my papers at home. If I can lay my hand on it after I arrive there I will send it to you.

Mr. [William A.] Harris of your State (member of the last Congress) has concluded to take charge of the [Washington] Spectator & intends to get and unite the Madison[ian] with it, and give a new name to the paper, if he can obtain it on fair terms, as he thinks he can. It is an important movement. I think well of his talents and highly of his character, and do not doubt he will make an able & sound editor. He starts under highly auspicious circumstances and has a fair prospect of rallying a strong support. I hope our friends will give him liberal patronage. Yours truly, J.C. Calhoun.

ALS in Vi, Robert M.T. Hunter Papers; variant PC in Charles Henry Ambler, ed., *Correspondence of Robert M.T. Hunter, 1826–1876*, p. 72. NOTE: Harris's new paper, the *Constitution*, began publication on October 18.

To JOSEPH W. LESE[S]NE, [Mobile]

Washington, 27th Sep[tembe]r 1844
My dear Sir, If I have long delayed the acknowledgement of your letter [*not found*], you must not attribute it to any want of respect, but to the very great pressure of official duties ever since it was received. In addition to the current duties of the office, I have had my attention much engrossed by several questions of much importance,

connected with our foreign relations, which have been not a little neglected for some years, especially as far as the South is concerned.

I have, however, so far got through my labours, as to send yesterday the last dispatch on subjects claiming special attention at present. The business of the office is now so well up, that I propose to leave tomorrow on a visit to Fort Hill, where I hope to spend the next month.

The opinion you express in your letter, as to the proper course for me, is that which I entertain, and have long acted on. Office of itself has no charms for me. If I know myself, I would not accept the highest, except as the means of rendering more extensive and durable services to the country. I am deeply impressed with the excellency of our system of Government, if fairly understood & carried out in practice. Its character has been greatly misunderstood and its powers perverted to the great oppression of one section, and the corruption of the other. The great object of my exertion, for many years, has been to bring the country to a more correct knowledge of its character & to correct the abuses of the Government. For these I have made many sacrifices and am prepared to make whatever others they may demand.

I embrace the occasion to tender to you and my other friends in Mobile my thanks for the elevated manner, in which you conducted the presidential canvass, while advocating my election. I would, at any time, far rather be defeated in a canvass conducted on principle, than to succeed by ["one" *interlined*] conducted simply in reference to victory. As now conducted, ["it is at once" *canceled*] it is at once corrupting & degrading. With a large majority, it is a mere struggle for spoils, taken from the plundered South. With great respect I am yours truly, J.C. Calhoun.

ALS in ScU-SC, John C. Calhoun Papers. NOTE: Lesesne (1811–1856) was a native of S.C. and a son-in-law of Thomas Cooper. In 1847 he became an Ala. judge.

From A[LPHONSE] PAGEOT, [French Minister to the U.S.]

Washington, September 27th 1844

Sir, In answer to the letter [of 9/20] of Mr. [A.] Folsom you had the goodness to communicate to me yesterday, I have no hesitation in saying that the Consul General of France at Hayti could, with propriety grant *unofficially,* his assisstance to him, with the Haytian Government, if it be not incompatible with previous instructions he may have received on the subject, or with the interest he has specially charge of. I am, with sentiments of high consideration Your ob[edi-en]t serv[an]t, A. Pageot.

ALS in DNA, RG 59 (State Department), Notes from Foreign Legations, France, vol. 12 (M-53:8, frames 715–716).

To Richard Pakenham, 9/27. Calhoun acknowledges receipt of Pakenham's note of 9/23 "relating to complaints of British subjects engaged in importing woollen goods into" the U.S. The papers have been referred to the Secretary of the Treasury [George M. Bibb] "for his consideration and decision." FC in DNA, RG 59 (State Department), Notes to Foreign Legations, Great Britain, 7:56–57 (M-99:36).

From G. T. RHODES

Hazelwood, Va. (Georgetown, D.C. P. Office)
September ["24" *canceled and* "27th" *interlined*], 1844
Sir: I take the liberty, very respectfully, to solicit from you some employment. From *you* I received my first appointment. I had the honor of serving under you from 1819 till you left the War Office for the Vice presidency, and I served with fidelity and advantage to the public. In the Engineer Department as principal clerk I then gave entire satisfaction to all my official superiors; and had you remained as the head of the War Department, I have good reason to think I would still occupy that post. I am sure at least that *you* would not have sanctioned my dismission from office without good cause and a *knowledge* of that cause.

Governor [James] Barbour, your successor, though an amiable and good man, was not a man of business, and in my case, from his own declaration afterwards made to his sister, Mrs. Daniel Bryan of Alexandria, acted very precipitately, not to say unjustly. He told his sister, that, had he known *who* it was, he would not have authorized my removal.

General [Alexander] Macomb, who made the representation to Governor Barbour on which I was displaced, had no earthly ground of complaint against me—as his own letters now filed in the Adjutant General's office prove—but my frequent absence from office without leave. This was all true enough, though on that occasion I had asked and obtained leave of absence, I well recollect, from Lt. [Edward H.] Courtenay, then General Macomb's aid[e], General Macomb himself at the moment not being in the office. Still, I overstaid all reasonable limit, and perhaps personally deserved the penalty inflicted. Had Governor Barbour called me before him, as he ought to have done before dismissing me, I would have told him the truth and thrown myself on his mercy. But though I really had no valid plea to offer for my long absence (several days), I might have had: I might have been unable to attend to duty from sickness or some other unavoidable cause. I would not, however, have deceived him an instant—for I have always felt an invincible love of truth—and would have told him nothing else—namely, that I had met with some friends at the races, had yielded to the temptations of pleasure and thus neglected my duty. But it was never charged and could not have been charged that I had been guilty of any act of inebriety or done any thing disreputable or ungentlemanly. On these points and my qualifications as a competent clerk, one of General Macomb's letters (which was afterwards got for me by Captain, now Major John L. Smith) is quite complimental.

I never made the slightest effort at restoration, either in person, or by my friends. I was mortified and indignant and became rather reckless—much to my subsequent suffering and distress. But I had in fact no chance of making a *timely* defence; for my discharge and the filling of the vacancy were simultaneous. The place was actually occupied by James C. Wilson, (brother-in-law to General Macomb) before I *received* my letter of dismission.

I wish not to be misunderstood, and must say that I do not pretend to justify my frequent absence without leave; but I could not justify General Macomb for his hot haste in putting into the vacancy a connection, who had nothing specially to recommend him to the patronage of government that I could ever hear of but his needy importunity. Had my father, a man of unblemished morals and adequate capacity, got a place in consequence of my ejectment from office, I might have considered my dismission, however sore a calamity it has since been to me personally, ["but" *canceled*] as a fit though severe punishment—an act of just retribution for neglect of duty. Towards the support of my father & family a portion of my public salary had regularly gone, and when I was dismissed they and I were prostrated together. My father survived the misfortune but a few months. I was dismissed in November 1827; he died in February following.

I might here mention a fact which, although it can now do no good to the father, might be a consideration in favor of the son. And that is this. Upon the discharge of Bell [*sic*; John H. Beall], a clerk in the Engineer Office, or about that time as well as I can now remember, Captain Smith who had the temporary command of the office in the absence of the Chief Engineer, appointed or was about to appoint my father to the place; but this intention on the part of Captain Smith who knew my father and thought he would make a good clerk (and I will venture to say he could not have got a better) was overruled by you on the ground of impropriety in having a son and father in the same office. Colonel [Benjamin] Fowler (now filling my place there) and his son Robert were in that office together for years, and it is not more than a twelvemonth probably since the latter left it. Robert, however, during your administration of the War Department, was a mere attaché at a per diem of $2.

To General Macomb, after my dismission, I never spoke, though I could hear that he continued to speak well of me. He could not have done otherwise. He had known me as an honorable, liberal man, who had done him personal service, on his reaching the City from Detroit, comparatively unknown here, with a large family and poor. He had been left out of the Army proper at the reduction of 1821 (if I recollect right), and was made Colonel of Engineers (Chief Engineer) to give him bread. Though myself uninformed on such topics, I had thought him a very meritorious officer, unjustly treated, and sympathized with his situation, and though an unimportant person myself—yet not without some influential friends—did what I could after he took charge of the Engineer Department, to make him at home there and to lessen ["the" *canceled and* "his" *interlined*] sense of mortification at being thrown out of the army.

I will not reflect on the memory of the dead, though I cannot feel much respect for the monkish dictum, nil de mortius nisi bonum, the observance of which, as every man of sense must know, would make history little better than a fable. Nisi *verum* might be well substituted for the latter part of the maxim. But I could not help thinking and feeling at the time—nor was I alone in the notion—that there was as much family selfishness in the motive of my dismission from office as patriotism or a due regard to the public interest.

I trust, Sir, you will pardon this long narrative, nor think me an egotist. Far from it. I have made the statement through respect for you: for I feel anxious to put myself right in the estimation of one, of whose moral purity I have always had the most exalted opinion, especially since the [Elijah] Mix contract affair, in which case I was called to give evidence before the Committee of investigation.

I am in perfect health of body and mind and well fitted for any clerical duty, but without employment and needy in the extreme. I have understood there is a good deal of extra labor occasionally required in the State Department, and I venture to ask some portion of it, or any employment there or elsewhere within your gift. I am sure you would never have occasion to regret your patronage. My habits & faculties are altogether favorable to business. Time and reflection have effectually weaned me from a taste for dissipated pleasure, which is but too apt to lead the ardent mind of youth and inexperience from the path of duty. I think I would be found on trial a valuable aid in any branch of the public service. I have had much experience in various departments of the government; write with much facility, and have great power of application, mental and manual. You would find me at least a very grateful, if not efficient agent—one that would render a full equivalent for his compensation. And should you wish it, I could furnish you with unexceptionable testimonials as to character and qualifications.

I suppose you occasionally see General [George] Gibson, Colonel [Joseph G.] Totten, and General [Roger] Jones. I mention these gentlemen because they were formerly officers under your immediate direction, and venture to refer to them in my behalf, and could name others, eminent in civil life, who would be much gratified by the success of this application.

Please answer this through the Georgetown post office. I could be at Washington, ready for action, in a few hours, and such a call would relieve me from a mountain's weight of misery.

I am writing with wretched pen and ink and must say this is not my business hand, but one which I frequently adopt, when using bad implements, on account of its greater legibleness. My ordinary business hand leans the other way.

I pray you again, Sir, to excuse the length and freedom of this communication, And am, with the highest respect, your ob[e]d[ien]t serv[an]t, G.T. Rhodes.

ALS in DNA, RG 59 (State Department), Applications and Recommendations, 1837–1845, Rhodes (M-687:27, frames 434–437).

To C[HARLES] S. SIBLEY, U.S. Attorney for the Middle District of Florida, Tallahassee

Department of State

Washington, 27th Sept. 1844

Sir: I have examined with care the evidence transmitted to this Department upon the subject of the charges preferred against you by Governor [Richard K.] Call of Florida, of maliciously prosecuting him by presenting two indictments against him, for nuisance and compromising a Criminal prosecution for money, and I am happy to inform you that the Conclusion at which I have arrived is, that the charges are wholly unfounded. I am Sir &c &c, Jno. C. Calhoun.

FC in DNA, RG 59 (State Department), Domestic Letters, 34:387 (M-40:32); PC in Carter, ed., *Territorial Papers*, 26:966–967.

From RICH[AR]D S. COXE

New York [City,] Sep[tembe]r 28, 1844

Sir, Since the date of my last I have received yours covering a draft for $150—and a blank receipt, which having signed I return in accordance with the request accompanying it.

Our inquiries have been continued and the result thus far has been the most unequivocal evidence of the violation of the neutrality of the United States. It fully appears that the two Mexican Steamers the Montezuma and the Guadalupe, sailed from Mexico for the United States, and having touched at Charlestown [S.C.] reached New York in June last. They did not put into any port of the United States under stress of weather or to avoid any enemy, but the original object of their visit was to receive such repairs and augmentation of strength as would render them more efficient for warlike purposes.

The Guadalupe is constructed of iron and was taken into dock for the purpose of cleaning her bottom which had become exceedingly foul, and to be painted. The Montezuma is built of wood. Before leaving Mexico she had been beached and by this accident her copper sheathing was partially injured. While in dock her copper was entirely removed and new copper put on. Much of her plank was also worm eaten and her bottom has been generally covered with new plank. The copper was furnished by Collins & Co. and cost about

$3000. The expenses of docking both vessels amounted to about $2400.

The Montezuma has received one new mast and the Guadalupe two. General repairs have been put upon the hull & rigging of both. The steam engine of each vessel has been not only completely repaired but essentially improved so as to be more efficient than ever.

The ammunition of both vessels has been much increased, they having taken on board sufficient powder, balls & shells, for six months service. I have also received information that other military stores are in preparation which are to be put on board smaller vessels and carried outside of the Hook where they will be transshipped to the Steamers.

The crews of both vessels have been much changed—increased in actual numerical force and several individuals shipped in the stead of others who came in them. Especially in the Engineer and Gunner's department have these alterations been made. The new additions to the crew do not consist of Mexicans transiently within the United States, but of Americans and Europeans.

Such is the general result of the information we have acquired. It is now the business of the government to determine whether any steps are to be taken in the case and what. Mr. [Ogden] Hoffman & myself concur in the opinion that the facts which have been developed amount to infractions of the Act of April 1818—but we differ as to some parts of that law. As your communication to Mr. H[offman] indicates an intention to take the opinion of the Att[orne]y Gen[era]l [John Nelson,] I have thought it advisable to inform you by the foregoing general statement of the facts which should be laid before him.

There can be no doubt that prosecutions may be sustained against the individuals who may have violated the various sections of the Act of 1818—but doubts have been suggested whether the ["4th" *canceled and* "3d, 5th" *interlined*] and 6th Sec[tion]s apply to foreign *national or public* vessels. The 5th Sec. clearly does—but that only covers the particular acts specially enumerated. I think the language of the 3d Sec. sufficiently comprehensive to include them.

If I am correct in this view then I think it equally clear that the 6th Sec. also comprehends them, and consequently that the case exists which authorises the President to direct the seizure. Nor does the question arising under this 6th Sec. depend exclusively upon that whether foreign national vessels are comprehended in the 3d.

I am not here supplied with the facilities to enable me fully to illustrate & enforce my views by argument, but I deem it proper thus to draw the attention of the Att[orne]y Gen[era]l to the points upon which a difference of opinion may arise. Very respectfully yours &c, Richd. S. Coxe.

ALS in DNA, RG 59 (State Department), Miscellaneous Letters (M-179:105, frames 441–443).

From FRANKLIN DEXTER

District Attorney's Office
Boston, Sept. 28th 1844

Sir, I have this morning received your letter of the 25th inst. directing an enquiry into the fact, stated in the public prints, that the House of Philo S. Shelton & Co. of Boston has contracted to supply the Mexican government with a quantity of tents, and that the contract is understood to have been made through British Agency.

I immediately addressed a note to Mr. Philo S. Shelton upon the subject requesting him to call upon me, which he did, and in the most express terms he denied that his house had been concerned directly or indirectly in any such transaction. I requested him to send me a note to that effect, and I have now the honor to enclose his note [of 9/28] which I have just received. If I should have any reason to believe that any such measures as are alluded to in your letter are in contemplation by anyone here I shall not fail to institute proper process to defeat them. I am very Respectfully Your Ob[edien]t Se[rvan]t, Franklin Dexter, U.S. Dist. Att[orne]y.

ALS with En in DNA, RG 59 (State Department), Miscellaneous Letters (M-179:105, frames 448–450).

From F[e]r[dinand] Gardner, U.S. Consul, Villa da Praia, St. Jago, Cape Verde Islands, 9/28. Gardner sends to Calhoun a decree of the Portuguese government which outlines changes in customs duties, specifies admitted and prohibited articles, and lists the Cape Verde ports to be opened or closed to foreign commerce. Gardner believes that the decree is in conflict with treaties between the U.S. and Portugal and requests Calhoun to investigate this aspect, although the decree relates specifically to British shipping. He encloses a printed version in Portuguese and an English translation of portions of it. ALS (No. 72) with Ens in DNA, RG 59 (State Department), Consular Despatches, Santiago, Cape Verde Islands (T-434:3).

From O[GDEN] HOFFMAN and RICH[AR]D S. COXE

U.S. Attorney's Office
New York [City], Sept. 28th 1844

Sir, We have received and carefully deliberated upon the contents of your communication addressed to Mr. Hoffman, under date of the 26th inst. After a careful consideration of the facts which have been collected in the authentic form of affidavits of competent witnesses, we concur in the opinion

1. That the fact is clearly established that there have been enlistments of men domiciled in the United States in the Port of New York, to serve on board the armed Steamers belonging to the republic of Mexico, now lying in this harbor.

2. That there has been an ["increase"(?) *canceled*] augmentation of the force of such vessels, as well by this addition to the crews, as by an increase of military stores, and by extensive repairs and additions to the hull, rigging, and machinery.

3. That these facts are established with sufficient distinctness to warrant the institution of criminal proceedings against the individuals by whom they have been committed.

The questions however, which arise upon these facts, and which admit of more doubt are

1st. Whether the facts above enumerated constitute a "fitting out and arming of these vessels" within the meaning of the 3d section, or whether the fitting out there stated, does not mean the original fitting out of a vessel never before employed in the line.

2d. Whether the commander and officers of a national vessel, belonging to a foreign power at peace with the United States, are amenable to the criminal jurisdiction of our Courts, for acts committed on board of such public vessel.

3d. Whether the 3d section of the Act of 1818, comprehends the case of such foreign national vessels, so as to subject them to forfeiture through the instrumentality of our Courts.

The phraseology employed by you in the last clause of your instructions "not to permit the vessels to depart, if the evidence be such that it would be a violation of our neutral obligations" appears to carry with it an expression of the opinion of the Department, that such departure may be prevented by legal process. In a case, however, involving such high national interest we should desire the distinct instructions of the Department, and therefore wish the opinion of the Attorney General [John Nelson] to be taken.

We beg leave further to remark, that restricted as we have necessarily been from the nature of the case from pursuing our inquiries, except in the most secret and guarded manner, we have strong reasons to believe that, whenever the necessity for this caution shall cease by the institution of public proceedings, the evidence which can be procured will be far more precise and distinct than it has yet been in our power to obtain.

Our information leads us also to the belief, that the vessels in question are not at this time prepared for sea, and that several days may elapse before they can be ready to sail. We beg, however, that we may be furnished with the instructions of the Department at the earliest practicable hour. We have the honor to be, Sir, With great respect Your ob[edien]t serv[an]ts, O. Hoffman, U.S. Att[orne]y, Richd. S. Coxe.

LS in DNA, RG 59 (State Department), Miscellaneous Letters (M-179:105, frames 443–444).

From ROBERT WALSH, "Private"

Paris, Sep[tembe]r 28th 1844

My Dear Sir, The very kind and flattering notice from y[ou; *ms. torn*] my nomination as Consul for Paris, reached this capital a day [*ms. torn*] too late for a return of acknowledgments by the Liverpool [*ms. torn*]er of the 19th inst. When I ventured to write to you about [*ms. torn*] situation, I did not even think of the office of Consul, inasm[uch] as it was occupied [by Lorenzo Draper]. From your silence, I inferred that it w[as] out of your power to meet my general wish, & I therefore m[ade] up my mind for a private career to the end of life. I cannot for a moment, doubt the elevation & liberality of your s[*ms. torn*] nor the favorable disposition, of President [John] Tyler. They exc[ite] in my breast the proper sentiments. No exertion will be wa[nting] on my part to render you finally satisfied with what you [*ms. torn*] done. An estrangement, of eight years, from all party feelings [&] connexions, enables me to view men & measures in clear & I [*ms. torn*] true lights. The correspondence, which you are pleased to mention so favorably, expressed my real impressions & conclusions on every subject, and could not be other than national. I do not yet know the latitude in which you may wish me to communicate with your department; but whatever the scope of topics, you may count on

freedom & Sincerity. The printed Inst[ruc]tions are not quite definite
on those heads.

The Situation in which I had every reason to suppose the Consulate to be, forces me to hesitate for two days. A particular investigation taught [me] that it was by no means eligible: but the desire
of corresponding to your friendly intentions; the instances of my
friends here; and the good will manifested towards me by the American press & by the Paris journals likewise, and the hope of being enabled to impart a due efficiency and consideration, overcame my
doubts and difficulties. You are probably aware that an Agency of
Claims with a Salary of two thousand dollars, was attatched to the
Consulate and that Congress suppressed this endowment. Its fees
and perquisites alone remained: these, according to the books of the
Vice Consul, did not, last year, produce two thousand dollars; they
have not exceeded that sum since 1840. A moiety of the proceeds
accrues to the functionary just mentioned. By the Regulations at
Washington, *made before the suppression of the Agency of Claims*,
no allowance is granted "for house or office-rent, stationery or other
ordinary expenses." These, howevever, cannot fall short, with me,
or three or hundred dollars per annum; I exclude house-rent, greater
of course. The office or[*ms. torn*] is in a dismal plight—a single room
on the ground floor; [*ms. torn*] volumes of American laws, some loose
public documents, [an im]perfect copy of Niles' Weekly Register,
two busts, and a box [or t]wo of records *en masse*: no furniture of its
own. I have al[read]y hired, at the rate of two hundred dollars per
annum, two [room]s as a bureau, in the Same hotel with my family
apart[men]t, in an excellent quarter. The Consulate is *notarial* and
statistical, here; it should not be a mercantile speculation or pecuniary job, but a business of intellect and knowledge, a reper[tory?] of
information relating to the public economy of France and [the]
United States: it could be rendered an important auxiliary, or comple-
ment, to the Legation. The Minister Plenipotentiary & the [Secr]e-
tary have to manage indispensable concerns—enough to en[gro]ss
their time & thoughts—apart from commercial tariffs, treaties, or-
dinances, quarantines, and a multitude of other matters af[fec]ting
the trade, navigation and legislation of the Union. The first [ne]ces-
sity for the Bureau is a collection of books and documents: [wi]thout
reference to the laws, not merely of Congress, ["but" *canceled and
then interlined*] of each of the States, the proper execution of notarial duties is impossible; and the communications of the Consul to
his government, under the Rules of the 5 Chapter of the General Instructions, can scarcely be adequate, without the command of digests,

texts & official expositions. You will, I trust, assist me in obtaining the American materials; the European will cost me money besides search and request. On the whole, the exchange of my [u]sual literary gains for the probable net-income of the Consulate is a personal sacrifice. The Signing of *passports* is burdensome for the Legation; it occupies diplomatic hours which could be more serviceably employed for our country. From my conversation with Mr. [William R.] King & Dr. [John L.] Martin, on the Subject, I am Sure that they would rejoice in seeing it transferred to the Consulate. A fee of one dollar on each passport, demandable only once a year from the Same person, would yield, perhaps, a thousand dollars; and it would not be felt by any number of the applicants, worth an estimate. I venture the suggestion [*ms. torn*] a transfer, in case of power in the President or Department of State. There is, I am informed, another regulation that might be fairly asked from Washington, which might contribute to the fulfilment of the ends of the Consulate & the Suitable remuneration of a functionary qualified and earnest for that purpose. The exports from Paris to the United States are very large. Not a few of the exporters send their invoices to the outports to be inspected and signed. It was an objection to my predecessor, Mr. [Lorenzo] Draper, that the dealers in the Same merchandise as himself, disliked to submit their invoices to a rival. This ground being removed, the government at Washington—I mean the Executive—might prescribe that all exporters resident in this capital, shall transact this business at the Paris Consulate. Your functionary bea[rs] the title of simple Consul. Most of the other powers have Consuls General—Austria, Russia, Sweden & Norway, the Two Sicilies, Sardinia, Holland, Portugal, Denmark, Tuscany, the Roma[n] States, Turkey, Greece, Brazil, the United Provinces of La Pla[ta]. Some have them at Havre: Austria has four in France: Fra[nce] has one in the United States. The European states have all fu[ll] legations, with counsellors. It has been remarked that our navy suffers in foreign consideration by the want of the dignity of [an?] Admiral. Our representation here would gain—the efficiency of the Consulate gain—were the Consul authorized to call himself merely, Consul General. It is not any personal vanity that prompts me to throw out this hint. We should keep the highest level according to the just pretensions of the United States. I must add that Some central jurisdiction or cognizance over the Consulates in France might serve the national interests. This point, however, may be reserved. All the Consuls here have fixed salaries; none of them are in trade: some of the great bankers hold the title of Consul General. Their bureaux are, of course, well-constituted. With Several of the great legations, the offices are immediately connected as indispensable departments to receive, record and digest commercial materials of every sort. I am about to examine the principal establishments, which are stocked & worked in a way to make us a little ashamed—with a view to a future interchange of the earliest information; of all events, documents, new aspects of affairs, that affect commercial interests. My personal intimacy with the chief functionaries of the ministries of Commerce, the Navy & the Treasury will facilitate the acquisition of whatever they can afford in furtherance of the duties and objects specified in the General Instructions. If I have troubled you with the foregoing details, it is because I could count, for indulgence, on your enlightened, patriotic & friendly aims. Pardon a few lines more, of seeming egotism. I was alarmed and deterred by the evil chance of rejection by the Senate, or removal by the next President whether Mr. [James K.] Polk or Mr. [Henry] Clay. Personal justice & public good together are not sure restraints on party resentments: the head of a party, sometimes, can recognize the claims alone, of coadjutors and votaries. In the event of Mr. Polk's success, you will, I trust, be persuaded to retain your present station. I shall look to you ["for" *canceled*] as a shield, in the hypothesis of [*ms. torn*] acknowledgment of my competency and assiduity. Mr. Clay [*ms. torn*], not long ago, professed warm regard for his old acquaintance; [nev]ertheless, there are importunities and calculations with which [he] may comply. There is one tribute to the common cause, which [*ms. torn*] fully paid in the four or five first years of my residence in Paris, [*ms. torn*]e vindication of American institutions, character and rights, [*ms. torn*] the journals; instant explanation & defence are frequently expedient; for, the government, polity, social order, aims, destinies, of the United S[tates] are misjudged, not more from jealousy, fear, malice, than from ignorance, and heedless presumption, or indifference. The legation will always have in me an alert assistant whose proficiency in the French language and personal relations with the conductors of the journals facilitate the duty. The Instructions of your Department enjoin that Consuls "should abstain from all participation in the political concerns of the countries to which they are appointed." A public elucidation of those of one's own country, in case of public misconception or misrepresentation, is widely different, and I presume, rarely incongruous or inexpedient.

For this occasion only I will carry further my encroachment on your high & important occupations. The article of the official *Moni-*

teur, of which I enclose a translation, comes from the personal favor of the eminent editor: the note in French is from the Secretary General of the Ministry of Agriculture & Commerce—who, indeed, is the efficient minister: he is an author of repute, & a member of the Chamber of Deputies and the Institute.

My family & myself had yesterday the pleasure of meeting your very intelligent Son-in-law & his interesting wife [Thomas G. and Anna Maria Calhoun Clemson], at dinner, at the table of our worthy minister Mr. King. They were as well & animated as you could wish them to be. Your very respectful & faithful Serv[an]t, Robert Walsh.

[Enclosure]
Alexis de Tocqueville to Robert Walsh

Paris ce 7 aout 1844

Mon cher Monsieur, Je désirerais beaucoup étudier pendant mon sejour à la campagne quelques documents qui puissent m'eclairer sur l'etat actuel des États-unis que j'ai un peur perdre de vue. Pouvez vous me guider dans cette traite[?] et me dire à quelle source il faut puiser. Il y a dans questions principalment que m'interessent ce ci moment, celle des l'oregon et celle des Texas. Comment me mettre bien au-courant de l'un ["des" *canceled*] et de l'autre? Si vous pouvez me donner quelques renseignement peut sur en point, vous me rendez un véritable service de cet je vais serais tres obligé.

Veuillez agrees l'expression de ma consideration la plus distinguée. Alexis de Tocqueville.

ALS with Ens in ScCleA. NOTE: Other Ens include an ALS from Al[phonse] Grün, editor of the *Moniteur Universel*, of 7/23, welcoming Walsh to his post as U.S. Consul, and informing him that his appointment will be announced in Grün's journal, and a translation of an article in the *Moniteur Universel* of 9/24 announcing Walsh's appointment and praising the literary talents of Walsh and other Tyler-appointed diplomats, including Washington Irving, Henry Wheaton, and Caleb Cushing. An EU in an unknown hand on de Tocqueville's letter to Walsh of 8/7 reads "Within 7 months of this year from Oct. to June, Mr. Walsh received at least thirty notes of this description from administrative functionaries, peers, Deputies—authors."

From Fran[cis]co Castellon, Brussels, 9/29. Castellon, a representative of the Honduran and Nicaraguan governments at Brussels, sends to Calhoun a copy of a letter from himself to Lord Aberdeen, dated 9/25, protesting that, according to European newspaper reports, British troops have occupied the port of Bluefields, on the Mosquito Coast of Nicaragua. In his letter to Aberdeen, Castellon narrates the history of Anglo-Spanish relations in Central America and the peaceful continuation of those relations with the now-independent Central American republics. Castellon protests "in the most solemn and formal manner to the cabinets of Europe and especially to the Government of the Republic of the United States" against the British occupation and also against Britain's recognition of the independence of the Mosquito Coast under the rule of a native Indian king. He especially denounces British naval actions against the island of Roatan, off the Honduran coast. Castellon tells Calhoun that these actions are especially ominous because Bluefields and Roatan "would be important on account of their topographical position in case the project of constructing the great ocean canal should be accomplished." Castellon calls upon the U.S. and European governments to respect the territorial rights of the Central American republics and to denounce and suppress British encroachments. A Clerk's EU on the ALS reads "Mr. [Robert] Greenhow. Wanted translation by tomorrow 10' O Clock." ALS (in French) and typescript (in English) in DNA, RG 59 (State Department), Notes from Foreign Legations, Central America, vol. 2 (T-34:2), received 11/25.

R[ichard] K. Crallé, Act[in]g Sec[retar]y [of State], to Albert Davy, U.S. Consul, Liverpool, 9/30. Joel W. White of Conn. having been appointed by President [John Tyler] to replace Davy, he is instructed to surrender to White the records of the consulate. FC in DNA, RG 59 (State Department), Consular Instructions, 12:98–99.

From DUFF GREEN, "Private"

Galveston, 30th Sep[tembe]r 1844

Sir, I enclose you a copy of a letter [of 9/30] to the officer commanding the Naval station at ["Mexico" *canceled*] Pensacola, which will explain the cause of my delay, & that I am about to sail in the Woodbury.

[Anson] Jones is elected President, but a majority of both houses of Congress are said to be decidedly in favor of annexation. [*Three words canceled.*] I am told that Jones declared himself favorable to annexation, and that the cause of his election was an apprehension that Burlesson [*sic*; Edward Burleson] if elected would invade Mexico and thus increase the embar[r]as[s]ments of the country. I find that there is little or no apprehension of any invasion unless it be by sea, and that then the most that can be done will be to bombard this town with her [Mexico's] war steamers. Will it not be well to have our fleet in readiness to forbid or to punish this?

There is much speculation as to what the Govt. of the United States will do.

I will write to you from Vera Cruz. Yours truly, Duff Green.

ALS with En in DNA, RG 59 (State Department), Diplomatic Despatches, Special Agents, vol. 13 (M-37:13, frames 13–16), received 11/14.

From R O B [E R] T M O N R O E H A R R I S O N

Consulate of the United States
Kingston Jamaica, 30th September 1844

Sir, I do myself the honor to inform you that an American Seaman by the name of William Colebrooke has just arrived here from a Small Port in Cuba whither he had gone in a Spanish vessel from the coast of Africa.

He states that he went out to the coast on the Brig "Cyrus" of Philadelphia with a Cargo of Sundries for a Spanish house on the River Cabinda and that Damas [*sic*; P.C. Dumas] the master of the Brig was induced to abandon her and give her up to the Commander of H.B. Majesty's Brig "Alert" owing to what he considered that officer[']s unjustifiable conduct in taking the Register and other papers of the Cyrus out of the vessel and taking them on board the Alert which then lay some distance at sea, under pretence of having them copied: thus exposing the Cyrus to be taken as a Pirate, in case the former vessel were by any accident driven to sea.

He further states that on the Return of the Alert's boat with the papers the next day, the Commander proposed to the Master of the "Cyrus" to return again to the command of his vessel which the latter refused.

The Seaman being ill with the African fever, is now in the Hospital here. With great respect I have the honor to be Sir Your very ob[edien]t and most humble Ser[van]t, Robt. Monroe Harrison.

LS (No. 303) in DNA, RG 59 (State Department), Consular Despatches, Kingston, vol. 9 (T-31:9), received 11/29.

From R[occo] Martuscelli, [Consul General of the Two Sicilies], New York [City], 9/30. Martuscelli apologizes for the tone and language of his letter to Calhoun of 8/18 [*sic*; 8/17]. "Je m'empresse de temoigner à V. E. tout mon regret pour la remarque qu'elle m'y fait d'avoir trouvé ma lettre du 18 ult. d'un ton et d'un langage peu convenable pour le Ministere des Finances." He has had good relations with the U.S. government for six years and has the greatest respect for the government and its officials. However, he reminds Calhoun of the subject of his previous notes [the unsettled claims of Dacorsi and De Martino]. A Clerk's EU reads "Apologizes for the style of his note, to which the Dept. took exceptions." LS (in French) in DNA, RG 59 (State Department), Notes from Foreign Legations, Two Sicilies, vol. 1 (M-55:1).

From STEWART NEWELL

> Consulate of the United States
> Galveston, Texas
> Sep[tember] 30th 1844

Sir, I have the honor to report to the Department that the U.S. Steamer "Union" Commander, [Henry H.] Bell Anchored off Velasco four days since in distress having Gen[era]l Duff Green on board as bearer of Despatches to Mexico, who landed from the "Union" at Velasco and proceeded to this place over land and will leave this Port tomorrow on board the U.S. Rev[enue] Sch[oone]r "Woodberry" for Vera Cruz.

The Union as I am informed having injured one of her Boilers so that it was observed to leak from a flaw or crack in it, and will perhaps be detained a few days to repair damage and arrive at this Port.

I have rendered Gen[era]l Green all the aid desired to hasten his departure with the Despatches, and shall be pleased to attend to any commands or instructions from the Department during his Abscence, as I am informed by him, he has been appointed U.S. Consul to this Port. I have the honor to be Most Respectfully Your Ob[edien]t Servant, Stewart Newell.

ALS (No. 6) in DNA, RG 59 (State Department), Consular Despatches, Galveston, vol. 2 (T-151:2), received 10/16.

From G[IDEON] T. SNOW

Consulate of the United States
of America, Pernambuco [Brazil]
September 30, 1844

Sir, Feeling a desire of furnishing your Department with every desirable information regarding the trade of this place I have made up an "Extra" return which I now enclose showing the total value of Imports from different countries during the year ending the 30th of last June, and specifying particularly the principal articles. By this you will perceive that there has been an excess of Import from the United States of Seventy three Thousand four hundred and forty seven dollars over the last year which is attributable to the increased consumption of our Domestic Manufactured goods which will no doubt go on increasing rapidly. You will also see that in Austria we have a powerful competitor in the Flour trade, and I have to remark that the best quality of Trieste [flour] is preferred to any thing which comes from our country.

Trusting the information conveyed in this Return will be acceptable I have the honour to remain, Sir Very respectfully Your ob[edien]t servant, G.T. Snow, Consul.

LS (No. 30) with En in DNA, RG 59 (State Department), Consular Despatches, Pernambuco, vol. 3 (T-344:3), received 11/13.

R[ichard] K. Crallé to Joel W. White, [Norwich, Conn.?], 9/30. Crallé notifies White of his appointment as U.S. Consul at Liverpool and sends him documents relevant to the conduct of the office. FC in DNA, RG 59 (State Department), Consular Instructions, 12:98.

"Ecuador," [by William Hunter, Jr., Clerk of the State Department, *ca.* 9/1844?]. This undated 20-page memorandum recounts the history of Ecuador and of U.S. relations with that country since 1830, when the republic of Colombia split into Ecuador, New Granada, and Venezuela. Efforts to secure compensation from Ecuador for its share of the claims of U.S. citizens, especially in the cases of the ships *Josephine* and *Ranger*, have been unsuccessful. A letter of 7/26/-1844 from [William M.] Blackford, the U.S. Chargé d'Affaires in New Granada, [received at the State Department on 9/14/1844], transmitted the latest refusal of Ecuador to negotiate. Claims of U.S. citizens against the former republic of Colombia constitute almost

$1,250,000. It appears impossible to ascertain accurately the amount of American trade with Ecuador. ADU in ScCleA.

"List of Senators," [State Department, *ca.* 9/1844?]. This undated 3-page manuscript document contains the names of the U.S. Senators in office *ca.* 9/1844 [between the first and second sessions of the 28th Cong.]. The document is perhaps a mailing list. Many of the names are checked off, and beside most is the name of a person, apparently a person who was supposed to communicate with the Senator listed. These names are —— Smith, J[oseph] A. Scoville, —— Buick[?], [Robert?] Beale, [Charles H.?] Winder, [Richard K.] Crallé, [J.B.] Ayres, [Caleb J.?] McNulty, "E.B.R.," and —— Fremont. DU in ScCleA.

SYMBOLS

◫

The following symbols have been used in this volume as abbreviations for the forms in which documents of John C. Calhoun have been found and for the repositories in which they are preserved. (Full citations to printed sources of documents can be found in the Bibliography.)

Abs   —abstract (a summary)
ADS   —autograph document, signed
ADU   —autograph document, unsigned
AEI   —autograph endorsement, initialed
AES   —autograph endorsement, signed
AEU   —autograph endorsement, unsigned
ALS   —autograph letter, signed
ALU   —autograph letter, unsigned
CC   —clerk's copy (a secondary ms. copy)
CCEx   —clerk's copy of an extract
CSmH   —Huntington Library, San Marino, Cal.
CU   —University of California-Berkeley
DLC   —Library of Congress, Washington
DNA   —National Archives, Washington
DS   —document, signed
DU   —document, unsigned
En   —enclosure
Ens   —enclosures
ES   —endorsement, signed
EU   —endorsement, unsigned
FC   —file copy (usually a letterbook copy retained by the sender)
LNHT   —Tulane University, New Orleans
LS   —letter, signed
LU   —letter, unsigned
M-   —(followed by a number) published microcopy of the National Archives
Me-Ar   —Maine State Archives, Augusta
MHi   —Massachusetts Historical Society, Boston
NcD   —Duke University, Durham, N.C.
NcU   —Southern Historical Collection, University of North Carolina at Chapel Hill
NNPM   —Pierpont Morgan Library, New York City
PC   —printed copy
PDS   —printed document, signed
PEx   —printed extract
PHarH   —Pennsylvania Historical and Museum Commission, Harrisburg
PHi   —Historical Society of Pennsylvania, Philadelphia

RG	—Record Group in the National Archives
RNR	—Redwood Library and Athenaeum, Newport, R.I.
ScC	—Charleston Library Society, Charleston, S.C.
ScCleA	—Clemson University, Clemson, S.C.
ScU-SC	—South Caroliniana Library, University of South Carolina, Columbia
T	—Tennessee State Library and Archives, Nashville
T-	—(followed by a number) published microfilm of the National Archives
Tx	—Texas State Library, Austin
TxDaHi	—Dallas Historical Society
TxU	—Barker Texas History Center, University of Texas at Austin
Vi	—Virginia State Library, Richmond
ViU	—University of Virginia, Charlottesville
Vt	—State Papers Division, Secretary of State, Montpelier, Vt.

BIBLIOGRAPHY

⫴

This Bibliography is limited to sources of and previous printings of John C. Calhoun documents in this volume.

Alexandria, D.C. and Va., *Gazette*, 1808–.

Ambler, Charles Henry, ed., *Correspondence of Robert M.T. Hunter, 1826–1876*, in the *American Historical Association Annual Report* for 1916 (2 vols. Washington: U.S. Government Printing Office, 1918), vol. II.

Anderson, S.C., *Gazette*, 1843–1855.

Boucher, Chauncey S., and Robert P. Brooks, eds., *Correspondence Addressed to John C. Calhoun, 1837–1849*, in the *American Historical Association Annual Report* for 1929 (Washington: U.S. Government Printing Office, 1930).

Bourne, Kenneth, ed., *British Documents on Foreign Affairs. Reports and Papers from the Foreign Office Confidential Print*. Part One, Series C. *North America, 1838–1914* (4 vols. Frederick, Md.: University Publications of America, 1986).

British and Foreign State Papers (170 vols. London: HMSO, 1812–1968), vols. 33 and 34.

Brown, J. Henry, *Brown's Political History of Oregon. Provisional Government. Treaties, Conventions, and Diplomatic Correspondence on the Boundary Question . . . with Original Documents*. Portland: Lewis & Dryden Printing Co., 1892.

Camden, S.C., *Journal*, 1826–1891?.

Carter, Clarence E., and John Porter Bloom, eds., *The Territorial Papers of the United States*. 28 vols. to date. Washington: U.S. Government Printing Office, 1934–.

Charleston, S.C., *Mercury*, 1822–1868.

Charleston, S.C., *Southern Patriot*, 1814–1848.

Columbia, S.C., *South-Carolinian*, 1838–1849?.

Columbus, Ga., *Times*, 1841–1870?.

Columbus, Ohio, *Ohio State Journal*, 1811–1904.

Concord, N.H., *Patriot*, 1808–1921.

Congressional Globe . . . 1833–1873 . . . . 46 vols. Washington: Blair & Rives and others, 1834–1873.

Correspondence Relative to the Negotiation of the Question of Disputed Right to the Oregon Territory, on the North-west Coast of America; Subsequent to the Treaty of Washington of August 9, 1842. Presented to Both Houses of Parliament by Command of Her Majesty, 1846. London: T.R. Harrison, n.d.

Crallé, Richard K., ed., *The Works of John C. Calhoun*. 6 vols. Columbia, S.C.: printed by A.S. Johnston, 1851, and New York: D. Appleton & Co., 1853–1857.

Davids, Jules, editorial director, *American Diplomatic and Public Papers: The United States and China,* Series I [1842–1860], 2 vols. Wilmington, Del.: Scholarly Resources Inc., 1973.

De Bow's Review. New Orleans, 1846–1880.

Edgefield, S.C., *Advertiser,* 1836–.

Garrison, George P., ed., *Diplomatic Correspondence of the Republic of Texas,* in the *American Historical Association Annual Report* for 1907, vol. II, and for 1908, vol. II. Washington: U.S. Government Printing Office, 1908–1911.

Greeley, Horace, *A History of the Struggle for Slavery Extension or Restriction in the United States, from the Declaration of Independence to the Present Day.* New York: Dix, Edwards & Co., 1856.

Greenville, S.C., *Mountaineer,* 1829–1901.

Hammond, George P., ed., *The Larkin Papers. Personal, Business, and Official Correspondence of Thomas Oliver Larkin, Merchant and United States Consul in California.* 11 vols. Berkeley: University of California Press, 1951–1968.

Holst, Hermann E., von, *John C. Calhoun.* Boston: Houghton Mifflin & Co., 1882.

Hon. J.C. Calhoun's Letter to the Hon. W.R. King. Charleston: printed by Walker & Burke, [1844].

Jackson, Miss., *Mississippian,* 1832–1865.

Jackson, Miss., *Southern Reformer,* 1843–1846.

Jameson, J. Franklin, ed., *Correspondence of John C. Calhoun,* in the *American Historical Association Annual Report* for 1899 (2 vols. Washington: U.S. Government Printing Office, 1900), vol. II.

Jollivet, Adolphe, *Documents Americains, Annexion du Texas, Emancipation des Noirs, Politique de l'Angleterre.* Paris: de l'Imprimerie de Bruneau, 1845.

London, England, *Times,* 1785–.

Manning, William R., ed., *Diplomatic Correspondence of the United States: Canadian Relations, 1784–1860.* 4 vols. Washington: Carnegie Endowment for International Peace, 1940–1945.

Manning, William R., ed., *Diplomatic Correspondence of the United States: Inter-American Affairs, 1831–1860.* 12 vols. Washington: Carnegie Endowment for International Peace, 1932–1939.

Merk, Frederick, *Slavery and the Annexation of Texas.* New York: Alfred A. Knopf, 1972.

Milledgeville, Ga., *Federal Union,* 1830–1872.

Moltmann, Gunter, "Eine Deutschland-Korrespondenz John C. Calhouns aus dem Jahre 1844," in *Jahrbuch fur Amerikastudien,* vol. 14 (1969), pp. 155–166.

New Orleans, La., *Louisiana Courier,* 1807–1860.

New York, N.Y., *Herald,* 1835–1924.

New York, N.Y., *National Anti-Slavery Standard,* 1840–1870.

Niles' Register. Baltimore, 1811–1849.

Norfolk and Portsmouth, Va., *American Beacon,* 1815–1861.

Oregon: The Claim of the United States to Oregon, as Stated in the Letters of the Hon. J.C. Calhoun and the Hon. J. Buchanan, (American Secretaries of State,) to the Right Hon. R. Pakenham, Her Britannic Majesty's Plenipotentiary. With an Appendix, Containing the Counter Statement of Mr. Paken-

ham to the American Secretaries of State, and a Map, Showing the Boundary Line Proposed by Each Party.* London: Wiley and Putnam, 1846.

Pendleton, S.C., *Messenger*, 1807–?.

Raleigh, N.C., *North Carolina Standard*, 1834–1870.

Richmond, Va., *Enquirer*, 1804–1877.

Sioussat, St. George L., ed., "Selected Letters, 1844–1845, from the Donelson Papers," in *Tennessee Historical Magazine*, vol. 3 (June, 1917), pp. 134–162.

"Some Letters of Tyler, Calhoun, Polk, Murphy, Houston, and Donelson," in *Tyler's Quarterly Historical and Genealogical Magazine*, vol. VI, no. 4 (April, 1925), pp. 221–249.

U.S. House of Representatives, *House Documents*, 28th, 29th, and 32nd Congresses.

U.S. House of Representatives, *House Journal*, 28th Congress.

U.S. Senate, *Journal of the Executive Proceedings of the Senate of the United States, 1789–1852.* 8 vols. Washington: U.S. Government Printing Office, 1887.

U.S. Senate, *Senate Documents*, 28th, 29th, and 32nd Congresses.

U.S. Senate, *Senate Journal*, 28th Congress.

Washington, D.C., *Constitution*, 1844–1845.

Washington, D.C., *Daily National Intelligencer*, 1800–1870.

Washington, D.C., *Madisonian*, 1837–1845.

Washington, D.C., *Spectator*, 1842–1844.

Washington, D.C., *The Globe*, 1830–1845.

INDEX

Ⅲ

Leipsic, Prussia: 172.
Leopold I (of Belgium): mentioned, 35, 318, 438, 567.
Lepsius, Karl Richard: mentioned, 503.
Lesesne, Joseph W.: to, 867.
Lester, C. Edwards: from, 239.
Levant, U.S.S.: 605, 607.
Levy, Jonas P.: mentioned, 256–257.
Levy, Uriah P.: mentioned, 257.
Lewis, Dixon H.: mentioned, 16, 53, 435.
Lewis, James: from, 579, 612.
Lewis, Joseph: mentioned, 521.
Lewis, Meriwether: mentioned, 697–698, 764, 767–768, 815.
Lewis, William B.: to, 11, 25.
Lexington, Ky., *Observer and Reporter*: mentioned, 796.
Library of Congress: documents in, 117, 124, 147, 251, 254, 365, 435, 494, 495, 632, 646, 794, 821, 829.
Lima, Miguel C.: mentioned, 692.
Lindsey, John: mentioned, 235.
Linens: 253, 442, 543.
Linn, Elizabeth Relfe: mentioned, 428.
Linn, Lewis F.: mentioned, 428.
Lionberger, Isaac: from, 26.
Lipman, Hymen L.: mentioned, 519.
Lippincott, Franklin: mentioned, 23; to, 710.
Lisboa, Gaspar José de: mentioned, 230.
Lisboa, João Francisco: mentioned, 396.
Litchfield County, Conn.: 682–683.
Littlehales, ——: mentioned, 63–64.
Little Rock, Ark.: 108, 295, 305.
Liverpool, England: 110, 126, 182, 185, 253, 271, 562, 777, 819–820, 835–836, 843–844, 854–855, 877, 882, 885.
Livingston, Jasper Hall: mentioned, 29; to, 135.
Livingston, T.B.: mentioned, 667.
Locofocos: 836.
London, England: xiv, 110, 146, 185–186, 191, 271, 383, 553–554, 645, 673. *See also* Everett, Edward.

London, England, *Chronicle*: mentioned, 788.
London, England, *Examiner*: mentioned, 756.
London, England, *Gazette*: mentioned, 548.
London, England, *Times*: documents in, 568, 665, 695, 763, 814; mentioned, 9, 387, 788.
Longacre, James B.: from, 542.
Longfellow, Alexander W.: mentioned, 516.
Loomis, Gustavus: mentioned, 197–198, 583.
Lopez, Carlos Antonio: mentioned, 524.
Loring, Richmond: mentioned, 287, 363; to, 290.
Los Angeles: 240.
Louis, Count of Aquila: mentioned, 693.
Louisiana: 156–158, 284, 404, 469, 477, 593, 627, 641. *See also* Fort Jesup, La.; New Orleans, La.; Sabine, port of.
Louisiana Purchase: 188, 210, 469–471, 654, 697, 699, 701, 745, 764–765, 816–818.
Louis Philippe: mentioned, 293, 334–336, 367, 483, 568, 592, 635, 788–789.
Louisville, Ky.: 116, 156, 174, 449.
Louisville, Ky., *City Gazette*: mentioned, 830.
Lumber: 134–135, 199–200, 282, 361, 514.
Lumpkin, Wilson: from, 144, 832.
Lushington, Stephen: mentioned, 449.
Luther, Martin: mentioned, 172.
Lyford, William G.: mentioned, 865.
Lyman, E., Jr.: from, 659.
Lynchburg, Va.: 406–408, 490, 511–513.
Lyon, ——: mentioned, 730.
Lyon, James G.: from, 434.
Lyon, Lucius: from, 309; mentioned, 370.

McAfee, Robert B.: mentioned, 513.
McCarthy, Florence: from, 835.